The 1981 Dow Jones-Irwin Business Almanac

The 1981 DOW JONES-IRWIN
Business Almanac

Edited by

Sumner N. Levine
State University of New York
at Stony Brook
and Editor
Financial Analyst's Handbook
and
The Investment Manager's Handbook

Executive Editor
Caroline Levine

Editorial Associates
Judy Atwood
Mary L. Westerling

DOW JONES-IRWIN
Homewood, Illinois 60430

ISBN 0-87094-232-8 (paperbound)
ISBN 0-87094-225-5 (casebound)
Library of Congress Catalog Card No. 76–53629

Printed in the United States of America

1 2 3 4 5 6 7 8 9 0 K 8 7 6 5 4 3 2 1

ARTICLES BY:

Roger G. Ibbotson. Professor, Graduate School of Business, University of Chicago, Chicago, IL

Geoffrey H. Moore. Director, Center for International Business Cycle Research, Rutgers University, Newark, NJ

Fred B. Renwick. Professor, Graduate School of Business Administration, New York University, New York, NY

Contents

Business in Review, 1
The 1980 Recession, *Geoffrey H. Moore*, 46

MAJOR LEGISLATION ENACTED, 51

REGULATORY AGENCIES, 55

Antitrust Division (Department of Justice), 55
Consumer Product Safety Commission (CPSC), 56
Economic Regulatory Administration (Department of Energy), 56
Federal Energy Regulatory Commission (Department of Energy), 57
Environmental Protection Agency (EPA), 57
Equal Employment Opportunity Commission (EEOC), 58
Federal Communications Commission (FCC), 59
Federal Maritime Commission (FMC), 61
Federal Trade Commission (FTC), 62
Food and Drug Administration (FDA), 66
Interstate Commerce Commission (ICC), 68
Labor-Management Services Administration (LMSA) (Department of Labor), 69
Occupation Safety and Health Administration (OSHA) (Department of Labor), 70
Office of Federal Contract Compliance (FCC) (Department of Labor), 71
Securities and Exchange Commission (SEC), 71
Standard Federal Regions, 75

FINANCE AND ACCOUNTING, 76

Accounting and Allied Financial Organizations, 76
Accounting Statements and Opinions, 77
How to Analyze and Understand Financial Statements, *Fred B. Renwick*, 80
Financial Statement Ratios by Industry, 95
Where to Go for Outside Financing, 124
Tax Shelters, 125
New Monetary Aggregates, 141

LARGEST CORPORATIONS, 144

The 100 Largest Industrial Corporations (ranked by sales), 144

The 100 Largest Industrial Corporations Outside the U.S. (ranked by sales), 150
The 25 Largest Industrial Companies in the World, 154
The 25 Largest Utilities (ranked by assets), 154
The Inc. 100 Fastest Growing Small Companies, 156

MANAGEMENT, 162

Basic Budgets for Profit Planning, 162
What Is the Best Selling Price?, 168
Cheaper Financing for Plant Expansion, 172
How to Cut Telephone Costs, 173
How to Do Business with the Government, 175

STOCK MARKET, 195

Securities Markets: Notable Dates, 195
Common Stock Prices and Yields, 198
Major Market Averages, 200
Dow Jones Industrial, Transportation, and Utility Averages, 202
Dow Jones Industrials, 204
The Constant-Dollar Dow, 205
Stock Market Averages by Industry Group, 207
Investment Returns on Stocks, Bonds, and Bills, *Roger G. Ibbotson*, 226
Vickers Favorite 50, 230
Summary of Favorite 50 by Industry, 232
Foreign Securities Listed on the New York Stock Exchange, 232
Margin Requirements, 233
Cash Dividends and Yields, 234
Shares Sold on Registered Exchanges, 235
Mutual Funds: Ten-Year Selected Performance, 236
50 Leading Stocks in Market Value (NYSE), 242
What is in a 10K and Other SEC Reports, 243
Investment and Financial Terms, 246

COMMODITIES MARKET, 266

Commodity Futures Trading Commission, 266
Commodity Exchanges, 267
Monthly Average Spot Price Charts of Selected Commodities, 268

Precious Metals and Currency Prices, 275
Dow Jones Commodity Indexes, 276

MONEY AND FINANCIAL
    INSTITUTIONS, 278

Interest Rates and Bond Yields, 278
Interest Rates: Money and Capital Markets, 280
Maximum Interest Rates Payable on Time and
    Savings Deposits at Federally Insured
    Institutions, 282
Prime Rate Charged by Banks on Short-Term
    Business Loans, 283
Terms of Lending at Commercial Banks, 284
Credit Ratings of Fixed Income and Money
    Securities, 286
Sources and Uses of Funds—Nonfarm,
    Nonfinancial Corporate Business, 293
Money Stock Measures and Liquid Assets, 294
Income Velocity of Money, 296
Current Assets and Liabilities of Nonfinancial
    Corporations, 297
Bank Loans, Investments, and Reserves, 298
New Security Issues of State and Local
    Governments, 300
New Security Issues of Corporations, 301
Funds Raised in U.S. Credit Markets, 302
Mortgage Debt Outstanding, 304
Consumer Installment Credit: Total
    Outstanding and Net Change, 306
Thrift Institutions and Life Insurance Com-
    panies: Selected Assets and Liabilities, 308

BANK AND OTHER FINANCIAL
    INSTITUTIONS, 310

25 Largest U.S. Commercial Banking
    Companies (ranked by assets), 310
25 Largest Commercial Banking Companies
    outside the United States, 312
300 Largest Commercial Banks in the U.S. by
    States, 314
25 Largest Diversified Financial Companies
    (ranked by assets), 318
25 Largest Life Insurance Companies (ranked
    by assets), 320

ADVERTISING AND THE MEDIA, 322

Top 100 National Advertisers, 322
Advertising Expenditures by Industry as a
    Percent of Sales and Gross Profit Margin, 324
World's Top 50 Ad Agencies, 326
Market Areas of Dominant Influence Ranked
    by TV Households, 327
Top U.S. Magazines: Circulation, 331

Retail Sales in 100 Top Markets, 333
Retail Trade: Trends and Projections,
    1974–1980, 336
Wholesale Trade: Trends and Projections,
    1974–1980, 337
Estimated and Projected Population, by Age
    and Sex, 1950 to 2010, and Zero Growth
    Projections, 1985 to 2050, 338

EMPLOYMENT WAGES AND
    PRODUCTIVITY, 340

Status of the Labor Force, 340
Selected Unemployment Rates, 342
Employment by Industry Division and Major
    Manufacturing Group, Seasonally Adjusted,
    344
Nonagricultural Employment, 346
Weekly Earnings, by Industry Division and
    Major Manufacturing Group, 348
Hours and Earnings, by Industry Division, 350
Productivity and Related Data, Private
    Business Sector, 352
Personal Income per Capita and per Square
    Mile, 354
Labor-Management Data, 355
Work Stoppages, 1947 to Date, 356
Wage and Benefit Settlements in Major Collec-
    tive Bargaining Units, 1975 to Date, 358
Effective Wage Adjustments Going into Effect
    in Major Collective Bargaining Units, 1975
    to Date, 359
Union Addresses and Membership, 360

PRICE DATA, 366

Consumer Price Index for All Urban Consumers
    and Revised CPI for Urban Wage Earners
    and Clerical Workers, U.S. City Average:
    General Summary and Groups, Subgroups,
    and Selected Items, 369
Consumer Prices, 380
Consumer Price Index—U.S. City Average, and
    Selected Areas, 382

ECONOMIC INDICATORS, 383

Composite Indexes and Their Components, 383
Summary of Recent Data and Current Changes
    for Principal Indicators, 384
Selected Business Statistics, 392

GROSS NATIONAL PRODUCT AND
    INCOME, 394

Gross National Product, 394
Gross National Product in 1972 Dollars, 396

Implicit Price Deflators for Gross National Product, 397
Changes in GNP and GNP Price Measures, 398
Selected Components of GNP, 399
Corporate Profits, 400
Gross Private Domestic Investment, 402
Expenditures for New Plant and Equipment, 404
Sources of Personal Income, 406
Disposition of Personal Income, 408
Personal Consumption Expenditures, 410
National Income, 411
Federal Sector, National Income Accounts Basis, 412
Federal Budget: Procedure and Timetable, 414

PRODUCTION, CONSTRUCTION, AND BUSINESS ACTIVITY, 418

Employment Status by Sex, Age, and Race, Seasonally Adjusted, 418
Industrial Production and Capacity Utilization, 420
Industrial Production—Major Market Groups and Selected Manufacturers, 422
New Private Housing and Vacancy Rates, 424
New Construction, 425
Business Sales and Inventories—Total and Trade, 426
Manufacturers' Shipments, Inventories, and Orders, 428

FEDERAL, STATE, AND LOCAL FINANCE, 430

Federal Budget Receipts and Outlays and Debt, 430
Federal Budget Receipts by Source and Outlays by Function, 432

INTERNATIONAL BUSINESS AND TRADE, 435

Financing Exports, 435
U.S. International Transactions, 436
Foreign Trade of the United States, 440
Unit Labor Costs and Productivity in Manufacturing, 447

INTERNATIONAL BUSINESS AND FINANCIAL COMPARISONS, 448

Treasury Bill Rates, 448
Representative Money-Market rates, 449
Commercial Paper Rates, United States and Canada, 450

Short-term Interest Rates, Selected Countries, 451
Long-term Government Bond Yields, Selected Countries, 452
Long-term Government Bond Yields, United Kingdom and France, 453
Foreign Government Bond Yields, 454
Foreign Corporate Bond Yields, 455
Economic and Business Indicators of Developed Countries, 456
Unemployment Rate, 457
Industrial Production, 458
Total Trade, 460
Gross Domestic Product, 462

WORLD POPULATION AND GNP BY COUNTRY, 463

Per Capita Gross National Product at Market Prices—Amount (1977) and Average Annual Growth Rates (1960–1977 and 1970–1977), 468

BUSINESS INFORMATION DIRECTORY, 470

General Sources, 470
Business and Economics Information, 470
Corporate Information, 471
Federal Government Developments, 471
Index Publications, 472
How to Follow Economic Indicators, 472
General Information Sources, 470
Useful Contacts for Business Information, 474
Information Sources in the U.S. Department of Commerce (By Subject), 478
State Information Guide, 482
International Information Sources, 511
District Offices of the U.S. Department of Commerce, 512
Regional Marketing Managers, 515
U.S. Export Development Offices, 517
Commercial Offices Overseas, Department of Commerce, 517
U.S. Department of State, 517
United States International Trade Commission, 517
Export-Import Bank, 518
Foreign Credit Insurance Association (FCIA), 518
Overseas Private Investment Corporation (OPIC), 518
International Organizations, 518
Commercial Organizations, 520
Sources of International Credit Information, 521

International Business Information Directory,
    521
  Japan, 521
  The People's Republic of China, 522
  USSR and Eastern Europe, 522
  Near East and North Africa, 524

Selected Business and Trade Organizations, 528
U.S. Customs Information, 537
Foreign Diplomatic Offices in the United
    States, 539

INDEX, 545

Business in Review

2 Key indicators of the economy signal an economic slide during 1980. The index declined 1.3 percent in November after falling a downward revised 1.4 percent in October. The revised drop was the largest since last April. Building permits contributed most to November's decline.

Ford raised car prices an average $149, or 1.9 percent. The boost is the second on 1980 model autos. The increases mean the new cars cost at least $425 more than their 1979 counterparts.

The farm price rise of 0.5 percent in December proves that markets have cooled since the sharp increases earlier in 1979. But the Agriculture Department said rising costs for farmers could bring new upward pressure on prices in 1980.

Gold soared as high as $534.50 an ounce Monday on buying triggered by unrest in Iran and Afghanistan. Its price closed at $533 in New York, up $15.20 from Friday's late quote.

3 Gold's price settled at a record $575.50 an ounce in New York, up $42.50, after climbing as high as $577. Dealers attributed the surge to the situation in Afghanistan and to a burst of pent-up enthusiasm following the New Year's Day market closings. At an IMF sale, 444,000 ounces of gold were sold at an average $562.85, a high. Silver rose $4.40 to $38.85, more than six times its year-ago price.

Fed Chairman Volcker declared that any interest rate decline shouldn't be considered a sign of easier monetary policy. He reemphasized the Fed's determination to maintain the battle against inflation through monetary restraint.

Petroleum spot prices seem to be softening, even as African members of OPEC appear to be rallying around Libya's new bid for higher official contract prices. Traders differed over what is happening in spot markets, but there was little trading.

U.S. auto output during December totaled 451,465 units, down 28 percent from the year ago and a bit lower than industry observers had expected. The output was the lowest since 1974.

Auto workers union officials said they expect to propose concessions for a new contract with Chrysler tomorrow and may be able to reach a tentative pact with the company almost immediately.

4 Gold's price, soared to $660 an ounce before closing at $625 in New York for a net daily gain of an unprecedented $49.50. Most gold experts were dumbfounded and U.S. and foreign government officials were tight-lipped. Analysts cited economic and political problems world-wide for the rise.

The dollar was pushed higher in foreign-exchange trading on strong intervention by central banks, including the Fed. The U.S. currency faced pressure due to tensions concerning Iran and Afghanistan and the speculator flight into precious metals.

New factory orders rose 0.9 percent in November to $147.79 billion after falling 0.4 percent in October. Despite the rise, a government economist saw the report as evidence of a weakening economy. He noted that a big jump in aircraft orders masked an 11.6 percent slide for the motor vehicle industry.

Ford will close temporarily 11 of its 13 U.S. car-making operations for one to two weeks beginning Monday to trim inventories. The closings, which will idle 34,600 workers, came as auto makers reported a 10 percent sales decline for mid-December.

A retail sales surge just before Christmas helped many big retailers post respectable sales figures for the month. But retailers see a sluggish first half. In December, K mart led major chains with a 12 percent sales gain; Sears had a disappointing 3.9 percent rise.

Credit demand surged at the end of 1979, Federal Reserve figures show. Analysts see demand tapering over the coming weeks. Business loans at New York City banks jumped $804 million in the week ended Wednesday, the fourth increase in five weeks.

Iranian oil-supply agreements have been concluded with European and Japanese companies that are based on a new pricing formula for establishing contract prices. Under the formula, the price for Iranian light, a top grade, will average $30 a barrel, up from $28.50 last month.

7   Grain prices are expected to fall because of the President's cutoff of grain exports to the Soviet Union, even though Carter has pledged to make up for the lost sales. Analysts see damage to both farmers and the economy. Futures markets in grain and related products won't open before Wednesday, on an order by the Commodity Futures Trading Commission.

Computer and oil-field equipment companies may suffer a decline in business following the new export limits for "high-technology" products, but businessmen doubt the move will have a significant effect on the Soviet economy.

Chrysler and the UAW tentatively agreed on a further $243 million in union concessions, moving it closer to completing terms of a federal financial aid package. But the auto maker said that there were unexpected problems in its long-range financing plan.

New-car sales fell 5.3 percent last month to 728,144 units. Domestic auto makers posted a 14 percent decline, while foreign producers reported a 39 percent gain to a record monthly total.

Some U.S. oil free of federal price controls, such as that from wells producing ten or fewer barrels a day, is fetching $35 to $40 a barrel, topping official OPEC contract prices of $24 to $34.

A tight credit policy is likely to be continued by the Fed, according to analysts, although estimates show that the growth of the nation's money supply slowed in 1979. Separately, Fed figures for the week ended December 26 show that the basic measure, M1, rose $2 billion and a broader gauge, M2, rose $2.5 billion.

8   Grain-supply contracts with the Soviets will be purchased from exporters by the U.S. for about $2.25 billion to ease the effect of the embargo. Separately, most of the nation's grain trade came to a near halt. Sales for immediate delivery were stalled by pricing confusion. U.S. futures markets are closed until tomorrow. In foreign markets prices fell sharply. U.S. livestock quotes plunged in anticipation that feed prices may decline.

Money-market analysts see higher interest rates stemming from U.S. pledges to purchase grain destined for the Soviet Union. Analysts said that such purchases would require further government financing, adding to credit strains in the market.

Limits on silver futures contracts were initiated by the Comex to avert a squeeze on deliverable supplies in coming months. Effective February 18, no trader may hold more than 500 contracts.

Home mortgage rates soared to record levels again in December, according to the Federal Home Loan Bank Board, and even higher rates are seen for future loans. The average effective interest rate on conventional mortgages for new home loans jumped 0.28 percentage point to 11.65 percent in early December.

9   The economy appears to have grown at a surprisingly brisk 2 percent to 3 percent annual rate in the fourth quarter, according to new Commerce Department estimates. The growth was linked to exports, construction outlays, and a rise in business inventories. The department's chief economist, Courtenay Slater, asserted that a recession still is on the way, however.

The stock market rallied, helped by the new government estimates of strong economic growth in the fourth period. Trading surged to more than 53 million shares. The Dow Jones industrial average posted its biggest gain in more than 14 months, rising 19.71 points to 851.71.

Carter's pay advisory committee moved to replace the voluntary 7 percent-a-year guideline for wage and benefit increases with a 7.5 percent-to-9.5 percent range. The proposal is to come before the committee January 22.

Consumer Installment credit expanded $2.41 billion in November, exceeding October's increase of $2.19 billion but far below September's record rise of $4.45 billion.

OPEC leaders said the dollar is likely to be replaced by year-end as the currency used for pricing OPEC's oil. It was predicted that a basket of currencies would be adopted to insulate OPEC revenues from the dollar's woes.

Home prices appear to be on the decline, according to Realtors, and the downturn may be more than temporary. A Realtors association said the median price of a single-family home fell $700 in November.

10   U.S. spot market prices for petroleum products have plunged due to weak demand, inflated prices and a mild winter. But consumer prices aren't likely to drop. Spot quotes cover just 10 per-

cent to 15 percent of petroleum sold. Crude oil prices on the open market are also lower.

The future of fuel oil for home heating, one of the oil industry's most popular products, is being threatened by sky-rocketing prices. Demand is down 5 percent to 10 percent, so far this winter.

Exxon has become the nation's biggest seller of gasoline, according to industry data, jumping ahead of Shell Oil and Indiana Standard. Exxon's gains have been helped by its links with Aramco, which accounts for the bulk of Saudi Arabia's oil output.

Corn, wheat, and soybean prices began their expected fall as trading resumed on futures exchanges. Besides reflecting uncertainty over the curb on grain shipments to the Soviets, the declines reflect new doubts over how Washington plans to indemnify exporters for their losses.

11 Producer prices for finished goods posted a rise of 0.8 percent last month, down from 1.3 percent in November and the smallest increase since last June. For the year, however, prices were up 12.5 percent, the biggest jump in five years. Little relief was seen for consumers in months ahead.

Business outlays are expected to rise 1 percent to 2 percent this year, after adjustment for inflation, far less than the 4½ percent to 5½ percent increase indicated for 1979. A government economist found the plans for 1980 consistent with a view of a mild economic downturn.

Ford, in a drastic production-cutting step, intends to close indefinitely its Los Angeles car-assembly plant February 8, laying off 1,670 workers. Ford said the plant, which makes full-sized cars, is being closed because smaller cars are more in demand.

New disclosure requirements were proposed by the SEC that would increase the amount of information that companies must tell holders. The SEC also proposed reducing the amount of company information that must be filed with the commission.

The Fed reported that the basic money supply, M1, grew 5.5 percent in 1979, up from an estimate of 5.1 percent. A broader gauge, M2, grew 8.3 percent, instead of 8 percent as earlier thought. The news had little effect on the money market.

14 Carter's budget and economic report, to be released late this month, will forecast a moderate recession this year, with unemployment rising to 7.5 percent in the fourth quarter and inflation remaining at the double-digit level. The President also will stick with his current anti-inflation policy.

The economy's expansion appears to be slowing. Government figures show that December's jobless rate rose to 5.9 percent from 5.8 percent in November, and that the economy created fewer jobs last year than in the prior two years. Also, while retail sales were up 1.1 percent last month, most of the gains reflect price boosts rather than increases in unit sales.

Honda's plan for a $200 million car-assembly facility near Columbus, Ohio, paves the way for other Japanese auto makers. It also accelerates the timing of any decision by Toyota and Nissan to make a similar move.

UAW President Douglas A. Fraser initiated a campaign to require Japanese auto makers to build cars in the U.S., a reversal of the auto union's traditional free-trade stance.

Exxon, in an internal study, concludes that any cessation of Iranian oil exports for three months or less could be handled by drawing from inventories and by speeding up oil tankers. But Exxon and other companies agree such a halt could affect prices.

15 Gold's price, climbed $25 an ounce to $671 on the Commodity Exchange in New York, a record for the market, reflecting concern over tensions in Iran and Afghanistan. Silver jumped $3.75 to a high of $42.50. In foreign-exchange trading the dollar gained, supporting the notion that gold's price rises reflect movements out of all currencies, rather than just the dollar.

A ruling that meals provided to employes are not wages subject to federal unemployment and Social Security taxes was left intact by the Supreme Court, a victory for Hotel Conquistador Inc. The decision may force the IRS to make hundreds of refunds.

16 The price of gold soared over $700 an ounce for the first time, settling in New York at $712.50. The surge was fueled partly by Treasury Secretary Miller's statement that the U.S. doesn't plan any gold sales in the current "unsettled" marketplace. Silver's price jumped to a record $47, then finished at $46.30. Platinum also reached a high, $877, before ending the day at $869.40. The dollar strengthened on foreign-currency markets in active trading.

U.S. auto makers' sales fell 5.3 percent in early January to 158,859 units, posting a smaller decline than had been anticipated. GM's totals were about even with last year. Sales were down 16.8 percent at Ford and 18.4 percent at Chrysler.

The Postal Service was pressured by the White House to scale down plans for an electronic mail system for businesses that generate large amounts of bills and other messages.

North Sea oil producers appear likely to settle on a first quarter reference price for crude oil of $29.75 a barrel, up 14 percent from the final quarter of 1979. The quote may be temporary, as North Sea sellers generally follow African producers, which still have a confusing mixture of prices.

The farm-credit market could tighten even further due to Carter's curb on grain shipments to Russia, analysts said. Loan repayments are likely to lag as the grain sales would have enabled farmers to pay off notes due in the first quarter.

Mexico's state oil company said it found an oil field with estimated reserves of 1.5 billion barrels. Separately, a group of U.S. companies began imports of Mexican natural gas at a rate of 300 million cubic feet daily.

17 Industrial output increased 0.3 percent last month, leaving the index with its smallest yearly gain since 1974. A government economist said the report showed signs of weakness. Many economists expect overall economic activity to decline in the first half.

Business inventories rose just 0.7 percent in November after increasing 0.9 percent in October, indicating that businesses continue to keep a close watch on their inventories. Some analysts said that as a result, any economic downturn this year may be a mild one.

Gold's price continued to climb, reaching a record $770 an ounce in New York before ending the day at $744, up $31.50 from the day before. The latest buying seemed to reflect signs that governments are taking an interest in the gold market. In foreign-exchange trading, the dollar generally retreated on some profit taking.

18 The price of gold touched a record $820 an ounce in frenzied trading, settling at $802 on the New York Commodity Exchange, up $58. Gold fever pushed up quotes for many other commodities. The Comex copper quote climbed to $1,199 a pound, triggering a 4.5-cent

price boost by Kennecott and Anaconda to $1.224, a record for a U.S. producer.

The U.S. response to the current wave of gold speculation has been muted, possibly indicating a change in U.S. policies. Also, other industrialized nations seem to have decided against intervening in the turbulent market.

U.S. auto makers said three additional car assembly plants and two truck facilities will be closed next week, bringing the number of closings to nine. About 35,000 workers will be idled, down from 80,000 this week.

The basic money supply, M1, fell $700 million in the week ended Jan. 9, less than had been expected by analysts. The surprising strength triggered a spurt in short-term interest rates. A broader measure of the supply, M2, was up $1.1 billion.

21 The economy is seen growing at a slow pace in the first quarter, which many analysts consider the best way to bring about a reduction in the inflation rate. In the 1979 fourth period, the nation's gross national product, adjusted for inflation, rose at a 1.4 percent annual rate, after moving up at a 3.1 percent pace in the third period.

Chrysler's Japanese lenders and the maker of the company's popular subcompact import cars, Mitsubishi, appear to be stepping up efforts to end ties with the troubled auto maker. The developments threaten Chrysler's recovery strategy.

The Fed at least unwittingly may have eased its credit brakes in recent weeks, economists said. The economists added that a surge in the availability of reserves threatens to renew ballooning of the nation's money supply and to cause even higher interest rates.

SEC officials agreed to settle a landmark case concerning how much a lawyer must disclose about wrongdoing by a corporate client. The SEC plans to drop its bid for sanctions against a firm if a federal judge clears a $1.3 million settlement of private suits against the lawyers.

22 A tax cut was rejected by the President in his written State of the Union message, which pledges continued efforts to fight inflation. The message sets a budget deficit for the year starting October 1 that is less than half the $33.2 billion deficit expected for fiscal 1980. Some of the new bills Carter wants passed are designed to reduce youth unemployment, establish a standby gasoline rationing plan, and convert utilities from oil to coal.

Gold's price hit $875 in New York, a high, settling at $825.50 an ounce, a record late quote and up $13.50 from Friday. At one point, the price fell $30 on news that the Comex had banned new positions in silver in all contract months. Silver finished at $44, down $2.80. The dollar rose in foreign-exchange trading.

Copper increased 11.5 cents a pound on the Comex, the biggest gain for a single day, to a price to $1.375. A record quote of $1.40 was set in 1974.

The consumer price index was defended by the Bureau of Labor Statistics as the best measure of inflation, but plans were announced to explore alternative methods of measuring price changes.

23 The price of gold plunged $143.50 an ounce in New York, its biggest decline ever, to $682. Despite the drop, most observers predicted gold will bounce back. Gold's tumble pushed down silver's price, which fell $10, a record single-day drop, to $34 an ounce. The slump in both metals followed Commodity Exchange curbs on silver trading and remarks by Fed Chairman Volcker supporting the Treasury's policy of gold sales.

Copper prices posted their biggest one-day loss ever, reflecting gold's record decline. On the Comex, copper fell 18 cents to $1.195.

Key parts of a "windfall profits" tax on oil producers were decided by House and Senate conferees. Larger oil companies would pay $204.8 billion during 1980 through 1990. Small independent producers would pay $22.5 billion. Still to be settled is how long the tax will last and how much money it will raise.

24 Chrysler, in another bid to lure customers, said it will announce a major new marketing program today. Details were not disclosed. There was speculation that the plan may include some earlier experiments. One program provided a "money-back guarantee" and another offered $50 to certain customers who came into showrooms for a test drive. Separately, Mitsubishi Motors agreed to temporarily resume shipments to Chrysler, even though Mitsubishi must finance at least the next shipment on its own.

New-car sales fell 24 percent in mid-January at U.S. auto makers, as expected. Chrysler posted a 24.1 percent decline; GM had a 23 percent drop.

Gold's price fluctuated on buying and profit taking, settling at $660 an ounce in New York, down $22 from the day before and bringing the metal's two-day decline to $165.50. Silver finished at $37.50 with a $3.50 gain. Speculators concerned about gold bought soft commodities, such as sugar and cotton. Sugar's quote has risen to 20 cents a pound, compared with 8 cents about six months ago.

Two big Pennsylvania banks, Equibank and National Central Bank, like smaller banks elsewhere, are withdrawing from the Federal Reserve System to pursue earnings opportunities available to non-member banks. The Fed fears the two banks' withdrawal could hamper its ability to set monetary policy.

Sea-Land Service, a unit of R. J. Reynolds, is resigning from 12 steamship groups that set rates on cargoes moving from Asia to the U.S. and Canada. The move, designed to increase Sea-Land's share of such trade, has jolted the groups involved.

25 Durable-goods orders inched up 0.6 percent last month to $75.86 billion, buoyed by a rise in aircraft orders. Bookings were down 1.6 percent in November. The latest report conforms with other year-end statistics indicating an economy that showed little signs of growth but continued to resist recession.

Gold trading was frenzied, with prices climbing $21 in New York to $681 an ounce after touching a low of about $655 in Hong Kong and a high of $735 in London. Commodity markets were somewhat unsettled, but price swings generally were narrower than in recent days. Sugar, cotton, and copper quotes climbed, however.

Ford said it will close temporarily 7 of its 13 car assembly plants next week. It cited dealer inventories and a parts shortage caused by a strike at Budd Co. About 15,600 workers will be idled, 7,000 fewer than this week.

Chrysler unveiled a package of innovative new-car merchandising ideas. The proposals include a $50 test-drive offer; an unprecedented 30-day "money-back guarantee"; two years of free scheduled maintenance; and membership in an independent road service club.

The Fed's injection of reserves into the banking network last Tuesday and Wednesday appears to have been prompted by technical factors. Separately, the basic money supply, M1, rose $1 billion in the week ended January 16 while a broader gauge, M2, rose $2.5 billion.

28   Consumer prices are likely to continue climbing, economists said, based on the momentum of last month's increase. In December, prices jumped 1.2 percent, the sharpest rise since February 1979, bringing the full-year increase to 13.3 percent, the steepest in 33 years.

Estimates of oil and gas reserves that may lie off the coast of Alaska were boosted sharply by the U.S. Geological Survey. The biggest increases in estimated reserves are in the Navarin Basin of the Bering Sea and in the Beaufort Basin of the Beaufort Sea.

29   Carter's budget for the 1981 fiscal year, starting October 1, sets a 9.3 percent increase in outlays to $615.8 billion and a slimmer deficit of $15.8 billion, which assumes several actions by Congress that are doubtful. The fiscal 1980 deficit is estimated at $39.8 billion. The election-year proposal provides a 12 percent rise in military spending and more aid for housing and youth-jobs programs. The budget is based on predictions of a mild recession in the first half and double-digit inflation.

Defense spending of $142.7 billion is slated by the President, reflecting concerns over Soviet aggression and unrest in the Middle East. Carter has pledged more money, however, to protect real growth targets if inflation is higher than expected. The request represents a 3.3 percent boost after adjustment for inflation.

Saudi Arabia raised the price of its Arab light grade, the OPEC benchmark crude, $2 a barrel to $26, as expected. Some in the industry were surprised that the boost was retroactive to January 1, however, because of a Saudi pledge to hold the price at $24 through January.

Gold's price edged up $4 an ounce in New York to $638 in quiet dealings. The dollar gained in foreign exchange trading. The currency was aided by Carter's budget message, which proposed a narrower deficit.

Japanese auto makers are coming under increasing U.S. pressure to establish manufacturing plants in the U.S. Officials are citing the strong possibility of legislative curbs on imports of Japanese-made cars.

30   U.S. Steel reported a fourth period loss of $561.7 million, believed the largest quarterly deficit posted by an American company. The loss reflects the $808.6 million cost of closedowns at 16 plants, which eliminated 13,000 jobs. Analysts had expected the loss, but they were surprised that U.S. Steel said it would continue its 40-cent-a-share quarterly dividend.

The merchandise trade deficit of the U.S. widened to $3.08 billion last month. The trade gap for 1979 narrowed to $24.69 billion from $28.4 billion in 1978, aided by strong exports. Government economists see a wider deficit in 1980, however, because of higher oil prices.

Gold jumped $64 an ounce in New York, settling at a price of $702 on trader expectations that the U.S. would report a wider trade deficit for December. The dollar fell on world currency markets.

Oil prices of Kuwait, Iraq, Qatar, and the United Arab Emirates were increased $2 a barrel, retroactive to January 1. The move, which may have been triggered by a boost by Saudi Arabia, stunned oil observers, who fear another round of price leapfrogging in OPEC.

FCC regulation of telecommunications companies would be curbed under legislation approved by the House Communications Subcommittee. The move is an attempt to step up competition in the industry.

Yields on long-term government obligations topped 11 percent for the first time in history. The bond market's mood darkened on worries about a wider U.S. trade deficit last month and oil prices.

31   The economy is headed for a "mild" recession in a dangerous inflationary environment, according to the economic report of the President and the annual report of his Council of Economic Advisers. Both documents reflect deep concerns that the 13 percent inflation of 1979 could become embedded if cautious fiscal and monetary policies are not pursued.

Treasury Secretary Miller and two other top economic officials told a Senate panel that the budget for fiscal 1981, beginning October 1, is not balanced because of the forecast of a recession and the need to increase defense spending. They warned inflation remains the major economic threat.

Key economic indicators, which skidded in October and November, were unchanged last month, leaving government economists uncertain as to whether they are signaling a recession or very slow growth. The Carter administration has forecast a "mild" recession this year.

Auto-production plans for February are expected to be down more than 20 percent from a year ago, instead of 15 percent as forecast previously. The latest moves could trim U.S. first quarter output to 1,760,000 cars, the second lowest for the period in recent years.

February 1980

1 New factory orders climbed 1.3 percent to $148.5 billion in December, after holding steady the month before, and showed a mixed pattern of increases and decreases in durable goods orders. Government economists said the report contained confusing signals on the direction of the economy.

General Motors plans to build two car-assembly plants by the mid-1980s for $1 billion to replace two less-efficient facilities in St. Louis and Pontiac, Michigan.

Ford intends to close 8 of its 13 U.S. car-assembly facilities temporarily next week to trim inventories, and Chrysler will close 1 of its 4 plants. The close-downs, and others announced earlier, will idle 32,475 workers for the week.

Standby oil-saving measures are expected to be announced next week by the Energy Department. The measurses include a mandatory four-day workweek and a ban on driving during one or more days each week.

Some petroleum refiners are balking at paying ever-rising crude oil prices in the current sluggish market. Nonetheless, OPEC producers may raise their prices further, possibly as soon as today.

The basic money supply, M1, declined $2.9 billion in the week ended January 23. A broader measure, M2, fell $2.6 billion. The news helped push down short-term interest rates. Separately, the Fed said it intends to begin issuing newly defined money measures next Friday.

4 Employment statistics for January indicate a widespread tightening throughout the labor market. Government economist said there isn't enough evidence yet of a serious downturn. Unemployment rose to 6.2 percent last month from 5.9 percent in December, bringing it to its highest level since July 1978.

The economy showed further signs of weakness last month and inflationary pressures were stronger, according to a survey of corporate purchasing managers. Many of the managers said they were confident, however, and reported "good business."

General Motors will begin today a $500 consumer rebate offer for certain 1979-model big cars and vans. The program may cost about $37.5 million and extends to March 10. It underscores auto makers' continuing problems with less fuel-efficient vehicles.

Sears, J. C. Penney, and other major retailers, hurt by high interest costs and the rising amount of unpaid debts, are tightening their consumer credit terms and seeking to increase their finance charge income.

5 Fed Chairman Volcker urged speedy congressional approval of legislation designed to stem the exodus of member banks from the Fed system. He warned that declining membership would weaken Fed control over monetary policy.

Gold's price fell $23.30 an ounce in New York to $660, largely due to a lack of buyers. The dollar declined in foreign-exchange dealings, especially against the British pound.

General motors reported that fourth quarter profit, reflecting a continuing U.S. sales slump, plunged more than 57 percent from record 1978 results to $426 million, or $1.46 a share. Analysts expect GM to be the only one of the Big Three auto makers to post a profit for the quarter. Full-year net fell about 17 percent to $2.89 billion, or $10.04 a share.

Eight strict fuel conservation measures that are in addition to nine standby measures announced by the Energy Department are being considered by energy officials. The proposals include a shortening of the school week and mandatory thermostat controls in homes.

6 Treasury Secretary Miller recommended that Congress pass a bill requiring most banks to meet uniform reserve requirements. The measure is designed to stem the Fed's loss of member banks, which have been leaving the system to escape reserve requirements.

Car sales rose 3.2 percent in January to an estimated 794,490 units, the first year-to-year increase in nine months. GM's sales were flat, while Ford and Chrysler posted declines of 23.1 percent and 22.9 percent. Imports made a strong showing.

The price of gold jumped $27 in New York to $687 an ounce, more than making up Monday's decline. On foreign-exchange markets, the dollar gained against most key currencies.

The freezing of Iranian assets is seen causing many international companies to restructure the way they finance overseas transactions to avoid such legal complications in other countries.

7 Gold jumped $26 an ounce in New York to $713 on trader expectations that the IMF auction would draw prices above $700. The dollar plunged on foreign-exchange markets, hitting its lowest level against the British pound since July.

The merchandise trade deficit on a balance-of-payments basis grew in the fourth quarter to $7.92 billion, the widest for any quarter last year, on higher prices for imports, especially oil. For 1979, the deficit was $29.13 billion, narrower than the $33.72 billion gap of 1978.

Home mortgage rates have declined lately from record levels of 13 percent or, in some areas, 14 percent, but economists generally do not expect rates to fall below 10½ percent this year. Lenders say inflation and higher costs of attracting savers will keep rates high.

Bond prices continued their unprecedented drop. Yields climbed to a record of about 12 percent on intermediate-term Treasury notes and 13 percent on prime-quality telephone debentures.

Chrysler arranged a $100 million short-term loan from Peugeot while it struggles to bring its sources of new financing into line. The loan could be the first step in a series of cooperative sales and production agreements with Peugeot.

An investigation of auto industry competition will be curtailed sharply by the FTC, and some subpoena demands that auto makers had contested will be withdrawn. The decision reflects, in part, criticism by Congress of some of the burdens the agency has imposed on businesses.

8 New money-supply definitions were adopted by the Fed to reflect more accurately the changing ways the public holds its funds. It appears the Fed will continue to focus on a relatively narrow concept of money. The definitions, which include several broader measures of money and overall liquidity, are not expected to alter the way monetary policy is conducted. M1, the most basic measure, is replaced with M1-A and a wider M1-B.

Chrysler reported a $375.8-million fourth quarter loss, pushing its full-year deficit to nearly $1.1 billion, a record. Sales fell 23 percent in the quarter to $3.05 billion and to $12 billion in the year from $13.67 billion in 1978.

GM and Chrysler each are closing 1 car-assembly operation next week and Ford is closing 5 of its 13 facilities to trim inventories. The closedowns, and several others, will idle a total 30,650 workers next week.

Consumer credit expanded $1.55 billion in December, or at a 6 percent annual rate, compared with a $2.41 billion increase in November. For the year, credit outstanding grew 13 percent to $311.34 billion from $275.63 billion in 1978.

Gold's price fell below $700 an ounce, posting a $23.50 decline in New York to $689.50. In foreign-exchange trading, the dollar rose against most key currencies in moderate dealings.

11 "Windfall profits" tax conferees hope to complete work on a bill to tax the profits of oil companies next week. Still to be decided are how to spend the $227 billion in tax money, which Senate energy tax credits to accept and which to reject, and, among other things, whether to make the levy retroactive to January 1.

Mortgage-rate ceilings on FHA and VA home loans were raised to 12 percent, effective today, from 11½ percent for single-family homes and 11 percent for multifamily dwellings. A federal housing official said that while the increases may seem too cautious when some rates are near 13 percent, he expects some stabilization in mortgage rates.

Chrysler is expected to announce another interim financing arrangement with Mitsubishi this week that would ensure the delivery of 40,000 Mitsubishi vehicles to the U.S. Also, E. F. Hutton is said to be close to agreeing to help underwrite all or part of a sale of $250 million in Chrysler debentures.

12 Retail sales increased an unexpectedly strong 2.3 percent last month, following a 0.5 percent rise in December. A top Commerce Department economist said strong consumer spending is not likely to continue. Another economist raised doubts that the economy will slip in the first quarter, as predicted.

Signs of a tighter credit policy were seen by some analysts, but others said there was not sufficient evidence of action by the Fed. The possibility of a credit tightening pushed up short-term interest rates; some rose more than ¼ percentage point.

Kodak's profit fell 11 percent in the fourth quarter to $294.7 million, or $1.82 a share, despite a 12 percent jump in sales to $2.52 billion. Earnings were hurt by higher prices for silver, used in photographic film, and for petroleum-based feedstocks.

Gold settled at $702 an ounce in New York, up $7.50. Gains early in the day were attributed to buying by holders of commitments to deliver gold. The dollar declined against most major currencies in foreign-exchange trading.

Copper's price reached a record $1.41 a pound on the New York Commodity Exchange, fueled by speculative demand. The new price spurred Asarco to raise its quote seven cents to $1.45, a record for a U.S. producer.

The bond market sell-off continued. Dealers said the market for long-term bonds is being pushed close to the point of temporarily ceasing to function. The Treasury's new 11¾ percent bonds of 2010 lost slightly more than 2¼ points, or $25 for every $1,000 of bonds, to 98 8/32 bid.

13 Business inventories rose 0.4 percent in December to $426.29 billion after climbing 0.8 percent in November. The latest increase reflects continued caution by businesses on inventory building. It suggests that, with inventories being watched so closely, any recession in 1980 will be brief.

The IRS is forcing businesses using lower-of-cost-or-market accounting to stop writing down their inventories in a manner that the Supreme Court has said violates IRS rules. The move could mean more than $1 million in added taxes for some companies.

Bethlehem Steel will raise the price of its carbon and high-strength steel plates, used in construction, shipbuilding, and other industries, about 5.5 percent, effective with shipments March 16.

Nissan and Toyota were urged by the Japanese government to curb exports to the United States and begin producing cars in America to ease trade frictions between the two countries.

Federal trade-adjustment assistance was approved for 1,800 Chrysler workers in Michigan who have lost work or face job cuts because of increased imports.

14 U.S. Steel signed a three-year contract with Nippon Steel that calls for the Japanese company to supply technical advice on ways U.S. Steel can increase the productivity of its ailing blast furnace operations. Separately, U.S. Steel raised the base price of its carbon, high-strength, and alloy plate $25 a ton, effective March 30.

SEC regulations designed to give investors and brokers better information about stock prices were approved by the commission. The rules would affect quotes on Nasdaq, the quotation system for over-the-counter stocks, and the way quotes are retrieved on quotation-display equipment.

The IRS is said to have a better capability to mount a crackdown on certain foreign corporate tax shelters. One of the industries on which the IRS has been focusing is pharmaceuticals. Some big U.S. drug concerns have extremely profitable units in Puerto Rico.

Car sales declined 22 percent in early February, reversing the 1 percent gain posted in the final third of last month. An industry analyst said there was a lot of erratic pressure in the marketplace, as various auto makers periodically tried to aid their dealers. GM reported a 15 percent drop, compared with a 17 percent rise in late January, and Ford sales fell 43 percent. Volume at Chrysler slipped 11 percent.

Nissan and Toyota told UAW President Douglas Fraser they would be "prudent" in their exports but insisted they would not impose voluntary restraints on shipments to the U.S. Fraser has been urging the auto makers to build cars in the U.S. and to curb exports to the American market.

15 Indiana Standard settled federal allegations of oil pricing violations. The company agreed to pay $100 million, forgo $180 million in potential future price boosts, cut gasoline and propane prices for certain customers, and increase outlays for domestic oil exploration and refinery improvements by $410 million.

Mobil Oil was fined $500,000 on criminal charges that it switched natural gas sales out of the interstate market without federal approval. Mobil had said it would not contest the charges.

Some of Algeria's oil customers are refusing to take any oil since the application of a $3-a-barrel "exploration" fee that makes Algerian crude the highest priced in OPEC, effectively selling at $37.21.

Gold prices skidded, falling $17.50 an ounce in New York to $670.50, on brightened hopes that the U.S. hostages in Iran might be released soon. On foreign-exchange markets, the dollar rose against most key currencies.

19 The economy remains strong and administration economists are worried that a recession might be avoided this year. The economists said the view of a stronger-than-expected economy fuels inflation by causing businesses to be firmer in pricing decisions than they otherwise would have been. Inflation fears were confirmed by statistics showing that producer prices for finished goods soared 1.6 percent last month, or at a 19.2 percent annual rate. Industrial output rose 0.3 percent.

Prime-rate increases are considered to be likely in the wake of the Fed's boost in its discount rate to 13 percent from 12 percent. The prime rate, generally at 15¼ percent, is expected to hit 15¾ percent in a few weeks. Analysts were surprised by the Fed's move. Corporate executives expect higher interest rates, but do not see a big impact on their operations.

The dollar continued to gain in foreign-exchange trading following the Fed's move. Trading was thin due to the Washington's birthday holiday. Gold's price fell in London to $661.50 an ounce from $665.25 in the morning meeting. On Friday, prices for most commodities fell. The stock market slumped. The Fed move was seen as insufficient to bring inflation under control. Bond market prices dropped, and even steeper declines are predicted.

20 The prime rate at most major banks was raised to a record 15¾ percent from 15¼ percent amid fears the Fed will be forced to take further credit-tightening measures following its discount rate boost to 13 percent. Rates on short-term securities posted increases ranging to more than one half of a percentage point.

Federal Reserve Board Chairman Volcker, worried that inflation may accelerate, told the House Banking Committee of the Fed's determination to slow monetary growth. He also unveiled new targets for money-supply expansion in 1980.

Housing starts, pressured by high interest rates, fell 6.4 percent last month to an annual rate of 1.4 million units, the lowest level of new housing construction since July 1976, the Commerce Department said. The department added that personal income grew 0.6 percent, with the help of several special factors.

Corporate-takeover rule changes that could make acquisitions more expensive were proposed by the SEC. The commission wants to make most offers for more than 10 percent of a company's stock subject to all disclosure requirements and holder protections under existing tender-offer laws.

21 The economy grew at an inflation-adjusted annual rate of 2.1 percent in the fourth quarter, instead of at the 1.4 percent pace reported last month. The revision suggested a strong economy. Government economists feared the statistics could lead to higher prices by fueling an inflation psychology.

A tax break on as much as $200 a year of income from interest or dividends, $400 for couples, was voted by conferees on the "windfall" tax on oil companies. The tax exclusion would not become available until 1981.

OPEC appears to have given up trying to restore order to short-term petroleum pricing until its next meeting, set for June 9. A special meeting may be held soon, however, on a long-term policy program that would include periodic and automatic price increases.

Bank interest-rate ceilings would be phased out over five years under a proposal endorsed by key federal bank regulators, who cited soaring inflation and interest rates. The Senate has approved a ten-year phase-out.

The new savings certificates held for 30 months are far more popular with consumers than the four-year certificates they replaced, according to a sampling of banks and savings and loan associations. But they still are second to 6-month certificates.

Gold climbed $29.50 an ounce in New York to $661.50 after hitting a low of $599. A dealer said the price turned around because the $600 level is an attractive buying price. The dollar posted declines in foreign-exchange trading.

22 A "windfall" tax on oil companies that would cut taxes for millions of individuals has been just about completed by conferees. The bill would raise less money than the President wanted and spread the burden differently, but Carter indicated he will sign it. The levy would start March 1. Revenue is targeted at $227.3 billion.

Wage and price council members studying last year's surge in oil-industry profits plan to report next week that 11 major companies violated federal anti-inflation price guidelines. The report is expected to lay part of the blame on the Energy Department.

Ford posted a fourth quarter net loss of $41 million. Losses in North American automotive operations offset strong results in other areas. Full-year net fell 26 percent to $1.17 billion, or $9.75 a share.

Four car-assembly plants in the U.S. will be closed temporarily next week, and AMC will reduce output indefinitely, by 50 units a day, at its Kenosha, Wisconsin, plant. The moves will idle 13,000 Ford and GM workers and 500 AMC employes.

Stocks plunged across a broad front. The Dow Jones Industrials fell 18.34 points to 868.52. The break was linked to concern over Iran and over comments by a respected Wall Street economist, Henry Kaufman of Salomon Brothers, urging "national emergency" moves against inflation. The remarks also hurt bond prices.

The dollar gained against most key currencies, aided by reports that Kaufman predicted higher interest rates. Gold fell $5 an ounce in New York to $656.50.

A prime rate increase to 16 percent from 15¾ percent currently seems almost certain, according to money analysts, because of the surging costs banks are encountering in raising funds. Some specialists predicted a 17 percent rate soon.

25 Strong economic growth and price increases are threatening to weaken business and labor support for Carter's moderate anti-inflation policies. Statistics for January show that consumer prices climbed 1.4 percent, or at a 16.8 percent annual rate, the sharpest rise since August 1973. Durable-goods orders jumped a surprisingly strong 4.3 percent.

Worsening inflation has spurred some prominent congressional Democrats to suggest that mandatory wage and price controls should at least be considered. The chances that Congress will act soon on such a program remain slim.

Bank loan demand could surge again, money experts warned, adding that chaotic conditions in bond markets may force borrowers to turn to banks for their financing needs. Analysts said an increase is possible despite the prime rate boost to 16¼ percent by some banks from 15¾ percent, and to a record 16½ percent by others.

High interest rates are causing headaches for businesses, but most major companies indicate that rates still do not seem stiff enough to alter their operations.

Short interest on the New York Stock Exchange jumped 18 percent to a record 60,021,211 shares in the month ended February 15. The one-month rise of 9,053,810 shares also set a high. Amex short interest climbed 13 percent to 8,010,580 shares.

26 Car sales fell 9.5 percent in mid-February to an estimated 217,604 units, continuing a pattern of recent months. Deliveries tumbled 2.2 percent at GM, nearly 21 percent at Ford, 26 percent at Chrysler, and an estimated 6.4 percent at AMC.

Mandatory wage and price controls, a wage-price freeze or credit controls would not be effective in combating inflation, Fed Chairman Volcker said. Volcker repeated the Fed's commitment to restrain monetary and credit growth.

Short-term interest rates jumped due to concern that the Fed may tighten its credit reins further. Several more banks raised their prime rate to 16½ percent from 16¼ percent, and some institutions raised their broker loan rate to 16½ percent from 15¾ percent.

27 Anti-inflation policies of the administration were defended by the President, but he indicated that they may be adjusted a bit. Carter again ruled out mandatory wage and price controls.

Higher interest rates for consumer loans and mortgages were announced by Citibank, and more banks raised their prime rate to 16½ percent. A prime rate increase within a month to 17 percent was predicted by John F. McGillicuddy, chairman of Manufacturers Hanover.

The Treasury sold $2.5 billion of five-year, 2½-month notes at an average return of 14.39 percent, a record for any note or bond ever sold by the department.

Gold declined $23.40 an ounce in New York to $625.50 in thin trading, which was attributed to a lack of new developments. On foreign-exchange markets, the dollar was mixed, falling against the Japanese yen and the British pound.

A "windfall" tax on oil producers that would raise $227 billion received final approval from House-Senate conferees after they agreed on aid to low-income people. A provision to help middle-income people pay for heat was dropped.

Domestic air fares were permitted by the CAB to rise 2½ percent because of higher costs, particularly for jet fuel. The increase is effective March 1.

28 March interest rates on popular new 2½-year money-market certificates were capped at 12 percent for thrift institutions and 11.75 percent for commercial banks by federal regulators. Rates of 13.75 percent and 13.5 percent would have been permitted March 1. Regulators feared a rate jump would have hurt many institutions.

A Treasury sale of $4 billion of 52-week bills brought a record average return of 13.527 percent. The coupon equivalent rate was 15.28 percent, the highest ever on a Treasury security.

Ceilings on interest rates for federally backed mortgages were raised for the second time in less than three weeks, to 13 percent from 12 percent.

Productivity in the private business sector fell at a 0.6 percent annual rate in last year's fourth quarter, the Labor Department said, instead of at the 1.6 percent pace reported a month ago.

29 Fiscal and monetary policies should follow a steady and moderate course, concluded the congressional Joint Economic Committee, and the government should devote more attention to expanding the economy's long-run potential. The panel's solution to inflation is more private investment and growth.

Wages and salaries climbed 2.4 percent in the fourth quarter, the largest three-month rise since the Labor Department's pay index was started in 1975. For the full year, wages rose 8.7 percent, also a record. Although the gains were large, they came during a year when consumer prices jumped 13 percent.

The merchandise trade deficit widened in January to $4.76 billion, the largest since February 1978, although oil imports declined. The trade gap was $4.07 billion in December and $2.73 billion in November.

March 1980

3 Rumors on credit controls are spurring some businesses to set up new lines of credit in anticipation of any controls. There is also concern that any controls would be ineffective in the corporate sector; consumer borrowing is seen a likely target.

Key economic indicators are not necessarily signaling the onset of a recession despite four consecutive months of declines, according to a Commerce Department economist. He said the monthly declines have been very small, averaging 0.4 percent. January's report showed a 0.7 percent drop.

A prime rate increase to 17 percent is seen likely this week as the banking industry's cost of gathering lendable funds continues to climb. The industry moved to a record 16¾ percent Friday.

4 Controls on auto loans and home mortgages are said to have been ruled out by senior Carter administration officials in the battle against inflation. Still being considered is the use of the Credit Control Act of 1969, under which the President may authorize the Fed to impose some credit controls.

Short-term interest rates posted the sharpest one-day jump on record following indications of a tougher Fed monetary policy and a $1 billion sale of Treasury bills by a foreign central bank. In resale trading, some Treasury issues touched a record of more than 15 percent bid.

Auto production declined 15 percent last month to 661,757 cars. The output by U.S. auto makers exceeded tentative targets set early in February.

A rise in the debt ceiling totaling $58 billion was sought by the Carter administration. Officials added they would trim the figure if the President decided to aim for a smaller deficit in either fiscal 1980 or 1981.

5 The prime rate was raised to a record 17¼ percent from 16¾ percent by the nation's major banks, led by Chase Manhattan. The increase, the fifth this year, reflects banks' high costs in obtaining funds for lending and investing. Many banks also boosted their broker-loan rate to 17 percent.

Bank-card and other charge-card issuers find the rising cost of borrowed money is rapidly approaching, and in some cases exceeding, the interest charges permitted under state laws. They are lobbying for higher usury-law ceilings; some may even drop card holders.

Car sales fell 6.7 percent last month to an estimated 808,465 units, posting a smaller-than-expected decline. Imports captured a record share of the U.S. market, more than 27 percent.

A new "synthetic fuels corporation" to

manage the proposed $20 billion federal energy program was approved by House-Senate conferees. The corporation would provide such incentives as federal loans and loan guarantees.

OPEC won't make another attempt to restore oil pricing unity until summer, according to Venezuela's energy minister, who also is OPEC's president. He cited stabilized production levels in OPEC countries and mild winter weather.

6 The Federal Reserve Board would be allowed to prescribe a level of reserves for nonmember banks as well as members under a bill approved by a congressional conference committee. The Fed has said the bill would enhance its ability to conduct monetary policy.

Some oil producers may cut output this year because of easing demand and bulging inventories world-wide, Saudi Arabia's oil minister suggested. He said that current Saudi output of 9.5 million barrels daily, increased by 1-million barrels early in 1979, is unlikely to continue through 1980.

7 Money market trading was nearly halted by uncertainty over the Carter administration's impending anti-inflation program, and interest rates surged. In the bond market, record returns were placed on new debt issues, depressing prices. Oil issues led a steep decline in the stock market. The Dow Jones industrial average skidded 16.81 points to 828.07.

Controls on credit-card lending may be imposed soon by the Carter administration, according to Senate Democratic Whip Alan Cranston. He sees the controls as part of a new anti-inflation package expected next week.

Department store sales were sluggish in February, but discount stores posted strong gains as consumers hunted for bargains. Volume rose 2 percent at Mobil's Montgomery Ward unit and 4.3 percent at Sears. K mart, which operates a discount chain, had an 18 percent increase.

A coal-conversion plan for electric utilities to reduce their use of oil and natural gas was approved by the President, over the objections of environmental aides who wanted tight curbs on the program. The proposal would provide $10 billion in funding.

10 The economy during February showed a continuation of the inflationary pressures that are pushing the Carter administration to toughen its anti-infla-

tion policies. Producer prices for finished goods rose 1.5 percent last month, or at an 18 percent annual rate, after climbing 1.6 percent in January. Unemployment fell to 6 percent from 6.2 percent.

Bank loan demand by business may accelerate, analysts said, despite a prime rate increase Friday at major banks to 17¾ percent from 17¼ percent. Analysts cited last week's near paralysis in the money market, an important source of financing. As interest rates soar, however, banks report that usury limits are beginning to impede corporate borrowing.

Mortgage rates were raised to 16½ percent from 15½ percent by American Savings & Loan, a unit of First Charter, and to 16 percent from 15½ percent by H. F. Ahmanson's Home Savings & Loan. The increases are the third in two weeks for both S&Ls.

11 Retail sales fell 0.7 percent last month to $78.98 billion following a 3.3 percent increase in January. The decline was the first since last October. Government economists were hard pressed to interpret the February report; one analyst speculated the drop could mean consumers just decided to pause after January.

Consumer credit expanded $1.37 billion in January, compared with a $1.35 billion expansion in December. In both months credit grew at a 5.3 percent annual rate.

Gold's price slumped $40.50 an ounce in New York to $558, its lowest level this year, as investors concentrated on current record interest rates, which make it expensive to finance speculation in gold and other commodities. Silver, platinum, and many other commodities also fell.

The dollar jumped sharply in foreign-exchange trading on high U.S. interest rates and trader expectations about a new Carter anti-inflation package.

The Treasury's sale of 13-week bills brought a record average return of 15.381 percent. For 26-week bills, the average return climbed to 14.956 percent, also a high.

12 A trucking deregulation measure that would make it easier for companies to enter the trucking business and for existing ones to expand was approved by the Senate Commerce Committee.

OPEC countries are planning major new oil production cuts on April 1. The reductions would include the lightest, highest-quality oil, such as that produced in North Africa, and the heavy, lower-quality crudes produced in Kuwait.

Gold, recovering slightly, jumped $8.50 in New York to $566.50 an ounce. On world currency markets, the dollar was narrowly mixed.

13 Capital spending is expected to rise a slim 1 percent to 2 percent in 1980, adjusted for inflation, according to a Commerce Department survey of businesses. The findings were unchanged from a previous survey. Business expects capital equipment prices to jump 10 percent, but a government economist said that estimates may be low.

Carter's anti-inflation package is running into some trouble, and the President has not decided when he will unveil it. Budget cuts deeper than the $12 billion to $13 billion proposed for fiscal 1981 are proving difficult, as are revenue raising measures. The fiscal 1981 budget deficit is estimated at $20 billion.

Bache Halsey plans to increase stock brokerage commissions an average 3 percent, effective tomorrow, and Lehman Brothers plans a 4 percent boost, effective March 21. The actions could trigger other rate increases on Wall Street.

Ceilings on government loans for mobile homes were raised to 17 percent from 15½ percent and for property improvements to 16½ percent from 15 percent. The increase is the third in five weeks.

Demand for steel and aluminum is unexpectedly strong, showing that many of the nation's industries have shrugged off high interest rates and continue to spend at relatively high levels. Steelmakers are being aided by foreign orders.

14 Wage-increase ceilings of between 7½ percent and 9½ percent were endorsed by the Carter administration. The higher limits are for the voluntary pay-restraint program's second year, which began October 1.

Prime-rate boosts to 18¼ percent were set by six major banks, led by New York's Chase Manhattan, reflecting sharp rises in banks' costs of raising money for relending. Some analysts predicted that the end is not in sight. Two Canadian banks also raised their prime lending rates for the first time since October, to 15¾ percent.

Henry Ford II will immediately step down as chairman of Ford Motor. He is succeeded by Philip Caldwell, who was president. The company named Donald E. Petersen to succeed Mr. Caldwell. Many had expected the presidency to go to William O. Bourke, who announced his resignation as an executive vice president.

Ford Motor will close three car-assembly plants next week in an effort to keep inventories in line with lagging sales.

Car sales dropped 8.6 percent in the first ten days of March, although they were somewhat higher than had been expected because of some special marketing efforts.

17 New anti-inflation proposals by the President that include credit restraints, budget restraints, budget cuts, a withholding tax on interest and dividends and a gasoline levy did not draw much of a positive reaction from business executives. Many thought the program was too little and too late. Stock market analysts anticipate a recession. Bond traders predict somewhat calmer markets. Gold and commodity trading is not likely to decline immediately. The Carter package generally drew praise overseas, but analysts were divided over possible market reaction in trading today.

The Fed's revamped policies to slow credit growth emphasize a switch to limiting the availability of credit rather than relying predominantly on high interest rates, although rates would rise initially. Among other things, banks are being asked to hold loan growth to a 6 percent-to-9 percent range this year.

Short-term interest rates are seen even more likely to climb following the new anti-inflation proposals, which include a 3-percentage-point surcharge to 16 percent on borrowings by large commercial banks at the Fed's discount window. Some bankers predict a 20 percent prime rate soon, up from the record 18½ percent level set Friday.

18 The dollar climbed in foreign currency trading on the promise of still higher U.S. interest rates resulting from Carter's anti-inflation package. Gold fell $57 an ounce in New York to $469. Prices of silver and other commodities also declined. Stocks were down across a broad front as the Dow Jones industrial average skidded 23.04 points, a five-month record, to 788.65. Bond prices rose slightly, but activity was light.

Money-market funds began reacting to the Fed's decision to require that a portion of their assets be placed in non-interest-bearing reserves. Merrill Lynch Ready Assets Trust and two other funds stopped taking new accounts.

Factories in the United States operated at 84.2 percent of capacity last month, the Federal Reserve Board reported, the same rate as in the previous two months.

19 Housing starts fell 6.3 percent last month to an annual rate of 1,334,000 units, the lowest level since December 1975. Apartment-unit construction jumped a surprising 56.1 percent. Other reports showed that the economy is slowing, but that activity is not slumping sharply. Personal income increased 0.3 percent. Businesses appear able to withstand a drop in consumer spending. Retail inventories fell 1.1 percent in January.

The prime rate was raised to 19 percent from 18¼ percent by Chase Manhattan. Several other major banks followed Chase. Analysts said boosts to 20 percent or higher are possible due to a new Fed provision requiring an increase in the reserves that banks must keep idle with the Fed.

Fed Chairman Volcker told the Senate Banking Committee that monetary policy would be tightened further if budget-cutting proposals fail to damp inflation.

The wage and price council, indicating concern over "disturbing" price increases, asked 250 companies to file price reports for last year's fourth quarter. Previously, the firms were told they could skip the reports.

20 Credit card issuing activities are slowing and spending limits are being trimmed by lenders and retailers following Carter's moves to slow consumer spending. J. C. Penney is boosting its minimum purchase requirement for time-payment accounts and Sears plans to increase minimum monthly payments on credit accounts.

Short-term interest rates tumbled as much as one-half percentage point on growing expectation that the economy will slip soon into recession. Several more major banks boosted their prime rate to 19 percent from 18½ percent.

Corporate profits rose 0.3 percent after taxes in the 1979 fourth quarter, the Commerce Department said, to an annual rate of $148.8 billion. Profits increased 6.5 percent in the third period. The department also announced the economy grew at an inflation-adjusted annual rate of 2 percent in the fourth quarter.

Gold surged $63.50 an ounce in New York to $550 as speculators took advantage of what they viewed as "bargain" prices. In foreign-exchange trading, the dollar declined on profit taking. Separately, Belgium's central bank raised its discount rate to 14 percent from 12 percent to bolster its franc.

The securities industry was warned by the SEC to stop a widespread practice under which brokers rebate commissions to money managers who give them business. The SEC maintained that such arrangements hurt money managers' clients.

21 The economy is growing at an annual rate of 2 percent in the current quarter, according to preliminary Commerce Department figures, the same rate as in the fourth period. But government economists believe that statistics mask some underlying weakness, and that output is being maintained partly because businesses are rebuilding inventories.

The U.S. current-account balance of payments deficit shrank to $317 million last year from $13.47 billion in 1978, reflecting a big increase in exports that more than offset a surge in oil imports.

Money-market interest rates soared after the Treasury announced it plans to sell more than $10 billion in short-term bills in the next two weeks. Rate increases came to more than three-quarters of a percentage point. The planned Treasury sale involves a total of $15.5 billion in securities and will raise $12.2 billion in new cash.

Retailers, fearing the Carter administration's credit controls will erode their profits, are encouraging cash sales and discouraging the use of credit. Even if some may raise prices to offset higher credit costs, many retailers likely will be forced to absorb the added expenses.

High gasoline prices, approaching $1.30 a gallon, have cut demand and pushed nation's inventories to their highest level ever. Industry observers predict more price increases.

24 The economy's future direction remains unclear following the Commerce Department's report on durable goods orders for February. Bookings rose 0.7 percent to $82.64 billion after climbing 5.5 percent in January. Government economists generally viewed the increase as an ambiguous signpost.

A tax cut stemming from any surplus in the fiscal 1981 budget may be suggested by congressional Democrats to win Republican support for their proposals to cut federal spending. Senate Democratic Leader Byrd plans to include the conditional pledge as part of a resolution he will introduce tomorrow.

Strong money-supply growth is seen by some economists for next month, and that possibility has them wondering whether the Fed will tighten its credit reins further in its fight against inflation.

New money-market funds, known as "clones," are planned by managers of funds as a way to keep expanding despite a recent Fed rule designed to slow the funds' exposive growth.

25 Residual fuel oil prices were reduced by Venezuela, a leading source of the heavy oil for the United States, and Exxon, a major marketer. Venezuela cut its quotes between 21 cents and $2 a barrel, and Exxon, citing slack demand, trimmed its U.S. East Coast postings $1 to $3.50 a barrel. In addition, export prices of light fuel oil and naphtha were lowered 4 percent by Venezuela.

The dollar reached its highest level in two and one-quarter years on world currency markets, aided by the prospect of even higher U.S. interest rates. Gold fell $15.30 an ounce in New York to $548. trading, the dollar declined on profit Separately, the U.S. is said to be interested in acquiring West German mark-denominated bonds or notes in exchange for some of its mark holdings.

Treasury bill rates soared amid fears of credit tightening by the Fed. In the secondary market, rates rose about ⅝ of a percentage point. At the Treasury's weekly sale, yields climbed to records, an average 16.532 percent for 13-week bills and 15.700 percent for 26-week issues.

Citibank said it has stopped issuing new MasterCard and Visa credit cards and has curtailed the availability of other types of consumer credit because of the Fed's credit restraint program. Mobile-home loans, home-improvement borrowings, and student loans will be hit particularly hard.

26 Consumer prices surged 1.4 percent, or at a 16.8 percent annual rate, in February, matching January. Gasoline prices again climbed more than 7 percent but food costs were unchanged. Most economists see inflation easing later this year, but they do not agree on how soon.

U.S. auto sales fell 16.2 percent in mid-March, totaling 249,235 units. Deliveries fell 18 percent at GM, 15.5 percent at Ford and 16.2 percent at Chrysler.

Volkswagen of America posted an 11.9 percent gain.

A balanced budget for the year starting October 1 was endorsed by the Senate, but senators rejected a plan by Sen. William Roth (R., Del.) to hold outlays to 21 percent of the projected gross national product for fiscal 1981.

The U.S. budget deficit widened in February to $9.35 billion from $5.1 billion last year. The deficit followed a January gap of $4.56 billion.

Boeing was named the prime contractor for the air-launched cruise missile, beating out General Dynamics' Convair division. Boeing will receive a $141 million contract this fiscal year. The missile could mean $2 billion to Boeing over the nine-year course of the production program.

27 Credit-restraint regulations may be amended by the Fed at a meeting Wednesday. One amendment would allow more growth in consumer credit by permitting creditors to choose a different base period from which to gauge credit growth. Another proposal would spell out how much notification a lender must give before altering a credit contract.

Wide-ranging controls on credit that will affect consumer and real estate loans the most were instituted by Bank of America to comply with Fed directions on limiting lending.

Money-market analysts were confused when the Fed allowed the rate on federal funds to soar to 25 percent. The latest trading range disclosed by the Fed was 11½ percent to 18 percent. Some analysts saw the climb as a sign of possible credit-tightening moves.

The Federal Home Loan Bank Board, in a move to free some S&L funds for investment, voted to reduce the liquidity reserve requirement for member savings and loan associations to 5 percent from 5.5 percent, effective April 1.

28 Silver prices plunged $5 an ounce to $10.80 on the New York Commodity Exchange on rumors, later denied, that the Hunt brothers were not able to meet a $100 million margin call by Bache Halsey Stuart on their huge holdings of silver futures contracts. As the silver market collapsed, the Hunts and their Arab associates had to scramble to cover heavy losses, setting off a chain reaction. Other commodities also plummeted; gold ended at $463, down $33.50.

The stock market gyrated wildly and

trading surged to almost 64 million shares following the news on the Hunts. In the money markets, investors flocked to Treasury bills, seeking a safe haven for their funds. The dollar climbed on international currency markets, aided by high U.S. interest rates and political and other pressures.

Uniform reserve requirements for all banks and a phase-out of interest-rate ceilings on deposits at banks and S&Ls were approved by the House. Fed Chairman Volcker has said the new requirements would strengthen the Fed's ability to conduct monetary policy.

The oil "windfall" tax cleared the Senate, 66 to 31. The President is likely to sign the bill soon, so the government can start collecting the $227 billion it is estimated the tax will raise this decade. The levy is retroactive to March 1.

Voluntary price guidelines were tightened by the wage and price council to delay price increases allowed under the anti-inflation program. Officials said they hoped the change would discourage anticipatory boosts spurred by fears of future inflation.

31 A new economic forecast of the Carter administration, to be announced today, anticipates a milder recession this year than was predicted in January, and considerably more inflation. The outlook matches that of most business economists, but some experts, noting recent anti-inflation moves, are speaking of a serious recession.

Increases in the prime rate, which hit a record 19½ percent Friday, may slow as credit demand eases in coming months, money analysts said. It was suggested that banks may toughen terms on loan agreements to try to slow the prime rate's rise.

Major forest-product companies based in the Pacific Northwest are being forced to make cutbacks because of high interest rates and a housing slump. Crown-Zellerbach is closing lumber and plywood operations at Joyce, Louisiana, indefinitely.

Building contracts fell 25 percent last month to $10.39 billion, the F. W. Dodge division of McGraw-Hill said, noting that February 1979's $13.87 billion total reflected two big nuclear power plant projects. Nonresidential construction gained 12 percent; residential building declined 5 percent.

Regulatory powers of the Fed would be expanded and higher interest rates on consumer deposits at banks and S&Ls

would be permitted under a bill cleared by the Senate and sent to Carter. The measure extends Fed reserve requirements to nonmember banks.

Agreement on a natural gas price was announced by the United States and Mexico, which forced the United States to accept a 23 percent increase, to $4.47 per 1,000 cubic feet. The price is identical to the latest Canadian quote.

April 1980

1 The silver market turmoil started by the Hunt family's problems continued. Engelhard Minerals agreed to cancel a $665 million contract to sell the Hunts 19 million ounces of silver at $35 an ounce. Instead, Engelhard will accept 8.5 million additional ounces of the metal and oil and gas interests valued at a total $395.2 million. The price of silver, which has hit $10.25, closed in commodity trading yesterday at $14.20. Separately, Bache disclosed its trading losses stemming from Hunt transactions may come to $50 million. In Washington, a House panel questioned stock and commodity market regulators on last week's silver tumult. Specialists expect the Hunts' silver losses may have dealt the final blow to the recent commodity speculation, already damped by high interest rates and fear of a recession.

A revised budget for the year starting October 1 that closely resembles proposals in Congress was unveiled by the President. Carter's plan projects a surplus of $16.5 billion, reflecting a big jump in revenue from an import fee on gasoline and a withholding tax on dividend and interest income.

Iran raised the price of its lighter grade of crude oil $2.50 a barrel, or 8 percent. The increase is the first by a member of OPEC for the second quarter.

2 New factory orders fell 0.6 percent in February to $155.23 billion. A government economist said the latest report showed little of the strength seen in January, when bookings jumped 4.3 percent. In addition, construction spending dropped 3.2 percent after a 3.3 percent gain the month before, reflecting weakness in the residential construction sector.

The prime rate was boosted to 19¾ percent from 19¼ percent by Chase Manhattan, which cited rising costs. The step reflects pressures on banks following Fed credit-restraint moves. Yesterday, however, the Fed acted to ease some of those pressures by injecting additional reserves into the banking network.

Bankers fear that a potential problem exists in the large new "commitments" for future loans lined up by corporations before the Fed's credit controls. Fulfilling the commitments would mean faster loan growth than the Fed has proposed.

Auto makers in the U.S. have set their lowest second quarter production schedules in 15 years, down 21 percent from 1979 to 1,939,000 cars. The plans reflect concerns that sales will not pick up this spring, normally a strong selling season.

Oil prices are being raised by members of OPEC, even though production has fallen as a result of stagnant demand. Nigeria is said to be increasing prices 51 cents a barrel, putting its top price at $34.72.

3 The prime rate was raised to a record 20 percent from 19½ percent by Chemical Bank, a move joined by other major institutions. The boost spurred questions from bankers on what constituted usurious interest. Money analysts expect intensive efforts by corporate treasurers on ways to cut their borrowing needs.

Canadian rates were boosted to keep pace with U.S. interest rates. The central bank's rate rose 0.71 percentage point to 16.2 percent, and the prime was lifted to 17.25 percent or 17.5 percent from 16.5 percent at several banks.

Federal Home Loan Bank Board officials disclosed that 266 of the 4,100 savings and loan institutions it regulates posted a net loss for 1979's second half. Soaring money costs are hurting S&Ls' profit margins.

Credit-control regulations were amended by the Fed to allow more growth in consumer debt and to require lenders to provide 30 days' notice before changing credit terms.

Interest rate ceilings on federally backed mortgages for single-family homes were increased to 14 percent from 13 percent. The boost is the third in two months.

The "windfall" oil tax bill was signed by the President, about a year after he proposed the levy. The tax will raise about $227 billion.

4 Auto makers, fearing a lackluster spring selling season, plan to temporarily close 13 of their 40 assembly plants starting next week, idling nearly 63,000 workers for one or two weeks. In addition, Chrysler is ordering a long-term production cut at one facility, which will affect 700 workers.

Car sales fell 16 percent last month to 892,200 units, reflecting a sharp drop in domestic-make autos and lower foreign-car deliveries due to dealer shortages. GM posted a decline of 16 percent; Ford and Chrysler each had a 26 percent drop.

Ford increased new-car prices an average $170 a vehicle, or 2.2 percent. GM earlier raised its prices by the same percentage, which worked out to $186 a car. Chrysler is expected to join the latest round of price boosts.

The prime rate was lifted to 20 percent from 19½ percent by more major banks, including Citibank, Marine Midland, and Irving Trust. In the money market, other short-term interest rates generally declined as trading slowed prior to the Easter holiday.

Savings and loan associations that belong to the Federal Home Loan Bank system will receive a $630 million infusion of funds, mostly in the form of early and fattened dividends, to ease money-rate pressures. In addition, federally chartered S&Ls were permitted to begin issuing flexiblerate, or rollover, mortgages.

7 The economy showed signs of weakening in March, government economists said following a report that the unemployment rate rose to 6.2 percent of the labor force from 6 percent in February. The economists added there were slight indications that inflation may ease in the months ahead, as producer prices for finished goods climbed 1.4 percent last month, compared with 1.5 percent in February.

Inflation and unemployment appeared to be growing again last month, a survey of corporate purchasing managers indicated. The survey found increasing pessimism about the nation's economy for the coming year and fewer reports of a rise in new orders.

Mortgage rates for new single-family homes took an unprecedented jump of 1.47 percentage points in early March, according to the Federal Home Loan Bank Board. The average rate was a record 14.6 percent in commitments for 25-year, fixed-rate conventional loans. Average sales prices of new and used homes declined.

The Fed's list of stocks traded over the

counter that fall under its margin, or credit, rules was expanded by 94, to 1,252.

8   Consumer credit expanded $2.91 billion in February, or at an 11 percent annual rate, after rising $1.37 billion in January, or at a 5.3 percent pace. The latest increase came before the Fed acted March 14 to curb the growth of consumer credit.

Gold jumped $34.40 an ounce to $521.50 following reports of heightened tension in Iran. The dollar declined against most other key currencies on foreign-exchange markets, but continued to rise against the Japanese yen.

Noncompetitive oil and gas leasing on federal lands, which mainly involves drawing bids in a random lottery, was permitted to resume by June 16, but under tighter regulations. It was suspended after the government decided that some lotteries were being rigged.

Home loan interest rates were boosted by Citibank, posting a new scale with rates ranging to as much as 19 percent. Home mortgage fees were increased one percentage point to 17½ percent for customers and to 18½ percent for noncustomers.

9   Federal banking regulators are considering asking Congress for authority to approve interstate bank acquisitions in emergency situations. Congress has requested that regulators suggest ways to prepare for possible hard times in the banking industry.

The dollar fell on currency markets, dropping 1.7 percent against the West German mark and 1.9 percent against the French franc. Traders cited nervousness over Iran. The price of gold jumped $17 an ounce to $538.50.

Bache said the Hunt family's $33 million debt to Bache has been reduced more than two thirds by a $22.6 million cash payment and liquidations of some silver-bullion collateral.

Charles Schultze, chairman of the Council of Economic Advisers, saw potential for a sharp reduction in the inflation rate during the second half. So far this year, consumer prices have been rising at an 18 percent to 20 percent annual rate.

Foreign direct investment transactions in the U.S. surged last year to 1,070 from 334 in 1978. The value of the transactions was not known, but the Commerce Department gave an estimate of $12.5 billion.

10   A downturn in the economy might be avoided, according to Carter's chief inflation fighter, Alfred Kahn, if wage and price boosts in coming months are moderate. But Labor Secretary Ray Marshall said indications are that the economy is in for a recession. One unusual sign of a possible recession is showing up. With unemployment in the auto industry up sharply, more workers than expected are seeking trade adjustment assistance.

The prime rate was lowered to 19¾ percent from 20 percent by UMB Bank & Trust, but money specialists generally shrugged off the move, noting the bank's relatively small size. In the money market, interest rates showed little change.

Toyota and Nissan indicated they will not build cars in the U.S. and will resist foreign and domestic pressure to do so until they decide that an American facility would be commercially feasible.

11   Retail sales, paced by a 7.2 percent decline in car sales, slumped 1.3 percent last month. Government economists said the report, following a 1.6 percent drop in February, adds strongly to indications that the economy is entering a recession.

Chain stores reported that business was slow in March, but discounters benefited as consumers battled to offset inflation. Volume was down 3.3 percent at Mobil's Montgomery Ward unit and was unchanged at Sears. K mart, the largest discounter, had a 13 percent increase.

Short-term interest rates tumbled as much as one-half percentage point in the money market, which may mean a cut in the banking industry's record prime rate of 20 percent. Some dealers said there was almost panic buying of Treasury bills and other debt securities.

Bond prices rose more than two points due to recession psychology and reports of a drop in retail prices. Citicorp redesigned a floating-rate note issue to take it beyond the reach of the small investor.

Auto makers plan to close temporarily or cut production at 9 of their 40 domestic assembly plants next week. The moves, which are intended to balance inventories, will idle 42,900 workers indefinitely.

Chrysler has told the federal government it can not meet all the requirements of a loan guarantee bill approved by Congress last year. The auto maker wants some changes in the requirements so that it can begin to draw on the aid.

14   Business inventories rose 0.07 percent to

$2.97 billion in February, after a revised 1.1 percent increase in January. The gain appeared mostly to reflect an inflationary boost in value rather than actual buildup. Economists view current conservative inventory policies as good news because businesses should be able to avert sharp production cuts to liquidate stocks in the event of a steep drop in spending.

Credit restraints could be eased by the Fed as early as this summer, because an economic slowdown and sluggish money-supply growth will give the Fed more leeway in fighting inflation. Underscoring sluggish money growth, M1-A, which indicates funds readily available for spending, fell $100 million to $374.3 billion in the week ended April 2. The unexpected drop sent money-market interest rates tumbling.

Chrysler will pay about $45 million to replace front fenders that the FTC says rust prematurely because of a design flaw. The amount, which the FTC says is the largest ever returned to consumers, covers repairs on 1976 and 1977 Dodge Aspens and Plymouth Volares.

Household Finance's termination of talks to buy a majority of Chrysler Financial is expected to deter further the auto maker's recovery efforts. Chrysler's major banks had insisted that the sale of the unit for as much as $320 million be completed before they would restructure the parent's debt.

15 Visa and MasterCard holders will be charged a 12-cent fee on each credit purchase and cash advance by Crocker National Bank of San Francisco. Citibank in New York increased by one percentage point the charges to merchants accepting the cards. That bank also instituted a $75 annual fee for those customers.

Tighter controls over commodities trading were urged by SEC Chairman Harold Williams. He told a House panel that he favored "suitability requirements," curbs on an investor's futures contract holdings, and margin requirements set by the Fed.

16 Industrial output slumped 0.8 percent in March, led by construction and home goods, after a downward-revised 0.2 percent drop in February. The Fed said the decline was the sharpest in nearly a year. The statistics join a string of indexes that show wide-spread economic weakness.

Corporate profits after taxes slid 0.9 percent in the 1979 final quarter to a $146.9

billion annual pace. The Commerce Department's earlier report had shown those earnings growing a slim 0.3 percent.

Money market interest rates fell as much as three-eighths percentage point amid mounting evidence of a recession. The drop increased pressure for a prime-rate reduction.

U.S. auto sales slipped 24 percent in early April to 183,988 domestically made units. Ford and Chrysler led the decline, followed by GM. VW of America's sales rose a bit.

17 A prime-rate cut of one-quarter percentage point to 19¾ was set by Chase Manhattan, which cited easing money costs. Some analysts saw the start of a downward drive in the key rate.

Housing starts plunged 21.8 percent in March to the lowest rate in nearly five years. It was the second-largest monthly drop on record, the Commerce Department said. Building permits also fell sharply, indicating the slump will worsen.

Bond markets will recover soon, said Treasury Secretary Miller. He based his outlook on public perceptions of controlled government spending and a cut in planned U.S. borrowing.

Prices soared on the bond markets after Henry Kaufman, a Salomon Bros. economist, issued a report that indicated interest rates are likely to turn down.

Factories operated at 83 percent of capacity in March, the lowest level in two years, down from 83.9 percent in February, the Fed said.

Credit cards issued by stores will start replacing bank cards, which are becoming hard to get and expensive to use, analysts say. Smaller stores stand to lose business because they rely on bank-issued cards.

18 Express mail delivery by the Postal Service within cities was approved by the U.S. Same-day and overnight deliveries will be offered experimentally until mid-1982.

Personal income grew 0.8 percent, or an adjusted $15.6 billion, in March, after rising 0.4 percent in February. A Commerce Department economist said the moderate rise reflected "incipient recession."

A recession has probably begun, the President said at his news conference, but it will be "mild and short." He said his top priority is still the fight against inflation and he defended his economic restraints as the best solution to long-term ills.

21 The prime rate was cut to 19½ percent Friday by many banks. Money analysts suggested that interest rates could continue to move lower. They noted the recent sharp slowing in the growth of the nation's money supply, below Fed targets.

The weakening economy could produce a recession that's deeper than the President is predicting, according to some Carter administration economists. A Commerce Department report showed that overall economic activity slowed to a 1.1 percent annual rate in the first quarter from the prior period's 2 percent pace.

Big international oil companies are expected by analysts to report first quarter earnings this week that are 75 percent to 100 percent higher than the year earlier. Exxon, Mobil, and Texaco are likely to post profit exceeding $1 billion.

Money-market funds appear to be growing at a slower rate in the wake of the Fed's "special deposit" rule. But fund managers predict that the funds' assets are likely to rise soon, as new funds that were formed in reaction to the Fed rule turn around.

22 Postal rate increases averaging 28 percent were proposed by the Postal Service, which cited inflation and higher labor costs. The proposal, which would generate $5 billion in additional annual revenue, would boost first-class mail rates to 20 cents for the first ounce from 15 cents.

Tax incentives to encourage wage and price restraint should be considered by the Carter administration, Wage and Price Council Chairman Kahn said. He added that the administration would consider such a move only after achieving a balanced budget.

Treasury bill yields again plunged at the latest auction of short-term issues, reflecting the sharp drop in money-market interest rates. Yields fell to 12.731 percent for 13-week bills and to 11.892 percent for 26-week issues.

Short interest in the month ended last Tuesday fell 9.9 percent on the New York Stock Exchange to 44,702,649 shares and 9.7 percent on the Amex to 6,773,790 shares.

23 Consumer prices climbed 1.4 percent last month, or at a 16.8 percent annual rate, matching February's increase. Still, government officials forecast a quick reduction in inflation later this year. The price report came as the economy showed a further sign of weakness, with durable goods orders posting a 3.2 percent drop for March, the steepest slide since July.

The stock market staged an explosive rally. The Dow Jones industrial average surged 30.89 points, its biggest gain since November 1, 1978, to 790.02. The rally was aided by steep declines in Treasury bill yields Monday. In the money market yesterday, short-term interest rates continued to fall.

GM earnings plunged 87 percent to $155 million, or 52 cents a share, in the first quarter, in line with analysts' forecasts. Sales fell 12 percent $15.7 billion. The results reflect sluggish U.S. sales and the cost of special sales-incentive programs.

Chrysler will eliminate 20 percent of its white-collar staff and support staff within the next few weeks, a move intended to save $200 million a year in overhead costs.

Steel production cuts may be necessary soon, according to some producers, because of a sharp decline in orders during the past few weeks. The drop is linked to high interest rates and falling car sales.

24 Exxon, the world's biggest oil company, set a U.S. record with first quarter earnings of nearly $1.93 billion, or $4.40 a share, more than double the year-earlier level. The company cautioned against using the increase as a basis for forecasting full-year results. Revenue jumped 47 percent to $27.65 billion.

Car sales plunged 33 percent in mid-April to an estimated 146,171 units, the lowest level for U.S. auto makers since 1975, when the industry was in the depths of a recession. GM posted a decline of 28 percent; Ford, 43 percent; Chrysler, 42 percent, and AMC, an estimated 23 percent. VW of America had a 5.6 percent gain.

The prime rate was cut to 19 percent from 19½ percent by Chase Manhattan. Other major banks are expected to join Chase soon. The reduction reflects a slowdown in loan demand and the lower cost of raising funds in money markets due to a sharp drop in short-term rates.

25 Borrowing costs for U.S. corporations plummeted on the belief that the Fed has eased its tight monetary policies. General Motors Acceptance Corp., a leading issuer, slashed the interest rate on some of its commercial paper to 12 percent from 13½ percent. Analysts cited declines in the federal funds rate, a key indicator, which has fallen to 15¾ percent, from about 19 percent recently, without action by the Fed.

Withdrawals at federally insured savings and loan associations exceeded deposits by $939 million in March, the Federal Home Loan Bank Board said. Mortgage lending was sluggish and depositors accelerated their switch to higher-yielding accounts. A net gain in savings was posted for February and January.

GM is considering cost-cutting measures that could include further reductions in its salaried work force. The auto maker disclosed that next week the total of hourly workers on indefinite layoff will climb to 90,000 from 82,000 currently.

28 The Hunt brothers and the family's Placid Oil Co. have mortgaged $3.2 billion of oil and gas properties, largely to meet debts incurred in last month's silver market collapse. The largest transaction involves a $2 billion note to secure loans from a group headed by Morgan Guaranty Trust and First National Bank in Dallas.

The prime rate remains at a high level, currently 19½ percent, at most banks, despite the sharp drop in other short-term interest rates. Citibank cut its fee to 19½ percent Friday from 19¾ percent. Money analysts speculated that profit-squeezed banks are boosting their earnings by propping up the prime rate and are using the fee to ration credit.

Interest rate declines were cited for a lowering in the interest ceiling on government-backed single-family mortgages to 13 percent from 14 percent. The drop is the first since October 1976. HUD Secretary Landrieu said that as many as 1 million more home buyers could qualify for mortgages at the new rate.

Productivity in the private-business sector increased at a 0.6 percent annual rate in the first quarter, the first rise in 15 months. The gain was due to a big jump in farm productivity.

General Motors' plans to lay off 10 percent of its salaried work force, or about 18,000 employes, will broaden the U.S. auto industry layoffs to the more than 250,000 layoffs reached during the depths of the 1974–75 recession.

Workers at Ford and GM were ruled eligible for special federal assistance because their jobs have been affected by increased imports. About 131,000 employes may apply for benefits.

29 Prime-rate cuts of a full percentage point to 18½ percent were announced by several banks, led by Morgan Guaranty Trust of New York. Other banks

trimmed their rate one-half percentage point to 19 percent. The moves reflected sliding short-term interest rates, which yesterday tumbled as much as three fourths of a percentage point.

Small-saver certificate rate ceilings were slashed for May by the Treasury to 10.5 percent from 11.75 percent for commercial banks and to 10.75 percent from 12 percent for thrift institutions. The rates are linked to 2½-year Treasury securities.

Ford posted a loss of $163.6 million for the first quarter, the second consecutive period in which North American operations pushed the company into the red. Earnings were hurt by depressed U.S. new-car sales and weaknesses in major foreign markets.

Basic domestic air fares will be allowed to rise 5.4 percent Thursday, the CAB said, citing rising fuel and other costs. The agency also said it will start letting fares reflect increasing nonfuel expenses every two months.

30 Merchandise trade figures of the U.S. for March show a narrowing in the deficit to $3.16 billion from February's record $5.57 billion, reflecting increased exports and reduced oil imports. The latest deficit brought the first quarter red-ink total to $13.49 billion, compared with $8.24 billion a year ago.

Venezuela's plans to increase residual fuel prices 50 cents a barrel later this week was linked to hedge buying by Japanese and U.S. oil companies. In addition, Venezuela is expected to lift export prices for light fuel oil.

The Fed further eased its grip on credit costs by allowing its interest rate on federal funds to drop to 13 percent, from an average of 14⅝ percent Monday. The stance buoyed investors in the short-term money market. Some analysts said that the Fed's posture could foster more cuts in the prime rate.

Exxon signed an accord with Saudi Arabia to build a $1.1 billion joint-venture polyethylene plant at Jubail, a port on the Red Sea.

May 1980

1 Key indicators of the economy plunged 2.6 percent in March, the largest drop in 5½ years, signalling that the economy began slipping into a recession near the end of the first quarter. New factory orders were down 0.9 percent in the

month, the sharpest decline since last July. In addition, the Labor Department reported a rise in the jobless rate for workers covered by unemployment insurance programs.

Chrysler, after intense negotiations, obtained a $150 million loan from Michigan, averting its most serious cash crisis yet.

The SEC turned down rule proposals that would have forced corporate lawyers to tell directors of wrongdoing by a client's employes. Several Commissioners indicated the agency may reexamine the rule later.

Farm prices dropped 4.5 percent last month, following a 1.7 percent decline in March. The Agriculture Department said April retail prices probably didn't reflect the drop, due to increased processing and distribution costs.

Short-term interests rates plunged in the money market, some by one-half percentage point, as foreign central banks bought $1.2 billion of U.S. Treasury bills. Analysts said a large portion of the purchases was related to support operations for the dollar.

The central bank of West Germany raised key interest rates to their highest level in ten years in an effort to damp inflation and stabilize interest rates. The discount rate was increased to 7.5 percent from 7 percent.

2 Securities houses would be required to set up separate firms for their commodities operations under a rule the SEC is considering proposing. The rule would be aimed at preventing commodity market reverses from jeopardizing the securities firms.

Sohio was ordered by an Energy Department official to increase gasoline prices in the Ohio area ten cents a gallon. The official said Sohio had been underselling its rivals.

Car production schedules of U.S. auto makers for the second quarter were cut more than 10 percent to an estimated 1,732,000 units. This would be the lowest second-period output in nearly 20 years. Further cuts may be necessary.

Construction outlays plunged 5.8 percent in March to a $229 billion annual rate, the sharpest monthly drop in 36 years. The decline followed a 2.8 percent slide in February.

Steel imports from seven Western European countries are injuring domestic steelmakers, the International Trade Commission ruled. The decisions mean the Commerce Department must proceed with investigations of dumping charges by U.S. Steel.

Carter contended his administration has "turned the corner" in fighting inflation. The President said there was progress toward lower interest rates, and predicted the inflation rate would drop significantly during the summer.

Saudi Arabia is said to be planning to announce an oil price boost at next week's OPEC meeting, but oil observers questioned whether the kingdom will move so quickly. It was indicated that Kuwait will boost some of its surcharges $2.50 a barrel, to a total surcharge of $8.00.

5 The unemployment rate increase for April, to an adjusted 7 percent of the work force, casts further doubt on the Carter administration's prediction that the recession will be mild. Last month's jump from March's 6.2 percent level was the sharpest since January 1975.

The Hunt brothers and the banks that helped finance the Hunts' silver purchases seem to be the chief beneficiaries of a $1.1 billion bailout plan, according to some members of Congress. Two subcommittees are investigating March's silver-market collapse. Banks will be asked about their role in the Hunts' silver transactions at Senate Banking Committee hearings May 29 and 30.

Sohio will not be forced to raise its gasoline prices about ten cents a gallon in Ohio as the Energy Department rescinded an order issued by one of its officials. Privately, officials said the revocation was politically motivated, due to the Ohio primary on June 3.

The Fed is seen by analysts to be facing mounting pressure to ease its tough credit restraints, in light of the economy's rapid deterioration. It relaxed its grip Friday, sending short-term interest rates plunging. The rate on 26-week Treasury bills fell to 9.35 percent from 10.35 percent.

Ford is attempting its second price increase in a month because of its deteriorated "profit situation." Its rivals are not likely to follow the move. The company boosted prices an average of $82 a unit, or 1.1 percent.

6 The prime rate was slashed to 17½ percent from 18½ percent by Morgan Guaranty Trust. Chase Manhattan and First National Bank of Chicago cut their rates one-half percentage point to 18 percent. The actions follow the steep drop in open-market interest rates in recent weeks.

Car sales fell about 27 percent last month to 740,000 units, a level that rivals the depth of the big industry slump in 1975.

GM cut its quarterly dividend to 60 cents a share from $1.15, and said it may report a loss for the second period. Separately, more than 9,000 GM workers in three states were found eligible for special federal assistance as a result of increased imports.

Reynolds Metals and Kaiser Aluminum rolled back some price increases. The companies said the rollbacks will bring them into compliance with the government's anti-inflation guidelines.

Boeing plans to slash production of commercial airliners 12 percent in 1981, a move that reflects the slump in airline traffic. First quarter earnings rose 29 percent to $139.8 million, or $1.45 a share.

Savings and loan associations with a federal charter will find it easier to open branches starting next January 1. The Federal Home Loan Bank Board said the S&Ls won't have to prove that a new branch is needed and that it probably will succeed.

7 Standard Brands proposed a $65-a-share offer for 45 percent of Liggett in a two-part takeover that would have a value of $565 million in convertible preferred stock and cash. Liggett, which has been fighting a proposed $50-a-share acquisition by Grand Metropolitan, welcomed the Standard Brands bid.

The Fed eliminated its three percentage point surcharge on the discount rate for large banks, citing the recent decline in money market rates. The basic 13 percent discount rate will remain unchanged.

Interest rates appear poised for another slide, according to analysts. Market rates fell yesterday as prices climbed on a signal that the Fed had eased its credit reins in the open market and the Fed decision to end the three-point surcharge.

Mortgage rates of some banks and savings institutions in California and Arizona were trimmed to as low as 14½ percent, but most institutions remained at 17 percent to 18 percent.

The dollar weakened further against some key currencies in foreign-exchange trading, falling 1.9 percent against the Japanese yen. The declines came as U.S. interest rates continued to slide. Gold fell $12.30 to $506.70.

Stock exchanges were authorized by the SEC to list an additional 63 put options. A put option gives a purchaser the right to sell 100 shares of the underlying stock at a fixed price during a specified time period.

Work on a $3 billion project in Iran for petrochemicals will resume soon, Mitsui & Co. said. The Japanese company is the chief promoter of the complex, and said it will send 300 technicians to finish the job. Work has been stalled for more than a year, despite similar previous statements by Mitsui.

8 Consumer credit growth slowed in March to $1.43 billion, or an annual rate of 5.5 percent, after increasing $2.3 billion, or 9 percent annually, in February. The March figures reflect credit-tightening steps taken by the Fed that month.

The prime rate was cut to 17 percent from 18 percent by Chase Manhattan Bank, undercutting other institutions that posted 17½ percent fees. Several banks coupled the reductions with a drop in broker-loan rates to 16½ percent from 17½ percent. The actions came as the Fed appeared to have loosened its grip on credit conditions in the money market.

Car sales at U.S. auto makers have taken a turn for the worse in recent weeks, deepening the nearly year-long recession at the companies and their suppliers. Some analysts see little chance of any strength returning to sales before October or November; a significant improvement could be a year away.

Chrysler reported a first-quarter loss of $448.8 million, its second largest quarterly deficit, reflecting lower-than-expected sales of $2.35 billion, higher interest costs, production cuts, and cash outlays for special marketing programs.

9 Major retail chains in April again failed to keep pace with the government-estimated inflation rate for general merchandise, about 7 percent. Sales fell 5.4 percent at Mobil's Montgomery Ward unit, 5 percent at Penney, and 4.3 percent at Sears.

Home sales skidded in March, leaving builders with 10.6 months' supply of unsold homes, the worst overhang in 17 years. New-home sales fell 17 percent to an annual rate of 446,000, the sharpest monthly drop in ten years.

Eight more car-assembly plants in the U.S. will be closed temporarily next week due to declining sales, idling 26,000 hourly workers. Four other car facilities also will be closed, and some truck production will be suspended.

Overall, 55,000 employes at vehicle plants will be on temporary layoff.

UAW President Douglas A. Fraser said the union will proceed with its campaign for limits on Japanese auto imports, adding that the UAW can not wait for the President and Congress to act.

Ford canceled $2.5 billion, or 19 percent, of its North American capital budget through 1984, in its cost-cutting program aimed at trimming losses.

The Fed acted to stem, at least temporarily, the drop in interest rates by draining reserves from the banking network when the federal funds rate fell to less than 10½ percent. Rates on short-term securities rose in many money-market sectors.

Oil producers in OPEC succeeded in part in establishing a long-term pricing and production strategy that could have a major impact on oil-consuming nations. The strategy would provide for regular price boosts tied to inflation and economic growth. Producers failed to come to complete grips with either output or prices for the long or short term.

12 Sweden's employers accepted a 6.8 percent wage boost proposed by mediators, resolving a week-long dispute in which 700,000 workers were locked out and 100,000 were on strike. The employers initially rejected the pact, and government pressure reportedly caused the switch. A similar pay package settled a public-sector labor conflict.

The slowdown in the rate of increases in producer prices for finished goods last month gave the Carter administration some encouraging news on inflation. Prices rose 0.5 percent, posting the smallest increase since May 1979. Economists' belief that economic activity will fall in the second quarter was bolstered by a report that retail sales dropped 1.2 percent.

An accounting rule requiring companies to disclose more details about pension commitments is to be issued today by the Financial Accounting Standards Board. Some experts believe the rule is overdue; others fear misleading figures.

13 The prime rate was cut to 16½ percent from 17½ percent by several major banks, and the broker-loan rate was slashed to 15 percent from 16½ percent. At the auction of six-month Treasury bills, used to set rates on popular money-market certificates, the average yield fell to 8.782 percent, the lowest level since October 1978. The decline

triggered a rule allowing savings banks to pay a higher return than commercial banks on the certificates.

The dollar declined against major currencies to a 2½-month low due to falling interest rates in the U.S. Gold dropped $5.10 to $507.70.

14 The oil import fee imposed by Carter, which would have boosted gasoline prices tomorrow, was overturned by a federal judge. The government will appeal the decision and request a stay of certain aspects of the ruling. The court decision could hurt a drive by Carter and Congress to balance the budget for fiscal 1981.

U.S. Steel plans to close three blast furnaces this weekend to bring production in line with reduced demand. Three other furnaces were closed last week. The latest action affects works in Gary, Indiana, Fairfield, Alabama, and Pittsburgh.

Airlines were permitted to raise domestic fares from 30 percent up to an unlimited amount without CAB approval. Carriers also were allowed expanded fare flexibility on some international routes.

Lockheed has just about given up hope that its L-1011 TriStar commercial aircraft program will prove profitable, Roy A. Anderson, chairman, said. But Anderson added that he sees profit on individual aircraft by sometime in 1982.

Bond and money markets rallied on sizable purchases of longer-term Treasury securities by the Fed. Some bond prices rose two points. In the short-term money market, interest rates on certain Treasury issues fell three-eighths of a percentage point.

Mortgage rates were cut by Citibank, to 14 percent from 15½ percent for the bank's customers, and by thrift institutions in Florida, Georgia, and Pennsylvania. Opinions were mixed on whether the reductions would boost demand.

15 Oil prices were increased 8 percent by Saudi Arabia in its third attempt to restore pricing unity to OPEC. The action, retroactive to April 1, boosts the kingdom's Arab light, OPEC's benchmark crude, $2 a barrel to $28. Saudi Arabia's latest effort is seen coming closer to healing the pricing split, mainly because oil markets are sluggish.

Car sales plummeted more than 42 percent in early May to an estimated 141,852 units, posting the steepest drop of this sales downturn. Deliveries were down 36 percent at GM, 51 percent at

Ford, 57 percent at Chrysler and 16 percent at VW of America.

Fed Chairman Volcker pledged to stick to current monetary policies despite a slowing economy. He said falling interest rates should not be considered a sign of a policy change. Volcker suggested that the board soon may dismantle its special credit-restraint program.

Further prime rate cuts are predicted by analysts, who cited banks' lower costs for gathering lendable funds. The specialists see a fee of 12 percent or lower within months, compared with 16½ percent to 17 percent currently.

The ceiling for mortgages backed by the federal government was slashed a record 1.5 percentage points to 11.5 percent, effective today. The reduction affects single-family homes. For multifamily homes, the ceiling remains at 13 percent.

Carter's oil-import fee was rejected in Senate and House panel votes following a federal judge's decision to bar the program. The Justice and Energy departments decided against asking the judge to allow the program to take effect while they appeal his ruling.

16 Car makers will close five car and six truck plants next week, idling 23,000 more hourly workers. The companies plan to build 105,189 cars this week, a 12 percent drop from last week and a 51 percent plunge from a year earlier.

19 Carter's economic policies, aimed at combating inflation despite recession, will face new tests in coming months. Industrial output fell 1.9 percent in April and housing starts slid at a 2.1 percent annual rate, dispelling any doubts about whether a slowdown has started. But it is still unclear how severe the recession will be.

Chrysler's decision to close its Lynch Road plant in Detroit and stop making full-size cars reflects its continuing efforts to trim operations back to profitability. The move will result in the layoff of 2,300 workers.

20 Personal income inched up less than 0.1 percent last month, the smallest rise in almost five years, reflecting sharp declines in production. Income was up 0.7 percent in March. Another report showed that personal consumption, adjusted for inflation, fell 0.9 percent in March, indicating concern about recession.

Major retailers' profits declined in the first quarter; Sears and J. C. Penney posted declines of about 60 percent. Retailers said they hope lower interest rates later this year will improve earnings.

The prime rate was cut to 16 percent from 16½ percent by Morgan Guaranty Trust. A handful of smaller banks followed Morgan. Analysts expect reductions by other major banks later in the week. The costs of long-term bond financing rose, however, as traders braced for a record supply of new corporate issues.

Oil prices were raised $2 a barrel by Libya and Indonesia, bringing their quotes for key grades to $36.72 a barrel and $34.75, respectively. Algeria also boosted its price $1 to $38.21. The increases appear likely to lead to a round of price increases in OPEC.

21 Partial deregulation of the trucking industry was approved by the House Surface Transportation Subcommittee. The proposal is somewhat more limited than a bill recently passed by the Senate.

The Fed apparently loosened its hold on interest rates, some analysts said, by reducing its interest rate floor on federal funds to about 9 percent from 10½ percent. Buoyed by the Fed's apparent relaxation, interest rates in the short-term money market dropped.

Corporate profits after taxes rose 5.9 percent in the first quarter after declining 0.9 percent in the fourth period. Also, the economy expanded at an inflation-adjusted 0.6 percent annual rate more slowly than previously believed. Carter officials tightened fiscal and monetary policies during the quarter.

Oil prices were increased $2 a barrel by Iraq and other Persian Gulf producers, indicating that Saudi Arabia's third attempt in six months to stabilize prices in OPEC has failed. Last week the Saudis boosted quotes $2 a barrel to $28 to bring it into line with others in the gulf.

22 Durable-goods orders fell 4.2 percent in April to $74.66 billion after declining 3.9 percent in March. The slowdown that had affected building materials seems to be spreading across the industrial sector, the Commerce Department said, adding that the report suggests further cutbacks in production.

Corporate purchasing managers indicated in a survey this month that the outlook for the U.S. economy is darkening rapidly. The percentage of managers reporting lower production soared to the highest level since before World War II.

The Fed gave implicit confirmation that it had reduced to about 9 percent from 10½ percent the lower end of its target interest rate band on federal funds, adding to pressures for a cut in its discount rate, currently a record 13 percent. Rates in money and capital markets continued to fall.

Officials of the Fed and the Federal Home Loan Bank Board told a Senate committee they believe the nation's banks and savings institutions are in good shape to weather a recession.

Banks and savings institutions would be able to raise interest rates on six-month money-market certificates as much as half a percentage point under proposals being considered by federal regulators. The aim would be to attract deposits, making more money available for lending.

Lower interest rates in the U.S. sent the dollar tumbling, spurring several central banks to intervene on the currency's behalf. Gold declined $5.10 to $505.50.

Work on an energy bill that will provide $20 billion in federal subsidies for synthetic-fuel plants and other projects was completed by House-Senate conferees. The measure would give the President the last part of his three-part energy package.

OPEC's customers will have to pay an additional $20 billion a year for oil because of Saudi Arabia's aborted effort to stabilize prices in the organization. The cost to consumers could be twice as much if the price boosts spread outside OPEC, which appears likely.

U.S. crude oil imports have dropped to the lowest level in four years, 4.8 million barrels daily, because of record inventories, said the American Petroleum Institute, a trade association.

23 The Fed, with signs of a recession multiplying, substantially eased credit restraints it imposed last March. Fed actions include reducing to 7.5 percent from 15 percent the noninterest-bearing "special requirement" for lenders offering consumer credit and for money-market mutual funds. The change likely will make the funds even more attractive to investors.

Money specialists expect an acceleration in the prime rate's downward drive following the partial dismantling of the Fed's curbs. Even before the announcement, several major banks cut their prime rate to 15½ percent from 16½ percent, undercutting the 16 percent fee posted Monday by Morgan.

Nigeria raised its oil price $2 a barrel, pushing its primary export crude to $36.71. The action sets the stage for a boost by North Sea producers, whose quotes are pegged to those of Nigeria, Algeria, and Libya.

Gasoline supply is expected to be abundant this Memorial Day weekend and all year, but fewer motorists may take to the road because gasoline prices have jumped 50 percent within the past year.

Carter's oil-import fee was dealt a heavy blow in the House, raising further doubts about whether it can survive in Congress. The House Ways and Means Committee approved a resolution to rescind the fee, designed to curb demand for gasoline by raising its price ten cents a gallon.

U.S. auto makers scheduled most of their assembly plants for operation next week, after weeks of drastic production cuts. Only AMC and Ford plan temporary closings, a total of one car and four truck plants, idling 14,720 workers.

Steel prices remain at surprisingly high levels considering the drop in demand. Analysts cite a lack of imports and increasing cost pressures on domestic steelmakers.

26 The economy may be headed for a potentially severe recession with an inflation rate that is unlikely to fall much below 10 percent. Economic adviser Charles Schultze said the recession may be somewhat larger than anticipated. While consumer prices in April rose 0.9 percent, compared with 1.4 percent in March, inflation fighter Alfred Kahn said factors in the slower rise are not "sustainable."

Machine-tool producers are beginning to feel the effects of a recession, but they maintain that there is not any sign of the steep drop in orders that occurred in late 1974. Last month bookings fell 22 percent from March to $415 million, according to a trade group.

Credit restrictions of banks, retailers, and other credit-card issuers are not likely to be eased soon, although the Fed relaxed last week some of the credit curbs it imposed in March. Banks and others cite the high cost of money and the cap on interest that can be charged.

The Fed may have to ease its grip on credit costs further to bolster the nation's sagging money supply, analysts said. An easier credit stance could drive the banking industry's prime rate down even further from about 16½ percent currently.

The lower limit on the Fed's federal funds rate was permitted to drop to 10½ percent, according to minutes of a May 6 Fed policy meeting. Officials were concerned over weak demand for money and the slowing economy.

The Hunt brothers tapped the U.S. banking system for nearly $1 billion in loans last winter, according to a special Fed report, despite federal efforts to curb speculative loans. Most of the loans went to finance silver debts.

U.S. auto sales in mid-May continued at the lowest daily rates in about two decades, plummeting 29 percent to an estimated 155,886 units. Deliveries fell 26 percent at GM, 33 percent at Ford, and 43 percent at Chrysler.

28 The prime rate was lowered to 14 percent by several major banks, led by Morgan Guaranty Trust, as the industry's cost of raising funds continued to fall. The reduction undercuts other banks that just last week trimmed their fee to 14½ percent. Morgan had been charging a 16 percent rate.

The dollar plunged to its lowest level in more than 1½ years on world currency markets because of declining U.S. interest rates. Gold's price jumped $14.10 to $523.80 an ounce.

Firestone posted a $52 million net loss for its second quarter, ended April 30, mostly due to plant closedown costs. The company also had an operating loss of $3 million, compared with a profit a year before.

Iran's oil output is said to have declined to about 500,000 barrels a day, and an Iranian oil ministry official was quoted as saying that non-Communist countries have not received any Iranian oil since May 17. The Islamic regime had set a target of 3 million barrels daily.

Uranium producers are hoping that scheduled production cutbacks in the U.S. and curbs on imports may help boost sagging uranium prices, which have fallen to $32 a pound from a three-year low of $41 in 1979.

29 The discount rate of the Federal Reserve was cut to 12 percent from a record 13 percent to reflect the recent sharp decline in short-term market interest rates. Analysts said the Fed action, which had been widely anticipated, could help the

bond market digest $1 billion in new issues, including a $600 million offering of AT&T.

Productivity in the private sector fell at an annual rate of 0.6 percent in the first quarter, according to the Labor Department, revising an earlier report of a rise at a 0.7 percent pace. Separately, initial claims for regular state unemployment insurance benefits jumped in the week ended May 17 to a record 675,000 from 616,000 the week before.

Slower oil demand and a drop in imports generally during April produced a U.S. merchandise trade deficit of $1.87 billion, the smallest in almost three years. Economists attributed the narrowed trade gap to the emerging recession.

An oil supply glut could cause a collapse in prices, according to Saudi Arabia's oil minister, unless OPEC restores pricing unity soon. He said the collapse will prove a "grave shock to the exporting countries."

U.S. Steel plans additional closings at its Edgar Thomson works in Pittsburgh because of declining steel demand. A total of 2,000 employes have been laid off in the latest and earlier cutbacks.

30 Wages and salaries increased 2.4 percent in the first quarter, matching the record quarter-to-quarter rise of last year's fourth period. At the end of the quarter, wages were up 9.1 percent from a year ago, the biggest 12-month jump since the index was started in 1975.

Auto makers, plagued by a deepening sales slump, plan to close temporarily all or part of 15 assembly plants next week for one to two weeks. The actions will idle 32,340 hourly workers. Ford plans the bulk of the closings.

The Hunt brothers said they are considering legal action against the Chicago Board of Trade, the Commodity Exchange in New York and some individual exchange members for "illegally" manipulating the silver market.

Stock prices plunged as the market entered the technical correction phase that traders have been nervous about all week. The Dow Jones industrials fell 14.07 points to 846.25. Traders also linked the decline to expectations of a dismal economic report by the government today.

Long-term bond yields climbed amid a flood of new corporate issues. Bond prices generally posted declines ranging to more than $10 for each $1,000 face amount of securities. Sales of

AT&T's $600 million of debentures slowed after a quick start.

June 1980

2 The recession may be more severe than the Carter administration expected, some economists indicated following a report that key economic indicators plunged a record 4.8 percent in April. The President conceded the recession has arrived sooner and is steeper than forecast, but said "corrective forces" already are at work that will make the recession "relatively short-lived."

Financier Kirk Kerkorian, who owns 47 percent of the two companies into which MGM is being divided, is expected to announce today terms of a tender offer for up to 5 percent more of the newly created movie concern's stock.

Commonwealth Edison said it is increasing its five-year $4.5 billion construction budget by $1 billion and postponing completion of three nuclear power projects as much as two years. More than $900 million of the rise is related to the projects.

Aluminum workers' new three-year contracts with major producers could make the workers the highest paid in the country's industrial sector. Assuming an 11 percent annual inflation rate, the average employe's pay would rise 42 percent over the life of the pact.

First National Bank of Chicago was misled concerning the silver collateral that Bache Group pledged in order to receive a $75 million loan shortly before the silver market crash, the bank's president told a Senate panel.

Capital markets will face another massive calendar of debt offerings this week as borrowers rush to take advantage of recent interest-rate declines. Prices are expected to fail further. About $2.2 billion in corporate issues is scheduled. Also, with the federal debt ceiling extended through Thursday, the Treasury announced plans to offer $16.2 billion in bills and notes.

Farm prices rose 0.9 percent in May, confirming economists' predictions that retail food prices, one of the few sectors unaffected by inflation, will be rising faster soon. Prices had fallen 4.5 percent in April and 1.7 percent in March.

Procter & Gamble won the competition for Crush's non-Canadian soft-drink properties with a bid of $53 million, sweetened from $46 million. P&G beat Dr. Pepper, whose bid Crush valued at about $51 million.

3 Steel production declined 6.9 percent last week from the previous week to 1,863,000 tons, the lowest point since 1971. The drop brought the industry's operating rate to 62.2 percent, compared with 95.8 percent a year ago.

Norfolk & Western and Southern railways plan a $2 billion merger in a move seen as a defensive response to other big rail consolidations announced since last January. The North-South union would give the U.S. five big and profitable rail systems in about three years.

Factory orders dropped 5.5 percent in April to $143.77 billion, posting the sharpest decline since December 1974. In another indication of further deterioration in economic activity, construction spending fell 3.6 percent to a $221.7 billion annual rate.

Interest rates pressed upward as the money and capital markets began offering about $2.2 billion in corporate issues and $1.5 billion of state and local government securities. Long-term bond prices tumbled an average of one point.

4 The nation is in a recession that began in January, declared the National Bureau of Economic Research, an authoritative nonprofit group. "It is clear that a peak has been reached and we are now in decline," said Martin Feldstein, president of the bureau and a professor of economics at Harvard. The average time from peak to trough of the six previous postwar recessions was just under a year.

Manufacturers Hanover was authorized by the Fed to acquire most of the nonbanking assets of financially ailing First Pennsylvania Corp. The purchase price was estimated at $100 million. In addition, Fed officials approved a reorganization plan for First Pennsylvania.

OECD delegates from 24 industrialized nations pledged at a meeting in Paris to seek to avoid a return to protectionism as a solution to current economic problems.

Interest rates, in a reversal, declined, helping money and capital markets absorb nearly $1 billion of long-term corporate and tax-exempt offerings. Analysts said investors are looking beyond technical factors and seeing a continued economic slowdown and even lower interest rates.

5 The prime rate was cut to 13 percent from

14 percent by Chase Manhattan. Other major banks joined Chase at 13 percent, bringing the key lending fee closer into line with other interest rates. Analysts expect further reductions in coming weeks. In money and capital markets, rates fell again. Stock prices rose on the prime-rate announcement. The Dow Jones industrial average jumped 14.25 points, posting its sharpest gain in six weeks.

Auto sales of U.S. and foreign companies declined more than expected in May from a year ago. Domestic makers' deliveries hit the lowest daily rate in more than 20 years. Volume slumped more than 33 percent to about 694,000 units.

The oil-import fee suffered a severe setback when House members voted for a resolution to rescind Carter's fee. The resolution was sent to the Senate, where opponents of the levy have been gathering for a similar showdown.

Inflation-fighting must remain the Carter administration's top priority despite the economic slump, Treasury Secretary Miller said. The official added that the administration wants to preserve the standby power under which Carter had the Fed impose credit controls in March.

Gold resumed its climb, surging $23.30 to $582.30 an ounce. On world-currency markets, the dollar generally gained, but the British pound recovered against the U.S. currency following its big sell-off Tuesday.

Home mortgage rates plunged a record 0.87 percentage point in the month ended in early May, the Federal Home Loan Bank Board said. Lenders were quoting an average rate of 15.72 percent for commitments to make 25-year conventional loans for 75 percent of a single-family home.

OECD nations' finance ministers maintained that strict monetary and fiscal controls should not be eased although global economic growth has slowed. Similarly, chief U.S. and European central bankers meeting in New Orleans backed stern anti-inflation policies.

Union Carbide is selling more than half its metals business for about $285 million to a group comprising Norway's largest closely held metals producer and Norwegian and Canadian investors.

6   Auto makers next week will close temporarily all or part of 15 car and truck facilities, idling 35,000 hourly workers. Ford will continue to have the largest number of temporary closedowns, 10 of its 17 U.S. operations.

The dollar resumed its slide in foreign-exchange trading, especially against the Japanese yen, due to lower interest rates for dollar deposits in Europe. Gold rose $4.70 to $587.

Commercial banks, suffering from sagging loan demand, appear to be rediscovering Treasury notes and bonds. The development could be a big plus for the Treasury market and help sustain the recent downward pressure on interest rates.

Kraft and Dart Industries, whose stocks have a combined market value of $2.5 billion, agreed to a tax-free merger. Holders are to exchange their common shares on a one-for-one basis for stock in the combined company, Dart & Kraft. The new concern's initial dividend would be at the $3.20 annual rate currently paid by Kraft. Dart's annual rate is $2.

The jobless rate for workers covered by unemployment insurance benefits jumped 0.6 percentage point in the five weeks ended May 17, a sign of continued worsening in the jobless outlook. The Labor Department is scheduled to report the May unemployment rate today, which may be up as much as 0.5 percentage point, to 7.5 percent.

SEC officials cleared a rule to allow stock exchange member firms to trade a limited number of exchange-listed securities over-the-counter.

9   Unemployment figures for May stirred speculation on how long the Carter administration will concentrate solely on fighting inflation. Joblessness climbed to 7.8 percent from 7 percent in April, to the highest level since November 1976. May producer price increases for finished goods slowed to a 0.3 percent pace, or 3.6 percent annually. Consumer credit fell a record $1.99 billion in April.

Campbell Soup is planning the first public debt offering in its 110-year history. The company filed a registration statement with the SEC covering the proposed sale of $100 million of notes, due 1990.

10   Interest rates plunged in money and capital markets on expectations that the Fed would loosen its credit reins to stem the deepening recession. At the Treasury's weekly auction, the average yield fell to 6.5 percent on 13-week bills, the lowest return since May 1978, and to 6.935 percent on 26-week bills, the lowest since April 1978.

Steel production fell 1.8 percent last week

from the previous seven days to 1,830,000 tons, bringing the industry's capacity utilization rate to 61.1 percent. Experts predicted further declines, with mills operating at about 50 percent of capacity sometime in July.

Aluminum producers, facing increased demand, are expanding, but their plans are causing concern among many users because a substantial share of the new smelters will be built outside the U.S. Customers fear an interruption of supplies.

New-home sales plummeted 21 percent in April from March to a 364,000-unit annual pace, the lowest level in nearly 14 years and just 50 percent of the year-earlier rate of 730,000 units. The housing slump fits into a picture of an overall drop in production and employment during the past few months.

The dollar declined to its lowest level since November 1978 in foreign-exchange trading because of sagging interest rates in the U.S. Central banks rushed to bolster the sagging currency.

Gold climbed $17.50 to $624 following heavy buying in Europe. Some New York buyers' dealers suspected the market may be in for a pause. Bullion's surge buoyed the silver market, pushing the metal up $1.08 to $17.88.

11   Tax cuts and perhaps additional spending later this year are being considered by the Carter administration, abandoning hopes of a balanced budget, if the recession worsens. The President told mayors seeking an antirecession package that he would act if the unemployment rate, 7.8 percent in May, continues to soar.

OPEC producers agreed on a new benchmark price of $32 barrel, suggesting possible increases of $1 to $3 for the bulk of OPEC oil starting July 1. Also suggested is a $4 boost for Saudi Arabia's crude. The Saudi oil minister indicated he will elaborate on the kingdom's position today.

Retail sales fell 1.5 percent last month, posting their fourth consecutive decline, because of a big drop in auto shipments. There were widespread signs of weakness in overall sales.

Ford is expected to receive a tentative Transportation Department ruling soon that could require it to make the largest vehicle recall in U.S. history. A department unit has made an initial finding that transmissions in 20 million vehicles can slip into reverse when the gear indicator is in the park position.

GM's 1979-model intermediate-size station wagons are the subject of a safety investigation by the Transportation Department because of a problem with shattering rear windows.

Supreme Court support for state laws that tax out-of-state income of corporations doing business within a state was reaffirmed in a case involving Exxon and Wisconsin.

12   Chrysler has run out of money to pay its bills. Payments to suppliers around the world have been halted, leaving Chrysler exposed to the possibility that suppliers could throw the company into formal bankruptcy proceedings. Federal and Chrysler officials are racing to arrange the first $500 million of promised U.S. aid.

Suppliers to the troubled auto maker, which could refuse to resume deliveries until they are paid, don't know what their next move will be. Many indicated a willingness to wait, but small businesses are already hurting badly.

Fed officials moved to ease credit conditions. The action got a quick response when First National Bank of Boston cut its prime rate to 12 percent from 13 percent. In some sectors of the money market, short-term interest rates fell one-half percentage point.

Budget conferees from the House and Senate agreed on a plan calling for $613.6 billion in outlays for the year beginning October 1 and a surplus of $200 million. The breakthrough came amid doubts that a balanced budget will be possible, mainly because of the rising unemployment rate.

Business inventories during April posted the sharpest rise in nearly a year, 1.3 percent, or $5.9 billion, as overall sales plunged at a record rate of 3.3 percent. The report was an ominous sign in an economy that seems to be declining rapidly.

OPEC's decision to set two new ceilings on oil prices, $32 a barrel and $37 a barrel, has spurred price boost proposals by Kuwait, Iraq, and Qatar. But because of producers' concern about an oil surplus, the jolt to consumers probably will be less than expected.

Oil consumers world-wide agreed the new OPEC price ceilings were too high and would undermine the world's economy. Energy Secretary Duncan termed the decision "irresponsible."

Ford's 1970–79 car and light-truck transmissions were found by the Transportation Department to have a safety defect that could lead to a major recall involving about 16 million vehicles.

13 The Fed lowered to 11 percent from 12 percent the discount rate it charges on loans to member banks, citing a decline in short-term interest rates. On May 28, the rate was cut to 12 percent from the record 13 percent set as part of the Fed's battle against inflation.

Citibank cut its prime rate to 12½ percent from 13 percent in a move that some skeptics said was designed to head off an industry-wide drop to 12 percent. In bond trading, prices soared on word that Salomon Brothers' chief economist, Henry Kaufman, forecast a continued steep drop in interest rates. The Fed's reduction also buoyed prices.

Auto makers will close temporarily next week eight car and four truck operations, bringing the total number of hourly workers idled to 33,200.

Banks and thrift institutions report a renewed interest in savings. The return of savers comes as a relief to the institutions, which have seen savings balances plummet as soaring interest rates lured deposits elsewhere, particularly to money-market funds.

16 Industrial output reports for April and May show that the recession, first evident in the housing and automotive industries, is affecting almost every sector of the economy. Production fell 2.1 percent last month, the steepest plunge since February 1975, after declining 2 percent in April.

The Hunt brothers will be forced to sell much of their silver over the next few years to pay off their $1.1 billion bailout loan, according to bankers who extended the credit.

17 The nation's factories operated at 78.9 percent of capacity last month; the lowest level in more than four years, according to the Federal Reserve Board. The decline was widespread throughout the manufacturing sector, although most severe in auto and construction-related factories.

Patent protection can be granted for a new living organism developed at GE, the Supreme Court ruled. The organism can break down crude oil, making it potentially a valuable aid in oil-spill cleanups. Some scientists said the ruling could lead to patent protection for major scientific experimentation with new life forms.

The decision that newly created microbes can be patented clears the way for a score of patent rulings. Among the organisms that universities and businesses want to patent are those that can make human insulin for treating diabetes and interferon for treating cancer and virus infections.

19 Economic activity appears to be contracting at an 8 percent annual rate in the current quarter, according to Carter administration economists. If the estimate proves correct, the decline would be the second steepest since World War II. Estimates for the first period were raised to show growth at an inflation-adjusted pace of 1.2 percent.

Treasury Secretary Miller conceded that the economic downturn has been sharper than the Carter administration had anticipated, but he said that by the end of 1980 there will be signs of a recovery.

20 Higher oil prices helped swell the deficit in the U.S. balance of payments, on a current-account basis, to $2.57 billion in the first quarter, the largest red-ink total since the third period of 1978. In last year's fourth quarter, the deficit was $1.80 billion.

The Social Security system could run short of funds in three years if the economy goes into a severe, prolonged slide, the system's trustees said. Trustees urged Congress to approve legislation permitting the transfer of money to the old-age fund from other funds.

Auto makers plan to close nine car and truck plants temporarily next week due to a lagging sales, laying off 27,950 hourly workers. Ford again reported the most extensive suspensions.

India won Carter's approval to buy reactor fuel, as members of Congress vowed a fight. Sen. John Glenn (D., Ohio) charged that the sale is incompatible with a 1978 law to guard against diversion of uranium into weapons. The Nuclear Regulatory Commission opposed the transaction but was overruled by the President.

State-run businesses can favor in-state customers, the Supreme Court reaffirmed in a ruling on a cement plant operated by the state of South Dakota. Justices concluded that a state acting like a private business should be able to operate freely.

23 Fed officials are seen likely by analysts to slow efforts to ease credit conditions in the weeks ahead. Analysts cite the need to avoid the risks of rekindling inflationary psychology and of undermining the dollar on currency markets.

U.S. grain exporters were permitted by

the Carter administration to resume selling foreign grain to the Soviet Union. Companies had been asked to halt such sales following the Soviet invasion of Afghanistan.

Carter's handling of the economy was approved by only one in ten chief executive officers in a *Wall Street Journal*/Gallup survey of business opinion. Company officials indicated they are most disturbed by the President's lack of leadership ability.

Auto parts suppliers, already hurt by the year-long car sales slump, were not particularly receptive to a letter from Ford asking them to consider a 1½ percent price cut starting July 1. Also, many of the same suppliers have not been paid by Chrysler because of a cash crunch.

Chrysler's success in pressuring its last few recalcitrant lenders into participating in a federal rescue package reflects the assistance of an army of suppliers, bankers, employes, and other company supporters.

24 Reduced oil consumption was pledged by the seven major industrial nations at the Venice meeting in an ambitious plan that depends heavily on coal. The agreement calls for participants to produce, by 1990, from nonoil sources the energy equivalent of between 15 million and 20 million barrels of oil daily.

The prime rate was cut to 11½ percent from 12 percent at Morgan Guaranty Trust although interest rates rose in money and capital markets. The increase in market rates came as financially ailing Chrysler prepared to offer today $500 million in notes. The notes will bear a 10.35 percent annual rate.

Home loan rates were lowered by several savings and loan associations. The largest federally chartered savings and loan in the U.S., California Federal Savings, cut its mortgage rate to 12 percent from 12½ percent to stimulate demand. Most thrifts remained at 12½ percent.

Alcoa is making its first aluminum production cut in response to the recent slowdown in demand. The producer will idle two units at its Point Comfort, Texas, facility, which will affect 200 employees.

26 Iraq is apparently the first member of OPEC to advise oil purchasers officially that its prices are rising $2 a barrel, effective next Tuesday. The boost puts its key grade at $31.96 a barrel. Also, Dubai is said to be planning a $2 increase, to $31.93.

Chrysler chairman Lee A. Iacocca said at a news conference that the approval of government debt guarantees is a turning point for the auto company, marking "the end of the most difficult phase."

27 A synthetic-fuels bill was sent to Carter after final congressional approval in the House. The $20 billion measure is designed to spur the production of 500,000 barrels of syn-fuels a day by 1987 and 2 million barrels by 1992.

Oil prices on the open market have fallen $1 to $2 a barrel this week, just as OPEC producers began a new round of increases in official prices. Industry observers attribute the drop to record inventories and stagnant demand.

Republican tax-cut pressures spurred Democrats in the Senate to back a resolution calling for such a proposal to reach the Senate floor by September 3. Within hours, though, Democrats killed the Republicans' election-year offering on the Senate floor.

The trucking industry will enter a period of great change in a few days. Carter will sign legislation soon that largely frees the carriers from federal controls. Industry analysts forecast that in a few years, there will be far fewer than the current 17,000 companies.

30 The economy continued to decline rapidly during June, according to a survey of corporate purchasing managers. More managers reported a drop in new orders than at any time in the past 30 years. Inflationary pressures appeared to have eased, however.

Construction contracts fell 31 percent in May, $11.1 billion, the F. W. Dodge division of McGraw-Hill said. The residential sector was hit the hardest, posting a 44 percent drop to $4.49 billion.

The money supply is expected by a group of economists to grow strongly this summer. A renewal of growth could help the economy, which has sunk into a recession, but could hurt money and bond markets by pushing up interest rates.

Most of the revenue-sharing money for states that the Senate Appropriations Committee had tried to delete would be restored under a vote in the Senate. The vote restores 75 percent of the funding.

Trade figures for May showed that the nation's deficit expanded to $3.96 billion, the widest trade gap since February. Exports plunged and imports, despite the recession, climbed.

"Fast track" energy legislation proposed by Carter to speed up energy projects by cutting through red tape faces a difficult time in a House-Senate conference committee after its resounding defeat in the House.

Gould, Inc., in a surprise move, is closing the operations of Gould Financial, its profitable financial unit. The closing apparently is aimed at reducing Gould Inc.'s overall debt.

A&P, which had projected a loss for the year ending next February 22, indicated that it expects to report a loss for the next two years.

July 1980

1 Key indicators of the economy fell 2.4 percent in May after declining a record 4.1 percent the month before. A top government economist warned of further weakness in the economy, particularly in the manufacturing sector. Declining industrial production and higher unemployment were seen for the next four or five months by a private forecaster.

Imports of color-television receivers from Taiwan and South Korea would be permitted to increase under agreements renewed by the U.S. A similar accord curbing imports from Japan was allowed to expire.

2 New factory orders fell 2.6 percent in May, their fourth consecutive decline, after dropping a sharp 5.9 percent in April. The latest report reflects a slight gain in nondurable goods. Separately, construction spending slid 3.6 percent during May to an annual rate of $218.5 billion.

A tax cut in 1981 was declared a certainty by House Speaker O'Neill, who added that Congress may act on a reduction before its fall adjournment. Separately, White House officials said a revision of budget and economic forecasts will assume a tax cut of $25 billion in 1981.

Mail rates for newspapers and magazines using the Postal Service's expedited "red-tag" service will increase sharply under a proposal endorsed by the service's board of governors. Users face an effective surcharge of 2.3 cents a piece.

Gold surged $22.10 an ounce to a four-month high of $669.50 due to demand from Arab and European buyers. In foreign-exchange trading, the dollar declined on a drop in interest rates for dollars deposited abroad.

Federal commodities market regulators raised questions about the way four futures exchanges fix settlement prices after complaints of conflicts of interest. The regulators took steps toward changing the practices.

Steelmakers in the U.S. will be increasingly vulnerable to foreign competition unless they get some federal help and change their attitudes on research and development spending, a congressional study concludes.

3 Bailouts for car dealers hurt by high interest rates and huge inventories are being discussed by the Small Business Administration. The SBA is considering bank loans carrying a 90 percent federal guarantee.

Oil-pricing moves by OPEC producers appear to be losing steam because of softening oil markets and buyer resistance. One producer, Venezuela, is planning an increase of just 60 cents a barrel and only on part of its output.

7 The Fed's decision to phase out credit restraints imposed last March pleased bankers, money-market fund managers and retailers. Retailers, however, do not expect the action to have much impact until later in 1980 because of the recession.

Proponents of easier credit appear likely to successfully argue their case when the Federal Open Market Committee, the Fed's policy-making arm, meets Wednesday, money specialists said. Experts predicted further reductions in short-term interest rates.

Unemployment is expected to resume its climb in coming months although the jobless rate for June declined, to 7.7 percent from 7.8 percent in May. One government analyst noted that job losses continued in manufacturing industries, and another analyst cited a drop in the average number of hours that employes worked.

Bethlehem Steel, citing market pressures, cut prices on 15 products used mostly in the recession-stricken auto and appliance industries an average 4.5 percent. The action follows similar moves by a smaller competitor, McLouth Steel.

AMC intends to raise prices today on its car and Jeep models an average $140, or 1.7 percent. AMC's boost comes after an increase last Tuesday by GM, the industry's price leader.

Savings and loan associations with a federal charter received regulatory permission to exercise broad credit-card issuing powers and to make unsecured loans to card holders, starting Thursday.

Norwegian oil and natural gas production in the North Sea was halted by a strike. About 2,000 workers are seeking 33 percent wage boosts, earlier retirement, and changes in safety procedures. Production losses total $30 million a day.

8   Aid for auto makers is expected to be offered today by the President. Carter plans to announce that he is easing some environmental regulations affecting car companies, providing low-interest loan aid for embattled dealers, and pledging development funds to areas hit hardest by plant closings and layoffs.

Penn Central Corp. agreed to acquire highly profitable GK Technologies for $45 a share or stock. An all-cash transaction would have a value of $630 million, but Penn Central said an accord provides that the maximum amount of cash it would pay would be $225 million.

Xerox, faced with a recession and Japanese competition, cut purchase prices on six low-priced copiers 6 percent to about 12 percent. Rental and lease prices were left unchanged.

A prime rate of 11½ percent became widespread as many banks lowered their lending charge from 12 percent. Spurring the moves was Fed plans to phase out the remaining elements of its credit restraint program, and sluggish loan demand. Many analysts see further rate reductions.

Interest rates rose on fears that the Fed will not ease its grip on credit significantly in the coming weeks. At the Treasury's auction, average yields rose to 8.209 percent for the 13-week bills and to 8.114 percent for the 26-week issue.

9   Producer prices rose 0.8 percent last month, or at a 9.6 percent annual rate, although energy prices fell for the first time in more than two years. The price index posted a 0.3 percent rise for May, equivalent to a 3.6 percent annual rate. Still, the second quarter advance was considerably slower than the rate of increase for the first period.

Bond price gyrations are creating a growing backlog of offerings, totaling $3 billion by one estimate. Market uncertainties continued yesterday as interest rates first rose on fears of a credit-tightening by the Fed, then fell after the possibility was dismissed.

Fed Chairman Volcker came out against any further moratorium on the purchase of U.S. banks by foreigners. The moratorium, which was contained in a bank-ing bill, expired July 1, but there had been discussions on reviving it.

Shell Oil said its Saudi Arabian affiliate and Saudi Basic Industries agreed to a $3 billion equally owned petrochemical complex to be located at Jubail. Each partner will provide $400 million of capital. The balance will be provided by the Saudi government and commercial banks.

OPEC's latest round of oil price boosts seems to have ended with only 6 out of the organization's 13 members posting increases. But industry observers warn that price rises could resume, should Saudi Arabia decide to change its pricing or production.

10   Consumer credit plunged a record $3.43 billion in May, or at an annual rate of 13 percent. The drop surpassed the decline of $1.99 billion, or 8 percent annually in April. Reports for both months reflected weakening demand for credit stemming from the recession and Fed actions in March to limit borrowing.

Demand for short-term credit by business grew at just a 0.9 percent annual pace in the second quarter, according to an analysis of Fed statistics, compared with a 21 percent rate in the first period.

New-home sales jumped 39.4 percent in May to a 488,000-unit yearly pace due to lower mortgage rates and price cuts by distressed builders. Despite the gain, builders still were left with a large inventory, indicating a slow recovery from the current slump.

General Motors announced plans to introduce a small electric-powered car in the 1984 model year that uses GM batteries and pledged its autos will average 31 miles a gallon by 1985. The company said it intends to test Gulf & Western's battery system for possible use in vans.

The New York Futures Exchange, the Big Board unit expected to open August 7, has impressed many commodity officials with the number of prospective traders it has attracted, about 160 so far.

Wholesale gasoline prices were reduced two cents to three cents a gallon by Gulf and three other major gasoline marketers, because of market conditions. The cuts do not signal a general decline in prices at the pump, however.

Energy Department officials gave out $200 million of federal grants for studies on possible synthetic fuels projects. The grants are the department's first under legislation recently signed by the President.

11   Retail sales climbed 1.5 percent last

month to $75.35 billion for the first in-
crease since January. A government
economist termed the June report encouraging, but cautioned that it was
preliminary and subject to revision.

Most chain stores reported slight volume
gains for their five-week June period,
and indicated they may be seeing the
bottom of the current slump. K mart and
Dayton-Hudson both had increases of
13.5 percent. Sears, the exception,
posted a 3.3 percent drop.

Chrysler has told the federal government
privately that it may need to tap as
much as $1 billion in debt guarantees
by the end of the year, about $250 mil-
lion more than had been expected.

Second work-turn operations at Chrysler's
St. Louis car-assembly facility will be
closed permanently next month when
the plant resumes production of mid-
sized models. About 2,100 hourly workers will be idled.

Steel discounts on a wide range of items
announced by Bethlehem Steel are being followed by at least five steelmakers.
One company, U.S. Steel, declined to
specify the size of its reductions, but
buyers said U.S. Steel planned to match
Bethlehem's average 4.5 percent price
cut.

14   Business inventories were down in May, a
development termed encouraging by a
government economist, who noted an
excessive buildup during April. The
latest report showed that inventories
decreased $425 million, or 0.1 percent,
the first decline in more than four years.

Ford apparently dismissed a proposal by
Toyota last month for a joint car-assembly venture in the U.S. Formal re-
jection of the idea is expected next
month, perhaps as early as August 1.

Major oil companies are likely to report a
surge of 25 percent to 50 percent in
second quarter net income, but probably will not post the spectacular gains
of the first period. The smaller rise is
being linked to softening markets and
the impact of the recession at more diversified concerns.

15   Gold plummeted $35.50 an ounce to $633
in New York, marking only the second
time the price has fallen that much in
the past four months. The decline was
spurred by a reiteration by Treasury
Secretary Miller that the U.S. might
resume gold sales. The dollar rose mod-
erately against most other major currencies on firmer U.S. and European
interest rates.

Building awards in 1980 are expected to

fall 17 percent to $137.3 billion from
$166.4 billion last year, F. W. Dodge
said in a revised forecast. In March 1980
the McGraw-Hill unit predicted volume would decline 10 percent. Dodge's
chief economist cited "the all-out effort
to reverse inflation at any cost" for the
dimmer outlook.

16   The New York Futures Exchange plan for
trading contracts based on 90-day
Treasury bills and 20-year Treasury
bonds was approved unanimously by
the Commodity Futures Trading Commission. The action allows the New
York Stock Exchange unit to open August 7, but a Chicago Board of Trade
court move may hinder the opening.

Gold plunged $24.50 an ounce to $608.50
in New York, marking a 9 percent decline in the past two days. The dollar
continued its climb against other major
currencies in quiet dealings.

Midland Bank Ltd. of London's plan to
take over Crocker National is expected
to spur other foreign bids for American
banks. A Crocker takeover is also seen
increasing debate on whether restrictions on U.S. bank mergers and interstate expansion should be eased.

17   The recession may end as early as October, many economists believe. But
unemployment is expected to rise even
after the slump ends as businesses plan
cutbacks in inventories and capital outlays. Inflation is seen likely to accelerate
in early 1981.

Brokerage firms, beginning tomorrow, can
execute orders in some listed stocks in
their offices rather than on the trading
floors. The experiment is part of the
SEC's drive toward a national market
system.

18   Housing starts, after a five-month slide,
climbed a record 30.4 percent in June
to an adjusted annual rate of 1,191,000
units, providing the strongest evidence
yet that the overall economy may soon
be recovering. Other economic statistics
showed that personal income increased
0.4 percent in June, the strongest performance since March, and that the nation's factories operated at 76.1 percent
of capacity last month, the lowest rate
since the fall of 1975.

Steel orders ended the steep decline that
began in mid-March, but there is little
optimism they will rise soon. One observer says the industry will be lucky to
increase its operating rate to more than
60 percent of capacity by year-end from
the current 52 percent.

The stock market reacted vigorously to

Reagan's nomination as the GOP's presidential candidate, pushing up the Dow Jones industrial average 10.66 points to 915.10, its highest level in almost three years. Reagan's nomination had little impact on the credit markets, where prices skidded.

The Savings and Loan industry is developing a desire to merge in a new era of deregulation. Experts predict 10 percent or more of the current 4,700 federally insured thrifts in the U.S. will disappear by 1985.

21 Kuwait's $982 million offer for a 14.6 percent stake in Getty Oil was rejected by J. Paul Getty's estate. The unanimous decision was based on massive tax complications involved in any sale and preserving future value for the estate's beneficiary, the J. Paul Getty Museum.

A coal-gas plant received a boost as Carter issued a $250 million federal loan guarantee to a group headed by American Natural Resources. The plant, to be built in Mercer County, North Dakota, should produce a maximum 137.5 million cubic feet of synthetic gas daily.

22 High inflation, rising unemployment and a continued slowdown in growth are forecast by the Carter administration in its midyear economic review. An official reaffirmed the administration's plans, at least for the present, to resist pressure for a tax cut in 1981, and instead to concentrate on fighting inflation.

The prime rate was cut to 11 percent from 11½ percent by Morgan Guaranty Trust and Bankers Trust. Other banks, facing sluggish loan demand, are expected to follow. One analyst saw the prime rate at 9 percent to 9½ percent by year-end.

Curbs on cable-television program offerings are expected to be scrapped by the FCC today. The anticipated moves would abolish ceilings on the number of "distant signals" that the systems may carry from TV stations outside the systems' local markets.

Federal spending cuts totaling $6.2 billion and revenue measures of $4.2 billion for fiscal 1981 were cleared for House floor action by the House Budget Committee.

23 An anti-inflation policy of monetary restraint will be continued by the Fed, Chairman Volcker said. The Fed official added that federal tax and spending policies should aim for the same goal, to avoid economic stimulus that could provoke another round of inflation.

Treasury Secretary Miller told the House Ways and Means Committee that any moves this year toward a tax cut may lead to faster increases in consumer prices. The remarks received the support of the panel's chairman, Al Ullman (D., Ore.).

Durable-goods orders declined 2.8 percent in June to $65.42 billion, posting the smallest drop since February. A government economist said the report suggested an easing in the sharp fall-off in business during April and May.

Petroleum prices on the spot market continued to fall, reflecting sluggish demand. Despite the soft markets, Qatar proceeded with its price increase of $2 a barrel, retroactive to July 1.

24 Consumer prices climbed 1 percent last month, or at a 12 percent annual rate, after increasing 0.9 percent in April and May. Still the latest rise was smaller than the 1.4 percent jump during the first quarter. The June report reflected moderation in food prices and the general effects of the recession.

The new-car sales rate dropped 24 percent in mid-July to 150,768 units in the aftermath of much-publicized rebate programs across several makes and model lines. Shipments fell 24 percent at GM, 36 percent at Ford and 30 percent at Chrysler.

25 General motors reported a second quarter loss of $412 million, the auto maker's biggest quarterly deficit ever. The deficit offset slim first period earnings, plunging GM into the red for the half. Separately, AMC had a fiscal third period red-ink total of $84.9 million, the largest in its history.

Ford said it will close six vehicle assembly plants for one to three weeks beginning Monday to reduce its inventories. About 15,600 hourly workers will be idled.

The prime rate was cut to 10¾ percent by several major banks. The lending charge is at its lowest level since November 1978. Analysts predict further reductions because of a decline in banks' borrowing costs and sluggish loan demand.

Home mortgage rates could fall to 11 percent by year-end from 12 percent to 13 percent currently, according to Jay Janis, Federal Home Loan Bank Board chairman. Janis also said that savings and loan associations are making a fine comeback.

More oil companies had big second quarter earnings gains but there were signs that sluggish markets may hurt the second half. Profit jumped 74 percent at Getty, 64 percent at Mobil, 62 percent at Gulf and 48 percent at Sun Co.

Pan Am reported a second quarter loss of $66.3 million, one of the biggest deficits in the airline industry. Delta's net fell slightly to $37.6 million, or $1.89 a share.

29   Grain price supports would be raised under a plan by the Carter administration that would require $1 billion in outlays. The administration, which has been under pressure to appease grumbling farmers, said the planned measures could raise prices about 5 percent.

Productivity in the nonfarm business sector fell at a 4.1 percent annual rate in the second quarter, posting the largest decline for that sector since 1974. The report reflects the effects of the recession on output and hours of paid work.

Bond prices slumped on trader concerns that heavy U.S. borrowings to cover budget deficits this year and next could disrupt markets and send interest rates soaring. Treasury Secretary Miller said the fears are unfounded.

30   Ford reported a record loss of $467.9 million for the second quarter, despite a series of cost-cutting measures. The deficit is believed to be the second highest quarterly loss sustained by a U.S. company. World-wide vehicle sales dropped 34 percent, pushing total volume down 23 percent to $9.27 billion.

Some crude-oil prices in the U.S. are beginning to fall because of sluggish petroleum markets. The biggest decline, $4 a barrel, is in prices charged by Standard Oil of Ohio for 250,000 barrels a day of Alaskan oil.

U.S. Steel's earnings on operations fell 46 percent in the second quarter to $80.7 million, or 93 cents a share. The company said that a retrenchment in steel operations last year resulted in a profit on steelmaking despite weak demand.

31   Chrysler reported a record loss of $536.1 million for the second quarter and a 33 percent sales decline to $2.12 billion. The deficit is close to what the auto maker had estimated. Separately, the Chrysler Loan Guarantee Board gave final approval to $300 million more in loan guarantees for the company.

Gasoline prices are beginning to fall slightly because of a growing glut of fuel. Among the major companies lowering prices are Cities Service, Texaco, Gulf Oil, and Conoco.

Farm prices surged 5.2 percent last month, the largest increase since 1974, as drought fears helped propel average prices for soybeans, corn, hogs, cattle, and broiler chickens.

Interest rates soared again in money and capital markets and prices plunged amid fears that the Fed has tightened its credit reins. Many economists concluded that the Fed is willing to accept a rise in the key rate on so-called federal funds.

August 1980

1   Key indicators of the economy climbed 2.5 percent in June, posting the first increase since June 1979. A government official said the report reinforces evidence that the low point of the recession may be reached sooner than expected. Private economists agreed that the rise was encouraging, but added that it is difficult to say when economic activity will pick up again.

Sears, Woolworth, and three other major retailers are being investigated by the FTC to see whether their ads were truthful about such things as "satisfaction-guaranteed" claims. The companies filed motions to limit subpoenas for their records.

Gulf Oil's plan for a government-backed, $1.4 billion synthetic fuels plant in Morgantown, West Virginia, is expected to get formal White House approval today but already has met with opposition. Citizens of the area are concerned over a toxic chemical spill at a pilot plant near Tacoma, Washington.

Standby gasoline rationing legislation survived attempts to kill it in the House and Senate. The plan would take effect if the nation ever anticipates a 20 percent oil shortage.

4   Most major oil companies and many independent petroleum refiners are lowering the prices they will pay for "uncontrolled" domestic crude oil because of sluggish markets. Most reductions are between $1 and $1.50 a barrel.

Purchasing agents confirmed the belief that the economy continues to weaken but at a "slightly slower" pace, according to the July survey by the National Association of Purchasing Management. The rate of new orders rose, inventories declined and inflation eased, the survey said.

Construction outlays dropped 2.3 percent in June to an adjusted $215 billion annual rate. The slower rate of decline suggests the economy is not slipping as rapidly as it was in March and April.

5 Chemical Bank increased to 11 percent from 10¾ percent its prime rate because of the recent sharp climb in its interest costs. Unless the spiral is reversed, analysts say, pressures could mount for an industry boost to at least 11¼ percent in the weeks ahead.

6 Some OPEC members are lowering the oil price premiums that previously were added to government contract selling prices. In other cases, the premiums, which had ranged as high as $11 a barrel, are being eliminated or ignored. Sluggish markets are cited.

Resumption of strategic petroleum stockpiling was ordered by Carter in compliance with the recently passed synthetic fuels legislation. The White House did not formally announce the action because it is concerned about angry reactions from oil-producing nations.

The Fed moved aggressively to drain reserves from the banking network yesterday as the key interest rate on federal funds plummeted to as low as 2 percent. That contrasts with an average rate of more than 10 percent on Monday.

8 Consumer credit dropped an adjusted $3.46 billion in June, or at a 13.5 percent annual rate. The record decline, reflecting the effects of the recession, was the third consecutive monthly decrease in debt outstanding. Analysts are uncertain what role the Fed's credit restraints played in reducing demand.

A stock price rally, led by oil and basic-industry issues, sent the Dow Jones industrial average to its highest level in almost 3½ years. Volume soared to nearly 62,000,000 shares, the ninth highest on record. The average closed at 950.94, up 12.71 points.

The Big Board's financial futures exchange got off to an impressive start, industry officials said. The New York Futures Exchange traded 3,581 contracts covering $358.1 million of bonds.

11 AT&T agreed to a three-year national labor contract with three unions providing an estimated 34.9 percent increase in total compensation. A union official said the pact would cost AT&T about $6 billion.

The housing industry recovered in June, but industry economists believe the recovery might soon stall. New-home sales climbed 16 percent to an adjusted annual rate of 535,000 units from May's revised 461,000. One economist says the halt in mortgage rate drops is bound to discourage home buyers.

Building awards in June dropped 18 percent to $12.42 billion from $15.15 billion a year earlier, F. W. Dodge said. Residential construction was hit hardest, declining 30 percent to $5.09 billion, but the McGraw-Hill unit's chief economist said a recovery is underway.

Home buyers will not be allowed to assume any of the Federal National Mortgage Association's conventional mortgages closed on or after October 1 unless they pass a credit check and agree to accept prevailing market interest rates. The new policy could make the assumption of mortgages more expensive in the future.

The auto industry's declining fortunes will not prevent the FTC from filing charges on defect disclosures against car makers, a top official said. The comment was made as the FTC filed a complaint against GM for alleged transmission failures.

A Labor Department rule change that narrowed the eligibility of workers for an additional 13 weeks of unemployment benefits beyond the normal 26 weeks was declared invalid by a federal district judge.

12 Retail sales climbed 2 percent last month after rising 1.4 percent in June. Government and private economists viewed the increase as a sign that consumer confidence may be rebounding, but were divided on whether the trend will continue at sufficient strength to bring an early end to the recession.

Corn crop estimates were trimmed by the Agriculture Department, which cited the drought in the Midwest. Low estimates also were set for cotton, sorghum, and soybeans. If the forecasts are correct, an official said, prices will rise substantially in 1980.

A new Energy Department report concludes that government policies have little effect, for either better or worse, on the nation's energy prospects for the next ten years. The finding is being criticized by some administration energy officials, who fear it could be used as a political weapon against Carter.

Gold fell $23 an ounce to $603.20. Many traders predicted further declines because of an absence of buyers. On world currency markets, the dollar fell slightly. Interest rates climbed in money and capi-

tal markets and prices plunged as dealers struggled with a huge supply of unsold debt securities. Also influencing
rates was a strong report on July retail
sales, sparking trader fears of increased
credit demands.

13 Penney's became the first major retailer
to report the steep profit decline that
many analysts are predicting for other
mass merchandisers in the July quarter.
The effect of the recession resulted in a
pretax loss of $6 million in Penney's
retail operations. Aided by insurance
operations, Penney's posted net income
of $5 million, or seven cents a share,
down 69 percent from last year.

Business inventories rose $1.37 billion,
or 0.3 percent, in June, setting the stage
for further weakness in the nation's
economy in coming months. The increase followed a rise of $857 million,
or 0.2 percent, in May.

Auto-leasing companies are being investigated by the FTC for possible violations of customers' rights. The agency
is looking into, among other things,
penalties imposed by leasing companies
on customers who fail to meet lease
terms.

An interest-rate decline in the key federal
funds rate, to as low as 8 percent at
one point from 9.19 percent on Monday,
spurred sales of new long-term debt offerings. In some sectors, prices, which
move inversely to yields, rose nearly $15
for every $1,000 face amount.

Nelson Bunker Hunt, who is being investigated by the SEC for a late filing on
Bache holdings of more than 5 percent,
disclosed that most of the Bache stock
was purchased through a joint account
with his brother. Previously, the Hunts
argued that they each bought 3.3 percent individually.

14 The wage and price council decided to
permit GE to switch to a special, higher
price standard because of "uncontrollable" labor-cost increases following a new contract. The decision marks
the first time the council has approved
a new standard for "uncontrollable"
new wage costs.

Merrill Lynch said it is considering a purchase of the Chicago White Sox base-
ball team. The securities firm indicated
it wants to offer the team as a limited
partnership.

15 Airlines may be granted far more flexibility to set international cargo rates than
they currently have. The CAB has in-
structed its staff to draft a rule that
would permit 5 percent to 20 percent

boosts without specific CAB approval.

A housing finance agency's $73.9 million
note sale was canceled by New York
State after it ran into an IRS roadblock.
The agency also decided to postpone
for a week the closing on a companion
$77.8 million bond issue.

Crude oil and petroleum imports continued to fall last month, according to oil
industry statistics, which showed a 25.3
percent drop from the year-earlier level.

18 Food-price increases stemming from
drought damage have dimmed the nation's chances of getting relief from
inflation during the current recession.
Higher food costs during July accounted
for nearly three-quarters of a producer-
price rise of 1.7 percent, the biggest
jump since November 1974.

Interest rates in money and capital markets are likely to face increased upward
pressure in the weeks ahead, analysts
said, due to fears of a renewed inflation
and signs of a slowing in the economy's
decline.

19 Housing starts rose 4.8 percent last month
after surging 33.3 percent in June, spurring analyst remarks that the housing
industry's recovery could stall unless
mortgage rates come down. Separately,
U.S. factories were operating at 74.2
percent of capacity in July, the lowest
level in five years. Personal income rose
1.4 percent, but the increase was due
primarily to higher payments for Social
Security and other government programs.

Stock prices fell on worries that interest
rates would rise following the jump in
the nation's money supply. The Dow
Jones industrial average posted its biggest loss in five months, declining 18.09
points to 948.63.

A prime rate boost to 11¼ percent from
11 percent appears likely as early as this
week, analysts said, because of higher
costs for bank borrowings.

Interest rates soared as money and capital
markets reacted to a record jump in the
nation's money supply. Bond prices
plunged almost two points in some
sectors.

20 Corporate profits, after taxes, plummeted
18.2 percent, or a record $28.7 billion,
in the second quarter from the first period, and indicated a continued weakness in manufacturing and employment.
The percentage decline is the third largest in the postWorld War II era.

The prime rate was raised to 11¼ percent
from 11 percent by Chase Manhattan.
Other banks are expected to follow, as

Chase's move reflects the recent rise in bank borrowing costs. That rise was evident yesterday in the secondary market for certificates of deposit.

Exports to the Soviet Union plunged to $693 million in the first half following the Carter administration's trade sanctions from $1.46 billion in 1979. The sanctions were imposed to show U.S. displeasure over the invasion of Afghanistan.

21 Durable goods orders rose 8.4 percent in July to $72.06 billion, posting the first increase since January and the biggest jump in nearly ten years. Government economists were encouraged by the figures, but cautioned that it is too early to tell whether they signal an end to the recession.

Short-interest soared a record 9,219,547 shares, or 14 percent, on the New York Stock Exchange in the month ended August 15 to a high of 73,533,020 shares. On the Amex, short interest fell 173,162 shares, or 2 percent, to 8,188,704 shares.

22 American Telephone, as part of its preparation for partial deregulation, announced a restructuring of top management and a $1 billion plan to buy out minority common shareholdings in four operating units.

Under deregulation, AT&T would split into two parts. One portion would be regulated, offering basic telecommunications services. The other would compete in unregulated markets, such as advanced data communications.

Tax cuts for businesses and individuals totaling $30 billion were approved for 1981 by the Senate Finance Committee, in defiance of the White House and House Democratic leadership. The panel pledged to sweeten its proposal today.

25 AT&T's plan to consolidate $28 billion of its pension money promises to make the year ahead a tense one for many of the 115 concerns, mostly banks, that manage the pension plans.

ABC settled an eight-year-old antitrust case by agreeing to loosen its grip on the prime-time entertainment programming of its television network stations. Similar settlements have been reached by CBS and NBC.

Lower housing costs helped keep consumer prices unchanged last month following an increase of 1 percent, or 12 percent annually, in June. Private economists predicted that rising interest rates and food prices will affect the overall price outlook in August.

26 The federal budget deficit grew by $15.06 billion in July because of the recession, compared with $7.21 billion in red ink a year earlier. The July figure brings the deficit so far this fiscal year to $58.72 billion.

Treasury bill yields rose at the weekly auction to their highest level since April 28 amid fears in money and capital markets that the Fed will clamp down on credit availability. The average rate climbed to 10.025 percent for 13-week bills and to 10.25 percent for the 26-week issue.

27 Sluggish gasoline sales have touched off a competitive scramble among leading oil companies. Sun Co. boosted the rebate that it gives service station owners and Ashland has cut wholesale prices in three cities.

Foreign direct investment in the United States increased a record 23 percent in 1979 to $52.26 billion, but was still below the level of U.S. direct investment abroad. U.S. investment abroad was up 14.8 percent to $192.65 billion.

Clayton Brokerage of St. Louis, a unit of Garnac Grain, will pay a $200,000 fine to settle charges by the Commodity Futures Trading Commission that the company participated in a plan to manipulate silver prices in 1978.

28 Productivity in the nonfarm business sector fell at a 2.9 percent annual rate in the second quarter, less than the 4.1 percent pace previously estimated. Overall private-business productivity declined for the sixth consecutive quarter, posting a 1.9 percent drop.

The trade deficit narrowed to $1.85 billion in July, the smallest red-ink total since March 1979. Sharply lower oil imports were cited.

A major gold find in California estimated at more than one million ounces was announced by Homestake Mining. The deposit, which is close to the surface, contains more than 6 million tons of ore with an average grade of 0.17 ounce of gold per ton. The gold was discovered in a remote area 70 miles west and north of Sacramento.

29 New economic proposals for 1981 were outlined by the President that would cut taxes $27.6 billion, with much of the relief going to business, and boost spending $4,29 billion over two years. For business, there are faster tax write-offs for plants and equipment and expanded investment tax credits. Offerings for individuals include an income tax credit.

The "revitalization" election-year plan spurred expressions of concern from some Democrats over what they considered was an inadequate level of spending. Republicans, who have urged bigger tax incentives for companies, criticized the plan's delayed nature.

Construction contracts awarded last month declined 15 percent from the year earlier to $13.47 billion, the F.W. Dodge unit of McGraw-Hill reported. An economist at the unit, however, noted that although the seasonally adjusted contracting index fell in July from 1979, it advanced from June and May levels.

A change in Chrysler's rescue legislation was suggested by a top Treasury official because of difficulties in selling the auto maker's government-backed notes. The official said the government should buy future issues under certain conditions.

Antitrust legislation would be extended to partnerships and unincorporated associations and individual ventures under a bill passed in the House.

September 1980

2 Business activity is expected to continue weakening in coming months despite the record jump in the government's index of leading indicators for July. The index climbed 4.6 percent, surpassing the previous record increase, set in June 1975.

3 New factory orders rose 5.7 percent in July, posting the first increase since January and the largest in almost ten years. A top government economist saw signs of a "prospective" recovery, but cautioned against assuming that a strong recovery is about to begin. Separately, July construction spending fell 0.9 percent, after declining 1.7 percent in June.

Auto production dropped 30 percent last month to 308,678 units. The output consisted mostly of 1980 models. The August figure reflects auto makers' intention to make certain that they aren't left with a glut of cars that might impede the introduction of 1981 models.

4 Interest rates fell again in money and capital markets after the Fed implicitly confirmed that its preferred trading range for federal funds is lower than what specialists had feared.

The stock market's rally continued, with volume climbing to 52,370,000 shares.

Analysts cited fading fears of a tighter credit policy. The Dow Jones industrial average rose 12.38 points to 953.16.

8 The economy combined strength in the labor force with high inflation last month. The unemployment rate, surprising economists, declined to a seasonally adjusted 7.6 percent of the work force from 7.8 percent in July. A 4.4 percent jump in consumer food prices sent producer prices for finished goods rising 1.4 percent in August, or at an 18 percent annual rate.

Purchasing agents indicated in a monthly survey that the economy is showing additional signs of recovering. The National Association of Purchasing Management survey showed a steep increase in the number of companies reporting an improvement in new orders in August.

Interest rates climbed in the nation's money and capital markets on fears the Fed may tighten credit. Short-term rates had increases of more than ¼ percentage point. A rise to 12 percent from 11½ percent in the banking industry's prime rate became widespread as a dozen big banks boosted the key fee.

The recession will "bottom out" sooner than expected, but government officials remain pessimistic that the economic recovery will be "sluggish." The report was made before the House Budget Committee by Charles Schultze, the President's key economic adviser, and James McIntyre, budget director.

Gold soared $30.70 an ounce to $680 in New York and hit nearly a seven-month high amid speculation that Saudi Arabia will soon increase its crude-oil prices. The dollar tumbled on world currency markets.

10 Banks and thrifts will be able to pay as much as 5¼ percent interest on checking accounts beginning next year, the Federal Depository Institutions Deregulation Committee ruled. But the panel left intact current interest rate ceilings on regular savings accounts.

New-home sales soared 23 percent in July to an adjusted annual rate of 659,000 units from June's revised 536,000. But industry officials predict the recovery will soon stall because of recent mortgage rate boosts.

11 Retail sales spurted 1.5 percent in August, following a revised 3.1 percent jump in July and marking the third consecutive monthly increase. Consumer debt extended in July climbed 18.4 percent. The latest government reports left some analysts cautiously predicting the recession may be the shortest since World War II.

Capital spending by businesses is expected to decline slightly this year after adjustment for inflation, a Commerce Department survey taken in July and August suggests. One analyst puts the decrease at 0.2 percent.

12 Business inventories rose $3.64 billion, or 0.8 percent, in July to an adjusted $450.67 billion. But sales climbed faster, up $8.5 billion, or 2.9 percent, to an adjusted $302.71 billion. The ratio of inventories to sales dropped for the first time in six months. Government economists said the figures indicated the recession is ending, but some private economists saw signs of continuing weakness.

The SEC was criticized by a House subcommittee for failing to bring about the national securities market envisioned by 1975 legislation. The intermarket trading system created by six stock exchanges has produced little of the competition that was intended, the panel said.

Savings and loan associations will be permitted to sell their housing-rehabilitation loans to Fannie Mae under a new ruling by the Federal Home Loan Bank Board. The move will let savings and loan associations raise extra capital, boosting mortgage lending.

Mortgage rates were raised to 13¾ percent from 13½ percent by two more California lenders—California Federal Savings & Loan Association and Gibraltar Savings & Loan.

Texaco reduced its estimate of proved U.S. natural gas reserves 10 percent to 8.8 trillion cubic feet. The reduction is Texaco's second in the past 12 months.

15 Oil producers will open their long-term strategy session today in Vienna with current pricing and production controversies still unsettled. Iran and several other OPEC members last night urged Saudi Arabia to reduce its output and boost its prices. But Saudi Arabia's oil minister said he wouldn't discuss the current price of oil until after the meeting.

The economy ended its decline in July or August and has started a recovery, Courtenay Slater, the Commerce Department's chief economist, said. But most private forecasts don't see a rise in real gross national output, adjusted for inflation, until the fourth quarter.

The Fed could be forced to tighten its credit reins if the sharp growth in the nation's money supply continues through September, economists and market analysts say. Many specialists believe the Fed's policy-making arm, which meets tomorrow, will maintain a moderate course for the time being.

16 Auto sales fell 20 percent on a daily rate basis for the first ten days of September to about 139,103 units from a year earlier. The decline was less than expected. General Motors' sales dropped 13 percent, Ford's 36 percent, Chrysler's 33 percent, and AMC's 14 percent. But Volkswagen's deliveries rose 72 percent.

OPEC members seemed to move toward a goal of matching oil production to demand to cope with current and possible future surpluses. But little progress was made at their meeting toward resolving differences on oil-pricing policies.

Sugar's price rose to its highest level in five years, about 37 cents a pound, on rumors that the Soviets were making a large purchase.

17 Industrial output rose an adjusted 0.5 percent in August, marking the first increase in seven months and providing the strongest evidence to date that economic recovery may be under way. Production had declined about 8.5 percent in the months between.

Interest rates dropped sharply in the nation's money and capital markets as investors were encouraged by figures showing a smaller-than-expected increase in industrial output last month.

Occidental Petroleum tentatively agreed to buy Firestone's plastics division for about $200 million in cash. Occidental's bid won over a competing offer from West Germany's Chemische Werke Huels.

Gold soared $15.60 an ounce to $679.50 in New York as a surge in Middle East buying of silver spilled over into the gold market. Silver rose $1.42 an ounce to $21.

Pay and price anti-inflation guidelines will probably be extended through December 31 as Carter is expected to accept recommendations for the extension by two advisory committees.

OPEC split on future oil-pricing and production policies. Algeria, Libya, and Iran stood apart from other cartel members, preventing the establishment of a long-term strategy plan after two days of debate.

18 Saudi Arabia will boost its oil prices $2 a barrel in a compromise aimed at papering over differences in OPEC. Other producers will "freeze" their prices at current levels until year-end. The price increase will apply to about one third of the cartel's total output of 27 million barrels a day.

Housing starts increased 12 percent in August to an adjusted annual rate of 1,399,000 units, marking the third consecutive month of recovery. But industry economists warned that high mortgage rates, already above 13 percent in most parts of the country, may have already started a relapse.

Stock prices soared on the prospect for stability in world oil prices. The Dow Jones industrial average spurted 15.36 points to close at 961.26, with trading just under 64 million shares.

19 Oil price unity could be restored by year-end, officials from most of OPEC believe. But sources said it will probably mean another price boost of $1 to $2 or more a barrel, effective January 1, for the Arab light oil produced in Saudi Arabia.

The U.S. and most other countries reacted with relief to Saudi Arabia's oil-price boost of $2 a barrel. The Energy Department said the boost would result in a slight rise in U.S. fuel prices. Economists agree that the latest cartel meeting won't have a significant impact on the U.S. economy.

Gasoline prices were slashed by five major oil companies because of sluggish markets and bulging inventories.

Personal income increased 0.8 percent in August to an adjusted annual rate of $2.138 trillion. Much of the gain came from boosts in private-industry payrolls. But consumer spending continued to rise at a faster pace than income is growing, up 1.2 percent to an annual rate of $1.685 trillion.

U.S. balance of payments, on a current-account basis, showed a narrower deficit in the second quarter of $2.50 billion, compared with a $2.64 billion deficit in the first quarter.

22 Real GNP plunged at a record annual rate of 9.6 percent in the April-to-June quarter, more than the previous estimate of 9 percent. But Courtenay Slater, the Commerce Department's chief economist, remained optimistic about prospects for recovery. Other economists worry that continued increases in interest rates could hamper an upturn. After-tax corporate profits in the second quarter slid more than expected, down 19.6 percent to an annual rate of $127.1 billion.

GM stock, estimated at $12 million, was stolen from the vault of Moseley Hallgarten during the summer in what Wall Street officials say may be the largest securities theft ever.

The Fed may be forced to tighten its credit stance soon because of the surge in the nation's money supply, some economists and analysts believe. The basic money stock soared $1.1 billion in the week ended September 10. Separately, the Fed's policy-making arm took steps last month to loosen the reins a bit in the third quarter on the money supply.

Oil production of OPEC will be reduced 10 percent to pare the current oversupply, Iran's oil minister said.

Multiemployer pension legislation was approved by Congress and creates incentives for companies to stay in such plans and provides penalties for those that abandon them. But some pension experts believe the bill might discourage other companies from joining.

24 Consumer prices rose an adjusted 0.7 percent in August, or at an 8.4 percent annual rate before compounding, providing evidence that the 1980 recession has done little to slow inflation. About half of the price boost was because of a surge in food prices. Separately, new factory orders for durable goods fell 2.3 percent last month to an adjusted $72.3 billion.

Unemployment benefits would be extended temporarily to 49 weeks from 39 weeks under a House Ways and Means measure. The full House may act on the $1.34 billion program later this week.

Stock prices plunged, with the Dow Jones industrial average falling 12.54 points to 962.03. The dive was triggered by news that Iraq bombed Iran's Abadan oil refinery. Trading surged to 64,390,000 shares.

25 American Motors, under a financial rescue plan, would be controlled effectively by Renault. The French auto maker would acquire, during the next two years, at least a 46.4 percent in AMC and would be able to boost its interest to more than 55 percent. The plan would pump $310 million to $385 million into AMC.

General Motors, in a move to raise cash, apparently is negotiating the sale of its Terex division, a maker of heavy-duty construction vehicles. The buyer is said to be IBH Holding of West Germany.

U.S. car sales dropped an unexpectedly steep 39 percent for mid-September to 137,413 autos. But at least part of the

decline was attributed to the introduction of new models in the next few days.

A rail-deregulation bill was quickly approved by House-Senate conferees. The
measure permits roads to raise freight
rates largely free of ICC control and
to sign rate-and-service contracts with
shippers and provides federal aid to
ailing carriers.

26 The discount rate was increased by the
Fed to 11 percent from 10 percent, in a
battle to slow the fast growth of the
nation's money supply. Interest rates
in money and capital markets soared
and bond prices plunged in the wake of
the Fed's announcement. Analysts predict the banking industry's prime rate
will rise, as early as today, to 12¾ percent from 12½ percent.

The 1980 Recession

Geoffrey H. Moore*

The economic slowdown that characterized the U.S. economy during 1979 was succeeded in 1980 by a recession. The slowdown, which ran from December 1978 to January 1980, was unusually long and generated much speculation on whether a recession—that is, a protracted, substantial, and widespread decline in economic activity—had or had not begun. By the spring of 1980 the uncertainty disappeared. The sharp decline that was taking place, and the antecedents that made its continuation likely, strongly supported the view that a recession was indeed underway. Early in June the National Bureau of Economic Research, which has become the arbiter on this

° Geoffrey H. Moore is director of the Center for International Business Cycle Research, Rutgers University, Newark, NJ 07102.

matter, made its pronouncement: The business cycle peak was January 1980. The decision was made long before the popular, but overly simplistic, definition of recession—namely, two successive quarters of decline in real GNP—could have been applied. The latest published GNP figure was for the first quarter of 1980, and it was at a record high. But monthly figures on economic activity had been dropping sharply, providing a basis for the diagnosis. Subsequent developments have confirmed it.

As soon as the recession became obvious, interest shifted to the question of how sharp and how long it would be and of what signs of an upturn might be expected. In appraising an ongoing recession it is helpful to make systematic comparisons with preceding recessions. A method for doing so is illustrated in Charts 1 and 2. The charts compare the current period,

CHART 1

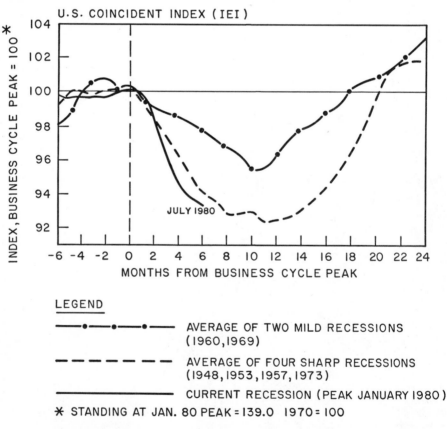

U.S. COINCIDENT INDEX (IEI)

JULY 1980

MONTHS FROM BUSINESS CYCLE PEAK

INDEX, BUSINESS CYCLE PEAK = 100 *

LEGEND

——•——•——•—— AVERAGE OF TWO MILD RECESSIONS (1960, 1969)

— — — — — — AVERAGE OF FOUR SHARP RECESSIONS (1948, 1953, 1957, 1973)

———————— CURRENT RECESSION (PEAK JANUARY 1980)

✱ STANDING AT JAN. 80 PEAK = 139.0 1970 = 100

Source: Center for International Business Cycle Research, Rutgers University.

CHART 2

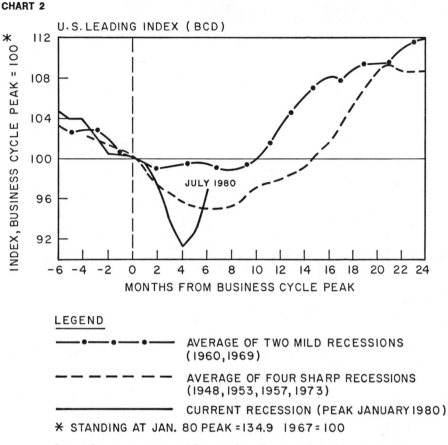

U·S·LEADING INDEX (BCD)

LEGEND

———•——•——•—— AVERAGE OF TWO MILD RECESSIONS (1960,1969)

— — — — — — AVERAGE OF FOUR SHARP RECESSIONS (1948,1953,1957,1973)

———————— CURRENT RECESSION (PEAK JANUARY 1980)

✱ STANDING AT JAN. 80 PEAK = 134.9 1967 = 100

Source: Center for International Business Cycle Research, Rutgers University.

starting six months before the January 1980 business cycle peak and ending 24 months after the peak, with the corresponding periods in earlier recessions. They distinguish the two recessions since 1948 that were especially mild (1960–61 and 1969–70) from the four that were deeper (1948–49, 1953–54, 1957–58, and 1973–75). The charts show the current development against the background of the average pattern of the two mild recessions and the average of the four sharp ones. In each case the level at the business cycle peak at the start of the recession is assigned a value of 100, with the figures before and after the peak shown as relatives on that base.

The coincident index in Chart 1 combines six important measures of economic performance into a single monthly series. Three of the components are dollar aggregates expressed in constant prices (gross national product, personal income, manufacturing, and trade sales) while three are expressed in physi-

cal units (industrial production, nonfarm employment, and unemployment rate). The index has the advantage of summing up these several aspects of the economy in a single number, ironing out some of their idiosyncrasies in the process. The turning points in this index have come very close to matching the dates of all the business cycle peaks and troughs since 1948, and in 1980 did so precisely. The relative severity of recessions, as well as their duration, is well measured by this index. As the chart shows, the decline in the current recession through July (the latest figure available at this writing) has been somewhat steeper than the average pattern of the four sharp recessions. The upturn in the average pattern came about a year after the recessions began, with recovery to the prerecession level taking about 20 months overall. As a rule, as the chart shows, periods of depressed activity (below preceding peak levels) have lasted longer when the recession was deep than when it was shallow.

CHART 3
GROWTH RATES IN COINCIDENT INDEX FOR MAJOR COUNTRIES EXCLUDING THE U.S.
DURING FIVE U.S. RECESSIONS, 1957–1980

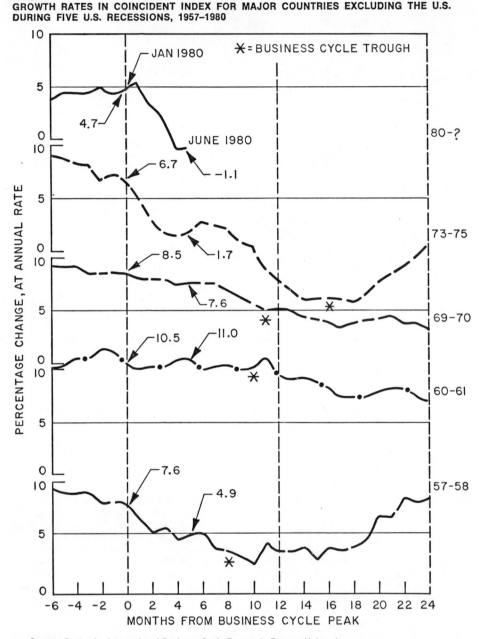

Source: Center for International Business Cycle Research, Rutgers University.
    The growth rate covers a six-month span, based on the ratio of the current month to the average of the preceding 12 months. The six countries are Canada, United Kingdom, West Germany, France, Italy and Japan.

The same kind of picture becomes visible several months earlier in Chart 2, which shows the movements of an index composed of a dozen "leading indicators." These indicators are of a kind that one would expect to move in advance of the measures of output, income, trade, and employment used in the coincident index—and which in fact have a rather consistent record of doing so. They have this property in part because they are more sensitive to favorable or unfavorable developments, such as fall or rise in interest rates or, credit ease or stringency. Some of the leading indicators represent prices in markets that promptly register such developments. In other cases the leading indicators represent the early stages of a process whose end result is the output of products or the employment or income generated by such output.

This means that there are a number of reasons why the leading indicators "lead," and since the composite index shown in the chart includes a group selected for these various reasons, the movements of the index itself "lead" for all these reasons. Although that circumstance complicates its interpretation, it has a salutary effect on the reliability of the index as compared with any single one of its components. The index is less affected by the erratic happenings and special developments that often upset the usual relationship that applies to one or another of its components. For example, new orders for products that are made to order have a leading relationship to the output of those products. But if a strike unexpectedly occurs in that industry, orders and output may be cut almost simultaneously, so that the usual lead-lag relationship is obscured. Again, when an industry has developed a large backlog of orders it may take a long time for a decline in new orders to be reflected in output, and a small fluctuation may not be reflected at all, whereas when the backlog is small the movements in new orders are likely to have a much quicker effect.

As the comparison of Charts 1 and 2 shows, the leading index was already declining when the 1980 recession started, antedating the decline in the coincident index. In past recessions, whether mild or severe, the leading index has bottomed out several months before the coincident index. Moreover, it has regained its level at the business cycle peak (crossing the 100 line in the chart) well before the coincident index reached this position. In the current recession the leading index fell more steeply from January through May 1980 than it did in the average of the four sharp recessions, but rebounded in June and July to an intermediate position. The rebound foreshadowed the end of the rapid decline in output and employment, but at this writing it is uncertain whether it is foreshadowing the end of the recession.

One of the factors that adds to this uncertainty is the development of recessionary tendencies in several of the major industrial countries. During 1979 and early 1980 strong economic expansion abroad fostered growth in U.S. exports, offsetting some of the weakness in domestic markets. The leading and coincident indexes available for Canada, the United Kingdom, West Germany, France, Italy, and Japan all showed greater strength than the corresponding indexes for the United States. By mid-1980, however, this situation was changing, with clear signs of recession in the United Kingdom and weakness developing in most of the other countries. International recessions are, as a rule, more severe than those that do not spread across many countries. Since 1957, for example, among the four U.S. recessions, those of 1957–58 and 1973–75 were international in scope and more severe than the two recessions of 1960–61 and 1969–70, which were largely confined to the United States.

This distinction is revealed in Chart 3, which shows the growth rate in coincident index for the six major industrial countries other than the U.S., during each of the U.S. recessions since 1957. The declines in the foreign growth rate were much sharper during the course of the U.S. recessions of 1957–58 and 1973–75 than in the 1960–61 or 1969–70 recessions. The disturbing fact is that between January and June 1980, the foreign growth rate had dropped more, and to a lower level, than it had in the corresponding periods of any of the preceding four U.S. recessions.

The 1980 recession had its origin in the developments produced by inflation and the reaction against it. The relationship is complex, but one of the simple facts that emerges from the history of business cycles and inflation is that the rate of inflation (that is to say, the rate at which the general level of prices advances) is closely related to the business cycle. Protracted and rapid advances in the volume of economic activity generate an increasingly rapid advance in prices. Slowdowns and recessions, on the other hand, are associated with declines in the rate of inflation. This proposition is demonstrated for four countries in Chart 4.

In each of the four countries, the increases in the rate of change of the consumer price index were associated with periods of rapid growth while all of the decreases in the inflation rate were associated with periods of slow growth or recession. With the 1980 recession in the United States the same relationship has reappeared. The rate of increase in the consumer price index, measured in the same way as in the chart, reached its high to date. (15.9 percent in March, some 15 months after the economic slowdown began (December 1978) and 3 months after the business cycle peak (January 1980). By July 1980 the rate had dropped to 11.7 percent. History, which has a reputation for repeating itself with a difference, was living up to its reputation. This time the difference is the high level of inflation from which the decline began. How long the decline lasts and the level of inflation that is ultimately reached will depend, as in the past, on the length of the 1980 recession and the nature of the recovery that follows.

CHART 4
DOES RECESSION SLOW INFLATION? EVIDENCE FROM FOUR COUNTRIES

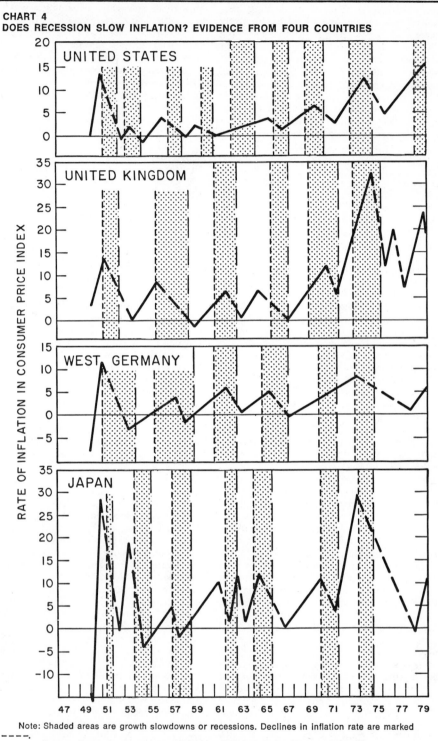

Note: Shaded areas are growth slowdowns or recessions. Declines in inflation rate are marked
----.

Source: Center for International Business Cycle Research, Rutgers University.

Major Legislation Enacted

Descriptions of major legislation passed by Congress in 1979 and 1980 are listed below in chronological order. Copies of enacted legislation may be obtained by ordering under the appropriate public law number from the Super- intendent of Documents, Government Printing Office, Washington, DC 20402. Alternatively, call 202-225-1772 or write the office of your own member of Congress for a copy of the bill.

Public Law Number	Description	Date Signed into Law
PL 96–3 (S 37)	Section of PL 95–630 relative to financial privacy repealed, extending authority for flexible regulation of interest rates on deposits and accounts in depository institutions.	March 7, 1979
PL 96–10 (HR 2283)	Amend the Council on Wage and Price Stability Act.	May 10, 1979
PL 96–18 (HR 3404)	Federal Reserve banks authorized to lend various obligations to the Treasury Secretary to meet the Treasury's short-term cash needs.	June 8, 1979
PL 96–19 (HR 2805)	Certain conforming and technical changes made in the financial disclosure provisions in the Ethics in Government Act.	June 13, 1979
PL 96–24 (HR 3915)	Effective date for automatic termination of insurance coverage for multiemployer pension plans advanced from July 1979 to May 1, 1980.	June 19, 1979
PL 96–25 (S 199)	Federal Maritime Commission's authority strengthened for dealing with illegal rebate practices in U.S. waterborne foreign trade.	June 19, 1979
PL 96–27 (HR 3879)	Funds authorized for independent audit of District of Columbia's government financial situation.	June 21, 1979
PL 96–28 (S 869)	Federal employees ethical standards clarified.	June 22, 1979
PL 96–30 (S 1317)	Antitrust exemption extended for oil companies participating in international energy programs.	June 30, 1979
PL 96–31 (S 984)	Provision made for authority to waive or reduce penalties where peanuts are marketed over the farm poundage quota.	July 7, 1979
PL 96–33 (HR 4556)	Authorization given to the Secretary of Health, Education, and Welfare to extend the conditional designations of state health planning agencies.	July 16, 1979
PL 96–35 (S 1007)	Funds for economic and military aid to Egypt and Israel authorized.	July 20, 1979
PL 96–37 (HR 3978)	Savings and loan associations exempted from Federal Trade Commission jurisdiction.	July 23, 1979
PL 96–39 (HR 4537)	Trade agreements by the United States in the Tokyo Round of Multilateral Trade Negotiations approved.	July 26, 1979
PL 96–41 (HR 2154)	Strategic and Critical Materials Stockpiling Act revised and updated to strengthen the congressional role in stockpiling matters and to make the act conform to present stockpiling policy.	July 30, 1979
PL 96–64 (S 1646)	Time extended for foreign banks to get required deposit insurance with regard to existing branches in the United States.	Sept. 10, 1979

MAJOR LEGISLATION ENACTED *(continued)*

Public Law Number	Description	Date Signed into Law
PL 96–88 (210)	Department of Education established.	Oct. 17, 1979
PL 96–90 (HR 1301)	American manufacturers allowed to ship lottery tickets as well as related materials to foreign countries with legal lotteries.	Oct. 23, 1979
PL 96–96 (HR 5386)	All states must bear equally any reduction In the 1980 appropriations for continuing education and community service programs.	Oct. 31, 1979
PL 96–102 (S 1030)	The President is granted authority to create an emergency energy program for the conservation of energy.	Nov. 5, 1979
PL 96–104 (HR 2515)	Temporary exemption provided from state usury ceilings on various agricultural and business loans.	Nov. 5, 1979
PL 96–127 (HR 4167)	Current price-support levels for dairy products extended through September 30, 1981.	Nov. 28, 1979
PL 96–129 (S 411)	Funds for the National Gas Pipeline Safety Act to clarify and expand the Department of Transportation authority over liquified natural gas and natural transportation safety and to establish a statutory framework of regulating the transportation of dangerous liquids authorized.	Nov. 30, 1979
PL 96–133 (S 1871)	Existing antitrust exemption for oil companies participating in the agreement on an international program on energy extended until June 30, 1980.	Nov. 30, 1979
PL 96–148 (S 901)	Initial cost-recovery provisions of the Clean Water Act repealed.	Nov. 20, 1979
PL 96–149 (S 1788)	Provision made for a small business permanent representative member of the National Consumer Cooperative Bank Board of Directors.	Dec. 19, 1979
PL 96–161 (HR 4998)	Federal Reserve Act requiring detailed minutes of Federal Open Market Committee meetings to be published on a deferred basis amended.	Dec. 28, 1979
PL 96–171 (HR 3948)	Federal Aviation Act of 1958 eliminating current age limitations on certain pilots of aircraft amended.	Dec. 29, 1979
PL 96–177 (HR 2727)	Methods for establishing quotas on the importation of certain meats modified to include certain meat products within such quotas.	Dec. 31, 1979
PL 96–181 (S 525)	Drug Abuse Office and Treatment Act of 1972 amended.	Jan. 2, 1980
PL 96–182 (HR 2043)	The Water Bank Act amended to authorize the agriculture secretary to adjust rates of payment regarding initial conservation agreements and to designate various areas as wetlands.	Jan. 2, 1980
PL 96–183 (HJ Res 467) ...	Urgent appropriations made for Chrysler Corporation loan guarantee program administrative expenses and to provide financial assistance (through fiscal year ending September 30, 1980) for the Chrysler Corporation.	Jan. 2, 1980
PL 96–185 (HR 5860)	Loan guarantees to Chrysler Corporation authorized.	Jan. 7, 1980
PL 96–186 (HJ Res 468) ...	Date for the submission of the President's Budget and Economic Report extended.	Jan. 8, 1980
PL 96–187 (HR 5010)	Federal Election Campaign Act Amendments of 1971 amended to make various changes with regard to the reporting and disclosure requirements.	Jan. 8, 1980
PL 96–188 (HJ 478)	Expiration date of the Defense Production Act of 1950 extended until March 28, 1980.	Jan. 28, 1980
PL 96–190 (S 423)	A national goal to develop and maintain effective fair, inexpensive, and expeditious mechanisms for resolution of consumer controversies established.	Feb. 12, 1980
PL 96–191 (HR 5076)	General Accounting Office Appeals Board to consider and act on appeals by employees on administrative actions.	Feb. 15, 1980

MAJOR LEGISLATION ENACTED *(continued)*

Public Law Number	Description	Date Signed into Law
PL 96–192 (S 1300)	Guidelines within the Civil Aeronautics Board established for matters concerning international routes and rates and for competitive goals provisions.	Feb. 15, 1980
PL 96–195 (S 1452)	Authority of the Commerce Secretary to issue war risk insurance extended through September 30, 1984.	Feb. 25, 1980
PL 96–209 (HR 4337)	Foreign Claims Settlement Commission of the United States transferred as a separate agency to the Department of Justice.	March 14, 1980
PL 96–210 (HR 5913)	Secretary of Commerce made permanent authority to accept negotiated contracts for government subsidized vessel construction.	March 17, 1980
PL 96–213 (HR 3398)	Target prices for the 1980 wheat and feed grains increased.	March 18, 1980
PL 96–221 (HR 4986)	Amends the Federal Reserve Act to authorize the automatic transfer of funds, to authorize negotiable order of withdrawal accounts at depository institutions, to authorize federally chartered savings and loan associations to establish remote service units, and to authorize federally insured credit unions to receive share draft deposits, and for other purposes.	March 31, 1980
PL 96–223 (HR 3919)	Crude Oil Windfall Profit Tax Act of 1979.	Apr. 2, 1980
PL 96–226 (HR 24)	Improves budget management and expenditure control by revising certain provisions relating to the Comptroller General and the Inspectors General of the Departments of Energy and Health, Education, and Welfare, and for other purposes.	Apr. 3, 1980
PL 96–234 (S 2427)	A bill to encourage greater participation in the farmer-held reserve program for corn and wheat, and for other purposes.	Apr. 11, 1980
PL 96–236 (HR 6029)	Provides for the implementation of the International Sugar Agreement, 1977, and for other purposes.	Apr. 22, 1980
PL 96–256 (HR 7471)	Extends the present public debt limit through June 5, 1980.	May 30, 1980
PL 96–259 (S 662)	Provides for increased participation by the United States in the Inter-American Development Bank, the Asian Development Bank, and the African Development Fund.	June 3, 1980
PL 96–272 (HR 3434)	A bill to amend the Social Security Act to make needed improvements in the child welfare and social services programs, to strengthen and improve the program of federal support for foster care of needy and dependent children, to establish a program of federal support to encourage adoptions of children with special needs, and for other purposes.	June 17, 1980
PL 96–275 (HR 6842)	Protects the confidentiality of Shippers' Export Declarations, standardizes export data submission and disclosure requirements.	June 17, 1980
PL 96–280 (SJ Res. 80)	Permits the supply of additional low-enriched uranium fuel under international agreements for cooperation in the civil uses of nuclear energy, and for other purposes.	June 18, 1980
PL 96–283 (HR 2759)	Promotes the orderly development of hard mineral resources in the deep seabed, pending adoption of an international regime relating thereto.	June 28, 1980
PL 96–294 (S 932)	Energy Security Act; Defense Production Act Amendments of 1980; United States Synthetic Fuels Corporation Act of 1980; Biomass Energy and Alcohol Fuels Act of 1980; Renewable Resources Act of 1980; Solar Energy and Energy Conservation Act of 1980; Geothermal Energy Act of 1980.	June 30, 1980

MAJOR LEGISLATION ENACTED *(concluded)*

Public Law Number	Description	Date Signed into Law
PL 96–302 (S 2698)	Provides authorizations for the Small Business Administration, and for other purposes.	July 2, 1980
PL 96–303 (HR 5997)	Provides for the distribution of the Code of Ethics for Government Services.	July 3, 1980
PL 96–308 (S 598)	Clarifies the circumstances under which territorial provisions in licenses to manufacture, distribute, and sell trademarked soft-drink products are lawful under the antitrust laws.	July 9, 1980
PL 96–310 (HR 7474)	Ocean Thermal Energy Conversion Research, Development, and Demonstration Act.	July 17, 1980
PL 96–316 (S 2240)	National Aeronautics and Space Administration Authorization Act, 1981.	July 30, 1980
PL 96–320 (S 2492)	Ocean Thermal Energy Conversion Act of 1980.	Aug. 3, 1980
PL 96–324 (HR 1198)	Clarifies authority to establish lines of demarcation dividing the high seas and inland waters.	Aug. 8, 1980
PL 96–327 (S 1916)	Authorizes operations by the Overseas Private Investment Corporation (OPIC) in the People's Republic of China.	Aug. 8, 1980
PL 96–334 (HJ Res. 589) ..	A joint resolution providing additional program authority for the Export-Import Bank.	Aug. 29, 1980

Regulatory Agencies

The following section provides compact summaries of the functions of the major regulatory agencies together with addresses and phone numbers. This information was abstracted from the latest United States Government Manual.

ANTITRUST DIVISION (DEPARTMENT OF JUSTICE)

CONSTITUTIONAL AVENUE AND TENTH STREET NW, WASHINGTON, DC 20530

INFORMATION: 202–737–8200

The Assistant Attorney General in charge of the Antitrust Division is responsible for enforcement of the federal antitrust laws. Such enforcement, which constitutes the principal function of the division, involves investigating possible antitrust violations, conducting grand jury proceedings, preparing and trying antitrust cases, prosecuting appeals, and negotiating and enforcing final judgments. The antitrust laws are enforced by criminal actions designed to punish violators for restraints on and monopolization of trade and by civil suits for injunctive relief aimed at maintaining or restoring competitive conditions in the system of free enterprise, which the antitrust laws protect.

In addition, the Antitrust Division represents the United States in judicial proceedings to review certain orders of the Interstate Commerce Commission, Federal Maritime Commission, Federal Communications Commission, and Nuclear Regulatory Commission, and directly represents the Secretary of the Treasury and the Civil Aeronautics Board in certain review proceedings. It also participates in cases of the Federal Trade Commission before the Supreme Court.

Other duties assigned to this division include studying, reporting, and advising on the competitive considerations involved in policies of government departments and agencies, and making recommendations with respect to such policies. Specific statutory responsibility to render such advice to other government bodies includes matters involved in NRC licensing of nuclear power reactors; activities connected with the nation's defense program, the Interstate Oil Compact, the development of nuclear energy, disposal of government-owned surplus property; and the filing of reports on the competitive factors involved in proposed bank mergers with the appropriate bank regulatory agencies. The division is also responsible for supporting competitive policies within the federal government. It does this through comment and testimony on pending legislative and other matters, participation in interagency committees (e.g., government patent policy, communications satellite policy, oil import policy, foreign trade policy), and formal intervention in regulatory proceedings (e.g., before the Interstate Commerce Commission, Civil Aeronautics Board, Federal Maritime Board, Federal Communications Commission, Securities and Exchange Commission). It also responds to requests from other agencies for advice respecting competitive aspects of activities within their jurisdiction.

The division represents the United States on the Restrictive Business Practices Committee of the Organization for Economic Cooperation and Development and, through the Department of State, maintains liaison with foreign governments on antimonopoly laws and policies. It also is charged with reporting annually to the President and the Congress on the nature and extent of identical bidding in public procurement.

The Consumer Affairs Section of the Antitrust Division is responsible for the institution of civil and criminal proceedings in cases referred to the Department of Justice by other

FIELD OFFICES (Antitrust Division)

City	Address
Atlanta, GA 30309	1776 Peachtree Street NW
Chicago, IL 60604	219 S. Dearborn Street
Cleveland, OH 44199	Celebreezze Federal Building
Dallas, TX 74202	East Cabell Federal Building
Los Angeles, CA 90012	U.S. Courthouse
New York, NY 10007	26 Federal Plaza
Philadelphia, PA 19106	U.S. Courthouse
San Francisco, CA 94102	Box 36046, 450 Golden Gate Avenue

agencies, such as the Food and Drug Administration and the Federal Trade Commission, which have primary responsibility for consumer protection activities. Such proceedings generally arise when a person has violated a statute enforced by these agencies or an order or rule issued by these agencies in the course of their consumer protection activities. Many of these proceedings involve acts or practices that are unfair and deceptive to consumers.

CONSUMER PRODUCT SAFETY COMMISSION (CPSC)

1111 18TH STREET NW
WASHINGTON, DC 20207
INFORMATION: 301-492-6590
Hotline: 800-638-8326 (in Maryland, 800-492-8363; in Alaska, Hawaii, Puerto Rico, and the Virgin Islands, 800-638-8333).

The commission has primary responsibility for establishing mandatory product safety standards, where appropriate, to reduce the unreasonable risk of injury to consumers from consumer products. In addition it has authority to ban hazardous consumer products. The Consumer Product Safety Act also authorizes the commission to conduct extensive research on consumer product standards, engage in broad consumer and industry information and education programs, and establish a comprehensive Injury Information Clearinghouse.

In addition to the new authority created by the act, the commission assumes responsibility for the Flammable Fabrics Act (67 Stat. 111; 15 U.S.C. 1191), the Poison Prevention Packaging Act (84 Stat. 1670), the Hazardous Substances Act (74 Stat. 372; 15 U.S.C. 1261), and the act of August 2, 1956 (70 Stat. 953; 15 U.S.C. 1211) which pro-

hibits the transportation of refrigerators without door safety devices.

The act also provides for petitioning of the commission by any interested person, including consumers or consumer organizations, to commence proceedings for the issuance, amendment, or revocation of a consumer product safety rule.

ECONOMIC REGULATORY ADMINISTRATION (DEPARTMENT OF ENERGY)

1000 INDEPENDENCE AVENUE, WASHINGTON, DC 20545
INFORMATION: 202-376-4000
202-254-8505

The Economic Regulatory Administration (ERA) administers the department's regulatory programs, other than those assigned to the Federal Energy Regulatory Commission. These functions include the oil pricing, allocation, and import programs designed to ensure price stability and equitable supplies of crude oil, petroleum products, and natural gas liquids among a wide range of domestic users.

The Economic Regulatory Administration ensures compliance with existing regulations and carries out new regulatory programs as assigned. ERA also administers other regulatory programs, including conversion of oil and gas-fired utility and industrial facilities to coal, natural gas import/export controls, natural gas curtailment priorities and emergency allocations, regional coordination of electric power system planning and reliability of bulk power supply, and emergency and contingency planning.

On behalf of the Secretary, ERA organizes and manages an active intervention program before the Federal Energy Regulatory Commission and other federal and state regulatory agencies in support of departmental policy objectives.

REGIONAL OFFICES (Consumer Product Safety Commission)

City	Address
Atlanta, GA 30309	1330 W. Peachtree Street NW
Boston, MA 02110	100 Summer Street
Chicago, IL 60604	230 S. Dearborn Street
Cleveland, OH 44114	55 Erieview Plaza
Dallas, TX 75242	1100 Commerce Street
Denver, CO 80202	Guaranty Bank Building, 817 17th Street
Kansas City, MO 64106	Traders National Bank Building, 1125 Grand Avenue
Los Angeles, CA 90010	3660 Wilshire Boulevard
Minneapolis, MN 55101	7th and Robert
New York, NY 10048	6 World Trade Center, Vesey Street
Philadelphia, PA 19106	400 Market Street
San Francisco, CA 94111	100 Pine Street
Seattle, WA 98174	3240 Federal Building, 915 Second Avenue

FEDERAL ENERGY REGULATORY COMMISSION (DEPARTMENT OF ENERGY)

825 N. Capitol Street NE, Washington, DC 20426

Information: 202–357–8055
Recorded News: 202–357–8555

An independent, five-member commission within the Department of Energy, the Federal Energy Regulatory Commission has retained many of the functions of the Federal Power Commission, such as the setting of rates and charges for the transportation and sale of natural gas and for the transmission and sale of electricity and the licensing of hydroelectric power projects. In addition, the authority to establish rates or charges for the transportation of oil by pipeline, as well as the valuation of such pipelines, has been assigned to the commission from the Interstate Commerce Commission.

REGIONAL REPRESENTATIVES (DOE)

The Secretary will be represented in each of the ten standard federal regions by regional representatives.

REGIONAL REGULATORY PROGRAMS (DOE)

The Department of Energy's regional allocation and compliance program will be conducted by the regional staff of the Office of Fuels Regulation, under the supervision and direction of the Administrator of the Economic Regulatory Administration and with the legal support of the General Counsel's field staff. These programs are separate from the outreach and other activities of the regional representatives.

The field activities of the Federal Energy Regulatory Commission will be separate from other department field activities but will have offices colocated with regional compliance or other department field offices in order to share common administrative support.

ENVIRONMENTAL PROTECTION AGENCY (EPA)

401 M Street SW, Washington, DC 20460
Information: 202–755–0707

AIR, NOISE, AND RADIATION PROGRAMS

The air activities of the agency include development of national programs, technical policies, and regulations for air pollution control; development of national standards for air quality, emission standards for new stationary sources, and emission standards for hazardous pollutants; technical direction, support, and evaluation of regional air activities; and provision of training in the field of air pollution control. Related activities include study, identification, and regulation of noise sources and control methods; technical assistance to states and agencies having radiation protection programs; and a national surveillance and inspection program for measuring radiation levels in the environment.

WATER AND WASTE MANAGEMENT PROGRAMS

EPA's water quality activities represent a coordinated effort to restore the nation's waters. The functions of this program include development of national programs, technical policies, and regulations for water pollution control and water supply; water quality standards and effluent guidelines development; technical direction, support, and evaluation of regional water activities; development of programs for technical assistance and technology transfer; provision of training in the field of water quality; analyses, guidelines, and standards for the land disposal of hazardous wastes; technical assistance in the development, management, and operation of waste management activities; and analyses on the recovery of useful energy from solid waste.

ENFORCEMENT

The Office of the Assistant Administrator for Enforcement provides policy direction to enforcement activities in air, water, pesticides, solid waste management, radiation, and noise control programs; plans and coordinates enforcement conferences, public hearings, and other legal proceedings; and engages in other activities related to enforcement of standards to protect the nation's environment.

RESEARCH AND DEVELOPMENT

The Office of the Assistant Administrator for Research and Development is responsible for a national research program in pursuit of technological controls of all forms of pollution. It directly supervises the research activities of EPA's national laboratories and gives technical policy direction to those laboratories that support the program responsibilities of EPA's regional offices. Close coordination of the various research programs is designed to yield a synthesis of knowledge from the biological, physical, and social sciences which

REGIONAL OFFICES (Environmental Protection Agency)

Region	Address
I	John F. Kennedy Federal Building, Boston, MA 02203
II	26 Federal Plaza, New York, NY 10007
III	Curtis Building, 6th and Walnut Streets, Philadelphia, PA 19106
IV	345 Cortland Street NE, Atlanta, GA 30308
V	230 S. Dearborn Street, Chicago IL 60604
VI	1201 Elm Street, Dallas, TX 75270
VII	324 E. 11th Street, Kansas City, MO 64106
VIII	1860 Lincoln Street, Denver, CO 80203
IX	215 Fremont, San Francisco, CA 94111
X	1200 6th Avenue, Seattle, WA 98101

can be interpreted in terms of total human and environmental needs. General functions include management of selected demonstration programs, planning for agency environmental quality monitoring programs, coordination of agency monitoring efforts with those of other federal agencies, the states, and other public bodies, and dissemination of agency research, development, and demonstration results.

REGIONAL OFFICES

EPA's ten regional offices represent the agency's commitment to the development of strong local programs for pollution abatement. The regional administrators are the agency's principal representatives in the regions in contacts and relationships with federal, state, interstate, and local agencies, industry, academic institutions, and other public and private groups. They are responsible for accomplishing within their regions the national program objectives established by the agency. They develop, propose, and implement an approved regional program for comprehensive and integrated environmental protection activities.

EQUAL EMPLOYMENT OPPORTUNITY COMMISSION (EEOC)

2401 E Street NW, Washington, DC 20506

Information: 202-634-6930

The commission's field offices receive written charges of job discrimination under title VII of the Equal Pay Act or the Age Discrimination in Employment Act. These charges may be against public and private employers exclusive of the federal government, labor organizations, joint labor-management apprenticeship programs, and public and private employment agencies. Members of the commission also may initiate charges alleging that a violation of Title VII has occurred.

Charges of Title VII violations must be filed with the commission within 180 days of the alleged violation (or up to 300 days where a state or local fair employment practices agency initially was contacted), and the commission is responsible for notifying persons so charged within 10 days of the receipt of a new charge. Before investigation, a charge must be deferred for 60 days to a local fair employment practices agency in states and municipalities where an enforceable fair employment practices law is in effect. The deferral period is 120 days for an agency that has been operating less than one year. Under a work-sharing agreement, executed between the commission and state and local fair employment practices agencies, the commission routinely will assume jurisdiction over certain charges of discrimination and proceed with its investigation rather than wait for the expiration of the deferral period.

The commission has instituted new procedural regulations that encourage settlement of charges of discrimination prior to a determination of decision by the agency on the merits of the charges. In addition, fact-finding conferences may be required as a part of the investigation and may assist in establishing the framework for a negotiated settlement. After an investigation, if there is reasonable cause to believe the charge is true, the district office attempts to remedy the alleged unlawful practices through the informal methods of conciliation, conference, and persuasion.

Unless an acceptable conciliation agreement has been secured, the commission may, after 30 days from the date the charge was filed, bring suit in an appropriate federal district court. (The Attorney General brings suit when a state government, governmental agency, or political subdivision is involved.) If the commission or the Attorney General does not proceed in this manner, at the conclusion of the administrative procedures, or earlier at the request of the charging party, a Notice of Right to Sue is issued, which allows the charging party to proceed within 90 days in a federal district court. In appropriate cases the commission may intervene in such civil action if the case is of general public interest. The investigation and conciliation of

DISTRICT OFFICES (Equal Employment Opportunity Commission)

District	Address
Atlanta, GA	75 Piedmont Ave. N.E. 30303
Baltimore, MD	711 W. 40th St. 21211
Birmingham, AL	2121 Eighth Ave. N. 35203
Charlotte, NC	403 N. Tryon St. 28202
Chicago, IL	536 S. Clark St. 60605
Cleveland, OH	1365 Ontario St. 44114
Dallas, TX	212 North St. Paul 75201
Denver, CO	1531 Stout St. 80202
Detroit, MI	231 W. Lafayette St. 48226
Houston, TX	2320 LaBranch 77004
Indianapolis, IN	46 E. Ohio St. 46204
Los Angeles, CA	3255 Wilshire Blvd. 90010
Memphis, TN	1407 Union Ave. 38104
Miami, FL	300 Biscayne Blvd. Way 33131
Milwaukee, WI	342 N. Water St. 53202
New Orleans, LA	600 South St. 70130
New York, NY	90 Church St. 10007
Philadelphia, PA	127 N. 4th St. 19106
Phoenix, AZ	201 N. Central Ave. 85073
San Francisco, CA	1390 Market St. 94102
Seattle, WA	710 2nd Ave. 98104
St. Louis, MO	1601 Olive St. 63103

charges having an industrywide or national impact are coordinated or conducted by the Office of Systemic Programs.

Under the provisions of Section 706 (f)(2), as amended by Section 5 of the Equal Employment Opportunity Act of 1972, if it is concluded after a preliminary investigation that prompt judicial action is necessary to carry out the purposes of the act, the commission or the Attorney General, in a case involving a state government, governmental agency, or political subdivision, may bring an action for appropriate temporary or preliminary relief pending final disposition of a charge.

The commission participates in the development of the law of employment discrimination through issuance of guidelines, publication of significant commission decisions, and involvement in litigation brought under Title VII and related statutes.

The commission has direct liaison with state and local governments, employer and union organizations, trade associations, civil rights organizations, and other agencies and organizations concerned with employment of minority group members and women. The commission engages in and contributes to the cost of research and other mutual interest projects with state and local agencies charged with the administration of fair employment practices laws.

Furthermore, the commission enters into work-sharing agreements with the state and local agencies in order to avoid duplication of effort by identifying specific charges to be investigated by the respective agencies.

FEDERAL COMMUNICATIONS COMMISSION (FCC)

1919 M STREET NW, WASHINGTON, DC 20554

INFORMATION: 202-632-7260

BROADCAST

The Broadcast Bureau administers the regulatory program for the following broadcast services: standard (AM), frequency modulation (FM), television (TV), instructional television fixed (ITFS), experimental, international shortwave, and related auxiliary services; issues construction permits, operating licenses, and renewals or transfers of licenses; and oversees compliance by broadcasters with statutes and commission policies.

CABLE TELEVISION

The commission's regulation of cable television includes rules relating to broadcast signal carriage, quality of service delivered, access to and use of cable channels for the delivery of nonbroadcast programs, and limitations on state and local restrictions on the delivery of interstate programing. The Cable Television Bureau administers the program for cable television and the associated microwave radio relay (CARS) service, including the registration of new cable television systems and enforcement of the rules through forfeiture or cease-and-desist procedures, and is responsible for maintaining relations with state and local authorities who share responsibility for the regulation of cable television systems.

COMMON CARRIER COMMUNICATIONS

In interstate and international common carrier communications by telephone, telegraph, radio, and satellite, the Common Carrier Bureau administers the program of regulation. Common carriers include companies, organizations, or individuals providing communications services to the public for hire, who must serve all who wish to use them at established rates. In rendering interstate and foreign communications services to the public, common carriers may use landline wire or cable facilities, point-to-point microwave radio (signals relayed by stations spaced at given intervals), land mobile radio (two-way telephone or one-way signaling communications between base and mobile units), or satellite systems. Communications services between the United States and overseas points by common carriers are provided by means of ocean cable, high-frequency radio, and satellite communications.

FIELD OFFICES (Federal Communications Commission)

City	Address
Anchorage, AL 99510	1011 E. Tudor Road
Atlanta, GA 30309	1365 Peachtree St. NE
Baltimore, MD 21201	Federal Building
Beaumont, TX 77701	Federal Building
Boston, MA 02109	Customhouse
Buffalo, NY 14202	Federal Building
Chicago, IL 60604	230 S. Dearborn Street
Cincinnati, OH 45231	8620 Winton Road
Dallas, TX 75242	1100 Commerce Street
Denver, CO 80202	1405 Curtis Street
Detroit, MI 48226	231 W. LaFayette Street
Honolulu, HI 96850	Federal Building
Houston, TX 77002	New Federal Office Building
Kansas City, MO 64133	Federal Building, 8800 E. 63rd Street
Long Beach, CA 90807	3711 Long Beach Boulevard
Miami, FL 33130	51 SW 1st Avenue
New Orleans, LA 70130	600 South Street
New York, NY 10014	201 Varick Street
Norfolk, VA 23502	870 N. Military Highway
Philadelphia, PA 19106	601 Market Street
Pittsburgh, PA	William Penn Highway, Monroeville 15146
Portland, OR 97204	1220 SW 3d Avenue
St. Paul, MN 55101	Federal Building and U.S. Courthouse
San Diego, CA	7840 El Cajon Boulevard, La Mesa 92041
San Francisco, CA 94111	Customhouse
San Juan, PR	747 Federal Building, Hato Rey, 00918
Savannah, GA 31412	125 Bull Street
Seattle, WA 98174	Federal Building
Tampa, FL 33607	1121 N. Westshore Boulevard
Washington, DC 20551	6525 Belcrest Road, Hyattsville, MD, 20788

LICENSING/GRANT RESPONSIBILITY (Federal Communications Commission)

Service	Bureau or Office
All broadcasting (radio and television)	Broadcast Bureau
Common carrier radio	Common Carrier Bureau
Section 214 of FCC Act	
Satellite	
Experimental radio	Office of Science and Technology
Type equipment	
Equipment certification	
Type approval	
Land mobile radio in Chicago, III. area	
Aviation radio	Private Radio Bureau
Amateur radio	
Ship radio	
Industrial radio	
Public safety radio	
Land transportation	
Citizens radio	
Amateur radio operator	
Registration of cable systems	Cable Television Bureau
Cable television relay radio	
Commercial radio operators	Field Operations Bureau

OTHER RADIO USES

The commission regulates the use of radio for many purposes other than broadcast and common carrier communication. The Private Radio Services Bureau administers the program of regulating the following radio services: aviation, marine, amateur, public fixed stations in Alaska, public safety (police, fire, etc.), industrial (manufacturers, petroleum, etc.), land transportation (railroad, taxicab, etc.), and citizens (private short-distance radiocommunications, signaling, control of objects, etc.), and of implementing the compulsory provisions of laws and treaties covering the use of radio for the safety of life at sea. The office of Science and Technology administers the program of regulating the experimental and low-power equipment.

ENFORCEMENT

Much of the investigative and enforcement work of the commission is carried out by its field staff. The Field Operations Bureau has 6 regional offices, 30 field offices, and 13 monitoring stations, in addition to a mobile network. The field staffs, in effect, are the commission's "eyes and ears" in detecting radio violations and enforcing rules and regulations. Monitoring stations maintain continuous surveillance of the radio spectrum, detecting unlicensed operation and activities or nonconforming transmission, and furnish radio bearings on ships and planes in distress.

FEDERAL MARITIME COMMISSION (FMC)

1100 L Street NW, Washington, DC 20573
Information: 202-523-5707

AGREEMENTS

The commission approves or disapproves agreements filed by common carriers, including conference agreements, interconference agreements, and cooperative working agreements between common carriers, terminal operators, freight forwarders, and other persons subject to the shipping laws, and reviews activities under approved agreements for compliance with the provisions of law and the rules, orders, and regulations of the commission.

PRACTICES

The commission regulates the practices of common carriers by water and other persons engaged in the foreign and domestic offshore commerce of the United States, and conferences of such common carriers in accordance with the requirements of the shipping statutes and the rules, orders, and regulations of the commission.

TARIFFS

The commission accepts or rejects tariff filings of domestic offshore carriers and common carriers engaged in the foreign commerce of the United States, or conferences of such carriers, in accordance with the requirements of the shipping statutes and the commission's rules and regulations. In the domestic offshore trade, the commission has the authority to set maximum or minimum rates or suspend rates. It approves or disapproves special permission applications submitted by domestic offshore carriers and carriers in the foreign commerce, or conferences of such carriers, for relief from the statutory and/or commission tariff requirements.

LICENSES

The commission issues or denies the issuance of licenses to persons, partnerships, corporations, or associations desiring to engage in ocean freight forwarding activities.

PASSENGER INDEMNITY

The commission administers the passenger indemnity provisions of the act of November 6, 1966 and issues or denies the issuance of certificates of financial responsibility of shipowners and operators to pay judgments for personal injury or death and to refund fares in the event of nonperformance of voyages.

WATER POLLUTION

The commission administers the vessel certification provisions of section 311(p)(1) of the Federal Water Pollution Control Act, as amended by the Clean Water Act of 1977 (91 Stat. 1566), section 204(c) of the Trans-Alaska Pipeline Authorization Act (87 Stat. 584), and section 305(a)(1) of the Outer Continental Shelf Lands Act Amendments of 1978 (92 Stat. 670) with respect to evidence of financial responsibility required from operators of vessels which may be subjected to liability for damages and removal of oil and hazardous substances discharged into U.S. waters.

INFORMAL COMPLAINTS

The commission reviews and determines the validity of alleged or suspected violations

DISTRICT OFFICES (Federal Maritime Commission)

District	Address
Atlantic	6 World Trade Center, Suite 603, New York, NY 10048
Gulf	P.O. Box 30550, 600 South Street, New Orleans, LA 70190
Pacific	625 Market Street, San Francisco, CA 94105
Puerto Rico	U.S. District Courthouse, Federal Office Building, Room 762, Carlos Chardon Street, Hato Rey, PR 00917
Great Lakes	610 Canal Street, Chicago, IL 60607

of the shipping statutes and rules and regulations of the commission by common carriers by water in the domestic offshore and the foreign commerce of the United States, terminal operators, freight forwarders, and other persons subject to the provisions of the shipping statutes. After investigation, it concludes such complaints by administrative action, formal proceedings, referral to the Department of Justice, or achieving voluntary agreement between the parties.

FORMAL ADJUDICATORY PROCEDURE

The commission conducts formal investigations on its own motion and adjudicates formal complaints pursuant to the Administrative Procedure Act.

RULE-MAKING

The commission promulgates rules and regulations to interpret, enforce, and assure compliance with the shipping statutes of common carriers by water and other persons subject to the statutes.

INVESTIGATION, AUDIT, AND FINANCIAL AND ECONOMIC ANALYSES

The commission prescribes and administers programs to assure compliance with the provisions of the shipping statutes of all persons subject thereto, including without limitation those for: the submission of regular and special reports, information, and data; the conduct of a plan for the field investigation and audit of activities and practices of common carriers by water in the domestic offshore trade and the foreign commerce of the United States, conferences of such carriers, terminal operators, freight forwarders, and other persons subject to the shipping statutes; and rate and related financial analysis studies, economic studies, and reports reflecting the various trade areas, the extent and nature of competition, commodities carried, and future commodity trends.

INTERNATIONAL AFFAIRS

The commission, in conjunction with the Department of State, conducts activities to effect the elimination of discriminatory practices on the part of foreign governments against United States flag shipping.

FEDERAL TRADE COMMISSION (FTC)

PENNSYLVANIA AVENUE AT SIXTH STREET NW, WASHINGTON, DC 20580

INFORMATION: 202–523–3625

The commission's principal functions are:

To promote free and fair competition in interstate commerce through prevention of general trade restraints such as price-fixing agreements, boycotts, illegal combinations of competitors, and other unfair methods of competition.

To safeguard the public by preventing the dissemination of false or deceptive advertisements of consumer products generally and food, drug, cosmetics, and therapeutic devices particularly, as well as other unfair or deceptive practices.

To prevent discriminations in price; exclusive dealing and tying arrangements; corporate mergers, acquisitions or joint ventures, when such practices or arrangements may substantially lessen competition or tend toward monopoly; interlocking directorates that may restrain competition; the payment or receipt of illegal brokerage; and discrimination among competing customers in the furnishing of or payment for services or facilities used to promote the resale of a product.

To bring about truthful labeling of textile and fur products.

To regulate packaging and labeling of certain consumer commodities within the purview of the Fair Packaging and Labeling Act to prevent consumer deception and to facilitate value comparisons.

To supervise the registration and operation of associations of American exporters engaged in export trade.

To petition for the cancellation of the registration of trademarks that were illegally registered or used for purposes contrary to the intent of the Trade-Mark Act of 1946.

To achieve true credit cost disclosure by consumer creditors (retailers, finance companies, nonfederal credit unions, and other creditors not specifically regulated by another government agency) as called for in the Truth in Lending Act; to assure a meaningful basis for informed credit decisions; and to regulate the issuance and liability of credit cards to prohibit their fraudulent use in interstate or foreign commerce.

To protect consumers against circulation of inaccurate or obsolete credit reports, and to insure that consumer reporting agencies exercise their responsibilities in a manner that is fair and equitable and in conformity with the Fair Credit Reporting Act.

To gather and make available to the Congress, the President, and the public, factual data concerning economic and business conditions.

ENFORCEMENT

The commission's law enforcement work falls into two general categories: actions to foster law observance voluntarily and formal litigation leading to mandatory orders against offenders.

For the most part, law observance is obtained through voluntary and cooperative action by way of staff level advice which is not binding on the commission, advisory opinions by the commission, trade regulation rules, and issuance of guides delineating legal requirements as to particular business practices.

The formal litigative proceedings are similar to those used in courts. Cases are instituted by issuance of a complaint charging a person, partnership, or corporation—the respondent—with violation of one or more of the statutes administered by the commission. Cases may be settled by consent orders or occasionally through informal administrative correction of minor violations. If the charges are not contested, or if in a contested case and after hearing the charges are found to be true, an order to cease and desist is issued requiring discontinuance of the unlawful practices.

LEGAL CASE WORK

Cases before the commission may originate through complaint by a consumer or a competitor; the Congress; or from federal, state, or municipal agencies. Also, the commission itself may initiate an investigation to determine possible violation of the laws administered by it. No formality is required in submitting a complaint. A letter giving the facts in detail is sufficient, but it should be accompanied by all evidence in possession of the complaining party in support of the charges made. It is the policy of the commission not to disclose the identity of any complainant, except as required by law.

Upon receipt of a complaint, various criteria are applied in determining whether the particular matter should be docketed for investigation. Within the limits of its resources, investigations are initiated which are considered to best support the commission's goals of maintaining competition and protecting consumers.

On completion of an investigation, there may be a staff recommendation for informal settlement of the case, issuance of a formal complaint, or closing the matter. In some cases, it is recommended that the commission seek an injunction in a U.S. district court to halt the use of allegedly unfair or deceptive practices until the commission's proceedings are completed.

If the commission decides to issue a complaint, the respondent is served with a copy of the complaint and proposed order. Prior to the hearings, respondent and commission counsel may negotiate a cease-and-desist order to which the respondent agrees to consent. If such a consent order is worked out, the respondent does not admit any violation of the law but agrees to discontinue the challenged practice.

If an agreement containing a consent order is not entered into, litigation usually ensues.

The case is heard by an administrative law judge who, after taking testimony at public hearings, issues an initial decision. This becomes the decision of the commission at the end of 30 days unless the respondent or the counsel supporting the complaint appeals the decision to the commission, or the commission by order stays the effective date or places the case on its own docket for review. In the commission's decision on such appeal or review, the initial decision is sustained, modified, or reversed. If it is sustained or modified, a cease-and-desist order is issued.

Under the Federal Trade Commission Act, the Clayton Act, and the Wool, Fur, and Textile Acts, the order to cease and desist, or to take other corrective action such as affirmative disclosure, divestiture, or restitution, becomes final 60 days after date of service upon the respondent, unless within that period the respondent petitions an appropriate United States court of appeals to review the order. In case of review, the order of the commission becomes final after affirmance by the court of appeals or by the Supreme Court of the United States, if taken to that court on certiorari. Violations of an order to cease and desist after it becomes final subject the offender to suit by the government in a United States district court for the recovery of a civil penalty of not more than $10,000 for each violation and, where the violation continues, each day of its continuance is a separate violation.

Under each of these statutes the respondent may apply to a court of appeals for review of an order and the court has power to affirm, modify, or set the order aside. Either party, on writ of certiorari, may apply to the Supreme Court for review of the action of the court of appeals.

In addition to the regular proceeding by complaint and order to cease and desist, the commission, after consultation with the Attorney General, may bring suit in a United States district court to enforce its subpoenas, to obtain preliminary injunctions, and to sue for civil penalties. The commission also has specific authority to enjoin the dissemination of advertisements of food, drugs, cosmetics, and devices intended for use in the diagnosis, prevention, or treatment of disease, whenever it has reason to believe that such a proceeding would be in the public interest. The preliminary injunctions remain in effect until an order to cease and desist is issued and becomes final, or until the complaint is dismissed by the commission or the order is set aside by the court on review.

Further, the dissemination of a false advertisement of a food, drug, device, or cosmetic, where the use of the commodity advertised may be injurious to health or where there is intent to defraud or mislead, constitutes a misdemeanor; and conviction subjects the offender to a fine of not more than $5,000, imprisonment of not more than six months, or both. Succeeding convictions may result in a fine of not more than $10,000, imprisonment of not more than one year, or both. The statute provides that the commission will certify this type of case to the Attorney General for institution of appropriate court proceedings.

COMPLIANCE ACTIVITIES

Through systematic and continuous review, the commission obtains and maintains compliance with its cease-and-desist orders. All respondents against whom such orders have been issued are required to file reports with the commission to substantiate their compliance. In the event compliance is not obtained or if the order is subsequently violated, civil penalty proceedings may be instituted. Violation of a commission order that has been affirmed by a decree of a U.S. court of appeals makes the respondent further subject to contempt proceedings in the court of appeals.

COOPERATIVE PROCEDURES

In carrying out the statutory directive to "prevent" the use in commerce of unfair practices, the commission makes extensive use of voluntary and cooperative procedures. Through these procedures business and industry may obtain authoritative guidance and a substantial measure of certainty as to what they may do under the laws administered by the commission.

Whenever it is practicable to do so, the commission will furnish an advisory opinion as to whether a proposed course of conduct, if pursued, would be likely to result in further action by the commission. Such opinions are binding on the commission but are subject to the right of the commission to reconsider and rescind the opinion should the public interest require. Information submitted will not be used as the basis for a proceeding against the requesting party without prior notice and opportunity to discontinue the course of action pursued in good faith in reliance upon the commission's advice.

Trade regulation rules express the experience and judgment of the commission, based on facts of which it has knowledge, concerning the substantive requirements of the statutes it administers. These rules may cover all applications of a particular statutory provision and may be nationwide in effect, or they may be limited to particular areas or industries or to particular products or geographic markets. Where a rule is related to an issue in an adjudicative proceeding thereafter instituted, the commission may rely upon such rule, provided that a fair hearing is afforded on the legality and propriety of applying the rule to a particular case.

Industry guides are administrative interpretations in laymen's language of laws administered by the commission for the guidance of the public in conducting its affairs in conformity with legal requirements. They provide the basis for voluntary and simultaneous abandonment of unlawful practices by members of a particular industry or industry in general. Failure to comply with the guides may result in corrective action by the commission under applicable statutory provisions.

CONSUMER PROTECTION

Consumer protection is one of the two main missions of the commission. In addition to preventing the use of unfair or deceptive advertising and marketing practices generally, the commission enforces a number of specific laws that help consumers.

One of the laws the commission enforces is the Consumer Credit Protection Act, which establishes, among other things, rules for the use of credit cards, the disclosure of the terms

REGIONAL OFFICES (Federal Trade Commission)

Region	Address
Atlanta—Alabama, Florida, Georgia, Kentucky, Mississippi, North Carolina, South Carolina, Tennessee	1718 Peachtree Street NE, Atlanta, GA 30309
Boston—Connecticut, Maine, Massachusetts, New Hampshire, Rhode Island, Vermont	150 Causeway Street, Boston, MA 02114
Chicago—Illinois, Indiana, Iowa, Minnesota, Missouri, Wisconsin	55 E. Monroe Street, Chicago, IL 60603
Cleveland—Michigan, Western New York, Ohio, Western Pennsylvania, Delaware, Maryland, West Virginia	118 St. Clair Avenue, Cleveland, OH 44144
Dallas—Arkansas, Louisiana, New Mexico, Oklahoma, Texas	2001 Bryan Street, Dallas, TX 75201
Denver—Colorado, Kansas, Montana, Nebraska, North Dakota, South Dakota, Utah, Wyoming	1405 Curtis Street, Denver, CO 80202
Los Angeles—Arizona, Southern California	11000 Wilshire Boulevard, Los Angeles, CA 90024
New York—New Jersey, Eastern New York	26 Federal Plaza, New York, NY 10007
San Francisco—Northern California, Hawaii, Nevada	450 Golden Gate Avenue, San Francisco, CA 94102
Seattle—Alaska, Idaho, Oregon, Washington	915 Second Avenue, Seattle, WA 98174
Honolulu—Field Station	300 Ala Moana Boulevard, Honolulu, HI 96850

on which open- and closed-end credit is granted, and the disclosure of the reasons a business uses in determining not to grant credit.

The Truth in Lending Act is one part of the Consumer Credit Protection Act. Its purpose is to ensure that every customer who has need for consumer credit is given meaningful information with respect to the cost of that credit. In most cases the credit cost must be expressed in the dollar amount of finance charges, and as an annual percentage rate computed on the unpaid balance of the amount financed. Other relevant credit information must also be disclosed so that the customer may compare the various credit terms available to him from different sources and avoid the uninformed use of credit. The act further provides a customer the right, in certain circumstances, to cancel a credit transaction that involves a lien on his residence. The Truth in Lending Act was amended in October 1970 to regulate the issuance, holder's liability, and fraudulent use of credit cards. New credit cards may be issued only in response to a request or application by the person who is to receive the card. Also, the liability to the cardholder for unauthorized use of a credit card is specifically limited to $50 if the cardholder has taken reasonable steps to notify the card issuer of the loss or theft. The act also establishes penalties for the fraudulent use of credit cards in interstate or foreign commerce when the aggregate retail value is $5,000 or more. The commission enforces the requirements of the Truth in Lending Act over finance companies, retailers, nonfederal credit unions, and other creditors not specifically regulated by another government agency, and persons or their agents who issue credit cards.

The Fair Credit Reporting Act, another part of the Consumer Protection Act, represents the first federal regulation of the vast consumer reporting industry, covering all credit bureaus, investigative reporting companies, detective and collection agencies, lenders' exchanges, and computerized information reporting companies. The purpose of this act is to insure that consumer reporting activities are conducted in a manner that is fair and equitable to the affected consumer, upholding his right to privacy against the informational demands of others. The consumer is given several important new rights, including the right to notice of reporting activities, the right to access to information contained in consumer reports, and the right to correction of erroneous information that may have been the basis for a denial of credit, insurance, or employment.

Under the Wool Products Labeling Act, the Textile Fiber Products Identification Act, and the Fur Products Labeling Act, the commission engages in compliance investigations, inspections, and industry counseling; issues registered identification numbers; and records continuing guaranties. The commission has published rules and regulations under these statutes, together with illustrations of acceptable labeling, which supply full information concerning their requirements. In connection with the Fur Act, the commission has issued a register of animal names, known as the *Fur Products Name Guide,* for use in properly describing furs and fur products.

ECONOMIC COMPETITION (ANTITRUST)

The second major mission of the commission is to encourage competitive forces in the American economy. Under the Federal Trade Commission Act, the commission seeks to prevent unfair practices that may keep one company from competing with others. Under the Federal Trade Commission Act and the Clayton Act, the commission attempts to prevent mergers of companies if the result may be to lessen competition. Under some circumstances, companies planning to merge must first give notice to the commission and the Department of Justice's Antitrust Division and provide certain information concerning the operations of the companies involved.

The commission also enforces the provisions of the Robinson-Patman Act, a part of the Clayton Act, which prohibits companies from discriminating among other companies that are its customers in terms of price or other services provided.

ECONOMIC FACT-FINDING

The commission makes economic and statistical studies of conditions and problems affecting competition in the economy. Reports of this nature may be in support of legislative proposals, in response to requests of the Congress and statutory directions, or for the information and guidance of the commission and the executive branch of the government as well as the public. Not only have the reports provided the basis for significant legislation, but by spotlighting uneconomic or otherwise objectionable trade practices, they have also led in many instances to voluntary changes in the conduct of business, with resulting benefits to both industry and the public.

The commission prepares quarterly reports on the financial position and operating results of the nation's manufacturing industries. These quarterly summaries present a composite income statement and balance sheet for all manufacturing corporations, classified by both industry and asset size.

The commission also prepares annual reports on current trends in merger activity, large mergers in manufacturing and mining, and rates of return for selected manufacturing industries.

FOOD AND DRUG ADMINISTRATION (FDA) (DEPARTMENT OF HEALTH, EDUCATION, AND WELFARE)

5600 FISHERS LANE, ROCKVILLE, MD 20852
INFORMATION: 301-443-1544

The name "Food and Drug Administration" was first provided by the Agriculture Appropriation Act of 1931, approved May 27, 1930 (46 Stat. 392), although similar law enforcement functions had been carried on under different organizational titles since January 1, 1907, when the Food and Drug Act of 1906 (34 Stat. 768; 21 U.S.C. 1-15) became effective.

The Food and Drug Administration's activities are directed toward protecting the health of the nation against impure and unsafe foods, drugs, and cosmetics, and other potential hazards.

BIOLOGICS

The Bureau of Biologics administers regulation of biological products shipped in interstate and foreign commerce; inspects manufacturers' facilities for compliance with standards; tests products submitted for release; establishes written and physical standards; approves licenses of manufacturers of biological products; conducts research related to the development, manufacture, testing, and use of new and old biological products; and evaluates claims for investigational new drugs that are biological products.

DRUGS

The Bureau of Drugs develops FDA policy with regard to the safety, effectiveness, and labeling of all drugs for human use; evaluates new drug applications and notices of claimed investigational exemption for new drugs; develops standards for the safety and effectiveness of all over-the-counter drugs; monitors the quality of marketed drugs through product testing, surveillance, and compliance programs; develops guidelines on good manufacturing practices; conducts research and develops scientific standards on the composition, quality, safety, and efficacy of human drugs; disseminates toxicity and treatment information on household products and medicines; evaluates applications for operation of activities using methadone or other drugs; directs the FDA antibiotic and insulin certification program.

FOODS

The Bureau of Foods conducts research and develops standards on the composition, quality, nutrition, and safety of foods, food additives, colors, and cosmetics; conducts research designed to improve the detection, prevention, and control of contamination that may be responsible for illness or injury conveyed by foods, colors, and cosmetics; coordinates and evaluates FDA's surveillance and compliance programs relating to foods, color, and cosmetics; reviews industry petitions and develops regulations for food standards to permit the safe use of color additives and food additives; collects and interprets data on nutrition, food additives, and environmental factors affecting the total chemical insult posed by food additives; and maintains a nutritional data bank.

RADIOLOGICAL HEALTH

The Bureau of Radiological Health carries out programs designed to reduce the exposure of man to hazardous ionizing and nonionizing radiation; develops standards for safe limits of radiation exposure; develops methodology for controlling radiation exposures; conducts research on the health effects of radiation exposure; and conducts an electronic product radiation control program to protect public health and safety, including the development and administration of performance standards to control the emission of radiation from electronic products and the undertaking by public and private organizations of research and investigation into the effects and control of such radiation emissions.

VETERINARY MEDICINE

The Bureau of Veterinary Medicine develops and conducts programs with respect to the safety and efficacy of veterinary preparations and devices; evaluates proposed use of veterinary preparations for animal safety and efficacy; and evaluates FDA's surveillance and compliance programs relating to veterinary drugs and other veterinary medical matters.

MEDICAL DEVICES

The Bureau of Medical Devices develops FDA policy regarding the safety, efficacy, and labeling of medical devices; evaluates medical device pre-market approval applications, product development protocols, and exemption requests for investigational devices; evaluates the safety, efficacy, and labeling of medical devices and recommends their classification into regulatory categories; develops safety and efficacy standards for medical devices and good manufacturing practice regulations; develops, coordinates, and evaluates FDA surveillance and compliance programs for medical devices; provides technical and other nonfinancial assistance to small manufacturers of medical devices; conducts research and testing activities relating to medical devices; collects and evaluates data on significant hazards to the public health which may be caused by the use of medical devices.

TOXICOLOGICAL RESEARCH

The National Center for Toxicological Research conducts research programs to study the biological effects of potentially toxic chemical substances found in man's environment, emphasizing the determination of the health effects resulting from long-term low-level exposure to chemical toxicants and the basic biological processes for chemical toxicants in animal organisms, and the development of improved methodologies and test protocols for evaluating the safety of chemical toxicants and the data that will facilitate the extrapolation of toxicological data from laboratory animals to man.

REGIONAL OPERATIONS

The Executive Director of Regional Operations executes direct line authority over FDA field activities; provides a central point to which headquarters officials can turn to for field support services; develops programs and plans for activities between FDA, state, and local agencies; and administers FDA's state-federal program policy.

REGIONAL OFFICES (Food and Drug Administration)

Region	Address
I	585 Commercial Street, Boston, MA 02109
II	830 Third Avenue, Brooklyn, NY 11232
III	U.S. Customhouse, 2nd and Chestnut Streets, Philadelphia, PA 19106
IV	1182 W. Peachtree Street NW, Atlanta, GA 30309
V	175 W. Jackson Boulevard, Chicago, IL 60604
VI	3032 Bryan Street, Dallas, TX 75204
VII	1009 Cherry Street, Kansas City, MO 64106
VIII	721 19th Street, Denver, CO 80202
IX	Federal Office Building, 50 U.N. Plaza, San Francisco, CA 94102
X	Federal Office Building, 909 First Avenue, Seattle, WA 98174

Field operations necessary for the enforcement of the laws under the jurisdiction of FDA are carried out within the 10 regional offices, 22 district offices, and 121 resident inspection posts throughout the United States and Puerto Rico.

INTERSTATE COMMERCE COMMISSION (ICC)

TWELFTH STREET AND CONSTITUTION AVENUE NW, WASHINGTON, DC 20423

INFORMATION: 202-275-7252

In broad terms and within prescribed legal limits, commission regulation encompasses transportation economics and service.

In the transportation economics area, the commission settles controversies over rates and charges among competing and like modes of transportation, shippers, and receivers of freight, passengers, and others. It rules upon applications for mergers, consolidations, acquisitions of control, and the sale of carriers and issuance of their securities. It prescribes accounting rules, awards reparations, and administers laws relating to railroad bankruptcy. It acts to prevent unlawful discrimination, destructive competition, and rebating. It also has jurisdiction over the use, control, supply, movement, distribution, exchange, interchange, and return of railroad equipment. Under certain conditions, it is authorized to direct the handling and movement of traffic over a railroad and its distribution over other lines of railroads.

In the transportation service area, the commission grants the right to operate to trucking companies, bus lines, freight forwarders, water carriers, and transportation brokers. It approves applications to construct and abandon railroad lines, and it rules upon discontinuances of passenger train service.

Although public hearings on matters before the commission may be held at any point throughout the country, final decisions are made at the Washington, D.C. headquarters in all formal proceedings. These cases include rulings upon rate changes, applications to engage in for-hire transport, carrier mergers, adversary proceedings on complaint actions, and punitive measures taken in enforcement matters.

Consumer protection programs involve assuring that the public obtains full measure of all transportation services to which entitlement is guaranteed by the Interstate Commerce Act. This law ensures that rates will be fair and service will be reasonable. Discrimination, preferential treatment, or prejudicial actions by carriers is illegal and instances of such violations should be brought to the attention of the commission at its headquarters or any field office.

The Office of Special Counsel was created by the commission in November 1978 to help determine the public interest in proceedings subject to ICC jurisdiction. The office can participate as a party or as an aid in the establishment of a record in those proceedings in which the public interest would be otherwise inadequately represented. The office has authority to appear before the commission, other agencies and the courts.

The Regional Rail Reorganization Act of

REGIONAL OFFICES (Interstate Commerce Commission)

Region	Address
1. Connecticut, Maine, Massachusetts, New Hampshire, New Jersey, New York, Rhode Island, Vermont	150 Causeway Street, Boston, MA 02114
2. Delaware, District of Columbia, Maryland, Ohio, Pennsylvania, Virginia, West Virginia	101 N. Seventh Street, Philadelphia, PA 19106
3. Alabama, Florida, Georgia, Kentucky, Mississippi, North Carolina, South Carolina, Tennessee	1776 W. Peachtree Street NW, Atlanta, GA 30309
4. Illinois, Indiana, Michigan, Minnesota, North Dakota, South Dakota, Wisconsin	219 S. Dearborn Street, Chicago, IL 60604
5. Arkansas, Iowa, Kansas, Louisiana, Missouri, Nebraska, Oklahoma, Texas	211 Main Street, Fort Worth, TX 76102
6. Alaska, Arizona, California, Colorado, Idaho, Montana, Nevada, New Mexico, Oregon, Utah, Washington, Wyoming	211 Main Street, San Francisco, CA 94105

1973 created in early 1974 a Rail Services Planning Office to assure that public interest is represented in the restructuring and revitalization of railroads in the Northeast and Midwest. The office was given permanent status by the Railroad Revitalization and Regulatory Reform Act of 1976 (90 Stat. 31; 45 U.S.C. 801 note). In addition to its other responsibilities, it provides planning support for the commission.

LABOR-MANAGEMENT SERVICES ADMINISTRATION (LMSA) (DEPARTMENT OF LABOR)

THIRD STREET AND CONSTITUTION AVENUE NW, WASHINGTON, DC 20216
INFORMATION: 202–523–7408

The Assistant Secretary for Labor-Management Relations has responsibility for the department's labor-management relations activities and serves as administrator of the Labor-Management Services Administration.

The Labor-Management Services Administration administers three laws and section 7120 of the Civil Service Reform Act of 1978. It also provides assistance to collective bargaining negotiators and keeps the Secretary posted on development in labor-management disputes of national scope.

LMSA provides technical assistance to state and local governments in matters concerning public employee labor relations and pursues research and policy development in the overall labor-management relations field.

VETERANS REEMPLOYMENT

Veterans reemployment rights are provided for in Title 38, Chapter 43 of the United States Code. LMSA helps veterans, reservists, national guardsmen, and rejectees exercise their reemployment rights pertaining to the job, seniority, status, and rate of pay they would have achieved had they not been away.

General information is provided to veterans and their preservice employers at the time the veteran is released from the armed forces.

Technical assistance and more specific information are provided to veterans and employers, aimed at voluntary resolution of reemployment problems. When such efforts are not successful, cases may be referred to the Department of Justice for legal action.

PENSION AND WELFARE PLANS

The Employee Retirement Income Security Act of 1974 (ERISA), approved September 2, 1974 (88 Stat. 829; 29 U.S.C. 1001 note), requires administrators of private pension and welfare plans to file copies of those plans with LMSA; to provide plan participants with easily understandable summaries of plans; and to report annually on the financial operation of the plans and bonding of persons charged with handling plan funds and assets. Such persons must also meet strict fiduciary responsibility standards administered by LMSA. Vesting, participation, and funding standards are administered by the Internal Revenue Service.

The Welfare and Pension Plans Disclosure Act (WPPDA) was repealed by ERISA on January 1, 1975, except that certain reporting provisions have been carried over by regulation.

LABOR ORGANIZATIONS

The Labor Management Reporting and Disclosure Act calls upon labor organizations

REGIONAL OFFICES (Labor-Management Services Administration)

Region	Address
New York—Maine, New Hampshire, Vermont, Rhode Island, Massachusetts, Connecticut, New York, New Jersey, Virgin Islands, Puerto Rico	1515 Broadway, New York, NY 10036
Philadelphia—Pennsylvania, Maryland, Delaware, Virginia, West Virginia	3535 Market Street, Philadelphia, PA 19104
Atlanta—Kentucky, Tennessee, North Carolina, South Carolina, Mississippi, Alabama, Florida, Georgia	1371 Peachtree Street NE, Atlanta, GA 30309
Chicago—Illinois, Wisconsin, Indiana, Minnesota, Michigan, Ohio	230 S. Dearborn Street, Chicago, IL 60604
Kansas City—Montana, Wyoming, Utah, Colorado, New Mexico, North Dakota, South Dakota, Nebraska, Kansas, Oklahoma, Texas, Iowa, Missouri, Arkansas, Louisiana	911 Walnut Street, Kansas City, MO 64106
San Francisco—Alaska, Hawaii, Idaho, Washington, Oregon, California, Nevada, Arizona	450 Golden Gate Avenue, San Francisco, CA 94102

REGIONAL OFFICES (Occupational Safety and Health Administration)

Region	Address
I	16–18 North Street, 1 Dock Square Building, Boston, MA 02109
II	1515 Broadway, New York, NY 10036
III	3535 Market Street, Philadelphia, PA 19104
IV	1375 Peachtree Street NE, Atlanta, GA 30309
V	230 S. Dearborn Street, Chicago, IL 60604
VI	555 Griffin Square Building, Dallas, TX 75202
VII	911 Walnut Street, Kansas City, MO 64106
VIII	1961 Stout Street, Denver, CO 80294
IX	450 Golden Gate Avenue, San Francisco, CA 94102
X	909 First Avenue, Seattle, WA 98174

REGIONAL OFFICES (Federal Contract Compliance)

Region	Address
I	John F. Kennedy Federal Building, Boston, MA 02203
II	1515 Broadway, New York, NY 10036
III	3535 Market Street, Philadelphia, PA 19104
IV	1371 Peachtree Street NE, Atlanta, GA 30309
V	230 S. Dearborn Street, Chicago, IL 60604
VI	555 Griffin Square Building, Dallas, TX 75202
VII	911 Walnut Street, Kansas City, MO 64106
VIII	1961 Stout Street, Denver, CO 80294
IX	450 Golden Gate Avenue, San Francisco, CA 94102
X	909 First Avenue, Seattle, WA 98104

to file with LMSA copies of their constitutions and bylaws and annual financial reports of their transactions for public view.

The act also prescribes rules for election of union officers, administration of trusteeships by labor organizations, rights of union members, and the handling of union funds.

Through technical assistance in all these areas LMSA seeks to obtain voluntary compliance with provisions of the act. Enforcement through the federal courts also is available under the law.

LABOR-MANAGEMENT RELATIONS SERVICES

Services offered by LMSA cover a broad range. They include assistance to employers and unions in meeting long-range, complicated problems caused by major economic and technological change; reporting on current and potentially critical dispute situations, analyzing data for immediate use in specific collective bargaining situations; providing staff assistance to presidential emergency boards and other ad hoc boards and commissions dealing with major disputes, such as in the transportation industry; making sure under Section 13(c) of the Urban Mass Transportation Act that protective arrangements exist so that the improvement of such systems with federal funds will not worsen the employment conditions of the workers; and exchanging information with, and giving technical assistance to, state and local governments and organizations of their employees to help them achieve sound labor-management relations.

DEVELOPMENT, RESEARCH, AND EVALUATION

Functions of LMSA in labor-management policy development and research include: review of collective bargaining performance and its contribution to meeting economic needs; development of policy for legislation and executive orders; study of impact of private policies affecting collective bargaining; and coordination of labor-management relations research activities. The evaluation function is the review of LMSA programs to assess their effectiveness and efficiency.

OCCUPATIONAL SAFETY AND HEALTH ADMINISTRATION (OSHA) (DEPARTMENT OF LABOR)

200 Constitution Avenue NW, Washington, DC 20210
Information: 202–523–8148

The Assistant Secretary for Occupational Safety and Health has responsibility for occupational safety and health activities.

The Occupational Safety and Health Administration, established pursuant to the Occupational Safety and Health Act of 1970 (84 Stat. 1590), develops and promulgates occupational safety and health standards; develops and issues regulations; conducts investigations and inspections to determine the status of compliance with safety and health standards and regulations; and issues citations and proposes penalties for noncompliance with safety and health standards and regulations.

OFFICE OF FEDERAL CONTRACT COMPLIANCE (FCC) (DEPARTMENT OF LABOR)

THIRD STREET AND CONSTITUTION AVENUE NW, WASHINGTON, DC 20210
INFORMATION: 202–393–2420

The Office of Federal Contract Compliance is responsible for establishing policies and goals and providing leadership and coordination of the government's program to achieve nondiscrimination in employment by government contractors and subcontractors and in federally assisted construction programs; administering programs to assure affirmative action by government contractors to employ and advance in employment Vietnamera veterans and handicapped workers; coordinating with the Equal Employment Opportunity Commission and the Department of Justice matters relating to Title VII of the Civil Rights Act of 1964; and maintaining liaison with other agencies having civil rights and equal employment opportunity activities.

SECURITIES AND EXCHANGE COMMISSION (SEC)

500 NORTH CAPITOL STREET, WASHINGTON, DC 20549
INFORMATION: 202–272–2650
FREEDOM OF INFORMATION ACT: 202–523–5530

FULL AND FAIR DISCLOSURE

The Securities Act of 1933 requires issuers of securities making public offerings of securities in interstate commerce or through the mails, directly or by others on their behalf, to file registration statements containing financial and other pertinent data about the issuer and the securities being offered. A similar requirement applies to such offerings on behalf of a controlling person of the issuer. Unless a registration statement is in effect with respect to such securities, it is unlawful to sell the securities in interstate commerce or through the mails. (There are certain limited exemptions, such as government securities, nonpublic offerings, and intrastate offerings, as well as offerings not exceeding $1,500,000 in amount, which comply with the commission's Regulation A.) The effectiveness of a registration statement may be refused or suspended after a public hearing, if the statement contains material misstatements or omissions, thus barring sale of the securities until it is appropriately amended. Registration of securities does not imply approval of the issue by the commission or that the commission has found the registration disclosures to be accurate. It does not insure investors against loss in their purchase but serves rather to provide information upon which investors may make an informed and realistic evaluation of the worth of the securities.

Persons responsible for filing false information with the commission subject themselves to the risk of fine or imprisonment or both; and persons connected with the public offering may be liable in damages to purchasers of the securities if the disclosures in the registration statement and prospectus are materially defective. Also, the above act contains antifraud provisions which apply generally to the sale of securities, whether or not registered (48 Stat. 74; 15 U.S.C. 77a et seq.).

REGULATION OF SECURITIES MARKETS AND PERSONS CONDUCTING A SECURITIES BUSINESS

The Securities Exchange Act of 1934 assigns to the commission broad regulatory responsibilities over the securities markets, the self-regulatory organizations within the securities industry, and persons conducting a business in securities. The commission is directed to facilitate the establishment of a national market system for securities and a national system for the clearance and settlement of securities transactions. Securities exchanges and certain clearing agencies are required to register with the commission, and associations of brokers or dealers are permitted to register with the commission. The Securities Exchange Act also provides for the establishment of the Municipal Securities Rulemaking Board to formulate rules for the municipal securities industry. The commission oversees the self-regulatory activities of the national securities exchanges and associations, registered clearing agencies, and the Municipal Securities Rulemaking Board. In addition, the commission regulates industry professionals, such as securities brokers and dealers, certain municipal securities professionals, and transfer agents.

The Securities Exchange Act authorizes national securities exchanges, national securities associations, clearing agencies, and the Municipal Securities Rulemaking Board to adopt rules that are designed, among other things to promote just and equitable principles of trade and to protect investors. The commission is required to approve or disapprove most proposed rules of these self-regulatory organizations and has the power to abrogate or amend existing rules of the national securities exchanges, national securities associations, and the Municipal Securities Rulemaking Board.

In addition, the commission has broad rulemaking authority over the activities of brokers, dealers, municipal securities dealers, securities information processors, and transfer agents. The commission may regulate such securities trading practices as short sales and stabilizing transactions. It may regulate the trading of options on national securities exchanges and the activities of members of exchanges who trade on the trading floors and may adopt rules governing broker-dealer sales practices in dealing with investors. The commission also is authorized to adopt rules concerning the financial responsibility of brokers and dealers and reports to be made by brokers and dealers. The Securities Exchange Act also empowers the Board of Governors of the Federal Reserve System to prescribe rules relating to the extension of credit by brokers and dealers for securities transactions. Such rules include the establishment of minimum margin requirements with respect to securities registered on national securities exchanges and certain securities traded over-the-counter (48 Stat. 881; U.S.C. 78a et seq.).

The Securities Exchange Act also requires the filing of registration applications and annual and other reports with national securities exchanges and the commission by companies whose securities are listed upon the exchanges, by companies that have assets of $1 million or more and 500 or more shareholders of record, and by companies that distributed securities pursuant to a registration statement declared effective by the commission under the Securities Act of 1933. Such applications and reports must contain financial and other data prescribed by the commission as necessary or appropriate for the protection of investors and to insure fair dealing. In addition, the solicitation of proxies, authorizations, or consents from holders of such registered securities must be made in accordance with rules and regulations prescribed by the commission. These rules provide for disclosures to securities holders of information relevant to the subject matter of the solicitation.

Disclosure of the holdings and transactions by officers, directors, and large (10 percent) holders of equity securities of companies is also required, and any and all persons who acquire more than 5 percent of certain equity securities are required to file detailed information with the commission and any exchange upon which such securities may be traded. Moreover, any person making a tender offer for certain classes of equity securities is required to file reports with the commission, if as a result of the tender offer such person would own more than 5 percent of the outstanding shares of the particular class of equity involved. The commission also is authorized to promulgate rules governing the repurchase by a corporate issuer of its own securities.

REGULATION OF MUTUAL FUNDS AND OTHER INVESTMENT COMPANIES

The Investment Company Act of 1940 provides for the registration with the commission of investment companies and subjects their activities to regulation to protect investors. The regulation covers sales and management fees, composition of boards of directors, and capital structure. Also, various transactions of investment companies, including transactions with affiliated interests, are prohibited unless the commission first determines that such transactions are fair. Under the act, the commission may institute court action to enjoin the consummation of mergers and other plans of reorganization of investment companies if such plans are unfair to security holders. It also may impose sanctions by administrative proceedings against investment company managements for violations of the act and other federal securities laws, and file court actions to enjoin acts and practices of management officials involving breaches of fiduciary duty involving personal misconduct and to disqualify such officials from office (54 Stat. 789; 15 U.S.C. 80a-1—80a-52).

REGULATION OF COMPANIES CONTROLLING ELECTRIC OR GAS UTILITIES

The Public Utility Holding Company Act of 1935 provides for regulation by the commission of the purchase and sale of securities and assets by companies in electric and gas utility holding company systems, their intra-system transactions and service and management arrangements. It limits holding companies to a single coordinated utility system and requires simplification of complex corporate and capital structures and elimination of unfair distribution of voting power among holders of system securities.

The issuance and sale of securities by holding companies and their subsidiaries, unless exempt (subject to conditions and terms which the commission is empowered to impose) as an issue expressly authorized by the state commission in the state in which the issuer is incorporated, must be found by the commission to meet statutory standards, namely: that the new security is reasonably adapted to the security structure and earning power of the issuer; that the proposed financing is necessary and appropriate to the economical and efficient operation of the

REGIONAL OFFICES (Securities and Exchange Commission)

Region	Address
1. New York, New Jersey	26 Federal Plaza, New York, NY 10007
2. Maine, Vermont, New Hampshire, Massachusetts, Connecticut, Rhode Island	150 Causeway Street, Boston, MA 02114
3. Tennessee, North Carolina, South Carolina, Mississippi, Alabama, Georgia, Florida, Louisiana (southeastern portion only)	1375 Peachtree Street NE, Atlanta, GA 30309
4. Minnesota, Wisconsin, Michigan, Iowa, Missouri, Illinois, Indiana, Ohio, Kentucky	219 S. Dearborn Street, Chicago, IL 60604
5. Kansas, Oklahoma, Texas, Arkansas, Louisiana (except southeastern portion)	411 W. 7th Street, Fort Worth, TX 76102
6. North Dakota, South Dakota, Colorado, Kansas, Utah, Wyoming, New Mexico	410 17th Street, Denver, CO 80202
7. California, Nevada, Arizona, Hawaii	10960 Wilshire Boulevard, Los Angeles, CA 90024
8. Washington, Oregon	915 Second Avenue, Seattle, WA 98174
9. Pennsylvania, West Virginia, Virginia, Maryland, Delaware	4015 Wilson Boulevard, Arlington, VA 22203

company's business; that the consideration received, and fees, commissions, and other remuneration paid, are fair; and that the terms and conditions of the sale are not detrimental to investors, consumers, or the public.

The purchase and sale of utility properties and other assets may not be made in contravention of rules, regulations, or orders of the commission regarding the consideration to be received, maintenance of competitive conditions, fees and commissions, accounts, disclosure of interest, and similar matters. In passing upon proposals for reorganization, merger, or consolidation, the commission must be satisfied that the objectives of the act generally are complied with and that the terms of the proposal are fair and equitable to all classes of security holders affected (49 Stat. 803; 15 U.S.C. 79–92z–6).

REGULATION OF INVESTMENT COUNSELORS AND ADVISERS

The Investment Advisers Act of 1940 provides that persons who, for compensation, engage in the business of advising others with respect to their security transactions must register with the commission. The act prohibits certain types of fee arrangements, makes unlawful practices of investment advisers involving fraud or deceit, and requires, among other things, disclosure of any adverse interests the advisers may have in transactions executed for clients. The act authorizes the commission to issue rules proscribing acts and practices that may operate as a fraud or deceit upon investors (54 Stat. 847; 15 U.S.C. 80b–1–80b–21).

REHABILITATION OF FAILING CORPORATIONS

Chapter X of the Bankruptcy Act provides for commission participation as adviser to federal courts in proceedings for the reorganization of insolvent corporations. An important aspect of this activity is the advice rendered to the parties and the court with respect to the fairness and feasibility of proposed plans of reorganization (52 Stat. 883; 11 U.S.C. 501–676).

INDEPENDENT REPRESENTATION OF THE INTERESTS OF HOLDERS OF DEBT SECURITIES

The interests of purchasers of publicly offered debt securities issued pursuant to trust indentures are safeguarded under the provisions of the Trust Indenture Act of 1939. This act, among other things, requires the exclusion from such indentures of certain types of exculpatory clauses and the inclusion of certain protective provisions. The independence of the indenture trustee, who is a representative of the debt holder, is assured by proscribing certain relationships that might conflict with the proper exercise of his duties (53 Stat. 1149; 15 U.S.C. 77aaa–77bbbb).

ENFORCEMENT ACTIVITIES

The commission's enforcement activities are designed to secure compliance with the federal securities laws administered by the commission and the rules and regulations adopted thereunder. These activities include measures to compel obedience to the disclosure requirements of the registration and other provisions of the acts; to prevent fraud and deception in the purchase and sale of securities; to obtain court orders enjoining acts and practices that operate as a fraud upon investors or otherwise violate the laws; to revoke the registrations of brokers, dealers, and investment advisers who willfully engage in such acts and practices; to suspend or expel from national securities exchanges or the National Association of Securities Dealers, Inc., any member or officer who has violated any provision of the federal securities laws; and to prosecute persons who have engaged in fraudulent activities or other willful violations of those laws. In addition, attorneys or accountants who violate the securities laws face possible loss of their privilege to practice before the commission. To this end, private investigations are conducted into complaints or other evidences of securities violations.

Evidence thus established of law violations in the purchase and sale of securities is used in appropriate administrative proceedings to revoke registration or in actions instituted in federal courts to restrain or enjoin such activities. Where the evidence tends to establish fraud or other willful violation of the securities laws, the facts are referred to the Attorney General for criminal prosecution of the offenders. The commission may assist in such prosecutions.

INVESTOR INFORMATION AND PROTECTION

Complaints and inquiries may be directed to the home office or to any regional office. Registration statements and other public documents filed with the commission are available for public inspection in the public reference room at the home office. Much of the information also is available in its New York, Chicago, and Los Angeles regional offices, and to a lesser extent in the other regional offices of the commission. Reproduction of the public material may be purchased from the commission at prescribed rates.

STANDARD FEDERAL REGIONS

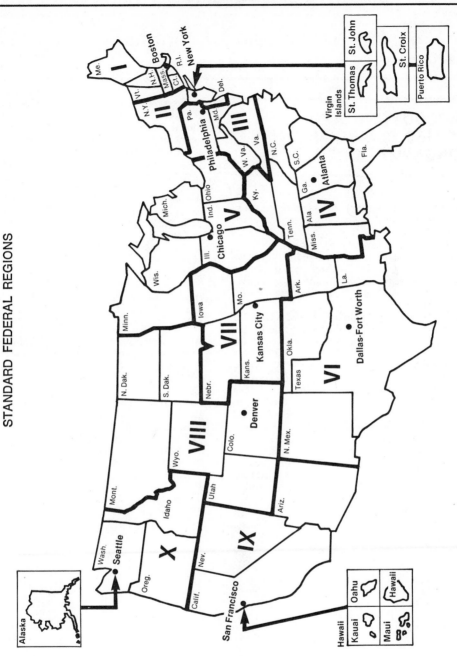

Finance and Accounting

ACCOUNTING AND ALLIED FINANCIAL ORGANIZATIONS

American Accounting Association (AAA): A private professional organization representing academic accounts. Address: 5717 Bessie Drive, Sarasota, FL 33581.

American Institute of Certified Public Accountants (AICPA): The largest private association of certified public accountants (CPAs). Address: 1211 Avenue of the Americas, New York 10036.

Cost Accounting Standards Board (CASB): A federal board established in 1970 for promulgating cost accounting standards for use by contractors with the federal government. Address: 441 G Street NW, Washington, DC 20548.

Financial Accounting Standards Board (FASB): The private body created to establish accounting standards. Established in July 1973, it succeeded the earlier Accounting Principles Board (APB). It is jointly sponsored by the AAA, AICPA, FEI, FAF, and NAA. The standards are officially recognized by the Securities and Exchange Commission (SEC). Address: High Ridge Park, Stamford, CT 06905.

Financial Executives Institute (FEI): An organization of corporate financial officers. Address: 633 Third Avenue, New York, NY 10017.

National Organization of State Boards of Accountancy (NOSBA): An organization representing state boards which license CPAs. Address: 1211 Avenue of the Americas, New York, NY 10036.

National Association of Accountants (NAA): An organization of businessmen and accountants. Address: 919 Third Avenue, New York, NY 10022.

The "Big Eight" Accounting Firms: The leading accounting firms within the profession. Clients of the Big Eight include 92 percent of the firms listed on the New York Stock Exchange and 76 percent of those listed on the American Stock Exchange. Listed in alphabetical order, the names and addresses of the Big Eight are:

Arthur Andersen & Co., 69 W. Washington Street, Chicago, IL 60602.

Arthur Young & Co., 277 Park Avenue, New York, NY 10017.

Coopers & Lybrand, 1251 Avenue of the Americas, New York, NY 10020.

Ernst & Ernst, 1300 Union Commerce Building, Cleveland, OH 44115.

Deloitte, Haskins & Sells, 1114 Avenue of the Americas, New York, NY 10036.

Peat, Marwick, Mitchell & Co., 345 Park Avenue, New York, NY 10022.

Price Waterhouse & Co., 1251 Avenue of the Americas, New York, NY 10020.

Touche Ross & Co., 1633 Broadway, New York, NY 10019.

ACCOUNTING STATEMENTS
AND OPINIONS

ACCOUNTING RESEARCH BULLETINS (ARB)

ARB Number and Title	Date
43. Restatement and revisions of accounting research bulletins ...	June 1953
44. Declining balance depreciation	July 1958
45. Long-term construction-type contracts	October 1955
46. Discontinuance for dating earned surplus	February 1956
47. Accounting for cost of pension plans	September 1956
48. Business combinations	January 1957
49. Earnings per share	April 1958
50. Contingencies	October 1958
51. Consolidated financial statements	August 1959

ACCOUNTING PRINCIPLES BOARD (APB) STATEMENTS

APB Statement Number and Title	Date
1. Statement by the Accounting Principles Board	April 13, 1962
2. Disclosure of supplemental financial information by diversified companies	September 1967
3. Financial statements restated for general price-level changes	June 1969
4. Basic concepts and accounting principles underlying financial statements of business enterprises	October 1970

ACCOUNTING PRINCIPLES BOARD (APB) OPINIONS

Opinions	Date Adopted
1. New depreciation guidelines and rules	November 1962
2. Accounting for the "investment credit"	December 1962
3. The statement of source and application of funds	October 1963
4. Accounting for the "investment credit" (amending No. 2)	March 1964
5. Reporting of leases in financial statements of lessee	September 1964
6. Status of Accounting Research Bulletins	October 1965
7. Accounting for leases in financial statements of lessors	May 1966
8. Accounting for the cost of pension plans	November 1966
9. Reporting the results of operations	December 1966
10. Omnibus opinion—1966	December 1966
Consolidated financial statements, poolings of interest—restatement of financial statements, tax allocation accounts—discounting, offsetting securities against taxes payable, convertible debt and debt issued with stock warrants, liquidation preference of preferred stock, installment method of accounting	
11. Accounting for income taxes	December 1967
Timing differences, operating losses, tax allocation within a period, other unused deductions and credits, financial reporting	
12. Omnibus opinion—1967	December 1967
Classification and disclosure of allowances, disclosure of depreciable assets and depreciation, deferred compensation contracts, capital changes, convertible debt and debt issued with stock warrants, amortization of debt discount and expense or premium	
13. Amending paragraph 6 of APB Opinion No. 9 application to commercial banks	March 1969
14. Accounting for convertible debt and debt issued with stock purchase warrants	March 1969
15. Earnings per share	May 1969
16. Business combinations	August 1970
17. Intangible assets	August 1970
18. The equity method of accounting for investments in common stock	March 1971

ACCOUNTING PRINCIPLES BOARD (APB) OPINIONS (*continued*)

Opinions	Date Adopted
19. Reporting changes in financial position	March 1971
20. Accounting changes	July 1971
Change in accounting principle, change in accounting estimate, change in the reporting equity, correction of an error in previously issued financial statements	
21. Interest on receivables and payables	August 1971
22. Disclosure of accounting policies	April 1972
23. Accounting for income taxes—special areas	April 1972
Undistributed earnings of subsidiaries, investments in corporate joint ventures, "bad debt reserves" of savings and loan associations, "policyholders' surplus" of stock life insurance companies	
24. Accounting for income taxes—investments in common	April 1972
Stock accounted for by the equity method (other than subsidiaries and corporate joint ventures)	
25. Accounting for stock issued to employees	October 1972
26. Early extinguishment of debt	October 1972
27. Accounting for lease transactions by manufacturer or dealer lessors	November 1972
28. Interim financial reporting	May 1973
29. Accounting for nonmonetary transactions	May 1973
30. Reporting the results of operations—reporting the effects of disposal of a segment of a business, and extraordinary, unusual and infrequently occurring events and transactions	June 1973
31. Disclosure of lease commitments by lessees	June 1973

FINANCIAL ACCOUNTING STANDARDS BOARD (FASB) STATEMENTS
(FASB succeeded APB in July 1973)

FASB Statement Number and Title	Date Adopted
1. Disclosure of foreign currency translation information	December 1973
2. Accounting for research and development costs	October 1974
3. Reporting accounting changes in interim financial statements (amendment of APB Opinion No. 28)	December 1974
4. Reporting gains and losses from extinguishment of debt (amendment of APB Opinion No. 30)	March 1975
5. Accounting for contingencies	March 1975
6. Classification of short-term obligations expected to be refinanced (amendment of ARB No. 43, Chapter 3A)	May 1975
7. Accounting and reporting by development stage enterprises	June 1975
8. Accounting for the translation of foreign currency transactions and foreign currency financial statements	October·1975
9. Accounting for income taxes—oil and gas producing companies (amendment of APB Opinions No. 11 and 23)	October 1975
10. Extension of "grandfather" provisions for business combinations (amendment of APB Opinion No. 16)	October 1975
11. Accounting for contingencies—transition method (amendment of FASB Statement No. 5)	December 1975
12. Accounting for certain marketable securities	December 1975
13. Accounting for leases	November 1976
14. Financial reporting for segments of a business enterprise	December 1976
15. Accounting by debtors and creditors for troubled debt restructurings	June 1977
16. Prior period adjustments	June 1977
17. Accounting for leases—initial direct costs (amendment of FASB Statement No. 13)	November 1977
18. Financial reporting for segments of a business enterprise—interim financial statements (amendment of FASB Statement No. 14)	November 1977
19. Financial accounting and reporting by oil and gas producing companies	December 1977
20. Forward exchange contracts (amendment of FASB Statement No. 8)	December 1977
21. Suspension of the reporting of earnings per share and segment information by nonpublic enterprises (amendment of APB Opinion No. 15 and FASB Statement No. 14)	April 1978

FINANCIAL ACCOUNTING STANDARDS BOARD STATEMENTS (*continued*)

FASB Statement Number and Title	Date Adopted
22. Changes in the provision of lease agreements resulting from re-fundings of tax-exempt debt (amendment of FASB Statement No. 13)	June 1978
23. Inception of the lease (amendment of FASB Statement No. 13)	August 1978
24. Reporting segment information in financial statements that are presented in another enterprise's financial report (amendment of FASB Statement No. 14)	December 1978
25. Suspension of certain accounting requirements for oil and gas producing companies (amendment of FASB Statement No. 19)	February 1979
26. Profit recognition on sales-type leases of real estate (amendment of FASB Statement No. 13)	April 1979
27. Classification of renewals or extensions of existing sales-type or direct financing leases (amendment of FASB Statement No. 13)	May 1979
28. Accounting for sales with leasebacks (amendment of FASB Statement No. 13)	May 1979
29. Determining contingent rentals (amendment of FASB Statement No. 13)	June 1979
30. Disclosure of information about major customers (amendment of FASB Statement No. 14)	August 1979
31. Accounting for tax benefits related to U.K. tax legislation concerning stock relief	September 1979
32. Specialized accounting and reporting principles and practices in AICPA Statements of Position and Guides on Accounting and Auditing Matters (amendment of APB Opinion No. 20)	September 1979
33. Financial reporting and changing prices	September 1979
34. Capitalization of interest cost	October 1979
35. Accounting and reporting by defined benefit pension plans	March 1980
36. Disclosure of pension information (amendment of APB Opinion No. 8)	May 1980
37. Balance sheet classification of deferred taxes (amendment of APB Opinion No. 11)	July 1980

How to Understand and Analyze Financial Statements*

Fred B. Renwick

Analyzing financial statements in corporate annual reports can be easy, fun, and rewarding, if you know what to look for. This short essay explains in a nutshell what to look for and how to analyze financial statements.

Only four statements are important to understand and analyze, namely:

- The *balance sheet,* which states the financial condition of the corporation as of one particular date: the date posted at the top of the statement.

- The *income statement,* which shows the amount of earnings for the year currently ending, and conveys information regarding the efficiency and profitability of the business.

- The *statement of retained earnings,* which gives further information regarding one of the lines on the balance sheet, and also shows the division of net income for the year between dividend payout to stockholders and earnings retained and reinvested in the business.

- The *statement of sources and uses of funds,* which gives further information regarding total current assets and total current liabilities as stated on the balance sheet; and shows the net changes during the year in working capital.

Additionally, corporate annual reports usually contain supplementary information which expands upon items in the four basic statements, and includes: (1) a letter or report of independent accountants and auditors addressed to stockholders and directors of the company certifying and validating the figures in the four statements, (2) notes which report material information regarding line items in each statement, (3) segment information which summarizes selected information by industry and geographic segments, (4) restatement pursuant to Financial Accounting Standards Board (FASB) *Statement of Financial Accounting Standards No. 33* to account for effects of inflation and changing prices on items in the four primary statements, and (5) a long-term (5 or 10-year) summary of selected items from the four primary statements.

The following section explains each statement in detail, Section II explains how to analyze the statements, Section III explains notes and supplementary information.

---

* See also the definition of financial terms, p. 246.

† Fred B. Renwick is Professor of Finance at the Graduate School of Business Administration, New York University, New York, N.Y.

I. FOUR FINANCIAL STATEMENTS: WHAT TO LOOK FOR

BALANCE SHEETS

Exhibit 1 shows a balance sheet for Universal Manufacturing Corporation (UMC), a hypothetical company which produces and distributes goods and services in the health industry. Universal's single line of business is divided into two industry segments: human and animal health products, and environmental health products and services.

Observe the format of Universal's balance sheet, the *report form,* where total assets, $26 million, are itemized first and total financing (total liabilities and stockholders' equity), $26 million, are itemized below the asset section. Some corporations prefer to use the *account form,* where assets are listed on the left side of the form and liabilities and owners' equity sections are listed to the right of the asset section. UMC is using the *report form.*

The balance sheet shows the ownership of total corporate assets as of the date of the statement. For example, the following calculation implies that if UMC's tangible assets were liquidated as of the date posted at the top of the balance sheet, $17.8 million would be available for distribution among the preferred and common stockholders.

Total assets owned by UMC	$26,000,000
Less: Intangibles	200,000
Total tangible assets owned by UMC	$25,800,000
Amount required to pay total liabilities	8,000,000
Amount remaining for the stockholders	$17,800,000

Further, the above example illustrates a critical point: the difference between *current market value* (the amount UMC's assets would really bring if sold) versus the *accounting book value* (the $17.8 million). Relationships exist between market and book values, but accounting statements (except for FASB *No. 33*) are factual reports of *book,* not *market,* values of corporate assets.

The following paragraphs explain each line entry on balance sheets.

Starting at the top of the balance sheet, after the name of the corporation, title, and date of the statement, total assets are itemized, with current assets (total, $13.6 million) always first.

Current assets consist of:

1. *Cash,* $350,000, which is what you would expect, namely pocket-book currency and

EXHIBIT 1

UNIVERSAL MANUFACTURING CORPORATION
Balance Sheet
December 31, 1981

Assets	1981	1980
Current assets	$ 350,000	$ 250,000
Cash		
Marketable securities at cost		
(market value: 1981, $2,980,000; 1980, $1,900,000)	2,850,000	1,830,000
Accounts receivable		
Less: Allowance for bad debt: 1981, $24,000; 1980, $21,000 ...	4,800,000	4,370,000
Inventories	5,600,000	4,950,000
Total current assets	$13,600,000	$11,400,000
Fixed assets (property, plant, and equipment)		
Land	$ 734,000	$ 661,000
Building	5,762,000	5,258,000
Machinery	11,435,000	10,011,000
Office equipment	614,000	561,000
	18,545,000	16,491,000
Less: Accumulated depreciation	6,435,000	5,671,000
Net fixed assets	12,110,000	10,820,000
Prepayments and deferred charges	90,000	61,600
Intangibles (goodwill, patent, trademarks)	200,000	200,000
Total assets	$26,000,000	$22,481,600

Liabilities	1981	1980
Current liabilities		
Accounts payable	$ 2,910,000	$ 2,300,000
Notes payable	1,420,000	730,000
Accrued expenses payable	430,000	350,000
Federal income taxes payable	1,240,000	1,320,000
Total current liabilities	$ 6,000,000	$ 4,700,000
Long-term liabilities		
First mortgage bonds, 8% interest, due 1995	$ 2,000,000	$ 2,000,000
Total liabilities	$ 8,000,000	$ 6,700,000

Stockholders' Equity

	1981	1980
Capital stock		
Preferred stock, 6% cumulative, $100 par value each;		
authorized, issued, and outstanding 13,600 shares	1,360,000	1,360,000
Common stock, 30 cents par value each; authorized, issued,		
and outstanding 760,000 shares	228,000	228,000
Capital surplus	1,112,000	1,112,000
Accumulated retained earnings	15,300,000	13,081,600
Total stockholders' equity	$18,000,000	$15,781,600
Total liabilities and stockholders' equity	$26,000,000	$22,481,600

coins in the treasurer's office, plus demand deposits at a commercial bank. Cash is synonymous with liquidity,

2. *Marketable securities,* $2.85 million, which usually are cash equivalents or highly liquid securities such as Treasury Bills of the federal government or negotiable certificates of deposit (CDs), or demand notes issued by large corporations,

3. *Accounts receivable,* $4.8 million, which consist of payments due from customers who purchased UMC's goods and services on credit and have not paid yet but are scheduled to pay within the next few months. Since a small fraction of customers might never pay (because of death, finan-

cial disaster, flood, or other catastrophe), an allowance is made, $24,000, pursuant to good accounting practices for bad debts,

4. *Inventories,* $5.6 million, which consist of (*a*) finished goods in stock and ready for sale or shipment, (*b*) work and merchandise in process, and (*c*) supplies and raw materials inventories; and are priced on the balance sheet at the lower of cost or market on either a first-in-first-out (Fifo) or last-in-first-out (Lifo) basis. Pricing policy is usually stated in a note.

Total current assets, $13.6 million, are the sum of the four aforecited figures and usually are earmarked for use within the coming 12 months. In other words, *current* means within the next 12 months.

Fixed assets (property, plant and equipment) are the permanent tangible capital owned by the business, and are listed *at cost* (original purchase price) next on the balance sheet; and consists of:

1. *Land,* $734,000, or ground upon which buildings or other assets such as forests, air or water rights, and the like are built,
2. *Building,* $5.762 million, which are structures such as offices, warehouses, and the like where business is conducted,
3. *Machinery,* $11.435 million, which are mechanical apparatuses for increasing productivity and economic efficiency,
4. *Office equipment,* $614,000, which is what you would expect, namely desks, typewriters, copiers, and the like.

Accumulated depreciation, $6.435 million, is the total depreciation (deterioration of property, plant, and equipment due to physical wear and tear) accumulated to date for accounting purposes against UMC's assets. It is important to know about three concepts of depreciation, namely: (1) depreciation calculated for tax purposes which is figured pursuant to the Tax Code to benefit from allowable accelerated rates of depreciation, (2) accounting depreciation, which can be either straight-line or accelerated and is usually explained in a note, (3) economic depreciation, which comes from technological obsolescence and deterioration in ability to continue generating future income at current rates due to changes in demand and markets for the goods and services produced by UMC. The balance sheet states only number two, accounting depreciation.

Net fixed assets, $12,110,000, are the sum of the four above figures, minus accounting depreciation; and are used by the business to generate future (beyond the coming 12 months) income.

Prepayments and deferred charges, $90,000, state total amounts paid in advance for assets not yet obtained (such as paid-up premiums on a fire insurance policy covering the next five years, or rental paid on computers for the next three years); and for benefits to be received in future years for expenditures already made (such as for research and development, moving the business to a new location, or expenses incurred in bringing a new product to market).

Intangibles, $200,000, are assets such as goodwill, trademarks, franchises, patents, copyrights, and the like which have no physical existence; yet are valuable in producing business income.

Total assets, $26 million, are current, plus fixed, plus prepayments and deferred charges, plus intangibles; and state the size of the business and are the total property owned by the business.

Look next at the lower part of the balance sheet, which concerns the financing of the business. Financing must come from either borrowing (liabilities) or ownership equity.

Underneath the asset section of the balance sheet (or on the right side if the company uses the account form), total current liabilities, $6 million, always are itemized next, then long-term liabilities, $2 million, then finally stockholders' equity of $18 million.

Total current liabilities consist of bills due and payable by UMC within the next 12 months, all of which fall into one of four categories:

1. *Accounts payable,* $2.91 million, which are bills currently owed and due to creditors,
2. *Notes payable,* $1.42 million, which are current obligations owed to a bank or other short-term lender,
3. *Accrued expenses payable,* $430,000, include wages due employees, fees to attorneys, current pension or retirement obligations, and the like,
4. *Federal income taxes payable,* $1.24 million, is the current tax payable to the Internal Revenue Service, and is sufficiently important to merit a line of its own on the corporate balance sheet.

Long-term liabilities, $2 million for UMC, can include straight debt (like UMC's which pays 8 percent interest and matures in 1995), convertible bonds (bonds which pay interest like straight bonds but are convertible upon demand of the bond owner into a stated number of shares of common stock), or "other" long-term debt (like pollution control and industrial revenue bonds or sinking-fund debentures). UMC has only straight debt outstanding.

Total liabilities, $8 million, are the sum of current and long-term liabilities and constitute the total financing obtained from borrowings.

Stockholders' equity, $18 million consists of:

1. *Capital stock,* $1.588 million, which includes both preferred stock and common stock but no convertible preferred stock and no warrants or rights to purchase either bonds or common stock,
2. *Capital surplus,* $1.112 million, which is the amount paid in by shareholders over the par or legal value of 30 cents for each common share,
3. *Accumulated retained earnings,* $15.3 million, which are earnings not paid out in dividends but have been retained and reinvested in the business. Further information regarding accumulated retained earnings since inception of the business is set

forth below in the *statement of retained earnings.*

Capital stock represents proprietary interest in the company, is represented by stock certificates authorized and issued by the company, and can belong to either of several classes, including:

1. *Preferred stock,* which has preference or takes priority over other shares regarding dividend payout (6 percent in UMC's case), and which can be cumulative, which means that if the company fails to pay dividends for whatever reason for any year, then the 6 percent of $100 or $6 per preferred share accumulates on the books and must be paid before common stockholders can receive future dividends. Total preferred stock authorized and issued by UMC is $100 per share times 13,600 shares or $1.36 million.

2. *Common stock,* which represents the remaining ownership of the company and is entitled to receive a dividend along with fluctuations in value of the stock. Par value is the legal stated value of each common share; so the par value (30 cents per share times 760,000 shares or $228,000) plus the additional amount or capital surplus ($1.112 million) together state the amount UMC received upon issuing 760,000 shares,

namely $1.34 million divided by 760,000 or $1.76 per share.

The bottom line, *total liabilities and stockholders equity,* states the financing of the corporation, and shows where UMC obtained the $26 million to buy the total assets itemized at the top of the balance sheet.

We turn next to income statements.

INCOME STATEMENTS

Exhibit 2 shows UMC's income statement, where the important items to look for, after the name of the company, the title, and date of the statement at the heading, are:

1. *Net sales,* which is where most of the business revenue comes from for most businesses, except rental and leasing companies, $23,850,000.
2. *Net Operating Income* (NOI) or profit before interest and taxes, which states profit from business operations, without regard to financing, $5,878,000.
3. *Total Income* before interest and taxes, which states the return on total capital available to the business during the year, $6,220,000.
4. *Less:* provision for federal income tax, $2,240,000.

EXHIBIT 2

UNIVERSAL MANUFACTURING CORPORATION
1981 and 1980
Consolidated Income Statement

	1981	1980
Net sales	$23,850,000	$19,810,000
Cost of sales and operating expenses		
Cost of goods sold	8,940,000	7,209,000
Depreciation	800,000	750,000
Selling and administrating expenses	8,232,000	6,814,000
Operating profit	$ 5,878,000	$ 5,037,000
Other income		
Dividends and interest	342,000	183,000
Total income	$ 6,220,000	$ 5,220,000
Less: Interest on bonds	160,000	160,000
Income before provision for federal income tax	$ 6,060,000	$ 5,060,000
Provision for federal income tax	2,240,000	1,980,000
Net profit for year	$ 3,820,000	$ 3,080,000
Common shares outstanding	760,000	760,000
Net earnings per share	$ 4.92	$ 3.95

Accumulated Retained Earnings Statement

	1981	1980
Balance January 1	$13,081,600	$11,413,200
Net profit for year	3,820,000	3,080,000
Total	$16,901,600	$14,493,200
Less: Dividends paid on		
Preferred stock	81,600	81,600
Common stock	1,520,000	1,330,000
Balance December 31	$15,300,000	$13,081,600

5. *Total Income,* after tax but before interest deduction, which states the after-tax profitability of the corporation and is widely used in computing cost of capital for a business enterprise, $3,980,000.

6. *Net income* (NI) or profit for the year, which states earnings after taxes and after all fixed charges. The net profit for the year is available for (a) dividend payout to preferred stockholders, (b) dividend payout to common stockholders, and (c) retention and reinvestment in the business, $3,820,000.

7. *Net earnings per share* (EPS), which equals total earnings available for distribution to common stockholders ($3.82 million minus 6% dividend owed on 13,600 shares of $100 par value preferred stock, or $3,738,400), divided by 760,000 common shares outstanding, $4.92.

$$\$3,820,000 - 0.06(13,600)(\$100) =$$
$$\$3,738,400$$
$$\$3,738,400/760,000 =$$
$$\$4.92 \text{ per share}$$

Cost of sales and operating expenses falls into one of three categories:

1. *Cost of goods sold,* which states the amount of labor, material, and other expenses in producing the items sold, $8,940,000.
2. *Depreciation expense,* which states the amount of capital (producer's durables) consumed in producing the goods and services sold and which must be replaced or restored to its original capacity, $800,000.
3. *Selling and administrating expenses,* which includes office expenses, executives salaries, salespersons salaries, advertising and promotion expenses and the like, $8,232,000.

Operating profit, also called net operating income, $5.878 million, is the income from business operations, and is an important indicator of how efficiently the fixed assets were employed during the year.

Other income, $342,000, is from UMC's marketable securities of $1.83 million at cost as of one year ago.

Total income, $6.22 million, is the sum of operating profit from the business and income from other sources.

Interest on bonds, $160,000, (8 percent of 2 million) is itemized next on the income statement, followed by:

Income after interest, before tax	$6,060,000
Provision for federal income tax	2,240,000
Net profit for the year	3,820,000
Net earnings per share	$4.92

We turn next to statements of accumulated retained earnings.

STATEMENTS OF ACCUMULATED RETAINED EARNINGS

The bottom part of Exhibit 2 contains the accumulated retained earnings statement for UMC, and shows at the beginning of the balance, since the starting date of the business to January 1 of the current year, $13,081,600—to which is added the net profit for the year, $3,820,000, to get total accumulated retained earnings of $16,901,600.

Dividends paid to stockholders are itemized next:

Preferred stock dividend: 6 percent of $1,360,000	$ 81,600
Common stock dividend: $2.00 per share declared times 760,000 shares	1,520,000
Total dividends paid	$1,601,600

Balance, December 31 (15.3 million) equals the difference between the total available ($16,901,600) and total dividends paid. Retained earnings are an important source of finance of corporate capital assets.

We turn next to statements of sources and uses of funds.

STATEMENT OF SOURCE AND APPLICATION OF FUNDS

Exhibit 3 is a statement of source and application or use of funds for UMC. Ordinarily, *funds* imply cash; but in a broader sense, *funds* include cash equivalents and substitutes for cash, such as short-term credit, notes, and account payable and accrued liabilities to meet the short-term financing needs of the business. So *funds* in the broader sense imply net *working capital,* which is the difference between current assets and current liabilities.

Sources of funds in general include transactions which increase the amount of working capital, such as:

1. Net profit from operations.
2. Sale or consumption of noncurrent assets.
3. Long-term borrowing.
4. Issuing additional shares of capital stock.
5. Annual depreciation.

Uses of funds in general include transactions which decrease working capital, such as:

1. Declaring cash dividends.
2. Repaying long-term debt.
3. Buying noncurrent assets.
4. Repurchasing outstanding capital stock.

In the case of UMC and Exhibit 3, funds were provided by net income, $3.82 million, and current depreciation expense, $800,000. Some analysts worry that depreciation is not cash, depreciation is a bookkeeping entry. But the capital was consumed in the process of pro-

EXHIBIT 3

Statement of Source and Application of Funds

	1981	
Funds were provided by		
Net income	$3,820,000	
Depreciation	800,000	
Total		$4,620,000
Funds were used for		
Dividends on preferred stock	$ 81,600	
Dividends on common stock	1,520,000	
Plant and equipment	1,720,300	
Sundry assets	398,100	
Total		$3,720,000
Increase in Working Capital		$ 900,000

Analysis of changes in working capital—1981

Changes in current assets		
Cash	$ 100,000	
Marketable securities	1,020,000	
Accounts receivable	430,000	
Inventories	650,000	
Total		$2,200,000
Changes in current liabilities		
Accounts payable	$ 610,000	
Notes payable	690,000	
Accrued expenses payable	80,000	
Federal income tax payable	(80,000)	
Total		$1,300,000

ducing the goods and services sold; so the business pays the cash to itself to ultimately replace the consumed capital. Depreciation expense is a source of funds.

Total funds provided for UMC are $4,620,000

Uses of funds are itemized next, where all uses fall into one of four categories:

Dividends on preferred stock	$ 81,600
Dividends on common stock	1,520,000
Plant and equipment	1,720,300
Sundry assets	398,100
Total uses or application of funds	$3,720,000

Increase in working capital, $900,000, is the difference between the total funds provided, $4.62 million, and the total funds used, $3.72 million.

An *analysis of changes in working capital* for the year is included in the statement of source and application of funds, and gives further information regarding the $900,000 increase in working capital, which is explained by analyzing changes in current assets together with changes in current liabilities.

Changes in current assets total $2.2 million, itemized as follows:

1. *Cash* increased from $250,000 to $350,000, giving a net change of $100,000,
2. *Marketable securities* increased from $1.83 million to $2.85 million, giving a net change of $1.02 million,
3. *Accounts receivable* increased from $4.37

million to $4.8 million, giving a net change of $430,000,
4. *Inventories* increased from $4.95 million to $5.6 million, giving a net change of $650,000.

Changes in current liabilities total $1.3 million, itemized as follows:

1. *Accounts payable* increased from $2.3 million to $2.91 million, giving a net change of $610,000,
2. *Notes payable* increased from $730,000 to $1.42 million, giving a net change of $690,000,
3. *Accrued expenses payable* increased from $350,000 to $430,000, giving a net change of $80,000,
4. *Federal income taxes payable* decreased from $1.32 million to $1.24 million, giving a net change of ($80,000).

The difference between the changes in current assets ($2.2 million) and changes in current liabilities ($1.3 million) equals the $900,000 increase in working capital.

We turn next to understanding more regarding how to analyze financial statements.

II. ANALYZING FINANCIAL STATEMENTS

The analysis of all four statements consists primarily of calculating ratios; but other methods including the time trend of the ratio, information theory, and flow-of-funds analysis are sometimes used. We shall limit our analysis to using ratios.[1]

In general, financial analysts, investors, creditors, and others look for two kinds of information regarding business enterprises:

1. *Risk,* including financial, business, market, and country or political risks,
2. *Return,* including productivity, efficiency, and profitability of corporate capital investments.

A third factor, *growth rate,* is important too, primarily because high steady growth is usually worth more than low or no growth.

BALANCE SHEET RATIOS

Balance sheet ratios belong to one of the three following categories:

1. *Liquidity and turnover ratios,* which indicate the ability of the corporation to pay current liabilities,
2. *Capitalization,* also called *leverage,* or *debt ratios,* which is the amount of borrowing relative to other factors such as total capitalization, total assets, or total equity,
3. *Net asset ratios,* which indicate the amount of assets backing each class of outstanding securities.

Liquidity ratios are calculated to judge whether the corporation owns sufficient cash and cash-equivalents or substitutes to comfortably pay short-term obligations, and include:
1. *Current liquidity,* the ability to pay current liabilities from current assets:

Current ratio:

$$\frac{\text{Current assets}}{\text{Current liabilities}} = \frac{\$13,600,000}{\$ 6,000,000} = 2.3 \text{ to } 1$$

In total dollar amounts, the numerator in the current ratio, minus the denominator, states *net working capital,* where

Total current assets $13,600,000
Less: Total current liabilities   6,000,000
Working capital .... $ 7,600,000

2. *Quick asset* (sometimes called *acid test*) ratio:

$$\frac{\text{Quick assets}}{\text{Current liabilities}} = \frac{\$8,000,000}{\$6,000,000} = 1.33$$

Where quick assets are total current assets minus inventories, because inventories usually are less liquid than either cash, marketable securities, or accounts receivable:

Total current assets ... $13,600,000
Less: Inventories   5,600,000
Quick assets $8,000,000
Less: Total current
     liabilities   6,000,000
Net quick assets $2,000,000

3. The *cash plus marketable securities ratio* indicates the firm's ability to pay current liabilities without relying on either inventories or accounts receivable:

$$\frac{\text{Cash plus marketable securities}}{\text{Total current liabilities}} = \frac{\$3,200,000}{\$6,000,000}$$
$$= 0.53$$

Liquidity and turnover of inventories ratios indicate how close inventories approximate true liquidity through total sales, and are the three following figures:
1. *Inventory as a percent of total current assets:*

$$\frac{\text{Inventory}}{\text{Total current assets}} = \frac{\$5,600,000}{\$13,600,000}$$
$$= 41.18 \text{ percent}$$

2. *Cost of goods sold,* including depreciation and capital consumption, *to average inventory ratio:*

$$\frac{\text{Cost of goods sold}}{\text{Inventory}} = \frac{\$9,740,000}{\$5,600,000} = 1.74$$

3. *Inventory turnover ratio:*

$$\frac{\text{Net sales}}{\text{Inventory}} = \frac{\$23,850,000}{\$5,600,000} = 4.26 \text{ times}$$

Liquidity of receivables ratios indicate how close accounts receivable approximate true liquidity through total sales, and are the two following figures:

1. *Average collection period ratio,* which indicates the number of day's sales in accounts receivables:

$$\frac{\text{Receivables} \times \text{Days in year}}{\text{Annual sales}} =$$
$$\frac{\$4,800,000 \times 360}{\$23,850,000} = 72.45$$

2. *Accounts receivable turnover ratio:*

$$\frac{\text{Annual sales}}{\text{Accounts receivable}} = \frac{\$23,850,000}{\$4,800,000} = 4.97$$

Liquidity and turnover of tangible and fixed asset ratios indicate relationships between total sales and total assets, and are given by the following two figures:
1. Fixed asset turnover ratio:

$$\frac{\text{Sales}}{\text{Net fixed assets}} = \frac{\$23,850,000}{\$12,110,000} = 1.97$$

---

[1] Comparison of these ratios with those typical of the industry is very helpful. Typical values are given on p. 95. More detailed tabulations are provided by Dun & Bradstreet and Robert Morris Associates.

2. Total asset turnover ratio:

$$\frac{\text{Net sales}}{\text{Average total tangible assets}} = \frac{\$23,850,000}{\$25,800,000}$$
$$= 0.9244$$

Capitalization ratios include:

1. Debt ratio:

$$\frac{\text{Total liabilities}}{\text{Total assets}} = \frac{\$8,000,000}{\$26,000,000} = 30.77 \text{ percent}$$

2. Current liabilities as a percent of total liabilities:

$$\frac{\text{Current liabilities}}{\text{Total liabilities}} = \frac{\$6,000,000}{\$8,000,000} = 75 \text{ percent}$$

3. Debt-to-net-worth ratio:

$$\frac{\text{Total liabilities}}{\text{Net Worth}} = \frac{\$8,000,000}{\$18,000,000} = 0.4444$$

4. Long-term debt capitalization ratio:

$$\frac{\text{Long-term debt}}{\text{Total capitalization}} = \frac{\$2,000,000}{\$19,800,000}$$
$$= 10.10 \text{ percent}$$

5. Preferred stock ratio:

$$\frac{\text{Preferred stock}}{\text{Total capitalization}} = \frac{\$1,360,000}{\$19,800,000}$$
$$= 6.87 \text{ percent}$$

6. Common stock ratio:

$$\frac{\text{Common stock plus accumulated earnings}}{\text{Total capitalization}} = \frac{\$16,440,000}{\$19,800,000}$$
$$= 83.03 \text{ percent}$$

7. Summary:

Total assets	$26,000,000	
Less: Intangibles	$ 200,000	
Less: Total current liabilities	$ 6,000,000	
Total capitalization	$19,800,000	100.00%
Bonds (long-term debt)	2,000,000	10.10
Preferred stock	1,360,000	6.87
Common stock (including capital surplus and retained earnings)	16,440,000	83.03

8. Long-term debt as a percent of total liabilities:

$$\frac{\text{Long-term debt}}{\text{Total liabilities}} = \frac{\$2,000,000}{\$8,000,000} = 25.00 \text{ percent}$$

Net asset value ratios include:

1. Net asset value per $1,000 bond; $9,900 per bond.

$$\frac{\text{Net tangible assets available to meet bondholders' claims}}{\text{Number of \$1,000 bonds outstanding}} = \frac{\$19,800,000}{2,000,000}$$

where the numerator is calculated as follows:

Total assets	$26,000,000
Less: Intangibles	200,000
Total tangible assets	$25,800,000
Less: Current liabilities	6,000,000
Net tangible assets available to meet bondholders' claims	$19,800,000

2. Net asset value per share of preferred stock: $1,308.82

$$\frac{\text{Net assets backing the preferred stock}}{\text{Number of shares of preferred stock outstanding}} = \frac{\$17,800,000}{13,600}$$

where the numerator is calculated as follows:

Total assets	$26,000,000
Less: Intangibles	200,000
Total tangible assets	$25,800,000
Less: Current liabilities	6,000,000
Less: Long-term liabilities	2,000,000
Net assets backing the preferred stock	$17,800,000

3. Net book value per share of common stock: $21.63

$$\frac{\text{Net assets available for the common stock}}{\text{Total number of shares outstanding}} = \frac{\$16,440,000}{760,000} = \$21.63$$

where the numerator is calculated as follows:

Total assets	$26,000,000
Less: Intangibles	200,000
Total tangible assets	$25,800,000
Less: Current liabilities	6,000,000
Less: Long-term liabilities	2,000,000
Less preferred stock	1,360,000
Net assets available for the common stock	$16,440,000

INCOME STATEMENT RATIOS

Income statement ratios belong to one of the two following categories:

1. *Coverage,* which analyzes financial risk by relating the financial charges of a corporation to its ability to service them.

2. *Productivity* or *capital efficiency ratios,* which relate income to total sales and to investment.

Coverage ratios include:

1. Interest coverage ratio: 38.875

$$\frac{\text{Net operating income before interest and taxes}}{\text{Interest charges on bonds}} = \frac{\$6,220,000}{\$160,000} = 38.875$$

2. Preferred dividend coverage ratio: 46.81

$$\frac{\text{Income available for paying preferred dividends}}{\text{Total dividends to preferred shareholders}} = \frac{\$3,820,000}{\$81,600} = 46.81$$

3. Earnings per common share: $4.92

$$\frac{\text{Earnings available for distribution to common shareholders}}{\text{Total number of common shares outstanding}} = \frac{\$3,738,400}{760,000} = \$4.92$$

where:

Net profit for the year	$3,820,000
Less: Dividend requirements on preferred stock	81,600
Earnings available for common stock	$3,738,400

4. Primary earnings for the year: $4.94

$$\frac{\text{Earnings for the year}}{\text{Common stock plus stock equivalents}} = \frac{\$3,820,000}{773,600} = \$4.94$$

Assuming the 13,600 preferred shares had been convertible and converted, on a share-for-share basis, into common stock.

13,600 + 760,000 = 773,600 common shares after conversion

5. Fully diluted earnings per share: $4.79

$$\frac{\text{Adjusted earnings}}{\text{Adjusted shares outstanding}} = \frac{\$3,900,000}{813,600}$$
$$= \$4.79$$

where:

Earnings for the year	$3,820,000
Plus: interest on convertible bonds	$ 160,000
Less: income tax applicable to interest deduction	80,000
Adjusted earnings for the year	$3,900,000
Common shares outstanding	760,000
Preferred convertible stock equivalent common shares	13,600
Twenty common shares per $1,000 convertible bond (2,000) outstanding	40,000
Adjusted shares outstanding	813,600

6. Summary:

Earnings per share	$4.92
Primary earnings	4.94
Fully diluted earnings ...	4.79

7. Price-earnings ratio: Approximately 15 times

$$\frac{\text{Market price of stock}}{\text{Earnings per share}} = \frac{\$72.25}{\$4.92} = 14.69$$

Productivity or capital efficiency ratios include:

1. Operating margin of profit: 24.65%.

$$\frac{\text{Operating profit}}{\text{Sales}} = \frac{\$5,878,000}{\$23,850,000} = 24.65\%$$

Previous year:

$$= \frac{\$5,037,000}{\$19,810,000} = 25.43\%$$

2. Operating cost ratio: 75.35%.

	Amount	Ratio
Net sales	$23,850,000	100.00%
Operating costs	17,972,000	75.35
Operating profit	$ 5,878,000	24.65%

3. Net profit ratio: 16.02%.

$$\frac{\text{Net profit for the year}}{\text{Net sales}} = \frac{\$3,820,000}{\$23,850,000} = 16.02\%$$

Previous year: 15.55%

$$= \frac{\$3,080,000}{\$19,810,000} = 15.55\%$$

RATIOS FROM STATEMENTS OF ACCUMULATED RETAINED EARNINGS

Retained earnings statements ratios belong to one of the two following categories:

1. Dividend payout ratio.
2. Earnings retention ratio.

The dividend payout ratio for UMC is: 40.66%.

$$\frac{\text{Dividends paid to common stockholders}}{\text{Income available for common stockholders}} = \frac{\$1,520,000}{\$3,738,400} = 40.66\%$$

where:

Net profit for the year	$3,820,000
Dividends on preferred stock	81,600
Earnings available for common ...	$3,738,400

The earnings retention ratio for UMC is: 59.34%.

$$\frac{\text{Earnings retained}}{\text{Earnings available for payout}} = \frac{\$2,218,400}{\$3,738,400} = 59.34\%$$

where:

Net profit for the year	$3,820,000
Less: Dividends paid on preferred stock	$ 81,600
Less: Dividends paid on common stock	1,520,000
Earnings retained	$2,218,400

Summary:

Dividend payout ratio	40.66%
Earnings retention ratio ...	59.34
Earnings available	100.00%

Dividends per share: $2.00.

$$\frac{\text{Total dividends paid to common shareholders}}{\text{Number of common shares outstanding}} = \frac{\$1,520,000}{760,000} = \$2.00$$

Balance December 31, $15,300,000.

RATIOS FROM STATEMENTS OF SOURCE AND APPLICATION OF FUNDS

Since an analysis was stated directly on the statement of source and use of funds in Exhibit 3, that part of the analysis is completed; however we still need to calculate profitability ratios which belong to one of the two following categories:

1. Return on assets.
2. Return on equity.

Return on assets ratios include:
  Return on total assets: 27.67%.

$$\frac{\text{Total income}}{\text{Last year's total assets}} = \frac{\$6,220,000}{\$22,481,600}$$
$$= 27.67\%$$

After tax return on total assets: 17.70%.

$$\frac{\text{Total income after tax but before interest}}{\text{Last year's total assets}} = \frac{\$3,980,000}{\$22,481,600}$$
$$= 17.70\%$$

where:

Total income	$6,220,000
Less: Provision for total taxes ..	2,240,000
After tax total income	$3,980,000

Return on equity ratio: 25.92%.

$$\frac{\text{Income available for distribution to common stockholders}}{\text{Last year's total equity of common stockholders}} = \frac{\$3,738,400}{\$14,421,600}$$
$$= 25.92\%$$

where:

Last year's total stockholder equity	$15,781,600
Less: Preferred stock value ...	1,360,000
Last year's common stock equity	$14,421,600

We turn next to further discussion of notes and supplemental information.

III. NOTES AND SUPPLEMENTAL INFORMATION

As explained in the introduction, financial statements in corporate annual reports usually are accompanied by:

- A *report of independent accountants and auditors* certifying the statements conform to generally accepted accounting principles and that generally accepted auditing standards and procedures were used.
- *Notes* which further explain details and disclose relevant information regarding line items on all four statements.
- *Segment information,* which summarizes selected items by business, industry, and geographic segment.
- A *restatement* of almost everything in current (in contrast with the traditional historical original purchase) prices, and to account for the effects of inflation on items reported in the standard statements.
- *Long-term record* summarizing selected items over a five- or ten-year time span.

REPORT OF INDEPENDENT ACCOUNTANTS

A typical report of independent accountants is addressed to the stockholders and board of directors of the corporation and will read as follows:

In our opinion, the accompanying consolidated financial statements, appearing on pages — through —, present fairly the financial position of Universal Manufacturing Corporation and its subsidiary companies at December 31, 1981 and 1980, and the results of their operations and changes in financial position for the years then ended, in conformity with generally accepted accounting principles consistently applied. Also, in our opinion, the five-year comparative consolidated summary of operations presents fairly the financial information included therein. Our examinations of these statements were made in accordance with generally accepted auditing standards and accordingly included such tests of the accounting records and such other auditing procedures as we considered necessary in the circumstances.

The report will be signed with the name and address of the accounting firm and dated.

NOTES TO FINANCIAL STATEMENTS

Notes disclose additional information regarding entries in all four primary statements, and usually are considered an integral part of the statements, included in and covered by the auditor's certification. Some corporations include the next three items to be discussed, segment information, effects of inflation, and long-term comparative summary of operations, in the notes. If included in some place other than the notes, then look for whether the statement was excluded from the auditor's audit.

EXHIBIT 4
SEGMENT REPORTING AND FOREIGN OPERATIONS

| | Industry Segments | | | Geographic Segments | | | | |
| | | | | | Foreign | | | |
	Segment No. 1	Segment No. 2	Consolidated	Domestic	OECD	Other	Eliminations	Consolidated
1981								
Sales, unaffiliated customers	$20,044,000	$3,806,000	$23,850,000	$12,647,000	$ 9,029,000	$2,175,000		$23,850,000
Sales, intersegment				2,171,000	346,000	21,000	($2,539,000)	
Total sales	$20,044,000	$3,806,000	$23,850,000	$14,818,000	$ 9,375,000	$2,196,000	($2,539,000)	$23,850,000
Pretax operating income	5,435,000	443,000	5,878,000	3,690,000	1,820,000	211,000	157,000	5,878,000
Identifiable assets at December 31	21,700,000	4,300,000	26,000,000	16,549,000	10,168,000	2,353,000	(3,070,000)	26,000,000
Depreciation expense	666,000	134,000	800,000					
Capital spending	1,884,300	234,100	2,118,400					
1980								
Sales, unaffiliated customers	$16,629,000	$3,181,000	$19,810,000	$10,519,000	$ 7,511,000	$1,780,000		$19,810,000
Sales, intersegment				2,614,000	246,000	14,000	($2,878,000)	
Total sales	$16,629,000	$3,181,000	$19,810,000	$13,133,000	$ 7,757,000	$1,794,000	($2,878,000)	$19,810,000
Pretax operating income	4,627,000	410,000	5,037,000	3,512,000	1,449,000	126,000	(50,000)	5,037,000
Identifiable assets at December 31	19,027,000	3,473,000	22,500,000	14,728,000	8,660,000	2,005,000	(2,893,000)	22,500,000
Depreciation expense	611,000	127,000	738,000					
Capital spending	1,751,000	190,000						
1979								
Sales, unaffiliated customers	$14,461,000	$2,779,000	$17,240,000	$ 9,504,000	$ 6,152,000	$1,584,000		$17,240,000
Sales, intersegment				2,677,000	155,000	3,000	($2,835,000)	
Total sales	$14,461,000	$2,779,000	$17,240,000	$12,181,000	$ 6,307,000	$1,587,000	($2,835,000)	$17,240,000
Pretax operating income	4,163,000	378,000	4,541,000	3,552,000	1,234,000	119,000	(364,000)	4,541,000
Identifiable assets at December 31	16,614,000	3,341,000	19,955,000	13,726,000	7,818,000	1,590,000	(3,179,000)	19,955,000
Depreciation expense	551,000	102,000	653,000					
Capital spending	1,969,000	238,000	2,207,000					

SEGMENT INFORMATION

Notes disclosing geographic area and industry segment information usually summarize selected items such as net sales, operating income, total assets, depreciation and amortization, and capital expenditures for industry segments (business segments or product groups) and foreign operations.

Exhibit 4 shows the segment information for UMC's two segments.

As you can see from Exhibit 4, industry segment number one, Human and Animal Health Products, accounts for 84 percent ($20,044,000 divided by $23,850,000) of total sales, and 92 percent ($5,435,000 divided by $5,878,000) of UMC's operating income; all supported by 83.46 percent ($21,700,000 divided by $26,000,000) of total assets. 11 percent ($234,100 divided by $2,118,400) of total capital expenditures were made in industry segment number two, Environmental Health Products and Services for the treatment of water and air pollution.

Exhibit 4 also shows, based on the following ratios, that UMC's business is roughly 60 percent domestic United States; 40 percent nondomestic:

Net Sales:

$$\frac{\text{United States}}{\text{Total company}} = \frac{\$14,818,000}{\$23,850,000} = 62.13\%$$

Operating income:

$$\frac{\text{United States}}{\text{Total company}} = \frac{\$3,690,000}{\$5,037,000} = 62.78\%$$

Total assets:

$$\frac{\text{United States}}{\text{Total company}} = \frac{\$16,549,000}{\$26,000,000} = 63.65\%$$

SUPPLEMENTAL INFORMATION ON INFLATION ACCOUNTING

Pursuant to Financial Accounting Standards Board (FASB) *Statement of Financial Accounting Standards No. 33*, public enterprises that have either (1) inventories and property, plant, and equipment (before deducting accumulated depreciation) amounting to more than $125 million or (2) total assets amounting to more than $1 billion (after deducting accumulated depreciation) are required to report supplementary information in addition to the primary financial statements. FASB *Standards No. 33* are:

For fiscal years ended on or after December 25, 1979, enterprises are required to report:

a. Income from continuing operations adjusted for the effects of general inflation.
b. The purchasing power gain or loss on net monetary items.

For fiscal years ended on or after December 25, 1979, enterprises are also required to report:

a. Income from continuing operations on a current cost basis.
b. The current cost amounts of inventory and property, plant, and equipment at the end of the fiscal year.
c. Increases or decreases in current cost amounts of inventory and property, plant, and equipment, net of inflation.

Enterprises are required to present a five-year summary of selected financial data, including information on income, sales and other operating revenues, net assets, dividends per common share, and market price per share. In the computation of net assets, only inventory and property, plant, and equipment need be adjusted for the effects of changing prices.

UMC, because of its "small company" asset size, would be exempt from FASB *No. 33*'s reporting requirement. However, exhibit 5 restates UMC's statement of income from continuing operations, restated for changing prices, for the year ending December 31, 1981; and UMC's five-year comparison of selected data adjusted for changing prices.

TEN-YEAR FINANCIAL SUMMARY

Long-term performance of UMC is summarized and reported on the ten-year financial summary statement, Exhibit 6.

The long-term view is used for detecting trends and changes in trends in important factors such as net sales, total assets, net operating income, earnings per share, and dividends per share. On balance, the trends for UMC look pretty good: upward.

EXHIBIT 5

SCHEDULE OF INCOME FROM CONTINUING OPERATIONS
AND OTHER CHANGES IN SHAREHOLDERS' EQUITY
ADJUSTED FOR EFFECTS OF CHANGING PRICES
For the Year Ended December 31, 1981

	As Reported (historical cost)	Adjusted for General Inflation (constant 1981 $)	Adjusted for Specific (current) Costs
Income from continuing operations			
Net sales	$23,850,000		
Other income	342,000		
Total revenue from continuing operations	$24,192,000	$24,192,000	$24,192,000
Costs and other deductions			
Depreciation expenses	800,000	1,076,000	1,115,000
Other costs and expenses	17,172,000	17,699,000	17,273,000
Interest expense	160,000	160,000	160,000
Federal and foreign income taxes	2,240,000	2,240,000	2,240,000
Total costs and other deductions	$20,372,000	$21,175,000	$20,788,000
Net income from continuing operations	$ 3,820,000	$ 3,017,000	$ 3,404,000
Purchasing power gain on net monetary liabilities (Net amounts owed)		1,000	1,000
Increase in current cost of inventories and property, plant and equipment during 1981			1,911,000
Less: effect of increase in general price level during 1981			2,788,000
Excess of increase in specific prices over increase in the general price level			($ 877,000)
Net income	$ 3,820,000		
Adjusted net income		$ 3,018,000	
Net change in shareholders' equity from above	$ 3,820,000	$ 3,018,000	$ 2,528,000

Summarized Balance Sheet
Adjusted for Changing Prices
At December 31, 1981

	As reported	Adjusted for General Inflation (constant 1981 $)	Adjusted for Specific (current) Costs
Assets			
Inventories	$ 5,600,000	$ 6,175,000	$ 5,670,000
Property, plant and equipment	12,110,000	13,354,000	16,327,000
All other assets	8,290,000	9,141,000	7,506,000
Total assets	$26,000,000	$28,670,000	$29,503,000
Total liabilities	8,000,000	7,600,000	7,600,000
Shareholders' equity	$18,000,000	$21,070,000	$21,903,000

EXHIBIT 5 *(concluded)*

Supplementary financial data
Five-Year Comparison of Selected Data
Adjusted for Changing Prices

	Years Ended December 31				
	1977	**1978**	**1979**	**1980**	**1981**
Sales					
As reported	$14,020,000	$15,610,000	17,240,000	$19,810,000	$23,850,000
1981 constant dollars	19,543,000	20,211,000	20,063,000	20,970,000	23,850,000
Net Income					
As reported					$ 3,820,000
1981 constant dollars					3,017,000
Current costs					3,404,000
Earnings per share					
As reported					$4.92
1981 constant dollars					3.86
Current costs					4.37
Common stock dividends declared per share					
As reported	$1.40	$1.43	$1.55	$1.75	$2.00
1981 constant dollars	1.95	1.85	1.80	1.85	2.00
Net assets at year-end					
As reported					$18,000,000
1981 constant dollars					21,070,000
Current costs					21,903,000
Purchasing power gain on net monetary liabilities					1,000
Market price per common share at year-end					
Actual	$69.25	68.13	$55.50	$67.63	$72.25
1981 constant dollars	90.50	84.95	64.80	72.45	68.50
Average consumer price index*	181.5	195.4	217.4	239.0	253.0

* Hypothetical, for illustrative purposes only.

EXHIBIT 6
TEN-YEAR FINANCIAL SUMMARY

	1981	1980	1979	1978	1977	1976	1975	1974	1973	1972
Net sales	$23,850,000	$19,810,000	$17,240,000	$15,610,000	$14,020,000	$12,604,000	$11,040,000	$9,426,000	$8,324,000	$7,611,000
Total income before tax	6,060,000	5,060,000	4,535,000	4,164,000	3,783,000	3,619,000	3,195,000	2,747,000	2,521,000	2,286,000
Net profit for the year	3,820,000	3,080,000	2,775,000	2,555,000	2,288,000	2,105,000	1,827,000	1,512,000	1,314,000	1,179,000
Earnings per share	4.92	3.95	3.56	3.28	2.94	2.71	2.36	1.95	1.70	1.53
Dividends per share	2.00	1.75	1.55	1.43	1.40	1.40	1.24	1.12	1.10	1.03
Net working capital	7,600,000	6,700,000	6,300,000	5,500,000	5,023,000	3,596,000	3,424,000	2,964,000	2,604,000	2,261,000
Total assets	26,000,000	22,481,600	19,934,000	17,594,000	15,390,000	12,433,000	9,890,000	8,348,000	7,365,000	6,643,000
Net plant and equipment	12,110,000	10,820,000	9,918,000	8,747,000	6,743,000	4,740,000	3,635,000	3,150,000	2,830,000	2,479,000
Long term debt	2,000,000	2,000,000	2,000,000	2,000,000	2,000,000	2,000,000	2,000,000	1,000,000	1,000,000	1,000,000
Preferred stock	1,360,000	1,360,000	1,360,000	1,360,000	1,360,000	1,360,000	1,360,000	1,360,000	1,360,000	1,360,000
Common stock and surplus	1,340,000	1,340,000	1,340,000	1,340,000	1,340,000	1,340,000	1,340,000	1,340,000	1,340,000	1,340,000
Book value per share	21.63									

FINANCIAL STATEMENT RATIOS BY INDUSTRY

Many quantitative indicators are used to assess the financial strength of an enterprise and the success of its operations. The simplest is to assemble related financial items, such as sales and profits, and express the relationship in the form of a ratio. Using these ratios, various aspects of company operations may be compared with the performance of other companies or groups of companies of similar size or in a similar line of business.

The Quarterly Financial Report's (QFR) ratio formatted income statement and balance sheet tables are expressed as a percent of net sales and total assets, respectively. The operating and financial characteristics of the respective industries and asset size groups are thus reduced to a common denominator to facilitate analysis.

The ratio tables include the following additional basic operating ratios:

1. *Annual rate of profit on stockholders' equity at end of the period* is a ratio obtained by dividing income for the quarter before or after domestic taxes [including branch income (loss) and equity in the earnings of nonconsolidated subsidiaries net of foreign taxes] by stockholders' equity at the end of the quarter; all multiplied by four to put the ratio on annual basis.

2. *Current assets to current liabilities* is a ratio obtained by dividing total current assets by total current liabilities. It is expressed as the number of times total current assets cover total current liabilities.

3. *Total cash, U.S. government and other securities to total current liabilities* is a ratio obtained by dividing total cash, U.S. government and other securities by total current liabilities. It is expressed as the number of times (usually less than one) that such assets cover total current liabilities.

4. *Total stockholders' equity to debt* is a ratio obtained by dividing total stockholders' equity by the total of short-term loans, current installments on long-term debt, and long-term debt due in more than one year. It is expressed as the number of times total stockholders' equity covers the total debt as defined above.

5. *Annual rate of profit on total assets* is a ratio obtained by dividing income, as defined in deriving the rate of profit on stockholders' equity, both before and after taxes, by total assets at the end of the quarter. The result is

Source: Quarterly Financial Report, Federal Trade Commission. The exhibits in this section are from the same FTC publication.

multiplied by four to put the ratio on an annual basis.

DESCRIPTION OF THE SAMPLE

The sample on which the QFR estimates for mining and wholesale and retail trade are based is a composite sample selected from two mutually exclusive sampling frames. Prior to the third quarter 1977, the sample drawn for manufacturing estimates was similarly based. The frame from which the major portion of the sample continues to be selected consists of the Internal Revenue Service file of those corporate entities which are required to file Form 1120 or 1120–S and which also have as their principal industrial activity manufacturing, mining, or wholesale or retail trade. The IRS file is sampled once each year. At the time the sample is selected, the file does not contain those corporate entities whose first income tax return has not been processed. In addition, several months elapse between the selection of this sample and its introduction into the QFR program. To keep the mining and wholesale and retail trade QFR sample as up to date as possible, a separate sample is drawn each calendar quarter from a frame comprising applications for a Federal Social Security Employer's Identification Number filed with the Social Security Administration (SSA) during the previous quarter by new corporations. In processing the composite list of sample companies, a screening technique is used to insure that corporations drawn from the SSA frame could not have been drawn from the IRS frame.

In sampling from the IRS frame, stratification by industry and size is employed, but in sampling from the SSA frame, stratification is by size alone. The measure of size used in the IRS frame is total assets, while the measure of size used in the SSA frame is number of employees. Beginning with the third quarter 1977, the stratum comprised of manufacturing firms with assets of less than $250,000 is estimated by multivariant techniques. The sampling fractions applied to the other various industry-size strata vary according to both industry and size. They range from approximately one out of 350 to one out of one. Nearly all corporations with assets greater than $10 million that fall into the industries covered are included in the sample. Thus, "large" corporations are permanent sample members, with a one out of one sampling fraction.

In those industry-size strata for which the sampling fraction is less than one out of one, a replacement scheme is utilized which provides that one eighth of the sample is replaced each quarter. Corporations removed are those that have been in the reporting group longest (usually eight quarters). Therefore, samples of small companies for adjacent quarters are seven-eighths identical; for quarters ending six

EXHIBIT 1: INCOME STATEMENT FOR CORPORATIONS IN ALL MANUFAC-
TURING, FOOD, TOBACCO, TEXTILE MILL PRODUCTS (ESIC industries 20, 21, 22)

	All Manufacturing*				
	1Q 1979	2Q 1979	3Q 1979	4Q 1979	1Q 1980
Income statement in ratio format	(percent of net sales)				
Net sales, receipts, operating revenues	100.0	100.0	100.0	100.0	100.0
Deduct: Depreciation, depletion, and amortization of property, plant, and equipment	2.9	2.8	2.9	2.8	3.0
Deduct: All other operating costs and expenses (net of purchase discounts)	89.1	88.6	89.6	90.2	89.7
Income (or loss) from operations	8.0	8.6	7.5	6.9	7.4
Nonoperating income (expense)	−0.1	−0.2	−0.2	−0.3	−0.4
Income (or loss) before income taxes	7.8	8.5	7.3	6.6	7.0
Net income (loss) of foreign branches and equity in earnings (losses) of nonconsolidated subsidiaries (net of foreign taxes) ..	1.2	1.3	1.4	1.4	1.5
Deduct: Current and deferred domestic income taxes	3.4	3.6	3.1	2.7	3.2
Income (or loss) after income taxes	5.6	6.1	5.7	5.3	5.3
Operating ratios					
Annual rate of profit on stockholders' equity at end of period:	(percent)				
Before income taxes	25.36	28.79	25.10	23.61	24.61
After taxes	15.74	18.09	16.25	15.70	15.44
Annual rate of profit on total assets:					
Before income taxes	12.98	14.72	12.71	11.85	12.27
After taxes	8.05	9.25	8.23	7.88	7.70

* During the first quarter of 1980 a considerable number of companies were reclassified by industry. To provide comparability, the four quarters of 1979 have been restated to reflect these reclassifications.

months apart they are six-eighths identical; for quarters ending nine months apart they are five-eighths identical; etc.

PRECISION OF THE ESTIMATES

More than 3,000 aggregates or ratios are estimated each quarter. Each estimate has its own standard deviation, which indicates the difference that can be expected due to sampling between the estimate and a comparable total based on a complete canvass. An estimate will differ from a comparable total based on a complete canvass by less than one standard deviation approximately 68 times out of 100, by less than two standard deviations approximately 95 times out of 100, and by less than two and one-half standard deviations approximately 99 times out of 100. The sample is designed so that one standard deviation of the estimate for the item, "Income before income taxes and extraordinary items," for all manufacturing corporations amounts to approximately one half of 1 percent of that estimated aggregate. For most of the manufacturing industry groups, one standard deviation of the estimate for the same item amounts to less than 5 percent of the estimated aggregate, while the comparable figure for mining is approximately 5 percent and for re-

tail trade and wholesale trade approximately 9 percent each.

Each report form received is reviewed by FTC accountants for adherence to generally accepted accounting principles and QFR guidelines. Should QFR requirements dictate a classification of data different from the reporting corporation's accounting, the accountant is responsible for reclassifying or adjusting the data item. If complex problems arise, reporting company officials are contacted to discuss proposed adjustments. In the review, the retained earnings reported in a company's balance sheet must be the same as the end-of-quarter retained earnings reported in the income statement, the retained earnings at the quarter's end must reconcile with those at the beginning of the quarter, and the retained earnings at the beginning of the quarter must be the same as at the end of the preceding quarter. Since corporations are added to and deleted from the sample each quarter, and since corporations are reclassified periodically by industry and size, *aggregated* estimates of retained earnings at the beginning of a quarter are seldom identical to the estimates of retained earnings at the end of the preceding quarter.

Food and Kindred Products*					Tobacco Manufacturers*					Textile Mill Products*				
1Q 1979	2Q 1979	3Q 1979	4Q 1979	1Q 1980	1Q 1979	2Q 1979	3Q 1979	4Q 1979	1Q 1980	1Q 1979	2Q 1979	3Q 1979	4Q 1979	1Q 1980
(percent of net sales)					(percent of net sales)					(percent of net sales)				
100.0	100.0	100.0	100.0	100.0	100.0	100.0	100.0	100.0	100.0	100.0	100.0	100.0	100.0	100.0
1.8	1.7	1.8	1.7	1.8	2.4	2.5	2.4	2.7	2.2	2.7	2.5	2.5	2.3	2.5
93.5	93.0	92.8	93.4	93.4	80.0	79.6	78.8	80.2	79.8	91.7	91.1	91.1	91.3	91.7
4.8	5.3	5.4	4.9	4.8	17.6	17.9	18.8	17.2	18.0	5.7	6.4	6.4	6.4	5.8
−0.5	−0.4	−0.5	−0.8	−0.7	−1.5	−3.3	−3.3	−4.8	−4.1	−0.9	−0.9	−0.4	−0.9	−0.8
4.3	4.9	4.9	4.1	4.2	16.1	14.6	15.4	12.4	13.8	4.8	5.6	6.0	5.6	5.0
0.4	0.6	1.0	0.5	0.5	2.1	3.1	4.9	4.7	6.1	0.0	0.1	0.1	0.0	0.1
1.9	2.0	2.0	1.5	1.7	7.3	6.9	7.2	6.4	6.8	2.3	2.4	2.4	2.4	2.2
2.8	3.4	3.9	3.1	3.0	11.0	10.9	13.1	10.8	13.1	2.6	3.3	3.7	3.2	2.8
(percent)					(percent)					(percent)				
20.30	24.72	26.11	20.87	20.25	30.71	29.98	33.58	29.30	32.30	16.81	21.87	21.95	21.90	19.59
12.19	15.59	17.24	13.81	12.80	18.52	18.40	21.63	18.43	21.24	9.02	12.83	13.40	12.52	10.92
9.85	12.11	12.73	10.10	9.83	15.30	15.66	16.90	14.26	16.30	8.82	11.32	11.42	11.28	10.02
5.92	7.64	8.40	6.68	6.21	9.23	9.61	10.89	8.97	10.72	4.73	6.64	6.97	6.45	5.58

EXHIBIT 2: BALANCE SHEET IN RATIO FORMAT FOR CORPORATIONS IN ALL MANUFACTURING, FOOD, TOBACCO, TEXTILE MILL PRODUCTS (ESIC industries 20, 21, 22).

ITEMS STATED AS A PERCENT OF TOTAL ASSETS

	All Manufacturing*				
	1Q 1979	2Q 1979	3Q 1979	4Q 1979	1Q 1980
Assets					
Cash on hand and in banks	3.7	3.4	3.3	3.6	3.2
U.S. government and other securities	2.4	2.5	2.1	2.1	2.0
Receivables	17.6	17.8	18.2	17.3	17.6
Inventories	20.7	20.8	20.7	20.6	21.0
Current assets not elsewhere specified	2.7	2.7	2.7	2.6	2.7
Total current assets	47.1	47.1	46.9	46.2	46.5
Land and depreciable fixed assets	63.6	63.6	62.9	63.1	62.8
Deduct: Accumulated depreciation, depletion, and amortization ..	28.7	28.6	28.1	27.5	27.4
Net property, plant, and equipment	35.0	35.0	34.8	35.5	35.3
Noncurrent assets not elsewhere specified, including investment in nonconsolidated entities, other long-term investments, intangibles, etc.	17.9	17.9	18.3	18.3	18.2
Total assets	100.0	100.0	100.0	100.0	100.0
Liabilities and stockholders' equity					
Short-term loans and current installments	4.7	4.9	5.3	5.0	5.4
Trade accounts and trade notes payable	9.3	9.4	9.6	10.1	9.8
Income taxes accrued, prior and current years, net of payments ...					
Federal	2.4	2.0	2.1	2.1	2.4
Other	0.4	0.4	0.4	0.4	0.4
Other current liabilities	9.6	9.6	9.6	9.5	9.7
Total current liabilities	26.3	26.4	27.0	27.0	27.6
Long-term debt due in more than one year					
Loans from banks	3.5	3.5	3.7	3.9	4.0
Other long-term debt	12.9	12.8	12.6	12.5	12.2
Noncurrent liabilities not elsewhere specified, including deferred income taxes	5.9	6.0	6.0	6.1	6.1
Minority stockholders' interest in consolidated domestic corporations	0.2	0.2	0.2	0.2	0.2
Total liabilities	48.8	48.9	49.4	49.8	50.1
Capital stock and other capital	13.9	13.5	13.2	13.0	12.8
Retained earnings	38.2	38.6	38.4	38.2	38.0
Deduct: Treasury stock, at cost	1.0	1.0	1.0	1.0	1.0
Stockholders' equity	51.2	51.1	50.6	50.2	49.9
Total liabilities and stockholders' equity	100.0	100.0	100.0	100.0	100.0
Balance sheet ratios		(times)			
Current assets to current liabilities	1.79	1.79	1.74	1.71	1.68
Total cash, U.S. government and other securities to total current liabilities	0.23	0.22	0.20	0.21	0.19
Total stockholders' equity to debt	2.42	2.41	2.36	2.34	2.31

* During the first quarter of 1980 a considerable number of companies were reclassified by industry. To provide comparability, the four quarters of 1979 have been restated to reflect these reclassifications.

Food and Kindred Products*					Tobacco Manufactures*					Textile Mill Products*				
1Q 1979	2Q 1979	3Q 1979	4Q 1979	1Q 1980	1Q 1979	2Q 1979	3Q 1979	4Q 1979	1Q 1980	1Q 1979	2Q 1979	3Q 1979	4Q 1979	1Q 1980
2.9	2.8	2.9	3.2	2.8	1.8	1.5	0.4	0.5	0.9	3.2	3.0	3.5	4.0	3.3
1.8	2.2	2.0	1.5	1.5	0.7	0.5	0.1	0.1	0.4	2.4	2.2	2.4	2.9	2.1
16.3	16.3	16.4	16.4	16.1	10.2	8.4	11.6	9.9	8.7	24.7	25.9	27.1	26.1	26.4
23.8	23.1	23.3	24.5	24.1	29.6	28.1	28.6	27.7	27.8	29.3	29.5	27.5	27.1	28.2
2.5	2.6	2.5	2.5	2.6	0.7	0.7	0.8	1.4	1.6	2.2	2.2	2.3	2.1	2.1
47.4	46.9	47.2	48.0	47.2	43.0	39.2	41.6	39.7	39.4	61.8	62.7	62.8	62.3	62.0
60.5	60.7	60.0	59.3	59.9	31.3	33.1	31.3	30.9	32.0	74.6	73.4	73.4	73.3	74.3
25.0	25.0	24.6	24.4	24.6	9.1	9.6	9.2	9.1	9.6	42.1	41.5	41.0	40.8	41.8
35.5	35.7	35.4	35.0	35.3	22.1	23.5	22.1	21.8	22.4	32.6	31.9	32.3	32.5	32.5
17.1	17.4	17.4	17.0	17.5	34.9	37.3	36.3	38.5	38.1	5.6	5.4	4.9	5.3	5.5
100.0	100.0	100.0	100.0	100.0	100.0	100.0	100.0	100.0	100.0	100.0	100.0	100.0	100.0	100.0
8.4	7.9	7.8	8.9	9.3	5.4	4.0	4.7	4.0	5.1	5.9	7.0	6.9	5.6	6.5
10.5	10.6	10.9	11.7	10.6	3.9	3.9	4.3	3.8	3.1	12.2	13.5	12.9	13.2	13.4
1.5	1.4	1.5	1.4	1.4	2.6	1.4	1.5	1.3	2.2	1.6	0.9	1.1	1.2	1.3
0.4	0.4	0.4	0.4	0.4	0.6	0.6	0.6	0.6	0.7	0.2	0.2	0.3	0.2	0.2
6.5	6.6	6.8	6.3	6.7	9.3	8.1	11.3	11.8	9.8	6.2	6.3	6.2	7.1	6.4
27.4	26.9	27.5	28.6	28.4	21.8	17.9	22.4	21.5	21.0	26.1	27.9	27.3	27.3	27.8
5.0	4.9	4.7	4.3	4.5	11.2	12.9	12.6	12.1	13.2	5.0	4.6	4.8	4.9	5.0
13.7	13.9	13.6	13.9	13.6	12.9	12.6	10.7	13.3	11.2	12.9	12.5	12.5	12.6	12.7
5.0	5.0	5.1	4.6	4.8	4.1	4.2	3.9	4.4	4.2	3.3	3.1	3.1	3.4	3.2
0.3	0.3	0.3	0.3	0.2	0.1	0.1	0.1	0.0	0.0	0.2	0.2	0.2	0.2	0.2
51.5	51.0	51.3	51.6	51.5	50.2	47.8	49.7	51.3	49.5	47.5	48.2	48.0	48.5	48.9
14.1	13.9	13.5	13.2	13.1	12.9	12.9	12.0	11.3	11.3	13.6	12.8	13.0	13.3	13.4
35.2	36.0	36.1	36.2	36.3	38.5	40.9	39.9	38.9	40.8	41.0	41.2	40.9	40.0	39.7
0.8	0.9	0.9	0.9	0.9	1.5	1.6	1.5	1.5	1.6	2.1	2.2	1.9	1.8	2.0
48.5	49.0	48.7	48.4	48.5	49.8	52.2	50.3	48.7	50.5	52.5	51.8	52.0	51.5	51.1
100.0	100.0	100.0	100.0	100.0	100.0	100.0	100.0	100.0	100.0	100.0	100.0	100.0	100.0	100.0
		(times)					(times)					(times)		
1.73	1.74	1.71	1.68	1.66	1.97	2.19	1.86	1.84	1.88	2.36	2.25	2.30	2.28	2.23
0.17	0.19	0.18	0.16	0.15	0.11	0.11	0.02	0.03	0.06	0.22	0.19	0.22	0.25	0.19
1.79	1.83	1.86	1.80	1.78	1.69	1.77	1.80	1.65	1.71	2.20	2.16	2.15	2.22	2.11

EXHIBIT 3: INCOME STATEMENT FOR CORPORATIONS IN PRINTING AND PUBLISHING, CHEMICALS, DRUGS (ESIC industries 27, 28, 28.1, 28.3)

	Printing and Publishing*				
	1Q 1979	2Q 1979	3Q 1979	4Q 1979	1Q 1980
Income statement in ratio format	(percent of net sales)				
Net sales, receipts, and operating revenues	100.0	100.0	100.0	100.0	100.0
Deduct: Depreciation, depletion, and amortization of property, plant, and equipment	2.6	2.5	2.6	2.4	2.7
Deduct: All other operating costs and expenses (net of purchase discounts)	87.7	86.2	85.9	87.4	88.4
Income (or loss) from operations	9.7	11.3	11.6	10.2	9.0
Nonoperating income (expense)	−0.3	−0.4	−0.3	−0.5	−0.1
Income (or loss) before income taxes	9.4	10.9	11.2	9.7	8.8
Net income (loss) of foreign branches and equity in earnings (losses) of nonconsolidated subsidiaries (net of foreign taxes) ..	0.4	0.4	0.6	0.4	0.3
Deduct: Current and deferred domestic income taxes	4.1	4.8	5.0	4.6	3.9
(Income (or loss) after income taxes	5.7	6.5	6.8	5.5	5.2
Operating ratios					
Annual rate of profit on stockholders' equity at end of period:	(percent)				
Before income taxes	27.78	33.78	34.73	30.89	26.52
After taxes	16.12	19.26	20.09	16.84	14.99
Annual rate of profit on total assets:					
Before income taxes	14.38	17.51	17.76	15.54	13.34
After taxes	8.35	9.98	10.27	8.47	7.54

* During the first quarter of 1980 a considerable number of companies were reclassified by industry. To provide comparability, the four quarters of 1979 have been restated to reflect these reclassifications.

† Included in Chemicals and Allied Products.

	Chemicals and Allied Products*					Industrial Chemicals and Synthetics*†					Drugs*†				
	1Q 1979	2Q 1979	3Q 1979	4Q 1979	1Q 1980	1Q 1979	2Q 1979	3Q 1979	4Q 1979	1Q 1980	1Q 1979	2Q 1979	3Q 1979	4Q 1979	1Q 1980
	(percent of net sales)					(percent of net sales)					(percent of net sales)				
	100.0	100.0	100.0	100.0	100.0	100.0	100.0	100.0	100.0	100.0	100.0	100.0	100.0	100.0	100.0
	3.7	3.6	3.7	3.9	3.5	5.0	4.9	5.0	5.4	4.6	2.2	2.4	2.4	2.3	2.4
	85.8	86.0	86.8	88.2	86.1	84.1	84.6	86.0	87.9	85.4	84.6	85.6	87.8	88.7	85.0
	10.5	10.4	9.6	7.9	10.5	10.9	10.5	9.0	6.7	10.0	13.2	11.9	9.9	9.0	12.6
	−0.1	0.0	−1.1	−0.2	−0.4	−0.4	−0.4	−2.1	−0.2	−1.0	0.6	1.3	0.6	1.5	1.5
	10.5	10.4	8.5	7.8	10.1	10.5	10.2	6.9	6.4	9.0	13.9	13.2	10.5	10.6	14.2
	1.9	1.9	2.2	2.3	2.2	1.1	1.1	1.5	1.5	1.6	6.2	6.7	6.9	6.4	6.4
	4.5	4.2	3.5	2.9	4.3	4.2	4.0	2.5	1.8	3.8	6.5	6.0	5.1	5.1	6.5
	7.9	8.0	7.2	7.0	8.0	7.3	7.3	5.9	6.1	6.8	13.5	13.8	12.4	11.9	14.0
	(percent)					(percent)					(percent)				
	27.47	27.76	23.65	21.75	27.66	26.57	26.51	18.97	17.56	24.97	30.70	29.14	25.96	25.56	31.67
	17.54	18.20	15.94	15.31	17.99	16.78	17.15	13.33	13.57	16.05	20.75	20.22	18.41	17.93	21.64
	14.66	15.03	12.65	11.57	14.69	13.39	13.49	9.43	8.66	12.37	18.70	18.07	15.97	15.64	19.27
	9.36	9.85	8.53	8.14	9.56	8.45	8.73	6.62	6.69	7.95	12.64	12.54	11.32	10.97	13.17

EXHIBIT 4: BALANCE SHEET IN RATIO FORMAT FOR CORPORATIONS IN PRINTING AND PUBLISHING, CHEMICALS, DRUGS (ESIC industries, 27, 28, 28.1, 28.3)

ITEMS STATED AS A PERCENT OF TOTAL ASSETS

	Printing and Publishing*				
	1Q 1979	2Q 1979	3Q 1979	4Q 1979	1Q 1980
Assets					
Cash on hand and in banks	5.8	5.3	5.2	5.7	5.3
U.S. government and other securities	3.9	3.1	2.6	2.9	3.2
Receivables	20.0	20.0	21.2	20.8	19.5
Inventories	12.2	12.6	12.1	11.7	12.3
Current assets not elsewhere specified	4.4	4.6	4.5	4.3	4.7
Total current assets	46.3	45.5	45.6	45.3	45.0
Land and depreciable fixed assets	54.3	54.8	54.0	53.9	54.7
Deduct: Accumulated depreciation, depletion, and amortization ..	23.4	23.4	22.8	22.5	22.7
Net property, plant, and equipment	30.9	31.4	31.2	31.5	31.9
Noncurrent assets not elsewhere specified, including investment in nonconsolidated entities, other long-term investments, intangibles, etc.	22.9	23.1	23.2	23.2	23.1
Total assets	100.0	100.0	100.0	100.0	100.0
Liabilities and stockholders' equity					
Short-term loans and current installments	4.3	4.9	5.4	4.9	4.6
Trade accounts and trade notes payable	8.8	8.8	8.8	9.2	8.7
Income taxes accrued, prior and current years, net of payments					
Federal	2.4	1.7	1.9	2.1	2.3
Other	0.4	0.3	0.4	0.4	0.4
Other current liabilities	7.7	7.9	7.8	7.7	7.4
Total current liabilities	23.7	23.5	24.3	24.3	23.5
Long-term debt due in more than one year					
Loans from banks	6.0	6.6	6.4	7.1	7.1
Other long-term debt	10.7	10.2	10.4	10.3	10.8
Noncurrent liabilities not elsewhere specified, including deferred income taxes	7.5	7.4	7.3	7.6	8.0
Minority stockholders' interest in consolidated domestic corporations	0.4	0.4	0.4	0.4	0.4
Total liabilities	48.2	48.2	48.9	49.7	49.7
Capital stock and other capital	12.9	12.5	12.0	11.6	11.3
Retained earnings	41.1	41.5	41.3	40.9	41.2
Deduct: Treasury stock, at cost	2.2	2.2	2.2	2.2	2.2
Stockholders' equity	51.8	51.8	51.1	50.3	50.3
Total liabilities and stockholders' equity	100.0	100.0	100.0	100.0	100.0
Balance sheet ratios		(times)			
Current assets to current liabilities	1.96	1.93	1.88	1.86	1.92
Total cash, U.S. government and other securities to total current liabilities	0.41	0.36	0.32	0.35	0.36
Total stockholders' equity to debt	2.47	2.40	2.29	2.25	2.24

* During the first quarter of 1980 a considerable number of companies were reclassified by industry. To provide comparability, the four quarters of 1979 have been restated to reflect these reclassifications.

† Included in Chemicals and Allied Products.

Chemicals and Allied Products*					Industrial Chemicals and Synthetics*†					Drugs*†				
1Q 1979	2Q 1979	3Q 1979	4Q 1979	1Q 1980	1Q 1979	2Q 1979	3Q 1979	4Q 1979	1Q 1980	1Q 1979	2Q 1979	3Q 1979	4Q 1979	1Q 1980
2.8	2.5	2.7	2.8	2.4	1.8	1.7	2.0	1.9	1.5	4.7	3.7	3.7	4.3	3.9
2.0	1.8	1.6	1.5	1.2	1.8	1.6	1.5	1.3	1.0	1.1	0.9	0.6	0.2	0.3
17.2	17.1	17.3	16.0	17.3	18.0	18.2	18.0	16.8	18.3	14.5	13.7	14.3	13.6	14.2
16.6	16.8	16.5	17.1	17.6	13.7	13.9	13.7	14.5	14.9	17.6	18.5	18.1	18.3	18.0
2.9	2.7	2.9	2.9	3.0	2.5	2.3	2.7	2.7	2.9	3.7	3.5	3.3	3.4	3.5
41.4	40.9	40.9	40.3	41.5	37.8	37.8	37.9	37.2	38.6	41.6	40.3	40.0	39.7	40.0
71.1	71.4	70.5	70.0	69.1	91.5	91.3	89.0	89.2	87.3	39.6	40.2	40.3	39.9	39.7
32.2	32.4	31.9	31.3	30.8	45.1	45.0	44.0	43.4	42.4	15.3	15.5	15.5	15.3	15.2
38.8	39.0	38.5	38.7	38.2	46.5	46.2	45.1	45.8	44.9	24.2	24.6	24.8	24.5	24.6
19.7	20.1	20.5	20.9	20.3	15.8	16.0	17.0	17.0	16.5	34.2	35.1	35.2	35.7	35.5
100.0	100.0	100.0	100.0	100.0	100.0	100.0	100.0	100.0	100.0	100.0	100.0	100.0	100.0	100.0
4.3	4.2	4.0	4.2	5.0	3.7	3.7	3.5	3.3	4.8	4.9	5.1	5.4	5.4	6.0
7.1	7.2	7.1	7.7	7.7	6.7	6.8	7.1	7.9	7.9	4.7	4.5	4.2	4.7	3.9
2.3	1.8	2.0	1.8	2.2	2.2	1.6	1.7	1.5	1.9	3.1	1.9	2.0	1.9	2.8
0.4	0.3	0.3	0.4	0.4	0.3	0.2	0.2	0.3	0.3	0.4	0.3	0.3	0.4	0.4
6.3	6.4	6.9	7.0	7.0	6.4	6.8	7.4	7.3	7.2	7.3	7.5	7.9	8.2	8.1
20.4	19.8	20.3	21.0	22.1	19.3	19.1	19.9	20.3	21.8	20.4	19.2	19.6	20.6	21.2
2.6	2.7	2.8	2.7	2.5	2.2	2.2	2.4	2.4	2.2	1.3	1.8	1.3	1.5	1.2
17.7	17.4	17.3	16.9	16.5	20.6	20.4	20.5	20.1	19.3	13.3	12.9	13.1	12.6	12.6
5.6	5.7	5.8	5.9	5.4	7.1	6.9	7.0	7.4	6.6	4.1	4.0	4.4	4.1	4.2
0.3	0.3	0.3	0.3	0.3	0.4	0.4	0.5	0.4	0.5	0.0	0.0	0.0	0.0	0.0
46.6	45.9	46.5	46.8	46.9	49.6	49.1	50.3	50.7	50.5	39.1	38.0	38.5	38.8	39.2
14.3	14.2	13.9	13.7	13.9	15.3	15.2	14.8	14.5	14.9	14.1	13.9	13.8	13.7	13.5
40.0	40.9	40.6	40.4	40.2	36.2	36.9	36.1	35.9	35.7	47.4	48.9	48.5	48.3	48.1
0.9	1.0	1.0	1.0	0.9	1.2	1.2	1.2	1.2	1.0	0.6	0.7	0.8	0.8	0.8
53.4	54.1	53.5	53.2	53.1	50.4	50.9	49.7	49.3	49.5	60.9	62.0	61.5	61.2	60.8
100.0	100.0	100.0	100.0	100.0	100.0	100.0	100.0	100.0	100.0	100.0	100.0	100.0	100.0	100.0
(times)					(times)					(times)				
2.03	2.07	2.02	1.92	1.87	1.96	1.98	1.90	1.83	1.77	2.04	2.10	2.04	1.92	1.89
0.23	0.22	0.21	0.20	0.16	0.18	0.18	0.17	0.16	0.11	0.28	0.24	0.22	0.22	0.20
2.17	2.24	2.21	2.23	2.21	1.90	1.93	1.88	1.90	1.89	3.12	3.14	3.13	3.14	3.06

EXHIBIT 5: INCOME STATEMENT FOR CORPORATIONS IN PAPER, PETRO-
LEUM, COAL, RUBBER, PLASTICS (ESIC industries, 26, 29, 30 and other nondurable manufacturing products)

	Paper and Allied Products*				
	1Q 1979	2Q 1979	3Q 1979	4Q 1979	1Q 1980
Income statement in ratio format	(percent of net sales)				
Net sales, receipts, and operating revenues	100.0	100.0	100.0	100.0	100.0
Deduct: Depreciation, depletion, and amortization of property, plant, and equipment	3.4	3.5	3.4	3.4	3.4
Deduct: All other operating costs and expenses (net of purchase discounts)	88.0	87.1	88.6	89.4	89.2
Income (or loss) from operations	8.6	9.4	8.0	7.2	7.4
Nonoperating income (expense)	0.4	−0.8	2.7	−0.8	−0.5
Income (or loss) before income taxes	8.9	8.7	10.8	6.5	6.9
Net income (loss) of foreign branches and equity in earnings (losses) of nonconsolidated subsidiaries (net of foreign taxes) ..	1.0	1.2	1.2	1.0	1.0
Deduct: Current and deferred domestic income taxes	3.3	3.2	3.7	2.0	2.5
Income (or loss) after income taxes	6.7	6.6	8.2	5.4	5.4
Operating ratios					
Annual rate of profit on stockholders' equity at end of period:	(percent)				
Before income taxes	24.18	24.96	29.73	18.51	19.44
After taxes	16.30	16.82	20.49	13.40	13.25
Annual rate of profit on total assets:					
Before income taxes	12.52	12.93	15.32	9.48	9.89
After taxes	8.44	8.71	10.56	6.86	6.74

* During the first quarter of 1980 a considerable number of companies were reclassified by industry. To provide comparability, the four quarters of 1979 have been restated to reflect these reclassifications.

	Petroleum and Coal Products*					Rubber and Miscellaneous Plastics Products*					Other Nondurable Manufacturing Products				
	1Q 1979	2Q 1979	3Q 1979	4Q 1979	1Q 1980	1Q 1979	2Q 1979	3Q 1979	4Q 1979	1Q 1980	1Q 1979	2Q 1979	3Q 1979	4Q 1979	1Q 1980
	(percent of net sales)					(percent of net sales)					(percent of net sales)				
	100.0	100.0	100.0	100.0	100.0	100.0	100.0	100.0	100.0	100.0	100.0	100.0	100.0	100.0	100.0
	4.3	4.3	3.9	3.4	3.3	2.8	2.7	2.7	2.7	2.9	1.1	1.0	0.9	1.0	1.1
	87.0	86.2	86.3	88.0	86.5	90.0	91.1	92.6	93.1	92.6	93.6	93.8	92.7	93.5	94.0
	8.7	9.5	9.8	8.5	10.3	7.2	6.2	4.7	4.1	4.5	5.3	5.2	6.3	5.5	5.0
	0.5	1.8	0.6	2.1	0.5	−0.9	−0.6	−0.9	−2.0	−1.3	−0.4	−0.5	−0.5	−0.7	−0.7
	9.2	11.3	10.4	10.6	10.7	6.4	5.7	3.8	2.2	3.2	4.9	4.7	5.8	4.9	4.3
	2.6	3.3	3.0	2.7	3.3	0.4	0.4	0.4	0.6	0.7	0.2	0.2	0.2	0.2	0.2
	3.9	5.0	4.4	3.8	5.0	2.6	2.2	1.5	1.1	1.5	2.2	2.2	2.4	2.3	2.2
	7.8	9.6	9.0	9.5	9.0	4.2	3.8	2.7	1.7	2.4	2.9	2.7	3.7	2.8	2.2
	(percent)					(percent)					(percent)				
	23.68	30.52	31.35	34.40	37.65	22.76	21.08	13.67	9.24	12.47	22.62	22.68	31.10	25.64	20.69
	15.75	20.13	21.09	24.55	24.28	14.08	13.39	8.78	5.58	7.68	12.62	12.66	19.01	14.26	10.49
	13.48	17.18	17.24	18.31	20.13	10.58	9.94	6.45	4.34	5.75	11.07	10.80	14.48	12.36	9.78
	8.97	11.33	11.60	13.07	12.99	6.55	6.31	4.14	2.62	3.54	6.18	6.03	8.85	6.87	4.96

EXHIBIT 6: BALANCE SHEET IN RATIO FORMAT FOR CORPORATIONS IN PAPER, PETROLEUM, COAL, RUBBER, PLASTICS (ESIC industries 26, 29, 30, and other nondurable manufacturing products)

ITEMS STATED AS A PERCENT OF TOTAL ASSETS

	Paper and Allied Products*				
	1Q 1979	2Q 1979	3Q 1979	4Q 1979	1Q 1980
Assets					
Cash on hand and in banks	3.5	3.3	3.7	3.6	3.4
U.S. government and other securities	1.8	1.6	1.7	1.3	1.3
Receivables	13.9	14.0	14.1	13.5	13.6
Inventories	14.2	14.3	13.8	14.1	14.2
Current assets not elsewhere specified	2.6	2.4	2.5	2.6	2.7
Total current assets	36.0	35.7	35.8	35.1	35.2
Land and depreciable fixed assets	83.3	83.4	81.7	81.9	81.0
Deduct: Accumulated depreciation, depletion, and amortization	34.4	34.3	32.9	32.5	31.9
Net property, plant, and equipment	49.0	49.1	48.8	49.3	49.2
Noncurrent assets not elsewhere specified, including investment in nonconsolidated entities, other long-term investments, intangibles, etc.	15.1	15.2	15.3	15.6	15.6
Total assets	100.0	100.0	100.0	100.0	100.0
Liabilities and stockholders' equity					
Short-term loans and current installments	3.2	3.6	3.3	3.4	3.7
Trade accounts and trade notes payable	6.9	7.0	7.2	7.2	6.9
Income taxes accrued, prior and current years, net of payments					
Federal	1.4	1.1	1.8	1.4	1.3
Other	0.4	0.4	0.4	0.4	0.4
Other current liabilities	6.3	6.0	6.1	5.8	6.1
Total current liabilities	18.2	18.2	18.7	18.4	18.4
Long-term debt due in more than one year					
Loans from banks	4.1	4.0	4.2	4.2	4.5
Other long-term debt	19.8	19.8	19.7	20.1	20.1
Noncurrent liabilities not elsewhere specified, including deferred income taxes	5.6	5.7	5.3	5.6	5.5
Minority stockholders' interest in consolidated domestic corporations	0.5	0.5	0.5	0.5	0.6
Total liabilities	48.2	48.2	48.5	48.8	49.1
Capital stock and other capital	15.2	14.8	14.3	14.1	14.3
Retained earnings	37.3	37.6	38.0	37.8	37.3
Deduct: Treasury stock, at cost	0.7	0.6	0.7	0.7	0.7
Stockholders' equity	51.8	51.8	51.5	51.2	50.9
Total liabilities and stockholders' equity	100.0	100.0	100.0	100.0	100.0
Balance sheet ratios			(times)		
Current assets to current liabilities	1.97	1.97	1.91	1.91	1.91
Total cash, U.S. government and other securities to total current liabilities	0.29	0.27	0.29	0.27	0.25
Total stockholders' equity to debt	1.91	1.89	1.89	1.84	1.80

* During the first quarter of 1980 a considerable number of companies were reclassified by industry. To provide comparability, the four quarters of 1979 have been restated to reflect these reclassifications.

	Petroleum and Coal Products*					Rubber and Miscellaneous Plastics Products*					Other Nondurable Manufacturing Products				
	1Q 1979	2Q 1979	3Q 1979	4Q 1979	1Q 1980	1Q 1979	2Q 1979	3Q 1979	4Q 1979	1Q 1980	1Q 1979	2Q 1979	3Q 1979	4Q 1979	1Q 1980
	3.1	2.7	2.6	2.9	3.2	2.7	2.6	2.1	2.6	2.3	5.5	5.0	4.9	6.0	5.3
	2.8	3.4	2.6	2.7	2.9	1.2	0.9	1.4	1.7	1.1	1.9	1.4	1.2	2.0	1.7
	10.5	11.3	12.4	12.7	12.7	24.2	24.1	23.7	22.0	22.4	29.0	28.4	32.3	30.0	28.8
	6.6	6.9	7.3	7.4	7.7	23.1	23.0	22.8	22.2	22.9	37.8	39.8	36.6	36.3	37.3
	1.4	1.3	1.4	1.4	1.5	2.4	2.4	2.5	2.7	2.5	3.4	3.4	3.2	3.3	3.8
	24.3	25.6	26.2	27.2	28.0	53.5	53.0	52.5	51.2	51.3	77.6	78.0	78.1	77.6	76.9
	85.2	83.2	80.6	79.6	78.5	62.1	63.0	63.2	64.7	65.0	30.1	29.7	29.0	28.8	29.8
	36.1	35.3	34.0	32.0	31.6	29.9	30.2	30.7	31.2	31.3	14.8	14.7	14.0	13.9	14.2
	49.1	47.9	46.6	47.7	46.9	32.3	32.8	32.4	33.4	33.7	15.4	15.0	15.0	15.0	15.5
	26.6	26.5	27.2	25.1	25.1	14.2	14.2	15.1	15.4	15.0	7.1	7.0	6.9	7.5	7.5
	100.0	100.0	100.0	100.0	100.0	100.0	100.0	100.0	100.0	100.0	100.0	100.0	100.0	100.0	100.0
	1.2	1.5	2.0	1.8	1.9	8.1	8.1	8.8	6.9	8.2	11.0	11.9	12.8	11.2	11.2
	9.0	10.0	11.0	12.4	12.0	10.6	10.3	9.7	10.3	10.5	16.1	17.7	16.9	16.7	17.5
	2.4	2.5	2.9	3.1	3.6	2.1	1.9	1.7	1.8	1.8	1.9	1.6	1.8	1.8	2.0
	0.4	0.4	0.5	0.5	0.5	0.3	0.2	0.3	0.3	0.3	0.3	0.2	0.3	0.4	0.4
	3.8	3.6	3.6	4.1	4.2	9.0	8.6	8.6	8.3	8.5	7.0	6.6	7.0	7.5	7.6
	16.9	18.0	19.9	21.7	22.1	30.0	29.1	29.1	27.7	29.3	36.3	38.1	38.9	37.8	38.5
	1.3	1.2	1.3	2.3	2.7	4.4	4.5	4.7	5.6	5.6	4.4	4.2	4.5	4.1	4.2
	12.7	12.2	11.8	10.9	9.9	14.1	14.1	14.0	14.2	13.7	8.0	7.9	7.9	7.7	7.7
	12.0	12.1	11.8	11.8	11.6	4.8	4.9	4.8	5.3	5.1	2.2	2.1	1.9	2.1	2.2
	0.2	0.2	0.2	0.2	0.1	0.2	0.2	0.2	0.2	0.2	0.2	0.2	0.1	0.1	0.1
	43.1	43.7	45.0	46.8	46.5	53.5	52.8	52.8	53.0	53.9	51.0	52.4	53.4	51.8	52.7
	13.2	12.6	11.9	11.0	10.6	12.5	12.5	12.6	12.4	11.6	13.5	13.2	12.4	12.9	12.7
	44.3	44.1	43.6	42.8	43.5	35.5	36.3	36.3	36.3	36.2	37.7	36.5	36.6	37.7	36.7
	0.6	0.5	0.5	0.5	0.6	1.5	1.6	1.8	1.7	1.7	2.2	2.0	2.5	2.3	2.1
	56.9	56.3	55.0	53.2	53.5	46.5	47.2	47.2	47.0	46.1	49.0	47.6	46.6	48.2	47.3
	100.0	100.0	100.0	100.0	100.0	100.0	100.0	100.0	100.0	100.0	100.0	100.0	100.0	100.0	100.0
			(times)					(times)					(times)		
	1.44	1.42	1.31	1.25	1.27	1.79	1.82	1.80	1.85	1.75	2.14	2.05	2.01	2.05	2.00
	0.35	0.34	0.26	0.26	0.28	0.13	0.12	0.12	0.15	0.12	0.20	0.17	0.16	0.21	0.18
	3.73	3.79	3.63	3.57	3.70	1.75	1.76	1.72	1.75	1.68	2.09	1.99	1.84	2.09	2.05

EXHIBIT 7: INCOME STATEMENT FOR CORPORATIONS IN STONE, CLAY, GLASS, PRIMARY METAL, IRON, STEEL, NONFERROUS METALS (ESIC industries 32, 33, 33.1–2, 33.5–6)

	Stone, Clay, and Glass Products*				
	1Q 1979	2Q 1979	3Q 1979	4Q 1979	1Q 1980
Income statement in ratio format	(percent of net sales)				
Net sales, receipts, and operating revenues	100.0	100.0	100.0	100.0	100.0
Deduct: Depreciation, depletion, and amortization of property, plant, and equipment	4.0	3.5	3.3	3.6	4.3
Deduct: All other operating costs and expenses (net of purchase discounts)	89.5	85.7	86.1	88.3	91.2
Income (or loss) from operations	6.5	10.7	10.6	8.1	4.5
Nonoperating income (expense)	−0.3	−0.2	−0.5	−0.7	−0.4
Income (or loss) before income taxes	6.2	10.5	10.1	7.5	4.1
Net income (loss) of foreign branches and equity in earnings (losses) of nonconsolidated subsidiaries (net of foreign taxes) ..	0.3	0.5	0.5	0.6	0.6
Deduct: Current and deferred domestic income taxes	3.2	4.1	3.8	3.0	2.2
Income (or loss) after income taxes	3.3	7.0	6.8	5.2	2.5
Operating ratios					
Annual rate of profit on stockholders' equity at end of period:	(percent)				
Before income taxes	15.53	30.88	30.45	21.76	11.18
After taxes	7.77	19.55	19.41	13.91	5.85
Annual rate of profit on total assets:					
Before income taxes	8.19	16.29	16.02	11.53	5.77
After taxes	4.09	10.31	10.21	7.37	3.02

* During the first quarter of 1980 a considerable number of companies were reclassified by industry. To provide comparability, the four quarters of 1979 have been restated to reflect these reclassifications.

† Included in Primary Metal Industries.

Primary Metal Industries*					Iron and Steel*†					Nonferrous Metals*†				
1Q 1979	2Q 1979	3Q 1979	4Q 1979	1Q 1980	1Q 1979	2Q 1979	3Q 1979	4Q 1979	1Q 1980	1Q 1979	2Q 1979	3Q 1979	4Q 1979	1Q 1980
(percent of net sales)					(percent of net sales)					(percent of net sales)				
100.0	100.0	100.0	100.0	100.0	100.0	100.0	100.0	100.0	100.0	100.0	100.0	100.0	100.0	100.0
2.9	2.9	2.9	3.0	3.0	3.1	2.9	3.0	3.1	3.2	2.7	2.7	2.9	2.8	2.6
90.2	88.9	91.0	91.8	89.9	91.4	89.7	91.9	93.2	91.8	87.8	87.4	89.1	89.2	86.7
6.9	8.2	6.1	5.2	7.1	5.6	7.3	5.1	3.7	5.1	9.5	10.0	8.0	8.0	10.7
−0.9	−0.8	−0.5	−3.9	−0.4	−0.7	−0.7	−0.2	−5.4	0.0	−1.2	−0.9	−0.9	−1.4	−1.2
6.0	7.4	5.7	1.3	6.7	4.8	6.6	4.9	−1.7	5.1	8.4	9.0	7.2	6.7	9.5
0.6	0.8	0.9	1.0	1.2	0.3	0.4	0.5	0.3	0.7	1.2	1.4	1.6	2.2	2.0
2.4	2.7	2.1	0.4	2.5	1.9	2.5	1.7	−0.6	1.9	3.3	3.3	2.8	2.2	3.5
4.2	5.4	4.4	1.9	5.4	3.2	4.6	3.7	−0.7	3.9	6.2	7.1	6.0	6.7	7.9
(percent)					(percent)					(percent)				
20.08	25.94	19.50	6.78	24.45	16.53	23.94	17.33	−4.33	18.79	26.10	29.25	23.07	24.17	33.08
12.72	17.23	13.26	5.71	16.75	10.20	15.55	11.74	−2.26	12.70	17.00	20.00	15.77	18.17	22.93
9.22	11.98	8.95	3.07	11.01	7.59	10.96	7.93	−1.93	8.30	12.00	13.72	10.64	11.21	15.34
5.84	7.96	6.09	2.58	7.54	4.68	7.12	5.37	−1.01	5.61	7.82	9.38	7.27	8.43	10.63

EXHIBIT 8: BALANCE SHEET IN RATIO FORMAT FOR CORPORATIONS IN STONE, CLAY, GLASS, PRIMARY METALS, IRON, STEEL, NONFERROUS METALS (ESIC industries 32, 33, 33.1–2, 33.5–6)

ITEMS STATED AS A PERCENT OF TOTAL ASSETS

	Stone, Clay, and Glass Products*				
	1Q 1979	2Q 1979	3Q 1979	4Q 1979	1Q 1980
ASSETS					
Cash on hand and in banks	4.1	4.1	4.5	4.6	3.6
U.S. government and other securities	2.0	1.8	1.9	2.5	1.5
Receivables	17.8	19.3	19.5	17.3	17.2
Inventories	16.6	16.0	15.0	15.2	16.5
Current assets not elsewhere specified	2.7	2.1	2.4	2.1	2.5
Total current assets	43.2	43.3	43.3	41.7	41.3
Land and depreciable fixed assets	83.1	82.7	81.7	82.6	82.6
Deduct: Accumulated depreciation, depletion, and amortization	36.9	36.4	35.6	34.9	34.8
Net property, plant, and equipment	46.2	46.3	46.1	47.7	47.8
Noncurrent assets not elsewhere specified, including investment in nonconsolidated entities, other long-term investments, intangibles, etc.	10.6	10.4	10.6	10.6	11.0
Total assets	100.0	100.0	100.0	100.0	100.0
Liabilities and stockholders' equity					
Short-term and current installments	4.2	4.7	4.9	4.3	5.1
Trade accounts and trade notes payable	7.5	7.8	7.8	7.6	7.4
Income taxes accrued, prior and current years, net of payments					
Federal	2.1	1.7	1.8	1.5	1.4
Other	0.4	0.3	0.3	0.3	0.3
Other current liabilities	6.1	6.6	6.4	6.1	6.4
Total current liabilities	20.4	21.1	21.3	19.8	20.7
Long-term debt due in more than one year					
Loans from banks	5.0	5.1	5.5	6.0	6.6
Other long-term debt	16.4	15.9	15.5	16.0	15.6
Noncurrent liabilities not elsewhere specified, including deferred income taxes	5.4	5.0	5.0	5.2	5.4
Minority stockholders' interest in consolidated domestic corporations	0.1	0.1	0.1	0.1	0.1
Total liabilities	47.3	47.3	47.4	47.0	48.4
Capital stock and other capital	14.9	14.5	14.5	15.0	14.4
Retained earnings	38.6	39.2	39.1	39.1	38.6
Deduct: Treasury stock, at cost	0.8	0.9	1.1	1.1	1.3
Stockholders' equity	52.7	52.7	52.6	53.0	51.6
Total liabilities and stockholders' equity	100.0	100.0	100.0	100.0	100.0
Balance sheet ratios			(times)		
Current assets to current liabilities	2.12	2.05	2.03	2.10	1.99
Total cash, U.S. government, and other securities to total current liabilities	0.30	0.28	0.30	0.36	0.25
Total stockholders' equity to debt	2.06	2.05	2.03	2.01	1.88

* During the first quarter of 1980 a considerable number of companies were reclassified by industry. To provide comparability, the four quarters of 1979 have been restated to reflect these reclassifications.

† Included in Primary Metal Industries.

	Primary Metal Industries*					Iron and Steel*†					Nonferrous Metals*†				
	1Q 1979	2Q 1979	3Q 1979	4Q 1979	1Q 1980	1Q 1979	2Q 1979	3Q 1979	4Q 1979	1Q 1980	1Q 1979	2Q 1979	3Q 1979	4Q 1979	1Q 1980
	2.3	2.4	2.4	3.0	2.5	2.5	2.8	2.6	3.2	2.5	1.9	1.8	2.1	2.6	2.6
	1.9	1.9	1.9	1.7	1.7	2.3	1.8	2.0	2.0	1.8	1.3	1.9	1.6	1.3	1.5
	18.2	18.5	18.4	17.3	18.7	18.6	18.9	18.8	17.4	19.2	17.6	17.8	17.9	17.2	18.0
	18.1	18.3	18.8	19.1	18.6	18.0	18.5	18.9	19.2	18.4	18.3	18.0	18.6	19.0	18.8
	1.6	1.5	1.6	1.5	1.6	1.5	1.3	1.4	1.1	1.4	1.9	1.8	2.0	2.1	1.9
	42.2	42.6	43.1	42.6	43.1	42.8	43.4	43.7	42.9	43.4	41.1	41.2	42.2	42.2	42.8
	87.0	86.4	85.6	85.4	83.7	96.3	95.5	95.2	95.1	93.7	71.3	71.0	69.7	69.6	67.8
	42.0	41.7	41.1	40.3	39.7	49.8	49.4	49.1	48.0	47.5	28.7	28.5	28.0	27.7	27.1
	45.0	44.7	44.5	45.1	44.1	46.4	46.0	46.2	47.1	46.3	42.7	42.5	41.7	41.8	40.6
	12.8	12.7	12.4	12.3	12.8	10.8	10.6	10.1	10.0	10.4	16.3	16.2	16.1	16.0	16.6
	100.0	100.0	100.0	100.0	100.0	100.0	100.0	100.0	100.0	100.0	100.0	100.0	100.0	100.0	100.0
	4.0	4.0	4.5	3.7	4.2	3.1	3.5	4.0	3.0	3.7	5.6	4.9	5.3	5.0	5.0
	8.9	9.0	8.8	9.3	9.2	9.5	9.3	9.0	9.4	9.3	7.9	8.4	8.6	9.2	9.2
	2.0	1.8	2.0	2.0	2.3	1.7	1.5	1.7	1.6	1.9	2.6	2.2	2.5	2.8	2.9
	0.4	0.3	0.4	0.4	0.4	0.3	0.3	0.4	0.4	0.4	0.4	0.4	0.4	0.4	0.4
	7.7	7.9	7.9	8.0	8.5	8.9	9.2	9.0	9.4	9.8	5.5	5.6	5.8	5.8	6.4
	22.9	23.1	23.6	23.5	24.5	23.5	23.9	24.2	23.7	25.0	21.8	21.6	22.6	23.1	23.8
	3.5	3.3	3.4	3.6	3.6	3.2	3.2	3.2	3.3	3.1	3.9	3.5	3.7	4.0	4.4
	20.2	20.4	20.1	20.2	19.4	19.7	20.0	19.7	20.7	20.2	21.1	21.1	20.7	19.3	18.1
	7.2	6.8	6.8	7.2	7.0	7.4	7.0	6.9	7.5	7.3	6.8	6.6	6.5	6.6	6.6
	0.3	0.3	0.3	0.4	0.4	0.2	0.2	0.3	0.3	0.2	0.4	0.4	0.4	0.6	0.6
	54.1	53.8	54.1	54.8	55.0	54.1	54.2	54.2	55.5	55.8	54.0	53.1	53.9	53.6	53.6
	14.1	13.7	13.4	13.1	12.8	13.5	13.2	13.0	12.9	12.6	14.9	14.6	13.9	13.4	13.0
	32.7	33.3	33.4	33.1	33.2	33.4	33.6	33.8	32.7	32.6	31.6	32.8	32.8	33.6	34.0
	0.9	0.9	0.9	0.9	0.9	1.0	1.0	1.0	1.1	1.1	0.6	0.6	0.6	0.6	0.6
	45.9	46.2	45.9	45.2	45.0	45.9	45.8	45.8	44.5	44.2	46.0	46.9	46.1	46.4	46.4
	100.0	100.0	100.0	100.0	100.0	100.0	100.0	100.0	100.0	100.0	100.0	100.0	100.0	100.0	100.0
	(times)					(times)					(times)				
	1.84	1.85	1.83	1.82	1.76	1.82	1.82	1.80	1.81	1.73	1.88	1.91	1.87	1.83	1.80
	0.18	0.19	0.18	0.20	0.17	0.20	0.19	0.19	0.22	0.17	0.15	0.17	0.16	0.17	0.17
	1.66	1.67	1.64	1.65	1.66	1.77	1.72	1.70	1.65	1.64	1.51	1.59	1.55	1.64	1.68

EXHIBIT 9: INCOME STATEMENT FOR CORPORATIONS IN FABRICATED METAL, MACHINERY, ELECTRICAL AND ELECTRONIC EQUIPMENT, INSTRUMENTS (ESIC industries 34, 35, 36, and 38)

	Fabricated Metal Products*				
	1Q 1979	2Q 1979	3Q 1979	4Q 1979	1Q 1980
Income statement in ratio format	(percent of net sales)				
Net sales, receipts, and operating revenues	100.0	100.0	100.0	100.0	100.0
Deduct: Depreciation, depletion, and amortization of property, plant, and equipment	2.2	2.1	2.1	2.2	2.3
Deduct: All other operating costs and expenses (net of purchase discounts)	90.1	89.2	90.4	91.0	90.3
Income (or loss) from operations	7.7	8.7	7.5	6.9	7.4
Nonoperating income (expense)	−0.5	−0.6	−0.5	−0.5	−0.3
Income (or loss) before income taxes	7.3	8.1	6.9	6.4	7.2
Net income (loss) of foreign branches and equity in earnings (losses) of nonconsolidated subsidiaries (net of foreign taxes)	0.4	0.5	0.6	0.5	0.6
Deduct: Current and deferred domestic income taxes	3.2	3.4	3.0	2.5	2.8
Income (or loss) after income taxes	4.5	5.2	4.5	4.4	5.0
Operating ratios					
Annual rate of profit on stockholders' equity at end of period:	(percent)				
Before income taxes	26.72	31.22	26.20	24.30	26.09
After taxes	15.63	18.85	15.84	15.42	16.64
Annual rate of profit on total assets:					
Before income taxes	13.10	15.19	12.74	11.81	12.72
After taxes	7.67	9.17	7.70	7.49	8.11

* During the first quarter of 1980 a considerable number of companies were reclassified by industry. To provide comparability, the four quarters of 1979 have been restated to reflect these reclassifications.

	Machinery, Except Electrical*					Electrical and Electronic Equipment*					Instruments and Related Products*				
	1Q 1979	2Q 1979	3Q 1979	4Q 1979	1Q 1980	1Q 1979	2Q 1979	3Q 1979	4Q 1979	1Q 1980	1Q 1979	2Q 1979	3Q 1979	4Q 1979	1Q 1980
	(percent of net sales)					(percent of net sales)					(percent of net sales)				
	100.0	100.0	100.0	100.0	100.0	100.0	100.0	100.0	100.0	100.0	100.0	100.0	100.0	100.0	100.0
	3.2	3.2	3.2	3.1	3.5	2.4	2.4	2.5	2.4	2.5	3.8	3.7	3.6	3.4	3.5
	86.1	86.1	86.7	87.5	87.2	89.4	88.7	89.9	90.0	89.6	84.8	84.9	84.8	86.3	86.2
	10.7	10.8	10.1	9.3	9.4	8.2	8.9	7.6	7.6	7.9	11.4	11.4	11.6	10.4	10.2
	−0.5	−0.5	−0.7	−0.9	−1.0	0.5	0.1	0.1	0.2	−0.2	1.4	1.5	0.6	1.2	1.2
	10.1	10.2	9.3	8.4	8.3	8.6	9.0	7.7	7.8	7.7	12.8	12.8	12.3	11.6	11.5
	1.4	1.6	1.6	2.3	1.4	1.0	0.9	1.0	1.2	1.0	1.8	1.9	2.0	2.0	1.9
	4.5	4.5	4.2	3.5	3.6	3.8	4.0	3.4	3.5	3.5	5.7	5.7	5.8	4.8	4.9
	7.1	7.3	6.8	7.2	6.0	5.8	5.8	5.3	5.5	5.1	8.8	9.0	8.4	8.7	8.5
	(percent)					(percent)					(percent)				
	26.86	28.92	25.78	25.68	22.70	28.39	31.64	27.04	28.52	27.01	27.42	28.47	27.42	26.59	25.57
	16.39	17.82	15.96	17.24	14.13	17.24	18.59	16.41	17.55	15.99	16.69	17.42	16.22	17.01	16.15
	14.53	15.53	13.81	13.46	11.76	13.58	14.79	12.46	13.12	12.40	17.12	17.97	17.18	16.68	15.95
	8.87	9.57	8.55	9.03	7.32	8.25	8.69	7.56	8.07	7.34	10.42	11.00	10.16	10.67	10.08

EXHIBIT 10: BALANCE SHEET IN RATIO FORMAT FOR CORPORATIONS IN FABRICATED METAL, MACHINERY, ELECTRICAL AND ELECTRONIC EQUIPMENT, INSTRUMENTS (ESIC industries 34, 35, 36, and 38)

ITEMS STATED AS A PERCENT OF TOTAL ASSETS

	Fabricated Metal Products*				
	1Q 1979	2Q 1979	3Q 1979	4Q 1979	1Q 1980
Assets					
Cash on hand and in banks	4.4	4.3	4.1	4.4	4.3
U.S. government and other securities	2.4	2.0	2.1	2.5	2.2
Receivables	24.4	24.7	24.5	23.2	23.8
Inventories	27.6	27.8	27.5	27.2	27.6
Current assets not elsewhere specified	2.3	2.2	2.2	2.2	2.3
Total current assets	61.1	60.9	60.3	59.5	60.1
Land and depreciable fixed assets	52.0	51.5	51.6	51.1	51.7
Deduct: Accumulated depreciation, depletion, and amortization	24.4	24.1	24.2	23.4	24.0
Net property, plant, and equipment	27.7	27.4	27.5	27.8	27.7
Noncurrent assets not elsewhere specified, including investment in nonconsolidated entities, other long term investments, intangibles, etc.	11.3	11.6	12.3	12.7	12.2
Total assets	100.0	100.0	100.0	100.0	100.0
Liabilities and stockholders' equity					
Short-term loans and current installments	6.2	7.0	6.9	6.3	6.7
Trade accounts and trade notes payable	11.7	11.6	11.2	11.6	10.8
Income taxes accrued, prior and current years, net of payments					
Federal	2.8	2.0	2.0	2.1	2.1
Other	0.5	0.3	0.3	0.3	0.3
Other current liabilities	11.4	11.2	11.2	11.1	11.8
Total current liabilities	32.5	32.2	31.5	31.4	31.7
Long-term debt due in more than one year					
Loans from banks	5.0	5.2	5.4	5.8	5.4
Other long-term debt	10.3	10.2	10.6	10.6	10.5
Noncurrent liabilities not elsewhere specified, including deferred income taxes	3.1	3.8	3.8	3.6	3.5
Minority stockholders' interest in consolidated domestic corporations	0.1	0.1	0.1	0.1	0.1
Total liabilities	51.0	51.4	51.4	51.4	51.3
Capital stock and other capital	12.4	12.1	12.0	12.2	12.3
Retained earnings	38.2	38.2	38.0	37.9	37.9
Deduct: Treasury stock, at cost	1.5	1.6	1.4	1.5	1.4
Stockholders' equity	49.0	48.6	48.6	48.6	48.7
Total liabilities and stockholders' equity	100.0	100.0	100.0	100.0	100.0
Balance sheet ratios		(times)			
Current assets to current liabilities	1.88	1.90	1.91	1.90	1.90
Total cash, U.S. government, and other securities to total current liabilities	0.21	0.20	0.20	0.22	0.21
Total stockholders' equity to debt	2.29	2.17	2.13	2.15	2.15

* During the first quarter of 1980 a considerable number of companies were reclassified by industry. To provide comparability, the four quarters of 1979 have been restated to reflect these reclassifications.

Machinery, Except Electrical*					Electrical and Electronic Equipment*					Instruments and Related Products*				
1Q 1979	2Q 1979	3Q 1979	4Q 1979	1Q 1980	1Q 1979	2Q 1979	3Q 1979	4Q 1979	1Q 1980	1Q 1979	2Q 1979	3Q 1979	4Q 1979	1Q 1980
3.7	3.1	2.9	3.3	2.8	4.2	4.3	4.4	4.3	3.5	3.4	2.9	2.3	3.5	2.6
2.2	2.0	1.8	2.0	1.8	3.6	3.0	2.6	2.5	2.4	5.0	3.9	3.8	4.5	3.7
19.9	20.4	20.3	20.0	20.4	21.6	22.4	22.5	21.7	21.9	19.0	18.9	20.0	19.2	19.4
24.9	25.0	24.9	24.6	25.0	28.2	29.1	28.7	28.6	29.1	23.0	23.9	23.1	22.7	23.9
3.2	3.2	3.3	2.9	3.1	4.3	4.5	4.5	4.1	4.4	4.4	4.4	4.4	4.2	4.5
53.9	53.7	53.2	52.8	53.1	62.0	63.2	62.8	61.2	61.4	54.7	54.0	53.5	54.1	54.1
49.4	49.8	50.0	50.1	50.4	41.8	42.8	42.6	42.6	41.9	55.3	55.4	55.2	55.3	55.0
22.0	21.9	21.9	21.4	21.5	19.7	20.1	19.8	19.2	18.9	27.2	27.1	26.9	26.6	26.3
27.4	27.8	28.1	28.7	28.9	22.2	22.6	22.8	23.4	23.0	28.0	28.3	28.3	28.8	28.7
18.6	18.5	18.7	18.5	18.0	15.8	14.2	14.4	15.4	15.7	17.3	17.6	18.2	17.1	17.2
100.0	100.0	100.0	100.0	100.0	100.0	100.0	100.0	100.0	100.0	100.0	100.0	100.0	100.0	100.0
6.5	7.1	7.8	7.4	7.8	5.0	5.6	5.6	4.9	5.4	4.2	3.8	3.7	3.3	4.0
8.1	8.5	8.4	9.3	8.8	9.1	9.1	9.1	9.9	9.2	6.0	6.0	6.0	6.3	6.2
2.7	2.1	2.2	2.2	2.5	2.5	2.0	2.0	1.8	2.2	2.6	1.4	2.0	2.0	2.3
0.5	0.5	0.5	0.4	0.5	0.4	0.4	0.4	0.4	0.4	0.4	0.3	0.4	0.4	0.4
10.4	10.3	10.0	9.8	9.8	18.4	19.1	19.0	18.2	18.7	8.5	9.0	9.1	9.3	9.2
28.2	28.5	28.8	29.0	29.4	35.4	36.2	36.1	35.3	36.0	21.8	20.5	21.2	21.4	22.1
4.1	4.1	4.1	4.4	4.5	2.4	2.3	3.1	3.7	3.2	2.4	3.0	3.1	3.1	3.0
10.0	9.9	10.0	10.5	10.3	9.8	9.9	9.7	9.7	9.6	9.9	9.6	9.1	8.8	8.7
3.6	3.7	3.5	3.7	3.9	4.3	4.5	4.7	5.1	5.0	3.5	3.7	3.8	3.8	3.7
0.1	0.1	0.1	0.1	0.1	0.3	0.3	0.3	0.3	0.3	0.0	0.1	0.1	0.1	0.1
45.9	46.3	46.4	47.6	48.2	52.2	53.3	53.9	54.0	54.1	37.5	36.9	37.3	37.3	37.6
17.4	17.0	16.5	16.1	16.1	17.2	15.8	15.4	15.1	15.2	14.7	14.7	14.3	14.4	14.3
37.3	37.3	37.7	37.0	36.3	32.1	32.5	32.1	32.2	31.8	48.3	48.8	48.9	48.8	48.4
0.7	0.7	0.7	0.6	0.6	1.5	1.6	1.5	1.3	1.1	0.5	0.5	0.5	0.5	0.3
54.1	53.7	53.6	52.4	51.8	47.8	46.7	46.1	46.0	45.9	62.5	63.1	62.7	62.7	62.4
100.0	100.0	100.0	100.0	100.0	100.0	100.0	100.0	100.0	100.0	100.0	100.0	100.0	100.0	100.0
(times)					(times)					(times)				
1.92	1.88	1.85	1.82	1.81	1.75	1.75	1.74	1.74	1.70	2.51	2.63	2.52	2.53	2.45
0.21	0.18	0.16	0.18	0.16	0.22	0.20	0.19	0.19	0.16	0.39	0.33	0.29	0.37	0.28
2.63	2.54	2.45	2.36	2.29	2.79	2.61	2.50	2.53	2.51	3.80	3.87	3.96	4.10	3.95

EXHIBIT 11: INCOME STATEMENT FOR CORPORATIONS IN TRANSPORTATION AND MOTOR VEHICLE EQUIPMENT, AIRCRAFT, GUIDED MISSILES (ESIC industries 37, 37.1, 37.7, other durable manufacturing products)

	Transportation Equipment*				
	1Q 1979	2Q 1979	3Q 1979	4Q 1979	1Q 1980
Income statement in ratio format	(percent of net sales)				
Net sales, receipts, and operating revenues	100.0	100.0	100.0	100.0	100.0
Deduct: Depreciation, depletion, and amortization of property, plant, and equipment	2.8	2.7	3.3	3.3	3.9
Deduct: All other operating costs and expenses (net of purchase discounts)	90.0	90.3	96.0	94.4	94.9
Income (or loss) from operations	7.2	7.0	0.7	2.3	1.2
Nonoperating income (expense)	0.0	−0.1	−0.1	−0.1	−0.3
Income (or loss) before income taxes	7.1	6.9	0.7	2.2	0.9
Net income (loss) of foreign branches and equity in earnings (losses) of nonconsolidated subsidiaries (net of foreign taxes) ..	1.7	1.7	1.6	1.8	1.6
Deduct: Current and deferred domestic income taxes	3.4	3.3	0.6	1.5	1.3
Income (or loss) after income taxes	5.5	5.3	1.7	2.5	1.2
Operating ratios					
Annual rate of profit on stockholders' equity at end of period:	(percent)				
Before income taxes	32.12	30.93	6.80	12.63	7.78
After taxes	19.95	19.10	5.15	7.87	3.83
Annual rate of profit on total assets:					
Before income taxes	14.73	14.29	3.11	5.87	3.44
After taxes	9.15	8.83	2.36	3.66	1.69

* During the first quarter of 1980 a considerable number of companies were reclassified by industry. To provide comparability, the four quarters of 1979 have been restated to reflect these reclassifications.
    † Included in Transportation Equipment.

Motor Vehicles and Equipment*†					Aircraft, Guided Missiles and Parts*†					Other Durable Manufacturing Products*				
1Q 1979	2Q 1979	3Q 1979	4Q 1979	1Q 1980	1Q 1979	2Q 1979	3Q 1979	4Q 1979	1Q 1980	1Q 1979	2Q 1979	3Q 1979	4Q 1979	1Q 1980
(percent of net sales)					(percent of net sales)					(percent of net sales)				
100.0	100.0	100.0	100.0	100.0	100.0	100.0	100.0	100.0	100.0	100.0	100.0	100.0	100.0	100.0
3.2	3.1	4.1	4.2	5.1	1.9	1.8	1.8	1.7	2.0	2.8	2.7	2.8	2.7	2.9
89.1	90.2	99.1	96.2	96.9	91.9	90.4	91.4	91.3	91.9	89.1	88.7	88.9	89.5	90.2
7.6	6.7	−3.2	−0.4	−2.0	6.3	7.8	6.8	7.0	6.1	8.1	8.7	8.3	7.8	6.9
0.0	0.1	−0.1	0.1	−0.4	0.4	0.1	0.5	0.0	0.2	−0.6	−0.7	−0.4	−1.1	−0.8
7.7	6.7	−3.2	−0.3	−2.4	6.6	7.8	7.3	7.0	6.3	7.5	8.0	7.9	6.7	6.1
2.0	2.0	2.1	2.1	2.0	1.1	1.2	1.0	1.2	1.0	0.2	0.3	0.2	0.3	0.1
3.5	3.2	−1.0	0.6	0.4	3.1	3.6	3.2	3.2	2.7	3.1	3.3	3.0	2.9	2.5
6.1	5.5	−0.2	1.2	−0.8	4.6	5.4	5.1	5.0	4.5	4.6	5.0	5.2	4.1	3.6
(percent)					(percent)					(percent)				
34.45	29.83	−3.14	5.44	−1.12	28.34	33.88	28.89	29.89	26.56	27.12	32.25	30.98	26.50	21.40
21.79	18.66	−0.51	3.51	−2.19	17.03	20.38	17.89	18.33	16.51	16.29	19.34	19.66	15.71	12.48
18.79	16.46	−1.72	3.07	−0.61	9.58	11.41	9.96	10.28	8.67	13.02	15.25	14.57	12.62	10.11
11.89	10.30	−0.28	1.98	−1.18	5.76	6.87	6.17	6.31	5.39	7.82	9.15	9.25	7.48	5.90

EXHIBIT 12: BALANCE SHEET IN RATIO FORMAT FOR CORPORATIONS IN TRANSPORTATION AND MOTOR VEHICLE EQUIPMENT, AIRCRAFT, GUIDED MISSILES (ESIC industries 37, 37.1, 37.7, other durable manufacturing products)

ITEMS STATED AS A PERCENT OF TOTAL ASSETS

	Transportation Equipment*				
	1Q 1979	2Q 1979	3Q 1979	4Q 1979	1Q 1980
Assets					
Cash on hand and in banks	5.6	4.9	4.3	4.5	3.4
U.S. government and other securities	2.9	3.6	2.2	2.1	1.9
Receivables	15.9	15.4	15.8	13.1	14.3
Inventories	29.4	29.4	30.2	30.5	31.1
Current assets not elsewhere specified	3.3	3.3	2.7	2.4	2.9
Total current assets	57.1	56.6	55.2	52.6	53.5
Land and depreciable fixed assets	50.0	50.4	50.8	52.5	52.2
Deduct: Accumulated depreciation, depletion, and amortization ..	25.8	25.8	25.5	26.0	25.7
Net property, plant, and equipment	24.2	24.6	25.3	26.5	26.6
Noncurrent assets not elsewhere specified, including investment in nonconsolidated entities, other long-term investments, intangibles, etc.	18.6	18.7	19.5	20.8	19.9
Total assets	100.0	100.0	100.0	100.0	100.0
Liabilities and stockholders' equity					
Short-term loans and current installments	2.1	2.5	3.1	3.7	4.2
Trade accounts and trade notes payable	11.5	10.8	11.4	10.5	10.9
Income taxes accrued, prior and current years, net of payments					
Federal	3.2	2.7	2.5	2.7	2.6
Other	0.4	0.4	0.4	0.4	0.3
Other current liabilities	21.9	22.7	22.0	21.1	22.3
Total current liabilities	39.1	38.9	39.4	38.4	40.3
Long-term debt due in more than one year					
Loans from banks	2.5	2.0	2.1	2.1	2.3
Other long-term debt	8.0	8.2	8.1	8.0	7.9
Noncurrent liabilities not elsewhere specified, including deferred income taxes	4.4	4.7	4.5	4.9	5.1
Minority stockholders' interest in consolidated domestic corporations	0.0	0.1	0.1	0.1	0.1
Total liabilities	54.1	53.8	54.2	53.6	55.8
Capital stock and other capital	9.4	9.2	9.7	10.1	9.8
Retained earnings	37.0	37.5	36.6	36.8	34.8
Deduct: Treasury stock, at cost	0.5	0.5	0.5	0.5	0.4
Stockholders' equity	45.9	46.2	45.8	46.4	44.2
Total liabilities and stockholders' equity	100.0	100.0	100.0	100.0	100.0
Balance sheet ratios			(times)		
Current assets to current liabilities	1.46	1.46	1.40	1.37	1.33
Total cash, U.S. government, and other securities to total current liabilities	0.22	0.22	0.16	0.17	0.13
Total stockholders' equity to debt	3.64	3.70	3.45	3.35	3.06

* During the first quarter of 1980 a considerable number of companies were reclassified by industry. To provide comparability, the four quarters of 1979 have been restated to reflect these reclassifications.
† Included in Transportation Equipment.

Motor Vehicles and Equipment*†					Aircraft, Guided Missiles and Parts*†					Other Durable Manufacturing Products*				
1Q 1979	2Q 1979	3Q 1979	4Q 1979	1Q 1980	1Q 1979	2Q 1979	3Q 1979	4Q 1979	1Q 1980	1Q 1979	2Q 1979	3Q 1979	4Q 1979	1Q 1980
4.9	4.0	2.4	3.3	2.6	7.9	7.4	8.1	6.7	4.9	4.5	4.7	4.7	5.1	4.9
3.1	4.3	2.4	2.8	1.9	3.2	2.9	2.0	1.5	2.1	1.2	1.4	1.3	1.6	1.6
17.2	16.6	17.7	13.1	14.8	12.6	12.3	11.6	11.8	11.9	20.4	21.1	21.6	20.2	19.3
22.0	21.2	22.2	21.5	20.6	44.3	45.7	45.3	46.0	48.8	25.0	24.2	23.5	22.9	23.5
3.9	4.0	3.2	2.7	3.7	2.2	2.1	2.0	1.9	1.9	3.4	3.4	3.3	3.6	3.8
51.1	50.1	47.9	43.4	43.7	70.1	70.4	69.1	67.9	69.5	54.4	54.9	54.4	53.4	53.1
57.2	58.2	59.7	63.8	63.5	34.7	34.4	33.5	33.9	33.8	63.5	62.9	62.0	63.1	63.6
30.2	30.4	30.6	32.4	32.3	19.0	18.7	17.8	17.6	17.2	25.8	25.4	24.9	25.4	25.3
27.0	27.8	29.0	31.4	31.2	15.7	15.7	15.7	16.3	16.6	37.7	37.5	37.1	37.8	38.3
21.8	22.1	23.0	25.2	25.1	14.1	13.9	15.3	15.8	13.8	7.9	7.6	8.5	8.8	8.6
100.0	100.0	100.0	100.0	100.0	100.0	100.0	100.0	100.0	100.0	100.0	100.0	100.0	100.0	100.0
1.5	2.0	3.0	4.2	4.5	1.5	1.5	2.3	2.2	3.1	9.3	10.1	10.2	9.1	9.4
13.3	12.3	12.8	10.6	12.4	8.5	8.3	8.7	9.6	9.2	10.2	9.9	10.1	9.7	9.7
2.2	1.4	0.9	0.9	0.9	5.2	5.3	5.4	5.7	5.6	2.1	1.7	1.7	1.6	1.8
0.4	0.4	0.3	0.3	0.2	0.5	0.5	0.5	0.4	0.5	0.3	0.2	0.2	0.3	0.3
14.7	15.4	14.9	13.4	13.5	37.9	38.3	36.9	35.7	37.0	6.0	6.0	6.0	6.2	5.9
32.1	31.5	31.9	29.5	31.5	53.4	53.8	53.7	53.6	55.4	27.9	28.1	28.3	26.9	27.1
2.2	1.4	1.5	1.5	1.6	2.3	2.1	2.1	2.0	2.4	6.8	6.9	7.7	7.6	7.8
6.2	6.6	6.4	6.8	6.9	7.8	7.8	7.1	6.9	6.4	13.1	13.1	12.5	13.2	13.6
4.9	5.2	5.1	5.5	5.8	2.6	2.6	2.6	3.0	3.1	4.1	4.3	4.2	4.3	4.1
0.0	0.1	0.2	0.2	0.2	0.0	0.0	0.0	0.0	0.0	0.1	0.3	0.3	0.3	0.3
45.5	44.8	45.1	43.5	46.0	66.2	66.3	65.5	65.6	67.4	52.0	52.7	53.0	52.4	52.7
8.3	8.3	8.5	8.9	8.7	10.9	10.5	11.5	11.3	10.9	13.6	13.2	12.8	13.0	13.1
46.6	47.3	46.9	48.0	45.7	23.3	23.6	23.4	23.5	22.1	36.4	36.0	36.1	36.5	36.1
0.3	0.4	0.4	0.5	0.4	0.5	0.4	0.4	0.4	0.3	2.0	2.0	1.8	1.8	1.9
54.5	55.2	54.9	56.5	54.0	33.8	33.7	34.5	34.4	32.6	48.0	47.3	47.0	47.6	47.3
100.0	100.0	100.0	100.0	100.0	100.0	100.0	100.0	100.0	100.0	100.0	100.0	100.0	100.0	100.0
(times)					(times)					(times)				
1.59	1.59	1.50	1.47	1.39	1.31	1.31	1.29	1.27	1.26	1.95	1.95	1.92	1.98	1.96
0.25	0.27	0.15	0.21	0.14	0.21	0.19	0.19	0.15	0.13	0.20	0.22	0.21	0.25	0.24
5.45	5.50	5.08	4.52	4.18	2.94	2.95	3.01	3.10	2.74	1.64	1.57	1.55	1.59	1.54

EXHIBIT 13: INCOME STATEMENT FOR CORPORATIONS IN MINING, RETAIL, WHOLESALE

	All Mining*				
	1Q 1979	2Q 1979	3Q 1979	4Q 1979	1Q 1980
Income statement in ratio format	(percent of net sales)				
Net sales, receipts, and operating revenues	100.0	100.0	100.0	100.0	100.0
Deduct: Depreciation, depletion, and amortization of property, plant, and equipment	9.4	9.6	8.6	8.8	9.3
Deduct: All other operating costs and expenses (net of purchase discounts)	79.7	77.7	75.5	76.1	77.8
Income (or loss) from operations	10.9	12.7	15.9	15.1	12.9
Nonoperating income (expense)	−1.5	−0.8	−0.4	−0.4	−1.1
Income (or loss) before income taxes	9.4	11.9	15.5	14.7	11.7
Net income (loss) of foreign branches and equity in earnings (losses) of nonconsolidated subsidiaries (net of foreign taxes) ..	1.4	1.3	1.5	1.3	2.1
Deduct: Current and deferred domestic income taxes............	4.1	4.4	5.7	5.1	5.6
Income (or loss) after income taxes	6.8	8.8	11.3	10.9	8.2
Operating ratios					
Annual rate of profit on stockholders' equity at end of period:	(percent)				
Before income taxes	19.57	23.70	31.55	29.89	24.28
After taxes	12.24	15.70	20.97	20.32	14.32
Annual rate of profit on total assets:					
Before income taxes	8.13	10.05	13.75	13.22	10.55
After taxes	5.09	6.66	9.14	8.99	6.22

* During the first quarter of 1980 a considerable number of companies were reclassified by industry. To provide comparability, the four quarters of 1979 have been restated to reflect these reclassifications.

	All Retail Trade*†					All Wholesale Trade*				
	1Q 1979	2Q 1979	3Q 1979	4Q 1979	1Q 1980	1Q 1979	2Q 1979	3Q 1979	4Q 1979	1Q 1980
	(percent of net sales)					(percent of net sales)				
	100.0	100.0	100.0	100.0		100.0	100.0	100.0	100.0	100.0
	1.2	1.1	1.1	1.1		0.7	0.7	0.7	0.7	0.7
	95.9	95.2	95.1	94.5		95.9	95.6	95.8	96.2	96.3
	2.9	3.7	3.8	4.4		3.4	3.7	3.5	3.1	3.0
	−0.4	−0.4	−0.4	−0.5		−0.3	−0.3	−0.3	−0.4	−0.4
	2.5	3.2	3.4	3.9		3.1	3.5	3.2	2.7	2.6
	0.1	0.1	0.1	0.2		0.2	0.1	0.2	0.2	0.2
	1.0	1.0	1.1	1.5		1.1	1.3	1.2	1.1	1.2
	1.6	2.3	2.3	2.6		2.0	2.3	2.2	1.8	1.7
	(percent)					(percent)				
	19.38	26.95	26.81	33.29		29.76	35.11	34.98	30.06	28.08
	12.24	18.43	17.86	21.42		18.96	22.59	22.30	18.16	16.42
	7.53	10.39	10.41	13.32		10.35	12.57	12.38	10.37	9.96
	4.75	7.10	6.93	8.57		6.60	8.09	7.90	6.27	5.82

EXHIBIT 14:   BALANCE SHEET IN RATIO FORMAT FOR CORPORATIONS IN MINING, RETAIL, WHOLESALE

ITEMS STATED AS A PERCENT

	All Mining*				
	1Q 1979	2Q 1979	3Q 1979	4Q 1979	1Q 1980
Assets					
Cash on hand and in banks	4.7	4.5	5.4	5.6	5.0
U.S. government and other securities	2.0	1.9	2.2	2.2	2.4
Receivables	12.5	13.0	13.2	13.6	13.3
Inventories	5.4	5.1	5.2	5.0	5.0
Current assets not elsewhere specified	2.2	2.2	2.1	2.8	3.1
Total current assets	26.7	26.7	28.1	29.2	28.8
Land and depreciable fixed assets	92.2	91.2	88.3	86.4	87.0
Deduct: Accumulated depreciation, depletion, and amortization ..	32.0	31.0	30.1	30.1	29.7
Net property, plant, and equipment	60.2	60.2	58.2	56.3	57.3
Noncurrent assets not elsewhere specified, including investment in nonconsolidated entities, other long-term investments, intangibles, etc.	13.0	13.2	13.7	14.4	13.9
Total assets	100.0	100.0	100.0	100.0	100.0
Liabilities and stockholders' equity					
Short-term loans and current installments	7.1	6.1	5.8	5.9	5.7
Trade accounts and trade notes payable	7.4	7.5	7.8	8.2	7.6
Income taxes accrued, prior and current years, net of payments					
Federal	0.9	0.7	1.2	1.4	1.1
Other	0.1	0.1	0.1	0.1	0.1
Other current liabilities	3.8	4.4	4.0	4.4	5.0
Total current liabilities	19.3	18.8	18.9	20.1	19.6
Long-term debt due in more than one year					
Loans from banks	11.4	13.0	13.7	12.8	14.8
Other long-term debt	18.0	16.7	15.0	14.5	14.0
Noncurrent liabilities not elsewhere specified, including deferred income taxes	9.4	8.9	8.4	8.1	7.9
Minority stockholders' interest in consolidated domestic corporations	0.3	0.3	0.3	0.3	0.3
Total liabilities	58.4	57.6	56.4	55.8	56.5
Capital stock and other capital	14.9	17.2	16.2	17.8	19.1
Retained earnings	27.8	26.3	28.4	27.4	25.4
Deduct: Treasury stock, at cost	1.2	1.0	1.1	1.0	1.0
Stockholders' equity	41.6	42.4	43.6	44.2	43.5
Total liabilities and stockholders' equity	100.0	100.0	100.0	100.0	100.0
Balance sheet ratios		(times)			
Current assets to current liabilities	1.38	1.42	1.48	1.45	1.47
Total cash, U.S. government, and other securities to total current liabilities	0.35	0.34	0.40	0.39	0.38
Total stockholders' equity to debt	1.14	1.19	1.26	1.34	1.26

 * During the first quarter of 1980 a considerable number of companies were reclassified by industry. To provide comparability, the four quarters of 1979 have been restated to reflect these reclassifications.
 † First quarter estimates for Retail Trade was published in the form of a press release during July 1980.

All Retail Trade*†					All Wholesale Trade*				
1Q 1979	2Q 1979	3Q 1979	4Q 1979	1Q 1980	1Q 1979	2Q 1979	3Q 1979	4Q 1979	1Q 1980
6.0	6.0	6.1	7.0		5.6	5.3	5.3	5.5	5.8
0.9	0.8	0.9	0.9		1.0	1.2	1.4	1.3	1.6
14.1	13.9	14.3	14.5		31.9	31.7	32.0	31.8	31.1
40.5	40.4	40.3	38.4		34.0	34.0	33.5	34.3	33.9
3.3	3.3	3.3	3.0		3.3	3.4	3.5	3.5	3.6
64.9	64.5	65.0	63.9		75.8	75.5	75.6	76.4	76.0
44.8	45.5	44.7	46.4		28.4	28.9	29.1	28.1	28.7
17.0	17.5	17.0	17.5		11.2	11.5	11.5	11.0	11.3
27.8	28.0	27.8	28.9		17.2	17.3	17.6	17.0	17.4
7.4	7.5	7.3	7.2		7.0	7.2	6.8	6.6	6.7
100.0	100.0	100.0	100.0		100.0	100.0	100.0	100.0	100.0
14.7	14.9	14.3	14.0		16.7	16.7	16.3	16.8	16.8
16.0	15.8	16.8	15.0		25.8	25.3	25.2	25.5	24.7
1.5	1.3	1.3	1.6		1.4	1.4	1.6	1.6	1.7
0.2	0.2	0.2	0.2		0.2	0.2	0.2	0.2	0.2
6.1	6.3	6.3	6.5		5.4	5.3	5.1	5.8	5.7
38.7	38.6	38.9	37.4		49.3	48.9	48.5	50.0	49.1
6.4	6.5	6.6	6.5		5.4	5.1	5.7	5.1	5.1
11.1	11.4	11.0	11.1		8.4	7.9	8.3	7.8	7.8
4.9	4.9	4.6	4.9		2.1	2.2	2.1	2.5	2.4
0.1	0.1	0.1	0.1		0.1	0.1	0.1	0.1	0.1
61.1	61.5	61.2	60.0		65.2	64.2	64.6	65.5	64.5
11.2	10.9	10.8	11.1		11.2	11.0	10.5	10.1	10.2
28.7	28.9	29.2	30.1		24.7	26.0	26.0	25.5	26.3
1.1	1.2	1.2	1.2		1.1	1.2	1.1	1.1	1.1
38.9	38.5	38.8	40.0		34.8	35.8	35.4	34.5	35.5
100.0	100.0	100.0	100.0		100.0	100.0	100.0	100.0	100.0
		(times)					(times)		
1.68	1.67	1.67	1.71		1.54	1.54	1.56	1.53	1.55
0.18	0.18	0.18	0.21		0.13	0.13	0.14	0.14	0.15
1.21	1.17	1.22	1.26		1.15	1.21	1.17	1.16	1.19

WHERE TO GO FOR OUTSIDE FINANCING

Alan J. Patricof*

With interest rates at record highs and the market for public issues still in a trough, small but growing companies should be looking at venture-capital firms as an alternative source of outside financing.

Point: After several slow years, venture-capital pools (98 percent of which take the form of limited partnerships) are showing renewed signs of life. *Reasons:*

Pension funds are channeling a small slice of their assets to venture capitalists as a means of diversifying their portfolios.

Major corporations are offering development funds to venture capitalists as a means of finding new products to market.

Result: In 1979, venture-capital firms funneled an estimated $300–$500 million into start-up and fast-growth situations. In 1980, observers expect that figure will double.

HOW TO TAKE ADVANTAGE

Draw up a business plan. Venture capitalists are eager to find companies with significant growth potential that are managed by high-caliber executives. They are not interested in inventions or projects. An average venture-capital firm will look at

* Alan Patricof Assoc., Inc., 1 E. 53 St., New York 10022.
Source: Reprinted from Boardroom Reports, Management's Source of Useful Information, 500 Fifth Avenue, New York, N.Y. 10036.

200 business plans in a year, but pick only a handful.

Sell the plan widely, but do not keep it on the market once a preliminary agreement is reached. A list of the 200 venture-capital firms in the U.S. and their areas of interest can be found in *Guide to Venture-Capital Sources.*[1]

Be prepared to spend time winning the confidence of any venture-capital firm attracted by the plan.

Execute as much of the company's business plan as possible *before* negotiating a deal. *Example:* Develop a backlog of product orders as quickly as possible. *Reason:* The more a company has to offer a venture-capital firm, the less equity it must surrender to get financing.

The kicker: Because each venture deal is different, there are no guidelines for what or how much an entrepreneur must give up in return for capital. *However,* different venture capitalists specialize in various kinds of deals. (*Examples:* Startups; working capital or debt financings; leveraged buy-outs; high technology or prosaic product lines.) Entrepreneurs with attractive business plans should be able to shop within the venture community to determine which group is appropriate for their particular project.

Rule of thumb: Entrepreneurs have to give up considerably more today than ten years ago. *Reason:* Venture capitalists can no longer easily turn over their investments by taking small growth companies public. They want to be compensated for the longer holding periods.

[1] Capital Publishing Corp., PO Box 348, Wellesley Hills, MA 02181, $49.50.

TAX SHELTERS

TAX SHELTER HIGHLIGHTS

Worthwhile *tax sheltered investments* offer both investment merit and tax benefits.

Tax shelter means turning dollars otherwise paid to Uncle Sam into assets or income, through: (1) *tax deferral,* (2) conversion of ordinary income into long-term capital gains, and (3) conversion and deferral—the conversion of this year's ordinary income into future years' long-term capital gains.

Limited partnerships are the best *tax-sheltered investment* for most investors because of limited liability and flow-through of tax losses.

As a tax shelter investor, you should have: (1) substantial net worth and assets, (2) sufficient current assets and liquidity, and (3) an understanding of tax-shelter risk.

The three major investment goals of tax shelter—*tax savings, tax-sheltered cash flow,* and *capital gains—cannot all be maximized simultaneously.*

Most tax shelters will involve *public programs* organized as *limited partnerships* in: newly constructed real estate, existing income producing real estate, net leased real estate, oil and gas drilling, equipment leasing, or agriculture.

Certain investors find specialized tax shelters/Keogh Plans, individual retirement accounts, annuities, corporate pension and profit-sharing plans, or municipal bonds well suited to their needs.

Selecting a tax shelter requires analysis of your own qualifications and characteristics, your investment goals and desired results.

Always consult your tax advisor before finalizing any tax-shelter investment decision.

INTRODUCTION

A tax shelter is any investment made more attractive by the timing of the profit or the way it is taxed. Before we go further, please do not worry that tax shelters are somehow illegal or immoral; they are not. And do not confuse *tax shelter* with *loophole.* Tax shelters are not loopholes at all.

Tax-sheltered investments are based on specific provisions of the tax laws enacted by Congress to encourage investment capital to flow directly into the basic areas of our economy such as housing, petroleum, manufacturing, and agriculture. In one sense *tax shelter* means in-

Source: *Tax Shelters,* Bache-Halsey Stuart Shields Incorporated.

vesting in vital industries in a way that permits you—rather than the companies you invest with —to keep the tax benefits . . . while retaining your opportunities for significant profits.

If you have a substantial net worth and your combined federal and state income taxes place you in at least the 50 percent tax bracket, you ought to consider some of the established ways to reduce the amount you have to pay the government on April 15.

A tax shelter should have two components. First and foremost, it has to be an investment with potential economic benefits. Any tax shelter that does not offer promise of being a worthwhile economic investment should be ignored. Without profit possibilities, chances are you would do just as well at tax time giving money to a favorite charity. In addition there has to be favorable tax treatment permitting you—and other properly qualified, high tax bracket investors—to reduce or defer your overall taxes.

VIEWPOINT

THE TAX SHELTER INDUSTRIES

The majority of investment-quality tax shelters are found in four areas:

Real estate.

Oil and gas.

Equipment leasing.

Agriculture.

In addition, there are several specialized tax-shelter areas which may interest you: Keogh Plans, annuities, pension and profit sharing plans, individual retirement accounts, and municipal bonds.

TAX SHELTER CONCEPTS

The idea behind tax shelters lies in turning dollars otherwise paid to Uncle Sam into income or into assets which may be sold for a profit. This process involves three concepts:

1. *Deferral:* Postponing payment of taxes from the current taxable year until a later year when you are in a lower tax bracket or have more cash.

2. *Conversion:* Obtaining current tax *deductions* against ordinary income while turning future revenues into income taxable at more favorable *capital gains* rates or lower rates derived from favorable tax features such as *depletion* or *depreciation.*

3. *Leverage:* Obtaining current deductions in excess of cash investment through the use of loans, either *nonrecourse loans* which increase *deductions* without increasing your investment or personal liability, or *recourse loans* for which you are personally liable. Non-

recourse loans currently apply only to real estate tax shelters. Since enactment of the Tax Reform Act of 1976 and the Revenue Act of 1978, recourse loans must be used for all tax shelters other than real estate if you are to have deductions in excess of 100 percent of your investment.

If you have unusually high income for one year, but do not expect to be at the same level in subsequent years, you may select a tax shelter emphasizing deferral. On the other hand, if your income continually puts you in a high tax bracket, you may want a shelter which will generate deductions for several years. In both cases the use of leverage may help you increase your tax benefits.

TAX SHELTER ORGANIZATIONS

Probably the most frequent question asked about tax shelters is: "Just what is a tax shelter?"

The answer: A tax shelter is a security, but not a stock, bond, or commodity. What you receive when you invest in a tax shelter is an interest in a *limited partnership, joint venture,* or, in rare instances, a *Subchapter S corporation.*

LIMITED PARTNERSHIP TAX SHELTERS

To fully understand a limited partnership, you need to study its five basic features: partnership, general partner, limited partners, limited liability, and flow-through of tax benefits. In addition, you should understand the difference between a "public" program and a "private" program.

THE PARTNERSHIP CONCEPT

A limited partnership is an undertaking between an individual and/or a company (called the *general partner*) that has investment expertise in a tax-shelter industry and a group of investors (called *limited partners*) seeking specific tax benefits, risks, and rewards. The general partner provides investment expertise; investors supply the money, or most of it. Tax benefits normally accrue to investors; profits are shared according to a stated formula designed to compensate company and investors for their respective contributions.

THE GENERAL PARTNER'S ROLE

Principal activities of the general partner include: assembling investors' capital, making investments, keeping partnership books, reporting results, and distributing any partnership profits.

"Making investments" involves purchasing direct interests in oil wells, real estate, leasable equipment, or various forms of agriculture on behalf of the limited partnership.

THE LIMITED PARTNER'S ROLE

Your function involves providing a share of the capital to finance initial selection and operation of partnership projects. You receive periodic progress reports and your share of partnership cash distributions. To preserve the tax status of the limited partnership, you and other limited partners must not take any active role in partnership management.

LIMITED LIABILITY

Your personal liability as a limited partner is legally limited to what you have actually invested or committed to invest plus your share of any undistributed profits. If something goes wrong (a major fire or an earthquake for example), the partnership's creditors can not attach your personal assets except to the extent of any recourse loans for which you have agreed to become personally liable.

FLOW-THROUGH OF TAX BENEFITS

The partnership itself pays no taxes; benefits pass directly to the partners. You include your share of partnership profits and losses (usually losses in the early years) on your own tax return. Later, if your partnership begins generating taxable profits, those profits are added to your other income.

PUBLIC AND PRIVATE PROGRAMS

Often, the general partner's role of "assembling investor's capital" means a formal offering registered with the SEC. Typically, these public programs involve a minimum $5,000 *subscription* with additional investment amounts available in *units* as small as $1,000. Assessments, if any, are limited to a stated amount or percentage of the original subscription. Public programs can be *blind pools,* an approach which gives the sponsor flexibility in selecting a diversified group of projects designed to meet partnership goals.

The substantial investor with much more income to shelter than the $5,000 minimum subscription required of most public programs may find a private program more suitable. Private offerings of tax shelters generally involve a large *subscription* with *units* of $50,000 or more. *Assessments* are more common than in public programs. The *offering amount* is typically less than $1 million; many are *specified property programs* involving one or a very few projects.

INVESTMENT GOALS

Before considering a *tax-sheltered partnership* you should determine whether your own financial and tax position justifies such an investment.

Before getting into tax shelters, you should conduct a "personal audit" to determine whether you have the prerequisites to become a tax-shelter investor and, more importantly, whether you can really benefit.

PREREQUISITES

As a tax-shelter investor, it's vital that you have: (1) substantial net worth and income, (2) sufficient current assets to avoid impairing other investment goals, and (3) an understanding of the risks and the lack of liquidity.

NET WORTH AND INCOME

The definition of *substantial* net worth and income varies from person to person and from tax shelter to tax shelter; however, there are some guidelines. Many states require that prospective tax-shelter investors meet "suitability requirements." For example, state regulators usually require that oil and gas investors have minimum net worth of $200,000 or net worth of $50,000 and some income taxed at a 50 percent rate. Tax shelters with lesser risk, for example, equipment leasing, have correspondingly lower suitability requirements.

CURRENT ASSETS

Another way to analyze whether you are "suitable" is to evaluate your current assets—possible sources of tax-shelter investment cash. Your investment should not come out of funds earmarked for college education or retirement. And you should not forego other investments. Tax-shelter funds should come out of current income, borrowings which you will repay out of current income, or current capital gains. Remember, your objective is sheltering current taxable income.

UNDERSTANDING RISK AND LIQUIDITY

The reasons for concern about current assets, income, and net worth relate to two characteristics of all tax shelters: investment risk and lack of liquidity.

It is difficult to quantify investment risk, but in every tax-sheltered investment there is underlying danger that oil wells will be dry, that apartments will not rent, that even companies with Triple A credit cannot meet lease payments, or that tax laws will change. Even if you have sufficient income, net worth, and available cash, you should understand that you may be faced with disappointing performance. "Investment risk" implies a range of returns—some great years, some less than great, some bad. With some tax shelters, you must be prepared to continue reinvesting for enough years to average your investment performance.

An understanding of *liquidity* is also required. Whatever shelter you choose, it may be at least six months before you begin receiving any cash distributions and up to two years before you can sell out and receive the *cash liquidating value* of your chosen partnership. Do not count on being able to sell a partnership interest like a stock or a bond on a moment's notice, even in an emergency.

If you meet the suitability requirements . . . if you have capital available from proper sources . . . if you are prepared to invest in your chosen tax-shelter industry long enough to smooth out the effect of investment risk . . . if you can live with the idea that it may be two years or longer before you get your money out . . . then you can probably benefit from a long-term tax-shelter investment program.

POSSIBLE BENEFITS

Once you have determined that tax shelters are suitable for your portfolio, you will have to decide what combination of the benefits offered by tax shelters fits your own investment goals:
(1) tax savings,
(2) tax-sheltered cash flow, or
(3) capital gains.

TAX SAVINGS

Reducing current taxes is the principal goal of most tax-shelter investors. Limited partnerships are usually structured to maximize tax *deductions* in the first year. The objective is to have *tax losses*, that is, a tax shelter that generates more deductions than income the first year or first few years. When combined with other income on your tax return, your share of partnership deductions offsets an equal amount of your taxable income from other sources on April 15. If you are in a 50 percent federal tax bracket, for example, each dollar of your share

**TAX DEDUCTIONS FROM SHELTER IN FIRST YEAR AS A
PERCENTAGE OF THE INVESTMENT**

	50% Deduct-ible	100% Deduct-ible	150% Deduct-ible	Nothing Deduct-ible
Taxable income*	$75,000	$75,000	$75,000	$75,000
Deductions from shelters	(5,000)	(10,000)	(15,000)	—
Revised taxable income	$70,000	$65,000	$60,000	$75,000
Tax due	$24,700	$22,200	$19,700	$27,200
Tax savings	$ 2,500	$ 5,000	$ 7,500	$ —
Net investment cost ($10,000 minus tax savings)	$ 7,500	$ 5,000	$ 2,500	$ —

*Personal service income after exemptions and itemized deductions.

of net partnership deductions generates *tax savings* of up to 50 cents.

Let us illustrate the effect of various degrees of deductibility in tax shelters. Assume you are in a 50 percent federal tax bracket, file a joint return, have $75,000 of taxable income and invest $10,000: (see table above)

The 50 percent deduction on a $10,000 investment, for example, saves $2,500 in taxes, so the net cost is only $7,500 even though you have $10,000 invested. The 100 percent and 150 percent deductible shelters produce tax savings of $5,000 and $7,500 respectively.

Try to resist the urge to conclude that the 150 percent deductible tax shelter is "best" because it saves the most taxes. It may be the best if reducing current taxes is your only goal. But remember, deductions in excess of your investment are achieved only through borrowing which utilizes either *nonrecourse loans* (in real estate) or *recourse loans* (all other tax shelters). You cannot deduct more than your share of partnership expenses; without borrowing, your partnership cannot expend more than you invest. Also remember, borrowing has to be repaid; this will involve additional risk especially if recourse loans are used. The funds used to make those repayments may increase your tax bill in later years and reduce your potential economic benefits.

TAX SHELTERED CASH FLOW

Any income received from a tax-shelter partnership may be partially or wholly offset by on-going deductions for depreciation, depletion, interest, and operating costs. Depreciation and depletion are particularly important because they are *noncash charges;* your taxable income is reduced by the deductions, but no cash is actually paid to anyone—it is only a bookkeeping transaction. Let us look at how one dollar of tax-sheltered income from a hypothetical tax-sheltered investment might yield *tax-sheltered cash flow:*

JOINT RETURN—50% TAX BRACKET

	Cash Flow	Tax Flow
Tax shelter gross income	$ 1.00	$ 1.00
Operating expenses	(0.46)	(0.46)
Operating income	$ 0.54	$ 0.54
Deductions:		
Depreciation (noncash)	—	(0.34)
Interest payments	(0.30)	(0.30)
Principal payments	(0.06)	—
Cash flow received	$ 0.18	
Taxable income (loss)		$(0.10)

In this example, you receive 18 cents in cash out of each dollar of gross income generated by your tax-sheltered investment. In addition, deductions reduce your taxable income from the same dollar to minus 10 cents which offsets 10 cents in taxable income from other sources and reduces your tax bill by 5 cents. Because deductions offset the tax liability, you receive 18 cents of tax-sheltered cash flow.

Some tax shelters yield fully tax-sheltered cash flow plus additional tax losses, as in the example above. Other shelters produce some deductions but not enough to absorb all the tax liability, thus partially sheltering your cash flow received. Still other shelters generate: (1) fully taxable cash flow, (2) tax losses but no cash flow, or (3) taxable income but no cash flow received, as in some high *leverage* situations requiring large loan repayments.

Because of the necessity to repay borrowed funds, leverage will reduce the possibility of receiving cash flow. Thus, a tax shelter offering maximum first year deductions through leverage will not generally satisfy a need for tax-sheltered cash flow in later years.

CAPITAL GAINS

If your partnership sells any assets, or if you sell your interest in a partnership, you have to pay a tax on your share of any profits.

If the assets sold are *capital assets,* the sale may qualify for taxation at long-term *capital gains* rates rather than ordinary income tax rates. Since long-term capital gains are taxed at a maximum rate of 28 percent against a 70 percent maximum rate for other types of income, capital gains may provide a significant degree of tax shelter.

Any investment plan seeking maximum tax savings in the first few years, or maximum tax-sheltered cash flow in later years, may limit capital gains possibilities. Here is why: In certain instances when *accelerated depreciation* or *intangible drilling costs* have been claimed as *deductions,* a portion of those deductions are subject to *recapture* as ordinary income in the year of the sale. This feature may limit capital gains, particularly if leverage has been employed.

In summary, you will not find a tax shelter that offers maximum tax savings, maximum tax-sheltered cash flow and maximum capital-gains opportunities. You will have to decide which tax-shelter investment goals are best for your situation. For example, if you have a very high annual income continuing for several years, some combination of tax savings and capital gains may be your goal. On the other hand, if you are nearing retirement, you may want to forego maximum tax savings in favor of tax-sheltered cash flow to augment your retirement fund; alternatively, you may decide to seek ways to defer your current taxes and pay them at your lower, post-retirement tax rate.

Whichever approach you take, the possible benefits from your chosen tax shelter may be lessened by certain aspects of the Tax Reform Act of 1976 and the Revenue Act of 1978. To insure that really substantial investors do not utilize tax shelters to avoid all taxes, Congress has enacted certain changes affecting the *minimum tax* on *tax-preference items* and the *maximum tax,* and has added a new alternative minimum tax.

Under the *minimum tax,* you pay additional income tax equal to 15 percent of your total *tax-preference items* (except that there is no minimum tax due on the first $10,000 of tax preferences or one half of your regular income tax, whichever is greater). There are seven tax-preference items; for purposes of the regular 15 percent minimum tax, three relate to tax shelters: (*a*) *accelerated depreciation of real property and leased personal property,* (*b*) *depletion,* and (*c*) *intangible drilling costs.* (See the definition of *tax-preference items* in the Glossary for details.)

Maximum tax relates to personal service income, that is, what is commonly called *earned income,* wages, salaries, professional fees, and certain payments for pensions, annuities, and deferred compensation. It is subject to a maximum tax of 50 percent; however, the amount of income eligible for the maximum tax is offset by the amount of the year's tax-preference items. The amount offset is taxable as unearned income at rates up to 70 percent. Under the Revenue Act of 1978, the nontaxed portion of long-term capital gains no longer offsets the personal service income eligible for maximum tax.

However, the Revenue Act of 1978 enacted the "alternative minimum tax" to replace the exemption of capital gains and adjusted itemized deduction tax preferences from the regular 15 percent minimum tax. This tax, which is imposed only if it exceeds the noncorporate taxpayer's regular tax (including the regular minimum tax), is computed by adding to regular taxable income the amount of the capital gains and adjusted itemized deduction preferences. This amount is subject to various rates, the maximum being 25 percent in excess of $80,000.

These three concepts are complex, but in general, the larger your taxable income and the more you invest in tax shelters, the more likely you will be affected.

THE MAJOR TAX SHELTERS

Many tax-shelter recommendations are concentrated in the areas of real estate, oil and gas, equipment leasing, and agriculture. This group offers: (1) a wide range of benefits satisfying virtually any tax-shelter investment goal; (2) a broad spectrum of risk/reward relationships; (3) a variety of offerings from which to select; and, (4) well established principles of taxation.

REAL ESTATE

Real estate is undoubtedly the most popular tax shelter. Because of its similarity to home ownership, it is easily understood.

The obvious distinction between a home and investment real estate is that tenants occupy investment buildings and make periodic lease or rental payments to cover costs of operations, maintenance, and debt retirement as well as profit. The not-so-obvious difference relates to taxation. Owners of investment real estate are allowed deductions for taxes, operating and maintenance expenses, interest on mortgage money, and depreciation on buildings (but not land). Homeowners are allowed deductions for taxes and interest paid on mortgages, thus making home ownership probably the most widely used tax shelter. However, homeowners are denied the other deductions.

TYPES OF PROGRAMS

Real estate is an umbrella term describing a variety of investments. Real estate limited partnerships involve raw land, office buildings, apartments, industrial parks, shopping centers, and mobile home parks, to name a few.

Generally real estate partnerships cluster in four areas: newly-constructed real estate, existing income-producing real estate, net leased real estate, and government-assisted housing.

Some real estate partnerships are *specified property programs;* others are *blind pool programs* involving properties selected after partnership operations begin.

Newly Constructed Real Estate. These programs construct new buildings or purchase new "first user" buildings. Typically, newly constructed real estate programs involve maximum *leverage* and employ *accelerated depreciation.* Because of more favorable *double-declining-balance* depreciation (at 200 percent of the straight-line depreciation rate), these programs usually concentrate on new apartment construction. Sometimes commercial properties (office buildings and shopping centers), which are limited to 150 percent declining-balance depreciation, are included for diversification.

High *leverage* from *nonrecourse loans* and accelerated depreciation mean tax losses of up to 50 percent of the amount invested the first year and in excess of 100 percent over the first five–ten years of the partnership.

New buildings (which might not rent easily) financed with high leverage imply high risk. Because of leverage, tax losses may continue for several years. Unusually attractive capital gains possibilities may be reduced by *recapture* of a portion of accelerated depreciation, particularly in the early years.

Interest and Taxes During Construction. The Tax Reform Act of 1976 enacted special rules regarding the deductibility of interest and taxes related to real property during construction periods. When fully operative, these rules will require that such interest and taxes be capitalized and amortized over a ten-year period, thereby reducing the deductions otherwise available from real estate ventures. There are transitional rules which apply this treatment to nonresidential real estate, residential real estate, and government-subsidized housing where the construction period begins after 1975, 1977, and 1981, respectively.

Existing Income-Producing Real Estate. These partnerships usually invest in existing commercial properties and apartments. Because of slower depreciation methods (125 percent declining-balance on apartments, straight-line on commercial) and lower leverage, most existing property programs offer lower tax losses in early years (10 percent to 20 percent the first year) and significant opportunities for tax-sheltered cash flow, hence the name *income-producing real estate.* Lower leverage on existing (hence more predictable) rental properties implies lesser risk. Established properties offer capital gains opportunities with fewer recapture problems because of lower accelerated depreciation.

Net-Leased Real Estate. These partnerships purchase office buildings, hotels, shopping centers, factory buildings, warehouses, and miniwarehouses, and so on, on a leveraged basis. Properties are leased to major corporations on a long term, "triple-net-lease" basis: the corporate tenant is responsible for a specified lease payment plus all taxes, insurance, maintenance, and other expenses during the life of the lease.

Tax losses the first year are minimal (remember, tenants pay operating costs; the partnership's only deductions are interest and straight-line depreciation). The real benefit in a net-lease program is the opportunity for a relatively low-risk investment yielding cash flow partially tax sheltered by depreciation (usually about 50 percent of the cash received over the life of the partnership is tax sheltered).

Government-Assisted Housing. These investments depend upon funding from various state and federal housing-finance programs; therefore, they are not always available. All involve construction or rehabilitation of properties for low-income, middle-income or elderly tenants. Accelerated depreciation plus extreme leverage (made possible by government loan guarantees and/or rent subsidies) create excellent tax loss possibilities, up to 200 percent the first year. Leverage and provisions of some federal laws may limit tax-sheltered cash flow; however, there will be a continuing stream of tax losses for several years. Recapture provisions severely reduce possibilities for early capital gains.

REAL ESTATE PARTNERSHIP OPERATIONS

All real estate limited partnerships function similarly—only the properties purchased and the tax treatment vary. Typically the general partner is a real estate developer, property management company, or real estate broker. The general partner subtracts a *management fee* and *organization and offering expenses.* Then he applies partnership *proceeds* to a group of properties which meet stated partnership objectives. First-year tax losses are derived from partnership and property operating expenses, depreciation, interest deductions, and so on.

After partnership properties are in operation, rental income is designated for property management, maintenance, and repayment of loans. (In partnerships involving net leases, the tenants pay all expenses except loan repayment.) Any excess is divided among the general and limited partners according to an established formula. Some general partners also receive compensation from brokerage commissions or property management fees.

OIL AND GAS

Oil and gas accumulate in pore spaces of underground rock formations. A given *reservoir*, as these accumulations are called, may be small or may contain millions of barrels of oil or billions of cubic feet of natural gas.

Because of the technology required, and because of "dry holes," the search for oil and gas is expensive. Industry statistics indicate that only about 1 exploratory well in 10 finds a new field and only 1 out of 40 or 50 is a significant commercial success. Because of high costs and risks, oil and gas companies are often forced to look outside for cash to finance drilling. Individual investors supply much of this drilling capital through tax-shelter limited partnerships.

Oil and gas investment represents perhaps the best all-around tax shelter. It offers opportunities for high first-year tax losses, partially tax-sheltered cash flow, and capital gains. Oil and gas is also the riskiest tax shelter because of "dry holes." However, diversifying partnership proceeds among numerous wells spreads the risk.

TYPES OF PROGRAMS

Limited partnerships that drill for oil and gas may be *blind pool programs* or *specified property programs*. Blind pools are most popular. Drilling programs are further classified according to risk. A few drill only exploratory or "wildcat wells." The majority seek to diversify risk by combining wildcats with 10 percent to 75 percent *development wells*—the wells which must be drilled over the extent of the reservoir before it can produce its maximum yield. Development drilling is considerably less risky. Roughly eight out of ten are completed as producers according to industry statistics; however, remember that a successful well may not be a profitable well. Development well sites result from someone's wildcat discovery. As you might suspect, they are expensive, limiting potential profitability of a balanced drilling partnership while lessening the risk.

General and administrative expenses, offering expenses, and *intangible drilling costs* combine to offer first-year tax losses of 70 percent to 90 percent of the amount invested. In one type of drilling program, the general partner pays all nondeductible costs, making 100 percent of your investment deductible.

Once successful wells are on stream, depletion partially shelters oil and gas gross income. You can deduct up to 22 percent of your share of this gross oil and gas income limited to the lesser of 65 percent of the partner's taxable income before the depletion allowance or 50 percent of the taxable income from each property in the partnership before the depletion allowance . . . as long as the wells produce. This percentage will decrease from 22 percent to 15 percent between 1980 and 1984.

Capital gains opportunities, reduced by *recapture* of a portion of *intangible drilling costs*, arise if the general partner exchanges partnership interests for common stock and you sell your stock profitably, or he offers a *cash liquidating value* which you accept.

DRILLING PROGRAM OPERATIONS

Drilling-partnership general partners are normally oil and gas producers seeking investors' capital to finance operations. After deducting the *front-end load*, the general partner typically drills as many wells as possible with available *proceeds*. While selecting wells which meet partnership objectives, he usually seeks diversification of risk, depth, and geological area. During drilling, progress reports are distributed frequently. After drilling is complete, any income is apportioned between the general partner and the investors (quarterly in most cases), according to an established formula.

EQUIPMENT LEASING

For industrial corporations, equipment leasing spreads large cash outlays over several years. In some instances, a lease may be classified as "off-the-balance-sheet" financing that does not hurt the corporation's borrowing capacity.

Virtually any industrial equipment can be leased: airplanes, computers, trucks, drilling rigs, entire factories, and railroad cars are examples.

Equipment-leasing partnerships all require: (1) investors to provide equity capital, (2) sponsors to supervise partnership operations, (3) lenders (banks or insurance companies) to provide loans, (4) users, and (5) leasable equipment.

Equipment leasing offers a lesser-risk approach to tax shelter. However, do not conclude that equipment leasing is riskless. The risk of user failure is always present; even companies with top credit ratings sometimes cannot meet obligations. Another risk is obsolescence. Tax laws require that a lease must have a shorter term than the equipment's useful life if certain tax benefits are to be retained. Thus, investors bear the risk of re-leasing or selling—even if technology has rendered the equipment obsolete. Also, upon successful sale, *recapture* of certain deductions may offset gains significantly.

TYPES OF PROGRAMS

The common type of equipment-leasing partnership offers deferral opportunities. Early-year tax losses result from *leverage* and *accelerated depreciation* (double-declining balance on new equipment or 150 percent declining balance on used equipment). Also, some equipment, a computer for example, has a very short useful life. *Useful life* is a tax concept related to depreciation. It may not coincide with the actual time equipment is used. For example, owners of railroad cars may elect to depreciate their equipment over a 12-year useful life even though the equipment may actually operate for several decades.

Accelerated depreciation and short useful life mean very high deductions in early years converting to taxable income when depreciation is exhausted—thereby deferring taxable income. Continuous reinvestment over several years creates an on-going deferral of taxable income.

LEASING-PARTNERSHIP OPERATIONS

The general partner typically deducts a management fee and offering expenses. Equipment is purchased using partnership proceeds and loans. The general partner typically receives a small portion of the lease payments plus a share of any equipment-sale proceeds; he may earn additional compensation by providing equipment maintenance for users. In equipment-leasing partnerships, the general partner is usually a company that specializes in equipment leasing.

AGRICULTURE

Agricultural tax shelters include cattle feeding, cattle and other livestock breeding, crops, and timber. With the exception of cattle feeding and breeding, none are widely available as *public programs*.

CATTLE FEEDING

Young *feeder cattle* are purchased with partnership *proceeds*. These cattle become collateral for recourse loans to purchase more cattle and grain for the feeding period. Interest and feed costs push total first-year deductions to 50 percent to 100 percent. When *finished cattle* are sold after four to six months, bank loans are repaid and the general partner's share is deducted. Any balance is ordinary income to the limited partners.

Because the holding period for cattle is 24 months, there are no capital gains. Disease and price fluctuations are major risks. Risks, however, can be partially offset, but not eliminated, with hedging and insurance.

BREEDING PROGRAMS

In addition to cattle, *breeding* refers to fur-bearing animals, other farm animals, and fish or shellfish. Although the "livestock" varies, program operations are similar. An initial "herd" is purchased. First-year tax losses can equal up to 50 percent to 90 percent; feed costs and depreciation are the principal deductions. Depreciation and investment-tax credit is available on the initial herd but not on offspring.

Sale of offspring generates income. Except for fish and shellfish programs, most females and superior males are retained to increase herd size and quality. Capital gains are available on livestock held more than 12 months (24 months for horses and cattle). Disease and price fluctuations are major risks. *Recapture* may reduce profitability.

CROPS

The list of potential crop partnerships covers virtually anything grown in an orchard, field, grove, or vineyard; fruits, nuts, grains, vegetables, and so on. Wine grapes, nuts, and citrus are the most popular program types.

Labor costs, interest, and operating expenses are deductible. By using leverage, first-year tax losses may approach 50 percent to 90 percent. Crop sales generate ordinary income. Depreciation may offer partially tax-sheltered cash flow. Risks depend on weather, price fluctuations, and whether new or mature properties are involved. Capital gains, subject to recapture restrictions, are primary investment objectives when the land on which the crops are grown is finally sold.

SUMMARY

Most investors satisfy their tax-shelter investment objectives through public or private programs organized as limited partnerships in newly-constructed real estate, existing income-producing real estate, net-leased real estate, government-assisted housing, oil and gas drilling, equipment leasing, or agriculture.

Each major tax shelter offers a specific package of possible tax and investment benefits. In addition, each shelter investment involves risk. Although some are riskier than others, there is always the danger that your rate of return from a given investment will be less than you anticipated or, in some instances, that you may suffer total loss. Always keep risk in mind as you consult your tax advisor about possible benefits.

SPECIALIZED TAX SHELTERS

In addition to the real estate, oil and gas, equipment leasing, and agriculture tax shelters, there are a number of personal and corporate investment vehicles which may apply to your financial situation; Keogh Plans, annuities, pension and profit sharing plans, individual retirement accounts, and municipal bonds. None of these tax shelters utilizes the limited partnership format.

KEOGH PLANS

If you are self-employed, depending on your income level, a defined-contribution Keogh Plan can help you set aside between $750 and $7,500 each year, tax-free, for your retirement. A defined-benefit Keogh Plan, when permissible in certain cases, may result in higher allowable contributions. Contributions to a Keogh Plan may be invested in a variety of investments: stocks, bonds, mutual funds, and so on; all growth and income accumulate tax free. After retirement, you pay tax on the money as you withdraw it from the plan.

ANNUITIES

An annuity is simply a contractual agreement between you and an insurance company that provides you with a very safe tax-advantaged accumulation vehicle. You pay no federal or state income tax on the earnings while they accumulate. You never have to worry about market fluctuations since both your principal and interest are 100 percent guaranteed by a major insurance company. Interest is credited daily, compounded automatically at competitive secure-dollar investment rates. You can withdraw money at any time and under specified conditions, without a penalty.

At retirement, you can choose an option that will provide you with income for a specified period of years . . . for life . . . beneficiary payments upon death . . . or income for your life and your spouse's life. The monthly payments you receive are partially tax sheltered because they represent, to a degree, return of your initial deposit. In addition, the interest portion of each monthly payment is taxable at your lower, post-retirement tax rate.

PENSION AND PROFIT-SHARING PLANS

Since enactment of the Employee Retirement Income Security Act of 1974 (ERISA), professionals (doctors, lawyers, accountants, architects, etc.) who incorporate can set up profit-sharing plans: generally up to 15 percent of the annual compensation paid each participant (limited to a maximum of $32,700 in 1979 and adjusted in later years by a cost-of-living adjustment factor) may be paid out free of corporate income tax. Pension-plan contributions, also free of corporate income tax, are limited based on an actuarial funding-formula compensation. Incorporated professionals may also establish pension plan contributions which are tax deductible. As in Keogh Plans, all growth and income accumulate tax free.

INDIVIDUAL RETIREMENT ACCOUNTS

ERISA also established a retirement plan for employed individuals. Any employee who is not participating in a qualified pension plan can establish his own *Individual Retirement Account*. Up to $1,500 or 15 percent of annual compensation (whichever is smaller) may be invested in an IRA each year. A married employee with a nonworking spouse can establish a joint IRA; contributions are limited to the lesser of $1,750 or 15 percent of compensation. If both spouses work, each can establish an IRA; the $1,500/15 percent limitation applies to each. All interest and appreciation in an IRA accumulate tax free. No withdrawals are permitted before age 59½; withdrawals must begin by age 70½. Withdrawals are taxed as ordinary income as received (at the lower post-retirement tax rate).

MUNICIPAL BONDS

Debt securities of state, cities, and special purpose "authorities" (turnpikes, sewer and water districts, etc.) pay interest that is free of federal and some state taxes. There are no tax losses, but 100 percent of the income is tax free, fully tax-sheltered cash flow. Municipal bonds may be purchased directly or by investing in one of several municipal-bond trusts or municipal-bond mutual funds which pool the funds of several investors and purchase diversified portfolios of bonds.

INVESTING IN TAX SHELTERS

SELECTING THE PROGRAM

Analyzing any program requires in-depth knowledge of partnership law, taxation, the industry, and the general partner's management and operations.

Some tenets that should guide you include:

Diversification. Pooling capital of several investors and spreading risk among several projects is a key benefit of limited partnerships.

Program Size. Too small a program may offer only limited diversification, or it may be excessively burdened by *front-end load.* Too large a program may force the sponsor into unwise decisions if he is under pressure to complete partnership projects before year-end.

Management. Decisions are based on integrity, past performance, experience in the operating area, financial stability, limited partnership experience, experience with comparable-size programs, and quality of investor communications.

Sharing Arrangement. The general partner's compensation should encourage superior performance. Compensation should be derived from operating profits, not front-end fees.

Tax Features. Well-accepted taxation principles avoid unnecessary "tax-risk." Programs promising excessive deductions or unreasonable expectation of investment returns are avoided.

Liquidity. Any liquidity is better than none; however, all tax shelters are, at best, illiquid. Emphasis is placed on the general partner's financial ability to provide liquidity at the appropriate time.

INVESTMENT APPLICATIONS

An integral part of selecting the "right" industry and "right" program is what you hope to accomplish by making the investment. Applications of tax-sheltered investments include: (1) saving taxes by sheltering high-level, recurring income, (2) reducing tax effects of major capital gains, (3) building retirement income, (4) increasing charitable contributions, (5) employing sophisticated estate-planning tactics, and (6) enhancing corporate tax planning.

RECURRING INCOME

The most familiar use of tax shelters is related to softening the burden of taxes on high-level, recurring income. If you are a high-salaried corporate executive, doctor, or lawyer, for example, you pretty well know that, short of some unpredictable economic or personal calamity, you will earn at least X dollars each year for the next Y years. You can use this knowledge and apply tax shelters to help offset your annual tax liability.

Let us assume that each year for the next ten years, you will file a joint return with $75,000 taxable income (after exemptions and itemized deductions). Also, assume you will make a 100 percent deductible, $10,000 annual tax-shelter investment and you are in the 50 percent federal tax bracket.

Over a ten-year period, you will invest $100,000, but because of tax savings you will be out of pocket only $50,000. You will have accomplished four things: (1) reduced your annual tax bill by $5,000, (2) invested $100,000 at an out-of-pocket cost of only $50,000, (3) purchased assets which can yield an investment return with dollars that normally go to pay taxes, and (4) spread your risk.

CAPITAL GAINS

Let us suppose that in one year you have, in addition to your $60,000 recurring taxable income, a $200,000 capital gain. A good rule of thumb is to consider investing 40 percent of a large capital gain in a tax shelter, in this case $80,000.

JOINT RETURN—50 PERCENT TAX BRACKET

	With Tax Shelter	Without Tax Shelter
Taxable Income*	$260,000	$260,000
Sixty percent capital gains deduction	(120,000)	(120,000)
Net taxable income	$140,000	$140,000
One hundred percent deductible tax shelter†	(80,000)	—
Revised taxable income	$ 60,000	$140,000
Tax due (including tax preference)	$ 32,000	$ 67,000
Tax savings	$ 35,100	
Net investment cost	$ 44,900	

* Personal service net income $60,000; capital gains $200,000.
† Assumes $40,000 of tax preference items.

This technique: (1) puts $80,000 to work for a net cost of 56 cents on the dollar, (2) reduces your tax bill 52 percent, and (3) still leaves you at least $120,000 cash remaining for your capital gain—a very powerful tax and investment planning tool.

Note: The alternative minimum tax is used in the computation of the With Tax Shelter example.

RETIREMENT PLANNING

If you are a few years from retirement, tax shelters—particularly those with a deferral feature—can help you take advantage of needed tax savings up to your retirement date. After retirement your tax shelter may yield ordinary income which will be taxed at your lower post-retirement tax rate.

CHARITY CONTRIBUTIONS

You invest in a tax-shelter limited partnership and hold it until the cash liquidating value or other fair market value is determined. Tax laws permit a deduction up to the fair market value of an asset contributed to a qualified charitable organization. Using this technique, you have the opportunity—assuming a successful tax-shelter investment—to take two deductions on the same dollars: first when you invest, then when you contribute. Your charity receives an income-producing asset free of any administrative responsibilities. Note, however, that charity giving is a very sensitive tax area requiring advance consultation with both your tax advisor and your charity.

ESTATE PLANNING

The same invest-hold-contribute technique used for charity giving can be used to transfer tax-shelter assets out of your estate to your children. This technique: (1) decreases your taxable estate and ultimately, reduces inheritance taxes; also, it (2) reduces overall family tax liability by shifting your high-bracket taxable income into your children's lower tax bracket. Like charity contributions, estate planning requires careful study by your tax advisor.

CORPORATE TAX PLANNING

Corporations—particularly closely-held entities—can employ tax shelters a number of creative ways, including: (1) sheltering recurring income; (2) utilizing tax benefits, then contributing the investment to employee-pension and profit-sharing plans; (3) avoiding the penalty tax on accumulated earnings; and (4) providing executive compensation through tax-shelter investment-loan plans.

INVESTMENT RETURNS

Because of risk, it is impossible to say what rate of return you may receive from a given tax-shelter program; losses or less-than-anticipated returns are always possible. However, with tax savings (which reduce your initial out-of-pocket investment costs), proper diversification, a proven management team, and, when feasible, a three- to five-year program of recurring investments, risks are significantly reduced.

As soon as possible, your general partner will begin distributing your share of any partnership profits—usually within six months to two years of the date you invest (longer when a highly leveraged partnership repays bank debt). After distributions begin, you will probably continue receiving them on a fairly regular basis; quarterly is the most common distribution pattern.

GLOSSARY

Note: Terms in *italics* are defined elsewhere in the glossary.

Accelerated depreciation Any method of *depreciation* which permits *deduction* of a greater percentage of the cost of an asset in early years of the asset's useful life with smaller deductions in later years. Two methods are widely used: (1) the "sum-of-the-years-digits" method and (2) the more popular "declining-balance" method. Under the declining balance, annual deductions are calculated as a percentage of the *straight-line depreciation* rate, that is, 200 percent declining balance (also called "double-declining balance") available for new residential construction; 150 percent declining balance, available for new commercial construction; 125 percent declining balance for existing improved real estate. Note that accelerated depreciation is usually a *tax preference item*.

Assessment Additional amounts of money which a *limited partner* in a *tax-sheltered partnership* may be required to furnish beyond his original *subscription*. A given program, depending on the terms, may be either "assessable" or "nonassessable." An assessable program may have limited or unlimited assessments. Assessments may be optional or mandatory.

"At-risk" limitations This limitation is designed to prevent noncorporate taxpayers from deducting losses in excess of their economic investment in the activity involved. These rules now apply to all activities except real estate and certain companies leasing equipment. In addition, where your amount of investment deemed to be "at risk" is reduced below zero (by distributions or change of status of liabilities from recourse to nonrecourse), income recognition may be required of deductions previously taken.

Blind pool program A *tax-sheltered partnership* which, at the time sale of *subscriptions* begins, does not have the *proceeds* of the offering allocated to specific projects or properties. (Contrast with *Specified property program.*)

Capital asset Any asset (property, equipment, livestock, etc.) which is: (1) used in a trade or business (except inventories or items held for sale to customers), (2) held for production of income, or (3) given the effect of a capital asset by a tax law provision. With certain exceptions, capital assets—including interests in *tax-shelter partnerships*—are subject to *capital-gains* treatment on any profit (or loss) arising from sale or exchange.

Capital gains Usually gain (or loss) from sale or exchange of any property is included in income and taxed at ordinary income tax rates. However, if the gain is from the sale or exchange of a *capital asset* owned for more than 12 months, the tax is calculated at the lower long-term capital-gains rate, generally no more than 28 percent. Almost all types of *tax-sheltered investments* except cattle feeding and equipment leasing offer some capital-gains opportunities. Certain types of real estate, and oil and gas offer the most potential. It has been said that capital gains offer the major source of tax relief. Note however that capital-gains benefits may be reduced by *recapture*. Note also that 60 percent of long-term capital gains may be taxed under the alternative minimum tax.

Cash liquidating value The amount, generally based on an evaluation of a qualified independent appraiser, which will be paid by the *general partner* for an interest in a *tax-sheltered partnership* upon exercise by a *limited partner* of his right to receive such value. Programs that offer cash liquidation can be described as offering "liquidity," as opposed to illiquid programs which do not have cash liquidating features.

Conversion Obtaining current tax *deductions* against ordinary income while turning future revenues into income taxable at more favorable *capital-gains* rates or lower rates derived from favorable tax features such as *depletion* or *depreciation*.

Deductions In this context, the interest, taxes, *depreciation, depletion,* and other expenses incurred in the trade or business of a *tax-sheltered partnership* which are passed on to the *limited partners* thereby reducing their taxable income and, ultimately, their tax liability. The "ordinary and necessary" expenses of any business are allowable as deductions; (1) *tax-sheltered intangible drilling costs* associated with oil and gas, (2) depreciation and interest costs associated with real estate, equipment leasing, and certain agricultural tax shelters, particularly when *leverage* is employed, and (3) the feed and maintenance costs associated with cattle feeding. Ideally, a *tax-sheltered partnership* will generate deductions in excess of income for the first year or first few years, thereby permitting program *limited partners* to recover part or all of their investments out of *tax losses.*

Deferral In this context, a form of tax shelter that results from an investment timed so that *deductions* take place during the investor's high-income years and taxable income is realized after retirement, in some other period of reduced income, or at a time when the tax will be more convenient to pay. Equipment leasing and certain types of real estate offer the best deferral opportunities.

Depletion A form of *deduction* that applies to "wasting-asset" interest. The purpose is to encourage exploration for new deposits by permitting recovery of exploration and development costs out of tax savings. The annual depletion deduction for any mineral property is the greater of "cost depletion" (based on the ratio of annual production to remaining reserves) and "percentage depletion" (a fixed annual percent). The major advantage of percentage depletion is that benefits are available each year a property produces income and do not cease when the cost of the property has been recovered. Oil and gas, timber, and minerals all offer some depletion. Percentage depletion on oil and gas is 22 percent of gross income from each property, limited to the lesser of 65 percent of the individual's taxable income or 50 percent of the taxable income from the property. However, beginning in 1981, this percentage decreases down to 15 percent ratably from 1981–84. Percentage depletion on other minerals ranges from 22 percent for sulfur down to 5 percent for clay and shale. Note that percentage depletion is a *tax preference item.*

Depreciation A form of *deduction* to permit recovery of the cost (less any salvage value) of an asset in the form of tax savings. This cost recovery is spread over the asset's "useful life" as an annual deduction from taxable income. Depreciation is most attractive in real estate, equipment leasing, and some types of cattle breeding, especially if *leverage* is employed. Tax laws permit choosing a constant annual depreciation amount over useful life (called straight-line depreciation) or, in some cases, one of several *accelerated-depreciation* methods.

Double-declining balance See: *Accelerated depreciation.*

Front-end load A slang term for the total of *organizational and offering expenses* plus *management fees:* that is, the total deductions from the *offering amount* to arrive at the *proceeds* of a *tax-sheltered partnership.* (See also: *Management fees.*)

General partner In this context, the manager or sponsor of a *tax-sheltered investment* which has been organized as a *limited partnership.* (See *Limited partnership* for details.)

Intangible drilling costs A tax *deduction* for certain expenditures incurred in drilling and completing oil and gas wells. "Intangibles" are the items which have no salvage value (commonly nonmaterial costs such as labor, chemicals, drill-site preparation, etc.). Intangibles frequently account for 50 percent to 80 percent of the cost of drilling and completing a given well. Note that intangible drilling costs on producing wells in excess of oil and gas net income is a *tax preference item.*

Joint venture A form of business organization. In this context, a *tax-sheltered investment* in which the manager and the investors share jointly in the ownership, management authority, and liability. (Contrast with *Limited partnership.*)

Leverage In this context, a method of increasing a tax shelter through borrowing (see *nonrecourse loans* and *recourse loans*) as a part of a *tax-sheltered investment.* The investor (in certain circumstances) is permitted *deductions* for interest, *management fees, depreciation,* and so on, on the amount he invests plus his pro-rata share of the amount the partnership borrows on a nonrecourse basis or any amounts for which he is personally liable on a recourse basis. Any properly-structured loans, therefore, serve to increase total deductions from income for tax purposes. Real estate offers excellent leverage possibilities, as do cattle breeding and equipment leasing.

Limited partner In this context, the purchaser of a *subscription* in a *tax-sheltered investment* which has been organized as a *limited partnership;* that is, an investor.

Limited partnership A form of business organization in which some partners exchange their right to participate in management for a limitation on their liability for partnership losses. Commonly, *limited partners* have liability only to the extent of their investment in the business plus their share of any undistributed profits. To establish limited liability, there must be at least one *general partner* who is fully liable for all claims against the business. Limited partnerships are a popular organizational form for *tax-sheltered investments* because of the ease with which tax benefits flow through the partnership to the individual partners. (Contrast with *Joint venture.*)

Liquidity See: *Cash liquidating value.*

Management fee An amount paid to the *general partner* of a *tax-sheltered partnership* to cover *organization and offering expenses* and/or to repay costs of operating and administrating the partnership, commonly expressed as a percentage of the total *offering amount.* Prior to the Tax Reform Act of 1976, the management fee was claimed as a *deduction* by many limited partnerships. Under present law, only the general partner's reimbursements to cover costs of operating and administrating the partnership are considered fully deductible. (See also: *Front-end load.*)

Maximum tax Individuals are taxed at a maximum rate of 50 percent on that portion of their taxable income attributable to personal-service income. However, the amount of income eligible for the maximum rate is offset by the amount of the year's *tax preference items.* The amount offset is taxable as unearned income at rates of up to 70 percent.

Minimum subscription The smallest dollar amount which an investor must initially commit in order to become a *limited partner* in a *tax-sheltered partnership,* usually one or more *units.* In a *public program* the minimum subscription is generally almost always $5,000. (See also: *Subscription.*)

Minimum tax Fifteen percent of total tax preference items which exceed the greater of $10,000 or one half the taxpayer's regular federal income tax liability. (See also: *Tax preference items.*)

Alternative minimum tax A tax on regular taxable income plus the long-term capital-gain preference (60 percent untaxed portion) plus adjusted itemized deductions in excess of 60 percent of adjusted gross income. The resulting "alternative minimum taxable income," after a specific exemption of $20,000, is subject to the following rates of tax: 10 percent on the first $40,000; 20 percent on the next $40,000 and 25 percent of any excess. This tax replaces the regular tax (including the 15 percent minimum tax) if it exceeds that tax.

Noncash charges *Deductions* for *depreciation and depletion* which are not actually paid to anyone, yet are subtracted from taxable income before calculating tax due. *Tax-sheltered partnerships* such as real estate and equipment leasing which employ *leverage* may be able to pyramid noncash charges to the point that limited partners receive *tax-sheltered cash flow* in the early years against which there is limited or no tax liability.

Nonrecourse loan In this context, any borrowing by a *tax-sheltered partnership*, structured in such a way that lenders can look only to specific assets pledged for repayment and not to the individual assets of the various partners. However, in the event of a foreclosure, if partnership cash and assets are not sufficient to repay the loan balance, the limited partners may be left with a substantial tax bill because of "forgiveness of debt." Real estate is the only tax-shelter area where nonrecourse financing is permitted. (Contrast with *recourse loan;* see also: *Leverage.*)

Offering amount The total dollar amount sought by a *general partner* from prospective *limited partners in a particular tax-sheltered partnership.*

Organization and offering expenses Those expenses incurred in connection with preparing a *tax-sheltered partnership* for registration with federal and/or state securities agencies and subsequently selling subscriptions to *limited partners.* Organizational and offering expenses typically include legal fees, printing costs, registration fees, sales commissions, and selling costs. (See also: *Management fee; Front-end load.*)

Private program A *tax-sheltered partnership* which is offered and sold pursuant to the private-offering exemption available under the Securities Act of 1933 and/or some registration exemption allowed under the securities laws of one or more states; that is, a program which is not registered with the Securities and Exchange Commission. (Contrast with *Public program.*)

Proceeds The dollar amount remaining for the general partner to conduct partnership operations after deduction of *organization and operating expenses* or other items of *front-end load* from the total amount committed.

Public program A *tax-sheltered partnership* which is registered with the Securities and Exchange Commission (SEC) and distributed in a public offering by broker dealers

and/or employees of the *general partner.* The principal differences between a public program and a *private program* relate to: (1) the number of *investors,* which may be several hundred in a public program, but which is limited, with certain exceptions, to 35 in a private program; (2) *minimum subscription: $5,000 in a public program, $50,000 or more in a private program; and (3) the fact that "private" investors are subject to stricter suitability standards.*

Recapture Upon profitable sale of certain assets, *capital gains* may be severely restricted when previously claimed *deductions* for *depreciation, farming losses, intangible drilling costs,* or *investment credit* are taken back into ordinary income (i.e., "recaptured"). Since ordinary income tax rates can run as high as 70 percent—versus 28 percent for capital gains—recapture can severely reduce or eliminate capital-gains benefits. The amount of recapture depends on the type of asset, holding period, type of depreciation (straight-line or accelerated), as well as dollar amount of gain versus the amount of "recaptured" deductions.

Recourse loan In this context, any borrowing by a *tax-shelter* investor for which he is personally liable. (Contrast with *Nonrecourse loan.*)

Specified property program A *tax-sheltered partnership* which, at the time sale of *subscriptions* begins, has the proceeds of the offering allocated to definite projects or properties which are described in detail in the prospectus or offering circular. (Contrast with *Blind pool program.*)

Straight-line depreciation See: *Depreciation.*

Subchapter S corporation A form of corporation with a limited number of qualified stockholders who elect to utilize a specific tax law provision which permits them to be taxed so the corporation pays no taxes and each stockholder reports his share of the corporate income (or loss) on his own tax return. (Also called a "tax option corporation.")

Subscription The total dollar amount for which a *limited partner* in a *tax-sheltered partnership* initially commits. Legally it represents the amount he is obligated to pay, exclusive of any *assessment* amount which he has the option to reject. (See also: *Unit.*)

Tax loss A situation that occurs when the *deductions* generated by a *tax-sheltered partnership* exceed program revenues. Thus, the limited partner's taxable income is lower, resulting in a tax saving. Ideally, a *tax-sheltered partnership* will generate enough tax losses the first year or first few years to permit the limited partners to recover their investment from "tax savings." However, *recapture* may ultimately limit these benefits.

Tax preference items Items of tax preference subject to the 15 percent *minimum tax* include: *accelerated depreciation* in excess of *straight-line depreciation* on real property and leased personal property, appreciation on certain stock options, excess intangible drilling costs on productive wells, and excess percentage depletion.

Tax savings See: *Tax losses.*

Tax-sheltered cash flow The situation that arises when *noncash charges* and other *deductions* exceed gross income from a tax-shelter partnership so that the program has cash to distribute to *limited partners* even though the cash they may receive involves no current tax liability or is taxed at a lower rate. Real estate and equipment-leasing programs employing *accelerated depreciation* and *leverage* are the best sources of tax-sheltered cash flow.

Tax-sheltered investment An investment that has an expectation of economic profit, made even more attractive because of the timing of the profit or the way it is taxed, generally having some or all of the following characteristics:

1. *Deferral* of taxes,
2. *Conversion of deductions* to possible future *capital gains*,
3. *Leverage*.

The flow-through of tax benefits is a material factor whether the entity is organized as a *limited partnership, joint venture,* or *Subchapter S corporation* and whether it is offered to investors as a *private program* or a *public program*. Common forms of tax-sheltered investments include: real estate, oil and gas, equipment leasing, and agriculture.

Tax-sheltered partnership A *tax-sheltered investment* organized as a *limited partnership*. Commonly, a tax-sheltered program is created to mutually benefit a *general partner* and a group of *limited partners*. It may be organized as a *public program* or a *private program*.

Unit The smallest dollar amount into which *subscriptions* in a *tax-shelter partnership* may be divided, usually $1,000 or $5,000. For example, a $1 million *public program* might consist of 200 units of $5,000 each. Alternately, it might consist of 1,000 units of $1,000 each. Each type would normally have a *minimum subscription* of $5,000.

This account has been prepared for informational purposes only and is not an offer to sell or the solicitation of an offer to buy any tax-sheltered investment or any other security.

The material contained in this description of tax-sheltered investments is based upon the provisions of the Internal Revenue Code of 1954, as presently amended, the existing applicable regulations, and current administrative rulings and practice. However, it is emphasized that no assurance can be given that legislative or administrative changes will not be forthcoming which would modify this description. Any such changes may or may not be retroactive with respect to transactions entered into prior to the effective date of such changes.

Investment in tax shelters may give rise to liability for state income, property, or inheritance taxes which are not discussed herein and may create the necessity for ancillary probate proceedings. Due to the complex tax and other legal considerations surrounding an investment in a tax shelter, each prospective investor is urged to consult with his own counsel before obligating himself to purchase an interest in a tax shelter.

MARRIED TAXPAYERS FILING JOINT RETURNS AND SURVIVING SPOUSES

If Taxable Income Is:	The Tax Is:
Not over $3,400	No tax.
Over $3,400 but not over $5,500	14% of excess over $3,400.
Over $5,500 but not over $7,600	$294, plus 16% of excess over $5,500.
Over $7,600 but not over $11,900	$630, plus 18% of excess over $7,600.
Over $11,900 but not over $16,000	$1,404, plus 21% of excess over $11,900.
Over $16,000 but not over $20,200	$2,265, plus 24% of excess over $16,000.
Over $20,200 but not over $24,600	$3,273, plus 28% of excess over $20,200.
Over $24,600 but not over $29,900	$4,505, plus 32% of excess over $24,600.
Over $29,900 but not over $35,200	$6,201, plus 37% of excess over $29,900.
Over $35,200 but not over $45,800	$8,162, plus 43% of excess over $35,200.
Over $45,800 but not over $60,000	$12,720, plus 49% of excess over $45,800.
Over $60,000 but not over $85,600	$19,678, plus 54% of excess over $60,000.
Over $85,600 but not over $109,400	$33,502, plus 59% of excess over $85,600.
Over $109,400 but not over $162,400	$47,544, plus 64% of excess over $109,400.
Over $162,400 but not over $215,400	$81,464, plus 68% of excess over $162,400.
Over $215,400	$117,504, plus 70% of excess over $215,400.

UNMARRIED INDIVIDUALS (other than surviving spouses)

If Taxable Income Is:	The Tax Is:
Not over $2,300	No tax.
Over $2,300 but not over $3,400	14% of excess over $2,300.
Over $3,400 but not over $4,400	$54, plus 16% of excess over 3,400.
Over $4,400 but not over $6,500	$314, plus 18% of excess over $4,400.
Over $6,500 but not over $8,500	$692, plus 19% of excess over $6,500.
Over $8,500 but not over $10,800	$1,072, plus 21% of excess over $8,500.
Over $10,800 but not over $12,900	$1,555, plus 24% of excess over $10,800.
Over $12,900 but not over $15,000	$2,059, plus 26% of excess over $12,900.
Over $15,000 but not over $18,200	$2,605, plus 30% of excess over $15,000.
Over $18,200 but not over $23,500	$3,565, plus 34% of excess over $18,200.
Over $23,500 but not over $28,800	$5,367, plus 39% of excess over $23,500.
Over $28,800 but not over $34,100	$7,434, plus 44% of excess over $28,800.
Over $34,100 but not over $41,500	$9,766, plus 49% of excess over $34,100.
Over $41,500 but not over $55,300	$13,392, plus 55% of excess over $41,500.
Over $55,300 but not over $81,800	$20,982, plus 63% of excess over $55,300.
Over $81,800 but not over $108,300	$37,677, plus 68% of excess over $81,800.
Over $108,300	$55,697, plus 70% of excess over $108,300.

NEW MONETARY AGGREGATES

Money supply data has been revised and expanded to reflect the Federal Reserve's redefinition of the monetary aggregates. The redefinition was prompted by the emergence in recent years of new monetary assets—for example, negotiable order of withdrawal (NOW) accounts and money-market mutual fund shares—and alterations in the basic character of established monetary assets—for example, the growing similarity of and substitution between the deposits of thrift institutions and those of commercial banks.

Four newly redefined monetary aggregates replace the old M-1 through M-5 measures, and a very broad measure of liquid assets has been adopted. The principle underlying these new monetary aggregates is that similar assets should be combined at the same level of aggregation:

M1-A is one of two narrow transactions measures. It is basically the same as the old M-1 aggregate (currency plus demand deposits at commercial banks), which had been called total money supply, except that it excludes demand deposits held by foreign commercial banks and official institutions.

M1-B, the other narrow measure, adds to M1-A interest-earning checkable deposits at all depositary institutions— namely NOW accounts, automatic transfer from savings (ATS) accounts, and credit-union-share draft balances—as well as a small amount of demand deposits at thrift institutions that cannot, using present data sources, be separated from interest-earning checkable deposits.

M-2 as redefined adds to M1-B overnight repurchase agreements (RPs) issued by commercial banks and certain overnight Eurodollars (those issued by Carribbean branches of member banks) held by U.S. nonbank residents, money-market mutual fund shares, and savings and small-denomination time deposits (those issued in denominations of less than $100,000) at all depository institutions. Depository institutions are commercial banks (including U.S. agencies and branches of foreign banks, Edge Act Corporations, and foreign investment companies), mutual savings banks, savings and loan associations, and credit unions.

Source: Survey of Current Business.

M-3 as redefined is equal to new M-2 plus large-denomination time deposits (those issued in denominations of $100,000 or more) at all depository institutions (including negotiable CDs) plus term RPs issued by commercial banks and savings and loan associations.

L, the very broad measure of liquid assets, equals new M-3 plus other liquid assets consisting of other Eurodollar holdings of U.S. nonbank residents, bankers acceptances, commercial paper, savings bonds, and marketable liquid Treasury obligations.

Consolidation adjustments have been made in the construction of each of the new measures, in order to avoid double counting of the public's monetary assets. A major consolidation adjustment involves the netting of deposits held by depository institutions with other depository institutions. In constructing M-1A, demand deposits held by commercial banks with other commercial banks have been removed. The procedure calls for the removal from M1-B of those demand deposit holdings of thrift institutions that are estimated to be used in servicing their checkable deposits, although at present the amount is negligible. Similarly, at the M-2 level all other demand deposit holdings of thrift institutions are deducted; currently that means all such demand deposits are netted from M-2. Savings and time deposits held by depositary institutions are also appropriately netted at the M-2 and M-3 levels. The other major kind of consolidation adjustment involves removing the assets held by money-market mutual funds from several components appearing in the M-2, M-3, and L measures. These institutions issue shares to the public and use the proceeds to acquire a variety of liquid assets that are components of the new M-2, M-3, and L measures. In order to avoid first counting these amounts as money-market mutual fund shares and then counting them again as money market fund holdings of RPs, CDs, commercial paper, and so forth, holdings of each of these assets by money market funds are subtracted from the relevant components.

The procedure for constructing the new seasonally adjusted aggregates has been to seasonally adjust each component with a standard option of the Census X-11 program—wherever possible—and then to sum the components to derive the appropriate total. Some components have not been seasonally adjusted. In some cases sufficient historical data is not yet available. In other cases the components are dominated by such a strong trend that seasonal adjustment is not likely to be successful.

A detailed explanation of the new measures was published in the February 1980 issue of the *Federal Reserve Bulletin*. Monthly data from 1959 to date and weekly data from 1970 to date are available from the Banking Section of the Division of Research and Statistics at the Federal Reserve Board, Washington, D.C. 20551.

MEANS OF FINANCING THE FEDERAL DEFICIT [1]

(In millions of dollars)

Description	1979 actual	1980 estimate	1981 estimate	1982 estimate	1983 estimate
Budget surplus or deficit (−)	−27,733	−39,754	−15,773	4.818	24,509
Deficit (−) of off-budget Federal entities [2]	−12,428	−16,766	−18,090	−15,078	−12,852
Total, surplus or deficit (−)	−40,162	−56,519	−33,862	−10,259	11,657
Means of financing other than borrowing from the public:					
Decrease or increase (−) in cash and monetary assets	2,131	10,103	....	....	....
Increase or decrease (−) in liabilities for:					
Checks outstanding, etc.[3]	735	265	−269	....	....
Deposit fund balances	2,662	898	584	....	....
Seigniorage on coins	992	953	447	993	1,079
Total, means of financing other than borrowing from the public	6,521	12,219	762	993	1,079
Total, requirements for borrowing from the public	−33,641	−44,300	−33,100	−9,266	12,735
Change in debt held by the public	33,641	44,300	33,100	9,266	−12,735

[1] Several amounts have been assumed to be zero in 1981 and 1982 because they are usually small and would be very difficult to estimate accurately.
[2] The off-budget Federal entities consist of the Rural Electrification and Telephone revolving fund, Rural Telephone Bank, Pension Benefit Guaranty Corporation, Federal Financing Bank, Postal Service fund, one program of the U.S. Railway Association, and the Energy Security Corporation.
[3] Besides checks outstanding, includes military payment certificates, accrued interest (less unamortized discount) payable on Treasury debt, and, as an offsetting change in assets, certain collections in transit.

PRESENT VALUE OF $1

Periods until Payment	1%	2%	4%	6%	8%	10%	12%	14%	15%	16%	18%	20%	22%	24%	25%	26%	28%	30%	35%	40%	45%	50%
1	0.990	0.980	0.962	0.943	0.926	0.909	0.893	0.877	0.870	0.862	0.847	0.833	0.820	0.806	0.800	0.794	0.781	0.769	0.741	0.714	0.690	0.667
2	0.980	0.961	0.925	0.890	0.857	0.826	0.797	0.769	0.756	0.743	0.718	0.694	0.672	0.650	0.640	0.630	0.610	0.592	0.549	0.510	0.476	0.444
3	0.971	0.942	0.889	0.840	0.794	0.751	0.712	0.675	0.658	0.641	0.609	0.579	0.551	0.524	0.512	0.500	0.477	0.455	0.406	0.364	0.328	0.296
4	0.961	0.924	0.855	0.792	0.735	0.683	0.636	0.592	0.572	0.552	0.516	0.482	0.451	0.423	0.410	0.397	0.373	0.350	0.301	0.260	0.226	0.198
5	0.951	0.906	0.822	0.747	0.681	0.621	0.567	0.519	0.497	0.476	0.437	0.402	0.370	0.341	0.328	0.315	0.291	0.269	0.223	0.186	0.156	0.132
6	0.942	0.888	0.790	0.705	0.630	0.564	0.507	0.456	0.432	0.410	0.370	0.335	0.303	0.275	0.262	0.250	0.227	0.207	0.165	0.133	0.108	0.088
7	0.933	0.871	0.760	0.665	0.583	0.513	0.452	0.400	0.376	0.354	0.314	0.279	0.249	0.222	0.210	0.198	0.178	0.159	0.122	0.095	0.074	0.059
8	0.923	0.853	0.731	0.627	0.540	0.467	0.404	0.351	0.327	0.305	0.266	0.233	0.204	0.179	0.168	0.157	0.139	0.123	0.091	0.068	0.051	0.039
9	0.914	0.837	0.703	0.592	0.500	0.424	0.361	0.308	0.284	0.263	0.225	0.194	0.167	0.144	0.134	0.125	0.108	0.094	0.067	0.048	0.035	0.026
10	0.905	0.820	0.676	0.558	0.463	0.386	0.322	0.270	0.247	0.227	0.191	0.162	0.137	0.116	0.107	0.099	0.085	0.073	0.050	0.035	0.024	0.017
11	0.896	0.804	0.650	0.527	0.429	0.350	0.287	0.237	0.215	0.195	0.162	0.135	0.112	0.094	0.086	0.079	0.066	0.056	0.037	0.025	0.017	0.012
12	0.887	0.788	0.625	0.497	0.397	0.319	0.257	0.208	0.187	0.168	0.137	0.112	0.092	0.076	0.069	0.062	0.052	0.043	0.027	0.018	0.012	0.008
13	0.879	0.773	0.601	0.469	0.368	0.290	0.229	0.182	0.163	0.145	0.116	0.093	0.075	0.061	0.055	0.050	0.040	0.033	0.020	0.013	0.008	0.005
14	0.870	0.758	0.577	0.442	0.340	0.263	0.205	0.160	0.141	0.125	0.099	0.078	0.062	0.049	0.044	0.039	0.032	0.025	0.015	0.009	0.006	0.003
15	0.861	0.743	0.555	0.417	0.315	0.239	0.183	0.140	0.123	0.108	0.084	0.065	0.051	0.040	0.035	0.031	0.025	0.020	0.011	0.006	0.004	0.002
16	0.853	0.728	0.534	0.394	0.292	0.218	0.163	0.123	0.107	0.093	0.071	0.054	0.042	0.032	0.028	0.025	0.019	0.015	0.008	0.005	0.003	0.002
17	0.844	0.714	0.513	0.371	0.270	0.198	0.146	0.108	0.093	0.080	0.060	0.045	0.034	0.026	0.023	0.020	0.015	0.012	0.006	0.003	0.002	0.001
18	0.836	0.700	0.494	0.350	0.250	0.180	0.130	0.095	0.081	0.069	0.051	0.038	0.028	0.021	0.018	0.016	0.012	0.009	0.005	0.002	0.001	0.001
19	0.828	0.686	0.475	0.331	0.232	0.164	0.116	0.083	0.070	0.060	0.043	0.031	0.023	0.017	0.014	0.012	0.009	0.007	0.003	0.002	0.001	
20	0.820	0.673	0.456	0.312	0.215	0.149	0.104	0.073	0.061	0.051	0.037	0.026	0.019	0.014	0.012	0.010	0.007	0.005	0.002	0.001	0.001	
21	0.811	0.660	0.439	0.294	0.199	0.135	0.093	0.064	0.053	0.044	0.031	0.022	0.015	0.011	0.009	0.008	0.006	0.004	0.002	0.001		
22	0.803	0.647	0.422	0.278	0.184	0.123	0.083	0.056	0.046	0.038	0.026	0.018	0.013	0.009	0.007	0.006	0.004	0.003	0.001	0.001		
23	0.795	0.634	0.406	0.262	0.170	0.112	0.074	0.049	0.040	0.033	0.022	0.015	0.010	0.007	0.006	0.005	0.003	0.002	0.001			
24	0.788	0.622	0.390	0.247	0.158	0.102	0.066	0.043	0.035	0.028	0.019	0.013	0.008	0.006	0.005	0.004	0.003	0.002	0.001			
25	0.780	0.610	0.375	0.233	0.146	0.092	0.059	0.038	0.030	0.024	0.016	0.010	0.007	0.005	0.004	0.003	0.002	0.001	0.001			
26	0.772	0.598	0.361	0.220	0.135	0.084	0.053	0.033	0.026	0.021	0.014	0.009	0.006	0.004	0.003	0.002	0.002	0.001				
27	0.764	0.586	0.347	0.207	0.125	0.076	0.047	0.029	0.023	0.018	0.011	0.007	0.005	0.003	0.002	0.002	0.001	0.001				
28	0.757	0.574	0.333	0.196	0.116	0.069	0.042	0.026	0.020	0.016	0.010	0.006	0.004	0.002	0.002	0.002	0.001	0.001				
29	0.749	0.563	0.321	0.185	0.107	0.063	0.037	0.022	0.017	0.014	0.008	0.005	0.003	0.002	0.002	0.001	0.001	0.001				
30	0.742	0.552	0.308	0.174	0.099	0.057	0.033	0.020	0.015	0.012	0.007	0.004	0.003	0.002	0.001	0.001	0.001	0.001				
40	0.672	0.453	0.208	0.097	0.046	0.022	0.011	0.005	0.004	0.003	0.001	0.001										
50	0.608	0.372	0.141	0.054	0.021	0.009	0.003	0.001	0.001	0.001												

Source: By permission, from Robert N. Anthony, Management Accounting: Text and Cases, rev. ed. (Homewood, Ill.: Richard D. Irwin, Inc., 1960), p. 656.

Largest Corporations

100 LARGEST INDUSTRIAL CORPORATIONS
(ranked by sales)

Rank 1979	Rank 1978	Company	Sales ($000)	Assets ($000)	Rank	Net Income ($000)	Rank	Stockholders' Equity ($000)	Rank
1	2	Exxon (New York)	79,106,471*	49,489,964	1	4,295,243	1	22,551,951	1
2	1	General Motors (Detroit)	66,311,200	32,215,800	2	2,892,700	3	19,179,300	2
3	4	Mobil (New York)	44,720,908	27,505,756	3	2,007,158	4	10,513,264	5
4	3	Ford Motor (Dearborn, Mich.)	43,513,700	23,524,600	5	1,169,300	11	10,420,700	6
5	5	Texaco (Harrison, N.Y.)	38,350,370	22,991,955	6	1,759,069	6	10,645,836	4
6	6	Standard Oil of California (San Francisco)	29,947,554	18,102,632	7	1,784,694	5	9,283,886	7
7	9	Gulf Oil (Pittsburgh)	23,910,000*	17,265,000	8	1,322,000	9	8,688,000	8
8	7	International Business Machines (Armonk, N.Y.)	22,862,776	24,529,974	4	3,011,259	2	14,961,235	3
9	8	General Electric (Fairfield, Conn.)	22,460,600	16,644,500	10	1,408,800	8	7,362,300	10
10	12	Standard Oil (Ind.) (Chicago)	18,610,347*	17,149,899	9	1,506,618	7	8,368,625	9
11	11	International Telephone & Telegraph (New York)	17,197,423	15,091,321	12	380,685	42	5,621,157	13
12	13	Atlantic Richfield (Los Angeles)	16,233,959	13,833,387	13	1,165,894	12	6,119,504	12
13	14	Shell Oil (Houston)	14,431,211*	16,127,016	11	1,125,561	13	7,003,616	11
14	15	U.S. Steel (Pittsburgh)	12,929,100	11,029,900	15	(293,000)	492	4,894,600	16
15	18	Conoco (Stamford, Conn.)[1]	12,647,998	9,311,171	17	815,360	17	3,783,111	21
16	16	E.I. du Pont de Nemours (Wilmington, Del.)	12,571,800	8,940,200	19	938,900	15	5,312,100	15
17	10	Chrysler (Highland Park, Mich.)	12,001,900	6,653,100	26	(1,097,300)	493	1,605,400	60
18	19	Tenneco (Houston)	11,209,000	11,631,000	14	571,000	24	3,345,000	24
19	17	Western Electric (New York)[2]	10,964,075	7,128,324	24	635,898	21	4,021,576	19
20	23	Sun (Radnor, Pa.)	10,666,000	7,460,600	23	699,900	19	3,769,900	22
21	33	Occidental Petroleum (Los Angeles)	9,554,795	5,560,330	35	561,646	26	1,463,362	70
22	26	Phillips Petroleum (Bartlesville, Okla.)	9,502,775	8,518,709	21	891,121	16	4,257,227	17
23	20	Procter & Gamble (Cincinnati)[3]	9,329,306	5,663,627	34	577,331	23	3,229,135	25
24	27	Dow Chemical (Midland, Mich.)	9,255,387	10,251,637	16	783,898	18	3,896,638	20
25	21	Union Carbide (New York)	9,176,500	8,802,600	20	556,200	27	4,042,500	18
26	32	United Technologies (Hartford)[4]	9,053,358	6,426,123	28	325,608	53	2,510,348	38
27	28	International Harvester (Chicago)[5]	8,392,042	5,247,475	39	369,562	44	2,149,073	43
28	22	Goodyear Tire & Rubber (Akron, Ohio)	8,238,676	5,371,239	38	146,184	129	2,163,350	42
29	40	Boeing (Seattle)	8,131,000	4,897,200	45	505,400	34	1,847,500	50
30	25	Eastman Kodak (Rochester, N.Y.)	8,028,231	7,554,128	22	1,000,764	14	5,390,603	14
31	42	LTV (Dallas)[6]	7,996,809	3,864,757	56	173,527	105	696,998	176
32	43	Standard Oil (Ohio) (Cleveland)	7,916,023	9,209,001	18	1,186,116	10	3,086,403	27
33	24	Caterpillar Tractor (Peoria, Ill.)	7,613,200	5,403,300	37	491,600	37	3,065,300	28
34	35	Union Oil of California (Los Angeles)	7,567,698*	6,013,149	32	500,604	36	2,956,877	30
35	31	Beatrice Foods (Chicago)[7]	7,468,373	3,669,095	60	261,010	62	1,836,972	51
36	30	RCA (New York)	7,454,600	5,990,200	33	283,800	58	1,759,800	53
37	29	Westinghouse Electric (Pittsburgh)	7,332,000	6,821,500	25	(73,900)‡	488	2,250,000	40
38	34	Bethlehem Steel (Bethlehem, Pa.)	7,137,200	5,165,900	40	275,700	59	2,570,400	35
39	47	R.J. Reynolds Industries (Winston-Salem, N.C.)[8]	7,133,100*	6,421,900	29	550,900	28	2,997,800	29
40	36	Xerox (Stamford, Conn.)	7,027,000	6,553,600	27	563,100	25	3,221,400	26

Employees		Net Income as Percent of Stockholders'				Earnings per Share					Total Return to Investors				Industry
		Sales		Equity					Growth Rate 1969–79		1979		1969–79 Average		
Number	Rank	%	Rank	%	Rank	1979($)	1978($)	1969($)	%	Rank	%	Rank	%	Rank	Code
169,096†	9	5.4	224	19.0	122	9.74	6.20	2.44‡	14.85	129	20.15	249	12.10	118	29
853,000†	1	4.4	307	15.1	290	10.04	12.24	5.95	5.37	375	2.89	383	4.53	289	40
213,500	6	4.5	299	19.1	120	9.46	5.31	2.14	16.02	101	65.91	68	15.22	68	29
494,579†	2	2.7	413	11.2	403	9.75	13.35	4.02	9.26	295	(14.78)	460	6.30	237	40
65,814	50	4.6	292	16.5	214	6.48	3.14	2.83	8.64	318	29.81	190	6.19	240	29
39,676	113	6.0	189	19.2	116	10.44	6.48	2.68	14.57	137	26.46	211	14.22	82	29
57,600	63	5.5	214	15.2	279	6.78	4.06	2.94	8.71	315	56.97	87	7.77	206	29
337,119	5	13.2	17	20.1	91	5.16	5.32	1.65	12.08	212	(9.12)	441	1.54	355	44
405,000†	3	6.3	176	19.1	119	6.20	5.39	1.54	14.94	125	13.16	308	6.28	238	36
52,282	75	8.1	100	18.0	160	10.23	7.36	2.27	16.25	96	44.59	124	17.05	49	29
368,000	4	2.2	435	6.8	451	2.65	4.66	2.90	(0.90)	423	2.58	390	(3.19)	418	36
50,341	80	7.2	127	19.1	121	9.48	6.60	2.05	16.55	93	45.59	121	9.49	169	29
36,384	129	7.8	112	16.1	237	7.32	5.45	2.16	12.98	184	75.41	51	14.46	79	29
171,654†	8	—		—		(3.41)	2.85	2.67	—		(10.12)	446	3.50	318	33
40,502	111	6.4	160	21.6	66	7.58	4.20	1.39	18.49	67	74.04	54	18.07	42	29
134,200†	13	7.5	120	17.7	176	6.42	5.39	2.45	-10.11	273	2.68	388	5.94	251	28
133,811†	14	—		—		(17.18)	(3.54)	1.87	—		(19.45)	468	(10.43)	452	40
107,000	21	5.1	251	17.1	195	5.30	4.53	2.31	8.66	317	35.53	158	11.40	128	29
168,000	10	5.8	199	15.8	254	n.a.	n.a.	n.a.	—		—		—		36
40,065	112	6.6	153	18.6	137	11.77	6.82	2.71	15.82	108	71.34	61	12.27	112	29
34,165	133	5.9	196	38.4	8	7.30	(0.39)	2.97	9.41	290	80.13	46	5.54	261	10
30,332	152	9.4	57	20.9	79	5.77	4.61	0.87	20.83	47	56.03	90	18.52	35	29
59,000	60	6.2	183	17.9	166	6.99	6.19	2.26	11.95	220	(12.74)	455	5.66	258	43
55,889	66	8.5	86	20.1	92	4.33	3.16	0.82	18.10	74	34.98	159	14.03	83	28
115,763	17	6.1	186	13.8	340	8.47	6.09	3.08	10.65	263	32.07	179	6.84	227	28
197,700	7	3.6	370	13.0	360	6.49	5.45	2.11	11.89	222	16.27	279	13.70	89	41
97,660	27	4.4	303	17.2	191	12.01	6.14	2.30	17.97	75	14.42	296	10.98	138	45
154,061†	11	1.8	444	6.8	452	2.02	3.12	2.19	(0.80)	421	(12.09)	452	(3.12)	417	30
98,300†	24	6.2	178	27.4	23	7.88	5.05	0.16	47.65	8	10.81	336	22.07	18	41
126,300	15	12.5	21	18.6	138	6.20	5.59	2.49	9.55	288	(13.14)	456	(2.74)	414	38
68,125	45	2.2	437	24.9	34	6.03	2.33	(10.15)‡	—		20.76	245	(10.62)	453	33
22,103	202	15.0	10	38.4	7	9.83	4.00	0.97	26.06	25	110.52	18	18.13	41	29
89,266†	30	6.5	159	16.0	241	5.69	6.56	1.67	13.04	182	(4.51)	419	9.71	162	45
16,957	248	6.6	149	16.9	198	5.76	4.37	2.30**	9.61	284	61.85	77	13.28	96	29
88,000	31	3.5	375	14.2	328	2.60	2.41	0.95	10.59	265	(4.74)	424	4.79	280	20
120,000	16	3.8	351	16.1	232	3.72	3.65	2.32	4.83	386	(9.39)	442	0.49	374	36
145,254†	12	—		—		(0.87)‡	2.81‡	1.91	—		26.90	208	1.11	362	36
97,700†	26	3.9	344	10.7	410	6.31	5.15	3.56	5.89	366	15.29	286	3.65	316	33
79,487	38	7.7	114	18.4	143	5.23	4.51	1.91	10.60	264	26.97	206	9.53	167	21
115,705	18	8.0	102	17.5	183	6.69	5.92	2.08	12.39	199	21.00	243	(3.38)	421	38

THE 100 LARGEST INDUSTRIALS *(continued)*

Rank 1979	1978	Company	Sales (000)	Assets ($000)	Rank	Net Income ($000)	Rank	Stockholders' Equity ($000)	Rank
41	49	Amerada Hess (New York)	6,769,941	4,899,237	44	507,116	33	1,900,209	48
42	38	Esmark (Chicago)[5]	6,743,167	2,389,872	99	92,423	193	833,774	150
43	52	Marathon Oil (Findlay, Ohio)	6,680,597*	4,321,133	50	323,222	54	1,688,787	55
44	44	Ashland Oil (Russell, Ky.)[9]	6,473,867*	3,113,214	70	526,253	29	967,501	126
45	37	Rockwell International (Pittsburgh)[9]	6,466,100	4,127,600	53	261,100	61	1,539,200	63
46	39	Kraft (Glenview, Ill.)	6,432,900	2,523,300	93	188,100	93	1,324,400	79
47	51	Cities Service (Tulsa)	6,276,500	4,773,000	47	347,500	48	2,227,400	41
48	45	Monsanto (St. Louis)	6,192,600	5,539,100	36	331,000	50	2,781,800	32
49	46	Philip Morris (New York)	6,144,091*	6,378,852	30	507,881	32	2,470,955	39
50	41	General Foods (White Plains, N.Y.)[10]	5,472,456	2,565,312	92	232,149	71	1,320,987	81
51	50	Minnesota Mining & Manufacuring (St. Paul)	5,440,370	4,574,888	49	655,211	20	2,950,472	31
52	58	Gulf & Western Industries (New York)[11,12]	5,288,247	5,160,193	41	227,438	74	1,501,358	65
53	48	Firestone Tire & Rubber (Akron, Ohio)[5]	5,284,200	3,457,100	63	112,900**	163	1,465,800	69
54	63	McDonnell Douglas (St. Louis)	5,278,531	3,380,604	65	199,103	86	1,378,207	76
55	59	W. R. Grace (New York)	5,266,629	3,728,853	57	222,580	76	1,572,282	61
56	53	Georgia-Pacific (Portland, Ore.)	5,207,000	4,118,000	54	327,000	52	1,794,000	52
57	60	PepsiCo (Purchase, N.Y.)	5,090,567	2,887,578	78	264,855	60	1,263,649	86
58	54	Armco (Middletown, Ohio)	5,035,127	3,260,163	68	221,040	78	1,715,271	54
59	56	Coca-Cola (Atlanta)	4,961,402	2,938,041	74	420,120	38	1,918,704	47
60	61	Deere (Moline, Ill.)[5]	4,933,104	4,179,232	52	310,637	56	1,974,346	46
61	57	Colgate-Palmolive (New York)	4,831,494	2,429,284	97	113,548	162	1,190,816	98
62	79	Getty Oil (Los Angeles)	4,831,005	6,031,920	31	604,434	22	3,429,018	23
63	65	Aluminum Co. of America (Pittsburgh)	4,785,583	4,711,251	48	504,569	35	2,529,091	37
64	78	Consolidated Foods (Chicago)[3,13]	4,720,266	2,089,471	121	111,408	168	785,296	158
65	55	Greyhound (Phoenix)	4,700,051	1,818,769	147	123,030	156	776,092	162
66	62	International Paper (New York)	4,605,000	4,843,400	46	525,300	30	2,586,300	34
67	64	Ralston Purina (St. Louis)[9]	4,600,600	2,183,100	112	128,100	147	1,038,500	116
68	70	TRW (Cleveland)	4,560,303	2,619,856	90	194,642	89	1,152,954	103
69	84	Allied Chemical (Morristown, N.J.)[14]	4,538,835	4,209,628	51	10,827	452	1,228,531	88
70	66	American Can (Greenwich, Conn.)	4,515,000	2,682,400	88	127,300	148	1,058,200	112
71	69	Weyerhaeuser (Tacoma, Wash.)	4,422,653	4,957,945	43	512,244	31	2,735,867	33
72	67	Continental Group (Stamford, Conn.)	4,369,700	3,595,300	62	189,200	91	1,266,700	84
73	68	Borden (New York)	4,312,533	2,462,760	95	134,015	139	1,185,075	99
74	144	Charter (Jacksonville, Fla.)	4,249,695	1,728,694	157	365,338	45	646,885	186
75	76	Signal Companies (Beverly Hills, Calif.)	4,241,200	2,850,500	82	203,700	80	1,183,700	100
76	71	National Steel (Pittsburgh)	4,234,458	3,160,279	69	126,466	149	1,413,853	73
77	96	Iowa Beef Processors (Dakota City, Neb.)[5]	4,216,370	416,789	377	42,747	317	238,831	348
78	80	Johnson & Johnson (New Brunswick, N.J.)	4,211,571	2,873,954	79	352,060	47	1,986,646	45
79	77	Honeywell (Minneapolis)	4,209,500	3,339,600	66	260,500	63	1,642,500	57
80	73	Sperry (New York)[10,15]	4,179,319	3,724,025	58	224,132	75	1,630,649	58
81	72	Litton Industries (Beverly Hills, Calif.)[11]	4,086,362	2,854,298	81	188,887	92	930,767	133
82	81	Lockheed (Burbank, Calif.)	4,069,800	2,112,900	117	56,500**	273	282,500	316
83	92	General Dynamics (St. Louis)	4,059,576	2,004,798	129	185,156	94	826,436	152
84	●	Union Pacific (New York)	3,989,474	5,086,883	42	382,486	40	2,558,229	36
85	82	Republic Steel (Cleveland)	3,987,381	2,749,872	85	121,158	158	1,489,198	66
86	74	Champion International (Stamford, Conn.)	3,907,928	3,040,485	72	247,120	65	1,535,028	64
87	91	Farmland Industries (Kansas City, Mo.)[16]	3,835,717	1,856,699	144	n.a.[17]		461,683	234
88	75	Bendix (Southfield, Mich.)[9]	3,828,700	2,311,000	105	162,600	114	1,035,600	117
89	83	American Brands (New York)	3,772,181*	3,670,578	59	347,331	49	1,609,481	59
90	86	General Mills (Minneapolis)[18]	3,745,000	1,835,200	145	147,000	127	916,200	136
91	106	IC Industries (Chicago)	3,734,600	3,617,800	61	173,700	104	1,206,500	94
92	88	Raytheon (Lexington, Mass.)	3,727,930	2,296,537	107	197,151	87	889,871	143
93	90	CPC International (Englewood Cliffs, N.J.)	3,698,689	2,067,644	125	178,651	98	988,988	123

Employees		Net Income as Percent of Stockholders'				Earnings per Share			Growth Rate 1969–79		Total Return to Investors				Industry Code
		Sales		Equity							1979		1969–79 Average		
Number	Rank	%	Rank	%	Rank	1979($)	1978($)	1969($)	%	Rank	%	Rank	%	Rank	
7,851†	400	7.5	119	26.7	25	12.15	3.42	1.86	20.64	50	82.36	43	9.30	172	29
44,000†	97	1.4	456	11.1	405	4.40	3.81	1.30	12.97	185	26.95	207	5.46	266	20
14,066	280	4.8	274	19.1	118	5.34	3.73	1.50	13.54	167	87.77	41	15.36	66	29
29,200	157	8.1	98	54.4	2	15.55	5.51	1.53	26.10	24	24.66	222	14.61	77	29
114,452	19	4.0	332	17.0	197	7.33	5.02	2.31	12.24	206	43.45	129	15.61	64	40
47,400	90	2.9	401	14.2	329	6.71‡	6.57	2.69	9.57	286	13.42	303	6.81	228	20
18,500	233	5.5	213	15.6	261	12.54	4.27	4.18	11.61	231	61.29	80	13.28	97	29
63,926	56	5.3	232	11.9	391	9.11	8.29	3.28	10.76	255	33.98	164	9.88	158	28
65,000	52	8.3	93	20.6	85	4.08	3.39	0.65	20.16	54	5.51	374	17.17	48	21
50,000	82	4.2	318	17.6	179	4.65	3.40	2.68**	5.67	373	10.58	337	2.95	334	20
87,738	32	12.0	26	22.2	53	5.59	4.83	1.61	13.26	175	(16.59)	462	1.58	353	38
102,160	23	4.3	310	15.1	284	4.62	3.53	1.15**	14.92	126	36.20	154	14.22	81	34
107,000	20	2.1	439	7.7	445	1.96**	(2.58)	2.01	(0.25)	416	(18.74)	467	(4.63)	432	30
82,736	35	3.8	353	14.4	318	5.06	4.14	3.06	5.16	380	11.92	322	8.58	189	41
82,100	36	4.2	320	14.2	333	5.02	4.23	2.31**	8.07	328	64.14	72	10.64	145	28
44,000	96	6.3	174	18.2	148	3.12	2.93	1.01	11.94	221	13.41	304	4.37	295	26
105,000	22	5.2	249	21.0	78	2.85	2.43	0.74	14.44	143	1.38	398	6.17	242	49
54,822	70	4.4	304	12.9	366	4.82	4.29	2.01	9.14	302	32.99	174	8.98	178	33
38,635	117	8.5	87	21.9	59	3.40	3.03	1.06	12.36	201	(16.90)	463	1.14	361	49
65,392	51	6.3	171	15.7	257	5.12	4.38	0.92	18.73	65	17.47	267	17.87	44	45
48,800†	85	2.4	430	9.5	422	1.39‡	2.15	0.85	5.04	382	(7.03)	432	3.11	331	43
14,616	272	12.5	20	17.6	172	7.34	3.98	1.47**	17.45	80	99.07	31	21.76	20	10
46,800†	91	10.5	42	20.0	99	14.29	8.90	3.72	14.41	144	20.37	246	5.10	274	33
94,500	29	2.4	429	14.2	331	3.60	3.21	2.06	5.74	371	17.46	268	0.77	368	20
52,315†	74	2.6	416	15.9	251	2.80	1.33	1.35	7.57	338	40.12	141	5.93	254	20
49,365	83	11.4	34	20.3	87	10.96	4.94	4.59	9.09	303	7.39	359	4.23	301	26
73,000	43	2.8	408	12.3	381	1.19	1.44	0.46	9.97	276	1.81	396	4.85	278	20
97,935	25	4.3	313	16.9	201	6.07	5.42	2.36	9.91	278	12.01	321	4.56	286	40
49,014	84	0.2	476	0.9	477	0.20	4.25	2.44	(22.13)	445	80.95	44	12.24	113	10
55,500†	67	2.8	406	12.0	388	6.44	5.32‡	3.49	6.32	362	7.09	364	5.54	262	34
47,844	87	11.6	32	18.7	131	4.02	2.85‡	1.07	14.15	147	33.29	171	6.94	225	26
53,887†	72	4.3	309	14.9	293	5.27	3.47	3.18	5.18	379	15.28	287	0.94	364	34
39,300†	114	3.1	391	11.3	402	4.31	4.38	1.04‡	15.28	121	0.66	402	5.63	260	20
8,000	398	8.6	82	56.5	1	14.83	1.17	0.10**	64.86	1	592.30	1	30.08	2	29
53,000	73	4.8	279	17.2	190	5.28	4.17	1.12	16.77	91	99.51	30	19.09	31	40
38,755†	115	3.0	397	8.9	432	6.56	5.85	4.76	3.26	402	0.34	403	2.66	338	33
9,700†	359	1.0	466	17.9	164	4.28	3.46	0.44	25.54	28	13.04	309	10.04	156	20
71,800	44	8.4	91	17.7	174	5.76	5.00	1.07	18.33	68	10.17	338	4.02	306	42
94,620	28	6.2	182	15.9	250	11.89	9.41	4.15	11.10	244	23.23	226	(2.42)	411	44
87,325	33	5.4	228	13.7	341	6.35	5.08	2.26	10.88	250	16.40	277	5.32	271	44
77,700	39	4.6	288	20.3	89	4.87	(2.60)	1.90	9.87	279	120.85	15	4.02	307	36
66,500	49	1.4	454	20.0	97	3.56**	4.21	(2.90)	—		76.92	50	7.18	220	41
81,600	37	4.6	295	22.4	48	6.85	(1.80)	0.10	52.61	5	94.04	32	19.02	32	41
33,077†	138	9.6	53	15.0	292	8.02	5.55	2.25	13.55	165	44.76	123	16.02	57	29
42,690†	105	3.0	393	8.1	442	7.49	6.86	4.96	4.21	395	17.03	273	4.25	299	33
43,182	101	6.3	170	16.1	235	4.70	3.32‡	1.98	9.03	308	18.39	260	2.06	349	26
10,100	351	—		—		n.a.	n.a.	n.a.	—		—		—		29
73,700	42	4.2	317	15.7	259	7.10	5.74	3.11**	8.60	321	19.26	253	11.09	134	40
54,690	71	9.2	59	21.6	64	12.00	7.93	3.65	12.64	193	43.93	126	13.56	92	21
64,229	54	3.9	340	16.0	239	2.92	2.72	1.03	10.98	248	(11.56)	450	6.37	236	20
64,989	53	4.7	286	14.4	321	9.52	5.23	3.02	12.17	207	9.34	345	4.45	292	20
67,230	46	5.3	236	22.2	54	6.30	4.83	1.18	18.23	71	47.52	113	17.65	47	36
41,000	108	4.8	275	18.1	157	7.51	6.20	2.42	11.99	219	28.54	199	12.39	110	20

THE 100 LARGEST INDUSTRIALS (continued)

Rank			Sales	Assets		Net Income		Stockholders' Equity	
1979	1978	Company	($000)	($000)	Rank	($000)	Rank	($000)	Rank
94	87	CBS (New York)	3,670,390	2,179,529	113	200,707	84	1,074,445	109
95	85	Inland Steel (Chicago)	3,635,225	2,725,473	86	131,108	144	1,311,619	82
96	93	Owens-Illinois (Toledo)	3,504,289	2,910,208	77	133,454	141	1,201,447	95
97	105	United Brands (New York)[3]	3,470,222	1,217,404	197	21,433	413	538,323	212
98	95	Dresser Industries (Dallas)[5]	3,457,400	2,503,800	94	228,000	73	1,422,300	71
99	94	American Home Products (New York)	3,401,301	2,090,674	120	396,039	39	1,322,012	80
100	89	Textron (Providence)	3,392,974	2,079,155	124	169,801	110	1,118,967	106

The definitions and concepts underlying the figures in this directory are explained at the end of the table.
n.a. Not available.
●Indicates that a corporation was not among the 500 or the Second 500 in 1978.
*Does not include excise taxes; see the explanation of "sales" at the end of the table.
**Reflects an extraordinary credit of at least 10 percent; see the explanations of "net income" and "earnings per share" at the end of the table.
†Average for the year; see the reference to "employees" at the end of the table.
‡Reflects an extraordinary charge of at least 10 percent; see the explanations of "net income" and "earnings per share" at the end of the table.
[1]Name changed from Continental Oil July 1, 1979.
[2]Company is wholly owned by American Telephone & Telegraph.
[3]Figures are for fiscal year ending June 30, 1979.
[4]Figures include Carrier (1978 rank: 139), acquired July 6, 1979.
[5]Figures are for fiscal year ending October 31, 1979.
[6]Figures include Lykes (1978 rank: 153), merged into LTV December 31, 1978.

NOTES TO THE FORTUNE DIRECTORY

Sales include service and rental revenues but exclude dividends, interest, and other non-operating revenues. All companies on the list must have derived more than 50 percent of their sales from manufacturing and/or mining. Sales of subsidiaries are included when they are consolidated; sales from discontinued operations are included when these figures are published. All figures are for the year ending December 31, 1979, unless otherwise noted. Sales figures do not include excise taxes collected by the manufacturer, and so the figures for some corporations—most of which sell gasoline, liquor, or tobacco—may be lower than those published by the corporations themselves. When they are at least 5 percent lower for this reason, there is an asterisk (*) next to the sales figure.

Assets are those shown at the company's year-end.

Net income is shown after taxes and after extraordinary credits or charges when any are shown on the income statement. A double asterisk (**) signifies an extraordinary credit reflecting at least 10 percent of the net income shown, a double dagger (‡) an extraordinary charge of at least 10 percent. Figures in parentheses indicate a loss.

Stockholders' equity is the sum of capital stock (excluding redeemable preferred), surplus, and retained earnings at the company's year-end.

Employees: The figure shown is a year-end total except when it is followed by a dagger (†), in which case it is an average for the year.

Earnings per share: For all companies, the figures shown for 1979 and 1978 are the "primary" earnings per share that appear on the company's income statement. These figures are based on a weighted average of the number of common shares and common-stock equivalents outstanding during the year. "Common-stock equivalents" generally include (a) convertible securities whose cash yield is less than two thirds of the prime rate at the time the securities were issued and (b) options and warrants when the effect of their inclusion in the computation would reduce the "primary" earnings per share. Weighted averages are used for 1969 where these are available; where they are not, figures are based on a simple average of 1968 and 1969 year-end shares outstanding. Per-share earnings for 1978 and 1969 are adjusted for stock splits and stock dividends. They are not restated for mergers, acquisitions, or accounting changes made after 1969. A double asterisk (**) signifies an extraordinary credit reflecting at least 10 percent of the net income shown, a double dagger (‡) an extraordinary charge of at least 10 percent. Results are listed as not available (n.a.) where the companies are cooperatives, joint ventures, or wholly owned subsidiaries of other companies. The growth rate is the average annual growth, compounded. No growth rate is given if the company had a loss in either 1969 or 1979.

Total return to investors includes both price appreciation and dividend yield, that is, to an investor in the company's stock. The figures shown assume sales at the end of 1979 of

Employees		Net Income as Percent of Stockholders'				Earnings per Share					Total Return to Investors				Industry Code
		Sales		Equity					Growth Rate 1969–79		1979		Average 1969–79		
Number	Rank	%	Rank	%	Rank	1979($)	1T78($)	1969($)	%	Rank	%	Rank	%	Rank	
38,714	116	5.5	220	18.7	133	7.21	7.15	2.55	10.95	249	8.42	353	6.06	248	48
37,341†	124	3.6	368	10.0	417	6.27	7.61	3.17	7.06	351	(1.63)	412	8.66	187	33
63,831	57	3.8	350	11.1	404	4.56	2.87‡	2.04	8.38	322	20.33	247	(0.20)	386	32
52,000	76	0.6	469	4.0	469	1.72	0.95	3.89**	(7.84)	440	12.17	318	(9.06)	446	20
55,200	68	6.6	152	16.0	242	5.88	5.22	1.45	15.03	123	43.40	130	18.33	37	45
50,269	81	11.6	30	30.0	16	2.51	2.21	0.78	12.40	198	2.22	393	4.29	297	42
64,000	55	5.0	259	15.2	282	4.51	4.47	2.14	7.74	332	9.76	341	5.13	272	34

[7]Figures are for fiscal year ending February 28, 1979.
[8]Figures include Del Monte (1978 rank: 184), merged into R.J. Reynolds Industries February 28, 1979.
[9]Figures are for fiscal year ending September 30, 1979.
[10]Figures are for fiscal year ending March 31, 1979.
[11]Figures are for fiscal year ending July 31, 1979.
[12]Figures includes Simmons (1978 rank: 416), acquired June 5, 1979.
[13]Figures include Hanes (1978 rank: 437), acquired January 29, 1979.
[14]Figures include Eltra (1978 rank: 254), merged into Allied Chemical November 5, 1979.
[15]Name changed from Sperry Rand July 31, 1979.
[16]Figures are for fiscal year ending August 31, 1979.
[17]Cooperatives provide only "net margin" figures, which are not comparable with the net income figures in these listings.
[18]Figures are for fiscal year ending May 31, 1979.
Source: Reprinted with permission from the 1980 FORTUNE Directory; © 1980 Time Inc.

stock owned at the end of 1969 or 1978. It has been assumed that any proceeds from cash dividends, the sale of rights and warrant offerings, and stock received in spin-offs were reinvested at the end of the year in which they were received. Returns are adjusted for stock splits, stock dividends, recapitalizations, and corporate reorganizations as they occur; however, no effort has been made to reflect the cost of brokerage commissions or of taxes. Results are listed as not available (n.a.) where shares are not publicly traded or traded on only a limited basis. Where companies have more than one class of shares outstanding, only the more widely held and actively traded has been considered.

Total-return percentages shown are the returns received by the hypothetical investor described above. The ten-year figures are annual averages, compounded. Where corporations were substantially reorganized—that is, because of mergers—the predecessor companies used in calculating total return are the same as those cited in the footnotes to the earnings-per-share figures.

Rankings: These refer to relative position within the Fortune list of the 500 largest U.S. industrial corporations.

Industry code numbers used in the directory indicate which industry represents the greatest volume of industrial sales for each company. The numbers refer to the industry groups below, which are based on categories established by the U.S. Office of Management and Budget and issued by the Federal Statistical Policy and Standards Office. They are the same industry groups as those shown in the tables

beginning on this page. The median figures in the tables refer only to results of companies among the 500; no attempt has been made to calculate medians in groups with less than four companies.

Code No.	Industry
10	Mining, crude-oil production
20	Food
21	Tobacco
22	Textiles, vinyl flooring
23	Apparel
25	Furniture
26	Paper, fiber, and wood products
27	Publishing, printing
28	Chemicals
29	Petroleum refining
30	Rubber, plastic products
31	Leather
32	Glass, concrete, abrasives, gypsum
33	Metal manufacturing
34	Metal products
36	Electronics, appliances
37	Shipbuilding, railroad, and transportation equipment
38	Measuring, scientific, photographic equipment
40	Motor vehicles
41	Aerospace
42	Pharmaceuticals
43	Soaps, cosmetics
44	Office equipment (includes computers)
45	Industrial and farm equipment
46	Jewelry, silverware
47	Musical instruments, toys, sporting goods
48	Broadcasting, motion-picture production and distribution
49	Beverages

THE 100 LARGEST INDUSTRIAL CORPORATIONS OUTSIDE THE U.S.
(ranked by sales)

Rank 1979	Rank 1978	Company	Country	Industry	Sales[1] ($000)	Assets[2] ($000)	Net Income[3] ($000)	Stockholders' Equity[4] ($000)	Employees
1	1	Royal Dutch/Shell Group	Neth.-Britain	Petroleum	59,416,560	59,568,944	6,474,283	23,107,896	163,000
2	2	British Petroleum	Britain	Petroleum	38,713,496	34,692,681	3,439,582	11,080,076	113,200
3	4	Unilever	Britain-Neth.	Food products	21,748,583	12,358,820	920,320	4,642,655	309,000
4	10	ENI[5]	Italy	Petroleum	18,984,960[6]	19,734,352[6]	89,040[6]	3,009,852[6]	121,257[6]
5	46	Fiat	Italy	Motor vehicles	18,300,000	n.a.	n.a.	n.a.	360,009
6	11	Française des Pétroles	France	Petroleum	17,305,220[6]	14,287,434[6]	1,137,282[6]	2,617,040[6]	43,500[6]
7	17	Peugeot-Citroën[7]	France	Motor vehicles	17,270,104	12,273,501	254,318	3,520,281	264,730
8	7	Volkswagenwerk	Germany	Motor vehicles	16,765,683	12,653,861	371,534	3,307,691	239,714
9	5	Philips' Gloeilampenfabrieken	Netherlands	Electronics, appliances	16,576,123	18,480,464	308.701	6,125,630	378,600
10	9	Renault[5]	France	Motor vehicles	16,117,376	n.a.	241,520	2,166,264	233,408
11	6	Siemens[8]	Germany	Electronics, appliances	15,069,575	17,023,483	361,938	4,402,459	334,000
12	12	Daimler-Benz	Germany	Motor vehicles	14,942,324	8,178,688	347,794	2,603,643	174,431
13	13	Hoechst	Germany	Chemicals	14,785,464[6]	12,749,906[6]	141,684[6]	2,760,003[6]	182,688[6]
14	14	Bayer	Germany	Chemicals	14,196,027[6]	13,819,348[6]	239,376[6]	2,818,853[6]	181,000[6]
15	16	BASF	Germany	Chemicals	14,138,872[6]	10,076,760[6]	338,040[6]	3,904,710[6]	117,168[6]
16	24	Petróleos de Venezuela[5]	Venezuela	Petroleum	14,115,899	13,091,916	2,907,291	9,975,027	33,242
17	8	Toyota Motor[9]	Japan	Motor vehicles	14,012,345[10]	6,613,272[10]	510,290[10]	3,830,162[10]	45,000[10]
18	22	Thyssen[8]	Germany	Steel and industrial products	13,636,918	9,932,732	87,262	1,841,675	155,800
19	26	Elf Aquitaine[5]	France	Petroleum	13,385,876	15,855,318	1,310,132	4,965,008	37,400
20	15	Nestlé	Switzerland	Food products, beverages	13,016,940	10,225,091	490,865	4,650,789	154,654
21	19	Nissan Motor[11]	Japan	Motor vehicles	12,652,060	10,011,877	331,206	3,200,298	94,141
22	23	Hitachi[11]	Japan	Electronics, appliances	12,632,844	13,286,220	484,190	3,612,588	141,132
23	20	Nippon Steel[11]	Japan	Metal refining—steel	12,595,259	16,412,735	243,562	2,199,304	78,582
24	21	Mitsubishi Heavy Industries[11]	Japan	Motor vehicles, industrial equipment	11,959,912	15,438,425	111,616	1,109,235	93,800
25	27	Imperial Chemical Industries	Britain	Chemicals	11,391,003	12,809,619	880,638	6,207,363	148,200

Rank		Company	Country	Industry					
26	18	Matsushita Electric Industrial[12]	Japan	Electronics, appliances	11,127,658	8,682,424	463,177	3,741,810	98,292
27	25	Petrobrás (Petróleo Brasileiro)[5]	Brazil	Petroleum	10,278,517	11,032,965	756,773	4,502,704	60,668
28	28	B.A.T. Industries	Britain	Tobacco	9,478,860*	8,984,925	398,940	3,747,047	185,000
29	34	Ruhrkohle	Germany	Mining—coal	8,856,975	7,164,611	3,249	346,175	134,216
30	29	Saint-Gobain-Pont-à-Mousson	France	Building materials, metal products	8,354,964	8,045,809	154,350	2,101,468	147,808
31	40	Toshiba[11]	Japan	Electronics, appliances	8,317,851	8,599,537	115,548	922,260	99,000
32	30	Générale d'Electricité	France	Electronics, appliances	8,233,537[6]	6,912,953[6]	73,255[6]	1,051,670[6]	149,500[6]
33	31	Montedison	Italy	Chemicals	8,199,258[6]	10,503,596[6]	22,193[6]	748,532[6]	114,712[6]
34	32	General Motors of Canada	Canada	Motor vehicles	8,032,990	1,902,705	210,703	711,035	38,000
35	35	Pechiney Ugine Kuhlmann	France	Metal refining—aluminum, steel	7,961,469	8,168,031	233,124	1,955,462	91,926
36	42	Rhône-Poulenc	France	Chemicals	7,944,278	7,811,294	186,019	1,868,816	106,695
37	72	Veba Oel	Germany	Petroleum, chemicals	7,930,643[6]	3,429,479[6]	50,367[6]	701,908[6]	23,356[6]
38	43	Petrofina	Belgium	Petroleum	7,827,034	7,224,435	283,382	1,590,217	23,000
39	66	Pemex (Petróleos Mexicanos)[5]	Mexico	Petroleum	7,290,691	n.a.	n.a.	n.a.	n.a.
40	49	Thomson-Brandt	France	Electronics, appliances	7,056,157	8,178,942	65,457	643,126	126,300
41	38	Fried. Krupp	Germany	Metal refining—steel; indus. equip.	6,981,574	5,246,775	n.a.	1,042,692	86,172
42	44	Canadian Pacific	Canada	Metal refining—steel; mining	6,957,492	9,416,618	433,791	2,557,295	109,700
43	375	British National Oil[5]	Britain	Petroleum	6,885,743	2,738,738	28,859	1,016,073	1,423
44	33	Mannesmann	Germany	Industrial equipment; metal products	6,824,905	5,335,509	79,820	1,360,754	105,842
45	63	Ford Motor	Britain	Motor vehicles	6,775,610	4,494,681	736,341	1,870,196	80,000
46	37	AEG-Telefunken	Netherlands	Electronics, appliances	6,513,250	5,474,754	(539,292)	680,113	125,000
47	50	ESTEL	Netherlands	Metal refining—steel; metal products	6,503,110	6,733,081	(86,614)	1,253,977	79,200
48	65	Esso	Germany	Petroleum	6,496,237	2,823,881	222,765	695,244	4,440
49	58	Schneider	France	Indus. equip.; metal refining—steel	6,411,887	14,090,895	2,422	389,420	105,000
50	41	British Steel[11,5]	Britain	Metal refining—steel	6,384,671	10,791,000	(600,796)	4,207,913	186,000
51	60	DSM[5]	Netherlands	Chemicals	6,358,581[6]	4,885,866[6]	44,446[6]	1,223,193[6]	31,750[6]
52	39	BL[5]	Britain	Motor vehicles	6,345,476	5,231,223	(306,632)	1,636,587	168,561
53	61	Michelin	France	Rubber products	6,244,467	7,603,053	128,540	1,949,863	n.a.
54	36	Ford Motor of Canada	Canada	Motor vehicles	6,103,129	2,001,195	8,537	719,359	39,200
55	53	Akzo Group	Netherlands	Chemicals	5,991,851	4,747,297	114,554	1,222,550	83,000
56	51	Dunlop Pirelli Union	Britain-Italy	Rubber products	5,982,611	n.a.	n.a.	n.a.	162,083
57	55	Nippon Kokan[11]	Japan	Metal refining—steel	5,971,254	11,375,071	48,932	907,259	40,905
58	48	Ford-Werke	Germany	Motor vehicles	5,957,469	2,275,416	263,739	612,104	57,772
59	52	Ciba-Geigy	Switzerland	Chemicals, pharmaceuticals	5,949,931	9,734,808	195,504	6,080,885	80,223
60	57	Robert Bosch	Germany	Motor-vehicle parts; electronics, appl.	5,888,788	4,471,182	102,260	1,208,687	121,395
61	54	National Coal Board[11,5]	Britain	Mining—coal	5,804,847	5,433,656	(37,671)	n.a.	300,000
62	45	Idemitsu Kosan[11]	Japan	Petroleum	5,773,182[10]	5,088,460[10]	1,843[10]	77,512[10]	7,870[10]
63	59	Gutehoffnungshütte[9]	Germany	Industrial and transportation equip.	5,757,910	5,253,485	47,453	734,326	84,288
64	56	Imperial Oil	Canada	Petroleum	5,484,040	3,984,075	420,864	2,088,323	14,966
65	67	Volvo	Sweden	Motor vehicles	5,475,432	4,984,859	97,161	641,127	65,054

THE 100 LARGEST INDUSTRIAL CORPORATIONS OUTSIDE THE U.S. *(concluded)*

Rank 1979	Rank 1978	Company	Country	Industry	Sales ($000)	Assets ($000)	Net Income ($000)	Stockholders' Equity ($000)	Employees
66	70	Sumitomo Metal Industries[11]	Japan	Metal refining—steel	5,341,660	9,040,333	84,980	759,546	42,746
67	75	Rio Tinto-Zinc	Britain	Mining—alum., lead, zinc, copper, iron	5,340,276	7,073,687	248,064	2,070,304	57,325
68	62	Brown Boveri	Switzerland	Electrical equipment	5,293,038[6]	n.a.	n.a.	n.a.	101,400[6]
69	87	Esso Petroleum	Britain	Petroleum	5,100,740	5,359,914	581,841	1,087,245	10,329
70	77	Honda Motor[13]	Japan	Motor vehicles	5,018,571	3,623,323	69,614	919,268	33,007
71	84	Mitsubishi Electric[11]	Japan	Electronics, appliances	4,952,475	4,702,533	108,682	770,188	64,154
72	79	Esso	France	Petroleum	4,858,965	2,379,679	49,503	426,408	4,940
73	68	General Electric Co.[11]	Britain	Industrial equipment, electronics	4,855,496	5,449,331	416,712	2,528,006	192,000
74	76	Kawasaki Steel[11]	Japan	Metal refining—steel	4,794,966[10]	8,059,921[10]	86,686[10]	797,949[10]	35,899[10]
75	73	Flick Group	Germany	Paper and wood products, chemicals	4,772,024	4,260,636	42,455	974,278	46,849
76	71	Imperial Group[11]	Britain	Tobacco	4,690,889*	4,225,445	503,445	2,218,479	101,800
77	86	Charbonnages de France[5]	France	Chemicals; mining—coal	4,422,372[6]	5,164,683[6]	18,249[6]	854,807[6]	84,900[6]
78	69	Kobe Steel[11]	Japan	Metal refining—steel	4,411,447[10]	5,908,918[10]	68,013[10]	634,275[10]	32,367[10]
79	74	Alcan Aluminum	Canada	Metal refining—aluminum	4,381,222	4,490,213	427,467	2,031,729	65,363
80	78	Hyundai Group	South Korea	Indus. equip., shipbldg., motor vehicles	4,303,841	4,503,521	29,353	975,130	103,766
81	82	Metallgesellschaft[8]	Germany	Metal refining—nonferrous	4,243,796	2,369,246	9,635	319,627	27,283
82	83	Guest, Keen & Nettlefolds	Britain	Motor-vehicle parts	4,161,281	3,686,925	69,602	1,725,106	104,324
83	96	Solvay	Belgium	Chemicals	4,127,872[6]	4,114,331[6]	137,777[6]	1,441,365[6]	46,214[6]
84	207	YPF (Yacimientos Petroliferos)[5]	Argentina	Petroleum	4,118,191	5,888,776	614,743	2,632,275	35,521
85	80	Ishikawajima-Harima Heavy Ind.[11]	Japan	Industrial equipment, shipbuilding	4,010,538	7,777,204	30,100	462,103	43,000
86	94	VÖEST-Alpine[5]	Austria	Metal refining—steel	3,990,571	5,894,793	(29,124)	907,496	80,203
87	106	Nippon Electric[11]	Japan	Electronics, appliances	3,942,699	4,442,921	39,396	472,001	60,481
88	●	Grand Metropolitan[8]	Britain	Beverages, food products	3,897,548	3,837,987	213,135	2,007,797	118,735
89	88	Salzgitter[8,5]	Germany	Metal refining—steel; shipbuilding	3,869,455	4,607,351	(1,997)	530,588	55,673
90	89	BSN-Gervais Danone	France	Food products; building materials	3,866,040	3,221,664	58,072	610,601	55,895

Rank	1978 Rank	Company	Country	Industry					
91	85	Toyo Kogyo[14]	Japan	Motor vehicles	3,859,794[10]	2,417,134[10]	34,841[10]	390,621[10]	26,809[10]
92	81	Maruzen Oil[11]	Japan	Petroleum	3,841,257	2,805,786	(1,781)	88,708	4,310
93	174	Kuwait National Petroleum[5]	Kuwait	Petroleum	3,832,233	1,765,676	562,497	548,093	3,580
94	●	Usinor	France	Metal refining—steel	3,791,875[6]	7,187,528[6]	n.a.	554,516[6]	40,200[6]
95	118	Sacilor	France	Metal refining—steel	3,764,164[6]	6,362,118[6]	(358,452)[6]	247,310[6]	29,878[6]
96	93	Italsider[5]	Italy	Metal refining—steel	3,743,941[10]	7,359,908[10]	(309,730)[10]	1,479,970[10]	52,731[10]
97	92	BMW (Bayerische Motoren Werke)	Germany	Motor vehicles	3,730,843	1,969,038	96,684	638,581	39,762
98	100	Toa Nenryo Kogyo	Japan	Petroleum	3,672,618	2,581,542	89,616	503,981	3,895
99	98	Bowater	Britain	Paper, pulp, wood products	3,656,240	2,268,860	109,284	799,326	37,600
100	90	IBM Deutschland	Germany	Office equipment (includes computers)	3,599,916	3,197,862	244,623	811,118	26,487

●Not on last year's list.

*Fortune estimate.

n.a. Not available.

[1]All companies on the list have derived more than 50 percent of their sales from manufacturing and/or mining. Sales do not include excise taxes or customs duties levied according to either volume or value of sales, and so the figures for some companies—most of which sell gasoline, liquor or tobacco—may be lower than those published by the companies themselves. Unless otherwise noted, figures exclude intercompany transactions and include consolidated subsidiaries more than 50 percent owned, either fully or on a prorated basis. Figures have been converted to dollars using an exchange rate that consists of the average rate in the official exchange market during each company's fiscal year (ending December 31, 1979, unless otherwise noted).

[2]Total shown at each company's year-end. Figures have been converted to dollars at the market rate prevailing at each company's year-end.

Source: Reprinted with permission from the 1980 FORTUNE Directory; © 1980 Time Inc.

[3]After taxes, minority interest, and extraordinary items. Figures have been converted to dollars at the average market rate prevailing during each company's fiscal year. Figures in parentheses are losses.

[4]Total at each company's year-end. Figures have been converted to dollars at the market rate prevailing at each company's year-end. Minority interest is not included.

[5]Government-owned.

[6]Also includes certain subsidiaries owned 50 percent or less, either fully or on a prorated basis.

[7]Figures include Chrysler France (1978 rank: 136) and Chrysler España (1978 rank: 423), acquired December 21, 1978.

[8]Figures are for fiscal year ending September 30, 1979.

[9]Figures are for fiscal year ending June 30, 1979.

[10]Parent only.

[11]Figures are for fiscal year ending March 31, 1979.

[12]Figures are for fiscal year ending November 20, 1979.

[13]Figures are for fiscal year ending February 28, 1979.

[14]Figures are for fiscal year ending October 31, 1979.

THE 25 LARGEST INDUSTRIAL COMPANIES IN THE WORLD

Rank 1979	Rank 1978	Company	Headquarters	Sales ($000)	Net Income ($000)
1	2	Exxon	New York	79,106,471	4,295,243
2	1	General Motors	Detroit	66,311,200	2,892,700
3	3	Royal Dutch/Shell Group	The Hague/London	59,416,560	6,474,283
4	5	Mobil	New York	44,720,908	2,007,158
5	4	Ford Motor	Dearborn, Mich.	43,513,700	1,169,300
6	7	British Petroleum	London	38,713,496	3,439,582
7	6	Texaco	Harrison, N.Y.	38,350,370	1,759,069
8	8	Standard Oil of California	San Francisco	29,947,554	1,784,694
9	13	Gulf Oil	Pittsburgh	23,910,000	1,322,000
10	10	International Business Machines	Armonk, N.Y.	22,862,776	3,011,259

(Continued on page 155)

THE 25 LARGEST UTILITIES
(ranked by assets)

Rank 1979	Rank 1978	Company	Assets[1] ($000)	Operating Revenues[2] ($000)	Rank	Net Income[3] ($000)	Rank	Stockholders' Equity[4] ($000)	Rank
1	1	American Telephone & Telegraph (New York)	113,768,836	45,408,078	1	5,674,248	1	44,921,072	1
2	2	General Telephone & Electronics (Stamford, Conn.)	18,405,965	9,957,817	2	645,070	2	4,405,518	3
3	3	Southern Company (Atlanta)	10,552,095	3,128,169	5	219,127	10	2,499,422	8
4	4	Pacific Gas & Electric (San Francisco)	10,310,763	4,372,220	3	458,234	3	4,491,707	2
5	6	Commonwealth Edison (Chicago)	9,172,615	2,720,922	10	296,678	6	3,024,343	5
6	5	American Electric Power (New York)	8,780,368	2,813,691	9	260,635	8	2,586,619	7
7	7	Consolidated Edison (New York)	7,133,210	3,332,786	4	323,912	5	3,390,205	4
8	8	Southern California Edison (Rosemead, Calif.)	6,977,237	2,563,974	11	346,219	4	2,722,955	6
9	10	Middle South Utilities (New Orleans)	6,503,068	1,823,059	22	182,058	19	1,664,060	17
10	9	Public Service Electric & Gas (Newark)	6,104,183	2,416,707	15	233,329	9	2,435,516	9
11	11	Virginia Electric & Power (Richmond)	5,960,584	1,703,309	25	196,467	14	2,078,136	11
12	12	Texas Utilities (Dallas)	5,821,933	1,756,289	24	211,151	11	1,830,472	14
13	13	Duke Power (Charlotte)	5,626,075	1,492,557	30	274,760	7	2,166,622	10
14	14	Consumers Power (Jackson, Mich.)	5,579,087	2,003,374	18	203,787	13	1,936,045	13
15	15	Philadelphia Electric	5,241,260	1,578,505	27	194,471	15	1,952,476	12
16	16	Detroit Edison	5,146,023	1,698,511	26	176,029	21	1,724,385	15
17	17	General Public Utilities (Parsippany, N.J.)	4,991,994	1,490,154	31	95,783	43	1,393,285	18
18	18	Florida Power & Light (Miami)	4,847,532	1,933,937	20	204,668	12	1,711,645	16
19	23	American Natural Resources (Detroit)	3,928,972	2,505,622	12	148,654	28	1,010,299	34
20	22	United Telecommunications (Westwood, Kan.)	3,872,977	1,792,078	23	182,887	17	1,093,998	30
21	21	Houston Industries	3,834,697	1,854,159	21	161,846	22	1,244,438	23
22	20	Pennsylvania Power & Light (Allentown, Pa.)	3,782,228	860,498	44	182,198	18	1,344,816	20
23	26	Central & South West (Dallas)	3,673,477	1,408,608	32	152,354	27	1,184,066	27
24	25	Carolina Power & Light (Raleigh)	3,647,913	925,910	42	153,244	26	1,331,168	21
25	19	Columbia Gas System (Wilmington)	3,626,036	2,851,733	8	153,281	25	1,097,886	29

n.a. Not available.

[1]Assets shown as of December 31, 1979, unless otherwise noted. Only assets of consolidated subsidiaries are included.

[2]Gross receipts from operations during the 1979 fiscal year, including any non-utility revenues from manufacturing, transportation, and so forth, and revenues from discontinued operations when they are published.

[3]After extraordinary items. Figures in parentheses indicate net losses.

Source: Reprinted with permission from the 1980 FORTUNE Directory; © 1980 Time Inc.

THE 25 LARGEST COMPANIES IN THE WORLD *(concluded)*

Rank 1979	Rank 1978	Company	Headquarters	Sales ($000)	Net Income ($000)
11	11	General Electric	Fairfield, Conn.	22,460,600	1,408,800
12	12	Unilever	London/Rotterdam	21,748,583	920,320
13	22	ENI	Rome	18,984,960	89,040
14	17	Standard Oil (Ind.)	Chicago	18,610,347	1,506,618
15	●	Fiat	Turin (Italy)	18,300,000	n.a.
16	23	Française des Pétroles	Paris	17,305,220	1,137,282
17	32	Peugeot-Citroën	Paris	17,270,104	254,318
18	15	International Telephone & Tel.	New York	17,197,423	380,685
19	19	Volkswagenwerk	Wolfsburg (Germany)	16,765,683	371,534
20	16	Philip's Gloeilampenfabrieken	Eindhoven (Netherlands)	16,576,123	308,701
21	24	Atlantic Richfield	Los Angeles	16,233,959	1,165,894
22	21	Renault	Paris	16,117,376	241,520
23	18	Siemens	Munich	15,069,575	361,938
24	25	Daimler-Benz	Stuttgart	14,942,324	347,794
25	26	Hoechst	Frankfurt	14,785,464	141,684

Source: Reprinted with permission from the 1980 *FORTUNE Directory;* © 1980 Time Inc.

Net Income as Percent of Equity %	Rank	Employees[5] Number	Rank	Earnings per Share[6] 1979($)	1978($)	1969($)	Growth Rate 1969–79[7] %	Rank	Total Return to Investors[8] 1979[9] %	Rank	1969–79 Average[10] %	Rank
12.6	20	1,029,905	1	8.04	7.74	4.00	7.23	9	(5.75)	46	7.44	13
14.6	9	226,824	2	4.20	4.26	2.23	6.54	15	8.52	18	6.18	17
8.8	48	26,540	5	1.51	1.45	1.82	(1.85)	49	(2.49)	39	0.86	45
10.2	39	26,877	4	3.55	3.20	2.58	3.24	29	13.74	14	4.04	30
9.8	42	16,400	11	2.51	3.30	3.00	(1.77)	48	(12.23)	48	2.03	43
10.1	40	22,557	7	2.29	2.26	2.20	0.40	40	(5.01)	41	3.36	35
9.6	46	23,074	6	4.51	4.29	2.37	6.65	13	15.42	10	8.01	10
12.7	17	12,917	13	4.56	3.52	2.35	6.85	12	5.02	22	5.33	20
10.9	29	11,959	16	2.13	2.46	1.86	1.36	37	(5.70)	45	1.72	44
9.6	45	13,176	12	2.85	2.95	2.60	0.92	38	5.93	20	5.68	19
9.5	47	9,625	22	1.63	1.88	1.73	(0.59)	45	(15.16)	49	0.56	48
11.5	26	12,628	14	2.45	2.54	1.52	4.89	22	2.56	29	0.80	46
12.7	18	20,130	8	2.88	2.61	2.05	3.46	28	(1.51)	37	2.34	41
10.5	34	12,068	15	3.24	3.21	2.79	1.51	36	(5.36)	43	3.62	33
10.0	41	9,544†	24	1.86	1.87	1.97	(0.57)	44	0.31	36	4.07	29
10.2	38	10,908	19	1.90	1.76	1.95	(0.26)	42	3.35	27	4.14	28
6.9	49	11,159	18	1.56	2.30	2.00	(2.45)	50	(43.86)	50	(0.45)	50
12.0	24	10,337	20	4.22	4.54	1.86	8.54	5	4.58	24	2.38	39
14.7	7	16,518	10	6.47	5.90	3.29	7.00	11	29.01	8	11.43	8
16.7	5	29,601	3	2.63	2.60	1.32	7.14	10	12.01	16	3.98	31
13.0	14	7,970	28	4.84	4.21	2.27	7.87	7	15.00	11	2.16	42
13.5	13	7,590	29	3.32	2.86	2.32	3.65	27	2.63	28	5.11	25
12.9	15	6,897	37	2.27	2.25	1.33	5.49	19	1.11	31	2.93	37
11.5	27	6,247	39	3.06	3.10	1.93	4.72	24	(1.65)	38	2.37	40
14.0	11	11,409	17	4.39	3.94	2.66	5.14	21	57.60	6	11.27	9

[4] Sum of capital stock (except redeemable preferred), surplus, and retained earnings at the end of the fiscal year. Common and preferred stock of subsidiaries have been excluded.

[5] Year-end total, unless followed by a dagger (†), in which case average for the year.

[6] Earnings per share have been computed as described in footnote 6, page 310.

[7] Average annual growth rate, compounded.

[8] Total return has been computed as described in footnote 8, page 311.

[9] Percentages shown are the returns received by the hypothetical investor described in footnote 9, page 311.

[10] Figures are for fiscal year ending September 30, 1979.

INC. 100 FASTEST GROWING SMALL COMPANIES

Rank 1980	Rank 1979	Company	Sales Growth 1975–79 Increase	Compound Annual Rate	Closing Date	1979 Sales ($000)	1975 Sales ($000)
1	4	Tandem Computers (Cupertino, Calif.)	9,534%	358%	9/30	$ 55,974	$ 581[1]
2	5	Cray Research (Mendota Heights, Minn.)	8,292	338	12/31	42,715	509[1]
3	☐	NBI (Boulder)	7,826	198	6/30	13,236	167
4	☐	Thousand Trails (Seattle)	5,961	179	12/31	21,396	353
5	2	Volunteer Capital (Brentwood, Tenn.)	5,119	169	12/31	51,878	994
6	☐	Cado Systems (Torrance, Calif.)	3,629	234	12/31	28,044	752[1]
7	3	Geneve (Greenwich, Conn.)	3,520*	145	12/31	72,400[3]	2,000
8	☐	Floating Point Systems (Portland, Ore.)	3,440	144	10/31	29,563	835
9	☐	DPF (Hartsdale, N.Y.)	2,464	125	5/31	577,749	22,537
10	☐	RSI (Greenville, S.C.)	2,215	119	8/31	57,854	2,499
11	☐	Printronlx (Irvine,Calif.)	2,040	178	3/30	20,563	961[1]
12	11	Texas American Oil (Midland, Tex.)	1,884*	111	12/31	113,400[2]	5,716
13	☐	Acton (Acton, Mass.)	1,513*	100	12/31	146,000[2]	9,052
14	1	Sonic Industries (Oklahoma City)	1,500	100	8/31	38,374	2,398
15	16	Salem National (Winston-Salem)	1,496	100	6/30	12,322	772
16	☐	Wespercorp (Anaheim, Calif.)	1,448	149	6/30	7,923	512
17	17	Econo-Therm Energy Systems (Minnetonka, Minn.)	1,405	97	2/28	19,945	1,325
18	☐	Xonics (Des Plaines, Ill.)	1,346	95	3/31	88,061	6,092
19	☐	Invesco International (Atlanta)	1,272*	92	12/31	21,000[2]	1,531
20	12	Prime Computer (Wellesley Hills, Mass.)	1,243	91	12/31	152,943	11,387
21	☐	FSC (Pittsburgh)	1,236	91	12/31	108,880	8,149
22	18	Tomlinson Oil (Wichita)	1,184	89	8/31	37,334	2,908
23	☐	Air Florida System (Miami)	1,178	89	7/30	44,234	3,462
24	☐	First Artists Production (Burbank, Calif.)	1,098	86	6/30	25,423	2,122
25	☐	Triad Systems (Sunnyvale, Calif.)	1,095	86	9/30	30,805	2,578
26	☐	Reeves Communlcations (New York)	1,087	86	6/30	30,502	2,570
27	☐	Telecom Equipment (Long Island City)	960	80	12/31	24,617	2,323
28	22	Rolm (Santa Clara, Calif.)	915	78	6/29	114,455	11,277
29	☐	Shopsmith (Vandalia, Ohio)	914	78	3/31	16,065	1,585
30	☐	Commodore (Syracuse, Ind.)	886	77	6/30	150,478	15,261
31	☐	Valtec (West Boylston, Mass.)	847	75	12/31	62,884	6,639
32	☐	Chuck Barris Productions (Hollywood, Calif.)	834	75	5/31	31,501	3,373
33	☐	Data Terminal Systems (Maynard, Mass.)	833	75	1/31	69,355	7,434
34	15	Carlsberg Capital (Santa Monica, Calif.)	824	74	5/31	55,152	5,966
35	39	Rampart General (Santa Ana, Calif.)	795	73	3/31	21,066	2,354
36	☐	Kenai (New York)	792	73	1/31	47,260	5,300
37	☐	Chem-Nuclear Systems (Bellevue, Wash.)	786	73	7/31	26,600	3,003
38	☐	Allied Technology (Troy, Ohio)	768	72	6/30	35,269	4,062
39	☐	Silco (Dallas)	747*	71	12/31	30,000[2]	3,542

156

1979 Net Income ($000)	1975 Net Income ($000)	1979 Net Income as % of Sales	No. of Employees	Acquisitions 1975–79	Date Inc.	CEO	Business Description
$ 4,920	$ (646)	8.8%	848	No	1974	J. G. Treybig	Mfr. multiple processor computer systems
7,819	(887)	18.3	524	No	1972	S. R. Cray	Mfr. large-scale computers
1,651	(7)	12.5	311	No	1973	T. S. Kavanagh	Mfr. word processing systems
2,790	(49)	13.0	394	No	1969	M. G. Kuolt II	Develops/operates campground resorts
1,734	189	3.3	3,750	Yes	1971	Earl Beasley, Jr.	Fast-food franchisee, fast-food chain
2,526	(107)[1]	9.0	97	No	1973	B. A. Lay	Mfr. small business computer systems
2,600[4]	400	4.8[5]	1,200	Yes	1971	R. J. Armstrong	Metal fabrication; molded plastics; mail order
2,008	(13)	6.8	646	No	1970	C. N. Winnningstad	Mfr. special-purpose computers
13,671	4,860	2.4	11,000	Yes	1961	B. J. Cohn	Computer leasing; wholesale baking
3,010	(1,177)	5.2	750	Yes	1972	C. C. Guy	Mfr. turf equip., heat transfer equip.; 3 motels
1,840	(96)	8.9	420	No	1974	R. A. Kleist	Mfr. computer line printers
2,285[4]	692	2.8[5]	172	Yes	1955	W. F. Judd	Oil and gas exploration, production, refining
5,500[2]	176	3.8	2,400	Yes	1960	S. J. Phillips	Mfr. snack foods; owner/operator cable TV
1,822	265	4.7	66	No	1973	M. D. Jirous	Restaurant equip. sales, operation, franchising
(383)	27	n.a.	140	No	1968	K. G. Langone	Leases truck tractors and trailers
845	30	10.7	135	No	1975	Randy Knapp	Mfr. controllers for mini- and microcomputers
(862)	(218)	n.a.	445	Yes	1961	M. F. Myers	Mfr. process and waste disposal systems
(11,490)	(1,297)	n.a.	1,000	Yes	1970	C. F. Haverty	Mfr. medical imaging products
(693)[4]	404	n.a.	150	No	1971	B. R. Davis	Coal mining
16,940	692	11.1	2,570	No	1972	K. G. Fisher	Mfr. computers and software packages
6,181	(3,204)	5.7	2,000	Yes	1969	G. G. Garland, Jr.	Mfr. equip. and chemicals for dry cleaning; refiner
3,674	(233)	9.8	46	No	1957	W. E. Tomlinson	Oil and gas exploration, production, refining
2,413	(718)	5.5	1,127	Yes	1972	C. E. Acker	Commercial airline
493	(33)	1.9	186	Yes	1969	E. E. Holly	Producer of movies and TV shows; mfr. shirts
3,297	172	10.7	480	No	1972	William Stevens	Mfr. microcomputer systems
2,288	194	7.5	238	Yes	1969	M. H. Green, Jr.	Producer/distributor of movies for TV and cinema
1,006	(426)	4.1	400	No	1970	S. R. Cohen	Designs/markets private telephone systems
11,343	582	9.9	2,239	Yes	1969	M. K. Oshman	Mfr. computers and telephone switching systems
738	127	4.6	520	No	1972	J. R. Folkerth	Mfr. power wookworking tools
4,040	(2,270)	2.7	3,000	Yes	1952	R. J. Gans	Mfr. mobile homes and recreational vehicles
3,569	158	5.7	965	Yes	1967	F. M. Drendel	Mfr. coaxial cable, fiber optics, lasers
5,244	83	16.6	100	No	1965	Chuck Barris	TV and film production ("Gong Show")
13,980	631	20.2	1,138	Yes	1970	R. F. Collings	Mfr. electronic terminals and cash registers
5,253	386	9.5	400	Yes	1955	R. P. Carlsberg	Financial services; real estate; construction
948	(25)	4.5	160	No	1966	W. V. Harris, Jr.	Mfr. fireplaces; residential housing
3,894	363	8.2	800	Yes	1973	Joel Friedman	Oil and gas exploration; oil field equip.
2,982	240	11.2	300	Yes	1969	B. W. Johnson	Radioactive disposal sites, waste transport
(858)	250	n.a.	400	Yes	1946	D. F. Aldrich	Subcontract mfr. electronic/electrical products
1,000[2]	39	3.3	750	Yes	1963	Stuart Hunt	Photoprocessing & finishing; land development

INC 100 *(continued)*

	Rank		Sales Growth 1975–79	Compound Annual Rate	Closing Date	1979 Sales ($000)	1975 Sales ($000)
1980	1979	Company	Increase				
40	☐	Cullinane (Wellesley, Mass.)	747	71	4/30	13,927	1,645
41	☐	Quality Care (Rockville Centre, N.Y.)	723	69	11/30	28,225	3,430
42	9	Lear Petroleum (Dallas)	718	69	9/30	78,314	9,576
43	84	Trans Delta (Fort Worth)	707	69	9/30	6,741	835
44	☐	Decision Systems (Mahwah, N.J.)	689	68	4/30	8,387	1,063
45	☐	Data Access Systems (Blackwood, N.J.)	681	67	8/31	28,153	3,603
46	☐	Excepticon (Lexington, Ky.)	677	67	6/30	10,827	1,394
47	☐	Siltec (Menlo Park, Calif.)	665	66	12/31	43,600	5,700
48	☐	Continuous Curve Contact Lenses (San Diego)	659	66	4/30	21,191	2,792
49	20	Jhirmack Enterprises (Redding, Calif.)	650	66	4/30	21,570	2,875
50	50	Dranetz Engineering Laboratories (South Plainfield, N.J.)	635	65	12/31	11,895	1,618
51	☐	Petroleum Equipment Tools (Houston)	635	65	12/31	58,134	7,911
52	☐	Auto-trol Technology (Denver)	594	62	12/31	33,540	4,835
53	38	Wainoco Oil (Houston)	576*	61	12/31	25,000	3,698
54	☐	UniShelter (Greenfield, Wis.)	568	61	4/30	16,700	2,500
55	☐	United Telecommunications (Latham, N.Y.)	565	61	12/31	20,816	3,130
56	☐	American Management Systems (Arlington, Va.)	547*	59	12/31	46,841[3]	7,238
57	☐	Emerson Radio (Secaucus, N.J.)	544	59	3/31	74,177	11,517
58	☐	GranTree Corp. (Portland, Oreg.)	529	58	10/31	83,081	13,218
59	☐	Southwest Airlines (Dallas)	508	57	12/31	136,114	22,372
60	☐	Computervision (Bedford, Mass.)	508	57	12/31	131,500	21,645
61	25	Western Standard (Riverton, Wyo.)	502	57	12/31	3,158	525
62	☐	Gulf Energy & Development (San Antonio)	499	56	12/31	54,589	9,115
63	☐	ADAC Laboratories (Sunnyvale, Calif.)	487	56	9/30	12,923	2,201
64	☐	Chessco Industries (Fairfield, Conn.)	464	54	6/29	13,592	2,410
65	☐	Heritage Communications (Des Moines)	460*	54	12/31	15,000[2]	2,679
66	☐	Computer Network (Washington, D.C.)	450	53	3/31	21,005	3,822
67	☐	Superior Foods (Dallas)	448	53	8/31	33,422	6,096
68	☐	Paradyne (Largo, Fla.)	434	52	12/31	41,441	7,765
69	46	Computer Task Group (Buffalo)	430*	52	12/31	18,000[2]	3,398
70	26	Galveston-Houston (Houston)	428	52	12/31	110,854	20,980
71	☐	MetPath (Teterboro, N.J.)	427	52	9/30	78,000	14,800
72	36	Verbatim (Sunnyvale, Calif.)	426	51	6/30	35,685	6,786
73	☐	Data Card (Minnetonka, Minn.)	424	51	3/31	44,400	8,467
74	☐	Berry Industries (Long Beach, Calif.)	415	51	12/30	21,615	4,200
75	☐	Haemonetics (Braintree, Mass.)	407	50	3/31	14,429	2,846
76	81	Penril (Rockville, Md.)	404	50	7/31	22,692	4,504
77	☐	Survival Technology (Bethesda, Md.)	394	49	7/31	11,717	2,374
78	☐	Liberty Homes (Goshen, Ind.)	384	48	12/31	109,198	22,542
79	☐	Interface Mechanisms (Lynwood, Wash.)	384	48	3/31	6,716	1,388
80	51	U.S. Surgical (Norwalk, Conn.)	375	48	12/31	60,876	12,822
81	☐	Continental Resources (Bedford, Mass.)	374	48	12/31	13,837	2,920
82	70	PaR Systems (St. Paul)	372	47	4/30	11,355	2,408
83	☐	Varadyne Industries (Santa Monica, Calif.)	357	46	6/30	10,050	2,198
84	☐	American Medical Buildings (Milwaukee)	357	46	12/31	26,983	5,903
85	82	Robinson-Nugent (New Albany, Ind.)	352	46	6/30	22,573	4,999
86	☐	Documation (Melbourne, Fla.)	351	46	2/2	58,720	13,011
87	☐	American Nucleonics (Westlake Village, Calif.)	350	46	8/31	4,500	1,000
88	☐	Knogo (Hicksville, N.Y.)	347	45	2/28	11,221	2,512

1979 Net Income ($000)	1975 Net Income ($000)	1979 Net Income as % of Sales	No. of Employees	Acqui- sitions 1975– 79	Date Inc.	CEO	Business Description
1,794	215	12.9	185	Yes	1968	J. J. Cullinane	Designs/markets software packages
514	126	1.8	550	Yes	1969	D. A. Schienman	Provides home health care services
5,007	362	6.4	161	Yes	1968	M. W. Woodard	Oil and gas exploration, production
(132)	182	n.a.	22	No	1959	S. P. Thurner	Oil and gas exploration, development
251	154	3.0	200	Yes	1960	Geo. Morgenstern	Computer software; micrographic retrieval sys.
3,415	424	12.1	245	Yes	1969	G. R. Cicconi	Supplier of data terminals and peripheral equip.
447	80	4.1	760	Yes	1969	John Swann	Residential care for retarded and disabled persons
2,600	212	6.0	800	Yes	1969	Robert Lorenzini	Mfr. silicon ingots and wafers, semicon. equip.
2,716	394	12.8	840	Yes	1960	Donald Brucker	Mfr. contact lenses and accessory care products
3,661	114	17.0	250	No	1968	Irene Redding	Mfr. hair and skin care products
1,663	13	14.0	200	No	1962	A. I. Dranetz	Mfr. electronic instruments and instrumentation
8,129	1,095	14.0	823	Yes	1967	D. M. Johnson	Rents equip. and tools to oil and gas drillers
3,438	350	10.3	540	No	1962	D. E. Smith	Mfr. computer-based design and drafting systems
6,015	1,132	24.1	234	No	1949	J. B. Ashmun	Oil and gas exploration, production
721	1	4.3	28	No	1961	J. A. Moseler	Residential developer; builder and realtor
803	89	3.9	384	No	1959	S. B. Ringel	Sells and services private telephone systems
1,414[4]	133	4.0[5]	1,000	No	1970	C. O. Rossotti	Computer applications, services; EDP consultant
3,151	(870)	4.2	500	No	1977	Stephen Lane	Mfr. home entertainment products
2,443	335	2.9	1,650	Yes	1959	W. M. Treece	Furniture rental and related retail sales
16,652	3,400	12.2	1,630	No	1967	H. D. Putnam	Commercial airline
12,960	(4,134)	9.9	2,200	No	1969	Martin Allen	Mfr. automation systems and software
137	(75)	4.3	250	No	1955	Roy Peck	Mineral exploration; resort facilities
5,552	1,161	10.2	185	No	1957	B. J. Beard	Oil and gas production; gas pipeline
1,278	(99)	9.9	247	No	1970	C. W. Cantoni	Mfr. computerized image processing systems
415	(70)	3.1	175	Yes	1969	Louis Radler	Mfr. specialty chemicals
1,100[2]	(581)	7.3	400	Yes	1971	J. M. Hoak, Jr.	Operates cable TV systems; display advertising
1,462	(502)	7.0	239	No	1967	Lee Johnson	Data processing and telecommuni- cations services
(280)	186	n.a.	380	Yes	1962	D. H. Neenach	Mfr. dough products; meat processor
4,117	(10)	9.9	950	No	1969	R. S. Wiggins	Mfr. electronic data communications equip.
293[4]	139	2.3[5]	515	No	1966	R. A. Marks	Data processing services
6,114	2,366	5.5	1,300	Yes	1936	N. M. Avery	Mfr. oil field equip.
1,150	1,560	1.5	2,235	Yes	1969	H. F. Enright	Clinical pathology and testing lab
2,344	520	6.6	1,543	No	1969	J. R. Anderson	Mfr. magnetic disk storage media
3,938	922	8.9	1,400	Yes	1969	W. K. Drake	Mfr. embossing equip. for plastic cards
272	(433)	1.3	450	Yes	1962	Arne Kalm	Oil field equip. and services; oil exploration
1,128	319	7.8	385	No	1971	G. F. Kingsley	Mfr. blood processing systems
1,453	837	6.4	570	Yes	1971	K. M. Miller	Mfr. devices for electronic signals
1,711	(433)	14.6	200	Yes	1969	Stanley Sarnoff	Mfr. injection devices, pharmaceutical items
5,104	(590)	4.7	1,000	No	1941	E. J. Hussey	Mfr. mobile homes
1,052	89	15.7	230	No	1969	D. C. Allais	Mfr. label printing and reading devices
5,138	889	8.4	902	Yes	1975	L. C. Hirsch	Mfr. surgical products, electronic monitors
765	83	5.5	180	No	1962	James McCann, Sr.	Rents, sells, services computer peripherals
915	139	8.1	240	No	1961	Karl Neumeier	Mfr. remote handling equip.
(289)	(360)	n.a.	400	No	1959	Russell DuBois	Mfr. ceramic capacitors and resistors
1,086	156	4.0	75	No	1965	J. W. Checota	Designs/builds medical buildings
2,927	130	13.0	325	No	1956	S. C. Robinson	Mfr. electromechanical components
6,358	1,600	10.8	1,980	Yes	1970	S. R. Halbert	Mfr. computer card equip. and line printers
481	(173)	10.7	90	No	1963	W. L. Foley	Mfr. antennas, electronic components
1,896	173	16.9	248	No	1966	A. J. Minasy	Mfr. electronic article surveillance systems

INC. 100 *(concluded)*

Rank 1980	Rank 1979	Company	Sales Growth 1975–79 Increase	Compound Annual Rate	Closing Date	1979 Sales ($000)	1975 Sales ($000)
89	95	CPT (Hopkins, Minn.)	345	45	6/30	34,071	7,660
90	59	Save-Way Industries (Hialeah, Fla)	344	45	12/31	41,762	9,402
91	67	Techtran Industries (Rocheser, N.Y.)	338	45	8/31	4,551	1,040
92	☐	Matrix (Northvale, N.J.)	334	44	8/31	13,950	3,214
93	☐	Comshare (Ann Arbor)	331	44	6/30	53,000	12,300
94	☐	Ann Stevens (New York)	330	44	6/30	6,398	1,487
95	☐	Crown Industries (Tampa)	328	44	9/30	63,543	14,852
96	71	Anacomp (Carmel, Ind.)	327	44	6/30	38,118	8,922
97	54	International Research & Development (Mattawan, Mich.)	326	44	12/31	14,012	3,291
98	☐	National Micronetics (West Hurley, N.Y.)	324	43	6/30	19,657	4,641
99	29	Winston Network (New York)	322*	43	12/31	32,796[3]	7,778
100	24	Golden Oil (Denver)	321	43	6/30	2,225	528

n.a. Not available.
*Based on estimated sales.
[1]1976 figure; no revenues in 1975.

HOW THE INC. 100 ARE SELECTED

To be included in The INC. 100, each company had to meet these criteria:

1. The company is an independent, publicly held corporation in a manufacturing, mining, or service industry. Utilities, banks, insurance companies, and other financial institutions are excluded.
2. The company's sales or revenues were less than $25 million in 1975.
3. The company shows a sales/revenues history of at least four years, with a demonstrated increase in its fiscal 1979 closing figure. Firms showing growth in the 1975–79 base period but a sales decline in the last year are excluded.

Sales and income figures were first gathered from prospectuses, annual reports, and various data bases and directories. Additional information was collected from stock reports, trade magazines, and general business publications. By applying the three criteria above, as well as a five-year growth rate of at least 200%—the benchmark established by the charter INC. 100—the number of companies that potentially qualified for listing was pared to less than 1,000. An editorial team led by research editor Elyse Friedman then conducted telephone interviews with corporate executives to verify the figures. Finally, after more than 600 calls, the 1980 INC. 100 were selected.

1979 Net Income ($000)	1975 Net Income ($000)	1979 Net Income as % of Sales	No. of Em- ployees	Acqui- sitions 1975– 79	Date Inc.	CEO	Business Description
3,515	654	10.3	451	No	1971	D. F. Scheff	Mfr. word processing machines
4,628	423	11.1	265	No	1963	Belvin Friedson	Mfr. barber and beauty supplies and appliances
140	6	3.1	104	Yes	1971	D. L. Decker	Mfr. computer terminals
1,165	216	8.4	250	Yes	1957	F. G. Bishop	Mfr. medical imaging equip. and graphics cameras
4,374	755	8.3	1,100	Yes	1966	R. L. Crandall	International computer services
281	37	4.4	33	No	1958	Gerald Goldman	Mfr. women's skirts and sportswear
2,147	768	3.4	775	Yes	1950	Robert Dressler	Mfr. building products, agricultural equip.
2,653	876	7.0	900	Yes	1968	R. D. Palamara	Computer and data processing services
890	349	6.4	500	No	1970	F. X. Wazeter	Consultants in toxicology and drug evaluation
2,265	(227)	11.5	800	No	1969	N. W. Buoymaster	Mrf. disk drive components
813[4]	(233)	3.3[5]	400	Yes	1968	Irwin Winston	Sells/services transit and poster advertising
14	28	0.6	5	No	1970	A. M. Alloway	Oil and gas exploration

[2]Company estimate.
[3]INC. estimate.
[4]Nine-month figure.
[5]Based on 9-month figures.

Management

Basic Budgets for Profit Planning

Charles J. Woefel

Because he is doing well, sometimes the owner-manager of a small manufacturing company does not take full advantage of proven management techniques that could further increase his profits. One such valuable management tool is a comprehensive budget system.

The purpose of this *Aid* is to set forth a simple framework of various budgets. Taken together, these budgets can lay out for you the information you need to compile reports, compare figures, analyze data, and be in a good position to plan future production and profits.

Today, most owner-managers recognize the various advantages of budgeting. Briefly, budgeting requires you to consider your basic objectives, policies, plans, resources, and so forth. It requires you to make sure your company is properly organized. It requires you and your key people to undertake a coordinated, comprehensive, and informative effort to achieve common objectives. It helps you insure that proper controls and evaluative procedures are established throughout your company. It encourages and motivates everyone concerned to put forth a good effort. It provides a plan so that all of you know where you are going—as well as why, how, when, and with whom. In short, the budgeting process is a valuable tool in planning for profits.

You can prepare a budget to cover practically any period of time. Usually a one-year budget is developed. In most cases it is projected on a quarterly basis, with each quarter detailed in months (sometimes even in weeks). Of considerable importance is the possibility that you can also prepare budgets for two, three, five, and ten years. Or even longer.

The series of simplified examples in this *Aid* will give you a good idea of the various interrelations developed in the budgeting process. (These figures are relative to one given set of values. Of course, different volumes of business would determine different costs and thus affect the realizable profits.) Using these concepts as a framework, you and your staff can set up your own comprehensive profit-planning budget.

In preparing a comprehensive budget picture, you start with the sales budget. Other budgets are related directly or indirectly to this budget. The following is a sales forecast in units:

SALES BUDGET—UNITS (for the year ended December 31, 19x1)

Territory	Total	1st Quarter	2d Quarter	3d Quarter	4th Quarter
East	26,000	5,000	6,000	7,000	8,000
West	11,000	2,000	2,500	3,000	3,500
	37,000	7,000	8,500	10,000	11,500

Assume you sell a single product and the sales price for it is $10. Your sales budget in terms of dollars would look like this:

SALES BUDGET—DOLLARS (for the year ended December 31, 19x1)

Territory	Total	1st Quarter	2d Quarter	3d Quarter	4th Quarter
East	$260,000	$50,000	$60,000	$ 70,000	$ 80,000
West	110,000	20,000	25,000	30,000	35,000
	$370,000	$70,000	$85,000	$100,000	$115,000

Source: *Small Business Administration Management Aid* by Charles J. Woefel, Southern Illinois University, Carbondale, Ill.

Say the estimated per unit cost of the product is $1.50 for direct material, $2.50 for direct labor, and $1.00 for manufacturing overhead.

By applying unit costs to the sales budget in units, you would come out with this budget:

COST OF GOODS SOLD BUDGET (for the year ended December 31, 19x1)

	Total	1st Quarter	2d Quarter	3d Quarter	4th Quarter
Direct material	$ 55,000	$10,500	$12,750	$15,000	$17,250
Direct labor	92,500	17,500	21,250	25,000	28,750
Mfg. overhead	37,000	7,000	8,500	10,000	11,500
	$185,000	$35,000	$42,500	$50,000	$57,500

Later on, before a cash budget can be compiled, you will need to know the estimated cash requirements for selling expenses. Therefore, you prepare a budget for selling expenses and another for cash expenditure for selling expenses (total selling expenses less depreciation):

SELLING EXPENSES BUDGET (for the year ended December 31, 19x1)

	Total	1st Quarter	2d Quarter	3d Quarter	4th Quarter
Commissions	$46,250	$ 8,750	$10,625	$12,500	$14,375
Rent	9,250	1,750	2,125	2,500	2,875
Advertising	9,250	1,750	2,125	2,500	2,875
Telephone	4,625	875	1,062	1,250	1,437
Depreciation—office	900	225	225	225	225
Other	22,225	4,150	5,088	6,025	6,963
	$92,500	$17,500	$21,250	$25,000	$28,750

SELLING EXPENSES BUDGET—CASH REQUIREMENTS (for the year ended December 31, 19x1)

	Total	1st Quarter	2d Quarter	3d Quarter	4th Quarter
Total selling expenses	$92,500	$17,500	$21,250	$25,000	$28,750
Less: Depreciation expense—office	900	225	225	225	225
Cash requirements	$91,600	$17,275	$21,025	$24,775	$28,525

Basic information for an estimate of administrative expenses for the coming year is easily compiled. Again, from that budget you can estimate cash requirements for those expenses to be used subsequently in preparing the cash budget.

ADMINISTRATIVE EXPENSES BUDGET (for the year ended December 31, 19x1)

	Total	1st Quarter	2d Quarter	3d Quarter	4th Quarter
Salaries	$22,000	$4,200	$5,100	$ 6,000	$ 6,900
Insurance	1,850	350	425	500	575
Telephone	1,850	350	425	500	575
Supplies	3,700	700	850	1,000	1,150
Bad debt expense	3,700	700	850	1,000	1,150
Other expenses	3,700	700	850	1,000	1,150
	$37,000	$7,000	$8,500	$10,000	$11,500

ADMINISTRATIVE EXPENSES BUDGET—CASH REQUIREMENTS (for the year ended December 31, 19x1)

	Total	1st Quarter	2d Quarter	3d Quarter	4th Quarter
Estimated adm. expenses .	$37,000	$7,000	$8,500	$10,000	$11,500
Less: Bad debt expense	3,700	700	850	1,000	1,150
Cash requirements	$33,300	$6,300	$7,650	$ 9,000	$10,350

Now, from the information budgeted so far, you can proceed to prepare the budget income statement. Assume you plan to borrow $10,000 at the end of the first quarter. Although payable at maturity of the note, the interest appears in the last three quarters of the year. The statement will resemble the following:

BUDGETED INCOME STATEMENT (for the year ended December 31, 19x1)

	Total	1st Quarter	2d Quarter	3d Quarter	4th Quarter
Sales	$370,000	$70,000	$85,000	$100,000	$115,000
Cost of goods sold	185,000	35,000	42,500	50,000	57,500
Gross margin	$185,000	$35,000	$42,500	$ 50,000	$ 57,500
Operating expense:					
Selling	$ 92,500	$17,500	$21,250	$ 25,000	$ 28,750
Administrative	37,000	7,000	8,500	10,000	11,500
Total	$129,500	$24,500	$29,750	$ 35,000	$ 40,250
Net income from operations	$ 55,500	$10,500	$12,750	$ 15,000	$ 17,250
Interest expense	450		150	150	150
Net income before income taxes	$ 55,050	$10,500	$12,600	$ 14,850	$ 17,100
Federal income taxes	27,525	5,250	6,300	7,425	8,550
Net income	$ 27,525	$ 5,250	$ 6,300	$ 7,425	$ 8,550

Estimating that 90 percent of your account sales are collected in the quarter in which they are made, that 9 percent are collected in the quarter following the quarter in which the sales were made, and that 1 percent of account sales are uncollectible, your accounts receivable budget of collections would look like this:

BUDGET OF COLLECTIONS OF ACCOUNTS RECEIVABLE (for the year ended December 31, 19x1)

	Total (net)	1st Quarter	2d Quarter	3d Quarter	4th Quarter
4th quarter sales 19x0	$ 6,000	$ 6,000			
1st quarter sales 19x1	69,300	63,000	$ 6,300		
2d quarter sales 19x1	84,150		76,500	$ 7,650	
3d quarter sales 19x1	99,000			90,000	$ 9,000
4th quarter sales 19x1	103,500				103,500
	$361,950	$69,000	$82,800	$97,650	$112,500

Going back to the sales budget in units, now prepare a production budget in units. Assume you have 2,000 units in the opening inventory and want to have on hand at the end of each quarter the following quantities: 1st quarter, 3,000 units; 2d quarter, 3,500 units; 3d quarter, 4,000 units; and 4th quarter, 4,500 units.

PRODUCTION BUDGET—UNITS (for the year ended December 31, 19x1)

	1st Quarter	2d Quarter	3d Quarter	4th Quarter
Sales requirements	7,000	8,500	10,000	11,500
Add: Ending inventory requirements	3,000	3,500	4,000	4,500
Total requirements	10,000	12,500	14,000	16,000
Less: Beginning inventory	2,000	3,000	3,500	4,000
Production requirements	8,000	9,000	10,500	12,000

Next, based on the production budget, prepart a budget to show the purchases needed during each of the four quarters. Expressed in terms of dollars, you do this by taking the production and inventory figures and multiplying them by the cost of material (previously estimated at $1.50 per unit). You could prepare a similar budget expressed in units.

BUDGET OF DIRECT MATERIALS PURCHASES (for the year ended December 31, 19x1)

	1st Quarter	2d Quarter	3d Quarter	4th Quarter
Required for production	$12,000	$13,500	$15,750	$18,000
Required for ending inventory	4,500	5,250	6,000	6,750
Total	$16,500	$18,750	$21,750	$24,750
Less: Beginning inventory	3,000	4,500	5,250	6,000
Required purchases	$13,500	$14,250	$16,500	$18,750

Now suppose you pay 50 percent of your accounts in the quarter of the purchase and 50 percent in the following quarter. Carry-over payables from last year were $5,000. Further, you always take the purchase discounts as a matter of good business policy. Since purchases net (less discount) were figured into the $1.50 cost estimate, purchase discounts do not appear in the budgets. Thus your payment on purchases budget will come out like this:

PAYMENT ON PURCHASES BUDGET (for the year ended December 31, 19x1)

	Total	1st Quarter	2d Quarter	3d Quarter	4th Quarter
4th quarter—19x1	$ 5,000	$ 5,000			
1st quarter—19x1	13,500	6,750	$ 6,750		
2nd quarter—19x1	14,250		7,125	$ 7,125	
3rd quarter—19x1	16,500			8,250	$ 8,250
4th quarter—19x1	9,375				9,375
Payments by quarters	$58,625	$11,750	$13,875	$15,375	$17,625

Taking the data for quantities produced from the production budget in units, calculate the direct labor requirements on the basis of units to be produced. (The number and cost of labor hours necessary to produce a given quantity can be set forth in supplemental schedules.)

DIRECT LABOR BUDGET—CASH REQUIREMENTS (for the year ended December 31, 19x1)

	Total	1st Quarter	2d Quarter	3d Quarter	4th Quarter
Quantity	39,500	8,000	9,000	10,500	12,000
Direct labor cost	$98,750	$20,000	$22,500	$26,250	$30,000

Now outline the items that comprise your factory overhead and prepare a budget like the following:

MANUFACTURING OVERHEAD BUDGET (for the year ended December 31, 19x1)

	Total	1st Quarter	2d Quarter	3d Quarter	4th Quarter
Heat and power	$10,000	$1,000	$2,500	$ 3,000	$ 3,500
Factory supplies	5,300	1,000	1,500	1,800	1,000
Property taxes	2,000	500	500	500	500
Depreciation	2,800	700	700	700	700
Rent	8,000	2,000	2,000	2,000	2,000
Superintendent	9,400	2,800	1,800	2,500	4,300
	$39,500	$8,000	$9,000	$10,500	$12,000

Figure the cash payments for manufacturing overhead by subtracting depreciation, which requires no cash outlay, from the totals above, and you will have the following breakdown:

MANUFACTURING OVERHEAD BUDGET—CASH REQUIREMENTS (for the year ended December 31, 19x1)

	Total	1st Quarter	2d Quarter	3d Quarter	4th Quarter
Production—units	39,500	8,000	9,000	10,500	12,000
Mfg. overhead expenses ..	$39,500	$8,000	$9,000	$10,500	$12,000
Less: Depreciation	2,800	700	700	700	700
Cash requirements	$36,700	$7,300	$8,300	$ 9,800	$11,300

Now comes the all important cash budget. You put it together by using the Collection of Accounts Receivable Budget; Selling Expenses Budget—Cash Requirements; Administrative Expenses Budget—Cash Requirements; Payment of Purchases Budget; Direct Labor Budget —Cash Requirements; and Manufacturing Budget—Cash Requirements.

Take $15,000 as the beginning balance and assume that dividends of $20,000 are to be paid in the fourth quarter.

CASH BUDGET (for the year ended December 31, 19x1)

	Total	1st Quarter	2d Quarter	3d Quarter	4th Quarter
Beginning cash balance .	$ 15,000	$15,000	$ 3,850	$ 13,300	$ 25,750
Cash collections	361,950	69,000	82,800	97,650	112,500
Total	$376,950	$84,000	$86,650	$110,950	$138,250
Cash payments					
Purchases	$ 58,625	$11,750	$13,875	$ 15,375	$ 17,625
Direct labor	98,750	20,000	22,500	26,250	30,000
Mfg. overhead	36,700	7,300	8,300	9,800	11,300
Selling expense	91,600	17,275	21,025	24,775	28,525
Adm. expenses	33,300	6,300	7,650	9,000	10,350
Federal income tax ...	27,525	27,525			
Dividends	20,000				20,000
Interest expense	450				450
Loan repayment	10,000				10,000
Total	$376,950	$90,150	$73,350	$ 85,200	$128,250
Cash deficiency		($6,150)			
Bank loan received	10,000	10,000			
Ending cash balance	$ 10,000	$ 3,850	$13,300	$ 25,750	$ 10,000

Now you are ready to prepare a budget balance sheet. Take the account balances of last year and combine them with the transactions reflected in the various budgets you have compiled. You will come out with a sheet resembling this:

**Budgeted Balance Sheet
December 31, 19x1**

Assets	19x1	19x0
Current assets:		
Cash	$ 10,000	$ 15,000
Accounts receivable	11,500	6,666
Less: Allowance for doubtful accounts	(1,150)	(666)
Inventory:		
Raw materials	6,750	3,000
Finished goods	22,500	10,000
Total current assets	$ 49,600	$ 34,000
Fixed assets:		
Land	$ 50,000	$ 50,000
Building	148,000	148,000
Less: Allowance for depreciation	(37,000)	(33,300)
Total fixed assets	$161,000	$164,700
Total assets	$210,600	$198,700

Liabilities and Shareholders' Equity

Current liabilities:		
Accounts payable	$ 9,375	$ 5,000
Shareholders' equity:		
Capital stock (10,000 shares; $10 par value)	$100,000	$100,000
Retained earnings	101,225	93,700
	$201,225	$193,700
Total liabilities and shareholders' equity	$210,600	$198,700

In order to make the most effective use of your budgets to plan profits, you will want to establish reporting devices. Throughout the time span you have set, you need periodic reports and reviews on both efforts and accomplishments. These let you know whether your budget plan is being attained and help you keep control throughout the process. It is through comparing actual performance with budgeted projections that you maintain control of the operations.

Your company should be structured along functional lines, with well-identified areas of responsibility and authority. Then, depending upon the size of your company, the budget reports can be prepared so as to correspond with the organizational structure of the company.

Two typical budget reports are shown below to demonstrate various forms these reports may take:

REPORT OF ACTUAL AND BUDGETED SALES
(for the year ended December 31, 19x1)

	Actual Sales	Budgeted Sales	Variations from budget (under)	
			Quarterly	Cumulative
1st quarter	$	$	$	$
2d quarter	$	$	$	$
3d quarter	$	$	$	$
4th quarter	$	$	$	$

BUDGETED REPORT ON SELLING EXPENSES
(for the year ended December 31, 19x1)

Budget This Month	Actual This Month	Variation This Month	Budget Year to Date	Actual Year to Date	Variations Year to Date	Remarks

What is the Best Selling Price?

Victor A. Lennon

SUMMARY

In setting prices, the goal should be to maximize profit. Although some owner-managers feel that an increased sales volume is needed for increased profits, volume alone does not mean more profit. The ingredients of profit are costs, selling price, and the unit sales volume. As in baking a cake, they must be in the proper proportions if the desired profit is to be obtained.

No one pricing formula will produce the greatest profit under all conditions. To price for maximum profit, the owner-manager must understand the different types of costs and how they behave. He also needs up-to-date knowledge of market conditions because the "right" selling price for a product under one set of market conditions may be the wrong price at another time.

The "best" price for a product is not necessarily the price that will sell the most units. Nor is it always the price that will bring in the greatest number of sales dollars. Rather the "best" price is one that will *maximize the profits* of the company.

The "best" selling price should be cost oriented and market oriented. It should be high enough to cover your costs and help you make a profit. It should also be low enough to attract customers and build sales volume.

A FOUR-LAYER CAKE

In determining the best selling price, think of price as being like a four-layer cake. The four elements in your price are: (1) direct costs, (2) manufacturing overhead, (3) nonmanufacturing overhead, and (4) profit.

Direct costs are fairly easy to keep in mind. They are the cost of the material and the direct labor required to make a new product. You have these costs for the new product only when you make it.

On the other hand, even if you don't make the new product, you have manufacturing overhead such as janitor service, depreciation of machinery, and building repairs, which must be charged to old products. Similarly, nonmanufacturing overhead such as selling and administrative expenses (including your salary) must be charged to your old products.

Source: *Small Business Administration Management Aid* by Victor A. Lennon, Lennon/Rose and Company, Inc.

DIRECT COSTING

The direct costing approach to pricing enables you to start with known figures when you determine the price for a new product. For example, suppose that you are considering a price for a new product whose direct costs—material and direct labor—are $3. Suppose further that you set the price at $5. The difference ($5 minus $3 = $2) is "contribution." For each unit sold, $2 will be available to help absorb your manufacturing overhead and your nonmanufacturing overhead and to contribute toward profit.

PRICE-VOLUME RELATIONSHIP

Any price above $3 will make some contribution toward your overhead costs which *are already there* whether or not you bring the new product to market. The amount of contribution will depend on the *selling price* which you select and on the *number of units* that you sell at that price. Look for a few moments at some figures which illustrate this price-volume-contribution relationship:

Selling price ...	$5	$4	$4
Projected sales in units	10,000	30,000	60,000
Projected dollar sales	$50,000	$120,000	$60,000
Direct costs ($3 per unit) ..	30,000	90,000	45,000
Contribution ...	$20,000	$ 30,000	$15,000

In this example, the $4 selling price, assuming that you can sell 30,000 units, would be the "best price" for your product. However, if you could sell only 15,000 units at $4, the best price would be $5. The $5 selling price would bring in a $20,000 contribution against the $15,000 contribution from 15,000 units at $4.

With these facts in mind, you can use a market-oriented approach to set your selling price. Your aim is to determine the combination of selling price and unit volume which will provide the greatest contribution toward your manufacturing overhead, nonmanufacturing overhead, and *profit*.

COMPLICATIONS

If you ran a nonmanufacturing company and could get as much of a product as you could sell, using the direct costing technique to determine your selling price would be fairly easy. Your success would depend on how well you could project unit sales volume at varying selling prices.

However, in a manufacturing company, various factors complicate the setting of a price. Usually, the quantity of a product that you can manufacture in a given time is limited. Also whether you ship directly to customers or manufacture for inventory has a bearing on your production and financial operation. Sometimes your production may be limited by manpower. Sometimes by equipment. Sometimes by the availability of raw materials. And sometimes by practices of your competition. You have to recognize such factors in order to maximize your profits.

The direct-costing concept enables you to key your pricing formula to that particular resource—manpower, equipment, or material—which is in the shortest supply. The Gail Manufacturing Company[1] provides an example of doing it.

ESTABLISH CONTRIBUTION PERCENTAGE

In order to use the direct costing approach, Mr. Gail had to establish a contribution percentage. He set it at 40 percent. From his past records, he determined that, over a 12-month period, a 40-percent contribution from each price would take care of his manufacturing overhead, his nonmanufacturing overhead, and profit. In arriving at this figure, he considered sales volume as well as his overhead costs.

Determining the contribution percentage is a *vital* step in using the direct costing approach to pricing. You should review your contribution percentage periodically to be sure that it covers *all* your overhead (including interest on money you may have borrowed for new machines or for building an inventory of finished products) and to be sure it provides for profit.

Mr. Gail's 40-percent contribution meant that his direct costs—material and indirect labor—would be 60 percent of the selling price (100 − 40 = 60). Here is an example of how he computed his minimum selling price:

Material	27¢
Direct labor	+ 10
	37¢

The 37 cents was 60 percent of the selling price which worked out to 62 cents (37 cents divided by 60 percent). The contribution was 25 cents (40 percent of selling price).

Selling price	62¢
Direct costs	− 37
	25¢

[1] All names in *Aids* are disguised.

In this approach, raw material is given the same importance as direct labor in determining the selling price.

VALUE OF MATERIAL

The value of the material used in manufacturing the product has a bearing on the contribution dollars that will accrue from each unit sold. Suppose, in the example above, that the material costs are only 15 cents instead of 27 cents while the direct labor costs remain the same—10 cents. Total direct costs would be 25 cents.

In order to get a maximum contribution of 40 percent—as Mr. Gail did—the direct costs must not exceed 60 percent of the selling price. To arrive at the selling price, divide the total direct cost by 60 percent (25 cents divided by 0.60). The selling price is 42 cents. With this new selling price, the contribution is 17 cents (42 cents minus 25 cents for direct costs).

The point to remember is that when the material costs are less, the contribution will be less. This is true even though the *same* amount of direct labor and the same amount of machine use is required to convert the raw material into the finished product.

CONTRIBUTION PER LABOR HOUR

What happens if Mr. Gail is unable to man his equipment fully at all times? In order to *maximize* profits, he must realize the same dollar contribution per direct labor dollar, *regardless* of the cost of materials. To do this, Mr. Gail could use the "contribution-per-labor-hour" formula for setting his selling prices.

In this formula, you determine a mark-on percentage to use on your direct labor costs. This mark-on will provide the required contribution as a percentage of selling price. For example, if direct labor is 10 cents and contribution is 25 cents, then contribution as a percentage of direct labor will be:

$$\frac{0.25}{0.10} = 250\%$$

The mark-on factor to use on direct labor costs is 250 percent of direct labor costs.

Now suppose that material cost is 15 cents and direct labor cost is 10 cents. The selling price would be 50 cents, figured as follows:

Material costs	15¢
Direct labor	+ 10
	25¢
Contribution	+ 25
Selling Price	= 50¢

The contribution-per-labor-hour approach assures Mr. Gail a 25-cent contribution for each 10 cents of labor (250 percent) used to make a product regardless of the value of the raw material used.

CONTRIBUTION PER POUND

If, and when, *raw materials* are in short supply and are the limiting factor, then the base to use is the dollar contribution per pound of material. This formula is similar to the one for contribution per labor hour. The difference is that you establish the contribution as a percentage of material cost rather than as a percentage of direct labor cost.

CONTRIBUTION PER MACHINE HOUR

Determining the contribution per machine hour can be a more involved task than figuring the contribution per pound. If different products are made on the same machine, each may use a *different* amount of machine time. This fact means that the total output of a certain machine in a given time period may vary. As a consequence, the dollar contribution per machine hour which a company realizes may vary from product to product. For example, products A, B, and C are made on the same machine and their contribution per machine hour is:

$28.80 for product A
$26.00 for product B
$20.00 for product C

When machine capacity is the *limiting factor,* you can maximize profit by using dollar contribution per machine hour when setting prices. When selling to customers, you should give priority to products which give the greatest dollar contribution per machine hour. In the above example, your salesmen would push product A over products B and C.

To use this pricing approach means that you have to establish a base dollar contribution per machine hour for each machine group. You do it by determining the total number of machine hours available in a given time period. You then relate these machine hours to the manufacturing and nonmanufacturing overhead to be absorbed in that period. For example:

Total machine hours available in 12
              months =   5,000
Total manufacturing and nonmanu-
        facturing overhead = $100,000
Contribution required per machine
hour to cover manufacturing and
    nonmanufacturing overhead = $20*
*$100,000 divided by 5,000 hours.

In this example, during periods when the company can sell the output of all of its available machine hours, it must realize a return of $20 per machine hour in order to cover its manufacturing and nonmanufacturing over-

head. When the full 5,000 hours are used, the $20-per-hour return will bring the company to its break-even point. When all of the company's available machine hours cannot be sold, its return per machine hour must be more than $20.

Notice that in the above example, only the breakeven point is considered. There is no provision for profit. How do you build profit into this pricing formula?

Return on investment is a good approach. If the Gail Manufacturing Company, for example, has $300,000 invested and wants a 10-percent return, its profit before taxes would have to be $30,000. Mr. Gail can relate this profit goal to the machine-hour approach by dividing the $30,000 by 5,000 (the available machine hours). This means that he needs $6 per machine hour as a mark-up for profit.

SELLING PRICE FOR PRODUCT C

Now suppose that Mr. Gail wants to use the contribution-per-machine-hour and profit-per-machine-hour approach to set a price for product C. For product C, the direct labor cost per unit is $1.80. Machine output (or units per hour) is 1.25, required contribution per machine hour is $20, and desired profit per machine hour is $6. The formula to set the unit selling price is:

Material cost	$21.37	
Direct labor	1.80	
Contribution per unit	16.00*	
Price before profit	$39.17	
Desired profit	4.80	($6 × 0.80*)
Desired selling price	$43.97	

*Calculated as follows: With a machine output of 1.25 units per hour, 0.80 of a machine hour is needed to produce one unit; the required contribution per machine hour is $20; therefore, $20 × 0.80 = $16.

If Mr. Gail is to get a 10-percent return on his investment before taxes, the selling price must be $43.97.

But suppose competitive factors mean that Mr. Gail cannot sell product C at $43.97. In such case, he might:

1. Not make product C if he can use the machine time to manufacture another product which will give his company its profit of 10 percent—provided, of course, that he has orders for the second product.

2. Reduce the selling price, if refusing orders for product C means that the machines will be idle. Any price greater than $39.17 will generate some profit which is better than no profit.

But suppose that $39.17 is also too high. Should Mr. Gail turn down all orders for product C at less than $39.17? Not necessarily. If he has no orders to run on the machines, he should accept orders for product C at less than $39.17

because $16 of that price are a contribution to his manufacturing and nonmanufacturing overhead. He has to pay these costs even when the machines are idle.

Keep in mind that the direct costing method of setting a price gives you flexibility. For example, Mr. Gail has to get $43.97 for product C in order to make his desired profit. But his price for that product can range from $23.17 to $43.97 (or higher, depending on market conditions).

Any price above $39.17 brings in some con-tribution toward profit. Mr. Gail can break even at $39.17. Any price between $39.17 and $23.17 brings in some contribution toward his overhead. And in a pinch, he can sell as low as $23.17 and recover his direct costs—material and direct labor.

However, Mr. Gail must use his flexibility with care. It takes only a few transactions at $23.17 (recovering only his direct costs) to keep him from maximizing his profits over a 12-month period.

Cheaper Financing for Plant Expansion

Joseph J. Feit, George R. Krouse, Richard A. Miller*

If a company needs to borrow money to build a new facility or expand an existing one, it may be able to *reduce* the interest cost *sharply* by using industrial revenue financing. *Bonus:* The company will probably be able to borrow the *full* amount, and it will have to put up little or no cash at all.

It works about the same as if the firm got a 15- or 20-year mortgage at 8 percent to 9 percent, with no down payment. (Interest is tax-free to the lender.) *The catch:* Considerable red tape and legal fees. That makes the process attractive mainly for projects that will cost $500,000 or more.

How industrial revenue financing works:

• The company finds a community that wants to attract new industry and jobs. It could be a small rural town or a major industrial city. In fact, the city where the company is now located may be willing to help the firm modernize or expand. *Point:* Even if the local community isn't pushing tax-free financing, don't be bashful. Ask if it's available. Help set up a revenue financing authority if there isn't one now. *Why?* The method generates local business at no cost to the locality.

How it's done:

• The *municipality* sells *tax-exempt* bonds or arranges low-interest bank financing to raise the money needed for the facility and *lends* it to the company. Depending on local law, the deal may cover the building only or the machinery and equipment, too. Repayments are set no higher than needed to cover the interest and repayment of the principal. Typically, when the bonds are paid off, the company owns the property free and clear.

° The law firm Simpson, Thacher & Bartlett, 1 Battery Park Pl., New York 10004.

Source: Reprinted from *Boardroom Reports*, Management's Source of Useful Information, 500 Fifth Avenue, New York, N.Y. 10036.

• *Restrictions:* Usually, the whole project can't involve more than $10 million. It is not possible to raise $9 million this way to finance part of a $15-million project. There are a few exceptions, including special situations such as a pollution-control facility.

• The process will probably take at least three months. Depending on the complexity of the transaction and the vigor of local legal requirements, it may take five or six months and a lot of management time for meetings and the preparation of many documents.

• *Fringe benefit:* If it's a two- or three-year building project, part of the money borrowed at 8 percent to 9 percent may be reinvested at 12 percent to 14 percent during the construction period. This "profit" can be applied to reduce the company's payment.

If the financing goes as high as several million dollars, a public offering of the bonds may be the best financing method. The cost of the offering will be 3 percent to 4 percent of the amount raised for a $1-to $3-million deal and proportionately less for a larger one. Much of the cost is paid out of the sale of the bonds and is therefore spread out over the life of the issues. The cost of the offering doesn't have to be paid upfront.

Some deals, especially those in the $100,000- to $1-million range, will probably be negotiated privately with one or two banks or institutional lenders. This way the offering costs less but the terms may be tougher. *Examples:* A faster repayment schedule or more restrictions on the company's freedom to do other borrowing.

How to find the money: First pick a plant site that is suitable. Then talk to the chamber of commerce or a good lawyer. Authorities should be eager to help if the facility will create jobs. If the local authorities won't cooperate, consider looking elsewhere.

How to Cut Telephone Costs

*Frank K. Griesinger**

Use direct dial. Calls placed before 8 A.M. or after 11 P.M., from Monday to Friday, and from 11 P.M. to 5 P.M. on Sunday, save 60 percent off of the peak-hour rates. Calls placed Monday to Friday, 5 P.M. to 11 P.M., and on Sunday evening, will save 35 percent.

What to do

Organize calls by time zones. Ask employees to work a later shift so they can place calls to *western* time zones after 5 P.M.

Consider having a busy western office call a busy eastern one *before* 8 A.M. *western time,* and leave the line "open" *all* day. *Cost:* About $55 a day.

Important: Direct-dial discount rates are *always* cheaper than the 10-hour minimum-measured-time WATS service, after 5 P.M. and before 8 A.M. Monday to Friday.

Counterpoint: For heavy telephone use between 8 A.M. and 5 P.M. *weekdays,* a WATS line may make sense. *How to tell:* If a line has between 20 and 90 hours of monthly calls, AT&T's ten-hour plus overtime WATS service will save money. *Maximum cost (for all states, except your state):* $245 for ten hours, plus $18.38 for each overtime hour.

For *more* than 90 hours (the "full business day"), WATS service is the most efficient. *Cost (countrywide, except your state):* $1,675 a month for 240 hours. *Good idea:* Let the company's data department have access to the line after 5 P.M. to use up the extra time.

Bargain: Check the competition. ITT-U.S. Transmission Service, MCI Communications, and SP Communications all offer measured and full-time direct-dial services, so shop around for the best rates.

Other ways to save

Consider a foreign-exchange service. If a company makes many calls from the home office in Chicago to a branch in Washington, it may make sense to bring a Washington number to the Chicago switchboard. *Result:* A call to any phone in the Washington area incurs only message-unit charges, plus a monthly mileage charge and a fee for the Washington business phone line. Usage is unlimited and calls can be placed from either city.

COST OF A FIVE-MINUTE CALL
NEW YORK CITY TO LOS ANGELES

1. Credit-card or collect, 8 A.M. to 5 P.M., Monday–Friday	$3.01
2. "Person to person," 8 A.M. to 5 P.M., Monday–Friday	$4.31
3. Direct-dial, 8 A.M. to 5 P.M., Monday–Friday	$2.06
4. Direct-dial, 5 P.M. to 11 P.M., Monday–Friday, and Sunday	$1.34
5. Direct-dial, 11 P.M. to 8 A.M., Monday–Friday, and from 11 P.M. Friday to 5 P.M. Sunday	$0.83
6. "Full business day" WATS call, using 100 of the 240-hour allowance.	$1.41
7. "Measured-time, ten-hour minimum" WATS call, using 30 hours of conversation monthly.	$1.70
8. MCI, SPC, or ITT-USTS public message service (quantity discounts and after-hours' rates may reduce cost). approximately	$1.82

Find alternatives to accepting collect calls. Collect, person-to-person calls add $1 to $1.30 to the high operator-handling surcharge. *Two solutions:*

1. WATS 800 number.

2. "Remote call forwarding" number. RCF allows customers in many cities to call you toll-free. *Cost:* About $16 a month, plus the direct-dial charge from the city of origin to your office. *Disadvantage:* Remote call forwarding is available only in those cities that have computerized central telephone exchanges.

Avoid hotel surcharges. Hotels frequently add their own operator-assistance fee to the normal cost of a phone call. *What to do:* Don't charge intrastate calls to your room number. Instead, use your credit card or tell the operator to charge the call to your residence telephone number. Both of these procedures will eliminate the hotel surcharge.

Avoid costly calls between a traveling executive and a secretary. Try using a WATS message service. Messages can be left as often as necessary and picked up by calling an 800 number. *Cost:* $75 a month, from the Cincinnati-based company ExecuCall, (800-543-3000 or, in Ohio, 800-582-1364).

Source: Reprinted from *Boardroom Reports,* Management's Source of Useful Information, 500 Fifth Avenue, New York, N.Y. 10036.
° Frank Griesinger Assoc., Superior Bldg., Suite 1412, Cleveland, Ohio 44114.

Government Builds New Data Center

NEW DATA CENTER IS CENTRAL SOURCE OF INFORMATION ON GOVERNMENT BUYING

The Federal Procurement Data Center is a new federal office which collects procurement data from the federal agencies. It keeps an automated central file of the information, and issues standard quarterly reports. Also, it can provide special reports to answer questions about government contracts.

The data center has just collected the procurement information for the first quarter it has studied—October 1 to December 31, 1978. The standard reports are becoming available, although a list of titles has not yet been prepared. The reports will break procurement transactions down by agency, product, type of transaction and similar components.

Standard reports probably will not be issued by company, but that information might have to be released under the Freedom of Information Act (it has not yet been tested).

Source: Washington Researchers, "The Information Report."

Single copies of standard reports are free. Requesting a copy will place you on a mailing list to be notified as new information is available.

Requests must be in writing, but general information can be obtained by telephone. Contact:

Federal Procurement Data Center
Washington Headquarters Service
Room 4B938
The Pentagon
Washington, DC 20301
202–695–0595

Special reports could cover questions like this: "Of all the cans of paint purchased last quarter by the federal government, what percentage were supplied by minority-owned firms?"

Charges for special reports will be based on computer time and staff time, but the rates were not yet available.

According to the data center, not all federal agencies supplied the procurement data for the first quarter, making the center's information about 70 percent accurate. It is expected that accuracy will increase in the next few quarters, as the system becomes more established.

The data center can be used as a central source of valuable federal contract information.

How to Do Business with the Government

SMALL BUSINESS ADMINISTRATION

The federal government is required by law to help and protect small business enterprise. In fiscal year 1976, the government contracted with small businesses for $12.4 billion worth of supplies and services, or 22.7 percent of its procurement dollars.

The Small Business Administration (SBA) was established in 1953 to help small businesses to obtain financing and to provide loans, within budget limitations, when private funding is not available. SBA reviews federal agency procurement requests for requirements that can be set aside for small businesses. It encourages agencies to break out certain sections from large contracts for small business firms. When a government contracting officer doubts the technical or financial capabilities of a small business, he must refer the matter to SBA. If, after studying the specific case, SBA is satisfied that the firm could perform, SBA awards a certificate of competency by which the contracting officer must abide.

MILITARY PROCUREMENT PROGRAMS

There are four basic methods of procurement for the armed forces:

Departmental programs.

Consolidated purchasing programs (interdepartmental).

Procurement by other government agencies (principally GSA).

Local sources of supply.

Specific information about these programs can be found in *Selling to the Military;* this publication is available from the Superintendent of Documents, U.S. Government Printing Office, Washington, DC 20402.

Source: "Doing Business with the Federal Government," U.S. Services Administration, Washington, D.C.

The following is an outline of military procurement.

DEPARTMENT OF DEFENSE

The Department of Defense (DOD) integrates policies and procedures and provides unified direction for the three military services (army, air force, and navy) and for the Defense Logistics Agency (DLA), formerly Defense Supply Agency (DSA). This policy control provides maximum national security through coordinated operations of DOD components.

The Office of the Secretary of Defense generally does not effect procurements. Individual military departments and defense agencies let contracts to supply their respective needs or the combined needs of DOD activities when the department or agency is designated as an executive agent.

The assistant secretary of defense, manpower, reserve affairs, and logistics formulates policy and procedures for military supply and related fields. This policy shapes the development of procurement systems and logistical relationships among military organizations. The assistant secretary's office also coordinates the procurement actions of major DOD activities.

The Armed Services Procurement Regulations (ASPR) contain military procurement policies and procedures authorized by Title 10 of the United States Code. Each military department and the DLA implement the ASPR in their own manuals and publications.

All military departments and the DLA have small business specialists at major procurement activities. These specialists are available to furnish detailed information on how to do business with DOD agencies.

DEPARTMENT OF THE ARMY

The U.S. Army Materiel Development and Readiness Command (DARCOM) is responsible for the materiel functions including research and development, testing and evaluation, procurement and production, storage and distribution, inventory management, maintenance, and disposals throughout the United States. DARCOM headquarters, formerly Army Materiel Command (AMC), is in Alexandria, Virginia. DARCOM consists of a nationwide network of 66 military installations and 73 activities.

Major subordinate commands are responsible for research, development, production, and procurement of each assigned commodity group.

Detailed listings of major army purchasing offices throughout the country appear in the Department of Defense publication *Selling to the Military*.

DEPARTMENT OF THE NAVY

The Naval Material Command, Arlington, Virginia, has chief responsibility for navy procurement. The Military Sealift Command, the Commandant of the Marine Corps, and the Office of Naval Research also conduct major procurement programs.

The Naval Material Command, Department of the Navy, Crystal Plaza, Arlington, Virginia (mail to Washington, DC 20360), has subordinate commands for air, electronics, sea, and supply systems as well as for facilities engineering. It makes limited procurements for the Marine Corps.

The Military Sealift Command contracts for ocean shipping services, including ship chartering and ocean towage, and contracts for repair of ocean-going ships.

The Office of Naval Research contracts for studies in electronics, materials, chemistry, physics, earth and ocean sciences, and biological and psychological sciences. It also coordinates the research programs of the navy's technical commands. The Bureau of Naval Personnel, Department of the Navy, Columbia Pike and Arlington Ridge Road, Arlington, Virginia (mail to Washington, DC 20370) is responsible for personnel research programs, special studies, and recruiting and training services. Naval Material Command supply activities handle procurement for the Bureau of Naval Personnel.

Major navy purchasing offices are listed in the Department of Defense publication *Selling to the Military*.

DEPARTMENT OF THE AIR FORCE

The Air Force Logistics Command buys all supplies and services for weapons support and other operational systems.

The Air Force Systems Command procures all air force systems and makes initial purchase of related support equipment. This command is also responsible for all research and development.

In general, all other air force commands purchase supplies and services needed to operate air force bases. In addition, the Military Airlift Command purchases services to provide airlift and air taxi service; the Air Training Command procures services for flight training; the Air Force Communications Service operates and maintains ground communication services; and the Aerospace Defense Command procures services in support of the analysis, operation, and maintenance of missile and aircraft warning systems.

THE DEFENSE LOGISTICS AGENCY

The Defense Logistics Agency (DLA), which was formerly the Defense Supply Agency, manages approximately 1.8 million general supply items for the military services. Some typical items DLA buys are food, clothing, textiles, medical and dental equipment, industrial and chemical equipment, electrical equipment and electronics, food preparation equipment, construction equipment, automotive equipment and fuel, and petroleum products and services.

The six DLA supply centers that buy and manage specific commodities are listed below.

Defense Construction Supply Center
3990 East Broad Street
Columbus, OH 43215
(614) 236-3541

Defense Electronics Supply Center
1507 Wilmington Pike
Dayton, OH 45444
(513) 296-5231

Defense Fuel Supply Center
Cameron Station, Building 8
5010 Duke Street
Alexandria, VA 22314
(202) 274-7428

Defense General Supply Center
Bellwood, Petersburg Pike
Richmond, VA 23297
(804) 275-3617 or 275-3287

Defense Industrial Supply Center
700 Robbins Avenue
Philadelphia, PA 19111
(215) 697-2747

Defense Personnel Support Center
2800 South 20th Street
Philadelphia, PA 19101
(215) 271-2321

Interested suppliers should contact the small business and economic utilization specialist of the appropriate supply center to obtain Standard Form 129, Bidder's Mailing List Application Form, and the appropriate commodity list. These forms should be completed and returned to the supply center so the company can be placed on the appropriate bidders mailing list.

Management and administration of most defense contracts are consolidated under DLA through the Defense Contract Administration Services (DCAS) regional offices. Firms interested in subcontracting should contact the small business and economic utilization specialist at the nearest DCAS regional office listed below.

Defense Contract Administration
Services Region
805 Walker Street
Marietta, GA 30060
(404) 424-6000, Ext. 231

Defense Contract Administration
Services Region
666 Summer Street
Boston, MA 02210
(617) 542-6000, Ext. 886

Defense Contract Administration
Services Region
O'Hare International Airport
P.O. Box 66475
Chicago, IL 60666
(312) 694-6390

Defense Contract Administration
Services Region
Federal Office Building
Room 1821
1240 E. Ninth Street
Cleveland, OH 44199
(216) 522-5122 or 522-5150

Defense Contract Administration
Services Region
500 South Ervay Street
Dallas, TX 75201
(214) 744-4581, Ext. 205

Defense Contract Administration
Services Region
11099 South La Cienega Blvd.
Los Angeles, CA 90045
(213) 643-0620 or 643-0621

Defense Contract Administration
Services Region
60 Hudson Street
New York, NY 10013
(212) 264-9090 or 264-9091

Defense Contract Administration
Services Region
2800 South 20th Street
P.O. Box 7478
Philadelphia, PA 19101
(215) 271-4006

Defense Contract Administration
Services Region
1136 Washington Avenue
St. Louis, MO 63101
(314) 268-6223

DLA, through the Defense Property Disposal Service (DPDS), has worldwide responsibility for disposal of military surplus personal property. DPDS maintains a centralized bidders mailing list at Battle Creek, Michigan.

To be placed on this list, individuals and firms should write to Defense Property Disposal Service, P.O. Box 1370, Battle Creek, MI 49016.

Additional information concerning DLA procurement is contained in the booklets *How to Do Business With DLA, An Introduction to DLA,* and *An Identification of Commodities Purchased by the DLA.* Copies of these publications are available from the Public Affairs Office or the Office of the Small Business and Economic Utilization Advisor, DLA, Cameron Station, 5010 Duke Street, Alexandria, VA 22314, (202) 274-6242.

GENERAL SERVICES ADMINISTRATION PROCUREMENT PROGRAMS

A large volume of goods and services utilized by civilian agencies and military departments is contracted for by the General Services Administration (GSA). GSA has six major subdivisions. They are the Automated Data and Telecommunications Service (ADTS), the Federal Preparedness Agency (FPA), the Federal Supply Service (FSS), the Federal Property Resources Service (FPRS), the National Archives and Records Service (NARS), and the Public Buildings Service (PBS). ADTS, FSS, and PBS make major procurements in their respective areas of responsibility. Business representatives interested in selling products and services to the government should contact the nearest GSA Business Service Center.

AUTOMATED DATA AND TELECOMMUNICATIONS SERVICE

Telecommunications. The Automated Data and Telecommunications Service (ADTS) operates the Federal Telecommunications System. It contracts for transmission facilities with common carriers and makes competitive procurements where possible. It also leases and purchases terminals for teletype, data, and facsimile transmission. Installation and maintenance services are also arranged. GSA regional offices obtain telephone services from local companies and from the interconnect industry.

Automatic Data Processing (ADP) Procurement. Public Law 89–306 directs GSA to coordinate and provide for the economic and efficient purchase, lease, and maintenance of automatic data processing equipment for use by federal agencies. The intent of this legislation was that GSA should act as the central purchasing manager of all ADP and related items for the government. Several procurement programs have been established to meet the government's ADP needs. However, because of the large number of procurements involved, it sometimes is necessary to delegate authority to federal agencies to conduct their own procurements.

ADP Schedules. Each year, GSA negotiates ADP schedules for most types of commercially available ADP equipment. These fixed priced, indefinite quantity contracts are used primarily for continued rental and maintenance of installed equipment and in acquiring special features. Under certain conditions, they also may be used to acquire additional equipment.

ADP Equipment Requirements Contracts. GSA awards requirements contracts for a variety of ADP equipment. These contracts cover such items as memory units, terminals, disk packs, punched card machines, and disk and tape drives. A Federal agency must use these contracts when the equipment available will meet the agency's requirement.

Teleprocessing Services. Government data processing requirements frequently can be satisfied by the use of teleprocessing services. GSA is establishing teleprocessing schedules and basic agreements that may be used by federal agencies to obtain the required teleprocessing services.

PUBLIC BUILDINGS SERVICE

Design Contracts. Within the Public Buildings Service (PBS), the Office of Construction Management, through its design and construction divisions in the GSA regional offices, contracts with architect-engineers for such projects as office buildings, courthouses, and research centers. These contracts are normally negotiated. Design contracts for air-conditioning systems, elevators, repairs, and alterations are also negotiated.

Negotiations are conducted following an evaluation of Standard Form 254, Architect-Engineer and Related Services Questionnaire, and photos of completed projects previously filed with the GSA regional and central offices. Generally, only architect-engineers in the geographic area of the project are considered. An exception may be made for projects of national significance.

The architect is responsible for furnishing complete design services. Subcontracts with consulting engineers are subject of GSA approval. If a project is basically of an engineering nature, the prime contract is negotiated with an engineering firm.

Topographic surveys, soil tests, and soil analyses are generally subcontracted by the architect-engineer. They are reimbursable items exclusive of the design fee.

The GSA regional offices commission murals and sculptures to be placed in public buildings. Artists are selected in cooperation with the National Endowment for the Arts (NEA). NEA-appointed panels, consisting of local civic and art-oriented representatives and the project architect, recommend artists to GSA. These recommendations provide the basis for the GSA selection process.

Construction Contracts. Contracts for construction or alteration are awarded to the lowest responsive and responsible bidder on the basis of competitive bids.

When competitive bids are solicited, a notice is placed in local newspapers, various trade journals, technical publications serving the construction industry, and *Commerce Business Daily.*

Each of GSA's PBS regional offices maintains mailing lists of interested prospective bidders. Firms may apply by contacting the nearest Business Service Center.

Leasing of Real Property. GSA leases space in urban centers in the 50 states of the United States, Puerto Rico, and the Virgin Islands for federal agencies. However, there are certain exceptions. The Departments of Agriculture, Commerce, and Defense may lease their own building space after GSA clearance. GSA does not lease space for post offices or in foreign countries.

Leases normally are obtained by negotiation. Occasionally, invitations for sealed bids are issued.

Maintenance and Repair of Government-Owned Buildings. The Office of Buildings Management operates buildings under the control of GSA. To perform these functions, it purchases such items as tools, hardware, paints and janitorial supplies (including uniforms), shop and cafeteria equipment, and office furniture.

Purchases from non-government sources are usually contracted for by authorized building managers. They may purchase equipment, supplies, and materials not to exceed $2,500 in any single instance and may contract for janitorial, window-cleaning and utility services, cafeteria operation, garbage removal, and dry cleaning.

Businesses interested in selling items to the Office of Buildings Management, performing building services, or buying wastepaper should contact the nearest GSA Business Service Center.

Real Property. GSA seeks appraisal, auctioneer, broker, and other contract services. Interested persons should write to the nearest GSA Business Service Center for the necessary applications.

Appraisal. GSA employs its own staff, independent appraisal companies, and individuals to report the estimated fair market value or the estimated fair annual rental of properties. A period of 30 to 90 days is usually required for appraisals, although the actual time is dependent upon the size and complexity of the properties. Appraisers are selected from the GSA Register of Available Real Estate Appraisers.

Interested appraisers should write to the nearest GSA Business Service Center and request GSA Form 1195, Application for Placement on GSA Register of Available Real Estate Appraisers.

Broker Services. Real estate brokers are employed in a manner similar to that used in private commerce. Under GSA procedures, brokers are also required to locate buyers and provide for wide public notice. Brokers are selected from those qualified who have informed GSA of their interest in performing brokerage services.

Surveying. Surveying and related cadastral services are obtained from civil engineers, surveyors, and land-development firms. Since this need is limited, GSA has not established a listing. Regional offices usually employ local surveyors under a selective professional services contract. Surveyors should inform the appropriate GSA Business Service Center of their interest.

Bid Bonds. Bid bonds are required for construction contracts in excess of $2,000. Standard Form 24, Bid Bond, a certified cashier's or bank check, or a money order can be accepted. Successful bidders must provide a performance bond for the total amount of the bid and a payment bond for half that amount.

To obtain these bonds, contact a surety or bonding company. The Small Business Administration can be of help.

Maintenance contracts do not require bid bonds.

FEDERAL SUPPLY SERVICE

The Federal Supply Service (FSS) is responsible for supplying thousands of common-use items such as office supplies and equipment, furniture, and books; hardware, refrigerators, air conditioners, and water coolers; automotive vehicles, other motor-propelled vehicles, and supporting supplies; laboratory, medical, photographic, and audio-video recording equipment and supplies.

The various programs under which procurements are made are described in the following sections.

Stock Program. Under this program, approximately 31,000 common-use items are stored in supply distribution facilities located for timely and cost-favorable service to customer agencies.

Agencies submit their requisitions to the GSA regional office serving their area. Orders are then directed to the appropriate supply distribution facility to be shipped from stock, unless the order is large enough to make direct delivery from the supplier more advantageous. Examples of items available under this program are paint, tools, and office supplies.

Federal Supply Schedules. Where economical to do so, an item may be purchased under the federal supply schedules program. The federal supply schedule program provides federal agencies with sources for approximately 700,000 products and services such as automotive parts and accessories, tires, batteries, furniture, electric lamps, appliances, photographic and duplicating equipment and supplies, athletic equipment, laboratory equipment and supplies, and audio and video recording equipment and supplies.

Schedules are indefinite quantity contracts usually established for a term of one year. They permit agencies to place orders directly with suppliers. Payment is made directly to the contractor by the ordering agency.

Solicitations for bids under the federal supply schedule program are advertised in *Commerce Business Daily*. Under certain conditions, contracts are negotiated in lieu of formal advertising procedures.

Consolidated Purchase Contracts. Items sometimes are not suitable for inclusion in either the stock or federal supply schedule programs. Agency requirements for those items are consolidated by GSA, and special definite quantity contracts are executed. Direct delivery is made from the contractor to the agency involved. These contracts are usually formally advertised but may be negotiated in certain circumstances.

Direct Order Purchasing. Upon request, GSA makes special procurements for agencies that:

Lack technical personnel or expertise.

Believe GSA can buy more advantageously because of its knowledge of the market.

Have special requirements, such as the Agency for International Development.

If the quantity of an order for a Federal supply schedule item exceeds the maximum order limitation, a special purchase may be made. Other special conditions and exceptions may necessitate direct-order purchasing.

Transportation. Upon request, FSS contracts for specialized transportation services such as conveyance by armored car. FSS contracts for metropolitan drayage where substantial tonnage is involved, for overseas shipments, and for packing, crating, and marking of government property. Bids for these services are normally requested through formal advertising procedures; some procurements are handled by negotiation.

Information relating to transportation procurements can be obtained from any GSA regional office. In some cases, individual agencies make their own arrangements.

Motor Pools. The Office of Transportation and Public Utilities, Motor Equipment Services Division, operates 100 motor pools in the 50 states of the United States and Puerto Rico. The Office of Procurement buys and rents vehicles for this operation and for other agencies. It buys parts, accessories, and services. Motor pools make some purchases locally. Contact the nearest GSA Business Service Center for more information about GSA motor pools.

Some agencies operate their own vehicles and should be contacted for more information.

Public Utilities. The Office of Transportation and Public Utilities, Public Utilities Management Division, contracts for utilities when available under an areawide utility contract. The using agency in the utility area will order utility services individually. Public utility services are generally provided only by regulated utility companies that are noncompetitive.

GSA has statutory authority to make contracts up to ten years in duration, but it usually contracts on an annual basis.

When areawide contracts are not available, individual utility contracts must be executed under existing rates and schedules. Purchases in excess of $10,000 per year are made by contract, while those for less can be made by purchase order. More specific descriptive information can be obtained by referring to Federal Property Management Regulation (FPMR) 101–36 and Federal Procurement Regulation (FPR) 1–4.4.

Personal Property. FSS, as well as individual agencies, contracts for the maintenance, repair, rehabilitation, and reclamation of personal property.

It lets service contracts for furniture, office machines, tires and tubes, refrigeration and air-conditioning equipment, household appliances, and fire extinguishers. Contracts are currently in effect for the reclamation or recycling of platinum, iridium, and silver from used aircraft sparkplugs and magneto points and for the recovery of silver from used photographic solutions and scrap film.

Small businesses provide most of the above services. However, GSA is required by law to utilize the workshops of Federal Prison Industries, Inc., and those workshops employing the blind and handicapped as a mandatory source of supply for many property rehabilitation requirements.

Information regarding these programs is available at all Business Service Centers (see Business Services Directory).

OTHER CIVILIAN AGENCY PROCUREMENT

Agencies publicize proposed procurements by means of news releases, paid advertising, *Commerce Business Daily,* and by mailing notices of requirements to known suppliers.

Most agencies, however, still rely on firms to demonstrate an interest by submitting Standard Form 129, Bidder's Mailing List Application. In this way, a prospective supplier will be placed only on the mailing list of the agency to which the application is submitted and only for the items listed.

Firms should not send company catalogs with requests to be placed on the mailing lists for all the items shown.

Before placing a firm on its bidders mailing list, an agency will often require additional information such as:

Production capability.

Description of items normally produced.

Number of employees.

Plant and transportation facilities.

Government contract experience.

Financial status.

Scope of the firm's operations.

Procurement by civilian agencies is generally decentralized so that regional and field offices may purchase their own supplies.

GSA procures common-use supplies. Requests to supply such items to other civilian agencies are usually referred to GSA.

The supply activities of those agencies that make substantial open-market purchases are described in the balance of this chapter.

DEPARTMENT OF AGRICULTURE

The purchasing activities and requirements of the U.S. Department of Agriculture (USDA) are varied; a wide range of supplies, services, and construction is purchased by over 200 local offices throughout the United States.

The department's Office of Operations exercises general responsibility for all phases of the department's procurement, supply, and property management functions and for the acquisition, management, utilization, and disposition of department-owned and leased real estate.

The department has prepared its own pamphlet, *Selling to the United States Department of Agriculture,* which outlines the department's procurement process, lists agencies and their procurement needs, and includes a directory of agency purchasing offices and their locations. This pamphlet, as well as information about the procurement requirements of the USDA agencies or subdepartments, is available without charge from the U.S. Department of Agriculture, Office of Operations (PGAMS), Room 131-W, Administration Building, Washington, DC 20250.

Four USDA agencies account for about 90 percent of the dollar value of USDA purchases, including the goods and services described below.

Agricultural Research Service (ARS). ARS buys special laboratory, scientific, and testing equipment; light trucks and laboratory-type trailers; farm equipment and supplies; refrigerating and dehumidifying equipment, and laboratory, scientific, and testing equipment, furniture, and supplies.

Its construction requirements include animal pens, insectaries, and greenhouses; storage sheds and laboratory buildings (including prefabricated types); windmills and wells; dock and harbor repairs; soil moisture tanks; fences; and roads, driveways, and parking areas.

ARS procurement is decentralized and on a regional level. For additional information, contact the Agricultural Research Service, U.S. Department of Agriculture, General Services Division, 6505 Belcrest Road, Hyattsville, MD 20782.

Animal and Plant Health Inspection Service (APHIS). APHIS buys laboratory supplies, vehicles, farm equipment, aircraft, office supplies and equipment, radio transmitting and receiving equipment, insecticides, data processing, and service and construction contracts.

For additional information about APHIS procurement, contact either of the following two offices.

Animal and Plant Health
 Inspection Service
U.S. Department of Agriculture,
 Administrative Services Division
Procurement and Property Branch
6505 Belcrest Road
Hyattsville, MD 20782

Animal and Plant Health
 Inspection Service
U.S. Department of Agriculture,
 Administrative Services Division
Administrative Operations Branch
123 East Grant Street
Minneapolis, MN 55403

Forest Service (FS). FS buys petroleum products; building and construction supplies; transportation equipment, including motor vehicles, aircraft, parachutes, and boats; engineering, laboratory test, scientific, photographic and radio equipment; refrigerators; heavy equipment including tractors, graders, compressors, concrete mixers, truck tractors, trailers, and cranes; explosives; chemicals and insecticides; seeds and fertilizers; hardware supplies, including hand tools, machine tools, barbed wire, and paints; and firefighting tools, lookout towers and binoculars.

Its public works projects include the construction of roads, bridges, and buildings. Forestry work projects include insect control, tree planting, range vegetation, and brush disposal.

FS procurement is decentralized and handled by regional and national forest staffs. For additional information, contact the Director of Administrative Services, Forest Service, U.S. Department of Agriculture, 1621 North Kent Street, Arlington, VA 22209.

Soil Conservation Service (SCS). SCS buys architect, engineering, and construction services (including core drilling); laboratory, photographic, radio, and soil sampling equipment; laboratory and office furniture and supplies, data processing equipment, office machines, and supplies; vehicles and other transportation equipment; and drafting and engineering equipment and supplies. It also purchases farm equipment and supplies such as feed, insecticides, and fertilizers.

Construction requirements include small dams, reservoirs, channels, debris basins, and other water use and control structures. The agency also rents construction equipment.

SCS procurement is decentralized and on the state level. For additional information, contact the Soil Conservation Service, U.S. Department of Agriculture, Administrative Services Division, Procurement Management Branch, Washington, DC 20250.

DEPARTMENT OF COMMERCE

This Department provides centralized procurement for a variety of supplies, equipment, and services for supporting nearly all the organizational elements of the department. Inquiries relative to these procurements, obtaining Bidder's Mailing List Application forms, procurement policies, or assistance and guidance should be directed to the Office of Administrative Services and Procurement, U.S. Department of Commerce, Washington, DC 20230.

Inquiries regarding business opportunities for minority business enterprises should be addressed to Market Development, Office of Minority Business Enterprise, Washington, DC 20230.

Certain specialized procurement needs of major purchasing activities located outside the

Washington, D.C., area may be directed to the following offices and addresses.

NATIONAL BUREAU OF STANDARDS (NBS)

Supply Division, Procurement Section
U.S. Department of Commerce
Building No. 301, Room B118
Gaithersburg, MD 20234

Contracting Officer
U.S. Department of Commerce
325 Broadway
Boulder, CO 80302

SOCIAL AND ECONOMIC STATISTICS ADMINISTRATION (SESA)

Property and Supply Branch
U.S. Department of Commerce
Federal Office Building 4
Room 1203
Suitland, MD 20233

MARITIME ADMINISTRATION (MARAD)

Eastern Regional Office
U.S. Department of Commerce
Federal Plaza
New York, NY 10020

Central Regional Office
U.S. Department of Commerce
701 Loyola Avenue
New Orleans, LA 70113

Western Regional Office
U.S. Department of Commerce
450 Golden Gate Avenue
San Francisco, CA 94102

NATIONAL OCEANIC AND ATMOSPHERIC ADMINISTRATION (NOAA)

Eastern Region
National Weather Service (NWS)
U.S. Department of Commerce
585 Stewart Avenue
Garden City, NY 11530

Southern Region
National Weather Service (NWS)
U.S. Department of Commerce
819 Taylor Street
Fort Worth, TX 76102

Central Region
National Weather Service (NWS)
U.S. Department of Commerce
601 East 12th Street
Kansas City, MO 64106

Western Region
National Weather Service (NWS)
U.S. Department of Commerce
Box 11188, Federal Building
125 South State Street
Salt Lake City, UT 84111

Alaska Region
National Weather Service (NWS)
U.S. Department of Agriculture
632 6th Avenue
Anchorage, AK 99501

Pacific Region
National Weather Service (NWS)
U.S. Department of Commerce
Bethel-Pauahi Building
1149 Bethel Street
Honolulu, HI 96813

Atlantic Marine Center
National Ocean Survey (NOS)
U.S. Department of Commerce
439 West York Street
Norfolk, VA 23510

Southeast Region
National Marine Fisheries Service (NMFS)
U.S. Department of Commerce
Federal Office Building
Sixth Floor
114 First Avenue, South
St. Petersburg, FL 33701

Northwest Region
National Marine Fisheries Service (NMFS)
U. S. Department of Commerce
Federal Building
14 Elm Street
Gloucester, MA 01930

National Climatic Center
Environmental Data Service (EDS)
U.S. Department of Commerce
Federal Building
Room 301-D
Asheville, NC 28801

Northwest Administrative Services Office (NASO)
U.S. Department of Commerce
Lake Union Building
1700 West Lake Avenue
Seattle, WA 98109

DEPARTMENT OF ENERGY

Created in the fall of 1977, this new federal department consolidates several previously separate units concerned with energy policies, strategies, and research and development. At present, each unit procures independently.

The Former Energy Research and Development Administration (ERDA). ERDA research and development projects concern fossil and nuclear fuels, solar and geothermal energy, and advanced energy systems. Other programs emphasize energy conservation technology, environment and safety, and national security.

The former ERDA procures supplies and services by contracting with industries, universities, and nonprofit institutions. Generally, procurements are coordinated either by headquarters or one of the eight field offices located in Albuquerque, N. Mex.; Chicago, Ill.; Idaho Falls, Idaho; Los Vegas, Nev.; Oak Ridge, Tenn.; Richland, Wash.; San Francisco, Calif.; and Aiken, S.C. (Savannah River Operations). The actual purchasing is performed, to a large extent, through subcontracts by major contractors, who operate government facilities.

The former ERDA contracts for basic and applied research, development, and demonstration for facility management, construction, architect-engineering, and other services, and for nuclear fuel processing, fabrication, and recovery. The bulk of procurements for material, equipment, and supplies is made up of small orders for standard, semistandard, and off-the-shelf items.

Selling to ERDA, Guide for the Submission of Research and Development Proposals by Individuals, and *Guide for the Submission of Research and Development Proposals by Educational Institutions* are available from the Office of Procurement, Energy Research and Development Administration, Washington DC 20545.

The Former Federal Energy Administration (FEA). Administration procurement requirements are primarily for research studies in the fields of energy policy and planning, economic impact, and production and use. With the exception of open-market procurement of supplies and materials by its regional offices, procurement is centralized in Washington, D.C. Competitive procurements are synopsized in the *Commerce Business Daily* and copies of requests for proposals may be viewed at all FEA regional offices as well as at headquarters.

Firms interested in FEA procurement requirements should contact the Office of Procurement, Federal Energy Administration, 12th Street and Pennsylvania Avenue, NW., Washington, DC 20461.

DEPARTMENT OF HEALTH, EDUCATION AND WELFARE

The Department of Health, Education and Welfare (DHEW) procures articles and services for staff and operational programs involving health, education, social security, and general welfare. The greatest dollar volume goes to the Public Health Service.

Since procurement responsibility is decentralized, businesses should direct inquiries to the constituent agencies of the department or to the regional office nearest them. The constituent agencies and their addresses are listed below.

Center for Disease Control
U.S. Department of Health, Education and Welfare
255 East Paces Ferry Road, NE
Atlanta, GA 30305

Food and Drug Administration
U.S. Department of Health, Education and Welfare
5600 Fishers Lane
Rockville, MD 20852

Health Resources Administration
U.S. Department of Health, Education and Welfare
5600 Fishers Lane
Rockville, MD 20852

Health Services Administration
U.S. Department of Health, Education and Welfare
5600 Fishers Lane
Rockville, MD 20852

Office of Human Dovelopment
U.S. Department of Health, Education and Welfare
Washington, DC 20201

National Institutes of Health
U.S. Department of Health, Education and Welfare
9000 Rockville Pike
Bethesda, MD 20014

Public Health Service
Alcohol, Drug Abuse and Mental Health Administration
U.S. Department of Health, Education and Welfare
5600 Fishers Lane
Rockville, MD 20852

Social and Rehabilitation Service
U.S. Department of Health, Education and Welfare
Switzer Building
Washington, DC 20201

Social Security Administration
U.S. Department of Health, Education and Welfare
6301 Security Boulevard
Baltimore, MD 21235

The regional offices are located in Atlanta, Ga.; Boston, Mass.; Chicago, Ill.; Dallas, Tex.; Denver, Colo.; Kansas City, Mo.; New York, N.Y.; Philadelphia, Pa.; San Francisco, Calif.; and Seattle, Wash.

Inquiries regarding procurement for the department as a whole should be addressed to the Director of Business Affairs, U.S. Department of Health, Education and Welfare, Washington, DC 20201.

For headquarters offices in downtown Washington, D.C., special administrative articles and services are bought by the Procurement and Contracts Section, Supply Operation Branch, Division of Administrative Services, Office of the Secretary, U.S. Department of Health, Education and Welfare, Washington, DC 20201.

The department has prepared its own pamphlet entitled *How To Do Business with DHEW*, which is available without charge from any of the regional offices or from the Director of Business Affairs. This pamphlet provides both general and detailed information about the department's procurement requirements and includes a directory of DHEW purchasing offices.

DEPARTMENT OF HOUSING AND URBAN DEVELOPMENT

The Department of Housing and Urban Development (HUD) administers programs concerning housing needs and the improvement and development of the nation's communities.

The headquarters office procures water and space heaters, ranges and refrigerators, lawn mowers, paint, screen wire, water closet seats, ash and garbage cans, hot-air furnace filters, window shades and cloth, and furniture. Inquiries should be directed to the Office of Procurement and Contracts, U.S. Department of Housing and Urban Development, 451 7th Street, SW., Washington, DC 20410.

Supplies and services for the rehabilitation, repair, management, maintenance, sale, or demolition of secretary-acquired properties are contracted for by the area and insuring offices of HUD if requirements are up to $10,000. Persons interested in being placed on HUD regional source lists should contact the appropriate regional office. These bidder source lists are not maintained at the national level. A list of regional and area insuring offices may be obtained by requesting HUD Form 788, Field Office Jurisdiction, from the Publications Services Center, U.S. Department of Housing and Urban Development, 451 7th Street, SW., Washington, DC 20410.

Flood Insurance Administration. The National Flood Insurance Program, federally subsidized, was authorized by Congress in 1968 to protect property owners who, up to that time, were unable to obtain coverage through the private insurance industry. The program for the first time made flood insurance available to individuals at affordable rates. In return for the federal subsidy, communities are required to adopt certain minimum flood-plain management measures to reduce or avert future flood damage. The Flood Insurance Administration is responsible for identifying and evaluating architect-engineer firms who propose to perform flood insurance studies that will identify the areas within a community that are subject to flooding. Interested architect-engineer firms should submit Standard Form 254, U.S. Government Architect-Engineer and Related Services Questionnaire, to the Flood Insurance Administration, U.S. Department of Housing and Urban Development, Engineering and Hydrology Division, 451 7th Street, SW., Washington, DC 20410.

DEPARTMENT OF THE INTERIOR

Most purchases are made by individual bureaus. Central office procurements are arranged by the Division of Property and Records, U.S. Department of the Interior, Washington, DC 20240.

National Park Service. The National Park Service contracts for physical improvements and concessions. A list of offices that issue bid invitations is available from the Division of Contracting and Property Management. Write to the National Park Service, U.S. Department of the Interior, Washington, DC 20240.

Geological Survey. Purchases include drafting, surveying, laboratory, office and electronic equipment, special photographic supplies, metals, lumber, machine parts, and hand tools.

The survey contracts for core and test hole drilling, aerial photography, and helicopter flights. Write the Branch of Procurement and Contracts, U.S. Geological Survey, Department of the Interior, 205 USGS National Center, 12201 Sunrise Valley Drive, Reston, VA 22092.

Bureau of Mines. Many of the Bureau purchases are related to laboratory needs and helium production. They are made at field research centers, laboratories, area and district offices, and helium plants.

Suppliers should file Standard Form 129, Bidder's Mailing List Application, at a field office. For a list of offices that issue bid invitations, write to the Chief, Division of Procurement and Property Management, Bureau of Mines, U.S. Department of the Interior, Washington, DC 20240.

Mining Enforcement and Safety Administration. Procurements are made in area and district offices. They include protective clothing for mine inspectors, mine safety equipment, furniture and office supplies, and contracts for services and training related to health and safety.

Inquiries or requests to be placed on mailing lists should be sent to the Division of Management Services, Mining Enforcement and Safety Administration, U.S. Department of the

Interior, 4015 Wilson Boulevard, Arlington, VA 22203.

Fish and Wildlife Service. The service buys small boats, outboard motors, construction and farming equipment, two-way radio transmitters and receivers, and fish foods.

Business representatives should send inquiries to the Procurement Officer, Fish and Wildlife Service, U.S. Department of the Interior, Washington, DC 20240, or to any one of its six regional offices.

Bureau of Indian Affairs. The Bureau purchases supplies and equipment for agriculture, building maintenance, and construction—especially roads and irrigation. It also buys subsistence items and school supplies.

Inquiries and requests for inclusion on mailing lists should be sent to the nearest office. They are listed in the Small Business Administration's *U.S. Government Purchasing and Sales Directory,* which can be purchased from the Superintendent of Documents, U.S. Government Printing Office, Washington, DC 20402.

Bureau of Reclamation. Inquiries about nonspecialized purchases should be sent to the nearest bureau office.

The Office of the Chief Engineer makes central procurements for electrical and mechanical equipment such as generators, turbines, transformers, and circuit breakers. For information about procurements of such equipment, write to the Chief Engineer, Bureau of Reclamation, U.S. Department of the Interior, Building 67, Denver Federal Center, Denver, CO 80225.

Bureau of Land Management. The central office (Washington, D.C.), state offices, and service centers purchase firefighting equipment, survey instruments, range-grass seed, brushland plows, range-land drills, and heavy equipment. They contract for plowing, seeding, and aerial spraying and for construction of earthfill dams, fences, and roads. When purchases exceed the open-market limitation ($2,000 or $2,500 for construction), bids are invited.

For more information, contact the Washington office or the nearest service center. The Small Business Administration's *U.S. Government Purchasing and Sales Directory* lists the addresses. The *Directory* can be purchased from the Superintendent of Documents, U.S. Government Printing Office, Washington, DC 20402.

Alaska Power Administration. The Alaska Power Administration makes procurements at its headquarters in Juneau, Alaska, at the hydroelectric power facilities at the Eklutna Project near Anchorage, Alaska, and at the Snettisham Project near Juneau, Alaska. Purchases are generally for the operation and maintenance of hydroelectric power plant and

facilities. Direct inquiries to the Administrator, Alaska Power Administration, U.S. Department of the Interior, P.O. Box 50, Juneau, AK 99802.

Bonneville Power Administration. The Bonneville Power Administration makes specialized purchases—usually from large manufacturers. Commodities are used in 115,000-230,000- 345,000- and 500,000-volt lines and substations. All purchases are made from the Procurement Office, Bonneville Power Administration, U.S. Department of the Interior, Portland, OR 97208.

Southeastern Power Administration. The Southeastern Power Administration makes procurements at its headquarters in Elberton, Georgia. Purchases are generally for administrative operations. The Southeastern Power Administration does not operate and maintain hydroelectric power facilities. Direct inquiries to the Administrator, Southeastern Power Administration, U.S. Department of the Interior, Samuel Elbert Building, Elberton, GA 30635.

Southwestern Power Administration. The Southwestern Power Administration purchases materials and supplies for the construction, maintenance, and operation of a 1,600-mile transmission system. Direct inquiries to the Administrator, Southwestern Power Administration, U.S. Department of the Interior, P.O. Drawer 1619, Tulsa, OK 74101.

DEPARTMENT OF JUSTICE

The various bureaus and services under this department are responsible for their own procurement, with the department itself only buying to meet the needs of headquarters offices. Requirements of the various bureaus include paper and paper products, fingerprint supplies, arms and ammunition, handcuffs and leg irons, medical supplies and equipment, and miscellaneous office supplies and equipment.

Bureau of Prisons. Prisons procure a range of general commodities since many of them are, in effect, self-contained cities. Purchases are made by the individual prisons from local sources of supply or from national supply houses.

Inquiries or applications for inclusions on mailing lists should be directed to specific penal institutions. Personal contacts by company representatives are recommended. They should be arranged sufficiently in advance to permit appropriate technicians and interested officials to be present, particularly for demonstrations of new or improved products.

Businesses making general inquiry about doing business with the federal prison system should write to the Bureau of the Prisons, U.S. Department of Justice, Washington, DC 20537.

Federal Prison Industries, Inc. This corporation purchases the raw materials required in the various prison workshops. Most procurements are by negotiated contract. Materials purchased include steel for steel furniture construction, wool and cotton for textile production, textiles for the production of clothing, leather for shoe production, bristles for making brushes, lumber for making furniture, and broom corn for brooms.

Federal prison products are for sale to government agencies only—usually through the facilities of the General Services Administration. Inquiries and requests to be put on mailing lists for solicitations of raw materials should be directed to the Purchasing Division, Federal Prison Industries, Inc., U.S. Department of Justice, Washington, DC 20537.

Drug Enforcement Administration (DEA). The procurement interests of this administration center on communications equipment, laboratory equipment, guns, ammunition, and automatic data processing development contracts directly applicable to law enforcement activities.

Inquiries with regard to DEA procurement should be made to the Drug Enforcement Administration, Administrative Services Division, U.S. Department of Justice, Washington, DC 20537.

Federal Bureau of Investigation (FBI). The major commodities purchased by this bureau are radio and electronic equipment, special laboratory equipment, guns and ammunition, and other types of law-enforcement supplies.

Inquiries with regard to FBI procurement, or visits of business representatives who are interested in selling their products, should be made to the Procurement and Administrative Services Section, Federal Bureau of Investigation, U.S. Department of Justice, Washington, DC 20535.

United States Marshals Service. Purchases by the United States Marshals Service include weapons, ammunition, communications equipment, and related services. They also lease special-purpose real estate.

Businesses desiring information on agency requirements should write to the Administrative Services Division, United States Marshals Service, U.S. Department of Justice, Washington, DC 20530.

DEPARTMENT OF THE TREASURY

The Department of the Treasury purchases supplies and services primarily through the procurement offices at its 12 bureau headquarters. Purchases are also made at many field-office locations. However, these are generally limited to housekeeping or off-the-shelf items.

The Bureaus of Government Financial Operations, Mint, Engraving and Printing, Customs Service, and Internal Revenue Service have the larger procurement activities of the treasury. They issue the majority of the department bid/proposal solicitations.

To determine whether a treasury procurement office has interest in your product or service, send a copy of Standard Form 129, Bidder's Mailing List Application, to the appropriate procurement office listed below. Those bureaus listed in darker type procure at the field office level.

Chief, Procurement and Personal Property
  Branch (Operations)
Office of the Secretary of the Treasury
U.S. Department of the Treasury
Main Treasury Building
Washington, DC 20220

Assistant Comptroller for Facilities
Bureau of Government Financial Operations
U.S. Department of the Treasury
Treasury Annex No. 1
Washington, DC 20226

Chief, Procurement and Property Branch
Bureau of Alcohol, Tobacco and Firearms
U.S. Department of the Treasury
Postal Service Building
Washington, DC 20226

Procurement Officer
Office of the Comptroller of the Currency
U.S. Department of the Treasury
Fifth Floor, East Building
L'Enfant Plaza
Washington, DC 20219

Administrative Officer
Federal Law Enforcement Training Center
U.S. Department of the Treasury
Brunswick, GA 31520

Chief, Procurement and Property
  Services Branch
Logistics Management Division
U.S. Customs Service
U.S. Department of the Treasury
Washington, DC 20229

Superintendent, Materials Management
  Division
Bureau of Engraving and Printing
U.S. Department of the Treasury
Engraving and Printing Annex
Washington, DC 20228

Chief, Contract and Procurement Section
Internal Revenue Service
U.S. Department of the Treasury
Washington, DC 20224

Chief, Procurement Division
Bureau of the Mint
U.S. Department of the Treasury
Washington, DC 20220

Chief, Procurement Section
Bureau of the Public Debt
U.S. Department of the Treasury
Engraving and Printing Annex
Washington, DC 20226

Chief, Office Services Section
United States Savings Bond Division
U.S. Department of the Treasury
Washington, DC 20226

Procurement Officer
United States Secret Service
U.S. Department of the Treasury
Washington, DC 20223

DEPARTMENT OF TRANSPORTATION

Procurement is decentralized throughout the Department of Transportation (DOT) as each of the operating administrations has in-house procurement capabilities. Specific information concerning each administration's requirements is contained in DOT Pamphlet 4200.1, *Contracting with the United States Department of Transportation*, which is available upon request from the Consumer Affairs Officer, U.S. Department of Transportation, 400 7th Street, SW., Washington, DC 20590.

The Office of the Secretary of Transportation, however, does contract with management consultant firms for studies of Department programs. Information concerning business opportunities with the Office of the Secretary may be obtained by contacting the Department of Transportation/OST, TAD-43, 400 7th Street, SW., Washington, DC 20590.

Federal Aviation Administration. The Federal Aviation Administration (FAA) makes procurements nationwide for aircraft and for equipment for communications, air navigation, and air traffic control. Purchases are made at headquarters for research and development and for major electronics systems. Further information may be obtained from any FAA regional office or the Procurement Management and Services Branch, Contracts Division, Federal Aviation Administration, U.S. Department of Transportation, Washington, DC 20591.

Federal Highway Administration. The Washington, D.C., procurement office of the Federal Highway Administration purchases road construction equipment, vehicles and parts, and support materials. It also contracts for research and development of safety standards and tests.

To be notified of contract opportunities, submit Standard Form 129, Bidder's Mailing List Application, to the Procurement Branch, Federal Highway Administration, U.S. Department of Transportation, 1717 H Street, NW., Washington, DC 20591.

U.S. Coast Guard. U.S. Coast Guard district offices and other units procure ship repairs and ship replacement parts, aircraft repairs and aircraft replacement parts, buoys and appendages, and materials and construction to support Coast Guard operating units.

The Washington, D.C., office procures vessels, aircraft, electronics equipment and supplies for new vessels, and research services. The contracts of the Department of the Navy and other military services are used when practical. Inquiries should be directed to the Commandant (FS-1), U.S. Coast Guard, U.S. Department of Transportation, 1300 E Street, NW., Washington, DC 20591.

Federal Railroad Administration. This Administration contracts for research in high-speed ground transportation concerning aerodynamics, vehicle propulsion, vehicle control, communications, and guideways. The procurement office is located in Room 211, Donohoe Building, 400 6th Street, SW., Washington, DC 20591.

The Alaska Railroad makes its own purchases. To sell to it, contact the Procurement Officer, Alaska Railroad, U.S. Department of Transportation, P.O. Box 7-2111, Anchorage, AK 99510.

Urban Mass Transportation Administration. Research contracts are the principal aim of procurement in this administration. Information may be obtained directly from the Urban Mass Transportation Administration (UMTA), U.S. Department of Transportation, Washington, DC 20591.

Saint Lawrence Seaway Development Corporation. The Saint Lawrence Seaway Development Corporation procures navigational lock-operating equipment and related maintenance parts and heavy construction equipment and spare parts. Information may be obtained from the Administrative Services Officer, Saint Lawrence Seaway Development Corporation, U.S. Department of Transportation, P.O. Box 520, Massena, NY 13662.

ENVIRONMENTAL PROTECTION AGENCY

The purchasing activities and requirements of the Environmental Protection Agency (EPA) are diversified because of the many types of programs for which the Agency is responsible.

First and foremost, EPA is a regulatory agency with responsibilities for establishing and enforcing environmental standards concerning air and water pollution, solid waste management, pesticides, radiation, noise, and toxic substances. Some of the data gathering and analysis required to develop effective standards and guidelines are obtained under contracts with experts or companies specializing in technical services. Most of the automated data processing equipment required is procured by negotiated contracts, these contracts may also cover software and support services.

EPA also requires construction, alteration, and repair of buildings, structures, and other real property. Construction is normally procured by means of formal advertising, and EPA has established an architect-engineer selection board.

For more detailed information on EPA procurements, write to one of the three major contracting offices listed below for the booklet *Contracting with EPA—A Guide for Prospective Contractors.*

Headquarters Contract Operations (PM-214)
U.S. Environmental Protection Agency
Washington, DC 20460

Contracts Management Division
U.S. Environmental Protection Agency
Cincinnati, OH 45268

Contracts Management Division
U.S. Environmental Protection Agency
Research Triangle Park, NC 27711

NATIONAL AERONAUTICS AND SPACE ADMINISTRATION

National Aeronautics and Space Administration (NASA) requirements range from highly complex research and development for aeronautics and space systems to basic supplies, support services, and construction. Its procurements to meet needs are decentralized.

The NASA Procurement Regulations, similar to the Armed Services Procurement Regulations, may be obtained by subscription from the Superintendent of Documents, U.S. Government Printing Office, Washington, DC 20402.

Detailed information on business opportunities may be obtained from the Office of Procurement, NASA Headquarters, Washington, DC 20546, or from any of the following field installations.

Ames Research Center
NASA
Moffett Field, CA 94035

Flight Research Center
NASA
Edwards, CA 93523

Goddard Space Flight Center
NASA
Greenbelt, MD 20771

Headquarters Contracts Division
NASA
Washington, DC 20546

Johnson Space Center
NASA
Houston, TX 77058

Kennedy Space Center
NASA
Kennedy Space Center, FL 32899

Langley Research Center
NASA
Hampton, VA 23365

Lewis Research Center
NASA
Cleveland, OH 44135

Marshall Space Flight Center
NASA
Huntsville, AL 35812

Wallops Flight Center
NASA
Wallops Island, VA 23337

Jet Propulsion Laboratory
NASA
Pasadena, CA 91103

National Space Technology Laboratories
NASA
Bay St. Louis, MS 39520

TENNESSEE VALLEY AUTHORITY

Purchases by the Tennessee Valley Authority (TVA) are primarily for construction and operation of electric power plants and transmission systems, construction of dams and locks, and development and experimental production of fertilizers. Items required include electrical generating equipment such as turbogenerators, steam-generating units, nuclear plant equipment, hydraulic turbines and generators, transformers, boilers, piping systems, and switchgear. Coal, coke, and nuclear fuel are bought. Electrical and electronic supplies, equipment, and spare parts, and communications equipment are stocked. Supplies procured include structural and milled steel, phosphate rock and chemicals, and items for medical, laboratory, and photographic purposes.

TVA has a centralized Division of Purchasing. Requests for information or for mailing list applications should be addressed to the Chief of the branch responsible for the equipment or supplies of interest at the Division of Purchasing, Tennessee Valley Authority, Chattanooga, TN 37401.

The Nuclear Procurement Branch buys nuclear fuel, turbogenerators, and nuclear steam-supply systems. The Equipment Procurement Branch is responsible for all other (nonnuclear) equipment. The Materials Procurement Branch buys construction and structural and building materials, architect-engineer services, and general supplies. The Fuels Procurement Branch buys coal and coke; and transportation services are bought by the Traffic Branch.

UNITED STATES POSTAL SERVICE

The Postal Service purchases both goods and services. Goods include mail-processing and mail-handling equipment; material transport and delivery service equipment; customer service equipment; office support requirements such as furniture, machines, equipment, and supplies; and custodial, protective, building, and vehicle maintenance equipment. Services bought are building protection and maintenance and vehicle maintenance and repair.

Procurements in excess of $10,000 are published in *Commerce Business Daily*, including those for facilities, architect-engineering services, and specific research and development programs and projects.

Further details concerning the Postal Service procurement programs are contained in *Selling to the Postal Service*, Publication 151, available without charge from the Office of Contracts, Documents, Processing Branch, Procurement and Supply Department, U.S. Postal Service, 475 L'Enfant Plaza, SW, Washington, DC 20260, or from any regional office. Information on procurements by the regional offices may be obtained by contacting the Contracts and Supply Management Branch at the appropriate address listed below.

Northeast Region
U.S. Postal Service
33rd Street and Eighth Avenue
New York, NY 10098

Eastern Region
U.S. Postal Service
1845 Walnut Street
Philadelphia, PA 19101

Central Region
U.S. Postal Service
433 West Van Buren Street
Chicago, IL 60699

Western Region
U.S. Postal Service
850 Cherry Avenue
San Bruno, CA 94099

Southern Region
U.S. Postal Service
5100 Poplar Avenue
Memphis, TN 38166

The Eastern Area Supply Center, U.S. Postal Service, VA Depot, Somerville, NJ 08877, purchases open-market items, such as wooden bulletin boards, mail chutes, scales, building supplies, cash boxes, carrier straps and accessories, conveyor belting, envelopes, impact cones, U.S. flags, office supplies, pack-ing materials, postmarking materials, rubber bands, seals, twine, corrugated paper cases, and other postal supplies.

The Western Area Supply Center, U.S. Postal Service, Topeka, KS 66624, purchases spare parts for electrical, electronic, vehicle, and mechanical equipment and assemblies.

Information on construction and leasing may be obtained from the General Manager, Facilities Procurement Division U.S. Postal Service, 475 L'Enfant Plaza, SW, Washington, DC 20260, or from the Director, Real Estate and Buildings in the appropriate region listed above.

To obtain information pertaining to the transportation of mail, write to the Director, Transportation Services Office, Logistics Department, U.S. Postal Service, 475 L'Enfant Plaza, SW, Washington, DC 20260.

To be placed on the appropriate bidder's mailing list, file a PS Form 7429, Bidder's Mailing List Application, and a Form 7429-A, Commodity and Geographic Location Check-Off, with the Data Automation Division, Bidder's Mailing Lists, Western Area Supply Center, U.S. Postal Service, Post Office Box 19065, Topeka, KS 66619.

VETERANS ADMINISTRATION

The Veterans Administration (VA) has a central purchasing office, the Marketing Center, P.O. Box 76, Hines, IL 60141. It buys medical supplies, textiles, food, paper products, prosthetics and orthopedic aids, and laundry equipment.

Some items are procured locally by VA field installations. These include perishable foodstuffs, laundry and maintenance services, repair services, pest extermination, and books.

The Department of Medicine and Surgery Supply Service awards management consultant contracts. Notices of contract opportunities appear in two information bulletins: 1 B 13-4, *Could You Use a Multimillion Dollar Customer?* and 1 B 13-5, *Let's Do Business*. They are available from the Department of Medicine and Surgery Supply Service, Veterans Administration, 810 Vermont Avenue, NW, Washington, DC 20420.

The Office of Construction awards contracts to private firms for design, construction, and building technology research. New facilities are built and old ones are improved to provide quality medical care for veterans. This office is also responsible for the design and construction activities of the National Cemetery System. Contracts are the lump-sum type. The Washington, D.C., office negotiates for all professional services (design work) and makes all construction contract awards.

Both buildings and cemetery projects are

advertised in *Commerce Business Daily.* Awards are made on the basis of competitive firms located in the geographic area of the bidding. Where possible, they are made to firms located in the geographic area of the project. Architects, engineers, and contractors should apply to the Assistant Administrator for Construction, Veterans Administration, 810 Vermont Avenue, NW, Washington, DC 20420.

GOVERNMENT SALES OF SURPLUS PROPERTY

PERSONAL PROPERTY

The General Services Administration and the Department of Defense are the principal agencies that sell surplus personal property. A few civilian agencies—including the Tennessee Valley Authority, the U.S. Postal Service, and the Maritime Administration—conduct their own sales.

Among the many thousands of items sold are motor vehicles and aircraft, medical equipment and supplies, plumbing and heating equipment, paper products, office machines and supplies and equipment, and industrial equipment. Goods may be used or unused, in good condition, requiring repair, or have value only as scrap.

As items become available for sale, public notice is given. "Invitation for Bid" are distributed to those who have expressed an interest in the types of property offered. Quantities are such that businesses of all sizes, as well as individuals, may participate without preference or priority. Sales are open to the public.

Sales generally are on a competitive basis. Bids must be responsive to the bid invitation and acceptable to the government. Prices and other factors are considered.

Mailing Lists and Catalogs. Each GSA regional office maintains its own mailing lists for sales of property located in the geographic area it serves. For general information about sales conducted by GSA or to be placed on the mailing list, write or call the GSA Business Service Center that serves the area where your business is located.

The Department of Defense maintains a centralized mailing list for sales of goods in the United States. This list is maintained by the Defense Surplus Bidders Control Office. Requests for inclusion on mailing lists should be mailed to DoD Surplus Sales, P.O. Box 1370, Battle Creek, MI 49016. Surplus property sales

catalogs describe the property, indicate dates and times for inspection, and provide other details.

Public Notice of Sales. Public notice of sales may be provided through newspaper, radio, or television announcements; by stories or advertisements; in trade journals and periodicals; through notices placed in public buildings; and through announcement in the *Commerce Business Daily,* which contains a listing of the larger current sales of personal property.

GSA publishes *Buying Government Surplus Personal Property,* which is available without charge from any Business Service Center.

Sale Methods. Any of the following may be used.

Sealed bids—Bids must be signed and returned to the office specified. If a deposit is required, it must be included. On the sale date, bids are opened publicly and awards made.

Public auction—Notice is given in newspapers or other media, and catalogs are provided. Traditional commercial auction methods are followed.

Spot bid—Generally, buyers place their bids in a box at the site, or submit them during the conduct of the sale. Awards are made on an item by item basis as the sale progresses. On some sales, provisions are made for those who cannot attend the sale to submit bids.

General Conditions of Sale. Sales brochures and announcements contain the instructions for bidding, payment, and property removal. Close attention should be paid to those instructions.

Deposits, usually 20 percent, are often required with sealed bids. They are promptly refunded to unsuccessful bidders.

Bidders should inspect the property carefully before placing bids. Property is offered "as is, where is."

REAL PROPERTY

Surplus real property is first available to local government and nonprofit institutions. If it cannot be used by them, competitive bids are sought.

GSA has the principal responsibility for surplus real property sales. However, special categories of land and improvements may be offered for sale by other agencies. The Veterans Administration sells houses that have been acquired through foreclosure on "GI bill" mortgages. The Department of Housing and Urban Development disposes of homes and other properties acquired because of defaults under mortgage insurance programs. Each agency is normally responsible for the sale of buildings and improvements on land in its custody.

GSA sells nearly every type of real estate found on the commercial market. In many cases, buyers may use the properties immediately.

Publicizing Real Property Sales. When government real property is for sale, the GSA regional office prepares a notice describing the property and how it will be sold. The notice is mailed to those who have shown an interest in buying similar property. A computerized mailing list is maintained in Denver, Colo., and bidders' applications are available at each of GSA's Business Service Centers.

Announcements are made in newspapers, magazines, trade journals, the *Commerce Business Daily,* and on radio and television. Specialists in the regional offices provide advice on current and future property sales.

Sale Methods. To determine the successful bidder, any of the following may be used.

Sealed bids—In response to an invitation, bids are submitted along with a deposit to the issuing regional office. On a specified date, bids are opened and read publicly. If the high bid is acceptable, an award is made—usually within 60 days. Deposits are returned promptly to all unsucessful bidders.

Public auction—Bidders must submit a predetermined and publicly announced deposit of earnest money. Award is made to the highest bidder whose offer is acceptable to the government.

Auction sales are usually conducted on the property site.

Brokers—Broker services are used principally in the sale of complex industrial facilities and other special-purpose properties. This method is used less frequently than sealed bids or auctions.

Advice to Buyers of Real Property. Give close attention to the instructions provided in the sales brochures and announcements.

Carefully inspect the property being offered for sale before bidding. It will be sold "as is, where is." Lack of information will not constitute grounds for adjustment of bids.

Be prepared to submit a deposit with your bid in the form and amount specified by the government. When credit terms are desired, make certain that the financial information necessary for credit is available. GSA generally follows commercial practices in extending credit.

STRATEGIC AND CRITICAL MATERIALS

The Strategic and Critical Materials Stock Piling Act provides for the acquisition and retention of certain materials in order to prevent a dependence upon foreign nations in times of national emergency. The Federal Preparedness Agency (FPA) in GSA is responsible for determining the quantity, quality, and type of materials to be stockpiled. Disposals of materials are made when the material in inventory is found to be in excess of national security needs. Disposal is subject in most cases to passage of legislation by Congress.

Disposals are made by the Office of Stockpile Disposal in the Federal Property Resources Service (FPRS) on a nonexclusive, nondiscriminatory basis. The materials are sold by sealed bids, auctions, negotiations, and other means.

Every reasonable effort is made to carry out a long-term disposal plan as formally announced. This allows industry to make developmental, research, and investment plans in anticipation of these disposals. However, market conditions and the impact of disposals on the economy must be taken into account. All sales are made by the Commissioner, FPRS, and the proceeds are returned to the General Fund of the U.S. Treasury. Sales of gold on behalf of the Treasury also are handled by the GSA Office of Stockpile Disposal.

For information on types and quantities of materials presently being sold from the stockpile, contact the appropriate GSA Business Service Center or the Office of Stockpile Disposal, General Services Administration, Room 2001, Washington, DC 20405. Usual materials available for sale include industrial chemicals, minerals, and concentrated ores; diamonds; rare and semirare metals; rare earths; and certain radioactive materials.

BUSINESS SERVICES DIRECTORY

Director or Manager	Mailing Address and Telephone	Area of Service
Director of Public Services	General Services Administration 18th and F Streets, NW, Rm. 6008 Washington, DC 20405 (202) 566-1240	Nationwide

Director or Manager	Mailing Address and Telephone	Area of Service
Deputy Director, Business Service Centers Staff	General Services Administration 18th & F Streets, NW, Rm. 6008 Washington, DC 20405 (202) 566-1240	Nationwide
Regional Director of Business Affairs	Business Service Center General Services Administration John W. McCormack Post Office and Courthouse Boston, MA 02109 (617) 223-2868	Connecticut, Maine, Massachusetts, New Hampshire, Rhode Island, and Vermont
Regional Director of Business Affairs	Business Service Center General Services Administration 26 Federal Plaza New York, NY 10007 (212) 264-1234	New Jersey, New York, Puerto Rico, and Virgin Islands
Regional Director of Business Affairs	Business Service Center General Services Administration 7th and D Streets, SW, Rm. 1050 Washington, DC 20407 (202) 472-1804	District of Columbia, Maryland, Virginia, and West Virginia
Manager	Mid-Atlantic Business Service Center General Services Administration 600 Arch Street Philadelphia, PA 19106 (215) 597-9613	Delaware and Pennsylvania
Regional Director of Business Affairs	Business Service Center General Services Administration 1776 Peachtree Street, NW Atlanta, GA 30309 (404) 881-4661	Alabama, Florida, Georgia, Kentucky, Mississippi, North Carolina, South Carolina, and Tennessee
Regional Director of Business Affairs	Business Service Center General Services Administration 230 South Dearborn Street Chicago, IL 60604 (312) 353-5383	Illinois, Indiana, Ohio, Michigan, Minnesota, and Wisconsin
Regional Director of Business Affairs	Business Service Center General Services Administration 1500 East Bannister Road Kansas City, MO 64131 (816) 926-7203	Iowa, Kansas, Missouri, and Nebraska
Regional Director of Business Affairs	Business Service Center General Services Administration 819 Taylor Street Fort Worth, TX 76102 (817) 334-3284	Arkansas, Louisiana, New Mexico, Oklahoma, and Texas
Manager	Gulf Coast Business Service Center General Services Administration Federal Office Building and Courthouse 515 Rusk Street Houston, TX 77002 (713) 226-5787	Gulf Coast from Brownsville, Texas, to New Orleans, Louisiana
Regional Director of Business Affairs	Business Service Center General Services Administration Building 41, Denver Federal Center Denver, CO 80225 (303) 234-2216	Colorado, Montana, North Dakota, South Dakota, Utah, and Wyoming
Regional Director of Business Affairs	Business Service Center General Services Administration 525 Market Street San Francisco, CA 94105 (415) 556-0877	

Director or Manager	Mailing Address and Telephone	Area of Service
Manager	Business Service Center General Services Administration 525 Market Street San Francisco, CA 94105 (415) 556-2122	California (northern), Hawaii, and Nevada (except Clark County)
Manager	Business Service Center General Services Administration 300 North Los Angeles Street Los Angeles, CA 90012 (213) 688-3210	Arizona, California (southern), and Nevada (Clark County only)
Regional Director of Business Affairs	Business Service Center General Services Administration 440 Federal Building 915 Second Avenue Seattle, WA 98174 (206) 442-5556	Alaska, Idaho, Oregon, and Washington

STANDARD INDUSTRIAL CLASSIFICATION CODES (SIC)

01–09 Agriculture, Forestry, and Fishing
- 01. Agricultural production—crops
- 02. Agricultural production—livestock
- 07. Agricultural services
- 08. Forestry
- 09. Fishing, hunting, and trapping

10–14 Mining
- 10. Metal mining
- 12. Bituminous coal and lignite mining
- 13. Oil and gas extraction
- 14. Mining and quarrying of nonmetallic minerals except fuels

15–17 Construction
- 15. Building construction—general contractors and operative builders
- 16. Construction other than building construction—general contractors
- 17. Construction—special trade contractors

20–39 Manufacturing
- 20. Food and kindred products
- 21. Tobacco manufacturers
- 22. Textile mill products
- 23. Apparel and other finished products made from fabrics and other similar materials
- 24. Lumber and wood products except furniture
- 25. Furniture and fixtures
- 26. Paper and allied products
- 27. Printing, publishing, and allied industries
- 28. Chemicals and allied products
- 29. Petroleum refining and related industries
- 30. Rubber and miscellaneous plastic products
- 31. Leather and leather products
- 32. Stone, clay, glass, and concrete products
- 33. Primary metal industries
- 34. Fabricated metal products, except machinery and transportation equipment
- 35. Machinery, except electrical
- 36. Electrical and electronic machinery, equipment, and supplies
- 37. Transportation equipment
- 38. Measuring, analyzing and controlling instruments; photographic, medical, and optical goods; watches and clocks
- 39. Miscellaneous manufacturing industries

40–49 Transportation, communications, Sanitary services, and utilities
- 40. Railroad transportation
- 41. Local and suburban transit and interurban highway passenger transportation
- 42. Motor freight transportation and warehousing
- 44. Water transportation
- 45. Transportation by air
- 46. Pipe lines, except natural gas
- 47. Transportation services
- 48. Communications
- 49. Electric, gas, and sanitary services

50–51 Wholesale trade
- 50. Wholesale trade—durable goods
- 51. Wholesale trade—nondurable goods

52–59 Retail trade
- 52. Building materials, hardware, garden supply, and mobile home dealers
- 53. General merchandise stores
- 54. Food stores
- 55. Automotive dealers and gasoline service stations
- 56. Apparel and accessory stores
- 57. Furniture, home furnishings, and equipment stores
- 58. Eating and drinking places
- 59. Miscellaneous retail

60–67 Finance, insurance, and real estate
- 60. Banking
- 61. Credit agencies other than banks
- 62. Security and commodity brokers, dealers, exchanges, and services
- 63. Insurance carriers
- 64. Insurance agents, brokers, and service
- 65. Real estate
- 67. Holding and other investment companies

70–89 Services
- 70. Hotels, rooming houses, camps, and other lodging places
- 72. Personal services
- 73. Business services
- 75. Automotive repair, services, and garages
- 76. Miscellaneous repair services
- 78. Motion pictures
- 79. Amusement and recreation services except motion pictures
- 80. Health services
- 82. Educational services
- 89. Miscellaneous services

Stock Market

SECURITIES MARKETS: NOTABLE DATES

1792　Original brokers' agreement subscribed to by 24 brokers (May 17).

1817　Constitution and the name "New York Stock Exchange Board" adopted (March 8).

1830　Dullest day in history of exchange—31 shares traded (March 16).

1840s　Outdoor trading in unlisted securities begins at Wall and Hanover Streets, moves to Wall and Broad, then shifts south along Broad Street.*

1863　Name changed to "New York Stock Exchange" (NYSE) (January 29).

1867　Stock tickers first introduced (November 15).

1868　Membership made salable (October 23).

1869　Gold speculation resulted in "Black Friday" (September 24).

1871　Continuous markets in stocks established.

1873　NYSE closed September 18–29.
Failure of Jay Cooke & Co. and others (September 18).
Trading hours set at 10 A.M. to 3 P.M.; Saturdays, 10 A.M. to noon (December 1).

1878　First telephones introduced in the exchange (November 13).

1881　Annunciator board installed for paging members (January 29).

1885　Unlisted Securities Department established (March 25).

1886　First million-share day—1,200,000 shares traded (December 15).

1908　E. S. Mendels forms New York Curb Agency in first departure from informal trading.*

1910　Unlisted Securities Department abolished (March 31).

1911　Trading rules established with formation of New York Curb Market Association.*

---

* Refers to American Exchange (AMEX) (formerly Curb Exchange).

† Applies to both the New York Stock Exchange and the American Exchange.

Sources: New York Stock Exchange *Fact Book* and American Stock Exchange *Data Book*.

1914　Exchange closed from July 31 through December 11—World War I.

1915　Stock prices quoted in dollars as against percent of par value (October 13).

1919　Separate ticker system installed for bonds (January 2).

1920　Stock Clearing Corporation established (April 26).

1921　New York Curb Market association moves indoors at 86 Trinity Place; name shortened to New York Curb Market and ticker service initiated (June 21).*

1927　Start of ten-share unit of trading for inactive stocks (January 3).

1929　Stock market crash; 16,410,000 shares traded (October 29).
New York Curb Market modifies its name to New York Curb Exchange.*

1930　Faster ticker—500 characters per minute—installed (September 2).

1931　Exchange building expanded; Telephone Quotation Department formed to send stock quotes to member firm offices.*

1933　New York Stock Exchange closed for bank holiday, March 4–14.

1934　Enactment of Securities Exchange Act of 1934 (June 6).

1938　First salaried president elected—Wm. McC. Martin, Jr. (June 30).

1946　Listed stocks outnumber unlisted stocks for first time since the 1934 act imposed restrictions on unlisted trading.*

1952　Trading hours changed: weekdays, 10 A.M. to 3:30 P.M. Closed Saturdays (September 29).*

1953　Name of New York Curb Exchange changed to American Stock Exchange.*

1958　First member corporation—Woodcock, Hess & Co. (June 4).
Mary C. Roebling becomes first woman governor.*

1962　Committee system of administration replaced by expanded paid staff reporting to president. Specialist system strengthened, surveillance of trading increased, listing and delisting standards introduced, and board restructured to give greater representation to commission and out-of-town brokers.*

1964   New member classification—Regis-
        tered Trader (August 3).

        New ticker—900 characters per min-
        ute—put into service (Decem-
        ber 1).†

        Am-Quote computerized telephone-
        quotation service was completed as
        first step in major automation pro-
        gram.°

1965   Fully automated quotation service in-
        troduced (March 8).

        Electronic Systems Center created
        (October 15).

        First women, Phyllis S. Peterson and
        Julia Montgomery Walsh, elected
        to regular membership.°

1966   New NYSE Stock Price Index inau-
        gurated (July 14).

        AMEX Price Change Index System
        introduced; computer complex in-
        stalled for ticker, surveillance, and
        compared-clearance operations.°

1967   First woman member admitted—
        Muriel F. Siebert (December 28).

1968   Ticker speed increased to maximum
        900 characters per minute; trans-
        mission begun to six European
        countries. Trading floor modern-
        ized; line capacity for communica-
        tions doubled. Visitors gallery ex-
        panded.°

1969   Central Certificate Service fully acti-
        vated (February 26).

1970   Public ownership of member firms ap-
        proved (March 26).

        Securities Investor Protection Corpo-
        ration Act signed (December 30).

1971   First negotiated commission rates ef-
        fective (April 5).

        First member organization listed—
        Merrill Lynch (July 27).

        AMEX incorporates and marks 50th
        anniversary of move indoors; Listed
        Company Advisory Committee
        formed, composed of nine chief
        executives of AMEX-listed com-
        panies.°

1972   NYSE reorganization, based on Mar-
        tin Report, approved (January 20).

        Board of Directors, with ten public
        members, replaced Board of Gov-
        ernors (July 13).

        Securities Industry Automation Cor-
        poration established with AMEX to
        consolidate facilities of both ex-
        changes (July 17).

        First salaried chairman took office—
        James J. Needham (August 28).

        Board of Governors reorganized to
        include ten public and ten industry
        representatives plus full-time sala-
        ried chairman as chief executive
        officer.°

1973   Depository Trust Company succeeded
        Central Certificate Service (May
        11).

        Chicago Board of Options Exchange
        opened with trading in 16 classes
        of call options (April 26).

        AMEX formally adopts affirmative
        action employment plan; Market
        Value Index System introduced to
        replace Price Change Index.°

1974   Trading hours extended to 4 P.M.
        (October 1).

        Consolidated tape begun; 15 stocks
        reported (October 18).

1975   Fixed commission system abolished
        (April 30).

        Full consolidated tape begun (June
        16).

        AMEX trades call options.°

        Trading begins in call options and
        odd lots of U.S. government instru-
        ments.°

1976   New data line installed, handling
        36,000 characters per minute (Jan-
        uary 19).

        Specialists began handling odd lots
        in their stocks (May 24).

        Varo, Inc.—first stock traded on both
        NYSE and AMEX (August 23).

        Competition between specialists be-
        gun (October 11).

1977   Independent audit committee on
        listed companies' boards required
        (January 6).

        Competitive Trader category for mem-
        bers approved (January 19).

        Foreign broker/dealers permitted to
        obtain membership (February 3).

        Full Automated Bond System in ef-
        fect (July 27).

1978   First 60 million share day in history
        (63,493,000 shares) (April 17).

        Intermarket Trading System (ITS)
        began.

        Registered Competitive Market-Maker
        category for members approved
        (May 2).

        First 65 million share day in history
        (66,370,000 shares) (August 3).

        Trading in Ginnie Maes inaugurated
        on the AMEX Commodities Ex-
        change (ACE)° (September 12).

        AMEX reached an index high of
        176.87 (September 13).

1979   Trading began at pilot post on the exchange floor. First stage in a $12-million upgrading of exchange facilities (January 29).

Board of Directors of NYSE approved plan for the creation of the New York Futures Exchange, a wholly owned subsidiary of NYSE. Futures contracts in seven financial instruments will be traded on the NYSE (March 1).

New York Commodities Exchange and NYSE terminated merger talks (March 15).

81,619,000 shares were traded on the NYSE, making it the heaviest trade day in exchange history (October 10).

1980   NYSE index reached an all time high of 70.10 (July 21).

NYSE Futures Exchange opened (August 7).

NYSE hit a record high of 83,520,000 shares traded on the Reagan-Bush Victory. The Dow finished 15.96 to 953.16 (November 5).

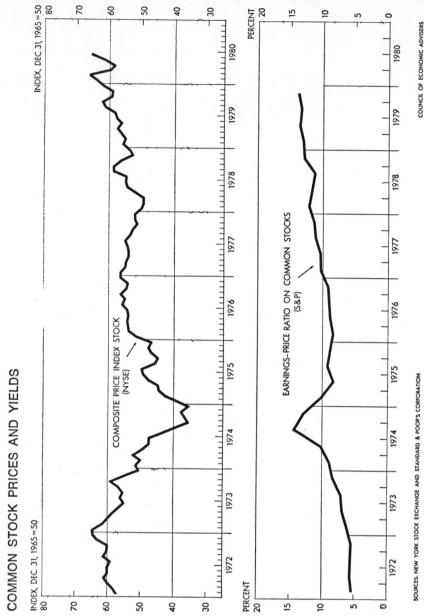

COMMON STOCK PRICES AND YIELDS

INDEX, DEC. 31, 1965 = 50

INDEX, DEC. 31, 1965 = 50

COMPOSITE PRICE INDEX STOCK
(NYSE)

PERCENT

EARNINGS-PRICE RATIO ON COMMON STOCKS
(S&P)

PERCENT

SOURCES: NEW YORK STOCK EXCHANGE AND STANDARD & POOR'S CORPORATION

COUNCIL OF ECONOMIC ADVISERS

Common stock prices [1]

| Period | New York Stock Exchange indexes (Dec. 31, 1965=50) [2] | | | | | Dow-Jones industrial average [3] | Standard & Poor's composite index (1941-43=10) [4] | Common stock yields (percent) [5] | |
	Composite	Industrial	Transportation	Utility	Finance			Dividend-price ratio	Earnings-price ratio
1974	43.84	48.08	31.89	29.79	49.67	759.37	82.85	4.47	11.59
1975	45.73	50.52	31.10	31.50	47.14	802.49	86.16	4.31	9.15
1976	54.46	60.44	39.57	36.97	52.94	974.92	102.01	3.77	8.90
1977	53.69	57.86	41.09	40.92	55.25	894.63	98.20	4.62	10.79
1978	53.70	58.23	43.50	39.22	56.65	820.23	96.02	5.28	12.03
1979	58.32	64.76	47.34	38.21	61.42	844.40	103.01	5.45	13.46
1979: June	57.61	63.57	47.54	38.44	61.87	838.65	101.73	5.53	13.58
July	58.38	64.24	48.85	38.88	64.43	836.95	102.71	5.50	----
Aug	61.19	67.71	52.48	39.26	68.40	873.55	107.36	5.30	----
Sept	61.89	69.17	52.21	38.39	67.21	878.50	108.60	5.31	13.38
Oct	59.27	66.68	48.09	36.58	61.64	840.39	104.47	5.56	----
Nov	59.02	66.45	47.61	36.55	60.64	815.78	103.66	5.71	----
Dec	61.75	69.83	50.59	37.29	63.21	836.14	107.78	5.53	13.77
1980: Jan	63.74	72.67	52.61	37.08	64.22	860.74	110.87	5.41	----
Feb	66.06	76.42	57.92	36.22	61.84	878.22	115.34	5.24	----
Mar	59.52	68.71	51.77	33.38	54.71	803.56	104.69	5.87	----
Apr	58.47	66.31	48.62	35.29	57.32	786.33	102.97	6.05	----
May	61.38	69.39	51.07	37.31	61.47	828.19	107.69	5.77	----
June	65.43	74.47	54.04	38.53	65.16	863.86	114.55	5.39	----
Week ended:									
1980: June 21	65.92	74.96	54.01	39.03	65.71	875.90	115.42	5.31	----
28	66.16	75.34	53.92	38.95	65.96	880.79	115.71	5.29	----
July 5	66.08	75.32	54.87	38.59	65.75	876.28	115.58	5.36	----
12	67.36	76.95	57.31	38.88	66.52	893.98	117.78	5.26	----
19	68.99	79.14	59.89	38.92	67.59	910.12	120.52	5.17	----
26	69.72	80.29	61.05	38.79	66.98	925.75	121.84	5.10	----

[1] Average of daily closing prices.
[2] Includes all the stocks (more than 1,500) listed on the NYSE.
[3] Includes 30 stocks.   [4] Includes 500 stocks.
[5] Standard & Poor's series. Dividend-price ratios based on Wednesday closing prices. Earnings-price ratios based on prices at end of quarter.

NOTE.—All data relate to stocks listed on the New York Stock Exchange (NYSE).

Sources: New York Stock Exchange, Dow-Jones & Company, Inc., and Standard & Poor's Corporation.

Source: *Economic Indicators*, Council of Economic Advisers.

MAJOR MARKET AVERAGES

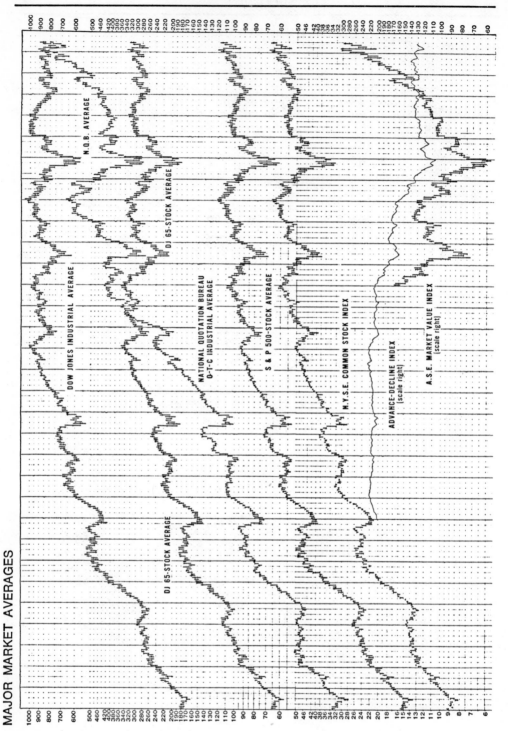

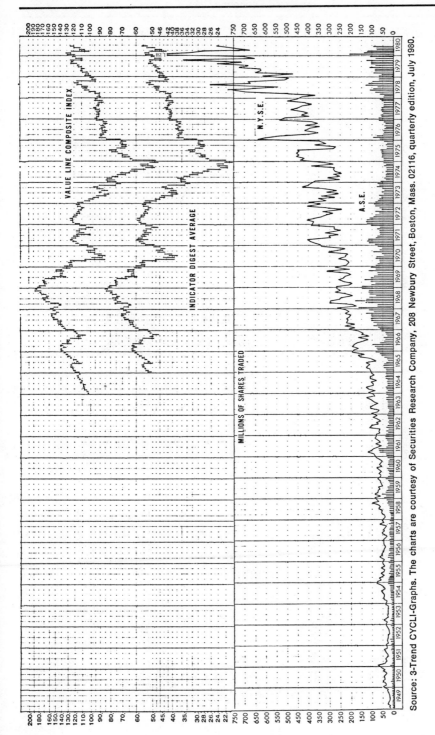

Source: 3-Trend CYCLI-Graphs. The charts are courtesy of Securities Research Company, 208 Newbury Street, Boston, Mass. 02116, quarterly edition, July 1980.

DOW JONES INDUSTRIAL, TRANSPORTATION, AND UTILITY AVERAGES

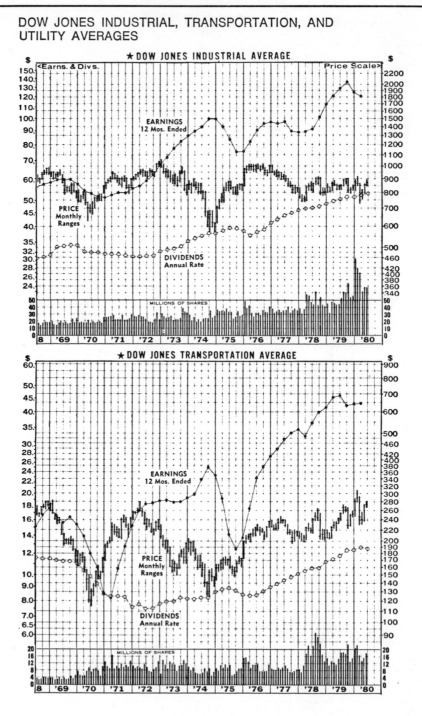

DOW JONES INDUSTRIAL, TRANSPORTATION, AND UTILITY
AVERAGES (*continued*)

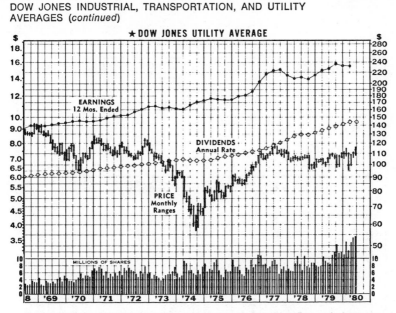

Source: 3-Trend CYCLI-Graphs. Charts courtesy of Securities Research Company,
208 Newbury Street, Boston, Mass. 02116, quarterly edition, July 1980.

DOW JONES INDUSTRIALS

	History — 52-Week		History — 5-Year		Earnings			P/E Ratio			Dvds	
	High $	Low $	High $	Low $	Last 12Mos $	% Ch %	5-Yr. Growth %	Today	5-Year Avg High	5-Year Avg Low	Indic. Amt $	Yield %
Dow Jones Ind.	936.18	759.13	1014.79	632.04	115.51	-6.11	11	8.1	10.7	7.8	55.76	6.0
Allied Chemical	61.38	36.00	61.38	27.00	6.72	19.36	11	7.1	9.4	6.4	2.20	4.2
Alum Co Am	70.88	48.38	70.88	27.13	14.42	19.67	56	4.8	12.7	7.9	3.20	4.7
Am Brands	83.38	58.50	83.38	30.50	13.51	57.28	28	6.1	8.1	6.3	6.10	7.4
Am Can	40.13	27.25	43.38	27.50	5.52	-15.98	8	5.8	7.6	6.1	2.90	9.1
Am Tel & Tel	59.13	45.00	65.63	44.75	8.06	1.26	11	6.4	9.4	7.9	5.00	9.6
Bethlehem Stl	26.88	19.00	48.00	18.25	4.82	-30.14	27	5.4	7.3	5.0	1.60	6.1
Dupont Corp	45.88	31.13	53.69	29.00	5.98	-3.86	31	7.2	14.1	10.0	2.75	6.4
Eastman Kodak	62.63	42.88	120.75	41.13	6.63	8.16	14	9.4	20.7	12.8	2.90	4.7
Exxon	72.75	52.00	72.75	32.50	11.98	75.92	18	5.9	8.7	6.7	5.60	8.0
Gen Electric	57.88	44.00	59.25	32.38	6.45	8.95	17	8.7	12.7	9.4	3.00	5.4
Gen Foods	37.00	23.50	37.00	18.38	5.19	6.13	14	5.8	9.0	6.6	2.20	7.3
Gen Motors	65.88	39.50	78.88	31.25	.64	-95.39	-21	81.8	8.1	5.5	4.40	8.4
Goodyear Tire	16.25	10.75	28.38	10.75	1.61	-47.90	-2	9.5	10.1	6.8	1.30	8.5
Inco Ltd	33.25	18.00	37.00	13.38	3.25	1525.00	-4	6.7	18.8	11.5	.82	3.7
Intl Bus Mach	72.50	50.38	80.50	39.31	5.35	-1.29	11	12.2	16.2	12.4	3.44	5.3
Intl Harvester	45.50	23.00	45.50	19.75	-7.69	-100.00	-21	NE	6.0	4.0	2.50	8.1
Intl Paper	47.13	30.50	79.75	30.50	5.08	-31.72	3	8.3	11.6	7.5	2.40	5.7
Johns Manville	27.75	18.25	38.25	18.25	4.06	-20.24	18	6.3	9.5	6.6	1.92	7.5
Merck & Co	79.00	58.25	85.75	47.38	5.43	19.08	14	14.2	20.5	15.0	2.30	3.0
Minn Mng Mfg	59.38	45.88	68.00	43.00	5.68	8.19	23	10.2	18.7	13.3	2.80	4.8
Owens-Illinois	28.13	17.63	31.63	16.00	4.21	4.47	10	6.1	8.5	6.1	1.40	5.5
Proct & Gambl	80.63	62.75	100.75	62.75	7.70	12.41	14	10.3	18.0	14.3	3.80	4.8
Sears, Roebuck	21.13	14.88	39.63	14.88	2.26	-20.70	8	8.3	14.5	10.6	1.36	7.3
Std Oil Cal	85.00	49.75	85.00	22.13	12.10	73.60	24	6.1	7.3	5.3	3.20	4.4
Texaco	41.63	24.75	41.63	21.13	7.58	109.39	23	4.6	8.4	6.7	2.40	6.6
Union Carbide	47.88	35.25	76.75	33.63	9.83	32.30	8	4.4	8.8	6.1	3.20	7.4
US Steel Corp	24.50	16.25	59.38	16.25	-3.77	-100.00	-35	NE	15.2	9.1	1.60	6.6
Unit Technols	52.75	36.25	52.75	15.63	6.06	15.65	17	8.0	10.0	6.5	2.20	4.5
Westinghouse	27.00	17.13	27.00	9.75	4.23	6.02	17	6.1	7.6	4.8	1.40	5.5
Woolworth FW	31.38	21.13	32.00	9.38	6.33	56.30	18	4.4	7.2	4.6	1.80	6.5

Source: The M/G Financial Weekly, Media General Financial Services, 301 E. Grace Street, Richmond, Va. 23261, August 4, 1980.

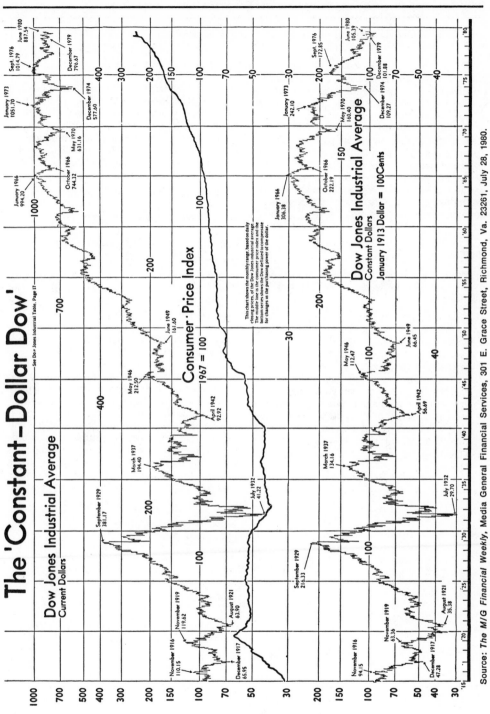

The 'Constant-Dollar Dow'

Dow Jones Industrial Average
Current Dollars

Consumer Price Index
1967 = 100

This chart shows the monthly range, based on daily closing prices, of the Dow Jones Industrial Average. The middle line is the consumer price index and the bottom series shows the Dow deflated to compensate for changes in the purchasing power of the dollar.

Dow Jones Industrial Average
Constant Dollars
January 1913 Dollar = 100 Cents

—See Dow Jones Industrial Table, Page 17

Source: *The M/G Financial Weekly*, Media General Financial Services, 301 E. Grace Street, Richmond, Va. 23261, July 28, 1980.

LISTING REQUIREMENTS FOR THE NEW YORK STOCK EXCHANGE

To be listed on the New York Stock Exchange, a company is expected to meet certain qualifications and to be willing to keep the investing public informed on the progress of its affairs. The company must be a going concern, or be the successor to a going concern. In determining eligibility for listing, particular attention is given to such qualifications as: 1) the degree of national interest in the company; 2) its relative position and stability in the industry; and 3) whether it is engaged in an expanding industry, with prospects of at least maintaining its relative position.

INITIAL LISTING

While each case is decided on its own merits, the Exchange generally requires the following as a minimum:

1. Demonstrated earning power under competitive conditions of $2.5 million before Federal income taxes for the most recent year and $2 million pretax for each of the preceding two years.
2. Net tangible assets of $16 million, but greater emphasis is placed on the aggregate market value of the common stock.
3. Market value of publicly held shares, subject to adjustment depending on market conditions, within the following limits:

Maximum $16,000,000
Minimum $ 8,000,000

Source: New York Stock Exchange *Fact Book* 1980.

Present (5/1/80) $16,000,000

(The market value requirement is subject to adjustment, based on the NYSE Index of Common Stock Prices. The base in effect as of May 1, 1980 is the Index on July 15, 1971 (55.06). The Index as of January 15 and July 15 of each year (if lower than the base) is divided by the base, and the resulting percentage is multiplied by $16 million to produce the adjusted market value standard. The adjustment formula is used only when the current Index is below the base.)

4. A total of 1,000,000 common shares publicly held.
5. 2,000 holders of 100 shares or more.

FOREIGN COMPANIES—ALTERNATE LISTING STANDARDS

To provide an alternate set of listing standards for companies organized outside the United States that meet the normal size and earnings yardsticks for NYSE listings, the Exchange will consider the acceptability of such companies' shares and shareholders on a worldwide basis.

In view of the widespread use of "bearer" shares in other countries, in contrast to the U.S. practice of registered shares, a company would find difficulty in certifying the requirement of 5,000 round-lot shareholders on a worldwide basis. Therefore, the Exchange will require that a member firm attest to the liquidity and depth of the market for the company's shares. These standards would apply only where a broad, liquid market for a company's shares in the company's home market exists.

STOCK MARKET AVERAGES BY INDUSTRY GROUP

These definitions apply to the following charts.

Price scale: The price ranges are always read from the scale at the right-hand side of each chart. This scale is equal to 15 times the earnings scale at the left, so when the price range bars and the earnings line coincide, it shows the price is at 15 times earnings. When the price is above the earnings line, the ratio of price to earnings is greater than 15 times earnings; when below, it is less.

Monthly price ranges represented by the solid vertical bars show the highest and lowest point of each month's transactions. Cross-bars indicate the month's closing price.

Monthly ratio-cator: The plottings for this line are obtained by dividing the closing price of the stock by the closing price of the Dow Jones Industrial Average on the same day. The resulting percentage is multiplied by a factor of 4.5 to bring the line closer to the price bars and is read from the right-hand scale. The plotting indicates whether the stock has kept pace, outperformed, or lagged behind the general market as represented by the DJIA.

Source: 3-Trend CYCLI-Graphs. The charts are courtesy of Securities Research Company, 208 Newbury Street, Boston, Mass. 02116, quarterly edition July 1980.

INDUSTRY GROUP AVERAGES*

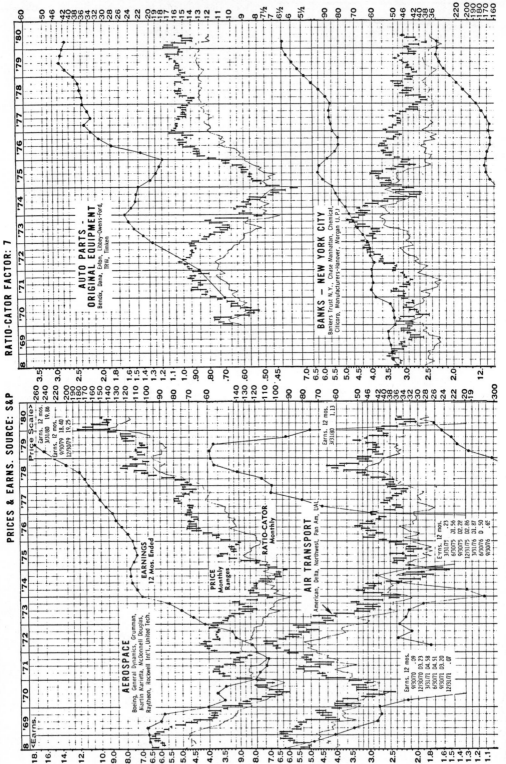

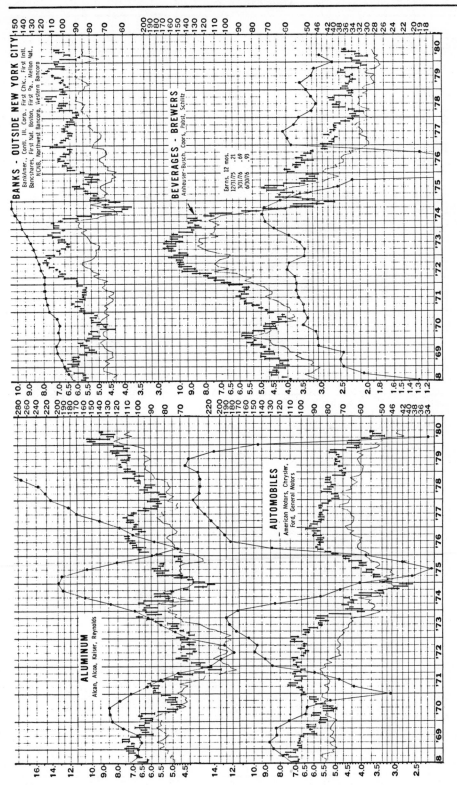

BANKS - OUTSIDE NEW YORK CITY
BankAmer., Contl. Ill. Corp., First Chic., First Intl.,
Bancshares, First Nat. Boston, First Pa., Mellon Nat.,
NCNB, Northwest Bancorp, Western Bancorp

BEVERAGES - BREWERS
Anheuser-Busch, Coors, Pabst, Schlitz

Earns. 12 mos.
12/31/75   .21
3/31/76   .69
6/30/76   .93

ALUMINUM
Alcan, Alcoa, Kaiser, Reynolds

AUTOMOBILES
American Motors, Chrysler,
Ford, General Motors

INDUSTRY GROUP AVERAGES (continued)

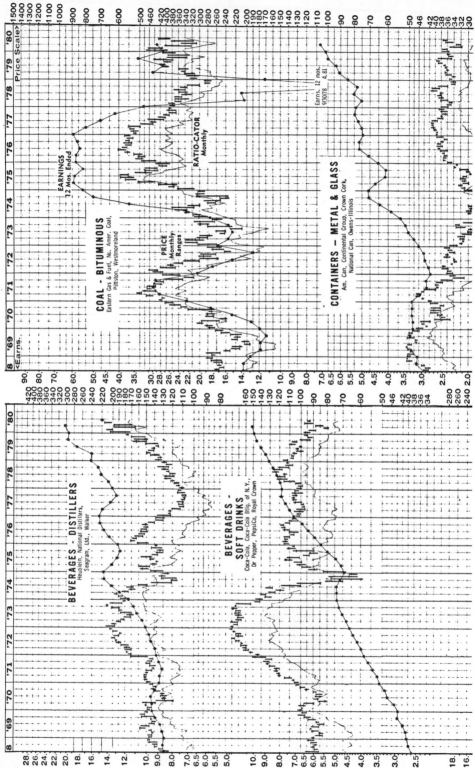

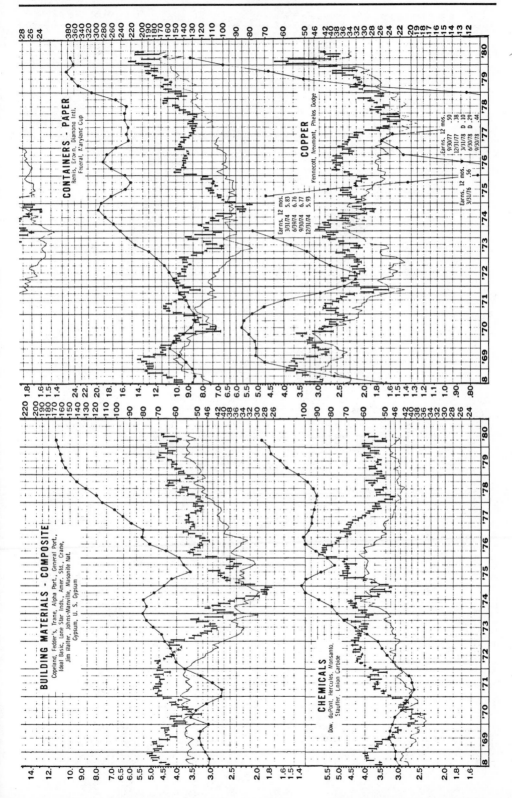

CONTAINERS - PAPER
Bemis, Brown, Diamond Intl.,
Federal, Maryland Cup

Earns, 12 mos.
3/31/74   5.83
6/30/74   6.76
9/30/74   6.77
12/31/74   5.93

COPPER
Kennecott, Newmont, Phelps Dodge

Earns, 12 mos.   .50
9/30/77   .38
12/31/77   D. .10
3/31/78   D. .29
6/30/78   .44
9/30/78

Earns, 12 mos.
3/31/76   .56

BUILDING MATERIALS - COMPOSITE
Copeland, Fedder's, Trane, Alpha Port., General Port.,
Ideal Basic, Lone Star Inds., Amer. Std., Crane,
Jim Walter, Johns-Manville, Masonite Nat.
Gypsum, U. S. Gypsum

CHEMICALS
Dow, duPont, Hercules, Monsanto,
Stauffer, Union Carbide

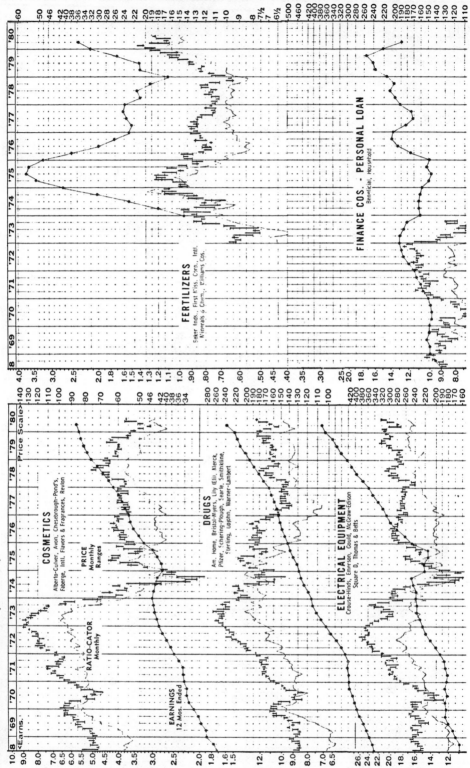

INDUSTRY GROUP AVERAGES *(continued)*

COSMETICS
Alberto-Culver, Avon, Chesebrough-Pond's, Faberge, Intl. Flavors & Fragrances, Revlon

PRICE
Monthly
Ranges

RATIO-CATOR
Monthly

EARNINGS
12 Mos. Ended

DRUGS
Am. Home, Bristol-Myers, Lily (Eli), Merck, Pfizer, Schering-Plough, Searle, Smithkline, Sterling, Upjohn, Warner-Lambert

ELECTRICAL EQUIPMENT
Crouse-Hinds, Emerson, Gould, McGraw-Edison, Square D, Thomas & Betts

FERTILIZERS
Beker Inds., First Miss. Corp., Intl. Minerals & Chem., Williams Cos.

FINANCE COS. - PERSONAL LOAN
Beneficial, Household

ELECTRONICS -
SEMICONDUCTORS/COMPONENTS
AMP, Intel, Motorola, Nat. Semiconductor,
Texas Instruments

FOODS—COMPOSITE
Beatrice Foods, Borden, CPC Int'l., Campbell Soup,
Carnation, Gen. Foods, Gen. Mills, Gerber Prod.,
Heinz (H. J.), Hershey Foods, Iowa Beef, Kellogg,
Kraft, Mayer (Oscar), Nabisco, Norton Simon,
Pillsbury, Quaker Oats, Ralston Purina, Standard
Brands, Stokely-Van Camp, Wrigley (Wm.)

FOREST PRODUCTS
Boise Cascade, Champion Int'l., Evans
Products, Georgia-Pacific, Louisiana-
Pacific, Potlatch Corp., Weyerhaeuser

ENTERTAINMENT
Columbia, Disney, MCA, MGM,
20th Century, Warner Comm.

INDUSTRY GROUP AVERAGES *(continued)*

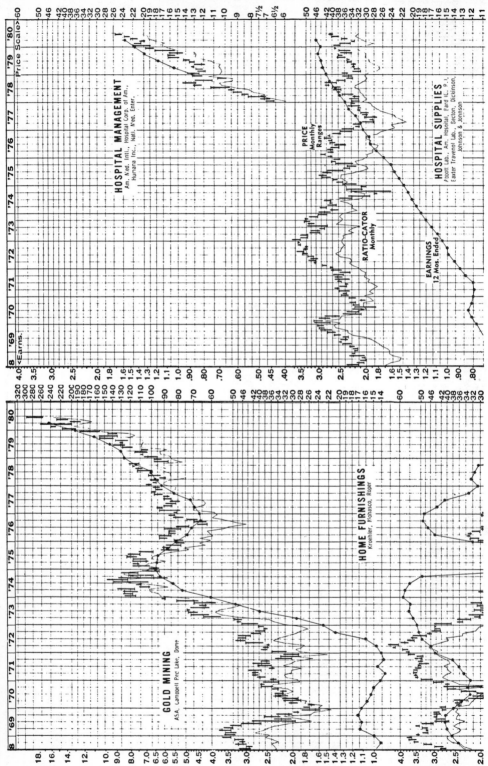

HOSPITAL MANAGEMENT
Am. Med. Intl., Hospital Corp. of Am.,
Humana Inc., Natl. Med. Enter.

HOSPITAL SUPPLIES
Abbott Lab., Am. Hospital, Bard (C. R.),
Baxter Travenol Lab., Becton, Dickinson,
Johnson & Johnson

HOME FURNISHINGS
Kroehler, Mohasco, Roper

GOLD MINING
ASA, Campbell Red Lake, Dome

PRICE
Monthly
Ranges

RATIO-CATOR
Monthly

EARNINGS
12 Mos. Ended

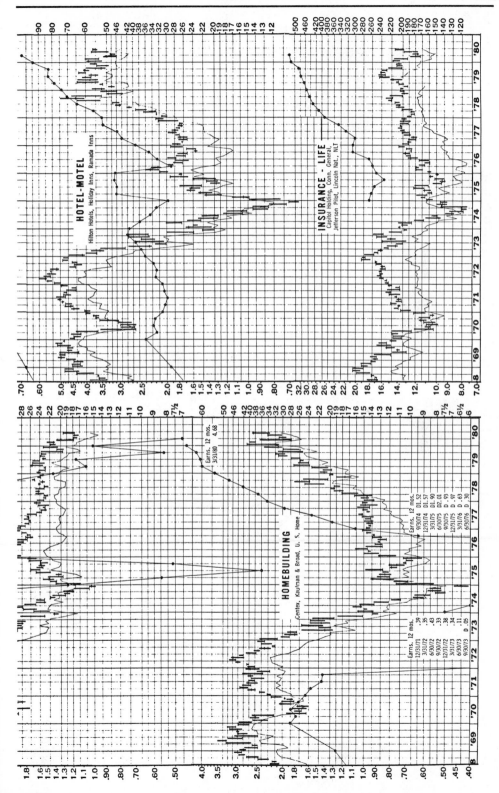

HOTEL - MOTEL
Hilton Hotels, Holiday Inns, Ramada Inns

INSURANCE - LIFE
Capitol Holding, Conn. General,
Jefferson Pilot, Lincoln Nat., NLT

HOMEBUILDING
Centex, Kaufman & Broad, U. S. Home

Earns. 12 mos.
3/31/80   4.68

Earns. 12 mos.
12/31/71   .39
3/31/72   .35
6/30/72   .43
9/30/72   .33
12/31/72   .38
3/31/73   .34
6/30/73   .11
9/30/73   D .05

Earns. 12 mos.
9/30/74   D1.52
12/31/74   D1.57
3/31/75   D1.90
6/30/75   D2.01
9/30/75   D .93
12/31/75   D .97
3/31/76   D .63
6/30/76   D .30

INDUSTRY GROUP AVERAGES *(continued)*

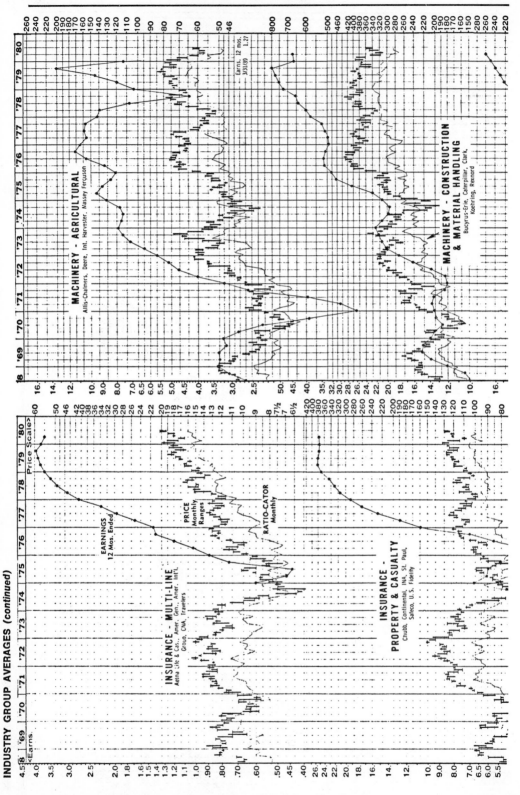

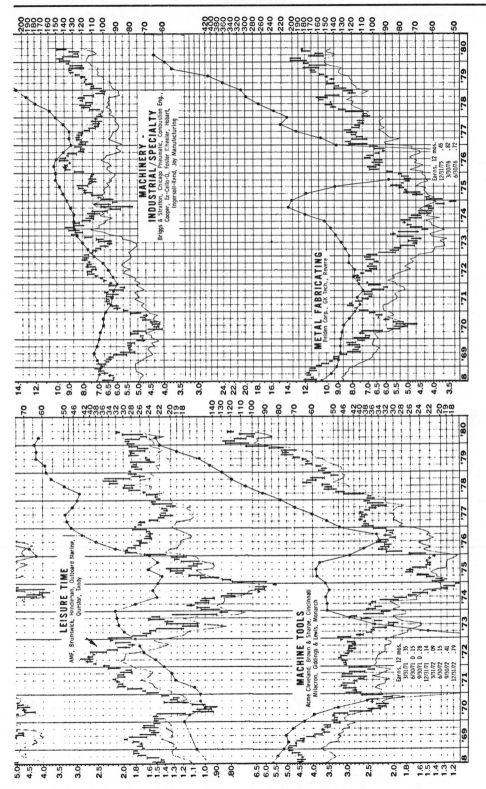

**MACHINERY -
INDUSTRIAL/SPECIALTY**
Briggs & Stratton, Chicago Pneumatic, Combustion Eng.,
Cooper, Ex-Cello-O, Foster Wheeler, Hobart,
Ingersoll-Rand, Joy Manufacturing

Earns. 12 mos.
12/31/75   .45
3/30/6   .82
6/30/6   .72

METAL FABRICATING
Belden Corp., GK Tech., Revere

LEISURE TIME
AMF, Brunswick, Handleman, Outboard Marine,
Questor, Tandy

MACHINE TOOLS
Acme Cleveland, Brown & Sharpe, Cincinnati
Milacron, Giddings & Lewis, Monarch

Earns. 12 mos.
3/31/71   .35
6/30/71 D .15
9/30/71 D .28
12/31/71   .14
3/31/72   .09
6/30/72   .15
9/30/72   .41
12/31/72   .79

INDUSTRY GROUP AVERAGES *(continued)*

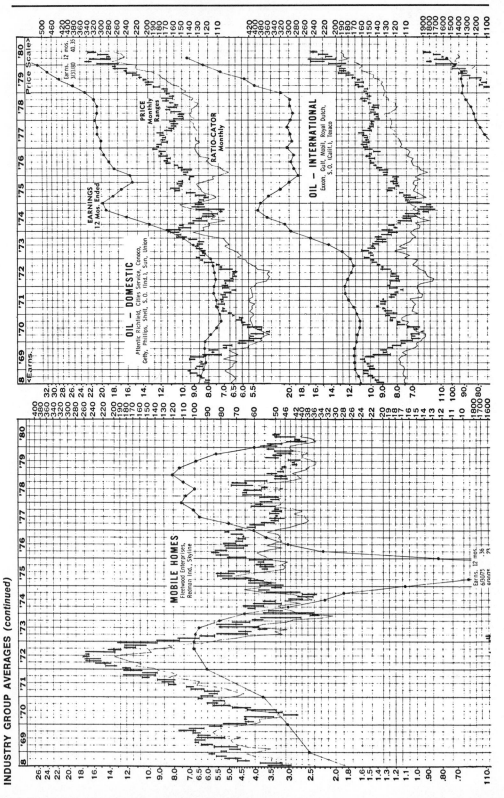

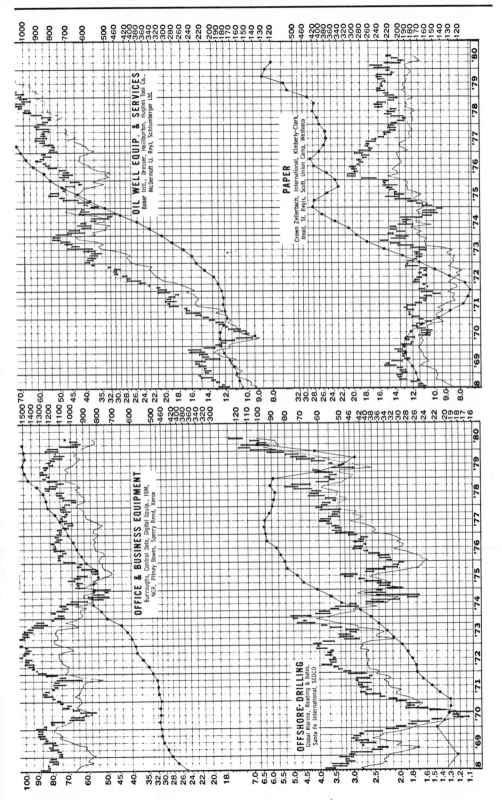

OIL WELL EQUIP. & SERVICES
Baker Intl., Dresser, Halliburton, Hughes Tool Co.,
McDermott (J. Ray), Schlumberger Ltd.

PAPER
Crown Zellerbach, International, Kimberly-Clark,
Mead, St. Regis, Scott, Union Camp, Westvaco

OFFICE & BUSINESS EQUIPMENT
Burroughs, Control Data, Digital Equip., IBM,
NCR, Pitney Bowes, Sperry Rand, Xerox

OFFSHORE-DRILLING
Global Marine, Reading & Bates,
Santa Fe International, SEDCO

INDUSTRY GROUP AVERAGES *(continued)*

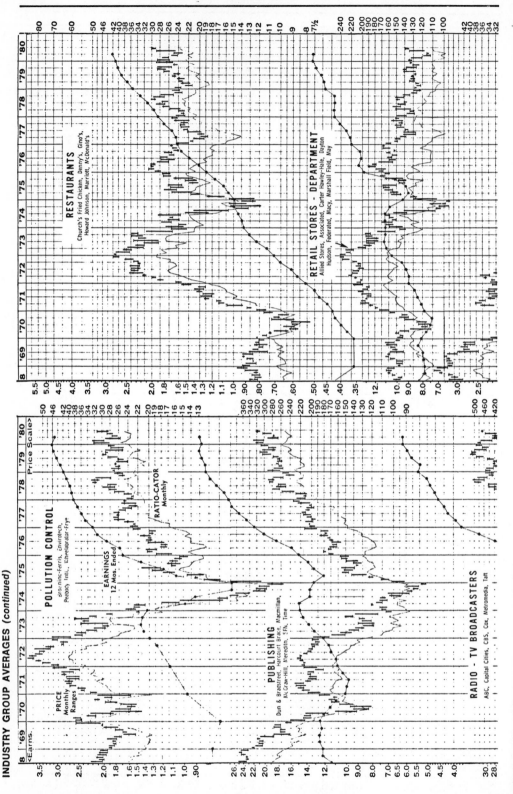

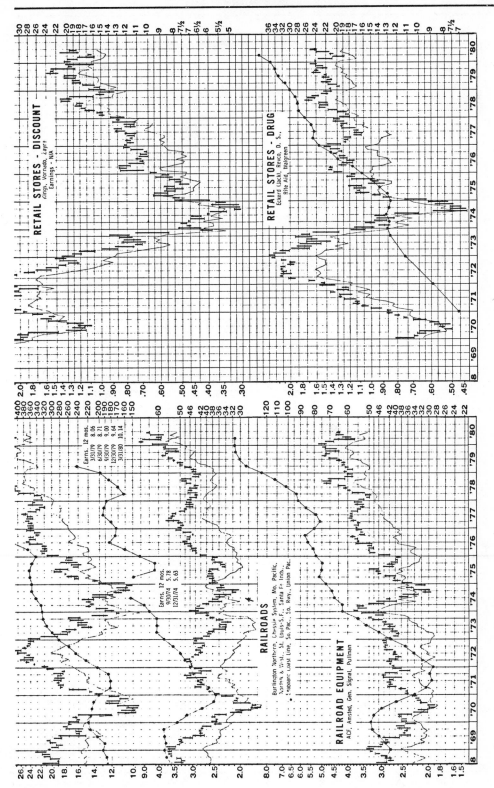

RETAIL STORES - DISCOUNT
Kings, Vornado, Zayr?
Earnings - N/A

RETAIL STORES - DRUG
Eckerd (Jack), Revco, D. S.,
Rite Aid, Walgreen

RAILROADS
Burlington Northern, Chessie System, Mo. Pacific,
Norfolk & West., St. Louis-S.F., Santa Fe Inds.,
Seaboard Coast Line, So. Pac., So. Rwy., Union Pac.

RAILROAD EQUIPMENT
ACF, Amsted, Gen. Signal, Pullman

Earns. 12 mos.
3/31/79   8.06
6/30/79   8.71
9/30/79   9.00
12/30/79   9.64
3/31/80   10.14

Earns. 12 mos.
9/30/74   5.78
12/31/74   5.63

INDUSTRY GROUP AVERAGES *(continued)*

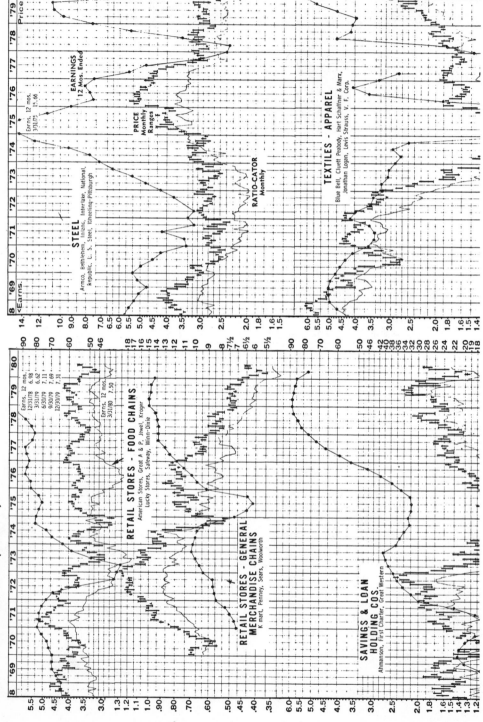

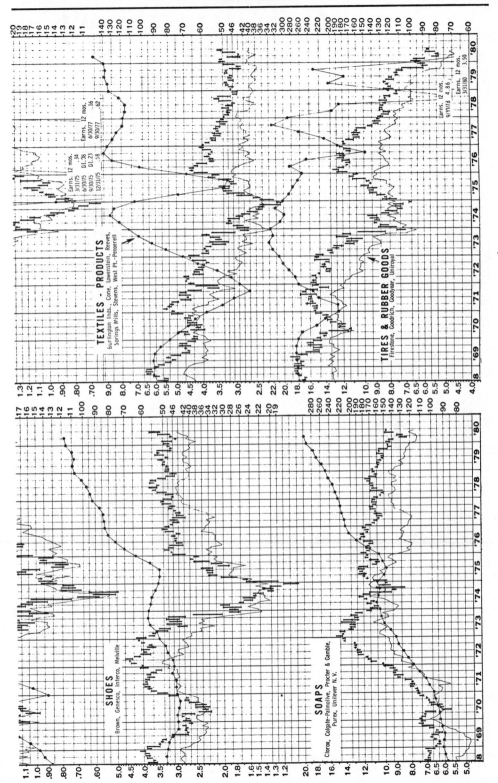

TEXTILES - PRODUCTS
Burlington Inds., Cone, Lowenstein, Reeves, Stevens, West Pt.-Pepperell Springs Mills, Stevens, West Pt.-Pepperell

Earns. 12 mos.
3/31/75   .34
6/30/75   D1.38
9/30/75   D1.23
12/31/75   .58

Earns. 12 mos.
6/30/77   .16
9/30/77   .62

TIRES & RUBBER GOODS
Firestone, Goodrich, Goodyear, Uniroyal

Earns. 12 mos.
9/11/78   4.86

Earns. 12 mos.
3/31/78   3.50
3/31/80   3.50

SHOES
Brown, Genesco, Interco, Melville

SOAPS
Clorox, Colgate-Palmolive, Procter & Gamble, Purex, Unilever N.V.

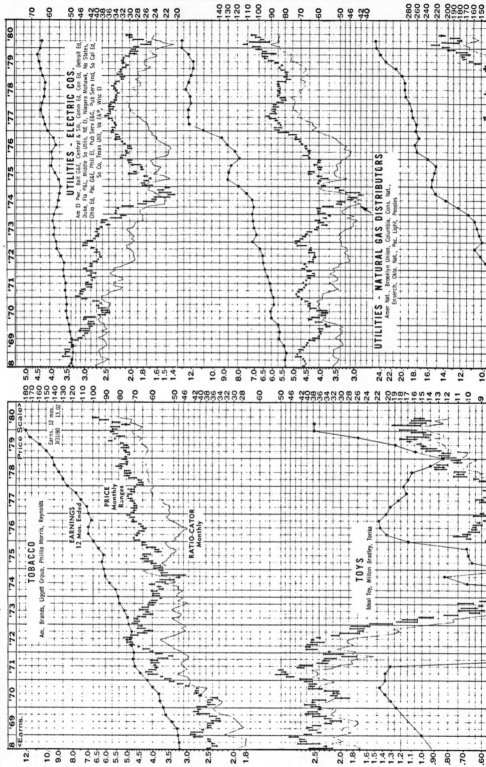

INDUSTRY GROUP AVERAGES (concluded)

UTILITIES - ELECTRIC COS.
Am El Pwr, Balt G&E, Central & Sw., Comm Ed, Con Ed, Detroit Ed,
Duke, Fla P&L, Middle So Utils, NE El, Niagara Mohawk, No States,
Ohio Ed, Pac G&E, Phil El, Pub Serv E&G, Pub Serv Ind, So Cal Ed,
So Co, Texas Util, Va E&P, Wisc El

UTILITIES - NATURAL GAS DISTRIBUTORS
Amer Nat., Brooklyn Union, Columbia, Cons. Nat.
Enserch, Okla. Nat., Pac. Light, Peoples

TOBACCO
Am. Brands, Liggett Group, Phillip Morris, Reynolds

EARNINGS
12 Mos. Ended

PRICE
Monthly
Ranges

RATIO-CATOR
Monthly

Price Scale

Earns. 12 mos.
3/31/80   13.02

TOYS
Ideal Toy, Milton Bradley, Tonka

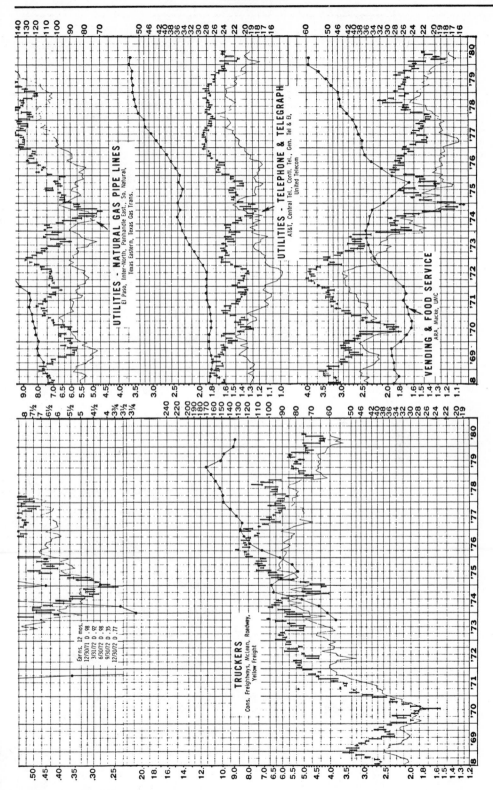

UTILITIES - NATURAL GAS PIPE LINES
El Paso, Inter-North, Panhandle East., So. Natural, Texas Eastern, Texas Gas Trans.

UTILITIES - TELEPHONE & TELEGRAPH
AT&T, Central Tel., Contl. Tel., Gen. Tel & El, United Telecom

VENDING & FOOD SERVICE
ARA, Macke, UMC

TRUCKERS
Cons. Freightways, McLean, Roadway, Yellow Freight

Earns. 12 mos.
12/30/71 D .98
3/31/72 D .92
6/30/72 D .98
9/30/72 D .35
12/30/72 D .77

Investment Returns on Stocks, Bonds, and Bills

Roger G. Ibbotson

Our look at history consists of examining the returns of five capital market sectors. We measure total returns (capital gains plus income) on common stocks, long-term corporate bonds, long-term government bonds, U.S. Trea- sury bills, and rates of inflation on consumer goods. Comparing the returns from the various sectors gives us insights into the returns avail- able from taking risk and the relationships between capital market returns and inflation.

EXHIBIT 1: WEALTH INDEXES OF INVESTMENTS IN THE U.S. CAPITAL MARKETS, 1926–1979

(assumed initial investment of $1.00 at year-end 1925, includes reinvestment income)

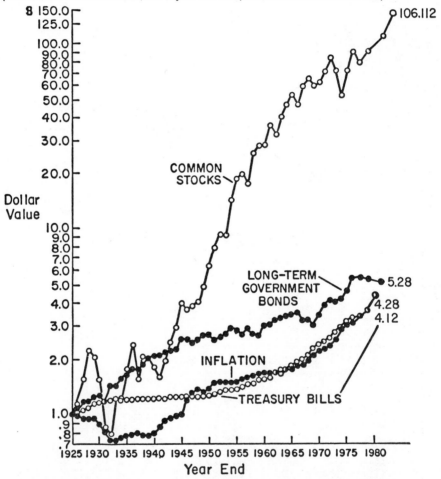

Source: Roger G. Ibbotson and Rex A. Sinquefield, *Stocks, Bonds, Bills, and Inflation: His- torical Returns (1926–1978),* Financial Analysts Research Foundation (Charlottesville, Va.: 1979 update).

THE RISKS AND REWARDS

We display graphically the rewards and risks available from the U.S. capital markets over the past 54 years. Exhibit 1 shows the growth of an investment in common stocks, long-term government bonds, and Treasury Bills as well as the increase in the inflation index over the 54-year period. Each of the series is initiated at $1 at year-end 1925. The vertical scale is logarithmic so that equal distances represent equal percentage changes anywhere along the axis. The graph vividly portrays that common stocks were the big winner over the entire period. If $1 were invested in stocks at year-end 1925 and all dividends reinvested, the dollar investment would have grown to $106.11 by year-end 1979. This phenomenal growth was not without substantial risk, especially during the earlier portion of the period. In contrast, long-term government bonds (with a constant 20-year maturity) exhibited much less risk, but grew to only $5.28.

A virtually riskless strategy (for those with short-term time horizons) has been to buy U.S. Treasury Bills. However, Treasury Bills have had a marked tendency to track inflation, with the result that their real (inflation adjusted) return is near zero for the entire 1926–1979 period. Note that the tracking is only prevalent over the latter portion of the period. During periods of deflation (such as the late 1920s and early 1930s) the Treasury bill returns were near zero, but not negative, since no one intentionally buys securities with negative yields. Beginning in the early 1940s, the yields (returns) on Treasury bills were pegged by the

government at low rates while high inflation was experienced. The government pegging ended with the U.S. Treasury-Federal Reserve Accord in March 1951.

We summarize the investment returns in Exhibit 2 by presenting the average annual returns over the 1926–1979 period. Common stocks returned a compounded (geometric mean) total return of 9.0 percent per year. The annual compound return from capital appreciation alone was 4.0 percent. After adjusting for inflation, annual compounded total returns were 6.1 percent per year.*

The average total return over any single year (arithmetic mean) for stocks was 11.3 percent, with positive returns recorded in nearly two-thirds of the years (36 out of 54 years). The risk or degree of return fluctuation is measured by standard deviation as 22.0 percent. The frequency distribution (histogram) counts the number of years the returns fell in each 5 percent return increment. Note the wide variations in common stock returns relative to the other capital market sectors. Annual stock

---

* Editor's note: Over the current decade the compounded growth rate for common stock with dividends reinvested has been considerably less than the long-term value of 9.0 percent. Thus from the beginning of 1970 to the end of 1979, the compounded growth rate has been 5.9 percent for common stock as compared to 6.2 percent for long-term corporate bonds and 6.3 percent for Treasury bills. All figures neglect taxes. The inflation rate during this period was 7.4 percent. After inflationary adjustments and income taxes, it is evident that all of these investments resulted in a net loss in terms of real income. Assuming a 40 percent tax rate and a 6 percent inflation rate, investments must earn 10 percent before taxes to break even.

EXHIBIT 2: BASIC SERIES, INVESTMENT TOTAL ANNUAL RETURNS, 1926–1979

Series	Geometric Mean	Arithmetic Mean	Standard Deviation	Distribution
Common Stocks	9.0%	11.3%	22.0%	
Long-Term Corporate Bonds	3.8%	3.9%	5.6%	
Long-Term Government Bonds	3.1%	3.3%	5.7%	
U.S. Treasury Bills	2.7%	2.7%	2.4%	
Inflation	2.7%	2.8%	5.0%	

-50%   0%   +50%

Source: Ibbotson and Sinquefield, *Stocks, Bonds, Bills, and Inflation.*

returns ranged from 54.0 percent in 1933 to —43.3 percent in 1931.

A simple example illustrates the difference between geometric and arithmetic means. Suppose $1 were invested in a common stock portfolio that experiences successive annual returns of +50 percent and —50 percent. At the end of the first year, the portfolio is worth $1.50. At the end of the second year, the portfolio is worth $0.75. The annual arithmetic mean is 0 percent, whereas the annual geometric mean (compounded return) is —13.4 percent. Naturally, it is the geometric mean that more directly measures the change in wealth over more than one period. On the other hand, the arithmetic mean is a better representation of typical performance over any single annual period.

The other capital market sectors also had returns commensurate with their risks. Long-term corporate bonds outperformed the default-free, long-term government bonds, which in turn outperformed the essentially riskless U.S. Treasury bills. Over the entire period the riskless U.S. Treasury bills had a return almost identical with the inflation rate. Thus, we again note that the real rate of interest (the inflation-adjusted riskless rate) has been on average very near 0 percent historically.

MEASUREMENT OF THE FIVE SERIES

The returns were computed by compounding monthly returns, with no adjustments made for transactions costs or taxes. We describe each of the five total return series which are listed annually in Exhibit 3.

COMMON STOCKS

The total return index is based upon Standard & Poor's (S&P) Composite Index with dividends reinvested monthly. To the extent that the 500 stocks currently included in the S&P Composite Index (prior to March 1957, there were 90 stocks) are representative of all stocks in the United States, the market value weighting scheme allows the returns of the index to correspond to the aggregate stock market returns in the U.S. economy.

LONG-TERM CORPORATE BONDS

We measure the total returns of a corporate bond index with approximately 20 years to maturity. We use Salomon Brothers' High-Grade Long-Term Corporate Bond Index from its beginning in 1969 through 1979. For the period 1946–68 we backdate Salomon Brothers' index using Salomon Brothers' monthly yield data and similar methodology. For the period 1926–45 we compute returns using Standard & Poor's monthly high-grade corporate composite bond yield data, assuming a 4 percent coupon and a 20-year maturity.

LONG-TERM GOVERNMENT BONDS

To measure the total returns of long-term U.S. government bonds, we use the bond data obtained from the U.S. Government Bond File (constructed by Lawrence Fisher) at the Center for Research in Security Prices (CRSP) at the University of Chicago. We attempt to maintain a 20-year bond portfolio whose returns do not reflect the potential tax benefits, impaired negotiability, or the special redemption or call privileges frequently characterizing government bond prices and yields.

U.S. TREASURY BILLS

For the U.S. Treasury bill index, we again use the data in the CRSP U.S. Government Bond File. We measure one-month holding period returns for the shortest-term bills not less than one month in maturity. Since U.S. Treasury bills were not initiated until 1929, we use short-term coupon bonds whenever bill quotes are unavailable.

CONSUMER PRICE INDEX

We utilize the Consumer Price Index (CPI) to measure inflation. The CPI is constructed by the U.S. Department of Labor, Bureau of Labor Statistics, Washington, D.C.

EXHIBIT 3: BASIC SERIES, INDEXES OF YEAR-END CUMULATIVE WEALTH, 1925–1979

| Year | Common Stocks | | Long-Term Government Bonds | | Long-Term Corporate Bonds | U.S. Treasury Bills | Consumer Price Index |
	Total Returns	Capital Appreciation Only	Total Returns	Capital Appreciation Only	Total Returns	Total Returns	Rates of Inflation
1925	1.000	1.000	1.000	1.000	1.000	1.000	1.000
1926	1.116	1.057	1.073	1.039	1.074	1.033	0.985
1927	1.535	1.384	1.174	1.095	1.154	1.065	0.965
1928	2.204	1.908	1.175	1.061	1.186	1.099	0.955
1929	2.018	1.681	1.215	1.059	1.225	1.152	0.957
1930	1.516	1.202	1.272	1.072	1.323	1.179	0.899
1931	0.859	0.636	1.204	0.981	1.299	1.192	0.814
1932	0.789	0.540	1.407	1.108	1.439	1.204	0.730
1933	1.214	0.792	1.406	1.073	1.588	1.207	0.734
1934	1.197	0.745	1.547	1.146	1.808	1.209	0.749
1935	1.767	1.053	1.624	1.170	1.982	1.211	0.771
1936	2.367	1.346	1.746	1.225	2.116	1.213	0.780
1937	1.538	0.827	1.750	1.194	2.174	1.217	0.804
1938	2.016	1.035	1.847	1.228	2.307	1.217	0.782
1939	2.008	0.979	1.957	1.271	2.399	1.217	0.778
1940	1.812	0.829	2.076	1.319	2.480	1.217	0.786
1941	1.602	0.681	2.095	1.305	2.548	1.218	0.862
1942	1.927	0.766	2.162	1.315	2.614	1.221	0.942
1943	2.427	0.915	2.207	1.310	2.688	1.225	0.972
1944	2.906	1.041	2.270	1.314	2.815	1.229	0.993
1945	3.965	1.361	2.513	1.423	2.930	1.233	1.015
1946	3.645	1.199	2.511	1.392	2.980	1.238	1.199
1947	3.853	1.199	2.445	1.327	2.911	1.244	1.307
1948	4.065	1.191	2.528	1.340	3.031	1.254	1.343
1949	4.829	1.313	2.691	1.395	3.132	1.268	1.318
1950	6.360	1.600	2.692	1.366	3.198	1.283	1.395
1951	7.888	1.863	2.586	1.281	3.112	1.302	1.477
1952	9.336	2.082	2.616	1.262	3.221	1.324	1.490
1953	9.244	1.944	2.711	1.270	3.331	1.348	1.499
1954	14.108	2.820	2.906	1.325	3.511	1.360	1.492
1955	18.561	3.564	2.868	1.271	3.527	1.381	1.497
1956	19.778	3.658	2.708	1.164	3.287	1.415	1.540
1957	17.648	3.134	2.910	1.208	3.573	1.459	1.587
1958	25.298	4.327	2.733	1.097	3.494	1.482	1.615
1959	28.322	4.694	2.671	1.029	3.460	1.526	1.639
1960	28.455	4.554	3.039	1.124	3.774	1.566	1.663
1961	36.106	5.607	3.068	1.092	3.956	1.600	1.674
1962	32.955	4.945	3.280	1.122	4.270	1.643	1.695
1963	40.469	5.879	3.319	1.092	4.364	1.695	1.723
1964	47.139	6.642	3.436	1.084	4.572	1.754	1.743
1965	53.008	7.244	3.460	1.047	4.552	1.823	1.777
1966	47.674	6.295	3.586	1.036	4.560	1.910	1.836
1967	59.104	7.560	3.257	0.895	4.335	1.991	1.892
1968	65.642	8.139	3.248	0.846	4.446	2.094	1.981
1969	60.059	7.210	3.083	0.754	4.086	2.232	2.102
1970	62.465	7.222	3.457	0.791	4.837	2.378	2.218
1971	71.406	8.001	3.914	0.843	5.370	2.482	2.292
1972	84.955	9.252	4.136	0.840	5.760	2.577	2.371
1973	72.500	7.645	4.090	0.775	5.825	2.756	2.579
1974	53.300	5.373	4.268	0.748	5.647	2.976	2.894
1975	73.130	7.068	4.661	0.754	6.474	3.149	3.097
1976	90.566	8.422	5.441	0.815	7.681	3.309	2.246
1977	84.076	7.453	5.405	0.751	7.813	3.479	3.466
1978	89.592	7.532	5.342	0.683	7.808	3.729	3.779
1979	106.112	8.459	5.277	0.615	7.481	4.115	4.281

Source: Ibbotson and Sinquefield, *Stocks, Bonds, Bills, and Inflation.*

VICKERS FAVORITE 50

| Rank By $ Value | | | | Stocks | $ Value (Mil.) | No. Funds Holding | No. of Shares Held | Net Chng. in Holdings | Net Chng. by Insiders | Percent of Outst. Stk. Held by Funds |
Mar. 31 1975	Mar. 31 1979	Dec. 31 1979	Mar. 31 1980							
1	1	1	1	International Business machines	994.30	268	17,834,991	−311,004	−1,380	3.1
2	3	3	2	Exxon Corp.	598.95	172	10,349,038	+854,303	−67	2.4
19	4	2	3	Schlumberger Ltd.	597.54	127	5,623,913	−243,928	+21,475	4.4
—	18	14	4	Alcan Aluminum Ltd.	492.77	98	9,568,276	−1,192,000	−1,000	23.7
14	6	7	5	Atlantic Richfield	407.73	139	9,579,468	+88,040	+3,376	4.2
—	11	10	6	Boeing Co.	363.41	81	6,824,636	−2,138,050	−18,117	7.1
37	21	16	7	Mobil Corp.	354.84	140	5,396,852	+1,033,500	+11,104	2.5
5	5	6	8	Philip Morris	348.49	94	10,137,864	−748,342	−43,600	8.1
7	7	5	9	Xerox Corp.	331.54	140	6,000,761	−348,177	+818	7.1
3	2	4	10	American Tel. & Tel.	322.15	139	6,625,203	−1,190,558	+1,210	0.9
38	16	9	11	Halliburton Co.	322.02	96	3,543,580	−98,950	−20	6.0
25	17	11	12	Digital Equipment	281.97	100	4,575,592	+321,924	−14,136	10.1
—	25	18	13	Union Oil Company of California	271.75	71	5,394,638	+404,741	+1,644	6.2
27	28	17	14	Standard Oil Company (Indiana)	247.84	88	4,907,730	−935,230	+6,930	1.6
—	14	8	15	Phillips Petroleum	244.12	79	5,954,203	−1,251,200	−0−	3.9
12	27	24	16	Texaco Inc.	237.85	122	7,153,272	+354,315	−24,014	2.6
18	12	13	17	General Electric	236.82	109	4,920,921	−118,744	−770	2.2
—	—	—	18	Murphy Oil Corp.*	231.11	34	2,743,200	−885,000	−8	22.1
11	10	15	19	General Motors Corp.	225.45	97	4,887,909	+40,347	+23,134	1.7
—	40	22	20	Gulf Oil Corp.	223.65	88	5,734,518	−203,400	−3,267	2.9
—	15	12	21	Smithkline Corp.	211.13	68	4,129,668	−288,561	+3,990	6.8
31	33	19	22	Conoco Inc.	202.94	68	4,547,774	−39,025	−15,176	4.2
—	29	21	23	Standard Oil Company of Ohio	197.86	91	4,548,548	−192,388	+10,019	1.9
39	20	35	24	Minnesota Mining & Manufacturing	191.41	88	3,847,378	+637,630	−2,500	3.3
—	30	30	25	Dome Petroleum Ltd.	188.89	53	3,580,800	−69,000	−16,500	7.3

				Company	Price		Shares	Change	%
36	34	32	26	Standard Oil Company of California	185.58	79	2,833,275	+374	1.7
16	24	25	27	Merck & Co.	179.07	91	2,652,903	−1,845	3.5
—	8	20	28	NCR Corp.	171.17	67	2,932,170	+11,126	11.2
4	—	33	29	Eastman Kodak	168.64	120	3,550,307	+723	2.2
44	9	23	30	E. I. DuPont DeNemours	166.66	65	4,813,167	+11,781	3.3
—	42	36	31	Hewlett Packard	162.02	57	2,576,816	−1,382	4.4
—	48	40	32	Aetna Life & Casualty Company	158.62	54	4,862,043	−10,400	6.0
—	—	—	33	MCA Inc.†	157.34	33	3,321,155	−36,751	14.2
—	—	46	34	Marathon Oil Co.	155.93	61	2,835,180	+3,460	4.7
31	—	26	35	Tenneco Inc.	154.22	79	4,486,476	+439	4.3
45	45	28	36	Pfizer Inc.	154.16	78	4,083,697	−2,100	5.6
8	—	38	37	Union Carbide Corp.	152.85	83	3,996,182	+785	6.0
—	—	—	38	Raytheon Co.†	150.45	71	2,104,229	−2,212	5.1
—	—	—	39	Allied Chemical Corp.†	149.58	57	3,361,316	+9,600	10.2
39	—	39	40	Superior Oil Co.	144.26	51	1,039,685	−0—	4.1
—	—	34	41	General Dynamics Corp.	143.79	43	2,142,100	−49,581	8.1
50	—	37	42	INA Corp.	142.97	40	4,846,345	+313	12.7
38	10	43	43	McDonald's Corporation	139.98	57	3,372,960	−83,900	8.4
32	—	47	44	Travelers Corp.	139.21	48	3,639,401	−29,959	8.6
—	—	49	45	Warner Communications Inc.	138.38	35	3,559,611	+279,875	9.9
—	46	—	46	Sperry Corp.†	134.49	59	2,907,939	+611,197	8.0
—	13	—	47	Schering Plough Corp.†	133.98	65	3,841,850	+992,760	7.2
23	—	42	48	Northwest Airlines Inc.	133.14	43	5,379,561	−48,200	24.9
—	—	—	49	Internorth Inc.*	131.17	21	2,417,880	−439,800	10.9
—	29	—	50	Honeywell Inc.	130.92	51	1,796,454	−345,700	8.1

Displaced Stocks: Abbott Laboratories, American Broadcasting Cos., Bristol Myers, Burroughs Corp., Ford Motor Co., Gulf Canada Ltd., Kaiser Aluminum & Chemical.

*Newcomer.

†Returnee.

Source: Vickers Guide to Investment Company Portfolios. Copyright © 1980 by Vickers Associates Inc. Reproduction hereof permitted only on written permission from Vickers Associates, Inc., Huntington, N.Y., the Copyright owner.

SUMMARY OF FAVORITE 50 BY INDUSTRY

DOLLAR VALUE OF STOCKS BY INDUSTRY TO TOTAL VALUE OF FAVORITE 50

Industry	3/31/80	12/31/79	3/31/79	3/31/75
Oil & Natural Gas	41.0%	37.8%	28.2%	19.8%
Office Equipment	15.8	18.5	22.8	20.7
Chemicals & Drugs	9.5	10.6	9.0	22.9
Electric & Electronics	5.6	4.9	3.2	3.2
Leisure	5.0	5.1	5.5	7.2
Aerospace	4.2	3.8	4.2	—
Metals & Mining	4.1	3.2	2.7	1.4
Miscellaneous	14.8	16.1	24.4	24.8
	100.0%	100.0%	100.0%	100.0%

FOREIGN SECURITIES LISTED ON THE NEW YORK STOCK EXCHANGE

Alcan Aluminum Limited
Aluminum (Canada)
ASA Limited
Investment company (Africa)
Bell Canada
Telecommunication services (Canada)
Benquet Consolidated, Inc.
Mining (Philippines)
British Petroleum Company Ltd.
Holding company-petroleum (Gt. Britain)
Campbell Red Lakes Mines, Ltd.
Mining (Canada)
Canadian Pacific Limited
Natural resources; transportation (Canada)
Carling O'Keefe Limited
Breweries (Canada)
Deltec International Limited
Foods, commodities (Gt. Britain)
Dome Mines, Limited
Mining (Canada)
EMI Limited
Electronics, records, entertainment
(Gt. Britain)
Genstar Limited
Building (Canada)
Honda Motor Co., Ltd.
Motorcycles; automobiles (Japan)
Hudson Bay Mining & Smelting Co.
Mining (Canada)
Intercontinental Diversified Corp.
Homesites, casinos (Panama)
Inco Ltd.
Mining (Canada)
KLM Royal Dutch Airlines
Airline (Netherlands)

Kubota, Ltd.
Agricultural machinery; pipe (Japan)
MacMillan Bloedel Ltd.
Forest products (Canada)
Massey-Ferguson Ltd.
Agricul. mach., diesel eng. (Canada)
Matsushita Electric Industrial Co., Ltd.
Electronic products (Japan)
McIntyre Mines Ltd.
Mining (Canada)
Norlin Corporation
Holding company-various (Panama)
Northern Telecom Ltd.
Telecommunication equipment (Canada)
Northgate Exploration Limited
Mining (Canada)
Pioneer Electronic Corporation
High fidelity stereo; audio (Japan)
Plessey Company Ltd.
Electronic equipment, systems (Gt. Britain)
Royal Dutch Petroleum Co.
Petroleum (Netherlands)
Schlumberger, N.V.
Petroleum (Netherlands Antilles)
Seagram Co. Ltd.
Distilleries (Canada)
"Shell" Transport and Trading Co., Ltd.
Petroleum (Gt. Britain)
Sony Corporation
Radios, recorders, televisions (Japan)
Unilever Limited
Foods, commodities (Gt. Britain)
Unilever, N.V.
Foods, commodities (Netherlands Antilles)
Walker (Hiram)-Gooderham & Worts, Ltd.
Distilleries (Canada)
Westcoast Transmission Co., Ltd.
Natural gas distributor (Canada)

MARGIN REQUIREMENTS

PERCENT OF MARKET VALUE AND EFFECTIVE DATES

Type of Security on Sale	Mar. 11, 1968	June 8, 1968	May 6, 1970	Dec. 6, 1971	Nov. 24, 1972	Jan. 3, 1974
Margin stocks............................	70	80	65	55	65	50
Convertible bonds......................	50	60	50	50	50	50
Short sales............................	70	80	65	55	65	50

Note: Regulations G, T, and U of the Federal Reserve Board of Governors, prescribed in accordance with the Securities Exchange Act of 1934, limit the amount of credit to purchase and carry margin stocks that may be extended on securities as collateral by prescribing a maximum loan value, which is a specified percentage of the market value of the collateral at the time the credit is extended. Margin requirements are the difference between the market value (100 percent) and the maximum loan value. The term "margin stocks" is defined in the corresponding regulation. Regulation G and special margin requirements for bonds convertible into stocks were adopted by the Board of Governors effective March 11, 1968.

Source: *Federal Reserve Bulletin.*

CASH DIVIDENDS AND YIELDS

	Common Stocks				Preferred Stocks			
Cal- endar Year	Number of Issues Listed at Year End	Number Paying Cash Dividends during Year	Estimated Aggregate Cash Payments (millions)	Median Yield*	Number of Issues Listed at Year End	Number Paying Cash Dividends during Year	Estimated Aggregate Cash Payments (millions)	Median Yield*
1929	842	554	$ 2,711	n.a.	n.a.	n.a.	n.a.	n.a.
1930	848	576	2,667					
1935	776	387	1,336					
1940	829	577	2,099	6.1%				
1945	881	746	2,275	3.6	388	341	$337	4.2%
1950	1,039	930	5,404	6.7	433	405	379	4.3
1951	1,054	961	5,467	6.5	441	406	380	4.6
1952	1,067	975	5,595	6.0	455	433	378	4.4
1953	1,069	964	5,874	6.3	461	443	383	4.7
1954	1,076	968	6,439	4.7	456	436	368	4.2
1955	1,076	982	7,488	4.6	432	412	336	4.2
1956	1,077	975	8,341	5.2	425	411	333	4.9
1957	1,098	991	8,807	6.1	424	409	335	4.9
1958	1,086	961	8,711	4.1	421	406	331	4.9
1959	1,092	953	9,337	3.8	415	403	337	5.1
1960	1,126	981	9,872	4.2	402	391	331	5.0
1961	1,145	981	10,430	3.3	396	381	341	4.8
1962	1,168	994	11,203	3.8	391	369	336	4.6
1963	1,194	1,032	12,096	3.6	378	359	342	4.6
1964	1,227	1,066	13,555	3.3	379	364	352	4.5
1965	1,254	1,111	15,302	3.2	373	358	388	4.7
1966	1,267	1,127	16,151	4.1	398	385	431	5.4
1967	1,255	1,116	16,866	3.2	445	432	596	5.8
1968	1,253	1,104	18,124	2.6	514	500	894	5.2
1969	1,290	1,121	19,404	3.6	499	487	1,142	6.8
1970	1,330	1,120	19,781	3.7	510	498	1,233	6.9
1971	1,399	1,132	20,256	3.2	528	499	1,360	6.7
1972	1,478	1,195	21,490	3.0	525	496	1,375	6.7
1973	1,536	1,276	23,627	5.0	522	497	1,487	8.0
1974	1,543	1,308	25,662	7.4	537	520	1,616	10.2
1975	1,531	1,273	26,901	5.0	580	552	1,682	9.3
1976	1,550	1,304	30,608	4.0	608	592	1,802	8.0
1977	1,549	1,360	36,270	4.5	628	619	1,954	8.4
1978	1,552	1,373	41,151	4.8	642	626	1,974	9.4
1979	1,536	1,359	46,937	5.0	656	644	2,225	10.9

*Based on cash payments during the year and price at end of year for dividend-paying stocks only.
n.a. Not available.
Source: New York Stock Exchange *Fact Book*, 1980.

SHARES SOLD ON REGISTERED EXCHANGES

Year	Number of Shares (mils.)			Percent of Total		
	NYSE	ASE	Other	NYSE	ASE	Other
1935	513.6	84.7	63.6	77.6%	12.8%	9.6%
1940	282.7	47.9	41.4	76.0	12.9	11.1
1945	496.0	152.4	96.1	66.6	20.5	12.9
1950	655.3	114.9	86.9	76.5	13.4	10.1
1955	820.5	243.9	148.0	67.7	20.1	12.2
1960	958.3	300.6	129.6	69.0	21.6	9.3
1961	1,292.3	525.3	192.9	64.3	26.1	9.6
1962	1,186.5	332.6	144.4	71.3	20.0	8.7
1963	1,350.9	336.3	151.4	73.5	18.3	8.2
1964	1,482.3	397.0	165.6	72.5	19.4	8.1
1965	1,809.4	582.2	195.3	69.9	22.5	7.5
1966	2,204.8	730.9	252.2	69.2	22.9	7.9
1967	2,885.8	1,290.2	327.8	64.1	28.6	7.3
1968	3,298.7	1,570.7	442.6	62.1	29.6	8.3
1969	3,173.6	1,341.0	448.8	63.9	27.0	9.0
1970	3,213.1	878.5	444.1	70.8	19.4	9.8
1971	4,265.3	1,049.3	601.1	72.1	17.7	10.2
1972	4,496.2	1,103.2	669.8	71.4	17.5	11.1
1973	4.336.6	740.4	653.2	75.7	12.9	11.4
1974	3,821.9	475.3	541.9	79.0	9.8	11.2
1975	5,056.5	540.9	637.6	81.1	8.7	10.2
1976	5,649.2	637.0	749.5	80.3	9.1	10.7
1977	5,613.3	651.9	758.2	79.9	9.3	10.8
1978	7,618.0	992.2	872.6	80.3	10.5	9.2
1979	8,675.3	1,161.3	1,026.2	79.9	10.7	9.4

Year	Market Value of Shares (mils.)			Percent of Total		
1935	$ 13,335	$ 1,205	$ 736	87.3%	7.9%	4.8%
1940	7,166	643	595	85.3	7.7	7.0
1945	13,462	1,728	1,036	83.0	10.6	6.4
1950	18,725	1,481	1,571	86.0	6.8	7.2
1955	32,745	2,593	2,530	86.5	6.8	6.7
1960	37,960	4,176	3,083	83.9	9.2	6.8
1961	52,699	6,752	4,352	82.6	10.6	6.8
1962	47,341	3,648	3,743	86.5	6.7	6.8
1963	54,887	4,755	4,678	85.3	7.4	7.3
1964	60,424	5,923	5,802	83.7	8.2	8.0
1965	73,200	8,612	7,402	82.0	9.7	8.3
1966	98,565	14,130	10,339	80.1	11.5	8.4
1967	125,329	23,111	13,318	77.5	14.3	8.2
1968	144,978	34,775	16,605	73.8	17.7	8.5
1969	129,603	30,074	15,621	73.9	17.2	8.9
1970	103,063	14,266	13,579	78.7	10.9	10.4
1971	147,098	17,664	20,169	79.5	9.6	10.9
1972	159,700	20,453	23,873	78.3	10.0	11.7
1973	146,451	10,430	21,156	82.3	5.9	11.9
1974	99,178	5,048	14,023	83.9	4.3	11.9
1975	133,819	5,678	17,595	85.2	3.6	11.2
1976	164,545	7,468	22,956	84.4	3.8	11.8
1977	157,250	8,532	21,421	84.0	4.6	11.4
1978	210,426	15,204	23,625	84.4	6.1	9.5
1979	251,098	20,596	28,279	83.7	6.9	9.4

Source: Securities & Exchange Commission in the New York Stock Exchange *Fact Book*, 1980.

MUTUAL FUNDS: TEN-YEAR SELECTED PERFORMANCE

Quarter Ended June 30	1980 Net Asset Value per share	1980 12 mos. Divs from Income	1980 12 mos. Disb. fr. Cap. Gns(a)	1979 Net Asset Value per share	1979 12 mos. Divs from Income	1979 12 mos. Disb. fr. Cap. Gns(a)	1978 Net Asset Value per share	1978 12 mos. Divs from Income	1978 12 mos. Disb. fr. Cap. Gns(a)	1977 Net Asset Value per share	1977 12 mos. Divs from Income	1977 12 mos. Disb. fr. Cap. Gns(a)
*Acorn Fund	23.72	.60	2.34	21.80	.42	1.33	17.93	.31	—	16.17	.21	—
Affiliated Fund	8.40	.48	.44	7.81	.42	.31	7.39	.37	.15	8.22	.35	.22
*Afuture Fund	14.29	—	—	13.77	.145	.102	11.15	.059	—	9.39	.033	—
American Birthright Trust	12.46	—	—	11.01	—	—	9.81	—	—	9.98	—	—
American Gen. Venture	19.11	.75	3.00	18.48	.41	2.53	16.87	.035	—	12.38	—	—
American Grth Fund (e)	9.16	.15	—	7.18	.27	—	6.19	.14	—	5.61	.155	—
*American Investors Fund	10.21	.09	—	7.67	—	—	6.40	.08	—	5.92	.05	—
American Inv. Inc. Fd.	11.56	1.23	.55	12.00	1.05	.16	11.77	1.05	.12	12.24	1.03	.31
American Mutual Fund	11.16	.54	.42	10.51	.51	.34	10.12	.49	.34	10.01	.48	.16
Anchor Growth Fund (b)	8.03	.25	—	7.33	.18	—	6.77	.22	—	6.48	.14	.28
Axe-Houghton Fund B	8.23	.45	.12	8.05	.43	.08	7.73	.40	.08	8.17	.41	.05
Axe-Houghton Inco Fund	4.51	.37	—	4.64	.36	—	4.70	.36	—	5.05	.315	—
Axe-Houghton Stock Fund	7.67	.28	—	6.34	.26	—	5.98	.06	—	5.95	.08	—
*D. L. Babson Income Trust	1.66	.143	—	1.67	.132	—	1.69	.12	—	1.80	.125	—
*Beacon Hill Mutual	10.27	.13	—	9.69	.12	—	9.40	.07	—	8.55	.06	—
Boston Foundation Fund	9.93	.71	—	9.69	.60	—	9.21	.535	—	9.63	.475	—
Broad Street Investing	11.47	.60	.80	11.12	.55	.59	10.74	.54	.60	11.82	.53	.77
Bullock Fund	14.72	.62	.45	13.55	.51	.35	12.48	.48	.28	13.02	.49	.26
Canadian Fund	9.53	.27	.78	8.88	.28	.38	7.31	.30	.29	7.69	.32	.30
*Capital Shares	10.38	.17	—	7.84	.12	—	6.94	.105	—	6.30	.094	—
Century Shares Trust	11.44	.53	.96	12.12	.44	.79	11.21	.35	.60	11.79	.14	.30
Charter Fund	18.39	.505	1.53	15.30	.281	3.836	16.31	.187	1.026	14.47	.125	—
Chase Fund of Boston	7.65	.16	—	6.77	.23	—	6.28	.23	—	6.38	.17	—
Chemical Fund	8.63	.27	.26	7.65	.235	.25	7.26	.21	.21	7.13	.185	.21
Colonial Fund	10.32	.55	—	9.57	.52	—	8.99	.43	—	9.42	.45	—
Colonial Growth Shares	6.56	.16	—	5.23	.16	—	4.59	.12	—	4.66	.10	—
Commerce Income Shares	8.80	.645	—	8.26	.59	—	8.03	.52	.082	8.93	.255	—
Composite Bond & Stock	9.06	.58	.19	8.95	.55	.15	8.51	.52	.10	9.09	.50	.09
Composite Fund	8.91	.31	6%S	8.26	.26	—	8.05	.22	—	7.48	.21	—
Comstock Fund	10.93	.43	—	8.62	.30	—	7.04	.22	—	6.11	.16	—
*Concord Fund	17.78	.56	—	16.13	.48	—	13.84	.39	—	13.14	.64	—
Decatur Income Fund	14.22	.78	.17	12.68	.75	—	11.85	.72	—	12.68	.63	—
Delaware Fund	13.40	.58	—	11.79	.55	—	11.41	.515	—	11.55	.435	—
*DeVegh Mutual Fund	41.30	.45	—	34.40	1.17	—	30.31	1.034	—	31.08	.88	—
Directors Capital Fund	2.26	—	—	3.00	—	—	3.94	—	—	4.32	.025	—
Dividend Shares	2.80	.145	.14	2.82	.12	.13	2.72	.12	.12	3.06	.12	.12
*Dodge & Cox Balanced Fund	23.16	1.35	.31	22.38	1.21	.20	20.85	1.15	.24	22.33	1.06	—
Dreyfus Fund	14.11	.57	.745	12.78	.445	.725	12.18	.47	.51	12.15	.42	.48
Eaton & Howard Balanced	8.12	.458	.13	7.58	.472	.29	7.69	.463	.13	8.39	.446	.15
Eaton & Howard Income	5.10	.535	—	5.63	.493	—	5.83	.478	—	6.24	.463	—
Eaton & Howard Stock	10.48	.43	—	9.24	.395	—	8.82	.382	—	9.16	.338	—
*Energy Fund	21.13	.66	.70	16.40	.57	.63	14.38	.47	.51	15.53	.46	.40
Enterprise Fund	9.92	.09	—	6.79	.095	—	5.70	.175	—	5.18	.10	—
*Evergreen Fund	29.17	.689	2.294	23.47	.04	4.18	21.67	.251	1.188	16 45	—	—
Fairfield Fund	13.24	.43	—	10.80	.32	—	10.03	.23	—	9.85	.19	—
*Fidelity Fund	17.21	.77	.68	16.03	.73	.79	15.63	.69	.38	16.33	.64	—
*Fidelity Trend Fund	25.89	.84	1.61	25.47	.515	—	22.84	.49	—	21.88	.40	—
*Financial Dynamics Fund	6.89	.42	—	5.97	.31	—	5.37	.153	—	5.07	.085	—
*Financial Industrial Fund	5.20	.254	.284	4.68	.222	.173	4.19	.186	.311	4.52	.159	—
*Financial Industrial Inco Fund	7.91	.51	.484	7.28	.50	.451	7.16	.41	.12	7.41	.135	.617
First Investors Discovery	7.49	.16	—	7.84	.085	—	6.79	.03	—	5.24	.01	—
First Invest. Fund For Inc.	7.45	.90	—	8.19	.81	.07	8.27	.78	.33	8.97	.85	.57
First Investors Stock	7.53	.773	—	8.08	.633	—	7.85	.57	—	8.54	.44	—
*44 Wall St Fund	16.86	—	3.25	16.72	—	—	12.30	—	—	8.37	—	—
Founders Mutual Fund	8.49	.406	.21	8.21	.371	.095	7.85	.351	.032	8.86	.322	.129
Frank'n C. Fds. Dy Tech (c)	10.83	.27	—	9.07	.11	—	8.41	.23	—	6.93	.14	—
Franklin Cust—Growth (c)	6.38	.045	—	6.33	.08	—	6.23	.08	—	5.28	.10	.107
Franklin Cust—Inc Shrs (c)	2.22	.13	—	1.94	.15	.045	1.79	.14	.025	1.76	.135	.022
Franklin Cust—Util Shrs (c)	4.54	.38	—	4.68	.34	—	4.79	.31	—	4.90	.295	—
Fundamental Investors (d)	7.49	.36	—	7.03	.28	—	6.62	.27	—	6.82	.25	.21
*General Securities	12.07	.275	.215	11.05	.291	.069	9.88	.20	—	9.56	.21	—
*Growth Industry Shrs	14.08	.206	.54	11.99	.19	—	10.11	.18	—	8.76	.13	—
*Guardian Mutual Fund	32.07	1.15	2.68	29.53	1.10	1.67	27.62	1.05	1.20	28.93	1.08	1.65
Guardian Pk Ave. Fd.	13.62	.81	1.57	13.31	.42	.68	12.71	.37	.46	11.85	.39	.62
Hamilton Fund H-DA	4.52	.206	—	4.23	.184	—	4.06	.215	—	4.17	.155	—
Heritage Fund	2.60	—	—	1.99	—	—	1.72	—	—	1.43	—	—

*Indicates no-load fund.

1976			1975			1974			1973			1972			1971			1970
Net Asset Value per share	12 mos. Divs from Income	12 mos. Disb. fr. Cap. Gns(a)	Net Asset Value per share	12 mos. Divs from Income	12 mos. Disb. fr. Cap. Gns(a)	Net Asset Value per share	12 mos. Divs from Income	12 mos. Disb. fr. Cap. Gns(a)	Net Asset Value per share	12 mos. Divs from Income	12 mos. Disb. fr. Cap. Gns(a)	Net Asset Value per share	12 mos. Divs from Income	12 mos. Disb. fr. Cap. Gns(a)	Net Asset Value per share	12 mos. Divs from Income	12 mos. Disb. fr. Cap. Gns(a)	Net Asset Value per share
12.65	.20	—	10.04	.18	—	8.07	.12	.04	8.95	.15	1.12	14.86	.08	.26	12.90	.17	—	7.31
8.33	.31	.12	7.22	.28	.03	5.79	.32	.17	6.21	.29	.20	6.92	.30	.24	7.42	.30	.15	5.78
9.57	.018	—	8.25	.01	—	7.18	—	—	8.60	—	1.87	11.15	—	—	10.82	—	—	4.9f
9.18	—	—	8.52	—	—	7.73	—	—	7.56	—	—	7.62	—	—	7.10	—	—	5.7
10.87	—	—	9.26	—	—	6.29	—	—	6.69	—	—	15.15	—	.37	12.25	—	—	
5.16	.18	—	4.67	.29	.53	4.82	.165	.12	5.92	.16	.085	6.22	.18	.63	6.72	.17	—	4.68
5.13	.06	—	5.06	.07	—	3.83	.05	—	4.53	—	—	6.01	.02	—	5.69	.04	—	4.35
11.08	.87	.36	10.00	—	—	—	—	—	—	—	—	—	—	—	—	—	—	
9.76	.46	—	8.35	.48	—	7.35	.37	.22	8.06	.36	.31	9.12	.36	.21	9.39	.36	—	6.86
7.37	.14	—	6.79	.17	—	5.91	.19	—	7.42	.12	—	12.06	.10	—	11.79	.20	—	8.20
7.55	.40	—	6.74	.47	.04	6.33	.37	.23	6.96	.31	.22	8.00	.35	.20	8.03	.36	—	6.14
4.80	.22	—	4.45	.26	—	4.03	.24	.15	4.56	.20	.24	5.68	.24	.21	5.87	.26	—	4.36
6.31	.16	—	5.86	.22	—	5.16	.16	.14	5.68	.08	.07	6.37	.16	.11	6.07	.26	.37	5.06
1.75	.128	—	1.74	.135	—	1.76	.14	—	1.90	.155	—	2.03	.095	—	2.00	.10	—	1.67
8.63	.05	—	8.34	.16	—	7.28	.15	—	8.70	—	.21	12.30	—	.70	10.76	.05	.62	7.36
9.25	.40	—	8.86	.42	—	7.94	.44	—	9.45	.45	.23	11.08	.39	.443	11.45	.56	—	8.58
12.62	.49	.77	11.55	.48	.14	10.50	.45	.69	13.29	.42	1.20	15.21	.42	.83	14.76	.42	.41	10.72
13.17	.47	.21	12.03	.47	.21	10.30	.39	.61	12.45	.28	.30	15.75	.35	.51	15.27	.39	.31	10.77
8.88	.33	.28	9.00	.33	.26	9.53	.225	.38	10.68	.19	.40	10.92	.225	.35	9.79	.245	.30	8.28
5.59	.084	—	4.95	.067	—	4.09	.12	—	5.30	.087	—	6.68	.133	—	6.55	.108	—	5.04
10.10	.31	—	10.36	.30	.29	9.17	.285	.51	12.44	.275	.54	14.37	.285	.35	13.46	.285	.30	8.94
11.93	.12	—	11.13	.138	—	9.08	.03	—	8.98	—	1.201	13.67	.133	—	9.04	.217	—	6.28
6.84	.14	—	6.87	.14	—	5.70	.18	—	7.81	.03	.36	12.01	.08	—	10.49	.12	—	6.49
8.36	.20	.198	8.71	.20	.15	8.46	.16	.455	10.42	.12	.52	10.80	.13	.50	9.42	.165	.378	7.16
9.92	.45	—	9.48	.51	—	8.93	.44	—	9.64	.43	.25	11.11	.44	.15	11.09	.45	—	8.73
5.17	.097	—	5.17	.115	—	4.91	.06	.03	5.81	.04	.20	7.19	.10	—	6.59	.11	—	4.43
9.15	.14	—	8.41	.33	—	6.89	.355	.29	8.40	.143	.583	10.98	.14	—	9.87	.21	—	7.46
8.72	.48	—	8.03	.48	—	7.26	.44	.20	8.22	.34	.30	8.87	.37	.38	9.36	.40	—	7.16
8.03	.26	—	7.93	.28	—	6.38	.28	—	7.11	.29	.30	9.28	.32	.40	10.14	.34	—	7.41
5.43	.10	—	4.55	.10	—	3.22	.08	—	3.12	.04	—	4.48	.10	—	4.41	.15	—	3.48
11.27	.16	—	8.84	.14	—	7.97	.11	—	8.94	—	—	11.45	.24	—	11.98	.22	—	9.06
11.63	.77	—	9.80	.65	—	8.36	.62	—	9.60	.60	.50	11.82	.60	.50	12.08	.625	.15	9.53
11.17	.41	—	9.47	.40	—	7.83	.36	.11	9.21	.33	.78	13.21	.37	.73	13.40	.50	.36	9.93
32.24	.79	—	31.29	1.018	—	25.75	.605	—	28.56	.71	—	34.87	.66	.75	34.73	.66	—	24.21
4.16	.054	—	3.83	.17	—	3.36	.187	—	4.96	—	1.226	8.05	—	.564	6.87	—	—	4.05
3.30	.125	.10	3.06	.125	.11	2.88	.115	.14	3.62	.11	.15	3.89	.11	.14	3.77	.115	.11	2.97
21.96	.95	—	19.61	.95	—	17.65	.87	.19	20.62	.80	.62	23.17	.81	.16	22.36	.83	.16	18.13
11.98	.36	—	10.91	.33	—	8.76	.25	—	10.44	.265	—	12.87	.31	.02	12.63	.38	—	9.30
8.78	.426	.09	8.36	.42	—	7.84	.415	.35	9.43	.409	.652	10.26	.431	.45	10.15	.466	.36	8.47
5.78	.44	—	5.48	.439	—	5.29	.43	.112	6.07	.425	.15	6.56	.424	.052	6.26	.295	.10	5.14
9.74	.292	—	9.68	.307	—	8.91	.303	.305	12.35	.31	.792	14.26	.347	.52	14.11	.393	.44	10.64
14.69	.46	—	12.84	.40	—	9.91	.28	.16	11.03	.25	.33	12.64	.32	.34	13.57	.41	.16	10.18
5.54	.11	—	5.29	.17	—	4.53	.12	—	5.40	.07	—	7.20	.10	—	6.73	.42	—	5.00
13.06	—	—	10.57	—	—	7.06	—	—	7.70	.045	1.267	12.50	—	—	—	—	—	
9.89	.24	—	8.14	.13	—	6.44	.10	—	7.51	—	—	11.95	.12	—	10.73	.16	—	7.46
16.00	.59	—	14.55	.60	—	12.53	.53	.17	14.95	.51	.45	17.18	.54	.24	16.13	.57	—	12.40
22.96	.375	—	20.78	.36	—	18.55	.32	—	22.40	.28	—	27.88	.49	—	29.94	.61	—	18.13
4.52	.07	—	4.29	.076	—	3.28	.08	—	3.87	.02	—	4.78	.05	—	4.45	.11	—	3.53
4.38	.128	—	3.84	.158	.077	3.49	.07	.06	4.28	.086	.031	4.27	.10	—	3.90	.14	—	3.13
7.21	.113	.354	6.38	.10	—	5.03	.10	—	5.53	.085	—	5.98	.08	—	5.91	.08	—	4.78
5.20	—	—	4.91	—	—	3.80	.05	—	5.05	—	—	8.97	—	—	7.79	—	—	—
8.39	.78	.04	7.27	.767	—	6.77	.738	—	8.29	.77	.06	9.84	.65	.02	9.57	.07	—	—
7.95	.22	—	7.10	.22	—	6.43	.23	—	7.55	.21	.39	9.93	.203	—	9.52	.215	—	6.84
7.11	—	—	5.74	—	—	3.65	—	—	3.72	—	.626	8.36	—	—	6.57	—	—	2.81
9.72	.275	.062	8.67	.289	.02	7.63	.205	—	8.70	.206	.104	9.44	.251	.021	8.83	.269	.002	6.52
6.93	.12	—	6.66	.10	—	5.97	—	—	7.35	.07	—	11.50	.05	—	8.88	.12	—	5.94
6.01	.11	.052	5.87	.075	.073	5.90	.05	.16	7.30	.02	.34	8.27	.04	—	6.68	.04	—	4.97
1.69	.139	.015	1.73	.139	.051	1.66	.14	.05	1.94	.14	.06	2.16	.14	.06	2.12	.14	—	1.73
4.11	.295	—	4.04	.245	—	3.27	.235	—	5.25	.225	—	5.21	.22	—	6.13	.22	—	5.17
7.29	.25	—	6.62	.28	—	5.90	.25	.25	7.38	.25	.49	9.33	.25	—	9.29	.25	—	6.91
9.18	.24	—	7.17	.24	—	5.54	.18	—	6.26	.12	—	8.63	.22	—	10.03	.263	.157	7.92
9.18	.095	—	9.04	.108	—	8.06	.10	.085	9.58	.105	.93	12.49	.14	.20	11.03	.165	.41	7.76
28.40	1.14	.17	24.18	1.08	.10	20.09	.78	.55	22.01	.75	1.22	25.79	.79	1.34	26.36	.83	.23	19.06
10.78	.41	.07	9.00	.31	—	7.46	.265	.14	7.52	.265	.12	9.45	—	—	—	—	—	—
4.47	.14	—	3.95	.14	—	3.43	.14	—	3.94	.15	—	4.59	.18	.065	4.75	.18	—	3.39
1.40	—	—	1.44	—	—	1.06	—	—	1.43	—	—	3.49	—	—	2.45	—	—	1.65

MUTUAL FUNDS: TEN-YEAR SELECTED PERFORMANCE (continued)

Quarter Ended June 30	1980 Net Asset Value per share	1980 12 mos. Divs from Income	1980 12 mos. Disb. fr. Cap. Gns(a)	1979 Net Asset Value per share	1979 12 mos. Divs from Income	1979 12 mos. Disb. fr. Cap. Gns(a)	1978 Net Asset Value per share	1978 12 mos. Divs from Income	1978 12 mos. Disb. fr. Cap. Gns(a)	1977 Net Asset Value per share	1977 12 mos. Divs from Income	1977 12 mos. Disb. fr. Cap. Gns(a)
*Herold Fund	140.66	—	—	112.88	—	—	102.91	—	—	97.44	—	—
IDS Growth Fund	9.33	.152	.54	7.31	.119	.164	6.69	.076	.067	5.69	.044	—
IDS New Dimension Fund	7.43	.186	—	5.83	.137	—	5.23	.081	—	4.75	.056	—
IDS Progressive Fund	3.90	.113	—	3.57	.115	—	3.41	.097	—	3.13	.065	—
International Investors	11.15	.373	—	4.88	.187	—	3.23	.143	—	2.42	.123	.01
Investment Co. of America	8.34	.355	.20	7.90	.275	.09	7.38	.245	.14	7.08	.24	.115
Invest. Trust of Boston	11.04	.32	.45	9.50	.37	.39	9.34	.31	.25	9.76	.34	.51
Investors Mutual	9.07	.615	—	8.97	.555	—	8.70	.543	—	9.16	.495	—
Investors Research Fund	6.09	.14	.799	6.19	.09	.561	6.23	.115	—	5.39	.06	—
Investors Selective	8.03	.649	—	8.83	.771	—	8.91	.727	.052	9.55	.699	0.28
Investors Stock Fund	20.05	1.03	—	19.00	.873	.16	17.61	.788	.15	18.89	.638	—
Investors Variable Pay	8.24	.307	—	7.49	.235	—	6.74	.176	—	6.49	—	—
ISI Trust Fund	11.23	.92	.94	12.05	.83	—	10.81	.70	—	10.59	.58	.07
Istel Fund	32.36	1.12	—	26.32	.75	—	21.12	.48	—	20.23	.77	—
*Ivest Fund	10.52	.34	—	9.76	.23	—	8.61	.16	—	7.92	.14	—
JP Growth Fund	11.84	.55	—	10.84	.40	.34	10.19	.35	—	10.56	.25	.34
Johnston Cap. Appreciation	24.47	1.14	.27	22.33	.85	—	20.39	.57	.04	19.90	.36	.44
Keystone Series B-1	16.02	1.62	—	16.73	1.44	—	17.01	1.36	—	18.14	1.39	—
Keystone Series B-2	17.87	1.92	—	18.86	1.66	—	19.06	1.63	—	20.04	1.63	—
Keystone Series B-4	7.54	.80	—	8.11	.76	—	8.21	.72	—	8.55	.72	—
Keystone Series K-1	7.45	.61	—	7.43	.59	—	7.44	.54	—	7.85	.54	—
Keystone Series K-2	6.05	.27	—	5.40	.25	—	5.18	.18	—	5.27	.13	—
Keystone Series S-1	18.63	.85	.85	18.39	.78	—	17.39	.65	.21	17.72	.63	.34
Keystone Series S-3	9.37	.53	.33	8.71	.34	.57	8.42	.07	—	7.81	.17	.80
Keystone Series S-4	7.26	.13	—	5.57	.10	—	4.81	.07	—	3.96	.06	—
Lexington Growth Fund	11.29	.27	4.90	14.13	.06	.145	12.00	.09	—	9.35	.05	—
Lexington Research Fund	17.16	.78	1.55	15.35	.56	.34	14.51	.56	—	14.87	.54	—
Life Insurance Investors	10.07	.94	—	11.22	.34	—	8.75	.23	.155	7.53	.19	.061
Lindner Fund	10.09	.448	1.377	10.79	.26	.23	9.27	.125	.225	6.90	.10	—
*Loomis Sayles Cap Dev	15.02	.36	1.65	13.68	.35	—	12.54	.27	—	10.84	.18	—
*Loomis Sayles Mutual	14.30	.78	—	13.38	.68	—	12.95	.61	—	13.16	.42	.08
Lord Abbett Inco. Fd.	2.95	.291	—	3.07	.238	.06	3.20	.24	.16	3.60	.22	.10
Magna Income Trust	8.21	.91	—	9.01	.87	—	9.15	.77	—	9.44	.70	—
Massachusetts Fund	12.18	.43	—	11.22	.61	—	10.57	.54	—	10.75	.50	—
Mass. Investors Grth. Stk.	11.03	.273	.381	9.39	.244	.283	8.78	.20	.264	8.47	.15	.256
Mass. Investors Trust	11.35	.535	.329	10.38	.473	.155	9.60	.43	.155	10.40	.394	.217
*Mathers Fund	21.06	.76	1.04	17.15	.79	1.79	16.28	.41	.32	13.96	.33	—
MIF Fund	7.98	.44	—	7.90	.40	—	7.68	.39	—	8.47	.33	.20
MIF Growth Fund	4.83	.15	—	4.16	.11	—	4.26	.09	—	3.87	.08	—
MONY Fund	10.54	.395	—	9.61	.335	—	9.08	.225	—	9.24	.165	—
Mutual Shares	41.11	1.08	3.92	38.66	.95	2.35	33.95	.60	1.35	30.41	.57	1.95
National Investors	7.55	.17	.45	6.89	.16	.30	6.40	.14	.27	6.36	.12	.24
National Sec—Balanced	9.77	.60	—	9.61	.56	—	9.24	.48	—	9.56	.44	—
National Sec—Bond	3.83	.425	—	4.22	.41	—	4.38	.39	—	4.64	.39	—
National Sec—Dividend	4.81	.30	.12	4.38	.285	—	4.13	.27	—	4.16	.255	.04
National Sec—Growth	6.40	.20	—	5.82	.185	—	5.62	.155	—	5.63	.13	—
National Sec—Income	5.80	.425	.12	5.73	.39	—	5.57	.365	—	5.61	.35	.04
National Sec—Pfd.	6.63	.63	—	7.17	.57	—	7.20	.51	—	7.81	.41	—
National Sec—Stock	9.00	.43	.32	8.52	.39	.10	7.79	.37	.04	8.28	.36	.12
Nation-Wide Securities	9.59	.56	.14	9.55	.53	.16	9.21	.53	.16	10.18	.51	.14
*Newton Growth Fund	16.04	.495	—	13.94	.395	—	12.85	.275	—	11.93	.185	—
*Nicholas Fund	14.09	.389	—	11.96	.31	—	10.15	.185	—	7.63	.07	—
*Northeast Investors Trust	12.53	.132	—	13.35	1.28	—	13.96	1.28	—	14.94	1.28	—
*One William Street Fund	16.93	.57	1.24	16.02	.48	.77	14.32	.325	.21	14.04	.27	.315
Oppenheimer Fund	9.02	.19	—	6.83	.435	—	5.90	.23	—	6.20	.18	—
O-T-C Securities Fund Inc.	24.74	.50	.55	19.20	.43	1.08	16.08	.37	.42	12.79	.39	.51
*Penn Square Mutual	7.86	.415	.41	7.63	.375	.35	7.49	.35	.31	8.19	.30	.37
*Pennsylvania Mutual	5.58	.16	.91	6.15	.075	—	5.46	.055	—	3.89	.124	—
Philadelphia Fund	9.49	.33	.52	8.40	.23	.75	8.17	.179	.341	7.43	.16	.31
Pilgrim Fund	14.89	.51	.33	12.86	.31	—	10.79	.15	—	9.05	.06	—
*Pine Street Fund	11.54	.675	.23	10.72	.59	.22	10.04	.502	.295	10.91	.417	.32
Pioneer Fund	18.07	.72	.615	16.20	.56	.48	14.33	.53	.475	14.35	.48	.45
Pioneer II Fund	10.68	.38	.60	10.14	.35	.75	9.71	.21	.265	8.01	.135	.31
Pligrowth Fund	14.48	.465	.055	11.91	.37	.06	11.05	.12	—	10.90	.295	.105
Plitrend Fund	12.29	.34	2.01	13.09	.27	.74	10.48	.225	.10	8.45	.225	.055
*T. Rowe Price Growth Stk	12.13	.419	—	11.35	.331	—	10.84	.277	—	10.20	.226	—
*Rowe Price New Era Fund	18.78	.495	3.37	13.63	.408	.36	10.74	.324	.246	11.09	—	—
*Rowe Price New Horizons	13.26	.232	.368	10.62	.157	—	9.70	.098	—	7.35	.071	—
*Provident Fund for Income	3.82	.28	—	3.78	.07	—	3.76	.27	—	4.04	.245	—

1976 Net Asset Value per share	12 mos. Divs from Income	12 mos. Disb. fr. Cap. Gns(a)	1975 Net Asset Value per share	12 mos. Divs from Income	12 mos. Disb. fr. Cap. Gns(a)	1974 Net Asset Value per share	12 mos. Divs from Income	12 mos. Disb. fr. Cap. Gns(a)	1973 Net Asset Value per share	12 mos. Divs from Income	12 mos. Disb. fr. Cap. Gns(a)	1972 Net Asset Value per share	12 mos. Divs from Income	12 mos. Disb. fr. Cap. Gns(a)	1971 Net Asset Value per share	12 mos. Divs from Income	12 mos. Disb. fr. Cap. Gns(a)	1970 Net Asset Value per share
93.91	—	—	90.33	1.43	—	76.80	.82	—	97.13	—	—	185.45	—	—	131.15	3.46	—	96.41
5.48	.028	—	5.45	.021	—	4.71	—	—	6.01	.113	.115	7.22	—	—	—	—	—	—
4.94	—	—	4.92	.061	—	4.25	.031	—	5.45	.015	—	7.52	—	—	5.28	.02	—	3.21
3.26	.074	—	3.14	.066	—	2.84	.047	—	4.11	.068	.717	6.06	—	—	4.58	.032	.15	3.02
2.88	.233	.023	5.96	.283	.023	5.77	.069	.023	4.38	.05	.02	2.77	.04	.013	1.87	.045	.276	1.66
7.14	.285	.035	6.38	.30	—	5.44	.21	.165	6.19	.195	.235	7.23	.195	.13	6.85	.195	—	5.00
10.76	.28	.41	10.03	.44	.20	8.85	.42	.35	10.91	.34	.90	12.10	.32	.30	12.27	.33	.30	9.44
8.99	.455	—	8.44	.438	—	7.77	.411	.053	9.52	.393	.23	10.42	.385	.168	10.06	.403	.025	8.13
5.53	.13	—	5.60	.14	—	4.28	.06	—	4.89	—	1.072	7.27	—	—	5.20	.09	—	4.05
9.04	.688	—	8.61	.723	—	8.50	.679	—	9.49	.626	—	9.58	.588	—	9.16	.575	—	8.61
19.58	.54	—	17.63	.558	—	15.56	.508	.08	19.03	.475	.29	21.20	.50	.155	19.73	.50	—	14.21
6.65	.137	—	6.72	.124	—	6.13	.112	—	8.51	.119	—	9.20	.147	—	7.82	.151	—	5.45
10.75	.84	.20	12.77	.94	2.14	14.21	.74	.085	13.34	.48	.238	12.80	.46	—	12.30	.23	—	
21.39	.62	—	21.17	.78	—	17.74	.63	.68	19.90	.30	.65	23.13	.30	.61	22.72	.48	.06	14.77
8.39	.09	—	8.02	.06	—	6.77	.15	—	8.98	.11	.205	12.60	.147	—	11.02	.10	—	7.69
11.17	.35	—	9.10	.40	—	7.82	.25	—	8.26	.17	.08	12.10	.19	.12	11.74	.338	—	
21.35	.36	.32	21.23	.47	—	18.80	.49	.25	23.04	.33	.80	28.61	.14	.59	23.60	.338	.37	16.32
17.35	1.40	—	16.90	1.73	—	17.51	1.44	—	18.95	1.37	—	19.09	1.34	—	18.64	1.31	—	17.79
18.84	1.63	—	17.25	1.70	—	17.73	1.57	—	20.07	1.60	—	20.78	1.57	—	19.61	1.47	—	18.43
7.91	.75	—	7.33	.77	—	7.14	.73	—	8.25	.73	—	9.13	.71	—	8.42	.68	—	7.78
7.48	.52	—	6.74	.53	—	6.05	.48	—	7.06	.48	—	8.19	.48	—	7.89	.47	—	6.69
5.55	.09	—	5.43	.10	—	4.49	.03	—	5.58	—	—	7.62	.04	—	5.74	.10	—	3.83
19.45	.44	—	19.25	.42	.30	17.33	.27	.37	22.56	.21	—	22.42	.34	—	19.71	.42	—	14.54
8.64	—	—	7.77	.18	—	5.83	—	—	7.09	.09	—	9.61	.09	—	8.50	.13	—	5.72
3.72	.04	—	3.33	—	—	2.81	—	—	3.69	—	—	6.87	—	—	5.22	.02	—	3.28
7.78	.04	—	6.54	.07	—	4.80	.05	—	5.78	.04	.75	11.03	—	1.09	10.40	.02	—	6.46
15.09	.43	—	12.96	.40	—	11.24	.25	—	12.68	.14	.76	17.30	.17	.55	16.65	.20	—	11.37
6.06	.17	.03	6.28	.15	.025	5.37	.125	.175	7.56	.115	.26	9.06	.10	.40	8.02	.12	—	5.53
5.42	.10	—	4.08	.11	—	4.00	.076	—	3.90	.072	1.148	5.30	.088	—	4.54	—	—	3.05
10.77	.13	—	10.76	.15	.37	10.07	.14	.37	12.41	.08	—	13.86	.16	—	11.89	.21	—	7.99
13.68	.43	—	13.15	.43	—	12.37	.46	—	14.39	.42	.42	15.30	.42	.35	14.74	.44	.35	11.26
3.31	.225	—	2.95	.18	—	2.62	.175	—	2.96	.17	.05	3.49	.16	.10	3.33	.16	—	2.86
8.65	.55	—	8.11	.60	—	7.61	.50	—	8.72	.47	—	9.14	.52	—	8.79	.53	—	7.65
10.54	.49	—	9.88	.50	—	9.14	.43	.23	11.25	.42	.35	12.10	.40	.28	11.36	.40	.18	8.81
9.77	.148	.224	10.33	.19	—	9.51	.196	.17	12.72	.176	.723	14.87	.176	.347	13.23	.21	.388	9.07
11.37	.345	.168	10.32	.405	—	9.23	.393	.15	10.89	.379	.618	12.59	.416	1.71	14.32	.457	.974	11.68
11.80	.24	—	10.23	.31	—	7.95	.25	—	10.50	.17	1.07	17.12	.32	—	13.75	.19	—	8.83
9.08	.33	—	7.66	.37	—	6.75	.35	.14	7.50	.33	.29	8.28	.33	.26	8.85	.36	.10	6.82
3.99	.08	—	3.58	.12	—	3.31	.11	.18	4.10	.08	.25	5.92	.08	.21	5.77	.10	.01	4.05
9.98	.148	—	9.67	.135	—	8.23	.065	—	10.09	.009	.351	13.47	.018	.252	11.91	.08	—	
25.97	.50	1.05	20.52	.85	—	15.87	.30	—	14.50	.43	—	16.78	.39	—	16.24	.45	—	11.35
6.84	.13	.14	6.65	.16	—	5.88	.12	.46	8.11	.10	.55	10.00	.10	.30	8.44	.13	.20	5.79
9.24	.38	—	7.93	.49	—	7.16	.49	—	8.53	.47	—	10.40	.48	.22	10.85	.49	.11	8.70
4.32	.39	—	4.09	.38	—	4.08	.38	—	4.77	.40	—	5.16	.38	—	4.94	.33	—	4.53
3.82	.25	—	3.28	.24	—	2.99	.205	.07	3.55	.20	.12	4.14	.21	.12	4.27	.22	.10	3.37
5.86	.13	—	5.64	.175	—	5.07	.195	—	6.38	.10	.45	9.94	.13	.35	9.44	.20	.25	6.92
5.13	.33	—	4.55	.325	—	4.16	.305	—	4.59	.30	.09	5.41	.29	.07	5.35	.28	.06	4.21
6.87	.40	—	5.60	.43	—	5.28	.39	—	6.03	.40	—	7.28	.39	.07	7.28	.36	—	5.62
7.99	.35	.10	6.86	.34	—	5.72	.32	.10	6.49	.32	.25	7.68	.32	.25	8.17	.34	.17	6.35
9.94	.50	.12	9.03	.50	.16	8.24	.47	.23	9.78	.49	.26	10.45	.49	.25	10.49	.49	.22	8.68
11.48	.24	—	11.68	.35	—	10.75	.13	—	12.14	—	.988	21.44	.05	—	15.36	.28	—	11.53
6.69	.05	—	6.35	.05	—	4.95	.024	—	7.08	—	—	13.09	—	.22	8.31	—	—	4.00
14.15	1.245	—	13.51	1.19	—	13.21	1.15	—	15.37	1.15	—	15.80	1.14	—	15.04	1.085	—	13.64
14.77	.30	.23	14.77	.395	—	13.25	.48	.53	15.87	.305	1.035	17.51	.255	.53	16.17	.295	—	11.52
6.67	.111	—	6.25	.25	—	5.58	.145	—	6.91	.084	.542	9.24	.145	.095	8.61	.20	—	5.88
11.09	.31	.43	10.07	.23	.35	9.42	.19	.18	9.71	.18	.32	12.05	.12	.23	10.67	.22	.15	9.42
8.36	.30	.28	7.19	.325	—	5.88	.255	.36	6.41	.24	.35	7.34	.25	.255	8.20	.296	.134	6.57
3.24	—	—	2.56	—	—	1.64	—	—	2.10	—	—	4.53	—	—	4.88	—	—	3.34
7.43	.178	.077	6.91	.147	.038	4.97	.086	.55	6.06	.07	.415	7.98	.079	.311	7.80	.179	.127	5.46
7.51	.085	—	7.03	.10	—	6.02	.06	—	7.74	.045	.035	11.02	.05	.54	10.05	.12	—	7.09
10.72	.39	.315	10.30	.445	—	8.76	.445	.178	9.67	.35	.275	10.84	.295	.60	11.46	.335	.64	8.53
13.91	.43	.22	11.81	.41	.155	9.79	.385	.58	11.28	.37	.60	12.23	.365	.525	11.97	.365	.27	9.18
6.65	.095	.095	5.29	.085	.173	4.45	.085	.12	4.26	.08	.84	6.13	.075	.19	5.02	.09	—	3.56
11.32	.345	.065	10.77	.385	.255	10.07	.27	.48	12.54	.19	.62	15.06	.175	.385	13.52	.32	.38	10.07
7.22	.21	.10	6.57	.178	.093	5.98	.25	.31	7.72	.16	—	8.72	.16	—	8.65	.16	—	6.07
11.27	.231	—	11.18	.229	—	10.10	.195	.23	12.77	.12	.54	16.43	.125	.315	13.94	.18	.20	9.20
11.24	.279	—	11.50	.286	—	10.12	.184	.105	10.77	.105	.138	11.63	.16	—	10.37	.16	—	8.08
7.18	.074	—	7.62	.091	—	6.39	.055	.031	8.84	.042	.692	14.97	.037	.207	9.99	.053	.153	6.11
3.68	.25	—	3.39	.26	.17	3.20	.25	.18	3.81	.25	.17	5.06	.22	.11	4.87	.24	.06	3.57

MUTUAL FUNDS: TEN-YEAR SELECTED PERFORMANCE (concluded)

Quarter Ended June 30	1980 Net Asset Value per share	1980 12 mos. Divs from Income	1980 12 mos. Disb. fr. Cap. Gns(a)	1979 Net Asset Value per share	1979 12 mos. Divs from Income	1979 12 mos. Disb. fr. Cap. Gns(a)	1978 Net Asset Value per share	1978 12 mos. Divs from Income	1978 12 mos. Disb. fr. Cap. Gns(a)	1977 Net Asset Value per share	1977 12 mos. Divs from Income	1977 12 mos. Disb. fr. Cap. Gns(a)
Puritan Fund	11.00	.72	.26	10.70	.675	.28	10.50	.665	.30	11.32	.615	.21
Putnam Fund	13.27	.87	.74	13.24	.69	.41	12.95	.66	.20	13.78	.60	.17
Putnam Growth Fund	12.13	.545	.925	11.04	.525	.66	10.49	.42	.35	10.56	.28	.415
Putnam Income Fund	6.74	.648	—	7.41	.76	—	7.69	.63	—	8.16	.63	—
Putnam Investors Fund	8.01	.305	.515	7.60	.27	.42	7.25	.215	.68	7.69	.135	.215
Research Capital Fund	9.55	.47	—	4.41	.13	—	3.04	.14	—	2.44	.165	—
*Revere Fund	7.07	.11	—	6.01	.10	—	5.20	—	—	5.66	.03	—
SAFECO Equity Fund	10.54	.463	.473	10.05	.42	.661	9.74	.345	.239	9.14	.299	.494
St. Paul Cap Fund	12.15	.275	—	9.24	.24	—	8.30	.24	—	8.06	.23	—
St. Paul Grth Fund	11.88	.12	1.51	10.14	.141	1.025	8.97	.14	—	7.49	.105	—
Scudder Int'l Invests	18.66	.493	1.356	16.19	.286	.496	14.93	.277	—	13.37	.148	—
*Scudder Special Fund	40.15	.72	—	33.75	.52	—	30.29	.45	—	24.30	.38	—
*Scudder Stvn & Clark C Stk	13.38	.42	—	10.63	.37	—	9.97	.32	—	9.57	.30	—
Scudder Income Fund	12.37	1.23	—	13.49	.107	—	13.61	1.04	.335	15.02	.78	—
Security Equity Fund	5.95	.21	.05	4.92	.08	—	4.42	.14	—	4.08	.06	—
Security Invest Fund	8.56	.56	.12	7.75	.50	.11	7.39	.48	.17	7.69	.44	.17
*Selected Amer. Shares	7.15	.375	—	7.01	.335	—	6.79	.285	—	7.13	.235	—
Sentinel Apex Fund	3.54	.118	—	3.66	.111	—	3.79	.09	—	3.53	.06	—
Sentinel Bal Fund	7.75	.53	—	7.42	.50	.08	7.50	.47	.05	8.16	.46	.10
Sentinel Com Stk Fund	12.95	.78	.28	11.90	.69	.15	11.46	.635	.20	12.54	.585	.33
*Sequoia Fund	22.58	.74	1.262	23.17	.38	.045	21.26	.34	.43	16.55	.35	—
Shareholders Tr of Boston	8.17	.27	—	7.32	.24	—	7.17	.37	—	7.50	.35	—
Sherman, Dean Fund	8.90	—	—	4.99	—	—	4.71	—	—	3.78	—	—
Sigma Capital Shares	12.68	.295	—	10.97	—	—	10.03	.099	—	9.07	.077	—
Sigma Investment Shares	11.35	.606	.151	10.48	.495	.145	9.98	.45	.201	10.42	.392	.181
Sigma Trust Shares	9.12	.685	—	9.10	.583	—	8.83	.539	—	8.86	.408	—
Sigma Venture Shares	10.96	.118	.517	9.33	—	—	8.84	.016	—	5.49	—	—
Sovereign Investors	13.73	.64	.10	12.08	.57	.10	11.42	.52	.10	12.12	.49	.23
Stein Roe & Farnham Bal	20.06	.87	—	18.67	.76	—	17.04	.68	—	17.54	.51	—
Stein Roe & Far Cap Oppt Fd	17.37	.25	.92	12.79	.25	—	9.78	.20	—	9.03	.17	—
*Stein Roe & Farnham Stk	16.65	.46	.23	13.45	.41	—	12.02	.34	—	12.21	.30	—
Strategic Invest Fd.	10.08	.404	—	4.37	.297	—	2.79	.189	—	2.05	.158	—
Surveyor Fund	13.72	.22	.21	10.72	—	—	9.58	.195	.18	8.89	.165	.15
*Technology Fund	10.75	.37	.43	8.84	.26	.20	8.05	.22	.10	7.55	.19	—
Templeton Growth Fund	6.54	.12	.38	5.95	.08	.09	5.13	.043	.02	4.12	.053	.237
*Twentieth Cent Growth Inv	8.53	—	1.24	6.61	—	1.07	6.11	—	.456	4.39	—	—
Union Income Fund	11.58	.99	.22	11.66	.90	.34	11.72	.86	.71	12.98	.86	.72
United Accumulative	7.87	.31	—	6.86	.29	—	6.42	.25	—	6.36	.21	—
United Income Fund	9.14	.59	.28	9.33	.51	.28	9.41	.52	.28	10.19	.50	.39
United Science Fund	8.12	.20	—	6.78	.17	—	6.22	.14	—	5.62	.11	—
United Services Fund	6.84	.33	—	2.90	.094	—	1.87	.136	—	1.48	.117	—
Value Line Fund	13.06	.26	—	9.97	.17	—	8.92	.13	—	7.23	.12	—
Value Line Income Fund	6.48	.345	.27	6.00	.315	—	5.31	.28	—	5.32	.28	—
Value Line Leveraged Grth	16.12	.40	3.26	16.11	.025	2.08	16.24	.045	—	10.36	—	—
Value Line Special Sit	8.33	.07	—	6.55	.03	—	5.48	.04	—	4.64	.02	—
Vance Sanders Investors	7.49	.375	.41	7.33	.34	.26	6.90	.33	—	7.41	.325	.13
Vance Sanders Common Stk	7.97	.21	.43	7.53	.16	.58	6.93	.14	.46	6.45	.11	—
Vance Sanders Special Fd	11.48	.40	1.82	11.06	.33	1.82	11.34	.17	—	8.35	.08	—
Wall Street Growth Fund	7.59	.24	—	6.91	.22	.02	6.19	.20	—	6.38	.05	—
Wash Mutual Investors	6.64	.38	.32	6.72	.35	—	6.42	.34	.09	6.81	.32	.18
Weingarten Equity Fd.	24.60	.15	3.15	·18.53	.19	—	15.76	.09	—	12.26	—	—
*Wellington Fund	9.91	.66	—	9.31	.54	.25	8.87	.50	.25	9.85	.49	.25
*Windsor Fund	10.17	.55	.85	10.47	.50	1.01	10.49	.45	.54	10.55	.38	.22
Wisconsin Fund	4.14	.451	—	4.65	.418	—	4.80	.333	—	5.35	.28	.22

Notes: (a) Capital gains distributions may include payments from other sources. (b) Paid 6% stock dividend in 1971; 8% in 1972. (c) Paid 5% stock dividend in 1970. (d) Paid 5% stock dividend in 1971. (e) Paid 10% stock dividend in 1972. All figures are adjusted for split-ups. Stock of record is used in determining in which period dividends and capital gains payments fall. To provide longer-term performance data, funds are not included in Quarterly Record until they have been offered publicly at least three years.
*Indicates no-load fund.
Source: *Baron's*, August 4, 1980.

1976 NAV per share	1976 12 mos. Divs from Income	1976 12 mos. Disb. fr. Cap. Gns(a)	1975 NAV per share	1975 12 mos. Divs from Income	1975 12 mos. Disb. fr. Cap. Gns(a)	1974 NAV per share	1974 12 mos. Divs from Income	1974 12 mos. Disb. fr. Cap. Gns(a)	1973 NAV per share	1973 12 mos. Divs from Income	1973 12 mos. Disb. fr. Cap. Gns(a)	1972 NAV per share	1972 12 mos. Divs from Income	1972 12 mos. Disb. fr. Cap. Gns(a)	1971 NAV per share	1971 12 mos. Divs from Income	1971 12 mos. Disb. fr. Cap. Gns(a)	1970 NAV per share
10.62	.585	.10	9.73	.565	.05	8.31	.56	.10	9.03	.53	.32	10.54	.61	.18	10.54	.50	—	8.31
13.69	.535	—	12.56	.52	—	11.84	.51	.535	14.94	.51	.91	16.38	.49	.27	14.82	.48	.20	11.40
10.69	.25	—	10.04	.305	—	8.67	.30	.375	10.57	.20	.61	12.60	.16	—	10.80	.30	—	7.88
7.62	.61	—	7.26	.60	—	6.90	.54	—	8.02	.46	—	8.38	.46	—	8.16	.46	—	6.54
8.01	.135	—	7.76	.21	—	7.27	.21	.655	9.62	.12	.77	10.72	.12	.16	8.49	.14	—	5.56
2.72	.26	—	5.75	.25	—	5.31	—	—	4.37	—	—	7.17	—	—	5.45	.10	—	3.83
5.21	.14	—	4.95	.145	—	5.10	.035	—	6.79	.11	.45	12.03	.64	.56	10.75	.12	—	8.31
9.35	.302	.054	7.76	.324	.107	6.49	.36	.037	8.09	.28	.47	9.28	.27	.42	9.52	.31	.18	7.17
8.46	.25	—	8.00	.40	—	7.35	.24	.445	9.35	.162	.628	11.15	.184	.303	10.14	.26	.04	7.42
7.44	.134	—	6.73	.31	—	5.74	.17	—	6.83	.03	.435	9.37	.038	—	8.03	.14	—	5.56
13.11	.14	—	12.99	.21	—	12.12	.16	.25	17.02	.022	1.757	15.57	.173	1.21	14.11	.25	—	11.77
23.46	.46	—	22.09	.47	—	20.82	.48	—	27.57	.80	.95	38.67	.97	—	34.96	.98	—	25.52
9.61	.31	—	8.77	.30	—	7.96	.23	—	10.11	.22	.18	11.44	.23	.14	10.73	.23	—	7.40
15.06	.63	—	13.91	.59	—	12.77	.56	—	16.03	.54	.26	16.74	.59	.13	15.67	.59	—	12.10
3.91	.07	—	3.46	.07	.04	2.81	.05	—	3.11	.04	—	4.50	.02	—	3.86	.04	—	2.38
6.83	.40	—	5.98	.50	—	5.27	.40	.20	6.53	.40	.35	8.03	.42	.33	8.19	.45	.30	6.37
7.02	.18	—	6.63	.18	—	6.20	.305	.055	7.77	.26	.51	9.89	.18	.33	10.03	.24	—	7.71
3.84	.055	.045	4.07	.06	—	3.85	.07	—	5.39	.05	.29	8.32	.055	.61	8.73	.10	—	5.78
7.47	.45	.20	7.21	.49	—	6.73	.43	.34	7.86	.39	.34	8.55	.35	.52	8.88	.39	—	7.60
12.13	.565	.30	11.10	.625	.12	9.51	.53	.39	10.95	.44	.38	12.12	.41	.62	13.04	.49	.20	10.51
12.45	.30	—	10.12	.38	—	7.55	.29	.799	9.05	.25	.63	12.01	.15	—	11.11	.26	.63	—
7.48	.08	—	6.62	.36	—	6.09	.37	—	6.78	.36	.32	9.14	.36	—	9.46	.336	—	6.60
3.12	—	—	3.42	—	—	2.43	—	—	2.19	—	—	3.31	.032	.014	3.37	—	—	2.24
8.12	.277	—	7.19	.098	—	5.50	.057	.048	7.09	.037	.323	10.97	.044	.296	10.05	.082	—	6.32
10.59	.327	.078	9.55	.379	—	8.12	.325	.28	10.10	.253	.702	12.12	.255	.595	11.64	.06	.445	8.76
8.12	.486	—	7.08	.461	—	6.47	.459	.156	7.83	.40	.385	9.42	.365	.28	9.15	.43	.18	7.26
4.87	—	—	4.29	—	—	3.15	—	.085	4.11	—	.168	6.67	.56	.01	4.90	.018	—	3.56
12.22	.48	.07	10.72	.46	.06	9.30	.42	.25	10.93	.38	.78	12.95	.40	.77	13.60	.50	.56	11.41
18.40	.56	—	18.07	.58	—	15.68	.51	.89	20.71	.42	.99	23.95	.44	.56	20.72	.53	—	15.09
8.27	.17	—	8.03	.14	—	7.38	.11	.24	9.78	.05	.36	11.71	.06	.10	10.00	.10	—	6.42
13.10	.28	—	12.80	.30	—	10.82	.23	.70	14.61	.14	.75	17.33	.16	.42	14.70	.22	—	10.17
2.52	.23	—	—	—	—	—	—	—	—	—	—	—	—	—	—	—	—	—
9.21	.15	.15	9.02	.18	.10	7.82	.21	—	9.45	.126	.10	14.39	.20	.46	13.91	.29	.24	10.01
7.59	.19	—	6.55	.18	—	5.44	.15	—	5.93	.12	.36	7.92	.18	.30	7.87	.20	.10	5.66
3.36	.04	.037	2.80	.048	.01	2.48	.038	.05	2.84	.02	.265	2.44	.023	.05	1.74	.025	.03	1.51
3.76	—	—	2.87	—	—	2.14	—	—	2.12	—	—	3.57	—	—	2.09	.026	—	1.64
12.57	.83	.29	11.41	.84	—	10.40	.55	.28	12.28	.43	1.12	15.17	.40	.37	13.35	.40	.36	10.48
6.51	.18	—	6.23	.16	—	5.53	.13	.05	6.93	.16	.20	8.18	.13	.19	7.66	.19	—	5.31
10.71	.40	.36	10.56	.42	.52	9.94	.40	.62	13.21	.37	.68	14.81	.36	.59	14.17	.47	.39	10.46
6.21	.10	—	6.19	.13	—	5.45	.11	—	6.63	.14	.16	8.48	.16	.11	8.07	.18	—	6.07
1.80	.195	—	4.62	—	—	4.88	—	—	6.41	—	—	13.17	—	—	10.28	—	—	7.92
6.93	.16	—	5.92	.135	—	4.55	.08	—	4.84	.08	—	6.77	.04	—	7.04	.075	—	4.80
4.85	.28	—	4.27	.28	—	3.60	.28	.02	4.32	.28	.07	4.99	.28	.05	5.26	.30	—	3.98
8.24	—	—	6.95	—	—	4.48	—	—	5.91	.14	—	10.48	—	—	—	—	—	—
3.98	.03	—	3.17	.025	—	2.39	—	—	2.93	—	—	5.56	—	—	5.81	.02	—	3.86
7.03	.325	—	6.42	.325	—	5.70	.315	.30	6.97	.315	.50	8.18	.315	.28	8.40	.17	.25	6.20
6.32	.13	—	6.20	.18	.21	5.78	.12	.67	7.02	.09	1.50	9.85	.125	.45	8.22	.315	.20	6.70
7.15	.08	—	6.65	.14	—	5.50	.13	—	6.63	.055	.31	10.27	.047	1.31	9.40	.065	—	5.19
6.20	.10	—	5.91	.18	—	5.46	.10	.65	7.17	—	.90	9.68	.17	1.00	8.83	.41	2.13	9.16
6.92	.305	.18	5.93	.305	.02	4.88	.275	.04	5.34	.245	.11	6.06	.245	.17	6.44	.245	.07	4.78
10.41	.05	—	10.73	—	—	8.18	—	—	10.28	—	1.38	15.13	—	—	11.59	.06	—	7.26
10.10	.48	.25	9.51	.50	.25	8.92	.47	.25	10.81	.44	.25	11.78	.44	—	11.63	.445	.25	9.45
9.84	.34	—	7.93	.31	—	6.02	.32	.14	7.12	.19	.53	9.12	.30	.54	9.96	.25	—	7.59
5.40	.16	—	5.05	.22	.10	4.68	.19	.04	5.38	.18	.26	6.69	.16	.435	6.69	.25	.24	5.61

50 LEADING STOCKS IN MARKET VALUE (NYSE)

Company	Millions of Shares, Dec. 31, 1979	
	Listed Shares	Market Value
Int'l Business Machines	583.9	$ 37,734
American Tel. & Tel.	700.8	36,529
Exxon Corp.	453.2	24,983
General Motors	291.4	14,605
Schlumberger, N.V.	133.6	12,524
Standard Oil Co. (Indiana)	152.2	12,002
General Electric	231.5	11,747
Mobil Corp.	212.2	11,726
Standard Oil of Calif.	171.0	9,638
Atlantic Richfield	114.6	9,208
Shell Oil	154.4	8,376
Texaco Inc.	274.3	7,920
Eastman Kodak	161.6	7,796
Phillips Petroleum	154.4	7,414
Gulf Oil	211.9	7,311
Getty Oil	88.5	6,529
Dow Chemical	200.4	6,436
Procter & Gamble	82.7	6,140
Minnesota Mining & Mfg.	118.0	5,944
du Pont de Nemours	145.8	5,886
Sears, Roebuck	324.6	5,844
Merck & Co.	75.9	5,501
Conoco	113.3	5,353
Standard Oil (Ohio)	60.3	5,327
Xerox Corp.	82.1	5,098
Halliburton Co.	58.9	5,009
Johnson & Johnson	61.3	4,857
Caterpillar Tractor	86.4	4,667
American Home Products	168.3	4,585
Morris (Philip) Inc.	124.5	4,484
Eli Lilly	73.3	4,380
Teledyne, Inc.	32.3	4,325
Coca-Cola Co.	124.0	4,292
Sun Company, Inc.	60.0	4,194
Tenneco Inc.	106.1	4,110
Weyerhaeuser Co.	128.6	4,084
General Tel. & Electronics	144.5	4,081
BankAmerica Corp.	147.5	4,074
Union Oil of California	86.6	3,877
SmithKline Corp.	60.9	3,827
Hewlett-Packard Co.	59.2	3,500
Reynolds (R.J.) Inds.	101.5	3,478
Union Pacific	47.7	3,449
Ford Motor	106.2	3,398
Superior Oil	25.5	3,366
Boeing Co.	65.1	3,294
Burroughs Corp.	41.1	3,223
Marathon Oil	61.4	3,072
Citicorp	128.6	3,038
International Tel. & Tel.	115.9	2,971
Total	7,508.0	$375,206

Source: New York Stock Exchange, *Fact Book*, 1980.

WHAT IS IN A 10K AND OTHER SEC REPORTS

PART I OF 10K

1. **Business.** Identifies principal products and services of the company, principal markets and methods of distribution and, if "material," competitive factors, backlog and expectation of fulfillment, availability of raw materials, importance of patents, licenses, and franchises, estimated cost of research, number of employees, and effects of compliance with ecological laws; if there is more than one line of business, for each of the last five fiscal years a statement of total sales and net income for each line which, during either of the last two fiscal years, accounted for 10 percent or more of total sales or pretax income.

2. **Summary of operations.** Summary of operations for each of the last five fiscal years and any additional years required to keep the summary from being misleading (per share earnings and dividends are included). Includes explanatory material describing reasons for changes in revenues, earnings, etc.

3. **Properties.** Location and character of principal plants, mines, and other important properties and if held in fee or leased.

4. **Parents and subsidiaries.** List or diagram of all parents and subsidiaries and for each named, the percentage of voting securities owned, or other basis of control.

5. **Legal proceedings.** Brief description of material legal proceedings pending; when civil rights statutes are involved, proceedings must be disclosed.

6. **Increases and decreases in outstanding securities.** Information for each security, including reacquired securities, new issues, securities issued in exchange for property, services or other securities, and new securities resulting from modification of outstanding securities.

7. **Approximate number of equity security holders.** Holders of record for each class of equity securities as of the end of the fiscal year.

Source: *The National Investment Library*, New York.

8. **Executive officers of the registrant.** List of all executive officers, nature of family relationship between them, positions and offices held.

9. **Indemnification of directors and officers.** General effect under which any director or officer is insured or indemnified against any liability which he may incur in his capacity as such.

10. **Financial statements and exhibits filed.** Complete, audited annual financial information, and a list of exhibits filed.

PART II OF 10K

11. **Principal security holders and security holdings of management.** Identification of owners of 10 percent or more of any class of securities and of securities held by directors and officers according to amount and percent of each class.

12. **Directors of the registrant.** Name, office, term of office, and specific background data on each.

13. **Remuneration of directors and officers.** List of each director and three highest paid officers with aggregate annual remuneration exceeding $40,000—and total paid all officers and directors.

14. **Options granted to management to purchase securities.** Options granted to or exercised by directors and officers since the beginning of the fiscal year.

15. **Interest of management and others in certain transactions.** Material changes in significant transactions of such things as assets, pension, retirement, savings or other similar plans, or unusual loans.

SCHEDULES TO 10K

I. Marketable securities. Other security investments.

II. Amounts due from directors, officers, and principal holders of equity securities other than affiliates.

III. Investments in securities of affiliates.

IV. Indebtedness of affiliates (not current).

V. Property, plant, and equipment.

VI. Reserves for depreciation, depletion, and amortization of property, plant, and equipment.

VII. Intangible assets.

VIII. Reserves for depreciation and amortization of intangible assets.

IX. Bonds, mortgages, and similar debt.

X. Indebtedness to affiliates (not current).

XI. Guarantees of securities of other issuers.

XII. Reserves.

XIII. Capital shares.

XIV. Warrants or rights.

XV. Other securities.

XVI. Supplementary profit and loss information.

XVII. Income from dividends (equity in net profit and loss of affiliates).

OTHER REPORTS

12-K. The 12-K annual report is filed with the SEC by certain companies which are regulated by, and file reports with, the Federal Power Commission, Interstate Commerce Commission, and Federal Communications Commission. It is similar in content to the 10-K.

10-Q. This is the quarterly financial report filed by most companies, which, although unaudited, provides a continuing view of a company's financial position during the year. It must be filed within 45 days of the close of a fiscal quarter.

8-K. This is a report of unscheduled material events or corporate changes deemed of importance to shareholders or to the SEC—changes in control of the registrant; acquisition or disposition of assets; legal proceedings; changes in securities (i.e., collateral for registered securities); defaults upon senior securities; increase or decrease in the amount of securities outstanding; options to purchase securities; revaluation of assets; submission of matters to a vote of security holders; and any newly enacted requirements affecting the company's business.

Proxy statement. Provides official notification to stockholders of matters to be brought to a vote at shareholders meeting.

Registration statement. Discloses fully, all financial and relevant facts on a company, needed by investors to evaluate proposed sale of securities. Very detailed.

TAX-FREE VERSUS TAXABLE INVESTMENTS

YOUR TOTAL TAX BRACKET* IS		3.00	3.50	4.00	4.25	4.50	4.75	5.00	5.25	5.50	5.75	6.00	6.25	6.50	6.75	7.00
								AFTER - TAX YIELDS								
27%	T	4.11	4.80	5.48	5.82	6.17	6.51	6.85	7.19	7.54	7.88	8.22	8.56	8.91	9.25	9.59
31%	A	4.35	5.07	5.80	6.16	6.53	6.89	7.25	7.61	7.98	8.34	8.70	9.06	9.43	9.79	10.15
36%	X	4.69	5.47	6.24	6.63	7.02	7.41	7.80	8.19	8.58	8.97	9.36	9.75	10.14	10.53	10.92
40%	A	5.00	5.83	6.68	7.10	7.52	7.93	8.35	8.77	9.19	9.60	10.02	10.44	10.86	11.27	11.69
45%	B	5.45	6.36	7.28	7.74	8.19	8.65	9.10	9.56	10.01	10.47	10.92	11.38	11.83	12.29	12.74
48%	L	5.77	6.73	7.68	8.16	8.64	9.12	9.60	10.08	10.56	11.04	11.52	12.00	12.48	12.96	13.44
50%	E	6.00	7.00	8.00	8.50	9.00	9.50	10.00	10.50	11.00	11.50	12.00	12.50	13.00	13.50	14.00
52%	EQUIV-ALENT	6.25	7.29	8.32	8.84	9.36	9.88	10.40	10.92	11.44	11.96	12.48	13.00	13.52	14.04	14.56
55%	YIELDS	6.67	7.78	8.88	9.44	9.99	10.55	11.10	11.66	12.21	12.77	13.32	13.88	14.43	14.99	15.54
57%		6.98	8.14	9.32	9.90	10.49	11.07	11.65	12.23	12.82	13.40	13.98	14.56	15.15	15.73	16.31
60%		7.50	8.75	10.00	10.63	11.25	11.88	12.50	13.13	13.75	14.38	15.00	15.63	16.25	16.88	17.50
61%		7.69	8.97	10.24	10.88	11.52	12.16	12.80	13.44	14.08	14.72	15.36	16.00	16.64	17.28	17.92
67%		9.09	10.61	12.12	12.88	13.64	14.39	15.15	15.91	16.66	17.42	18.18	18.94	19.70	20.45	21.21

This table gives the approximate yields which taxable securities must earn in various income brackets to produce after-tax yields equal to those on tax-free bonds yielding from 3.00% to 7.00%. This table is computed on the theory that the taxpayer's highest rate is applicable to the entire amount of any increase or decrease in his taxable income resulting from a switching from taxable to tax-free securities or vice versa.

* Federal and state income tax.

INVESTMENT AND FINANCIAL TERMS*†

Abandonment value The amount that can be realized by liquidating a project before its economic life has ended.*

Accelerated depreciation Depreciation methods that write off the cost of an asset at a faster rate than the write-off under the straight-line method. The three principal methods of accelerated depreciation are: (1) sum-of-the-years'-digits, (2) double-declining balance, and (3) units-of-production.*

Accruals Continuing recurring short-term liabilities. Examples are accrued wages, accrued taxes, and accrued interest.

Accrued interest Interest accrued on a bond since the last interest payment was made. The buyer of the bond pays the market price plus accrued interest. Exceptions include bonds that are in default and income bonds. (See: *Flat income bond*.)†

Aging schedule A report showing how long accounts receivable have been outstanding. It gives the percent of receivables not past due and the percent past due by, for example, one month, two months, or other periods.*

Amortization Accounting for expenses or charges as applicable rather than as paid. Includes such practices as depreciation, depletion, write-off of intangibles, prepaid expenses, and deferred charges.†

Amortize To liquidate on an installment basis; an amortized loan is one in which the principal amount of the loan is repaid in installments during the life of the loan.*

Annual report The formal financial statement issued yearly by a corporation. The annual report shows assets, liabilities, earnings—how the company stood at the close of the business year, how it fared profit-wise during the year and other information of interest to shareowners.†

Annuity A series of payments of a fixed amount for a specified number of years.*

Arbitrage The process of selling overvalued and buying undervalued assets so as to bring

about an equilibrium where all assets are properly valued. One who engages in arbitrage is called an arbitrager.*

Arrearage Overdue payment; frequently omitted dividend on preferred stock.

Assets Everything a corporation owns or due to it: Cash, investments, money due it, materials and inventories, which are called current assets; buildings and machinery, which are known as fixed assets; and patents and good will, called intangible assets. (See: Liabilities)†

Assignment A relatively inexpensive way of liquidating a failing firm that does not involve going through the courts.*

Auction market The system of trading securities through brokers or agents on an exchange such as the New York Stock Exchange. Buyers compete with other buyers while sellers compete with other sellers for the most advantageous price. Most transactions are executed with public customers on both sides since the specialist buys or sells for his own account primarily to offset imbalances in public supply and demand. (See: *Dealers, Quotation, Specialist*.)†

Averages Various ways of measuring the trend of securities prices, one of the most popular of which is the Dow-Jones average of 30 industrial stocks listed on the New York Stock Exchange.

Formulas—some very elaborate—have been devised to compensate for stock splits and stock dividends and thus give continuity to the average.

In the case of the Dow-Jones industrial average, the prices of the 30 stocks are totaled and then divided by a divisor which is intended to compensate for past stock splits and stock dividends and which is changed from time to time. As a result point changes in the average have only the vaguest relationship to dollar price changes in stocks included in the average. Currently, the divisor is 1.465. (See: *NYSE common stock index, Point, Split*.)†

Balance sheet A condensed financial statement showing the nature and amount of a company's assets, liabilities and capital on a given date. In dollar amounts the balance sheet shows what the company owned, what it owed, and the ownership interest in the company of its stockholders. (See: *Assets, Earnings report*.)†

Balloon payment When a debt is not fully amortized, the final payment is larger than the preceding payments and is called a *balloon* payment.*

Bankruptcy A legal procedure for formally liquidating a business, carried out under the jurisdiction of courts of law.*

Bear market A declining market. (See: *Bull market*.)†

Bearer bond A bond which does not have the

---

* Entries from *Managerial Finance*, 6th edition, by J. Fred Weston and Eugene F. Brigham.

† Entries from *The Language of Investing Glossary*.

Sources: From *Managerial Finance*, 6th ed., by J. Fred Weston and Eugene F. Brigham. Copyright © 1978 by the Dryden Press, a division of Holt, Rinehart & Winston. Copyright © 1962, 1966, 1969, 1972, 1975 by Holt, Rinehart & Winston. Reprinted by permission of Holt, Rinehart, & Winston.

The *Language of Investing Glossary* published by The New York Stock Exchange, Inc.

owner's name registered on the books of the issuer and which is payable to the holder. (See: *Coupon bond, Registered bond.*)†

Beta coefficient Measures the extent to which the returns on a given stock move with "the stock market."°

Bid and asked Often referred to as a quotation or quote. The bid is the highest price anyone has declared that he wants to pay for a security at a given time, the asked is the lowest price anyone will take at the same time. (See *Quotation.*)†

Block A large holding or transaction of stock —popularly considered to be 10,000 shares or more.†

Blue chip A company known nationally for the quality and wide acceptance of its products or services, and for its ability to make money and pay dividends.†

Blue-sky laws A popular name for laws various states have enacted to protect the public against securities frauds. The term is believed to have originated when a judge ruled that a particular stock had about the same value as a patch of blue sky.†

Board room A room for registered representatives and customers in a broker's office where opening, high, low, and last prices of leading stocks used to be posted on a board throughout the market day. Today such price displays are normally electronically controlled although most board rooms have replaced the board with the ticker and/or individual quotation machines.†

Bond A long-term debt instrument.°

Book A notebook the specialist in a stock uses to keep a record of the buy and sell orders at specified prices, in sequence of receipt, which are left with him by other brokers. (See *Specialist.*)†

Book value The accounting value of an asset. The book value of a share of common stock is equal to the net worth (common stock plus retained earnings) of the corporation divided by the number of shares of stock outstanding.°

Break-even analysis An analytical technique for studying the relation between fixed cost, variable cost, and profits. A break-even *chart* graphically depicts the nature of break-even analysis. The break-even *point* represents the volume of sales at which total costs equal total revenues (that is, profits equal zero).°

Broker An agent, who handles the public's orders to buy and sell securities, commodities, or other property. For this service a commission is charged. (See: *Commission broker, dealer.*)†

Brokers' loans Money borrowed by brokers from banks or other brokers for a variety of uses. It may be used by specialists and to help finance inventories of stock they deal in; by brokerage firms to finance the underwriting of new issues of corporate and municipal securities; to help finance a firm's own investments; and to help finance the purchase of securities for customers who prefer to use the broker's credit when they buy securities. (See: *Margin.*)†

Bull market An advancing market. (See: *Bear market.*)†

Business risk The basic risk inherent in a firm's operations. Business risk plus financial risk resulting from the use of debt equals total corporate risk.°

Call (1) An option to buy (or "call") a share of stock at a specified price within a specified period. (2) The process of redeeming a bond or preferred stock issue before its normal maturity.°

Call premium The amount in excess of par value that a company must pay when it calls a security.°

Call price The price that must be paid when a security is called. The call price is equal to the par value plus the call premium.°

Call privilege A provision incorporated into a bond or a share of preferred stock that gives the issuer the right to redeem (call) the security at a specified price.°

Callable A bond issue, all or part of which may be redeemed by the issuing corporation under definite conditions before maturity. The term also applies to preferred shares which may be redeemed by the issuing corporation.†

Capital asset An asset with a life of more than one year that is not bought and sold in the ordinary course of business.°

Capital budgeting The process of planning expenditures on assets whose returns are expected to extend beyond one year.°

Capital gain or capital loss Profit or loss from the sale of a capital asset. A capital gain, under current federal income tax laws, may be either short-term (12 months or less) or long-term (more than 12 months). A short-term capital gain is taxed at the reporting individuals's full income tax rate. A long-term capital gain is subject to a lower tax. The capital gains provisions of the tax law are complicated. You should consult your tax advisor for specific information.†

Capital market line A graphical representation of the relationship between risk and the required rate of return on an efficient portfolio.°

Capital markets Financial transactions involving instruments with maturities greater than one year.°

Capital rationing A situation where a constraint is placed on the total size of the capital investment during a particular period.°

Capital stock All shares representing ownership of a business, including preferred and common. (See: *Common stock, Preferred stock.*)†

Capital structure   The permanent long-term financing of the firm represented by long-term debt, preferred stock, and net worth (net worth consists of capital, capital surplus, and retained earnings). Capital structure is distinguished from *financial structure*, which includes short-term debt plus all reserve accounts.°

Capitalization   Total amount of the various securities issued by a corporation. Capitalization may include bonds, debentures, preferred and common stock, and surplus. Bonds and debentures are usually carried on the books of the issuing company in terms of their par or face value. Preferred and common shares may be carried in terms of par or stated value. Stated value may be an arbitrary figure decided upon by the directors or may represent the amount received by the company from the sale of the securities at the time of issuance. (See: *Par.*)†

Capitalization rate   A discount rate used to find the present value of a series of future cash receipts; sometimes called *discount rate.*°

Carry-back; carry forward   For income tax purposes, losses than can be carried backward or forward to reduce federal income taxes.°

Cash budget   A schedule showing cash flows (receipts, disbursements, and net cash) for a firm over a specified period.°

Cash cycle   The length of time between the purchase of raw materials and the collection of accounts receivable generated in the sale of the final product.°

Cash flow   Reported net income of a corporation *plus* amounts charged off for depreciation, depletion, amortization, extraordinary charges to reserves, which are bookkeeping deductions and not paid out in actual dollars and cents. (See: *Amortization, Depletion, Depreciation.*)†

Cash sale   A transaction on the floor of the Stock Exchange which calls for delivery of the securities the same day. In "regular way" trades, the seller is to deliver on the fifth business day except for bonds, which is the next day. (See: *Regular way delivery.*)†

Certainty equivalents   The amount of cash (or rate of return) that someone would require *with certainty* to make him indifferent between this certain sum (or *rate of return*) and a particular uncertain, risky sum (or rate of return).°

Certificate   The actual piece of paper which is evidence of ownership of stock in a corporation. Watermarked paper is finely engraved with delicate etchings to discourage forgery. Loss of a certificate may at the least cause a great deal of inconvenience—at the worst, financial loss.†

Characteristic line   A linear least-squares regression line that shows the relationship between an individual security's return and returns on "the market." The slope of the characteristic line is the beta coefficient.°

Chattel mortgage   A mortgage on personal property (not real estate). A mortgage on equipment would be a chattel mortgage.°

Closed-end investment company   (See: *Investment company*).

Coefficient of variation   Standard deviation divided by the mean: CV.°

Collateral   Assets that are used to secure a loan.°

Collateral trust bond   A bond secured by collateral deposited with a trustee. The collateral is often the stocks or bonds of companies controlled by the issuing company but may be other securities.†

Commercial paper   Unsecured, short-term promissory notes of large firms, usually issued in denominations of $1 million or more. The rate of interest on commercial paper is typically somewhat below the prime rate of interest.°

Commission   The broker's basic fee for purchasing or selling securities or property as an agent.†

Commission broker   An agent who executes the public's orders for the purchase or sale of securities or commodities.†

Commitment fee   The fee paid to a lender for a formal line of credit.°

Common stock   Securities which represent an ownership interest in a corporation. If the company has also issued preferred stock, both common and preferred have ownership rights. The preferred normally is limited to a fixed dividend but has prior claim on dividends and, in the event of liquidation, assets. Claims of both common and preferred stockholders are junior to claims of bondholders or other creditors of the company. Common stockholders assume the greater risk, but generally exercise the greater control and may gain the greater reward in the form of dividends and capital appreciation. The terms common stock and capital stock are often used interchangeably when the company has no preferred stock.†

Compensating balance   A required minimum checking account balance that a firm must maintain with a commercial bank. The required balance is generally equal to 15 to 20 percent of the amount of loans outstanding. Compensating balances can raise the effective rate of interest on bank loans.°

Competitive trader   A member of the Exchange who trades in stocks on the Floor for an account in which he has an interest. Also known as a Registered Trader.†

Composite cost of capital   A weighted average

of the component costs of debt, preferred stock, and common equity. Also called the *weighted-average cost of capital,* but it reflects the cost of each additional dollar raised, not the average cost of all capital the firm has raised throughout its history.°

Composition An informal method of reorganization that voluntarily reduces creditors' claims on the debtor firm.°

Compound interest An interest rate that is applicable when interest in succeeding periods is earned not only on the initial principal but also on the accumulated interest of prior periods. Compound interest is contrasted to *simple interest,* in which returns are not earned on interest received.°

Compounding The arithmetic process of determining the final value of a payment or series of payments when compound interest is applied.°

Conditional sales contract A method of financing new equipment by paying it off in installments over a one-to-five-year period. The seller retains title to the equipment until payment has been completed.°

Conglomerate A corporation that has diversified its operations, usually by acquiring enterprises in widely varied industries.†

Consolidated balance sheet A balance sheet showing the financial condition of a corporation and its subsidiaries. (See: *Balance sheet.*)†

Consolidated tape Under the Consolidated Tape Plan, the NYSE and AMEX ticker systems became the "Consolidated Tape", Network A and Network B respectively, on June 16, 1975. Network A reports transactions in NYSE listed securities that take place on the NYSE or any of the participating regional stock exchanges and other markets. Each transaction is identified according to its originating market. Similarly, transactions in AMEX-listed securities, and certain other securities listed on regional stock exchanges, are reported and identified on Network B.†

Consolidated tax return An income tax return that combines the income statement of several affiliated firms.°

Continuous compounding (discounting) As opposed to discrete compounding, interest is added continuously rather than at discrete points in time°

Conversion price The effective price paid for common stock when the stock is obtained by converting either convertible preferred stocks or convertible bonds. For example, if a $1,000 bond is convertible into 20 shares of stock, the conversion price is $50 ($1,000/20).°

Conversion ratio or conversion rate The number of shares of common stock that may be obtained by converting a convertible bond or share of convertible preferred stock.°

Convertibles Securities (generally bonds or preferred stocks) that are exchangeable at the option of the holder for common stock of the issuing firm.°

Correlation coefficient Measures the degree of relationship between two variables.°

Correspondent A securities firm, bank, or other financial organization which regularly performs services for another in a place or market to which the other does not have direct access. Securities firms may have correspondents in foreign countries or on exchanges of which they are not members. Correspondents are frequently linked by private wires. Member organizations of the N.Y.S.E. with offices in New York City may also act as correspondents for out-of-town member organizations which do not maintain New York City offices.†

Cost of capital The discount rate that should be used in the capital budgeting process.°

Coupon bond Bond with interest coupons attached. The coupons are clipped as they come due and are presented by the holder for payment of interest. (See: *Bearer bond, Registered bond.*)†

Coupon rate The stated rate of interest on a bond.°

Covariance The correlation between two variables multiplied by the standard deviation of each variable:

$$\text{Cov} = r_{xy}\sigma_x\sigma_y.°$$

Covenant Detailed clauses contained in loan agreements. Covenants are designed to protect the lender and include such items as limits on total indebtedness, restrictions on dividends, minimum current ratio, and similar provisions.°

Covering Buying a security previously sold short. (See: *Short sale, Short covering.*)†

Cumulative dividends A protective feature on preferred stock that requires all past preferred dividends to be paid before any common dividends are paid.°

Cumulative preferred A stock having a provision that if one or more dividends are omitted, the omitted dividends must be paid before dividends may be paid on the company's common stock.†

Cumulative voting A method of voting for corporate directors which enables the shareholder to multiply the number of his shares by the number of directorships being voted on and cast the total for one director or a selected group of directors. A 10-share holder normally casts 10 votes for each of, say 12 nominees to the board of directors. He thus has 120 votes. Under the cumulative voting principle he may do that or he may cast 120 (10×12) votes for only one nominee, 60 for two, 40 for three, or any other distribution he chooses. Cumulative voting is required under the corporate laws of some states, is permitted in most others.†

Curb exchange Former name of the American Stock Exchange, second largest exchange in the country. The term comes from the market's origin on a street in downtown New York.†

Current assets Those assets of a company which are reasonably expected to be realized in cash, or sold, or consumed during the normal operating cycle of the business. These include cash, U.S. government bonds, receivables and money due usually within one year, and inventories.†

Current liabilities Money owed and payable by a company, usually within one year.†

Current return (See: *Yield.*)

Cut-off point In the capital budgeting process, the minimum rate of return on acceptable investment opportunities.*

Day order An order to buy or sell which, if not executed expires at the end of the trading day on which it was entered.†

Dealer An individual or firm in the securities business acting as a principal rather than as an agent. Typically, a dealer buys for his own account and sells to a customer from his own inventory. The dealer's profit or loss is the difference between the price he pays and the price he receives for the same security. The dealer's confirmation must disclose to his customer that he has acted as principal. The same individual or firm may function, at different times, either as broker or dealer. (See: *NASD, Specialist.*)†

Debenture A long-term debt instrument that is not secured by a mortgage on specific property.*

Debit balance In a customer's margin account that portion of purchase price of stock, bonds, or commodities covered by credit extended by the broker to the margin customer.†

Debt ratio Total debt divided by total assets.*

Decision tree A device for setting forth graphically the pattern of relationship between decisions and chance events.*

Default The failure to fulfill a contract. Generally, default refers to the failure to pay interest or principal on debt obligations.*

Degree of leverage The percentage increase in profits resulting from a given percentage increase in sales. The degree of leverage may be calculated for financial leverage, operating leverage, or both combined.*

Depletion accounting Natural resources, such as metals, oil and gas, and timber, which conceivably can be reduced to zero over the years, present a special problem in capital manage-

ment. Depletion is an accounting practice consisting of charges against earnings based upon the amount of the asset taken out of the total reserves in the period for which accounting is made. A bookkeeping entry, it does not represent any cash outlay nor are any funds earmarked for the purpose.†

Depository trust company (DTC) A central securities certificate depository through which members effect security deliveries between each other via computerized bookkeeping entries thereby reducing the physical movement of stock certificates.†

Depreciation Normally, charges against earnings to write off the cost, less salvage value, of an asset over its estimated useful life. It is a bookkeeping entry and does not represent any cash outlay nor are any funds earmarked for the purpose.†

Devaluation The process of reducing the value of a country's currency stated in terms of other currencies; for example, the British pound might be devalued from $2.30 for one pound to $2.00 for one pound*

Director Person elected by shareholders to establish company policies. The directors appoint the president, vice presidents, and all other operating officers. Directors decide, among other matters, if and when dividends shall be paid. (See: *Management, Proxy.*)†

Discount The amount by which a preferred stock or bond may sell below its par value. Also used as a verb to mean "takes into account" as the price of the stock has discounted the expected dividend cut. (See: *Premium.*)†

Discount rate The interest rate used in the discounting process; sometimes called *capitalization rate.*

Discounted cash flow techniques Methods of ranking investment proposals. Included are (1) internal rate of return method, (2) net present value method, and (3) profitability index or benefit/cost ratio.*

Discounting The process of finding the present value of a series of future cash flows. Discounting is the reverse of compounding.*

Discounting of accounts receivable Short-term financing where accounts receivable are used to secure the loan. The lender does not *buy* the accounts receivable but simply uses them as collateral for the loan. Also called *assigning accounts receivable.*

Discretionary account An account in which the customer gives the broker or someone else discretion, which may be complete or within specific limits, either to the purchases, or sale of securities or commodities including selection, timing, amount, and price to be paid or received.†

Diversification Spreading investments among

different companies in different fields. Another type of diversification is also offered by the securities of many individual companies because of the wide range of their activities. (See: *Investment trust*.)†

Dividend The payment designated by the board of directors to be distributed pro rata among the shares outstanding. On preferred shares, it is generally a fixed amount. On common shares, the dividend varies with the fortunes of the company and the amount of cash on hand, and may be omitted if business is poor or the directors determine to withhold earnings to invest in plant and equipment. Sometimes a company will pay a dividend out of past earnings even if it is not currently operating at a profit.†

Dividend yield The ratio of the current dividend to the current price of a share of stock.*

Dollar cost averaging A system of buying securities at regular intervals with a fixed dollar amount. Under this system the investor buys by the dollars' worth rather than by the number of shares. If each investment is of the same number of dollars, payments buy more when the price is low and fewer when it rises. Thus temporary downswings in price benefit the investor if he continues periodic purchases in both good times and bad and the price at which the shares are sold is more than their average cost. (See: *Formula investing*.)†

Double taxation Short for *double taxation of dividends*. The federal government taxes corporate profits once as corporate income; any part of the remaining profits distributed as dividends to stockholders may be taxed again as income to the recipient stockholder.†

Dow theory A theory of market analysis based upon the performance of the Dow-Jones industrial and transportation stock price averages. The theory says that the market is in a basic upward trend if one of these averages advances above a previous important high, accompanied or followed by a similar advance in the other. When the averages both dip below previous important lows, this is regarded as confirmation of a basic downward trend. The theory does not attempt to predict how long either trend will continue, although it is widely misinterpreted as a method of forecasting future action.†

Down tick (See: *Up tick*.)

Du Pont system A system of analysis designed to show the relationship between return on investment, asset turnover, and the profit margin.*

Earnings report A statement—also called an *income statement*—issued by a company showing its earnings or losses over a given period. The earnings report lists the income earned, ex-

penses, and the net result. (See: *Balance sheet*.)†

EBIT Acronym for *earnings before interest and taxes*.*

Economical ordering quantity (EOQ) The optimum (least cost) quantity of merchandise which should be ordered.*

EPS Acronym for *earnings per share*.*

Equipment trust certificate A type of security, generally issued by a railroad, to pay for new equipment. Title to the equipment, such as a locomotive, is held by a trustee until the notes are paid off. An equipment trust certificate is usually secured by a first claim on the equipment.†

Equity The net worth of a business, consisting of capital stock, capital (or paid-in) surplus, earned surplus (or retained earnings), and occasionally, certain net worth reserves. *Common equity* is that part of the total net worth belonging to the common stockholders. *Total equity* would include preferred stockholders. The terms *common stock, net worth*, and *common equity* are frequently used interchangeably.†

Exchange acquisition A method of filling an order to buy a large block of stock on the floor of the exchange. Under certain circumstances, a member-broker can facilitate the purchase of a block by soliciting orders to sell. All orders to sell the security are lumped together and crossed with the buy order in the regular auction market. The price to the buyer may be on a net basis or on a commission basis.†

Exchange distribution A method of selling large blocks of stock on the floor of the exchange. Under certain circumstances, a member-broker can facilitate the sale of a block of stock by soliciting and getting other member-brokers to solicit orders to buy. Individual buy orders are lumped together and crossed with the sell order in the regular auction market. A special commission is usually paid by the seller; ordinarily the buyer pays no commission.†

Exchange rate The rate at which one currency can be exchanged for another; for example, $2.30 can be exchanged for one British pound.†

Excise tax A tax on the manufacture, sale, or consumption of specified commodities.*

Exdividend A synonym for "without dividend." The buyer of a stock selling exdividend does not receive the recently declared dividend. Every dividend is payable on a fixed date to all shareholders recorded on the books of the company as of a previous date of record. For example, a dividend may be declared as payable to holders of record on the books of the company on a given Friday. Since five business days are allowed for delivery of stock in a "regular way" transaction on the New York Stock Exchange, the exchange would declare the stock "exdividend" as of the opening of the market on the preceding Monday. That means anyone who bought it on and after Monday would not be entitled to that dividend. When stocks go ex-dividend, the stock tables include the symbol "x" following the name. (See: *Cash sale, Net change, Transfer.*)†

Ex-dividend date   The date on which the right to the current dividend no longer accompanies a stock. (For listed stock, the ex-dividend date is four working days prior to the date of record.)°

Exercise price   The price that must be paid for a share of common stock when it is bought by exercising a warrant.°

Expected return   The rate of return a firm expects to realize from an investment. The expected return is the mean value of the probability distribution of possible returns.°

Ex-rights   The date on which stock purchase rights are no longer transferred to the purchaser of the stock.°

Extension   An informal method of reorganization in which the creditors voluntarily postpone the date of required payment on past-due obligations.°

External funds   Funds acquired through borrowing or by selling new common or preferred stock.°

Extra   The short form of *extra dividend*. A dividend in the form of stock or cash in addition to the regular or usual dividend the company has been paying.†

Face value   The value of a bond that appears on the face of the bond, unless the value is otherwise specified by the issuing company. Face value is ordinarily the amount the issuing company promises to pay at maturity. Face value is not an indication of market value. Sometimes referred to as par value. (See: *Par.*)†

Factoring   A method of financing accounts receivable under which a firm sells its accounts receivable (generally without recourse) to a financial institution (the *factor*).°

Field warehousing   A method of financing inventories in which a "warehouse" is established at the place of business of the borrowing firm.°

Financial accounting standards board (FASB)   A private (nongovernment) agency which functions as an accounting standards-setting body.°

Financial intermediation   Financial transactions which bring savings surplus units together with savings deficit units so that savings can be redistributed into their most productive uses.°

Financial lease   A lease that does not provide for maintenance services, is not cancellable,

and is fully amortized over the life of the lease.°

Financial leverage   The ratio of total debt to total assets. There are other measures of financial leverage, especially ones that relate cash inflows to required cash outflows.°

Financial markets   Transactions in which the creation and transfer of financial assets and financial liabilities take place.°

Financial risk   That portion of total corporate risk, over and above basic business risk, that results from using debt.°

Financial structure   The entire right side of the balance sheet—the way in which a firm is financed.°

Fiscal year   A corporation's accounting year. Due to the nature of their particular business, some companies do not use the calendar year for their bookkeeping. A typical example is the department store which finds December 31 too early a date to close its books after the Christmas rush. For that reason many stores wind up their accounting year January 31. Their fiscal year, therefore, runs from February 1 of one year through January 31 of the next. The fiscal year of other companies may run from July 1 through the following June 30. Most companies, though, operate on a calendar year basis.†

Fisher effect   The increase in the nominal interest rates over real (purchasing power adjusted) interest rates reflecting anticipated inflation.°

Fixed charges   Costs that do not vary with the level of output, especially fixed financial costs such as interest, lease payments, and sinking fund payments.°

Flat income bond   This term means that the price at which a bond is traded includes consideration for all unpaid accruals of interest. Bonds which are in default of interest or principal are traded flat. Income bonds, which pay interest only to the extent earned are usually traded flat. All other bonds are usually dealt in "and interest," which means that the buyer pays to the seller the market price plus interest accrued since the last payment date.†

Float   The amount of funds tied up in checks that have been written but are still in process and have not yet been collected.°

Floating exchange rates   Exchange rates may be fixed by government policy (*pegged*) or allowed to *float* up or down in accordance with supply and demand. When market forces are allowed to function, exchange rates are said to be floating.°

Floor   The huge trading area–about two-thirds the size of a football field—where stocks and bonds are bought and sold on the New York Stock Exchange.†

Floor broker A member of the Stock Exchange who executes orders on the floor of the exchange to buy or sell any listed securities. (See: *Commission broker, Two-dollar broker.*)†

Flotation cost The cost of issuing new stocks or bonds.°

Formula investing An investment technique. One formula calls for the shifting of funds from common shares to preferred shares or bonds as the market, on average, rises above a certain predetermined point—and the return of funds to common share investments as the market average declines. (See: *Dollar cost averaging.*)†

Free and open market A market in which supply and demand are freely expressed in terms of price. Contrasts with a controlled market in which supply, demand, and price may all be regulated.†

Fundamental research Analysis of industries and companies based on factors such as sales, assets, earnings, products or services, markets, and management. As applied to the economy, fundamental research includes consideration of gross national product, interest rates, unemployment, inventories, savings, and so on. (See: *Technical research.*)†

Funded debt Usually long-term, interest-bearing bonds or debentures of a company. Could include long-term bank loans. Does *not* include short-term loans, preferred, or common stock.†

Funding The process of replacing short-term debt with long-term securities (stocks or bonds).°

General mortgage bond A bond which is secured by a blanket mortgage on the company's property, but which may be outranked by one or more other mortgages.†

General purchasing power reporting A proposal by the FASB that the current values of nonmonetary items in financial statements be adjusted by a general price index.°

Gilt-edged High-grade bond issued by a company which has demonstrated its ability to earn a comfortable profit over a period of years and pay its bondholders their interest without interruption.†

Give up A term with many different meanings. For one, a member of the exchange on the floor may act for a second member by executing an order for him with a third member. The first member tells the third member that he is acting on behalf of the second member and "gives up" the second member's name rather than his own. For another, if you have an account with Doe & Company but you're in a town where Doe has no office, you go to another member firm, tell them you have an account with Doe & Company and would like to buy some stock. After verifying your account with Doe & Company, the firm may execute your order and tell the broker who sells the stock that the firm is acting on behalf of Doe & Company. They give up the name of Doe & Company to the selling broker. Or the firm may simply wire your order to Doe & Company who will execute it for you.†

Good delivery Certain basic qualifications must be met before a security sold on the exchange may be delivered. The security must be in proper form to comply with the contract of sale and to transfer title to the purchaser.†

Good 'til cancelled order (GTC) or open order An order to buy or sell which remains in effect until it is either executed or cancelled.†

Goodwill Intangible assets of a firm established by the excess of the price paid for the going concern over its book value.°

Government bonds Obligations of the U.S. government, regarded as the highest grade issues in existence.†

Growth stock Stock of a company with a record of growth in earnings at a relatively rapid rate.†

Guaranteed bond A bond which has interest or principal, or both, guaranteed by a company other than the issuer. Usually found in the railroad industry when large roads, leasing sections of trackage owned by small railroads, may guarantee the bonds of the smaller road.†

Guaranteed stock Usually preferred stock on which dividends are guaranteed by another company; under much the same circumstances as a bond is guaranteed.†

Hedge (See: *Arbitrage, Puts & Calls, Short sale*).†

Holding company A corporation which owns the securities of another, in most cases with voting control.†

Hurdle rate In capital budgeting, the minimum acceptable rate of return on a project. If the expected rate of return is below the hurdle rate, the project is not accepted. The hurdle rate should be the marginal cost of capital.°

Hypothecation The pledging of securities as collateral—for example, to secure the debit balance in a margin account.†

Improper accumulation Earnings retained by a business for the purpose of enabling stockholders to avoid personal income taxes.°

Inactive stock An issue traded on an exchange or in the over-the-counter market in which there is a relatively low volume of transactions. Volume may be no more than a few hundred shares a week or even less. On the New York Stock Exchange many inactive stocks are traded in 10-share units rather than the customary 100. (See: *Round lot.*)†

In-and-out Purchase and sale of the same security within a short period—a day, a week, even a month. An in-and-out trader is generally more interested in day-to-day price fluctuations than dividends or long-term growth.†

Income bond Generally income bonds promise to repay principal but to pay interest only when earned. In some cases unpaid interest on an income bond may accumulate as a claim against the corporation when the bond becomes due. An income bond may also be issued in lieu of preferred stock.†

Incremental cash flow Net cash flow attributable to an investment project.*

Incremental cost of capital The average cost of the increment of capital raised during a given year.*

Indenture A written agreement under which bonds and debentures are issued, setting forth maturity date, interest rate, and other terms.†

Independent broker Members on the floor of the NYSE who execute orders for other brokers having more business at that time than they can handle themselves, or for firms who do not have their exchange member on the floor. Formerly known as *two-dollar brokers* from the time when these independent brokers received $2 per hundred shares for executing such orders. Their fees are paid by the commission brokers. (See: *Commission broker.*)†

Index A statistical yardstick expressed in terms of percentages of a base year or years. For instance, the Federal Reserve Board's index of industrial production is based on 1967 as 100. An index is not an average. (See: *Averages, NYSE common stock index.*)†

Insolvency The inability to meet maturing debt obligations.*

Institutional Investor An organization whose primary purpose is to invest its own assets or those held in trust by it for others. Includes pension funds, investment companies, insurance companies, universities, and banks.†

Interest Payments a borrower pays a lender for the use of his money. A corporation pays interest on its bonds to its bondholders. (See: *Bond, dividend.*)†

Interest factor (IF) Numbers found in compound interest and annuity tables.*

Internal financing Funds made available for capital budgeting and working-capital expansion through the normal operations of the firm; internal financing is approximately equal to retained earnings plus depreciation.*

Internal rate of return (IRR) The rate of return on an asset investment. The internal rate of return is calculated by finding the discount rate that equates the present value of future cash flows to the cost of the investment.*

Intrinsic value That value which, in the mind of the analyst, is justified by the facts. It is often used to distinguish between the *true value* of an asset (the intrinsic value) and the asset's current market price.*

Investment The use of money for the purpose of making more money, to gain income or increase capital, or both. Safety of principal is an important consideration. (See: *Speculation.*)†

Investment banker Also known as an *underwriter.* He is the middleman between the corporation issuing new securities and the public. The usual practice is for one or more investment bankers to buy outright from a corporation a new issue of stocks or bonds. The group forms a syndicate to sell the securities to individuals and institutions. Investment bankers also distribute very large blocks of stocks or bonds—perhaps held by an estate. Thereafter the market in the security may be over-the-counter, on a regional stock exchange, the American Exchange, or the New York Stock Exchange. (See: *Over-the-counter, primary distribution, syndicate.*)†

Investment company A company or trust which uses its capital to invest in other companies. There are two principal types: the closed-end and the open-end, or mutual fund. Shares in closed-end investment companies, some of which are listed on the New York Stock Exchange, are readily transferable in the open market and are bought and sold like other shares. Capitalization of these companies remains the same unless action is taken to change, which is seldom. Open-end funds sell their own new shares to investors, stand ready to buy back their old shares, and are not listed. Open-end funds are so called because their capitalization is not fixed; they issue more shares as people want them.†

Investment counsel One whose principal business consists of acting as investment adviser and a substantial part of his business consists of rendering investment supervisory services.†

Investment tax credit Business firms can deduct as a credit against their income taxes a specified percentage of the dollar amount of new investments in each of certain categories of assets.*

Investors service bureau A facility of the New York Stock Exchange which answers written inquiries from individual investors on all aspects of securities investing. Major areas of inquiries involve: finding local brokerage firms which take small orders or accounts, explaining investing methods and listed securities, clarifying exchange operations, providing instructions for tracing dubious securities.†

Issue Any of a company's securities, or the act of distributing such securities.†

Legal list A list of securities in which mutual

savings banks, pensions funds, insurance companies, and other fiduciary institutions are permitted to invest.*

Leverage The effect on the per-share earnings of the common stock of a company when large sums must be paid for bond interest or preferred stock dividends, or both, before the common stock is entitled to share in earnings. Leverage may be advantageous for the common stock when earnings are good but may work against the common when earnings decline. Example: Company A has 1,000,000 shares of common stock outstanding, no other securities. Earnings drop from $1,000,000 to $800,000 or from $1 to 80 cents a share, a decline of 20 percent. Company B also has 1,000,000 shares of common but must pay $500,000 annually in bond interest. If earnings amount to $1,000,000, there is $500,000 available for the common or 50 cents a share. But earnings drop to $800,000 so there is only $300,000 available for the common, or 30 cents a share—a drop of 40 percent. Or suppose earnings of the company with only common stock increased from $1,000,000 to $1,500,000—earnings per share would go from $1 to $1.50, or an increase of 50 percent. But if earnings of the company which had to pay $500,000 in bond interest increased that much—earnings per common share would jump from 50 cents to $1 a share, or 100 percent. When a company has common stock only, no leverage exists because all earnings are available for the common, although relatively large fixed charges payable for lease of substantial plant assets may have an effect similar to that of a bond issue.†

Leverage factor The ratio of debt to total assets.*

Liabilities All the claims against a corporation. Liabilities include accounts and wages and salaries payable, dividends declared payable, accrued taxes payable, fixed or long-term liabilities such as mortgage bonds, debentures, and bank loans. (See: *Assets, balance sheet.*)†

Lien A lender's claim on assets that are pledged for a loan.*

Limit, limited order, or limited price order An order to buy or sell a stated amount of a security at a specified price, or at a better price, if obtainable after the order is represented in the Trading Crowd.†

Line of credit An arrangement whereby a financial institution (bank or insurance company) commits itself to lend up to a specified maximum amount of funds during a specified period. Sometimes the interest rate on the loan is specified, at other times, it is not. Sometimes a commitment fee is imposed for obtaining the line of credit.*

Liquidation The process of converting securities or other property into cash. The dissolution of a company, with cash remaining after sale of its assets and payment of all indebtedness being distributed to the shareholders.†

Liquidity Refers to a firm's cash position and its ability to meet maturing obligations.*

Listed stock The stock of a company which is traded on a securities exchange, and for which a listing application and a registration statement, giving detailed information about the company and its operations, have been filed with the Securities and Exchange Commission, unless otherwise exempted, and the exchange itself. The various stock exchanges have different standards for listing. Some of the guides used by the New York Stock Exchange for an original listing are national interest in the company, a minimum of 1-million shares publicly held among not less than 2,000 round-lot stockholders. The publicly held common shares should have a minimum aggregate market value of $16 million. The company should have net income in the latest year of over $2.5-million before federal income tax and $2-million in each of the preceding two years.†

Load The portion of the offering price of shares of open-end investment companies in excess of the value of the underlying assets which cover sales commissions and all other costs of distribution. The load is usually incurred only on purchase, there being, in most cases, no charge when the shares are sold (redeemed).†

Lock-box plan A procedure used to speed up collections and to reduce float.*

Locked in An investor is said to be locked in when he has a profit on a security he owns but does not sell because his profit would immediately become subject to the capital gains tax. (See: *Capital gain.*)†

Long Signifies ownership of securities: "I am long 100 U.S. Steel" means the speaker owns 100 shares. (See: *Short position, short sale.*)†

Management The board of directors, elected by the stockholders, and the officers of the corporation, appointed by the board of directors.†

Manipulation An illegal operation. Buying or selling a security for the purpose of creating a false or misleading appearance of active trading or for the purpose of raising or depressing the price to induce purchase or sale by others.†

Margin The amount paid by the customer when he uses his broker's credit to buy a security. Under Federal Reserve regulations, the initial margin required in past years has ranged from 50 percent of the purchase price all the way to 100 percent. (See: *Brokers' loans, Equity, Margin call.*)†

Margin call A demand upon a customer to put up money or securities with the broker. The call is made when a purchase is made; also if a customer's equity in a margin account declines below a minimum standard set by the exchange or by the firm. (See: *Margin.*)†

Margin—profit on sales The *profit margin* is the percentage of profit after tax to sales.°

Marginal cost The cost of an additional unit. The marginal cost of capital is the cost of an additional dollar of new funds.°

Marginal efficiency of capital A schedule showing the internal rate of return on investment opportunities.°

Marginal revenue The additional gross revenue produced by selling one additional unit of output.°

Market order An order to buy or sell a stated amount of a security at the most advantageous price obtainable. (See: *Good 'til cancelled order, Limit order, Stop order.*)†

Market price In the case of a security, market price is usually considered the last reported price at which the stock or bond sold.†

Matched and lost When two bids to buy the same stock are made on the trading floor simultaneously, and each bid is equal to or larger than the amount of stock offered, both bids are considered to be on an equal basis. So the two bidders flip a coin to decide who buys the stock. Also applies to offers to sell.†

Maturity The date on which a loan or a bond or debenture comes due and is to be paid off.†

Member corporation A securities brokerage firm, organized as a corporation, with at least one member of the New York Stock Exchange, Inc., who is an officer and a holder of voting stock in the corporation. (See: *Member firm.*)†

Member firm A securities brokerage firm organized as a partnership and having at least one general partner who is a member of the New York Stock Exchange, Inc. (See: *Member corporation.*)†

Member organization This term includes New York Stock Exchange Member Firm *and* Member Corporation. (See: *Member corporation, Member firm.*)†

Merger Any combination that forms one company from two or more previously existing companies.°

Money market Financial markets in which funds are borrowed or lent for short periods (i.e., less than one year). (The money market is distinguished from the capital market, which is the market for long-term funds.)°

Mortgage A pledge of designated property as security for a loan.°

Mortgage bond A bond secured by a mortgage on a property. The value of the property may or may not equal the value of the so-called mortgage bonds issued against it. (See: *Bond, Debenture.*)†

Municipal bond A bond issued by a state or a political subdivision, such as county, city, town, or village. The term also designates bonds issued by state agencies and authorities. In general, interest paid on municipal bonds is exempt from federal income taxes and state and local income taxes within the state of issue.†

Mutual fund (See: *Investment company.*)

NASD The National Association of Securities Dealers, Inc. An association of brokers and dealers in the over-the-counter securities business. The association has the power to expel members who have been declared guilty of unethical practices. NASD is dedicated to—among other objectives—"adopt, administer and enforce rules of fair practice and rules to prevent fraudulent and manipulative acts and practices, and in general to promote just and equitable principles of trade for the protection of investors."†

NASDAQ An automated information network which provides brokers and dealers with price quotations on securities traded over-the-counter. NASDAQ is an acronym for National Association of Securities Dealers Automated Quotations.†

Negotiable Refers to a security, title to which is transferable by delivery. (See: *Good delivery.*)†

Net asset value A term usually used in connection with investment companies, meaning net asset value per share. It is common practice for an investment company to compute its assets daily, or even twice daily, by totaling the market value of all securities owned. All liabilities are deducted, and the balance divided by the number of shares outstanding. The resulting figure is the net asset value per share. (See: *Assets, Investment company.*)†

Net change The change in the price of a security from the closing price on one day and the closing price on the following day on which the stock is traded. The net change is ordinarily the last figure on the stock price list. The mark + 1⅛ means up $1.125 a share from the last sale on the previous day the stock traded.†

Net present value (NPV) method A method of ranking investment proposals. The NPV is equal to the present value of future returns, discounted at the marginal cost of capital, minus the present value of the cost of the investment.°

Net worth The capital and surplus of a firm —capital stock, capital surplus (paid-in capital), earned surplus (retained earnings), and, occasionally, certain reserves. For some purposes, preferred stock is included; generally, net worth refers only to the common stockholders' position.°

New issue A stock or bond sold by a corporation for the first time. Proceeds may be issued to retire outstanding securities of the company, for new plant or equipment, or for additional working capital.†

Nominal interest rate The contracted or stated interest rate, undeflated for price-level changes.°

Noncumulative A preferred stock on which unpaid dividends do not accrue. Omitted dividends are, as a rule, gone forever. (See: *Cumulative preferred.*)†

Normal probability distribution A symmetrical, bell-shaped probability function.°

NYSE common stock index A composite index covering price movements of all common stocks listed on the "Big Board." It is based on the close of the market December 31, 1965 as 50.00 and is weighted according to the number of shares listed for each issue. The index is computed continuously and printed on the ticker tape each half hour. Point changes in the index are converted to dollars and cents so as to provide a meaningful measure of changes in the average price of listed stocks. The composite index is supplemented by separate indexes for four industry groups: industrials, transportation, utilities, and finances. (See: *Averages.*)†

Objective probability distributions Probability distributions determined by statistical procedures.°

Odd lot An amount of stock less than the established 100-share unit or 10-share unit of trading: from 1 to 99 shares for the great majority of issues, 1 to 9 for so-called inactive stocks. (See: *Round lot, Inactive stock.*)†

Off-board This term may refer to transactions over-the-counter in unlisted securities, or to a transaction involving listed shares which was not executed on a national securities exchange. (See: *Over-the-counter, Secondary distribution.*)†

Offer The price at which a person is ready to sell. Opposed to bid, the price at which one is ready to buy. (See: *Bid and asked.*)†

Open order (See: *Good 'til cancelled order.*)

Open-end investment company (See: *Investment company.*)

Operating leverage The extent to which fixed costs are used in a firm's operation. Break-even analysis is used to measure the extent to which operating leverage is employed.°

Opportunity cost The rate of return on the best *alternative* investment that is available. It is the highest return that will *not* be earned if the funds are invested in a particular project. For example, the opportunity cost of *not* invest-

ing in bond A yielding 8 percent might be 7.99 percent, which could be earned on bond B.°

Option A right to buy (call) or sell (put) a fixed amount of a given stock at a specified price within a limited period of time. The purchaser hopes that the stock's price will go up (if he bought a call) or down (if he bought a put) by an amount sufficient to provide a profit greater than the cost of the contract and the commission and other fees required to exercise the contract. If the stock price holds steady or moves in the opposite direction, the price paid for the option is lost entirely. There are several other types of options available to the public but these are basically combinations of puts and calls. Individuals may write (sell) as well as purchase options and are thereby obliged to deliver or buy the stock at the specified price.

There are also listed call option markets on the Chicago Board Options Exchange, the American, Midwest, Pacific, and PBW Stock Exchanges. These differ from the over-the-counter market in that trading is limited to selected issues, expiration of contracts is standardized at four dates during the year, exercise prices are set at multiples of 5 below 50 and multiples of 10 above 50, and option prices are determined through a continuous competitive-auction market system.†

Orders good until a specified time A market or limited price order which is to be represented in the Trading Crowd until a specified time, after which such order or the portion thereof not executed is to be treated as cancelled.†

Ordinary income Income from the normal operations of a firm. Operating income specifically excludes income from the sale of capital assets.°

Organized security exchanges Formal organizations having tangible, physical locations. Organized exchanges conduct an auction market in designated ("listed") investment securities. For example, the New York Stock Exchange is an organized exchange.°

Overbought An opinion as to price levels. May refer to a security which has had a sharp rise or to the market as a whole after a period of vigorous buying, which it may be argued, has left prices "too high."†

Overdraft system A system where a depositor may write checks in excess of his balance, with his bank automatically extending a loan to cover the shortage.°

Oversold An opinion—the reverse of overbought. A single security or a market which, it is believed, has declined to an unreasonable level.†

Over-the-counter A market for securities made up of securities dealers who may or may not be members of a securities exchange. Over-the-counter is mainly a market made over the telephone. Thousands of companies have insufficient shares outstanding, stockholders, or earnings to warrant application for listing on the New York Stock Exchange, Inc. Securities of these companies are traded in the over-the-counter market between dealers who act either as principals or as brokers for customers. The over-the-counter market is the principal market for U.S. government and municipal bonds. (See: *NASD, NASDAQ, Off-board.*)†

Paper profit An unrealized profit on a security still held. Paper profits become realized profits only when the security is sold. (See: *Profit taking.*)†

Par In the case of a common share, par means a dollar amount assigned to the share by the company's charter. Par value may also be used to compute the dollar amount of the common shares on the balance sheet. Par value has little significance so far as market value of common stock is concerned. Many companies today issue no-par stock but give a stated per share value on the balance sheet. In the case of preferred shares and bonds, however, par is important. It often signifies the dollar value upon which dividends on preferred stocks, and interest on bonds, are figured. The issuer of a 6 percent bond promises to pay that percentage of the bond's par value annually. (See: *Capitalization, Transfer tax.*)†

Par value The nominal or face value of a stock or bond.*

Participating preferred A preferred stock which is entitled to its stated dividend and, also, to additional dividends on a specified basis upon payment of dividends on the common stock.†

Passed dividend Omission of a regular or scheduled dividend.†

Payback period The length of time required for the net revenues of an investment to return the cost of the investment.*

Payout ratio The percentage of earnings paid out in the form of dividends.*

Pegging A market stabilization action taken by the manager of an underwriting group during the offering of new securities. He does this by continually placing orders to buy at a specified price in the market.*

Penny stocks Low-priced issues often highly speculative, selling at less than $1 a share. Frequently used as a term of disparagement, although a few penny stocks have developed into investment-caliber issues.†

Percentage order A limited price order to buy (or sell) a stated amount of a specified stock after a fixed number of shares of such stock have traded.†

Perpetuity A stream of equal future payments expected to continue forever.*

Pledging of accounts receivable Short-term borrowing from financial institutions where the loan is secured by accounts receivable. The lender may physically take the accounts receivable but typically has recourse to the borrower; also called *discounting of accounts receivable.*°

Point In the case of shares of stock, a point means $1. If ABC shares rises 3 points, each share has risen $3. In the case of bonds a point means $10, since a bond is quoted as a percentage of $1,000. A bond which rises 3 points gains 3 percent of $1,000, or $30 in value. An advance from 87 to 90 would mean an advance in dollar value from $870 to $900 for each $1,000 bond. In the case of market averages, the word point means merely that and no more. If, for example, the Dow-Jones Industrial averages rises from 870.25 to 871.25, it has risen a point. A point in this average, however, is not equivalent to $1. (See: *Averages.*)†

Pooling of interest An accounting method for combining the financial statements of firms that merge. Under the pooling-of-interest procedure, the assets of the merged firms are simply added to form the balance sheet of the surviving corporation. This method is different from the "purchase" method, where goodwill is put on the balance sheet to reflect a premium (or discount) paid in excess of book value.*

Portfolio Holdings of securities by an individual or institution. A portfolio may contain bonds, preferred stocks, and common stocks of various types of enterprises.†

Portfolio effect The extent to which the variation in returns on a combination of assets (a "portfolio") is less than the sum of the variations of the individual assets.*

Portfolio theory Deals with the selection of optimal portfolios; that is, portfolios that provide the highest possible return for any specified degree of risk.*

Preemptive right A provision contained in the corporate charter and bylaws that gives holders of common stock the right to purchase on a pro rata basis new issues of common stock (or securities convertible into common stock).*

Preferred stock A class of stock with a claim on the company's earnings before payment may be made on the common stock and usually entitled to priority over common stock if the company liquidates. Usually entitled to dividends at a specified rate—when declared by the board of directors and before payment of a dividend on the common stock—depending upon the terms of the issue. (See: *Cumulative preferred, Participating preferred.*)†

Premium The amount by which a preferred stock, bond, or option may sell above its par value. In the case of a new issue of bonds or stocks, premium is the amount the market price rises over the original selling price. Also refers to a charge sometimes made when a stock is borrowed to make delivery on a short sale. May refer, also, to redemption price of a bond or preferred stock if it is higher than face value. (See: *Disount, Short sale.*)†

Present value (PV) The value today of a future payment, or stream of payments, discounted at the appropriate discount rate.°

Price-earnings ratio The price of a share of stock divided by earnings per share for a twelve-month period. For example, a stock selling for $50 a share and earning $5 a share is said to be selling at a price-earnings ratio of 10 to 1.†

Primary distribution Also called primary offering. The original sale of a company's securities. (See: *Investment banker, Secondary distribution.*)†

Prime rate The lowest rate of interest commercial banks charge very large, strong corporations.°

Principal The person for whom a broker executes an order, or a dealer buying or selling for his own account. The term *principal* may also refer to a person's capital or to the face amount of a bond.†

Pro forma A projection. A *pro forma* financial statement is one that shows how the actual statement will look if certain specified assumptions are realized. *Pro forma* statements may be either future or past projections. An example of a backward *pro forma* statement occurs when two firms are planning to merge and shows what their consolidated financial statements would have looked like if they had been merged in preceding years.°

Profit center A unit of a large, decentralized firm that has its own investments and for which a rate of return on investment can be calculated.°

Profit margin The ratio of profits after taxes to sales.°

Profitability index (PI) The present value of future returns divided by the present value of the investment outlay.°

Profit-taking Selling stock which has appreciated in value since purchase, in order to realize the profit which has been made possible. The term is often used to explain a downturn in the market following a period of rising prices. (See: *Paper profit.*)†

Progressive tax A tax that requires a higher percentage payment on higher incomes. The personal income tax in the United States, which is at a rate of 14 percent on the lowest increments of income to 70 percent on the highest increments, is progressive.°

Prospectus The official selling circular that must be given to purchasers of new securities registered with the Securities and Exchange Commission so investors can evaluate those securities before or at the time of purchase. It highlights the much longer Registration Statement filed with the commission. It warns the issue has not been approved (or disapproved) by the commission and discloses such material information as the issuer's property and business, the nature of the security offered, use of proceeds, issuer's competition and prospects, management's experience, history, and remuneration, and certified financial statements. A preliminary version of the prospectus, used by brokers to obtain buying indications from investors, is called a *red herring*. This is because of a front-page notice (printed in red ink) that the preliminary prospectus is "subject to completion or amendment" and "shall not constitute an offer to sell. . ."†

Proxy A document giving one person the authority or power to act for another. Typically, the authority in question is the power to vote shares of common stock.°

Proxy statement Information required by SEC to be given stockholders as a prerequisite to solicitation of proxies for a security subject to the requirements of Securities Exchange Act.†

Prudent man rule An investment standard. In some states, the law requires that a fiduciary, such as a trustee, may invest the fund's money only in a list of securities designated by the state—the so-called legal list. In other states, the trustee may invest in a security if it is one which a prudent man of discretion and intelligence, who is seeking a reasonable income and preservation of capital, would buy.†

Pure (or primitive) security A security that pays off $1 if one particular state of the world occurs and pays off nothing if any other state of the world occurs.°

Put An option to sell a specific security at a specified price within a designated period.°

Puts and calls (See: *Option.*)

Quotation Often shortened to *quote*. The highest bid to buy and the lowest offer to sell a security in a given market at a given time. If you ask your broker for a "quote" on a stock, he may come back with something like "45¼ to 45½." This means that $45.25 is the highest price any buyer wanted to pay at the time the quote was given on the floor of the exchange and that $45.50 was the lowest price which any seller would take at the same time. (See: *Bid and asked.*)†

Rally A brisk rise following a decline in the

general price level of the market, or in an individual stock.†

Rate of return The internal rate of return on an investment.°

Record date The date on which you must be registered as a shareholder on the stock book of a company in order to receive a declared dividend or, among other things, to vote on company affairs. (See: *Ex dividend, Transfer*.)†

Recourse arrangement A term used in connection with accounts-receivable financing. If a firm sells its accounts receivable to a financial institution under a recourse agreement, then, if the accounts receivable cannot be collected, the selling firm must repurchase the account from the financial institution.°

Redemption price The price at which a bond may be redeemed before maturity, at the option of the issuing company. Redemption value also applies to the price the company must pay to call in certain types of preferred stock. (See: *Callable*.)†

Rediscount rate The rate of interest at which a bank may borrow from a Federal Reserve Bank.°

Refinancing Same as refunding. New securities are sold by a company and the money is used to retire existing securities. Object may be to save interest costs, extend the maturity of the loan, or both.°

Refunding Sale of new debt securities to replace an old debt issue.°

Registered bond A bond which is registered on the books of the issuing company in the name of the owner. It can be transferred only when endorsed by the registered owner. (See: *Bearer bond, Coupon bond*.)†

Registered representative Present name for the older term *customer's man*. In a New York Stock Exchange Member Organization, a *registered representative* is an employee who has met the requirements of the exchange as to background and knowledge of the securities business. Also known as an *account executive* or *customer's broker*.†

Registrar Usually a trust company or bank charged with the responsibility of preventing the issuance of more stock than authorized by a company. (See: *Transfer*.)†

Registration Before a public offering may be made of new securities by a company, or of outstanding securities by controlling stockholders—through the mails or in interstate commerce—the securities must be registered under the Securities Act of 1933. The registration statement is filed with the SEC by the issuer. It must disclose pertinent information relating to the company's operations, securities, management, and purpose of the public offering. Securities of railroads under jurisdiction of the Interstate Commerce Commission, and certain other types of securities, are exempted. On security offerings involving less than $300,000, less information is required.

Before a security may be admitted to dealings on a national securities exchange, it must be registered under the Securities Exchange Act of 1934. The application for registration must be filed with the exchange and the SEC by the company issuing the securities. It must disclose pertinent information relating to the company's operations, securities, and management.†

Regression analysis A statistical procedure for predicting the value of one variable (dependent variable) on the basis of knowledge about one or more other variables (independent variables).°

Regular way delivery Unless otherwise specified, securities sold on the N.Y. Stock Exchange are to be delivered to the buying broker by the selling broker and payment made to the selling broker by the buying broker on the fifth business day after the transaction. Regular way delivery for bonds is the following business day. (See: *Transfer*.)†

Regulation T The federal regulation governing the amount of credit which may be advanced by brokers and dealers to customers for the purchase of securities. (See: *Margin*.)†

Regulation U The federal regulation governing the amount of credit which may be advanced by a bank to its customers for the purchase of listed stocks. (See: *Margin*.)†

Reinvestment rate The rate of return at which cash flows from an investment are reinvested. The reinvestment rate may or may not be constant from year to year.°

REIT Real Estate Investment Trust, an organization similar to an investment company in some respects but concentrating its holdings in real estate investments. The yield is generally liberal since REIT's are required to distribute as much as 90 percent of their income. (See: *Investment company*.)†

Reorganization When a financially troubled firm goes through reorganization, its assets are restated to reflect their current market value, and its financial structure is restated to reflect any changes on the asset side of the statement. Under a reorganization the firm continues in existence; this is contrasted to bankruptcy, where the firm is liquidated and ceases to exist.°

Replacement-cost accounting A requirement under SEC release no. 190 (1976) that large companies disclose the replacement costs of inventory items and depreciable plant.°

Required rate of return The rate of return that stockholders expect to receive on common stock investments.°

Residual value The value of leased property at the end of the lease term.*

Retained earnings That portion of earnings not paid out in dividends. The figure that appears on the balance sheet is the sum of the retained earnings for each year throughout the company's history.*

Return (See: *Yield.*)

Rights When a company wants to raise more funds by issuing additional securities, it may give its stockholders the opportunity, ahead of others, to buy the new securities in proportion to the number of shares each owns. The piece of paper evidencing this privilege is called a right. Because the additional stock is usually offered to stockholders below the current market price, rights ordinarily have a market value of their own and are actively traded. In most cases they must be exercised within a relatively short period. Failure to exercise or sell rights may result in actual loss to the holder. (See: *Warrant.*)†

Rights offering A securities flotation offered to existing stockholders.*

Risk The probability that actual future returns will be below expected returns. It is measured by standard deviation or coefficient of variation of expected returns.*

Risk-adjusted discount rates The discount rate applicable for a particular risky (uncertain) stream of income: the riskless rate of interest plus a risk premium appropriate to the level of risk attached to the particular income stream.*

Risk premium The difference between the required rate of return on a particular risky asset and the rate of return on a riskless asset with the the same expected life.*

Risk-return trade-off function (See *Security market line.*)

Round lot A unit of trading or a multiple thereof. On the NYSE the unit of trading is generally 100 shares in stocks and $1,000 par value in the case of bonds. In some inactive stocks, the unit of trading is ten shares.†

Sale and leaseback An operation whereby a firm sells land, buildings, or equipment to a financial institution and simultaneously executes an agreement to lease the property back for a specified period under specific terms.*

Salvage value The value of a capital asset at the end of a specified period. It is the current market price of an asset being considered for replacement in a capital budgeting problem.*

Scale order An order to buy (or sell) a security which specifies the total amount to be bought (or sold) and the amount to be bought (or sold) at specified price variations.†

Seat A traditional figure-of-speech for a membership on an exchange. Price and admission requirements vary.†

SEC The Securities and Exchange Commission, established by Congress to help protect investors. The SEC administers the Securities Act of 1933, the Securities Exchange Act of 1934, the Securities Act Amendments of 1975, the Trust Indenture Act, the Investment Company Act, the Investment Advisers Act, and the Public Utility Holding Company Act.†

Secondary distribution Also known as a secondary offering. The redistribution of a block of stock, sometimes after it has been sold by the issuing company. The sale is handled off the NYSE by a securities firm or group of firms and the shares are usually offered at a fixed price which is related to the current market price of the stock. Usually the block is a large one, such as might be involved in the settlement of an estate. The security may be listed or unlisted. (See: *Exchange distribution, Investment banker, Primary distribution, Special offering, Syndicate.*)†

Securities and exchange commission (See *SEC.*)

Securities, junior Securities that have lower priority in claims on assets and income than other securities (*senior securities*). For example, preferred stock is junior to debentures, but debentures are junior to mortgage bonds. Common stock is the most junior of all corporate securities.*

Securities, senior Securities having claims on income and assets that rank higher than certain other securities (*junior securities*). For example, mortgage bonds are senior to debentures, but debentures are senior to common stock.*

Security market line A graphic representation of the relation between the required return on a security and the product of its risk times a normalized market measure of risk. Risk-return relationships for individual securities or investments.*

Seller's option A special transaction on the NYSE which gives the seller the right to deliver the stock or bond at any time within a specified period, ranging from not less than 6 business days to not more than 60 days. (See: *Delivery.*)†

Selling group A group of stock brokerage firms formed for the purpose of distributing a new issue of securities; part of the investment banking process.*

Sensitivity analysis Simulation analysis in which key variables are changed and the resulting change in the rate of return is observed. Typically, the rate of return will be more sensitive to changes in some variables than it will in others.*

Serial bond An issue which matures in part at periodic stated intervals.†

Service lease A lease under which the lessor maintains and services the asset.°

Settlement Conclusion of a securities transactions in which a customer pays a debit balance he owes a broker or receives from the broker the proceeds from a sale. The term also applies to continuous daily netting out of transactions among brokerage houses, usually through centralized securities clearing corporations. (See: *Regular delivery, Cash sale, Depository trust company*.)†

Short covering Buying stock to return stock previously borrowed to make delivery on a short sale.†

Short position Stocks sold short and not covered as of a particular date. On the NYSE, a tabulation is issued once a month listing all issues on the exchange in which there was a short position of 5,000 or more shares and issues in which the short position had changed by 2,000 or more shares in the preceding month. *Short position* also means the total amount of stock an individual has sold short and has not covered, as of a particular date.†

Short sale A person who believes a stock will decline and sells it though he does not own any has made a short sale. For instance: You instruct your broker to sell short 100 shares of ABC. Your broker borrows the stock so he can deliver the 100 shares to the buyer. The money value of the shares borrowed is deposited by your broker with the lender. Sooner or later you must cover your short sale by buying the same amount of stock you borrowed for return to the lender. If you are able to buy ABC at a lower price than you sold it for, your profit is the difference between the two prices—not counting commissions and taxes. But if you have to pay more for the stock than the price you received, that is the amount of your loss. Stock exchange and federal regulations govern and limit the conditions under which a short sale may be made on a national securities exchange. Sometimes a person will sell short a stock he already owns in order to protect a paper profit. This is known as selling short against the box. (See: *Up tick*).†

SIAC Securities Industry Automation Corporation, an independent organization established by the New York and American Stock Exchanges as a jointly owned subsidiary to provide automation, data processing, clearing, and communications services.†

Simulation A technique whereby probable future events are simulated on a computer. Estimated rates of return and risk indexes can be generated.°

Sinking fund A required annual payment designed to amortize a bond or a preferred stock issue. The sinking fund may be held in the form of cash or marketable securities, but more generally the money put into the sinking fund is used to retire each year some of the securities in question.°

SIPC Securities Investor Protection Corporation, which provides funds for use, if necessary, to protect customers' cash and securities which may be on deposit with a SIPC member firm in the event the firm fails and is liquidated under the provisions of the SIPC Act. SIPC is not a government agency. It is a nonprofit membership corporation created, however, by an act of Congress.†

Small business administration (SBA) A government agency organized to aid small firms with their financing and other problems.°

Special bid A method of filling an order to buy a large block of stock on the floor of the New York Stock Exchange. In a special bid, the bidder for the block of stock—a pension fund, for instance, will pay a special commission to the broker who represents him in making the purchase. The seller does not pay a commission. The special bid is made on the floor of the exchange at a fixed price which may not be below the last sale of the security or the current bid in the regular market, whichever is higher. Member firms may sell this stock for customers directly to the buyer's broker during trading hours.†

Special offering Opposite of special bid. A notice is printed on the ticker tape announcing the stock sale at a fixed price usually based on the last transaction in the regular auction market. If there are more buyers than stock, allotments are made. Only the seller pays the commission. (See: *Secondary distribution*.)†

Specialist A member of the New York Stock Exchange, Inc., who has two functions: First, to maintain an orderly market, insofar as reasonably practicable, in the stocks in which he is registered as a specialist. In order to maintain an orderly market, the exchange expects the specialist to buy or sell for his own account, to a reasonable degree, when there is a temporary disparity between supply and demand. Second, the specialist acts as a broker's broker. When a commission broker on the exchange floor receives a limit order, say, to buy at $50 a stock then selling at $60—and he cannot wait at the post where the stock is traded to see if the price reaches the specified level. So he leaves th order with the specialist, who will try to execute it in the market if and when the stock declines to the specified price. At all times the specialist must put his customers' interests above his own. There are about 400 specialists on the NYSE. (See: *Book, Limited order*.)†

Speculation The employment of funds by a speculator. Safety of principal is a secondary factor. (See: *Investment*.)†

Speculator   One who is willing to assume a relatively large risk in the hope of gain. The speculator may buy and sell the same day or speculate in an enterprise which he does not expect to be profitable for years.†

Split   The division of the outstanding shares of a corporation into a larger number of shares. A 3-for-1 split by a company with 1 million shares outstanding results in 3 million shares outstanding. Each holder of 100 shares before the 3-for-1 split would have 300 shares, although his proportionate equity in the company would remain the same; 100 parts of 1 million are the equivalent of 300 parts of 3 million. Ordinarily splits must be voted by directors and approved by shareholders. (See: *Stock dividends.*)†

Standard deviation   A statistical term that measures the variability of a set of observations from the mean of the distribution (σ.)*

State-preference model   A framework in which decisions are based on probabilities of payoffs under alternative states of the world.*

Stock ahead   Sometimes an investor who has entered an order to buy or sell a stock at a certain price will see transactions at that price reported on the ticker tape while his own order has not been executed. The reason is that other buy and sell orders at the same price came in to the specialist ahead of his and had priority. (See: *Book, Specialist.*)†

Stock dividend   A dividend paid in securities rather than cash. The dividend may be additional shares of the issuing company, or shares of another company (usually a subsidiary) held by the company. (See: *Ex-dividend, Split.*)†

Stock split   An accounting action to increase the number of shares outstanding; for example, in a 3-for-1 split, shares outstanding would be tripled and each stockholder would receive three new shares for each one formerly held. Stock splits involve no transfer from surplus to the capital account.*

Stockholder of record   A stockholder whose name is registered on the books of the issuing corporation.†

Stop limit order   A stop order which becomes a limit order after the specified stop price has been reached. (See: *Limit order, Stop order.*)†

Stop order   An order to buy at a price above or sell at a price below the current market. Stop buy orders are generally used to limit loss or protect unrealized profits on a short sale. Stop sell orders are generally used to protect unrealized profits or limit loss on a holding. A stop order becomes a market order when the stock sells at or beyond the specified price and, thus, may not necessarily be executed at that price.†

Stopped stock   A service performed—in most cases by the specialist—for an order given him by a commission broker. Let's say XYZ just sold at $50 a share. Broker A comes along with an order to buy 100 shares at the market. The lowest offer is $50.50. Broker A believes he can do better for his client than $50.50, perhaps might get the stock at $50.25. But he doesn't want to take a chance that he'll miss the market —that is, the next sale might be $50.50 and the following one even higher. So he asks the specialist if he will stop 100 at ½ ($50.50). The specialist agrees. The specialist guarantees Broker A he will get 100 shares at 50½ if the stock sells at that price. In the meantime, if the specialist or broker A succeeds in executing the order at $50.25, the stop is called off. (See: *Specialist.*)†

Street   The New York financial community in the Wall Street area.†

Street name   Securities held in the name of a broker instead of his customer's name are said to be carried in a *street name.* This occurs when the securities have been bought on margin or when the customer wishes the security to be held by the broker.†

Subjective probability distributions   Probability distributions determined through subjective procedures without the use of statistics.*

Subordinated debenture   A bond having a claim on assets only after the senior debt has been paid off in the event of liquidation.*

Subscription price   The price at which a security may be purchased in a rights offering.

Switch order or contingent order   An order for the purchase (sale) of one stock and the sale (purchase) of another stock at a stipulated price difference.†

Switching   Selling one security and buying another.†

Syndicate   A group of investment bankers who together underwrite and distribute a new issue of securities or a large block of an outstanding issue.†

Synergy   A situation where "the whole is greater than the sum of its parts"; in a synergistic merger, the postmerger earnings exceed the sum of the separate companies' premerger earnings.*

Systematic risk   That part of a security's risk that cannot be eliminated by diversification.*

Take-over   The acquiring of one corporation by another—usually in a friendly merger but sometimes marked by a "proxy fight." In "unfriendly" take-over attempts, the potential buying company may offer a price well above current market values, new securities, and other inducements to stockholders. The management of the subject company might ask for a better price or fight the take-over or merger with another company. (See: *Proxy.*)†

Tangible assets Physical assets as opposed to intangible assets such as goodwill and the stated value of patents.°

Technical research Analysis of the market and stocks based on supply and demand. The technician studies price movements, volume, and trends and patterns which are revealed by charting these factors, and attempts to assess the possible effect of current market action on future supply and demand for securities and individual issues. (See: *Fundamental research*.)†

Tender offers A situation wherein one firm offers to buy the stock of another, going directly to the stockholders, frequently over the opposition of the management of the firm whose stock is being sought.°

Term loan A loan generally obtained from a bank or an insurance company with a maturity greater than one year. Term loans are generally amortized.°

Thin market A market in which there are comparatively few bids to buy or offers to sell, or both. The phrase may apply to a single security or to the entire stock market. In a thin market, price fluctuations between transactions are usually larger than when the market is liquid. A thin market in a particular stock may reflect lack of interest in that issue or a limited supply of or demand for stock in the market. (See: *Bid and asked, Liquidity, Offer*.)†

Third market Trading of stock exchange listed securities in the over-the-counter market by non-exchange-member brokers and all types of investors.†

Ticker The instruments which display prices and volume of securities transactions worldwide within minutes after each trade.†

Time order An order which becomes a market or limited price order at a specified time.†

Tips Supposedly "inside" information on corporation affairs.†

Trade credit Interfirm debt arising through credit sales and recorded as an account receivable by the seller and as an account payable by the buyer.°

Trader One who buys and sells for his own account for short-term profit. (See *Investor, Speculator*.)†

Trading floor (See: *Floor*.)

Trading post One of 23 trading locations on the floor of the New York Stock Exchange at which stocks assigned to that location are bought and sold. About 75 stocks are traded at each post.†

Transfer This term may refer to two different operations. One is the delivery of a stock certificate from the seller's broker to the buyer's broker and legal change of ownership, normally accomplished within a few days. The other is to record the change of ownership on the books of the corporation by the transfer agent. When the purchaser's name is recorded on the books of the company, dividends, notices of meetings, proxies, financial reports, and all pertinent literature sent by the issuer to its securities holders are mailed direct to the new owner. (See: *Registrar, Street name*.)†

Transfer agent A transfer agent keeps a record of the name of each registered shareowner, his or her address, the number of shares owned, and sees that certificates presented to his office for transfer are properly cancelled and new certificates issued in the name of the transferee. (See: *Registrar, Transfer*.)†

Treasury stock Common stock that has been repurchased by the issuing firm.° It may be held in the company's treasury indefinitely, reissued to the public, or retired. Treasury stock receives no dividends and has no vote while held by the company.†

Trust receipt An instrument acknowledging that the borrower holds certain goods in trust for the lender. Trust receipt financing is used in connection with the financing of inventories for automobile dealers, construction equipment dealers, appliance dealers, and other dealers in expensive durable goods.°

Trustee The representative of bondholders who acts in their interest and facilitates communication between them and the issuer. Typically these duties are handled by a department of a commercial bank.°

Turnover rate The volume of shares traded in a year as a percentage of total shares listed on an exchange, outstanding for an individual issue, or held in an institutional portfolio.

Underwriter (See: *Investment banker*.)

Underwriting (1) The entire process of issuing new corporate securities. (2) The insurance function of bearing the risk of adverse price fluctuations during the period in which a new issue of stock or bonds is being distributed.°

Underwriting syndicate A syndicate of investment firms formed to spread the risk associated with the purchase and distribution of a new issue of securities. The larger the issue, the more firms typically are involved in the syndicate.°

Unlisted A security not listed on a stock exchange. (See: *Over-the-counter*.)†

Unlisted Securities Securities that are traded in the over-the-counter market period.°

Unlisted trading privileges On some exchanges a stock may be traded at the request of a member without any prior application by the company itself. The company has no agreement to conform with standards of the exchange. Today admission of a stock to unlisted trading privileges requires SEC approval of an application filed by the exchange. The information in the application must be made available by the exchange to the public. No unlisted stocks are traded on the New York Stock Exchange. (See: *Listed stock.*)†

Unsystematic risk That part of a security's risk associated with random events; unsystematic risk can be eliminated by proper diversification.°

Up tick A term used to designate a transaction made at a price higher than the preceding transaction. Also called a *plus-tick*. A stock may be sold short only on an up tick, or on a "zero-plus" tick. A *zero-plus* tick is a term used for a transaction at the same price as the preceding trade but higher than the preceding different price.

Conversely, a *down tick*, or *minus* tick, is a term used to designate a transaction made at a price lower than the preceding trade. A *zero minus* tick is a transaction made at the same price as the preceding sale but lower than the preceding different price.

A plus sign, or a minus sign, is displayed throughout the day next to the last price of each company's stock traded at each trading post on the floor of the New York Stock Exchange. (See: *Short sale.*)†

Utility theory A body of theory dealing with the relationships among money income, utility (or "happiness"), and the willingness to accept risk.°

Value additivity principle Neither fragmenting cash flows or recombining them will affect the resulting values of the cash flows.°

Volume The number of shares traded in a security or an entire market during a given period. Volume is usually considered on a daily basis and a daily average is computed for longer periods.†

Voting right The stockholder's right to vote his stock in the affairs of his company. Most common shares have one vote each. Preferred stock usually has the right to vote when preferred dividends are in default for a specified period. The right to vote may be delegated by the stockholder to another person. (See: *Cumulative voting, Proxy.*)†

Warrant A long-term option to buy a stated number of shares of common stock at a specified

price. The specified price is generally called the *exercise price.*°

Weighted cost of capital A weighted average of the component costs of debt, preferred stock, and common equity. Also called the *composite cost of capital.*°

When issued A short form of "when, as, and if issued." The term indicates a conditional transaction in a security authorized for issuance but not as yet actually issued. All "when issued" transactions are on an "if" basis, to be settled if and when the actual security is issued and the exchange or National Association of Securities Dealers rules the transactions are to be settled.†

Wire house A member firm of an exchange maintaining a communications network linking either its own branch offices, offices of correspondent firms, or a combination of such offices.†

Working capital Refers to a firm's investment in short-term assets—cash, short-term securities, accounts receivable, and inventories. *Gross working capital* is defined as a firm's total current assets. *Net working capital* is defined as current assets minus current liabilities. If the term *working capital* is used without further qualification, it generally refers to gross working capital.°

Working control Theoretically, ownership of 51 percent of a company's voting stock is necessary to exercise control. In practice—and this is particularly true in the case of a large corporation—effective control sometimes can be exerted through ownership, individually or by a group acting in concert, of less than 50 percent.†

Yield Also known as return. The dividends or interest paid by a company expressed as a percentage of the current price. A stock with a current market value of $40 a share paying dividends at the rate of $2.00 is said to return 5 percent ($2 ÷ $40). The current return on a bond is figured the same way. A 3 percent $1,000 bond selling at $600 offers a current yield return of 5 percent ($30 ÷ $600). (See: *Dividend, Interest.*)†

Yield to maturity The yield of a bond to maturity takes into account the price discount from or premium over the face amount. It is greater than the current yield when the bond is selling at a discount and less than the current yield when the bond is selling at a premium.†

Commodities Market

COMMODITY FUTURES TRADING COMMISSION

Federal laws regulating commodity futures trading are enforced by the Commodity Futures Trading Commission.

National Office

Commodity Futures Trading Commission
2033 K Street, NW
Washington, DC 20581
Telephone: 202–254–7556

Regional Offices

Eastern Region
One World Trade Center, Suite 4747
New York, NY 10048
Telephone: 212–466–2071

Central Region
233 So. Wacker Drive, 46th Floor
Chicago, IL 60606
Telephone: 312–353–5990

510 Grain Exchange Building
Minneapolis, MN 55415
Telephone: 612–725–2025

Southwestern Region
4901 Main Street, Room 208
Kansas City, MO 64112
Telephone: 816–374–2994

Western Region
Two Embarcadero Center, Suite 975
San Francisco, CA 94111
Telephone: 415–556–7503

The function of the Commodity Futures Trading Commission (CFTC) is to strengthen the regulation of futures trading, and to bring under regulation all agricultural and other commodities, including lumber and metals, which are traded on commodity exchanges. Major purposes of the trading regulation are to pre-

Source: U.S. Government Manual.

vent price manipulation, market corners, and the dissemination of false and misleading commodity and market information affecting commodity prices. Other responsibilities are to protect market users against cheating, fraud, and abusive practices in commodity transactions and to safeguard the handling of traders' margin money and equities by establishing minimum financial requirements for futures commission merchants and by preventing the misuse of such funds by brokers.

The Commodity Futures Trading commission was established as an independent agency by the Commodity Futures Trading Commission Act of 1974 (88 Stat. 1389; 7 U.S.C. 4a).

As the successor to the Commodity Exchange Authority under the Department of Agriculture, this new Commission has been given several new authorities and responsibilities under the Commodity Exchange Act, which makes more effective regulation of the commodity futures markets possible. For example, the Commission regulates all commodity futures, whereas many commodities were not regulated under prior law. The act also requires the registration of additional persons involved in futures trading that had not been previously registered, such as commodity trading advisors, commodity pool operators, and persons associated with futures commission merchants. The CFTC also is empowered to regulate option and leverage transactions in commodities. The Commodity Exchange Act requires futures trading to be conducted on contract markets designated by the Commission. In order to obtain designation, a contract market must demonstrate that the market will not be contrary to the public interest. Once designation has been granted, a contract market must provide, among other things, settlement procedures for customers' claims and grievances. Further, the Commission is authorized to impose sanctions, such as fines and penalties, for violations under the act; to enjoin practices in violation of the act; and, finally, to litigate its own cases.

COMMODITY EXCHANGES

AMEX Commodities Exchange, Inc.
86 Trinity Place
New York, NY 10006
212–938–6191

Chicago Board of Trade (CBOT)
141 W. Jackson Boulevard
Chicago, IL 60604
312–435–3500

Chicago Mercantile Exchange (CME)
444 W. Jackson Boulevard
Chicago, IL 60606
312–648–1000

Commodity Exchange, Inc. of New York
(COMEX)
4 World Trade Center
New York, NY 10048
212–938–2000

International Monetary Market of the Chicago
Mercantile Exchange; merged with CME.

Kansas City Board of Trade (KCBT)
4800 Main Street
Kansas City, MO 64112
816–753–7363

Mid-America Commodity Exchange
175 W. Jackson Boulevard
Chicago, IL 60604
312–435–0606

Minneapolis Grain Exchange (MGE)
159 Grain Exchange Building
Minneapolis, MN 55415
612–338–6212

New Orleans Commodity Exchange
308 Board of Trade Place
New Orleans, LA 70130
504–524–2184

New York Coffee and Sugar & Cocoa Exchange
4 World Trade Center
New York, NY 10048
212–938–2800

New York Cotton Exchange (NYCE) and the
Citrus, Petroleum and Wool Associates
4 World Trade Center
New York, NY 10100
212–938–2650

New York Futures Exchange, Inc.
30 Broad Street
New York, NY 10005
212–623–4949

New York Mercantile Exchange (NYME)
4 World Trade Center
New York, NY 10048
212–938–2222

MONTHLY AVERAGE SPOT PRICE CHARTS OF SELECTED COMMODITIES

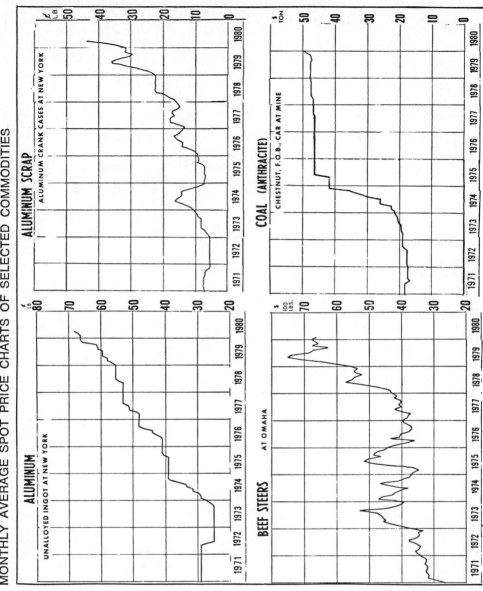

ALUMINUM
UNALLOYED INGOT AT NEW YORK

ALUMINUM SCRAP
ALUMINUM CRANK CASES AT NEW YORK

BEEF STEERS
AT OMAHA

COAL (ANTHRACITE)
CHESTNUT, F.O.B., CAR AT MINE

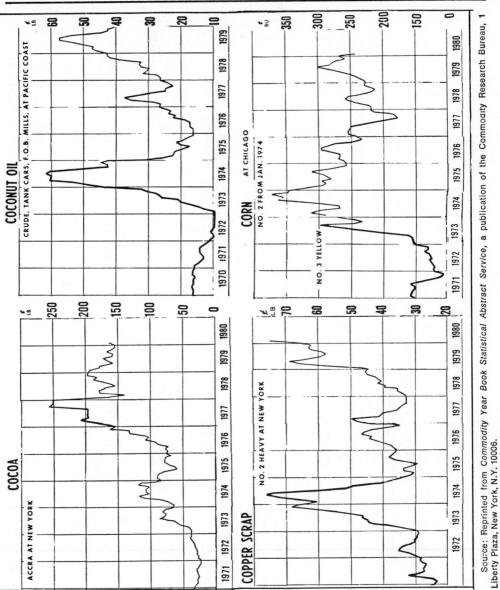

COCONUT OIL
CRUDE, TANK CARS, F.O.B. MILLS, AT PACIFIC COAST

CORN AT CHICAGO
NO. 2 FROM JAN. 1974
NO. 3 YELLOW

COCOA
ACCRA AT NEW YORK

COPPER SCRAP
NO. 2 HEAVY AT NEW YORK

Source: Reprinted from *Commodity Year Book Statistical Abstract Service*, a publication of the Commodity Research Bureau, 1 Liberty Plaza, New York, N.Y. 10006.

MONTHLY AVERAGE SPOT PRICE CHARTS (continued)

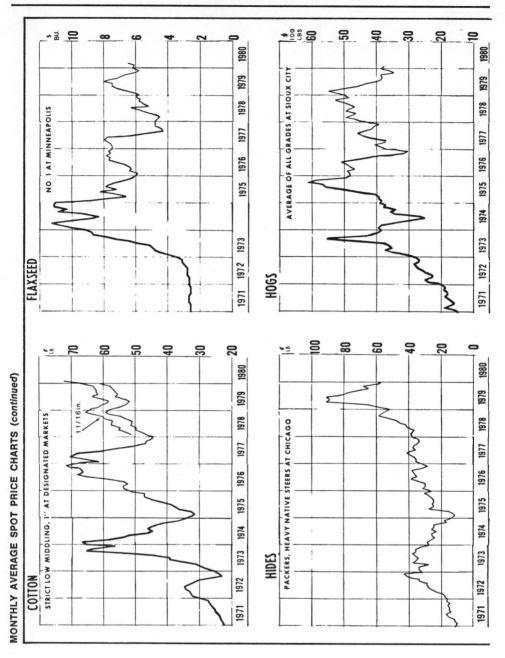

COTTON

STRICT LOW MIDDLING, 1" AT DESIGNATED MARKETS

11/16 in.

FLAXSEED

NO. 1 AT MINNEAPOLIS

HIDES

PACKERS, HEAVY NATIVE STEERS AT CHICAGO

HOGS

AVERAGE OF ALL GRADES AT SIOUX CITY

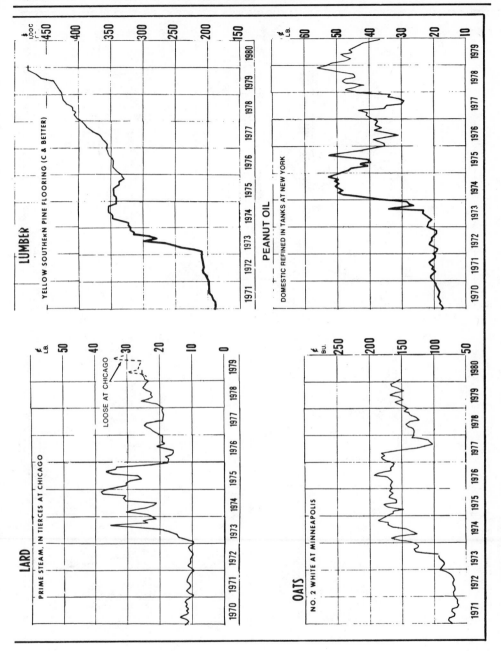

LUMBER
YELLOW SOUTHERN PINE FLOORING (C & BETTER)

LARD
PRIME STEAM, IN TIERCES AT CHICAGO

LOOSE AT CHICAGO

PEANUT OIL
DOMESTIC REFINED IN TANKS AT NEW YORK

OATS
NO. 2 WHITE AT MINNEAPOLIS

MONTHLY AVERAGE SPOT PRICE CHARTS *(continued)*

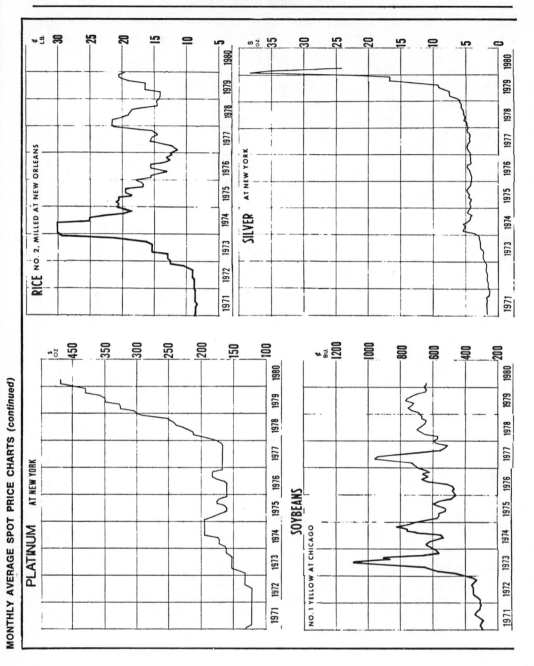

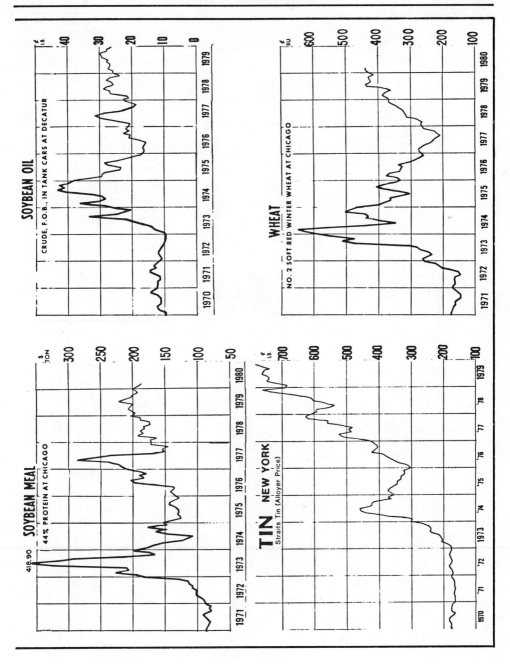

SOYBEAN OIL
CRUDE, F.O.B., IN TANK CARS AT DECATUR

WHEAT
NO. 2 SOFT RED WINTER WHEAT AT CHICAGO

SOYBEAN MEAL
44% PROTEIN AT CHICAGO

TIN NEW YORK
Straits Tin (Alloyer Price)

Producer Price Indexes, for special commodity groupings

[1967 = 100 unless otherwise specified]

Commodity grouping	Annual average 1978	1979 Apr.	May	June	July	Aug.	Sept.	Oct.	Nov.	Dec.[1]	1980 Jan.	Feb.	Mar.	Apr.
All commodities - less farm products	208.4	228.0	230.1	232.0	235.4	237.5	241.4	245.3	247.0	249.5	255.4	260.5	262.6	264.3
All foods	206.4	227.7	226.4	223.8	225.4	224.7	228.5	226.9	230.0	232.2	231.1	235.7	234.7	231.7
Processed foods	206.7	227.8	227.5	224.7	226.4	224.8	230.8	228.9	231.8	234.2	233.3	238.5	236.8	234.0
Industrial commodities less fuels	197.2	214.7	216.0	217.0	219.0	220.3	222.0	225.9	226.9	228.5	234.3	237.5	238.4	239.9
Selected textile mill products (Dec. 1975 = 100)	108.8	112.3	112.8	113.5	114.0	115.1	115.8	116.4	117.0	117.2	118.8	119.4	121.1	122.1
Hosiery	106.3	112.5	112.5	112.7	114.1	113.0	112.7	113.3	114.6	115.3	119.5	119.6	119.9	120.7
Underwear and nightwear	158.9	167.3	167.7	168.3	168.5	170.8	170.8	171.2	171.6	172.9	175.7	177.8	181.8	182.0
Chemicals and allied products, including synthetic rubber and manmade fibers and yarns	190.5	204.1	207.6	209.5	215.0	218.6	220.9	224.3	226.3	228.7	235.8	238.2	242.1	248.4
Pharmaceutical preparations	140.6	150.0	150.1	151.7	151.7	152.0	153.6	155.6	155.4	156.9	159.2	160.4	161.7	165.9
Lumber and wood products, excluding millwork and other wood products	298.3	326.4	325.1	321.7	325.3	333.9	341.0	337.3	323.3	310.8	308.6	314.0	312.2	284.5
Special metals and metal products	209.6	232.7	232.4	233.7	235.5	234.9	236.4	243.4	244.5	246.3	253.5	255.7	254.8	255.6
Fabricated metal products	216.2	232.9	234.6	235.7	237.4	239.8	241.1	244.0	244.6	245.3	247.3	248.3	251.3	256.0
Copper and copper products	155.6	212.1	199.0	193.0	191.9	197.1	200.5	212.2	213.8	217.1	227.2	258.2	240.9	224.7
Machinery and motive products	190.4	204.1	205.3	206.0	207.7	207.2	208.5	213.4	214.3	215.9	219.3	220.6	222.2	226.1
Machinery and equipment, except electrical	214.3	230.0	231.8	232.6	235.1	236.2	238.2	240.8	242.5	244.8	248.4	250.4	252.9	257.5
Agricultural machinery, including tractors	216.3	230.8	232.1	233.8	235.8	238.4	243.6	246.3	250.8	251.5	255.2	256.0	257.7	259.7
Metalworking machinery	228.8	251.2	254.3	256.8	260.1	261.7	265.6	269.5	272.7	276.0	282.1	284.8	288.1	294.3
Numerically controlled machine tools (Dec. 1971 = 100)	179.1	192.7	195.7	195.8	202.2	204.2	206.5	208.5	208.8	211.2	213.2	215.6	216.8	223.9
Total tractors	228.7	245.4	247.7	248.2	251.2	253.8	256.0	261.2	262.5	266.2	271.6	273.5	274.3	278.4
Agricultural machinery and equipment less parts	212.7	226.7	228.1	229.5	231.4	233.7	238.4	241.0	244.9	245.8	249.3	250.4	252.1	254.2
Farm and garden tractors less parts	216.1	228.5	230.5	231.8	233.9	237.6	244.1	247.6	250.5	251.1	255.3	256.7	258.8	261.0
Agricultural machinery excluding tractors less parts	216.7	233.0	233.6	235.7	237.6	239.2	243.5	245.4	251.3	252.0	255.4	256.6	257.0	259.0
Industrial valves	232.3	252.4	255.0	255.8	257.0	258.2	260.1	261.8	263.1	266.1	270.1	272.2	276.1	283.5
Industrial fittings	232.7	255.5	259.3	260.4	260.8	262.3	264.3	272.6	276.8	276.8	276.8	280.4	282.8	289.9
Abrasive grinding wheels	208.1	220.3	221.6	222.8	222.8	224.6	224.6	239.0	239.0	239.0	239.0	240.0	240.0	258.4
Construction materials	228.3	250.0	250.3	250.3	252.3	254.3	256.6	258.5	256.7	255.4	259.1	262.2	264.6	262.1

[1] Data for December 1979 have been revised to reflect the availability of late reports and corrections by respondents. All data are subject to revision 4 months after original publication.

Source: *Monthly Labor Review,* U.S. Department of Labor, Bureau of Labor Statistics.

PRECIOUS METALS AND CURRENCY PRICES

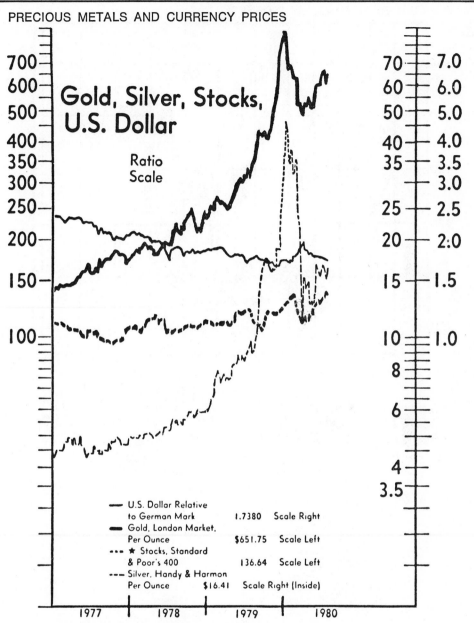

Gold, Silver, Stocks, U.S. Dollar

Ratio Scale

— U.S. Dollar Relative
to German Mark   1.7380   Scale Right
— Gold, London Market,
Per Ounce $651.75   Scale Left
•••★ Stocks, Standard
& Poor's 400   136.64   Scale Left
--- Silver, Handy & Harmon
Per Ounce $16.41   Scale Right (Inside)

1977   1978   1979   1980

Source: *The M/G Financial Weekly,* Media General Financial Services, 301 East Grace Street, Richmond, Va. 23261, July 28, 1980.

DOW JONES COMMODITY INDEXES

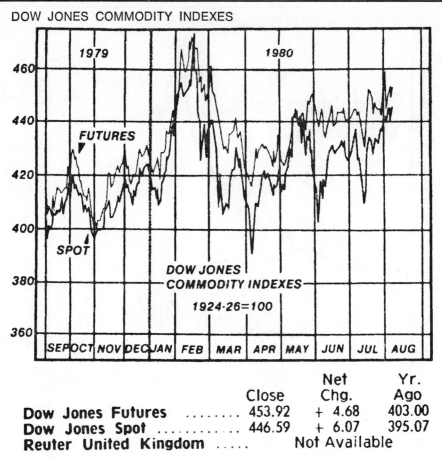

	Close	Net Chg.	Yr. Ago
Dow Jones Futures	453.92	+ 4.68	403.00
Dow Jones Spot	446.59	+ 6.07	395.07
Reuter United Kingdom	Not Available		

Source: *The Wall Street Journal*, August 11, 1980.

Confused About Mail Order Rules? Brochures Might Have The Answers

Many companies now are getting into the mail order business, and can run into problems if they are not familiar with federal laws that regulate this type of trading.

The United States Postal Service has two publications that can help—*Business Reply Mail, Regulations Applications—Annual Renewals* and *Packaging For Mailing*. Both are free, and can be ordered from:

Mail Classification
Main Post Office, Room 1010
Washington, DC 20012
202-523-2234

Another helpful source is the Federal Trade Commission, which protects consumers from mail order problems. Consumers and companies alike can benefit from the free brochure, *Unordered Merchandise*, and a free two-page fact sheet called Mail Order Gifts.

For only one copy contact:

Public Reference
Federal Trade Commission
6th & Pennsylvania Avenue, Room 130
Washington, DC 20580
202-523-3598

For more than one copy, write or call:

Distribution and Duplication
Federal Trade Commission
6th & Pennsylvania Avenue, Room 720
Washington, DC 20580
202-523-3667

Metric Conversion Clearinghouse

If metric conversion is affecting your industry or markets, free information and expertise is available from: U.S. Metric Board, 1815 North Lynn St., #600, Arlington, VA 22207, 301-921-2318.

Source: Washington Researchers' *The Information Report*, 918 16th St. N.W., Washington, D.C. 20006.

Money and Financial Institutions

INTEREST RATES AND BOND YIELDS

PERCENT PER ANNUM

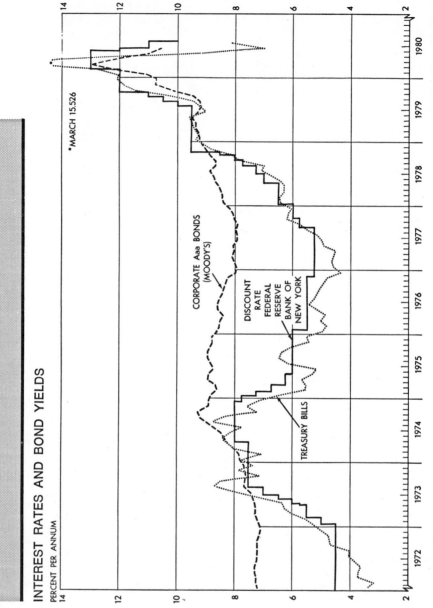

*MARCH 15.526

CORPORATE Aaa BONDS (MOODY'S)

DISCOUNT RATE FEDERAL RESERVE BANK OF NEW YORK

TREASURY BILLS

SOURCE: SEE TABLE BELOW

COUNCIL OF ECONOMIC ADVISERS

[Percent per annum]

Period	U.S. Treasury security yields: 3-month bills [1]	Constant maturities [2]: 3-year	Constant maturities [2]: 10-year	High-grade municipal bonds (Standard & Poor's) [3]	Corporate Aaa bonds (Moody's)	Prime commercial paper, 4–6 months [4]	Discount rate (N.Y. F.R. Bank) [5]	Prime rate charged by banks [5]	New-home mortgage yields (FHLBB) [6]
1974	7.886	7.82	7.56	6.09	8.57	9.87	7.83	10.81	8.92
1975	5.838	7.49	7.99	6.89	8.83	6.33	6.25	7.86	9.01
1976	4.989	6.77	7.61	6.49	8.43	5.35	5.50	6.84	8.99
1977	5.265	6.69	7.42	5.56	8.02	5.60	5.46	6.83	9.01
1978	7.221	8.29	8.41	5.90	8.73	7.99	7.46	9.06	9.54
1979	10.041	9.71	9.44	6.39	9.63	[4] 10.91	10.28	12.67	10.77
1979: June	9.045	8.95	8.91	5.99	9.29	9.71	9½–9½	11¾–11½	10.66
July	9.262	8.94	8.95	6.05	9.20	9.82	9½–10	11½–11¾	10.78
Aug	9.450	9.14	9.03	6.10	9.23	10.39	10–10½	11¾–12¼	11.01
Sept	10.182	9.69	9.33	6.40	9.44	11.60	10½–11	12¼–13½	11.02
Oct	11.472	10.95	10.30	6.98	10.13	13.23	11–12	13½–15	11.21
Nov	11.868	11.18	10.65	7.19	10.76	[4] 13.26	12–12	15¼–15½	11.37
Dec	12.071	10.71	10.39	7.09	10.74	12.80	12–12	15½–15¼	11.64
1980: Jan	12.036	10.88	10.80	7.21	11.09	12.66	12–12	15¼–15¼	11.87
Feb	12.814	12.84	12.41	8.04	12.38	13.60	12–13	15¼–16¾	11.93
Mar	15.526	14.05	12.75	9.09	12.96	16.50	13–13	16¾–19½	12.62
Apr	14.003	12.02	11.47	8.40	12.04	14.93	13–13	19½–19½	13.03
May	9.150	9.44	10.18	7.37	10.99	9.29	13–12	*18½–14	13.68
June	6.995	8.92	9.78	7.60	10.58	8.03	12–11	14–12	12.69
July	8.126	----	----	----	----	----	11–	12–	----
Week ended:									
1980: June 28	7.077	8.96	9.80	7.77	10.53	7.89	11–11	12–12	----
July 5	8.149	9.15	10.11	7.88	10.84	8.26	11–11	12–12	----
12	8.209	9.16	10.18	7.93	10.94	8.21	11–11	12–11½	----
19	8.169	9.19	10.20	8.00	11.09	8.30	11–11	11½–11½	----
26	7.880	9.23	10.20	8.13	11.11	8.26	11–11	11½–11	----
Aug 2	8.221	----	----	----	----	----	11–	11–	----

[1] Rate on new issues within period.
[2] Yields on the more actively traded issues adjusted to constant maturities by the Treasury Department.
[3] Weekly data are Wednesday figures.
[4] Beginning November 1, 1979, data are for 6 months paper.
[5] Average effective rate for year; opening and closing rate for month and week.
[6] Effective rate (in the primary market) on conventional mortgages, reflecting fees and charges as well as contract rate and assumed, on the average, repayment at end of 10 years. Rates beginning January 1973 not strictly comparable with prior rates.
* Range of 18½–19.

Sources: Department of the Treasury, Board of Governors of the Federal Reserve System, Federal Home Loan Bank Board, Moody's Investors Service, and Standard & Poor's Corporation.

Source: *Economic Indicators*, Council of Economic Advisers.

INTEREST RATES: MONEY AND CAPITAL MARKETS
AVERAGES, PERCENT PER ANNUM

Instrument	1977	1978	1979	1980 Feb.	1980 Mar.	1980 Apr.	1980 May	1980, week ending May 3	May 10	May 17	May 24	May 31
Money market rates												
1 Federal funds[1]	5.54	7.94	11.20	14.13	17.19	17.61	10.98	15.12	12.96	10.85	10.71	9.46
Commercial paper[2,3]												
2 1-month	5.42	7.76	10.86	13.62	16.55	16.10	9.60	12.76	10.31	9.44	9.13	8.19
3 3-month	5.54	7.94	10.97	13.78	16.81	15.78	9.49	12.44	10.04	9.38	9.12	8.19
4 6-month	5.60	7.99	10.91	13.60	16.50	14.93	9.29	11.88	9.60	9.26	8.95	8.15
Finance paper, directly placed[2,3]												
5 1-month	5.38	7.73	10.78	13.58	16.30	15.70	9.30	12.20	9.93	9.31	8.79	8.00
6 3-month	5.49	7.80	10.47	13.05	15.36	14.05	9.09	11.42	9.90	8.95	8.62	7.81
7 6-month	5.50	7.78	10.25	12.39	14.70	13.68	9.01	11.15	9.73	8.93	8.64	7.81
8 Prime bankers acceptances, 90-day[3,4]	5.59	8.11	11.04	14.01	17.10	15.63	9.60	12.46	10.04	9.60	9.08	8.42
Certificates of deposit, secondary market[5]												
9 1-month	5.48	7.88	11.03	13.93	16.81	16.23	9.77	12.97	10.30	9.65	9.42	8.35
10 3-month	5.64	8.22	11.22	14.30	17.57	16.14	9.79	12.89	10.26	9.70	9.43	8.43
11 6-month	5.92	8.61	11.44	14.58	17.74	15.80	9.78	12.67	10.07	9.71	9.43	8.60
12 Eurodollar deposits, 3-month[6]	6.05	8.74	11.96	15.33	18.72	17.81	11.20	15.33	12.96	11.16	11.09	9.78
U.S. Treasury bills[3,7]												
Secondary market												
13 3-month	5.27	7.19	10.07	12.86	15.20	13.20	8.58	10.47	9.14	8.53	8.15	7.70
14 6-month	5.53	7.58	10.06	12.86	15.03	12.88	8.65	10.38	9.09	8.68	8.26	7.87
15 1-year	5.71	7.74	9.75	12.46	14.03	11.97	8.66	9.99	9.00	8.72	8.34	8.03
Auction average[8]												
16 3-month	5.265	7.221	10.041	12.814	15.526	14.003	9.150	10.788	9.728	8.604	8.953	7.675
17 6-month	5.510	7.572	10.017	12.721	15.100	13.618	9.149	10.790	9.495	8.782	8.923	7.753
Capital market rates												
U.S. TREASURY NOTES AND BONDS												
Constant maturities[9]												
18 1-year	6.09	8.34	10.67	13.92	15.82	13.30	9.39	10.94	9.77	9.44	9.02	8.68
19 2-year	6.45	8.34	10.12	13.42	14.88	12.50	9.45	10.61	9.60	9.48	9.21	9.07
20 2½-year[10]				14.00	14.65	11.25	9.05					
21 3-year	6.69	8.29	9.71	12.84	14.05	12.02	9.44	10.49	9.57	9.44	9.23	9.14
22 5-year	6.99	8.32	9.52	12.60	13.47	11.84	9.95	10.63	9.94	9.94	9.89	9.79
23 7-year	7.23	8.36	9.48	12.53	13.00	11.49	10.09	10.54	10.02	10.16	10.08	9.98
24 10-year	7.42	8.41	9.44	12.41	12.75	11.47	10.18	10.57	10.08	10.25	10.16	10.14
25 20-year	7.67	8.48	9.33	12.21	12.49	11.42	10.44	10.78	10.32	10.49	10.50	10.37
26 30-year		8.49	9.29	12.13	12.34	11.40	10.36	10.77	10.30	10.40	10.38	10.25

27	Composite[11] 3 to 5 years[12]	6.85	8.30	9.58	12.52	13.41	.....	.....	.....	.....	.....	.....	.....
28	Over 10 years (long-term)	7.06	7.89	8.74	11.55	11.87	10.83	9.82	10.15	9.70	9.87	9.86	9.77
	STATE AND LOCAL NOTES AND BONDS												
	Moody's series[13]												
29	Aaa	5.20	5.52	5.92	7.28	8.16	7.95	6.80	7.15	6.60	6.60	6.80	6.85
30	Baa	6.12	6.27	6.73	8.12	10.30	9.19	8.02	8.25	8.00	7.85	8.00	8.00
31	Bond Buyer series[14]	5.68	6.03	6.52	8.16	9.17	8.63	7.59	7.96	7.11	7.44	7.72	7.73
	CORPORATE BONDS												
32	Seasoned issues, all industries[15]	8.43	9.07	10.12	12.92	13.73	13.21	12.11	12.60	12.11	12.04	12.10	12.00
	By rating group												
33	Aaa	8.02	8.73	9.63	12.38	12.96	12.04	10.99	11.38	10.93	10.96	11.02	10.90
34	Aa	8.24	8.92	9.94	12.73	13.51	13.06	11.91	12.39	11.91	11.80	11.92	11.82
35	A	8.49	9.12	10.20	12.99	13.97	13.55	12.35	12.94	12.41	12.28	12.33	12.16
36	Baa	8.97	9.45	10.69	13.57	14.45	14.19	13.17	13.68	13.20	13.10	13.11	13.10
	Aaa utility bonds[16]												
37	New issue	8.19	8.96	10.03	13.57	14.00	12.90	11.53	12.10	11.38	11.43	11.50	11.52
38	Recently offered issues	8.19	8.97	10.02	13.35	13.90	12.91	11.64	12.05	11.55	11.65	11.60	11.55
	MEMO: Dividend/price ratio[17]												
39	Preferred stocks	7.60	8.25	9.07	10.55	11.26	11.06	10.20	10.60r	10.13	10.22	10.29	10.16
40	Common stocks	4.56	5.28	5.46	5.24	5.77	6.05	5.77	5.94	5.82	5.83	5.82	5.58

1. Weekly figures are seven-day averages of daily effective rates for the week ending Wednesday; the daily effective rate is an average of the rates on a given day weighted by the volume of transactions at these rates.

2. Beginning November 1977, unweighted average of offering rates quoted by at least five dealers (in the case of commercial paper), or finance companies (in the case of finance paper). Previously, most representative rate quoted by those dealers and finance companies. Before November 1979, maturities for data shown are 30-59 days, 90-119 days, and 120-179 days for commercial paper; and 30-59 days, 90-119 days, and 150-179 days for finance paper.

3. Yields are quoted on a bank-discount basis.

4. Average of the midpoint of the range of daily dealer closing rates offered for domestic issues.

5. Five-day average of rates quoted by five dealers (three-month series was previously a seven-day average).

6. Averages of daily quotations for the week ending Wednesday.

7. Except for auction averages, yields are computed from daily closing bid prices.

8. Rates are recorded in the week in which bills are issued.

9. Yield on the more actively traded issues adjusted to constant maturities by the U.S. Treasury, based on daily closing bid prices.

Source: Federal Reserve Bulletin.

10. Each figure is an average of only five business days near the end of the month. The rate for each month is used to determine the maximum interest rate payable in the following month on small saver certificates. (See table 1.16).

11. Unweighted averages for all outstanding notes and bonds in maturity ranges shown, based on daily closing bid prices. "Long-term" includes all bonds neither due nor callable in less than 10 years, including several very low yielding "flower" bonds.

12. The three- to five-year series has been discontinued.

13. General obligations only, based on figures for Thursday, from Moody's Investors Service.

14. Twenty issues of mixed quality.

15. Averages of daily figures from Moody's Investors Service.

16. Compilation of the Board of Governors of the Federal Reserve System. Issues included are long-term (20 years or more). New-issue yields are based on quotations on date of offering; those on recently offered issues (included only for first 4 weeks after termination of underwriter price restrictions). on Friday close-of-business quotations.

17. Standard and Poor's corporate series. Preferred stock ratio based on a sample of ten issues: four public utilities, four industrials, one financial, and one transportation. Common stock ratios on the 500 stocks in the price index.

MAXIMUM INTEREST RATES PAYABLE ON TIME AND SAVINGS DEPOSITS AT FEDERALLY INSURED INSTITUTIONS

PERCENT PER ANNUM

Type and maturity of deposit	Commercial banks				Savings and loan associations and mutual savings banks			
	In effect May 31, 1980		Previous maximum		In effect May 31, 1980		Previous maximum	
	Percent	Effective date	Percent	Effective date	Percent	Effective date	Percent	Effective date
1 Savings	5¼	7/1/79	5	7/1/73	5½	7/1/79	5¼	(1)
2 Negotiable order of withdrawal accounts [2]	5	1/1/74	(3)	....	5	1/1/74	(3)	....
Time accounts [4]								
Fixed ceiling rates by maturity								
3 30–89 days	5¼	8/1/79	5	7/1/73	(3)	....	(3)	....
4 90 days to 1 year	5¾	1/1/80	5½	7/1/73	6	1/1/80	5¾	(1)
5 1 to 2 years [5]	} 6	7/1/73	} 5½	1/21/70	} 6½	(1)	} 5¾	1/21/70
6 2 to 2½ years [5]			5¾	1/21/70			6	1/21/70
7 2½ to 4 years [5]	6½	7/1/73	5¾	1/21/70	6¾	(1)	6	1/21/70
8 4 to 6 years [6]	7¼	11/1/73	(7)	....	7½	11/1/73	(7)	....
9 6 to 8 years [6]	7½	12/23/74	7¼	11/1/73	7¾	12/23/74	7½	11/1/73
10 8 years or more [6]	7¾	6/1/78	(3)	....	8	6/1/78	(3)	....
11 Issued to governmental units (all maturities)[8]	8	6/1/78	7¾	12/23/74	8	6/1/78	7¾	12/23/74
12 Individual retirement accounts and Keogh (H.R. 10) plans (3 years or more)[8,9]	8	6/1/78	7¾	7/6/77	8	6/1/78	7¾	7/6/77
Special variable ceiling rates by maturity								
13 6-month money market time deposits[10]	(11) (12)	(11) (12)	(11) (13)	(11) (13)	(11) (12)	(11) (12)	(11) (13)	(11) (13)
14 2½ years or more								

1. July 1, 1973, for mutual savings banks; July 6, 1973, for savings and loan associations.

2. For authorized states only, federally insured commercial banks, savings and loan associations, cooperative banks, and mutual savings banks in Massachusetts and New Hampshire were first permitted to offer negotiable order of withdrawal (NOW) accounts on Jan. 1, 1974. Authorization to issue NOW accounts was extended to similar institutions throughout New England on Feb. 27, 1976, and in New York State on Nov. 10, 1978, and in New Jersey on Dec. 28, 1979.

3. No separate account category.

4. For exceptions with respect to certain foreign time deposits see the FEDERAL RESERVE BULLETIN for October 1962 (p. 1279), August 1965 (p. 1084), and February 1968 (p. 167).

5. No minimum denomination. Until July 1, 1979, a minimum of $1,000 was required for savings and loan associations, except in areas where mutual savings banks permitted lower minimum denominations. This restriction was removed for deposits maturing in less than 1 year, effective Nov. 1, 1973.

6. No minimum denomination. Until July 1, 1979, minimum denomination was $1,000 except for deposits representing funds contributed to an Individual Retirement Account (IRA) or a Keogh (H.R. 10) plan established pursuant to the Internal Revenue Code. The $1,000 minimum requirement was removed for such accounts in December 1975 and November 1976 respectively.

7. Between July 1, 1973, and Oct. 31, 1973, there was no ceiling for certificates maturing in 4 years or more with minimum denominations of $1,000; however, the amount of such certificates that an institution could issue was limited to 5 percent of its total time and savings deposits. Sales in excess of that amount, as well as certificates of less than $1,000, were limited to the 6½ percent ceiling on time deposits maturing in 2½ years or more.

Effective Nov. 1, 1973, ceilings were reimposed on certificates maturing in 4 years or more with minimum denomination of $1,000. There is no limitation on the amount of these certificates that banks can issue.

8. Accounts subject to fixed rate ceilings. See footnote 6 for minimum denomination requirements.

9. Effective January 1, 1980, commercial banks are permitted to pay the same rate as thrifts on IRA and Keogh accounts and accounts of governmental units when such deposits are placed in the new 2½ year or more variable ceiling certificates or in 26-week money market certificates regardless of the level of the Treasury bill rate.

10. Must have a maturity of exactly 26 weeks and a minimum denomination of $10,000, and must be nonnegotiable.

11. Commercial banks, savings and loan associations, and mutual savings banks were authorized to offer money market time deposits effective June 1, 1978. The ceiling rate for commercial banks on money market time deposits entered into

before June 5, 1980, is the discount rate (auction average) on most recently issue. six-month U.S. Treasury bills. Until Mar. 15, 1979, the ceiling rate for savings and loan associations and mutual savings banks was ¼ percentage point higher than the rate for commercial banks. Beginning March 15, 1979, the ¼-percentage-point interest differential is removed when the six-month Treasury bill rate is 9 percent or more. The full differential is in effect when the six-month bill rate is 8¾ per cent or less. Thrift institutions may pay a maximum 9 percent when the six-month bill rate is between 8¾ and 9 percent. Also effective March 15, 1979, interest compounding was prohibited on six-month money market time deposits at all offering institutions. The maximum allowable rates in May for commercial banks were as follows: May 1, 10.790; May 8, 9.495; May 15, 8.782; May 22, 8.923; and May 29, 7.753. The maximum allowable rates in May for thrift institutions were as follows: May 1, 10.790; May 8, 9.495; May 15, 9.000; May 22, 9.000; and May 29, 8.003. [NOTE. Effective for all six-month money market certificates issued beginning June 5, 1980, the interest rate ceilings will be determined by the discount rate (auction average) of most recently issued six-month U.S. Treasury bills as follows:

Bill rate	Commercial bank ceiling	Thrift ceiling
8.75 and above	bill rate + ¼ percent	bill rate + ¼ percent
8.50 to 8.75	bill rate + ¼ percent	9.00
7.50 to 8.50	bill rate + ¼ percent	bill rate + ½ percent
7.25 to 7.50	7.75	bill rate + ½ percent
Below 7.25	7.75	7.75

The prohibition against compounding interest in these certificates continues. In addition, during the period May 29, 1980, through Nov. 1, 1980, commercial banks may renew maturing six-month money market time deposits for the same depositor at the thrift institution ceiling interest rate.]

12. Effective Jan. 1, 1980, commercial banks, savings and loan associations, and mutual savings banks were authorized to offer variable-ceiling nonnegotiable time deposits with no required minimum denomination and with maturities of 2½ years or more. The maximum rate for commercial banks is ¾ percentage point below the yield on 2½ year U.S. Treasury securities; the ceiling rate for thrift institutions is ¼ percentage point higher than that for commercial banks. Effective Mar. 1,

Source: *Federal Reserve Bulletin.*

1980, a temporary ceiling of 11¾ per cent was placed on these accounts at commercial banks; the temporary ceiling is 12 percent at savings and loan associations and mutual savings banks. [NOTE. Effective for all variable ceiling nonnegotiable time deposits with maturities of 2½ years or more issued beginning June 2, 1980, the ceiling rates of interest will be determined as follows:

Treasury yield	Commercial bank ceiling	Thrift ceiling
12.00 and above	11.75	12.00
9.50 to 12.00	Treasury yield – ¼ percent	Treasury yield
Below 9.50	9.25	9.50

Interest may be compounded on these time deposits. The ceiling rates of interest at which these accounts may be offered will vary biweekly.]

13. Between July 1, 1979, and Dec. 31, 1979, commercial banks, savings and loan associations, and mutual savings banks were authorized to offer variable ceiling accounts with no required minimum denomination and with maturities of 4 years or more. The maximum rate for commercial banks was 1¼ percentage points below the yield on 4-year U.S. Treasury securities; the ceiling rate for thrift institutions was ¼ percentage point higher than that for commercial banks.

NOTE. Before Mar. 31, 1980, the maximum rates that could be paid by federally insured commercial banks, mutual savings banks, and savings and loan associations were established by the Board of Governors of the Federal Reserve System, the Board of Directors of the Federal Deposit Insurance Corporation, and the Federal Home Loan Bank Board under the provisions of 12 CFR 217, 329, and 526, respectively. Title II of the Depository Institutions Deregulation and Monetary Control Act of 1980 (P.L. 96–221) transferred the authority of the agencies to establish maximum rates of interest payable on deposits to the Depository Institutions Deregulation Committee. The maximum rates on time deposits in denominations of $100,000 or more with maturities of 30–89 days were suspended in June 1970; such deposits maturing in 90 days or more were suspended in May 1973. For information regarding previous interest rate ceilings on all types of accounts, see earlier issues of the FEDERAL RESERVE BULLETIN, the Federal Home Loan Bank Board *Journal*, and the *Annual Report* of the Federal Deposit Insurance Corporation.

Month	Average rate	Month	Average rate
1979—Jan.	11.75	1979—Sept	12.90
Feb.	11.75	Oct.	14.39
Mar.	11.75	Nov.	15.55
Apr.	11.75	Dec.	15.30
May	11.75	1980—Jan.	15.25
June	11.65	Feb.	15.63
July	11.54	Mar.	18.31
Aug.	11.91	Apr.	19.77
		May	16.57

PRIME RATE CHARGED BY BANKS ON SHORT-TERM BUSINESS LOANS
PERCENT PER ANNUM

Effective date	Rate	Effective Date	Rate
1979—Dec. 7	15¼	1980—Apr. 2	20
1980—Feb. 19	15¾	18	19½
22	16¼-16½	May 1	18½-19
29	16¾	2	18½
Mar. 4	17¼	7	17½
7	17¾	16	16½
14	18½	23	14½
19	19	30	14
28	19½		

Source: *Federal Reserve Bulletin.*

TERMS OF LENDING AT COMMERCIAL BANKS (survey of loans made, February 4–9, 1980)

Item	All sizes	Size of loan (in thousands of dollars)					
		1–24	25–49	50–99	100–499	500–999	1,000 and over
SHORT-TERM COMMERCIAL AND INDUSTRIAL LOANS							
1 Amount of loans (thousands of dollars)	9,920,415	768,933	485,280	526,248	1,709,993	659,611	5,770,349
2 Number of loans	135,532	100,191	14,735	8,270	9,789	1,032	1,515
3 Weighted-average maturity (months)	2.5	3.4	3.4	3.2	3.3	3.1	1.9
4 Weighted-average interest rate (percent per annum)	15.67	15.06	15.54	15.91	16.23	16.34	15.50
5 Interquartile range[1]	14.87–16.43	13.65–16.99	13.80–17.27	14.99–17.39	15.40–17.27	15.73–17.00	14.84–16.21
Percentage of amount of loans							
6 With floating rate	50.8	19.0	39.4	46.3	58.1	61.0	53.3
7 Made under commitment	47.8	19.8	29.0	37.2	50.0	59.6	52.0
8 With no stated maturity	25.6	10.7	18.1	22.9	21.1	34.4	28.7
LONG-TERM COMMERCIAL AND INDUSTRIAL LOANS							
9 Amount of loans (thousands of dollars)	1,866,260		287,223		254,459	120,692	1,223,885
10 Number of loans	21,710		20,016		1,243	186	264
11 Weighted-average maturity (months)	43.2		32.3		42.8	50.9	45.1
12 Weighted-average interest rate (percent per annum)	15.32		15.42		15.40	15.70	15.24
13 Interquartile range[1]	15.25–16.25		14.00–16.94		15.25–16.70	15.25–16.90	15.25–15.86
Percentage of amount of loans							
14 With floating rate	65.6		20.0		46.0	76.5	79.3
15 Made under commitment	71.4		29.0		72.9	74.9	80.7
CONSTRUCTION AND LAND DEVELOPMENT LOANS							
16 Amount of loans (thousands of dollars)	855,640	102,387	97,606	178,002	278,768		198,877
17 Number of loans	18,763	11,371	2,806	2,645	1,788		152
18 Weighted-average maturity (months)	13.1	17.5	4.5	2.8	20.7		14.5
19 Weighted-average interest rate (percent per annum)	15.79	15.80	14.47	14.96	16.80		15.78
20 Interquartile range[1]	13.85–17.99	14.08–17.45	12.55–16.09	13.80–16.10	16.25–18.11		13.50–18.01
Percentage of amount of loans							
21 With floating rate	39.3	26.5	18.4	16.5	35.4		82.2
22 Secured by real estate	95.4	93.1	99.4	99.0	94.7		92.5
23 Made under commitment	60.6	62.8	78.4	69.2	42.4		68.7
24 With no stated maturity	9.0	7.2	4.2	4.8	10.8		13.4
Type of construction							
25 1- to 4-family	54.2	75.6	88.7	74.1	34.7		36.0
26 Multifamily	5.3	3.0	2.7	4.0	9.1		3.8
27 Nonresidential	40.4	21.4	8.6	22.0	56.1		60.3

LOANS TO FARMERS	All sizes	1–9	10–24	25–49	50–99	100–249	250 and over
28 Amount of loans (thousands of dollars)	1,142,204	149,134	177,200	184,658	221,694	195,259	214,259
29 Number of loans	63,877	41,030	11,985	5,443	3,490	1,485	443
30 Weighted-average maturity (months)	7.2	8.1	7.6	6.6	7.1	8.3	5.7
31 Weighted-average interest rate (percent per annum)	14.14	13.49	13.58	13.72	13.76	14.77	15.25
32 Interquartile range[1]	13.39–15.03	12.89–14.37	12.55–14.67	13.21–14.28	13.42–14.20	13.65–15.75	13.90–16.36
By purpose of loan							
33 Feeder livestock	14.41	13.35	12.99	14.08	14.14	14.64	15.40
34 Other livestock	13.48	14.19	14.81	13.76	12.44	*	*
35 Other current operating expenses	14.28	13.52	13.81	14.09	14.32	14.73	14.79
36 Farm machinery and equipment	13.00	13.17	13.10	12.05	13.75	14.02	*
37 Other	14.60	13.35	13.52	14.06	14.16	16.39	15.86

1. Interest rate range that covers the middle 50 percent of the total dollar amount of loans made.

2. Fewer than 10 sample loans.

Source: *Federal Reserve Bulletin.*

▲ Revised; data published in the April 1980 BULLETIN were not final.

NOTE. For more detail, see the Board's E.2(416) statistical release.

CREDIT RATINGS OF FIXED INCOME AND MONEY SECURITIES

KEY TO STANDARD & POOR'S MUNICIPAL BOND RATINGS

Standard & Poor's municipal bond ratings cover obligations of states and political subdivisions. Ratings are assigned to general obligation and revenue bonds. General obligation bonds are usually secured by all resources available to the municipality and the factors outlined in the rating definitions below are weighed in determining the rating. Because revenue bonds in general are payable from specifically pledged revenues, the essential element in the security for a revenue bond is the quantity and quality of the pledged revenues available to pay debt service. Although an appraisal of most of the same factors that bear on the quality of general obligation bond credit is usually appropriate in the rating analysis of a revenue bond, other factors are important, including particularly the competitive position of the municipal enterprise under review and the basic security covenants. Although a rating reflects our judgment as to the issuer's capacity for the timely payment of debt service, in certain instances it may also reflect a mechanism or procedure for an assured and prompt cure of a default, should one occur, i.e., an insurance program, federal or state guaranty, or the automatic withholding and use of state aid to pay the defaulted debt service.

AAA

Prime—These are obligations of the highest quality. They have the strongest capacity for timely payment of debt service.

General obligation bonds—In a period of economic stress, the issuers will suffer the smallest declines in income and will be least susceptible to autonomous decline. Debt burden is moderate. A strong revenue structure appears more than adequate to meet future expenditure requirements. Quality of management appears superior.

Revenue bonds—Debt service coverage has been, and is expected to remain, substantial. Stability of the pledged revenues is also exceptionally strong, due to the competitive position of the municipal enterprise or to the nature of the revenues. Basic se-

Source: *Fixed Income Investor,* Standard & Poor's Corporation.

curity provisions (including rate covenant, earnings test for issuance of additional bonds, debt service reserve requirements) are rigorous. There is evidence of superior management.

AA

High grade—The investment characteristics of general obligation and revenue bonds in this group are only slightly less marked than those of the prime quality issues. Bonds rated AA have the second strongest capacity for payment of debt service.

A

Good grade—Principal and interest payments on bonds in this category are regarded as safe. This rating describes the third strongest capacity for payment of debt service. It differs from the two ratings as shown below.

General obligation bonds—There is some weakness, in the local economic base, in debt burden, in the balance between revenues and expenditures, or in quality of management. Under certain adverse circumstances, any one such weakness might impair the ability of the issuer to meet debt obligations at some future date.

Revenue bonds—Debt service coverage is good, but not exceptional. Stability of the pledged revenues could show some variations because of increased competition or economic influences on revenues. Basic security provisions, while satisfactory, are less stringent. Management performance appears adequate.

BBB

Medium grade—This is the lowest investment grade security rating.

General obligation bonds—Under certain adverse conditions, several of the above factors could contribute to a lesser capacity for payment of debt service. The difference between A and BBB ratings is that the latter shows more than one fundamental weakness, or one very substantial fundamental weakness, whereas the former shows only one deficiency among the factors considered.

Revenue bonds—Debt service coverage is only fair. Stability of the pledged revenues could show substantial variations, with the revenue flow possibly being subject to erosion over time. Basic security provisions are no more than adequate. Management performance could be stronger.

BB

Lower medium grade—Bonds in this group have some investment characteristics, but they no longer predominate. For the most part this rating indicates a speculative, non-investment grade obligation.

B

Low grade—Investment characteristics are virtually nonexistent, and default could be imminent.

D

Defaults—Payment of interest and/or principal is in arrears.

NCR

No contract rating—No ratings are assigned to new offerings unless a contract is applied for.

Provisional ratings—The letter "p" following a rating indicates the rating is provisional, where payment of debt service requirements will be largely or entirely dependent upon the timely completion of the project.

For both municipal and corporate bond ratings, in order to provide more detailed indications of credit quality, traditional bond letter ratings may be modified by the addition of a plus or a minus sign, when appropriate, to show relative standing within the major rating categories, the only exceptions being in the AAA–Prime grade category and in the lesser categories below BB.

KEY TO STANDARD & POOR'S CORPORATE BOND RATINGS

Bank-quality bonds—Under present commercial bank regulations bonds rated in the top four categories (AAA, AA, A, BBB, or their equivalent) generally are regarded as eligible for bank investment.

AAA

Bonds rated AAA are highest grade obligations. They possess the ultimate degree of protection as to principal and interest. In the market they move with interest rates, and hence provide the maximum safety on all counts.

AA

Bonds rated AA also qualify as high-grade obligations, and in the majority of instances differ from AAA issues only in small degree. Here, too, prices move with the long-term money market.

Source: *Fixed Income Investor,* Standard & Poor's Corporation.

A

Bonds rated A are regarded as upper medium grade. They have considerable investment strength but are not entirely free from adverse effects of changes in economic and trade conditions. Interest and principal are regarded as safe. They predominantly reflect money rates in their market behavior, but also, to some extent, economic conditions.

BBB

The BBB, or medium grade, category is on the borderline between definitely sound obligations and those where the speculative element begins to predominate. These bonds have adequate asset coverage and normally are protected by satisfactory earnings. Their susceptibility to changing conditions, particularly to depressions, necessitates constant watching. In the market, the bonds are more responsive to business and trade conditions than to interest rates. This group is the lowest that qualifies for commercial bank investment.

BB

Bonds given a BB rating are regarded as lower medium grade. They have only minor investment characteristics. In the case of utilities, interest is earned consistently but by narrow margins. In the case of other types of obligors, charges are earned on average by fair margin, but in poor periods deficit operations are possible.

B

Bonds rated CCC and CC are outright Payment of interest cannot be assured under difficult economic conditions.

CCC–CC

Bonds rated CCC and C are outright speculations, with the lower rating denoting the more speculative. Interest is paid, but continuation is questionable in periods of poor trade conditions. In the case of CC ratings, the bonds may be on an income basis and payment may be small.

C

The rating of C is reserved for income bonds on which no interest is being paid.

DDD–D

All bonds rated DDD, DD, and D are in default, with the rating indicating the relative salvage value.

NR—not rated.

Canadian corporate bonds are rated on the same basis as American corporate issues. The ratings measure the intrinsic value of the bonds, but they do not take into account exchange and other uncertainties.

KEY TO STANDARD & POOR'S PREFERRED STOCK RATINGS

Quality ratings on preferred stocks are expressed by symbols like those used in rating bonds. They are independent of Standard & Poor's bond ratings, however, in the sense that they are not necessarily graduated downward from the ratings accorded the issuing company's debt. They represent a considered judgment of the relative security of dividends but are not indicative of the protection of principal from market fluctuations. These ratings are as follows:

AAA	Prime	BB	Lower grade
AA	High grade	B	Speculative
A	Sound	C	Nonpaying
BBB	Medium grade		

To provide more detailed indications of credit quality, the traditional preferred stock letter ratings may be modified by the addition of a + or −, when appropriate, to show relative standing within the major rating categories, the only exceptions being in the AAA–Prime grade category and the lesser categories below BB.

KEY TO STANDARD & POOR'S COMMERCIAL PAPER RATINGS

These ratings are graded into four classifications ranging from A for the highest quality designations to B, C, and D for the lowest. Issuers rated A are further refined by the use of the numbers 1, 2, and 3, to denote relative strength within this highest classification, from A-1 down to A-3.

The requirements a company must meet to qualify for a given rating are as follows:

A RATING

1. Liquidity ratios are adequate to meet cash requirements.
   Liquidity ratios are basically as follows, broken down by the type of issuer:
   Industrial Company: acid-test ratio, current ratio, cash flow as a percent of current liabilities, short-term debt as a percent of current liabilities, short-term debt as a percent of current assets.

Source: *Fixed Income Investor,* Standard & Poor's Corporation.

Utility: current liabilities as a percent of revenues, cash flow as a percent of current liabilities, short-term debt as a percent of capitalization.
Finance Company: current ratio, current liabilities as a percent of net receivables, current liabilities as a percent of total liabilities.

2. The long-term senior debt rating is A or better; in some instances BBB credits may be allowed if other factors outweigh the BBB.
3. The issuer has access to at least two additional channels of borrowing.
4. Basic earnings and cash flow have an upward trend with allowances made for unusual circumstances.
5. Typically, the issuer's industry is well established and the issuer has a strong position within its industry.
6. The reliability and quality of management are unquestioned.

The relative strength or weakness of the above factors determines whether the issuer's commercial paper is rated A-1, A-2, or A-3.

B RATING

1. Liquidity ratios are good but not necessarily as high as in the A category.
2. The long-term senior debt rating is no less than BB.
3. Typically, the earnings growth record may be unimpressive and the potential of the company may not be fully developed. However, there is still demonstrated earning power.
4. The issuer has at least one alternative borrowing channel available.
5. The reliability and quality of management are at least average.

C RATING

1. There are wide swings in liquidity ratios from year to year.
2. The long-term senior debt rating is not of investment quality.
3. Maintenance of a satisfactory level of earnings is in some doubt due to management's ability, the burden of debt, competition, and other factors.
4. The flow of information and cooperation from management is barely acceptable and analysts may seriously question reliability and quality.

D RATING

Every indication is that the company will shortly be in default.

KEY TO MOODY'S MUNICIPAL BOND RATINGS

Aaa

Bonds which are rated Aaa are judged to be of the best quality. They carry the smallest degree of investment risk and are generally referred to as "gilt edge." Interest payments are protected by a large or by an exceptionally stable margin and principal is secure. While the various protective elements are likely to change, such changes as can be visualized are most unlikely to impair the fundamentally strong position of such issues.

Aa

Bonds which are rated Aa are judged to be of high quality by all standards. Together with the Aaa group they comprise what are generally known as high grade bonds. They are rated lower than the best bonds because margins of protection may not be as large as in Aaa securities or fluctuation of protective elements may be of greater amplitude or there may be other elements present which make the long-term risks appear somewhat larger than in Aaa securities.

A

Bonds which are rated A possess many favorable investment attributes and are to be considered as upper medium grade obligations. Factors giving security to principal and interest are considered adequate, but elements may be present which suggest a susceptibility to impairment sometime in the future.

Baa

Bonds which are rated Baa are considered as medium grade obligations; i.e., they are neither highly protected nor poorly secured. Interest payments and principal security appear adequate for the present but certain protective elements may be lacking or may be characteristically unreliable over any great length of time. Such bonds lack outstanding investment characteristics and in fact have speculative characteristics as well.

Ba

Bonds which are rated Ba are judged to have speculative elements; their future cannot be considered as well-assured. Often the protection of interest and principal payments

Source: *Moody's Bond Record,* Moody's Investor Service, Inc.

may be very moderate, and thereby not well safeguarded during both good and bad times over the future. Uncertainty of position characterizes bonds in this class.

B

Bonds which are rated B generally lack characteristics of the desirable investment. Assurance of interest and principal payments or of maintenance of other terms of the contract over any long period of time may be small.

Caa

Bonds which are rated Caa are of poor standing. Such issues may be in default or there may be present elements of danger with respect to principal or interest.

Ca

Bonds which are rated Ca represent obligations which are speculative in a high degree. Such issues are often in default or have other marked shortcomings.

C

Bonds which are rated C are the lowest rated class of bonds, and issues so rated can be regarded as having extremely poor prospects of ever attaining any real investment standing.

CON. (. . .)

Bonds for which the security depends upon the completion of some act or the fulfillment of some condition are rated conditionally. These are bonds secured by (a) earnings of projects under construction, (b) earnings of projects unseasoned in operating experience, (c) rentals which begin when facilities are completed, or (d) payments to which some other limiting condition attaches. Parenthetical rating denotes probable credit stature upon completion of construction or elimination of basis of condition.

Those bonds in the A and Baa groups which Moody's believes possess the strongest investment attributes are designated by the symbols A1 and Baa1.

KEY TO MOODY'S SHORT-TERM LOAN RATINGS

MIG 1

Loans bearing this designation are of the best quality, enjoying strong protection from established cash flows of funds for their servicing or from established and broad-based access to the market for refinancing, or both.

MIG 2

Loans bearing this designation are of high quality, with margins of protection ample although not so large as in the preceding group.

MIG 3

Loans bearing this designation are of favorable quality, with all security elements accounted for but lacking the undeniable strength of the preceding grades. Market access for refinancing, in particular, is likely to be less well established.

MIG 4

Loans bearing this designation are of adequate quality, carrying specific risk but having protection commonly regarded as required of an investment security and not distinctly or predominantly speculative.

KEY TO MOODY'S CORPORATE BOND RATINGS

Aaa

Bonds which are rated Aaa are judged to be of the best quality. They carry the smallest degree of investment risk and are generally referred to as "gilt edge." Interest payments are protected by a large or by an exceptionally stable margin and principal is secure. While the various protective elements are likely to change, such changes as can be visualized are most unlikely to impair the fundamentally strong position of such issues.

Aa

Bonds which are rated Aa are judged to be of high quality by all standards. Together with the Aaa group they comprise what are generally known as high grade bonds. They are rated lower than the best bonds because margins of protection may not be as large as in Aaa securities or fluctuation of protective elements may be of greater amplitude or there may be other elements present which make the long-term risks appear somewhat larger than in Aaa securities.

A

Bonds which are rated A possess many favorable investment attributes and are to be

Source: *Moody's Bond Record*, Moody's Investor Service, Inc.

considered as upper medium grade obligations. Factors giving security to principal and interest are considered adequate, but elements may be present which suggest a susceptibility to impairment sometime in the future.

Baa

Bonds which are rated Baa are considered as medium grade obligations; i.e., they are neither highly protected nor poorly secured. Interest payments and principal security appear adequate for the present but certain protective elements may be lacking or may be characteristically unreliable over any great length of time. Such bonds lack outstanding investment characteristics and in fact have speculative characteristics as well.

Ba

Bonds which are rated Ba are judged to have speculative elements; their future cannot be considered as well-assured. Often the protection of interest and principal payments may be very moderate, and thereby not well safeguarded during both good and bad times over the future. Uncertainty of position characterizes bonds in this class.

B

Bonds which are rated B generally lack characteristics of the desirable investment. Assurance of interest and principal payments or of maintenance of other terms of the contract over any long period of time may be small.

Caa

Bonds which are rated Caa are of poor standing. Such issues may be in default or there may be present elements of danger with respect to principal or interest.

Ca

Bonds which are rated Ca represent obligations which are speculative in a high degree. Such issues are often in default or have other marked shortcomings.

C

Bonds which are rated C are the lowest rated class of bonds, and issues so rated can be regarded as having extremely poor prospects of ever attaining any real investment standing.

KEY TO MOODY'S PREFERRED STOCK RATINGS

Moody's Rating Policy Review Board extended its rating services to include quality designations on preferred stocks on October 1, 1973. The decision to rate preferred stocks, which Moody's had done prior to 1935, was prompted by evidence of investor interest. Moody's believes that its rating of preferred stocks is especially appropriate in view of the ever-increasing amount of these securities outstanding, and the fact that continuing inflation and its ramifications have resulted generally in the dilution of some of the protection afforded them as well as other fixed-income securities.

Because of the fundamental differences between preferred stocks and bonds, a variation of our familiar bond rating symbols is being used in the quality ranking of preferred stocks. The symbols, presented below, are designed to avoid comparison with bond quality in absolute terms. It should always be borne in mind that preferred stocks occupy a junior position to bonds within a particular capital structure.

Preferred stock rating symbols and their definitions are as follows:

aaa

An issue which is rated aaa is considered to be a top-quality preferred stock. This rating indicates good asset protection and the least risk of dividend impairment within the universe of preferred stocks.

aa

An issue which is rated aa is considered a high-grade preferred stock. This rating indicates that there is reasonable assurance that earnings and asset protection will remain relatively well maintained in the foreseeable future.

a

An issue which is rated a is considered to be an upper medium grade preferred stock. While risks are judged to be somewhat greater than in the aaa and aa classifications, earnings and asset protection are, nevertheless, expected to be maintained at adequate levels.

baa

An issue which is rated baa is considered to be medium grade, neither highly protected

Source: *Moody's Bond Record,* Moody's Investors Service, Inc.

nor poorly secured. Earnings and asset protection appear adequate at present but may be questionable over any great length of time.

ba

An issue which is rated ba is considered to have speculative elements and its future cannot be considered well assured. Earnings and asset protection may be very moderate and not well safeguarded during adverse periods. Uncertainty of position characterizes preferred stocks in this class.

b

An issue which is rated b generally lacks the characteristics of a desirable investment. Assurance of dividend payments and maintenance of other terms of the issue over any long period of time may be small.

caa

An issue which is rated caa is likely to be in arrears on dividend payments. This rating designation does not purport to indicate the future status of payments.

KEY TO MOODY'S COMMERCIAL PAPER RATINGS*

Moody's evaluates the salient features that affect a commercial paper issuer's financial and competitive position. Our appraisal includes, but is not limited to, the review of such factors as: quality of management, industry strengths and risks, vulnerability to business cycles, competitive position, liquidity measurements, debt structure, operating trends and access to capital markets. Differing degrees of weight are applied to these factors as deemed appropriate for individual situations.

Issuers rated in all three Prime categories are judged to be investment grade.

PRIME-1

Commercial paper issuers rated PRIME-1 are judged to be of the best quality. Their short-term debt obligations carry the smallest degree of investment risk. Margins of support

* The term "commercial paper" as used by Moody's means unsecured promissory obligations having a maximum maturity of 270 days, proceeds of which are normally employed to support current transactions or for bridge financing. Moody's makes no representation as to whether such commercial paper is by any other definition "commercial paper" or is exempt from registration under the Securities Act of 1933, as amended.

for current indebtedness are large or stable with cash flow and asset protection well assured. Current liquidity provides ample coverage of near-term liabilities and unused alternative financing arrangements are generally available. While protective elements may change over the intermediate or longer term, such changes are most unlikely to impair the fundamentally strong position of short-term obligations.

PRIME-2

Issuers in the commercial paper market rated PRIME-2 are of high quality. Protection for short-term note holders is assured with liquidity and value of current assets as well as cash generation in sound relationship to current indebtedness. They are rated lower

Source: *Moody's Bond Record,* Moody's Investors Service, Inc.

than the best commercial paper issuers because margins of protection may not be as large or because fluctuations of protective elements over the near or intermediate term may be of greater amplitude. Temporary increases in relative short and overall debt load may occur. Alternative means of financing remain assured.

PRIME-3

Commercial paper issuers rated PRIME-3 possess favorable investment attributes for short-term commitment. Liquidity considerations and cash generation provide satisfactory support for short-term debt repayment. While near-term investors are well-protected, elements may be present which suggest improvement or deterioration in support at sometime in the future. Alternative financing strategies have been outlined.

SOURCES AND USES OF FUNDS—NONFARM, NONFINANCIAL CORPORATE BUSINESS
QUARTERLY DATA AT SEASONALLY ADJUSTED ANNUAL RATES ($ billions)

Period	Sources							Uses			Discrepancy (sources less uses)
	Total	Internal[1]	External					Total	Purchase of physical assets[2]	Increase in financial assets	
			Total	Credit market funds			Other				
				Total	Long-term	Short-term					
1970	104.4	58.9	45.5	40.7	34.2	6.5	4.9	95.9	80.3	15.6	8.5
1971	127.8	68.6	59.3	45.2	41.9	3.3	14.1	119.6	86.0	33.5	8.2
1972	161.6	80.8	80.8	58.2	45.3	12.9	22.6	145.8	100.3	45.6	15.8
1973	200.0	83.8	116.2	73.0	49.2	23.8	43.1	185.6	123.3	62.3	14.4
1974	191.3	75.7	115.6	82.1	51.6	30.6	33.4	179.0	134.7	44.4	12.2
1975	150.0	106.8	43.2	37.9	44.1	-6.3	-5.3	133.0	99.9	33.2	16.9
1976	209.7	125.3	84.4	60.7	49.1	11.6	23.8	183.3	139.0	44.3	26.4
1977	242.3	139.9	102.3	79.9	53.0	26.9	22.4	216.8	169.9	46.9	25.5
1978	295.7	148.8	146.9	94.7	61.5	33.2	52.2	274.3	195.9	78.3	21.4
1979	339.0	158.3	180.7	113.6	70.0	43.6	67.0	324.9	223.8	101.1	14.1
1978: I	259.6	135.0	124.5	94.7	51.2	43.5	29.8	232.5	177.0	55.0	27.0
II	297.7	150.5	147.2	92.7	65.2	27.5	54.5	281.3	203.2	78.1	16.4
III	303.5	153.8	149.7	90.4	63.1	27.3	59.3	284.4	199.9	84.4	19.1
IV	322.1	155.9	166.2	101.1	66.5	34.6	65.1	298.9	203.6	95.2	23.2
1979: I	336.7	154.4	182.3	112.0	66.3	45.7	70.3	324.7	214.0	110.7	12.1
II	320.8	159.0	161.8	127.1	76.9	50.2	34.6	302.6	230.9	71.7	18.2
III	385.0	161.6	223.4	129.1	75.3	53.8	94.3	371.3	229.9	141.4	13.8
IV	310.2	158.2	152.0	89.3	63.2	26.1	62.7	297.9	220.3	77.6	12.3
1980: I p	364.4	153.3	211.1	124.6	70.0	54.6	86.5	352.2	229.5	122.7	12.2

[1] Undistributed profits (after inventory valuation and capital consumption adjustments), capital consumption allowances, and foreign branch profits.
[2] Plant and equipment, residential structures, inventory investment, and mineral rights from U.S. Government.

Source: Board of Governors of the Federal Reserve System.

Source: Economic Indicators, Council of Economic Advisers.

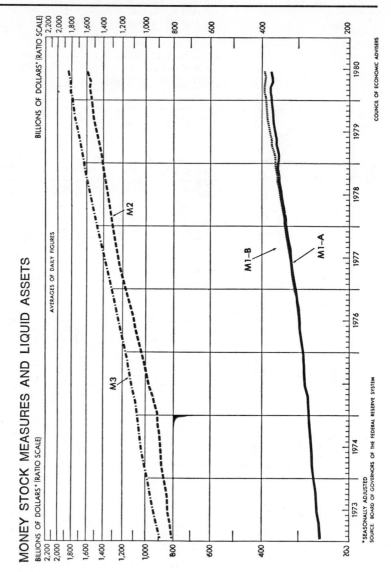

MONEY STOCK MEASURES AND LIQUID ASSETS

BILLIONS OF DOLLARS* (RATIO SCALE)

AVERAGES OF DAILY FIGURES

M3

M2

M1-B

M1-A

BILLIONS OF DOLLARS* (RATIO SCALE)

*SEASONALLY ADJUSTED
SOURCE: BOARD OF GOVERNORS OF THE FEDERAL RESERVE SYSTEM

COUNCIL OF ECONOMIC ADVISERS

[Averages of daily figures; billions of dollars, seasonally adjusted]

Period	M1-A Currency plus demand deposits	M1-B M1-A plus other checkable deposits at banks and thrift institutions	M2 M1-B plus overnight RPs and Eurodollars, MMMF shares, and savings and small time deposits at commercial banks and thrift institutions[1]	M3 M2 plus large time deposits and term RPs at commercial banks and thrift institutions	L M3 plus other liquid assets	Percent change[2] M1-A	Percent change[2] M1-B	Percent change[2] M2	Percent change[2] M3
1973: Dec	264.1	264.4	858.1	976.1	1,137.2	5.4	5.5	7.0	11.2
1974: Dec	275.3	275.7	906.2	1,058.6	1,242.8	4.2	4.3	5.6	8.5
1975: Dec	287.9	289.0	1,022.4	1,161.0	1,369.6	4.6	4.8	12.8	9.7
1976: Dec	305.0	307.7	1,166.7	1,299.7	1,523.5	5.9	6.5	14.1	11.9
1977: Dec	328.4	332.5	1,294.1	1,460.3	1,715.5	7.7	8.1	10.9	12.4
1978: Dec	351.6	359.9	1,401.5	1,623.6	1,927.7	7.1	8.2	8.3	11.2
1979: Dec	369.7	386.4	1,525.5	1,775.5	2,141.1	5.1	7.4	8.8	9.4
1979: June	359.4	373.9	1,465.9	1,695.2	2,048.8	4.5	7.9	9.4	9.0
July	362.0	377.4	1,478.3	1,709.2	2,063.8	6.9	9.9	10.3	9.7
Aug	364.0	379.9	1,491.8	1,725.8	2,081.3	8.2	10.9	11.0	10.4
Sept	365.9	382.2	1,502.9	1,745.5	2,110.0	8.0	10.3	9.8	11.3
Oct	366.6	382.9	1,510.1	1,757.8	2,120.4	6.0	7.3	9.4	10.9
Nov	368.0	384.2	1,516.4	1,765.4	2,126.4	7.2	8.3	8.3	10.5
Dec	369.7	386.4	1,525.5	1,775.5	2,141.1	5.8	6.8	7.7	9.7
1980: Jan	370.8	388.1	1,534.5	1,786.9	2,155.2	4.9	5.8	7.5	9.3
Feb	373.7	391.3	1,546.7	1,804.5	2,175.9	5.4	6.1	6.8	9.3
Mar	373.1	391.2	1,553.1	1,811.1	2,190.2	4.0	4.8	5.3	7.7
Apr	367.6	386.6	1,549.8	1,811.1	2,201.0	.5	1.9	6.1	6.2
May	367.8	386.2	1,562.3	1,824.4	2,216.9	-.1	1.0	7.9	6.8
June p	371.3	390.9	1,584.5	1,842.9		.9	2.3		7.7

[1] Total M2 excludes demand deposits held by thrift institutions at commercial banks, not shown separately in components.

[2] Annual changes are from December to December and monthly changes are from 6 months earlier at a seasonally adjusted annual rate.

Source: *Economic Indicators*, Council of Economic Advisers.

NOTE.—See page 27 for components.
See *Federal Reserve Bulletin*, February 1980, for details on series.
Source: Board of Governors of the Federal Reserve System.

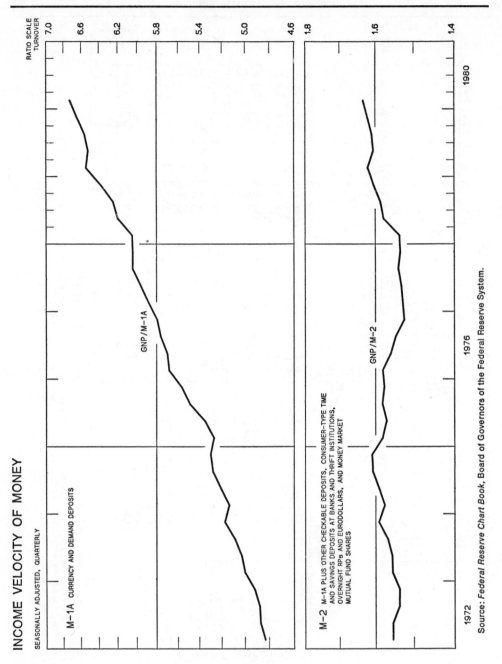

INCOME VELOCITY OF MONEY

SEASONALLY ADJUSTED, QUARTERLY

RATIO SCALE
TURNOVER

7.0
6.6
6.2
5.8
5.4
5.0
4.6
1.8
1.6
1.4

M–1A CURRENCY AND DEMAND DEPOSITS

GNP/M–1A

M–2 M–1A PLUS OTHER CHECKABLE DEPOSITS, CONSUMER-TYPE TIME
AND SAVINGS DEPOSITS AT BANKS AND THRIFT INSTITUTIONS,
OVERNIGHT RPs AND EURODOLLARS, AND MONEY MARKET
MUTUAL FUND SHARES

GNP/M–2

1972
1976
1980

Source: *Federal Reserve Chart Book*, Board of Governors of the Federal Reserve System.

CURRENT ASSETS AND LIABILITIES OF NONFINANCIAL CORPORATIONS
($ billions, except as noted)

End of period	Current assets						Current liabilities			Net working capital	Current ratio [1]
	Total	Cash	U.S. government securities	Notes and accounts receivable	Inventories	Other current assets	Total	Notes and accounts payable	Other current liabilities		
SEC series: [2]											
1970	492.3	50.2	7.7	206.1	193.3	35.0	304.9	211.3	93.6	187.4	1.615
1971	529.6	53.3	11.0	221.1	200.4	43.8	326.0	220.5	105.5	203.6	1.625
1972	599.3	59.0	10.6	248.2	225.7	55.8	375.6	282.9	92.7	223.7	1.595
1973	697.8	66.3	12.8	288.5	263.9	66.4	450.9	340.3	110.7	246.9	1.548
1974	790.7	71.1	12.3	322.1	313.6	71.7	530.4	402.3	128.1	260.3	1.491
FTC-FRB series: [3]											
1974	735.4	73.2	11.1	265.8	319.5	65.9	453.4	269.8	183.6	282.0	1.622
1975	759.0	82.1	19.0	272.1	315.9	69.9	451.6	264.2	187.4	307.4	1.681
1976	826.3	87.3	23.6	293.3	342.9	79.2	492.7	282.0	210.6	333.6	1.677
1977	900.9	94.3	18.7	325.0	375.6	87.3	546.8	313.7	233.1	354.1	1.648
1978	1,028.1	103.7	17.8	381.9	428.3	96.3	661.9	375.1	286.8	366.2	1.553
1978: I	925.0	88.8	18.6	337.4	390.5	89.7	574.2	325.2	249.0	350.7	1.611
II	954.2	91.3	17.3	356.0	399.3	90.3	593.5	338.0	255.6	360.6	1.608
III	992.6	91.7	16.1	376.4	415.5	92.9	626.0	356.2	269.7	366.6	1.586
IV	1,028.1	103.7	17.8	381.9	428.3	96.3	661.9	375.1	286.8	366.2	1.553
1979: I	1,078.6	102.4	19.2	405.3	452.6	99.1	701.6	392.6	309.0	377.0	1.537
II	1,110.6	100.1	20.8	419.0	469.2	101.5	723.9	410.8	313.2	386.7	1.534
III	1,169.6	103.6	17.8	448.9	492.7	106.7	773.7	443.1	330.6	395.9	1.512
IV	1,199.9	116.2	17.8	451.7	503.9	110.3	803.7	460.8	342.8	396.3	1.493

[1] Total current assets divided by total current liabilities.
[2] Based on data from *Statistics of Income,* Department of the Treasury.
[3] Based on data from *Quarterly Financial Report for Manufacturing, Mining, and Trade Corporations,* Federal Trade Commission.

Source: *Economic Indicators,* Council of Economic Advisers.

NOTE.—SEC series not available after 1974.
See *Federal Reserve Bulletin,* July 1978, for details regarding the series.
Sources: Board of Governors of the Federal Reserve System, Federal Trade Commission, and Securities and Exchange Commission.

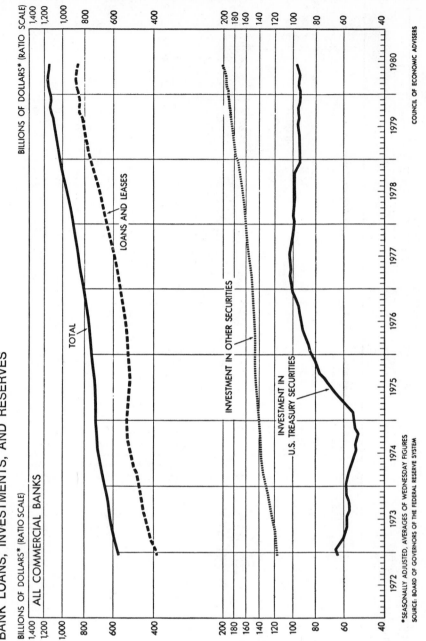

BANK LOANS, INVESTMENTS, AND RESERVES

BILLIONS OF DOLLARS* (RATIO SCALE)

ALL COMMERCIAL BANKS

TOTAL

LOANS AND LEASES

INVESTMENT IN OTHER SECURITIES

INVESTMENT IN
U.S. TREASURY SECURITIES

BILLIONS OF DOLLARS* (RATIO SCALE)

*SEASONALLY ADJUSTED, AVERAGES OF WEDNESDAY FIGURES
SOURCE: BOARD OF GOVERNORS OF THE FEDERAL RESERVE SYSTEM

COUNCIL OF ECONOMIC ADVISERS

[Billions of dollars, seasonally adjusted, except as noted]

| Period | All commercial banks [1] | | | | | All member banks [3] | | | | |
| | Total loans and investments | Loans and leases | | Investments | | Reserves | | | Borrowings (millions of dollars, unadjusted) | |
		Total [2]	Commercial and industrial loans	U.S. Treasury securities	Other securities	Total	Non-borrowed	Required	Total	Seasonal
1973: Dec	647.8	460.3	165.6	58.7	128.8	34.98	33.68	34.68	1,298	41
1974: Dec	713.6	519.9	197.3	53.7	140.0	36.66	35.94	36.41	703	32
1975: Dec	744.6	516.9	189.8	82.1	145.7	34.67	34.54	34.40	127	13
1976: Dec	804.3	554.8	191.2	100.6	149.0	34.90	34.85	34.63	62	12
1977: Dec	891.1	632.1	211.2	99.5	159.6	36.00	35.43	35.81	558	54
1978: Dec	1,014.3	747.8	246.5	93.4	173.1	41.16	40.29	40.93	874	134
1979: Dec	1,132.5	847.2	290.5	93.8	191.5	43.57	42.10	43.13	1,473	82
1979: June	1,080.0	803.1	270.4	94.8	182.1	40.53	39.11	40.31	1,396	188
July	1,092.2	813.4	275.5	95.3	183.5	40.78	39.61	40.57	1,179	168
Aug	1,102.8	823.3	279.9	94.1	185.4	41.11	40.03	40.89	1,097	177
Sept	1,122.8	840.0	285.9	95.2	187.6	41.43	40.09	41.24	1,344	169
Oct	1,129.1	845.0	288.6	95.3	188.8	42.20	40.18	41.93	2,022	161
Nov	1,128.6	843.8	288.3	94.3	190.5	43.06	41.15	42.81	1,906	146
Dec	1,132.5	847.2	290.5	93.8	191.5	43.57	42.10	43.13	1,473	82
1980: Jan	1,144.8	858.5	295.6	93.2	193.1	43.44	42.20	432.0	1,241	75
Feb	1,162.7	872.7	301.1	94.8	195.2	43.35	41.70	43.14	1,655	96
Mar	1,165.2	874.7	302.7	94.5	196.0	43.68	40.85	43.47	2,824	150
Apr	1,161.0	871.6	301.3	93.2	196.2	44.91	42.45	44.64	2,443	156
May	1,154.9	860.5	297.6	94.6	199.7	44.46	43.44	44.28	1,028	64
June [4]	1,152.4	853.9	296.6	97.0	201.5	43.98	43.60	43.77	365	12

[1] Data are averages of Wednesday figures.
[2] Excludes loans to commercial banks in the United States.
[3] Data are averages of daily figures. Member bank reserves series reflects actual reserve requirement percentages with no adjustment to eliminate the effect of changes in Regulations D and M.

[4] Data for loans and investments are estimates.

Source: Board of Governors of the Federal Reserve System.

Source: *Economic Indicators*, Council of Economic Advisers.

NEW SECURITY ISSUES OF STATE AND LOCAL GOVERNMENTS
MILLIONS OF DOLLARS

Type of issue or issuer, or use	1977	1978	1979	1979				1980	
				Sept.	Oct.	Nov.	Dec.	Jan.p	Feb.p
1 All issues, new and refunding[1]	46,769	48,607	43,490	2,479	4,229	4,172	3,583	3,013	2,350
Type of issue									
2 General obligation	18,042	17,854	12,109	699	1,037	805	855	1,151	987
3 Revenue	28,655	30,658	31,256	1,773	3,180	3,355	2,712	1,856	1,353
4 Housing Assistance Administration[2]	...	...	...	...	...	...	...	...	...
5 U.S. government loans	72	95	125	7	12	12	16	6	10
Type of issuer									
6 State	6,354	6,632	4,314	113	294	274	569	699	327
7 Special district and statutory authority	21,717	24,156	23,434	1,404	2,749	2,697	2,102	1,379	1,202
8 Municipalities, counties, townships, school districts	18,623	17,718	15,617	955	1,174	1,189	896	929	811
9 Issues for new capital, total	36,189	37,629	41,505	2,436	4,171	3,702	3,186	3,000	2,340
Use of proceeds									
10 Education	5,076	5,003	5,130	218	311	298	408	220	366
11 Transportation	2,951	3,460	2,441	38	562	97	214	172	176
12 Utilities and conservation	8,119	9,026	8,594	336	1,426	515	409	547	326
13 Social welfare	8,274	10,494	15,968	1,082	1,191	2,042	1,724	1,285	1,050
14 Industrial aid	4,676	3,526	3,836	382	427	369	157	51	68
15 Other purposes	7,093	6,120	5,536	380	254	381	274	725	354

1. Par amounts of long-term issues based on date of sale.
2. Only bonds sold pursuant to the 1949 Housing Act, which are secured by contract requiring the Housing Assistance Administration to make annual contributions to the local authority.

SOURCE. Public Securities Association
Source: *Federal Reserve Bulletin.*

NEW SECURITY ISSUES OF CORPORATIONS
MILLIONS OF DOLLARS

Type of issue or issuer, or use	1977	1978	1979	1979					1980	
				Aug.	Sept.	Oct.	Nov.	Dec.	Jan.	Feb.
1 All issues¹	53,792	47,230	51,102	4,083	4,308	4,561	3,834	3,774	5,740	4,114
2 Bonds	42,015	36,872	39,690	2,859	3,021	3,532	2,589	2,441	4,397	2,518
Type of offering										
3 Public	24,072	19,815	25,815	1,973	2,167	2,669	1,583	1,500	2,450	1,426
4 Private placement	17,943	17,057	13,877	886	854	863	1,006	941	1,947	1,092
Industry group										
5 Manufacturing	12,204	9,572	9,590	806	1,095	1,334	322	265	774	831
6 Commercial and miscellaneous	6,234	5,246	3,939	413	361	214	207	455	503	244
7 Transportation	1,996	2,007	3,054	171	175	296	257	187	313	153
8 Public utility	8,262	7,092	8,058	137	620	1,107	663	743	1,338	568
9 Communication	3,063	3,373	4,198	336	418	433	854	55	483	518
10 Real estate and financial	10,258	9,586	10,853	996	353	147	287	737	987	205
11 Stocks	11,777	10,358	11,410	1,224	1,287	1,029	1,245	1,333	1,343	1,596
Type										
12 Preferred	3,916	2,832	3,650	401	698	195	465	289	290	88
13 Common	7,861	7,526	7,760	823	589	834	780	1,044	1,053	1,508
Industry group										
14 Manufacturing	1,189	1,241	1,686	360	394	151	158	231	324	380
15 Commercial and miscellaneous	1,834	1,816	2,623	266	218	98	286	430	313	426
16 Transportation	456	263	255	142	4		2		59	58
17 Public utility	5,865	5,140	5,218	366	527	662	607	365	506	627
18 Communication	1,379	264	-303		83	47	2	1		39
19 Real estate and financial	1,049	1,631	1,324	91	61	70	190	306	140	65

1. Figures, which represent gross proceeds of issues maturing in more than one year, sold for cash in the United States, are principal amount or number of units multiplied by offering price. Excludes offerings of less than $100,000, secondary offerings, undefined or exempted issues as defined in the Securities Act of 1933, employee stock plans, investment companies other than closed-end, intra-corporate transactions, and sales to foreigners.

Source: *Federal Reserve Bulletin.*

SOURCE. Securities and Exchange Commission.

FUNDS RAISED IN U.S. CREDIT MARKETS
BILLIONS OF DOLLARS; QUARTERLY DATA ARE AT SEASONALLY ADJUSTED ANNUAL RATES

Transaction category, sector	1974	1975	1976	1977	1978	1979	1977 H1	1977 H2	1978 H1	1978 H2	1979 H1	1979 H2
						Nonfinancial sectors						
1 Total funds raised	**191.3**	**210.8**	**271.9**	**338.5**	**400.3**	**395.2**	**298.1**	**378.9**	**384.5**	**416.1**	**383.2**	**408.5**
2 Excluding equities	**187.4**	**200.7**	**261.1**	**335.4**	**398.2**	**390.9**	**296.9**	**373.8**	**387.1**	**409.3**	**380.5**	**402.5**
By sector and instrument												
3 U.S. government	11.8	85.4	69.0	56.8	53.7	37.4	46.1	67.4	61.4	46.0	27.3	47.4
4 Treasury securities	12.0	85.8	69.1	57.6	55.1	38.8	46.7	68.6	62.3	47.9	29.6	47.9
5 Agency issues and mortgages	-.2	-.4	-.1	-.9	-1.4	-1.4	-.6	-1.2	-.9	-1.9	-2.3	-.5
6 All other nonfinancial sectors	179.5	125.4	202.9	281.8	346.6	357.9	252.0	311.5	323.1	370.2	355.9	361.2
7 Corporate equities	3.8	10.1	10.8	3.1	2.1	4.4	1.2	5.1	-2.6	6.8	2.7	6.0
8 Debt instruments	175.6	115.3	192.0	278.6	344.5	353.5	250.8	306.4	325.7	363.4	353.2	355.2
9 Private domestic nonfinancial sectors	164.1	112.1	182.0	267.9	314.4	335.9	241.5	294.2	302.5	326.3	340.2	333.1
10 Corporate equities	4.1	.9	10.5	2.7	2.6	3.5	.5	4.9	-1.8	7.0	2.8	4.1
11 Debt instruments	160.0	102.1	171.5	265.1	311.8	332.4	241.0	289.3	304.3	319.2	337.4	329.0
12 Debt capital instruments	98.0	98.4	123.5	175.6	196.6	201.9	158.7	192.5	188.0	205.1	202.6	201.5
13 State and local obligations	16.5	16.1	15.7	23.7	28.3	21.4	22.3	25.0	27.8	28.7	17.4	25.3
14 Corporate bonds	19.7	27.2	22.8	21.0	20.1	21.2	16.6	25.4	20.6	19.6	23.2	19.4
Mortgages												
15 Home	34.8	39.5	63.7	96.4	104.5	110.2	89.7	103.1	99.8	109.2	111.0	109.4
16 Multifamily residential	6.9	*	1.8	7.4	10.2	8.9	6.4	8.4	9.3	11.2	8.1	9.8
17 Commercial	15.1	11.0	13.4	18.4	23.3	25.0	14.8	21.9	21.2	25.4	25.7	24.7
18 Farm	5.0	4.6	6.1	8.8	10.2	10.2	9.0	8.7	9.3	11.1	17.1	13.0
19 Other debt instruments	62.0	3.8	48.0	89.5	115.2	130.5	82.3	96.7	116.3	114.1	134.8	127.4
20 Consumer credit	9.9	9.7	25.6	40.6	50.6	42.3	36.6	44.5	50.1	51.0	47.3	37.2
21 Bank loans n.e.c.	31.7	-12.3	4.0	27.0	37.3	50.0	27.3	26.7	43.1	31.4	47.7	53.5
22 Open market paper	6.6	-2.6	4.0	2.9	5.2	10.9	3.4	2.4	5.3	5.1	10.8	10.9
23 Other	13.7	9.0	14.4	19.0	22.2	27.3	14.9	23.2	17.8	26.5	29.0	25.8
24 By borrowing sector	164.1	112.1	182.0	267.9	314.4	335.9	241.5	294.2	302.5	326.3	340.2	333.1
25 State and local governments	15.5	13.7	15.2	20.4	23.6	18.0	15.7	25.0	21.0	26.1	14.4	21.6
26 Households	51.2	49.5	90.7	139.9	162.6	164.2	129.4	150.4	156.1	169.1	167.7	160.5
27 Farm	8.0	8.8	9.0	14.7	18.1	24.6	15.7	13.8	15.3	20.8	23.4	25.8
28 Nonfarm noncorporate	7.7	2.0	5.4	12.5	15.4	15.5	13.4	12.5	16.3	14.5	15.0	16.1
29 Corporate	81.7	38.1	59.8	80.3	94.7	113.6	67.3	92.4	93.7	95.8	119.6	109.2
30 Foreign	15.4	13.3	20.8	13.9	32.3	22.0	10.5	17.3	20.6	43.9	15.7	28.1
31 Corporate equities	-.2	.3	.3	.4	-.5	.9	.6	.2	-.8	-.2	-.1	1.9
32 Debt instruments	15.7	13.2	20.5	13.5	32.8	21.1	9.9	17.1	21.4	44.1	15.8	26.2
33 Bonds	2.1	6.2	8.6	5.1	4.0	4.1	4.4	5.7	5.0	3.0	3.5	4.7
34 Bank loans n.e.c.	4.7	3.9	6.8	3.1	18.3	2.9	-.4	6.5	9.3	27.3	3.1	2.3
35 Open market paper	7.3	.3	1.9	2.4	6.6	11.2	2.7	2.2	3.6	9.6	6.1	16.3
36 U.S. government loans	1.6	2.8	3.3	3.0	3.9	3.0	3.1	2.9	3.6	4.2	3.1	2.8

Financial sectors

	39.2	12.7	24.1	54.0	81.4	86.2	47.7	60.3	80.7	82.1	87.9	84.5
37 Total funds raised	**39.2**	**12.7**	**24.1**	**54.0**	**81.4**	**86.2**	**47.7**	**60.3**	**80.7**	**82.1**	**87.9**	**84.5**
By instrument												
38 U.S. government related	23.1	13.5	18.6	26.3	41.4	52.4	22.6	29.9	38.5	44.3	45.9	58.9
39 Sponsored credit agency securities	16.6	2.3	3.3	7.0	23.1	24.3	7.1	6.8	21.9	24.3	21.7	26.8
40 Mortgage pool securities	5.8	10.3	15.7	20.5	18.3	28.1	17.9	23.1	16.6	20.1	24.2	32.0
41 Loans from U.S. government	.7	.9	-.4	-1.2	.0	.0	-2.3	.0	.0	.0	.0	.0
42 Private financial sectors	16.2	-.8	5.5	27.7	40.0	33.8	25.1	30.4	42.2	37.8	41.9	25.7
43 Corporate equities	.6	-1.4	1.0	.9	1.7	.9	.9	.8	2.2	1.1	2.7	-1.0
44 Debt instruments	15.9	2.9	4.4	26.9	38.3	32.9	24.2	29.6	40.0	36.7	39.2	26.7
45 Corporate bonds	2.1	2.3	5.8	10.1	7.5	6.9	10.2	10.1	8.5	6.4	8.9	5.0
46 Mortgages	-1.3	-3.7	2.1	3.1	.9	-1.2	3.1	3.0	2.1	-.3	-.4	-1.9
47 Bank loans n.e.c.	-4.6	1.1	-3.7	-.3	2.8	-.4	-1.8	1.2	2.5	3.1	-1.4	.6
48 Open market paper and repurchase agreements	3.8		2.2	9.6	14.6	18.4	9.8	9.5	13.5	15.7	24.4	12.4
49 Loans from Federal Home Loan Banks	6.7	-4.0	-2.0	4.3	12.5	9.2	2.9	5.8	13.2	11.8	7.7	10.6
By sector												
50 Sponsored credit agencies	17.3	3.2	2.6	5.8	23.1	24.3	4.7	6.8	21.9	24.3	21.7	26.8
51 Mortgage pools	5.8	10.8	15.7	20.5	18.3	28.1	17.9	23.1	16.6	20.1	24.2	32.0
52 Private financial sectors	16.2	-.8	5.5	27.7	40.0	33.8	25.1	30.4	42.2	37.8	41.9	25.7
53 Commercial banks	1.2	1.2	2.3	1.1	1.3	1.6	.8	1.5	1.5	1.1	1.3	1.8
54 Bank affiliates	3.5	-.3	-.1	1.3	6.7	4.5	1.3	1.2	5.8	7.6	6.2	2.9
55 Savings and loan associations	4.8	-2.3	.9	9.9	14.3	9.8	8.3	11.5	16.4	12.2	9.9	9.7
56 Other insurance companies	.9	.1	1.0	1.0	1.1	1.0	1.1	1.0	1.1	1.1	1.0	.9
57 Finance companies	6.0	.5	6.4	17.6	18.6	19.2	16.7	18.5	18.9	18.2	24.3	14.2
58 REITs	.6	-1.4	-2.4	-2.2	-1.0	-.2	-2.4	-2.0	-1.0	-1.0	-.5	.1
59 Open-end investment companies	-.7	-.1	-1.0	-.9	-1.0	-2.1	-.6	-1.3	-.5	-1.5	-.3	-3.9

All sectors

	230.5	223.5	296.0	392.5	481.7	481.4	345.8	439.2	465.2	498.3	471.0	493.1
50 Total funds raised, by instrument	**230.5**	**223.5**	**296.0**	**392.5**	**481.7**	**481.4**	**345.8**	**439.2**	**465.2**	**498.3**	**471.0**	**493.1**
61 Investment company shares	-.7	-.1	-1.0	-.9	-1.0	-2.1	-.6	-1.3	-.5	-1.5	-.3	-3.9
62 Other corporate equities	4.8	10.8	12.9	4.9	4.7	7.3	2.6	7.2	.1	9.4	5.7	8.9
63 Debt instruments	226.4	212.8	284.1	388.5	478.0	476.2	343.8	433.3	465.5	490.4	465.6	488.1
64 U.S. government securities	34.3	98.2	88.1	84.3	95.2	89.9	71.2	97.4	100.0	90.4	73.4	106.3
65 State and local obligations	16.5	16.1	15.7	23.7	28.3	21.4	22.3	25.0	27.8	28.7	17.4	25.3
66 Corporate and foreign bonds	23.9	36.4	37.2	36.1	31.6	32.2	31.2	41.1	34.2	29.1	35.5	29.1
67 Mortgages	60.5	57.2	87.1	134.0	149.0	158.1	122.9	145.1	141.6	156.4	161.4	154.8
68 Consumer credit	9.9	9.7	25.6	40.6	50.6	42.3	36.6	44.5	50.1	51.0	47.3	37.2
69 Bank loans n.e.c.	41.0	-12.2	7.0	29.8	58.4	52.5	25.1	34.4	54.9	61.8	49.5	56.3
70 Open market paper and RPs	17.7	-1.2	8.1	15.0	26.4	40.5	15.9	14.0	22.4	30.4	41.3	39.7
71 Other loans	22.7	8.7	15.3	25.2	38.6	39.5	18.5	31.8	34.6	42.5	39.8	39.2

Source: *Federal Reserve Bulletin.*

MORTGAGE DEBT OUTSTANDING
MILLIONS OF DOLLARS, END OF PERIOD

Type of holder, and type of property	1977	1978	1979	1979 Q1	1979 Q2	1979 Q3	1979 Q4	1980 Q1
1 All holders	1,023,505	1,172,754	1,333,550r	1,206,213	1,252,426	1,295,935r	1,333,550r	1,362,802
2 1- to 4-family	656,566	761,843	872,068r	784,546	816,940	846,287r	872,068r	890,189
3 Multifamily	111,841	121,972	130,713r	123,965	125,916	128,270r	130,713r	132,795
4 Commercial	189,274	212,746	238,412r	217,495	224,499	232,208r	238,412r	243,839
5 Farm	65,824	76,193	92,357r	80,207	85,071	89,170r	92,357r	95,979
6 Major financial institutions	745,011	848,095	939,487r	865,974	894,385	920,231r	939,487r	951,898
7 Commercial banks[1]	178,979	213,963	245,998r	220,063	229,564	239,627r	245,998r	251,198
8 1- to 4-family	105,115	126,966	145,975r	130,585	136,223	142,195r	145,975r	149,061
9 Multifamily	9,215	10,912	12,546r	11,223	11,708	12,221r	12,546r	12,811
10 Commercial	56,898	67,056	77,096r	68,968	71,945	75,099r	77,096r	78,725
11 Farm	7,751	9,029	10,381r	9,287	9,688	10,112r	10,381r	10,601
12 Mutual savings banks	88,104	95,157	98,908r	96,136	97,155	97,929	98,908r	99,151
13 1- to 4-family	57,637	62,252	64,706r	62,892	63,559	64,065	64,706r	64,865
14 Multifamily	15,304	16,529r	17,180r	16,699	16,876	17,010	17,180r	17,223
15 Commercial	15,110	16,319	16,963r	16,488	16,662	16,795	16,963r	17,004
16 Farm	53	57	59	57	58	59	59	59
17 Savings and loan associations	381,163	432,808	475,797	441,358	456,543	468,307	475,797	479,078
18 1- to 4-family	310,686	356,114	394,436	363,723	377,516	387,992	394,436	397,156
19 Multifamily	32,513	36,053	37,588	36,677	37,071	37,277	37,588	37,847
20 Commmercial	37,964	40,641	43,773	40,958	41,956	43,038	43,773	44,075
21 Life insurance companies	96,765	106,167	118,784	108,417	111,123	114,368	118,784	122,471
22 1- to 4-family	14,727	14,436	16,193	14,507	14,489	14,884	16,193	16,850
23 Multifamily	18,807	19,000	19,274	19,080	19,102	19,107	19,274	19,590
24 Commercial	54,388	62,232	71,137	63,908	66,055	68,513	71,137	73,618
25 Farm	8,843	10,499	12,180	10,922	11,477	11,864	12,180	12,413
26 Federal and related agencies	70,006	81,853	97,293	86,689	90,095	93,143	97,293	104,045
27 Government National Mortgage Association	3,660	3,509	3,852	3,448	3,425	3,382	3,852	3,919
28 1- to 4-family	1,548	877	763	821	800	780	763	749
29 Multifamily	2,112	2,632	3,089	2,627	2,625	2,602	3,089	3,170
30 Farmers Home Administration	1,353	926	1,274	956	1,200	1,383	1,274	2,757
31 1- to 4-family	626	288	417	302	363	163	417	1,139
32 Multifamily	275	320	71	180	75	299	71	408
33 Commercial	149	101	174	283	278	262	174	409
34 Farm	303	217	612	191	484	659	612	801

35	Federal Housing and Veterans Administration	5,212	5,419	5,764	5,522	5,597	5,672	5,764	5,833
36	1- to 4-family	1,627	1,641	1,863	1,693	1,744	1,795	1,863	1,908
37	Multifamily	3,585	3,778	3,901	3,829	3,853	3,877	3,901	3,925
38	Federal National Mortgage Association	34,369	43,311	51,091	46,410	48,206	49,173	51,091	53,990
39	1- to 4-family	28,504	37,579	45,488	40,702	42,543	43,534	45,488	48,394
40	Multifamily	5,865	5,732	5,603	5,708	5,663	5,639	5,603	5,596
41	Federal Land Banks	22,136	25,624	31,277	26,893	28,459	29,804	31,277	33,311
42	1- to 4-family	670	927	1,552	1,042	1,198	1,374	1,552	1,708
43	Farm	21,466	24,697	29,725	25,851	27,261	28,430	29,725	31,603
44	Federal Home Loan Mortgage Corporation	3,276	3,064	4,035	3,460	3,208	3,729	4,035	4,235
45	1- to 4-family	2,738	2,407	3,059	2,685	2,489	2,850	3,059	3,210
46	Multifamily	538	657	976	775	719	879	976	1,025
47	Mortgage pools or trusts2	70,289	88,633	119,278	94,551	102,259	110,648	119,278	124,097
48	Government National Mortgage Association	44,896	54,347	76,401	57,955	63,000	69,357	76,401	80,905
49	1- to 4-family	43,555	52,732	74,546	56,269	61,246	67,535	74,546	78,934
50	Multifamily	1,341	1,615	1,855	1,686	1,754	1,822	1,855	1,971
51	Federal Home Loan Mortgage Corporation	6,610	11,892	15,180	12,467	13,708	14,421	15,180	15,454
52	1- to 4-family	5,621	9,657	12,149	10,088	11,096	11,568	12,149	12,359
53	Multifamily	989	2,235	3,031	2,379	2,612	2,853	3,031	3,095
54	Farmers Home Administration	18,783	22,394	27,697	24,129	25,551	26,870	27,697	27,738
55	1- to 4-family	11,397	13,400	14,884	13,883	14,329	14,972	14,884	14,926
56	Multifamily	759	1,116	2,163	1,465	1,764	1,763	2,163	2,159
57	Commercial	2,945	3,560	4,328	3,660	3,833	4,054	4,328	4,495
58	Farm	3,682	4,318	6,322	5,121	5,625	6,081	6,322	6,158
59	Individual and others3	138,199	154,173	177,492r	158,999	165,687	171,913r	177,492r	182,762
60	1- to 4-family	72,115	82,567	96,037r	85,354	89,345	92,580r	96,037r	98,930
61	Multifamily	20,538	21,393	23,436r	21,637	22,094	22,921r	23,436r	23,975
62	Commercial	21,820	22,837	24,941r	23,230	23,770	24,447r	24,941r	25,513
63	Farm	23,726	27,376	33,078r	28,778	30,478	31,965r	33,078r	34,344

1. Includes loans held by nondeposit trust companies but not bank trust departments.

2. Outstanding principal balances of mortgages backing securities insured or guaranteed by the agency indicated.

3. Other holders include mortgage companies, real estate investment trusts, state and local credit agencies, state and local retirement funds, noninsured pension funds, credit unions, and U.S. agencies for which amounts are small or separate data are not readily available.

NOTE. Based on data from various institutional and governmental sources, with some quarters estimated in part by the Federal Reserve in conjunction with the Federal Home Loan Bank Board and the Department of Commerce. Separation of nonfarm mortgage debt by type of property, if not reported directly, and interpolations and extrapolations when required, are estimated mainly by the Federal Reserve. Multifamily debt refers to loans on structures of five or more units.

Source: *Federal Reserve Bulletin.*

CONSUMER INSTALLMENT CREDIT:¹ TOTAL OUTSTANDING AND NET CHANGE
MILLIONS OF DOLLARS

Holder, and type of credit	1977	1978	1979	1979			1980			
				Oct.	Nov.	Dec.	Jan.	Feb.	Mar.	Apr.
				Amounts outstanding (end of period)						
1 Total	230,829	275,629	311,122	305,217	307,641	311,122	308,984	308,190	307,621	306,131
By major holder										
2 Commercial banks	112,373	136,189	149,604	149,152	149,057	149,604	148,868	148,249	147,315	145,405
3 Finance companies	44,868	54,298	68,318	65,692	67,164	68,318	68,724	69,545	70,421	71,545
4 Credit unions	37,605	45,939	48,186	48,770	48,673	48,186	47,270	46,707	46,521	45,731
5 Retailers²	23,490	24,876	27,916	24,860	25,732	27,916	26,985	26,309	25,841	25,746
6 Savings and loans	7,354	8,394	10,361	10,073	10,241	10,361	10,320	10,543	10,755	10,887
7 Gasoline companies	2,963	3,240	4,316	4,174	4,281	4,316	4,433	4,467	4,421	4,503
8 Mutual savings banks	2,176	2,693	2,421	2,496	2,493	2,421	2,384	2,370	2,347	2,314
By major type of credit										
9 Automobile	82,911	102,468	115,022	114,876	115,121	115,022	114,761	115,007	115,281	115,014
10 Commercial banks	49,577	60,564	65,229	65,973	65,646	65,229	64,824	64,544	64,047	62,978
11 Indirect paper	27,379	33,850	37,209	37,469	37,334	37,209	37,020	36,949	36,821	36,325
12 Direct loans	22,198	26,714	28,020	28,504	28,312	28,020	27,804	27,595	27,226	26,653
13 Credit unions	18,099	21,967	23,042	23,322	23,275	23,042	22,604	22,335	22,246	21,868
14 Finance companies	15,235	19,937	26,751	25,581	26,200	26,751	27,333	28,128	28,988	30,168
15 Revolving	39,274	47,051	55,330	50,883	52,060	55,330	54,420	53,522	52,662	52,217
16 Commercial banks	18,374	24,434	28,954	27,600	27,827	28,954	28,841	28,575	28,241	27,889
17 Retailers	17,937	19,377	22,060	19,109	19,952	22,060	21,146	20,480	20,000	19,825
18 Gasoline companies	2,963	3,240	4,316	4,174	4,281	4,316	4,433	4,467	4,421	4,503
19 Mobile home	15,141	16,042	17,409	17,244	17,349	17,409	17,387	17,476	17,596	17,668
20 Commercial banks	9,124	9,553	9,991	10,013	10,036	9,991	9,968	9,974	9,978	9,965
21 Finance companies	3,077	3,152	3,390	3,295	3,321	3,390	3,415	3,428	3,475	3,523
22 Savings and loans	2,538	2,848	3,516	3,418	3,475	3,516	3,502	3,578	3,650	3,694
23 Credit unions	402	489	512	518	517	512	502	496	494	486
24 Other	93,503	110,068	123,361	122,214	123,111	123,361	122,416	122,185	122,082	121,232
25 Commercial banks	35,298	41,638	45,430	45,566	45,548	45,430	45,235	45,156	45,049	44,573
26 Finance companies	26,556	31,209	38,177	36,816	37,643	38,177	37,976	37,989	37,958	37,854
27 Credit unions	19,104	23,483	24,632	24,930	24,881	24,632	24,164	23,876	23,781	23,377
28 Retailers	5,553	5,499	5,856	5,751	5,780	5,856	5,839	5,829	5,841	5,921
29 Savings and loans	4,816	5,546	6,845	6,655	6,766	6,845	6,818	6,965	7,106	7,193
30 Mutual savings banks	2,176	2,693	2,421	2,496	2,493	2,421	2,384	2,370	2,347	2,314

Net change (during period)[3]

	35,278	44,810	35,491	2,186	2,407	1,349	1,372	2,295	1,437	-1,985
31 Total	35,278	44,810	35,491	2,186	2,407	1,349	1,372	2,295	1,437	-1,985
By major holder										
32 Commercial banks	18,645	23,813	13,414	771	283	218	433	783	17	-2,237
33 Finance companies	5,948	9,430	14,020	1,076	1,340	1,087	1,096	1,376	1,174	984
34 Credit unions	6,436	8,334	2,247	-152	-44	-455	-324	-373	-215	-743
35 Retailers[2]	2,654	1,386	3,040	335	477	282	120	53	243	-65
36 Savings and loans	1,111	1,041	1,967	76	143	165	7	306	204	83
37 Gasoline companies	132	276	1,076	122	218	115	50	166	48	14
38 Mutual savings banks	352	530	-273	-42	-10	-63	-10	-16	-34	-21
By major type of credit										
39 Automobile	15,204	19,557	12,554	487	533	682	972	881	395	-645
40 Commercial banks	9,956	10,987	4,665	203	-76	122	83	22	-412	-1,335
41 Indirect paper	5,307	6,471	3,359	237	40	260	72	48	-86	-698
42 Direct loans	4,649	4,516	1,306	-34	-116	-138	11	-26	-326	-637
43 Credit unions	2,861	3,868	1,075	-79	-24	-213	-134	-177	-82	-373
44 Finance companies	2,387	4,702	6,814	363	633	773	1,023	1,036	889	1,063
45 Revolving	6,248	7,776	8,279	664	799	432	289	575	611	-388
46 Commercial banks	4,015	6,060	4,520	253	136	24	109	383	395	-260
47 Retailers	2,101	1,440	2,683	289	445	293	130	26	168	-142
48 Gasoline companies	132	276	1,076	122	218	115	50	166	48	14
49 Mobile home	565	897	1,366	150	103	108	120	198	128	36
50 Commercial banks	387	426	437	105	33	-22	68	57	17	-30
51 Finance companies	-189	74	238	27	19	84	48	32	57	41
52 Savings and loans	297	310	668	21	52	51	10	115	57	33
53 Credit unions	70	87	23	-3	-1	-5	-6	-6	-3	-8
54 Other	13,261	16,580	13,292	885	972	127	-9	641	303	-988
55 Commercial banks	4,287	6,340	3,792	210	190	94	173	321	17	-612
56 Finance companies	3,750	4,654	6,968	686	688	230	25	308	228	-120
57 Credit unions	3,505	4,379	1,149	-70	-19	-237	-184	-190	-130	-362
58 Retailers	553	-54	357	46	32	-11	-10	27	75	77
59 Savings and loans	814	731	1,299	55	91	114	-3	191	147	50
60 Mutual savings banks	352	530	-273	-42	-10	-63	-10	-16	-34	-21

1. The Board's series cover most short- and intermediate-term credit extended to individuals through regular business channels, usually to finance the purchase of consumer goods and services or to refinance debts incurred for such purposes, and scheduled to be repaid (or with the option of repayment) in two or more installments.

2. Includes auto dealers and excludes 30-day charge credit held by travel and entertainment companies.

3. Net change equals extensions minus liquidations (repayments, charge-offs, and other credit); figures for all months are seasonally adjusted.

NOTE. Total consumer noninstallment credit outstanding—credit scheduled to be repaid in a lump sum, including single-payment loans, charge accounts, and service credit—amounted to $70.9 billion at the end of 1979, $64.7 billion at the end of 1978, $58.6 billion at the end of 1977, and $55.4 billion at the end of 1976.

Source: *Federal Reserve Bulletin*.

THRIFT INSTITUTIONS AND LIFE INSURANCE COMPANIES: SELECTED ASSETS AND LIABILITIES
MILLIONS OF DOLLARS, END OF PERIOD

Account	1977	1978	1979						1980			
			July	Aug.	Sept.	Oct.	Nov.	Dec.r	Jan.r	Feb.r	Mar.	Apr.p
						Savings and loan associations						
1 Assets	459,241	523,542	561,037	566,493	570,479	576,251	578,922	579,307	582,252	585,685	589,498	591,024
2 Mortgages	381,163	432,808	460,620	464,609	468,307	472,198	474,678	475,797	476,448	477,303	479,078	480,113
3 Cash and investment securities[1]	39,150	44,884	49,496	50,007	49,301	49,220	48,180	46,541	48,473	50,168	50,899	50,588
4 Other	38,928	45,850	50,721	51,877	52,871	54,833	56,064	56,969	57,331	58,214	59,521	60,323
5 Liabilities and net worth	459,241	523,542	561,037	566,493	570,479	576,251	578,922	579,307	582,252	585,685	589,498	591,024
6 Savings capital	386,800	430,953	456,657	457,856	462,626	464,489	465,646	470,171	472,236	473,862	478,265	472,423
7 Borrowed money	27,840	42,907	48,437	50,437	52,738	54,268	54,433	55,375	55,233	55,276	57,346	57,454
8 FHLBB	19,945	31,990	35,286	36,009	37,620	39,223	39,638	40,441	40,364	40,337	42,413	42,742
9 Other	7,895	10,917	13,151	14,428	15,118	15,045	14,795	14,934	14,869	14,939	14,933	14,712
10 Loans in process	9,911	10,721	11,309	11,047	10,909	10,766	10,159	9,511	8,735	8,269	8,079	7,676
11 Other	9,506	9,904	11,681	15,712	12,497	14,673	16,324	11,684	13,315	15,385	12,683	14,272
12 Net worth[2]	25,184	29,057	31,131	31,441	31,709	32,055	32,360	32,566	32,733	32,893	33,125	33,199
13 MEMO: Mortgage loan commitments outstanding[3]	19,875	18,911	22,360	22,282	22,397	20,930	18,029	16,007	15,559	16,744	15,844	13,960
						Mutual savings banks[4]						
14 Assets	147,287	158,174	162,598	163,388	163,431	163,133	163,205	163,405	163,252	164,270	165,107	n.a.
Loans												
15 Mortgage	88,195	95,157	97,238	97,637	97,973	98,304	98,610	98,908	98,940	99,220	99,151	
16 Other	6,210	7,195	10,282	10,430	9,982	9,510	9,449	9,253	9,804	10,044	10,131	
Securities												
17 U.S. government[5]	5,895	4,959	7,992	7,921	7,891	7,750	7,754	7,658	7,387	7,436	7,629	
18 State and local government[5]	2,828	3,333	3,154	3,149	3,150	3,100	3,003	2,930	2,887	2,853	2,824	
19 Corporate and other[6]	37,918	39,732	37,171	37,125	37,076	37,210	37,036	37,086	37,114	37,223	37,493	
20 Cash	2,401	3,665	2,540	2,866	3,020	2,909	3,010	3,156	2,703	3,012	3,361	
21 Other assets	3,839	4,131	4,220	4,260	4,339	4,351	4,343	4,412	4,417	4,481	4,518	
22 Liabilities	147,287	158,174	162,598	163,388	163,431	163,133	163,205	163,405	163,252	164,270	165,107	
23 Deposits	134,017	142,701	145,757	145,713	146,252	145,096	144,828	146,006	145,044	145,171	146,328	
24 Regular[7]	132,744	141,170	143,843	143,731	144,258	143,263	143,064	144,070	143,143	143,284	144,214	
25 Ordinary savings	78,005	71,816	67,537	66,733	65,676	62,672	61,156	61,123	59,252	58,234	56,948	
26 Time and other	54,739	69,354	76,306	76,998	78,572	80,591	81,908	82,947	83,891	85,050	87,266	
27 Other	1,272	1,531	1,914	1,982	2,003	1,834	1,764	1,936	1,901	1,887	2,115	
28 Other liabilities	3,292	4,565	5,578	6,350	5,790	6,600	6,872	2,220	2,557	3,127	2,607	
29 General reserve accounts	9,978	10,907	11,264	11,324	11,388	11,437	11,504	163,405	11,544	11,615	11,643	
30 MEMO: Mortgage loan commitments outstanding[8]	4,066	4,400	4,214	4,071	4,123	3,749	3,619	3,182	2,919	2,618	2,397	

Life insurance companies

Line	Item												
31	**Assets**	351,722	389,924	414,120	418,350	421,660	423,760	427,496	431,453	436,378	439,119	n.a.	n.a.
	Securities												
32	Government	19,553	20,009	20,468	20,472	20,379	20,429	20,486	20,294	20,281	20,317		
33	United States[9]	5,315	4,822	5,228	5,229	5,067	5,075	5,122	4,984	4,896	4,953		
34	State and local	6,051	6,402	6,243	6,258	6,295	6,339	6,354	6,392	6,417	6,516		
35	Foreign[10]	8,187	8,785	8,997	8,985	9,017	9,015	9,010	8,918	8,968	8,850		
36	Business	175,654	198,105	212,876	215,252	216,500	216,183	217,856	218,284	222,475	223,998		
37	Bonds	141,891	162,587	175,854	176,920	177,698	178,633	179,158	178,828	182,305	183,383		
38	Stocks	33,763	35,518	37,022	38,332	38,802	37,550	38,698	39,456	40,170	40,615		
39	Mortgages	96,848	106,167	112,120	113,102	114,368	115,991	117,253	118,784	120,083	121,100		
40	Real estate	11,060	11,764	12,351	12,738	12,740	12,816	12,906	13,047	13,076	13,241		
41	Policy loans	27,556	30,146	32,390	32,713	33,046	33,574	34,220	34,761	35,261	35,784		
42	Other assets	21,051	23,733	23,915	24,073	24,627	24,767	24,775	26,283	25,202	24,677	n.a.	n.a.

Credit unions

Line	Item												
43	**Total assets/liabilities and capital**	53,755	62,348	64,840	65,547	66,280	65,063	65,419	65,854	64,506	64,857	65,678	65,190
44	Federal	29,564	34,760	35,413	35,724	36,151	35,537	35,670	35,934	35,228	35,425	36,091	35,834
45	State	24,191	27,588	29,427	29,823	30,129	29,526	29,749	29,920	29,278	29,432	29,587	29,356
46	Loans outstanding	41,845	50,269	52,083	52,970	53,545	53,533	56,267	53,125	52,089	51,626	51,337	50,344
47	Federal	22,634	27,687	28,379	28,848	29,129	29,020	30,613	28,698	28,053	27,783	27,685	27,119
48	State	19,211	22,582	23,704	24,122	24,416	24,513	25,654	24,426	24,036	23,843	23,652	23,225
49	Savings	46,516	53,517	56,393	56,583	57,255	55,739	55,797	56,232	55,447	55,790	56,743	56,338
50	Federal (shares)	25,576	29,802	30,732	30,761	31,097	30,366	30,399	30,530	30,040	30,256	30,948	30,851
51	State (shares and deposits)	20,940	23,715	25,661	25,822	26,158	25,373	25,398	25,702	25,407	25,534	25,795	25,487

1. Holdings of stock of the Federal Home Loan Banks are included in "other assets."

2. Includes net undistributed income, which is accrued by most, but not all, associations.

3. Excludes figures for loans in process, which are shown as a liability.

4. The NAMSB reports that, effective April 1979, balance sheet data are not strictly comparable with previous months. Beginning April 1979, data are reported on a net-of-valuation-reserves basis. Prior to that date, data were reported on a gross-of-valuation-reserves basis.

5. Beginning April 1979, includes obligations of U.S. government agencies. Prior to that date, this item was included in "Corporate and other."

6. Includes securities of foreign governments and international organizations and, prior to April 1979, nonguaranteed issues of U.S. government agencies.

7. Excludes checking, club, and school accounts.

8. Commitments outstanding (including loans in process) of banks in New York State as reported to the Savings Banks Association of the state of New York.

9. Direct and guaranteed obligations. Excludes federal agency issues not guaranteed, which are shown in the table under "Business" securities.

10. Issues of foreign governments and their subdivisions and bonds of the International Bank for Reconstruction and Development.

NOTE. *Savings and loan associations*: Estimates by the FHLBB for all associations in the United States. Data are based on monthly reports of federally insured associations and annual reports of other associations. Even when revised, data for current and preceding year are subject to further revision.

Mutual savings banks: Estimates of National Association of Mutual Savings Banks for all savings banks in the United States.

Life insurance companies: Estimates of the American Council of Life Insurance for all life insurance companies in the United States. Annual figures are annual-statement asset values, with bonds carried on an amortized basis and stocks at year-end market value. Adjustments for interest due and accrued and for differences between market and book values are not made on each item separately but are included, in total, in "other assets."

Credit unions: Estimates by the National Credit Union Administration for a group of federal and state-chartered credit unions that account for about 30 percent of credit union assets. Figures are preliminary and revised annually to incorporate recent benchmark data.

Source: *Federal Reserve Bulletin.*

Banks and Other Financial Institutions

25 LARGEST U.S. COMMERCIAL BANKING COMPANIES
(ranked by assets)

1979	1978	Company	Assets[1] ($000)	Deposits ($000)	Loans[2] ($000)	Number of Employees[3]
1	1	BankAmerica Corp. (San Francisco)	108,389,318	84,984,746	57,096,295	80,959
2	2	Citicorp (New York)	106,370,619	70,290,725	62,536,389	51,600
3	3	Chase Manhattan Corp. (New York)	64,708,018	48,456,210	39,749,569	32,510
4	4	Manufacturers Hanover Corp. (New York)	47,675,446	38,156,078	25,230,815	21,165
5	5	J. P. Morgan & Co. (New York)	43,487,679	30,278,552	22,158,171	10,831
6	6	Chemical New York Corp.	39,375,293	28,986,820	20,337,991	17,494
7	7	Continental Ilinois Corp. (Chicago)	35,790,119	24,007,200	22,861,532	11,770
8	9	Bankers Trust New York Corp.	30,952,922	22,436,852	15,975,911	12,671
9	10	First Chicago Corp.	30,181,800	21,106,060	15,563,358	10,207
10	8	Western Bancorp. (Los Angeles)	29,687,134	23,631,073	16,813,824	29,097†
11	11	Security Pacific Corp. (Los Angeles)	24,923,382	18,450,827	16,145.246	23,701†
12	12	Wells Fargo & Co. (San Francisco)	20,593,124	15,831,015	14,735,678	17,461
13	14	Irving Bank Corp. (New York)[10]	16,702,433	13,525,148	7,275,544	8,700
14	15	Crocker National Corp. (San Francisco)	16,138,650	12,516,820	10,433,489	16,311
15	13	Marine Midland Banks (Buffalo)	15,728,156	12,509,007	9,007,151	9,901†
16	17	First National Boston Corp.	13,759,850	8,965,353	7,003,981	10,600
17	16	Mellon National Corp. (Pittsburgh)	13,507,677	9,503,209	6,772,074	6,712
18	18	Northwest Bancorp. (Minneapolis)	12,415,823	9,573,230	7,443,593	12,552
19	19	First Bank System (Minneapolis)	12,118,450	8,982,846	6,785,968	9,090†
20	20	First International Bancshares (Dallas)	11,503,940	8,920,587	5,866,489	5,330†
21	23	Republic of Texas Corp. (Dallas)	10,797,651	7,646,570	5,351,834	5,270
22	22	National Detroit Corp.	9,506,400	6,896,142	4,543,246	6,496
23	25	First City Bancorp. of Texas (Houston)	9,504,717	7,597,333	4,497,802	5,847
24	24	Texas Commerce Bancshares (Houston)	9,259,500	7,226,326	4,888,897	5,431
25	26	Bank of New York Co.	8,994,425	6,870,299	4,294,434	5,833

n.a. Not available.

[1] As of December 31, 1979.

[2] Net of unearned discount and loan loss reserve. Figure does not include direct lease financing.

[3] Year-end total unless followed by a dagger (†), in which case average for the year.

[4] After extraordinary items. Figures in parentheses indicate net losses. A double asterisk (**) signifies an extraordinary credit reflecting at least 10% of the net income shown; a double dagger (‡) signifies an extraordinary charge of at least 10%.

[5] Sum of capital stock (except redeemable preferred), surplus, and retained earnings at the end of the year.

[6] For all companies, the figures shown for 1979 and 1978 are the 'primary' earnings per share that appear in the company's income statement. These figures are based on a weighted average of the number of common shares and common-stock equivalents outstanding during the year. 'Common-stock equivalents' generally include (a) convertible securities whose cash yield is less than two-thirds of the prime rate at the time the securities were issued and (b) options and warrants when the effect of their inclusion in the computation would reduce the 'primary' earnings per share. Weighted averages are used for 1969 where these are available; where they are not, figures are based on a simple average of 1968 and 1969 year-end shares outstanding. Per-share earnings for 1978 and 1969 are adjusted for stock splits and stock dividends. They are not restated for mergers, acquisitions, or accounting changes made after 1969.

Source: Reprinted by permission from the 1980 *FORTUNE Directory;* © 1980 Time Inc.

Net Income[1] ($000)	Stockholders' Equity[5] ($000)	Net Income As Percent Of Equity	Earnings per Share[6]				Total Return to Investors[8]	
			1979($)	1978($)	1969($)	Growth Rate: 1969—79[7] (percent)	1979[9] (percent)	1968–79 Average[9] (percent)
600,203	3,461,978	17.3	4.10	3.41	1.11	13.96	12.20	9.33
541,447	3,597,988	15.0	4.34	3.79	1.10	14.71	6.45	7.20
303,019	2,026,533	15.0	8.81	5.53	2.93	11.64	39.66	2.73
211,605	1,554,952	13.6	6.42	5.59	2.47	10.02	3.59	5.16
288,127	1,949,253	14.8	7.07	6.32	1.91	13.98	7.44	8.39
134,706	1,190,229	11.3	8.53	7.05	4.47	6.68	6.43	1.95
195,807	1,362,902	14.4	4.99	4.49	1.39	13.63	16.67	11.0*
113,738	778,600	14.6	9.30	6.40	3.99	8.83	29.56	2.03
112,041	1,186,520	9.4	2.83	3.29	1.46	6.84	(12.50)	6.31
203,342	1,221,961	16.6	5.38	4.36	1.99	10.46	36.55	6.96
163,580	1,042,407	15.7	5.94	5.18	2.15	10.70	18.72	6.26
123,416	834,095	14.8	5.45	4.91	1.75	12.03	5.12	5.72
68,339	507,235	13.5	7.77	6.27	3.35	8.78	26.74	3.85
116,898	644,000	18.2	8.94	5.66	3.03	11.43	26.96	4.70
39,848	480,331	8.3	3.18	2.26**	3.70	(1.50)	30.32	(0.04)
84,224	649,114	13.0	6.84	5.12	2.88	9.04	12.00	4.66
96,362	825,548	11.7	4.92	4.19	2.12	8.78	14.91	6.25
106,642	718,733	14.8	4.13	3.56	1.37	11.67	6.59	7.49
101,691	701,067	14.5	6.80	6.01	2.34	11.26	12.27	7.57
97,923	593,222	16.5	4.79	4.05	1.01	16.84	20.08	12.22
72,400	501,998	14.4	4.08	3.41	1.00	15.10	21.51	8.33
75,604	607,991	12.4	6.24	5.66	2.80	8.34	10.80	7.85
68,478	449,438	15.2	5.34	4.54	1.62[11]	12.67	21.51	10.01
82,380	495,273	16.6	5.70	4.71	1.16	17.26	25.67	15.81
43,560	358,971	12.1	7.05	6.19	3.53	7.16	14.74	3.36

[7] Average annual growth rate, compounded.

[8] Total return includes both price appreciation and dividend yield, i.e., to an investor in the company's stock. The figures shown assume sales at the end of 1979 of stock owned at the end of 1969 or 1978. It has been assumed that any proceeds from cash dividends, the sale of rights and warrant offerings and stock received in spin-offs were reinvested at the end of the year in which they were received. Returns are adjusted for stock splits, stock dividends, recapitalizations, and corporate reorganizations as they occur; however, no effort has been made to reflect the cost of brokerage commissions or of taxes. Results are listed as not available where shares are not publicly traded or traded on only a limited basis. Where corporations have more than one class of shares outstanding, only the more widely held and actively traded have been considered.

[9] Percentages are the returns received by the hypothetical investor described in footnote 8. The ten-year figures are annual averages compounded. Where corporations were substantially reorganized—e.g., because of mergers—the predecessor companies used in calculating total return are the same as those cited in the footnotes dropped from the earnings-per-share figures.

[10] Name changed from Charter New York Corp. on October 17, 1979.

[11] Figure is for First City National Bank of Houston.

25 LARGEST COMMERCIAL BANKING COMPANIES OUTSIDE THE UNITED STATES

Rank 1979	Rank 1978	Bank	Country	Assets[1] ($000)	Increase (Decrease) from Prior Year In U.S. Dollars	Increase (Decrease) from Prior Year In Local Currencies
1	1	Caisse Nationale de Crédit Agricole[7]	France	105,061,750	22.16	17.70
2	3	Banque Nationale de Paris[7]	France	98,920,326	26.68	22.05
3	2	Deutsche Bank[8]	Germany	92,044,349	14.70	8.77
4	4	Crédit Lyonnais[7]	France	91,141,741	23.24	18.74
5	6	Société Générale[7]	France	84,966,762	27.13	22.48
6	5	Dai-Ichi Kangyo Bank[9,10]	Japan	73,264,223	(0.25)	18.58
7	11	Dresdner Bank[8]	Germany	70,276,749	15.23	9.28
8	15	Barclays Bank	Britain	67,291,542	38.01	27.00
9	19	National Westminster Bank	Britain	64,218,254	41.80	30.49
10	7	Fuji Bank[9,10]	Japan	63,596,000	(2.06)	16.43
11	8	Sumitomo Bank[9,10]	Japan	61,906,132	(2.91)	15.42
12	9	Mitsubishi Bank[9,10]	Japan	61,511,874	(2.07)	16.42
13	13	Westdeutsche Landesbank Girozentrale[7,8]	Germany	60,011,611	17.08	11.03
14	10	Sanwa Bank[9,10]	Japan	59,969,573	(2.90)	15.43
15	17	Commerzbank[8]	Germany	58,110,028	20.17	13.96
16	21	Financière de Suez[12]	France	53,365,769	20.90	16.48
17	27	Norinchukin Bank[13]	Japan	52,489,197	39.20	26.95
18	12	Industrial Bank of Japan[9,10]	Japan	51,461,906	(3.55)	14.65
19	14	Bank of Tokyo[8,13]	Japan	50,846,340	4.12	15.47
20	16	Banco do Brasil[7]	Brazil	49,014,444	0.58	104.49
21	48	Financière de Paris et des Pays-Bas[12]	France	48,287,295	77.40	70.92
22	24	Bayerische Vereinsbank[8]	Germany	48,069,168	15.20	9.25
23	30	Banca Nazionale del Lavoro[7]	Italy	45,673,042	22.21	18.27
24	26	Algemene Bank Nederland	Netherlands	45,613,131	18.00	13.81
25	28	Rabobank	Netherlands	45,365,959	20.52	16.24

[1]Asset figures have been converted into U.S. dollars using the market rate prevailing at each bank's fiscal year-end, which is December 31, 1979, unless otherwise noted. Figures for subsidiaries are included if they are more than 50 percent owned, unless otherwise noted. Dalwa Bank (No. 42). Mitsubishi Trust & Banking (No. 46), and Sumitomo Trust & Banking (No. 49) include holdings of major trusts in their assets.

[2]Deposit figures have been converted into U.S. dollars using the market rate as of each bank's fiscal year-end. Figures for all German banks include their own bonds; so do the figures for Norinchukin Bank (No 17), Industrial Bank of Japan (No. 18), Bank of Toyko (No. 19), and Long-Term Credit Bank of Japan (No. 35). Banco do Brasil (No. 20) includes funds for refinancing. Figures for Swiss banks include medium-term notes.

[3]Loan figures have been converted into U.S. dollars using the market rate prevailing at each bank's fiscal year-end. Figures include loans to banks and money at call or available on short notice.

[4]Net-income figures have been converted into U.S. dollars using the average rate in the official exchange market during the bank's fiscal year. Net income is after taxes and excludes minority interest.

Source: Reprinted by permission from the 1980 FORTUNE Directory; © 1980 Time Inc.

Deposits[2] ($000)	Rank	Loans[3] ($000)	Net Income[4] ($000)	Stockholders' Equity[5] ($000)	Offices[6]	Employees
80,997,231	5	86,117,956	387,842	6,438,331	10,025	65,000[11]
96,197,509	1	67,701,568	130,867	1,361,785	2,326	55,988
84,512,299	3	72,855,654	225,446	2,805,991	1,355	43,942
89,147,570	2	70,597,049	90,689	1,211,634	2,312	46,810
82,481,788	4	61,101,985	147,739	1,356,161	2,508	44,040
51,535,539	11	43,417,005	131,305	1,552,748	331	24,418
66,040,463	6	54,411,345	146,262	1,879,219	1,135	31,370
58,346,550	8	54,263,401	739,524	3,895,686	5,000	110,000
58,883,427	7	54,151,588	700,479	3,447,105	3,838	69,648[11]
45,297,164	14	36,518,852	143,629	1,612,308	254	19,286
43,617,066	16	34,982,800	137,392	1,608,749	265	18,453
43,634,131	15	34,577,630	142,548	1,544,501	237	18,969
56,609,896	9	47,613,802	100,733	1,398,415	13	7,335
42,728,828	17	34,148,292	128,214	1,368,047	244	17,601
55,273,633	10	50,162,868	77,038	1,566,034	885	21,656
31,859,542	32	42,046,149	138,280	1,537,851	1,630	34,674
47,635,922	12	26,172,490	43,895	326,292	37	3,102
42,053,694	18	31,138,198	121,375	1,198,082	24	5,037
30,935,961	36	20,988,685	111,223	1,002,795	64	14,256
26,927,604	48	42,635,975	1,649,315	3,254,268	1,585	84,546
23,632,760	50	39,827,093	133,859	1,694,579	991	25,889
45,305,534	13	42,583,874	71,953	1,015,759	486	11,966
39,706,693	21	24,855,822	36,133	1,546,632	354	19,900
40,230,969	19	39,072,939	135,779	1,192,692	911	27,530
34,010,144	31	34,935,347	164,640	1,857,566	3,094	25,339

[5]Stockholders' equity figures have been converted into U.S. dollars using the market rate prevailing at each bank's fiscal year-end. Equity is the sum of capital stock, surplus, and retained earnings. Figures for all French banks are before appropriation of profits.

[6]Includes head office, branches, and agencies.

[7]Government-owned.

[8]Excludes certain subsidiaries that are more than 50 percent owned.

[9]Figures are for fiscal year ending September 30, 1979.

[10]Parent company only.

[11]Average for the year.

[12]Includes certain subsidiaries owned 50 percent or less.

[13]Figures are for fiscal year ending March 31, 1979.

300 LARGEST COMMERCIAL BANKS IN THE U.S. BY STATES

ALABAMA

Rank 12/31/79		Deposits 12/31/79
110	First National Bank, Birmingham	1,337,183,000
149	Birmingham Trust National Bank	949,997,652
224	Central Bank of Alabama NA, Decatur	601,618,792
265	Central Bank of Birmingham	510,485,527
278	First National Bank, Mobile	483,711,635
283	Merchants National Bank, Mobile	478,634,000
290	First Alabama Bank of Montgomery NA	470,361,944

ALASKA

287	National Bank of Alaska, Anchorage	474,288,000

ARIZONA

28	Valley National Bank, Phoenix	4,330,638,000
46	First National Bank, Phoenix	2,869,573,000
84	Arizona Bank, Phoenix	1,620,597,261
245	United Bank of Arizona, Phoenix	538,435,526

CALIFORNIA

1	Bank of America NT&SA, San Francisco	86,061,884,000
10	Security Pacific National Bank, Los Angeles	18,456,636,000
11	Wells Fargo Bank NA, San Francisco	16,131,409,000
12	Crocker National Bank, San Francisco	12,539,557,000
15	United California Bank, Los Angeles	11,674,927,000
26	Union Bank, Los Angeles	4,511,678,000
47	California First Bank of San Francisco	2,866,617,000
53	Bank of California NA, San Francisco	2,402,474,000
61	Lloyds Bank California, Los Angeles	2,145,997,358
90	Sumitomo Bank of California, San Francisco	1,504,857,769
136	City National Bank, Beverly Hills	1,068,541,800
195	Chartered Bank of London, San Francisco	680,485,202
198	Central Bank, Oakland	672,355,000
217	Golden State Sanwa Bank, San Francisco	617,873,000
222	Manufacturers Bank, Los Angeles	605,043,714
223	Barclays Bank of California, San Francisco	604,758,951
237	Imperial Bank, Los Angeles	553,671,549
250	Hibernia Bank, San Francisco	534,040,679
260	Bank of the West, San Jose	516,676,000
263	California Canadian Bank, San Francisco	512,206,000
269	San Diego Trust & Savings Bank	507,410,000

COLORADO

109	First National Bank, Denver	1,341,469,000
120	United Bank of Denver NA	1,214,877,000
193	Colorado National Bank, Denver	691,602,000
220	Central Bank of Denver	610,317,000

CONNECTICUT

63	Connecticut Bank & Trust Co., Hartford	2,104,575,470
66	Hartford National Bank & Trust Co.	2,079,450,000

INDIANA

Rank 12/31/79		Deposits 12/31/79
77	American Fletcher Nat'l Bank & Trust Co., Indianapolis	1,803,329,000
91	Indiana National Bank, Indianapolis	1,501,827,000
117	Merchants National Bank & Trust Co., Indianapolis	1,257,386,000
243	Lincoln National Bank & Trust Co., Fort Wayne	539,759,321
274	Gary National Bank	495,131,335

IOWA

201	Iowa-Des Moines National Bank	663,886,000

KANSAS

211	Fourth National Bank & Trust Co., Wichita	644,849,000

KENTUCKY

92	First National Bank, Louisville	1,495,080,994
111	Citizens Fidelity Bank & Trust Co., Louisville	1,329,397,000
199	Liberty National Bank & Trust Co., Louisville	667,713,694
240	First Security National Bank & Trust Co., Lexington	544,132,415

LOUISIANA

108	Whitney National Bank, New Orleans	1,355,007,851
171	Hibernia National Bank, New Orleans	781,551,000
180	First National Bank of Commerce, New Orleans	742,753,000
228	First National Bank, Shreveport	577,088,830
241	Commercial National Bank, Shreveport	542,156,903
252	Louisiana National Bank, Baton Rouge	529,949,000
294	American Bank & Trust Co., Baton Rouge	464,798,932

MARYLAND

49	Maryland National Bank, Baltimore	2,724,903,639
83	Equitable Trust Co., Baltimore	1,651,920,000
87	First National Bank, Baltimore	1,562,694,000
124	Suburban Trust Co., Hyattsville	1,181,550,578
155	Union Trust Co., Baltimore	991,462,000
255	Citizens Bank & Trust Co., Riverdale	525,448,669
292	Mercantile-Safe Deposit & Trust Co., Baltimore	468,327,000

MASSACHUSETTS

17	First National Bank, Boston	8,727,284,000
78	New England Merchants National Bank, Boston	1,794,277,140
93	Shawmut Bank of Boston NA	1,484,470,000
100	State Street Bank & Trust Co., Boston	1,412,382,000
157	BayBank Middlesex, Burlington	900,832,454
246	Worcester County National Bank, Worcester	537,718,000
282	BayBank Norfolk County Trust Co., Dedham	479,670,741
285	Arlington Trust Co., Lawrence	478,109,000
296	Third National Bank of Hampden County, Springfield	460,542,640

143	Union Trust Co., New Haven	996,675,316
148	Colonial Bank, Waterbury	958,403,700
213	Connecticut National Bank, Bridgeport	620,858,540
216	State National Bank, Bridgeport	618,960,268
247	Citytrust, Bridgeport	537,358,465
289	First Bank, New Haven	471,983,034

DELAWARE

150	Wilmington Trust Co.	940,963,284
226	Bank of Delaware, Wilmington	596,321,469
281	Delaware Trust Co., Wilmington	479,932,000

DISTRICT OF COLUMBIA

59	Riggs National Bank, Washington, D.C.	2,183,307,000
76	American Security Bank, Washington, D.C.	1,850,588,000
179	National Bank of Washington, D.C.	744,718,885
244	Union First National Bank, Washington, D.C.	539,614,865

FLORIDA

64	Southeast First National Bank, Miami	2,096,651,000
194	Sun First National Bank, Orlando	688,071,089
261	First National Bank of Florida, Tampa	513,966,000
268	Landmark First National Bank, Ft. Lauderdale	508,288,317
271	Flagship National Bank, Miami	497,270,295

GEORGIA

42	Citizens & Southern National Bank, Atlanta	3,240,019,000
73	First National Bank, Atlanta	1,937,536,000
122	Trust Company National Bank, Atlanta	1,191,598,000
191	Fulton National Bank, Atlanta	694,694,000

HAWAII

| 80 | Bank of Hawaii, Honolulu | 1,756,844,000 |
| 105 | First Hawaiian Bank, Honolulu | 1,372,391,165 |

IDAHO

102	Idaho First National Bank, Boise	1,408,920,077
139	First Security Bank of Idaho NA, Boise	1,036,785,000
284	Bank of Idaho NA, Boise	478,389,310

ILLINOIS

7	Continental Illinois National Bank & Trust Co., Chicago	23,751,206,000
9	First National Bank, Chicago	21,169,959,000
24	Harris Trust & Savings Bank, Chicago	4,929,378,046
31	Northern Trust Co., Chicago	3,919,959,000
74	American National Bank & Trust Co., Chicago	1,895,400,000
172	LaSalle National Bank, Chicago	781,196,000
258	Central National Bank, Chicago	521,839,000

MICHIGAN

20	National Bank of Detroit	6,603,652,000
40	Manufacturers National Bank, Detroit	3,330,826,000
45	Detroit Bank & Trust	3,057,172,000
96	Michigan National Bank, Lansing	1,430,388,000
104	Michigan National Bank, Detroit	1,389,059,000
134	Old Kent Bank & Trust Co., Grand Rapids	1,080,462,000
163	Bank of the Commonwealth, Detroit	868,234,816
164	Citizens Commercial & Savings Bank, Flint	842,075,304
165	City National Bank, Detroit	841,424,000
200	Genesee Merchants Bank & Trust Co., Flint	667,556,000
234	Security Bank & Trust Co., Southgate	561,235,000
293	First National Bank & Trust Co., Kalamazoo	465,431,000
300	Union Bank & Trust Co. NA, Grand Rapids	453,118,000

MINNESOTA

50	Northwestern National Bank, Minneapolis	2,683,480,000
56	First National Bank, Minneapolis	2,204,755,000
82	First National Bank, St. Paul	1,703,238,610

MISSISSIPPI

| 128 | Deposit Guaranty National Bank, Jackson | 1,146,082,872 |
| 140 | First National Bank, Jackson | 1,008,589,853 |

MISSOURI

70	First National Bank, St. Louis	1,951,492,000
71	Mercantile Trust Co. NA, St. Louis	1,949,100,000
167	Commerce Bank of Kansas City NA	828,607,000
186	United Missouri Bank of Kansas City NA	717,374,000
189	First National Bank, Kansas City	702,800,000
196	Boatmen's National Bank, St. Louis	678,227,000

NEBRASKA

| 225 | Omaha National Bank | 600,276,627 |
| 286 | First National Bank & Trust Co., Lincoln | 476,082,859 |

NEVADA

| 89 | First National Bank of Nevada, Reno | 1,531,956,000 |
| 202 | Valley Bank, Las Vegas | 663,539,778 |

NEW JERSEY

88	First National State Bank, Newark	1,558,657,000
113	United Jersey Bank, Hackensack	1,287,970,000
123	Midlantic National Bank, Newark	1,182,287,000
154	New Jersey National Bank, Trenton	918,254,000
156	National Community Bank, Rutherford	906,327,862
161	First Peoples Bank of N.J., Haddon Twp.	871,531,824

300 LARGEST COMMERCIAL BANKS IN THE U.S., BY STATES (continued)

NEW JERSEY (continued)

Rank 12/31/79		Deposits 12/31/79
162	Fidelity Union Trust Co., Newark	871,041,000
173	New Jersey Bank NA, West Paterson	772,433,000
183	Heritage Bank NA, Cherry Hill	726,369,000
185	Garden State National Bank, Paramus	719,737,000
188	National State Bank, Elizabeth	709,383,334
204	First National Bank, Totowa	657,314,887
218	First Jersey National Bank, Jersey City	617,488,493
238	Bank of New Jersey, Camden	552,520,000
248	First National Bank of South Jersey, Pleasantville	535,854,445
249	Central Jersey Bank & Trust Co., Freehold	534,618,634
264	Trust Company of New Jersey, Jersey City	510,606,000
276	American National Bank & Trust, Morristown	486,693,000
279	Citizens First National Bank, Ridgewood	483,487,000
280	Colonial First National Bank, Red Bank	483,027,916

NEW MEXICO

Rank 12/31/79		Deposits 12/31/79
197	Albuquerque National Bank	675,708,572
297	First National Bank, Albuquerque	457,085,493

NEW YORK

Rank 12/31/79		Deposits 12/31/79
2	Citibank NA	70,556,239,000
3	Chase Manhattan Bank NA	49,354,530,000
4	Manufacturers Hanover Trust Co.	37,800,269,000
5	Morgan Guaranty Trust Co.	30,297,926,000
6	Chemical Bank	29,022,808,000
8	Bankers Trust Co.	22,042,970,000
13	Marine Midland Bank NA, Buffalo	12,537,171,000
14	Irving Trust Co.	11,956,008,000
18	Bank of New York	6,870,337,363
34	European American Bank & Trust Co.	3,723,887,000
36	National Bank of North America	3,634,318,000
41	Republic National Bank	3,300,267,885
48	Bank of Tokyo Trust Co.	2,864,983,356
52	Lincoln First Bank NA, Rochester	2,406,016,000
58	Citibank (New York State) NA, Buffalo	2,193,900,000
94	Bank Leumi Trust Co.	1,479,097,771
95	United States Trust Co.	1,446,471,000
98	Manufacturers & Traders Trust Co., Buffalo	1,420,469,275
116	J. Henry Schroder Bank & Trust Co.	1,276,347,000
153	Key Bank NA, Albany	923,463,000
170	Fuji Bank & Trust Co.	788,717,392
181	Industrial Bank of Japan Trust Co.	738,927,000
184	Long Island Trust Co., Garden City	723,862,207
192	State Bank of Albany	694,129,008
207	UBAF Arab American Bank	653,857,160
210	Oneida National Bank & Trust Co. of Central N.Y., Utica	645,029,717
229	Security Trust Co., Rochester	569,071,273
230	Liberty National Bank & Trust Co., Buffalo	567,528,003
235	Brown Brothers Harriman & Co.	559,913,102

PENNSYLVANIA (continued)

Rank 12/31/79		Deposits 12/31/79
67	Equibank, Pittsburgh	2,053,221,000
75	Provident National Bank, Philadelphia	1,888,720,000
86	American Bank & Trust Co., Reading	1,575,238,000
103	Industrial Valley Bank & Trust Co., Philadelphia	1,403,779,000
106	Hamilton Bank, Lancaster	1,369,657,060
107	Continental Bank, Norristown	1,355,474,000
142	Union National Bank, Pittsburgh	1,003,613,459
166	Commonwealth National Bank, Harrisburg	837,016,000
174	First National Bank, Allentown	768,615,236
206	Northeastern Bank of Pennsylvania, Mt. Pocono'	655,581,000
214	Central Penn National Bank, Philadelphia	620,310,000
236	First Eastern Bank NA, Wilkes-Barre	555,967,857
239	Southeast National Bank of Pennsylvania, Chester	548,351,000
257	United Penn Bank, Wilkes-Barre	522,860,000
259	First Valley Bank, Lansford	519,773,703
267	Dauphin Deposit Bank & Trust Co., Harrisburg	509,382,412
277	Merchants National Bank, Allentown	484,397,961
291	Pennsylvania Bank & Trust Co., Warren	469,507,000

PUERTO RICO

Rank 12/31/79		Deposits 12/31/79
68	Banco Popular de Puerto Rico, San Juan	2,045,838,263
135	Banco de Ponce	1,070,612,680

RHODE ISLAND

Rank 12/31/79		Deposits 12/31/79
62	Industrial National Bank of Rhode Island, Providence	2,118,613,000
119	Rhode Island Hospital Trust National Bank, Providence	1,214,996,000
130	Old Stone Bank, Providence	1,121,383,000

SOUTH CAROLINA

Rank 12/31/79		Deposits 12/31/79
129	South Carolina National Bank, Columbia	1,137,570,000
177	Citizens & Southern National Bank, Charleston	751,241,394
190	Bankers Trust of South Carolina, Columbia	698,566,000
203	First National Bank of S.C., Columbia	662,857,331

SOUTH DAKOTA

Rank 12/31/79		Deposits 12/31/79
273	National Bank of South Dakota, Sioux Falls	495,625,000

TENNESSEE

Rank 12/31/79		Deposits 12/31/79
114	First Tennessee Bank NA, Memphis	1,281,773,644
125	First American National Bank, Nashville	1,172,507,000
132	Third National Bank, Nashville	1,101,098,000
137	Commerce Union Bank, Nashville	1,059,672,461
175	Union Planters National Bank, Memphis	765,284,277
231	National Bank of Commerce, Memphis	567,196,000
242	American National Bank & Trust Co., Chattanooga	539,872,712
288	United American Bank, Knoxville	472,539,000

266	Barclays Bank of New York	509,875,000
275	Key Bank of Central N.Y., Syracuse	491,520,140
298	Empire National Bank, Middletown	456,640,000

NORTH CAROLINA

27	North Carolina National Bank, Charlotte	4,496,863,000
33	Wachovia Bank & Trust Co. NA, Winston-Salem	3,825,123,086
57	First Union National Bank, Charlotte	2,203,989,000
101	Northwestern Bank, North Wilkesboro	1,410,471,145
126	First-Citizens Bank & Trust Co., Raleigh	1,168,048,255
251	Branch Banking & Trust Co., Wilson	533,234,000
295	Southern National Bank, Lumberton	464,308,819

OHIO

35	BancOhio National Bank, Columbus	3,675,688,000
44	AmeriTrust Co., Cleveland	3,172,243,225
54	National City Bank, Cleveland	2,362,257,000
69	Central National Bank, Cleveland	1,983,093,000
72	Huntington National Bank, Columbus	1,942,502,000
115	Society National Bank, Cleveland	1,279,717,167
141	First National Bank, Cincinnati	1,007,927,000
144	Union Commerce Bank, Cleveland	986,721,250
145	Bank One of Columbus NA	972,712,000
147	Central Trust Co. NA, Cincinnati	966,440,000
169	Fifth Third Bank, Cincinnati	789,802,000
178	Winters National Bank & Trust Co., Dayton	749,786,000
182	First National Bank, Akron	729,013,794
209	Toledo Trust Co.	647,234,255
253	Provident Bank, Cincinnati	529,640,000

OKLAHOMA

118	First National Bank & Trust Co., Oklahoma City	1,231,789,605
131	Liberty National Bank & Trust Co., Oklahoma City	1,106,957,734
158	Bank of Oklahoma NA, Tulsa	899,699,000
159	First National Bank & Trust Co., Tulsa	882,480,000
299	Fidelity Bank NA, Oklahoma City	453,410,112

OREGON

37	First National Bank of Oregon, Portland	3,609,058,000
38	United States National Bank of Oregon, Portland	3,512,586,000
221	Oregon Bank, Portland	607,557,136

PENNSYLVANIA

16	Mellon Bank NA, Pittsburgh	9,820,249,000
23	First Pennsylvania Bank NA, Philadelphia	5,296,466,000
30	Philadelphia National Bank	4,062,963,000
32	Pittsburgh National Bank	3,914,323,000
43	Girard Bank, Philadelphia	3,226,601,000
60	Fidelity Bank, Philadelphia	2,163,890,000

TEXAS

21	Republic National Bank, Dallas	5,980,729,000
22	First National Bank, Dallas	5,980,102,000
25	First City National Bank, Houston	4,783,904,481
29	Texas Commerce Bank NA, Houston	4,112,822,000
79	Mercantile National Bank, Dallas	1,760,726,000
97	Bank of the Southwest NA, Houston	1,422,098,053
133	Fort Worth National Bank	1,096,175,550
138	First National Bank, Fort Worth	1,042,636,930
151	Allied Bank of Texas, Houston	934,868,862
160	Frost National Bank, San Antonio	881,769,023
168	Houston National Bank	825,168,000
205	First National Bank of Midland	656,873,065
212	Austin National Bank	621,091,000
215	National Bank of Commerce, San Antonio	619,377,046
233	First International Bank in Houston NA	564,073,000
256	Capital Bank, Houston	525,366,000
262	Capital National Bank, Austin	513,728,049
270	El Paso National Bank	505,496,142
272	First National Bank, Amarillo	496,149,724

UTAH

99	First Security Bank of Utah NA, Ogden	1,415,015,000
127	Zions First National Bank, Salt Lake City	1,160,371,000
208	Walker Bank & Trust Co., Salt Lake City	651,761,000

VIRGINIA

51	United Virginia Bank, Richmond	2,503,893,000
65	Virginia National Bank, Norfolk	2,084,153,000
81	First & Merchants National Bank, Richmond	1,735,648,000
85	Bank of Virginia, Richmond	1,583,865,626
152	First National Exchange Bank, Roanoke	925,080,391
187	First American Bank of Virginia, McLean	714,721,507
232	First Virginia Bank, Falls Church	565,626,098
254	Fidelity American Bank NA, Lynchburg	529,202,000

WASHINGTON

19	Seattle-First National Bank	6,639,876,000
39	Rainier National Bank, Seattle	3,459,760,214
112	Pacific National Bank of Washington, Seattle	1,316,711,000
121	Peoples National Bank, Seattle	1,204,433,397
146	Old National Bank, Spokane	969,712,446
219	Puget Sound National Bank, Tacoma	612,302,001

WISCONSIN

55	First Wisconsin National Bank, Milwaukee	2,280,915,000
176	M & I Marshall & Ilsley Bank, Milwaukee	761,907,000
227	Marine National Exchange Bank, Milwaukee	580,657,000

Source: Compiled by American Banker. Copyright 1980. Reprinted with permission of the American Banker, February 29, 1980.

25 LARGEST DIVERSIFIED FINANCIAL COMPANIES (ranked by assets)

Rank 1979	Rank 1978	Company	Assets[1] ($000)	Revenues[2] ($000)	Net Income[3] ($000)	Stockholders' Equity[4] ($000)
1	1	Aetna Life & Casualty (Hartford)	30,228,463	11,446,880	585,418	2,868,449
2	2	Travelers Corp. (Hartford)	19,159,864	7,888,901	395,046	2,355,831
3	3	American Express (New York)	17,108,200	4,666,500	345,300	1,832,600
4	5	H. F. Ahmanson (Los Angeles)	12,137,253	1,211,220	117,137	830,973
5	6	Merrill Lynch & Co. (New York)	10,556,100	2,051,996	118,743	784,245
6	8	First Charter Financial (Beverly Hills)	9,548,833	846,313	90,848	782,423
7	7	Great Western Financial (Beverly Hills)	9,453,989	878,354	93,071	638,357
8	4	INA (Philadelphia)	8,987,035	4,551,372	261,637	1,526,009
9	9	Loews (New York)	8,842,683	4,065,475	208,580	1,040,754
10	12	Transamerica (San Francisco)	7,983,535	4,044,647	240,202	1,324,953
11	11	Lincoln Natnonal (Fort Wayne, Ind.)	7,770,900	2,445,099	165,009	1,198,060
12	10	Continental (New York)	7,458,312	3,252,707	273,585	1,894,095
13	13	American General Insurance (Houston)	6,548,192	1,886,052	218,650	1,002,309
14	14	Imperial Corp. of America (San Diego)	6,520,823	583,152	74,180	481,930
15	21	Beneficial (Wilmington)	6,031,300	982,900	101,100	930,500
16	18	American International Group (New York)	5,727,499	2,327,542	259,835	1,245,807
17	19	Household Finance (Prospect Heights, Ill.)	5,668,300	836,100	161,200	1,239,000
18	16	Walter E. Heller International (Chicago)	5,566,491	610,982	40,361	312,732
19	17	Avco Corp. (Greenwich, Conn.)[10]	5,300,401	1,932,155	132,283	889,689
20	15	C.I.T. Financial (New York)	5,083,467	627,117	146,983	987,523
21	20	First Boston (New York)	4,890,917	145,495	17,245	127,213
22	22	St. Paul Companies	4,101,210	1,783,056	162,968	935,715
23	25	Gibraltar Financial Corp. of California (Beverly Hills)	4,041,477	361,339	29,632	208,834
24	23	Golden West Financial (Oakland, Calif.)	3,888,766	365,220	36,495	180,523
25	24	U.S. Fidelity & Guaranty (Baltimore)	3,679,842	2,136,231	229,089	1,042,926

n.a. Not available.

[1] Total assets shown as of December 31, 1979, unless otherwise noted. Only assets of consolidated subsidiaries are included. Holding companies that own commercial banks or life-insurance companies are listed here only when these subsidiaries represent less than 80 percent of assets.

[2] Total income during the year, including any consolidated nonfinancial revenues from manufacturing, retailing, etc., and revenues from discounted operations when published. All companies on the list must have derived more than 50 percent of their revenues from two or more kinds of financial business and be publicly held.

[3] After extraordinary items and realized capital gains and losses. Figures in parentheses indicate net loss. A double asterisk (**) signifies an extraordinary credit reflecting at least 10 percent of the net income shown; a double dagger (‡) signifies an extraordinary charge of at least 10 percent.

Source: Reprinted by permission from the 1980 FORTUNE Directory; © 1980 Time Inc.

Net Income as Percent of Equity	Number of Employees[5]	Earnings Per Share				Total to Investors[8]	
		1979($)	1978($)	1969($)	Growth Rate 1969–79[7] (percent)	1979[9] (percent)	1969–79 Average[9] (percent)
20.4	37,540	7.25	6.19	0.89	23.34	35.36	13.92
16.8	29,166	9.20	8.43	1.58	19.27	18.25	4.84
18.8	40,732	4.83	4.31	1.27**	14.29	8.59	6.18
14.1	4,300	5.11	5.13	1.73	11.44	22.84	—
15.1	26,860	3.26	2.00	0.94	13.24	31.14	—
11.6	2,290	3.05	3.55	0.95	12.37	26.61	4.70
14.6	2,243	4.15	4.01	0.97	15.65	28.67	7.15
17.1	35,280	6.78	5.64	1.67	15.04	37.57	9.29
20.0	29,400	18.19	14.47	2.20	23.52	49.88	8.80
18.1	29,000	3.66	3.15	1.31	10.82	8.42	1.29
13.8	16,625	7.09	6.39	2.61	10.51	29.94	6.35
14.4	23,239	5.10	5.39	1.30	14.65	16.84	8.43
21.8	9,000	8.79	7.30	0.82	26.77	41.38	8.80
15.4	1,500	5.24	4.96	0.99	18.13	65.00	8.20
10.9	13,500	4.24	4.19	2.72	4.54	24.92	4.04
20.9	19,400	6.93	5.13	0.58	28.15	18.03	12.35
13.0	12,000	3.33	3.18	1.94	5.55	12.00	1.33
12.9	4,599	3.40	2.97	1.41	9.20	45.66	5.12
14.9	27,102	8.56	8.96	3.12	10.62	26.33	3.12
14.9	19,675	n.a.	n.a.	n.a.	—	74.50	10.03
13.6	1,326	3.78	0.31	1.27	11.52	8.47	3.29
17.4	9,713	7.77	8.56	1.92	15.00	27.96	10.24
14.2	1,200	2.12	2.24	0.56	14.24	15.63	8.29
20.2	1,123	2.61	2.99	0.30	24.15	40.51	—
22.0	8,588	8.28	7.77	1.34	19.98	33.77	12.95

[4] Sum of capital stock (except redeemable preferred), surplus, and retained earnings at the end of the fiscal year.

[5] Year-end total unless followed by a dagger (†), in which case average for the year.

[6] Earnings per share have been computed as described in footnote 6, page 310.

[7] Average annual growth rate, compounded.

[8] Total return has been computed as described in footnote 8, page 311.

[9] Percentages shown are the returns received by the hypothetical investor described in footnote 9, page 311. The ten-year figures are annual averages compounded. Where corporations were substantially reorganized—e.g., because of mergers—the predecessor companies used in calculating total return are the same as those cited in the footnotes dropped from the earnings-per-share figures.

[10] Figures are for fiscal year ending November 30, 1979.

25 LARGEST LIFE INSURANCE COMPANIES
(ranked by assets)

Rank 1979	Rank 1978	Company	Assets[1] ($000)	Premium and Annuity Receipts[2] ($000)	Rank	Net Investment Income ($000)	Rank
1	1	Prudential (Newark)*	54,734,107	8,007,951	1	3,313,429	1
2	2	Metropolitan (New York)*	44,967,563	5,934,722	2	3,088,872	2
3	3	Equitable Life Assurance (New York)*	30,839,211	4,576,910	4	1,808,988	3
4	6	Aetna Life (Hartford)[7]	18,548,768	4,729,187	3	1,227,687	5
5	4	New York Life*	18,479,224	2,598,658	6	1,235,376	4
6	5	John Hancock Mutual (Boston)*	17,318,502	2,170,657	8	1,150,511	6
7	7	Connecticut General Life (Bloomfield)	12,240,721	2,434,535	7	842,235	7
8	8	Travelers (Hartford)[8]	11,816,987	3,642,396	5	800,696	8
9	9	Northwestern Mutual (Milwaukee)*	10,553,947	1,246,917	11	702,921	9
10	10	Massachusetts Mutual (Springfield)*	8,340,825	1,222,180	12	542,418	11
11	11	Teachers Insurance & Annuity (New York)	8,297,558	1,135,270	13	657,703	10
12	12	Mutual of New York*	7,412,472	1,024,812	15	484,474	12
13	14	Bankers Life (Des Moines)*	6,764,447	1,441,554	9	476,310	13
14	13	New England Mutual (Boston)*	6,314,187	940,021	17	429,110	14
15	15	Mutual Benefit (Newark)*	5,181,444	791,509	18	336,796	15
16	16	Connecticut Mutual (Hartford)*	4,968,917	612,729	21	320,818	17
17	17	Lincoln National Life (Fort Wayne)[9]	4,730,167	1,296,836	10	323,099	16
18	18	Penn Mutual (Philadelphia)*	3,652,186	383,693	29	239,483	18
19	20	Continental Assurance (Chicago)[10]	3,029,916	948,833	16	162,025	24
20	21	Western & Southern (Cincinnati)*	2,911,687	311,484	38	191,288	21
21	22	State Farm Life (Bloomington, Ill.)	2,905,358	556,390	22	203,909	19
22	19	National Life & Accident (Nashville)	2,790,166	371,161	31	197,869	20
23	23	Phoenix Mutual (Hartford)*	2,753,070	488,682	25	178,175	22
24	25	Pacific Mutual (Newport Beach, Calif.)*	2,623,865	732,841	20	178,141	23
25	24	Occidental of California (Los Angeles)[11]	2,555,514	1,044,851	14	147,701	27

Data for all companies are on the 'statutory' accounting basis required by state insurance regulatory authorities.

n.a. Not available.

* Indicates mutual company.

[1] As of December 31, 1979.

[2] Includes premium receipts from life, accident, and health policies, annuities, separate accounts, and contributions to deposit administration funds.

[3] After dividends to policyholders and federal income taxes, excluding capital gains and losses. Figures in parentheses indicate a loss.

Source: Reprinted by permission from the 1980 *FORTUNE Directory;* © 1980 Time Inc.

Net Gain From Operations[3]			Life Insurance in Force[4]		Increase in Life Insurance in Force[5]		Percent of Increase		Employees[6]	
($000)	Mutual	Stock	($000)	Rank	($000)	Rank	Increase	Rank	Number	Rank
278,398	1		367,283,576	1	36,919,838	1	11.2	30	61,942	1
233,912	2		323,588,876	2	36,054,625	2	12.5	22	51,000	2
77,024	5		183,491,377	3	17,785,117	3	10.7	32	25,470	4
194,373		1	127,618,848	4	15,354,208	4	13.7	18	17,756	7
151,444	3		111,892,459	6	10,550,165	6	10.4	34	19,889	6
144,365	4		125,594,445	5	12,778,186	5	11.3	27	20,400	5
137,199		3	73,574,843	8	9,390,626	7	14.6	12	9,346	9
159,933		2	95,652,561	7	7,898,677	8	9.0	38	39,488	3
64,241	6		51,667,387	10	6,296,695	12	13.9	17	6,410	20
56,907	7		44,526,715	13	4,316,146	14	10.7	31	9,243	11
40,164		13	6,195,971	44	759,359	38	14.0	16	1,666	44
37,778	10		33,936,777	16	3,035,704	19	9.8	36	7,566	17
21,131	18		31,150,903	17	3,987,482	15	14.7	10	5,502	24
55,136	8		28,194,982	19	2,846,856	21	11.2	28	6,648	19
39,243	9		34,698,250	14	4,596,149	13	15.3	9	5,594	23
27,354	14		23,387,951	21	2,568,909	26	12.3	23	4,868	25
52,182		8	51,133,832	11	7,257,646	9	16.5	6	8,327	14
19,365	19		16,662,221	26	1,273,947	29	8.3	40	3,882	27
19,562		17	21,825,415	23	916,535	36	4.4	45	n.a.	
27,853	13		14,148,074	32	398,050	45	2.9	47	7,872	16
89,057		5	45,285,839	12	7,158,770	10	18.8	5	15,435	8
91,049		4	16,415,708	29	233,269	47	1.4	48	7,966	15
32,435	11		26,121,663	20	2,691,432	23	11.5	26	3,135	31
24,160	15		16,312,955	30	3,068,678	18	23.2	3	3,067	32
54,477		7	62,827,919	9	6,555,719	11	11.7	25	6,126	21

[4] Face value of all life policies as of December 31, 1979.
[5] Change between December 31, 1978, and December 31, 1979.
[6] Includes home office, field force, and full-time agents. Year-end total unless followed by a dagger (†), in which case average for the year.
[7] Company is wholly owned by Aetna Life & Casualty (No. 1 on the Diversified-Financial list).
[8] Company is wholly owned by Travelers Corp. (No. 2 on the Diversified-Financial list).
[9] Company is wholly owned by Lincoln National Corp. (No. 11 on the Diversified-Financial list).
[10] Company is 82 percent owned by Loews (No. 9 on the Diversified-Financial list).
[11] Company is wholly owned by Transamerica. (No. 10 on Diversified-Financial list).

TOP 100 NATIONAL ADVERTISERS, 1979

All numbers in thousands

COMPANY	TOTAL	MAGAZINES	NEWSPAPER SUPPS	SPOT RADIO	NETWORK RADIO	OUTDOOR	SPOT TV	NETWORK TV	TOTAL TV	% TV
1. Procter & Gamble Co.	$509,118.9	$40,640.4	$2,641.5	$2,465.5	$—	$—	$173,761.6	$289,609.8	$463,371.4	91.0
2. General Foods Corp.	354,697.2	41,241.0	5,075.2	6,452.9	5,034.0	199.3	93,457.0	203,237.8	296,694.8	83.6
3. General Motors Corp.	338,834.2	67,634.4	5,570.0	24,858.7	8,517.1	7,919.4	106,743.9	117,590.7	224,334.6	66.2
4. Ford Motor Co.	216,453.2	31,138.5	10.7	12,211.3	1,865.8	4,960.2	69,250.7	97,016.0	166,266.7	76.8
5. Philip Morris, Inc.	211,697.0	64,650.8	12,198.0	4,629.2	—	26,814.5	16,813.6	86,590.9	103,404.5	48.8
6. R.J. Reynolds Industries, Inc.	202,393.4	114,869.3	36,258.3	2,472.7	—	26,515.7	6,924.7	15,352.7	22,277.4	11.0
7. American Home Products Corp.	184,880.8	10,266.0	394.3	4,132.4	5,056.8	—	42,465.8	122,565.5	165,031.3	89.3
8. General Mills, Inc.	176,149.6	14,985.8	905.4	2,720.5	504.6	60.7	71,324.4	85,648.2	156,972.6	89.1
9. Bristol-Myers Co.	163,059.9	19,849.2	1,081.5	1,054.4	437.4	—	23,650.4	116,987.0	140,637.4	86.2
10. Chrysler Corp.	147,576.7	13,925.9	101.3	21,819.4	2,146.9	2,064.8	37,928.6	69,589.8	107,518.4	72.9
11. McDonald's Corp.	142,568.9	1,748.7	—	646.6	7,079.4	2,383.1	75,334.2	62,456.3	137,790.5	96.6
12. American Telephone & Telegraph Co.	139,779.9	25,287.2	425.0	9,204.5	—	796.3	42,084.0	54,903.5	96,987.5	69.4
13. PepsiCo, Inc.	137,473.9	2,161.7	—	4,897.1	—	940.2	57,152.2	72,322.7	129,474.9	94.2
14. Lever Brothers Co.	128,316.6	15,207.2	446.3	427.0	—	244.4	40,282.6	71,709.1	111,991.7	87.3
15. Seagram Co., Ltd.	120,896.9	84,877.1	7,489.3	6.2	—	8,030.3	6,161.2	14,332.8	20,494.0	17.0
16. Coca-Cola Co.	118,614.2	3,786.2	413.7	6,133.2	3,438.5	3,098.7	46,700.1	58,482.3	105,182.4	88.7
17. Anheuser-Busch Cos. Inc.	111,067.7	7,013.9	571.6	19,567.1	—	1,660.0	15,772.5	63,044.1	78,816.6	71.0
18. Johnson & Johnson	105,910.5	15,901.5	1,438.7	151.5	307.8	9.6	4,673.1	83,736.1	88,409.2	83.5
19. Ralston Purina Co.	103,192.5	10,834.2	526.8	2,729.5	—	19.5	19,711.8	69,062.9	88,774.7	86.0
20. Sears Roebuck & Co.	102,812.5	13,819.6	98.7	308.2	5,434.3	121.9	17,053.5	65,976.3	83,029.8	80.8
21. Pillsbury Co.	100,963.7	6,018.0	42.9	1,199.7	531.4	710.8	39,595.9	53,396.4	92,992.3	92.1
22. Colgate-Palmolive Co.	94,912.4	9,086.6	1,067.1	3,541.0	4,284.8	6.6	27,751.5	52,928.2	80,679.7	85.0
23. Warner-Lambert Co.	94,355.9	5,353.6	676.9	476.5	912.1	50.0	19,821.2	63,692.9	83,514.1	88.5
24. Kraft, Inc.	89,960.5	21,428.1	257.6	1,957.1	4,068.5	1,103.5	28,087.9	36,214.2	64,302.1	71.5
25. Sterling Drug, Inc.	87,513.9	11,168.5	1,221.3	1,878.4	—	40.5	5,360.4	63,776.3	69,136.7	79.0
26. Heublein, Inc.	84,603.5	14,861.6	110.0	4,371.0	566.6	8,885.6	20,782.8	35,025.9	55,808.7	66.0
27. Kellogg Co.	82,583.5	3,216.0	455.0	1,678.4	—	10.0	21,681.0	55,543.1	77,224.1	93.5
28. Loews Corp.	81,608.7	35,745.1	12,305.2	436.7	—	24,848.3	2,705.4	5,568.0	8,273.4	10.1
29. Nestle Enterprises, Inc.	81,061.3	8,663.0	488.0	458.7	847.2	123.8	29,037.2	41,443.4	70,480.6	86.9
30. Gillette Co.	80,932.3	12,171.8	76.8	—	—	21.0	15,916.1	52,746.6	68,662.7	84.8
31. B A T Industries, Ltd.	80,656.8	36,081.4	7,593.3	170.3	—	30,872.8	5,939.0	—	5,939.0	7.4
32. Toyota Motor Co., Ltd.	79,429.0	9,823.1	62.8	3,615.6	658.1	1,846.9	42,332.5	21,090.0	63,422.5	79.8
33. Time, Inc.	74,046.3	27,243.1	1,277.1	638.8	1,390.2	43.5	38,240.9	5,212.7	43,453.6	58.7
34. Nabisco, Inc.	71,810.5	6,744.9	491.1	592.4	149.7	—	13,868.5	49,963.9	63,832.4	88.9
35. Consolidated Foods Corp.	64,355.3	8,351.1	326.4	404.7	911.8	104.0	18,570.7	35,686.6	54,257.3	84.3
36. Schering-Plough Corp.	60,366.4	10,752.1	17.0	—	5,439.3	1,903.6	8,363.0	33,891.4	42,254.4	70.0
37. Quaker Oats Co.	60,040.5	10,011.7	499.7	255.4	460.2	61.3	12,736.1	36,016.1	48,752.2	81.2
38. Esmark, Inc.	59,613.2	3,925.5	473.4	61.0	288.7	38.4	14,437.1	40,389.1	54,826.2	92.0
39. Revlon, Inc.	59,234.0	10,638.8	144.3	1,246.9	1,289.6	5.2	19,115.5	26,793.7	45,909.2	79.2
40. General Electric Co.	59,144.1	20,383.6	1,991.8	835.1	842.0	64.1	10,164.9	24,862.6	35,027.5	59.2
41. CBS, Inc.	58,771.6	28,532.9	6,103.9	672.6	4,519.8	821.8	13,344.3	4,776.3	18,120.6	30.8
42. Norton Simon, Inc.	58,614.0	14,737.6	1,074.5	711.5	—	2,436.2	18,123.7	21,530.5	39,654.2	67.7
43. Nissan Motor Co., Ltd.	57,686.9	8,065.7	88.4	5,697.9	—	1,279.0	21,865.0	20,690.9	42,555.9	73.8
44. Richardson-Merrell, Inc.	56,910.6	3,324.6	—	1,699.7	1,028.3	—	11,682.4	39,175.6	50,858.0	89.4
45. International Telephone & Telegraph Corp.	56,486.7	7,131.3	397.2	1,004.8	194.8	547.6	11,359.6	35,851.4	47,211.0	83.6
46. Eastman Kodak Co.	55,036.7	10,565.7	149.5	145.6	1,921.6	775.7	3,413.2	34,065.9	37,479.1	68.1
47. William Wrigley Jr. Co.	54,677.2	418.4	24.4	1,899.1	1,462.7	—	26,070.2	24,802.4	50,872.6	93.0
48. Chesebrough-Pond's, Inc.	54,505.3	11,014.5	1,068.1	331.4	2,354.9	—	7,251.1	32,485.3	39,736.4	72.9
49. Mars, Inc.	53,406.8	1,927.8	189.4	—	—	65.3	24,666.7	26,557.6	51,224.3	95.9
50. RCA Corp.	52,916.8	21,773.2	968.2	894.6	553.3	409.1	6,370.8	21,947.6	28,318.4	53.5

		Total									%
51	Jos. Schlitz Brewing Co.	52,643.1	901.6	9.1	4,327.4	—	684.9	15,291.2	31,428.9	46,720.1	88.7
52	Gulf & Western Industries, Inc.	51,149.5	7,972.6	597.5	1,046.2	460.3	1,169.0	20,101.8	19,802.1	39,903.9	78.0
53	Mobil Corp.	50,822.0	3,994.4	1,853.1	2,183.5	—	148.2	36,931.6	5,711.2	42,642.8	83.9
54	U.S. Government	49,808.4	18,788.3	1,272.7	6,882.1	2,735.7	707.4	2,288.2	17,134.0	19,422.2	39.0
55	Clorox Co.	47,055.3	4,770.1	—	—	—	—	2,706.4	39,578.8	42,285.2	89.9
56	J.C. Penney Co., Inc.	46,885.6	7,458.9	11.6	140.1	866.7	133.9	16,908.9	21,365.5	38,274.4	81.6
57	Volkswagenwerk A.G.	46,858.1	13,306.8	—	58.0	—	475.8	12,520.9	20,496.6	33,017.5	70.5
58	American Brands, Inc.	46,751.0	31,399.3	—	39.8	156.1	10,287.0	1,530.5	3,329.1	4,859.6	10.4
59	Bayer A.G.	45,498.6	2,966.6	9.2	328.1	1,486.9	1,443.6	5,588.0	33,685.4	39,273.4	86.3
60	American Motors Corp.	44,711.7	5,389.1	—	99.9	—	287.8	21,692.0	17,242.9	38,934.9	87.1
61	Liggett Group, Inc.	44,572.1	21,527.7	2,126.6	1,976.2	841.1	4,157.5	3,712.5	10,230.5	13,943.0	31.3
62	Beecham Group, Ltd.	44,336.5	2,795.8	159.1	479.3	—	—	6,361.9	34,540.4	40,902.3	92.3
63	Morton-Norwich Products, Inc.	44,196.8	4,412.7	35.7	117.7	3,224.2	45.2	7,339.2	29,022.1	36,361.3	82.3
64	American Cyanamid Co.	41,326.2	7,187.0	74.4	128.9	—	14.2	11,317.0	22,604.7	33,921.7	82.1
65	Campbell Soup Co.	40,156.2	6,324.7	525.1	1,071.9	2,064.7	214.9	8,866.2	21,088.7	29,954.9	74.6
66	CPC International, Inc.	39,801.8	4,254.7	262.8	3.3	—	474.4	15,528.5	19,281.4	34,809.9	87.5
67	H.J. Heinz Co.	39,060.8	3,232.9	634.9	—	—	33.0	9,640.2	25,516.5	35,156.7	90.0
68	Noxell Corp.	39,033.4	9,649.9	1.7	570.9	—	—	4,105.8	24,705.1	28,810.9	73.8
69	K mart Corp.	37,095.1	5,164.3	—	5,731.6	—	30.2	16,281.6	8,087.7	24,369.3	65.7
70	E.I. Du Pont De Nemours & Co., Inc.	36,953.0	16,615.3	1,575.2	254.4	1,799.7	9.6	2,736.0	15,762.5	18,498.5	50.1
71	Squibb Corp.	36,486.1	2,777.4	123.6	1,666.4	3,981.7	9.3	8,465.1	19,462.6	27,927.7	76.5
72	Polaroid Corp.	35,826.0	5,631.8	196.3	5.1	—	—	2,901.9	27,090.9	29,992.8	83.7
73	American Express Co.	35,692.9	6,252.4	12.9	533.6	—	27.0	10,191.9	18,675.1	28,867.0	80.9
74	Trans World Corp.	35,438.1	2,343.1	253.4	2,863.6	553.1	144.4	25,660.3	3,620.2	29,280.5	82.6
75	Greyhound Corp.	34,423.2	4,748.4	14.9	845.6	3,117.0	—	5,465.0	20,232.3	25,697.3	74.7
76	Mattel, Inc.	34,252.8	1,678.8	50.8	—	—	163.7	19,727.9	12,631.6	32,359.5	94.5
77	MCA, Inc.	33,122.9	1,539.4	10,621.0	38.2	286.5	394.3	13,390.9	6,852.6	20,243.5	61.1
78	SmithKline Corp.	31,757.4	6,011.7	72.1	129.5	5,294.1	—	3,893.0	16,357.0	20,250.0	63.8
79	Warner Communications, Inc.	31,716.9	2,107.8	156.7	977.6	150.1	444.2	12,996.4	14,884.1	27,880.5	87.9
80	S.C. Johnson & Son, Inc.	31,647.3	7,502.0	619.3	301.4	328.0	246.0	4,159.7	18,490.9	22,650.6	71.6
81	A.H. Robins Co., Inc.	31,204.7	1,435.0	—	3,563.2	—	.9	29,321.1	447.1	29,768.8	95.4
82	Levi Strauss & Co.	29,471.0	2,895.7	42.0	240.3	—	.3	5,628.0	17,341.8	22,969.8	77.9
83	Transamerica Corp.	27,652.1	1,779.3	—	2,037.5	487.8	181.0	8,943.6	16,020.1	24,963.7	90.3
84	Beatrice Foods Co.	27,565.8	4,847.1	38.8	57.2	157.7	39.0	14,869.7	5,576.0	20,445.7	74.2
85	Toyo Kogyo Co., Ltd.	27,413.6	4,958.8	—	—	—	96.5	7,318.3	14,982.8	22,301.1	81.4
86	Scott Paper Co.	26,840.7	1,934.7	283.1	336.3	—	23.6	16,474.4	7,788.6	24,263.0	90.4
87	Honda Motor Co., Ltd.	26,675.1	9,005.5	128.9	221.8	—	1,521.5	2,148.8	13,648.6	15,797.4	59.2
88	Milton Bradley Co.	26,644.1	817.0	—	—	—	—	25,052.0	775.1	25,827.1	96.9
89	North American Philips Corp.	26,434.4	2,969.8	121.8	—	—	1.0	8,549.6	14,792.2	23,341.8	88.3
90	Brown-Forman Distillers Corp.	26,347.8	13,021.6	337.8	—	—	4,794.1	2,547.9	5,646.4	8,194.3	31.1
91	Ciba-Geigy, Ltd.	26,207.5	665.3	46.5	473.0	470.1	—	3,119.8	21,902.9	25,022.7	95.5
92	Pfizer, Inc.	26,019.9	8,803.0	188.2	46.4	—	1.7	2,014.2	14,496.3	16,510.5	63.5
93	Hershey Foods Corp.	25,979.2	2,000.8	181.2	32.7	—	33.2	10,508.8	13,222.5	23,731.3	91.3
94	Union Carbide Corp.	25,809.2	956.3	377.3	383.0	—	.6	1,676.2	22,415.8	24,092.0	93.3
95	UAL, Inc.	25,724.2	4,517.6	34.8	5,323.2	—	207.4	8,742.8	6,898.4	15,641.2	60.8
96	Borden, Inc.	24,998.2	4,504.4	131.6	234.4	1,331.2	122.2	7,710.7	10,963.7	18,674.4	74.7
97	Royal Crown Cos., Inc.	24,740.9	121.1	—	159.8	—	181.1	19,132.9	5,146.0	24,278.9	98.1
98	Standard Brands, Inc.	24,557.0	5,597.8	194.8	3,053.4	44.4	185.7	8,422.8	7,058.1	15,480.9	63.0
99	International Business Machines Corp.	24,425.0	4,930.2	69.5	—	774.9	20.9	902.6	17,726.9	18,629.5	76.3
100	Columbia Pictures Industries, Inc.	23,850.3	953.3	—	1,839.8	—	76.0	9,554.1	11,427.1	20,981.2	88.0

Sources: BAR, LNA, RAB

NOTES (1) Where available dealer, dealer association, distributor & bottler expenditures have been included.
(2) Newspaper ad expenditure figures for all companies not available at press time.
(3) Newspaper Supplement data includes Family Weekly, Parade, The New York Times Magazine, and the New York News Magazine.

Source: Television Bureau of Advertising, Inc.

ADVERTISING EXPENDITURES BY INDUSTRY AS A PERCENT OF SALES AND GROSS PROFIT MARGIN

INDUSTRY	SIC	A&P AS % Sales 1979	Margin 1979
Agriculture production-crops	100	2.2	5.4
Agriculture produc-livestock	200	.6	1.6
Metal mining	1000	.1	.2
Copper ores	1020	.2	1.0
Lead & zinc ores	1030	.0	.1
Gold ores	1040	0.0	0.0
Coal & lignite mining	1210	.0	.1
Crude petroleum & natural gas	1310	.2	.3
Drilling oil & gas wells	1380	.2	.6
Misc nonmetallic minerals	1490	N/A	N/A
General building contractors	1520	1.1	5.1
Operative builders	1530	2.7	9.0
Construction-not bldg constr	1600	.2	1.2
Construction-spl contractors	1700	1.5	2.0
Food & kindred products	2000	3.5	11.3
Meat products	2010	1.2	9.5
Dairy products	2020	4.1	22.2
Canned-preserved fruits-vegs	2030	2.0	8.5
Flour & other grain mill pds	2040	2.0	10.4
Bakery products	2050	1.5	3.8
Cane sugar refining	2060	2.4	5.8
Fats & oils	2070	.2	3.1
Alcoholic bev & soft drinks	2080	5.4	15.8
Food preparations NEC	2090	1.0	2.8
Cigarets	2110	6.6	15.7
Cigars	2120	2.2	4.7
Textile mill products	2200	.6	2.9
Floor covering mills	2270	2.0	4.3
Apparel & other finished pds	2300	1.8	6.6
Lumber & wood products	2400	.8	3.4

INDUSTRY	SIC	A&P AS % Sales 1979	Margin 1979
Pottery products NEC	3260	1.9	5.8
Concrete gypsum & plaster	3270	.9	4.9
Abrasive asbestos & misc min	3290	.5	2.0
Blast furnaces & steel works	3310	.2	1.3
Iron & steel foundries	3320	N/A	N/A
Prim smelt-refin nonfer mtl	3330	.1	1.3
Second smelt-refin nonfer mt	3340	.2	.8
Rolling & draw nonfer metal	3350	.5	2.4
Misc primary metal products	3390	.4	1.7
Metal cans & shipping cont	3410	2.1	8.6
Hardware NEC	3420	1.6	4.5
Heating equip & plumbing fix	3430	2.4	10.0
Misc metal work	3440	1.4	4.3
Bolts-nuts-screws-riv-washrs	3450	.5	1.4
Ordnance & accessories	3480	2.9	10.9
Valves pipe fittings ex bras	3490	.9	2.9
Engines & turbines	3510	.9	2.9
Farm-garden machinery & eqp	3520	2.2	12.3
Construction machinery & eqp	3530	.9	3.9
Metalworking machinery & eqp	3540	1.2	3.4
Special industry machinery	3550	1.6	4.2
General industrial mach & eq	3560	1.1	3.3
Office computing & acctg mcn	3570	1.2	2.6
Refrig & service ind machine	3580	1.7	9.6
Elec & elect mach eq & supp	3600	1.5	6.5
Elec transmission & distr eq	3610	1.0	3.3
Industrial controls	3620	.9	2.3
Household appliances	3630	5.5	17.7
Electric lighting-wiring eqp	3640	1.7	4.2

INDUSTRY	SIC	A&P AS % Sales 1979	Margin 1979
Sanitary services	4950	.2	.6
Steam supply	4960	N/A	N/A
Wnsl-autos & parts	5010	1.2	5.0
Whsl-lumber & constr matl	5030	1.0	6.7
Whsl-sporting & recrea goods	5040	2.3	10.7
Whsl-metals & minerals	5050	.5	1.4
Whsl-elec apparatus & equip	5060	1.6	7.5
Whsl-hardwr plum heat equip	5070	1.2	13.7
Whsl-machinery & equipment	5080	1.3	4.9
Whsl-scrap & waste materials	5090	8.3	20.3
Whsl-drugs & proprietary	5120	1.4	3.1
Whsl-groceries & related pds	5140	.6	2.4
Whsl-nondurable goods NEC	5190	.8	3.6
Retail-lumber & bldg matrl	5210	2.2	8.7
Retail-mobile home dealers	5270	1.3	7.2
Retail-department stores	5310	3.0	9.8
Retail-variety stores	5330	2.1	8.0
Retail-grocery stores	5410	1.1	5.2
Retail-auto dlrs & gas statn	5500	1.9	9.3
Retail-apparel & acces stores	5600	2.7	7.0
Retail-womens ready to wear	5620	2.5	7.9
Retail-shoe stores	5660	2.2	5.4
Retail-furniture stores	5710	5.8	15.8
Retail-hshld appliance store	5720	2.9	13.9
Retail-eating places	5810	3.3	15.8
Retail-drug stores	5910	1.7	8.1
Retail-jewelry stores	5940	3.6	12.5
Retail-mail order houses	5960	10.7	24.0
Retail-fuel & ice dealers	5980	N/A	N/A

Category	SIC	A&P/SALES	A&P GROSS MARGIN
Wood buildings-mobile homes	2450	1.0	4.9
Household furniture	2510	1.6	8.7
Office furniture	2520	.9	3.2
Paper & allied products	2600	.8	2.5
Convert paper-paperbd pd NEC	2640	2.0	5.6
Paperboard containers-boxes	2650	.4	1.2
Printing publishing & allied	2700	3.0	5.0
Newspapers publishing-print	2710	2.0	11.6
Periodicals publishing-print	2720	3.5	14.7
Books publishing & printing	2730	4.9	9.4
Commercial printing	2750	1.0	3.0
Manifold business forms	2760	.5	1.3
Greeting card publishing	2770	1.7	3.0
Service indus for print trde	2790	.0	.0
Chemicals & allied prods	2800	2.6	6.2
Indl inorganic chemicals	2810	2.2	5.4
Plastic matr & synthic resin	2820	.5	.5
Drugs	2830	5.6	11.7
Soap & detergent & cosmetics	2840	10.2	18.5
Paints-varnishes-lacquers	2850	1.7	5.3
Industrial organic chemicals	2860	.6	2.8
Agriculture chemicals	2870	1.2	2.2
Misc chemical products	2890	2.8	6.7
Petroleum refining	2910	.7	2.9
Paving & roofing materials	2950	1.3	5.1
Rubber & misc plastic prods	3000	1.1	5.0
Fabricated rubber prods nec	3060	.4	2.3
Misc plastic products	3070	3.7	4.1
Footwear except rubber	3140	2.3	7.1
Leather goods NEC	3190	1.9	4.3
Flat glass	3210	.3	1.0
Glass containers	3220	4.0	11.3
Cement hydraulic	3240	.1	.3
Structural clay products	3250	.6	1.6
Radio-tv receiving sets	3650	5.7	16.4
Tele & telegraph apparatus	3660	1.9	5.6
Electronic components & acce	3670	1.1	3.2
Electrical machy & eqp NEC	3690	2.9	12.0
Motor vehicles & car bodies	3710	1.3	9.3
Aircraft & parts	3720	.7	4.0
Ship-boat building repairing	3730	2.0	11.5
Railroad equipment	3740	.2	.7
Motorcycles bicycles & parts	3750	1.3	9.0
Guided missiles & space vehc	3760	.1	
Travel trailers & campers	3790	1.0	10.9
Engr lab & research equip	3810	1.1	2.8
Measuring & controlling inst	3820	2.0	4.2
Optical instruments & lenses	3830	2.1	4.7
Surg & med instruments & app	3840	1.5	3.5
Photographic equip & suppl	3860	2.2	5.7
Watches clocks & parts	3870	1.6	6.4
Jewelry-precious metals	3910	4.3	9.2
Musical instruments	3930	2.6	7.6
Toys & amusement sport goods	3940	5.3	14.4
Pens-pencil & oth office mat	3950	4.6	11.6
Misc manufacturing	3990	1.8	5.0
Railroads-line haul operating	4010	.5	2.8
Intercity & rural hywy trans	4130	.5	1.8
Trucking-local & long dist	4210	1.1	2.0
Water transportation	4400	.1	.2
Air transportation-certified	4510	1.5	7.2
Pipe lines ex natural gas	4610	N/A	N/A
Transportation services	4700	1.0	6.7
Telephone communication	4810	.1	.2
Radio-tv broadcasters	4830	2.5	4.5
Communication services NEC	4890	1.5	7.8
Natural gas transmission	4920	.2	.9
Water supply	4940	.0	.0
Retail-stores NEC	5990	2.7	9.6
Savings & loan associations	6120	.7	1.9
Personal credit institutions	6140	2.9	6.8
Business credit institutions	6150	8.5	9.1
Finance-services	6190	3.4	14.1
Security & commodity brokers	6200	1.4	4.9
Insurance agents & brokers	6400	.9	2.0
Real estate	6500	1.4	7.2
Subdivid develop ex cemetery	6550	1.7	7.0
Miscellaneous investing	6790	5.9	15.1
Hotel-motels	7010	3.0	12.9
Serv-personal	7200	3.6	11.4
Serv-linen supply	7210	.6	2.0
Serv-advertising agencies	7310	.2	1.5
Serv-bldg cleang & mainten	7340	.2	1.3
Serv-computer & data process	7370	1.4	5.6
Serv-R&D labs & info service	7390	3.2	9.9
Serv-automotive repair & ser	7500	1.3	3.2
Serv-motion picture prodctn	7810	4.3	18.4
Serv-motion picture theatres	7830	3.1	19.1
Serv-racing incl track oper	7940	3.2	20.8
Serv-misc amusement & recrea	7990	3.9	14.9
Serv-nursing personal care	8050	4.6	7.2
Serv-hospitals	8060	.8	2.4
Serv-educational	8200	5.8	17.6
Serv-engineering & architec	8910	1.2	3.1
Conglomerates	9990	1.2	4.6

Legend:
A&P = Advertising & Promotion
SIC = Standard Industrial Classification
N/A = No data available for this value
NEC = Not Elsewhere Classified
A&P/SALES = A&P EXPENDITURES/NET SALES
A&P GROSS MARGIN = A&P Expenditures (NET SALES-COST OF GOODS SOLD)

SOURCE: Schonfeld & Associates Inc., 120 South LaSalle Street Chicago, Illinois 60603, (312) 236-5846

Source: Reprinted with permission from Advertising Age, July 14, 1980, Crain Communications Inc., 1980. Reprinted by permission of Schonfeld & Associates, Inc., Chicago.

WORLD'S TOP 50 AD AGENCIES IN 1979

Figures shown here in millions are based on total equity interest in foreign shops. AA must stress that this table represents only estimates due to reporting procedures of a few agencies that varied slightly from those requested.

Rank	Agency	Gross Income	Billings
1	Dentsu	$352.8	$2,437
2	J. Walter Thompson	253.9	1,693
3	McCann-Erickson	252.3	1,687
4	Young & Rubicam	247.6	1,921
5	Ogilvy & Mather	206.2	1,393
6	Ted Bates	181.0	1,177
7	SSC&B	153.2	1,021.6
8	BBDO	144.8	985.5
9	Leo Burnett	141.1	950.7
10	Foote, Cone & Belding	137.6	918.1
11	*D'Arcy-MacManus & Masius	128.0	853.6
12	Hakuhodo	127.4	896.3
13	Grey Advertising	106.3	710.0
14	Doyle Dane Bernbach	104.0	701.0
15	†Benton & Bowles	95.4	640.4
16	Campbell-Ewald	84.2	561.9
17	Compton	77.7	524.6
18	Eurocom	77.2	519.7
19	Dancer Fitzgerald Sample	$68.4	$469.9
20	Naito Issui Sha	65.0	370.3
21	N W Ayer	63.9	428.4
22	Daiko Advertising	62.5	491.8
23	Wells, Rich, Greene	56.6	377.6
24	Marsteller	54.3	362.5
25	Needham, Harper & Steers	50.4	336.2
26	Kenyon & Eckhardt	49.2	328.3
27	Norman, Craig & Kummel	48.0	323.1
28	William Esty Co.	45.6	304.0
29	Bozell & Jacobs Intl.	45.2	304.0
30	Intermarco-Farner	43.5	291.6
31	Dai-Ichi Kikaku	38.4	272.6
32	KM&G Intl.	37.7	245.1
33	Tokyu	34.4	239.9
34	Yomiko	30.7	172.9
35	Cunningham & Walsh	$29.3	$225.2
36	Publicis Conseil	29.2	201.2
37	Ross Roy	26.9	179.0
38	Asahi Kokoku Sha	26.0	165.4
39	Campbell-Mithun	23.8	158.4
40	MPM/Casabranca	23.1	86.7
41	Wunderman, Ricotta & Kline	22.7	151.2
42	TBWA	22.6	150.8
43	Dai-Ichi	22.2	158.1
44	Alcantara Machado Periscinoto	20.8	83.1
45	Asahi Tsushin	20.8	143.9
46	††Groupe Roux Seguela Cayzac & Goudard	18.9	97.3
47	William Wilkens & Co	18.6	93.7
48	Nationwide Ad Service	18.2	69.8
49	Orikomi	18.1	134.6
50	GGK	17.8	118.4

*D'Arcy-MacManus & Masius figures exclude de Garmo, which was merged into the D'Arcy New York office in January.

†Figures include 20% ownership in Gestion et Recherche Publicitaire. a French agency group comprising B&B Publicite. Feldman. Calleux and Concurrence

††Groupe RSCG includes the main Paris agency. RSCG plus Chevassus & Vadon. Dire. Immediat and four smaller units

Source: Reprinted with permission from *Advertising Age*, April 14, 1980, Crain Communications Inc., 1980. Reprinted by permission of Schonfeld & Associates, Inc., Chicago.

MARKET AREAS OF DOMINANT INFLUENCE RANKED BY TV HOUSEHOLDS

JANUARY 1979—ARBITRON TELEVISION

Rank	ADI Market	Region	TV Households
1	New York	MA	6,375,500
2	Los Angeles	P	3,882,800
3	Chicago	ENC	2,806,600
4	Philadelphia	MA	2,364,000
5	San Francisco	P	1,830,700
6	Boston	NE	1,788,300
7	Detroit	ENC	1,590,700
8	Washington, DC	SA	1,363,900
9	Cleveland	ENC	1,304,200
10	Dallas-Ft. Worth	WSC	1,115,300
	Cumulative total 33.1%		24,422,000
11	Pittsburgh	MA	1,098,900
12	Houston	WSC	1,009,500
13	St. Louis	WNC	971,900
14	Minneapolis-St. Paul	WNC	962,800
15	Miami	SA	946,900
16	Atlanta	SA	902,500
17	Tampa-St. Petersburg	SA	875,900
18	Seattle-Tacoma	P	854,000
19	Baltimore	SA	797,500
20	Indianapolis	ENC	762,800
	Cumulative total 45.5%		33,604,700
21	Denver	M	694,000
22	Portland, OR	P	672,500
23	Hartford-New Haven	NE	670,400
24	Sacramento-Stockton	P	648,500
25	Milwaukee	ENC	638,700
26	Cincinnati	ENC	635,300
27	Kansas City	WNC	629,300
28	San Diego	P	624,500
29	Buffalo	MA	624,200
30	Nashville	ESC	575,200
	Cumulative total 54.2%		40,017,300
31	Providence	NE	559,700
32	Columbus, OH	ENC	546,200
33	Phoenix	M	540,300
34	Charlotte	SA	530,900
35	Memphis	ESC	524,000
36	New Orleans	WSC	511,400
37	Greenville-Spartanburg-Asheville	SA	504,800
38	Oklahoma City	WSC	475,300
39	Grand Rapids-Kalamazoo-Battle Crk.	ENC	472,900

Key:

NE	New England	**ENC**	East North Central	**WSC**	West South Central
	Maine		Ohio		Arkansas
	New Hampshire		Indiana		Louisiana
	Vermont		Illinois		Oklahoma
	Massachusetts		Michigan		Texas
	Rhode Island		Wisconsin		
	Connecticut			**M**	Mountain
		ESC	East South Central		Montana
MA	Middle Atlantic		Kentucky		Idaho
	New York		Tennessee		Wyoming
	New Jersey		Alabama		Colorado
	Pennsylvania		Mississippi		New Mexico
					Arizona
SA	South Atlantic	**WNC**	West North Central		Utah
	Delaware		Minnesota		Nevada
	Maryland		Iowa		
	D.C.		Missouri	**P**	Pacific
	Virginia		North Dakota		Washington
	West Virginia		South Dakota		Oregon
	North Carolina		Nebraska		California
	South Carolina		Kansas		Alaska
	Georgia				
	Florida				

Source: *Spot Television Planning Guide*, Television Bureau of Advertising, Inc.

JANUARY 1979—ARBITRON TELEVISION (continued)

40	Orlando-Daytona Beach	SA	468,100
	Cumulative total 61.1%		45,150,900
41	Wilkes Barre-Scranton	MA	456,100
42	Raleigh-Durham	SA	451,800
43	Louisville	ESC	449,200
44	Charleston-Huntington	SA	443,400
45	Albany-Schenectady-Troy	MA	437,200
46	Dayton	ENC	432,300
47	Harrisburg-York-Lancaster-Lebanon	MA	430,800
48	Norfolk-Portsmth-Newport Nws-Hmpt.	SA	429,000
49	Salt Lake City	M	423,900
50	Birmingham	ESC	421,500
	Cumulative total 67.0%		49,526,100
51	San Antonio	WSC	406,700
52	Tulsa	WSC	397,800
53	Greensboro-Winston Salem-High Point	SA	397,600
54	Wichita-Hutchinson	WNC	393,300
55	Flint-Saginaw-Bay City	ENC	385,500
56	Richmond	SA	381,600
57	Toledo	ENC	381,400
58	Little Rock	WSC	378,800
59	Shreveport-Texarkana	WSC	360,900
60	Knoxville	ESC	349,200
	Cumulative total 72.2%		53,358,900
61	Syracuse	MA	340,800
62	Mobile-Pensacola	ESC	337,700
63	Des Moines	WNC	337,100
64	Jacksonville	SA	324,700
65	Rochester, NY	MA	323,200
66	Green Bay	ENC	320,000
67	Roanoke-Lynchburg	SA	319,300
68	Omaha	WNC	314,700
69	Fresno	P	304,100
70	Cedar Rapids-Waterloo	WNC	296,000
	Cumulative total 76.6%		56,576,500
71	Springfield-Decatur-Champaign	ENC	288,800
72	Johnstown-Altoona	MA	287,500
73	Chattanooga	ESC	283,600
74	Davenport-Rock Island-Moline	ENC	282,800
75	Spokane	P	282,300
76	Paducah-Cape Girardeau-Harrisburg	WSC	278,000
77	Albuquerque	M	276,200
78	South Bend-Elkhart	ENC	269,800
79	Portland-Poland Spring	NE	267,300
80	Youngstown	ENC	251,100
	Cumulative total 80.3%		59,343,900
81	West Palm Beach	SA	244,300
82	Lincoln-Hastings-Kearney	WNC	240,600
83	Jackson, MS	ESC	239,400
84	Bristol-Kingsport-Johnson City	ESC	239,100
85	Springfield, MO	WNC	234,200
86	Springfield, MA	NE	219,400
87	Evansville	ENC	214,000
88	Peoria	ENC	211,800
89	Lexington	ESC	211,000
90	Burlington-Plattsburgh	NE	208,000
	Cumulative total 83.4%		61,605,700
91	Tucson	M	203,700
92	Sioux Falls-Mitchell	WNC	201,000
93	Lansing	ENC	196,900
94	Greenville-New Bern-Washington	SA	196,000
95	Baton Rouge	W	194,300
96	Huntsville-Decatur-Florence	ESC	191,000
97	Austin, TX	WSC	190,700
98	Ft. Wayne	ENC	189,200
99	Columbia, SC	SA	188,800
100	Rockford	ENC	180,900
	Cumulative total 86.0%		63,538,200

101	Fargo	WNC	'	180,600
102	Waco-Temple	WSC		179,700
103	Colorado Springs-Pueblo	M		179,600
104	Madison	ENC		175,200
105	El Paso	WSC		172,500
106	Monroe-El Dorado	WSC		170,900
107	Duluth-Superior	WNC		165,400
108	Augusta	SA		160,500
109	Terre Haute	ENC		160,200
110	Wichita Falls-Lawton	WSC		160,000
	Cumulative total 88.3%			65,242,800
111	Wheeling-Steubenville	ENC		156,800
112	Salinas-Monterey	P		154,100
113	Joplin-Pittsburg	WNC		153,400
114	Savannah	SA		152,200
115	Lafayette, LA	WSC		151,500
116	Snta Brbra-Snt Maria-Sn Luis Obispo	P		150,900
117	Amarillo	WSC		150,100
118	Traverse City-Cadillac	ENC		149,300
119	Montgomery	ESC		147,700
120	Beaumont-Port Arthur	WSC		146,900
	Cumulative total 90.4%			66,755,700
121	Columbus, GA	SA		146,300
122	Binghamton	MA		145,000
123	Sioux City'	WNC		144,900
124	Charleston, SC	SA		144,200
125	Lubbock	WSC		143,000
126	La Crosse-Eau Claire	ENC		140,000
127	Yakima	P		139,000
128	Eugene	P		136,200
129	Wilmington	SA		135,300
130	Wausau-Rhinelander	ENC		134,100
	Cumulative total 92.3%			68,163,700
131	Topeka	WNC		134,000
132	Bluefield-Beckley-Oak Hill	SA		133,500
133	Corpus Christi	WSC		133,000
134	Rochester-Mason City-Austin	WNC		132,800
135	Erie	MA		132,600
136	Columbus-Tupelo	ESC		131,100
137	Las Vegas	M		129,900
138	McAllen-Brownsville	WSC		126,500
139	Columbia-Jefferson City	WNC		125,300
140	Tallahassee	SA		124,200
	Cumulative total 94.0%			69,466,600
141	Boise	M		122,800
142	Ft. Myers	SA		120,800
143	Minot-Bismarck-Dickinson	WNC		118,900
144	Quincy-Hannibal	ENC		117,900
145	Chico-Redding	P		114,500
146	Bangor	NE		112,800
147	Macon	SA		112,000
148	Reno	WSC		111,500
149	Odessa-Midland	WSC		110,300
150	Albany, GA	SA		106,100
	Cumulative total 95.6%			70,614,200
151	Utica	MA		102,400
152	Alexandria, MN	WNC		100,300
153	Missoula-Butte	M		99,600
154	Bakersfield	P		99,000
155	Abilene-Sweetwater	WSC		97,100
156	Medford	P		96,900
157	Dothan	WSC		90,900

JANUARY 1979—ARBITRON TELEVISION *(continued)*

158	Tyler	WSC	89,400
159	Florence, SC	SA	83,900
160	Elmira	MA	81,300
	Cumulative total 96.8%		71,555,000
161	Billings	M	79,600
162	Ft. Smith	WSC	79,400
163	Idaho Falls-Pocatello	M	78,200
164	Watertown-Carthage	MA	76,700
165	Clarksburg-Weston	SA	74,900
166	Rapid City	WNC	74,700
167	Laurel-Hattiesburg	ESC	73,000
168	Salisbury	SA	69,900
169	Meridian	ESC	68,100
170	Anchorage	P	64,600
	Cumulative total 97.8%		72,294,100
171	Alexandria, LA	WSC	64,400
172	Jonesboro	WSC	63,400
173	Lake Charles	WSC	62,700
174	Ardmore-Ada	WSC	62,600
175	Great Falls	M	59,600
176	Cheyenne	M	55,000
177	Gainsville	SA	53,300
178	Casper-Riverton	M	51,200
179	Marquette	ENC	51,200
180	Panama City	SA	51,200
	Cumulative total 98.6%		72,868,700
181	St. Joseph	WNC	50,100
182	Roswell	M	50,000
183	Biloxi-Gulfport-Pascagoula	ESC	49,000
184	El Centro-Yuma	P	48,800
185	Eureka	P	48,500
186	Mankato	WNC	45,900
187	Palm Springs	P	45,200
188	Grand Junction	M	42,700
189	Tuscaloosa	ESC	39,500
190	Jackson, TN	ESC	38,600
	Cumulative total 99.2%		73,327,000
191	Anniston	ENC	37,800
192	Greenwood-Greenville	ESC	36,000
193	Lafayette, IN	ENC	35,600
194	Lima	ENC	35,100
195	Twin Falls	M	34,700
196	San Angelo	WSC	32,600
197	Bellingham	P	32,300
198	Bowling Green	ESC	31,900
199	Harrisonburg	SA	31,800
200	Parkersburg	SA	30,100
	Cumulative total 99.7%		73,664,900
201	Presque Isle	NE	28,700
202	Ottumwa-Kirksville	WNC	27,800
203	Zanesville	ENC	27,700
204	Laredo	WSC	25,400
205	Farmington	M	21,000
206	Victoria	WSC	19,100
207	Flagstaff	M	18,500
208	Selma	ESC	17,300
209	North Platte	WNC	14,400
210	Helena	M	14,000
211	Alpena	ENC	13,700
212	Miles City-Glendive	M	8,600
	Cumulative total 100.0%		73,901,100

TOP U.S. MAGAZINES: CIRCULATION

	Circulation	
	1979*	1978†
TV Guide	19,043,358	19,495,113
Reader's Digest	17,888,680	17,978,238
National Geographic Magazine	10,413,639	10,134,530
Better Homes and Gardens	8,097,651	8,039,983
Family Circle	7,753,604	8,380,582
Women's Day	7,560,329	8,083,799
McCall's	6,526,745	6,536,728
Ladies' Home Journal	5,502,149	6,031,430
Good Housekeeping	5,271,172	5,361,950
Playboy	5,249,010	5,248,309
National Enquirer	5,024,180	5,362,022
Penthouse	4,711,849	4,612,958
Redbook	4,303,944	4,463,315
Time	4,272,888	4,272,495
Newsweek	2,934,530	2,925,694
Cosmopolitan	2,747,042	2,700,364
Senior Scholastic	2,649,291	2,736,079
American Legion	2,592,065	2,598,931
Sports Illustrated	2,274,819	2,272,905
People Weekly	2,262,611	2,476,876
U.S. News & World Report	2,042,910	2,037,177
Field and Stream	2,021,381	2,029,949
Glamour	1,879,402	1,918,606
Southern Living	1,862,667	1,632,619
V.F.W. Magazine	1,829,180	1,830,259
Smithsonian	1,812,084	1,707,295
Popular Science	1,800,319	1,822,762
Outdoor Life	1,709,872	1,752,056
Hustler	1,700,873	1,508,297
Today's Education	1,694,024	1,685,507
Mechanics Illustrated	1,680,245	1,660,484
Elks Magazine	1,644,470	1,631,725
Popular Mechanics	1,642,570	1,624,074
True Story	1,604,178	1,645,565
Workbasket	1,569,788	1,845,352
Midnight Globe	1,552,579	1,801,770
Boys' Life	1,516,405	1,508,788
Parents' Magazine	1,456,311	1,517,644
Seventeen	1,450,625	1,450,083
Sunset	1,403,481	1,372,122
Ebony	1,262,619	1,241,303
Nation's Business	1,256,270	1,186,452
Sport	1,207,633	1,269,038
Psychology Today	1,177,988	1,178,516
House & Garden	1,084,277	1,073,109
'Teen	1,059,325	974,069
Vogue, incorporating Vanity Fair	1,019,847	1,007,513
Golf Digest	974,645	943,520
Mademoiselle	958,035	1,017,907
Family Handyman	953,305	880,573
Grit	899,515	1,009,288
Hot Rod	986,927	833,166
House Beautiful	867,096	834,246
Oui	862,979	907,542
Scouting	845,193	935,102
Apartment Life	833,950	827,059
Popular Photography	824,213	820,459
Decorating & Craft Ideas	815,145	798,461
Junior Scholastic	811,772	913,603
Family Health	806,860	933,928
Weight Watchers Magazine	800,842	822,164
Business Week	793,519	781,072
Motor Trend	756,933	752,697
Playgirl	748,953	661,642
Rolling Stone	720,380	620,544
Car & Driver	719,746	742,719
Jet	718,798	678,005
Scientific American	714,914	691,922

TOP U.S. MAGAZINES: CIRCULATION *(continued)*

	Circulation	
	1979*	1978†
Golf, incorporating *Golfing*	709,564	709,619
Forbes	676,537	667,224
Saturday Evening Post	666,087	534,534
Fortune	663,443	661,962
Esquire	659,543	664,348
Gourmet	656,004	655,837
National Lampoon	647,600	569,373
Signature	641,099	604,509
Harper's Bazaar	633,675	592,305
Modern Photography	621,420	610,426
Essence	600,739	600,429
Lutheran, The	580,886	579,967
Catholic Digest	544,235	543,700
Sports Afield	534,104	532,636
Saturday Review	519,214	532,246
Flower & Garden Magazine	501,567	522,618
New Yorker	500,274	498,128

* Figures in this column are based on the total average paid circulation for the six months ending December 31, 1979.

† Figures in this column are based on the total average paid circulation for the six months ending December 31, 1978.

Source: Audit Bureau of Circulation's *FAS-FAX Report,* December 31, 1978, March 15, 1979, December 31, 1979, March 14, 1980.

RETAIL SALES IN 100 TOP MARKETS*

SMSA	Group rank for total retail sales	% U.S. sales	% change 1977 vs. 1972	Food	Eating and drinking	Drug, proprietary stores	Gasoline service stations	General merchandise	Apparel, accessory stores	Furniture, home furnishings	Auto dealers	Bldg. mat'l, hardware, mobile homes
Los Angeles-Long Beach, Cal.	1	3.57	66.2	$6,028,868	$2,918,664	$1,014,124	$1,841,236	$3,760,940	$1,518,058	$1,530,507	$5,700,819	$1,088,417
Chicago, Ill.	2	3.43	58.9	5,073,791	2,660,092	1,022,647	1,817,443	3,702,351	1,756,263	1,269,375	5,306,147	1,063,199
New York, N.Y.	3	3.28	28.4	6,530,903	2,939,493	770,912	1,133,826	3,526,903	2,277,147	1,304,749	2,883,759	636,392
Detroit, Mich.	4	2.14	63.1	3,614,003	1,463,101	544,862	1,269,058	2,379,701	986,473	809,616	4,144,852	756,734
Philadelphia, Pa.	5	2.01	52.3	3,544,881	1,419,651	455,202	1,035,835	2,143,419	951,658	701,722	2,934,608	553,707
Boston, Mass.	6	1.75	52.3	3,127,354	1,410,708	438,201	872,458	1,796,104	839,173	537,625	2,173,421	579,952
San Francisco-Oakland, Cal.	7	1.65	70.5	2,839,920	1,472,176	562,738	763,695	1,769,290	689,928	708,725	2,417,937	499,421
Washington, D.C.-Md.-Va.	8	1.54	61.7	2,441,619	1,176,762	536,694	915,954	1,761,846	666,795	567,748	2,500,069	417,605
Dallas-Fort Worth, Tex.	9	1.34	76.0	2,139,669	923,647	354,964	707,463	1,481,409	497,037	451,427	2,665,463	418,603
Houston, Tex.	10	1.33	101.4	2,277,448	908,518	284,867	638,789	1,634,854	489,992	460,001	2,602,973	471,585
Nassau-Suffolk, N.Y.	11	1.24	43.8	2,295,364	768,014	242,350	654,042	1,363,314	554,451	455,042	1,528,893	357,070
St. Louis, Mo.	12	1.09	68.8	1,909,296	776,971	256,745	724,690	1,406,362	379,563	370,353	1,860,488	397,364
Minneapolis-St. Paul, Minn.	13	1.03	78.9	1,425,091	726,873	218,490	615,071	1,441,860	361,662	361,677	1,672,979	546,944
Anaheim-Santa Ana-Garden Grove, Cal.	14	1.03	110.2	1,582,838	838,985	233,838	531,193	1,181,473	332,803	451,500	1,728,022	511,495
Pittsburgh, Pa.	15	1.01	64.8	1,742,328	661,382	246,449	583,877	1,385,171	387,510	340,247	1,685,198	340,141
Atlanta, Ga.	16	0.96	71.1	1,453,530	710,608	222,977	578,555	1,306,917	295,188	306,258	1,610,324	406,390
Cleveland, O.	17	0.93	66.9	1,627,371	651,530	263,216	571,752	1,212,128	340,866	309,507	1,595,329	259,894
Baltimore, Md.	18	0.90	54.5	1,649,319	731,304	246,338	554,103	1,048,081	332,972	298,822	1,329,229	206,114
Newark, N.J.	19	0.83	44.9	1,648,486	584,286	170,372	452,849	633,296	418,565	352,531	1,223,090	241,528
Denver-Boulder, Colo.	20	0.83	88.7	1,335,795	663,503	170,847	401,438	913,480	310,678	329,559	1,435,507	389,462
San Diego, Cal.	21	0.83	102.1	1,273,025	649,813	204,957	435,150	1,045,272	275,045	382,980	1,341,956	435,984
Miami, Fla.	22	0.78	65.4	1,296,456	688,625	225,423	368,255	927,329	393,006	295,578	1,329,467	166,599
Seattle-Everett, Wash.	23	0.81	95.8	1,327,424	703,836	245,222	387,131	825,588	327,361	321,332	1,290,903	375,275
Phoenix, Ariz.	24	0.71	106.5	1,267,823	556,621	200,197	348,852	745,694	203,149	327,554	1,256,226	331,278
San Jose, Cal.	25	0.68	97.0	1,084,041	465,990	189,833	336,365	792,079	248,466	322,357	1,168,395	305,642
Kansas City, Mo.-Kan.	26	0.67	72.4	1,000,224	471,742	134,413	417,862	885,584	255,158	215,087	1,272,234	232,405
Riverside-San Bernardino-Ontario, Cal.	27	0.65	100.8	1,103,414	477,172	172,642	401,856	737,539	197,120	219,103	1,064,819	427,246
Milwaukee, Wis.	28	0.64	67.7	1,069,924	498,360	139,968	349,731	810,544	224,450	265,672	1,042,829	215,769
Cincinnati, O.	29	0.64	73.9	1,136,663	517,196	174,755	437,015	875,544	195,799	232,645	992,945	201,252
Tampa-St. Petersburg, Fla.	30	0.64	69.5	1,152,992	513,561	185,036	328,854	778,076	183,745	252,334	1,073,449	265,628

RETAIL SALES IN 100 TOP MARKETS (continued)

SMSA	Group rank for total retail sales	% U.S. sales	% change 1977 vs. 1972	Food	Eating and drinking	Drug, proprietary stores	Gasoline service stations	General merchandise	Apparel, accessory stores	Furniture, home furnishings	Auto dealers	Bldg. matl., hardware, mobile homes
Portland, Ore.	31	0.64	100.2	923,985	519,885	136,198	323,208	886,680	228,651	276,795	1,084,316	237,181
Indianapolis, Ind.	32	0.61	80.6	908,873	402,121	158,211	411,595	711,962	172,724	197,665	1,071,451	230,666
Fort Lauderdale-Hollywood, Fla.	33	0.58	112.0	1,064,464	526,278	161,898	269,599	687,716	235,953	262,834	828,413	164,248
Columbus, O.	34	0.53	69.6	837,760	412,365	113,673	326,187	705,371	167,760	194,364	975,281	194,394
Buffalo, N.Y.	35	0.52	49.4	1,024,102	396,768	161,462	239,989	656,069	211,892	161,110	827,431	154,029
New Orleans, La.	36	0.51	73.2	1,040,247	404,157	143,740	231,957	617,209	264,936	181,033	750,787	147,306
Sacramento, Cal.	37	0.50	101.2	883,790	379,878	157,496	278,098	554,002	160,110	216,850	860,719	264,171
Hartford-New Britain-Bristol, Conn.	38	0.48	59.0	879,575	359,141	131,847	296,246	495,483	202,419	152,235	657,292	164,358
Oklahoma City, Okla.	39	0.44	92.5	713,673	314,787	68,830	203,325	478,903	228,164	168,848	902,221	190,732
Rochester, N.Y.	40	0.43	54.7	789,868	275,367	124,852	222,666	431,366	142,454	129,955	738,501	151,962
San Antonio, Tex.	41	0.42	84.5	674,526	343,642	76,509	214,647	589,855	165,350	160,139	785,881	167,605
Louisville, Ky.	42	0.42	68.6	717,206	321,345	111,860	275,709	510,537	137,430	160,913	729,011	165,634
Memphis, Tenn.	43	0.40	64.8	692,899	238,572	93,400	256,977	474,833	168,030	145,770	758,976	134,416
Salt Lake City-Ogden, Utah	44	0.40	91.4	627,242	245,080	91,630	226,877	483,275	129,394	190,497	746,653	212,448
Nashville-Davidson, Tenn.	45	0.40	86.2	651,478	267,508	93,098	255,701	429,299	141,655	134,934	830,215	151,051
Bridgeport-Stamford-Norwalk-Danbury, Conn.	46	0.40	55.4	703,296	245,512	84,208	216,977	348,462	192,117	149,927	515,525	179,623
Birmingham, Ala.	47	0.39	81.6	697,836	224,354	93,267	213,503	409,953	197,908	134,733	744,208	156,032
Greensboro-Winston-Salem-High Point, N.C.	48	0.37	77.9	607,955	233,523	96,511	224,392	368,779	152,507	157,229	691,716	167,073
Dayton, O.	49	0.37	59.5	616,898	267,889	63,418	259,892	509,664	101,372	142,205	645,975	132,007
Toledo, O.	50	0.36	67.2	629,959	277,890	82,229	266,054	446,047	107,525	120,660	671,733	121,881
Flint, Mich.	51	0.36	133.7	440,228	165,409	309,783	157,187	357,307	98,649	107,220	597,015	115,748
Honolulu, Hawaii	52	0.35	88.4	503,947	433,266	152,461	136,053	605,874	171,783	79,944	396,195	50,903
Albany-Schenectady-Troy, N.Y.	53	0.33	53.3	635,842	245,615	77,289	189,320	349,180	139,954	99,486	485,826	123,265
Providence-Warwick-Pawtucket, R.I.	54	0.33	44.1	616,730	234,734	91,459	199,254	334,572	138,777	102,150	454,314	130,248
Tulsa, Okla.	55	0.33	105.5	578,205	199,309	56,057	165,978	342,137	164,265	133,784	675,400	157,894
New Haven-Waterbury-Meriden, Conn.	56	0.33	49.3	640,148	241,891	74,750	197,625	363,790	148,828	115,670	435,802	106,599
Orlando, Fla.	57	0.33	90.9	535,213	226,077	84,686	224,330	359,231	81,889	110,391	635,973	124,809
Norfolk-Virginia Beach-Portsmouth, Va.	58	0.31	74.3	540,992	216,257	74,387	179,646	398,061	128,579	121,838	580,295	109,760
Charlotte-Gastonia, N.C.	59	0.30	70.9	524,968	181,413	84,187	154,703	358,298	128,884	107,392	614,338	125,467
Jacksonville, Fla.	60	0.30	54.4	507,340	198,068	107,970	214,605	280,158	103,695	91,916	608,730	106,392
Akron, O.	61	0.30	61.8	560,283	221,051	61,624	188,049	356,645	90,966	90,836	499,458	170,807
Richmond, Va.	62	0.30	72.2	489,215	199,800	87,666	233,661	320,477	109,368	102,834	477,911	85,679
Grand Rapids, Mich.	63	0.29	74.9	413,437	205,919	34,999	157,082	426,949	128,389	129,709	532,410	158,353
Gary-Hammond-East Chicago, Ind.	64	0.29	72.5	540,549	205,126	91,592	216,829	306,909	107,697	106,601	503,239	111,226
West Palm Beach-Boca Raton, Fla.	65	0.29	96.0	535,091	191,482	84,574	140,241	278,103	130,326	139,694	472,926	137,353
Allentown-Bethlehem-Easton, Pa.	66	0.28	69.0	536,956	187,218	65,361	144,257	332,961	87,911	100,202	413,982	104,928
Northeastern Pennsylvania	67	0.27	55.7	513,224	177,124	70,114	150,752	330,461	95,923	89,210	375,654	110,310
Syracuse, N.Y.	68	0.27	58.3	558,678	194,437	110,699	144,827	254,354	109,930	88,924	440,067	86,153
Worcester-Fitchburg-Leominster, Mass.	69	0.26	54.3	506,190	171,169	65,962	153,873	286,121	98,544	86,025	359,535	92,847
New Brunswick-Perth Amboy, N.J.	70	0.26	57.0	521,354	176,872	52,692	161,203	355,512	142,420	83,794	284,603	89,427

Rank	City										
71	Omaha, Neb.	0.26	67.0	408,119	220,879	71,122	157,113	353,982	89,795	129,859	447,596	82,432
72	Fresno, Cal.	0.25	104.2	435,234	164,616	96,049	135,992	257,821	82,897	105,353	427,529	128,961
73	Wilmington, Del.	0.24	59.4	424,550	159,240	69,613	155,584	302,108	91,717	101,773	351,003	94,416
74	Raleigh-Durham, N.C.	0.24	80.1	416,002	162,112	56,485	152,504	288,969	98,012	82,575	401,985	87,432
75	Springfield-Chicopee-Holyoke, Mass.	0.23	53.1	464,245	165,327	55,686	143,323	220,779	94,840	66,855	309,082	100,755
76	Long Branch-Asbury Park, N.J.	0.23	63.9	477,504	184,006	53,642	139,372	213,339	94,437	86,856	343,893	81,283
77	Youngstown-Warren, O.	0.23	62.8	404,472	147,758	58,059	158,059	340,536	76,048	85,128	391,985	73,502
78	Tucson, Ariz.	0.23	89.4	428,370	163,194	62,867	142,940	272,588	63,253	91,099	416,522	98,136
79	Austin, Tex.	0.23	103.5	377,671	195,620	44,699	119,625	191,983	112,473	91,915	441,177	130,031
80	Knoxville, Tenn.	0.23	91.7	366,352	134,912	57,089	143,763	297,502	76,218	81,547	412,376	128,441
81	Greenville-Spartanburg, S.C.	0.22	68.7	421,595	144,185	65,543	141,243	225,524	86,937	81,540	353,536	122,473
82	Harrisburg, Pa.	0.22	71.5	388,521	146,222	57,637	144,987	228,300	80,415	71,460	333,081	81,998
83	Albuquerque, N.M.	0.21	96.8	310,903	160,039	52,461	120,988	241,149	83,181	103,749	431,718	89,876
84	Oxnard-Simi Valley-Ventura, Cal.	0.21	93.1	408,651	143,899	65,733	114,285	218,377	61,468	79,237	389,844	93,082
85	Lansing-East Lansing, Mich.	0.21	68.5	315,694	148,745	29,829	128,864	303,139	79,220	72,467	420,126	87,271
86	Wichita, Kan.	0.21	91.8	302,473	157,265	38,477	110,077	241,260	97,997	77,099	422,286	103,833
87	Baton Rouge, La.	0.21	93.1	389,006	110,513	52,300	101,335	291,254	64,074	79,770	402,974	88,887
88	Paterson-Clifton-Passaic, N.J.	0.20	39.4	323,586	132,162	34,989	92,389	274,100	121,195	76,034	241,332	56,122
89	Tacoma, Wash.	0.19	95.4	302,782	143,253	52,863	116,189	219,398	62,365	81,546	356,384	93,658
90	Canton, O.	0.19	81.8	340,997	131,906	38,155	110,271	227,770	69,085	65,313	361,363	80,972
91	Davenport, Ia.-Rock Island-Moline, Ill.	0.19	83.9	287,869	151,879	53,338	130,891	231,809	61,846	69,370	340,698	93,077
92	El Paso, Tex.	0.19	91.8	272,263	126,036	40,720	89,462	287,335	94,146	89,893	329,830	71,784
93	Fort Wayne, Ind.	0.19	74.4	279,094	149,052	54,262	118,013	238,435	70,366	74,365	358,106	66,804
94	New Bedford-Fall River, Mass.	0.18	55.7	350,170	128,680	45,001	99,643	207,087	76,095	68,020	247,372	56,085
95	Chattanooga, Tenn.	0.18	62.5	308,684	104,212	44,887	122,207	197,989	64,821	59,935	338,444	80,802
96	Mobile, Ala.	0.18	87.4	335,080	119,076	43,670	105,227	201,766	62,792	58,670	327,696	90,998
97	Johnson City-Kingsport-Bristol, Tenn.	0.17	89.8	305,555	89,404	35,899	106,341	193,629	62,483	57,468	340,100	127,679
98	Columbia, S.C.	0.17	81.3	279,176	110,284	33,980	107,541	222,557	61,641	55,384	321,176	93,852
99	Jersey City, N.J.	0.17	35.3	368,207	127,876	42,963	93,862	121,396	128,496	59,369	178,758	41,923
100	Charleston, S.C.	0.16	88.3	315,691	88,953	35,808	95,153	207,231	59,079	51,529	266,436	91,413

* Compiled by Marketing Economics Institute's "Marketing Economics Guide."
Source: Reprinted with permission from *Advertising Age*, December 19, 1979, Crain Communications Inc., 1979.

RETAIL TRADE: TRENDS AND PROJECTIONS, 1974–1980

MILLIONS OF CURRENT DOLLARS EXCEPT AS NOTED

Item	1974	1975	1976	1977	1978	1979[1]	Percent change 1978–79	1980[1]	Percent change 1979–80[2]
Retail Trade total (SIC 52–59)									
Sales	534,511	580,445	642,507	724,020	798,818	878,700	10.0	966,570	10.0
Total employment (000)	12,794	12,824	13,431	13,903	14,496	14,931	3.0	15,304	2.5
Non-supervisory workers (000)	11,540	11,552	12,113	12,508	13,060	13,451	3.	13,787	2.5
Average hourly earnings (Dec.—$)	3.18	3.40	3.65	3.92	4.31	—	—	—	—
Year-to-year percent change in average hourly earnings (Dec.–Dec.)	8.2	6.9	7.4	7.4	9.9	—	—	—	—
Department stores (SIC 5311)									
Sales	54,115	57,442	62,900	71,583	79,732	86,908	9.0	94,729	9.0
Total employment (000)	1,718	1,658	1,702	1,747	1,891	1,929	2.0	1,958	1.5
Non-supervisory workers (000)	1,557	1,522	1,575	1,623	1,774	1,823	2.8	1,850	1.5
Average hourly earnings (Dec.—$)	3.09	3.31	3.52	3.85	4.17	—	—	—	—
Year-to-year percent change in average hourly earnings (Dec.–Dec.)	8.0	7.1	6.3	9.4	8.3	—	—	—	—
Eating and Drinking Places (SIC 5812–5813)									
Sales	45,193	51,427	58,008	63,891	70,083	76,390	9.0	83,265	9.0
Total employment (000)	3,199	3,332	3,624	3,853	4,260	4,494	5.5	4,674	4.0
Non-supervisory workers (000)	2,989	3,115	3,380	3,585	3,931	4,147	5.5	4,313	4.0
Average hourly earnings (Dec.—$)	2.34	2.58	2.82	2.99	3.31	—	—	—	—
Year-to-year percent change in average hourly earnings (Dec.–Dec.)	8.8	10.3	9.3	6.0	10.7	—	—	—	—
Apparel stores total (SIC 56)									
Sales	24,910	26,700	32,200	34,341	37,828	41,233	9.0	44,738	9.5
Total employment (000)	797	784	805	821	884	911	3.0	920	1.0
Non-supervisory workers (000)	703	687	704	712	765	783	2.4	791	1.0
Average hourly earnings (Dec.—$)	2.85	3.09	3.32	3.53	3.85	—	—	—	—
Year-to-year percent change in average hourly earnings (Dec.–Dec.)	9.6	8.4	7.4	6.3	9.1	—	—	—	—

[1] Estimates by Industry and Trade Administration (BDBD).
[2] Forecast.

Source: Bureau of the Census (sales data), Bureau of Labor Statistics (employment and earnings), and Industry and Trade Administration (BDBD) (estimates).

Source: *1980 U.S. Industrial Outlook*, U.S. Department of Commerce.

WHOLESALE TRADE: TRENDS AND PROJECTIONS 1974–1980

SALES IN MILLIONS OF DOLLARS

SIC		1974	1975	1976	1977	1978	1979[1]	Percent change 1978–79	1980[2]	Percent change 1979–80
50–51	Merchant wholesalers, total[3]	550,036	535,596	580,894	642,104	754,105	882,793	17	997,556	13
	Durable goods, total	237,044	220,094	246,732	285,605	349,916	409,951	17	455,046	11
501	Motor vehicles, equipment	38,266	38,951	44,889	54,046	68,298	79,940	17	92,730	16
502	Furniture, furnishings	8,288	8,136	9,594	11,026	12,966	14,438	11	15,639	9
503	Lumber, other construction materials	18,789	16,576	20,920	26,181	32,223	38,000	18	39,520	4
506	Electrical goods	25,405	23,546	27,868	31,745	38,325	43,384	13	45,987	6
507	Hardware, plumbing equipment	18,106	16,814	19,174	22,404	25,868	29,352	13	31,406	7
508	Machinery, equipment, supplies	63,047	65,911	71,378	82,003	97,877	114,376	17	128,101	12
	Nondurable goods, total	312,992	315,502	334,162	356,498	404,189	472,842	17	539,040	14
511	Paper, paper products	12,338	11,498	13,444	15,482	17,586	20,049	14	22,054	10
512	Drugs, sundries	8,600	9,284	10,144	10,868	11,526	12,794	11	14,073	10
513	Apparel, piece goods	15,315	15,715	17,567	19,595	25,076	27,584	10	29,791	8
514	Groceries and related products	88,786	95,022	99,791	110,766	125,091	146,581	17	168,568	15
518	Beer, wine, spirits	18,133	20,055	21,587	23,371	27,028	29,731	10	32,109	8
	Total employment (000)[4]	4,433	4,415	4,546	4,697	4,898	5,075	4	5,180	2

[1] Estimated by Industry and Trade Administration (BDBD).
[2] Forecasts.
[3] Because some trade lines are excluded, wholesalers by type of business do not add to durable and nondurable totals.
[4] Includes employees in other distributive lines (about 25 percent of total) not defined as merchant wholesalers.

Source: Bureau of the Census (sales data). Bureau of Labor Statistics (hourly earnings and employment). Estimates and forecasts by Industry and Trade Administration (BDBD).

Source: *U.S. Industrial Outlook*, 1980, U.S. Department of Commerce.

ESTIMATED AND PROJECTED POPULATION, BY AGE AND SEX, 1950 TO 2010, AND ZERO GROWTH PROJECTIONS, 1985 TO 2050

In thousands, except percent. As of July 1. Includes Armed Forces abroad. The base date for the projections is 1976. These projections were prepared using the "cohort-component" method. Series I, II, and III assume a slight improvement in mortality, an annual net immigration of 400,000, and completed cohort fertility rates (i.e., average number of lifetime births per 1,000 women) that move toward the following levels: I—2,700; II—2,100; III—1,700. Series II—X differs from Series II only in that it assumes no net immigration. The Series II and Series II—X fertility assumption represents "replacement level" fertility (i.e., the level of fertility at which the population would exactly replace itself in the absence of net immigration).

YEAR, SERIES, AND SEX	Total, all ages	Under 5 years	5-13 years	14-17 years	18-21 years	22-24 years	25-34 years	35-44 years	45-54 years	55-64 years	65 years and over	16 years and over	18 years and over	21 years and over	Median age (yr.)
TOTAL															
1950	152,271	16,410	22,423	8,444	8,947	7,129	24,036	21,637	17,453	13,396	12,397	109,141	104,994	98,341	30.2
1960	180,671	20,341	32,965	11,219	9,555	6,573	22,919	24,221	20,578	15,625	16,675	121,835	116,146	108,856	29.4
1970	204,878	17,148	36,636	15,910	14,707	9,980	25,294	23,142	23,310	18,664	20,087	142,956	135,184	124,031	27.9
1975	213,559	15,879	33,440	16,934	16,484	11,120	30,919	22,816	23,769	19,777	22,420	155,724	147,306	134,776	28.8
1977	216,863	15,241	32,228	16,957	16,784	11,648	33,161	23,544	23,392	20,401	23,507	161,047	152,610	139,727	29.4
1978	218,548	15,361	31,378	16,639	17,085	11,859	33,936	24,383	23,184	20,068	24,054	163,588	155,170	142,306	29.7
Percent of total:															
1950	100.0	10.8	14.7	5.5	5.9	4.7	15.8	14.2	11.5	8.8	8.1	71.7	69.0	64.6	(X)
1960	100.0	11.3	18.2	6.2	5.3	3.6	12.7	13.4	11.4	8.6	9.2	67.4	64.3	60.3	(X)
1970	100.0	8.4	17.9	7.8	7.2	4.9	12.3	11.3	11.4	9.1	9.8	69.8	66.0	60.5	(X)
1975	100.0	7.4	15.7	7.9	7.7	5.2	14.5	10.7	11.1	9.3	10.5	72.9	69.0	63.1	(X)
1977	100.0	7.0	14.9	7.7	7.8	5.4	15.3	10.9	10.8	9.4	10.8	74.3	70.4	64.4	(X)
1978	100.0	7.0	14.4	7.6	7.8	5.4	15.5	11.2	10.6	9.5	11.0	74.9	71.0	65.1	(X)
Projections:															
1985——I	238,878	22,887	31,012												30.7
——II	232,880	18,803	29,098	14,392	15,442	12,411	39,859	31,376	22,457	21,737	27,305	177,607	170,587	159,218	31.5
——III	228,879	16,235	27,665												32.0
1990——I	254,715	24,616	38,591												31.4
——II	243,513	19,437	32,568	12,771	14,507	10,642	41,086	36,592	25,311	20,776	29,824	185,082	178,737	167,787	32.8
——III	236,264	16,211	28,546												33.7
2000——I	282,837	23,638	44,725	19,698	17,692	10,336						204,408	194,776	181,139	32.5
——II	260,378	17,852	35,080	16,045	14,990	9,663	34,450	41,344	35,875	23,257	31,822	199,324	191,400	179,893	35.5
——III	245,876	14,158	28,915	13,831	13,006	9,219						195,865	188,972	178,989	37.3
2010——I	315,248	29,126	45,417	19,865	20,728	15,038	42,076					230,814	220,841	205,257	31.1
——II	275,335	19,221	33,067	15,439	16,319	12,043	36,246	34,685	40,551	32,926	34,837	215,392	207,608	195,361	36.6
——III	250,892	13,763	25,540	12,557	13,498	10,191	32,344					205,389	199,032	188,929	40.2
MALE															
1950	75,849	8,362	11,415	4,269	4,484	3,525	11,804	10,706	8,715	6,714	5,856	53,893	51,803	48,460	29.8
1960	89,320	10,339	16,762	5,682	4,810	3,284	11,327	11,872	10,142	7,559	7,542	59,413	56,536	52,859	28.5
1970	100,269	8,742	18,667	8,101	7,437	5,000	12,521	11,316	11,251	8,828	8,407	68,714	64,759	59,121	26.6
1975	104,213	8,114	17,048	8,624	8,344	5,567	15,347	11,150	11,490	9,345	9,184	74,709	70,426	64,088	27.6
1977	105,722	7,791	16,438	8,555	8,585	5,828	16,472	11,497	11,328	9,653	9,576	77,236	72,938	66,422	28.2
1978	106,502	7,855	16,005	8,486	8,651	5,934	16,862	11,909	11,239	9,782	9,778	78,446	74,155	67,649	28.5

Projections:															
1985—I	116,441	11,726	15,869												29.5
II	11[illegible],366	9,632	14,888	7,346	7,820	6,208	19,825	15,374	10,915	10,346	11,012	85,079	81,500	75,750	30.3
III	111,315	8,315	14,154												30.8
1990—I	124,232	12,618	19,772												30.2
II	118,490	9,963	16,685	6,533	7,358	5,320	20,424	17,964	12,299	9,945	11,999	88,553	85,310	79,758	31.6
III	114,775	8,309	14,624												32.5
2000—I	138,091	12,121	22,928	10,090	9,002	5,188						97,882	92,952	86,018	30.8
II	126,588	9,153	17,981	8,218	7,626	4,849	17,124	20,261	17,518	11,141	12,717	95,292	91,236	85,386	34.1
III	119,162	7,259	14,819	7,083	6,616	4,624						93,529	90,001	84,926	36.0
2010—I	154,121	14,943	23,292	10,180	10,558	7,564	21,012					110,813	105,705	97,775	29.5
II	133,710	9,855	16,946	7,907	8,306	6,049	18,076	16,971	19,770	15,851	13,978	102,987	99,003	92,775	34.8
III	121,213	7,051	13,079	6,426	6,865	5,113	16,109					97,909	94,658	89,524	38.6
FEMALE															
1950	76,422	8,048	11,008	4,175	4,463	3,603	12,233	10,931	8,738	6,682	6,541	55,248	53,191	49,881	30.5
1960	91,352	10,002	16,203	5,537	4,745	3,289	11,591	12,349	10,436	8,067	9,133	62,422	59,610	55,997	30.3
1970	104,609	8,406	17,968	7,809	7,270	4,980	12,772	11,826	12,059	9,838	11,681	74,243	70,425	64,910	29.3
1975	109,346	7,765	16,392	8,310	8,140	5,554	15,571	11,667	12,279	10,432	13,236	81,014	76,880	70,688	30.0
1977	111,141	7,450	15,790	8,229	8,372	5,820	16,689	12,047	12,064	10,748	13,930	83,811	79,672	73,306	30.6
1978	112,046	7,507	15,373	8,153	8,434	5,925	17,074	12,474	11,945	10,886	14,276	85,142	81,014	74,657	31.0
Projections:															
1985—I	122,437	11,161	15,144												31.9
II	119,514	9,171	14,210	7,046	7,621	6,204	20,034	16,002	11,542	11,390	16,293	92,528	89,087	83,468	32.7
III	117,564	7,919	13,512												33.2
1990—I	130,483	11,998	18,820												32.7
II	125,023	9,474	15,883	6,238	7,148	5,321	20,663	18,626	13,012	10,831	17,824	96,530	93,427	88,029	33.9
III	121,489	7,902	13,923												34.8
2000—I	144,746	11,517	21,797	9,607	8,690	5,148						106,525	101,825	95,121	34.1
II	133,790	8,699	17,099	7,827	7,363	4,815	17,326	21,084	18,356	12,116	19,105	104,032	100,165	94,508	36.8
III	126,714	6,899	14,096	6,748	6,390	4,595						102,336	98,971	94,063	38.5
2010—I	161,128	14,183	22,125	9,684	10,170	7,474	21,063					120,001	115,136	107,482	32.8
II	141,625	9,367	16,121	7,533	8,013	5,994	18,171	17,713	20,782	17,075	20,858	112,405	108,605	102,586	38.3
III	129,678	6,712	12,462	6,131	6,633	5,078	16,235					107,480	104,374	99,405	41.7
SERIES II–X ILLUSTRATIVE PROJECTIONS [1]															
1980	220,497	15,782	29,951	15,645	16,978	12,222	35,720	25,545	22,604	21,140	24,910	167,215	159,119	146,333	30.3
1985	228,912	18,283	28,423	14,136	15,153	12,165	38,842	30,856	22,218	21,593	27,244	174,960	168,071	156,916	31.7
1990	237,028	18,680	31,353	12,361	14,076	10,288	39,636	35,556	24,861	20,526	29,690	180,780	174,634	164,005	33.0
2000	248,372	16,698	33,014	15,147	14,106	9,037	32,295	39,369	34,570	22,684	31,451	190,991	183,513	172,675	36.0
2025	267,418	17,207	32,525	14,530	13,977	9,777	33,405	35,535	29,773	32,067	48,621	210,317	203,156	192,561	38.4
2050	269,411	17,499	32,314	14,367	14,125	10,084	33,882	34,351	31,438	31,522	49,829	212,335	205,230	194,556	38.6
Percent distribution in ultimate stationary population	100.0	6.5	11.7	5.2	5.2	3.8	12.7	12.5	12.2	11.2	19.0	79.2	76.6	72.8	38.9

X Not applicable. [1] Series II–X, which would reach zero growth around the middle of the twenty-first century, is one of many possible approaches to zero growth. Immediate cessation of net immigration, combined with replacement level fertility would not lead to immediate zero growth because the U.S. has a relatively young age structure (due to the post-World War II baby boom) which provides momentum for continued growth. Immediate zero growth in 1978 (assuming no dramatic change in mortality) would require an annual total fertility rate of about 900 with net immigration at the current level, or about 1,000 with no net immigration. Total fertility rate in 1978 was about 1,800.

Source: U.S. Bureau of the Census, *Current Population Reports*, series P–25, Nos. 310, 311, 519, 704, and 800.

Source: *Statistical Abstract of the United States*, U.S. Department of Commerce, Bureau of Census.

Employment Wages and Productivity

STATUS OF THE LABOR FORCE

MILLIONS OF PERSONS*

SEASONALLY ADJUSTED

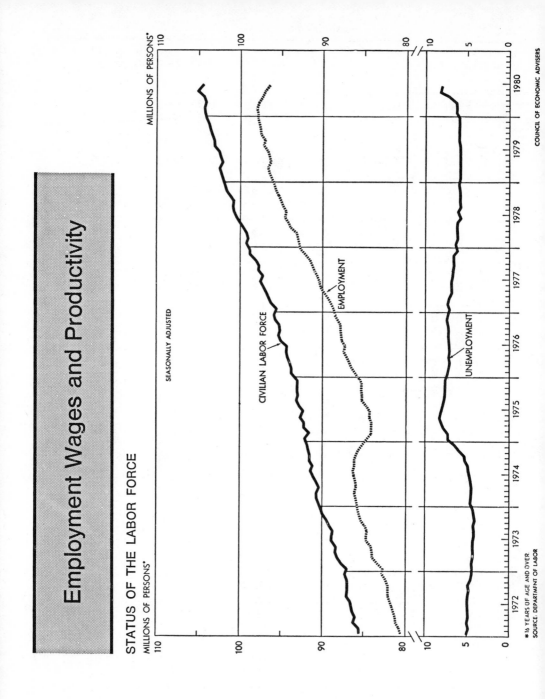

MILLIONS OF PERSONS*

CIVILIAN LABOR FORCE

EMPLOYMENT

UNEMPLOYMENT

*16 YEARS OF AGE AND OVER
SOURCE: DEPARTMENT OF LABOR

COUNCIL OF ECONOMIC ADVISERS

[Thousands of persons 16 years of age and over, except as noted]

Period	Noninstitutional population	Unadjusted		Seasonally adjusted								
		Civilian employment	Unemployment	Total labor force (including Armed Forces)	Civilian labor force	Civilian employment		Nonagricultural		Unemployment		Labor force participation rate (percent) [2]
						Total	Agricultural	Total	Part-time for economic reasons [1]	Total	15 weeks and over	
1974	150,827	85,935	5,076	93,240	91,011	85,935	3,492	82,443	2,709	5,076	937	61.8
1975	153,449	84,783	7,830	94,793	92,613	84,783	3,380	81,403	3,490	7,830	2,483	61.8
1976	156,048	87,485	7,288	96,917	94,773	87,485	3,297	84,188	3,272	7,288	2,339	62.1
1977	158,559	90,546	6,855	99,534	97,401	90,546	3,244	87,302	3,297	6,855	1,911	62.8
1978*	161,058	94,373	6,047	102,537	100,420	94,373	3,342	91,031	3,216	6,047	1,379	63.7
1979	163,620	96,945	5,963	104,996	102,908	96,945	3,297	93,648	3,281	5,963	1,202	64.2
1979: June	163,469	97,917	6,235	104,552	102,476	96,652	3,243	93,409	3,284	5,824	1,152	64.0
July	163,685	98,891	6,104	105,175	103,093	97,184	3,267	93,917	3,274	5,909	1,067	64.3
Aug	163,891	98,226	6,137	105,218	103,128	97,004	3,315	93,689	3,298	6,124	1,185	64.2
Sept	164,106	97,576	5,798	105,586	103,494	97,504	3,364	94,140	3,167	5,990	1,152	64.3
Oct	164,468	98,158	5,781	105,688	103,595	97,474	3,294	94,180	3,315	6,121	1,195	64.3
Nov	164,682	97,943	5,776	105,744	103,652	97,608	3,385	94,223	3,392	6,044	1,191	64.2
Dec	164,898	98,047	5,836	106,088	103,999	97,912	3,359	94,553	3,519	6,087	1,230	64.3
1980: Jan	165,101	96,145	7,043	106,310	104,229	97,804	3,270	94,534	3,513	6,425	1,334	64.4
Feb	165,298	96,264	6,993	106,346	104,260	97,953	3,326	94,626	3,406	6,307	1,286	64.3
Mar	165,506	96,546	6,805	106,184	104,094	97,656	3,358	94,298	3,418	6,438	1,363	64.2
Apr	165,693	96,566	6,846	106,511	104,419	97,154	3,242	93,912	3,816	7,265	1,629	64.3
May	165,886	96,709	7,318	107,230	105,142	96,988	3,379	93,609	4,349	8,154	1,722	64.6
June	166,105	97,776	8,291	106,634	104,542	96,537	3,191	93,346	3,999	8,006	1,766	64.2

[1] Persons at work. Economic reasons include slack work, material shortages, inability to find full-time work, etc.

[2] Total labor force as percent of noninstitutional population 16 years of age and over.

*Data beginning 1978 not strictly comparable with earlier data because of revisions in the household survey, which added about 250,000 to labor force and to employment.

Source: Economic Indicators, Council of Economic Advisers.

Source: Department of Labor, Bureau of Labor Statistics.

SELECTED UNEMPLOYMENT RATES

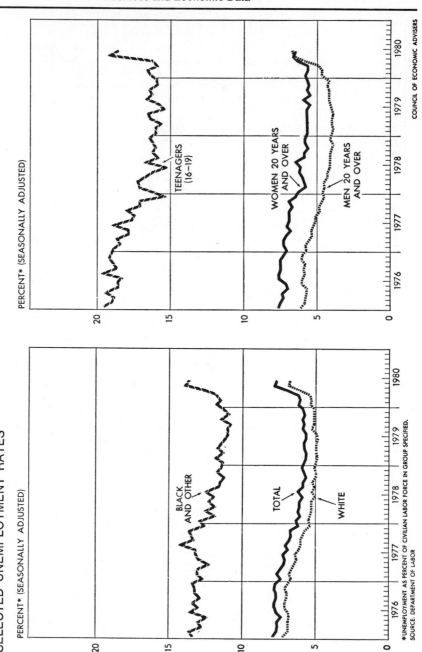

PERCENT* (SEASONALLY ADJUSTED)

PERCENT* (SEASONALLY ADJUSTED)

BLACK AND OTHER

TOTAL

WHITE

TEENAGERS (16-19)

WOMEN 20 YEARS AND OVER

MEN 20 YEARS AND OVER

*UNEMPLOYMENT AS PERCENT OF CIVILIAN LABOR FORCE IN GROUP SPECIFIED.
SOURCE: DEPARTMENT OF LABOR

COUNCIL OF ECONOMIC ADVISERS

[Monthly data seasonally adjusted]

Period	Total (all civilian workers)	By sex and age			By race		By selected groups				Labor force time lost (percent)[1]
		Men 20 years and over	Women 20 years and over	Both sexes 16–19 years	White	Black and other	Experienced wage and salary workers	Household heads	Full-time workers	Part-time workers	
1974	5.6	3.8	5.5	16.0	5.0	9.9	5.3	3.3	5.1	8.6	6.1
1975	8.5	6.7	8.0	19.9	7.8	13.9	8.2	5.8	8.1	10.3	9.1
1976	7.7	5.9	7.4	19.0	7.0	13.1	7.3	5.1	7.3	10.1	8.3
1977	7.0	5.2	7.0	17.7	6.2	13.1	6.6	4.5	6.5	9.8	7.6
1978	6.0	4.2	6.0	16.3	5.2	11.9	5.6	3.7	5.3	9.0	6.5
1979	5.8	4.1	5.7	16.1	5.1	11.3	5.4	3.6	5.5	8.7	6.3
1979: June	5.7	4.0	5.7	15.4	4.9	11.2	5.3	3.5	5.2	8.6	6.3
July	5.7	4.1	5.5	15.8	5.0	11.0	5.4	3.6	5.3	8.3	6.4
Aug	5.9	4.2	5.9	16.6	5.3	11.0	5.7	3.7	5.3	8.4	6.2
Sept	5.8	4.2	5.5	16.2	5.1	10.8	5.5	3.7	5.3	8.9	6.4
Oct	5.9	4.2	5.7	16.4	5.1	11.5	5.6	3.8	5.4	8.3	6.4
Nov	5.8	4.3	5.6	15.9	5.1	10.9	5.5	3.8	5.4	8.5	6.4
Dec	5.9	4.2	5.7	16.0	5.1	11.3	5.5	3.7	5.4	8.5	6.4
1980: Jan	6.2	4.7	5.8	16.3	5.4	11.8	5.8	4.2	5.7	8.7	6.7
Feb	6.2	4.6	5.7	16.5	5.3	11.5	5.7	4.0	5.6	8.9	6.6
Mar	6.2	4.9	5.7	15.9	5.4	11.8	5.9	4.3	5.8	8.3	6.8
Apr	7.0	5.9	6.3	16.2	6.2	12.6	6.7	4.9	6.6	8.3	7.5
May	7.8	6.6	6.6	19.2	6.9	13.9	7.6	5.3	7.5	9.3	8.8
June	7.7	6.7	6.5	18.5	6.8	13.6	7.4	5.3	7.4	8.8	8.3

Unemployment rate (percent of civilian labor force in group)

[1] Aggregate hours lost by the unemployed and persons on part-time for economic reasons as percent of potentially available labor force hours.

Source: *Economic Indicators*, Council of Economic Advisers.

Source: Department of Labor, Bureau of Labor Statistics.

EMPLOYMENT BY INDUSTRY DIVISION AND MAJOR MANUFACTURING GROUP, SEASONALLY ADJUSTED

NONAGRICULTURAL PAYROLL DATA, IN THOUSANDS

Industry division and group	1979									1980			
	Apr.	May	June	July	Aug.	Sept.	Oct.	Nov.	Dec.	Jan.	Feb.	Mar. ᴾ	Apr. ᴾ
TOTAL	89.036	89.398	89.626	89.713	89.762	89.803	89.982	90.100	90.241	90.652	90.845	90.799	90.320
MINING	940	944	949	956	968	973	979	983	991	1.000	1.009	1.010	1.016
CONSTRUCTION	4.559	4.648	4.662	4.688	4.674	4.671	4.694	4.714	4.783	4.893	4.831	4.698	4.558
MANUFACTURING	21.066	21.059	21.063	21.079	20.957	20.949	20.899	20.836	20.881	20.890	20.892	20.889	20.615
Production workers	15.134	15.112	15.096	15.090	14.956	14.957	14.894	14.829	14.865	14.848	14.826	14.822	14.556
Durable goods	12.752	12.739	12.760	12.786	12.714	12.737	12.650	12.587	12.615	12.601	12.655	12.658	12.395
Production workers	9.146	9.119	9.123	9.124	9.044	9.066	8.972	8.908	8.931	8.894	8.926	8.934	8.672
Lumber and wood products	761	762	757	753	752	758	760	751	740	737	740	729	685
Furniture and fixtures	490	487	485	488	484	480	482	483	483	484	481	481	477
Stone, clay, and glass products	714	715	715	711	710	708	709	704	706	708	709	704	687
Primary metal industries	1.260	1.254	1.257	1.256	1.245	1.236	1.226	1.223	1.208	1.208	1.210	1.205	1.195
Fabricated metal products	1.732	1.730	1.737	1.730	1.714	1.716	1.723	1.726	1.725	1.712	1.724	1.722	1.690
Machinery, except electrical	2.466	2.471	2.484	2.500	2.492	2.496	2.455	2.438	2.444	2.512	2.511	2.516	2.513
Electric and electronic equipment	2.101	2.106	2.124	2.131	2.092	2.117	2.125	2.125	2.140	2.149	2.147	2.160	2.151
Transportation equipment	2.084	2.077	2.057	2.073	2.079	2.086	2.025	1.994	2.019	1.938	1.980	1.984	1.845
Instruments and related products	689	688	693	694	695	692	696	694	698	700	703	707	705
Miscellaneous manufacturing	455	449	451	450	451	448	449	449	452	453	450	450	447

	8.314 / 5.988	8.320 / 5.993	8.303 / 5.973	8.293 / 5.966	8.243 / 5.912	8.212 / 5.891	8.249 / 5.922	8.249 / 5.921	8.266 / 5.934	8.289 / 5.954	8.237 / 5.900	8.231 / 5.888	8.220 / 5.884
Nondurable goods / Production workers	(see header)												
Food and kindred products	1,728	1,725	1,720	1,707	1,696	1,691	1,707	1,710	1,715	1,707	1,705	1,698	1,686
Tobacco manufactures	69	70	69	68	64	65	65	60	62	64	65	65	65
Textile mill products	892	893	892	892	886	884	887	889	893	891	891	893	894
Apparel and other textile products	1,325	1,324	1,312	1,324	1,302	1,294	1,299	1,292	1,297	1,309	1,312	1,312	1,308
Paper and allied products	717	714	715	718	717	714	715	714	713	718	717	718	714
Printing and publishing	1,234	1,236	1,242	1,250	1,247	1,245	1,252	1,262	1,263	1,273	1,278	1,279	1,277
Chemicals and allied products	1,111	1,114	1,119	1,116	1,111	1,110	1,113	1,114	1,119	1,123	1,121	1,122	1,125
Petroleum and coal products	213	213	212	212	213	215	217	217	217	219	163	160	181
Rubber and miscellaneous plastics products	781	784	775	777	764	751	751	749	745	745	744	744	732
Leather and leather products	244	247	247	229	243	243	243	242	242	240	241	240	238
TRANSPORTATION AND PUBLIC UTILITIES	5,024	5,130	5,190	5,169	5,194	5,180	5,218	5,229	5,223	5,212	5,210	5,212	5,186
WHOLESALE AND RETAIL TRADE	20,088	20,129	20,116	20,122	20,126	20,169	20,243	20,308	20,254	20,428	20,521	20,498	20,367
WHOLESALE TRADE	5,138	5,156	5,180	5,182	5,185	5,190	5,209	5,235	5,218	5,248	5,274	5,280	5,250
RETAIL TRADE	14,950	14,973	14,936	14,940	14,941	14,979	15,034	15,073	15,036	15,180	15,247	15,218	15,117
FINANCE, INSURANCE, AND REAL ESTATE	4,915	4,936	4,958	4,972	5,003	4,997	5,018	5,039	5,056	5,081	5,092	5,103	5,108
SERVICES	16,880	16,954	17,051	17,092	17,141	17,191	17,257	17,298	17,357	17,442	17,522	17,540	17,546
GOVERNMENT	15,564	15,598	15,637	15,635	15,699	15,673	15,674	15,693	15,696	15,706	15,768	15,849	15,924
Federal	2,758	2,770	2,788	2,785	2,813	2,762	2,770	2,771	2,771	2,791	2,823	2,884	2,952
State and local	12,806	12,828	12,849	12,850	12,886	12,911	12,904	12,922	12,925	12,915	12,945	12,965	12,972

Source: *Monthly Labor Review*, U.S. Department of Labor, Bureau of Labor Statistics.

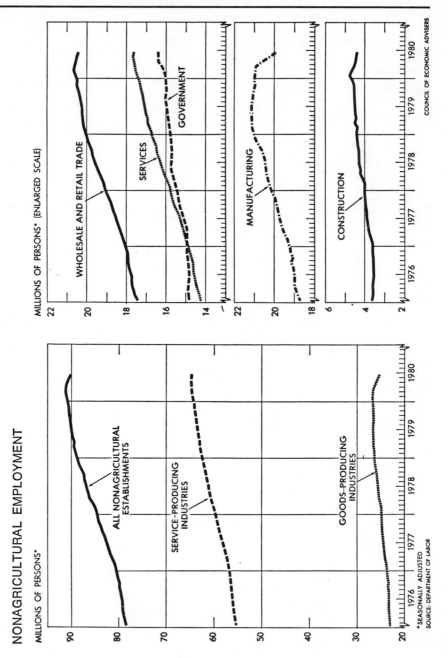

NONAGRICULTURAL EMPLOYMENT

MILLIONS OF PERSONS*

ALL NONAGRICULTURAL ESTABLISHMENTS

SERVICE-PRODUCING INDUSTRIES

GOODS-PRODUCING INDUSTRIES

*SEASONALLY ADJUSTED
SOURCE: DEPARTMENT OF LABOR

MILLIONS OF PERSONS* (ENLARGED SCALE)

WHOLESALE AND RETAIL TRADE

SERVICES

GOVERNMENT

MANUFACTURING

CONSTRUCTION

COUNCIL OF ECONOMIC ADVISERS

[Thousands of wage and salary workers;[1] seasonally adjusted]

| Period | Total nonagricultural employment | Goods-producing industries | | Manufacturing | | | Service-producing industries | | | | | Government | |
		Total[2]	Construction	Total	Durable goods	Nondurable goods	Total	Transportation and public utilities	Wholesale and retail trade	Finance, insurance, and real estate	Services	Federal	State and local
1974	78,265	24,794	4,020	20,077	11,925	8,152	53,471	4,725	16,987	4,148	13,441	2,724	11,446
1975	76,945	22,600	3,525	18,323	10,688	7,635	54,345	4,542	17,060	4,165	13,892	2,748	11,937
1976	79,382	23,352	3,576	18,997	11,077	7,920	56,030	4,582	17,755	4,271	14,551	2,733	12,138
1977	82,471	24,346	3,851	19,682	11,597	8,086	58,125	4,713	18,516	4,467	15,303	2,727	12,399
1978	86,697	25,585	4,229	20,505	12,274	8,231	61,113	4,923	19,542	4,724	16,252	2,753	12,919
1979	89,886	26,504	4,483	21,062	12,772	8,290	63,382	5,141	20,269	4,974	17,078	2,773	13,147
1979: June	89,909	26,557	4,472	21,132	12,837	8,295	63,352	5,168	20,217	4,970	17,074	2,783	13,140
July	90,054	26,582	4,491	21,128	12,841	8,287	63,472	5,156	20,254	4,989	17,114	2,784	13,175
Aug	90,222	26,528	4,499	21,055	12,782	8,273	63,694	5,182	20,301	5,019	17,152	2,811	13,229
Sept	90,283	26,554	4,507	21,071	12,822	8,249	63,729	5,185	20,352	5,017	17,192	2,762	13,221
Oct	90,441	26,554	4,529	21,043	12,764	8,279	63,887	5,203	20,414	5,033	17,264	2,769	13,204
Nov	90,552	26,504	4,553	20,966	12,693	8,273	64,048	5,216	20,479	5,049	17,308	2,773	13,223
Dec	90,678	26,590	4,615	20,983	12,706	8,277	64,088	5,212	20,448	5,064	17,362	2,773	13,229
1980: Jan	91,031	26,715	4,745	20,971	12,681	8,290	64,316	5,202	20,529	5,091	17,462	2,791	13,241
Feb	91,186	26,623	4,659	20,957	12,715	8,242	64,563	5,198	20,637	5,101	17,540	2,826	13,261
Mar	91,144	26,476	4,529	20,938	12,707	8,231	64,668	5,202	20,610	5,115	17,580	2,886	13,275
Apr	90,951	26,121	4,467	20,642	12,442	8,200	64,830	5,178	20,531	5,119	17,618	3,115	13,269
May p	90,602	25,746	4,441	20,282	12,139	8,143	64,856	5,162	20,496	5,139	17,668	3,094	13,297
June p	90,088	25,367	4,377	19,969	11,905	8,064	64,721	5,143	20,422	5,153	17,618	3,077	13,308

[1] Includes all full- and part-time wage and salary workers in nonagricultural establishments who worked during or received pay for any part of the pay period which includes the 12th of the month. Excludes proprietors, self-employed persons, domestic servants, and personnel of the Armed Forces. Total derived from this table not comparable with estimates of nonagricultural employment of the civilian labor force, shown on p. 11, which include proprietors, self-employed persons, and domestic servants; which count persons as employed when they are not at work because of industrial disputes; and which are based on a sample of the working-age population, whereas the estimates in this table are based on reports from employing establishments.

[2] Includes mining, not shown separately.

NOTE.—Annual data revised beginning 1977; seasonally adjusted data, beginning 1975.

Source: Department of Labor, Bureau of Labor Statistics.

Source: Economic Indicators, Council of Economic Advisers.

WEEKLY EARNINGS, BY INDUSTRY DIVISION AND MAJOR MANUFACTURING GROUP
GROSS AVERAGES, PRODUCTION OR NONSUPERVISORY WORKERS ON PRIVATE NONAGRICULTURAL PAYROLLS

Industry division and group	Annual average		1979									1980			
	1978	1979	Apr.	May	June	July	Aug.	Sept.	Oct.	Nov.	Dec.	Jan.	Feb.	Mar. P	Apr. P
TOTAL PRIVATE	$203.70	$219.91	$211.65	$216.20	$219.71	$221.76	$222.84	$225.90	$225.62	$226.06	$229.40	$225.34	$227.39	$229.15	$228.50
MINING	332.11	364.64	363.80	361.66	367.62	355.28	365.49	372.80	374.51	380.19	383.25	384.09	383.62	387.10	387.00
CONSTRUCTION	318.32	341.69	320.21	340.01	346.03	348.35	354.16	360.43	356.82	346.75	355.05	332.40	340.80	348.00	351.36
MANUFACTURING	249.27	268.94	254.41	265.86	269.06	267.73	267.60	274.04	274.85	277.14	285.07	277.01	278.20	280.99	278.56
Durable goods	270.44	290.50	273.14	288.46	291.51	288.86	287.65	295.39	295.80	297.43	308.26	297.82	300.24	304.21	300.85
Lumber and wood products	222.88	240.16	230.69	236.41	247.63	245.46	248.58	253.43	248.35	241.72	245.00	236.98	244.09	243.21	234.24
Furniture and fixtures	183.92	195.32	185.25	189.85	195.94	191.52	196.86	202.02	204.36	205.02	210.27	202.37	204.52	206.98	205.74
Stone, clay, and glass products	262.91	283.86	276.60	284.08	288.39	285.94	287.73	291.07	291.90	294.82	296.78	282.71	285.91	294.35	295.00
Primary metal industries	342.76	371.36	371.96	365.56	370.66	373.35	371.28	378.31	372.19	376.88	379.55	378.51	384.21	383.26	383.51
Fabricated metal products	259.94	278.26	256.86	275.54	279.21	274.04	276.62	282.74	285.36	286.59	298.33	286.64	287.65	292.73	289.12
Machinery except electrical	284.34	306.39	286.13	302.33	308.28	302.82	303.56	313.41	309.92	314.67	327.42	318.31	319.97	323.23	320.58
Electric and electronic equipment	234.55	254.29	237.07	249.64	253.13	248.29	252.49	261.63	261.14	266.26	274.23	268.13	269.74	271.20	269.00
Transportation equipment	333.80	351.44	313.05	356.10	352.29	349.70	341.82	349.61	358.07	354.14	379.14	352.08	357.14	365.31	361.89
Instruments and related products	233.54	251.74	241.20	249.29	248.68	248.25	247.44	252.75	257.86	264.55	269.98	269.37	267.81	268.37	268.66
Miscellaneous manufacturing	181.97	196.06	186.50	192.50	194.61	194.66	196.06	199.25	201.22	203.94	207.23	207.62	206.80	208.74	207.20

Nondurable goods	217.88	235.80	225.38	231.08	234.04	236.38	237.98	241.96	241.92	245.92	249.77	244.92	243.90	245.70	246.13
Food and kindred products	230.26	250.17	241.41	246.31	247.56	251.83	253.08	257.00	254.40	261.70	264.37	261.49	258.96	261.19	261.80
Tobacco manufactures	233.55	254.22	255.68	265.69	265.98	246.56	247.78	255.71	249.48	273.39	278.08	266.66	273.43	287.27	290.60
Textile mill products	173.72	187.80	172.93	181.25	184.32	185.54	192.23	196.66	197.06	200.72	202.11	200.41	199.92	201.23	195.13
Apparel and other textile products	140.26	149.25	142.04	147.42	149.88	149.74	149.88	151.51	153.36	153.79	157.60	156.64	153.33	158.95	157.79
Paper and allied products	279.71	303.31	287.87	295.10	302.74	304.73	307.57	312.56	312.68	318.32	325.38	318.65	318.42	318.52	322.24
Printing and publishing	244.40	259.13	247.30	254.76	257.31	258.06	263.03	266.82	264.75	268.71	273.18	267.84	268.25	271.19	268.28
Chemicals and allied products	293.72	317.26	314.25	312.25	314.75	316.92	319.77	323.11	326.09	331.33	333.80	331.93	332.38	334.40	336.54
Petroleum and coal products	376.27	410.41	414.42	410.34	404.49	414.10	407.66	425.10	418.51	428.74	411.87	342.23	372.24	370.93	410.06
Rubber and miscellaneous plastics products	225.77	241.38	229.31	238.95	240.54	239.19	237.60	244.22	247.86	247.44	252.75	251.88	249.38	250.57	248.06
Leather and leather products	144.32	154.40	147.55	152.15	155.45	154.61	154.45	157.87	157.32	159.71	162.63	163.68	164.86	164.16	164.26
TRANSPORTATION AND PUBLIC UTILITIES	302.80	326.38	307.32	314.42	321.20	329.20	335.30	337.16	337.16	342.50	342.00	338.12	341.02	342.61	344.12
WHOLESALE AND RETAIL TRADE	153.64	164.96	162.50	162.00	165.16	168.17	167.99	167.75	167.38	167.83	170.42	170.35	170.98	172.48	171.30
WHOLESALE TRADE	228.14	247.93	243.18	244.68	247.26	249.21	249.35	252.59	253.24	255.57	261.19	258.72	259.58	261.89	262.27
RETAIL TRADE	130.20	139.07	137.39	136.50	139.50	142.07	141.93	140.61	139.54	140.45	142.91	142.44	142.44	143.22	142.15
FINANCE, INSURANCE, AND REAL ESTATE	178.36	191.66	190.37	188.44	188.96	192.56	191.50	195.29	194.93	197.29	199.84	201.47	204.57	207.69	206.18
SERVICES	163.67	175.27	171.93	171.28	173.38	176.16	175.96	178.22	178.65	180.60	183.68	183.63	185.25	186.23	186.23

Source: *Monthly Labor Review*, U.S. Department of Labor, Bureau of Labor Statistics.

HOURS AND EARNINGS, BY INDUSTRY DIVISION, 1949–1979
GROSS AVERAGES, PRODUCTION OR NONSUPERVISORY WORKERS ON NONAGRICULTURAL PAYROLLS

Year	Total private			Mining			Construction			Manufacturing		
	Average weekly earnings	Average weekly hours	Average hourly earnings	Average weekly earnings	Average weekly hours	Average hourly earnings	Average weekly earnings	Average weekly hours	Average hourly earnings	Average weekly earnings	Average weekly hours	Average hourly earnings
1949	$50.24	39.4	$1.275	$62.33	36.3	$1.717	$67.56	37.7	$1.792	$53.88	39.1	$1.378
1950	53.13	39.8	1.335	67.16	37.9	1.772	69.68	37.4	1.863	58.32	40.5	1.440
1951	57.86	39.9	1.45	74.11	38.4	1.93	76.96	38.1	2.02	63.34	40.6	1.56
1952	60.65	39.9	1.52	77.59	38.6	2.01	82.86	38.9	2.13	66.75	40.7	1.64
1953	63.76	39.6	1.61	83.03	38.8	2.14	86.41	37.9	2.28	70.47	40.5	1.74
1954	64.52	39.1	1.65	82.60	38.6	2.14	88.91	37.2	2.39	70.49	39.6	1.78
1955	67.72	39.6	1.71	89.54	40.7	2.20	90.90	37.1	2.45	75.30	40.7	1.85
1956	70.74	39.3	1.80	95.06	40.8	2.33	96.38	37.5	2.57	78.78	40.4	1.95
1957	73.33	38.8	1.89	98.25	40.1	2.45	100.27	37.0	2.71	81.19	39.8	2.04
1958	75.08	38.5	1.95	96.08	38.9	2.47	103.78	36.8	2.82	82.32	39.2	2.10
1959	78.78	39.0	2.02	103.68	40.5	2.56	108.41	37.0	2.93	88.26	40.3	2.19
1960	80.67	38.6	2.09	105.04	40.4	2.60	112.67	36.7	3.07	89.72	39.7	2.26
1961	82.60	38.6	2.14	106.92	40.5	2.64	118.08	36.9	3.20	92.34	39.8	2.32
1962	85.91	38.7	2.22	110.70	41.0	2.70	122.47	37.0	3.31	96.56	40.4	2.39
1963	88.46	38.8	2.28	114.40	41.6	2.75	127.19	37.3	3.41	99.23	40.5	2.45
1964	91.33	38.7	2.36	117.74	41.9	2.81	132.06	37.2	3.55	102.97	40.7	2.53
1965	95.45	38.8	2.46	123.52	42.3	2.92	138.38	37.4	3.70	107.53	41.2	2.61
1966	98.82	38.6	2.56	130.24	42.7	3.05	146.26	37.6	3.89	112.19	41.4	2.71
1967	101.84	38.0	2.68	135.89	42.6	3.19	154.95	37.7	4.11	114.49	40.6	2.82
1968	107.73	37.8	2.85	142.71	42.6	3.35	164.49	37.3	4.41	122.51	40.7	3.01
1969	114.61	37.7	3.04	154.80	43.0	3.60	181.54	37.9	4.79	129.51	40.6	3.19
1970	119.83	37.1	3.23	164.40	42.7	3.85	195.45	37.3	5.24	133.33	39.8	3.35
1971	127.31	36.9	3.45	172.14	42.4	4.06	211.67	37.2	5.69	142.44	39.9	3.57
1972	136.90	37.0	3.70	189.14	42.6	4.44	221.19	36.5	6.06	154.71	40.5	3.82
1973	145.39	36.9	3.94	201.40	42.4	4.75	235.89	36.8	6.41	166.46	40.7	4.09
1974	154.76	36.5	4.24	219.14	41.9	5.23	249.25	36.6	6.81	176.80	40.0	4.42
1975	163.53	36.1	4.53	249.31	41.9	5.95	266.08	36.4	7.31	190.79	39.5	4.83
1976	175.45	36.1	4.86	273.90	42.4	6.46	283.73	36.8	7.71	209.32	40.1	5.22
1977	189.00	36.0	5.25	301.20	43.4	6.94	295.65	36.5	8.10	228.90	40.3	5.68
1978	203.70	35.8	5.69	332.11	43.3	7.67	318.32	36.8	8.65	249.27	40.4	6.17
1979	219.91	35.7	6.16	364.64	43.0	8.48	341.69	36.9	9.26	268.94	40.2	6.69

Year	Transportation and public utilities			Wholesale and retail trade			Finance, insurance, and real estate			Services		
1949	...	...	...	$42.93	40.5	$1.060	$47.63	37.8	$1.260	...	...	...
1950	...	...	...	44.55	40.5	1.100	50.52	37.7	1.340	...	...	...
1951	...	...	...	47.79	40.5	1.18	54.67	37.7	1.45	...	...	...
1952	...	...	...	49.20	40.0	1.23	57.08	37.8	1.51	...	...	...
1953	...	...	...	51.35	39.5	1.30	59.57	37.7	1.58	...	...	...
1954	...	...	...	53.33	39.5	1.35	62.04	37.6	1.65	...	...	...
1955	...	...	...	55.16	39.4	1.40	63.92	37.6	1.70	...	...	...
1956	...	...	...	57.48	39.1	1.47	65.68	36.9	1.78	...	...	...
1957	...	...	...	59.60	38.7	1.54	67.53	36.7	1.84	...	...	...
1958	...	...	...	61.76	38.6	1.60	70.12	37.1	1.89	...	...	...
1959[1]	...	...	...	64.41	38.8	1.66	72.74	37.3	1.95	...	...	...
1960	...	...	...	66.01	38.6	1.71	75.14	37.2	2.02	...	...	...
1961	...	...	...	67.41	38.3	1.76	77.12	36.9	2.09	...	...	...
1962	...	...	...	69.91	38.2	1.83	80.94	37.3	2.17	...	...	...
1963	...	...	...	72.01	38.1	1.89	84.38	37.5	2.25	...	...	...
1964	$118.78	41.1	$2.89	74.66	37.9	1.97	85.79	37.3	2.30	$70.03	36.1	$1.94
1965	125.14	41.3	3.03	76.91	37.7	2.04	88.91	37.2	2.39	73.60	35.9	2.05
1966	128.13	41.2	3.11	79.39	37.1	2.14	92.13	37.3	2.47	77.04	35.5	2.17
1967	130.82	40.5	3.23	82.35	36.6	2.25	95.72	37.1	2.58	80.38	35.1	2.29
1968	138.85	40.6	3.42	87.00	36.1	2.41	101.75	37.0	2.75	83.97	34.7	2.42
1969	147.74	40.7	3.63	91.39	35.7	2.56	108.70	37.1	2.93	90.57	34.7	2.61
1970	155.93	40.5	3.85	96.02	35.3	2.72	112.67	36.7	3.07	96.66	34.4	2.81
1971	168.82	40.1	4.21	101.09	35.1	2.88	117.85	36.6	3.22	103.06	33.9	3.04
1972	187.86	40.4	4.65	106.45	34.9	3.05	122.98	36.6	3.36	110.85	33.9	3.27
1973	203.31	40.5	5.02	111.76	34.6	3.23	129.20	36.6	3.53	117.29	33.8	3.47
1974	217.48	40.2	5.41	119.02	34.2	3.48	137.61	36.5	3.77	126.00	33.6	3.75
1975	233.44	39.7	5.88	126.45	33.9	3.73	148.19	36.5	4.06	134.67	33.5	4.02
1976	256.71	39.8	6.45	133.79	33.7	3.97	155.43	36.4	4.27	143.52	33.3	4.31
1977	278.90	39.9	6.99	142.52	33.3	4.28	165.26	36.4	4.54	153.45	33.0	4.65
1978	302.80	40.0	7.57	153.64	32.9	4.67	178.36	36.4	4.90	163.67	32.8	4.99
1979	326.38	39.9	8.18	164.96	32.6	5.06	191.66	36.3	5.28	175.27	32.7	5.36

[1] Data include Alaska and Hawaii beginning in 1959.

Source: *Monthly Labor Review*, U.S. Department of Labor, Bureau of Labor Statistics.

PRODUCTIVITY AND RELATED DATA, PRIVATE BUSINESS SECTOR

1967=100; quarterly data seasonally adjusted

Period	Output[1]		Hours of all persons[2]		Output per hour of all persons		Compensation per hour[3]		Unit labor costs		Implicit price deflator[4]	
	Private business sector	Non-farm business sector	Private business sector	Non-farm business sector	Private business sector	Non-farm business sector	Private business sector	Non-farm business sector	Private business sector	Non-farm business sector	Private business sector	Non-farm business sector
1967	100.0	100.0	100.0	100.0	100.0	100.0	100.0	100.0	100.0	100.0	100.0	100.0
1968	105.1	105.3	101.7	102.0	103.3	103.2	107.6	107.4	104.1	104.0	103.9	104.0
1969	108.3	108.5	104.5	105.4	103.6	103.0	115.0	114.2	111.0	110.9	108.8	108.7
1970	107.3	107.4	102.8	104.0	104.4	103.2	123.3	121.9	118.2	118.1	113.9	114.0
1971	110.3	110.2	102.3	103.6	107.8	106.4	131.6	130.1	122.0	122.3	118.9	119.2
1972	117.5	117.8	105.4	107.0	111.5	110.1	139.8	138.4	125.4	125.7	123.2	122.9
1973	124.4	124.9	109.5	111.5	113.6	112.0	151.3	149.2	133.2	133.2	130.3	127.9
1974	121.4	121.8	110.2	112.2	110.2	108.6	165.2	163.0	149.8	150.1	143.1	141.4
1975	118.7	118.8	105.4	107.2	112.6	110.7	181.7	179.3	161.3	161.9	157.5	156.4
1976	126.4	126.9	108.4	110.8	116.6	114.6	197.6	194.2	169.5	169.5	165.5	164.8
1977	133.8	134.3	112.7	115.4	118.7	116.4	213.3	209.6	179.7	180.1	174.8	174.5
1978	140.7	141.5	118.0	121.0	119.3	116.9	231.4	227.5	194.0	194.6	187.2	186.1
1979	144.1	144.9	121.8	125.3	118.3	115.7	253.1	247.9	214.0	214.4	203.8	202.1
1978: III	141.8	142.7	118.4	121.6	119.7	117.4	233.7	229.5	195.2	195.6	188.9	187.8
IV	144.0	145.0	120.2	123.3	119.8	117.6	238.4	234.4	199.0	199.3	192.9	191.4
1979: I	144.4	145.5	121.5	124.8	118.9	116.6	244.8	240.2	205.9	206.0	197.2	195.1
II	143.4	144.2	121.3	124.9	118.3	115.4	250.4	244.9	211.7	212.1	202.0	200.3
III	143.8	144.6	122.0	125.7	117.8	115.0	255.7	249.9	217.0	217.3	206.1	204.7
IV	144.8	145.5	123.0	126.2	117.7	115.2	260.3	255.6	221.1	221.8	209.7	208.4
1980: I	144.8	145.6	123.1	126.7	117.7	114.9	267.6	262.2	227.5	228.2	214.5	213.7
II p	140.1	140.7	120.0	123.7	116.7	113.7	275.3	269.0	235.8	236.6	220.4	220.3

Percent change; quarterly data at seasonally adjusted annual rates

Period												
1967	2.0	1.9	-0.0	0.3	2.0	1.6	5.3	5.4	3.3	3.8	2.9	3.3
1968	5.1	5.3	1.7	2.0	3.3	3.2	7.6	7.4	4.1	4.0	3.9	4.0
1969	3.0	3.0	2.7	3.3	.2	-.2	6.9	6.4	6.6	6.7	4.7	4.5
1970	-.9	-1.1	-1.6	-1.3	.7	.2	7.2	6.8	6.4	6.5	4.7	4.9
1971	2.8	2.6	-.5	.4	3.3	3.6	6.7	6.7	3.3	3.5	4.4	4.5
1972	6.6	6.9	3.1	3.2	3.4	3.6	6.2	6.4	2.8	2.7	3.6	3.1
1973	6.9	6.0	3.9	4.6	1.9	1.7	8.2	7.8	6.2	6.0	5.8	4.1
1974	-2.4	-2.5	.6	.6	-3.0	-3.1	9.2	9.2	12.5	12.7	9.8	10.5
1975	2.3	2.5	-4.3	-4.4	2.1	2.0	10.0	10.0	7.7	7.9	10.1	10.6
1976	6.5	6.6	2.9	3.3	3.5	3.5	8.8	8.3	5.0	4.7	5.0	5.4
1977	5.8	5.8	3.9	4.2	1.8	1.5	8.0	7.9	6.0	6.3	5.6	5.9
1978	5.2	5.4	4.7	4.9	.5	.5	8.5	8.0	8.0	8.0	7.1	6.6
1979	2.4	2.4	3.3	3.5	-.8	-1.1	9.4	9.0	10.3	10.2	8.9	8.6
1978: III	4.2	4.5	2.0	2.1	2.1	2.4	8.8	8.5	6.6	5.9	6.9	7.0
IV	6.4	6.8	6.1	6.0	.3	.7	8.4	8.7	8.1	7.9	8.7	7.8
1979: I	-1.2	-1.2	4.5	4.7	-3.1	-3.3	11.0	10.2	14.6	14.0	9.3	8.1
II	-2.9	-3.6	-.9	.4	-2.0	-3.9	9.5	8.1	11.8	12.5	10.1	11.0
III	-1.1	-1.2	2.5	2.7	-1.4	-1.5	8.7	8.5	10.3	10.1	8.3	9.0
IV	2.8	2.5	3.1	1.7	-.3	.8	7.5	9.5	7.8	8.6	7.2	7.4
1980: I	-.2	-.2	-.5	1.3	-.3	-1.1	11.7	10.7	12.1	12.0	9.4	10.6
II p	-12.5	-12.8	-9.7	-9.1	-3.1	-4.1	12.0	10.8	15.5	15.6	11.5	13.0

1 Output refers to gross domestic product originating in the sector in 1972 dollars.
2 Hours of all persons in private industry engaged in the sector, including hours of proprietors and unpaid family workers. Estimates based primarily on establishment data.
3 Wages and salaries of employees plus employers' contributions for social insurance and private benefit plans. Also includes an estimate of wages, salaries, and supplemental payments for the self-employed.
4 Current dollar gross domestic product divided by constant dollar gross domestic product.

NOTE.—Percent changes are from preceding period and are based on original data; they therefore may differ slightly from percent changes based on indexes shown here. Data revised beginning 1977.

Source: Department of Labor, Bureau of Labor Statistics.
Source: Economic Indicators, Council of Economic Advisers.

PERSONAL INCOME PER CAPITA AND PER SQUARE MILE 1960–1978

DATA EXCLUDE FEDERAL EMPLOYEES OVERSEAS AND, BEGINNING 1978, U.S. RESIDENTS EMPLOYED BY PRIVATE U.S. FIRMS ON TEMPORARY FOREIGN ASSIGNMENT

| DIVISION AND STATE | PER CAPITA INCOME IN CURRENT DOLLARS | | | | | | | | | | | | Income per sq. mi. of land area, 1978 ($1,000) |
| | Total (dol.) | | | | Income rank | | | | Percent of U.S. | | | | |
	1960	1970	1975	1978	1960	1970	1975	1978	1960	1970	1975	1978	
U.S.____	2,201	3,893	5,861	7,810	(X)	(X)	(X)	(X)	100	100	100	100	481
N.E._____	2,419	4,245	6,030	7,967	(X)	(X)	(X)	(X)	110	109	103	102	1,551
Maine____	1,825	3,250	4,766	6,333	36	36	46	46	83	83	81	81	224
N.H.____	2,172	3,720	5,417	7,277	21	20	31	32	99	96	92	93	702
Vt._____	1,864	3,447	4,924	6,541	34	32	40	42	85	89	84	84	344
Mass____	2,436	4,276	6,077	8,063	9	10	13	14	111	110	104	103	5,949
R.I._____	2,182	3,878	5,709	7,526	19	16	25	26	99	100	97	96	6,706
Conn____	2,839	4,871	6,799	8,914	1	1	2	4	129	125	116	114	5,681
M.A._____	2,549	4,390	6,358	8,206	(X)	(X)	(X)	(X)	116	113	108	105	3,012
N.Y.____	2,703	4,605	6,519	8,267	6	4	9	13	123	118	111	106	3,067
N.J.____	2,699	4,684	6,794	8,818	7	2	3	6	123	120	116	113	8,591
Pa._____	2,239	3,879	5,841	7,733	16	15	20	21	102	100	100	99	2,021
E.N.C._____	2,367	4,050	6,047	8,167	(X)	(X)	(X)	(X)	108	104	103	105	1,380
Ohio____	2,322	3,949	5,778	7,812	12	14	22	20	105	101	99	100	2,049
Ind____	2,149	3,709	5,609	7,696	22	22	28	23	98	95	96	98	1,146
Ill____	2,617	4,446	6,735	8,745	8	8	4	7	119	114	115	112	1,764
Mich____	2,327	4,041	5,991	8,442	11	12	14	10	106	104	102	108	1,365
Wis_____	2,178	3,712	5,616	7,597	20	21	27	25	99	95	96	97	653
W.N.C._____	2,022	3,657	5,719	7,632	(X)	(X)	(X)	(X)	92	94	98	98	256
Minn____	2,065	3,819	5,779	7,847	25	18	21	18	94	98	99	100	397
Iowa____	1,960	3,643	5,894	7,873	30	29	17	¹7	89	94	101	101	408
Mo____	2,091	3,654	5,476	7,342	23	28	30	31	95	94	93	94	517
N. Dak__	1,681	3,077	5,888	7,478	40	42	18	28	76	79	100	96	70
S. Dak__	1,758	3,108	5,009	6,841	39	40	37	35	80	80	85	88	62
Nebr____	2,009	3,657	5,882	7,391	26	27	19	29	91	94	100	95	151
Kans____	2,085	3,725	5,958	8,001	24	19	16	¹15	95	96	102	102	230
S.A._____	1,837	3,562	5,480	7,260	(X)	(X)	(X)	(X)	83	91	93	93	940
Del____	2,735	4,468	6,547	8,604	4	7	8	8	124	115	112	110	2,529
Md____	2,319	4,267	6,403	8,306	13	11	10	12	105	110	109	106	3,479
D.C.____	2,829	4,644	7,262	10,022	(X)	(X)	(X)	(X)	129	119	124	128	102,000
Va.____	1,882	3,677	5,772	7,624	33	¹24	23	24	86	94	98	98	987
W. Va.__	1,592	3,038	4,962	6,456	43	45	38	45	72	78	85	83	499
N.C.____	1,577	3,200	4,940	6,607	¹44	38	39	41	72	82	84	85	755
S.C.____	1,396	2,951	4,665	6,242	48	47	47	48	63	76	80	80	603
Ga.____	1,645	3,300	5,029	6,700	42	35	36	37	75	85	86	86	587
Fla.____	1,962	3,698	5,631	7,505	29	23	26	27	89	95	96	96	1,192
E.S.C._____	1,490	2,936	4,648	6,326	(X)	(X)	(X)	(X)	68	75	79	81	495
Ky.____	1,576	3,076	4,887	6,615	46	43	42	40	72	79	83	85	584
Tenn____	1,577	3,079	4,804	6,489	¹44	41	44	44	72	79	82	83	684
Ala____	1,510	2,892	4,635	6,247	47	48	48	47	69	74	79	80	461
Miss____	1,196	2,547	4,047	5,736	50	50	50	50	54	65	69	73	291
W.S.C._____	1,785	3,323	5,293	7,259	(X)	(X)	(X)	(X)	81	85	90	93	374
Ark____	1,358	2,791	4,510	6,183	49	49	49	49	62	72	77	79	260
La.____	1,650	3,023	4,803	6,640	41	46	45	38	75	78	82	85	586
Okla__	1,850	3,341	5,280	6,951	35	34	34	34	84	86	90	89	291
Tex____	1,894	3,507	5,584	7,697	32	31	29	22	86	90	95	99	382
Mt_____	2,054	3,557	5,508	7,443	(X)	(X)	(X)	(X)	93	91	94	95	89
Mont____	1,983	3,395	5,388	7,051	28	33	33	33	90	87	92	90	38
Idaho____	1,812	3,243	5,179	6,813	38	37	35	36	82	83	88	87	72
Wyo____	2,210	3,672	6,123	9,096	17	26	12	2	100	94	104	116	40
Colo____	2,247	3,838	5,987	8,001	15	17	15	¹15	102	99	102	102	206
N. Mex__	1,815	3,045	4,843	6,505	37	44	43	43	82	78	83	83	65
Ariz____	1,994	3,614	5,391	7,374	27	30	32	30	91	93	92	94	153
Utah____	1,954	3,169	4,900	6,622	31	39	41	39	89	81	84	85	105
Nev____	2,793	4,583	6,625	9,032	2	6	6	3	127	118	113	116	54
Pac_____	2,608	4,317	6,518	8,730	(X)	(X)	(X)	(X)	118	111	111	112	291
Wash____	2,352	3,997	6,298	8,450	10	13	11	9	107	108	107	108	479
Oreg____	2,195	3,677	5,769	7,839	18	¹24	24	19	100	94	98	100	199
Calif____	2,710	4,423	6,575	8,850	5	9	7	5	123	114	112	113	1,262
Alaska__	2,740	4,638	9,636	10,851	3	3	1	1	124	119	164	139	8
Hawaii__	2,300	4,599	6,708	8,380	14	5	5	11	104	118	114	107	1,154

X Not applicable.   ¹ In order to have the lowest rank equal to the number of States, the following numbers are omitted: 16, 24, and 45; and the following States share the same rank: Colo. and Kans., 15; Oreg. and Va., 24; and N.C. and Tenn., 44.

Source: U.S. Bureau of Economic Analysis, *Survey of Current Business*, October 1978 and April 1979; and unpublished data.

Source: *Statistical Abstract of the United States*, U.S. Department of Commerce, Bureau of the Census.

LABOR–MANAGEMENT DATA

Definitions are applicable to the exhibits on pages 356 and 359.

Data on wage changes apply to private nonfarm industry agreements covering 1,000 workers or more. Data on wage and benefit changes *combined* apply only to those agreements covering 5,000 workers or more. First-year wage settlements refer to pay changes going into effect within the first 12 months after the effective date of the agreement. Changes over the life of the agreement refer to total agreed upon settlements (exclusive of potential cost-of-living escalator adjustments) expressed at an average annual rate. Wage-rate changes are expressed as a percent of straight-time hourly earnings, while wage and benefit changes are expressed as a percent of total compensation.

Effective wage-rate adjustments going into effect in major bargaining units measure changes actually placed into effect during the reference period, whether the result of a newly negotiated increase, a deferred increase negotiated in an earlier year, or a cost-of-living escalator adjustment. Average adjustments are affected by workers receiving no adjustment, as well as by those receiving increases or decreases.

Work stoppages include all known strikes or lockouts involving six workers or more and lasting a full shift or longer. Data cover all workers idle one shift or more in establishments directly involved in a stoppage. They do not measure the indirect or secondary effect on other establishments whose employees are idle owing to material or service shortages.

WORK STOPPAGES, 1947 TO DATE

| Month and year | Number of stoppages | | Workers involved | | Days idle | |
	Beginning in month or year	In effect during month	Beginning in month or year (thousands)	In effect during month (thousands)	Number (thousands)	Percent of estimated working time
1947	3,693	....	2,170	....	34,600	.30
1948	3,419	....	1,960	....	34,100	.28
1949	3,606	....	3,030	....	50,500	.44
1950	4,843	....	2,410	....	38,800	.33
1951	4,737	....	2,220	....	22,900	.18
1952	5,117	....	3,540	....	59,100	.48
1953	5,091	....	2,400	....	28,300	.22
1954	3,468	....	1,530	....	22,600	.18
1955	4,320	....	2,650	....	28,200	.22
1956	3,825	....	1,900	....	33,100	.24
1957	3,673	....	1,390	....	16,500	.12
1958	3,694	....	2,060	....	23,900	.18
1959	3,708	....	1,880	....	69,000	.50
1960	3,333	....	1,320	....	19,100	.14
1961	3,367	....	1,450	....	16,300	.11
1962	3,614	....	1,230	....	18,600	.13
1963	3,362	....	941	....	16,100	.11
1964	3,655	....	1,640	....	22,900	.15
1965	3,963	....	1,550	....	23,300	.15

Year / Month						
1966	4,405	....	1,960	....	25,400	.15
1967	4,595	....	2,870	....	42,100	.25
1968	5,045	....	2,649	....	49,018	.28
1969	5,700	....	2,481	....	42,869	.24
1970	5,716	....	3,305	....	66,414	.37
1971	5,138	....	3,280	....	47,589	.26
1972	5,010	....	1,714	....	27,066	.15
1973	5,353	....	2,251	....	27,948	.14
1974	6,074	....	2,778	....	47,991	.24
1975	5,031	....	1,746	....	31,237	.16
1976	5,648	....	2,420	....	37,859	.19
1977	5,506	....	2,040	....	35,822	.17
1978	4,230	....	1,623	....	36,922	.17
1979: April	512	....	426	....	5,126	.27
May	556	....	132	....	3,682	.19
June	536	....	137	....	2,989	.16
July	471	....	168	....	3,001	.16
August	463	....	119	....	3,152	.15
September	464	....	135	....	2,319	.13
October	443	....	230	....	2,968	.15
November	257	....	91	....	2,720	.15
December	134	....	42	....	1,976	.11
1980: January p	352	441	207	292	3,142	.16
February p	354	590	114	332	3,025	.17
March p	396	631	123	310	2,705	.14
April	425	663	116	231	2,786	.14

Source: *Monthly Labor Review*, U.S. Department of Labor, Bureau of Labor Statistics.

WAGE AND BENEFIT SETTLEMENTS IN MAJOR COLLECTIVE BARGAINING UNITS, 1975 TO DATE

IN PERCENT

Sector and measure	Annual average					Quarterly average						
						1978		1979				1980 P
	1975	1976	1977	1978	1979	III	IV	I	II	III	IV	I
Wage and benefit settlements, all industries:												
First-year settlements	11.4	8.5	9.6	8.3	9.0	7.2	6.1	2.8	10.5	9.0	8.5	8.6
Annual rate over life of contract	8.1	6.6	6.2	6.3	6.6	5.9	5.2	5.3	7.8	6.1	6.0	6.4
Wage rate settlements, all industries:												
First-year settlements	10.2	8.4	7.8	7.6	7.4	7.5	7.4	5.7	8.9	6.8	6.3	7.8
Annual rate over life of contract	7.8	6.4	5.8	6.4	6.0	6.4	5.9	6.6	7.2	5.1	5.3	6.3
Manufacturing:												
First-year settlements	9.8	8.9	8.4	8.3	6.9	8.4	9.5	8.7	9.7	6.3	5.6	7.0
Annual rate over life of contract	8.0	6.0	5.5	6.6	5.4	7.2	7.4	7.7	8.1	4.7	4.2	5.6
Nonmanufacturing (excluding construction):												
First-year settlements	11.9	8.6	8.0	8.0	7.6	7.4	6.4	3.2	8.5	9.4	7.8	9.1
Annual rate over life of contract	8.0	7.2	5.9	6.5	6.2	5.9	5.1	5.6	5.8	6.5	7.4	7.1
Construction:												
First-year settlements	8.0	6.1	6.3	6.5	8.8	7.0	8.4	9.7	8.7	9.7	7.5	9.6
Annual rate over life of contract	7.5	6.2	6.3	6.2	8.3	7.2	7.1	8.2	8.3	8.5	7.6	9.3

Source: *Monthly Labor Review*, U.S. Department of Labor, Bureau of Labor Statistics.

EFFECTIVE WAGE ADJUSTMENTS GOING INTO EFFECT IN MAJOR COLLECTIVE BARGAINING UNITS, 1975 TO DATE

IN PERCENT

Sector and measure	Average annual changes					Average quarterly changes									
						1978				1979				1980 P	
	1975	1976	1977	1978	1979	I	II	III	IV	I	II	III	IV	I	
Total effective wage rate adjustment, all industries	8.7	8.1	8.0	8.2	9.1	1.3	2.6	2.7	1.4	1.4	2.6	3.3	1.6	1.3	
Change resulting from—															
Current settlement	2.8	3.2	3.0	2.0	3.0	.5	.6	.5	.4	.2	1.1	1.0	.5	.3	
Prior settlement	3.7	3.2	3.2	3.7	3.0	.6	1.4	1.2	.5	.6	1.0	1.0	.4	.5	
Escalator provision	2.2	1.6	1.7	2.4	3.1	.3	.6	1.0	.5	.6	.5	1.2	.7	.6	
Manufacturing	8.5	8.5	8.4	8.6	9.6	1.4	2.2	2.9	1.9	1.5	2.3	3.2	2.4	1.6	
Nonmanufacturing	8.9	7.7	7.6	7.9	8.8	1.3	2.9	2.5	1.1	1.4	2.8	3.4	1.0	1.1	

NOTE: Because of rounding and compounding, the sums of individual items may not equal totals.
Source: *Monthly Labor Review*, U.S. Department of Labor, Bureau of Labor Statistics.

UNION ADDRESSES
AND MEMBERSHIP

Actors and Artists of America; Associated
(AFL-CIO)
1500 Broadway
New York, NY 10036
Membership: 82,800

Actors' Equity Association
1500 Broadway
New York, NY 10036
Membership: 18,500

Air Line Pilots Association (AFL-CIO)
Pilot Division
1625 Massachusetts Avenue NW
Washington, DC 20036
Membership: 27,536

Aluminum Workers International Union
(AFL-CIO)
Paul Brown Building
818 Olive Street
St. Louis, MO 63101
Membership: 30,000

American Federation of Television and Radio
Artists
1350 Avenue of the Americas
New York, NY 10019
Membership: 29,672

Asbestos Workers; International Association of
Heat and Frost Insulators and (AFL-CIO)
505 Machinists Building
1300 Connecticut Avenue NW
Washington, DC 20036
Membership: 18,470

Association of Flight Attendants
1625 Massachusetts Avenue NW
Washington, DC 20036
Membership: 24,000

Automobile, Aerospace and Agricultural Im-
plement Workers of America; International
Union, United (Ind.)
8000 E. Jefferson Avenue
Detroit, MI 48214
Membership: 1,358,354

Bakery, Confectionery & Tobacco Workers' International Union of America (AFL-CIO)
1828 L Street NW
Washington, DC 20036
Membership: 164,040

Source: *Directory of National Unions and Employee Associations*, 1979, Supplement to Bulletin 2044. Bureau of Labor Statistics, U.S. Department of Labor.

Barbers, Beauticians, and Allied Industries,
International Association (AFL-CIO)
7050 W. Washington Street
Indianapolis, IN 46214
Membership: 38,000

Boilermakers, Iron Ship Builders, Blacksmiths,
Forgers and Helpers; International Brother-
hood of (AFL-CIO)
New Brotherhood Building
8th Street at State Avenue
Kansas City, KS 66101
Membership: 144,500

Brick and Clay Workers of America; The
United (AFL-CIO)
3377 W. Broad Street
Columbus, OH 43204
Membership: 16,000

Bricklayers, and Allied Craftsmen; International Union of (AFL-CIO)
815 15th Street NW
Washington, DC 20005
Membership: 134,744

Broadcast Employees and Technicians; National Association of (AFL-CIO)
7101 Wisconsin Avenue
Bethesda, MD 20012
Membership: 6,000

Carpenters and Joiners of America; United
Brotherhood of (AFL-CIO)
101 Constitution Avenue NW
Washington, DC 20001
Membership: 831,780

Cement, Lime and Gypsum Workers International Union: United (AFL-CIO)
7830 W. Lawrence Avenue
Chicago, IL 60656
Membership: 36,049

Chemical Workers Union; International
(AFL-CIO)
1655 W. Market Street
Akron, OH 44313
Membership: 71,816

Classified School Employees; American Association of (Ind.)
1645 Schrock Road
Columbus, OH 43229
Membership: 89,000

Clothing and Textile Workers Union; Amalgamated (AFL-CIO)
15 Union Square
New York, NY 10003
Membership: 532,000

Communications Workers of America (AFL-
CIO)
1925 K Street NW
Washington, DC 20006
Membership: 483,238

Distillery, Rectifying, Wine and Allied Workers' International Union of America (AFL-CIO)
66 Grand Avenue
Englewood, NJ 07631
Membership: 29,500

Distributive Workers of America (Ind.)
13 Astor Place
New York, NY 10003
Membership: 40,000

Education Association; National (Ind.)
1201 16th Street NW
Washington, DC 20036
Membership: 1,886,532

Electrical, Radio and Machine Workers; International Union of (AFL-CIO)
1126 16th Street NW
Washington, DC 20036
Membership: 237,693

Electrical, Radio, and Machine Workers of America; United (Ind.)
11 E. 51st Street
New York, NY 10022
Membership: 165,000

Electrical Workers; International Brotherhood of (AFL-CIO)
1125 15th Street NW
Washington, DC 20005
Membership: 923,560

Elevator Constructors; International Union of (AFL-CIO)
Clarke Building
5565 Sterrett Place
Columbia, MD 21044
Membership: 19,000

Farm Workers of America; United (AFL-CIO)
La Paz
Keene, CA 93531
Membership: 18,000

Fire Fighters; International Association of (AFL-CIO)
1750 New York Avenue NW
Washington, DC 20006
Membership: 174,350

Firemen and Oilers; International Brotherhood of (AFL-CIO)
VFM Building
200 Maryland Avenue NE
Washington, DC 20002
Membership: 45,000

Food and Commercial Workers International Union, United (AFL-CIO)
1775 K Street NW
Washington, DC 20006
Membership: 1,238,103

Furniture Workers of America; United (AFL-CIO)
1910 Airlane Drive
Nashville, TN 37210
Membership: 27,042

Garment Workers of America; United (AFL-CIO)
200 Park Avenue South
New York, NY 10003
Membership: 25,000

Glass Bottle Blowers Association of the United States and Canada (AFL-CIO)
608 E. Baltimore Pike
Media, PA 19603
Membership: 83,200

Glass and Ceramic Workers of North America; United (AFL-CIO)
556 E. Town Street
Columbus, OH 43215
Membership: 34,527

Glass Workers' Union of North America; American Flint (AFL-CIO)
1440 S. Byrne Road
Toledo, OH 43614
Membership: 32,718

Government Employees; American Federation of (AFL-CIO)
1325 Massachusetts Avenue NW
Washington, DC 20005
Membership: 260,000

Government Employees; National Association of (Ind.)
285 Dorchester Avenue
Boston, MA 02127
Membership: 153,527

Grain Millers; American Federation of (AFL-CIO)
4949 Olson Memorial Highway
Minneapolis, MN 55422
Membership: 38,000

Graphic Arts International Union (AFL-CIO)
1900 L Street NW
Washington, DC 20036
Membership: 93,224

Hatters, Cap and Millinery Workers International Union: United (AFL-CIO)
105 Madison Avenue
New York, NY 10016
Membership: 10,000

Hotel and Restaurant Employees and Bartenders International Union (AFL-CIO)
120 E. 4th Street
Cincinnati, OH 45202
Membership: 432,171

Industrial Workers of America; International Union Allied (AFL-CIO)
3520 W. Oklahoma Avenue
Milwaukee, WI 53215
Membership: 82,005

Iron Workers; International Association of Bridge, Structural and Ornamental (AFL-CIO)
1750 New York Avenue NW
Washington, DC 20006
Membership: 179,670

Jewelry Workers' Union; International (AFL-CIO)
8 W. 40th Street
New York, NY 10018
Membership: 10,000

Laborers' International Union of North America (AFL-CIO)
905 16th Street NW
Washington, DC 20006
Membership: 627,406

Ladies' Garment Workers' Union; International (AFL-CIO)
1710 Broadway
New York, NY 10019
Membership: 365,346

Lathers; International Union of Wood, Wire and Metal (AFL-CIO) (Merged into United Brotherhood of Carpenters and Joiners of America)

Laundry and Dry Cleaning International Union (AFL-CIO)
Carlton House
550 Grant Street
Pittsburgh, PA 15219
Membership: 18,362

Leather Goods, Plastic and Novelty Workers' Union; International (AFL-CIO)
265 W. 14th Street
New York, NY 10011
Membership: 30,000

Letter Carriers National Association of (AFL-CIO)
100 Indiana Avenue NW
Washington, DC 20001
Membership: 227,221

Locomotive Engineers; Brotherhood of (Ind.)
1112 Brotherhood of Locomotive Engineers Building
Cleveland, OH 44114
Membership: 38,000

Longshoremen's and Warehousemen's Union; International (Ind.)
1188 Franklin Street
San Francisco, CA 90109
Membership: 58,000

Longshoremen's Association; International (AFL-CIO)
17 Battery Place
New York, NY 10004
Membership: 80,000

Machinists and Aerospace Workers; International Association of (AFL-CIO)
1300 Connecticut Avenue NW
Washington, DC 20036
Membership: 917,266

Maintenance of Way Employees; Brotherhood of (AFL-CIO)
12050 Woodward Avenue
Detroit, MI 48203
Membership: 119,184

Marine and Shipbuilding Workers of America; Industrial Union of (AFL-CIO)
1126 16th Street NW
Washington, DC 20036
Membership: 22,600

Maritime Union of America; National (AFL-CIO)
346 W. 17th Street
New York, NY 10011
Membership: 50,000

Meat Cutters and Butcher Workmen of North America; Amalgamated (AFL-CIO) (Merged with Retail Clerks International to form United Food and Commercial Workers International Union)

Metal Polishers, Buffers, Platers and Allied Workers International Union (AFL-CIO)
5578 Montgomery Road
Cincinnati, OH 45212
Membership: 10,000

Mine Workers of America; United (Ind.)
900 15th Street NW
Washington, DC 20005
Membership: 277,000

Molders' and Allied Workers' Union; International (AFL-CIO)
1225 E. McMillan Street
Cincinnati, OH 45206
Membership: 70,800

Musicians; American Federation of (AFL-CIO)
1500 Broadway
New York, NY 10036
Membership: 330,000

Newspaper Guild, The (AFL-CIO)
1125 15th Street NW
Washington, DC 20005
Membership: 32,235

Nurses' Association; American (Ind.)
2420 Pershing Road
Kansas City, MO 64108
Membership: 199,691

Office and Professional Employees International Union (AFL-CIO)
265 W. 14th Street
New York, NY 10011
Membership: 98,500

Oil, Chemical and Atomic Workers International Union (AFL-CIO)
P.O. Box 2812
1636 Champa Street
Denver, CO 80201
Membership: 177,370

Operating Engineers; International Union of (AFL-CIO)
1125 17th Street NW
Washington, DC 20036
Membership: 420,000

Painters and Allied Trades of the United States and Canada; International Brotherhood of (AFL-CIO)
United Unions Building
1750 New York Avenue NW
Washington, DC 20006
Membership: 195,000

Paperworkers International Union; United (AFL-CIO)
163-03 Horace Harding Expressway
Flushing, NY 14272
Membership: 300,000

Pattern Makers' League of North America (AFL-CIO)
1925 N. Linn
Arlington, VA 22209
Membership: 10,500

Plant Guard Workers of America; International Union, United (Ind.)
25510 Kelly Road
Roseville, MI 48066
Membership: 41,000

Plasterers' and Cement Masons' International Association of the United States and Canada; Operative (AFL-CIO)
1125 17th Street NW
Washington, DC 20036
Membership: 58,000

Plumbing and Pipe Fitting Industry of the United States and Canada; United Association of Journeymen and Apprentices of the (AFL-CIO)
901 Massachusetts Avenue NW
Washington, DC 20001
Membership: 228,000

Police, Fraternal Order of (Ind.)
G–3136 W. Pasadena Avenue
Flint, MI 48504
Membership: 135,000

Postal Supervisors; National Association of (Ind.)
P.O. Box 23456, L'Enfant Plaza Station
Washington, DC 20024
Membership: 34,356

Postal Workers Union; American (AFL-CIO)
817 14th Street NW
Washington, DC 20005
Membership: 251,551

Pottery and Allied Workers, International Brotherhood of (AFL-CIO)
(affiliated with Seafarer's International Union)

Printing and Graphic Communications Union, International (AFL-CIO)
1730 Rhode Island Avenue NW
Washington, DC 20036
Membership: 109,000

Professional Air Traffic Controllers Organization
2100 M Street NW
Washington, DC 20037
Membership: 21,000

Railroad Signalmen; Brotherhood of (AFL-CIO)
601 W. Golf Road
Mt. Prospect, IL 60056
Membership: 12,416

Railway, Airline and Steamship Clerks, Freight Handlers, Express and Station Employees; Brotherhood of (AFL-CIO)
3 Research Place
Rockville, MD 20850
Membership: 212,293

Railway Carmen of the United States and Canada; Brotherhood (AFL-CIO)
Carmen's Building
4929 Main Street
Kansas City, MO 64112
Membership: 95,157

Retail Clerks International Union (AFL-CIO)
(merged with Amalgamated Meat Cutters and Butcher Workmen of North America to form United food and Commercial Workers International Union)

Retail, Wholesale and Department Store Union (AFL-CIO)
101 W. 31st Street
New York, NY 10001
Membership: 200,000

Retail Workers Union, United (Ind.)
9865 W. Roosevelt Road
Westchester, IL 60153
Membership: 21,500

Roofers, Waterproofers and Allied Workers Association; United Union of (AFL-CIO)
1125 17th Street NW
Washington, DC 20036
Membership: 30,000

Rubber, Cork, Linoleum and Plastic Workers of America; United (AFL-CIO)
URWA Building
South High Street
Akron, OH 44308
Membership: 211,161

Screen Actors Guild
7750 Sunset Boulevard
Hoollywood, CA 90046
Membership: 46,000

Seafarers' International Union of North America (AFL-CIO)
675 4th Avenue
Brooklyn, NY 11232
Membership: 83,669

Service Employees' International Union (AFL-CIO)
2020 K Street NW
Washington, DC 20006
Membership: 575,000

Sheet Metal Workers' International Association (AFL-CIO)
United Unions Building
1750 New York Avenue NW
Washington, DC 20006
Membership: 153,000

Shoe Workers of America; United (AFL-CIO) (merged into Amalgamated Clothing and Textile Workers)

Shoe Workers' Union, Boot and (AFL-CIO) (merged with the Retail Clerks International Association)

State, County and Municipal Employees, American Federation of (AFL-CIO)
1625 L Street NW
Washington, DC 20036
Membership 957,000

Steelworkers of America, United (AFL-CIO)
Five Gateway Center
Pittsburgh, PA 15222
Membership: 1,300,000

Stove, Furnace and Allied Appliance Workers' International Union of North America (AFL-CIO)
2929 S. Jefferson Avenue
St. Louis, MO 63118
Membership: 8,600

Teachers, American Federation of (AFL-CIO)
11 DuPont Circle NW
Washington, DC 20036
Membership: 446,045

Teamsters, Chauffeurs, Warehousemen and Helpers of America, International Brotherhood of (Ind.)
25 Louisiana Avenue NW
Washington, DC 20001
Membership: 1,888,895

Technical Engineers, International Federation of Professional and (AFL-CIO)
1126 16th Street NW
Washington, DC 20036
Membership: 19,500

Telecommunications International Union (Ind.)
P.O. Box 5462
Hamden, CT 16518
Membership: 50,000

Telegraph Workers, United (AFL-CIO)
701 Gude Drive
Rockville, MD 20850
Membership: 11,850

Textile Workers of America, United (AFL-CIO)
420 Common Street
Lawrence, MA 01842
Membership: 39,981

Textile Workers Union of America (AFL-CIO) (merged into Clothing and Textile Workers Union)

Theatrical Stage Employees and Moving Picture Machine Operators of the United States and Canada, International Alliance of (AFL-CIO)
1515 Broadway
Suite 601
New York, NY 10036
Membership: 63,003

Tile, Marble, Terrazzo Finishers and Shopmen International Union
801 N. Pitt Street
Alexandria, VA 22314
Membership: 7,000

Tobacco Workers International Union (AFL-CIO) (merged with Bakery and Confectionery Workers' International Union of America to form the Bakery, Confectionery & Tobacco Workers International Union)

Transit Union; Amalgamated (AFL-CIO)
5025 Wisconsin Avenue NW
Washington, DC 20016
Membership: 150,000

Transport Workers Union of America (AFL-CIO)
1980 Broadway
New York, NY 10023
Membership: 150,000

Transportation Union, United (AFL-CIO)
14600 Detroit Avenue
Cleveland, OH 44107
Membership: 265,000

Typographical Union, International (AFL-CIO)
P.O. Box 157
Colorado Springs, CO 80901
Membership: 103,949

Upholsters' International Union of North America (AFL-CIO)
25 N. Fourth Street
Philadelphia, PA 19106
  Membership: 53,000

Utility Workers Union of America (AFL-CIO)
815 16th Street NW
Washington, DC 20006
  Membership: 60,000

Western Pulp and Paper Workers, Association of (Ind)
1430 Southwest Clay
Portland, OR 97201
  Membership: 20,202

Woodworkers of America, International (AFL-CIO)
1622 N. Lombard Street
Portland, OR 97217
  Membership: 108,717

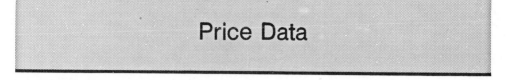

Price Data

Definitions are applicable to the exhibits on pages 369–79 and 382.

Price data are gathered by the Bureau of Labor Statistics from retail and primary markets in the United States. Price indexes are given in relation to a base period (1967 = 100, unless otherwise noted).

DEFINITIONS

The **Consumer Price Index** is a monthly statistical measure of the average change in prices in a fixed market basket of goods and services. Effective with the January 1978 index, the Bureau of Labor Statistics began publishing CPI's for two groups of the population. One index, a new CPI for All Urban Consumers, covers 80 percent of the total noninstitutional population; and the other index, a revised CPI for Urban Wage Earners and Clerical Workers, covers about half the new index population. The All Urban Consumers index includes, in addition to wage earners and clerical workers, professional, managerial, and technical workers, the self-employed, short-term workers, the unemployed, retirees, and others not in the labor force.

The CPI is based on prices of food, clothing, shelter, fuel, drugs, transportation fares, doctor's and dentist's fees, and other goods and services that people buy for day-to-day living. The quantity and quality of these items are kept essentially unchanged between major revisions so that only price changes will be measured. Prices are collected from over 18,000 tenants, 24,000 retail establishments, and 18,000 housing units for property taxes in 85 urban areas across the country. All taxes directly associated with the purchase and use of items are included in the index. Because the CPI's are based on the expenditures of two population groups in 1972–73, they may not accurately reflect the experience of individual families and single persons with different buying habits.

Though the CPI is often called the "Cost-of-Living Index," it measures only price change, which is just one of several important factors affecting living costs. Area indexes do not measure differences in the level of prices among cities. They only measure the average change in prices for each area since the base period.

Producer Price Indexes measure average changes in prices received in primary markets of the United States by producers of commodities in all stages of processing. The sample used for calculating these indexes contains about 2,800 commodities and about 10,000 quotations per month selected to represent the movement of prices of all commodities produced in the manufacturing, agriculture, forestry, fishing, mining, gas and electricity, and public utilities sectors. The universe includes all commodities produced or imported for sale in commercial transactions in primary markets in the United States.

Producer Price Indexes can be organized by stage of processing or by commodity. The stage of processing structure organizes products by degree of fabrication (that is, finished goods, intermediate or semifinished goods, and crude materials). The commodity structure organizes products by similarity of end-use or material composition.

To the extent possible, prices used in calculating Producer Price Indexes apply to the first significant commercial transaction in the United States, from the production or central marketing point. Price data are generally collected monthly, primarily by mail questionnaire. Most prices are obtained directly from producing companies on a voluntary and confidential basis. Prices generally are reported for the Tuesday of the week containing the 13th day of the month.

In calculating Producer Price Indexes, price changes for the various commodities are averaged together with implicit quantity weights representing their importance in the total net selling value of all commodities as of 1972. The detailed data are aggregated to obtain indexes for stage of processing groupings, commodity groupings, durability of product groupings, and a number of special composite groupings.

Price indexes for the output of selected SIC industries measure average price changes in commodities produced by particular industries, as defined in the *Standard Industrial Classification Manual 1972* (Washington, U.S. Office of Management and Budget, 1972). These indexes are derived from several price series, combined to match the economic activity of the specified industry and weighted by the value of shipments in the industry. They use data from comprehensive industrial censuses conducted by the U.S. Bureau of the Census and the U.S. Department of Agriculture.

NOTES ON THE DATA

Beginning with the May 1978 issue of the *Review*, regional CPI's cross classified by population size, were introduced. These indexes will enable users in local areas for which an index is not published to get a better approximation of the CPI for their area by using the appropriate population size class measure for their region. The cross-classified indexes will be published bimonthly.

For further details about the new and the revised indexes and a comparison of various aspects of these indexes with the old unrevised CPI, see *Facts About the Revised Consumer Price Index*, a pamphlet in the Consumer Price Index Revision 1978 series. See also *The Consumer Price Index: Concepts and Content Over the Years*, Report 517, revised edition (Bureau of Labor Statistics, May 1978).

For interarea comparisons of living costs at three hypothetical standards of living, see the family budget data published in the *Handbook of Labor Statistics, 1977*, Bulletin 1966 (Bureau of Labor Statistics, 1977), tables 122–133. Additional data and analysis on price changes are provided in the *CPI Detailed Report* and *Producer Prices and Price Indexes*, both monthly publications of the Bureau.

As of January 1976, the Wholesale Price Index (as it was then called) incorporated a revised weighting structure reflecting 1972 values of shipments. From January 1967 through December 1975, 1963 values of shipments were used as weights.

For a discussion of the general method of computing consumer, producer, and industry price indexes, see *BLS Handbook of Methods for Surveys and Studies*, Bulletin 1910 (Bureau of Labor Statistics, 1976), chapters 13–15. See also John F. Early, "Improving the Measurement of Producer Price Change," *Monthly Labor Review*, April 1978, pp. 7–15. For industry prices, see also Bennett R. Moss, "Industry and Sector Price Indexes," *Monthly Labor Review*, August 1965, pp. 974–82.

Source: *Monthly Labor Review*, U.S. Department of Labor, Bureau of Labor Statistics.

Producer Price Indexes, by durability of product

[1967 = 100]

Commodity grouping	Annual average 1978	1979 Apr.	May	June	July	Aug.	Sept.	Oct.	Nov.	Dec.¹	1980 Jan.	Feb.	Mar.	Apr.
Total durable goods	204.9	223.9	224.7	225.8	227.6	228.0	230.1	234.6	235.3	237.0	243.4	246.4	246.6	247.2
Total nondurable goods	211.9	234.1	236.9	238.8	243.7	245.8	251.1	253.7	256.2	259.3	263.0	270.0	273.1	274.0
Total manufactures	204.2	223.1	225.0	226.5	229.8	231.7	235.2	239.0	240.6	242.6	248.2	252.7	254.8	256.5
Durable	204.7	222.7	223.8	224.6	226.6	227.2	229.4	234.0	234.6	236.2	242.2	245.0	245.2	246.2
Nondurable	203.0	222.8	225.6	227.8	232.5	235.9	241.0	244.0	246.6	249.0	253.8	260.7	264.7	267.3
Total raw or slightly processed goods	234.6	266.1	268.2	269.7	274.3	272.1	276.9	278.7	281.0	285.9	287.5	295.9	295.6	290.4
Durable	209.6	272.5	262.9	272.8	265.4	259.8	255.7	259.2	265.8	267.8	282.7	305.2	302.5	286.0
Nondurable	235.6	264.7	267.6	268.5	274.0	272.0	277.5	279.2	281.2	286.3	286.9	294.2	294.0	289.7

¹ Data for December 1979 have been revised to reflect the availability of late reports and corrections by respondents. All data are subject to revision 4 months after original publication.

Source: *Monthly Labor Review*, U.S. Department of Labor, Bureau of Labor Statistics.

CONSUMER PRICE INDEX FOR ALL URBAN CONSUMERS AND REVISED CPI FOR URBAN WAGE EARNERS AND CLERICAL WORKERS, U.S. CITY AVERAGE: GENERAL SUMMARY AND GROUPS, SUBGROUPS, AND SELECTED ITEMS (1967 = 100 unless otherwise specified)

General summary	All Urban Consumers							Urban Wage Earners and Clerical Workers (revised)						
		1979			1980				1979			1980		
	Mar.	Oct.	Nov.	Dec.	Jan.	Feb.	Mar.	Mar.	Oct.	Nov.	Dec.	Jan.	Feb.	Mar.
All items	209.1	225.4	227.5	229.9	233.2	236.4	239.8	209.3	225.6	227.6	230.0	233.3	236.5	239.9
Food and beverages	224.4	232.1	233.1	235.5	237.5	238.6	241.0	225.1	232.3	233.1	235.7	237.8	239.0	241.2
Housing	217.6	237.7	240.8	243.6	247.3	250.5	254.5	217.5	237.7	240.7	243.6	247.3	250.5	254.4
Apparel and upkeep	164.3	171.0	171.7	172.2	171.0	171.9	176.0	164.2	170.8	171.3	171.4	169.8	171.5	175.1
Transportation	198.1	222.7	224.9	227.7	233.5	239.6	243.7	198.7	223.4	225.7	228.3	234.1	240.2	244.3
Medical care	233.9	245.9	248.0	250.7	253.9	257.9	260.2	233.7	247.2	249.1	251.7	254.9	258.7	260.9
Entertainment	184.8	192.0	192.8	193.4	195.3	197.8	200.6	184.0	191.4	192.0	192.3	193.9	196.2	199.5
Other goods and services	192.8	202.3	202.9	204.0	206.3	208.1	208.9	192.6	201.4	202.0	203.0	206.0	207.7	208.3
Commodities	200.5	215.6	217.4	219.4	222.4	225.2	228.0	200.9	215.8	217.4	219.4	222.3	225.3	228.1
Commodities less food and beverages	187.0	204.9	206.9	208.8	212.0	215.5	218.4	187.0	205.0	206.9	208.7	212.0	215.7	218.7
Nondurables less food and beverages	187.8	214.9	216.6	219.0	224.6	231.8	237.5	188.4	216.6	218.1	220.5	226.3	234.1	239.8
Durables	184.9	196.0	198.4	199.8	201.3	202.1	203.0	184.5	194.8	196.9	198.2	199.6	200.3	201.2
Services	225.1	243.6	246.2	249.3	253.1	256.8	261.3	225.1	244.0	246.7	249.6	253.6	257.3	261.7
Rent, residential	171.3	181.4	182.1	182.9	184.1	185.6	186.6	171.2	181.2	181.9	182.7	183.9	185.5	186.4
Household services less rent	253.7	280.7	284.6	289.2	295.1	300.2	307.3	254.3	282.3	286.3	291.1	297.2	302.4	309.6
Transportation services	206.7	218.5	221.5	224.2	226.8	229.6	233.4	207.4	218.6	221.5	224.0	226.6	229.3	232.7
Medical care services	251.8	265.3	267.6	270.7	274.4	279.0	281.5	251.3	266.8	268.8	271.8	276.6	279.8	282.2
Other services	195.0	205.7	206.5	207.1	209.0	211.1	212.9	195.0	206.4	207.3	207.4	209.3	211.4	213.5
Special indexes:														
All items less food	203.8	221.8	224.1	226.4	229.9	233.5	237.1	203.7	222.0	224.2	226.4	230.0	233.7	237.3
All items less mortgage interest costs	204.1	218.3	219.8	221.7	224.3	227.1	229.8	204.5	218.7	220.1	222.0	224.7	227.6	230.2
Commodities less food	185.9	203.4	205.4	207.2	210.4	213.8	216.7	185.9	203.5	205.4	207.1	210.3	214.0	216.9
Nondurables less food	185.7	211.3	212.9	215.2	220.5	227.3	232.6	186.3	212.9	214.4	216.7	222.1	229.4	234.8
Nondurables less food and apparel	200.0	234.8	236.8	240.1	248.6	258.2	264.1	200.5	236.3	238.2	241.5	250.2	260.1	266.3
Nondurables	206.9	224.5	225.8	228.2	232.0	236.3	240.3	206.7	225.3	226.5	229.0	232.9	237.4	241.4
Services less rent	235.0	255.1	258.2	261.6	266.1	270.2	275.4	235.0	255.7	258.8	262.1	266.7	270.8	275.9
Services less medical care	220.8	239.6	242.3	245.3	249.2	252.7	257.4	220.8	239.9	242.6	245.5	249.5	253.1	257.7
Domestically produced farm foods	220.7	224.1	224.5	225.7	229.2	229.1	231.2	221.0	224.0	224.4	225.5	229.0	229.2	231.0
Selected beef cuts	253.4	257.3	256.5	263.2	265.7	267.2	270.2	255.6	259.1	259.2	265.2	268.1	267.2	270.2
Energy	241.2	307.5	307.8	313.7	327.9	344.6	355.0	241.7	310.2	310.7	317.0	331.5	348.7	359.6
All items less energy	206.9	219.2	221.4	223.6	225.9	228.0	230.8	207.1	218.8	221.0	223.0	225.3	227.3	230.0
All items less food and energy	200.4	213.6	216.1	218.1	220.6	222.8	225.7	200.2	213.0	215.4	217.3	219.6	221.8	224.6
Commodities less food and energy	180.3	189.6	191.4	192.6	193.7	194.9	196.5	180.0	188.7	190.4	191.4	192.4	193.5	195.1
Energy commodities	239.5	329.0	332.5	340.0	361.5	385.0	398.5	240.0	333.8	341.5	348.0	368.8	386.4	400.3
Services less energy	223.7	241.3	244.6	247.6	251.6	255.2	259.6	223.7	241.7	245.1	248.0	252.2	255.7	260.0
Purchasing power of the consumer dollar, 1967 = $1	$0.478	$0.444	$0.440	$0.435	$0.429	$0.423	$0.417	$0.478	$0.443	$0.439	$0.435	$0.429	$0.423	$0.417

CONSUMER PRICE INDEX—U.S. CITY AVERAGE (continued)

Columns 2–8 are **All Urban Consumers**; columns 9–15 are **Urban Wage Earners and Clerical Workers (revised)**. Within each group the first column is Mar. (1979); the next three (Oct., Nov., Dec.) are **1979**; the last three (Jan., Feb., Mar.) are **1980**.

General summary	Mar.	Oct.	Nov.	Dec.	Jan.	Feb.	Mar.	Mar.	Oct.	Nov.	Dec.	Jan.	Feb.	Mar.
FOOD AND BEVERAGES	224.4	232.1	233.1	235.5	237.5	238.6	241.0	225.1	232.3	233.1	235.7	237.8	239.0	241.2
Food	230.4	238.2	239.1	241.7	243.8	244.9	247.3	231.1	238.3	239.1	241.8	244.0	245.2	247.5
Food at home														
Cereals and bakery products	229.9	235.4	236.0	238.7	240.6	241.3	243.6	230.0	234.8	235.4	238.3	240.1	241.1	243.1
Cereals and cereal products (12/77 = 100)	213.5	227.0	228.7	231.6	234.2	236.8	238.6	214.1	227.9	229.7	232.3	234.7	237.4	239.3
Flour and prepared flour mixes (12/77 = 100)	113.7	120.8	121.1	122.9	125.0	125.8	126.6	113.9	121.4	122.1	123.8	126.1	127.2	127.7
Cereal (12/77 = 100)	114.9	124.0	122.8	123.8	125.7	125.7	126.6	115.2	125.0	124.6	125.1	126.9	127.3	127.5
Rice, pasta, and commeal (12/77 = 100)	114.1	119.7	119.7	122.8	123.7	124.9	126.0	114.4	119.3	119.9	122.9	124.2	125.5	126.6
Bakery products (12/77 = 100)	112.2	120.4	121.0	122.4	123.5	125.1	126.1	112.1	120.8	121.3	122.7	123.6	125.1	126.2
White bread	187.0	202.5	204.5	207.4	208.6	210.7	212.0	187.6	203.2	203.9	206.6	209.7	212.0	212.1
Other breads (12/77 = 100)	112.6	120.5	121.3	123.3	123.8	124.6	125.6	114.2	123.8	124.2	126.0	126.9	127.5	129.3
Fresh biscuits, rolls, and muffins (12/77 = 100)	113.1	119.4	121.2	123.1	124.8	126.2	127.0	112.4	118.7	120.8	122.3	123.1	124.3	124.9
Fresh cakes and cupcakes (12/77 = 100)	110.5	117.6	119.4	120.3	121.7	122.8	124.4	110.6	118.1	119.1	120.1	120.8	122.2	123.2
Cookies (12/77 = 100)	113.5	116.6	117.1	117.8	119.7	119.9	120.4	114.6	118.3	118.4	119.6	121.5	124.0	125.6
Crackers and bread and cracker products (12/77 = 100)	112.1	115.0	114.5	116.2	117.5	119.9	120.2	112.5	115.0	116.1	116.3	118.4	121.0	121.8
Fresh sweetrolls, coffeecake, and donuts (12/77 = 100)	110.7	118.9	119.9	121.5	122.2	123.8	125.0	112.4	120.7	121.9	123.4	124.1	125.4	126.2
Frozen and refrigerated bakery products and fresh pies, tarts, and turnovers (12/77 = 100)	113.8	122.5	123.7	124.8	125.7	127.2	127.9	112.3	118.8	120.8	121.4	122.5	123.8	124.0
Meats, poultry, fish, and eggs	237.0	230.3	230.2	235.5	238.0	236.2	237.8	236.9	229.7	230.0	235.1	237.5	236.4	237.1
Meats, poultry, and fish	241.7	235.9	235.2	239.8	243.0	242.6	243.8	241.5	235.3	235.0	239.2	242.5	242.8	243.0
Meats	244.2	238.6	237.4	242.3	244.1	244.1	245.7	243.9	238.1	237.3	241.8	243.7	244.3	245.0
Beef and veal	252.1	256.2	255.5	262.2	264.6	266.2	269.1	254.2	257.5	257.7	263.7	266.7	268.9	270.8
Ground beef other than canned	264.6	263.4	264.2	271.2	274.1	273.3	275.3	264.4	265.8	266.0	273.0	272.7	276.2	278.7
Chuck roast	270.8	263.3	263.1	268.1	274.7	277.7	286.2	279.3	268.3	273.1	274.2	283.6	288.7	293.4
Round roast	228.0	230.3	229.1	238.1	241.9	244.5	244.2	230.1	233.0	232.7	240.5	245.1	245.8	244.5
Round steak	236.5	242.2	241.9	247.5	249.8	252.3	254.2	234.4	239.4	239.7	246.2	249.4	250.5	251.1
Sirloin steak	233.4	250.4	247.0	250.8	250.9	251.1	254.3	230.0	249.6	247.4	253.5	253.5	253.0	256.0
Other beef and veal (12/77 = 100)	141.7	147.1	146.3	150.2	151.8	152.2	153.8	143.1	147.0	146.6	149.9	151.9	152.8	153.7
Pork	233.4	204.3	201.0	205.0	206.4	202.8	202.6	232.2	204.7	201.5	205.6	206.8	204.1	203.0
Bacon	227.9	190.5	186.3	193.6	194.5	190.1	187.6	229.2	194.4	188.7	195.8	195.3	193.8	189.4
Pork chops	223.6	195.1	188.8	187.8	192.1	189.7	190.7	224.1	194.9	188.1	189.1	194.8	191.0	190.5
Ham other than canned (12/77 = 100)	108.0	94.8	95.9	102.5	99.1	95.7	95.8	106.8	94.0	95.4	100.9	96.5	95.2	94.7
Sausage	285.4	257.6	254.5	256.5	256.6	255.1	257.6	280.5	258.1	255.8	258.3	260.3	258.3	259.8
Canned ham	236.7	218.2	214.8	218.9	220.8	219.5	219.3	235.8	215.8	214.6	219.1	219.3	218.9	217.4
Other pork (12/77 = 100)	132.2	115.2	112.9	112.6	116.2	114.3	113.6	130.8	115.1	112.7	112.7	116.2	114.6	113.7

Other meats	233.9	240.7	242.0	243.0	243.2	244.7	245.6	231.3	238.0	238.5	239.5	239.3	240.9	241.5
Frankfurters	234.5	236.8	238.9	239.3	239.0	242.7	244.6	232.7	237.7	237.2	238.7	239.5	242.1	242.8
Bologna, liverwurst, and salami (12/77 = 100)	129.0	134.2	133.8	134.4	134.1	135.6	135.5	127.8	130.7	130.4	130.8	130.5	132.3	132.2
Other lunchmeats (12/77 = 100)	120.7	120.3	121.6	121.5	121.2	120.7	121.8	118.0	118.8	119.5	119.4	118.7	118.6	118.8
Lamb and organ meats (12/77 = 100)	125.4	137.7	138.3	140.0	141.6	142.4	142.3	126.7	138.8	139.8	141.7	142.5	143.4	144.3
Poultry	189.9	170.3	166.7	176.2	187.8	182.6	180.7	188.7	168.3	170.1	173.9	184.3	181.1	177.4
Fresh whole chicken	191.5	159.7	175.2	175.2	191.1	183.6	179.5	187.7	157.7	163.3	169.8	183.8	178.9	172.5
Fresh and frozen chicken parts (12/77 = 100)	121.6	110.1	110.8	112.3	120.7	116.8	116.8	121.6	108.4	110.7	111.8	120.1	117.0	116.3
Other poultry (12/77 = 100)	123.0	120.3	115.9	116.9	119.3	118.8	118.2	122.2	119.8	119.8	117.4	120.1	119.4	117.7
Fish and seafood	294.0	311.5	312.2	312.6	316.7	320.4	322.6	292.6	306.5	307.5	309.1	315.4	317.9	320.2
Canned fish and seafood (12/77 = 100)	108.3	115.2	116.8	117.1	118.5	120.3	120.4	107.9	114.5	116.0	116.5	118.4	119.7	119.5
Fresh and frozen fish and seafood (12/77 = 100)	114.2	120.7	120.1	120.2	121.9	123.0	124.3	113.7	118.1	117.8	118.5	121.2	122.0	123.5
Eggs	181.3	161.3	170.1	185.9	178.2	157.2	164.5	182.0	160.3	169.6	186.6	177.0	156.7	164.3
Dairy products	201.5	213.3	216.0	216.9	218.4	219.5	220.3	202.3	214.0	216.3	217.4	218.9	219.8	221.1
Fresh milk and cream (12/77 = 100)	113.8	120.3	121.9	122.7	123.2	123.7	124.1	114.2	120.4	121.8	122.6	123.2	123.6	124.2
Fresh whole milk	186.5	197.6	200.4	201.2	202.3	203.2	204.0	187.4	197.4	199.7	200.9	201.8	202.7	203.8
Other fresh milk and cream (12/77 = 100)	113.6	119.2	120.6	122.0	122.1	122.7	122.7	113.3	119.8	121.1	122.2	122.8	123.0	123.1
Processed dairy products (12/77 = 100)	114.0	120.9	122.3	122.5	123.8	124.5	125.1	114.5	121.7	123.0	123.3	124.5	125.1	126.2
Butter	194.5	213.3	214.4	214.0	216.9	218.3	218.3	196.2	216.6	217.1	216.6	219.8	220.9	220.9
Cheese (12/77 = 100)	114.6	121.0	122.7	122.6	123.5	124.2	124.9	114.6	121.1	122.5	122.7	123.6	124.4	125.5
Ice cream and related products (12/77 = 100)	113.4	120.4	121.4	122.6	124.0	124.6	125.1	114.8	121.9	123.4	124.3	125.6	125.6	127.2
Other dairy products (12/77 = 100)	111.0	116.4	117.8	117.9	119.8	120.9	121.6	111.6	116.9	118.2	118.3	120.4	121.3	121.9
Fruits and vegetables	225.9	232.0	229.5	230.2	229.8	228.3	228.3	225.4	230.2	230.2	228.3	227.2	225.9	230.1
Fresh fruits and vegetables	230.5	235.5	230.1	230.1	227.2	223.1	222.9	230.9	233.6	236.7	228.5	224.9	226.6	227.4
Fresh fruits	226.2	260.4	242.7	234.9	236.6	235.8	245.4	223.2	260.6	238.3	233.3	232.7	234.7	245.4
Apples	219.1	212.7	207.2	221.8	230.4	239.6	250.2	237.3	212.9	207.7	202.2	230.1	237.6	249.0
Bananas	194.7	209.0	209.0	219.9	236.2	238.5	243.9	192.3	199.7	206.5	220.0	219.5	228.4	240.8
Oranges	261.4	306.7	293.9	256.7	236.2	231.1	238.1	252.0	290.3	283.3	249.5	231.3	228.4	240.9
Other fresh fruits (12/77 = 100)	115.5	143.9	127.5	121.1	121.6	121.4	127.4	115.8	149.7	125.7	121.6	122.7	121.3	126.9
Fresh vegetables	234.6	212.2	218.4	225.7	212.2	211.2	215.5	237.9	209.4	216.4	199.6	217.9	199.8	211.3
Potatoes	200.1	191.1	195.7	207.0	203.8	203.3	203.3	201.0	183.8	191.7	199.6	200.9	199.8	200.3
Lettuce	281.3	262.9	244.2	227.5	197.6	199.8	208.3	293.2	264.2	239.0	231.3	193.2	191.7	203.8
Tomatoes	182.7	194.4	225.3	227.9	216.7	184.9	201.4	187.7	194.1	254.8	255.4	213.2	184.3	197.2
Other fresh vegetables (12/77 = 100)	136.6	140.0	119.1	128.0	132.0	125.1	125.4	137.1	112.5	118.9	128.1	130.5	123.9	123.0
Processed fruits and vegetables	222.7	230.1	231.0	232.3	234.7	236.2	237.2	221.3	228.3	228.6	230.0	231.8	233.9	235.0
Processed fruits (12/77 = 100)	115.9	120.4	121.2	121.8	122.9	123.4	123.9	115.9	120.3	121.1	121.3	122.4	123.6	123.9
Frozen fruit and fruit juices (12/77 = 100)	114.1	116.3	116.6	116.8	117.2	117.6	117.7	114.4	115.2	115.7	115.9	116.5	117.8	116.5
Frut juices and other than frozen (12/77 = 100)	113.3	119.8	122.1	123.6	125.1	126.0	127.2	113.4	119.8	122.4	123.5	124.8	126.3	127.4
Canned and dried fruits (12/77 = 100)	120.3	124.6	124.2	124.2	125.3	125.5	125.5	119.8	124.0	124.0	123.5	124.8	125.3	125.9
Processed vegetables (12/77 = 100)	107.9	110.9	110.9	111.7	113.0	114.0	114.6	107.0	109.8	109.4	110.5	111.2	112.2	113.0
Frozen vegetables (12/77 = 100)	107.1	110.2	110.2	110.6	111.9	113.0	112.6	106.5	110.2	109.6	110.8	111.4	111.7	111.9

CONSUMER PRICE INDEX—U.S. CITY AVERAGE (continued)

General summary	All Urban Consumers							Urban Wage Earners and Clerical Workers (revised)						
		1979			1980				1979			1980		
	Mar.	Oct.	Nov.	Dec.	Jan.	Feb.	Mar.	Mar.	Oct.	Nov.	Dec.	Jan.	Feb.	Mar.
FOOD AND BEVERAGES Continued														
Food Continued														
Food at home Continued														
Fruits and vegetables Continued														
Cut corn and canned beans except lima (12/77=100)	111.6	113.6	113.4	114.4	114.5	115.2	116.0	110.0	111.9	111.8	113.0	112.7	113.4	115.4
Other canned and dried vegetables (12/77=100)	106.4	109.9	110.0	110.9	112.9	113.9	114.8	105.2	108.5	108.1	109.1	110.4	111.9	112.3
Other foods at home	262.4	278.0	279.6	281.1	283.5	288.0	292.0	262.2	276.5	278.3	279.9	282.6	287.3	290.9
Sugar and sweets	272.1	283.1	283.2	284.6	289.8	297.5	313.5	272.4	282.2	281.9	284.1	289.6	297.1	314.1
Candy and chewing gum (12/77=100)	115.0	119.9	120.1	120.1	121.3	122.4	123.8	115.3	119.6	119.8	119.9	121.2	122.2	123.9
Sugar and artificial sweeteners (12/77=100)	114.5	119.0	116.2	117.2	122.2	131.5	153.0	114.8	116.9	116.2	117.6	122.7	131.6	153.8
Other sweets (12/77=100)	109.5	115.9	116.4	117.5	118.7	119.5	120.4	108.7	114.8	114.6	116.6	117.5	118.5	119.3
Fats and oils (12/77=100)	219.5	231.9	232.3	233.0	233.9	235.9	236.8	219.8	231.9	232.8	233.7	234.9	236.5	236.8
Margarine	235.5	244.4	246.2	247.7	248.3	247.9	248.8	234.6	244.9	246.7	247.8	248.8	247.9	248.3
Nondairy substitutes and peanut butter (12/77=100)	110.0	115.1	115.1	115.7	115.3	116.4	117.9	110.3	114.6	115.0	115.8	116.1	117.2	118.5
Other fats, oils, and salad dressings (12/77=100)	113.0	121.1	121.0	121.1	121.9	123.6	123.7	113.4	121.0	121.3	121.5	122.3	123.8	123.4
Nonalcoholic beverages	347.1	372.1	374.3	375.4	378.5	384.5	387.1	346.9	368.2	370.7	372.3	375.6	383.0	384.4
Cola drinks, excluding diet cola	233.8	246.4	247.5	247.2	249.5	255.9	259.3	232.9	242.0	243.6	243.4	245.5	253.6	254.4
Carbonated drinks, including diet cola (12/77=100)	113.8	118.5	118.4	118.7	119.9	122.3	123.5	111.6	116.1	115.6	116.4	116.4	120.2	121.1
Roasted coffee	348.3	434.4	438.1	440.7	443.2	439.6	437.6	349.8	424.4	430.8	435.3	440.1	436.8	432.3
Freeze dried and instant coffee	332.7	366.5	370.2	374.3	378.2	382.2	381.7	332.1	365.3	369.3	372.9	376.8	380.4	380.3
Other noncarbonated drinks (12/77=100)	112.5	114.8	115.7	116.3	116.8	118.3	118.6	111.3	113.5	114.8	115.5	116.2	117.5	118.1
Other prepared foods	202.9	213.4	215.3	217.4	218.8	221.8	224.1	203.0	213.4	215.7	217.2	219.1	221.7	224.0
Canned and packaged soup (12/77=100)	109.2	113.4	114.3	115.9	116.5	118.1	118.0	109.1	113.3	114.8	116.3	116.8	117.9	117.6
Frozen prepared foods (12/77=100)	113.9	123.1	124.5	125.6	126.0	126.6	128.2	113.9	120.0	122.9	123.9	125.1	125.5	127.1
Snacks (12/77=100)	112.0	119.6	120.4	121.3	121.8	123.4	124.1	112.4	120.6	121.7	122.2	122.8	124.7	125.3
Seasonings, olives, pickles, and relish (12/77=100)	114.8	118.8	118.9	120.1	121.4	123.6	124.9	113.5	117.6	118.2	119.0	121.1	123.1	124.0
Other condiments (12/77=100)	110.7	115.8	116.8	119.5	120.8	123.7	126.0	111.1	117.0	118.5	120.2	121.4	124.6	126.6
Miscellaneous prepared foods (12/77=100)	112.2	117.2	119.0	118.9	119.6	120.7	122.2	112.4	116.7	118.6	118.7	119.7	120.5	122.2
Other canned and packaged prepared foods (12/77=100)	112.7	116.7	117.7	118.6	119.4	121.2	122.2	112.7	116.9	118.0	118.6	119.5	120.3	122.0
Food away from home	236.0	249.6	251.3	253.4	256.1	258.3	260.9	237.9	251.3	252.7	255.1	258.0	260.1	262.7
Lunch (12/77=100)	115.2	121.3	122.3	123.3	124.6	125.9	127.0	116.4	122.2	123.2	124.0	125.7	126.7	127.6
Dinner (12/77=100)	114.2	121.6	122.4	123.4	124.8	125.8	127.0	114.6	122.4	123.0	124.2	125.6	126.8	128.1
Other meals and snacks (12/77=100)	113.7	119.5	120.2	121.4	122.5	123.2	124.9	114.9	120.5	120.9	122.5	123.7	124.4	126.2

Category														
Alcoholic beverages	169.2	176.0	177.4	178.0	179.3	180.4	181.7	169.6	176.9	178.0	178.7	179.7	181.1	182.8
Alcoholic beverages at home (12/77=100)	109.9	114.6	115.6	116.0	116.8	117.4	118.2	110.8	115.7	116.5	117.0	117.6	118.3	119.3
Beer and ale	166.1	175.1	176.9	177.8	179.0	179.9	182.0	166.6	175.2	176.9	177.6	178.8	179.9	181.7
Whiskey	124.8	129.4	130.7	130.8	131.6	132.6	132.8	126.1	131.0	131.9	132.0	132.9	133.8	134.4
Wine	190.8	198.0	198.1	199.1	201.6	202.5	204.1	194.2	202.5	201.5	204.0	203.8	206.1	208.4
Other alcoholic beverages (12/77=100)	104.4	105.9	107.0	106.9	107.1	107.3	107.4	103.8	105.9	106.2	106.4	106.4	106.7	107.2
Alcoholic beverages away from home (12/77=100)	112.4	115.9	116.4	116.8	118.0	119.2	120.0	110.0	114.2	114.9	115.2	115.9	117.6	119.1
HOUSING	217.6	237.7	240.8	243.6	247.3	250.5	254.5	217.5	237.7	240.7	243.6	247.3	250.5	254.4
Shelter	228.0	251.5	255.9	259.4	264.0	267.2	271.6	228.5	252.4	256.9	260.4	265.1	268.3	272.7
Rent, residential	*71.3	181.4	182.1	182.9	184.1	185.6	186.6	171.2	181.2	181.9	182.7	183.9	185.5	186.4
Other rental costs	226.3	241.6	243.1	244.9	251.1	255.7	258.6	226.3	241.3	242.6	244.4	251.1	255.6	258.6
Lodging while out of town	237.4	254.2	256.2	258.4	267.0	272.8	276.8	236.7	253.0	254.6	256.9	266.1	271.6	275.7
Tenants' insurance (12/77=100)	106.4	114.1	114.6	115.1	116.2	117.8	118.6	106.6	114.7	115.0	115.5	116.8	118.5	119.3
Homeownership	248.2	276.7	282.4	286.9	292.5	296.3	302.0	249.2	278.3	284.1	288.7	294.6	298.4	304.0
Home purchase	212.7	233.4	237.3	239.9	242.1	243.0	244.0	212.7	233.6	237.7	240.2	242.3	243.0	243.8
Financing, taxes, and insurance	287.7	330.5	340.1	348.3	359.8	367.7	379.9	289.5	333.5	343.5	351.6	363.4	371.6	384.1
Property insurance	299.8	319.9	320.8	323.1	327.7	335.7	335.7	300.0	321.9	322.6	324.5	328.8	335.2	337.4
Property taxes	181.1	185.1	185.1	186.0	186.7	188.2	188.2	182.5	186.5	186.6	187.4	188.2	189.9	199.9
Contracted mortgage interest cost	344.2	408.1	423.1	435.3	452.8	464.0	483.0	344.5	408.8	424.2	436.1	453.7	465.0	484.1
Mortgage interest rates	159.2	172.0	175.4	178.3	183.7	187.5	194.4	159.2	172.0	175.6	178.4	183.8	187.8	194.8
Maintenance and repairs	247.5	264.7	266.4	268.3	270.6	273.7	278.8	248.4	265.3	266.5	268.9	271.9	274.4	278.2
Maintenance and repair services	267.8	287.0	288.8	290.4	293.2	297.1	303.2	269.3	289.4	290.3	292.8	295.9	293.3	303.5
Maintenance and repair commodities	200.1	212.5	214.0	216.6	217.6	218.9	221.4	201.5	211.9	213.6	215.8	218.4	219.5	222.3
Paint and wallpaper, supplies, tools, and equipment (12/77=100)	109.7	117.4	118.8	121.6	122.5	123.5	125.0	111.1	116.6	118.1	120.3	122.2	122.3	123.6
Lumber, awnings, glass, and masonry (12/77=100)	109.7	116.0	115.5	115.4	115.9	115.8	117.6	110.6	116.2	117.2	118.1	118.6	119.3	119.9
Plumbing, electrical, heating, and cooling supplies (12/77=100)	105.7	112.8	113.4	114.7	114.7	115.3	116.4	106.7	113.8	114.0	114.5	117.0	117.9	119.3
Miscellaneous supplies and equipment (12/77=100)	108.2	113.3	113.8	114.3	115.4	116.4	117.0	106.9	111.9	112.2	112.3	113.2	114.5	118.2
Fuel and other utilities	225.9	252.9	252.0	255.1	258.6	263.8	268.0	226.0	253.4	252.4	255.7	259.2	264.4	268.7
Fuels	264.0	310.3	307.0	311.8	318.0	327.1	333.9	263.7	310.1	306.9	311.8	318.1	327.0	333.9
Fuel oil, coal, and bottled gas	339.5	470.8	477.4	488.0	514.0	539.1	553.4	340.0	471.7	478.2	489.0	515.1	540.3	554.1
Fuel oil	346.4	491.2	497.2	507.3	534.4	561.9	577.9	346.9	491.9	497.7	508.1	534.9	562.5	577.9
Other fuels (6/78=100)	99.3	118.5	121.7	126.0	132.7	136.6	138.3	99.2	118.8	122.2	126.6	133.7	137.9	139.5
Gas (piped) and electricity	244.0	272.5	267.3	270.8	273.0	278.8	284.0	243.6	272.2	267.1	270.7	273.0	278.5	283.9
Electricity	208.7	228.7	221.5	224.7	226.6	238.3	237.9	208.9	228.8	221.5	224.9	226.8	233.9	238.1
Utility (piped) gas	286.2	329.1	328.9	332.6	335.1	336.8	343.9	284.3	327.4	327.8	331.1	333.8	335.4	342.6

CONSUMER PRICE INDEX—U.S. CITY AVERAGE (continued)

General summary	All Urban Consumers							Urban Wage Earners and Clerical Workers (revised)						
	1979				1980			1979				1980		
	Mar.	Oct.	Nov.	Dec.	Jan.	Feb.	Mar.	Mar.	Oct.	Nov.	Dec.	Jan.	Feb.	Mar.
HOUSING Continued														
Fuel and other utilities Continued														
Other utilities and public services	158.8	158.8	161.0	161.9	161.5	161.3	161.9	158.9	158.9	160.9	161.8	161.5	161.4	161.9
Telephone services	131.2	131.2	133.3	134.3	133.4	132.8	133.2	132.1	131.3	133.3	134.2	133.4	132.8	133.1
Local charges (12/77 100)	100.4	98.7	101.8	103.2	102.6	102.7	103.3	100.5	98.8	101.8	103.2	102.6	102.7	103.2
Interstate toll calls (12/77 = 100)	98.3	98.4	98.4	98.4	97.7	97.4	97.4	98.3	98.4	98.4	98.4	97.7	97.5	97.5
Intrastate toll calls (12/77 = 100)	100.7	101.7	101.5	101.5	100.8	98.8	98.7	100.6	101.5	101.3	101.3	100.6	98.7	98.6
Water and sewerage maintenance	240.7	245.6	247.1	247.2	250.0	252.3	253.9	241.2	245.8	247.2	247.3	250.5	253.0	254.7
Household furnishings and operations	187.4	193.3	195.1	195.8	196.9	199.0	201.3	186.3	191.7	193.2	193.9	194.9	196.8	199.2
Housefurnishings	161.2	165.2	166.6	166.9	167.6	169.3	171.5	160.8	164.4	165.5	165.9	166.5	167.9	170.4
Textile housefurnishings	172.3	177.8	178.9	178.6	176.7	182.9	187.2	174.3	177.2	178.4	177.3	175.3	181.2	185.3
Household linens (12/77 = 100)	105.8	107.7	108.8	108.3	105.4	110.1	113.9	105.5	107.4	108.3	107.2	106.0	109.8	113.2
Curtains, drapes, slipcovers, and sewing materials (12/77 = 100)	109.1	114.2	114.4	114.6	115.1	118.2	119.7	112.4	114.1	114.5	114.4	113.2	116.6	118.2
Furniture and bedding	174.1	180.0	182.2	182.8	184.0	185.2	189.2	173.7	180.3	182.1	182.7	183.6	184.3	187.9
Bedroom furniture (12/77 = 100)	110.1	116.4	117.7	118.3	119.1	120.5	122.5	109.7	114.8	115.9	116.0	116.8	117.5	119.2
Sofas (12/77 = 100)	105.1	107.3	107.9	108.2	108.2	108.5	110.9	104.8	109.6	111.7	111.6	110.6	110.3	110.2
Living room chairs and tables (12/77 = 100)	103.3	106.2	107.7	108.1	108.9	110.0	110.8	104.7	107.5	108.6	109.2	109.4	111.2	111.9
Other furniture (12/77 = 100)	112.4	115.0	116.8	117.1	118.1	118.3	122.6	112.2	114.7	115.3	115.9	117.8	117.5	121.3
Appliances including TV and sound equipment	134.8	136.9	137.5	137.5	137.8	138.3	138.8	134.5	135.7	136.2	136.9	137.2	137.8	139.0
Television and sound equipment (12/77 = 100)	103.8	104.9	105.0	105.3	105.3	105.4	105.7	103.3	104.1	104.4	104.8	104.9	104.9	105.5
Television	103.0	103.4	103.6	103.6	103.7	103.7	104.0	102.0	102.0	102.4	102.2	102.2	102.3	102.9
Sound equipment (12/77 = 100)	105.6	107.4	107.4	107.8	107.8	108.1	108.3	105.5	106.9	107.1	108.0	108.2	108.2	108.7
Household appliances	154.0	156.9	158.2	157.9	158.5	159.4	160.2	153.8	155.6	156.2	157.1	157.7	158.8	160.7
Refrigerators and home freezer	151.7	153.3	156.0	156.7	156.7	156.5	157.9	155.2	157.9	158.1	159.0	159.4	159.7	161.4
Laundry equipment (12/77 = 100)	108.2	112.1	112.1	113.6	114.1	115.0	116.8	108.0	113.0	112.2	112.8	113.8	114.7	116.6
Other household appliances (12/77 = 100)	108.8	109.8	110.8	109.9	110.5	111.3	111.2	107.4	107.2	107.6	108.2	108.6	109.5	110.7
Stoves, dishwashers, vacuums, and sewing machines (12/77 = 100)	109.3	109.0	111.1	108.6	110.0	112.0	111.6	108.4	106.9	107.1	108.1	109.2	110.5	111.1
Office machines, small electric appliances, and air conditioners (12/77 = 100)	108.2	110.7	112.1	114.4	111.1	110.5	110.2	106.2	107.6	108.2	108.3	107.8	108.4	110.2
Other household equipment (12/77 = 100)	108.6	111.2	112.4	113.0	114.6	114.5	117.3	107.7	108.0	111.6	111.8	113.3	114.4	116.0
Floor and window coverings, infants' laundry cleaning and outdoor equipment (12/77 = 100)	108.6	109.8	111.1	111.7	113.1	112.7	116.4	103.5	105.5	107.7	107.4	108.9	109.4	110.8
Clocks, lamps, and decor items (12/77 = 100)	105.3	108.6	110.0	110.2	111.6	114.9	114.9	105.8	107.1	108.2	107.3	109.4	109.8	112.3
Tableware, serving pieces, and nonelectric kitchenware (12/77 = 100)	112.3	115.4	116.8	117.2	119.9	121.4	122.6	110.7	114.7	115.2	115.2	117.3	118.9	120.8
Lawn equipment, power tools, and other hardware (12/77 = 100)	105.9	108.5	109.0	110.3	110.6	111.7	112.2	107.6	111.0	111.1	112.5	113.0	114.2	115.0

Item														
Housekeeping supplies	218.4	224.8	228.3	229.2	231.1	235.0	238.0	218.1	223.9	226.7	227.2	228.8	232.8	235.5
Soaps and detergents	210.3	217.9	220.6	221.2	224.1	228.9	232.1	209.0	216.3	218.2	219.7	222.2	226.5	230.0
Other laundry and cleaning products (12/77 = 100)	109.0	113.7	114.1	114.7	116.1	117.2	117.0	109.1	113.5	113.7	114.5	115.6	117.1	116.9
Cleansing and toilet tissue, paper towels and napkins (12/77 = 100)	115.1	117.2	119.2	120.5	120.6	121.2	123.9	115.2	117.9	119.6	120.9	121.8	123.4	125.8
Stationery, stationery supplies, and gift wrap (12/77 = 100)	106.8	109.5	111.3	111.9	111.6	112.7	113.8	106.1	108.6	109.2	109.3	109.0	112.3	113.6
Miscellaneous household products (12/77 = 100)	110.3	114.3	115.6	116.9	117.7	119.4	120.9	109.0	112.7	114.1	114.7	115.0	116.6	118.3
Lawn and garden supplies (12/77 = 100)	108.5	110.0	113.8	112.5	114.4	119.4	121.4	110.0	108.8	113.2	109.9	111.3	113.3	114.0
Housekeeping services	242.9	254.6	256.6	258.1	260.0	261.6	263.6	241.6	253.9	255.9	257.5	259.2	261.1	262.7
Postage	257.3	257.3	257.3	257.3	257.3	257.3	257.3	257.2	257.2	257.2	257.2	257.2	257.2	257.2
Moving, storage, freight, household laundry, and drycleaning services (12/77 = 100)	115.5	118.8	120.4	121.2	122.9	124.2	125.4	111.7	119.7	121.2	122.3	123.3	124.6	126.1
Appliance and furniture repair (12/77 = 100)	107.6	112.3	112.9	113.4	114.0	114.7	115.8	106.7	112.1	112.9	113.4	114.4	115.5	116.0
APPAREL AND UPKEEP	164.3	171.0	171.7	172.2	171.0	171.9	176.0	164.2	170.8	171.3	171.4	169.8	171.5	175.1
Apparel commodities	159.2	165.2	165.9	166.1	164.3	165.1	169.2	159.3	165.3	165.7	165.7	163.6	165.2	168.7
Apparel commodities less footwear	157.1	162.3	162.9	163.0	161.1	161.8	166.2	157.3	162.4	162.7	162.6	160.2	161.9	165.7
Men's and boys'	158.7	164.2	165.4	165.4	162.8	162.7	165.6	159.4	164.4	163.5	165.0	162.4	162.9	166.0
Men's (12/77 = 100)	100.3	103.5	104.3	104.3	102.6	102.3	104.3	101.2	103.8	104.5	104.2	102.3	102.4	104.4
Suits, sport coats, and jackets (12/77 = 100)	97.6	101.6	101.2	100.9	98.8	98.2	99.9	96.3	99.1	98.7	96.8	94.9	94.4	96.4
Coats and jackets (12/77 = 100)	94.4	97.8	98.1	98.0	95.5	93.6	96.9	99.0	99.5	99.7	99.1	95.6	92.2	96.9
Furnishings and special clothing (12/77 = 100)	105.2	109.9	112.4	112.3	112.2	112.7	115.0	104.2	109.1	110.0	109.9	109.3	111.1	113.2
Shirts (12/77 = 100)	104.0	108.5	109.7	110.5	108.6	109.3	111.9	104.4	108.3	109.4	111.5	108.3	109.4	112.0
Dungarees, jeans, and trousers (12/77 = 100)	99.5	99.5	100.5	100.4	98.2	97.7	98.7	101.7	102.8	104.0	103.4	102.2	102.2	102.7
Boys' (12/77 = 100)	101.4	106.3	106.6	106.6	105.6	106.3	107.5	101.7	105.3	105.6	105.8	104.7	105.9	107.5
Coats, jackets, sweaters, and shirts (12/77 = 100)	96.8	103.9	103.2	102.4	99.3	102.5	102.5	100.4	102.8	103.4	103.1	99.8	101.9	105.0
Furnishings (12/77 = 100)	105.7	110.8	111.5	111.9	111.5	110.9	112.0	105.5	110.1	109.7	110.2	109.7	109.5	110.7
Suits, trousers, sport coats, and jackets (12/77 = 100)	103.4	106.5	107.4	107.8	108.2	109.5	109.8	102.6	104.7	105.8	106.2	106.6	107.7	108.2
Women's and girls'	151.8	155.5	151.5	154.6	151.5	155.1	155.5	151.2	154.8	154.5	153.5	149.9	151.3	154.9
Women's (12/77 = 100)	101.5	103.4	103.0	102.8	100.8	100.8	103.8	101.8	103.3	103.0	102.3	100.1	101.4	103.7
Coats and jackets	169.3	173.9	173.3	170.0	166.4	163.1	167.6	175.5	174.1	172.4	167.9	165.0	162.4	167.0
Dresses	164.3	167.2	164.3	165.3	161.3	160.6	169.3	158.7	159.1	156.8	155.7	150.0	151.2	157.5
Separates and sportswear (12/77 = 100)	100.0	99.6	98.6	98.6	96.1	97.1	99.8	98.6	100.4	100.7	99.5	97.1	99.2	101.0
Underwear, nightwear, and hosiery (12/77 = 100)	104.2	106.6	108.1	108.2	108.6	110.2	110.0	104.8	107.9	108.9	109.3	109.1	110.6	115.5
Suits (12/77 = 100)	92.2	95.2	95.8	95.8	91.0	88.2	91.6	97.5	99.9	97.5	98.1	94.0	96.8	100.2
Girls' (12/77 = 100)	98.3	97.1	102.8	100.3	100.5	98.9	101.8	95.3	101.5	101.7	101.4	97.9	97.3	100.1
Coats, jackets, dresses, and suits (12/77 = 100)	99.3	103.6	103.9	100.3	97.5	95.7	97.7	95.2	97.9	97.3	97.7	97.9	92.6	100.1
Separates and sportswear (12/77 = 100)	94.4	102.8	102.6	100.6	99.9	98.2	98.9	95.2	97.9	104.3	102.9	99.8	98.1	99.8
Underwear, nightwear, hosiery, and accessories (12/77 = 100)	103.8	106.7	107.2	107.3	106.1	105.6	108.4	102.5	103.9	104.2	104.4	104.4	103.5	107.8

CONSUMER PRICE INDEX—U.S. CITY AVERAGE (continued)

General summary	All Urban Consumers Mar.	1979 Oct.	1979 Nov.	1979 Dec.	1980 Jan.	1980 Feb.	1980 Mar.	Urban Wage Earners and Clerical Workers (revised) Mar.	1979 Oct.	1979 Nov.	1979 Dec.	1980 Jan.	1980 Feb.	1980 Mar.
APPAREL AND UPKEEP – Continued														
Apparel commodities – Continued														
Apparel commodities less footwear – Continued														
Infants' and toddlers'	216.1	224.8	226.3	227.1	224.9	226.6	231.4	217.7	228.7	228.7	230.5	229.1	232.7	237.3
Other apparel commodities	166.6	175.5	177.8	180.9	184.4	191.4	199.9	168.9	178.7	179.8	182.9	185.5	191.8	197.8
Sewing materials and notions (12/77 = 100)	102.5	102.2	100.8	102.4	103.2	106.3	107.1	101.4	100.8	99.7	100.8	101.2	105.7	107.2
Jewelry and luggage (12/77 = 100)	109.9	118.3	121.0	123.1	126.1	131.2	138.6	112.8	122.3	123.8	126.2	128.4	132.3	137.2
Footwear	171.6	182.6	183.8	184.3	183.7	184.6	187.0	170.4	181.9	183.2	183.8	183.3	183.9	186.3
Men's (12/77 = 100)	109.2	116.7	117.7	117.3	117.8	118.3	119.0	109.2	118.0	119.1	119.4	119.3	119.4	120.9
Boys' and girls' (12/77 = 100)	107.3	113.0	114.0	115.8	117.3	117.9	119.5	106.4	113.0	114.5	114.7	116.9	118.0	119.5
Womens' (12/77 = 100)	106.4	113.5	113.9	113.8	111.6	112.1	114.2	105.0	111.1	111.2	111.8	109.4	109.5	110.9
Apparel services	200.0	212.5	214.2	216.6	220.7	222.9	225.9	199.0	210.8	212.0	213.4	216.9	219.8	223.5
Laundry and drycleaning other than coin operated (12/77 = 100)	116.4	125.2	126.3	127.1	129.3	130.6	132.5	115.8	124.7	125.7	126.6	129.0	130.6	132.3
Other apparel services (12/77 = 100)	109.8	114.0	114.7	117.0	119.6	120.7	122.1	109.6	112.9	113.3	113.7	115.1	116.9	119.6
TRANSPORTATION	198.1	222.7	224.9	227.7	233.5	239.6	243.7	198.7	223.4	225.7	228.3	234.1	240.2	244.3
Private	198.1	223.1	225.0	227.5	233.5	239.8	244.0	198.5	223.7	225.7	228.2	234.1	240.4	244.6
New cars	162.7	167.5	170.6	171.7	173.9	175.3	175.0	162.4	167.4	170.9	171.7	174.1	175.4	175.4
Used cars	195.4	199.9	198.2	198.2	197.2	195.3	195.2	194.5	199.9	198.4	198.3	197.2	195.3	195.2
Gasoline	220.6	303.8	306.9	313.9	334.6	357.6	370.9	221.2	305.2	308.3	315.6	335.9	359.0	372.7
Automobile maintenance and repair	236.3	249.1	250.8	252.6	255.1	258.2	260.9	236.8	249.4	251.1	253.4	256.2	258.2	261.7
Body work (12/77 = 100)	113.1	120.6	121.6	123.3	125.0	126.5	127.3	114.0	120.4	121.7	123.1	124.3	126.1	127.2
Automobile drive train, brake, and miscellaneous mechanical repair (12/77 = 100)	113.0	119.4	120.1	120.6	121.8	123.2	124.1	113.9	120.2	120.8	121.8	123.6	124.8	126.1
Maintenance and servicing (12/77 = 100)	112.3	117.5	118.4	119.2	120.2	121.3	123.1	111.8	117.3	118.2	119.3	120.4	121.3	122.8
Power plant repair (12/77 = 100)	111.5	117.8	118.5	119.2	120.4	122.5	123.5	111.8	118.0	118.6	119.6	120.9	123.1	124.0
Other private transportation	193.4	203.7	205.5	207.5	209.8	212.6	216.5	193.9	204.0	206.3	208.4	206.6	213.6	217.1
Other private transportation commodities	169.0	182.0	183.4	185.6	184.4	191.2	192.7	170.0	181.6	183.9	186.4	188.0	191.7	193.2
Motor oil, coolant, and other products (12/77 = 100)	107.8	115.9	117.4	118.1	120.9	123.9	126.4	107.4	115.9	118.1	119.3	122.4	124.0	126.1
Automobile parts and equipment (12/77 = 100)	109.4	117.9	118.7	120.3	121.9	123.5	124.3	110.3	117.6	119.0	120.6	121.4	123.9	124.7
Tires	150.7	160.7	161.5	163.8	165.8	168.5	170.1	151.3	161.1	163.0	165.7	166.3	170.6	172.5
Other parts and equipment (12/77 = 100)	110.2	121.8	123.0	124.4	126.6	127.3	127.2	112.2	120.0	121.5	122.4	124.0	125.0	124.4

Other private transportation services	225.7	221.5	218.7	216.3	214.3	211.9	202.2	225.0	220.4	217.6	215.3	213.4	211.4	201.8
Automobile insurance	243.8	239.7	236.8	235.2	233.9	233.7	223.5	244.0	240.2	237.1	235.3	233.9	233.8	223.4
Automobile finance charges (12/77 = 100)	135.2	131.3	129.4	126.5	124.1	119.4	112.0	137.4	132.1	129.9	127.2	124.6	120.4	112.6
Automobile rental, registration, and other fees (12/77 = 100)	111.6	110.9	109.8	109.2	108.9	108.6	105.6	110.8	109.8	109.1	108.5	108.3	107.9	105.3
State registration	145.5	145.3	144.1	144.0	144.0	143.9	143.7	145.3	145.2	144.2	144.1	144.1	144.0	143.9
Drivers' license (12/77 = 100)	104.4	104.5	104.5	104.2	104.2	104.2	104.3	104.7	104.8	104.7	104.5	104.5	104.5	104.5
Vehicle inspection (12/77 = 100)	120.2	119.7	118.3	118.3	116.5	115.5	112.8	119.7	119.0	117.5	117.5	115.6	114.6	112.0
Other vehicle related fees (12/77 = 100)	127.0	125.4	123.8	122.2	121.3	120.8	112.7	122.0	119.6	118.8	117.6	117.1	116.4	110.1
Public	226.1	223.9	221.9	219.1	214.0	207.3	192.1	232.1	229.5	226.8	223.0	216.5	209.1	191.5
Airline fare	259.3	255.2	251.0	245.8	232.4	220.7	191.4	259.9	255.4	251.1	245.5	232.1	220.6	191.8
Intercity bus fare	290.2	288.2	284.8	282.3	279.9	275.5	247.3	290.7	288.5	284.7	282.2	279.8	276.0	248.0
Intracity mass transit	198.6	197.6	196.7	195.7	195.1	191.0	186.6	200.8	199.7	198.5	196.4	195.6	191.3	186.8
Taxi fare	251.2	249.3	248.9	243.9	242.4	238.7	215.6	245.6	244.0	243.1	238.5	237.0	233.6	211.1
Intercity train fare	237.1	237.0	237.1	236.6	232.1	221.4	201.9	237.2	237.2	237.2	236.3	231.0	221.1	201.4
MEDICAL CARE	260.9	258.7	254.9	251.7	249.1	247.2	233.7	260.2	257.9	253.9	250.7	248.0	245.9	233.9
Medical care commodities	164.4	162.7	161.0	159.9	158.5	157.4	151.7	163.5	162.1	160.5	159.2	157.8	156.6	150.7
Prescription drugs	152.0	150.7	148.8	147.4	146.2	145.2	139.9	150.9	149.8	147.9	146.4	145.5	144.5	139.2
Anti-infective drugs (12/77 = 100)	120.1	119.8	118.2	116.8	115.5	114.8	110.5	117.9	117.2	115.8	114.6	113.9	113.5	109.7
Tranquilizers and sedatives (12/77 = 100)	122.2	121.0	119.7	118.3	116.9	115.6	112.8	122.2	121.3	119.9	118.4	117.1	115.8	112.6
Circulatones and diuretics (12/77 = 100)	114.7	114.2	113.0	112.3	111.6	110.6	108.2	113.3	113.4	112.4	111.4	111.0	109.7	106.8
Hormones, diabetic drugs, biologicals, and prescription and supplies (12/77 = 100)	129.6	127.8	124.8	123.1	122.6	122.2	115.5	130.0	128.7	126.0	123.8	123.2	122.5	116.1
Pain and symptom control drugs (12/77 = 100)	121.3	120.1	119.0	118.2	117.5	116.3	111.1	120.5	119.7	118.8	117.8	116.8	115.6	110.6
Supplements, cough and cold preparations, and respiratory agents (12/77 = 100)	116.5	115.2	114.2	113.7	112.8	112.6	109.1	115.5	113.7	112.6	112.1	111.9	111.3	107.9
Nonprescription drugs and medical supplies (12/77 = 100)	118.0	116.6	115.6	115.1	114.0	113.2	109.0	117.3	116.3	115.3	114.6	113.4	112.5	108.1
Eyeglasses (12/77 = 100)	114.5	112.6	111.4	110.5	110.4	110.0	106.1	114.1	112.9	111.5	110.9	110.9	110.2	105.5
Internal and respiratory over-the-counter drugs	183.0	180.8	179.0	178.5	176.6	175.2	168.5	182.2	180.4	179.1	177.9	175.4	173.7	166.8
Nonprescription medical equipment and supplies (12/77 = 100)	116.1	115.6	115.0	114.2	112.7	111.8	108.1	115.1	114.6	113.8	113.1	111.8	111.0	107.4
Medical care services	282.2	279.8	275.6	271.8	268.8	266.8	251.3	281.5	279.0	274.4	270.7	267.6	265.3	251.8
Professional services	247.8	245.5	241.7	238.3	235.9	234.9	222.7	245.3	242.9	238.9	235.9	233.0	231.6	221.7
Physicians' services	266.2	264.1	260.3	256.5	255.5	254.4	238.2	262.3	260.2	256.0	252.5	250.8	249.7	237.5
Dental services	235.7	233.4	229.5	226.1	222.7	221.2	212.2	234.1	231.5	227.4	224.5	220.7	218.5	210.3
Other professional services (12/77 = 100)	119.3	117.4	115.9	114.8	112.2	112.1	108.8	119.5	118.1	116.6	115.1	112.8	112.7	108.9
Other medical care services	324.4	322.1	317.3	313.0	309.3	305.9	286.1	325.3	322.7	317.4	312.8	309.5	306.2	288.2
Hospital and other medical services (12/77 = 100)	127.7	126.8	124.9	123.2	121.8	120.5	113.7	128.8	127.8	125.6	123.8	122.6	121.3	114.7
Hospital room	401.2	398.8	393.9	388.7	383.6	379.4	358.5	405.8	403.4	395.3	389.4	385.1	380.2	361.3
Other hospital and medical care services	126.9	125.9	123.8	122.1	120.8	119.5	112.7	127.8	126.5	124.7	122.9	122.0	120.8	113.9

CONSUMER PRICE INDEX—U.S. CITY AVERAGE (concluded)

General summary	All Urban Consumers							Urban Wage Earners and Clerical Workers (revised)						
	1979	1979	1979	1979	1980	1980	1980	1979	1979	1979	1979	1980	1980	1980
	Mar.	Oct.	Nov.	Dec.	Jan.	Feb.	Mar.	Mar.	Oct.	Nov.	Dec.	Jan.	Feb.	Mar.
ENTERTAINMENT	184.8	192.0	192.8	193.4	195.3	197.8	200.6	184.0	191.4	192.0	192.3	193.9	196.2	199.5
Entertainment commodities	185.7	193.1	194.0	195.2	197.6	200.4	203.4	184.4	190.7	191.3	192.4	194.2	196.9	200.3
Reading materials (12/77 = 100)	108.6	113.8	114.5	115.1	116.7	117.4	119.4	108.3	113.3	114.2	114.8	116.2	117.0	119.1
Newspapers	209.7	217.7	222.4	223.5	226.8	227.7	232.4	209.3	217.4	222.2	223.3	226.4	227.3	232.0
Magazines, periodicals, and books (12/77 = 100)	110.9	117.2	116.0	116.8	118.1	119.2	120.8	110.9	117.2	115.8	116.6	117.8	118.9	120.7
Sporting goods and equipment (12/77 = 100)	106.6	111.2	111.7	112.2	113.8	115.9	117.2	104.4	106.7	106.9	107.7	108.6	108.8	112.4
Sport vehicles (12/77 = 100)	107.0	111.5	.....	112.9	.....	117.4	118.7	104.2	104.6	104.6	105.8	.....	109.1	110.8
Indoor and warm weather sport equipment (12/77 = 100)	105.1	107.5	107.8	107.5	107.6	108.3	109.5	103.1	106.0	106.1	106.3	106.4	107.8	109.3
Bicycles	157.3	167.1	167.1	167.1	170.5	174.5	177.2	156.5	166.9	167.4	167.0	170.5	174.9	177.8
Other sporting goods and equipment (12/77 = 100)	104.9	110.0	110.3	111.0	111.8	112.4	112.9	103.8	109.8	110.2	111.3	111.9	112.6	113.4
Toys, hobbies, and other entertainment (12/77 = 100)	107.1	110.8	111.2	112.1	113.2	115.1	116.9	107.3	111.0	111.2	111.8	112.6	114.3	116.4
Toys, hobbies, and music equipment (12/77 = 100)	108.1	110.7	110.5	111.2	112.1	114.1	115.7	107.7	110.1	109.8	109.9	110.9	112.3	114.9
Photographic supplies and equipment (12/77 = 100)	106.3	109.4	109.9	109.7	110.8	114.1	118.2	105.8	109.3	109.6	110.1	111.2	114.2	116.9
Pet supplies and expense (12/77 = 100)	106.0	112.1	113.5	115.5	116.8	117.6	118.2	107.3	113.9	114.6	116.1	116.7	117.9	119.0
Entertainment services	183.9	190.8	191.5	191.1	192.5	194.5	197.0	184.3	193.5	194.3	193.0	194.4	196.0	199.1
Fees for participant sports (12/77 = 100)	108.4	113.2	113.8	113.8	114.6	116.0	117.5	108.3	114.9	115.2	115.0	115.6	116.3	118.8
Admissions (12/77 = 100)	112.3	115.7	116.1	116.6	117.9	118.3	119.1	111.7	116.8	117.3	117.8	119.4	119.7	120.2
Other entertainment services (12/77 = 100)	106.8	110.0	110.0	108.6	109.1	111.4	113.2	107.3	111.4	112.0	109.0	109.3	111.8	113.9
OTHER GOODS AND SERVICES	192.8	202.3	202.9	204.0	206.3	208.1	208.9	192.6	201.4	202.0	203.0	206.0	207.7	208.3

	185.8	191.3	191.5	192.1	196.7	198.1	198.4	185.8	191.2	191.4	192.1	197.1	198.3	198.6
Tobacco products														
Cigarettes	188.4	193.8	194.0	194.7	199.7	200.9	201.2	188.6	193.9	194.1	194.8	200.3	201.3	201.6
Other tobacco products and smoking accessories (12/77 = 100)	108.9	113.0	112.8	113.2	113.9	115.6	116.3	108.1	112.3	112.4	112.7	113.4	114.8	115.7
Personal care	192.1	199.8	200.9	203.0	204.2	206.5	208.1	191.5	199.4	200.5	203.3	204.4	206.6	207.7
Toilet goods and personal care appliances	186.1	192.5	193.1	195.8	196.4	198.6	200.2	185.9	191.6	192.4	194.5	196.2	198.3	199.6
Products for the hair, hairpieces and wigs (12/77 = 100)	105.9	111.9	112.2	113.0	114.2	116.1	116.6	105.5	111.1	111.4	112.4	114.0	114.9	114.9
Dental and shaving products (12/77 = 100)	110.6	114.1	115.6	117.3	117.8	118.6	119.2	109.3	112.7	113.9	114.7	115.3	116.8	118.4
Cosmetics, bath and nail preparations, manicure and eye makeup implements (12/77 = 100)	108.6	110.7	111.4	113.0	112.9	114.2	115.1	107.9	110.1	110.2	112.1	112.9	114.0	114.8
Other toilet goods and small personal care appliances (12/77 = 100)	107.7	110.9	109.9	112.1	112.1	112.9	114.7	110.1	111.7	112.3	113.1	114.0	115.6	116.6
Personal care services	197.9	207.0	208.5	210.0	211.6	214.2	215.7	197.3	207.3	208.6	210.2	212.7	215.0	215.8
Beauty parlor services for women	199.6	208.3	210.3	212.1	213.3	216.1	217.9	199.6	209.1	210.2	212.0	214.2	216.6	217.8
Haircuts and other barber shop services for men (12/77 = 100)	110.3	115.9	116.1	116.8	118.1	119.3	119.7	109.3	115.4	116.3	117.1	118.8	120.0	120.1
Personal and educational expenses	208.1	224.0	224.2	224.6	226.3	228.0	228.3	208.6	224.2	224.4	224.8	226.2	227.8	228.2
School books and supplies	191.6	202.3	202.3	202.5	206.0	206.5	206.9	194.1	205.8	205.9	206.0	209.8	210.4	210.7
Personal and educational services	212.5	229.4	229.6	229.9	231.4	233.3	233.6	212.5	229.0	229.3	229.7	230.6	232.5	232.9
Tuition and other school fees	108.6	118.1	118.1	118.1	118.3	118.5	118.6	108.5	118.2	118.2	118.2	118.4	118.6	118.7
College tuition (12/77 = 100)	108.8	117.3	117.3	117.3	117.6	117.8	117.9	108.8	117.3	117.3	117.3	117.6	117.8	117.9
Elementary and high school tuition (12/77 = 100)	107.5	120.9	120.9	120.9	120.9	120.9	120.9	107.4	120.7	120.7	120.7	120.7	120.7	120.7
Personal expenses (12/77 = 100)	110.6	115.8	116.3	117.3	120.1	124.4	125.0	110.6	114.9	115.5	116.3	117.7	121.4	122.1
Special indexes:														
Gasoline, motor oil, coolant, and other products	218.7	299.8	302.9	309.7	329.9	352.5	365.5	219.2	301.2	304.3	311.4	331.3	353.8	367.2
Insurance and finance	257.1	288.9	296.0	302.1	310.5	316.7	326.3	257.1	288.5	295.8	301.6	310.0	316.2	325.6
Utilities and public transportation	205.1	220.7	220.5	223.5	225.0	227.9	230.9	205.3	220.7	220.3	223.0	224.4	227.2	230.2
Housekeeping and home maintenance services	262.5	278.7	280.6	282.2	284.7	287.6	292.0	262.7	279.9	281.3	283.4	266.0	288.7	292.0

Source: *Monthly Labor Review*, U.S. Department of Labor, Bureau of Labor Statistics.

CONSUMER PRICES

INDEX, 1967=100 (RATIO SCALE)

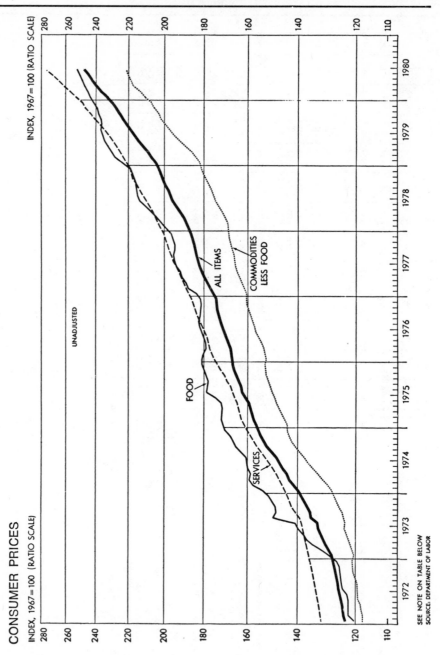

INDEX, 1967=100 (RATIO SCALE)

UNADJUSTED

ALL ITEMS

COMMODITIES LESS FOOD

FOOD

SERVICES

SEE NOTE ON TABLE BELOW
SOURCE: DEPARTMENT OF LABOR

[1967=100]

Period	Unadjusted — All items	Unadjusted — Food	Unadjusted — Commodities less food	Unadjusted — Services	Seasonally adjusted — All commodities	SA Food — All	SA Food — Food at home	SA Food — Food away from home	SA Commodities less food — All	SA Commodities less food — Durable	SA Commodities less food — Non-durable	SA — Services
1972	125.3	123.5	119.4	133.3	120.9	123.5	121.6	131.1	119.4	118.9	119.8	133.3
1973	133.1	141.4	123.5	139.1	129.9	141.4	141.4	141.4	123.5	121.9	124.8	139.1
1974	147.7	161.7	136.6	152.1	145.5	161.7	162.4	159.4	136.6	130.6	140.9	152.1
1975	161.2	175.4	149.6	166.6	158.2	175.4	175.8	174.3	149.1	145.5	151.7	166.6
1976	170.5	180.8	156.6	180.4	165.2	180.8	179.5	186.1	156.6	154.3	158.3	180.4
1977	181.5	192.2	165.1	194.3	174.7	192.2	190.2	200.3	165.1	163.2	166.5	194.3
1978	195.4	211.4	174.7	210.9	187.1	211.4	210.2	218.4	174.7	173.9	174.3	210.9
1979	217.4	234.5	195.1	234.2	208.4	234.5	232.9	242.9	195.1	191.1	198.7	234.2
1979: June	216.6	235.4	194.7	232.1	207.4	234.2	232.4	242.2	193.7	190.0	197.2	232.6
July	218.9	236.9	197.0	234.7	209.6	235.3	233.0	244.3	196.2	191.5	201.1	235.1
Aug	221.1	236.3	199.5	237.6	211.5	235.5	232.5	246.1	198.7	193.1	205.2	237.7
Sept	223.4	237.1	201.8	240.7	214.0	237.9	235.4	247.5	201.2	194.2	208.6	240.5
Oct	225.4	238.2	203.4	243.6	215.8	239.8	237.1	249.9	202.9	195.7	210.3	243.5
Nov	227.5	239.1	205.4	246.2	217.9	241.4	238.5	252.0	205.1	198.4	212.0	246.1
Dec	229.9	241.7	207.2	249.3	220.4	244.8	242.3	254.4	207.3	200.3	215.0	249.5
1980: Jan	233.2	243.8	210.4	253.1	223.5	244.8	241.8	256.9	211.5	202.5	221.8	252.9
Feb	236.4	244.9	213.8	256.8	226.1	244.7	240.9	258.6	215.2	203.5	228.4	256.8
Mar	239.8	247.3	216.7	261.3	228.8	247.1	243.5	260.6	217.9	204.0	233.8	261.6
Apr	242.5	249.1	218.6	265.3	230.0	248.4	244.5	262.5	219.0	205.1	235.1	265.6
May	244.9	250.4	220.2	269.2	230.8	249.2	245.1	263.8	219.8	206.3	235.5	269.8
June	247.6	252.0	221.4	274.2	231.6	250.5	246.0	266.1	220.4	207.4	235.8	274.7

NOTE.—Data beginning January 1978 relate to all urban consumers. Earlier data relate to urban wage earners and clerical workers.

Source: Department of Labor, Bureau of Labor Statistics.
Source: Economic Indicators, Council of Economic Advisers.

CONSUMER PRICE INDEX—U.S. CITY AVERAGE, AND SELECTED AREAS

1967 = 100 UNLESS OTHERWISE SPECIFIED

Area[1]	All Urban Consumers							Urban Wage Earners and Clerical Workers (revised)						
	1979 Mar.	Oct.	Nov.	Dec.	1980 Jan.	Feb.	Mar.	1979 Mar.	Oct.	Nov.	Dec.	1980 Jan.	Feb.	Mar.
U.S. city average[2]	209.1	225.4	227.5	229.9	233.2	236.4	239.8	209.3	225.6	227.6	230.0	233.3	236.5	239.9
Anchorage, Alaska (10/67=100)	201.0	...	213.7	223.3	218.2	...	223.5	200.5	...	211.8	227.0	215.9	...	220.2
Atlanta, Ga.	...	220.8	...	223.3	...	230.3	...	...	223.5	...	227.0	...	233.5	...
Baltimore, Md.	209.1	...	227.2	...	234.4	...	245.0	210.4	...	227.9	...	234.5	...	243.9
Boston, Mass.	205.1	...	222.7	221.2	227.3	227.9	234.2	204.3	...	222.5	220.7	226.9	227.9	234.2
Buffalo, N.Y.	...	218.7	...	221.2	...	227.9	...	...	218.6	...	220.7	...	227.9	...
Chicago, Ill.-Northwestern Ind.	206.6	221.8	225.9	228.4	230.3	232.7	235.5	206.2	221.7	225.6	227.8	229.9	232.5	235.2
Cincinnati, Ohio-Ky.-Ind.	215.7	...	233.4	...	239.5	...	247.8	216.7	...	235.6	...	241.0	...	249.7
Cleveland, Ohio	...	224.7	...	232.5	...	243.5	...	...	225.5	...	233.2	...	244.1	...
Dallas-Ft. Worth, Tex.	...	228.2	...	234.1	...	241.7	...	...	228.0	...	233.3	...	240.9	...
Denver-Boulder, Colo.	223.0	...	245.9	...	247.3	...	255.2	225.0	...	248.6	...	250.9	...	259.4
Detroit, Mich.	211.6	227.2	231.3	233.2	237.2	240.4	242.9	211.6	226.9	230.8	232.2	236.4	239.9	242.4
Honolulu, Hawaii	...	210.5	...	214.8	...	220.9	...	...	211.1	...	215.5	...	221.3	...
Houston, Tex.	...	244.2	...	248.7	...	255.9	...	...	241.8	...	246.0	...	251.9	...
Kansas City, Mo.-Kansas	...	229.9	...	233.7	...	238.7	...	...	227.9	...	232.4	...	236.6	...
Los Angeles-Long Beach, Anaheim, Calif.	203.8	221.8	224.2	228.0	232.6	237.6	241.3	204.4	224.0	225.8	229.9	235.0	240.0	243.9
Miami, Fla. (11/77=100)	111.2	...	119.4	...	123.3	...	127.7	112.4	...	120.5	...	124.9	...	128.8
Milwaukee, Wis.	207.6	...	229.8	229.2	236.4	235.5	242.7	209.5	...	232.5	229.7	240.8	235.9	247.8
Minneapolis-St. Paul, Minn.-Wis.	206.4	231.2	221.3	234.0	226.1	237.9	231.2	206.3	233.0	220.7	234.8	225.5	239.6	230.8
New York, N.Y.-Northeastern N.J.	203.5	219.9	220.0	222.9	224.4	228.0	229.0	206.3	219.3	221.1	222.4	225.8	227.7	231.3
Northeast, Pa. (Scranton)	...	...	...	...	...	...	...	206.6	...	221.1	...	225.8	...	235.1
Philadelphia, Pa.-N.J.	204.8	220.1	222.4	223.7	227.2	231.1	234.6	206.8	221.3	223.8	224.6	228.0	231.6	235.1
Pittsburgh, Pa.	...	226.0	...	229.2	...	235.5	...	...	226.1	...	229.7	...	235.9	...
Portland, Oreg.-Wash.	215.4	...	236.6	...	244.6	...	253.6	215.8	...	236.7	...	243.5	...	251.7
St. Louis, Mo.-Ill.	208.4	...	225.7	...	232.7	...	238.1	207.0	...	226.3	...	233.5	...	238.5
San Diego, Calif.	221.4	...	247.8	...	254.0	...	258.3	218.6	...	244.8	...	251.0	...	255.6
San Francisco-Oakland, Calif.	...	221.5	...	230.2	...	240.7	...	...	220.8	...	229.0	...	240.0	...
Seattle-Everett, Wash.	207.0	...	227.6	...	236.0	...	243.8	205.8	...	225.5	...	233.8	...	241.3
Washington, D.C.-Md.-Va.	212.6	...	225.4	...	231.9	...	238.8	213.4	...	226.7	...	233.0	...	239.2

[1] The areas listed include not only the central city but the entire portion of the Standard Metropolitan Statistical Area, as defined for the 1970 Census of Population, except that the Standard Consolidated Area is used for New York and Chicago.

[2] Average of 85 cities.

Source: *Monthly Labor Review*, U.S. Department of Labor, Bureau of Labor Statistics.

Economic Indicators

COMPOSITE INDEXES AND THEIR COMPONENTS

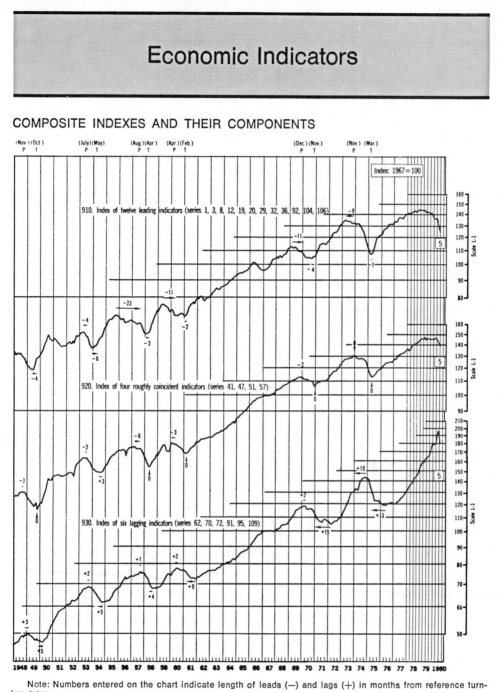

Note: Numbers entered on the chart indicate length of leads (—) and lags (+) in months from reference turning dates.

Source: *Business Conditions Digest*, U.S. Department of Commerce, Bureau of Economic Analysis.

SUMMARY OF RECENT DATA AND CURRENT CHANGES FOR PRINCIPAL INDICATORS

Series number	Series title	Timing classification[3]	Unit of measure	Avg. 1978	Avg. 1979	3d Q 1979	4th Q 1979	1st Q 1980	Mar. 1980	Apr. 1980	May 1980	Mar. to Apr. 1980	Apr. to May 1980	3d Q to 4th Q 1979	4th Q 1979 to 1st Q 1980
	I. CYCLICAL INDICATORS														
	A. Composite Indexes														
910	Twelve leading indicators	L,L,L	1967=100	141.8	140.1	140.4	136.4	134.1	131.8	126.4	123.4	-4.1	-2.4	-2.8	-1.7
920	Four coincident indicators	C,C,C	....do....	140.1	145.0	144.9	144.9	144.7	143.1	140.4	138.3	-1.9	-1.5	0.	-0.1
930	Six lagging indicators	Lg,Lg,Lg	....do....	143.1	166.4	167.2	177.6	183.3	190.4	196.1	179.3	3.0	-8.6	6.2	3.2
	Leading Indicator Subgroups:														
913	Marginal employment adjustments	L,L,L	....do....	98.1	96.7	95.9	96.3	95.7	94.3	90.0	88.1	-4.6	-2.1	0.4	-0.6
914	Capital investment commitments	L,L,L	....do....	115.7	113.6	113.7	112.8	111.8	109.7	106.6	106.2	-2.8	-0.4	-0.8	-0.9
915	Inventory investment and purchasing	L,L,L	....do....	106.2	105.9	105.5	102.7	102.1	101.6	99.9	97.4	-1.7	-2.5	-2.7	-0.6
916	Profitability	L,L,L	....do....	93.2	91.7	91.8	90.4	NA	NA	NA	NA	NA	NA	-1.5	NA
917	Money and financial flows	L,L,L	....do....	149.0	145.3	147.6	140.2	137.8	137.9	135.1	133.8	-2.0	-1.0	-5.0	-1.7
	B. Cyclical Indicators by Economic Process														
	B1. Employment and Unemployment														
	Marginal Employment Adjustments:														
*1	Average workweek, prod. workers, mfg.	L,L,L	Hours.	40.4	40.2	40.2	40.2	40.1	39.8	39.6	39.4	-0.5	-0.5	0.	-0.2
21	Avg. weekly overtime, prod. workers, mfg.[2]	L,C,L	....do....	3.6	3.3	3.8	3.2	3.2	3.2	3.0	2.9	-0.3	-0.1	0.2	0.
2	Accession rate, per 100 employees, mfg.[2]	L,L,L	Percent.	4.1	3.9	3.8	3.8	3.9	3.6	3.0	2.6	-0.6	-0.1	0.2	-0.1
5	Avg. weekly initial claims (inverted[4])	L,C,L	Thousands.	339	381	391	404	406	440	569	635	-29.3	-11.6	-3.3	-0.5
*3	Layoff rate, per 100 employ., mfg. (inv.[4])[2]	L,L,L	Percent.	0.9	1.1	1.3	1.2	1.4	1.5	2.8	3.5	-1.3	-0.7	0.1	-0.2
4	Quit rate, per 100 employees, mfg.[2]	L,Lg,U	....do....	2.1	2.0	1.9	2.0	2.0	1.9	1.6	1.4	-0.3	-0.2	0.1	0.
	Job Vacancies:														
60	Ratio, help-wanted advertising to persons unemployed[2]	L,Lg,U	Ratio.	0.738	0.786	0.775	0.789	0.699	0.670	0.500	0.409	-0.170	-0.091	0.014	-0.090
46	Help-wanted advertising	L,Lg,U	1967=100.	149	158	156	161	150	145	122	112	-15.9	-8.2	3.2	-6.8
	Comprehensive Employment:														
48	Employee hours in nonagri. establishments	U,C,C	A.r., bil. hrs.	164.08	169.13	169.55	170.21	171.34	170.93	169.70	168.81	-0.7	-0.5	0.4	0.7
42	Persons engaged in nonagri. activities	U,C,C	Thousands.	91,031	93,648	93,915	94,319	94,486	94,298	93,912	93,609	-0.4	-0.3	0.4	0.2
*41	Employees on nonagri. payrolls	C,C,C	....do....	86,446	89,497	89,759	90,108	90,772	90,819	90,508	90,328	-0.3	-0.2	0.4	0.7
40	Employees in mfg., mining, construction	L,C,U	....do....	25,597	26,579	26,638	26,587	26,705	26,600	26,210	25,693	-1.5	-2.0	-0.2	0.4
90	Ratio, civilian employment to total population of working age[2]	U,Lg,U	Percent.	53.59	59.25	59.33	59.31	59.17	59.00	58.63	58.47	-0.37	-0.16	-0.02	-0.14
	Comprehensive Unemployment:														
37	Total unemployed (inverted[4])	L,Lg,U	Thousands.	6,047	5,963	6,008	6,084	6,390	6,438	7,265	8,154	-12.8	-12.2	-1.3	-5.0
43	Unemployment rate, total (inverted[4])[2]	L,Lg,U	Percent.	6.0	5.8	5.8	5.9	6.1	6.2	7.0	7.8	-0.8	-0.8	-0.1	-0.2
45	Avg. weekly insured unemploy. rate (inv.[4])[2]	L,Lg,U	....do....	3.2	3.0	2.9	3.0	3.2	3.3	3.7	4.3	-0.4	-0.6	-0.1	-0.2
*91	Avg. duration of unemployment (inverted[4])	Lg,Lg,Lg	Weeks.	11.9	10.8	10.5	10.5	10.7	11.0	11.3	10.5	-2.7	7.1	0.	-1.9
44	Unemploy. rate, 15 weeks and over (inv.[4])[2]	Lg,Lg,Lg	Percent.	1.4	1.2	1.1	1.2	1.3	1.3	1.6	1.6	-0.3	0.	-0.1	-0.1

Note: Columns grouped under "Basic data[1]" (Average 1978–1979; 3d Q 1979; 4th Q 1979; 1st Q 1980; Mar., Apr., May 1980) and "Percent change" (Mar. to Apr. 1980; Apr. to May 1980; 3d Q to 4th Q 1979; 4th Q 1979 to 1st Q 1980).

B2. Production and Income

Comprehensive Output and Income:

No.	Series	Unit	Code												
50	GNP in 1972 dollars	A.r., bil. dol.	C,C,C	1399.2	1431.6	1433.3	1440.3	1444.7	1174.1	1165.8	1161.6	...	...	0.5	0.3
52	Personal income in 1972 dollars	....do.	C,C,C	1145.2	1178.3	1179.3	1186.6	1182.2	1017.5	1009.3	1003.9	-0.7	-0.4	0.6	-0.4
*51	Pers. income less transfer pay., 1972 dollars	....do.	C,C,C	995.7	1024.1	1021.3	1029.1	1024.3	...	...	...	-0.8	-0.5	0.8	-0.5
53	Wages and salaries in mining, mfg., and construction, 1972 dollars	....do.	C,C,C	243.5	246.0	243.9	241.5	238.5	236.5	231.5	227.7	-2.1	-1.6	-1.0	-1.2

Industrial Production:

No.	Series	Unit	Code												
*47	Industrial production, total	1967=100	C,C,C	146.1	152.2	152.3	152.2	152.2	151.6	148.6	145.5	-2.0	-2.1	-0.1	0.
73	Industrial production, durable mfrs.	....do.	C,C,C	139.7	146.3	145.8	145.1	144.0	143.2	138.9	135.0	-3.0	-2.8	-0.5	-0.8
74	Industrial production, nondurable mfrs.	....do.	C,L,L	156.9	163.9	164.3	164.4	165.2	164.3	161.8	159.6	-1.5	-1.4	-0.5	0.5
49	Value of goods output, 1972 dollars	A.r., bil. dol.	C,C,C	639.5	653.1	651.3	655.1	659.7	...	...	...	...	...	0.6	0.7

Capacity Utilization:

No.	Series	Unit	Code												
82	Capacity utilization rate, mfg., FRB[2]	Percent.	L,C,U	84.4	85.6	85.4	84.6	83.7	...	...	...	...	...	-0.8	-0.9
83	Capacity utilization rate, mfg., BEA[2]	....do.		84	82	82	81	80	...	...	...	...	...	-1	-1
84	Capacity utilization rate, materials, FRB[3]	....do.	L,C,U	85.6	87.2	87.2	86.3	85.4	...	...	...	...	...	-0.9	-0.9

B3. Consumption, Trade, Orders, and Deliveries

Orders and Deliveries:

No.	Series	Unit	Code												
6	New orders, durable goods	Bil. dol.	L,L,L	70.19	77.20	75.66	76.54	80.01	77.55	72.22	66.95	-6.9	-7.3	1.2	4.5
7	New orders, durable goods, 1972 dollars	....do.	L,L,L	41.48	41.40	40.18	39.43	39.66	38.33	35.59	33.05	-7.1	-7.1	-1.9	0.6
*8	New orders, cons. goods and mtls., 1972 dol.	....do.	L,L,L	37.16	36.50	35.77	34.87	34.78	33.15	30.34	28.64	-8.5	-5.6	-2.5	-0.3
25	Chg. in unfilled orders, durable goods[5]	....do.	L,L,L	3.68	3.26	1.52	2.05	2.33	1.62	0.02	-2.38	-1.60	-2.40	0.53	0.28
96	Mfrs.' unfilled orders, durable goods[5]	Bil. dol., EOP	L,Lg,U	228.82	267.88	261.74	267.88	274.88	274.88	274.90	272.52	0.	-0.9	2.3	2.6
32	Vendor performance[2] ⑪	Percent.	L,L,L	64	63	55	49	45	45	40	32	-5	-8	-6	-4

Consumption and Trade:

No.	Series	Unit	Code												
56	Manufacturing and trade sales	Bil. dol.	C,C,C	254.26	288.36	292.99	300.02	309.57	305.66	295.63	NA	-3.3	NA	2.4	3.2
*57	Manufacturing and trade sales, 1972 dollars	....do.	C,C,C	156.32	159.82	160.03	158.89	158.76	154.50	150.81	NA	-2.4	NA	-0.7	-0.1
75	Industrial production, consumer goods	1967=100	C,C,U	149.1	150.5	149.6	149.0	148.2	147.9	145.2	142.7	-1.8	-1.7	-0.4	-0.5
54	Sales of retail stores	Mil. dol.	C,L,U	66,741	73,837	74,886	76,385	77,997	76,534	74,774	73,658	-2.3	-1.5	2.0	2.1
59	Sales of retail stores, 1972 dollars	....do.	U,L,U	44,314	44,800	45,072	44,879	44,344	42,972	41,750	41,012	-2.8	-1.8	-0.4	-1.2
55	Personal consumption expend., autos	A.r., bil. dol.	L,C,C	68.0	69.2	67.9	66.8	71.5	56.5	52.8	51.7	...	...	-1.6	7.0
58	Index of consumer sentiment ⑩	I Q 1966=100	L,L,L	79.4	66.0	63.9	62.1	63.5	...	...	...	-6.5	-2.1	-2.8	2.3

B4. Fixed Capital Investment

Formation of Business Enterprises:

No.	Series	Unit	Code												
*12	Net business formation	1967=100	L,L,L	132.9	131.7	131.5	132.4	133.9	130.7	NA	NA	NA	NA	0.7	1.1
13	New business incorporations	Number.	L,L,L	39,996	43,714	44,084	44,956	43,887	42,630	NA	NA	NA	NA	2.0	-2.4

SUMMARY OF RECENT DATA AND CURRENT CHANGES FOR PRINCIPAL INDICATORS (continued)

Series title	Timing classification[3]	Unit of measure	Average 1978	Average 1979	3d Q 1979	4th Q 1979	1st Q 1980	Mar. 1980	Apr. 1980	May 1980	Mar. to Apr. 1980	Apr. to May 1980	3d Q to 4th Q 1979	4th Q to 1st Q 1980	Series number
I. CYCLICAL INDICATORS—Con.															
B4. Fixed Capital Investment—Con.															
Business Investment Commitments:															
10. Contracts and orders, plant and equipment	L,L,L	Bil. dol.	22.01	25.25	24.28	25.77	26.06	26.27	24.20	21.36	-7.9	-11.7	6.1	1.1	10
*20. Contr. and orders, plant and equip., 1972 dol.	L,L,L	...do...	13.60	14.54	13.65	14.51	14.23	14.13	13.01	11.70	-7.9	-10.1	6.3	-1.9	20
24. New orders, cap. goods indus., nondefense	L,L,L	...do...	18.30	21.64	21.30	21.70	22.64	22.59	22.16	19.76	-1.9	-10.8	1.9	4.3	24
27. New orders, capital goods industries, nondefense, 1972 dollars	L,L,L	...do...	11.41	12.68	12.14	12.52	12.57	12.35	12.02	10.92	-2.7	-9.2	3.1	0.4	27
9. Construction contracts, commercial and industrial buildings, floor space	L,C,U	Mil. sq. ft.	80.73	90.34	88.17	86.02	90.91	82.84	72.90	62.72	-12.0	-14.0	-2.4	5.7	9
11. New capital appropriations, mfg.	U,Lg,U	Bil. dol.	16.78	22.41	22.55	23.48	30.48	...	...	...	...	...	4.1	29.8	11
97. Backlog of capital appropriations, mfg.[5]	C,Lg,Lg	Bil. dol., EOP	63.43	77.10	73.58	77.10	85.12	...	...	...	...	...	4.8	10.4	97
Business Investment Expenditures:															
61. Business expend., new plant and equipment	C,Lg,Lg	A.r., bil. dol.	153.82	177.09	179.33	186.95	191.36	...	...	...	...	...	4.2	2.4	61
69. Machinery and equipment sales and business construction expenditures	C,Lg,Lg	...do...	230.16	270.75	276.55	282.77	299.28	299.54	289.75	NA	-3.3	NA	2.2	5.8	69
76. Industrial production, business equip.	C,Lg,U	1967=100	160.3	171.3	172.2	172.9	175.5	175.8	174.2	172.1	-0.9	-1.2	0.4	1.5	76
86. Nonresid. fixed investment, total, 1972 dol.	C,Lg,C	A.r., bil. dol.	140.1	148.8	150.7	150.5	151.2	...	...	...	...	...	-0.1	0.5	86
Residential Construction Commitments and Investment:															
28. New private housing units started, total	L,L,L	A.r., thous.	2,020	1,744	1,809	1,593	1,263	1,041	1,039	920	-0.2	-11.5	-11.9	-20.7	28
*29. New building permits, private housing	L,L,L	1967=100	145.4	123.8	131.4	108.0	91.7	78.2	63.7	66.6	-18.5	4.6	-17.8	-15.1	29
89. Fixed investment, residential, 1972 dol.	L,L,L	A.r., bil. dol.	60.1	56.7	56.5	55.8	51.7	...	...	...	...	...	-1.2	-7.3	89
B5. Inventories and Inventory Investment															
Inventory Investment:															
30. Chg. in business inventories, 1972 dol.[2]	L,L,L	...do...	14.1	9.7	7.1	1.4	0.3	...	...	...	...	...	-5.7	-1.1	30
*36. Change in inventories on hand and on order, 1972 dollars (smoothed[6])[2]	L,L,L	...do...	19.02	10.62	13.16	-7.51	-10.72	-10.64	-7.49	NA	3.15	NA	-20.67	-3.21	36
31. Chg. in book value, mfg. and trade invent.[2]	L,L,L	...do...	43.2	46.3	46.2	31.9	43.9	30.5	70.8	NA	40.3	NA	-14.3	12.0	31
38. Chg. in mtl. stocks on hand and on order[2]	L,L,L	Bil. dol.	2.05	2.5o	1.73	2.09	2.08	1.21	-0.36	NA	-1.57	NA	-0.36	-0.01	38
Inventories on Hand and on Order:															
71. Mfg. and trade inventories, total[5]	Lg,Lg,Lg	Bil. dol., EOP	380.35	426.64	418.66	426.64	439.32	439.32	445.22	NA	1.3	NA	1.9	3.0	71
*70. Mfg. and trade invent., total, 1972 dol.[5]	Lg,Lg,Lg	...do...	249.59	257.32	257.63	257.32	256.88	256.88	258.34	NA	0.6	NA	-0.1	-0.2	70
65. Mfrs.' inventories of finished goods[5]	Lg,Lg,Lg	...do...	63.88	70.53	69.87	70.53	73.94	73.94	75.76	NA	2.5	NA	0.9	4.8	65
77. Ratio, inventories to sales, mfg. and trade, constant dollars[2]	Lg,Lg,Lg	Ratio.	1.57	1.60	1.62	1.62	1.66	1.66	1.71	NA	0.05	NA	0.	0.	77
78. Materials and supplies, stocks on hand and on order[5]	L,Lg,Lg	Bil. dol., EOP	1o8.52	199.20	192.93	199.20	205.43	205.43	205.07	NA	-0.2	NA	3.2	3.1	78

B6. Prices, Costs, and Profits

Series	Code	Unit	1	2	3	4	5	6	7	8	9	10	11	12	Ref
Sensitive Commodity Prices:															
*92. Chg. in sensitive prices (smoothed⁶)²	L,L,L	Percent.	0.07	0.32	-1.17	-1.24	-0.10	1.07	2.31	2.49	2.42	2.10	2.08	1.23	92
23. Industrial materials prices ⑪	U,L,L	1967=100	3.7	3.2	-7.8	-4.7	278.5	301.9	316.9	318.5	307.1	297.6	293.0	231.0	23
Stock Prices:															
*19. Stock prices, 500 common stocks ⑩	L,L,L	1941-43=10	4.7	-0.9	4.6	-1.6	107.69	102.97	104.69	110.30	105.30	106.22	103.01	96.02	19
Profits and Profit Margins:															
16. Corporate profits after taxes	L,L,L	A.r., bil. dol.	7.6	-0.9	…	…	…	…	…	158.0	146.9	148.3	144.1	121.5	16
18. Corp. profits after taxes, 1972 dollars	L,L,L	…do.	4.8	-2.5	…	…	…	…	…	88.8	84.7	86.9	85.7	78.5	18
79. Corp. profits after taxes, with IVA and CCA	L,C,L	…do.	-9.6	-7.5	…	…	…	…	…	72.6	80.3	86.8	85.6	83.1	79
80. …do……in 1972 dol.	L,C,L	…do.	-11.7	-8.9	…	…	…	…	…	41.4	46.9	51.5	51.6	54.2	80
15. Profits (after taxes) per dol. of sales, mfg.²	L,L,L	Cents	0.2	-0.4	…	…	…	…	…	5.6	5.4	5.8	5.7	5.4	15
26. Ratio, price to unit labor cost, nonfarm bus	L,L,L	1967=100	-0.4	-0.2	…	…	…	…	…	93.6	94.0	94.2	94.3	95.6	26
Cash Flows:															
34. Net cash flow, corporate	L,L,L	A.r., bil. dol.	4.9	-0.3	…	…	…	…	…	238.8	227.7	228.3	222.3	194.1	34
35. Net cash flow, 1972 dollars	L,L,L	…do.	3.0	-2.3	…	…	…	…	…	131.3	127.5	130.5	128.8	121.5	35
Unit Labor Costs and Labor Share:															
63. Unit labor cost, private business sector	Lg,Lg,Lg	1967=100	2.9	1.9	…	…	…	…	…	227.5	221.1	217.0	214.0	194.0	63
68. Labor cost (cur. dol.) per unit of gross domestic product (1972), nonfin. corp.	Lg,Lg,Lg	Dollars	2.6	2.2	…	1.2	…	…	…	1.182	1.152	1.127	1.115	1.020	68
*62. Labor cost per unit of output, mfg.	Lg,Lg,Lg	1967=100	3.0	2.2	1.2	1.2	192.2	190.0	187.7	185.3	179.9	176.0	175.4	164.1	62
64. Compensation of employees as percent of national income²	Lg,Lg,Lg	Percent.	0.4	0.2	…	…	…	…	…	76.4	76.0	75.8	75.8	75.7	64

B7. Money and Credit

Series	Code	Unit	1	2	3	4	5	6	7	8	9	10	11	12	Ref
Money:															
85. Change in money supply (M1-B)²	L,L,L	Percent.	0.05	-0.38	1.15	-1.18	-0.03	-1.18	0.	0.41	0.36	0.74	0.60	0.66	85
102. Change in money supply (M2)²	L,C,U	…do.	0.09	-0.33	0.87	-0.53	0.72	-0.15	0.38	0.59	0.50	0.83	0.71	0.67	102
*104. Chg. in total liquid assets (smoothed⁶)²	L,L,L	…do.	-0.15	-0.25	-0.08	-0.08	0.58	-0.66	0.74	0.64	0.79	1.04	0.95	0.97	104
105. Money supply (M1-B), 1972 dollars	L,L,L	Bil. dol.	-2.5	-1.9	-0.9	-2.1	197.9	199.7	203.9	206.2	211.4	215.5	215.6	222.5	105
106. Money supply (M2), 1972 dollars	L,L,L	…do.	-2.1	-1.4	-0.1	-1.1	799.4	800.6	809.1	816.3	834.0	846.0	846.2	864.4	106
Velocity of Money:															
107. Ratio, GNP to money supply (M1-B)²	C,C,C	Ratio.	0.070	0.080	…	…	…	…	…	6.460	6.390	6.310	6.330	6.125	107
108. Ratio, pers. income to money supply (M2)²	C,Lg,C	…do.	0.010	0.016	…	…	1.326	1.333	1.333	1.332	1.322	1.306	1.310	1.273	108
Credit Flows:															
33. Change in mortgage debt²	L,L,L	A.r., bil. dol.	-3.92	-12.14	NA	-21.49	NA	47.59	69.08	73.96	77.88	90.02	86.56	90.83	33
112. Change in business loans²	L,L,L	…do.	34.21	-42.43	-41.43	3.99	-38.96	2.47	-1.52	29.93	-4.28	38.15	22.88	14.27	112
113. Change in consumer installment debt²	L,L,L	…do.	-3.36	-13.57	NA	-41.06	NA	-23.82	17.24	20.41	23.77	37.34	35.50	44.35	113
110. Total private borrowing	L,L,L	…do.	23.1	-30.3	…	…	…	…	…	364.03	295.83	424.67	358.07	346.63	110

SUMMARY OF RECENT DATA AND CURRENT CHANGES FOR PRINCIPAL INDICATORS (continued)

Series title	Unit of measure	Timing classification[3]	Basic data[1] Average 1978	Average 1979	3d Q 1979	4th Q 1979	1st Q 1980	Mar. 1980	Apr. 1980	May 1980	Percent change Mar. to Apr. 1980	Apr. to May 1980	3d Q to 4th Q 1979	4th Q to 1st Q 1980	Series number
I. CYCLICAL INDICATORS—Con.															
B7. Money and Credit—Con.															
Credit Difficulties:															
14. Liabilities of business failures (inv.[4])①	Mil. dol.	L,L,L	221.33	NA	228.61	NA	NA	NA	NA	NA	NA	NA	NA	NA	14
39. Delinquency rate, instal. loans (inv.[4])[2][5]	Percent, EOP	L,L,L	2.45	2.64	2.59	2.64	2.53	2.53	NA	NA	NA	NA	-0.05	0.11	39
Bank Reserves:															
93. Free reserves (inverted[4])①	Mil. dol.	L,U,U	-679	-1,131	-1,077	-1,527	-1,701	-2,638	-2,352	-893	-286	-1,459	450	174	93
94. Borrowing from the Federal Reserve①	do.	L,Lg,U	872	1,338	1,207	1,800	1,907	2,824	2,443	1,028	-381	-1,415	593	107	94
Interest Rates:															
119. Federal funds rate[2]①	Percent	L,Lg,Lg	7.94	11.20	10.95	13.58	15.05	17.19	17.61	10.98	0.42	-6.63	2.63	1.47	119
114. Treasury bill rate[2]①	do.	C,Lg,Lg	7.22	10.04	9.63	11.80	13.46	15.53	14.00	9.15	-1.53	-4.85	2.17	1.66	114
115. Treasury bond yields[2]①	do.	C,Lg,Lg	7.89	8.74	8.48	9.61	11.53	11.87	10.83	9.82	-1.04	-1.01	1.13	1.54	115
116. Corporate bond yields[2]①	do.	Lg,Lg,Lg	8.98	10.05	9.64	11.33	12.99	14.08	13.36	11.61	-0.72	-1.75	1.69	1.66	116
117. Municipal bond yields[2]①	do.	U,Lg,Lg	6.02	6.52	6.28	7.20	8.23	9.17	8.63	7.59	-0.54	-1.04	0.92	1.03	117
118. Mortgage yields, residential[2]①	do.	Lg,Lg,Lg	9.75	10.89	10.80	NA	NA	14.63	13.45	11.99	-1.18	-1.46	NA	NA	118
67. Bank rates on short-term bus. loans[2]①	do.	Lg,Lg,Lg	9.80	13.18	12.31	15.81	15.67	...	...	...	...	...	3.50	-0.14	67
*109. Average prime rate charged by banks[2]①	do.	Lg,Lg,Lg	9.06	12.67	12.12	15.08	16.40	18.31	19.77	16.57	1.46	-3.20	2.96	1.32	109
Outstanding Debt:															
66. Consumer installment debt[5]	Bil. dol., EOP	Lg,Lg,Lg	267.63	303.13	297.19	303.13	308.24	308.24	306.25	NA	-0.6	NA	2.0	1.7	66
*72. Commercial and industrial loans outstanding, weekly reporting large comm. banks	Bil. dol.	Lg,Lg,Lg	126.31	147.06	152.40	154.92	161.16	162.07	162.28	159.03	0.1	-2.0	1.7	4.0	72
*95. Ratio, consumer install. debt to pers. income[2]	Percent	Lg,Lg,Lg	14.34	14.99	15.07	15.04	14.90	14.89	14.82	NA	-0.07	NA	-0.03	-0.14	95
II. OTHER IMPORTANT ECONOMIC MEASURES															
B. Prices, Wages, and Productivity															
B1. Price Movements															
310. Implicit price deflator, GNP	1972=100		152.0	165.5	167.2	170.6	174.5	...	...	...	...	...	2.0	2.3	310
320. Consumer prices (CPI), all items①	1967=100		195.4	217.4	221.1	227.1	236.5	239.8	242.5	244.9	1.1	1.0	2.9	3.9	320
320c. Change in CPI, all items, S/A[2]	Percent		0.7				1.4	1.4	0.9	0.9	-0.5	0.1	0.3	0.3	320
322. CPI, food	1967=100		211.4	234.5	236.2	242.0	245.5	247.1	248.4	249.2	0.5	0.3	2.5	1.4	322
330. Producer prices (PPI), all commodities①	do.		209.3	235.6	239.1	247.5	258.7	261.5	262.3	263.7	0.3	0.5	3.5	4.5	330
331. PPI, crude materials	do.		240.2	282.2	287.1	298.2	302.5	300.7	290.3	294.1	-3.5	1.3	3.9	1.4	331
332. PPI, intermediate materials	do.		215.5	242.8	247.1	257.5	270.9	273.4	273.8	274.9	0.1	0.4	4.2	5.2	332
333. PPI, capital equipment	do.		199.1	216.7	218.5	223.0	229.9	231.6	235.9	236.0	1.9	0.4	2.1	3.1	333
334. PPI, finished consumer goods	do.		192.6	215.7	218.4	227.5	237.4	241.2	241.2	242.1	0.	0.4	4.2	4.4	334

No.	Series	Unit												
B2. Wages and Productivity														
340	Average hourly earnings, production workers, private nonfarm economy	...do....	212.9	229.8	232.5	237.2	242.8	245.3	246.4	247.9	0.4	0.6	2.0	2.4
341	Real average hourly earnings, production workers, private nonfarm economy	...do....	109.0	105.6	105.2	104.0	102.4	102.0	101.5	101.2	-0.5	-0.3	-1.1	-1.5
345	Average hourly compensation, nonfarm economy	...do....	227.1	260.8	249.5	254.9	261.0	·	·	·	...	...	...	...
346	Real avg. hourly comp., nonfarm business	...do....	116.2	113.7	113.0	111.8	110.1	·	·	·	...	...	...	...
370	Output per hour, private business sector	...do....	119.3	118.3	118.0	117.9	117.6	·	·	·	...	...	...	...
C. Labor Force, Employment, and Unemployment														
441	Total civilian labor force	Millions	100.42	102.91	103.24	103.75	104.19	104.09	104.42	105.14	0.3	0.7	0.5	0.4
442	Total civilian employment	...do....	94.37	96.94	97.23	97.66	97.80	97.66	97.15	96.99	-0.5	-0.2	0.4	0.1
37	Number of persons unemployed	Thousands	6,047	5,963	6,008	6,084	6,390	6,438	7,265	8,154	12.8	12.2	1.3	5.0
444	Unemployed males, 20 years and over	...do....	2,252	2,223	2,274	2,315	2,593	2,696	3,246	3,671	20.4	13.1	1.9	11.9
445	Unemployed females, 20 years and over	...do....	2,236	2,213	2,209	2,235	2,271	2,255	2,534	2,670	12.4	5.4	1.2	1.6
446	Unemployed persons, 16-19 years of age	...do....	1,559	1,528	1,524	1,531	1,526	1,487	1,485	1,813	-0.1	22.1	0.5	-0.3
	Labor Force Participation Rates:														
451	Males, 20 years and over[2]	Percent	79.8	79.8	79.9	79.6	79.5	79.4	79.5	79.9	0.1	0.4	-0.3	-0.1
452	Females, 20 years and over[2]	...do....	49.6	50.6	50.9	51.0	51.0	51.0	51.5	51.5	0.5	0.	0.1	0.2
453	Both sexes, 16-19 years of age[2]	...do....	58.0	58.1	57.5	58.2	57.6	57.3	56.3	57.9	-1.0	1.6	0.7	-0.6
D. Government Activities — D1. Receipts and Expenditures														
501	Federal Government receipts	A.r., bil. dol.	432.1	497.6	504.8	524.7	538.4				...	...	3.9	2.6
502	Federal Government expenditures[2]	...do....	459.8	509.0	516.1	540.4	561.3				...	...	4.7	3.9
500	Federal Government surplus or deficit[2]	...do....	-27.7	-11.4	-11.3	-15.7	-22.9				...	...	-4.4	-7.2
511	State and local government receipts	...do....	331.6	354.6	359.8	368.7	375.3				...	...	2.5	1.8
512	State and local government expenditures[2]	...do....	303.6	330.0	334.5	342.9	350.6				...	...	2.5	2.2
510	State and local govt. surplus or deficit[2]	...do....	27.4	24.6	25.3	25.8	24.6				...	...	0.5	-1.2
D2. Defense Indicators														
517	Defense Department obligations	Mil. dol.	10,360	11,132	11,891	11,325	13,246	14,757	13,639	NA	-7.6	NA	-4.8	17.0
525	Military prime contract awards	...do....	5,157	5,356	5,927	5,159	6,149	5,781	5,571	NA	NA	NA	-13.0	19.2
548	New orders, defense products	...do....	3,467	3,284	3,199	3,623	3,876	4,594	4,948	4,970	7.7	0.4	13.3	7.0
564	National defense purchases	A.r., bil. dol.	99.0	108.3	109.0	114.6	119.6				...	...	5.1	4.4
E. U.S. International Transactions — E1. Merchandise Trade														
602	Exports, total except military aid	Mil. dol.	11,955	15,136	15,742	16,783	17,705	18,534	18,468	NA	-0.4	NA	6.6	5.5
604	Exports of agricultural products	...do....	2,483	2,896	3,101	3,368	3,430	3,331	3,285	NA	-1.4	NA	8.6	1.8
606	Exports of nonelectrical machinery	...do....	2,500	3,009	3,139	3,221	3,391	3,423	3,571	NA	4.3	NA	2.6	5.3
612	General imports, total	...do....	14,333	17,195	17,830	19,083	21,064	20,607	19,308	NA	-6.3	NA	7.0	10.4
614	Imports of petroleum and products	...do....	3,278	4,676	5,101	5,968	6,782	6,991	5,185	NA	-25.8	NA	17.0	13.6
616	Imports of automobiles and parts	...do....	1,725	1,853	1,926	1,887	1,965	1,960	1,710	NA	-12.8	NA	-2.0	4.1

SUMMARY OF RECENT DATA AND CURRENT CHANGES FOR PRINCIPAL INDICATORS (concluded)

Series title	Unit of measure	Average 1977	Average 1978	Average 1979	4th Q 1978	1st Q 1979	2d Q 1979	3d Q 1979	4th Q 1979	1st Q 1980	% chg 2d Q to 3d Q 1979	% chg 3d Q to 4th Q 1979	% chg 4th Q 1979 to 1st Q 1980	Series number
II. OTHER IMPORTANT ECONOMIC MEASURES—Con.														
E2. Goods and Services Movements Except Transfers Under Military Grants														
618. Merchandise exports	Mil. dol.	30,204	35,514	45,514	38,900	41,805	42,815	47,198	50,237	54,708	10.2	6.4	8.9	618
620. Merchandise imports	do.	37,922	43,953	52,881	45,715	46,919	50,085	54,258	59,462	65,583	6.6	9.6	10.3	620
622. Merchandise trade balance[2]	do.	-7,718	-8,440	-7,367	-6,815	-5,114	-8,070	-7,060	-9,225	-10,875	1,010	-2,165	-1,650	622
651. Income on U.S. investments abroad	do.	8,147	10,743	16,492	12,851	14,263	15,250	18,050	18,407	20,548	18.4	2.0	11.6	651
652. Income on foreign investment in the U.S.	do.	3,650	5,518	8,365	6,343	7,225	7,980	8,731	9,524	10,425	9.4	9.1	9.5	652
668. Exports of goods and services	do.	46,177	55,260	71,627	61,131	65,667	67,763	74,773	78,305	85,325	10.3	4.7	9.0	668
669. Imports of goods and services[2]	do.	48,543	57,560	70,408	60,638	62,935	67,873	72,267	78,555	86,016	6.5	8.7	9.5	669
667. Balance on goods and services[2]	do.	-2,366	-2,301	1,220	493	2,732	-110	2,506	-250	-691	2,616	-2,756	-441	667
A. National Income and Product														
A1. GNP and Personal Income														
50. GNP in 1972 dollars	A.r., bil. dol.	1340.5	1399.2	1431.6	1426.6	1430.6	1422.3	1433.3	1440.3	1444.7	0.8	0.5	0.3	50
200. GNP in current dollars	do.	1899.5	2127.6	2368.8	2235.2	2292.1	2329.8	2396.5	2456.9	2520.8	2.9	2.5	2.6	200
213. Final sales, 1972 dollars	do.	1327.4	1385.1	1421.9	1414.6	1418.4	1404.1	1426.0	1439.0	1444.4	1.6	0.9	0.4	213
224. Disposable personal income, current dollars	do.	1305.1	1458.4	1624.3	1524.8	1572.2	1601.7	1640.0	1683.1	1737.4	2.4	2.6	3.2	224
225. Disposable personal income, 1972 dollars	do.	929.5	972.6	994.8	991.5	996.6	993.0	993.4	996.2	998.5	0.	0.3	0.2	225
217. Per capita GNP in 1972 dollars	A.r., dollars	6,180	6,401	6,494	6,506	6,512	6,460	6,494	6,509	6,514	0.5	0.2	0.1	217
227. Per capita disposable pers. income, 1972 dol.	do.	4,285	4,449	4,512	4,522	4,536	4,510	4,501	4,502	4,502	-0.2	0.	0.	227
A2. Personal Consumption Expenditures														
231. Total, 1972 dollars	A.r., bil. dol.	861.7	900.8	924.5	920.3	921.8	915.0	925.9	935.4	936.5	1.2	1.0	0.1	231
233. Durable goods, 1972 dollars	do.	138.2	146.7	147.1	152.1	150.2	144.8	146.9	146.7	145.4	1.5	-1.0	-0.9	233
238. Nondurable goods, 1972 dollars	do.	332.7	343.3	349.1	351.9	348.1	344.1	349.2	355.1	354.0	1.5	1.7	-0.3	238
239. Services, 1972 dollars	do.	390.8	410.8	428.3	416.3	423.5	426.1	429.9	433.6	437.0	0.9	0.9	0.8	239
230. Total, current dollars	do.	1210.0	1350.8	1509.8	1415.4	1454.2	1475.9	1528.6	1580.4	1629.5	3.6	3.4	3.1	230
232. Durable goods, current dollars	do.	178.8	200.3	213.0	212.1	213.8	208.7	213.4	216.2	220.2	2.3	1.3	1.9	232
236. Nondurable goods, current dollars	do.	481.3	530.6	596.9	558.1	571.1	581.2	604.7	630.7	652.0	4.0	4.3	3.4	236
237. Services, current dollars	do.	549.8	619.8	699.8	645.1	669.3	686.0	710.6	733.5	757.3	3.6	3.2	3.2	237
A3. Gross Private Domestic Investment														
241. Total, 1972 dollars	do.	200.1	214.3	215.2	217.4	217.2	221.7	214.2	207.7	203.2	-3.4	-3.0	-2.2	241
243. Total fixed investment, 1972 dollars	do.	186.9	200.2	205.5	205.5	204.9	203.5	207.1	206.4	202.9	1.8	-0.4	-1.6	243
30. Change in business inventories, 1972 dol.[2]	do.	13.1	14.1	9.7	12.0	12.3	18.1	7.1	1.4	0.3	-11.0	-5.7	-1.1	30
240. Total, current dollars	do.	303.3	351.5	387.2	370.5	373.8	395.4	392.3	387.2	387.7	-0.8	-1.3	0.1	240
242. Total fixed investment, current dollars	do.	281.3	329.1	369.0	349.8	354.6	361.9	377.8	381.7	383.0	4.4	1.0	0.3	242
245. Chg. in bus. inventories, current dol.[2]	do.	21.9	22.3	18.2	20.6	19.1	33.4	14.5	5.6	4.7	-18.9	-8.9	-0.9	245

¹ Basic data.

A4. Government Purchases of Goods and Services

Series														
261. Total, 1972 dollars ....do......	268.5	273.2	274.3	276.0	274.7	272.4	273.1	277.1	280.0	0.3	1.5	1.0	261
263. Federal Government, 1972 dollars ....do......	100.6	98.6	99.4	99.3	101.1	98.1	97.4	101.1	104.3	-0.7	3.8	3.2	263
267. State and local governments, 1972 dollars.........do......	167.9	174.6	174.9	176.6	173.6	174.3	175.6	176.0	175.7	0.7	0.2	-0.2	267
260. Total, current dollars ....do......	396.2	435.6	476.4	453.8	460.1	466.6	477.8	501.2	517.2	2.4	4.9	3.2	260
262. Federal Government, current dollars ....do......	144.4	152.6	166.6	159.0	163.6	161.7	162.9	178.4	186.2	0.7	9.5	4.4	262
266. State and local governments, current dollars ....do......	251.8	283.0	309.8	294.8	296.5	304.9	314.9	322.8	331.0	3.3	2.5	2.5	266

A5. Foreign Trade

Series														
256. Exports of goods and services, 1972 dollars ....do......	98.4	108.9	119.9	113.8	117.0	116.0	122.2	124.3	131.7	5.3	1.7	6.0	256
257. Imports of goods and services, 1972 dollars ....do......	88.2	97.9	102.3	101.0	100.0	102.9	102.1	104.1	106.7	-0.8	2.0	2.5	257
255. Net exports of goods and serv., 1972 dol.[2] ....do......	10.3	11.0	17.6	12.9	17.0	13.2	20.1	20.1	25.0	6.9	0.	4.9	255
252. Exports of goods and services, current dol. ....do......	175.9	207.2	257.5	224.9	238.5	243.7	267.3	280.4	308.1	9.7	4.9	9.9	252
253. Imports of goods and services, current dol. ....do......	185.8	217.5	262.1	229.4	234.4	251.9	269.5	292.4	321.7	7.0	8.5	10.0	253
250. Net exports of goods and serv., current dol.[2] ....do......	-9.9	-10.3	-4.6	-4.5	4.0	-8.1	-2.3	-11.9	-13.6	5.8	-9.6	-1.7	250

A6. National Income and Its Components

Series														
220. National income ....do......	1525.8	1724.3	1924.8	1820.0	1869.0	1897.9	1941.9	1990.4	2035.4	2.3	2.5	2.3	220
280. Compensation of employees ....do......	1156.9	1304.5	1459.2	1364.8	1411.2	1439.7	1472.8	1513.2	1555.2	2.3	2.7	2.8	280
282. Proprietors' income with IVA and CCA ....do......	100.2	116.8	130.8	125.7	129.0	129.3	130.3	134.5	130.0	0.8	3.2	-3.3	282
286. Corporate profits with IVA and CCA ....do......	150.0	167.7	178.2	184.8	178.9	176.6	180.8	176.4	175.0	2.4	-2.4	-0.8	286
284. Rental income of persons with CCA ....do......	24.7	25.9	26.9	27.1	27.3	26.8	26.6	27.0	27.0	-0.7	1.5	0.	284
288. Net interest ....do......	94.0	109.5	129.7	117.6	122.6	125.6	131.5	139.2	148.1	4.7	5.9	6.4	288

A7. Saving

Series														
290. Gross saving (private and govt.) ....do......	276.1	324.6	363.9	346.9	362.2	374.3	367.3	351.9	346.6	-1.9	-4.2	-1.5	290
295. Business saving ....do......	230.7	253.0	275.9	264.7	266.0	274.6	281.9	281.0	279.2	2.7	-0.3	-0.6	295
292. Personal saving ....do......	65.0	72.0	73.8	71.5	79.2	85.9	70.3	59.7	64.4	-18.2	-15.1	7.9	292
298. Government surplus or deficit[2] ....do......	-19.5	-0.3	13.2	10.8	15.8	12.7	14.0	10.0	1.7	1.3	-4.0	-8.3	298
293. Personal saving rate[2] ....Percent..	5.0	4.9	4.5	4.7	5.0	5.4	4.3	3.5	3.7	-1.1	-0.8	0.2	293

NOTE: Series are seasonally adjusted except for those indicated by Ⓤ, which appear to contain no seasonal movement. Series indicated by an asterisk (*) are included in the major composite indexes. Dollar values are in current dollars unless otherwise specified. For complete series titles (including composition of the composite indexes) and sources, see "Titles and Sources of Series" at the back of BCD. NA = not available. a = anticipated. EOP = end of period. A.r. = annual rate. S/A = seasonally adjusted (used for special emphasis). IVA = inventory valuation adjustment. CCA = capital consumption adjustment. NIA = national income accounts.

[1] For a few series, data shown here have been rounded to fewer digits than those shown elsewhere in BCD. Annual figures published by the source agencies are used if available.
[2] Differences rather than percent changes are shown for this series.
[3] The three-part timing code indicates the timing classification of the series at peaks, at troughs, and at all turns: L = leading; C = roughly coincident; Lg = lagging; U = unclassified.
[4] Inverted series. Since this series tends to move counter to movements in general business activity, signs of the changes are reversed.
[5] End-of-period series. The annual figures (and quarterly figures for monthly series) are the last figures for the period.
[6] This series is a weighted 4-term moving average (with weights 1, 2, 2, 1) placed at the terminal month of the span.
Source: Business Conditions Digest, U.S. Department of Commerce, Bureau of Economic Analysis.

SELECTED BUSINESS STATISTICS
SEASONALLY ADJUSTED WHERE APPLICABLE—SHADED AREA DENOTES RECESSIONS/DEPRESSIONS

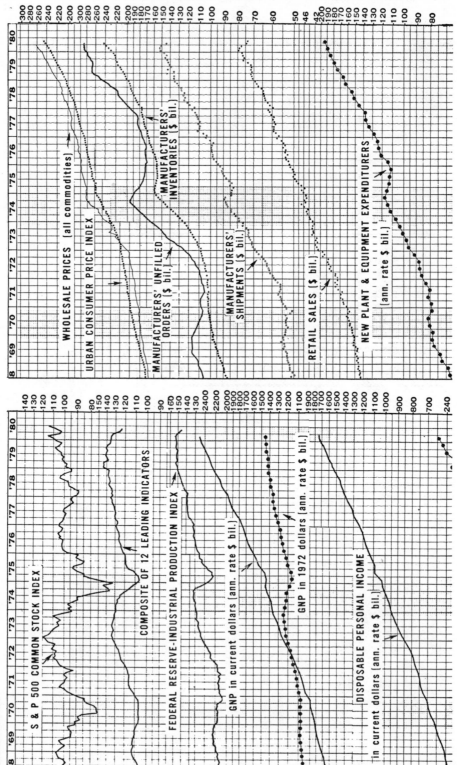

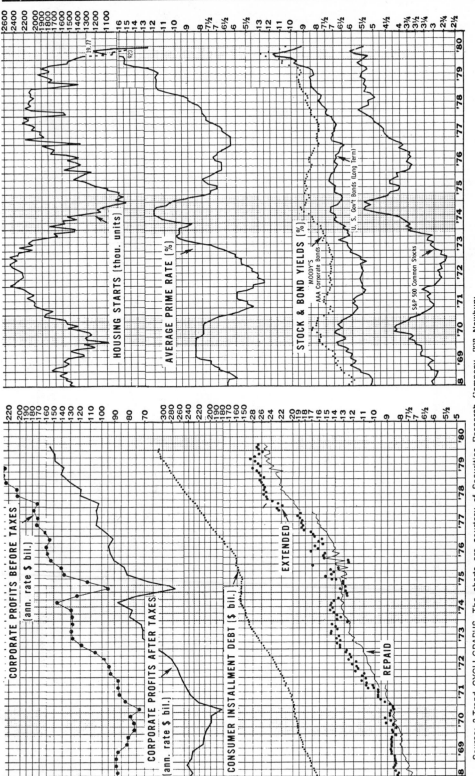

HOUSING STARTS (thou. units)

AVERAGE PRIME RATE (%)

STOCK & BOND YIELDS (%)

MOODY'S
AAA Corporate Bonds

U. S. Gov't Bonds (Long Term)

S&P 500 Common Stocks

CORPORATE PROFITS BEFORE TAXES
(ann. rate $ bil.)

CORPORATE PROFITS AFTER TAXES
(ann. rate $ bil.)

CONSUMER INSTALLMENT DEBT ($ bil.)

EXTENDED

REPAID

Source: 3-Trend CYCLI-GRAPHS. The charts are courtesy of Securities Research Company, 208 Newbury Street, Boston, Mass., quarterly edition, 1980.

Gross National Product and Income

GROSS NATIONAL PRODUCT

BILLIONS OF DOLLARS (RATIO SCALE)

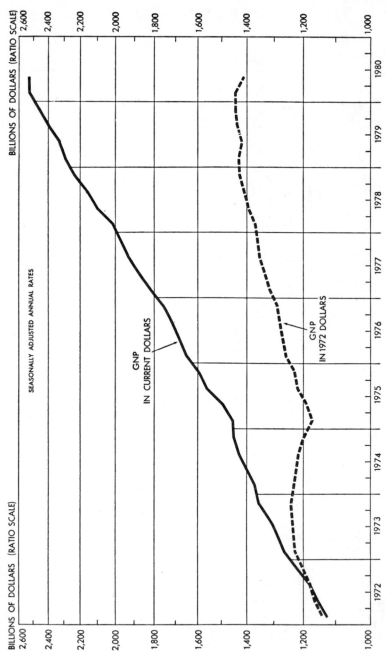

SEASONALLY ADJUSTED ANNUAL RATES

GNP
IN CURRENT DOLLARS

GNP
IN 1972 DOLLARS

BILLIONS OF DOLLARS (RATIO SCALE)

SOURCE: DEPARTMENT OF COMMERCE

COUNCIL OF ECONOMIC ADVISERS

[Billions of current dollars; quarterly data at seasonally adjusted annual rates]

Period	Gross national product	Personal consumption expenditures	Gross private domestic investment	Exports and imports of goods and services			Government purchases of goods and services					Final sales
				Net exports	Exports	Imports	Total	Federal			State and local	
								Total	National defense	Non-defense		
1969----	935.5	579.7	146.2	1.8	54.7	52.9	207.9	97.5	76.3	21.2	110.4	926.2
1970----	982.4	618.8	140.8	3.9	62.5	58.5	218.9	95.6	73.5	22.1	123.2	978.6
1971----	1,063.4	668.2	160.0	1.6	65.6	64.0	233.7	96.2	70.2	26.0	137.5	1,057.1
1972----	1,171.1	733.0	188.3	-3.3	72.7	75.9	253.1	102.1	73.5	28.6	151.0	1,161.7
1973----	1,306.6	809.9	220.0	7.1	101.6	94.4	269.5	102.2	73.5	28.7	167.3	1,288.6
1974----	1,412.9	889.6	214.6	6.0	137.9	131.9	302.7	111.1	77.0	34.1	191.5	1,404.0
1975----	1,528.8	979.1	190.9	20.4	147.3	126.9	338.4	123.1	83.7	39.4	215.4	1,539.6
1976----	1,702.2	1,089.9	243.0	8.0	163.3	155.4	361.3	129.7	86.4	43.3	231.6	1,692.1
1977----	1,899.5	1,210.0	303.3	-9.9	175.9	185.8	396.2	144.4	93.7	50.6	251.8	1,877.6
1978----	2,127.6	1,350.8	351.5	-10.3	207.2	217.5	435.6	152.6	99.0	53.6	283.0	2,105.2
1979----	2,368.8	1,509.8	387.2	-4.6	257.5	262.1	476.4	166.6	108.3	58.4	309.8	2,350.6
1978: III--	2,159.6	1,369.3	356.2	-6.8	213.8	220.6	440.9	152.3	99.0	53.3	288.6	2,139.5
IV--	2,235.2	1,415.4	370.5	-4.5	224.9	229.4	453.8	159.0	101.2	57.8	294.8	2,214.5
1979: I---	2,292.1	1,454.2	373.8	4.0	238.5	234.4	460.1	163.6	103.4	60.2	296.5	2,272.9
II--	2,329.8	1,475.9	395.4	-8.1	243.7	251.9	466.6	161.7	106.0	55.7	304.9	2,296.4
III--	2,396.5	1,528.6	392.3	-2.3	267.3	269.5	477.8	162.9	109.0	53.9	314.9	2,381.9
IV--	2,456.9	1,580.4	387.2	-11.9	280.4	292.4	501.2	178.4	114.6	63.8	322.8	2,451.4
1980: I---	2,520.8	1,629.5	387.7	-13.6	308.1	321.7	517.2	186.2	119.6	66.6	331.0	2,516.1
II p--	2,523.4	1,628.2	366.9	1.3	307.3	306.0	527.0	192.5	123.6	68.9	334.5	2,511.7

Source: Department of Commerce, Bureau of Economic Analysis.

Source: Economic Indicators, Council of Economic Advisers.

GROSS NATIONAL PRODUCT IN 1972 DOLLARS

BILLIONS OF 1972 DOLLARS; QUARTERLY DATA AT SEASONALLY ADJUSTED ANNUAL RATES

Period	Gross national product	Personal consumption expenditures	Gross private domestic investment			Net exports	Exports of goods and services		Government purchases of goods and services			Final sales
			Nonresidential fixed	Residential fixed	Change in business inventories		Exports	Imports	Total	Federal	State and local	
1969	1,078.8	655.4	114.3	43.2	10.6	-1.3	62.2	63.5	256.7	121.8	134.9	1,068.2
1970	1,075.3	668.9	110.0	40.4	4.3	1.4	67.1	65.7	250.2	110.7	139.5	1,071.0
1971	1,107.5	691.9	108.0	52.2	6.6	-.6	67.9	68.5	249.4	103.9	145.5	1,100.9
1972	1,171.1	733.0	116.8	62.0	9.4	-3.3	72.7	75.9	253.1	102.1	151.0	1,161.7
1973	1,235.0	767.7	131.0	59.7	16.5	7.6	87.4	79.9	252.5	96.6	155.9	1,218.5
1974	1,217.8	760.7	130.6	45.0	8.0	15.9	93.0	77.1	257.7	95.8	161.8	1,209.9
1975	1,202.3	774.6	113.6	38.8	-9.8	22.6	90.0	67.5	262.6	96.5	166.1	1,212.1
1976	1,273.0	820.6	119.0	47.8	6.6	15.8	96.1	80.4	263.3	96.4	166.9	1,266.4
1977	1,340.5	861.7	129.3	57.7	13.1	10.3	98.4	88.2	268.5	100.6	167.9	1,327.4
1978	1,399.2	900.8	140.1	60.1	14.1	11.0	108.9	97.9	273.2	98.6	174.6	1,385.1
1979	1,431.6	924.5	148.8	56.7	9.7	17.6	119.9	102.3	274.3	99.4	174.9	1,421.9
1978: III	1,407.3	905.3	141.6	60.2	12.2	13.3	111.9	98.5	274.7	98.5	176.2	1,395.1
IV	1,426.6	920.3	145.5	60.0	12.0	12.9	113.8	101.0	276.0	99.3	176.6	1,414.6
1979: I	1,430.6	921.8	147.2	57.7	12.3	17.0	117.0	100.0	274.7	101.1	173.6	1,418.4
II	1,422.3	915.0	146.9	56.7	18.1	13.2	116.0	102.9	272.4	98.1	174.3	1,404.1
III	1,433.3	925.9	150.7	56.5	7.1	20.1	122.2	102.1	273.1	97.4	175.6	1,426.2
IV	1,440.3	935.4	150.5	55.8	1.4	20.1	124.3	104.1	277.1	101.1	176.0	1,439.0
1980: I	1,444.7	936.5	151.2	51.7	.3	25.0	131.7	106.7	280.0	104.3	175.7	1,444.4
IIp	1,410.8	913.6	143.9	41.1	2.3	29.3	128.7	99.4	280.6	106.6	174.0	1,408.5

Source: *Economic Indicators*, Council of Economic Advisers.

IMPLICIT PRICE DEFLATORS FOR GROSS NATIONAL PRODUCT

1972 = 100; QUARTERY DATA ARE SEASONALLY ADJUSTED

Period	Gross national product	Personal consumption expenditures				Gross private domestic investment		Exports and imports of goods and services		Government purchases of goods and services	
		Total	Durable goods	Non-durable goods	Services	Nonresidential fixed	Residential fixed	Exports	Imports	Federal	State and local
1969	86.72	88.5	93.1	89.4	86.1	86.6	87.7	87.9	83.3	80.0	81.9
1970	91.36	92.5	95.5	93.6	90.5	91.3	90.6	93.1	89.1	86.4	88.3
1971	96.02	96.6	99.0	96.6	95.8	96.4	94.9	96.6	93.5	92.6	94.5
1972	100.00	100.0	100.0	100.0	100.0	100.0	100.0	100.0	100.0	100.0	100.0
1973	105.80	105.5	101.6	107.9	104.7	103.8	110.8	116.2	118.2	105.8	107.3
1974	116.02	116.9	108.4	123.8	113.6	115.3	122.3	148.3	171.0	115.9	118.4
1975	127.15	126.4	117.7	133.4	123.2	132.2	132.8	163.6	188.0	127.5	129.7
1976	133.71	132.8	124.3	138.1	131.2	138.5	142.5	169.9	193.3	134.6	138.8
1977	141.70	140.4	129.4	144.7	140.7	146.6	159.3	178.7	210.7	143.6	150.0
1978	152.05	150.0	136.5	154.6	150.9	157.8	179.7	190.3	222.1	154.8	162.1
1979	165.46	163.3	144.8	171.0	163.4	171.3	201.4	214.8	256.2	167.6	177.1
1978: III	153.45	151.3	137.9	155.7	152.3	159.6	183.1	191.1	223.9	154.6	163.8
IV	156.68	153.8	139.4	158.6	155.0	162.3	189.5	197.6	227.2	160.1	166.9
1979: I	160.22	157.8	142.4	164.1	158.0	165.4	192.6	203.9	234.5	161.9	170.8
II	163.81	161.3	144.1	168.9	161.3	169.6	199.2	210.1	244.9	164.8	174.9
III	167.20	165.1	145.3	173.2	165.3	173.8	205.5	218.7	264.0	167.2	179.3
IV	170.58	169.0	147.4	177.6	169.2	176.2	208.7	225.7	280.8	176.4	183.5
1980: I	174.48	174.0	151.5	184.1	173.3	180.3	213.4	234.0	301.5	178.5	188.4
IIp	178.86	178.2	153.6	187.5	178.0	184.7	217.6	238.7	307.7	180.7	192.2

Source: Department of Commerce, Bureau of Economic Analysis.

Source: *Economic Indicators*, Council of Economic Advisers.

CHANGES IN GNP AND GNP PRICE MEASURES

PERCENT CHANGE FROM PREVIOUS PERIOD; QUARTERLY DATA AT SEASONALLY ADJUSTED ANNUAL RATES

Period	Gross national product					Gross domestic product				
	Current dollars	Constant (1972) dollars	Implicit price deflator	Chain price index	Fixed-weighted price index (1972 weights)	Current dollars	Constant (1972) dollars	Implicit price deflator	Chain price index	Fixed-weighted price index (1972 weights)
1968	9.1	4.4	4.5	4.4	4.3	9.1	4.4	4.5	4.4	4.4
1969	7.7	2.6	5.0	5.0	5.0	7.8	2.6	5.1	5.0	5.0
1970	5.0	-.3	5.4	5.3	5.2	5.0	-.3	5.3	5.3	5.2
1971	8.2	3.0	5.1	5.0	4.9	8.1	2.8	5.1	5.0	4.9
1972	10.1	5.7	4.1	4.1	4.0	10.1	5.8	4.1	4.1	4.0
1973	11.6	5.5	5.8	6.0	6.0	11.5	5.4	5.7	5.9	5.9
1974	8.1	-1.4	9.7	9.9	10.2	7.9	-1.3	9.3	9.6	9.3
1975	8.2	-1.3	9.6	9.4	9.3	8.5	-1.1	9.7	9.4	9.6
1976	11.3	5.9	5.2	5.6	5.6	11.2	5.7	5.1	5.6	5.6
1977	11.6	5.3	6.0	6.3	6.4	11.5	5.3	5.9	6.2	6.4
1978	12.0	4.4	7.3	7.4	7.5	12.0	4.4	7.3	7.4	7.5
1979	11.3	2.3	8.8	8.9	9.3	11.2	2.3	8.7	8.8	9.3
1978: III	10.9	3.5	7.2	8.2	8.3	11.1	3.6	7.2	8.2	8.3
IV	14.8	5.6	8.7	8.6	8.9	14.8	5.6	8.7	8.7	8.9
1979: I	10.6	1.1	9.3	9.7	9.9	10.1	.9	9.1	9.6	9.9
II	6.7	-2.3	9.3	8.8	9.5	6.9	-2.1	9.2	8.7	9.4
III	11.9	3.1	8.5	8.9	10.0	11.5	3.2	8.0	8.4	9.6
IV	10.5	2.0	8.4	8.5	9.4	10.7	2.4	8.1	8.1	9.1
1980: I	10.8	1.2	9.5	9.6	10.9	10.5	1.4	9.0	9.2	10.6
IIᵖ	.4	-9.1	10.4	8.3	8.9	-.1	-9.4	10.3	8.3	8.9

NOTE.—Annual changes from previous year and quarterly changes from previous quarter.

Source: *Economic Indicators*, Council of Economic Advisers.

Source: Department of Commerce, Bureau of Economic Analysis.

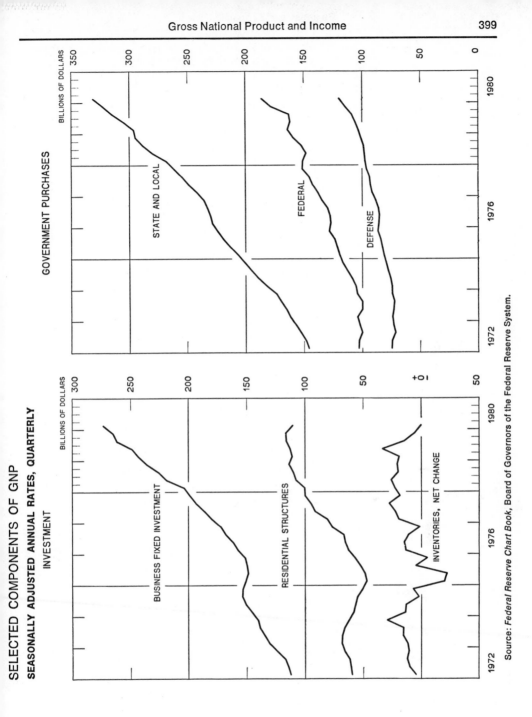

SELECTED COMPONENTS OF GNP
SEASONALLY ADJUSTED ANNUAL RATES, QUARTERLY

INVESTMENT

GOVERNMENT PURCHASES

Source: *Federal Reserve Chart Book*, Board of Governors of the Federal Reserve System.

CORPORATE PROFITS

BILLIONS OF DOLLARS

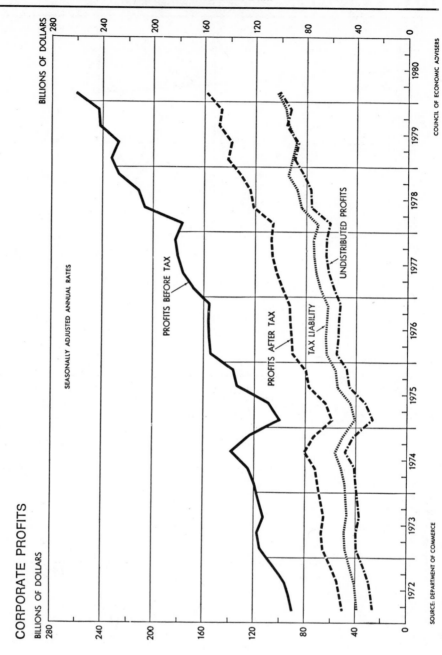

SEASONALLY ADJUSTED ANNUAL RATES

BILLIONS OF DOLLARS

PROFITS BEFORE TAX

PROFITS AFTER TAX

TAX LIABILITY

UNDISTRIBUTED PROFITS

SOURCE: DEPARTMENT OF COMMERCE

COUNCIL OF ECONOMIC ADVISERS

[Billions of dollars; quarterly data at seasonally adjusted annual rates]

Period	Profits (before tax) with inventory valuation adjustment [1]						Profits before tax	Tax liability	Profits after tax			Inventory valuation adjustment
	Total [2]	Domestic industries										
		Total	Financial	Nonfinancial					Total	Dividends	Undistributed profits	
				Total [3]	Manufacturing	Wholesale and retail trade						
1969	77.9	74.2	11.3	62.9	36.8	10.1	83.4	39.7	43.8	22.6	21.2	−5.5
1970	66.4	62.6	12.6	50.1	27.1	9.4	71.5	34.5	37.0	22.9	14.1	−5.1
1971	76.9	72.4	14.1	58.2	32.4	11.7	82.0	37.7	44.3	23.0	21.3	−5.0
1972	89.6	84.7	15.4	69.3	40.6	13.3	96.2	41.5	54.6	24.6	30.0	−6.6
1973	97.2	90.4	16.2	74.1	44.1	14.7	115.8	48.7	67.1	27.8	39.3	−18.6
1974	86.5	76.9	14.0	62.5	36.6	12.9	126.9	52.4	74.5	31.0	43.6	−40.4
1975	107.9	101.8	13.0	88.9	48.3	20.7	120.4	49.8	70.6	31.9	38.7	−12.4
1976	141.3	133.1	17.8	115.3	65.7	23.3	156.0	63.8	92.2	37.5	54.7	−14.6
1977	162.0	152.1	23.8	128.3	73.5	24.1	177.1	72.6	104.5	42.1	62.4	−15.2
1978	180.8	170.6	29.7	140.9	81.7	23.0	206.0	84.5	121.5	47.2	74.3	−25.2
1979	194.9	181.6	33.2	148.5	88.8	23.7	236.6	92.5	144.1	52.7	91.4	−41.8
1978: III	189.0	178.8	30.6	148.3	85.1	25.5	212.0	87.5	124.6	47.8	76.8	−23.0
IV	198.6	189.0	32.1	156.9	90.6	25.8	227.4	95.1	132.3	49.7	82.6	−28.8
1979: I	193.3	181.4	31.9	149.6	94.1	18.6	233.3	91.3	142.0	51.5	90.5	−39.9
II	191.3	179.6	32.0	147.7	90.6	22.4	227.9	88.7	139.3	52.3	87.0	−36.6
III	198.3	182.5	33.8	148.7	86.4	26.5	242.3	94.0	148.3	52.8	95.5	−44.0
IV	196.5	183.0	35.0	148.0	84.0	27.1	243.0	96.1	146.9	54.4	92.5	−46.5
1980: I	197.2	181.1	34.7	146.5	93.0	16.5	260.4	102.4	158.0	56.7	101.3	−63.2
II p										58.1		−27.8

[1] See p. 411 for profits with inventory valuation and capital consumption adjustments.
[2] Includes rest of the world, not shown separately.
[3] Includes industries not shown separately.

Source: Department of Commerce, Bureau of Economic Analysis.
Source: *Economic Indicators*, Council of Economic Advisers.

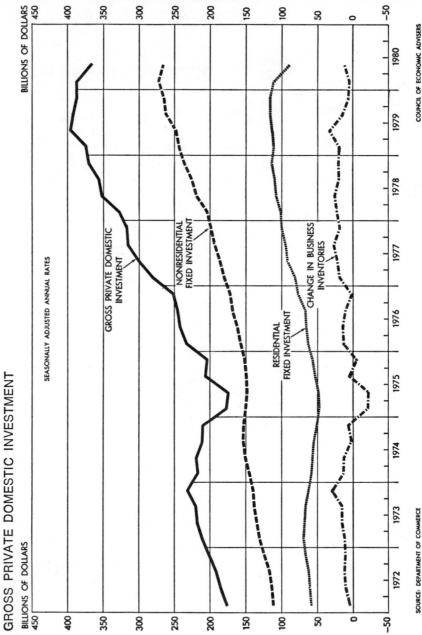

GROSS PRIVATE DOMESTIC INVESTMENT

BILLIONS OF DOLLARS

SOURCE: DEPARTMENT OF COMMERCE

COUNCIL OF ECONOMIC ADVISERS

BILLIONS OF DOLLARS

SEASONALLY ADJUSTED ANNUAL RATES

GROSS PRIVATE DOMESTIC INVESTMENT

NONRESIDENTIAL FIXED INVESTMENT

RESIDENTIAL FIXED INVESTMENT

CHANGE IN BUSINESS INVENTORIES

[Billions of dollars; quarterly data at seasonally adjusted annual rates]

Period	Gross private domestic investment	Nonresidential fixed investment						Residential fixed investment				Change in business inventories	
		Total	Structures		Producers' durable equipment			Total	Non-farm structures	Farm structures	Producers' durable equipment	Total	Non-farm
			Total	Non-farm	Total	Non-farm							
1969	146.2	98.9	35.7	34.3	63.3	58.9		37.9	36.3	0.7	0.9	9.4	9.2
1970	140.8	100.5	37.7	36.1	62.8	58.1		36.6	35.1	.6	.9	3.8	3.7
1971	160.0	104.1	39.3	37.8	64.7	59.9		49.6	47.9	.7	1.0	6.4	5.1
1972	188.3	116.8	42.5	41.1	74.3	69.1		62.0	60.3	.7	1.1	9.4	8.8
1973	220.0	136.0	49.0	46.9	87.0	80.1		66.1	64.3	.6	1.2	17.9	14.7
1974	214.6	150.6	54.5	51.8	96.2	88.2		55.1	52.7	1.2	1.1	8.9	10.8
1975	190.9	150.2	53.8	51.3	96.4	87.4		51.5	49.5	.9	1.1	−10.7	−14.3
1976	243.0	164.9	57.3	54.7	107.6	97.4		68.1	65.7	1.1	1.3	10.0	12.1
1977	303.3	189.4	62.6	59.8	126.8	116.3		91.9	88.8	1.5	1.6	21.9	20.7
1978	351.5	221.1	76.5	73.3	144.6	132.6		108.0	104.4	1.8	1.8	22.3	21.3
1979	387.2	254.9	92.6	88.9	162.2	147.8		114.1	110.2	1.9	2.0	18.2	16.5
1978: III	356.2	225.9	79.7	76.4	146.3	133.5		110.2	106.4	1.9	1.9	20.0	18.5
IV	370.5	236.1	84.4	81.1	151.8	138.9		113.7	110.0	1.9	1.9	20.6	19.3
1979: I	373.8	243.4	84.9	81.2	158.5	146.1		111.2	107.8	1.5	1.9	19.1	18.8
II	395.4	249.1	90.5	86.8	158.6	144.5		112.9	109.1	1.8	2.0	33.4	32.6
III	392.3	261.8	95.0	91.4	166.7	150.0		116.0	112.0	2.0	2.0	14.5	12.6
IV	387.2	265.2	100.2	96.3	165.1	150.4		116.4	112.1	2.3	2.1	5.6	2.1
1980: I	387.7	272.6	103.3	99.6	169.4	155.9		110.4	105.9	2.3	2.2	4.7	4.4
II ᵖ	366.9	265.9	102.7	99.0	163.2	149.6		89.3	85.7	1.8	1.9	11.7	12.4

Source: Department of Commerce, Bureau of Economic Analysis.

Source: Economic Indicators, Council of Economic Advisers.

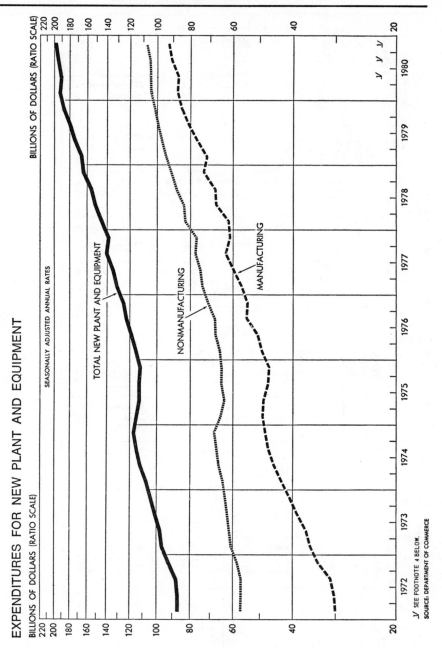

EXPENDITURES FOR NEW PLANT AND EQUIPMENT

BILLIONS OF DOLLARS (RATIO SCALE)

BILLIONS OF DOLLARS (RATIO SCALE)

SEASONALLY ADJUSTED ANNUAL RATES

TOTAL NEW PLANT AND EQUIPMENT

NONMANUFACTURING

MANUFACTURING

1/ SEE FOOTNOTE 4 BELOW.
SOURCE: DEPARTMENT OF COMMERCE

[Billions of dollars; quarterly data at seasonally adjusted annual rates]

Period	Total[1]	Expenditures for plant and equipment									Starts of plant and equipment projects[3]	
		Manufacturing			Nonmanufacturing						Manufacturing	Public utilities
		Total	Durable goods	Non-durable goods	Total	Mining	Transportation	Public utilities	Communication	Commercial and other[2]		
1972	88.44	31.35	15.64	15.72	57.09	2.42	5.72	17.00	11.89	20.07	35.21	28.60
1973	99.74	38.01	19.25	18.76	61.73	2.74	6.03	18.71	12.85	21.40	47.57	38.13
1974	112.40	46.01	22.62	23.39	66.39	3.18	6.66	20.55	13.96	22.05	52.49	45.74
1975	112.78	47.95	21.84	26.11	64.82	3.79	7.57	20.14	12.74	20.60	48.24	34.50
1976	120.49	52.48	23.68	28.81	68.01	4.00	7.45	22.28	13.30	20.99	51.05	29.66
1977	135.80	60.16	27.77	32.39	75.64	4.50	6.93	25.80	15.45	22.97	66.73	32.54
1978	153.82	67.62	31.66	35.96	86.19	4.78	8.05	29.48	18.16	25.71	72.44	34.93
1979	177.09	78.92	38.23	40.69	98.17	5.56	10.12	32.56	20.56	29.35	87.30	21.70
1980[4]	194.63	89.55	43.11	46.45	105.08	6.18	10.95	32.94	22.51	32.51		
1979: I	165.94	71.56	34.00	37.56	94.38	5.46	10.08	32.35	18.75	27.73	21.98	3.27
II	173.48	76.42	36.86	39.56	97.06	5.31	9.71	33.24	20.29	28.51	19.56	5.75
III	179.33	80.22	39.72	40.50	99.12	5.42	10.29	33.33	20.41	29.66	20.87	8.00
IV	186.95	85.19	41.30	43.88	101.76	6.06	10.74	31.52	22.71	30.72	24.71	4.13
1980: I	191.36	87.32	42.30	45.01	104.04	6.02	10.32	34.35	22.48	30.86	25.52	12.20
II[4]	191.00	86.82	42.18	44.64	104.18	6.72	11.16	32.87	63.43	--	--	--
III[4]	195.54	90.97	43.70	47.28	104.56	5.88	10.98	32.71	55.00	--	--	--
IV[4]	199.41	92.14	44.06	48.07	107.27	6.14	11.21	32.16	57.76	--	--	--

[1] Excludes agricultural business; real estate operators; medical, legal, educational, and cultural service; and nonprofit organizations. These figures do not agree precisely with the nonresidential fixed investment data in gross national product estimates, mainly because those data include investment by farmers, professionals, nonprofit institutions, and real estate firms, and certain outlays charged to current account.

Source: Economic Indicators, Council of Economic Advisers.

[2] Includes trade, service, construction, finance, and insurance.
[3] Starts are estimated by adding changes in carryover to expenditures during given period.
[4] Planned capital expenditures as reported by business in late April and May 1980. Plans are adjusted when necessary for systematic bias.

Source: Department of Commerce, Bureau of Economic Analysis.

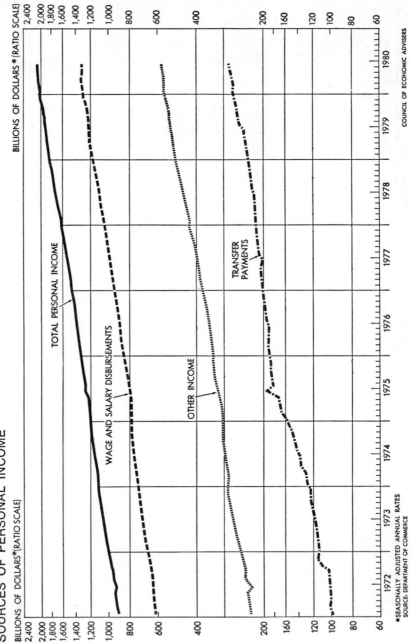

SOURCES OF PERSONAL INCOME
BILLIONS OF DOLLARS*(RATIO SCALE)

BILLIONS OF DOLLARS*(RATIO SCALE)

TOTAL PERSONAL INCOME

WAGE AND SALARY DISBURSEMENTS

OTHER INCOME

TRANSFER PAYMENTS

*SEASONALLY ADJUSTED ANNUAL RATES
SOURCE: DEPARTMENT OF COMMERCE

COUNCIL OF ECONOMIC ADVISERS

[Billions of dollars; monthly data at seasonally adjusted annual rates]

Period	Total personal income	Wage and salary disbursements[1]	Other labor income[1 2]	Proprietors' income[3]		Rental income of persons[4]	Dividends	Personal interest income	Transfer payments[5]	Less: Personal contributions for social insurance	Non-farm personal income[6]
				Farm	Nonfarm						
1972	942.5	633.8	42.0	18.0	58.1	21.5	24.6	74.6	104.1	34.2	917.3
1973	1,052.4	701.3	48.7	32.0	60.4	21.6	27.8	84.1	118.9	42.2	1,011.9
1974	1,154.9	764.6	55.6	25.4	60.9	21.4	31.0	103.0	140.8	47.7	1,119.3
1975	1,255.5	805.9	65.1	23.5	63.5	22.4	31.9	115.5	178.2	50.5	1,220.8
1976	1,381.6	890.0	77.4	18.3	71.0	22.1	37.5	127.0	193.8	55.6	1,350.6
1977	1,531.6	984.0	91.8	19.6	80.5	24.7	42.1	141.7	208.4	61.3	1,498.1
1978	1,717.4	1,103.3	106.5	27.7	89.1	25.9	47.2	163.3	224.1	69.6	1,674.2
1979	1,924.2	1,227.6	122.7	32.8	98.0	26.9	52.7	192.1	252.0	80.7	1,873.4
1979: June	1,905.1	1,220.5	121.8	33.4	95.8	27.2	52.6	189.4	244.7	80.2	1,853.7
July	1,933.2	1,229.8	123.3	32.8	97.9	27.3	52.5	191.8	258.5	80.8	1,882.3
Aug	1,946.5	1,236.5	124.9	31.0	99.5	27.3	52.7	194.4	261.2	81.0	1,897.3
Sept	1,960.1	1,247.9	126.4	28.8	100.9	25.0	53.0	197.1	262.7	81.7	1,913.8
Oct	1,981.2	1,257.4	128.0	31.0	101.1	26.8	53.6	200.7	264.8	82.2	1,931.8
Nov	2,005.5	1,271.3	129.6	33.0	102.1	27.0	54.2	205.4	265.9	83.0	1,953.9
Dec	2,028.3	1,282.9	131.2	33.4	103.0	27.2	55.2	210.3	268.8	83.6	1,976.1
1980: Jan	2,046.5	1,293.0	132.8	31.3	103.9	27.2	55.8	214.1	275.0	86.7	1,995.9
Feb	2,055.7	1,304.2	134.4	27.9	102.3	26.6	56.6	217.2	273.5	87.1	2,008.3
Mar	2,070.0	1,314.0	136.0	24.0	100.8	27.2	57.5	220.3	276.1	85.9	2,026.2
Apr [p]	2,071.5	1,309.0	137.5	23.0	98.9	27.4	58.1	224.8	278.0	85.1	2,028.5
May [p]	2,077.7	1,309.1	138.8	22.0	96.7	27.1	58.5	229.4	282.9	86.7	2,035.5
June [p]	2,085.7	1,309.9	140.1	21.5	95.6	27.4	59.2	233.7	285.6	87.3	2,043.8

[1] The total of wage and salary disbursements and other labor income differs from compensation of employees (see p. 411) in that it excludes employer contributions for social insurance and the excess of wage accruals over wage disbursements.

[2] Consists of employer contributions to private pension, health, and welfare funds; workmen's compensation; directors' fees; and a few other minor items.

Source: Department of Commerce, Bureau of Economic Analysis.
Source: *Economic Indicators,* Council of Economic Advisers.

[3] With inventory valuation and capital consumption adjustments.
[4] With capital consumption adjustment.
[5] Consists mainly of social insurance benefits, direct relief, and veterans payments.
[6] Personal income exclusive of farm proprietors' income, farm wages, farm other labor income, and agricultural net interest.

DISPOSITION OF PERSONAL INCOME

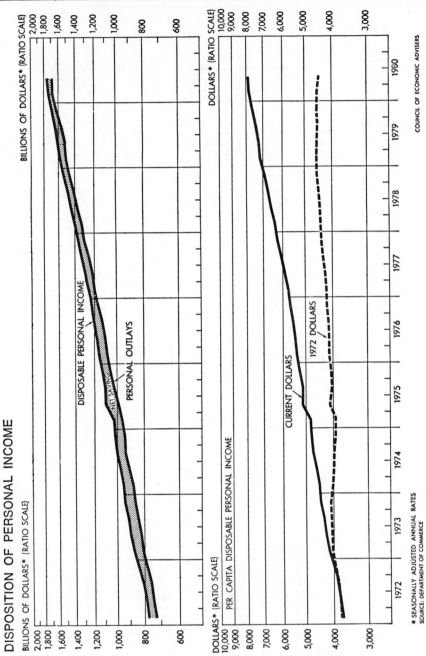

BILLIONS OF DOLLARS* (RATIO SCALE)

DISPOSABLE PERSONAL INCOME

NET SAVINGS

PERSONAL OUTLAYS

BILLIONS OF DOLLARS* (RATIO SCALE)

2,000
1,800
1,600
1,400
1,200
1,000
800
600

DOLLARS* (RATIO SCALE)

PER CAPITA DISPOSABLE PERSONAL INCOME

CURRENT DOLLARS

1972 DOLLARS

DOLLARS* (RATIO SCALE)

10,000
9,000
8,000
7,000
6,000
5,000
4,000
3,000

1972 1973 1974 1975 1976 1977 1978 1979 1980

* SEASONALLY ADJUSTED ANNUAL RATES
SOURCE: DEPARTMENT OF COMMERCE

COUNCIL OF ECONOMIC ADVISERS

Period	Personal income	Less: Personal tax and nontax payments	Equals: Disposable personal income	Less: Personal outlays[1]	Equals: Personal saving	Per capita disposable personal income		Per capita personal consumption expenditures		Percent change in real per capita disposable personal income	Saving as percent of disposable personal income	Population (thousands)[2]
	Billions of dollars					Dollars						
						Current dollars	1972 dollars	Current dollars	1972 dollars			
1971	859.1	116.3	742.8	685.5	57.3	3,588	3,714	3,227	3,342	2.6	7.7	207,053
1972	942.5	141.2	801.3	751.9	49.4	3,837	3,837	3,510	3,510	3.3	6.2	208,846
1973	1,052.4	150.8	901.7	831.3	70.3	4,285	4,062	3,849	3,648	5.9	7.8	210,410
1974	1,154.9	170.3	984.6	913.0	71.7	4,646	3,973	4,197	3,589	−2.2	7.3	211,945
1975	1,255.5	168.8	1,086.7	1,003.0	83.6	5,088	4,025	4,584	3,627	1.3	7.7	213,566
1976	1,381.6	197.1	1,184.5	1,115.9	68.6	5,504	4,144	5,064	3,813	3.0	5.8	215,203
1977	1,531.6	226.4	1,305.1	1,240.2	65.0	6,017	4,285	5,579	3,973	3.4	5.0	216,898
1978	1,717.4	259.0	1,458.4	1,386.4	72.0	6,672	4,449	6,179	4,121	3.8	4.9	218,594
1979	1,924.2	299.9	1,624.3	1,550.5	73.8	7,367	4,512	6,848	4,193	1.4	4.5	220,464
					Seasonally adjusted annual rates							
1978: III	1,742.5	266.0	1,476.5	1,405.6	70.9	6,748	4,461	6,258	4,137	3.3	4.8	218,814
IV	1,803.1	278.2	1,524.8	1,453.4	71.5	6,954	4,522	6,455	4,197	5.6	4.7	219,286
1979: I	1,852.6	280.4	1,572.2	1,493.0	79.2	7,157	4,536	6,619	4,196	1.2	5.0	219,690
II	1,892.5	290.7	1,601.7	1,515.8	85.9	7,275	4,510	6,704	4,156	−2.3	5.4	220,166
III	1,946.6	306.6	1,640.0	1,569.7	70.3	7,430	4,501	6,926	4,195	−.8	4.3	220,715
IV	2,005.0	321.9	1,683.1	1,623.4	59.7	7,606	4,502	7,142	4,227	.1	3.5	221,285
1980: I	2,057.4	320.0	1,737.4	1,672.9	64.4	7,834	4,502	7,348	4,223	0	3.7	221,768
II p	2,078.3	324.3	1,754.0	1,671.1	82.9	7,892	4,428	7,326	4,111	−6.4	4.7	222,255

[1] Includes personal consumption expenditures, interest paid by consumers to business, and personal transfer payments to foreigners (net).
[2] Includes Armed Forces abroad. Annual data are for July 1 through 1973 and are averages of quarterly data beginning 1974. Quarterly data are average for the period.

Source: Department of Commerce (Bureau of Economic Analysis and Bureau of the Census).
Source: Economic Indicators, Council of Economic Advisers.

PERSONAL CONSUMPTION EXPENDITURES

BILLIONS OF DOLLARS EXCEPT AS NOTED; QUARTERLY DATA AT SEASONALLY ADJUSTED ANNUAL RATES

Period	Total personal consumption expenditures	Durable goods			Nondurable goods				Services	Retail sales of new passenger cars (millions of units)	
		Total durable goods [1]	Motor vehicles and parts	Furniture and household equipment	Total nondurable goods [1]	Food	Clothing and shoes	Gasoline and oil		Domestics	Imports
1969	579.7	85.5	37.7	35.0	247.0	126.1	45.1	20.4	247.2	8.5	1.1
1970	618.8	84.9	34.9	36.7	264.7	136.3	46.6	22.0	269.1	7.1	1.3
1971	668.2	97.1	43.8	39.4	277.7	140.6	50.5	23.4	293.4	8.7	1.6
1972	733.0	111.2	50.6	44.8	299.3	150.4	55.1	24.9	322.4	9.3	1.6
1973	809.9	123.7	55.5	50.7	333.8	168.1	61.3	27.8	352.3	9.7	1.8
1974	889.6	122.0	48.0	54.9	376.3	189.8	65.3	36.4	391.3	7.5	1.4
1975	979.1	132.6	53.4	58.0	408.9	209.6	70.1	39.5	437.5	7.1	1.6
1976	1,089.9	157.4	70.0	64.0	443.9	227.1	75.9	42.9	488.5	8.6	1.5
1977	1,210.0	178.8	81.6	70.9	481.3	246.7	82.4	46.7	549.8	9.1	2.1
1978	1,350.8	200.3	91.2	77.6	530.6	271.7	91.2	50.9	619.8	9.3	2.0
1979	1,509.8	213.0	91.5	85.6	596.9	302.0	99.2	65.1	699.8	8.3	2.3
1978: III	1,369.3	203.5	92.4	78.9	536.7	274.5	92.7	51.5	629.1	9.4	2.0
IV	1,415.4	212.1	94.9	82.7	558.1	283.9	96.8	55.0	645.1	9.3	1.9
1979: I	1,454.2	213.8	97.7	82.1	571.1	292.9	95.5	58.4	669.3	9.3	2.3
II	1,475.9	208.7	89.1	84.2	581.2	296.7	96.9	60.2	686.0	8.0	2.5
III	1,528.6	213.4	89.8	87.3	604.7	303.1	101.0	68.3	710.6	8.6	2.2
IV	1,580.4	216.2	89.4	88.9	630.7	315.6	103.6	73.4	733.5	7.5	2.4
1980: I	1,629.5	220.2	92.9	88.2	652.0	322.6	103.9	83.6	757.3	7.9	2.8
II ᵖ	1,628.2	197.0	71.9	86.6	654.4	324.0	106.6	84.7	776.8	5.5	2.2

[1] Total includes other items not shown separately.

Source: Economic Indicators, Council of Economic Advisers.

Source: Department of Commerce, Bureau of Economic Analysis.

NATIONAL INCOME

BILLIONS OF DOLLARS; QUARTERLY DATA AT SEASONALLY ADJUSTED ANNUAL RATES

Period	National income	Compensation of employees [1]	Proprietors' income with inventory valuation and capital consumption adjustments — Farm	Proprietors' income — Non-farm	Rental income of persons with capital consumption adjustment	Corporate profits with inventory valuation and capital consumption adjustments — Total	Profits with inventory valuation adjustment and without capital consumption adjustment — Total	Profits before tax	Inventory valuation adjustment	Capital consumption adjustment	Net interest
1969	767.9	571.4	13.9	52.3	18.1	81.4	77.9	83.4	−5.5	3.5	30.8
1970	798.4	609.2	13.9	51.2	18.6	67.9	66.4	71.5	−5.1	1.5	37.5
1971	858.1	650.3	14.3	53.4	20.1	77.2	76.9	82.0	−5.0	.3	42.8
1972	951.9	715.1	18.0	58.1	21.6	92.1	89.6	96.2	−6.6	2.5	47.0
1973	1,064.6	799.2	32.0	60.4	21.4	99.1	97.2	115.8	−18.6	1.9	52.3
1974	1,136.0	875.8	25.4	60.9	22.4	83.6	86.5	126.9	−40.4	−2.9	69.0
1975	1,215.0	931.1	23.5	63.5	22.7	95.9	107.9	120.4	−12.4	−12.0	78.6
1976	1,359.8	1,037.8	18.3	71.0	24.7	126.8	141.3	156.0	−14.6	−14.5	83.8
1977	1,525.8	1,156.9	19.6	80.5	25.9	150.0	162.0	177.1	−15.2	−12.0	94.0
1978	1,724.3	1,304.5	27.7	89.1	26.9	167.7	180.8	206.0	−25.2	−13.1	109.5
1979	1,924.8	1,459.2	32.8	98.0	27.0	178.2	194.9	236.6	−41.8	−16.7	129.7
1978: III	1,752.5	1,321.1	26.1	91.3	26.8	175.2	189.0	212.0	−23.0	−13.8	111.9
IV	1,820.0	1,364.8	31.3	94.4	27.1	184.8	198.6	227.4	−28.8	−13.8	117.6
1979: I	1,869.9	1,411.2	34.2	94.8	27.3	178.9	193.3	233.3	−39.9	−14.5	122.6
II	1,897.9	1,439.7	33.7	95.5	26.8	176.6	191.3	227.9	−36.6	−14.7	125.6
III	1,941.9	1,472.8	30.9	99.4	26.6	180.8	198.3	242.3	−44.0	−17.6	131.5
IV	1,990.4	1,513.2	32.5	102.1	27.0	176.4	196.5	243.0	−46.5	−20.1	139.2
1980: I p	2,035.4	1,555.2	27.7	102.3	27.0	175.0	197.2	260.4	−63.2	−22.2	148.1

[1] Includes employer contributions for social insurance.

Source: *Economic Indicators*, Council of Economic Advisers.

Source: Department of Commerce, Bureau of Economic Analysis.

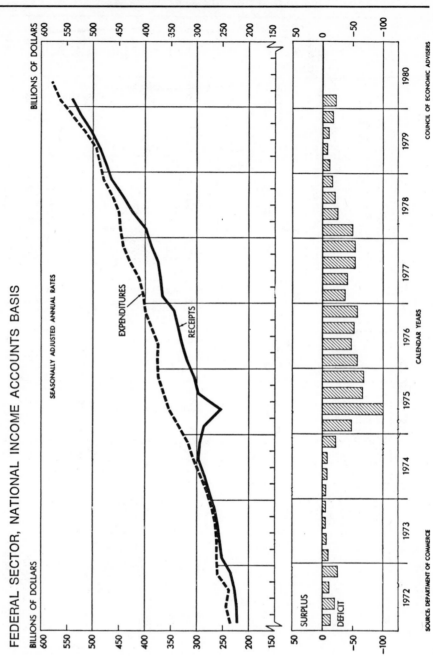

FEDERAL SECTOR, NATIONAL INCOME ACCOUNTS BASIS

[Billions of dollars; quarterly data at seasonally adjusted annual rates]

Period	Federal Government receipts					Federal Government expenditures							Surplus or deficit (−), national income and product accounts
	Total	Personal tax and nontax receipts	Corporate profits tax accruals	Indirect business tax and nontax accruals	Contributions for social insurance	Total	Purchases of goods and services	Transfer payments	Grants-in-aid to State and local governments	Net interest paid	Subsidies less current surplus of Government enterprises	Less: Wage accruals less disbursements	
Fiscal year:													
1976	313.9	137.0	51.7	24.3	100.9	371.1	125.7	156.5	57.6	25.2	6.2	0.0	−57.3
1977	366.0	166.0	59.1	24.5	116.4	411.4	140.3	169.6	66.3	28.4	6.9	.0	−45.5
1978	414.7	186.3	67.7	27.2	133.5	450.1	150.7	182.0	74.7	33.1	9.6	.0	−35.4
1979	483.7	223.5	78.4	29.4	152.4	493.6	162.4	201.7	79.3	40.4	9.8	.0	−9.9
Calendar year:													
1976	331.4	147.2	54.6	23.4	106.3	385.0	129.7	161.7	61.1	26.8	5.8	.0	−53.6
1977	375.4	169.6	61.8	25.1	118.9	421.7	144.4	172.7	67.5	29.0	8.1	.0	−46.3
1978	432.1	194.9	72.0	28.1	137.0	459.8	152.6	185.4	77.3	34.8	9.7	.0	−27.7
1979	497.6	230.0	78.2	30.0	159.3	509.0	166.6	209.8	80.4	43.1	9.1	.0	−11.2
1978: III	442.1	200.9	74.6	28.4	138.2	462.6	152.3	188.8	77.6	35.6	8.4	.2	−20.4
IV	463.5	211.0	81.2	29.3	142.0	479.7	159.0	192.1	80.7	37.1	10.9	.0	−16.3
1979: I	475.0	213.0	77.2	29.4	155.5	486.8	163.6	196.8	77.8	40.0	8.3	−.2	−11.7
II	485.8	223.4	74.9	29.9	157.5	492.9	161.7	201.9	77.7	42.6	9.0	.0	−7.0
III	504.8	235.2	79.4	30.0	160.2	516.1	162.9	217.6	81.8	43.5	10.2	.0	−11.3
IV	524.7	248.5	81.4	30.7	164.1	540.4	178.4	222.7	84.3	46.2	8.8	.0	−15.7
1980: I	538.4	246.1	86.8	33.8	171.7	561.3	186.2	230.0	86.0	50.2	8.9	.0	−22.9
II ᵖ	---	249.2	---	43.0	171.7	579.0	192.5	236.1	86.4	54.5	9.4	.0	---

Sources: Department of Commerce (Bureau of Economic Analysis), Department of the Treasury, and Office of Management and Budget.

Source: *Economic Indicators*, Council of Economic Advisers.

FEDERAL BUDGET: PROCEDURE AND TIMETABLE
Congressional Budget Timetable

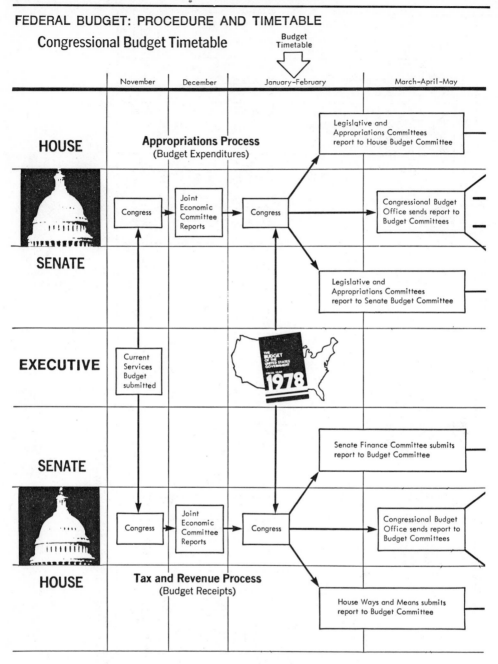

Budget Timetable

	November	December	January–February	March–April–May

HOUSE

Appropriations Process
(Budget Expenditures)

Legislative and Appropriations Committees report to House Budget Committee

Congress → Joint Economic Committee Reports → Congress

Congressional Budget Office sends report to Budget Committees

SENATE

Legislative and Appropriations Committees report to Senate Budget Committee

EXECUTIVE

Current Services Budget submitted

THE BUDGET OF THE UNITED STATES GOVERNMENT 1978

SENATE

Senate Finance Committee submits report to Budget Committee

Congress → Joint Economic Committee Reports → Congress

Congressional Budget Office sends report to Budget Committees

HOUSE

Tax and Revenue Process
(Budget Receipts)

House Ways and Means submits report to Budget Committee

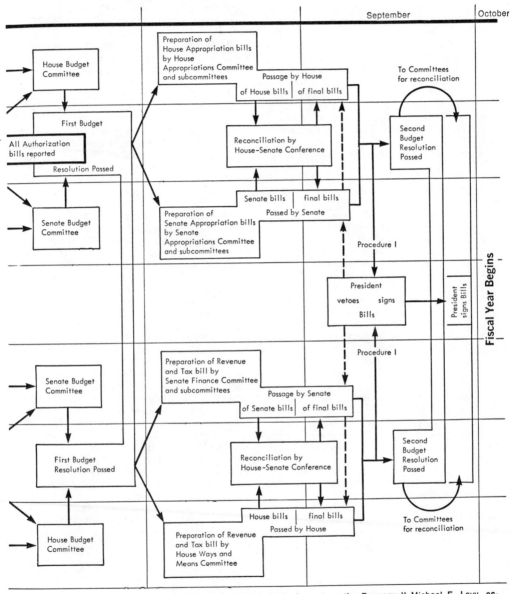

September | October

House Budget Committee

First Budget

All Authorization bills reported

Resolution Passed

Senate Budget Committee

Preparation of House Appropriation bills by House Appropriations Committee and subcommittees

Passage by House

of House bills | of final bills

To Committees for reconciliation

Reconciliation by House–Senate Conference

Second Budget Resolution Passed

Senate bills | final bills

Passed by Senate

Preparation of Senate Appropriation bills by Senate Appropriations Committee and subcommittees

Procedure I

President

vetoes   signs

Bills

President signs Bills

Fiscal Year Begins

Procedure I

Senate Budget Committee

Preparation of Revenue and Tax bill by Senate Finance Committee and subcommittees

Passage by Senate

of Senate bills | of final bills

First Budget Resolution Passed

Reconciliation by House–Senate Conference

Second Budget Resolution Passed

House bills | final bills

Passed by House

To Committees for reconciliation

House Budget Committee

Preparation of Revenue and Tax bill by House Ways and Means Committee

Source: The Conference Board, "The Federal Budget: Its Impact on the Economy," Michael E. Levy, assisted by Delos R. Smith.

CONGRESSIONAL BUDGET ACT OF 1974: THE NEW BUDGET PROCESS IN TEN STEPS

1. To give Congress an earlier and better start in reviewing and reshaping the budget, the Executive Branch must submit a "current services budget" by November 10th for the new fiscal year that starts the following October 1st. The current services budget should project the spending required to maintain ongoing programs throughout the following fiscal year at existing commitment levels, or at commitment levels specified by existing legislation based on current economic assumptions. The Joint Economic Committee should review and assess the current services budget and report to Congress by December 31st.

2. The President will continue to submit his new budget to Congress in late January or early February. In addition to the traditional budget totals and breakdowns, the budget document must include a list of existing "tax expenditures"—i.e., estimates of revenues lost to the Treasury through preferential tax treatment—as well as any proposed changes in tax expenditures. The budget must also contain estimates of expenditures for programs for which funds are appropriated one year in advance and five-year budget projections of all federal spending under existing programs.

3. Reports of all standing committees to the House and Senate Budget Committees of the spending plans of those committees on all matters under their jurisdiction, including spending under new legislation, are required by March 15th for the upcoming fiscal year.

4. An annual report of the Congressional Budget Office to the Budget Committees on alternative budget levels and national budget priorities is required on or before April 1st.

5. By April 15th, the Budget Committees must report concurrent resolutions to the House and Senate floors, and Congress will have to clear the initial budget resolution by May 15th. This initial budget resolution sets target totals for appropriations, outlays, taxes, the budget surplus or deficit, and the federal debt. Within these overall targets, the resolution will break down appropriations and outlays by the functional categories used in the President's budget document, as well as by classifications used by the appropriations subcommittees for the 13 appropriations bills. The resolution will include any recommended changes in tax revenues and in the level of the federal debt ceiling.

6. Committees report bills or resolutions authorizing new budget authority by May 15th.

7. The basic appropriations process proceeds within the Appropriations Committees, but is subject to targets of the budget resolution.

8. Scorekeeping reports will be issued periodically by the Congressional Budget Office on the status of budget authority, revenue, outlays and debt legislation, comparing the amounts and changes in such legislation with the First Congressional Budget Resolution.

9. Subject to prior authorization, all appropriations bills have to be cleared by the middle of September—no later than the seventh day after Labor Day. By September 15th, after finishing action on all appropriations and other spending bills, Congress must adopt a second, and final, budget resolution that may either affirm or revise the budget targets set by the initial resolution. This resolution must provide for a final budget reconciliation by changing either one or more of the following: (1) appropriations (both for the upcoming fiscal year or carried over from previous fiscal years) and/or entitlements; (2) revenues; and (3) the public debt. The final resolution will direct the committees that have jurisdiction over these matters to report the necessary legislative changes. The Budget Committees will then combine these changes and report them to the floor in the form of a reconciliation bill.

If Congress has withheld all appropriations and entitlement bills from the President until passage of the final reconciliation bill, then this bill becomes the final budget legislation, subject to Presidential signature (or veto). If, on the other hand, each individual appropriations bill has been signed by the President upon passage by the Congress, the final reconciliation bill—upon signature by the President—supersedes all the previously passed individual bills.

10. The new fiscal year begins on October 1st.

COMPARISON OF TRENDS IN FEDERAL DEBT AND GROSS NATIONAL PRODUCT

(Dollar amounts in billions)

Fiscal year	Gross Federal debt	Debt outstanding, end of year				GNP	Debt held by public as percent of GNP
		Held by					
		Federal Government accounts	The public				
			Total	Federal Reserve System	Other		
1954	270.8	46.3	224.5	25.0	199.5	363.6	61.7
1955	274.4	47.8	226.6	23.6	203.0	380.0	59.6
1956	272.8	50.5	222.2	23.8	198.5	411.0	54.1
1957	272.4	52.9	219.4	23.0	196.4	432.7	50.7
1958	279.7	53.3	226.4	25.4	200.9	442.1	51.2
1959	287.8	52.8	235.0	26.0	209.0	473.3	49.7
1960	290.9	53.7	237.2	26.5	210.7	497.3	47.7
1961	292.9	54.3	238.6	27.3	211.4	508.3	46.9
1962	303.3	54.9	248.4	29.7	218.7	546.9	45.4
1963	310.8	56.3	254.5	32.0	222.4	576.3	44.2
1964	316.8	59.2	257.6	34.8	222.8	616.2	41.8
1965	323.2	61.5	261.6	39.1	222.5	657.1	39.8
1966	329.5	64.8	264.7	42.2	222.5	721.1	36.7
1967	341.3	73.8	267.5	46.7	220.8	774.4	34.5
1968	369.8	79.1	290.6	52.2	238.4	829.9	35.0
1969 [1]	367.1	87.7	279.5	54.1	225.4	903.7	30.9
1970 [2]	382.6	97.7	284.9	57.7	227.2	959.0	29.7
1971	409.5	105.1	304.3	65.5	238.8	1,019.3	29.9
1972	437.3	113.6	323.8	71.4	252.3	1,110.5	29.2
1973 [3]	468.4	125.4	343.0	75.2	267.9	1,237.5	27.7
1974	486.2	140.2	346.1	80.0	265.4	1,359.2	25.5
1975	544.1	147.2	396.9	85.0	311.9	1,457.3	27.2
1976 [4]	631.9	151.6	480.3	94.7	385.6	1,621.0	29.6
TQ	646.4	148.1	498.3	96.7	401.6	1,715.8	29.0
1977	709.1	157.3	551.8	105.0	446.8	1,843.3	29.9
1978	780.4	169.5	610.9	115.5	495.5	2,060.4	29.7
1979	833.8	189.2	644.6	115.6	529.0	2,313.4	27.9
1980 estimate	892.8	203.9	688.9	NA	NA	2,518.0	27.4
1981 estimate	939.4	217.4	722.0	NA	NA	2,764.4	26.1
1982 estimate	972.6	241.3	731.3	NA	NA	3,107.6	23.5
1983 estimate	988.8	270.3	718.5	NA	NA	3,513.0	20.5

NA = Not available.

[1] During 1969, 3 Government-sponsored enterprises became completely privately owned, and their debt was removed from the totals for the Federal Government. At the dates of their conversion, gross Federal debt was reduced $10.7 billion, debt held by Government accounts was reduced $0.6 billion, and debt held by the public was reduced $10.1 billion.

[2] Gross Federal debt and debt held by the public increased $1.6 billion due to a reclassification of the Commodity Credit Corporation certificates of interest from loan assets to debt.

[3] A procedural change in the recording of trust fund holdings of Treasury debt at the end of the month increased gross Federal debt and debt held in Government accounts by about $4.5 billion.

[4] Gross Federal debt and debt held by the public increased $0.5 billion due to a retroactive reclassification of the Export-Import Bank certificates of beneficial interest from loan assets to debt.

Source: Special Analysis of the Budget.

Production, Construction, and Business Activity

EMPLOYMENT STATUS BY SEX, AGE, AND RACE, SEASONALLY ADJUSTED
NUMBERS IN THOUSANDS

Employment status	Annual average		1979									1980			
	1978	1979	Apr.	May	June	July	Aug.	Sept.	Oct.	Nov.	Dec.	Jan.	Feb.	Mar.	Apr.
TOTAL															
Total noninstitutional population[1]	161,058	163,620	163,008	163,260	163,469	163,685	163,891	164,106	164,468	164,682	164,898	165,101	165,298	165,506	165,693
Total labor force	102,537	104,996	104,280	104,476	104,552	105,475	105,218	105,586	105,688	105,744	106,088	106,310	106,346	106,184	106,511
Civilian noninstitutional population[1]	158,941	161,532	160,926	161,182	161,393	161,604	161,801	162,013	162,375	162,589	162,809	163,020	163,211	163,416	163,601
Civilian labor force	100,420	102,908	102,198	102,398	102,476	103,093	103,128	103,494	103,595	103,652	103,999	104,229	104,260	104,094	104,419
Employed	94,373	96,945	96,254	96,495	96,652	97,184	97,004	97,504	97,474	97,608	97,912	97,804	97,953	97,656	97,154
Agriculture	3,342	3,297	3,215	3,246	3,243	3,267	3,315	3,364	3,294	3,385	3,359	3,270	3,326	3,358	3,242
Nonagricultural industries	91,031	93,648	93,039	93,249	93,409	93,917	93,689	94,140	94,180	94,223	94,553	94,534	94,626	94,298	93,912
Unemployed	6,047	5,963	5,944	5,903	5,824	5,909	6,124	5,990	6,121	6,044	6,087	6,425	6,307	6,438	7,265
Unemployment rate	6.0	5.8	5.8	5.8	5.7	5.7	5.9	5.8	5.9	5.8	5.9	6.2	6.0	6.2	7.0
Not in labor force	58,521	58,623	58,728	58,784	58,917	58,511	58,673	58,519	58,780	58,937	58,810	58,791	58,951	59,322	59,182
Men, 20 years and over															
Civilian noninstitutional population[1]	67,006	68,293	67,997	68,123	68,227	68,319	68,417	68,522	68,697	68,804	68,940	69,047	69,140	69,238	69,329
Civilian labor force	53,464	54,486	54,239	54,288	54,370	54,579	54,597	54,735	54,760	54,709	54,781	54,855	55,038	54,996	55,114
Employed	51,212	52,264	52,049	52,158	52,201	52,325	52,311	52,453	52,443	52,374	52,478	52,279	52,531	52,300	51,868
Agriculture	2,361	2,350	2,295	2,301	2,305	2,327	2,375	2,377	2,371	2,438	2,427	2,387	2,435	2,394	2,320
Nonagricultural industries	48,852	49,913	49,754	49,857	49,896	49,998	49,936	50,076	50,072	49,936	50,051	49,892	50,096	49,906	49,548
Unemployed	2,252	2,223	2,190	2,130	2,169	2,254	2,286	2,282	2,317	2,335	2,303	2,577	2,507	2,696	3,246
Unemployment rate	4.2	4.1	4.0	3.9	4.0	4.1	4.2	4.2	4.2	4.3	4.2	4.7	4.6	4.9	5.9
Not in labor force	13,541	13,807	13,758	13,835	13,857	13,740	13,820	13,787	13,937	14,095	14,159	14,192	14,102	14,242	14,215

Women, 20 years and over

Civilian noninstitutional population[1]	77,981	77,876	77,766	77,656	77,542	77,426	77,308	77,124	77,006	76,897	76,784	76,670	76,532	76,860	75,489
Civilian labor force	40,137	39,751	39,857	39,878	39,659	39,445	39,362	39,239	39,304	39,033	38,653	38,619	38,415	38,910	37,416
Employed	37,602	37,496	37,604	37,574	37,402	37,248	37,112	37,075	37,000	36,873	36,457	36,411	36,216	36,698	35,180
Agriculture	552	582	567	540	582	612	572	628	600	585	583	577	572	591	586
Nonagricultural industries	37,051	36,914	37,037	37,034	36,820	36,636	36,540	36,447	36,400	36,288	35,874	35,834	35,644	36,107	34,593
Unemployed	2,534	2,255	2,254	2,304	2,257	2,197	2,250	2,164	2,304	2,160	2,196	2,208	2,199	2,213	2,236
Unemployment rate	6.3	5.7	5.7	5.8	5.7	5.6	5.7	5.5	5.9	5.5	5.7	5.7	5.7	5.7	6.0
Not in labor force	37,844	38,125	37,909	37,778	37,883	37,981	37,946	37,885	37,702	37,864	38,131	38,051	38,117	37,949	38,073

Both sexes, 16-19 years

Civilian noninstitutional population[1]	16,291	16,302	16,305	16,317	16,326	16,360	16,370	16,367	16,377	16,387	16,381	16,389	16,397	16,379	16,447
Civilian labor force	9,168	9,346	9,365	9,497	9,559	9,498	9,473	9,520	9,227	9,481	9,453	9,491	9,544	9,512	9,540
Employed	7,683	7,859	7,818	7,952	8,032	7,986	7,919	7,976	7,693	7,986	7,994	7,926	7,989	7,984	7,981
Agriculture	370	381	325	344	350	335	351	359	340	355	355	368	348	356	395
Nonagricultural industries	7,313	7,478	7,493	7,608	7,682	7,651	7,568	7,617	7,353	7,631	7,639	7,558	7,641	7,628	7,586
Unemployed	1,485	1,487	1,547	1,545	1,527	1,512	1,554	1,544	1,534	1,495	1,459	1,565	1,555	1,528	1,559
Unemployment rate	16.2	15.9	16.5	16.3	16.0	15.9	16.4	16.2	16.6	15.8	15.4	16.5	16.3	16.1	16.3
Not in labor force	7,123	6,956	6,940	6,820	6,767	6,862	6,897	6,847	7,150	6,906	6,928	6,898	6,853	6,867	6,907

White

Civilian noninstitutional population[1]	143,254	143,115	142,951	142,806	142,645	142,461	142,296	141,981	141,822	141,661	141,492	141,331	141,123	141,614	139,580
Civilian labor force	92,083	91,821	91,977	91,852	91,579	91,242	91,147	91,082	90,759	90,659	90,215	90,120	89,996	90,602	88,456
Employed	86,385	86,822	87,081	86,895	86,894	86,571	86,454	86,425	85,976	86,120	85,775	85,632	85,497	86,025	83,836
Unemployed	5,698	4,999	4,896	4,957	4,685	4,671	4,693	4,657	4,783	4,539	4,440	4,488	4,499	4,577	4,620
Unemployment rate	6.2	5.4	5.3	5.4	5.1	5.1	5.1	5.1	5.3	5.0	4.9	5.0	5.0	5.1	5.2
Not in labor force	51,171	51,294	50,975	50,954	51,066	51,219	51,149	50,900	51,161	51,107	51,213	51,313	51,200	51,011	51,124

Black and other

Civilian noninstitutional population[1]	20,346	20,301	20,261	20,214	20,163	20,128	20,079	20,032	19,979	19,943	19,901	19,850	19,802	19,918	19,361
Civilian labor force	12,319	12,266	12,362	12,453	12,432	12,391	12,512	12,404	12,343	12,386	12,260	12,219	12,191	12,306	11,964
Employed	10,771	10,823	10,937	10,979	11,024	11,044	11,076	11,063	10,982	11,023	10,887	10,816	10,767	10,920	10,537
Unemployed	1,549	1,443	1,424	1,474	1,408	1,347	1,436	1,341	1,361	1,363	1,373	1,403	1,424	1,386	1,427
Unemployment rate	12.6	11.8	11.5	11.8	11.3	10.9	11.5	10.8	11.0	11.0	11.2	11.5	11.7	11.3	11.9
Not in labor force	8,027	8,035	7,899	7,761	7,731	7,737	7,567	7,264	7,639	7,579	7,629	7,674	7,627	7,612	7,397

Note: The monthly data in this table have been revised to reflect seasonal experience through 1979.
[1] Population figures are not seasonally adjusted.
Source: *Monthly Labor Review*, U.S. Department of Labor.

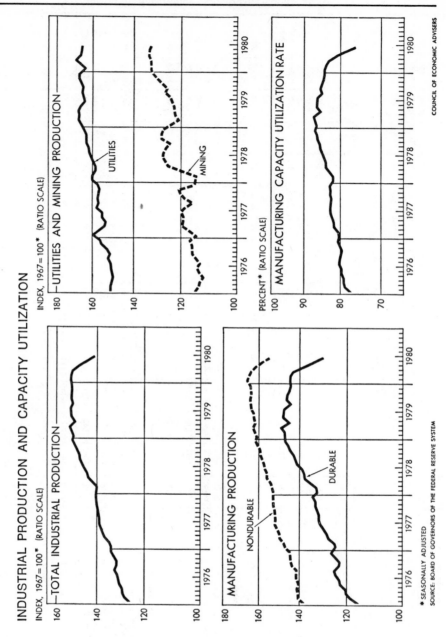

INDUSTRIAL PRODUCTION AND CAPACITY UTILIZATION

INDEX, 1967=100* (RATIO SCALE)

TOTAL INDUSTRIAL PRODUCTION

INDEX, 1967=100* (RATIO SCALE)

UTILITIES AND MINING PRODUCTION

UTILITIES

MINING

MANUFACTURING PRODUCTION

NONDURABLE

DURABLE

PERCENT* (RATIO SCALE)

MANUFACTURING CAPACITY UTILIZATION RATE

COUNCIL OF ECONOMIC ADVISERS

* SEASONALLY ADJUSTED
SOURCE: BOARD OF GOVERNORS OF THE FEDERAL RESERVE SYSTEM

[Seasonally adjusted]

Period	Total industrial production		Industry production indexes, 1967 = 100					Manufacturing capacity utilization rate, percent [1]			
	Index, 1967= 100	Per- cent change from year earlier	Manufacturing			Mining	Utili- ties	Federal Reserve series		Com- merce series [2]	Whar- ton series [3]
			Total	Dur- able	Non- dur- able			Total manu- factur- ing	Mate- rials		
1967 proportion	*100.00*		*87.95*	*51.98*	*35.97*	*6.36*	*5.69*				
1973	129.8	8.4	129.8	127.1	133.8	114.7	145.4	87.6	91.8	86	93.0
1974	129.3	.4	129.4	125.7	134.6	115.3	143.7	83.8	87.1	83	90.3
1975	117.8	-8.9	116.3	109.3	126.4	112.8	146.0	72.9	73.4	77	79.5
1976	130.5	10.8	130.3	122.3	141.8	114.2	151.7	79.5	81.1	81	85.6
1977	138.2	5.9	138.4	130.0	150.5	118.2	156.5	81.9	82.7	83	88.2
1978	146.1	5.7	146.8	139.7	156.9	124.0	161.4	84.4	85.6	84	91.1
1979	152.2	4.2	153.2	146.3	163.3	125.3	166.1	85.7	87.2	83	92.7
1979: June	152.6	4.4	153.9	147.6	163.0	123.9	164.2	86.2	87.6	83	92.9
July	152.8	3.9	154.1	147.2	164.1	124.7	164.8	86.1	87.9	---	---
Aug	151.6	2.4	152.4	144.2	164.3	126.4	165.5	84.9	86.9	---	---
Sept	152.4	2.6	153.5	145.9	164.0	125.8	165.3	85.3	86.8	82	92.4
Oct	152.2	1.7	153.2	145.7	164.0	128.1	166.1	84.9	86.6	---	---
Nov	152.1	1.0	153.0	145.0	164.5	130.0	167.4	84.6	86.4	---	---
Dec	152.2	.3	152.8	144.5	164.7	131.6	167.0	84.3	86.0	81	91.8
1980: Jan	152.6	.7	153.4	144.7	166.1	132.6	163.9	84.4	86.0	---	---
Feb	152.3	.2	152.7	144.1	165.1	132.8	166.1	83.8	85.4	---	---
Mar	151.7	-.9	151.9	143.3	164.4	132.9	169.6	83.1	84.9	80	91.4
Apr	148.3	-1.7	148.2	138.7	161.8	133.6	166.1	80.8	82.4	---	---
May *p*	144.7	-5.1	144.3	134.2	158.6	133.4	165.9	78.4	79.5	---	---
June *p*	141.2	-7.5	140.3	130.0	155.1	132.9	165.7	76.1	76.5	---	---

[1] Output as percent of capacity.
[2] Annual data are averages of four monthly indexes.
[3] Quarterly data entered in last month of quarter. Annual data are averages of quarterly data.

Sources: Board of Governors of the Federal Reserve System, Department of Commerce (Bureau of Economic Analysis), and Wharton School of Finance.

Source: *Economic Indicators*, Council of Economic Advisers.

INDUSTRIAL PRODUCTION—MAJOR MARKET GROUPS AND SELECTED MANUFACTURES
1967 = 100, SEASONALLY ADJUSTED

Period	Total	Products								Materials	Supplementary group: Energy total
		Final Products						Intermediate products			
		Consumer goods			Equipment		Total	Construction supplies			
		Total	Durable goods	Nondurable goods	Total	Business					
1967 proportion	*47.82*	*27.68*	*7.89*	*19.79*	*20.14*	*12.63*	*12.89*	*6.42*	*39.29*	*12.23*
1970	105.3	109.0	106.1	110.1	100.1	107.0	112.9	111.0	109.2	117.0
1971	106.3	114.7	118.8	113.1	94.7	104.1	116.7	116.8	111.3	119.5
1972	115.7	124.4	133.8	120.6	103.8	118.0	126.5	128.4	122.3	125.2
1973	124.4	131.5	146.2	125.6	114.5	134.2	137.2	139.8	133.9	128.3
1974	125.1	128.9	135.3	126.3	120.0	142.4	135.3	134.5	132.4	125.5
1975	118.2	124.0	121.4	125.1	110.2	128.2	123.1	116.3	115.5	125.5
1976	127.6	137.1	141.9	135.2	114.6	135.4	137.2	132.6	131.7	129.1
1977	135.9	145.3	154.0	141.9	123.0	147.8	145.1	140.6	138.6	132.9
1978	142.2	149.1	159.2	145.1	132.8	160.3	154.1	151.7	148.3	135.4
1979	147.0	150.5	155.5	148.5	142.2	171.3	160.0	156.9	156.0	137.8
1979: June	147.6	151.8	158.6	149.1	141.9	171.5	159.5	156.3	156.5	137.2
July	147.1	150.8	157.2	148.2	142.1	171.4	159.4	156.4	157.6	137.1
Aug	145.6	148.2	147.5	148.5	141.8	171.5	160.6	157.3	156.0	136.8
Sept	147.2	149.7	151.8	148.9	143.9	173.6	159.8	156.3	156.3	136.8
Oct	146.8	149.9	152.6	148.6	142.9	172.0	159.8	156.8	156.3	137.2
Nov	146.6	148.9	149.2	148.7	143.6	172.5	159.8	156.7	156.4	139.0
Dec	147.0	148.5	146.6	149.2	145.0	174.1	159.9	156.0	156.2	138.1
1980: Jan	147.0	148.2	142.4	150.5	145.4	175.0	160.8	156.4	156.7	137.8
Feb	147.4	148.5	144.5	150.1	146.0	175.8	159.3	154.3	155.9	139.0
Mar	147.1	147.8	144.0	149.3	146.1	175.9	157.7	152.4	155.4	139.6
Apr	145.0	144.9	136.6	148.3	145.2	174.3	151.5	141.3	151.2	137.6
May [p]	142.7	141.9	129.4	146.8	143.8	172.3	146.8	134.6	146.4	137.0
June [p]	140.8	140.6	128.2	145.5	141.2	168.3	142.3	128.5	141.3	135.7

[1967=100, seasonally adjusted]

Period	Durable manufactures								Nondurable manufactures			
	Primary metals		Fabricated metal products	Non-electrical machinery	Electrical machinery	Transportation equipment		Lumber and products	Apparel products	Printing and publishing	Chemicals and products	Foods
	Total	Iron and steel				Total	Motor vehicles and parts					
1967 proportion	*6.57*	*4.21*	*5.93*	*9.15*	*8.05*	*9.27*	*4.50*	*1.64*	*3.31*	*4.72*	*7.74*	*8.75*
1970	106.6	104.7	102.4	104.4	108.1	89.5	92.3	105.6	101.4	107.0	120.4	108.9
1971	100.2	96.1	103.5	100.2	107.7	97.9	118.6	113.8	104.7	107.1	125.9	112.8
1972	112.1	107.1	112.1	116.0	122.2	108.2	135.5	120.8	109.4	112.7	143.6	116.8
1973	126.7	122.3	124.7	133.7	143.1	118.3	148.8	126.0	117.3	118.2	154.5	120.9
1974	123.1	119.8	124.2	140.1	143.8	108.7	128.2	116.2	114.3	118.3	159.4	124.0
1975	96.4	95.8	109.9	125.1	116.5	97.4	111.1	107.6	107.6	113.3	147.2	123.4
1976	109.7	104.8	123.9	134.5	134.8	111.1	142.0	123.2	125.7	122.5	170.9	133.0
1977	111.1	103.8	123.0	143.6	145.4	122.2	161.1	131.2	134.2	127.6	185.7	138.8
1978	119.9	113.2	131.0	153.6	159.4	132.5	169.9	136.3	134.2	131.5	197.4	142.7
1979	121.2	113.2	141.6	163.6	175.0	135.3	160.0	136.9	130.7	136.9	210.4	147.9
1979: June	124.3	118.1	149.3	164.5	175.1	139.4	169.6	136.8	132.0	136.9	207.8	149.5
July	127.1	119.0	149.3	165.3	174.4	135.5	160.2	135.2	129.7	135.6	210.5	149.4
Aug	121.0	112.0	147.6	166.2	171.7	124.7	138.5	138.0	130.1	137.7	213.1	148.1
Sept	121.7	115.0	146.5	165.1	176.7	131.7	150.6	138.6	131.2	137.1	212.0	148.8
Oct	118.0	108.2	147.5	162.3	177.3	133.7	150.6	138.7	128.5	137.2	211.4	148.6
Nov	117.2	108.0	146.9	162.8	179.5	128.2	139.9	136.1	128.8	136.2	215.1	148.3
Dec	115.4	106.6	146.1	162.9	181.2	125.9	135.4	131.7	128.3	137.8	216.5	148.9
1980: Jan	116.4	107.2	145.0	166.9	181.7	122.4	127.6	131.6	127.2	138.9	217.7	150.0
Feb	111.9	103.4	145.3	166.1	179.7	126.2	135.4	130.2	128.0	139.9	216.0	150.2
Mar	113.6	106.0	144.7	166.0	179.5	124.3	131.7	125.4	128.0	139.2	214.5	150.3
Apr	106.9	97.4	141.9	163.3	177.3	114.9	115.0	106.5	126.0	136.5	210.2	149.0
May ᵖ	98.0	84.2	136.1	161.9	172.0	110.3	106.6	100.6	----	135.5	204.7	149.3
June ᵖ	90.4	----	130.6	157.5	165.9	109.0	106.9	----	----	134.0	----	149.3

Source: Board of Governors of the Federal Reserve System.
Source: *Economic Indicators*, Council of Economic Advisers.

NEW PRIVATE HOUSING AND VACANCY RATES
THOUSANDS OF UNITS OR HOMES, EXCEPT AS NOTED

| Period | New private housing units | | | | | | New private homes | | Vacancy rate for rental housing units (percent) [2] |
| | Units started, by type of structure | | | | Units authorized | Units completed | Homes sold | Homes for sale at end of period [1] | |
	Total	1 unit	2-4 units	5 or more units					
1972	2,356.6	1,309.2	141.3	906.2	2,218.9	2,003.9	718	409	5.6
1973	2,045.3	1,132.0	118.3	795.0	1,819.5	2,100.5	634	418	5.8
1974	1,337.7	888.1	68.1	381.6	1,074.4	1,728.5	519	346	6.2
1975	1,160.4	892.2	64.0	204.3	939.2	1,317.2	549	313	6.0
1976	1,537.5	1,162.4	85.9	289.2	1,296.2	1,377.2	646	353	5.6
1977	1,987.1	1,450.9	121.7	414.4	1,690.0	1,657.1	819	402	5.6
1978	2,020.3	1,433.3	125.0	462.0	1,800.5	1,867.5	817	414	5.0
1979	1,745.1	1,194.1	122.0	429.0	1,551.8	1,870.8	709	[3]398	5.3
Seasonally adjusted annual rates									
1979: June	1,910	1,276	123	511	1,639	1,837	698	418	5.3
July	1,764	1,222	130	412	1,563	1,776	768	416	------
Aug	1,788	1,237	152	399	1,622	1,747	738	414	------
Sept	1,874	1,237	123	514	1,695	1,963	716	412	5.4
Oct	1,710	1,139	129	442	1,478	1,819	674	407	------
Nov	1,522	980	114	428	1,287	1,831	617	399	------
Dec	1,548	1,055	110	383	1,247	1,880	571	398	5.2
1980: Jan	1,419	1,002	127	290	1,271	1,787	584	396	------
Feb	1,330	786	101	443	1,168	1,832	548	384	------
Mar	1,041	617	91	333	968	1,669	458	379	5.0
Apr ᵖ	1,030	628	100	302	789	1,891	350	366	------
May ᵖ	913	628	86	199	825	1,535	488	350	------
June ᵖ	1,191	747	67	377	1,059	------	------	------	5.4

[1] Seasonally adjusted.
[2] Quarterly data entered in last month of quarter.
[3] New series beginning March 1979.

NOTE.—Units authorized beginning 1978 relate to 16,000 permit-issuing places; data for 1972-77 are for 14,000 places and for 1971, for 13,000 places.

Source: Department of Commerce, Bureau of the Census.

Source: *Economic Indicators*, Council of Economic Advisers.

NEW CONSTRUCTION

Period	Total new construction expenditures	Private					Federal, State, and local	Construction contracts[2]	
		Total	Residential		Commercial and industrial	Other		Total value index (1972=100)	Commercial and industrial floor space (millions of square feet)
			Total[1]	New housing units					
			Billions of dollars						
1973	137.9	105.4	59.7	50.1	21.7	24.0	32.5	109.2	1,010
1974	138.5	100.2	50.4	40.6	23.8	25.9	38.3	103.0	840
1975	134.5	93.7	46.5	34.4	20.8	26.4	40.9	101.9	555
1976	151.1	111.9	60.5	47.3	19.9	31.5	39.1	121.0	592
1977	174.0	135.8	81.0	65.7	22.5	32.4	38.2	153.6	739
1978	205.5	159.6	93.4	75.8	29.6	36.6	45.9	174.1	977
1979	229.0	179.9	99.0	78.6	39.9	41.0	49.0	182.9	1,050
	Seasonally adjusted annual rates							Seasonally adjusted	Seasonally adjusted annual rates
1979: May	223.0	175.3	96.2	76.8	38.8	40.2	47.7	178	1,045
June	225.7	179.0	97.7	78.4	40.3	41.0	46.7	177	1,009
July	231.0	181.3	98.5	79.0	41.4	41.4	49.7	181	1,062
Aug	231.6	182.0	98.9	79.3	40.3	42.8	49.6	163	1,006
Sept	235.3	184.3	100.4	80.4	41.1	42.9	50.9	185	1,106
Oct	239.9	187.3	101.5	79.9	42.9	42.9	52.6	171	1,118
Nov	239.4	187.4	101.8	79.0	43.5	42.0	52.0	156	1,010
Dec	244.0	191.2	102.1	78.5	45.3	43.8	52.9	183	969
1980: Jan	259.6	198.1	105.8	80.7	47.4	44.9	61.5	190	1,253
Feb	248.8	191.7	101.5	75.1	46.4	43.8	57.0	171	1,026
Mar p	237.1	180.6	94.0	68.4	43.8	42.8	56.5	155	994
Apr p	226.6	172.4	84.5	60.7	44.5	43.4	54.2	130	875
May p	218.5	165.7	78.4	55.1	43.8	43.6	52.8	125	753

[1] Includes nonhousekeeping residential construction and additions and alterations, not shown separately.

[2] F. W. Dodge series. Relates to 50 States beginning 1969 for value index and beginning 1971 for floor space.

Source: Economic Indicators, Council of Economic Advisers.

NOTE.—New construction expenditures data prior to 1973 not comparable with later data; series revised beginning 1977.

Sources: Department of Commerce (Bureau of the Census) and McGraw-Hill Information Systems Company, F. W. Dodge Division.

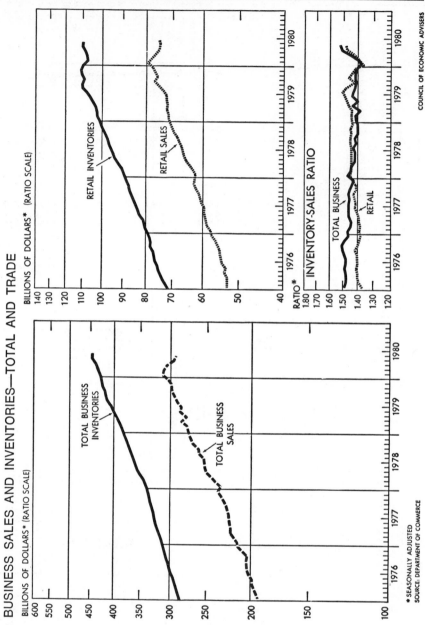

BUSINESS SALES AND INVENTORIES—TOTAL AND TRADE

BILLIONS OF DOLLARS* (RATIO SCALE)

BILLIONS OF DOLLARS* (RATIO SCALE)

TOTAL BUSINESS INVENTORIES

TOTAL BUSINESS SALES

RETAIL INVENTORIES

RETAIL SALES

INVENTORY-SALES RATIO

RATIO*

TOTAL BUSINESS

RETAIL

COUNCIL OF ECONOMIC ADVISERS

* SEASONALLY ADJUSTED
SOURCE: DEPARTMENT OF COMMERCE

Millions of dollars, seasonally adjusted

Period	Total business — Sales[2]	Total business — Inventories[3]	Wholesale — Sales[2]	Wholesale — Inventories[3]	Retail Sales[2] — Total	Retail Sales[2] — Durable goods stores	Retail Sales[2] — Nondurable goods stores	Retail Inventories[3] — Total	Retail Inventories[3] — Durable goods stores	Retail Inventories[3] — Nondurable goods stores	Inventory-sales ratio[4] — Total business[1]	Inventory-sales ratio[4] — Retail
1972	130,049	203,161	29,584	39,786	37,422	12,369	25,054	55,079	24,238	30,841	1.50	1.40
1973	152,237	234,162	36,822	46,254	42,461	14,409	28,052	63,237	28,418	34,819	1.43	1.40
1974	175,741	285,518	45,836	56,537	45,083	14,118	30,965	71,067	32,861	38,206	1.47	1.48
1975	180,263	285,035	44,633	55,113	49,013	15,247	33,766	71,744	33,356	38,388	1.58	1.44
1976	202,001	310,736	48,408	61,307	54,784	18,150	36,633	79,273	37,841	41,432	1.48	1.38
1977	224,786	337,432	53,509	67,998	60,435	20,724	39,711	89,210	42,970	46,240	1.44	1.39
1978	254,297	380,643	62,842	80,771	66,741	23,458	43,283	101,538	50,100	51,438	1.41	1.43
1979	288,449	427,040	73,611	89,920	73,837	25,680	48,158	108,862	53,087	55,775	1.41	1.45
1979: May	286,413	401,945	72,338	84,904	72,292	25,319	46,973	106,160	53,611	52,549	1.40	1.47
June	283,772	406,720	72,629	85,406	72,093	24,718	47,375	107,372	54,413	52,959	1.43	1.49
July	289,993	413,581	74,778	87,662	73,121	25,247	47,874	109,799	55,829	53,970	1.43	1.50
Aug	293,167	417,324	75,588	88,474	74,871	26,137	48,734	110,181	55,876	54,305	1.42	1.47
Sept	296,775	418,588	76,495	88,499	76,666	27,048	49,618	110,748	54,068	54,680	1.41	1.42
Oct	298,619	423,037	77,489	89,146	75,583	25,656	49,927	110,415	54,523	55,892	1.42	1.46
Nov	299,154	426,190	78,407	89,324	76,421	25,679	50,742	110,383	54,415	55,968	1.42	1.44
Dec	302,386	427,040	78,947	89,920	77,150	25,943	51,207	108,862	53,087	55,775	1.41	1.41
1980: Jan	312,730	431,815	81,178	91,085	79,464	27,268	52,196	108,436	52,130	56,306	1.38	1.36
Feb	310,571	435,321	79,689	91,508	79,993	26,369	51,624	108,717	52,232	56,485	1.40	1.39
Mar	305,657	439,325	79,042	91,708	76,534	24,296	52,238	109,095	52,276	56,819	1.44	1.43
Apr	295,277	445,528	76,670	92,736	75,011	22,821	52,190	110,252	52,490	57,762	1.51	1.47
May	291,962	445,385	76,182	92,376	74,265	22,537	51,728	109,607	51,666	57,941	1.53	1.48
June ᵖ					75,345	23,095	52,250					

1 The term "business" also includes manufacturing.
2 Monthly average for year and total for month.
3 Book value, end of period, seasonally adjusted.
Source: Economic Indicators, Council of Economic Advisers.

4 For annual periods, ratio of weighted average inventories to average monthly sales; for monthly data, ratio of inventories at end of month to sales for month.
Source: Department of Commerce (Bureau of Economic Analysis and Bureau of the Census).

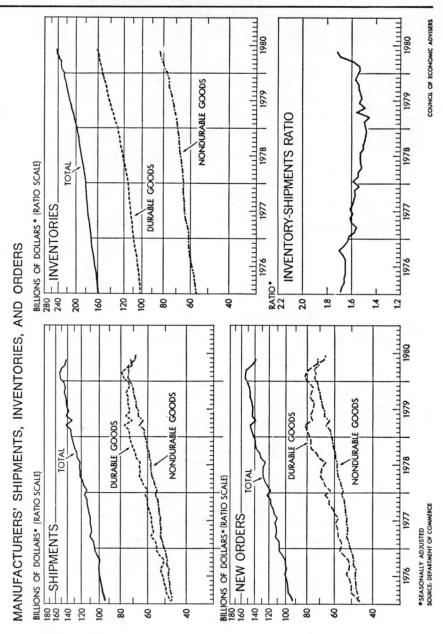

MANUFACTURERS' SHIPMENTS, INVENTORIES, AND ORDERS

BILLINGS OF DOLLARS* (RATIO SCALE)

SHIPMENTS

TOTAL

DURABLE GOODS

NONDURABLE GOODS

BILLIONS OF DOLLARS* (RATIO SCALE)

INVENTORIES

TOTAL

DURABLE GOODS

NONDURABLE GOODS

BILLIONS OF DOLLARS* (RATIO SCALE)

NEW ORDERS

TOTAL

DURABLE GOODS

NONDURABLE GOODS

RATIO*

INVENTORY-SHIPMENTS RATIO

*SEASONALLY ADJUSTED
SOURCE: DEPARTMENT OF COMMERCE

COUNCIL OF ECONOMIC ADVISERS

Millions of dollars, seasonally adjusted

Period	Manufacturers' shipments [1] Total	Durable goods	Non-durable goods	Manufacturers' inventories [2] Total	Durable goods	Non-durable goods	Manufacturers' new orders [1] Total	Durable goods Total	Capital goods industries, non-defense	Non-durable goods	Manufacturers' unfilled orders [3]	Manufacturers' inventory-shipments ratio [4]
1973	72,954	39,703	33,251	124,672	81,426	43,245	76,183	42,853	11,089	33,330	159,468	1.58
1974	84,821	44,253	40,568	157,915	101,866	56,048	87,157	46,740	12,737	40,417	187,574	1.65
1975	86,617	43,678	42,939	158,178	101,766	56,412	85,082	41,957	10,772	43,125	169,126	1.83
1976	98,810	50,697	48,113	170,156	109,095	61,061	99,184	51,047	12,501	48,137	173,646	1.66
1977	110,842	58,010	52,832	180,224	115,751	64,472	112,451	59,562	15,084	52,889	193,561	1.59
1978	124,714	66,505	58,210	198,334	129,456	68,878	128,488	70,145	18,308	58,344	239,321	1.52
1979	141,000	73,981	67,019	228,258	151,689	76,569	144,335	77,215	21,643	67,120	279,710	1.52
1979: June	139,050	72,797	66,253	213,942	141,480	72,462	142,386	76,028	21,704	66,359	267,837	1.54
July	142,094	73,875	68,220	216,120	143,141	72,979	142,620	74,585	21,227	68,035	268,362	1.52
Aug	142,708	74,363	68,345	218,669	144,658	74,011	143,615	74,762	21,077	68,854	269,269	1.53
Sept	143,614	74,201	69,414	221,341	146,048	75,293	147,378	77,647	21,578	69,731	273,033	1.54
Oct	145,547	75,544	70,003	223,476	148,136	75,340	146,610	76,521	21,073	70,089	274,097	1.54
Nov	144,326	73,751	70,574	226,483	150,476	76,007	146,996	75,903	21,754	71,092	276,767	1.57
Dec	146,289	74,191	72,098	228,258	151,689	76,569	149,232	77,199	22,285	72,033	279,710	1.56
1980: Jan	152,088	77,948	74,140	232,294	154,043	78,251	155,588	81,467	23,859	74,121	283,211	1.53
Feb	152,889	79,159	73,730	235,096	155,314	79,782	154,603	81,021	21,480	73,582	284,924	1.54
Mar	150,081	75,925	74,156	238,522	157,127	81,395	152,065	77,546	22,590	74,519	286,907	1.59
Apr	143,596	72,207	71,389	242,540	159,877	82,663	143,313	72,416	22,162	70,897	286,629	1.69
May	141,515	69,443	72,072	243,402	160,607	82,795	138,920	67,328	19,589	71,592	284,033	1.72
June p		68,240						65,423	19,096			

[1] Monthly average for year and total for month. Shipments are the same as sales.
[2] Book value, end of period.
[3] End of period.
[4] For annual periods, ratio of weighted average inventories to average monthly shipments; for monthly data, ratio of inventories at end of month to shipments for month.

Source: Economic Indicators, Council of Economic Advisers.

Source: Department of Commerce, Bureau of the Census.

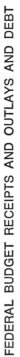

Federal, State, and Local Finance

FEDERAL BUDGET RECEIPTS AND OUTLAYS AND DEBT

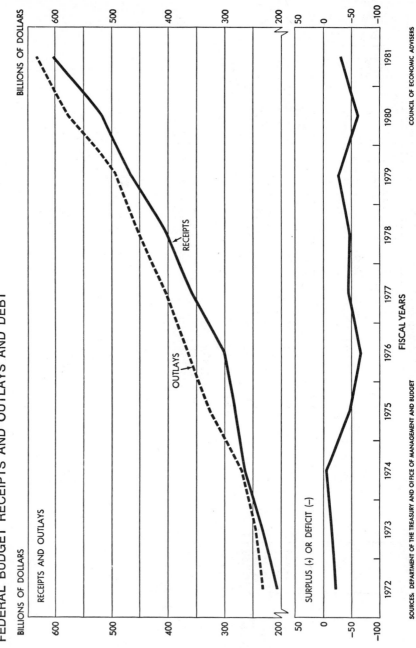

BILLIONS OF DOLLARS

BILLIONS OF DOLLARS

RECEIPTS AND OUTLAYS

OUTLAYS

RECEIPTS

SURPLUS (+) OR DEFICIT (-)

FISCAL YEARS

COUNCIL OF ECONOMIC ADVISERS

SOURCES: DEPARTMENT OF THE TREASURY AND OFFICE OF MANAGEMENT AND BUDGET

[Billions of dollars]

Period	Receipts	Outlays	Surplus or deficit (−)	Federal debt (end of period)	
				Total[1]	Held by the public
Fiscal year or period:					
1970	193.7	196.6	−2.8	382.6	284.9
1971	188.4	211.4	−23.0	409.5	304.3
1972	208.6	232.0	−23.4	437.3	323.8
1973	232.2	247.1	−14.8	468.4	343.0
1974	264.9	269.6	−4.7	486.2	346.1
1975	281.0	326.2	−45.2	544.1	396.9
1976	300.0	366.4	−66.4	631.9	480.3
Transition quarter	81.8	94.7	−13.0	646.4	498.3
1977	357.8	402.7	−45.0	709.1	551.8
1978	402.0	450.8	−48.8	780.4	610.9
1979	465.9	493.7	−27.7	833.8	644.6
1980 (estimates):					
Third Concurrent Resolution, June 12, 1980	525.7	572.7	−47.0		
Mid-Session Review, July 1980[2]	517.9	578.8	−60.9		
1981 (estimates):					
First Concurrent Resolution, June 12, 1980	613.8	613.6	.2		
Mid-Session Review, July 1980[2]	604.0	633.8	−29.8		
Cumulative total, first 9 months:					
Fiscal year 1979	346.0	368.8	−22.8	812.2	632.2
Fiscal year 1980	384.9	428.6	−43.7	884.4	688.0

[1] Excludes non-interest-bearing public debt securities held by IMF.
[2] Estimates from *Mid-Session Review of the 1981 Budget*, Office of Management and Budget, July 21, 1980.

Sources: Department of the Treasury and Office of Management and Budget, except as noted.
Source: *Economic Indicators*, Council of Economic Advisers.

FEDERAL BUDGET RECEIPTS BY SOURCE AND OUTLAYS BY FUNCTION

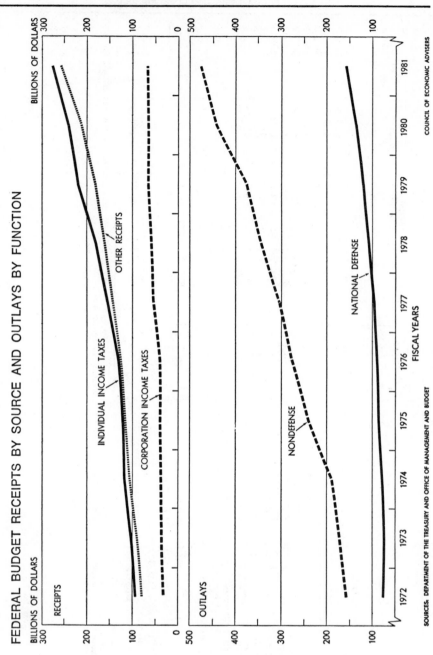

BILLIONS OF DOLLARS

SOURCES: DEPARTMENT OF THE TREASURY AND OFFICE OF MANAGEMENT AND BUDGET

COUNCIL OF ECONOMIC ADVISERS

[Billions of dollars]

Period	Receipts				Outlays						
	Total	Individual income taxes	Corporation income taxes	Other	Total	National defense		International affairs	Health and income security	Interest	Other
						Total	Department of Defense, military				
Fiscal year or period:											
1970	193.7	90.4	32.8	70.5	196.6	78.6	77.1	4.3	56.1	18.3	39.3
1971	188.4	86.2	26.8	75.4	211.4	75.8	74.5	4.1	70.1	19.6	41.8
1972	208.6	94.7	32.2	81.7	232.0	76.6	75.1	4.7	81.4	20.6	48.8
1973	232.2	103.2	36.2	92.8	247.1	74.5	73.2	4.1	91.8	22.8	53.9
1974	264.9	119.0	38.6	107.4	269.6	77.8	77.6	5.7	106.5	28.0	51.6
1975	281.0	122.4	40.6	118.0	326.2	85.6	84.9	6.9	136.3	30.9	66.5
1976	300.0	131.6	41.4	127.0	366.4	89.4	87.9	5.6	160.9	34.5	76.1
Transition quarter	81.8	38.8	8.5	34.5	94.7	22.3	21.9	2.2	41.5	7.2	21.5
1977	357.8	157.6	54.9	145.2	402.7	97.5	95.6	4.8	176.7	38.0	85.7
1978	402.0	181.0	60.0	161.1	450.8	105.2	103.0	5.9	189.9	44.0	105.9
1979	465.9	217.8	65.7	182.4	493.7	117.7	115.0	6.1	209.8	52.6	107.5
1980 (estimates)[1]	517.9	240.7	65.5	211.7	578.8	135.6	132.6	10.9	250.4	64.3	117.6
1981 (estimates)[1]	604.0	278.2	66.4	259.4	633.8	157.5	153.9	10.3	293.8	67.6	104.6
Cumulative total, first 9 months:											
Fiscal year 1979	346.0	160.2	52.7	133.2	368.8	85.5	84.9	4.2	155.4	41.1	82.7
Fiscal year 1980	384.9	177.8	52.2	154.9	428.6	100.9	98.7	8.0	181.7	50.2	87.9

[1] Estimates from *Mid-Session Review of the 1981 Budget*, Office of Management and Budget, July 21, 1980.

Sources: Department of the Treasury and Office of Management and Budget. Source: *Economic Indicators*, Council of Economic Advisers.

1981 FEDERAL GOVERNMENT HOLIDAYS: NO POSTAL SERVICE

January 1	New Year's Day
February 16	Washington's Birthday (observed)
May 25	Memorial Day (observed)
July 4	Independence Day
September 1	Labor Day
October 13	Columbus Day (observed)
November 11	Veterans' Day
26	Thanksgiving
December 25	Christmas

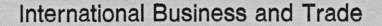

FINANCING EXPORTS

Many sources of financial assistance are available to exporters. First, of course, is your own working capital or bank line of credit. Use of your own facilities may, however, restrict your total cash availability even if you were to establish a separate export line of credit with your bank.

Commercial Banks More than 250 U.S. banks have qualified international banking departments with specialists familiar with particular foreign countries and experts in different types of commodities and transactions. These banks, located in all major U.S. cities, maintain correspondent relationships with smaller banks throughout the United States. This banking network enables any exporter to find assistance (for himself or his overseas customer) for his export financing needs. The larger banks also maintain correspondent relationships with banks in most foreign countries or operate their own overseas branches, providing a direct channel to overseas customers.

Factoring Houses Exporters should also be aware of factoring houses that deal in accounts receivable of American exporters. Although possibly charging higher fees, they will purchase your receivables, often without recourse, assuring you of prompt payment for your export sale.

Export Management Companies Export management companies not only will act as your export representative, but some of these professional export houses also will carry the financing for the export sale, again assuring you of immediate payment and removing from your company any foreign credit risk. For names of export management companies in your area, you may contact your local Department of Commerce district office.

Eximbank The U.S. Government also participates in the financing of America's exports. The Export-Import Bank of the United States (Eximbank) offers direct loans for large projects and equipment sales that usually require longer term financing. It cooperates with commercial banks in the United States and abroad in providing a number of· financial arrangements to help U.S. exporters offer credit to their overseas buyers. It provides export credit guarantees to commercial banks that finance export sales; and, through the Foreign Credit Insurance Association (FCIA), provides insurance to American exporters which enables them to extend credit terms to their overseas buyers. In all cases, the Bank must find a "reasonable assurance of repayment" as a precondition of participating in the transaction.

Eximbank regulations and conditions of assistance are, of course, subject to change. For more information, consult your commercial bank, or write directly to the Export-Import Bank of the United States, 811 Vermont Avenue, NW., Washington, D.C. 20571. Telex 89–461.

Foreign Credit Insurance Association The FCIA administers the U.S. export credit insurance program on behalf of its member insurance companies and the Government-owned Eximbank. The private insurers cover the normal commercial credit risks, mainly the insolvency of or the prolonged payment default by the overseas buyer. Eximbank assumes all liability for the political risks including, in addition to exchange transfer delay, such hazards as war, revolution, or similar hostilities; unforeseen withdrawal or nonrenewal of a license to export or import; requisition, expropriation, confiscation, or intervention in the business of the buyer by a governmental authority; transport or insurance charges caused by interruption or diversion of shipment; and certain other government acts which may prevent or unduly delay payment and which are beyond the control of the seller or the buyer.

One of FCIA's major forms of coverage is the master policy, designed to provide under one policy substantially automatic coverage for all of an exporter's sales to overseas buyers both short- and medium-term, on credit terms ranging up to 5 years. The policy may provide political risks coverage only, or comprehensive risks coverage.

For information on other types of policies offered by FCIA, exporters should consult with FCIA at One World Trade Center, 9th Floor, New York, N.Y. 10048.

Source: Excerpted from *A Basic Guide to Exporting*, U.S. Department of Commerce.

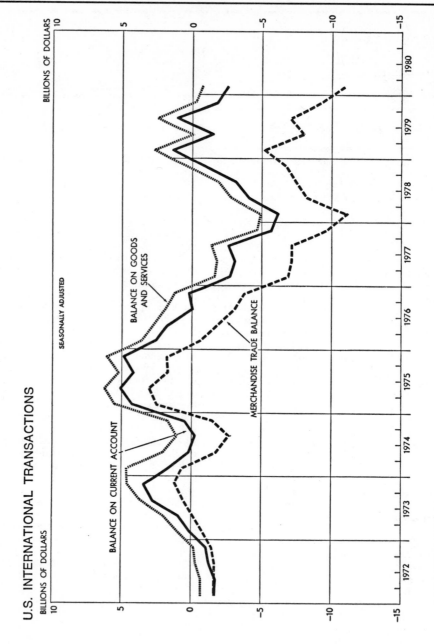

U.S. INTERNATIONAL TRANSACTIONS

BILLIONS OF DOLLARS

BILLIONS OF DOLLARS

SEASONALLY ADJUSTED

BALANCE ON GOODS AND SERVICES

BALANCE ON CURRENT ACCOUNT

MERCHANDISE TRADE BALANCE

10 5 0 -5 -10 -15

1972 1973 1974 1975 1976 1977 1978 1979 1980

SOURCE: DEPARTMENT OF COMMERCE

COUNCIL OF ECONOMIC ADVISERS

[Millions of dollars; quarterly data seasonally adjusted]

Period	Merchandise [1][2] Exports	Merchandise [1][2] Imports	Merchandise [1][2] Net balance	Investment income [2] Receipts	Investment income [2] Payments	Investment income [2] Net	Net military transactions	Net travel and transportation receipts	Other services, net [3]	Balance on goods and services [1]	Remittances, pensions, and other unilateral transfers [1]	Balance on current account
1972	49,381	−55,797	−6,416	14,764	−6,572	8,192	−3,420	−3,063	2,766	−1,941	−3,854	−5,795
1973	71,410	−70,499	911	21,808	−9,655	12,153	−2,070	−3,158	3,184	11,021	−3,881	7,140
1974	98,306	−103,649	−5,343	25,587	−12,084	15,503	−1,653	−3,184	3,986	9,309	−7,186	2,124
1975	107,088	−98,041	9,047	25,351	−12,564	12,787	−746	−2,792	4,598	22,893	−4,613	18,280
1976	114,745	−124,051	−9,306	29,286	−13,311	15,975	559	−2,558	4,711	9,382	−4,998	4,384
1977	120,816	−151,689	−30,873	32,587	−14,598	17,989	1,628	−3,293	5,086	−9,464	−4,605	−14,068
1978	142,054	−175,813	−33,759	42,972	−22,073	20,899	886	−3,188	5,959	−9,204	−5,055	−14,259
1979	182,055	−211,524	−29,469	65,970	−33,460	32,510	−1,275	−2,695	5,806	4,878	−5,666	−788
1978: III	36,828	−44,336	−7,508	10,557	−5,717	4,840	139	−910	1,506	−1,933	−1,233	−3,166
IV	38,900	−45,715	−6,815	12,851	−6,343	6,508	3	−774	1,571	493	−1,313	−820
1979: I	41,805	−46,919	−5,114	14,263	−7,225	7,038	−29	−611	1,448	2,732	−1,324	1,408
II	42,815	−50,885	−8,070	15,250	−7,980	7,270	−102	−637	1,428	−110	−1,383	−1,493
III	47,198	−54,258	−7,060	18,050	−8,731	9,319	−443	−834	1,524	2,506	−1,407	−1,099
IV	50,237	−59,462	−9,225	18,407	−9,524	8,883	−700	−613	1,405	−250	−1,552	−1,802
1980: I p	54,708	−65,583	−10,875	20,548	−10,425	10,123	−700	−778	1,539	−691	−1,876	−2,567

[1] Excludes military grants.
[2] Adjusted from Census data for differences in timing and coverage.
[3] Fees and royalties from U.S. direct investments abroad or from foreign direct investments in the United States are excluded from investment income and included in other services, net.

Source: Department of Commerce, Bureau of Economic Analysis.
Source: Economic Indicators, Council of Economic Advisers.

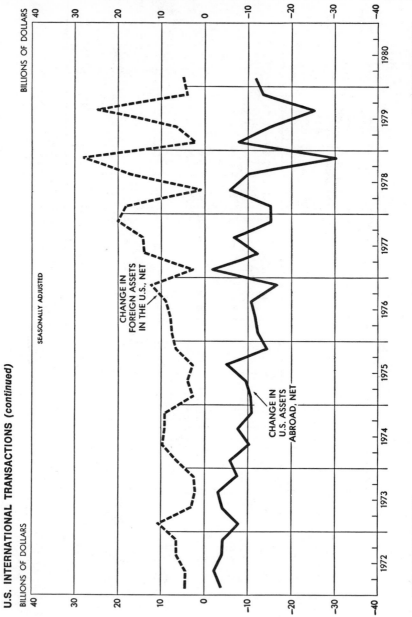

U.S. INTERNATIONAL TRANSACTIONS *(continued)*

BILLIONS OF DOLLARS

SOURCE: DEPARTMENT OF COMMERCE

COUNCIL OF ECONOMIC ADVISERS

[Millions of dollars; quarterly data seasonally adjusted, except as noted]

Period	U.S. assets abroad, net [increase/capital outflow (−)]				Foreign assets in the U.S., net [increase/capital inflow (+)][2]				Allocations of special drawing rights (SDR)	Statistical discrepancy		U.S. official reserve assets[1] (unadjusted, end of period)
	Total	U.S. official reserve assets[1][2]	Other U.S. Government assets	U.S. private assets[2]	Total	Foreign official assets		Other foreign assets		Total (sum of the items with sign reversed)	Of which: Seasonal adjustment discrepancy	
						Total	Assets of foreign official reserve agencies					
1972	−14,497	−4	−1,568	−12,925	21,461	10,475	10,293	10,986	710	−1,879	------	13,151
1973	−22,874	158	−2,644	−20,388	18,388	6,026	5,090	12,362	------	−2,654	------	14,378
1974	−34,745	−1,467	366	−33,643	34,241	10,546	10,244	23,696	------	−1,620	------	15,883
1975	−39,703	−849	−3,474	−35,380	15,670	7,027	5,509	8,643	------	5,753	------	16,266
1976	−51,269	−2,558	−4,214	−44,498	36,518	17,693	13,066	18,826	------	10,367	------	18,747
1977	−35,793	−375	−3,693	−31,725	50,741	36,575	35,416	14,167	------	−880	------	19,312
1978	−61,191	732	−4,644	−57,279	64,096	33,293	31,072	30,804	------	11,354	------	18,650
1979	−61,748	−1,107	−3,783	−56,858	37,575	−14,271	−13,556	51,845	1,139	23,822	------	18,928
1978: III	−9,977	115	−1,386	−8,706	17,069	4,777	4,556	12,292	------	−3,926	−2,850	18,850
IV	−30,418	182	−991	−29,609	28,048	18,368	16,673	9,680	------	3,190	1,998	18,650
1979: I	−7,768	−3,585	−1,102	−3,081	2,201	−8,744	−8,616	10,945	1,139	3,020	74	21,658
II	−15,279	343	−991	−14,631	6,407	−10,095	−10,216	16,502	------	10,364	1,167	21,246
III	−25,215	2,779	−766	−27,228	24,941	5,789	5,573	19,152	------	−825	−3,641	18,534
IV	−13,487	−644	−925	−11,918	4,025	−1,221	−297	5,246	------	11,264	2,400	18,928
1980: I p	−11,817	−3,246	−1,461	−7,110	5,016	−7,765	−7,722	12,781	1,152	8,215	−115	21,448

[1] Consists of gold, special drawing rights (SDR), convertible currencies, and the U.S. reserve position in the IMF.
[2] Quarterly data are not seasonally adjusted.

Sources: Department of Commerce (Bureau of Economic Analysis) and Department of the Treasury.

FOREIGN TRADE OF THE UNITED STATES

Value of exports ($ millions)	Annual		1979				
	1978	1979	Mar.	Apr.	May	June	July
Exports (mdse.), incl. reexports, total* ..	¹143,662.8	181,801.6	15,586.7	14,267.3	14,818.9	15,365.9	14,731.8
Eccl. Dept. of Defense shipments	¹143,577.5	181,636.8	15,584.4	14,257.0	14,812.9	15,344.5	14,725.7
Seasonally adjusted†	—	—	14,297.3	13,978.8	14,083.1	14.817.3	15.691.1
By geographic regions:							
Africa	5,887.1	6,299.2	524.2	458.4	497.3	529.5	480.0
Asia	39,629.9	48,771.1	4,197.9	3,827.6	3.737.0	4,052.6	4,375.5
Australia and Oceania	3,464.3	4,318.8	334.9	336.4	361.5	352.6	315.6
Europe	43,607.7	60,014.0	5,302.9	4,595.4	4,998.8	4,885.5	4,609.6
Northern North America	28,375.2	33,096.7	3,052.8	2.804.8	2,919.6	2,941.0	2,527.7
Southern North America	11,026.2	14,886.5	1,152.7	1,178.4	1,179.1	1,330.3	1,119.0
South America	10,992.3	13,569.4	1,021.2	971.3	1,007.3	1,176.9	1,222.0
By leading countries:							
Africa:							
Egypt	1,134.1	1,433.3	173.3	113.5	140.7	122.5	82.8
Republic of South Africa	1,081.1	1,413.0	103.6	108.2	108.9	122.3	122.0
Asia; Australia and Oceania:							
Australia, including New Guinea ..	2,944.1	3,649.4	285.5	286.5	312.2	294.9	259.5
India	947.9	1,167.0	98.3	74.0	57.7	73.6	82.6
Pakistan	495.7	529.1	53.9	60.1	24.6	38.1	70.2
Malaysia	728.4	932.1	77.8	66.7	76.4	89.4	74.9
Indonesia	751.4	981.5	74.8	71.2	107.3	79.4	109.2
Philippines	1,041.2	1,570.1	115.1	130.9	130.2	112.1	147.9
Japan	12,885.1	17,579.3	1,609.7	1,317.2	1,257.7	1,505.2	1,584.8
Europe:							
France	4,166.2	5,586.7	546.6	470.7	410.4	438.6	392.5
German Democratic Republic (formerly E. Germany)	170.4	356.0	32.9	26.2	33.1	31.1	9.2
Federal Republic of Germany (formerly W. Germany)	6,956.8	8,482.3	811.2	647.6	679.5	650.9	610.1
Italy	3,360.6	4,358.5	406.3	363.5	378.5	364.9	273.5
Union of Soviet Socialist Republics	2,252.3	3,607.1	271.0	273.7	234.6	352.4	364.5
United Kingdom	7,116.0	10,634.8	962.1	864.5	866.6	766.5	903.5
North and South America:							
Canada	28,373.7	33,095.8	3,052.8	2,804.6	2,919.6	2,940.9	2,527.7
Latin American republics, total‡ ..	20,185.2	26,256.6	1,974.0	1,969.1	2,001.2	2,320.9	2,169.9
Argentina	841.8	1,889.9	99.2	112.1	143.0	124.9	155.4
Brazil	2,980.6	3,441.6	272.9	232.9	228.9	254.6	321.8
Chile	724.6	885.5	53.1	50.3	56.9	86.6	81.0
Colombia	1,045.9	1,409.3	99.2	102.3	108.9	181.6	128.0
Mexico	6,680.3	9,847.2	711.1	763.2	755.3	905.3	718.9
Venezuela	3,727.7	3,931.3	330.1	353.4	312.9	343.6	353.9
Exports of U.S. merchandise, total §	141,125.6	178,578.0	15,300.1	14,020.8	14,534.9	15,102.6	14,496.0
Excluding military grant-aid	141,040.3	178,413.2	15,297.8	14,010.5	14,529.0	15,081.1	14,489.9
Agricultural products, total	29,384.1	34,745.4	2,877.3	2,651.5	2,509.1	2,760.6	2,715.2
Nonagricultural products, total	111,741.4	143,832.6	12,422.8	11,369.4	12,025.8	12,342.0	11,780.8
By commodity groups and principal commodities:							
Food and live animals‡	¹18,311.3	22,245.4	1,581.0	1,528.1	1,584.8	1,905.2	2,053.3
Meats and preparations (incl. poultry)	958.4	1,126.9	94.7	86.8	90.0	106.9	87.5
Grains and cereal preparations ...	11,633.8	14,450.5	929.9	960.8	1,039.4	1,225.3	1,397.2
Beverages and tobacco	¹2,292.8	2,336.7	223.2	202.3	183.1	175.8	176.4
Crude materials, inedible, exc. fuels‡	¹15,555.1	20,755.3	1,837.5	1,668.0	1,626.7	1,605.2	1,434.6
Cotton, raw, excl. linters and waste	1,739.6	2,198.4	188.7	198.1	174.7	197.2	133.5
Soybeans, exc. canned or prepared	5,210.4	5,707.7	644.4	517.1	349.4	319.0	260.3
Metal ores, concentrates, and scrap	1,839.1	3,324.6	226.6	211.9	296.3	248.1	296.1
Mineral fuels, lubricants, etc‡	¹3,880.6	5,615.9	435.7	467.0	471.2	499.8	534.0
Coal and related products	2,122.6	3,496.0	258.8	279.6	325.9	316.7	330.0
Petroleum and products	1,563.7	1,913.6	152.3	169.1	139.3	157.4	188.4

	1979				1980			
Aug.	**Sept.**	**Oct.**	**Nov.**	**Dec.**	**Jan.**	**Feb.**	**Mar.**	**Apr.**
15,009.4	14,939.6	17,283.2	17,320.3	16,984.6	16,360.9	16,970.8	19,685.0	—
14,975.1	14,919.6	17,275.5	17,301.2	16,954.2	16,343.9	16,958.6	19,671.4	—
15,713.3	15,822.4	16,680.0	16,928.1	16,741.6	17,347.7	17,233.0	18,534.4	—
536.2	477.8	640.6	624.2	599.4	555.0	—	—	—
4,271.7	4,088.0	4,303.8	4,320.4	4,568.2	4,046.8	—	—	—
313.6	341.4	414.5	439.7	438.7	362.1	—	—	—
4,784.2	4,817.0	5,608.3	6,310.7	5,831.3	6,214.1	—	—	—
2,519.4	2,777.3	3,347.3	2,895.3	2,507.7	2,598.6	—	—	—
1,333.9	1,188.7	1,446.0	1,360.1	1,529.0	1,480.2	—	—	—
1,183.4	1,161.7	1,385.5	1,273.3	1,446.6	1,104.2	—	—	—
98.5	78.5	115.9	179.5	121.0	150.5	—	—	—
109.2	125.3	146.5	128.3	149.4	136.5	—	—	—
258.2	283.0	344.6	381.7	370.5	308.2	—	—	—
172.0	106.6	92.9	88.5	149.1	86.0	—	—	—
45.0	45.5	28.2	15.3	32.7	25.7	—	—	—
79.9	84.6	86.1	87.8	89.2	85.0	—	—	—
107.7	99.4	73.0	73.8	89.4	102.6	—	—	—
134.1	131.7	134.4	146.5	174.3	123.7	—	—	—
1,449.2	1,539.9	1,521.2	1,597.5	1,606.3	1,525.8	—	—	—
439.9	488.8	544.4	533.4	509.3	717.0	—	—	—
17.4	26.2	34.0	61.7	67.8	17.2	—	—	—
673.5	680.9	832.6	813.6	849.4	962.3	—	—	—
346.0	296.3	413.2	411.8	474.9	441.2	—	—	—
341.3	312.5	325.8	378.3	426.4	174.0	—	—	—
860.8	848.4	1,000.7	1,113.0	863.9	947.1	—	—	—
2.519.4	2,777.1	3,347.3	2,895.3	2,507.7	2,598.5	—	—	—
2,343.9	2,182.9	2,631.3	2,453.5	2,736.0	2,359.0	—	—	—
145.6	151.9	307.2	199.0	219.3	176.1	—	—	—
324.7	347.7	329.4	341.8	392.4	273.5	—	—	—
92.9	72.6	99.8	93.5	88.4	77.0	—	—	—
119.5	95.4	128.1	127.0	148.2	123.9	—	—	—
924.9	799.7	968.4	954.3	1,008.5	982.8	—	—	—
315.6	311.6	343.8	289.4	430.1	287.2	—	—	—
14,748.5	14,686.3	16,998.7	16,966.8	16,662.1	16,031.5	—	—	—
14,714.1	14,666.3	16,991.0	16,947.7	16,631.6	16,014.5	—	—	—
2,735.4	2,734.7	3,507.9	3,783.9	3,681.5	3,276.9	—	—	—
12,013.0	11,951.6	13,490.8	13,182.8	12,980.6	12,754.6	—	—	—
2,055.9	2,056.5	2,384.3	2,194.9	2,273.8	2,107.9	2,046.5	2,212.3	—
88.1	99.2	103.9	93.6	120.2	84.2	—	—	—
1,399.7	1,376.7	1,599.4	1,442.9	1,523.7	1,301.9	—	—	—
178.1	141.8	184.0	281.6	283.6	152.4	204.1	335.3	—
1,539.4	1,555.6	1,940.8	2,323.0	2,160.6	2,109.7	2,169.6	2,375.4	—
148.7	136.5	127.8	214.1	311.9	256.1	—	—	—
313.9	313.8	640.0	834.5	564.7	606.4	—	—	—
290.0	292.5	280.2	385.8	412.8	404.8	—	—	—
496.3	438.0	567.4	521.5	542.8	481.4	435.6	566.9	—
328.3	272.3	389.2	319.1	319.8	233.5	—	—	—
148.8	150.6	167.3	186.2	196.4	219.3	186.9	234.9	—

FOREIGN TRADE OF THE UNITED STATES *(continued)*

Value of exports ($ millions)	Annual		1979				
	1978	1979	Mar.	Apr.	May	June	July
Exports of U.S. merchandise *(continued)*							
Oils and fats, animal and vegetable ..	¹1,521.3	1,845.0	171.3	129.6	104.4	187.6	157.6
Chemicals	¹12,622.8	17,306.2	1,522.3	1,289.8	1,320.8	1,513.2	1,433.2
Manufactured goods‡	¹12,416.8	16,235.2	1,384.1	1,228.5	1,355.0	1,468.1	1,230.3
Textiles	2,225.2	3,189.4	263.8	238.8	266.8	286.9	243.7
Iron and steel	1,716.3	2,342.0	198.8	184.5	183.8	208.4	194.0
Nonferrous base and metals	1,047.8	1,609.4	129.3	126.3	141.4	153.2	116.9
Machinery and transport equipment, total	¹59,255.4	70,403.8	6,325.1	5,843.9	6,047.2	5,984.1	5,651.0
Machinery, total‡	37,017.5	44,741.0	3,971.7	3,580.2	3,806.1	3,875.1	3,556.8
Agricultural	2,151.6	2,635.5	275.3	259.9	267.5	235.0	224.7
Metalworking	1,188.3	1,391.4	119.6	106.7	139.3	129.0	120.0
Construction, excav. and mining	1,318.4	1,233.8	117.6	107.9	105.4	114.4	105.7
Electrical	6,966.6	8,635.0	748.3	703.6	738.7	750.2	673.7
Transport equipment, total	22,250.3	25,750.4	2,354.4	2,264.8	2,243.0	2,125.9	2,095.7
Motor vehicles and parts	13,237.3	15,076.5	1,395.4	1,259.0	1,451.5	1,399.9	1,037.2
Miscellaneous manufactured articles	¹10,177.5	12,639.6	1,133.2	965.3	1,071.7	1,074.8	997.6
Commodities not classified	¹5,006.7	9,030.3	684.5	688.1	764.1	667.4	821.8
Value of imports ($ millions)							
General imports, total	171,978.0	206,326.5	15,764.8	16,172.0	16,511.5	17,435.6	17,115.0
Seasonally adjusted†	—	—	15,357.5	15,841.4	16,438.3	16,835.4	16,806.1
By geographic regions:							
Africa	16,898.1	24,376.5	1,651.1	1,835.0	1,795.7	1,808.4	2,053.1
Asia	58,264.0	66,740.4	4,803.7	5,233.8	4,946.8	5,772.2	5,677.3
Australia and Oceania	2,350.4	3,072.0	253.0	277.7	263.7	285.2	264.5
Europe	37,984.5	43,548.2	3,458.9	3,574.2	3,569.8	3,986.1	3,784.9
Northern North America	33,546.2	38,122.3	3,373.6	2,968.5	3,508.1	3,096.4	2,914.5
Southern North America	12,624.4	17,287.8	1,285.8	1,239.4	1,418.2	1,395.7	1,362.6
South America	10,302.6	13,172.5	938.1	1,042.9	1,008.7	1,091.4	1,057.8
By leading countries:							
Africa:							
Egypt	105.0	381.0	35.1	14.9	21.4	55.1	19.5
Republic of South Africa	2,258.7	2,616.5	196.8	214.1	256.9	203.0	208.9
Asia; Australia and Oceania:							
Australia, including New Guinea ..	1,727.7	2,236.2	189.4	208.1	187.8	201.6	187.1
India	979.4	1,037.7	85.4	96.8	93.6	92.8	92.4
Pakistan	83.7	120.0	11.6	11.3	11.4	12.0	10.2
Malaysia	1,519.1	2,145.6	201.2	147.4	166.1	196.5	151.6
Indonesia	3,606.9	3,620.6	249.5	339.0	226.4	332.0	289.0
Philippines ....:	1,207.2	1,488.8	120.9	95.8	118.3	128.2	101.3
Japan	24,457.7	26,242.9	1,985.1	2,300.6	2,092.0	2,319.9	2,183.3
Europe:							
France	4,051.0	4,770.8	356.4	362.3	409.6	416.7	414.4
German Democratic Republic (formerly E. Germany)	35.3	36.2	2.6	4.2	3.3	4.1	2.2
Federal Republic of Germany (formerly W. Germany)	9,961.5	10,955.3	858.0	981.9	938.8	1,002.6	941.9
Italy	4,102.1	4,918.1	425.0	403.3	367.1	492.9	498.2
Union of Soviet Socialist Republics	539.1	872.4	23.2	28.7	71.9	75.4	44.2
United Kingdom	6,513.9	8,028.7	671.0	653.4	656.0	697.4	710.4
North and South America:							
Canada	33,525.0	38,099.3	3,370.6	2,968.3	3,507.3	3,094.2	2,912.0
Latin American republics, total‡ ..	18,556.0	24,782.2	1,830.4	1,939.1	2,011.1	2,089.1	1,899.8
Argentina	563.4	587.1	45.9	47.5	59.8	67.1	42.6
Brazil	2,825.7	3,118.8	206.9	240.6	219.7	258.6	232.3
Chile	385.3	439.8	35.4	33.0	46.9	35.2	45.3
Colombia	1,044.2	1,209.4	118.4	115.0	104.4	79.1	88.4
Mexico ...,...................	6,093.9	8,813.4	656.6	666.1	725.6	710.0	621.5
Venezuela	3,545.1	5,165.9	347.0	475.9	393.6	392.9	476.0
By commodity groups and principal commodities:							
Agricultural products, total	14,961.6	16,881.0	1,435.9	1,490.9	1,382.3	1,509.0	1,267.4
Nonagricultural products, total	157,016.5	189,445.5	14,329.0	14,681.1	15,129.2	15,926.7	15,847.6

	1979				1980			
Aug.	Sept.	Oct.	Nov.	Dec.	Jan.	Feb.	Mar.	Apr.
140.1	163.7	146.6	166.4	158.7	139.6	142.5	228.1	—
1,546.8	1.589.6	1,652.7	1,439.2	1,607.5	1,617.1	1,537.8	1,880.4	—
1,341.6	1,360.7	1,565.6	1,507.6	1,536.9	1,647.9	1,734.7	1,882.6	—
262.5	283.1	311.2	288.2	302.6	268.6	—	—	—
201.8	202.1	226.0	203.9	227.9	178.0	—	—	—
124.1	114.2	142.6	148.1	171.8	171.2	—	—	—
5,600.7	5,645.4	6,348.6	6,168.2	6,355.2	5,612.9	6,540.7	7,444.5	—
3,665.0	3,677.6	4,067.3	3,885.3	4,170.8	3,872.8	—	—	—
214.9	194.2	224.9	193.9	178.0	208.1	—	—	—
108.1	111.2	110.1	121.1	125.3	97.5	—	—	—
123.6	100.3	125.7	89.5	89.4	83.2	—	—	—
709.2	738.6	790.6	741.5	788.6	783.3	—	—	—
1,957.2	1,976.9	2,283.9	2,284.3	2,212.6	1,744.1	—	—	—
1,019.6	1,200.5	1,454.3	1,345.9	1,154.1	1,130.2	—	—	—
1,038.9	1,080.0	1,157.4	1,173.2	1,157.5	1,575.9	1,408.5	1,542.7	—
776.3	635.0	1,043.5	1,172.0	555.0	659.7	455.2	833.7	—
17,931.0	18,075.5	19,243.3	18,658.1	19,797.2	20,138.9	20,638.6	21,060.4	—
18,277.2	18,407.1	19,037.1	18,548.4	19,665.0	20,944.8	21,640.4	20,607.1	—
2,193.1	2,514.3	2,571.3	2,147.6	2,727.0	2,421.0	—	—	—
6,156.5	6,002.0	6,466.8	5,849.1	5,908.6	6,642.1	—	—	—
260.9	232.1	190.1	290.5	304.0	295.7	—	—	—
3,784.2	3,385.7	3,589.6	4,001.1	4,436.4	4,092.6	—	—	—
2,886.2	3,164.5	3,438.0	3,544.1	3,428.5	3,463.4	—	—	—
1,480.3	1,580.8	1,813.2	1,561.0	1,772.7	1,916.5	—	—	—
1,169.3	1,192.9	1,173.6	1,264.2	1,218.6	1,306.9	—	—	—
9.9	51.0	61.5	56.9	31.3	21.0	—	—	—
264.3	255.8	251.8	238.5	167.3	342.5	—	—	—
181.7	178.2	129.5	205.0	218.7	233.1	—	—	—
96.6	90.1	88.1	74.0	59.4	92.2	—	—	—
8.0	9.5	9.5	7.8	8.2	11.8	—	—	—
182.8	185.3	257.0	175.1	171.7	276.8	—	—	—
384.7	341.8	377.2	306.0	258.4	511.8	—	—	—
149.3	129.5	146.5	134.2	149.5	149.1	—	—	—
2,276.1	2,188.7	2,299.8	2,349.1	2,135.5	2,496.5	—	—	—
395.9	367.4	381.5	489.8	470.8	489.9	—	—	—
2.7	2.9	2.2	2.2	4.9	4.7	—	—	—
1,024.0	766.2	803.2	1,016.5	1,070.6	989.3	—	—	—
403.3	351.5	389.3	413.8	492.3	397.3	—	—	—
110.3	90.8	132.7	103.3	147.8	41.8	—	—	—
703.4	667.1	712.8	789.0	807.5	782.3	—	—	—
2,881.9	3,162.3	3,437.8	3,541.6	3,426.4	3,463.1	—	—	—
2,113.9	2,150.1	2,342.9	2,296.7	2,468.5	2,515.5	—	—	—
56.4	42.9	34.2	35.7	50.7	36.6	—	—	—
321.1	264.5	215.0	312.6	287.8	294.3	—	—	—
50.4	33.9	28.9	35.2	51.8	37.6	—	—	—
97.1	81.0	115.9	110.4	107.2	109.3	—	—	—
756.8	767.0	943.1	782.8	937.0	948.9	—	—	—
406.7	524.3	464.9	477.4	462.8	537.7	—	—	—
1,314.1	1,257.6	1,255.2	1,542.6	1,656.4	1,649.7	1,367.2	1,536.2	—
16,616.9	16,817.9	17,988.2	17,115.5	18,140.8	18,489.2	—	—	—

FOREIGN TRADE OF THE UNITED STATES (concluded)

Value of imports ($ millions)	Annual 1978	Annual 1979	1979 Mar.	1979 Apr.	1979 May	1979 June	1979 July
General imports (continued)							
Food and live animals‡	¹13,521.5	15,170.6	1,242.6	1,325.7	1,245.1	1,357.3	1,172.9
Cocoa beans	667.0	554.9	51.4	45.0	27.7	44.0	37.7
Coffee	3,728.2	3,819.7	282.4	339.6	274.6	279.5	305.6
Meats and preparations	1,856.0	2,539.3	242.3	242.3	231.3	269.9	205.2
Sugar	723.0	974.3	62.2	57.6	122.5	120.5	67.5
Beverages and tobacco	¹2,221.3	2,565.6	221.9	205.3	217.1	210.9	204.2
Crude materials, inedible, exc. fuels‡	¹9,293.8	10,650.5	859.3	870.1	1,006.0	960.9	919.1
Metal ores	2,811.6	3,247.1	211.1	251.6	302.6	298.8	306.4
Paper base stocks	1,166.9	1,546.7	129.4	111.7	156.8	122.9	125.6
Textile fibers	247.8	231.2	19.8	18.8	19.4	20.8	20.5
Rubber	684.7	897.1	82.3	100.5	61.7	95.3	67.8
Mineral fuels, lubricants, etc.	¹42,095.8	60,060.9	3,947.9	4,240.6	4,165.9	4,528.2	5,075.0
Petroleum and products	39,104.2	56,046.0	3,673.8	4,015.0	3,802.1	4,236.3	4,757.8
Oils and fats, animal and vegetable	¹511.0	739.8	55.7	44.2	40.6	61.6	35.0
Chemicals	¹6,430.0	7,485.0	655.1	648.7	698.3	663.6	570.9
Manufactured goods‡	¹27,234.9	30,065.1	2,424.0	2,251.0	2,596.4	2,669.8	2,481.2
Iron and steel	7,259.3	7,446.3	479.9	479.8	678.0	644.1	626.9
Newsprint	2,100.7	2,322.1	209.3	183.0	186.7	189.5	185.7
Nonferrous metals	5,122.8	6,320.1	562.6	444.4	522.8	562.1	507.9
Textiles	2,200.1	2,216.4	185.9	182.9	189.3	200.6	179.6
Machinery and transport equipment	¹47,590.2	53,678.4	4,438.3	4,750.0	4,509.3	4,712.5	4,328.6
Machinery, total‡	24,403.8	28,044.8	2,289.6	2,313.7	2,291.1	2,536.0	2,402.0
Metalworking	946.7	1,442.4	105.5	113.4	119.7	135.4	121.8
Electrical	5,170.7	6,558.1	547.1	482.5	523.9	607.1	564.4
Transport equipment	23,186.1	25,633.6	2,148.8	2,436.2	2,218.3	2,176.5	1,926.6
Automobiles and parts	20,631.2	22,074.6	1,871.7	2,162.9	1,943.1	1,920.8	1,673.5
Miscellaneous manufactured articles	¹19,061.5	21,006.0	1,569.2	1,549.5	1,584.5	1,864.4	1,967.9
Commodities not classified	¹4,018.5	4,904.7	350.8	287.0	448.3	406.4	360.2
Indexes (1967 = 100)							
Exports (U.S. mdse., excl. military grant-aid):							
Unit value	224.7	255.5	255.1	257.1	256.8	264.2	265.6
Quantity	204.9	227.9	234.8	213.3	221.5	223.5	213.5
Value	460.3	582.2	598.8	548.4	568.8	590.3	567.2
General imports:							
Unit value	291.3	347.4	319.4	320.5	328.1	335.3	345.2
Quantity	221.2	221.7	221.6	226.4	225.8	232.9	221.8
Value	644.4	770.1	707.6	725.6	740.9	781.0	765.7
Shipping weight and value							
Waterborne trade:							
Exports (incl. reexports):							
Shipping weight (000 sh. tons)	300,032	357,792	28,239	27,463	28,288	31,650	31,768
Value (mil. $)	77,268	97,579	8,176	7,381	7,775	8,384	8,009
General imports:							
Shipping weight (000 sh. tons)	592,949	597,254	45,937	51,080	48,529	51,744	51,439
Value (mil. $)	115,480	140,093	10,028	11,030	10,703	12,170	11,921

Notes: Unless otherwise stated in footnotes, data through 1976 and descriptive notes are as shown in the 1977 edition of Business Statistics.

Beginning January 1978, data are based on a new classification system and include nonmonetary gold; the overall total, and the commodity groups (but not the items within the groups) have been revised back to January 1977 to reflect these changes.

* Data may not equal the sum of the geographic regions, or commodity groups and principal commodities, because of revisions to the totals not reflected in the component items.

	1979				1980			
Aug.	Sept.	Oct.	Nov.	Dec.	Jan.	Feb.	Mar.	Apr.
1,177.1	1,163.2	1,185.5	1,449.5	1,470.9	1,466.1	1,203.4	1,351.0	—
50.3	17.6	30.1	31.3	25.3	35.2	—	—	—
300.8	357.5	297.1	378.1	453.2	477.0	—	—	—
165.8	157.0	162.3	221.8	232.6	228.7	—	—	—
67.3	70.0	108.0	133.3	60.3	63.6	—	—	—
198.7	222.5	217.8	247.8	258.5	178.6	198.5	212.9	—
958.3	942.0	852.5	878.1	853.7	882.4	892.6	988.7	—
302.9	313.9	251.9	287.6	301.4	304.6	—	—	—
138.8	119.5	138.1	144.3	135.4	148.3	—	—	—
21.7	16.1	16.5	19.3	18.7	24.2	—	—	—
74.0	77.3	62.7	59.0	62.7	99.9	—	—	—
5,460.4	6,084.4	6,558.7	5,410.7	6,836.2	6,558.6	7,741.9	7,391.7	—
5,108.2	5,742.7	6,226.0	4,999.9	6,300.2	6,046.3	—	—	—
66.3	56.8	72.4	69.4	97.6	58.2	32.7	42.3	—
648.1	612.1	609.9	708.5	697.1	696.1	726.8	786.2	—
2,627.6	2,484.0	2,693.4	2,721.3	2,739.9	2,916.3	2,815.6	2,909.9	—
729.3	697.3	645.8	716.7	690.1	580.9	—	—	—
199.5	173.5	194.7	220.1	220.4	216.5	—	—	—
508.1	490.8	626.0	574.0	693.0	808.0	—	—	—
188.7	182.3	173.9	177.3	207.9	203.8	—	—	—
4,314.3	4,183.5	4,569.4	4,815.0	4,608.9	4,982.8	4,741.9	5,104.2	—
2,395.4	2,362.6	2,455.1	2,455.9	2,366.3	2,519.4	—	—	—
123.5	108.7	123.1	156.3	147.2	145.9	—	—	—
584.2	610.2	621.6	568.7	604.7	604.0	—	—	—
1,918.9	1,821.0	2,114.4	2,359.1	2,242.5	2,463.4	—	—	—
1,671.6	1,566.2	1,758.2	1,989.9	1,880.7	2,009.5	—	—	—
2,046.4	1,871.3	1,991.9	1,826.6	1,688.1	1,879.8	1,668.3	1,806.7	—
433.7	455.8	491.9	531.0	546.3	520.0	616.8	466.8	—
269.8	266.5	273.4	272.6	274.8	277.0	276.7	278.7	—
213.5	215.4	243.3	243.4	237.0	226.4	236.0	271.1	—
576.0	574.1	665.2	663.4	651.1	627.1	652.9	755.8	—
351.8	362.8	372.2	379.9	388.9	399.5	416.6	425.0	—
228.0	215.0	231.3	219.9	227.6	224.0	221.6	221.8	—
801.5	779.9	860.9	835.5	885.2	894.7	923.1	942.5	—
32,714	30,101	35,324	32,673	34,644	—	—	—	—
8,191	8,072	9,350	9,345	9,751	—	—	—	—
50,891	51,846	52,068	44,458	51,748	—	—	—	—
12,721	12,556	12,944	12,504	13,684	—	—	—	—

† Effective February 1979 *Survey,* seasonally adjusted data have been revised to reflect sums of commodity components; comparable data for periods prior to 1977 will be shown in the 1979 *Business Statistics.*

‡ Includes data not shown separately.

§ Data may not equal the sum of geographic regions, or commodity groups and principal commodities, because of revisions to the totals not reflected in the components.

Source: *Survey of Current Business,* Bureau of Economic Analysis.

DISPOSABLE PERSONAL INCOME, SAVINGS, AND RATIO OF SAVINGS TO INCOME

Period	United States	Other Countries						
		France	F.R. Germany	Italy	Nether- lands	United Kingdom	Japan	Canada
Disposable personal income (1967 = 100)								
1970	126.0	136.9	133.3	134.8	139.7	125.3	157.4	125.2
1975	199.6	268.2	214.0	302.5	258.5	267.1	367.5	257.4
1976	217.5	302.0	226.5	363.6	297.8	307.2	415.9	291.2
1977	239.7	341.6	239.3	445.2	324.7	348.2	455.2	321.2
1978	267.8	388.7	254.7		351.6	403.5	494.3	357.0
1979	298.3	436.8p	275.1			479.2		399.4
1980								
Savings (1967 = 100)								
1970	123.7	135.5	165.0	150.0	134.3	134.4	161.6	105.0
1975	204.4	292.6	297.6	412.1	256.8	447.0	470.4	443.7
1976	167.7	290.0	283.2	469.9	297.7	494.5	529.2	469.2
1977	158.9	347.9	277.9	609.9	285.4	552.7	545.9	507.6
1978	176.0	415.5	298.9		309.7	685.8	564.4	586.3
1979	180.4	438.5p	341.3			905.3		648.8
1980								
Ratio of savings to disposable personal income (percent)								
1970	7.4	16.7	14.6	18.8	14.0	9.0	18.1	5.3
1975	7.7	18.6	16.4	23.0	14.5	14.0	22.5	10.9
1976	5.8	16.4	14.7	21.8	14.6	13.4	22.4	10.2
1977	5.0	17.3	13.7	23.1	12.8	13.3	21.1	10.0
1978	4.9	18.2	13.8		12.9	14.1	20.1	10.4
1979	4.5	17.1	14.6			15.7		10.3
1980								

Savings data are calculated by deducting outlays—such as personal consumption expenditures, interest paid, and transfer payments to foreigners—from disposable personal income.
Source: *International Economic Indicators*, U.S. Department of Commerce.

UNIT LABOR COSTS AND PRODUCTIVITY IN MANUFACTURING
Indexes: 1967 = 100

Period	United States	Other Countries France	F.R. Germany	Italy	Nether-lands	United Kingdom	Japan	Canada
Unit labor costs in U.S. dollars								
1970	116.5	96.7	125.7	119.2	108.7	104.8	113.2	111.7
1975	152.4	206.2	268.5	245.1	245.4	196.2	284.8	165.6
1976	158.2	195.1	265.4	212.5	238.8	182.4	285.3	185.7
1977	166.6	207.0	299.4	234.9	268.7	195.3	326.7	182.5
1978	179.4	242.6	359.0	270.4	311.8	242.2	408.7	174.3
1979	192.9							
1980								
Unit labor costs in national currencies								
1970	116.5	108.6	115.0	119.8	109.1	120.3	112.0	108.1
1975	152.4	179.4	165.4	256.2	171.9	242.9	233.4	156.2
1976	158.2	189.3	167.5	282.7	175.1	278.0	233.5	169.7
1977	166.6	206.8	174.3	332.3	183.1	307.8	241.6	179.8
1978	179.4	221.9	180.6	367.7	187.0	347.2	235.2	184.1
1979	192.9							
1980								
Output per man-hour								
1970	105.0	121.2	116.1	121.7	134.0	110.0	146.5	114.7
1975	118.8	150.7	151.3	152.9	181.1	126.1	174.6	133.7
1976	124.0	163.6	160.3	165.9	199.1	129.2	188.7	140.4
1977	127.7	171.7	169.0	167.8	206.7	128.2	197.3	148.1
1978	128.3	180.2	175.1	172.7	217.3	130.5	212.9	155.0
1979	130.3							
1980								

Indexes of unit labor costs and hourly compensation are adjusted for changes in exchange rates in order to express them in U.S. dollars.
Source: *International Economic Indicators*, U.S. Department of Commerce.

International Business and Financial Comparisons

TREASURY BILL RATES
BOND-EQUIVALENT YIELDS, AT OR NEAR END OF MONTH

	1976 Dec	1977 Dec	1978 Dec	1979 Nov	1979 Dec	1980 Jan	1980 Feb	1980 Mar	1980 Apr	1980 May	1980 Jun
United States	4.41	6.33	9.42	11.68	12.39	12.96	14.92	15.85	10.29	8.05	7.90
Canada	8.14	7.17	10.46	13.62	13.66	13.50	13.55	15.24	15.15	11.58	10.24
Japan	5.68	4.15	3.39	5.17	5.68	5.68	5.68	5.68	5.68	6.82	6.82
Australia	8.73	8.35	8.35	9.02	9.31	9.33	9.52	10.77	11.12	10.83	10.79
United Kingdom	13.98	6.42	12.01	16.75	16.45	16.93	16.71	16.95	16.73	16.75	16.29
Belgium	10.00	9.25	9.25	14.30	14.40	14.40	15.00	17.50	17.00	15.50	13.75
Ireland	14.28	6.74	11.83	16.36	16.37	16.08	16.45	16.76	16.88	16.69	16.57
Italy	17.38	12.81	12.81	13.05	15.62	13.17	15.62	15.87	16.12	15.53	15.86
Netherlands	5.63	6.00	9.50	14.00	12.75	10.75	10.50	10.75	10.25	10.87	10.37
Sweden	9.75	9.21	5.84	9.74	9.74	10.79	10.79	10.78	10.78	12.89	12.89
Argentina*	78.92	109.06	82.55	70.43	71.04	63.77	61.83	59.76	58.55	64.01	70.26
Brazil	38.58	38.08	41.21	27.33	27.84	24.62	23.85	25.90	27.33	24.62	33.84
Korea	n.a.	16.88	17.01	19.53	19.53	22.01	22.01	22.01	22.01	22.01	22.01
Mexico	n.a.	n.a.	12.75	16.85	17.89	18.71	19.30	21.38	22.33	n.a.	n.a.
New Zealand	4.00	7.50	10.50	11.25	11.25	11.25	11.25	11.25	11.25	11.25	11.25
Philippines	9.78	10.04	12.08	12.64	12.63	12.56	12.33	12.31	12.31	12.31	12.46
Singapore	2.99	3.17	4.01	5.65	6.18	6.77	6.74	6.92	7.21	7.10	6.85
South Africa	7.94	8.17	7.61	3.90	4.30	4.29	4.38	4.39	4.47	4.78	4.72

* revised

Source: Reprinted, with permission, from *World Financial Markets*, a publication of Morgan Guaranty Trust Company, New York.

REPRESENTATIVE MONEY-MARKET RATES

BOND EQUIVALENT YIELDS ON MAJOR SHORT-TERM (MOSTLY 3–4 MONTH) MONEY-MARKET INSTRUMENTS OTHER THAN TREASURY BILLS, AT OR NEAR END OF MONTH

	1976 Dec	1977 Dec	1978 Dec	1979 Nov	1979 Dec	1980 Jan	Feb	Mar	Apr	May	Jun
United States	4.75	6.84	10.57	12.90	13.70	13.49	15.45	18.44	13.70	7.90	8.03
Canada	8.62	7.25	10.62	13.65	14.15	13.80	13.75	16.00	15.40	11.75	11.50
Japan	6.75	5.89	4.64	8.14	8.01	8.02	9.86	12.68	12.12	12.53	10.87
Australia	9.75	9.75	9.10	10.50	10.30	10.30	10.40	11.75	14.00	13.50	13.00
United Kingdom	14.38	6.50	12.50	16.81	17.00	17.75	18.31	18.12	17.12	17.00	17.00
Belgium	10.50	9.50	9.25	14.35	14.45	14.50	15.00	17.50	17.00	15.75	14.00
France	10.00	9.19	6.44	12.37	12.62	12.19	13.62	13.69	12.56	12.37	12.25
Germany	4.80	3.60	3.70	9.50	8.70	8.85	9.50	9.80	9.97	10.20	9.95
Ireland	14.69	6.75	13.00	17.75	18.12	18.00	18.37	19.12	18.75	17.88	17.50
Italy	16.63	11.75	11.37	13.62	17.12	17.75	17.62	17.87	16.50	17.12	17.25
Netherlands	5.88	6.25	10.50	14.75	13.00	11.37	12.87	11.25	10.37	11.25	10.62
Spain	11.36	12.06	22.80	12.80	13.20	13.40	13.40	15.50	17.50	18.70	16.90
Switzerland	1.84	2.02	0.50	4.50	6.12	6.00	5.25	7.37	6.37	5.62	5.87
Hong Kong	5.50	5.73	11.82	13.25	14.37	15.37	15.50	15.87	14.75	12.12	8.75
Korea	16.99	16.88	17.01	19.53	19.53	22.01	22.01	22.01	22.01	22.01	22.01
New Zealand	10.37	11.87	12.00	16.25	16.00	16.20	15.75	16.00	15.25	14.25	13.50
Philippines	15.47	11.96	11.48	10.13	10.41	10.33	9.99	11.49	11.79	11.06	12.22
Singapore	3.75	4.81	7.38	8.25	10.12	10.12	10.25	11.50	11.31	10.75	9.75
South Africa	9.73	9.00	7.85	4.12	4.72	4.61	4.93	5.03	5.55	5.34	5.24

Source: Reprinted, with permission, from *World Financial Markets*, a publication of Morgan Guaranty Trust Company of New York.

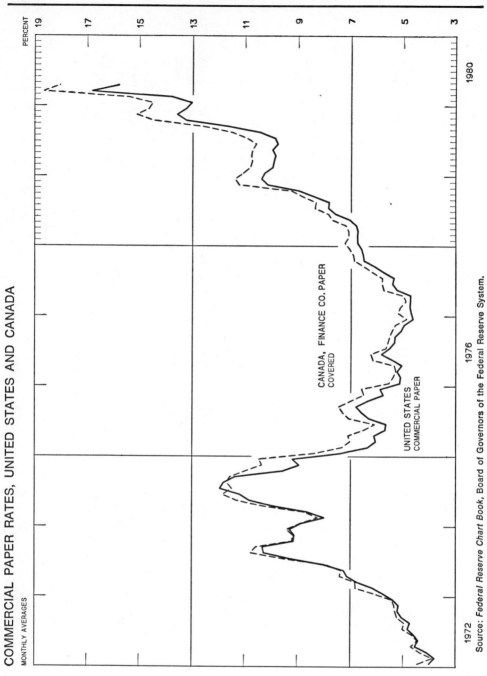

COMMERCIAL PAPER RATES, UNITED STATES AND CANADA

MONTHLY AVERAGES

PERCENT

19

17

15

13

11

9

7

5

3

CANADA, FINANCE CO. PAPER
COVERED

UNITED STATES
COMMERCIAL PAPER

1972

1976

1980

Source: *Federal Reserve Chart Book,* Board of Governors of the Federal Reserve System.

SHORT-TERM INTEREST RATES, SELECTED COUNTRIES

MONTHLY AVERAGES

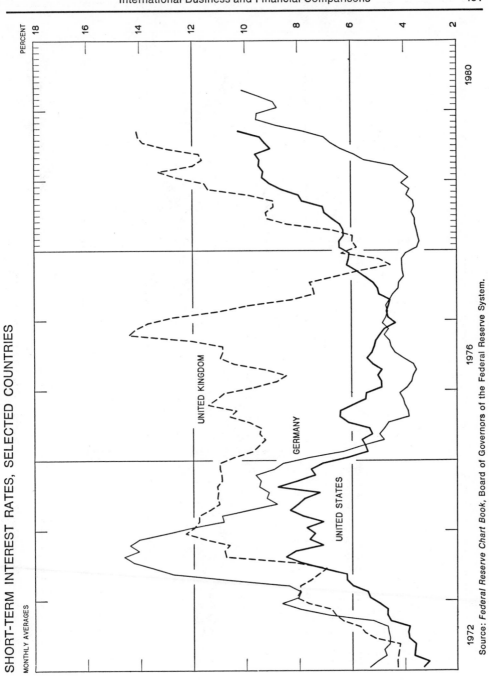

UNITED KINGDOM

GERMANY

UNITED STATES

1972

1976

1980

PERCENT

18

16

14

12

10

8

6

4

2

Source: *Federal Reserve Chart Book*, Board of Governors of the Federal Reserve System.

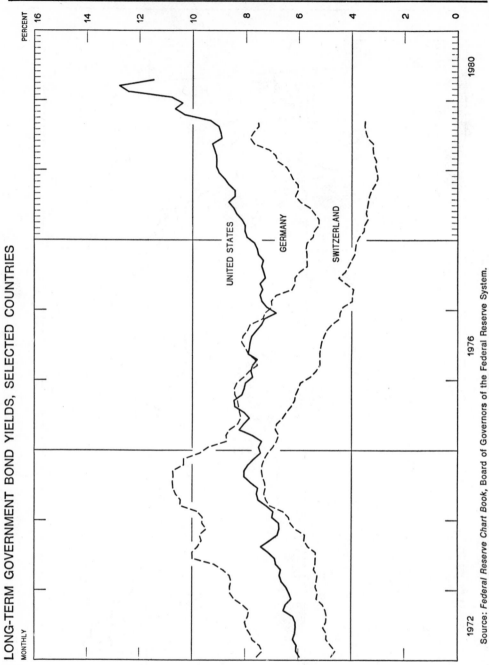

LONG-TERM GOVERNMENT BOND YIELDS, SELECTED COUNTRIES

MONTHLY

PERCENT

UNITED STATES

GERMANY

SWITZERLAND

1972

1976

1980

Source: *Federal Reserve Chart Book*, Board of Governors of the Federal Reserve System.

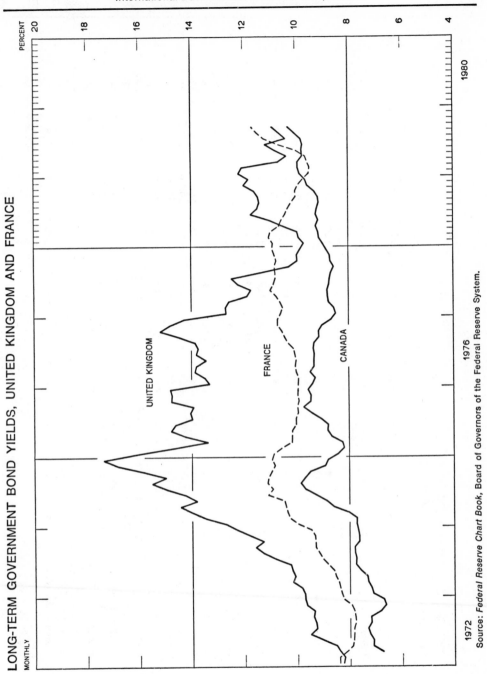

LONG-TERM GOVERNMENT BOND YIELDS, UNITED KINGDOM AND FRANCE

MONTHLY

PERCENT

UNITED KINGDOM

FRANCE

CANADA

1972   1976   1980

Source: *Federal Reserve Chart Book*, Board of Governors of the Federal Reserve System.

FOREIGN GOVERNMENT BOND YIELDS
LONG-TERM ISSUES, AT OR NEAR END OF MONTH

	1976 Dec	1977 Dec	1978 Dec	1979 Nov	1979 Dec	1980 Jan	Feb	Mar	Apr	May	Jun
United States	7.20	7.97	9.00	10.09	10.20	11.11	12.60	12.50	10.38	10.24	9.90
Canada	8.47	8.77	9.68	10.94	11.32	12.13	12.91	13.20	12.01	11.39	11.29
Japan	8.61	6.40	6.40	8.78	8.63	8.56	9.17	9.76	9.65	8.75	8.45
Australia	10.50	9.50	8.90	10.40	10.45	10.65	11.50	11.75	11.85	11.85	11.80
United Kingdom	14.31	10.53	12.75	13.98	13.83	13.30	13.89	13.98	13.44	13.30	13.06
Belgium	9.30	8.76	8.80	11.00	11.13	11.42	11.93	12.45	12.02	12.26	11.84
France	11.04	11.07	9.94	12.09	12.59	12.52	14.11	14.44	13.94	13.49	13.34
Germany	7.28	5.52	6.65	7.81	7.91	8.13	8.86	9.72	8.93	8.20	8.00
Italy	13.92	10.82	10.89	11.31	11.28	11.39	11.56	11.63	11.63	11.64	11.80
Netherlands	8.40	8.11	8.48	9.18	9.29	9.41	10.37	11.45	10.59	9.97	9.95
Austria	8.55	9.00	7.91	8.27	8.20	8.20	8.51	8.93	9.50	9.52	9.26
Denmark	14.57	16.83	17.27	18.04	18.28	18.55	19.71	20.37	20.57	20.27	20.90
Finland	10.92	10.25	9.19	9.49	9.58	9.94	10.13	10.38	10.59	10.46	n.a.
Ireland	15.49	11.30	13.44	16.64	16.64	15.95	15.95	15.95	16.20	16.19	15.78
Norway	7.25	8.37	8.19	10.19	10.04	10.10	10.15	10.20	10.26	10.31	10.16
Sweden	9.61	9.84	10.09	11.04	11.22	10.92	11.24	11.26	11.33	11.31	n.a.
Switzerland	4.43	3.75	3.03	4.04	4.20	4.48	5.03	5.09	4.96	4.82	4.72
Argentina*	63.02	181.65	112.18	70.93	47.94	42.58	45.02	54.02	59.98	47.21	57.33
New Zealand	8.70	10.00	10.02	12.96	12.98	13.44	13.45	13.57	13.47	13.75	n.a.
Philippines	13.41	13.40	13.40	13.30	13.20	13.40	13.40	13.40	13.40	13.40	13.40
South Africa	11.00	10.75	9.85	9.34	9.44	9.38	9.33	9.32	9.56	9.69	9.85
Venezuela	7.04	7.24	7.24	7.33	7.29	7.38	7.25	7.33	7.40	7.45	7.45

* revised

Source: Reprinted, with permission, from *World Financial Markets*, a publication of Morgan Guaranty Trust Company of New York.

FOREIGN CORPORATE BOND YIELDS
LONG-TERM ISSUES, AT OR NEAR END OF MONTH

	1976 Dec	1977 Dec	1978 Dec	1979 Nov	1979 Dec	1980 Jan	Feb	Mar	Apr	May	Jun
United States	7.35	8.30	9.25	10.50	10.75	11.88	12.88	13.75	10.75	11.20	10.63
Canada	9.58	9.71	10.34	11.72	12.07	12.80	13.35	13.90	12.84	12.29	12.14
Japan	8.81	6.68	6.94	8.34	8.34	8.12	8.12	8.75	9.50	8.68	8.23
Australia	12.00	11.00	10.25	11.65	11.65	11.90	12.60	12.75	13.10	13.25	13.15
United Kingdom	15.96	11.88	13.53	14.89	14.96	14.25	14.55	14.99	14.66	14.39	13.98
Belgium	11.88	9.85	9.58	11.70	11.93	11.82	12.22	n.a.	n.a.	n.a.	n.a.
France	11.39	12.09	10.27	12.33	12.92	12.91	14.57	14.80	14.37	14.39	14.16
Germany	7.47	5.92	6.80	8.40	8.20	8.10	8.50	9.60	10.00	9.40	8.90
Italy	16.90	10.71	10.12	9.90	10.22	10.22	10.56	11.12	11.85	12.14	14.12
Netherlands	8.22	7.90	8.62	9.50	9.95	9.78	10.54	12.05	10.85	10.43	9.96
Norway	7.65	8.59	8.37	10.94	10.53	10.71	10.75	10.80	10.85	10.91	10.46
Spain	10.86	11.58	12.17	11.40	11.77	11.34	11.18	11.19	11.45	10.89	10.83
Sweden	9.82	9.83	10.03	9.81	10.21	10.43	10.78	10.85	11.00	11.07	11.71
Switzerland	5.50	4.96	4.85	5.44	5.53	5.61	5.63	6.06	5.77	5.56	5.64
Korea	21.70	19.60	24.00	31.00	32.50	32.50	31.00	31.00	31.00	31.00	30.50
Mexico	15.56	17.56	20.37	22.43	21.99	23.00	23.55	24.49	26.26	24.70	n.a.
Venezuela	10.37	10.39	12.43	14.06	14.55	13.63	13.87	14.86	15.94	14.40	12.81

Source: Reprinted, with permission, from *World Financial Markets*, a publication of Morgan Guaranty Trust Company of New York.

ECONOMIC AND BUSINESS INDICATORS OF DEVELOPED COUNTRIES*

Unless otherwise specified in the tables, the following definitions apply. Industrial production: Covers mining, manufacturing and electricity, gas and water (major divisions 2 and 4 of the International Standard Industrial Classification), but not building or civil engineering. Indexes are adjusted for number of working days in the month. Employment: Includes members of the armed forces. International liquidity: Reserve position in IMF includes oil facility lending.

CONVENTIONAL SIGNS

In graphs:
S = Affected by strike.
B = Break in continuity of series.
In tables:
(e) = Secretariat estimates.

---

* All exhibits in this section are reproduced with permission from *Main Economic Indicators*, Organisation for Economic Co-operation and Development, Paris, May 1980.
Note: Captions on data in this section taken from the O.E.C.D. *Main Economic Indicators* appear in both French and English.

. = For data: not available.
    For rates of change: either rate over 100 percent or not calculated because data affected by strike or other special event.
— = Nil or negligible.
• = Decimal point.
In tables and graphs:
$ = U.S. dollar.
Cent = U.S. cent.
£ = Pound sterling.

ABBREVIATIONS

O.E.C.D. MAIN COUNTRY GROUPINGS
E.E.C.: European Economic Community: Belgium, Denmark, France, Germany, Ireland, Italy, Luxembourg, the Netherlands, and the United Kingdom.

O.E.C.D.-Europe: All European member countries of O.E.C.D., i.e., countries in E.E.C. plus Austria, Finland, Greece, Iceland, Norway, Portugal, Spain, Sweden, Switzerland, and Turkey.

North America: Canada and the United States.

O.E.C.D.-Total: All member countries of O.E.C.D., i.e., countries in O.E.C.D.-Europe and in North America plus Japan, Australia, and New Zealand.

OTHER
Orig. = Series prior to seasonal adjustment.
Adj. = Series adjusted for seasonal variations.
Billion = Thousand million.
Tons = Metric tons.

UNEMPLOYMENT RATE

Adjusted for seasonal variations — Chiffres corrigés des variations saisonnières
3-month moving averages — Moyennes mobiles de 3 mois

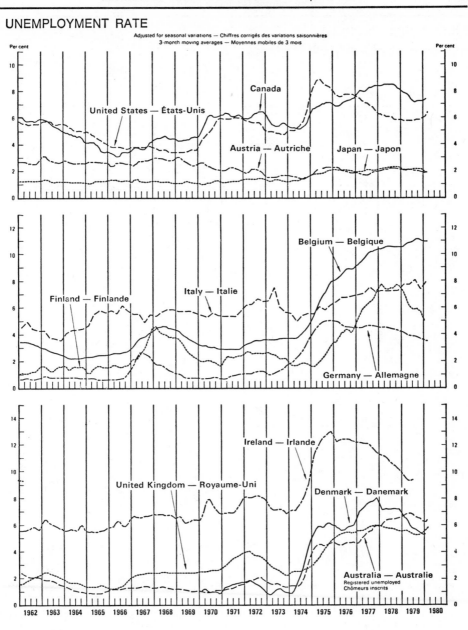

INDUSTRIAL PRODUCTION
DEVIATION FROM LONG-TERM TREND

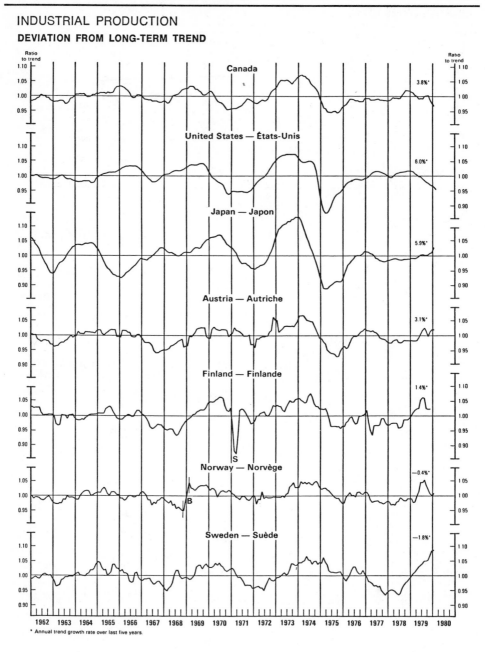

* Annual trend growth rate over last five years.

INDUSTRIAL PRODUCTION *(continued)*

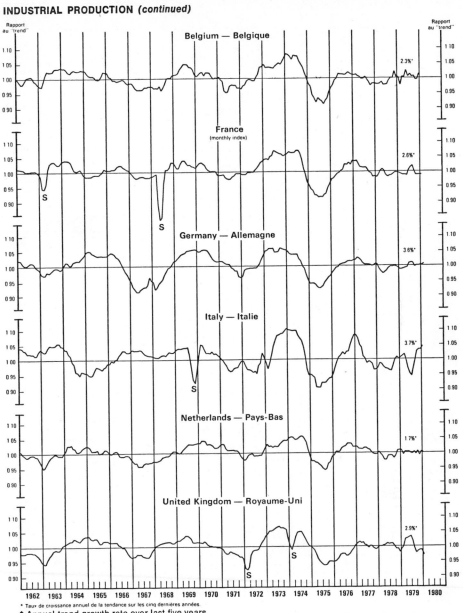

* Taux de croissance annuel de la tendance sur les cinq dernières années.
* Annual trend growth rate over last five years.

TOTAL TRADE

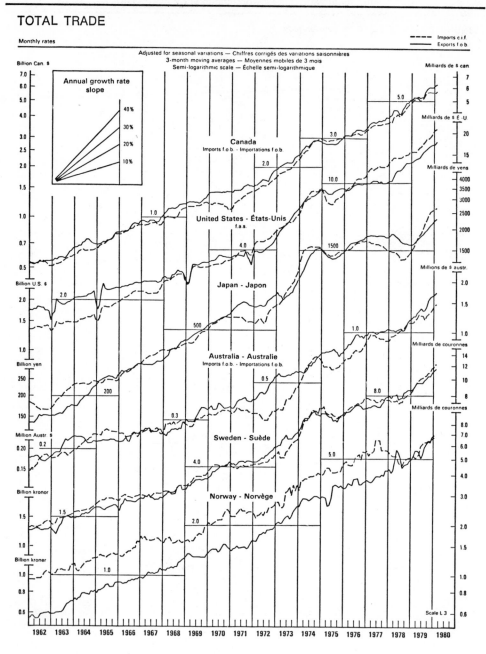

Monthly rates

Imports c.i.f
Exports f.o.b

Adjusted for seasonal variations — Chiffres corrigés des variations saisonnières
3-month moving averages — Moyennes mobiles de 3 mois
Semi-logarithmic scale — Échelle semi-logarithmique

Billion Can. $ Milliards de $ can

Annual growth rate slope

Canada
Imports f.o.b. - Importations f.o.b.

United States - États-Unis
f.a.s.

Japan - Japon

Australia - Australie
Imports f.o.b. - Importations f.o.b.

Sweden - Suède

Norway - Norvège

1962 1963 1964 1965 1966 1967 1968 1969 1970 1971 1972 1973 1974 1975 1976 1977 1978 1979 1980

Scale L.3

TOTAL TRADE (continued)

- - - - Importations c.a.f
———— Exportations f.o.b

Taux mensuels

Adjusted for seasonal variations — Chiffres corrigés des variations saisonnières
3-month moving averages — Moyennes mobiles de 3 mois
Semi-logarithmic scale — Échelle semi-logarithmique

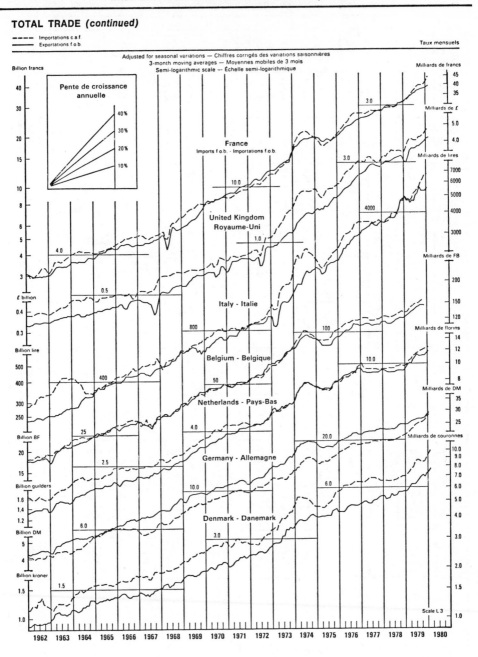

GROSS DOMESTIC PRODUCT[1]

	at 1975 prices and 1975 exchange rates — aux prix et aux taux de change de 1975 (Billion dollars/Milliards de dollars)							Volume (2) 1979/1978 annual % / % annuel	at current prices and exchange rates — aux prix et taux de change courants (Billion dollars/Milliards de dollars)			
	1970	1974	1975	1976	1977	1978	1979[3]	1979/1978	1976	1977	1978	1979[3]
Canada	128.62	162.12	163.94	173.24	177.83	184.19	189.3	2.75	195.82	199.68	205.32	222.8
United States - États-Unis	1361.14	1541.25	1526.51	1612.72	1695.24	1770.51	1805.9	2	1695.53	1889.16	2112.37	2349.0
Japan - Japon	393.15	495.09	501.87	534.31	563.13	596.21	632.0	6	564.66	693.84	973.91	1021.6
Australia - Australie	72.39	85.22	87.20	90.47	91.46	93.64	98.1	4.75	95.87	95.90	109.12	120.5
New Zealand - Nouvelle-Zélande	11.50	13.72	13.96	13.97	13.60	13.93	14.0	0.25	13.96	14.87	18.39	21.1
Austria - Autriche	31.12	38.26	37.68	40.02	41.50	42.11	44.3	5.25	40.56	47.95	58.05	68.9
Belgium - Belgique	52.69	64.02	62.88	66.20	66.98	68.65	70.7	3	68.10	79.19	96.91	111.5
Denmark - Danemark	33.61	37.86	37.69	40.32	41.10	41.52	42.6	2.5	41.37	46.36	55.89	65.6
Finland - Finlande	22.76	27.52	27.70	27.77	27.87	28.26	30.3	7.25	29.76	31.53	33.87	41.6
France	278.53	338.19	338.82	355.59	365.60	379.50	390.9	3	349.90	381.64	471.59	566.9
Germany - Allemagne	379.41	428.16	420.25	441.93	454.06	468.53	488.4	4.25	445.92	515.59	638.88	755.8
Greece - Grèce	16.28	19.63	20.82	22.14	22.90	24.33	25.2	3.5	22.55	26.16	31.59	37.5
Iceland - Islande	0.96	1.29	1.29	1.33	1.41	1.48	1.5	2.5	1.50	1.96	2.18	2.4
Ireland - Irlande	6.82	8.01	8.10	8.34	8.80	9.33	9.6	3.25	8.07	9.38	12.18	14.9
Italy - Italie	170.45	199.30	192.05	203.32	207.40	212.69	221.2	4	188.23	215.30	260.11	318.6
Luxembourg	2.00	2.54	2.30	2.36	2.40	2.51	2.6	4	2.53	2.82	3.51	4.1
Netherlands - Pays-Bas	70.89	83.66	82.80	87.21	89.65	91.77	94.8	3.25	90.84	106.92	130.78	151.8
Norway - Norvège	22.67	26.95	28.45	30.39	31.49	32.59	33.5	2.75	31.29	35.77	39.98	45.3
Portugal	11.88	15.39	14.72	15.63	16.48	17.01	17.5	3	15.38	16.25	17.80	20.2
Spain - Espagne	80.13	103.70	104.84	107.99	110.82	113.60	115.3	1.5	108.13	119.89	147.09	197.4
Sweden - Suède	62.95	68.79	69.33	70.22	68.34	70.23	73.0	4	74.24	78.30	87.30	103.3
Switzerland - Suisse	52.15	58.56	54.30	53.53	54.84	54.93	55.1	0.25	56.79	60.66	84.55	94.1
Turkey - Turquie	25.07	33.01	35.95	38.99	40.70	41.94	42.3	1.0	41.05	47.79	52.47	66.1
United Kingdom - Royaume Uni	207.01	231.65	229.41	237.82	240.95	248.50	249.7	0.5	221.17	247.31	309.21	391.2
O.E.C.D.-Total - O.C.D.E. Total	3494.18	4083.90	4062.84	4275.81	4434.55	4607.95	4747.8	3.0	4403.20	4964.23	5953.03	6792.2
North America - Amérique du Nord	1489.76	1703.37	1690.45	1785.96	1873.07	1954.70	1995.2	2.1	1891.35	2088.84	2317.69	2571.8
O.E.C.D.-Europe - O.C.D.E.-Europe	1527.38	1786.50	1769.36	1851.01	1893.48	1949.48	2008.5	3.0	1837.37	2070.79	2533.92	3057.2
E.E.C. - C.E.E.	1201.42	1393.38	1374.30	1443.10	1476.93	1523.00	1570.5	3.1	1416.12	1604.52	1979.05	2380.4

[1] Sources: National Accounts of O.E.C.D. Countries, 1977 Vol. 1, countries submissions and Secretariat estimates.
[2] Various base years, GDP/GNP Growth rate.
[3] Provisional figures.

World Population and GNP by Country

WORLD POPULATION DATA

Region or Country[1]	Population Estimate Mid-1980 (millions)[2]	Birth Rate[3]	Death Rate[3]	Rate of Natural Increase (annual, %)[4]	Number of Years to Double Population[5]	Population Projected for 2000 (millions)[6]	Infant Mortality Rate[7]	Total Fertility Rate[8]	Population under Age 15 (%)	Population over Age 64 (%)	Life Expectancy at Birth (years)[9]	Urban Population (%)[10]	Projected Ultimate Population Size (millions)[11]	Per Capita Gross National Product (US$)[12]
WORLD	4,414	28	11	1.7	41	6,156	97	3.8	35	6	61	39	9,832	2,040
MORE DEVELOPED[1]	1,131	16	9	0.6	111	1,272	20	2.0	24	11	72	69	1,372	6,260
LESS DEVELOPED[1]	3,283	32	12	2.0	34	4,884	110	4.4	39	4	57	29	8,460	560
AFRICA	472	46	17	2.9	24	832	140	6.4	45	3	49	26	2,051	530
NORTHERN AFRICA	110	42	13	3.0	23	186	121	6.2	44	3	54	42	370	790
Algeria	19.0	48	13	3.4	20	36.9	142	7.3	47	4	56	55	93.6	1,260
Egypt	42.1	38	10	2.7	26	64.9	90	5.3	40	4	55	44	90.0	400
Libya	3.0	47	13	3.5	20	5.7	130	7.4	49	4	55	60	11.7	6,910
Morocco	21.0	43	14	3.0	23	37.3	133	6.9	46	2	55	42	70.9	670
Sudan	18.7	48	18	3.1	22	31.8	141	6.6	44	3	46	20	88.8	320
Tunisia	6.5	33	8	2.5	28	9.7	125	5.7	44	4	57	50	14.4	950
WESTERN AFRICA	141	49	19	3.0	23	262	159	6.8	46	3	46	21	711	460
Benin	3.6	49	19	3.0	23	6.6	149	6.7	46	4	46	14	15.0	230
Cape Verde	0.3	28	9	1.8	38	0.4	105	3.0	36	4	60	20	0.6	160
Gambia	0.6	48	23	2.4	28	1.0	217	6.4	41	2	41	16	2.4	230
Ghana	11.7	48	17	3.1	22	21.2	115	6.7	47	3	48	36	56.6	390
Guinea	5.0	46	21	2.5	27	8.2	175	6.2	44	3	44	23	22.6	210
Guinea-Bissau	0.6	41	23	1.8	39	0.9	208	5.5	39	4	41	26	1.7	200
Ivory Coast	8.0	48	18	2.9	24	14.0	154	6.7	45	2	46	32	36.1	840
Liberia	1.9	50	17	3.2	21	3.5	148	6.7	48	2	48	29	8.6	460
Mali	6.6	49	22	2.7	26	11.6	190	6.7	48	1	39	17	27.9	120
Mauritania	1.6	50	22	2.8	25	2.9	187	6.9	42	6	42	23	7.2	270
Niger	5.5	51	22	2.9	24	10.0	200	7.1	47	3	42	11	23.7	220
Nigeria	77.1	50	18	3.2	22	148.9	157	6.9	47	2	48	20	434.7	560
Senegal	5.7	48	22	2.6	27	9.7	160	6.5	44	3	42	32	23.5	340
Sierra Leone	3.5	46	19	2.6	26	6.0	136	6.4	41	5	46	16	13.6	210
Togo	2.5	49	19	3.0	23	4.7	163	6.7	46	3	46	15	11.9	320
Upper Volta	6.9	48	22	2.6	27	11.8	182	6.5	44	3	42	5	24.2	160
EASTERN AFRICA	135	48	19	3.0	23	244	132	6.6	46	3	47	13	629	240
Burundi	4.5	47	20	2.7	25	7.8	140	6.3	44	2	42	5	19.9	140
Comoros	0.3	40	18	2.2	31	0.4	148	5.2	43	3	46	11	1.4	180
Djibouti	0.4	48	24	2.5	28	0.6	—	—	—	—	—	70	—	450
Ethiopia	32.6	50	25	2.5	28	55.3	162	6.7	45	3	39	13	136.5	120
Kenya	15.9	53	14	3.9	18	32.3	83	8.1	50	2	56	10	93.8	320
Madagascar	8.7	45	19	2.6	27	15.1	102	6.1	43	3	46	16	39.1	250
Malawi	6.1	51	19	3.2	22	11.5	142	7.0	44	4	46	9	31.3	180
Mauritius	0.9	27	7	2.0	34	1.3	35	3.1	37	4	67	44	1.8	830
Mozambique	10.3	45	19	2.6	27	17.9	148	6.1	45	2	46	8	44.0	140
Reunion	0.5	26	6	1.9	36	0.7	41	2.8	38	4	65	56	1.2	3,060
Rwanda	5.1	50	19	3.0	23	9.6	127	6.9	47	3	46	4	24.7	180
Seychelles	0.1	26	8	1.8	38	0.1	43	4.5	42	6	65	37	—	1,060
Somalia	3.6	48	20	2.8	25	6.3	177	6.1	44	2	43	31	17.0	130
S. Rhodesia (Zimbabwe)	7.4	47	14	3.4	21	14.0	129	6.6	47	3	54	20	37.2	480
Tanzania	18.6	47	16	3.1	22	35.0	125	6.5	46	3	50	13	93.9	230
Uganda	13.7	45	14	3.0	23	25.5	120	6.1	45	3	52	7	57.9	—
Zambia	5.8	49	17	3.2	22	10.7	144	6.9	46	3	48	39	28.6	480

WORLD POPULATION DATA (continued)

Region or Country[1]	Population Estimate Mid-1980 (millions)[2]	Birth Rate[3]	Death Rate[3]	Rate of Natural Increase (annual, %)[4]	Number of Years to Double Population[5]	Population Projected for 2000 (millions)[6]	Infant Mortality Rate[7]	Total Fertility Rate[8]	Population under Age 15 (%)	Population over Age 64 (%)[9]	Life Expectancy at Birth (years)[9]	Urban Population (%)[10]	Projected Ultimate Population Size (millions)[11]	Per Capita Gross National Product (US$)[12]
MIDDLE AFRICA	**54**	**45**	**20**	**2.6**	**27**	**87**	**167**	**6.0**	**43**	**3**	**45**	**29**	**218**	**300**
Angola	6.7	48	23	2.4	28	11.2	203	6.4	44	3	41	22	29.2	300
Cameroon	8.5	42	19	2.3	30	13.1	157	5.7	41	4	44	29	31.5	460
Central African Rep.	2.2	42	19	2.2	31	3.6	190	5.5	41	4	42	42	8.3	250
Chad	4.5	44	21	2.3	30	7.4	165	5.9	42	4	44	18	17.4	140
Congo	1.6	45	19	2.6	27	2.5	180	6.0	43	3	46	39	6.9	540
Equatorial Guinea	0.4	42	19	2.3	30	0.6	165	5.7	42	4	46	51	1.2	
Gabon	0.6	33	22	1.1	62	0.8	178	4.3	33	6	44	32	1.3	3,580
Sao Tome and Principe	0.1	45	11	3.4	21	0.1	64	–	–	–	–	24	–	490
Zaire	29.3	46	19	2.8	25	48.1	160	6.1	45	3	46	30	121.9	210
SOUTHERN AFRICA	**32**	**39**	**11**	**2.8**	**25**	**52**	**101**	**5.2**	**42**	**4**	**59**	**44**	**124**	**1,380**
Botswana	0.8	51	17	3.4	21	1.4	97	6.5	50	3	56	12	4.5	620
Lesotho	1.3	40	16	2.4	29	2.1	111	5.4	40	4	50	4	5.1	280
Namibia	1.0	44	15	2.9	24	1.7	142	5.9	44	3	51	32	4.5	1,080
South Africa	28.4	38	10	2.8	25	46.3	97	5.1	42	4	60	48	107.5	1,480
Swaziland	0.6	47	19	2.8	25	0.9	168	6.4	48	3	46	8	2.7	590
ASIA	**2,563**	**28**	**11**	**1.8**	**39**	**3,578**	**103**	**3.9**	**37**	**4**	**58**	**27**	**5,573**	**760**
SOUTHWEST ASIA	**98**	**40**	**12**	**2.7**	**25**	**164**	**117**	**5.8**	**43**	**4**	**56**	**46**	**281**	**2,280**
Bahrain	0.4	44	9	3.6	20	0.7	78	7.4	44	3	63	78	1.1	4,100
Cyprus	0.6	19	8	1.1	64	0.7	17	2.1	25	10	73	53	1.0	2,110
Gaza	0.4	53	18	3.5	20	0.7	137	–	48	5	52	87	–	–
Iraq	13.2	47	13	3.4	20	24.5	104	7.0	48	4	55	66	49.1	1,860
Israel	3.9	25	7	1.8	38	5.5	15	3.5	33	8	73	87	7.5	4,120
Jordan	3.2	46	13	3.3	21	5.9	97	7.0	48	3	56	42	11.8	1,050
Kuwait	1.3	42	5	3.7	19	3.1	39	7.0	44	2	69	56	5.3	14,890
Lebanon	3.2	34	10	2.5	28	4.9	65	4.7	43	5	65	60	7.6	–
Oman	0.9	49	19	3.0	23	1.7	142	7.2	45	3	47	5	3.2	2,570
Qatar	0.2	44	14	3.0	23	0.4	138	7.2	45	3	48	69	0.8	12,740
Saudi Arabia	8.2	49	18	3.0	23	15.5	150	7.2	45	3	48	24	30.8	8,040
Syria	8.6	45	13	3.2	21	16.2	114	7.4	49	4	57	49	32.7	930
Turkey	45.5	35	10	2.5	28	69.6	119	5.0	40	4	58	45	97.8	1,210
United Arab Emirates	0.8	44	14	3.0	23	1.6	138	7.2	34	3	48	65	2.5	14,230
Yemen, North	5.6	48	25	2.3	30	9.5	160	6.8	47	4	45	11	20.4	580
Yemen, South	1.9	48	21	2.7	26	3.4	155	7.0	49	4	45	33	6.9	420
MIDDLE SOUTH ASIA	**938**	**37**	**16**	**2.2**	**32**	**1,422**	**137**	**5.5**	**42**	**3**	**51**	**21**	**2,566**	**180**
Afghanistan	15.9	48	21	2.7	26	26.4	226	6.9	45	3	37	11	65.8	240
Bangladesh	90.6	46	20	2.6	27	156.7	153	6.3	44	3	46	9	334.5	90
Bhutan	1.3	43	21	2.2	31	2.0	147	6.2	42	3	43	4	4.0	100
India	676.2	34	15	1.9	36	976.2	134	5.3	41	3	52	21	1,642.8	180
Iran	38.5	44	14	3.0	23	66.1	112	6.3	44	4	58	47	101.0	–
Maldives	0.1	50	23	2.7	26	0.2	119	–	44	2	–	11	–	150
Nepal	14.0	44	20	2.4	29	22.0	133	6.4	40	3	43	4	51.4	120
Pakistan	86.5	44	16	2.8	25	152.0	142	6.3	46	3	52	26	334.6	230
Sri Lanka	14.8	28	7	2.2	32	20.0	42	3.4	39	4	63	22	30.3	190

WORLD POPULATION DATA (continued)

Region or Country[1]	Population Estimate Mid-1980 (millions)[2]	Birth Rate[3]	Death Rate[3]	Rate of Natural Increase (annual, %)[4]	Number of Years to Double Population[5]	Population Projected for 2000 (millions)[6]	Infant Mortality Rate[7]	Total Fertility Rate[8]	Population under Age 15 (%)	Population over Age 64 (%)[9]	Life Expectancy at Birth (years)[9]	Urban Population (%)[10]	Projected Ultimate Population Size (millions)[11]	Per Capita Gross National Product (US$)[12]
SOUTHEAST ASIA	354	36	13	2.2	31	539	96	4.7	42	3	53	21	915	400
Brunei	0.2	28	4	2.4	29	0.3	20	5.1	43	3	66	64	—	10,640
Burma	34.4	39	14	2.4	29	53.7	140	5.5	40	4	52	24	92.3	150
Dem. Kampuchea	6.0	33	15	1.8	39	9.1	150	4.7	42	3	44	12	36.5	—
East Timor	0.8	44	21	2.3	30	1.1	175	6.1	42	3	42	12	—	—
Indonesia	144.3	35	15	2.0	34	210.6	91	4.1	42	2	50	18	356.8	360
Laos	3.7	44	20	2.4	29	5.7	175	6.2	42	3	39	15	11.1	90
Malaysia	14.0	31	6	2.5	28	20.7	44	4.4	41	3	61	27	29.5	1,090
Philippines	47.7	34	10	2.4	28	78.1	80	5.0	43	3	61	32	127.9	510
Singapore	2.4	17	5	1.2	59	3.0	12	1.9	31	4	71	100	3.7	3,260
Thailand	47.3	32	9	2.3	30	75.5	68	4.5	43	3	60	13	104.7	490
Vietnam	53.3	41	18	2.3	30	80.9	115	5.8	41	4	48	19	149.4	170
EAST ASIA	1,173	18	6	1.2	57	1,453	51	2.3	31	6	65	32	1,812	1,200
China[13]	975	18	6	1.2	58	1,212.3	56	2.3	32	6	64	26	1,530.0	460
Hong Kong	4.8	18	5	1.2	56	6.2	12	2.6	29	6	72	92	7.3	3,040
Japan	116.8	15	6	0.9	79	129.4	8	1.8	24	8	75	76	133.4	7,330
Korea, North	17.9	33	8	2.4	28	27.4	70	4.5	40	4	62	33	42.9	730
Korea, South	38.2	23	7	1.6	44	51.1	38	3.2	38	4	62	48	64.1	1,160
Macao	0.3	30	8	2.2	32	0.3	78	—	38	5	—	97	—	1,460
Mongolia	1.7	37	8	2.9	24	2.7	70	5.3	43	3	62	47	3.9	940
Taiwan	17.8	25	5	2.0	35	23.8	25	3.1	35	4	71	77	29.6	1,400
NORTH AMERICA	247	16	8	0.7	98	289	13	1.8	23	11	73	74	296	9,650
Canada	24.0	15	7	0.8	88	29.0	12	1.9	26	8	73	76	30.3	9,170
United States	222.5	16	9	0.7	99	260.4	13	1.8	22	11	73	74	265.5	9,700
LATIN AMERICA	360	34	8	2.6	26	595	85	4.5	42	4	64	61	955	1,380
MIDDLE AMERICA	91	38	7	3.1	22	168	72	5.3	46	3	64	59	274	1,180
Costa Rica	2.2	31	4	2.7	26	3.4	28	3.8	44	4	70	41	4.7	1,540
El Salvador	4.8	40	7	3.3	21	8.6	51	6.0	46	3	62	39	13.7	600
Guatemala	7.0	43	12	3.1	23	12.3	76	5.7	45	3	58	36	23.2	910
Honduras	3.8	47	12	3.5	20	7.1	103	7.1	48	3	57	31	15.3	480
Mexico	68.2	37	6	3.1	22	128.9	70	5.2	46	3	65	65	203.5	1,290
Nicaragua	2.6	47	12	3.4	20	4.8	122	6.6	48	3	55	49	9.3	840
Panama	1.9	28	6	2.2	31	2.9	47	4.1	44	4	70	51	4.5	1,290
CARIBBEAN	30	28	8	1.9	36	42	72	3.8	40	5	65	50	66	1,160
Bahamas	0.2	25	5	2.0	34	0.3	25	3.5	44	4	69	58	0.4	2,620
Barbados	0.3	16	8	0.9	80	0.3	27	2.2	32	10	70	44	0.4	1,940
Cuba	10.0	18	6	1.2	59	12.7	25	2.5	37	6	72	64	16.5	810
Dominica	0.1	21	5	1.6	43	0.1	20	—	—	—	58	27	—	440
Dominican Republic	5.4	37	9	2.8	25	8.5	96	5.4	48	3	60	49	15.1	910
Grenada	0.1	27	6	2.2	32	0.1	24	—	—	—	63	15	0.2	530
Guadeloupe	0.3	17	6	1.1	65	0.4	35	3.2	32	6	69	48	—	2,850
Haiti	5.8	42	16	2.6	26	9.9	130	5.9	41	4	51	24	16.3	260
Jamaica	2.2	29	7	2.2	31	2.8	15	3.7	46	6	70	41	5.3	1,110
Martinique	0.3	16	7	0.9	80	0.4	32	3.0	32	6	69	50	—	3,950
Netherland Antilles	0.3	28	7	2.2	32	0.4	25	3.1	38	6	62	48	—	3,150
Puerto Rico	3.5	23	6	1.7	42	4.5	20	2.4	36	6	73	62	—	2,720
St. Lucia	0.1	35	7	2.8	25	0.1	36	—	50	5	67	17	—	630
Trinidad and Tobago	1.2	25	6	1.9	37	1.4	29	2.6	38	4	67	49	2.2	2,910

WORLD POPULATION DATA (continued)

Region or Country[1]	Population Estimate Mid-1980 (millions)[2]	Birth Rate[3]	Death Rate[3]	Rate of Natural Increase (annual, %)[4]	Number of Years to Double Population[5]	Population Projected for 2000 (millions)[6]	Infant Mortality Rate[7]	Total Fertility Rate[8]	Population under Age 15 (%)	Population over Age 64 (%)	Life Expectancy at Birth (years)[9]	Urban Population (%)[10]	Projected Ultimate Population Size (millions)[11]	Per Capita Gross National Product (US$)[12]
TROPICAL SOUTH AMERICA	198	36	9	2.7	26	333	98	4.6	42	3	62	60	551	1,430
Bolivia	5.3	44	19	2.5	28	8.9	168	6.8	42	4	47	34	19.4	510
Brazil	122.0	36	8	2.8	25	205.1	109	4.4	41	3	64	61	341.0	1,570
Colombia	26.7	29	8	2.1	33	42.2	77	3.9	45	3	62	60	55.2	870
Ecuador	8.0	42	10	3.1	22	14.6	70	6.3	44	4	60	43	25.7	910
Guyana	0.9	28	7	2.1	33	1.2	50	3.9	40	4	69	40	2.0	550
Paraguay	3.3	39	8	3.1	22	5.6	64	5.8	45	3	64	40	9.2	850
Peru	17.6	40	12	2.8	25	29.2	92	5.3	44	3	56	62	54.6	740
Suriname	0.4	30	7	2.3	30	0.7	30	—	46	4	67	66	1.8	2,110
Venezuela	13.9	36	6	3.0	23	25.7	45	4.9	43	3	66	75	40.1	2,910
TEMPERATE SOUTH AMERICA	41	24	9	1.5	45	51	44	2.9	30	7	68	80	64	1,750
Argentina	27.1	26	9	1.6	43	32.9	45	2.9	28	8	69	80	41.0	1,910
Chile	11.3	21	7	1.4	48	15.2	40	3.0	35	5	66	80	18.6	1,410
Uruguay	2.9	21	10	1.1	65	3.5	46	2.7	27	10	69	83	4.5	1,610
EUROPE	484	14	10	0.4	176	521	19	2.0	24	12	72	69	560	5,650
NORTHERN EUROPE	82	13	11	0.1	476	84	13	1.8	23	14	72	74	90	6,140
Denmark	5.1	12	10	0.2	385	5.3	9	1.7	22	14	74	67	5.4	9,920
Finland	4.8	14	9	0.4	161	5.1	9	1.7	22	11	72	59	5.2	6,820
Iceland	0.2	19	6	1.2	57	0.3	11	2.3	30	9	76	87	0.3	8,320
Ireland	3.3	22	10	1.1	61	4.0	16	3.4	31	11	71	52	5.5	3,470
Norway	4.1	13	10	0.3	248	4.4	9	1.8	24	14	75	44	4.5	9,510
Sweden	8.3	11	11	0.0	1,386	8.6	8	1.7	21	15	75	83	8.2	10,210
United Kingdom	55.8	12	12	0.1	1,155	56.5	14	1.7	23	14	72	78	60.1	5,030
WESTERN EUROPE	153	12	11	0.1	918	158	12	1.6	22	14	72	82	163	8,970
Austria	7.5	11	12	-0.1	—	7.6	15	1.6	23	15	72	52	7.8	7,030
Belgium	9.9	12	12	0.1	990	10.7	12	1.7	22	14	71	95	10.4	9,070
France	53.6	14	10	0.3	198	57.5	11	1.9	24	14	73	73	60.7	8,270
Germany, West	61.1	9	12	-0.2	—	59.8	15	1.4	21	15	72	92	60.8	9,600
Luxembourg	0.4	11	12	-0.0	—	0.4	11	1.5	20	13	70	68	0.4	10,410
Netherlands	14.1	13	8	0.4	159	15.5	10	1.5	25	11	75	88	15.8	9,290
Switzerland	6.3	11	9	0.2	301	6.4	10	1.5	22	13	73	55	6.8	12,100
EASTERN EUROPE	110	18	11	0.7	102	121	23	2.3	23	11	71	59	135	3,670
Bulgaria	8.9	16	10	0.5	139	9.5	22	2.3	22	11	71	60	10.4	3,200
Czechoslovakia	15.4	18	12	0.7	100	17.2	19	2.4	23	12	70	67	19.0	4,720
Germany, East	16.7	14	14	0.0	—	16.6	13	1.8	21	16	72	76	17.7	5,660
Hungary	10.8	16	13	0.3	267	11.2	24	2.2	21	13	70	52	11.8	3,450
Poland	35.5	19	9	1.0	71	40.9	22	2.3	24	10	71	57	46.8	3,660
Romania	22.3	20	10	1.0	69	25.7	31	2.6	25	10	70	48	29.7	1,750
SOUTHERN EUROPE	140	15	9	0.7	105	157	24	2.3	26	11	71	60	172	3,290
Albania	2.7	30	8	2.2	32	3.8	87	4.2	37	5	69	34	5.7	740
Greece	9.6	16	9	0.7	98	10.6	19	2.3	24	12	73	65	10.9	3,270
Italy	57.2	12	9	0.3	224	61.3	18	1.9	24	12	72	67	62.6	3,840
Malta	0.3	17	10	0.8	92	0.4	16	2.0	25	9	71	94	0.4	2,160
Portugal	9.9	17	10	0.7	99	11.6	39	2.5	28	10	69	29	13.6	2,020
Spain	37.8	17	8	0.9	75	43.9	16	2.6	28	10	72	70	50.0	3,520
Yugoslavia	22.4	17	9	0.9	80	25.7	34	2.2	26	9	68	39	28.6	2,390

WORLD POPULATION DATA (concluded)

Region or Country[1]	Population Estimate Mid-1980 (millions)[2]	Birth Rate[3]	Death Rate[3]	Rate of Natural Increase (annual, %)[4]	Number of Years to Double Population[5]	Population Projected for 2000 (millions)[6]	Infant Mortality Rate[7]	Total Fertility Rate[8]	Population under Age 15 (%)	Population over Age 64 (%)	Life Expectancy at Birth (years)[9]	Urban Population (%)[10]	Projected Ultimate Population Size (millions)[11]	Per Capita Gross National Product (US$)[12]
USSR	266	18	10	0.8	82	311	31	2.4	24	10	70	62	360	3,700
OCEANIA	23	20	9	1.1	61	30	42	2.8	31	8	69	71	37	6,020
Australia	14.6	16	8	0.8	86	17.9	12	2.1	27	9	73	86	18.5	7,920
Fiji	0.6	27	4	2.3	30	0.8	41	4.0	41	2	71	37	1.2	1,440
New Zealand	3.2	16	8	0.8	83	3.9	14	2.2	29	9	72	83	4.6	4,790
Papua-New Guinea	3.2	41	16	2.5	27	5.1	106	6.0	44	4	50	13	9.3	560
Samoa, Western	0.2	37	7	3.0	23	0.2	40	5.8	50	3	63	21	0.5	—
Solomon Islands	0.2	41	10	3.1	22	0.4	78	6.2	44	3	57	9	—	430

Pop. 1980   Birth Rate   Death Rate   Nat. Inc.   Doub. Time   Pop. 2000   Inf. Mort.   TFR   Pop. < 15   Pop. > 64   Life Expec.   Urb. Pop.   Ult. Pop.   GNP p.c.

General Notes

World Population Data Sheets of various years **should not be used as a time series.** Because every attempt is made to use the most recent and most accurate information, data sources vary and changes in numbers and rates from year to year may reflect improved source material, revised data, or a later base year for computation, rather than yearly changes.

Sources of data. Aside from population estimates and projections (see footnotes 2 and 6), number of years to double population (footnote 5), and per capita Gross National Product (footnote 12), most of the data in this Data Sheet were reported in the following United Nations (UN) publications: Demographic Yearbook, 1977 and 1978; Population and Vital Statistics Report, Data Available as of 1 January 1980, Statistical Papers, Series A, Vol. XXXII, No. 1; and World Population Trends and Prospects by Country, 1950-2000: Summary Report of the 1978 Assessment, ST/ESA/SER.R/33, 1979. Other sources were: U.S. Bureau of the Census, World Population: 1977, 1978, and World Population: 1979 (forthcoming); unpublished reports of the Census Bureau's Foreign Demographic Analysis Division; World Bank, Population Projections 1975-2000 and Long-term (Stationary Population), prepared by K. C. Zachariah and My Thi Vu of the Bank's Population and Human Resources Division, July 1979; Country Reports of the World Fertility Survey; official country publications; and special studies.

Figures for the regions and the world: Population totals (columns 1 and 6) take into account small areas not listed on the Data Sheet. These totals may also not equal the sums of their parts because of independent rounding. All other regional and world figures are weighted averages for countries for which data are available.

Footnotes

[1] The Data Sheet lists all geopolitical entities with a population larger than 200,000 and all members of the United Nations (UN) regardless of population size. Classification of "more developed" and "less developed" regions follows the latest (1979) practice of the UN. The "more developed" regions comprise all of Europe, North America (Canada and the United States), Australia, New Zealand, Japan, and the USSR. Cyprus, Israel, and Turkey, formerly included in the "more developed" region of Southern Europe, are now included by the UN with their region of location, Southwest Asia, and are thereby considered "less developed."

[2] Based on a population total from a very recent census or on the most recent official country or UN estimate; for almost all countries the estimate was for mid-1978. Each estimate was updated by the Population Reference Bureau to mid-1980 by applying the same rate of growth as indicated by population change during part or all of the period since 1970.

[3] Annual number of births or deaths per 1,000 population. For the more developed countries with complete or nearly complete registration of births and deaths, nearly all the rates shown pertain to 1977 or 1978. For most less developed countries with incomplete registration, the rates refer to the 1975-80 period. These rates were used in the medium variant estimates and projections as assessed by the UN in 1978 (UN, World Population Trends and Prospects. . . .). These figures should be considered as rough approximations only. Some estimates were obtained from published reports of the U.S. Bureau of the Census, the World Bank, the World Fertility Survey, government statistical offices, and special studies.

[4] Birth rate minus the death rate. Since the rates were based on unrounded birth and death rates, some rates do not exactly equal the difference between the birth and death rates shown because of rounding.

[5] Based on the current unrounded rate of natural increase and assuming no change in the rate.

[6] For most countries, projected by the Population Reference Bureau by applying the 1980-2000 growth rate implied by the UN medium variant projections to the country's estimated mid-1980 population total. For the United States, the projection shown is from the most recent Series II projection published by the U.S. Bureau of the Census. This projection assumes that birth rates in the U.S. will rise somewhat during the balance of this century until a total fertility rate (see footnote 8) of 2.1 is reached.

[7] Annual number of deaths to infants under one year of age per 1,000 live births. For countries with complete or nearly complete registration of births and deaths, nearly all rates pertain to 1977 or 1978. For many less developed countries with incomplete registration, rates are the latest available estimates generally obtained from the sources noted above.

[8] The total fertility rate (TFR) indicates the average number of children that would be born to each woman in a population if each were to live through her childbearing lifetime (usually considered ages 15-49) bearing children at the same rate as women of those ages actually did in a given year. A TFR of 2.1 to 2.5, depending upon mortality conditions, indicates "replacement level" fertility—the level at which a country's population would eventually stop growing (or declining), leaving migration out of account. Most TFRs shown here refer to the 1975-80 period and are from UN, World Population Trends and Prospects. . . .

[9] Average number of years a newborn child could be expected to live if current mortality conditions were to continue throughout his or her lifetime. For the more developed countries with reliable mortality data, nearly all estimates shown pertain to part or all of the 1970-77 period. For most of the less developed countries with unreliable mortality data, estimates refer to some part of the period since 1970 and were prepared by one of the following organizations: the UN Population Division; the Population Division of the U.S. Bureau of the Census; or the World Bank's Population and Human Resources Division. Estimates of life expectancy for most less developed countries should be considered as rough approximations only.

[10] Percentage of total population living in areas termed urban by that country.

[11] This column has been included in this year's edition of the Data Sheet in order to illustrate each country's potential population growth and the ultimate size that could eventually be achieved. These projections were prepared by K. C. Zachariah and My Thi Vu of the World Bank (Population Projections, 1975-2000 . . .) and are not forecasts of what will necessarily happen, but could happen as a result of "long run implications of recent trends under a series of highly stylized assumptions." Specifically, the projections assume that fertility in all countries will someday arrive at replacement level (a TFR then of about 2.1) and remain there. For less developed countries, this is assumed to occur in the middle of the 21st century in Africa and somewhat earlier in Asia and Latin America. For more developed countries the arrival at replacement level fertility is placed about the year 2000. This assumes that the TFR will increase to 2.1 by that time in the many developed countries where fertility is now below replacement level. The projections also assume that immigration will have no appreciable impact on the population growth of a particular country; this assumption tends to lower the "ultimate population" of the United States and a few other countries which can be expected to receive immigrants in the future. Several regional totals were adjusted by the Population Reference Bureau in order to agree with the geographical classifications used on the Data Sheet.

[12] Data refer to 1978 and are provisional. All data for individual countries are from the World Bank, World Bank Atlas: Population, Per Capita Product, and Growth Rates, 1979.

[13] Opinions vary widely on demographic measures for China. Those shown here come from official sources quoted in the Guangming Daily and People's Daily and UN sources noted above. Their accuracy is unknown. The projected population for 2000 shown here could be high in light of China's recently announced policy to encourage the one-child family and reduce population growth to zero by 2000.

Source: 1980 World Population Data Sheet, courtesy of the Population Reference Bureau, Inc.

PER CAPITA GROSS NATIONAL PRODUCT AT MARKET PRICES—AMOUNT (1977) AND AVERAGE ANNUAL GROWTH RATES (1960–1977 AND 1970–1977)

COUNTRIES WITH POPULATIONS OF 1 MILLION OR MORE. GNP PER CAPITA ROUNDED TO NEAREST U.S. $10

Country	GNP Per Capita Amount 1977 (U.S. $)	Real Growth Rate (%) 1970–77	Country	GNP Per Capita Amount 1977 (U.S. $)	Real Growth Rate (%) 1970–77
Kuwait	12,690	−0.9	Ecuador	820	6.1
Switzerland	11,080	0.1	Ivory Coast	770	1.1
Sweden	9,340	1.2	Colombia	760	3.8
Denmark	9,160	2.3	Cuba[2,3]	750	−1.2
United States	8,750	2.0	Paraguay	750	4.3
Germany, Federal Republic of	8,620	2.2	Peru	720	1.8
Norway	8,570	3.9	Korea, Democratic People's Republic of[2,3]	680	5.3
Canada	8,350	3.4	Albania	660	4.1
Belgium	8,280	3.5	Morocco	610	4.2
Netherlands	7,710	2.2	El Salvador	590	2.1
France	7,500	3.1	Nigeria	510	4.4
Australia	7,290	1.6	Papua New Guinea	510	2.5
Saudi Arabia[1]	7,230	13.0	Yemen Arab Republic[2]	510	n.a.
Libya	6,520	−4.5	Congo, People's Republic of the	500	0.8
Japan	6,510	3.6	Bolivia	480	2.9
Austria	6,450	3.8	Philippines	460	3.7
Finland	6,190	2.8	Rhodesia[2]	460	−0.1
German Democratic Republic[2,3]	5,070	4.9	Zambia	460	−0.2
United Kingdom	4,540	1.6	Thailand	430	4.1
New Zealand	4,480	0.9	Cameroon	420	1.0
Czechoslovakia[2,3]	4,240	4.3	Honduras	420	0.0
Israel	3,760	2.0	China, People's Republic of[2,3]	410	4.5
Italy	3,530	2.0	Liberia	410	1.1
USSR[2,3]	3,330	4.4	Senegal	380	0.4
Poland[2,3]	3,290	6.3	Ghana	370	−2.0
Spain	3,260	3.6	Yemen, People's Democratic Republic of[7]	350	11.2
Hungary[2,3]	3,100	5.1	Egypt, Arab Republic of	340	5.2
Ireland	3,060	2.1	Sudan[2]	330	2.5
Greece	2,950	4.0	Indonesia	320	5.7
Bulgaria[2,3]	2,830	5.7	Kenya	290	0.9
Singapore[4]	2,820	6.6	Angola[2]	280	−3.4
Venezuela	2,630	3.2	Togo	280	5.3
Hong Kong	2,620	5.8	Mauritania	270	−0.1
Trinidad and Tobago	2,620	1.5	Lesotho[2]	250	9.9
Puerto Rico	2,450	0.1	Central African Republic[2]	240	0.9
Yugoslavia	2,100	5.1	Haiti	230	2.1
Argentina	1,870	1.8	Madagascar	230	−2.7
Portugal	1,840	3.1	Afghanistan	220	2.7
Iraq	1,570	7.1	Benin	210	0.5
Romania[5]	1,530	9.9	Tanzania[8]	210	2.1
Uruguay	1,450	1.3	Zaire	210	−1.4
Brazil	1,410	6.7	Guinea	200	2.5
South Africa	1,400	1.1	Pakistan	200	0.8
Costa Rica	1,390	3.2	Sierra Leone	200	−1.3
Chile	1,250	−1.8	Niger	190	−1.8
Panama	1,200	−0.1	India	160	1.1
China, Republic of	1,180	5.5	Rwanda	160	1.3
Mexico	1,160	1.2	Sri Lanka	160	1.3
Algeria	1,140	2.1	Malawi	150	3.1
Turkey	1,110	4.5	Burma	140	1.3
Jamaica	1,060	−2.0	Mozambique[2]	140	−4.3
Korea, Republic of	980	7.6	Upper Volta	140	1.6
Malaysia	970	4.9	Burundi	130	0.6
Jordan[6]	940	6.5	Chad	130	−1.0
Mongolia[2,3]	870	1.6	Mali	120	1.9
Nicaragua	870	2.5	Somalia[2]	120	−1.1
Syrian Arab Republic	860	6.1	Ethiopia	110	0.2
Dominican Republic	840	4.6	Nepal	110	2.4
Tunisia	840	6.5			
Guatemala	830	3.3			

PER CAPITA GROSS NATIONAL PRODUCT AT MARKET PRICES *(concluded)*

Country	GNP Per Capita		Country	GNP Per Capita	
	Amount 1977 (U.S. $)	Real Growth Rate (%) 1970–77		Amount 1977 (U.S. $)	Real Growth Rate (%) 1970–77
Bhutan[2]	90	—0.3	Lebanon	n.a.	n.a.
Lao People's Democratic			Kampuchea, Democratic	n.a.	n.a.
Republic	90	n.a.	Uganda	n.a.	n.a.
Bangladesh	80	—0.2	Viet Nam	n.a.	n.a.
Iran	n.a.	n.a.			

n.a.—Not available.
[1] GNP per capita growth rate relates to 1963–77.
[2] Estimates of GNP per capita and its growth rate are tentative.
[3] For estimation of GNP per capita, see Technical Note *World Bank Atlas*, 1979, p. 22.
[4] Excluding the expatriate community, the GNP per capita amounts to US $2,290.
[5] This estimate is not comparable to those for the other centrally planned economies. It has been arrived at, following the *World Bank Atlas* methodology, by adjusting official Romanian national accounts data and converting them to U.S. dollars at the effective exchange rate for foreign trade transactions.
[6] GNP per capita relates to East Bank only. GNP per capita growth rate relates to 1972–77.
[7] GNP per capita growth rate relates to 1973–77.
[8] Mainland Tanzania.
Source: *World Bank Atlas* (Washington, DC: World Bank, 1979).

Business Information Directory

GENERAL INFORMATION SOURCES

Government publications referred to below may be obtained from the Government Printing Office (GPO), Washington, DC, 20402, unless otherwise indicated.

GENERAL SOURCES

The *United States Government Manual* is an annual publication. It describes the organization, purposes, and programs of most government agencies and lists top personnel. Available from the GPO.

Washington Information Directory is an annual publication listing, by topic, organizations and publications which provide information on a wide range of subjects. It also lists congressional committee assignments, regional federal offices, embassies, and state and local officials. Published by the Congressional Quarterly, Inc., 1414 22nd Street NW, Washington, DC 20037.

Statistical Abstracts of the United States, published annually, is the standard summary on the social, political, and economic statistics of the United States. It includes data from both government and private sources. Appendix II gives a comprehensive list of sources. (GPO)

Professional and trade organizations and publications are a major source of contacts and information. Key directories to these sources are listed below.

Encyclopedia of Associations, published by Gale Research Co., Book Tower, Detroit, MI 48226.

The World Guide to Trade Associations gives a comprehensive national and international listing of associations. Published by R. R. Bowker Co., 1180 Avenue of the Americas, New York, NY 10036.

Ulrich's International Periodical Directory covers both domestic and foreign periodicals. Published by R. R. Bowker Co., 1180 Avenue of the Americas, New York, NY 10036.

Standard Periodical Directory covers U.S. and Canadian periodicals. Published by Oxbridge Communications, Inc., 183 Madison Avenue, New York, NY 10016.

Ayer's Directory of Newspapers and Periodicals provides titles of trade newspapers and periodicals. Published by Ayer Press, W.

Washington Square, Philadelphia, PA 19106.

Standard Rate and Data Service provides information on periodical circulation and advertising rates. Published by Standard Rates and Data Service, Inc., 5201 Old Orchard Road, Skokie, IL 60076.

Listings of trade directories are given in the following guides:

Guide to American Directories, published by B. Klein Publications, Inc., P.O. Box 8503, Coral Springs, FL 33065.

Trade Directories of the World provides an international listing of directories. Published by Croner Publications, 211–03 Jamaica Avenue, Queens Village, NY 11428.

Encyclopedia of Business Information, a comprehensive single-volume source, is updated periodically. Available from Gale Research Co., Book Tower, Detroit, MI 48226.

BUSINESS AND ECONOMICS INFORMATION

Business and economic information is provided by the following key references.

Survey of Current Business is a major publication which is supplemented on a weekly basis with *Current Statistics*. The publication contains articles as well as comprehensive statistics on all aspects of the economy, including data on the GNP, employment, wages, prices, finance, foreign trade, and production by industrial sector. (GPO)

Business Conditions Digest is a monthly with an extensive collection of charts and tables on the national income and products, leading coincident and lagging cyclical indicators, foreign trade, prices, wages, analytical ratios, and international production and stock prices. (GPO)

Economic Indicators is a monthly summary-type publication prepared by the Council of Economic Advisers. It contains charts and tables on natural output, income, spending, employment, unemployment, wages, industrial production, construction, prices, money, credit, federal finance, and international statistics. (GPO)

Federal Reserve Bulletin is a monthly issued by the Federal Reserve System, containing articles and very extensive tabulated data on all aspects of the monetary situation, credit, mortgage markets, interest rates, and stock and bond yields. A monthly *Chart Book* is available which contains charts of financial and monetary data. Both are available from the Division of Administrative Services, Board of Governors, Federal Reserve System, Washington, DC 20551.

Monthly Labor Review. This monthly publication provides articles and statistics on employment, productivity, wages, earnings, prices, wage settlements, and work stoppages. (GPO)

U.S. Industrial Outlook is an annual providing evaluations and projections of all major industrial and commercial segments of the domestic economy. (GPO)

Quarterly Financial Report of Manufacturing Corporations is issued by the Securities and Exchange Commission and the Federal Trade Commission. It covers corporate financial statistics including sales, profits, assets, and financial ratios, classified by industry group and size. (GPO)

Current Industrial Reports are a series of over 100 monthly, quarterly, semiannual, and annual reports on major products manufactured in the United States. For subscription, contact the Bureau of the Census, U.S. Department of Commerce, Washington, DC 20233. (GPO)

Annual Survey of Manufacturers. General statistics of manufacturing activity for industry groups, individual industries, states, and geographical regions are provided. (GPO)

County Business Patterns is an annual publication on employment and payrolls, which includes a separate paperbound report for each state. (GPO)

Foreign Trade is a Bureau of the Census publication giving monthly reports on U.S. foreign trade. (GPO)

Population: Current Report is a series of monthly and annual reports covering population changes and socioeconomic characteristics of the population. (GPO)

Retail Sales: Current Business Report is a weekly report which provides retail statistics. (GPO)

Wholesale Trade, Sales and Inventories: Current Business Report provides a monthly report on wholesale trade. (GPO)

Directory of Marketing Research Houses and Services is an annual available from the American Marketing Association, 420 Lexington Avenue, New York, NY 10022.

CORPORATE INFORMATION

The major sources of information on publicly held corporations (as well as government and municipal issues) are: *Moody's Investor Services, Inc.,* owned by Dun & Bradstreet, 99 Church Street, New York, NY 10007, and *Standard & Poor's Corp.,* owned by McGraw-Hill, 345 Hudson Street, New York, NY 10014.

Standard & Poor's *Corporate Records* and Moody's *Manuals* are large multivolume works published annually and kept up to date with daily (for Standard & Poor's) or semiweekly (for Moody's) reports. The services provide extensive coverage of industrials, public utilities, transportation, banks, and financial companies. Also included are municipal and government issues.

In addition, the above corporations provide computerized data services and magnetic tapes. Compustat tapes, containing major corporate financial data, are available from Investor's Management Services, Inc., Denver, CO, a subsidiary of Standard & Poor's. Time-sharing access to Compustat and other financial data bases is available through Interactive Data Corporation, Waltham, MA.

The 10-K and other corporate reports are filed with the Securities and Exchange Commission and are available at local SEC offices, investor relations departments of publicly traded companies, as well as various private services, such as Disclosure Inc., Reliance Group, 120 Broadway, New York, NY 10005, which provides a complete microfiche service.

Major trade directories include the *Thomas Register of American Manufacturers* (published by Thomas Publishing Company, 1 Pennsylvania Plaza, New York, NY) and Dun & Bradstreet's *Reference Book of Manufacturers.*

Thomas Register includes in one volume an alphabetical listing of manufacturers, giving address, phone number, product, subsidiaries, plant location, and an indication of assets.

Dun & Bradstreet's *Reference Book* covers similar information, including sales and credit. Dun & Bradstreet also publishes directories on transportation and apparel trades, the *Million Dollar Directory* (a listing of firms with a net worth of $1 million or more), and a *Middle Market Directory* (a listing of firms with a net worth of $500,000 to $1 million).

FEDERAL GOVERNMENT DEVELOPMENTS

Commerce Business Daily. This daily provides information on contract awards and subcontract opportunities, Defense Department awards, and surplus sales. (GPO)

Federal Register. This daily provides information on federal agency regulations and other legal documents (GPO).

CQ Weekly Report. This major service follows every important piece of legislation through both houses of Congress and reports on the political and lobbying pressures being applied. Available from the Congressional Quarterly Service, 1414 22nd Street, Washington, DC 20037.

Daily Report for Executives. A daily series of reports giving Washington developments that affect all aspects of business operations. Available from the Bureau of National Affairs, Inc., 1231 25th Street NW, Washington, DC 20037.

Two major services, the *Bureau of National Affairs, Inc.* (address above) and the *Commerce Clearing House, Inc.* (4025 West Peterson Avenue, Chicago, IL 60646), publish a large number of valuable weekly looseleaf reports covering developments in all aspects of law, government regulations, and taxation.

INDEX PUBLICATIONS

Indexes of a wide variety of articles appearing in periodicals, trade presses, and financial services dealing with corporations, industry, and finance are given in the following:

Business Periodicals Index published by H. W. Wilson Co., 950 University Avenue, Bronx, NY.

Funk and Scott Index of Corporations and Industries, published by Predicast, Inc., 11001 Cedar Street, Cleveland, OH 44141.

Major newspaper indexes are:

New York Times Index published by the New York Times Company, 229 W. 43rd Street, New York, NY 10036 (semimonthly, cumulates annually).

Wall Street Journal Index published by Dow Jones & Co. Inc., 22 Cortland Street, New York, NY 10007 (monthly).

HOW TO FOLLOW ECONOMIC INDICATORS

In the current turbulence of the economy, fluctuations in economic conditions are increasingly significant. Researchers investigating markets and economic developments should monitor the nation's economic indicators closely. The indicators are surveys performed by the government, illustrating the country's economic health. The following list describes several of the indicators and tells how to follow them.

Consumer Price Index—This covers changes in the cost of goods to consumers. Press releases

Source: *The Information Reports,* Washington Researchers, 918 16th Street NW, Washington, DC 20006.

reporting on it are issued monthly by the Department of Labor's Bureau of Labor Statistics. To be put on a mailing list to receive the reports, write:

Bureau of Labor Statistics
441 G St. NW, Room 1539
Washington, DC 20212

To receive data from the index within 24 hours of release, subscribe to the Consumer Price Index Mailgram service, for $95 per year, from:

National Technical Information Service
5285 Port Royal Road
Springfield, VA 22161
703–557–4650

Producer Price Index—Formerly called the *Wholesale Price Index,* this measures changes in prices received in primary markets by producers. It is calculated monthly. To regularly receive free releases, write the Bureau of Labor Statistics at the address above.

Composite Index of Leading Economic Indicators—The Commerce Department's Bureau of Economic Analysis compiles this each month from 12 major economic indicators. It is published in *Business Conditions Digest,* which can be purchased for $40 per year from:

Superintendent of Documents
Government Printing Office
Washington, DC 20402
202–783–3238

To receive the numbers only, contact:

Bureau of Economic Analysis
Department of Commerce
Washington, DC 20230
202–523–0589

Personal Consumption Expenditure Deflator —This is the Commerce Department's version of the Consumer Price Index. It is prepared monthly by the Bureau of Economic Analysis, and it tends to appear more optimistic than the Consumer Price Index. Its findings are released in a regular Personal Income and Outlays news release. The bureau will supply single copies of this free upon request, and will put those associated with the media (the bureau isn't too rigid in its definition of "media") on the mailing list. Contact the Bureau of Economic Analysis at the address above, or at this telephone number: 202–523–0777.

The data also are available in the *Survey of Current Business,* a monthly journal of research. The charge is $22 yearly mailed second class and $35 per year mailed first class. Contact the Government Printing Office at the address and telephone number listed above.

State and Metropolitan Area Unemployment—The index measures changes in the unemployment situation. A free release is available monthly from the Bureau of Labor Statistics.

Unemployment Insurance Claims Weekly Report—A weekly release, the report gives the number of persons receiving unemployment insurance benefits. Obtain the release free from:

Division of Information
Employment and Training Administration
Department of Labor
601 D St. NW
Washington, DC 20213
202–376–6172

Employment Cost Index—A quarterly study, this measures wage and salary rates and changes. A free release can be obtained by writing the Bureau of Labor Statistics.

Employment Situation—Also from the Bureau of Labor Statistics, this monthly study surveys households to determine total employment. Releases are free.

Money Supply—The Federal Reserve Board issues a free release on the nation's money supply each week. Ask for report H-6 from:

Publications Services
Federal Reserve Board
Washington, DC 20551
202–452–3244

Consumer Credit—A free report on consumer credit is issued monthly by the Federal Reserve Board. Write or call the office above and request report G-19.

Value of New Construction Put in Place—The Census Bureau charts the dollar amount of new construction in this monthly report (published in what is called the C-30 series).

The price is $11 annually or 90 cents per issue. The information, however, is first available in press releases on the first working date of each month at 1:30 P.M. for the press and 2 P.M. for the general public. Contact:

Bureau of the Census
Construction Statistics Division
Construction Progress Branch
Washington, DC 20233
301–763–5717

Monthly Retail Trade Report—The Census Bureau compiles this index of retail sales and accounts receivable. The figures are published in *Current Business Reports,* which can be purchased from the Government Printing Office for $1.30 per monthly issue or $25 annually. The annual subscription includes monthly reports, advance monthly reports, and an annual report. Ask for the publication by title and say it is part of the BR Series.

Survey of U.S. Export and Import Merchandise Trade—This gives the value of exports and imports, and also lists oil and petroleum products. Reports are 30 cents per copy and $14.95 annually from:

Subscriber Services Section
Bureau of the Census
Washington, DC 20233
301–763–5140

Only written requests are accepted by the Bureau of Labor Statistics, and they should include the name of the index. The bureau will place interested persons on mailing lists to receive releases regularly. But, because of staff limitations, sometimes it takes several months to be placed on the lists.

USEFUL CONTACTS FOR BUSINESS INFORMATION

Association addresses of any organization may be obtained by writing the Director of Information Central, American Society of Association Executives, 1571 "Eye" Street NW, Washington, DC 20005, or calling 202–626–2723.

Congressional action information can be obtained from several sources. The Bill Status Office will provide information on whether legislation has been introduced, who sponsored it, and its current status. For House action, call 202–225–1772; for Senate action, call 202–224–2971.

Cloakrooms of both houses will provide details on what is happening on the floor of the chamber. House cloakrooms: Democrat 202–225–7330; Republican 202–225–7350. Senate cloakrooms: Democrat 202–224–4691; Republican 202–224–6191.

Corporate reports filed with the SEC can be ordered at 45¢ per page from the National Investment Library, 32 Union Square, New York, NY 10005; or call 212–254–1700.

Service also provided by Disclosure Inc., 4827 Rugby Avenue, Bethesda, MD 20014, or call 301–951–0100.

The Commerce Department's ombudsman operates throughout the entire government complex to assist both business and consumers. Services include dissemination of information and reports such as *Outlook '80*. Write Office of Business Liaison, U.S. Department of Commerce, Washington, DC 20230, or call 202–377–3176.

European Community country information is available free from the European Community Information Service, 2100 M Street NW, Washington, DC 20037; or call 202–862–9500.

Economic data and indicators provided on a weekly, monthly, or quarterly basis may be obtained as released. Telephone numbers of the offices publishing and producing the information are given in the table below.

Department and Information	Telephone Number
Agriculture Department	
To order publications	202–447–2791
Agricultural prices	202–447–3570
Bureau of Economic Analysis	
Business Conditions Digest	202–523–0535
Gross national product (preliminary)	202–523–0824
Personal income	202–523–0813
Merchandise trade balance, balance of payments basis	202–523–0668
Bureau of Labor Statistics	
To order publications	202–523–1327
Consumer price index	202–272–5002
Employment situation	202–523–1581
Wholesale price index	202–272–5110
Census Bureau	
To order publications	202–449–1600
Construction expenditures	202–763–5717
Manufacturers shipments, inventories, and orders	202–763–2502
Housing starts	202–763–7842
Advance report on durable goods, manufacturers shipments, and orders	202–763–2502
Advance monthly retail sales	202–763–7660
Export and import merchandise trade	202–763–5140
Monthly wholesale trade	202–763–7007
Federal Reserve	
To order publications	202–452–3245
Money stock measures	202–452–3591
Consumer credit	202–452–2410
Industrial production and related data	202–452–3153
Capacity utilization in manufacturing	202–452–3197
Joint Economic Committee	202–224–3081
To obtain latest economic information (employment, housing starts, price indices, retail sales, industrial production)	

Economic news and highlights of the day are provided by phone from the Department of Commerce; call 202–393–1847.

The Energy Information Center will provide free information on energy and related matters. Write National Energy Information Center, Forrestal Building, 1000 Independence Avenue SW, Washington, D.C. 20585.

Industry information statistics and details on specific industries can be obtained from the Bureau of Industrial Economics Department of Commerce, Washington, DC 20230; or call 202–377–4356.

Technical and scientific information is provided by the National Technical Information Service of the Department of Commerce, 8001 Forbes Place, Springfield, VA 22161, which handles requests about government-sponsored research of all kinds. For $125 it will research a subject. If a search has been done, a copy will be provided for $30. Call 703–557–4642. For rush orders, call 703–557–4650.

The reference section of the Library of Congress, Science and Technology Division, 10 First Street SE, Washington, DC 20540, provides answers to specific questions; call 202–287–5580. The National Referral Center provides names, addresses, and descriptions of information resources; call 202–287–5670.

Population information on all aspects of national and world population is provided by the Population Reference Bureau, Inc., 1337 Connecticut Avenue NW, Washington, DC 20036; or call 202–785–4664.

Smithsonian Institution Science Information Exchange provides, at a fee to cover costs, information both on individuals currently working in specific fields and on sources of research support; it also covers general research trends. Write 1730 M Street NW, Washington, DC 20036; or call 202–634–3933.

The Washington Information Research Service provides reports and guidance to information on a fee basis. Write Washington Researchers, 918 16th Street NW, Washington, DC 20006, or call 202–828–4800.

Foreign trade information as well as general business data are provided by the World Trade Information Center, One World Trade Center, New York, NY 10048, which maintains extensive data banks. The charge for a preliminary search is about $25. Call 212–466–3063.

Federal Information Centers (FICS) located in key cities throughout the country are a joint venture of the U.S. General Services Administration and the U.S. Civil Services. Each center is a focal point for obtaining information about the federal government and often about state and local governments. A member of the center's staff can either provide information or direct inquiries to an expert who can. Some centers have specialists who speak foreign languages. The coordinator of the FICS is located at 18th and F Streets, NW, Washington, DC 20405; call 202–566–1937. The Federal Information Centers and their telephone numbers are listed below.

Alabama
Birmingham: 322–8591. Toll-free tieline to Atlanta, GA.
Mobile: 438–1421. Toll-free tieline to New Orleans, LA.

Alaska
Anchorage: (907) 271–3650. Federal Building and U.S. Courthouse, 701 C Street 99513

Arizona
Phoenix: (602) 261–3313. Federal Building, 230 N. First Avenue 85025.
Tucson: 622–1511. Toll-free tieline to Phoenix, AZ.

Arkansas
Little Rock: 378–6177. Toll-free tieline to Memphis, TN.

California
Los Angeles: (213) 688–3800. Federal Building, 300 N. Los Angeles Street 90012.
Sacramento: (916) 440–3344. Federal Building, U.S. Courthouse, 650 Capitol Mall 95814.
San Diego: (714) 293–6030. 880 Front Street 92188.
San Francisco: (415) 556–6600. Federal Building, U.S. Courthouse, 450 Golden Gate Avenue 94102.
San Jose: 275–7422. Toll-free tieline to San Francisco, CA.
Santa Ana: 836–2386. Toll-free tieline to Los Angeles, CA.

Colorado
Colorado Springs: 471–9491. Toll-free tieline to Denver, CO.
Denver: (303) 837–3602. Federal Building, 1961 Stout Street 80204.
Pueblo: 544–9523. Toll-free tieline to Denver, CO.

Connecticut
Hartford: 527–2617. Toll-free tieline to New York, NY.
New Haven: 624–4720. Toll-free tieline to New York, NY.

District of Columbia
Washington: (202) 755–8660. Seventh and D Streets SW, Room 5716, 20407.

Florida
Fort Lauderdale: 522–8531. Toll-free tieline to Miami, FL.
Jacksonville: 354–4756. Toll-free tieline to St. Petersburg, FL.

Miami: (305) 350–4155. Federal Building, 51 Southwest First Avenue 33130.

Orlando: 422–1800. Toll-free tieline to St. Petersburg, FL.

St. Petersburg: (813) 893–3495. William C. Cramer Federal Building, 144 First Avenue S. 33701.

Tampa: 229–7911. Toll-free tieline to St. Petersburg, FL.

West Palm Beach: 833–7566. Toll-free tieline to Miami, FL.

Northern Florida (Sarasota, Manatee, Polk, Osceola, Orange, Seminole, and Volusia counties and north): (800) 282–8556. Toll-free line to St. Petersburg, FL.

Southern Florida (Charlotte, De Soto, Hardee, Highlands, Okeechobee, Indian River, and Brevard counties and south): (800) 432–6668. Toll-free line to Miami, FL.

Georgia
Atlanta: (404) 526–6891. Federal Building, 75 Spring Street NE 30303.

Hawaii
Honolulu: (808) 546–8620. Federal Building, 300 Ala Moàna Boulevard, P.O. Box 50091, 96850.

Illinois
Chicago: (312) 353–4242. Everett McKinley Dirksen Building, 219 S. Dearborn Street 60604.

Indiana
Gary/Hammond: 883–4110. Toll-free tieline to Indianapolis, IN.

Indianapolis: (317) 269–7373. Federal Building, 575 North Pennsylvania 46204.

Iowa
Des Moines: (515) 284–4448. Federal Building, 210 Walnut Street 50309.

Other Iowa locations: (800) 532–1556. Toll-free line to Des Moines, IA.

Kansas
Topeka: (913) 295–2866. Federal Building and U.S. Courthouse, 444 S.E. Quincy 66683.

Other Kansas locations: (800) 432–2934. Toll-free line to Topeka, KS.

Kentucky
Louisville: (502) 582–6261. Federal Building, 600 Federal Place 40202.

Louisiana
New Orleans: (504) 589–6696. Federal Building, Room 1210, 701 Loyola Avenue 70113.

Maryland
Baltimore: (301) 962–4980. Federal Building, 31 Hopkins Plaza 21201.

Massachusetts
Boston: (617) 223–7121. J. F. K. Federal Building, Cambridge Street, Lobby, 1st Floor 02203.

Michigan
Detroit: (313) 226–7016. McNamara Federal Building, 477 Michigan Avenue 48226.

Grand Rapids: 451–2628. Toll-free tieline to Detroit, MI.

Minnesota
Minneapolis: (612) 725–2073. Federal Building and U.S. Courthouse, 110 S. Fourth Street 55401.

Missouri
Kansas City: (816) 374–2466. Federal Building, 601 East Twelfth Street 64106.

St. Louis: (314) 425–4106. Federal Building, 1520 Market Street 63103.

Other Missouri locations within area code 314: (800) 392–7711. Toll-free line to St. Louis, MO.

Other Missouri locations within area codes 816 and 417: (800) 892–5808. Toll-free line to Kansas City, MO.

Nebraska
Omaha: (402) 221–3353. Federal Building, U.S. Post Office, and Courthouse, 215 N. 17th Street 68102.

Other Nebraska locations: (800) 642–8383. Toll-free line to Omaha, NB.

New Jersey
Newark: (201) 645–3600. Federal Building, 970 Broad Street 07102.

Paterson/Passaic: 523–0717. Toll-free tieline to Newark, NJ.

Trenton: 396–4400. Toll-free tieline to Newark, NJ.

New Mexico
Albuquerque: (505) 766–3091. Federal Building and U.S. Courthouse, 500 Gold Avenue SW 87101.

Santa Fe: 983–7743. Toll-free tieline to Albuquerque, NM.

New York
Albany: 463–4421. Toll-free tieline to New York, NY.

Buffalo: (716) 846–4010. Federal Building, 111 West Huron Street 14202.

New York: (212) 264–4464. Lobby, Federal Building, 26 Federal Plaza 10278.

Rochester: 546–5075. Toll-free tieline to Buffalo, NY.

Syracuse: 476–8545. Toll-free tieline to Buffalo, NY.

North Carolina
Charlotte: 376–3600. Toll-free tieline to Atlanta GA.

Ohio
Akron: 375–5638. Toll-free tieline to Cleveland, OH.

Cincinnati: (513) 684–2801. Federal Building, 550 Main Street 45202.

Cleveland: (216) 522–4040. Federal Building, 1240 E. Ninth Street 44199.

Columbus: 221–1014. Toll-free tieline to Cincinnati, OH.

Dayton: 223–7377. Toll-free tieline to Cincinnati, OH.

Toledo: 241–3223. Toll-free tieline to Cleveland, OH.

Oklahoma

Oklahoma City: (405) 231–4868. U.S. Post Office and Courthouse, 201 N.W. 3rd Street 73102.

Tulsa: 584–4193. Toll-free tieline to Oklahoma City, OK.

Oregon

Portland: (503) 221–2222. Federal Building, 1220 S.W. Third Avenue 97204.

Pennsylvania

Allentown/Bethlehem: 821–7785. Toll-free tieline to Philadelphia, PA.

Philadelphia: (215) 597–7042. Federal Building, 600 Arch Street 19106.

Pittsburgh: (412) 644–3456. Federal Building, 1000 Liberty Avenue 15222.

Scranton: 346–7081. Toll-free tieline to Philadelphia, PA.

Rhode Island

Providence: 331–5565. Toll-free tieline to Boston, MA.

Tennessee

Chattanooga: 265–8231. Toll-free tieline to Memphis, TN.

Memphis: (901) 534–3285. Clifford Davis Federal Building, 167 N. Main Street 38103.

Nashville: 242–5056. Toll-free tieline to Memphis, TN.

Texas

Austin: 472–5494. Toll-free tieline to Houston, TX.

Dallas: 767–8585. Toll-free tieline to Fort Worth, TX.

Fort Worth: (817) 334–3624. Fritz Garland Lanham Federal Building, 819 Taylor Street 76102.

Houston: (713) 226–5711. Federal Building, U.S. Courthouse, 515 Rusk Avenue 77002.

San Antonio: 224–4471. Toll-free tieline to Houston, TX.

Utah

Ogden: 399–1347. Toll-free tieline to Salt Lake City, UT.

Salt Lake City: (801) 524–5353. Federal Building, Lobby, 125 S. State Street 84138.

Virginia

Newport News: 244–0480. Toll-free tieline to Norfolk, VA.

Norfolk: (804) 441–3101. Federal Building, 200 Granby Mall, Room 120 23510.

Richmond: 643–4928. Toll-free tieline to Norfolk, VA.

Roanoke: 982–8591. Toll-free tieline to Norfolk, VA.

Washington

Seattle: (206) 442–0570. Federal Building, 915 Second Avenue 98174.

Tacoma: 383–5230. Toll-free tieline to Seattle, WA.

Wisconsin

Milwaukee: 271–2273. Toll-free tieline to Chicago, IL.

INFORMATION SOURCES IN THE U.S. DEPARTMENT OF COMMERCE (By subject)

Subject	Source	Telephone Number
Aeronautical charting	NOAA	301–443–8708
Agricultural census	CEN	301–568–1200
Air-quality research	NOAA	303–499–1000
Appliance labeling	NBS	301–921–3181
Applied technology	NBS	301–921–3181
Arab boycott	ITA	202–377–3259
Atmospheric remote sensing	NOAA	303–499–1000
Atmospheric research	NOAA	303–499–1000
Atomic, nuclear, isotopic research	NBS	301–921–3181
Automation technology	NBS	301–921–3181
Balance of payments	BEA	202–523–0777
Broadcast news	SEC	202–377–5610
Building technology	NBS	301–921–3181
Business censuses	CEN	301–763–7273
Business development loans	EDA	202–377–5113
Business Conditions Digest	BEA	202–523–0777
Capital equipment	ITA	202–377–3259
Censuses	CEN	301–568–1200
Climate monitoring	NOAA	303–499–1000
Coal gasification	NBS	301–921–3181
Coastal zone management	NOAA	202–634–4239
Commerce Technical Advisory Board (CTAB)	S&T	202–377–5065
Commodity statistics	ITA	202–377–3259
Computer science and technology	NBS	301–921–3181
Construction and forest products	ITA	202–377–3259
Consumer goods	ITA	202–377–3259
Consumer products safety	NBS	301–921–3181
Corporate profits	BEA	202–523–0777
Decennial (1980 Census)	CEN	301–568–1200
Disaster research	NBS	301–921–3181
Domestic Business Development, Bureau of	ITA	202–377–3259
East-west trade	ITA	202–377–3259
Economic affairs	OCE	202–377–2235
Economic censuses	CEN	301–568–1200
Economic development programs	EDA	202–377–5113
Education statistics	CEN	301–568–1200
Energy (conservation)	NBS	301–921–3181
Energy (inventions)	NBS	301–921–3181
Environment (pollution)	NBS	301–921–3181
Environment affairs	S&T	202–377–4335
Environment data services	NOAA	302–634–7305
Environmental research	NOAA	303–499–1000
Environmental satellites	NOAA	301–443–8243
Employment and unemployment surveys	CEN	301–568–1200
Exports awards	ITA	202–377–2253
Export Development, Bureau of	ITA	202–377–2253
Export information	ITA	202–377–2253
Export licenses	ITA	202–377–4654
Expositions (international)	USTS	202–377–4987
Failure analysis	NBS	301–921–3181
Federal economic indicators	OCE	202–377–2235
Field operations	ITA	202–377–2253
Fire protection (see also Research and Education)	NBS	301–921–3181
Flash floods	NOAA	301–427–7622
Foreign investment statistics	BEA	202–523–0777
Foreign trade analysis	ITA	202–377–2253
Foreign trade statistics	CEN	301–568–1200
Freedom of information	SEC	202–377–5659
Frequency allocations (federal use)	NTIA	202–395–5800
Geodetic surveys	NOAA	301–443–8708

INFORMATION SOURCES IN THE U.S. DEPARTMENT OF COMMERCE *(continued)*

Subject	Source	Telephone Number
Government finances (state and local)	CEN	301–568–1200
Grants to local government	EDA	202–377–5113
Great Lakes research	NOAA	303–499–1000
Gross national product	BEA	202–523–0777
Health	NBS	301–921–3181
Housing and construction statistics	CEN	301–568–1200
Hurricane research	NOAA	303–499–1000
Hurricane warning	NOAA	301–427–7622
Hydrology, Office of	NOAA	301–427–7622
Import programs	ITA	202–377–3259
Income, family	CEN	301–568–1200
Income, personal (national and regional)	BEA	202–523–0777
Industry surveys	CEN	301–568–1200
Information policy	NTIA	202–395–5800
Input-output analysis	BEA	202–523–0777
Interdepartment Radio Advisory Committee (IRAC)	NTIA	202–395–5800
International finance, investment, and marketing	ITA	202–377–2253
International investment statistics	BEA	202–523–0777
Investment services	ITA	202–377–2253
Laser information	NBS	301–921–3181
Law enforcement standards	NBS	301–921–3181
Leading economic indicators	BEA	202–523–0777
Manufacturing industry (by commodity)	ITA	202–377–3259
Marine ecosystem studies	NOAA	303–499–1000
Marine mammals	NOAA	202–634–7281
Marine technology	NOAA	301–443–8243
Maritime technology	MARAD	202–377–2746
Materials research	NBS	301–921–3181
Meteorological center	NOAA	301–427–7622
Metric	NBS	301–921–3181
Minority business programs	OMBE	202–377–3024
National marine fisheries	NOAA	202–634–7281
Nautical charts	NOAA	301–443–8708
News releases and speeches	SEC	202–377–4901
Occupation and industry statistics	CEN	301–568–1200
Ombudsman for business	ITA	202–277–3259
Overseas business opportunities	ITA	202–377–2253
Patent and trademarks	PTO	703–557–3428
Patents, government-owned, foreign filing	NTIS	703–557–4735
Plant and equipment expenditures	BEA	202–523–0777
Pollution abatement and control expenditures	BEA	202–523–0777
Population information	CEN	301–568–1200
Product standards	S&T	202–377–3221
Public works projects	EDA	202–377–5113
Publications, sales and distribution	SEC	202–377–5494
Radiation measurements	NBS	301–921–3181
Recent Department of Commerce Publications	SEC	202–377–4233
Regional Economic Statistics	BEA	202–523–0777
Regional Planning Commissions	SEC	202–377–4901
Research (economic)	OCE	202–377–2235
Research and data (fire)	NFPCA	202–634–7663
Research (maritime)	MARAD	202–377–2746
Resource and Trade Assistance, Bureau of	ITA	202–377–3259
Retail, wholesale, and service trade statistics	CEN	301–763–7273
Satellites	NOAA	301–443–8243
Science and technology	S&T	202–377–5065
Sea grants	NOAA	202–634–4034
Secretarial statements	SEC	202–377–4901
Service industries (statistics)	ITA	202–377–3259
Ship operations shipbuilding	MARAD	202–377–2746
Solar forecasts	NOAA	303–499–1000
Solar standards, research	NBS	301–921–3181
Space environment research	NOAA	303–499–1000
Spectrum management	NTIA	202–395–5800
Standard reference materials	NBS	301–921–3181
Statistical reporter	OFSPS	202–673–7965
Stratospheric research	NOAA	303–499–1000

INFORMATION SOURCES IN THE U.S. DEPARTMENT OF COMMERCE *(concluded)*

Subject	Source	Telephone Number
Survey of current business	BEA	202–523–0777
Technical document sales (all government agencies)	NTIS	202–557–4600
Technical help to exporters	NTIS	703–557–4733
Technology transfer to developing countries	NTIS	202–724–3370
Telecommunications applicators	NTIA	202–395–5800
Telecommunications policy (international and domestic)	NTIA	202–395–5800
Telecommunications research	NTIA	202–395–5800
Telecommunications technology	NTIA	202–395–5800
Textiles	ITA	202–377–3259
Time and frequency (standards)	NBS	303–323–3198
Tornado and severe storms research	NOAA	303–499–1000
Tornado warning	NOAA	301–427–7622
Tourism, international and domestic	USTS	202–377–4987
Trade adjustment assistance	EDA	202–377–5133
Trade fairs, trade centers and missions	ITA	202–377–2253
Trademarks	PAT	703–557–3428
Trade negotiations	ITA	202–377–2253
Trade zone board	ITA	202–377–3259
Transportation equipment	ITA	202–377–3259
Travel to and in United States	USTS	202–377–4987
Weather modification (cloud seeding)	NOAA	303–499–1000
Weather service	NOAA	301–427–7622
Weights and measures	NBS	301–921–3181

Abbreviations

BEA	Bureau of Economic Analysis
CEN	Bureau of the Census
EDA	Economic Development Administration
ITA	Industry and Trade Administration
MARAD	Maritime Administration
NBS	National Bureau of Standards
NFPCA	National Fire Prevention and Control Administration
NOAA	National Oceanic and Atmospheric Administration
NTIA	National Telecommunications and Information Administration
NTIS	National Technical Information Service
OCE	Office of Chief Economist
OFSPS	Office of Federal Stat. Policy and Standards
OMBE	Office of Minority Business Enterprise
PTO	Patent and Trademark Office
SEC	Office of the Secretary
S&T	Office of the Assistant Secretary for Science and Technology
USTS	United States Travel Service

ADDRESSES OF U.S. DEPARTMENT OF COMMERCE INFORMATION SOURCES

Office of Assistant Secretary for Science and Technology
Main Commerce Building
14th and Constitution Avenues
Washington, DC 20230
Telephone: 202–377–3653

Office of the Chief Economist
Main Commerce Building
14th and Constitution Avenues
Washington, DC 20230
Telephone: 202–377–2235

Bureau of the Census
Federal Office Building No. 3
Suitland, MD 20230
Telephone: 301–568–1200

Bureau of Economic Analysis
Tower Building
1401 K Street NW
Mailing Address:
U.S. Department of Commerce
14th and Constitution Avenues
Washington, DC 20230
Telephone: 202–523–0777

Industry and Trade Administration
Main Commerce Building
14th and Constitution Avenues
Washington, DC 20230
Telephone: 202–377–3808

Economic Development Administration
Main Commerce Building
14th and Constitution Avenues
Washington, DC 20230
Telephone: 202–377–5113

Maritime Administration
Main Commerce Building
14th and Constitution Avenues
Washington, DC 20230
Telephone: 202–377–2746

National Bureau of Standards
Administration Building
National Bureau of Standards
Washington, DC 20234
Telephone: 301–921–3112

National Oceanic and Atmospheric Administration
11400 Rockville Pike
Rock-Wall Building
Rockville, MD 20852
Telephone: 202–965–1752

National Technical Information Service
Pennsylvania Building
425 13th Street NW
Washington, DC 20004
Telephone: 202–724–3382

Office of Minority Business Enterprise
Main Commerce Building
14th and Constitution Avenues
Washington, DC 20230
Telephone: 202–377–3024

Office of Telecommunications and Information Administration
1800 G Street NW
Washington, DC 20504
Telephone: 202–377–1832

Patent and Trademark Office
Crystal Plaza Building 3
2021 Jefferson Davis Highway
Arlington, VA 20231
Telephone: 703–557–3428

United States Travel Service
Main Commerce Building
14th and Constitution Avenues
Washington, DC 20230
Telephone: 202–377–4987

STATE
INFORMATION GUIDE

Regional Directories

Central Atlantic States Manufacturing Directory, T. K. Sanderson Organization, 200 E. 25 Street, Baltimore, MD 21218

Commercial Classified Directory and Buyers Guide 1977, Commercial Classified Publishers, Inc., 225 Broadway, New York, NY 10007

Daltons' Greater Philadelphia Industrial Directory, Dalton Corp., 2925 N. Broad Street, Philadelphia, PA 19132

Directory of Central Atlantic States Manfacturers, Manufacturers' News, Inc., 3 E. Huron Street, Chicago, IL 60611; George D. Hall Company, 20 Kilby Street, Boston, MA 02109

Directory of New England Manufacturers, The, George D. Hall Company, 20 Kilby Street, Boston, MA 02109

Eastern Manufacturers' and Industrial Directory, Bell Directory Publishers, Inc., 2112 Broadway, New York, NY 10023

Midwest Manufacturers' and Industrial Directory, Industrial Directory Publishers, 1002 Park Avenue Building, Detroit, MI 48226

New England Apparel Directory, Register Publication, Inc., 99 Chauncey Street, Boston, MA 02111

New England Industrial Service Directory, George D. Hall Company, 20 Kilby Street, Boston, MA 02109

New England Manufacturers Directory, Manufacturers' News, Inc., 3 E. Huron Street, Chicago, IL 60611

State Sales Guides, Dun & Bradstreet, Inc., 99 Church Street, New York, NY 10007

Survey of Industries in Texarcana (Arkansas-Texas), Texarkana Chamber of Commerce, Box 1468, Texarkana, AK 75501

Alabama

STATE CAPITOL, MONTGOMERY, AL 36130
(205) 832–3511

° Refers throughout this section to the Small Business Administration regional office.

† Refers throughout this section to the Small Business Administration field office.

INFORMATION OFFICES

Commerce/Economic Development
Alabama Development Office
State Capitol
Montgomery, AL 36130

Taxation
Department of Revenue
Administrative Building
Montgomery, AL 36130

State Chamber of Commerce
Alabama Chamber of Commerce
468 S. Perry Street
P. O. Box 76
Montgomery, AL 36101

Small Business Administration
908 S. 20th Street†
Birmingham, AL 35205

PUBLICATIONS

Economic Abstract of Alabama, (irregular publication), University of Alabama, Center for Business and Economic Research, University, AL 35486

Estimates of Population of Alabama Counties and Metropolitan Areas, (annual), Superintendent of Documents, U.S. Government Printing Office, Washington, DC 20402.

Alabama Business (income statistics, annual), Center for Business and Economic Research, P.O. Box AK, University, AL 35486

Alabama Labor Market (employment statistics, monthly), Department of Industrial Relations, Montgomery, AL 36130.

INDUSTRIAL AND BUSINESS DIRECTORIES

Alabama Directory of Mining and Manufacturing, Alabama Development Office, State Capitol, Montgomery, AL 36130

Alabama Industrial Directory, Manufacturers' News, Inc., 3 E. Huron Street, Chicago, IL 60611; State Industrial Directories Corp., 2 Penn Plaza, New York, NY 10001

Alabama International Trade Directory, Alabama State Chamber of Commerce, P.O. Box 76, Montgomery, AL 36101

Birmingham Industrial Directory, Birmingham Chamber of Commerce, 1914 6th Avenue, Birmingham, AL 35203

Alaska

STATE CAPITOL, JUNEAU, AK 99811
(907) 465–2111

INFORMATION OFFICES

Commerce/Economic Development
Department of Commerce & Economic Development
Pouch D
Juneau, AK 99811
Taxation
Department of Revenue
Pouch S
Juneau, AK 99811
State Chamber of Commerce
Alaska State Chamber of Commerce
310 2nd Street
Juneau, AK 99801
Small Business Administration
Anchorage, Alaska†
1016 W. 6th Avenue
Anchorage, AK 99501

Fairbanks, Alaska
101 12th Avenue
Fairbanks, AK 99701

PUBLICATIONS

Alaska Economy, Department of Commerce and Development, Division of Economic Enterprise, Juneau, AK 99801

Alaska Statistical Review, Department of Economic Development, Division of Economic Enterprise, Juneau, AK 99801

Alaska Population by Area (population statistics, annual), Department of Labor, Research and Analysis, Box 1149, Juneau, AK 99811

Alaska Review of Business and Economic Conditions Series (income statistics, five times a year), Institute of Social, Economic and Government Research, University of Alaska, Fairbanks, AK 99701

Alaska Economic Trends (employment statistics, monthly), Department of Labor, Research and Analysis, Box 1149, Juneau, AK 99811

Alaska's Manpower Outlook—1970s Regional Population and Employment Estimates 1961–1980 (employment statistics, annual), Employment Security Division, Department of Labor, Juneau, AK 99801

INDUSTRIAL AND BUSINESS DIRECTORIES

Alaska Directory of Commercial Establishments, Manufacturers' News, Inc., 3 E. Huron Street, Chicago, IL 60611; State Industrial Directories Corp., 2 Penn Plaza, New York, NY 10001

Alaska Petroleum and Industrial Directory, 409 W. Northern Lights Boulevard, Anchorage, AK 99603

Arizona

STATE CAPITOL, PHOENIX, AZ 85007
(602) 255–4900

INFORMATION OFFICES

Commerce/Economic Development
Office of Economic Planning and Development
1700 W. Washington Avenue
Phoenix, AZ 85007
Taxation
Department of Revenue
State Capitol
Phoenix, AZ 85007
State Chamber of Commerce
Arizona State Chamber of Commerce
3216 N. Third Street
Phoenix, AZ 85012
Small Business Administration
3030 N. Central Avenue†
Phoenix, AZ 85012

PUBLICATIONS

Arizona Statistical Review, Valley National Bank, Economic Research Department, P.O. Box 71, Phoenix, AZ 85001

Statistical Abstract of Arizona, University of Arizona, Division of Economic Business Research, College of Business and Public Administration, Tucson, AZ 85724

Arizona Basic Economic and Manpower Data (annual), Arizona Department of Economic Security, P.O. Box 6123, Phoenix, AZ 85005

Arizona Review (income statistics, monthly), Division of Economic and Business Research, University of Arizona, Tucson, AZ 85724

Arizona Newsletter (income statistics, monthly), Arizona Department of Economic Security, Research Institute Statistics Bureau, P.O. Box 6123, Phoenix, AZ 85005

Phoenix Area Manpower Newsletter (income statistics, monthly), Arizona Department of Economic Security, Research Institute Statistics Bureau, P.O. Box 6123, Phoenix, AZ 85005

Tucson Area Manpower Newsletter (income statistics, monthly), Arizona Department of Economic Security, Research Institute Statistics Bureau, P.O. Box 6123, Phoenix, AZ 85005

Arizona Indicator (income statistics, monthly), Arizona Department of Economic Security, Research Institute Statistics Bureau, P.O. Box 6123, Phoenix, AZ 85005

Manpower Newsletter (employment statistics, monthly), Unemployment Compensations Division, Employment Security Commission, Phoenix, AZ 85005

INDUSTRIAL AND BUSINESS DIRECTORIES

Arizona Directory of Industries, Manufacturers' News, 3 E. Huron Street, Chicago, IL 60611

Arizona Directory of Manufacturers, Manufacturers' News, Inc., 3 E. Huron Street, Chicago, IL 60611; State Industrial Directories Corp., 2 Penn Plaza, New York, NY 10001

Arizona Exports and Imports, Office of Economic Planning and Development, 1700 W. Washington Avenue, Phoenix, AZ 85007

Arizona USA International Trade Directory, Arizona State Department of Economic Planning and Development, 1700 W. Washington Avenue, Phoenix, AZ 85007

Directory of Arizona Manufacturers, Phoenix Chamber of Commerce, Phoenix, AZ 85001

Arkansas

STATE CAPITOL, LITTLE ROCK, AR 72201
(501) 371–3000

INFORMATION OFFICES

Commerce/Economic Development
Department of Commerce
1501 N. University Avenue
Little Rock, AR 72207
Department of Economic Development
One State Capitol Mall
Little Rock, AR 72201
Taxation
Division of Revenue Services
Department of Finance and Administration
7th and Wolfe Streets
Little Rock, AR 72201
State Chamber of Commerce
Arkansas State Chamber of Commerce
911 Wallace Building
Little Rock, AR 72201
Small Business Administration
611 Gaines Street†
Little Rock, AR 72201

PUBLICATIONS

Arkansas Business Economic Review (population statistics, quarterly), Bureau of Business and Economic Research, University of Arkansas, Fayetteville, AR 72701

Annual Estimates of Total Personal and Per Capita Income (annual), Industrial Research and Extension Center, University of Arkansas, P.O. Box 3017, Little Rock, AR 72203

Arkansas Current Employment Development (monthly), Employment Security Division, Department of Labor, Little Rock, AR 72203

Employment and Payroll (quarterly), Employment Security Division, Department of Labor, Little Rock, AR 72203

INDUSTRIAL AND BUSINESS DIRECTORIES

Arkansas Almanac, Arkansas Almanac, Inc., Little Rock, AR 72114

Arkansas Directory of Industries, Manufacturers' News, 3 E. Huron Street, Chicago, IL 60611

Directory of Arkansas Manufacturers, Arkansas Department of Economic Development, One State Capitol Mall, Little Rock, AR 72201; State Industrial Directories Corp., 2 Penn Plaza, New York, NY 10001

California

STATE CAPITOL, SACRAMENTO, CA 95814
(916) 332–9900

INFORMATION OFFICES

Commerce/Economic Development
Economic and Business Development
1120 N Street
Sacramento, CA 95814
Taxation
Franchise Tax Board
920 23d Street
Sacramento, CA 95814

Board of Equalization
1020 N Street
Sacramento, CA 95814
State Chamber of Commerce
California Chamber of Commerce
455 Capitol Mall
P.O. Box 1736
Sacramento, CA 95808
Small Business Administration
450 Golden Gate Avenue°
San Francisco, CA 94102

211 Main Street†
San Francisco, CA 94105

1229 N Street
Fresno, CA 93712

350 S. Figueroa Street†
Los Angeles, CA 90071

880 Front Street†
San Diego, CA 92188

2800 Cottage Way
Sacramento, CA 95825

PUBLICATIONS

California Statistical Abstract, Department of Finance, Budget Division, Sacramento, CA 95814

California's Population (annual), Population Research Unit, Department of Finance, Sacramento, CA 95814

The UCLA Forecast for the Nation and California (income statistics, annual), UCLA Business Forecasting Project, Graduate School of Management, UCLA, Los Angeles, CA 90024

California Economic Indicators (income statistics, quarterly), California Department of Finance, 1025 P Street, Sacramento, CA 95814

California Employment and Payroll (quarterly), Employment Development Department, 800 Capitol Mall, Sacramento, CA 95814

California Labor Market Bulletin Statistical Supplement (employment statistics, monthly) Employment Development Department, 800 Capital Mall, Sacramento, CA 95814

Taxable Sales in California (sales statistics, quarterly), State Board of Equalization, P.O. Box 1799, Sacramento, CA 95814

California-The Future, Office of Business and Industrial Development, P.O. Box 1499, Sacramento, CA 95805

INDUSTRIAL AND BUSINESS DIRECTORIES

California Handbook, Center for California Public Affairs, 226 W. Foothill Boulevard, Claremont, CA 91711

California International Business Directory, Center for International Business, 333 S. Flower Street, Los Angeles, CA 90071

California Manufacturers Register, Time-Mirror Press, 1115 S. Boyle Avenue, Los Angeles, CA 90023; Manufacturers' News, Inc., 3 E. Huron Street, Chicago, IL 50611; State Industrial Directories Corp., 2 Penn Plaza, New York, NY 10001

Los Angeles Area Chamber of Commerce Southern California Business Directory and Buyers Guide, Los Angeles Chamber of Commerce, 404 S. Bixel Street, Los Angeles, CA 95113

San Francisco Manufacturers Directory, San Francisco Chamber of Commerce, 333 Pine Street, San Francisco, CA 94577

Colorado

STATE CAPITOL, DENVER, CO 80203
(303) 839–5000

INFORMATION OFFICES

Commerce/Economic Development
Division of Commerce and Development
Department of Local Affairs
Centennial Building
1313 Sherman Street
Denver, CO 80203

Taxation
Administrative Division
Department of Revenue
1375 Sherman Street
Denver, CO 80203

State Chamber of Commerce
Colorado Association of Commerce and Industry
1390 Logan Street
Denver, CO 80203

Small Business Administration
721 19th Street
Denver, CO 80202

721 19th Street†
Denver, CO 80202

PUBLICATIONS

Economic Growth at a Glance (population statistics, annual), Denver Chamber of Commerce, 1301 Walton Street, Denver, CO 80202

Annual Report—Colorado Department of Revenue (income statistics, annual), Colorado Department of Revenue, 1375 Sherman Street, Denver, CO 80203

Colorado's Current Monthly Estimate of Nonfarm Employment (monthly), Colorado Division of Employment, 251 East 12th Avenue, Denver, CO 80203

Colorado Manpower Review (employment statistics, monthly), Colorado Division of Employment, 251 East 12th Avenue, Denver, CO 80203

Sales Tax Statistical Summary (annual), Department of Revenue, Denver, CO 80203

INDUSTRIAL AND BUSINESS DIRECTORIES

Colorado Inaustrial Capability Register, Public Affairs Department, Colorado Interstate Gas Co., P.O. Box 1087, Colorado Springs, CO 80901

Directory of Colorado Manufacturers, Business Research Division, University of Colorado, Boulder, CO 80309; State Industrial Directories Corp. 2 Penn Plaza, New York, NY 10001

Connecticut

INFORMATION OFFICES

Commerce/Economic Development
Department of Economic Development
210 Washington Street
Hartford, CT 06106
Taxation
Department of Revenue Statistics
92 Farmington Avenue
Hartford, CT 06115
State Chamber of Commerce
Connecticut Business and Industry Association
60 Washington Street
Hartford, CT 06106
Small Business Administration
1 Financial Plaza†
Hartford, CT 06103

PUBLICATIONS

Connecticut Market Data, Connecticut Department of Economic Development, Hartford, CT 06106
Weekly Health Bulletin (population statistics, annual), Public Health, Education Section, State Department of Health, State Office Building, Hartford, CT 06115
Connecticut Area Trends in Employment and Unemployment (income statistics, annual), Research and Information, Connecticut Labor Department, Hartford, CT 06115
Labor Situation (employment statistics, monthly), Employment Security Division, Department of Labor, Wethersfield, CT 06109
Sales and Use Tax Information (sales statistics, quarterly), State Tax Department, 92 Farmington Avenue, Hartford, CT 06115

INDUSTRIAL AND BUSINESS DIRECTORIES

Classified Business Directory—State of Connecticut, Connecticut Directory Co., Inc., 322 Main Street, Stamford, CT 06901
Connecticut Classified Business Directory,

Connecticut Directory Co., Inc., 322 Main Street, Stamford, CT 06901
Connecticut State Industrial Directory, Manufacturers' News, 3 E. Huron Street, Chicago, IL 06011; State Industrial Directories Corp., 2 Penn Plaza, New York, NY 10001
Directory of Connecticut Manufacturing Establishments, Connecticut Department of Labor, 200 Folly Brook Boulevard, Wethersfield, CT 06109

Delaware

INFORMATION OFFICES

Commerce/Economic Development
Department of Community Affairs and Economic Development
Division of Economic Development and Minority Business Enterprise
630 State College Road
Dover, DE 19901
Taxation
Department of Finance
Division of Revenue
601 Delaware Avenue
Wilmington, DE 19899
State Chamber of Commerce
Delaware State Chamber of Commerce, Inc.
1102 West Street
Wilmington, DE 19801
Small Business Administration
844 King Street
Wilmington, DE 19801

PUBLICATIONS

Comparison of Corporate Taxes in Delaware, New York, Pennsylvania and Maryland, Division of Economic Development, P.O. Box 1401, Dover, DE 19901
Dimensions on Delaware, Office of Management, Budget and Planning, Townsend Building, Dover, DE 19901
Estimates of the Population of Delaware Counties (population statistics, annual), Superintendent of Documents, U.S. Government Printing Office, Washington, DC 20402
Delaware Economic Indicators (income statistics, quarterly), Office of Management, Budget and Planning, Townsend Building, Dover, DE 19901

Employment, Hours and Earnings (employment statistics, monthly), University Plaza office, Chapman Road and Route 273, Newark, DE 19702

INDUSTRIAL AND BUSINESS DIRECTORIES

Delaware Directory of Commerce and Industry, Delaware State Chamber of Commerce, 1102 West Street, Wilmington, DE 19801

Delaware State Industrial Directory, State Industrial Directories Corp., 2 Penn Plaza, New York, NY 10001

Florida

STATE CAPITOL, TALLAHASSEE, FL 32301
(904) 488–1234

INFORMATION OFFICES

Commerce/Economic Development
Department of Commerce
Collins Building
Tallahassee, FL 32301

Division of Economic Development
Department of Commerce
Collins Building
Tallahassee, FL 32301
Taxation
Department of Revenue
Carlton Building
Tallahassee, FL 32301
State Chamber of Commerce
Florida State Chamber of Commerce
P.O. Box 5497
Tallahassee, FL 32301
Small Business Administration
2222 Ponce de Leon Boulevard†
Coral Gables, FL 33134

700 Twiggs Street
Tampa, FL 33602

400 W. Bay Street†
Jacksonville, FL 32202

701 Clematis Street
West Palm Beach, FL 33402

PUBLICATIONS

Florida Statistical Abstract (population, income statistics, annual), University of Florida, Bureau of Economic and Business Research, 221 Matherly Hall, Gainesville, FL 32611

Economic Report of the Governor (quarterly income statistics, annual), Office of the Governor, Office of Planning and Budgeting,

The Capitol, Tallahassee, FL 32301

Florida Employment Statistics (monthly), Department of Labor and Employment Security, Division of Employment Security, Caldwell Building, Tallahassee, FL 32301

Annual Report of the Comptroller (sales statistics, annual), Department of Banking and Finance, Office of Comptroller, The Capitol, Tallahassee, FL 32301

Population Studies (quarterly), University of Florida, Bureau of Economic and Business Research, 221 Matherly Hall, Gainesville, FL 32611

INDUSTRIAL AND BUSINESS DIRECTORIES

Directory of Florida Industries, Manufacturers' News, Inc., 3 E. Huron Street, Chicago, IL 60611; Florida State Chamber of Commerce, P.O. Box 5497, Tallahassee, FL 32301; State Industrial Directories Corp., 2 Penn Plaza, New York, NY 10001

Florida Industries Guide, McHenry Publishing Co., Inc., Box 935, Orlando, FL 32802

Georgia

STATE CAPITOL, ATLANTA, GA 30334
(404) 656–2000

INFORMATION OFFICES

Commerce/Economic Development
Department of Industry and Trade
1400 N. Omni Boulevard
Atlanta, GA 30303
Taxation
Department of Revenue
270 Washington Street, SW
Atlanta, GA 30334
State Chamber of Commerce
Georgia Chamber of Commerce
1200 Commerce Building
Atlanta, GA 30303
Small Business Administration
1720 Peachtree Street NW
Atlanta, GA 30309

PUBLICATIONS

Georgia Statistical Abstract, University of Georgia, Division of Research, College of Business Administration, Athens, GA 30602

Georgia Vital Statistics (population statistics, annual), Management and Analysis Unit, Department of Human Resources, 47 Trinity Avenue, SW, Atlanta, GA 30334

Georgia Statistical Abstract (income statistics, annual), Division of Research, College of Business Administration, University of Georgia, Athens, GA 30602

Employment and Earnings (employment statistics, annual), Employment Security Agency, Department of Labor, Atlanta, GA 30303

Employment and Wages Insured by the Georgia Employment Security Law (quarterly), Employment Security Agency, Department of Labor, Atlanta, GA 30303

INDUSTRIAL AND BUSINESS DIRECTORIES

Directory of Associations in Georgia, 1974–1975, Basic Data Research, Industrial Development Division, Engineering Experiment Station, Atlanta, GA 30332

Georgia Manufacturing Directory, Georgia Department of Industry and Trade, P.O. Box 1776, Atlanta, GA 30332

Georgia World Trade Directory, Georgia Chamber of Commerce, 1200 Commerce Building, Atlanta, GA 30303

Industrial Sites in Georgia, Georgia Power, Box 4545R, Atlanta, GA 30302

Hawaii

STATE CAPITOL BUILDING, HONOLULU, HI 96813
(808) 548–2211

INFORMATION OFFiCES

Commerce/Economic Development
Department of Planning and Economic Development
250 S. King Street
Honolulu, HI 96813
Taxation
Department of Taxation
425 Queen Street
Honolulu, HI 96813
State Chamber of Commerce
Chamber of Commerce of Hawaii
735 Bishop Street
Dillingham Building
Honolulu, HI 96813
Small Business Administration
300 Ala Moana†
Honolulu, HI 96850

PUBLICATIONS

State of Hawaii Data Book, A Statistical Abstract (income statistics, annual), State of Hawaii Department of Planning and Economic Development, P.O. Box 2359, Honolulu, HI 96804

Labor—Area News (employment statistics, monthly), Department of Labor, Industrial Relations, Honolulu, HI 96813

Employment and Payrolls in Hawaii (annual), Department of Labor, Industrial Relations, Honolulu, HI 96813

INDUSTRIAL AND BUSINESS DIRECTORIES

Directory of Manufacturers, State of Hawaii, Chamber of Commerce of Hawaii, Dillingham Building, 735 Bishop Street, Honolulu, HI 96813

Hawaii Business Directory, Hawaii Business Directory, Inc., Box 2057, Honolulu, HI 96805

Hawaii Directory of Manufacturers, Manufacturers' News, Inc., 3 E. Huron Street, Chicago, IL 60611; State Industrial Directories Corp., 2 Penn Plaza, New York, NY 10001

Idaho

STATE CAPITOL, BOISE, ID 83720
(208) 334–2470

INFORMATION OFFICES

Commerce/Economic Development
Division of Economic and Community Affairs
Capitol Building
Boise, ID 83720
Taxation
Department of Revenue and Taxation
Capitol Building
Boise, ID 83720
State Chamber of Commerce
Idaho Association of Commerce and Industry
805 Idaho Street
Boise, ID 83720
Small Business Administration
1005 Main Street†
Boise, ID 83701

PUBLICATIONS

Estimates of the Population of Idaho Counties (population statistics, annual), Superintendent of Documents, U.S. Government Printing Office, Washington, DC 20402

Annual Wages in Idaho (employment statistics, annual), Department of Employment, State of Idaho, P.O. Box 7189, Boise, ID 83707

Distribution by Industry of Covered Workers in Idaho (employment statistics, annual), Department of Employment, State of Idaho, P.O. Box 7189, Boise, ID 83707

Distribution by Industry of Wages Paid for Covered Employment in Idaho (annual), Department of Employment, State of Idaho, P.O. Box 7189, Boise, ID 83707

Idaho Manpower Review (employment statistics, monthly), Department of Employment, State of Idaho, P.O. Box 7189, Boise, ID 83707

Monthly Employment by Industry and County (quarterly), Department of Employment, State of Idaho, P.O. Box 7189, Boise, ID 83707

Centerpoint; Focus on Business and Economics (quarterly), Center for Business and Research, University of Idaho, Moscow, ID 83843

INDUSTRIAL AND BUSINESS DIRECTORIES

Manufacturing Directory of Idaho, Center for Business and Research, University of Idaho, Moscow, ID 83843

Idaho Prospectus, Bureau of Tourism and Industrial Development, Capitol Building, Boise, ID 83720

Illinois

STATE HOUSE, SPRINGFIELD, IL 62706
(217) 782-2000

INFORMATION OFFICES

Commerce/Economic Development
Department of Commerce and Community Affairs
222 S. College Street
Springfield, IL 62706
Taxation
Department of Revenue
1515 S. 9th Street
Springfield, IL 62708
State Chamber of Commerce
Illinois State Chamber of Commerce
20 N. Wacker Drive
Chicago, IL 60606
Small Business Administration
219 S. Dearborn Street†
Chicago, IL 60604
1 North Old State Capitol Plaza
Springfield, IL 62701

PUBLICATIONS

Vital Statistics of Illinois (population statistics, annual), Illinois Department of Health, 535 W. Jefferson Street, Springfield, IL 62706

Employment and Annual Payrolls of Firms (annual), Illinois Bureau of Employment Security, Department of Labor, Chicago, IL 60605

Illinois Employment Report (monthly), Illinois Bureau of Employment Security, Department of Labor, Chicago, IL 62605

Illinois Economic Data Book, Department of Commerce and Community Affairs, 222 S. College Street, Springfield, IL 62706

Report of Department of Revenue (sales statistics, annual), Department of Revenue, Springfield, IL 62706

Monthly Economic Data Sheets (monthly), Department of Commerce and Community Affairs, 222 S. College Street, Springfield, IL 62706

INDUSTRIAL AND BUSINESS DIRECTORIES

Chicago Buyers' Guide, Chicago Association of Commerce and Industry, 130 S. Michigan Avenue, Chicago, IL 60603

Chicago Cook County and Illinois Industrial Directory, National Publishing Corp., 3150 Des Plaines Avenue, Des Plaines, IL 60018

Chicago Geographic Edition, Manufacturers' News, Inc., 3 E. Huron Street, Chicago, IL 60611; State Industrial Directories Corp., 2 Penn Plaza, New York, NY 10001

Illinois Industrial Directory, Illinois Industrial Directories National Publishing Corp., 3150 Des Plaines Avenue, Des Plaines, IL 60018

Illinois Manufacturers Directory, Manufacturers' News, Inc., 3 E. Huron Street, Chicago, IL 60611; State Industrial Directories Corp., 2 Penn Plaza, New York, NY 10001

Illinois Services Directory, Manufacturers' News, Inc., 3 E. Huron Street, Chicago, IL 60611

International Buyers' Directory to Illinois Products, Department of Business and Economic Development, 222 S. College Street, Springfield, IL 62706

Indiana

STATE HOUSE, INDIANAPOLIS, IN 46204
(317) 633-4740

INFORMATION OFFICES

Commerce/Economic Development
Department of Commerce
440 N. Meridian Street
Indianapolis, IN 46204
Taxation
Department of Revenue
State Office Building
Indianapolis, IN 46204

State Board of Tax Commissioners
201 State Office Building
Indianapolis, IN 46204
State Chamber of Commerce
Indiana State Chamber of Commerce, Inc.
201–212 Board of Trade Building
Indianapolis, IN 46204
Small Business Administration
575 N. Pennsylvania Street†
Indianapolis, IN 46204

PUBLICATIONS

Statistical Abstract of Indiana Counties, Indiana State Chamber of Commerce, Indianapolis, IN 46200
Estimates of Population of the Indiana Counties (population statistics, annual), Superintendent of Documents, Government Printing Office, Washington, DC 20402
Indiana Business Review (income statistics, annual), Division of Research, School of Business, Indiana University, Bloomington, IN 47401
Data Supplement to the Indiana Business Review (quarterly), Division of Research, School of Business, Indiana University, Bloomington, IN 47401
Covered Employment and Payrolls (employment statistics, quarterly), Employment Security Division, Research and Statistics Section, Indianapolis, IN 46204
Indiana Labor Market Information (employment statistics, quarterly), Employment Security Division, Research and Statistics Section, Indianapolis, IN 46204
Indiana Fact Book, Indiana State Planning Service Agency, Harrison Office Building, Indianapolis, IN 46204

INDUSTRIAL AND BUSINESS DIRECTORIES

Indiana Industrial Directory, Manufacturers' News, Inc., 3 E. Huron Street, Chicago, IL 60611; Indiana State Chamber of Commerce, 201–212 Board of Trade Building, Indianapolis, IN 46204; State Industrial Directories Corp., 2 Penn Plaza, New York, NY 10001

Iowa

STATE CAPITOL, DES MOINES, IA 50319
(515) 281–5011

INFORMATION OFFICES

Commerce/Economic Development
Development Commission
250 Jewett Building

914 Grand Avenue
Des Moines, IA 50309
Taxation
Department of Revenue
Lucas Building
East 21st and Walnut Streets
Des Moines, IA 50319
Small Business Administration
210 Walnut Street†
Des Moines, IA 50309

PUBLICATIONS

Statistical Profile of Iowa, Iowa Development Commission, Research Division, Des Moines, IA 50319
Iowa Detailed Report of Vital Statistics (population statistics, annual), Records and Statistics Division, Iowa State Department of Health, Lucas State Office Building, Des Moines, IA 50319
The Construction of Personal Income Estimates for Counties: A Study in Economic Statistics (income statistics), Bureau of Business and Economic Research, College of Business Administration, The University of Iowa, Iowa City, IA 52242
Iowa Employment and Earnings (employment statistics, monthly), Iowa Employment Security Commission, Des Moines, IA 50310
Report of Iowa Employment Security Commission (annual), Iowa Employment Security Commission, Des Moines, IA 50319
Retail Sales and Use Tax Annual Report (sales statistics, quarterly), Research and Statistics Division, Iowa Department of Revenue, Lucas State Office Building, Des Moines, IA 50319

INDUSTRIAL AND BUSINESS DIRECTORIES

Directory of Iowa Manufacturers, Iowa Development Commission, 250 Jewett Building, 914 Grand Avenue, Des Moines, IA 50319

Kansas

STATE HOUSE, TOPEKA, KS 66612
(913) 296–0111

INFORMATION OFFICES

Commerce/Economic Development
Department of Economic Development
503 Kansas Avenue
Topeka, KS 66603

Taxation
  Department of Revenue
  State Office Building
  Topeka, KS 66612
State Chamber of Commerce
  Kansas Association of Commerce and Industry
  500 First National Tower
  1 Townsite Plaza
  Topeka, KS 66603
Small Business Administration
  110 E. Waterman Street†
  Wichita, KS 67202

  1150 Grand Avenue
  Kansas City, MO 64160

PUBLICATIONS

Kansas Statistical Abstract, University of Kansas, Center for Public Affairs, 601 Blake Hall, Lawrence, KS 66045
Kansas Data for Site Selection, Kansas Department of Economic Development, 503 Kansas Avenue, Topeka, KS 66603
Fifty Interesting Facts About Kansas, Kansas Association of Commerce and Industry, 500 First National Tower, Topeka, KS 66603
Annual Economic Report of the Governor (income statistics, annual), Division of the Budget, State Capitol Building, Topeka, KS 66612
Annual Manpower Planning Report (employment statistics, annual), Research and Analysis Section, Department of Human Resources, 401 Topeka Boulevard, Topeka, KS 66603
Area Manpower Reviews (employment statistics, bienniel), Research and Analysis Section, Department of Human Resources, 401 Topeka Boulevard, Topeka, KS 66603
Kansas Facts, Kansas Department of Economic Development, 503 Kansas Avenue, Topeka, KS 66603

INDUSTRIAL AND BUSINESS DIRECTORIES

Directory of Kansas Manufacturers and Products, Kansas Department of Economic Development, 503 Kansas Avenue, Topeka, KS 66603; State Industrial Directories Corp., 2 Penn Plaza, New York, NY 10001
Directory of Manufacturers, Wichita, Kansas, Wichita Area Chamber of Commerce, 350 West Douglas, Wichita, KS 67202

Kentucky

STATE CAPITOL, FRANKFORT, KY 40601
(502) 564–3130

INFORMATION OFFICES

Commerce/Economic Development
  Department of Commerce
  Capitol Plaza Tower
  Frankfort, KY 40601
Taxation
  Department of Revenue
  Capitol Annex
  Frankfort, KY 40601
State Chamber of Commerce
  Kentucky Chamber of Commerce
  Versailles Road
  Frankfort, KY 40601
Small Business Administration
  600 Federal Place†
  Louisville, KY 40202

PUBLICATIONS

Deskbook of Kentucky Economic Statistics, Department of Commerce, Frankfort, KY 40601
Kentucky Vital Statistics (population statistics, annual), Kentucky Vital Statistics, Kentucky Department for Human Resources, 275 E. Main Street, Frankfort, KY 40601
Kentucky Employment Statistics (monthly), Department for Human Resources, Frankfort, KY 40601
Number of Workers in Manufacturing Industries and Total Wages Covered by Kentucky Unemployment Insurance Law Classified by Industry and County (quarterly), Department for Human Resources, Frankfort, KY 40601
Department of Revenue Annual Report (sales statistics, annual), Department of Revenue, Frankfort, KY 40601

INDUSTRIAL AND BUSINESS DIRECTORIES

Exporters Directory, Kentucky Department of Commerce, Capitol Plaza Tower, Frankfort, KY 40601
Kentucky Directory of Manufacturers, Department of Commerce, Capitol Plaza Tower, Frankfort, KY 40601; and from Manufacturers' News, 3 E. Huron Street, Chicago, IL 60611; State Industrial Directories Corp., 2 Penn Plaza, New York, NY 10001

Louisiana

STATE CAPITOL, BATON ROUGE, LA 70804
(504) 389–6601

INFORMATION OFFICES

Commerce/Economic Development
  Department of Commerce and Industry

State Land and Natural Resources Building
Baton Rouge, LA 70804
Taxation
Department of Revenue
Capitol Annex
Baton Rouge, LA 70804
State Chamber of Commerce
Louisiana Association of Business and Industry
P.O. Box 3988
Baton Rouge, LA 70821
Small Business Administration
1001 Howard Avenue†
New Orleans, LA 70113

500 Fannin Street
Shreveport, LA 71101

PUBLICATIONS

Statistical Abstract of Louisiana, University of New Orleans, Division of Business and Economic Research, New Orleans, LA 70122

Vital Statistics of Louisiana (population statistics, annual), Louisiana Health and Human Resources Administration, Division of Health, Public Health Statistics, P.O. Box 60630, New Orleans, LA 70160

The Louisiana Economy (income statistics, annual), Research Division, College of Administration and Business, Louisiana Tech University, Ruston, LA 71272

Employment and Total Wages Paid by Employees Subject to the Louisiana Employment Security Law (employment statistics, quarterly), Department of Employment Security, Baton Rouge, LA 70804

Louisiana Labor Market (monthly), Department of Employment Security, Baton Rouge, LA 70804

INDUSTRIAL AND BUSINESS DIRECTORIES

Louisiana Directory of Manufacturers, Department of Commerce and Industry, State Land and Natural Resources Building, Baton Rouge, LA 70804; and from Manufacturers' News, Inc., 3 E. Huron Street, Chicago, IL 60611; State Industrial Directories Corp., 2 Penn Plaza, New York, NY 1001

Louisiana International Trade Directory, International House, New Orleans, LA 70150

Maine

State House, Augusta, ME 04333
(207) 289–1110

INFORMATION OFFICES

Commerce/Economic Development
State Development Office
State House
Augusta, ME 04333
Private Development Associations
Maine Development Foundation
1 Memorial Circle
Augusta, ME 04330

Maine Capital Corporation
1 Memorial Circle
Augusta, ME 04330
Taxation
Bureau of Taxation
Department of Finance and Administration
State Office Building
Augusta, ME 04333
State Chamber of Commerce
Maine State Chamber of Commerce
477 Congress Street
Portland, ME 04111
Small Business Administration
40 Western Avenue†
Augusta, ME 04430

PUBLICATIONS

Maine Economic Data Book, Department of Commerce and Industry, Augusta, ME 04330

Maine Vital Statistics (population statistics, annual), Department of Health and Welfare, Augusta, ME 04330

Employment, Wages Contribution Under Employment Security Program (employment statistics, annual), Employment Security Commission in the State Department of Manpower Affairs, Union Street, Augusta, ME 04330

Maine Manpower (employment statistics, monthly), Employment Security Commission in the State Department of Manpower Affairs, Union Street, Augusta, ME 04330

Sales and Use Tax Assessments (sales statistics, monthly), Bureau of Taxation, Sales Tax Division, State Office Building, Augusta, ME 04330

Facts About Industrial Maine, Maine State Development Office, Augusta, ME 04330

INDUSTRIAL AND BUSINESS DIRECTORIES

Doing Business in Maine, State Development Office, Augusta, ME 04333

Maine Marketing Directory, State Development Office, Augusta, ME 04333

Maine Register, Tower Publishing Company, 163 Middle Street, Portland, ME 04111

Portland Directory, Tower Publishing Company, 163 Middle Street, Portland, ME 04111

Maryland

STATE HOUSE, ANNAPOLIS, MD 21404
(301) 269-3091

INFORMATION OFFICES

Commerce/Economic Development
Department of Economic and Community
Development
1748 Forest Drive
Annapolis, MD 21401
Taxation
Comptroller of the Treasury
State Treasury Building
Calvert Street
Annapolis, MD 21404
State Chamber of Commerce
Maryland State Chamber of Commerce
60 West Street
Annapolis, MD 21401
Small Business Administration
8600 LaSalle Road†
Towson, MD 21204

PUBLICATIONS

Maryland Statistical Abstract, Department of
Economic and Community Development,
2525 Riva Road, Annapolis, MD 21401
Maryland Population Estimates and Projections
(population statistics, annual), State Department of Health and Hygiene, 201 W. Preston Street, Baltimore, MD 21201
Labor Market Information Review (employment statistics, quarterly) Maryland Department of Human Resources, Office of Program and Planning Evaluation, 1100 Eutau
Street, Baltimore, MD 21201

INDUSTRIAL AND BUSINESS DIRECTORIES

Directory of Maryland Exporters-Importers,
Maryland Department of Economics and
Community Development, 2525 Riva Road,
Annapolis, MD 21401
Directory of Maryland Manufacturers, Maryland Department of Economic and Community Development, 2525 Riva Road,
Annapolis, MD 21401
Maryland State Industrial Directory, State
Industrial Directories Corp., 2 Penn Plaza,
New York, NY 10001

Massachusetts

STATE HOUSE, BOSTON, MA 02133
(617) 727-2121

INFORMATION OFFICES

Commerce/Economic Development
Executive Office of Economic Affairs
State House, Room 212
Boston, MA 02133

Department of Commerce and Development
Leverett Saltonstall Building
100 Cambridge Street
Boston, MA 02202
Taxation
Department of Revenue
Leverett Saltonstall Building
100 Cambridge Street
Boston, MA 02202
Small Business Administration
150 Causeway Street†
Boston MA 02114

302 High Street
Holyoke, MA 01050

PUBLICATIONS

Business Incentives, Department of Commerce
and Development, Boston, MA 02202
Annual Report of Vital Statistics of the Commonwealth of Massachusetts (population
statistics, annual), Office of Health Statistics, Lemuel Shattuck Hospital, 170 Morton Street, Jamaica Plain, MA 02130
City and Town Monographs (income statistics, annual), Massachusetts Department of
Commerce and Development, 100 Cambridge Street, Boston, MA 02202

INDUSTRIAL AND BUSINESS DIRECTORIES

*Directory of Directors in the City of Boston
and Vicinity,* Bankers Service Co., 14 Beacon Street, Boston, MA 02108
Directory of Massachusetts Manufacturers,
George D. Hall Company, 20 Kilby Street,
Boston, MA 02109
Massachusetts Directory of Manufacturers,
Manufacturers' News, Inc., 3 E. Huron
Street, Chicago, IL 60611
Massachusetts State Industrial Directory,
State Industrial Directories Corp., 2 Penn
Plaza, New York, NY 10001

Michigan

STATE CAPITOL, LANSING, MI 48913
(517) 373-1837

INFORMATION OFFICES

Commerce/Economic Development
Department of Commerce
525 W. Ottawa Street

P.O. Box 30225
Lansing, MI 48909
Taxation
Bureau of Collection
Department of Treasury
Treasury Building
Lansing, MI 48922
State Chamber of Commerce
Michigan State Chamber of Commerce
501 S. Capitol Avenue
Lansing, MI 48933
Small Business Administration
477 Michigan Avenue†
Detroit, MI 48226

540 W. Kaye Avenue
Marquette, MI 49885

PUBLICATIONS

Michigan Statistical Abstract, Michigan State University, Graduate School of Business Administration, Division of Research, East Lansing, MI 48823
County Population Data (population statistics, annual), Department of Management and Budget, Information Systems Division, Lewis Cass Building, Lansing, MI 48909
Michigan Statistical Abstract (income statistics, biennial), Bureau of Business and Economic Research, Michigan State University, East Lansing, MI 48824
Annual Report of Michigan Employment Security (employment statistics, monthly), Employment Security Commission, Detroit, MI 48202
Michigan Manpower Review (employment statistics, monthly), Employment Security Commission, Detroit, MI 48202
County Economic Profiles (statistics on income, population, manufacturing, selected services and retail trade), Office of Economic Development, P.O. Box 30225, Lansing, MI 48909
Annual Report of Michigan Department of Treasury Annual Report (sales statistics, annual), Michigan Department of Treasury, Lansing, MI 48922
Research and Statistical Bulletin (sales statistics, monthly), Michigan Department of Treasury, Lansing, MI 48922
Quarterly Report of the Michigan Department of Treasury, Lansing, MI 48922

INDUSTRIAL AND BUSINESS DIRECTORIES

Directory of Michigan Manufacturers, Manufacturers' News, Inc., 3 E. Huron Street, Chicago, IL 60611; Manufacturers Publishing Co., 8543 Puritan Avenue, Detroit, MI 48238
Harris Michigan Manufacturers Industrial Directory, Harris Publishing Company, 33140 Aurora Road, Cleveland, OH 44139

Michigan State Industrial Directory, State Industrial Directories Corp., 2 Penn Plaza, New York, NY 10001

Minnesota

State Capitol, St. Paul, MN 55155
(612) 296–6013

INFORMATION OFFICES

Commerce/Economic Development
Department of Commerce
Metro Square Building
St. Paul, MN 55101

Department of Economic Development
480 Cedar Street
St. Paul, MN 55101

Division of Small Business and Finance Agency
480 Cedar Street
St. Paul, MN 55101
Taxation
Department of Revenue
Centennial Office Building
St. Paul, MN 55145
State Chamber of Commerce
Minnesota Association of Commerce and Industry
Hanover Building
480 Cedar Street
St. Paul, MN 55101
Small Business Administration
12 S. 6th Street†
Minneapolis, MN 55402

PUBLICATIONS

Minnesota Vital Statistics (population statistics, annual), Section of Health Statistics, Department of Health, 717 Delaware Street, SE, Minneapolis, MN 55440
Employment Trends, A Manpower Analysis (employment statistics, monthly), Minnesota Department of Economic Security, Communications and Publication, 390 N. Robert Street, St. Paul, MN 55101
Minnesota Statistical Profile, Minnesota Department of Economic Development, 480 Cedar Street, St. Paul, MN 551011

INDUSTRIAL AND BUSINESS DIRECTORIES

Minnesota Directory of Manufacturers, Manufacturers' News, Inc., 3 E. Huron Street, Chicago, IL 60611; Documents Section, State of Minnesota, 140 Centennial Building, St. Paul, MN 55155; State Industrial

Directories Corp., 2 Penn Plaza, New York, NY 10001

Mississippi

New Capitol, Jackson, MS 39205
(601) 354-7011

INFORMATION OFFICES

Commerce/Economic Development
Mississippi Department of Economic Development
P.O. Box 849
Jackson, MS 39205

Department of Agriculture and Commerce
1604 Sillers Building
Jackson, MS 39205
Taxation
Tax Commission
102 Woolfolk Building
Jackson, MS 39201
State Chamber of Commerce
P.O. Box 1849
Standard Life Building
Jackson, MS 39205
Small Business Administration
111 Fred Haise Boulevard
Biloxi, MS 39530

200 E. Pascagoula Street†
Jackson, MS 39201

PUBLICATIONS

Mississippi Statistical Abstract, State University, College of Business and Industry, Division of Research, Mississippi State, MS 39762
Annual Bulletin of Vital Statistics (population statistics, annual), State Board of Health, Statistical Services Unit, P.O. Box 1700, Jackson, MS 39205
Mississippi Business Review (income statistics, annual), Division of Business Research, College of Business and Industry, Mississippi State University, P.O. Box 5288, State College, MS 39762
Mississippi Covered Employment and Wages (employment statistics, monthly), Mississippi Employment Security Commission, P.O. Box 1699, Jackson, MS 39205
Monthly Employment and Quarterly Wages of Workers Covered by the Mississippi Employment Law (annual), Mississippi Employment Security Commission, P.O. Box 1699, Jackson, MS 39205
Quarterly Bulletin on Employment and Wages of Workers Covered by the Mississippi Employment Security Law (quarterly), Mississippi Employment Security Commission, Jackson, MS 39205

Annual Service Bulletin (sales statistics, annual), State Tax Commission, P.O. Box 960, Jackson, MS 39205
Mississippi Industrial Development Brochure, Mississippi Department of Economic Development, P.O. Box 849, Jackson, MS 39205

INDUSTRIAL AND BUSINESS DIRECTORIES

Mississippi International Trade Directory, Mississippi Marketing Council, Box 849, Sillers State Office Building, Jackson, MS 39205
Mississippi Manufacturers Directory, Manufacturers' News, Inc., 3 E. Huron Street, Chicago, IL 60611; Public Information Office, Mississippi Research and Development Center, Jackson, MS 39205; State Industrial Directories Corp., 2 Penn Plaza, New York, NY 10001

Missouri

State Capitol, Jefferson City, MO 65101
(314) 751-2151

INFORMATION OFFICES

Commerce/Economic Development
Department of Consumer Affairs, Regulation and Licensing
1014 Madison Street
Post Office Box 118
Jefferson City, MO 65102
Taxation
Department of Revenue
Division of Taxation
Jefferson State Office Building
Post Office Box 629
Jefferson City, MO 65105
State Chamber of Commerce
Missouri Chamber of Commerce
428 East Capitol Avenue
Post Office Box 149
Jefferson City, MO 65102
Small Business Administration
911 Walnut Street
Kansas City, MO 64106

1150 Grand Avenue†
Kansas City, Missouri 64106

Mercantile Tower†
1 Mercantile Center
St. Louis, Missouri 63101

PUBLICATIONS

Data for Missouri Counties, University of Missouri, Extension Division Publications, 206 Whitten Hall, Columbia, MO 65211 (Available, 1982)

Missouri Vital Statistics (population statistics, annual), Missouri Center for Health Statistics, Broadway State Office Building, Post Office Box 570, Jefferson City, MO 65102

Missouri State and Area Labor Trends (employment statistics, monthly), Missouri Division of Employment Security, Post Office Box 59, Jefferson City, MO 65104

Manual Combined Financial Report of the Department of Revenue and the State Treasurer (annual), Department of Revenue, Division of Taxation and Collection, Post Office Box 629, Jefferson City, MO 65105

Report of Collections (monthly), Department Cashier, Department of Revenue, Division of Taxation and Collection, Post Office Box 629, Jefferson City, MO 65105

INDUSTRIAL AND BUSINESS DIRECTORY

Contacts Influential: Commerce and Industrial Directory (for Kansas City Area), Contacts Influencial, Inc., 6347 Brookside Boulevard, Suite 204, Kansas City, MO 64113

Montana

State Capitol, Helena, MT 59601
(406) 449–3111

INFORMATION OFFICES

Commerce/Economic Development
 Governor's Office of Commerce and Small Business Development
 State Capitol Building
 Helena, MT 59601

 Department of Community Affairs
 Research and Information Division
 1424 9th Avenue
 Helena, MT 59601
State Chamber of Commerce
 Montana Chamber of Commerce
 P.O. Box 1730
 Helena, MT 59601
Small Business Administration
 301 South Park†
 Helena, MT 59601

PUBLICATIONS

Montana Data Book, Department of Community Affairs, Division of Research and Information, Helena, MT 59601

Unpublished estimates on population, Department of Labor and Industry, Employment Security Division, Helena, MT 59601

Montana Personal Income Series (income statistics, annual), Department of Community Affairs, Division of Research and Information, Helena, MT 59601

Montana Labor Market Supplements (employment statistics, annual), Department of Labor and Industry, Employment Security Division, Research and Analysis Section, Helena, MT 59601

try, Employment Security Division, Research and Analysis Section, Helena, MT 59601

Montana County Profiles (county reports, regional summaries, periodically updated), Department of Community Affairs, Division of Research and Information, Helena, MT 59601

INDUSTRIAL AND BUSINESS DIRECTORIES

Montana Directory of Manufacturers, Research and Information Systems Division, Department of Community Affairs, State Capitol, Helena, MT 59601

Nebraska

State Capitol, Lincoln, NB 68509
(402) 471–3111

INFORMATION OFFICES

Commerce/Economic Development
 Department of Economic Development
 301 Centennial Mall South
 Lincoln, NB 68509
Taxation
 Department of Revenue
 301 Centennial Mall South
 Lincoln, NB 68509
State Chamber of Commerce
 Nebraska Association of Commerce and Industry
 P.O. Box 81556
 Lincoln, NB 68501
Small Business Administration
 19th and Farnam Streets†
 Empire State Building
 Omaha, NB 68102

PUBLICATIONS

Nebraska Statistical Handbook, Nebraska Department of Economic Development, Division of Research, Box 94666, Lincoln, NB 68509

Nebraskans' Book, Nebraska Department of Economic Development, Division of Research, P.O. Box 94666, Lincoln, NB 68508

Business in Nebraska (income statistics, annual), Bureau of Business Research, University of Nebraska, Lincoln, NB 68588

Nebraska Work Force Trends (employment statistics, monthly), Department of Labor, Division of Employment, Lincoln, NB 68501

INDUSTRIAL AND BUSINESS DIRECTORIES

Directory of Nebraska Manufacturers and Their Products, Manufacturers' News, Inc., 3 E. Huron Street, Chicago, IL 60611

Directory of Nebraska Manufacturers, State Department of Economic Development, Lincoln, NB 68509

Manufacturers and Wholesales Directory, Lincoln Chamber of Commerce, 200 Lincoln Building, Lincoln, NB 68508

Nevada

LEGISLATIVE BUILDING, CARSON CITY, NV 89710
(702) 885–5627

INFORMATION OFFICES

Commerce/Economic Development
Department of Commerce
321 Nye Building
Carson City, NV 89710

Department of Economic Development
Capitol Complex
Carson City, NV 89710

Taxation
Tax Commission
1340 S. Curry Street
Carson City, NV 89710

State Chamber of Commerce
Nevada Chamber of Commerce Association
P.O. Box 2806
Reno, NV 89505

Small Business Administration
301 E. Stewart†
Las Vegas, NV 89101

50 S. Virginia Street
Reno, NV 89505

PUBLICATIONS

Nevada Community Profiles, Department of Economic Development, Carson City, NV 89710

Nevada Manpower Report (employment statistics, monthly), Employment Security Department, Carson City, NV 89710

Nevada Employment and Payroll (annual), Employment Security Department, Carson City, NV 89710

County Data Files (irregular update), Department of Economic Development, Carson City, NV 89710

INDUSTRIAL AND BUSINESS DIRECTORIES

Nevada Industrial Directory, Department of Economic Development, Capitol Complex, Carson City, NV 89710

Nevada Directory of Business, Manufacturers' News, Inc., 3 E. Huron Street, Chicago, IL 60611

New Hampshire

STATE HOUSE, CONCORD, NH 03301
(603) 271–1110

INFORMATION OFFICES

Commerce/Economic Development
Department of Resources and Economic Development
Division of Economic Development
6 Loudon Road
Concord, NH 03301

Taxation
Board of Taxation
61 S. Spring Street
Concord, NH 03301

State Chamber of Commerce
Business and Industry Association of New Hampshire
23 School Street
Concord, NH 03301

Small Business Administration
55 Pleasant Street†
Concord, NH 03301

PUBLICATIONS

Resident Population Figures (population statistics, annual), Office of State Planning, Concord, NH 03301

Employment and Unemployment in New Hampshire (monthly), Department of Employment Security, Concord, NH 03301

Employment and Wage by County (quarterly), Department of Employment Security, Concord, NH 03301

Economic Conditions in New Hampshire (employment statistics, quarterly), Department of Employment Security, Concord, NH 03301

INDUSTRIAL AND BUSINESS DIRECTORIES

Made in New Hampshire, New Hampshire Office of Industrial Development, Department of Resources, Concord, NH 03301

New Hampshire Register, Tower Publishing Company, 163 Middle Street, Portland, ME 04111

New Jersey

STATE HOUSE, TRENTON, NJ 08625
(609) 292-2121

INFORMATION OFFICES

Commerce/Economic Development

Department of Labor and Industry
John Fitch Plaza
Trenton, NJ 08625

Division of Travel and Tourism
P.O. Box 400
Trenton, NJ 08625

Economic Development Authority
P.O. Box 1446
Trenton, NJ 08625

Taxation

Division of Taxation
West State and Willow Streets
Trenton, NJ 08625

State Chamber of Commerce

New Jersey State Chamber of Commerce
5 Commerce Street
Newark, NJ 07102

Small Business Administration

970 Broad Street†
Newark, NJ 07102

1800 E. Davis Street
Camden, NJ 08104

PUBLICATIONS

Facts and Facets of New Jersey, Division of Economic Development, P.O. Box 2766, Trenton, New Jersey 08625

New Jersey Population Estimates (population statistics, annual), Division of Planning and Research, Office of Demographic and Economic Analysis, P.O. CN-388, Trenton, New Jersey 08625

County Profiles, Division of Economic Development, P.O. Box 2766, Trenton, New Jersey 08625

Covered Employment Trends in New Jersey (employment statistics, annual), Division of Planning and Research, P.O. Box CN-383, Trenton, New Jersey 08625

New Jersey Covered Employment Trends by Geographic Areas of the State, Division of Planning and Research, Office of Labor Statistics, P.O. Box CN-383, Trenton, New Jersey 08625

New Jersey Employment and the Economy, Division of Planning and Research, P.O. Box CN-056, Trenton, New Jersey 08625

New Jersey Economic Indicators, Division of Planning and Research, P.O. Box CN-056, Trenton, New Jersey 08625

Industrial Development Network, Division of Economic Development, P.O. Box 2766, Trenton, New Jersey 08625

INDUSTRIAL AND BUSINESS DIRECTORIES

New Jersey State Industrial Directory, Manufacturers' News, Inc., 3 E. Huron Street, Chicago, IL 60611; State Industrial Directories Corp., 2 Penn Plaza, New York, NY 10001

New Mexico

STATE CAPITOL, SANTA FE, NM 87503
(505) 827-4011

INFORMATION OFFICES

Commerce/Economic Development

Economic Development Division
Bataan Memorial Building
Santa Fe, NM 87503

Taxation

Bureau of Revenue
Manuel Lujan Sr. Building
Santa Fe, NM 87501

State Chamber of Commerce

Association of Commerce and Industry of New Mexico
117 Quincy NE
Albuquerque, NM 87108

Small Business Administration

5000 Marble Avenue NE†
Albuquerque, NM 87110

PUBLICATIONS

New Mexico Statistical Abstract, University of New Mexico, Bureau of Business Research, Albuquerque, NM 87131

New Mexico Blue Book (population statistics, biennial), Office of the Secretary of State, 400 Legislative Executive Building, Santa Fe, NM 87503

Income and Employment in New Mexico, Selected Years (New Mexico Studies in Business and Economics, No. 22—income statistics, biennial), Bureau of Business and Economic Research, University of New Mexico, Albuquerque, NM 87131

New Mexico Socio and Economic Statistics (income statistics, published irregularly), New Mexico State Planning Office, Executive Legislative Building, Santa Fe, NM 87503

New Mexico Manpower Review (employment statistics, monthly), Research and Statistics Section, Employment Security Commission of New Mexico, P.O. Box 1928, Albuquerque, NM 87103

*The State of New Mexico Bureau of Revenue
Receipts and Disbursements Monthly
Statement* (sales statistics, monthly), Bu-
reau of Revenue, Santa Fe, NM 87503

INDUSTRIAL AND BUSINESS DIRECTORIES

*Directory of New Mexico Manufacturing and
Mining,* Manufacturers' News, Inc., 3 E.
Huron Street, Chicago, IL 60611; New
Mexico Commerce and Industry Department,
Bataan Memorial Building, Santa Fe, NM
87503; State Industrial Directories Corp., 2
Penn Plaza, New York, NY 10001

New York

STATE CAPITOL, ALBANY, NY 12224
(518) 474–8390

INFORMATION OFFICES

Commerce/Economic Development
  Department of Commerce
  99 Washington Avenue
  Albany, NY 12245

    Division of Industrial and Corporate De-
    velopment

    99 Washington Avenue
    Albany, NY 12245

    Office of Development Planning
    Executive Chamber
    Albany, NY 12224
Taxation
  State Tax Commission
  Department of Taxation and Finance
  State Campus Building #9
  Albany, NY 12227
State Chamber of Commerce
  New York State Business Council
  150 State Street
  Albany, NY 12207
Small Business Administration
  26 Federal Plaza†
  New York, NY 10007

  111 W. Heron Street
  Buffalo, NY 14202

  100 S. Clinton Street†
  Syracuse, NY 13202

  180 State Street
  Elmira, NY 14901

  Twin Towers Building
  Albany, NY 12207

  425 Broad Hollow Road
  Melville, NY 11746

  100 State Street
  Rochester, NY 14014

PUBLICATIONS

New York State Statistical Yearbook, Division
  of Budget, Albany, NY 12207
Vital Statistics of New York State (popula-
  tion statistics, annual), Office of Biosta-
  tistics, State Department of Health, Albany, NY 12208
*Personal Income in Areas and Counties of New
  York State* (income statistics, annual),
  Quarterly Summary of Business Statistics
  (variety of economic time series); *Business
  Trends in NY State* (analysis of economic
  trends, monthly); *Best Business Advantages;
  Report to Business; Your Business.* New York
  State Department of Commerce, 99 Washington Avenue, Albany, NY 12245
New York Employment Review (employ-
  ment statistics, monthly), Division of Re-
  search and Statistics, 370 7th Avenue, New
  York, NY 10001

INDUSTRIAL AND BUSINESS DIRECTORIES

*New York and Surrounding Territory Classi-
  fied Business Directory,* New York Direc-
  tory Co., Inc., 1440 Broadway, New York,
  NY 10018
New York Classified Business Directory, New
  York Directory Co., Inc., 1440 Broadway
  New York, NY 10018
New York State Industrial Directory, State
  Industrial Directories Corp., 2 Penn Plaza,
  New York, NY 10001; Manufacturers'
  News, Inc., 3 E. Huron Street, Chicago,
  IL 60611
Directory of Minority Business Enterprise,
  Minority Business Development Bureau,
  New York State Department of Commerce,
  230 Park Avenue, New York, NY 10169

North Carolina

STATE LEGISLATIVE BUILDING, RALEIGH, NC
27602
(919) 733–1110

INFORMATION OFFICES

Commerce/Economic Development
  Department of Commerce
  430 N. Salisbury Street
  Raleigh, NC 27611
Taxation
  Department of Revenue
  2 S. Salisbury Street
  Raleigh, NC 22760

State Chamber of Commerce
North Carolina Citizen's Association
P.O. Box 2508
Raleigh, NC 27602
Small Business Administration
230 S. Tryon Street†
Charlotte, NC 28202
215 S. Evans Street
Greenville, NC 27834

PUBLICATIONS

North Carolina State Statistical Abstract, Department of Administration, Office of the State Budget and Association for Coordinating Interagency Statistics, Raleigh, NC 27601

Vital Statistics (population statistics, annual), North Carolina State Board of Health, Division of Administration Service, Public Health Statistical Section, Raleigh, NC 27611

Statistics of Taxation (income statistics, biennial), Tax Research Division, North Carolina Department of Revenue, Raleigh, NC 27640

North Carolina Insured Employment and Wage Payments (employment statistics, quarterly), Bureau of Employment Security Research, Employment Security Commission, P.O. Box 25903, Raleigh, NC 27611

North Carolina Insured Employment and Wage Payments (annual), Bureau of Employment Security Research, Employment Security Commission, P.O. Box 25903, Raleigh, NC 27611

Labor Force Estimates by County Area and State (annual), Bureau of Employment Security Research, Employment Security Commission, P.O. Box 25903, Raleigh, NC 27611

Statistics of Taxation (sales statistics, biennial), Division of Tax Research, North Carolina Department of Revenue, Revenue Building, Raleigh, NC 27640

INDUSTRIAL AND BUSINESS DIRECTORIES

Directory of North Carolina Manufacturing Firms, North Carolina Department of Commerce, Raleigh, NC 27611; State Industrial Directories Corp., 2 Penn Plaza, New York, NY 10001; Manufacturers' News, Inc., 3 E. Huron Street, Chicago, IL 60611

North Dakota

STATE CAPITOL, BISMARCK, ND 58505
(701) 224–2000

INFORMATION OFFICES

Commerce/Economic Development
Department of Business and Industrial Development
513 E. Bismarck Avenue
Bismarck, ND 58505
Taxation
Tax Department
State Capitol
Bismarck, ND 58505
State Chamber of Commerce
Greater North Dakota Association—State Chamber of Commerce
P.O. Box 2467
Fargo, ND 58102
Small Business Administration
657 2d Avenue N.†
Fargo, ND 58102

PUBLICATIONS

North Dakota Growth Indicators, Business and Industrial Development Department, Bismarck, ND 58505

Population estimates are available annually from Business and Industrial Development Department, 513 E. Bismarck Avenue, Bismarck, ND 58505

Area Report of Employment and Total Wages by County and Industry (employment statistics, quarterly), Employment Security Bureau, Bismarck, ND 58505

Prairie Employer Review (employment statistics, monthly), Job Service North Dakota, P.O. Box 1537, Bismarck, ND 58505

INDUSTRIAL AND BUSINESS DIRECTORIES

North Dakota Business Directory, Box 736, W. Fargo, ND 58078

North Dakota Manufacturers Directory, North Dakota Business and Industrial Development, 513 E. Bismarck Avenue, Bismarck, ND 58505; Manufacturers' News, Inc., 3 E. Huron Street, Chicago, IL 60611; State Industrial Directories Corp., 2 Penn Plaza, New York, NY 10001

Strictly Business, Frontier Directory Co., Inc., 222 W. Bowen Avenue, Bismarck, ND 58501

Ohio

STATE HOUSE, COLUMBUS, OH 43215
(614) 466–2000

INFORMATION OFFICES

Commerce/Economic Development
Ohio Department of Economic and Community Development

30 E. Broad Street
Columbus, OH 43216
Taxation
Department of Taxation
30 E. Broad Street
Columbus, OH 43215
State Chamber of Commerce
Ohio Chamber of Commerce
Huntington Bank Building
17 South High Street
Columbus, OH 43215
Small Business Administration
550 Main Street
Cincinnati, OH 45202

1240 E. 9th Street†
Cleveland, OH 44199

85 Marconi Boulevard†
Columbus, OH 43215

PUBLICATIONS

Profit in Ohio, Department of Economic and Community Development, Office of Industrial Development, Columbus, OH 43216
Population Estimates for Ohio (population statistics, annual), Department of Economics and Community Development, Human Resources Development Division, Bureau of Research and Analysis, 30 E. Broad Street, Columbus, OH 43216
Bulletin of Business Research (income statistics, monthly), Center for Business and Economic Research, The Ohio State University, 1775 College Road, Columbus, OH 43210
Ohio Labor Market Information (employment statistics, monthly), Ohio Bureau of Employment Services, 1455 Front Street, Columbus, OH 43216
Ohio Labor Market Information (employment statistics, quarterly), Ohio Bureau of Employment Services, 1455 Front Street, Columbus, OH 43216
Annual Report of Ohio Department of Taxation (sales statistics, annual), Department of Taxation, Columbus, OH 43215

INDUSTRIAL AND BUSINESS DIRECTORIES

Akron, Ohio Membership Directory and Buyers Guide, Akron Area Chamber of Commerce, Windsor Publications, 20229 Erwin Street, Woodland Hills, CA 91364
Directory of Manufacturers in the Toledo Area, Toledo Area Chamber of Commerce, 218 Huron Street, Toledo, OH 43604
Directory of Ohio Manufacturers, Harris Publishing Co., 33140 Aurora Road, Cleveland, OH 44139; Manufacturers' News, Inc., 3 E. Huron Street, Chicago, IL 60611
Manufacturers Directory, Columbus Area Chamber of Commerce, 50 W. Broad Street, Columbus, OH 43215

Ohio and International Trade, Division of International Trade, Department of Economic and Community Development, 30 E. Broad Street, Columbus, OH 43216

Oklahoma

STATE CAPITOL, OKLAHOMA CITY, OK 73105
(405) 521–2011

INFORMATION OFFICES

Commerce/Economic Development
Department of Industrial Development
4024 N. Lincoln
Oklahoma City, OK 73152
Department of Economic and Community Affairs
5500 N. Western Avenue
Oklahoma City, OK 73118
Taxation
Tax Commission
M. C. Connors Building
Oklahoma City, OK 73105
State Chamber of Commerce
Oklahoma State Chamber of Commerce
4020 North Lincoln
Oklahoma City, OK 73105
Small Business Administration
200 N.W. 5th Street†
Oklahoma City, OK 73102
U.S. Department of Commerce, Industry and Trade Administration, 4024 N. Lincoln, Oklahoma City, OK 73105

PUBLICATIONS

Statistical Abstract of Oklahoma, University of Oklahoma, Center for Economic and Management Research, Norman, OK 73019
Oklahoma Population Estimates (population statistics, annual), Research and Planning Division, Oklahoma Employment Security Commission, Will Rogers Memorial Office Building, Oklahoma City, OK 73105
Oklahoma Business Bulletin (income statistics, monthly), Center for Economic and Management Research, Norman, OK 73019
Oklahoma Labor Market (employment statistics, monthly), Employment Security Commission, Oklahoma City, OK 73105
Oklahoma Labor Newsletter (employment statistics, monthly), Employment Security Commission, Oklahoma City, OK 73105
Oklahoma Sales Tax Statistical Report (sales statistics, annual), Oklahoma Tax Commission, Oklahoma City, OK 73105

INDUSTRIAL AND BUSINESS DIRECTORIES

Oklahoma Directory of Manufacturers and Products, Industrial Development Department, P.O. Box 53424, Oklahoma City, OK 73152

Tulsa Area Manufacturers Directory, Metro Tulsa Chambers of Commerce, 616 S. Boston Avenue, Tulsa, OK 74119

Oregon

STATE CAPITOL, SALEM, OR 97310
(503) 378-3131

INFORMATION OFFICES

Commerce/Economic Development
Department of Commerce
Labor and Industries Building
Salem, OR 97310
Department of Economic Development
155 Cottage Street, N.E.
Salem, OR 97310
Taxation
Department of Revenue
204 State Office Building
Salem, OR 97310
Associated Oregon Industries, Inc.
1149 Court Street, NE
Salem, OR 97301
Small Business Administration
1220 SW Third Avenue
Portland, OR 97204

PUBLICATIONS

Oregon Blue Book (population statistics, annual), State Capitol Building, Room 136, Salem, OR 97310

Oregon Covered Employment and Payrolls by Industry and County (employment statistics, quarterly), Department of Employment, Salem, OR 97310

Oregon's Labor Market (monthly), Department of Employment, Salem, OR 97310

INDUSTRIAL AND BUSINESS DIRECTORIES

International Trade Directory of Oregon and Southern Washington, Chamber of Commerce, 824 SW 5th Avenue, Portland, OR 97204

Oregon Manufacturers Directory, Department of Economic Development, 155 Cottage Street, N.E., Salem, OR 97310; State Industrial Directories Corp., 2 Penn Plaza, New York, NY 10001; Manufacturers' News, Inc., 3 E. Huron Street, Chicago, IL 60611

Pennsylvania

MAIN CAPITOL BUILDING, HARRISBURG, PA 17120
(717) 787-2121

INFORMATION OFFICES

Department of Commerce
Department of Commerce
419 S. Office Building
Harrisburg, PA 17120

Bureau of Economic Development
Department of Commerce
425 S. Office Building
Harrisburg, PA 17120

Bureau of Economic Assistance
Department of Commerce
412 S. Office Building
Harrisburg, PA 17120

Small Business Action Center
Department of Commerce
400 S. Office Building
Harrisburg, PA 17120
Taxation
Department of Revenue
Strawberry Square
Harrisburg, PA 17120
State Chamber of Commerce
Pennsylvania Chamber of Commerce
222 N. Third Street
Harrisburg, PA 17101
Small Business Administration
231 St. Asaphs Road†
1 Bala Cynwyd Plaza
Bala Cynwyd, PA 19004

1500 N. 2nd Street
Harrisburg, PA 17102

1000 Liberty Avenue†
Pittsburgh, PA 15222

Penn Place
20 Pennsylvania Avenue
Wilkes-Barre, PA 18702

PUBLICATIONS

Pennsylvania Statistical Abstract, Department of General Services, Bureau of Management Services, State Book Store, P.O. Box 1365, Harrisburg, PA 17125

A Business Guide to Pennsylvania, Department of Commerce, Bureau of Economic Development, Harrisburg, PA 17120

Investors Handbook (annual), Department of Commerce, Bureau of Statistics, Research and Planning, Harrisburg, PA 17120

Industrial Census Series (annual), Department of Commerce, Bureau of Statistics, Research and Planning, Harrisburg, PA 17120, including *Statistics for Manufacturing Industries, Statistics by Industry and Size of Establishment,* and *County Industry Reports.*

Pennsylvania Economic Chartbook (quarterly), Department of Commerce, Bureau of Statistics, Research and Planning, Harrisburg, PA 17120

Estimates of the Total and Household Population for Counties by Age, Sex and Race (annual), Governor's Office of Budget and Administration, Bureau of Management Services, Harrisburg, PA 17105

Employment and Wages of Workers Covered by the Pennsylvania Unemployment Compensation Law by County and Industry (employment statistics, annual), Department of Labor and Industry, Bureau of Employment Security, Harrisburg, PA 17121

Pennsylvania Employment and Earnings (monthly), Department of Labor and Industry, Bureau of Employment Security, Harrisburg, PA 17121

Statistical Data Sheet (employment statistics, quarterly), Department of Labor and Industry, Bureau of Employment Security, Harrisburg, PA 17121

INDUSTRIAL AND BUSINESS DIRECTORIES

Directory of Pennsylvania Manufacturing Exporters, Department of Commerce, Bureau of Statistics, Research and Planning, Harrisburg, PA 17120

Industrial Directory of the Commonwealth of Pennsylvania, Department of General Services, Bureau of Management Services, State Book Store, Box 1365, Harrisburg, PA 17125

Rhode Island

State House, Providence, RI 02903
(401) 277-2000

INFORMATION OFFICES

Commerce/Economic Development
Department of Economic Development
7 Jackson Walkway
Providence, RI 02903
Taxation
Division of Taxation
Department of Administration
CIC Complex
Providence, RI 02908
State Chamber of Commerce
Rhode Island Chamber of Commerce
206 Smith Street
Providence, RI 02908

Small Business Administration
57 Eddy Street†
Providence, RI 02903

PUBLICATIONS

Rhode Island Basic Economic Statistics, Department of Economic Development, 7 Jackson Walkway, Providence, RI 02903

Employment Bulletin (employment statistics, monthly), Division of Statistics and Census, Department of Labor, Providence, RI 02903

Sales Tax Collection by City or Town and County (sales statistics, monthly), Rhode Island Office of Admission Processing and Methods, State House, Providence, RI 02901

Sales Tax Collection by Kind of Business (monthly), Rhode Island Office of Admission Processing and Methods, State House, Providence, RI 02901

INDUSTRIAL AND BUSINESS DIRECTORIES

Rhode Island Directory of Manufacturers and List of Nonmanufacturing Establishments, Department of Economic Development, 7 Jackson Walkway, Providence, RI 02903

Rhode Island State Industrial Directory, State Industrial Directories Corp., 2 Penn Plaza, New York, NY 10001

South Carolina

State House, Columbia, SC 29211
(803) 758-0221

INFORMATION OFFICES

Commerce/Economic Development
South Carolina State Development Board
1301 Gervais Street
Columbia, SC 29201
Taxation
Tax Commission
John C. Calhoun Office Building
Columbia, SC 29201
State Chamber of Commerce
South Carolina Chamber of Commerce
1002 Calhoun Street
Columbia, SC 29201
Small Business Administration
1801 Assembly Street†
Columbia, SC 29201

PUBLICATIONS

South Carolina Statistical Abstract, Budget and Control Board, Division of Research and Statistical Services, Columbia, SC 29201

Annual Report of the State Board of Health (population statistics, annual), Division of Vital Statistics, State Board of Health, State Office Building, Columbia, SC 29201

Average Monthly Coverage Employment and Total Payroll (employment statistics, annual), Employment Security Commission, Columbia, SC 29202

The South Carolina Labor Market (employment statistics, monthly), Employment Security Commission, Columbia, SC 29202

Report to the Governor and General Assembly (sales statistics, annual), South Carolina Tax Commission, Columbia, SC 29201

Economic Report for South Carolina, Budget and Control Board, Division of Research and Statistical Services, Columbia, SC 29201

INDUSTRIAL AND BUSINESS DIRECTORIES

Industrial Directory of South Carolina, South Carolina State Development Board, 1301 Gervais Street, Columbia, SC 29201

South Carolina International Trade Directory, South Carolina State Development Board, 1301 Gervais Street, Columbia, SC 29201

South Dakota

STATE CAPITOL, PIERRE, SD 57501
(605) 224-3011

INFORMATION OFFICES

Commerce/Economic Development
Department of Commerce and Consumer Affairs
State Capitol
Pierre, SD 57501

Department of Economic and Tourism Development
State Office Building #2
Pierre, SD 57501

Division of Industrial Development
S. Cliff Street
Sioux Falls, SD 57103

Taxation
Department of Revenue
Capitol Lake Plaza
Pierre, SD 57501

State Chamber of Commerce
Greater South Dakota Association
P. O. Box 190
Pierre, SD 57501

Small Business Administration
8th and Main Avenue†
Sioux Falls, SD 57102

515 9th Street
Rapid City, SD 57701

PUBLICATIONS

South Dakota Economic and Business Abstract, University of South Dakota, Business Research Bureau, Vermillion, SD 57069

Annual estimates of population statistics are available from the Department of Manpower Affairs, Employment Security Division, 607 N. Fourth Street, Pierre, SD 57501

Annual Report of Employment Security Department of South Dakota (employment statistics, annual), South Dakota Department of Manpower Affairs, Employment Security Division, 607 N. 4th Street, Aberdeen, SD 57401

Labor Bulletin: An Analysis of Current Labor Statistics in South Dakota (monthly), South Dakota Department of Manpower Affairs, Employment Security Division, 607 N. 4th Street, Aberdeen, SD 57401

South Dakota Facts, University of South Dakota, Business Research Bureau, Vermillion, SD 57069

INDUSTRIAL AND BUSINESS DIRECTORIES

Directory of South Dakota Industries, Manufacturers' News, Inc., 3 E. Huron Street, Chicago, IL 60611

South Dakota Manufacturers and Processors Directory, South Dakota Industrial Development Division, 620 S. Cliff Street, Sioux Falls, SD 57104; State Industrial Directories Corp., 2 Penn Plaza, New York, NY 10001

Tennessee

STATE CAPITOL, NASHVILLE, TN 37219
(615) 741-3011

INFORMATION OFFICES

Commerce/Economic Development
Department of Economic and Community Development

1007 Andrew Jackson·Building
Nashville, TN 37219
Taxation
Department of Revenue
927 Andrew Jackson Building
Nashville, TN 37219
State Chamber of Commerce
State Chamber Division of the Tennessee
Taxpayers Association
1070 Capitol Hill Building
Nashville, TN 37219
Small Business Administration
502 S. Gay Street
Knoxville, TN 37902

404 James Robertson Parkway†
Nashville, TN 37219

167 N. Main Street
Memphis, TN 38103

PUBLICATIONS

Tennessee Statistical Abstract, University of
Tennessee, Center for Business and Economic Research, Knoxville, TN 37916
Tennessee Survey of Business (population
statistics, annual), Center for Business and
Economic Research, University of Tennes-
see, Knoxville, TN 37916
Population statistics are available from Sta-
tistical Service, State Department of Pub-
lic Health, Cordell Hull Office Building,
Nashville, TN 37219
Mid-South Quarterly Business Review (in-
come statistics, quarterly), Bureau of Busi-
ness and Economic Research, College of
Business Administration, Memphis State
University, Memphis, TN 38111
*Basic Employment Security Data—State of
Tennessee with County Data* (employ-
ment statistics, annual), Department of
Employment Security, Nashville, TN 37219
The Labor Market Report (employment sta-
tistics, monthly), Department of Employ-
ment Security, Nashville, TN 37219
Comparative Statement of Collected Revenue
(sales statistics, monthly), Department of
Revenue, Nashville, TN 37242
Sales and Use Tax (sales statistics, monthly),
Department of Revenue, Nashville, TN
37242
Tennessee Pocket Data Book, University of
Tennessee, Center for Business and Eco-
nomic Research, Knoxville, TN 37916

INDUSTRIAL AND BUSINESS DIRECTORIES

Directory of Tennessee Industries, Manufacturers' News, Inc., 3 E. Huron Street, Chicago, IL 60611; State Industrial Directories
Corp., 2 Penn Plaza, New York, NY 10001

Tennessee Directory of Manufacturers, Industrial Development Division, Andrew
Jackson Building, Nashville, TN 37219

Texas

STATE CAPITOL, AUSTIN, TX 78701
(512) 475–2323

INFORMATION OFFICES

Commerce/Economic Development
Industrial Commission
410 East 5th Street
Austin, TX 78711
Taxation
Comptroller of Public Accounts
104 LBJ State Office Building
Austin, TX 78711
State Chamber of Commerce
Texas State Chamber of Commerce
77001 N. Lamar
Suite 302
Austin, TX 78752

Tourist Development Agencies
P.O. Box 12008
Austin, TX 78711

Lower Rio Grand Valley Chamber of Com-
merce
P.O. Box 975
Weslaco, TX 75896

South Texas Chamber of Commerce
6222 NW IH 19
San Antonio, TX 78201

East Texas Chamber of Commerce
P.O. Box 1592
Longview, TX 75601

West Texas Chamber of Commerce
P.O. Box 1516
Abilene, TX 79604
Small Business Administration
1720 Regal Row°
Dallas, TX 75235

1100 Commerce Street†
Dallas, TX 75202

4100 Rio Bravo
El Paso, TX 79902

500 Dallas Street†
Houston, TX 77002

222 E. Van Buren Street†
Lower Rio Grand Valley
Harlingen, TX 78550

3105 Leopard Street†
Corpus Christi, TX 78408

1205 Texas Avenue†
Lubbock, TX 79401

727 E. Durango†
San Antonio, TX 78206

PUBLICATIONS

Texas Almanac, Dallas Morning News, Dallas, TX 75201

Population Estimates for Texas (annual), Population Research Center, University of Texas, Austin, TX 78712

Annual population estimates are available from the Division of Vital Statistics, State Department of Health, Austin, TX 78756

Employment, Establishments and Wages Covered by the Texas Unemployment Compensation Act (quarterly), Texas Employment Commission, Austin, TX 78701

A Brief Guide to Business Regulations and Services in Texas. Texas Industrial Commission, P.O. Box 12728, Austin, TX 78711

Texas Facts: The Book on Profitable Plant Locations, Texas Industrial Commission, 714 Sam Houston Office Building, Austin, TX 78711

Texas Labor Market Employment Trends and Outlook (monthly), Texas Employment Commission, Austin, TX 78701

Texas Industrial Update (monthly), Texas Industrial Commission, P.O. Box 12728, Austin, TX 78711

INDUSTRIAL AND BUSINESS DIRECTORIES

Dallas Business Guide, Dallas Chamber of Commerce, Fidelity Tower, Dallas, TX 75201

Directory of Texas Manufacturers, Bureau of Business Research, University of Texas, Austin, TX 78712; State Industrial Directories Corp., 2 Penn Plaza, New York, NY 10001

Fort Worth Directory of Manufacturers, Fort Worth Area Chamber of Commerce, 700 Throckmorton Street, Fort Worth, TX 76102

Texas Exporter-Importer Directory, Gulf International Trades, Box 52717, Houston, TX 77052

Texas Manufacturers Directory, Manufacturers' News, Inc., 3 E. Huron Street, Chicago, IL 60611

Utah

STATE CAPITOL, SALT LAKE CITY, UT 84114
(801) 533–4000

INFORMATION OFFICES

Commerce/Economic Development
Trade Commission
Department of Business Regulation
330 E. 4th South Street
Salt Lake City, UT 84111

Department of Community and Economic Development
Division of Economic and Industrial Development
#2 Arrow Press Square, Suite 200
165 South West Temple
Salt Lake City, UT 84101

Taxation
Tax Commission
200 State Office Building
Salt Lake City, UT 84134

Small Business Administration
125 S. State Street
Salt Lake City, UT 84138

PUBLICATIONS

Statistical Abstract, University of Utah, Bureau of Economic and Business Research, Salt Lake City, UT 84112

Utah Economic and Business Review (population statistics, annual), Utah Population Work Committee, Utah Committee on Industrial and Unemployment Planning, 174 Social Hall Avenue, Salt Lake City, UT 84111

Personal Income in Utah and Utah's Counties (income statistics, three to four years), Bureau of Economic and Business Research, University of Utah, Salt Lake City, UT 84112

Utah Department of Employment Security Annual Report (employment statistics, annual), Department of Employment Security, Salt Lake City, UT 84147

Employment News Letter (monthly), Department of Employment Security, Salt Lake City, UT 84147

Statistical Review of Government in Utah, Utah Foundation, 32 First South Street, Salt Lake City, UT 84111

Utah Shines, Division of Economic and Industrial Development, #2 Arrow Press Square, 165 South West Temple, Salt Lake City, UT 84101

INDUSTRIAL AND BUSINESS DIRECTORIES

Directory of Utah Manufacturers, Manufacturers' News, Inc., 3 E. Huron Street, Chicago, IL 60611; Department of Employment Security, 1234 S. Main Street, Salt Lake City, UT 84147

Vermont

STATE HOUSE, MONTPELIER, VT 05602
(802) 828-1110

INFORMATION OFFICES

Commerce/Economic Development
Agency of Development and Community Affairs
Department of Economic Development
109 State Street
Montpelier, VT 05602
Taxation
Department of Taxes
Agency of Administration
109 State Street
Montpelier, VT 05602
State Chamber of Commerce
Vermont State Chamber of Commerce
P.O. Box 37
Montpelier, VT 05602
Small Business Administration
87 State Street†
Montpelier, VT 05602

PUBLICATIONS

Vermont Facts and Figures, Department of Budget and Management, Montpelier, VT 05602
The Vermont Labor Market (employment statistics, monthly), Department of Employment Security, Montpelier, VT 05602

INDUSTRIAL AND BUSINESS DIRECTORIES

Vermont Directory of Manufacturers, Vermont Agency of Development and Community Affairs, Montpelier, VT 05602
Vermont State Industrial Directory, Manufacturers' News, Inc., 3 E. Huron Street, Chicago, IL 60611; State Industrial Directories Corp., 2 Penn Plaza, New York, NY 10001
Vermont Yearbook, The National Survey, Chester, VT 05143

Virginia

STATE CAPITOL, RICHMOND, VA 23219
(804) 786-0000

INFORMATION OFFICES

Commerce/Economic Development
Division of Industrial Development
1010 State Office Building
Richmond, VA 23219
Department of Conservation and Economic Development
1100 State Office Building
Richmond, VA 23219
Taxation
Department of Taxation
2200 W. Broad Street
Richmond, VA 23219
State Chamber of Commerce
Virginia State Chamber of Commerce
611 E. Franklin Street
Richmond, VA 23219
Small Business Administration
400 N. 8th Street†
Richmond, VA 23240

PUBLICATIONS

Estimates of Population, Virginia Counties and Cities (annual), Tayloe Murphy Institute, Graduate School of Business Administration, University of Virginia, Charlottesville, VA 22903
Personal Income Estimates for Virginia (annual), Tayloe Murphy Institute, Graduate School of Business Administration, University of Virginia, Box 3430, Charlottesville, VA 22903
Personal Income Estimates for Virginia SMSAs and Non-SMSAs Counties (annual), Tayloe Murphy Institute, Graduate School of Business Administration, University of Virginia, Box 3430, Charlottesville, VA 22903
Personal Income Estimates for Virginia Counties and Cities (annual), Tayloe Murphy Institute, Graduate School of Business Administration, University of Virginia, Box 3430, Charlottesville, VA 22903
Covered Employment and Wages (employment statistics, quarterly), Manpower Research Division, Virginia Employment Commission, Richmond, VA 23214
Trends in Employment, Hours and Earnings in Virginia (monthly), Manpower Research Division, Virginia Employment Commission, Richmond, VA 23214

INDUSTRIAL AND BUSINESS DIRECTORIES

Industrial Directory of Virginia, Chamber of Commerce, 611 E. Franklin Street, Richmond, VA 23219
Virginia Industrial Directory, Manufacturers' News, Inc., 3 E. Huron Street, Chicago, IL 60611; State Industrial Directories Corp., 2 Penn Plaza, New York, NY 10001

Washington

LEGISLATIVE BUILDING, OLYMPIA, WA 98501
(206) 753-5000

INFORMATION OFFICES

Commerce/Economic Development
Department of Commerce and Economic Development
101 General Administration Building
Olympia, WA 98504

Taxation
Department of Revenue
General Administration Building
Olympia, WA 98504

State Chamber of Commerce
Association of Washington Business
1414 S. Cherry Street
Olympia, WA 98501

Small Business Administration
710 2d Avenue*
Seattle, WA 98104

915 2d Avenue†
Seattle, WA 98174

651 U.S. Courthouse†
Spokane, WA 99120

PUBLICATIONS

The Research Council's Handbook, Washington State Research Council, Olympia, WA 98504

Vital Statistics Summary (population statistics, annual), Bureau of Vital Statistics, Health Service Division, 214 General Administration Building, Olympia, WA 98504

Estimates of Personal Income for SMSAs and Non-SMSAs Counties—State of Washington (income statistics, annual), Office of Program and Fiscal Management, Population Studies Division, House Office Building, Olympia, WA 98504

Employment and Payrolls in Washington State by County and Industry (employment statistics, quarterly), Employment Security Department, Olympia, WA 98504

The Washington Labor Market (monthly), Employment Security Department, Olympia, WA 98504

Annual Report of the Tax Commission (sales statistics, annual), Washington State Department of Revenue, General Administration Building, Olympia, WA 98504

State of Washington Pocket Data Book, Washington State Office of Program Planning and Fiscal Management, Olympia, WA 98504

INDUSTRIAL AND BUSINESS DIRECTORIES

Washington Manufacturers Register, Times Mirror Press, 1115 S. Boyle, Los Angeles, CA 90023

Washington State International Trade Directory, Washington State Department of

Commerce and Economic Development, Olympia, WA 98504

Washington State Manufacturers Directory, Manufacturers' News, Inc., 3 E. Huron Street, Chicago, IL 60611

West Virginia

STATE CAPITOL, CHARLESTON, WV 25305
(304) 348-3456

INFORMATION OFFICES

Commerce/Economic Development
Governor's Office of Economic and Community Development
State Office Building R-150
Charleston, WV 25305

Taxation
Tax Department
West Wing
State Capitol
Charleston, WV 25305

State Chamber of Commerce
P.O. Box 2789
1101 Kanawha Valley Building
Charleston, WV 25301

Small Business Administration
Charleston National Plaza
Charleston, WV 25301

109 N. 3d Street†
Clarksburg, WV 26301

PUBLICATIONS

The Statistical Handbook, West Virginia Research League, Inc., Charleston, WV 25414

Annual population estimates are available from the Division of Resource Management, Agricultural Economics Committee, West Virginia University, Morgantown, WV 26505

West Virginia Work Force Annual Average (employment statistics, annual), Research and Statistics Division, 112 California Avenue, Charleston, WV 25305

Employment Wages Covered by West Virginia Unemployment Compensation Law (annual), Research and Statistics Division, 112 California Avenue, Charleston, WV 25305

West Virginia Statistical Handbook, West Virginia University, Bureau of Business Research, Morgantown, WV 26505

West Virginia Economic Profile, Governor's Office of Economic and Community Development, State Office Building #6, Charleston, WV 25305

INDUSTRIAL AND BUSINESS DIRECTORIES

West Virginia Manufacturing Directory, Governor's Office of Economic and Community Development, State Office Building #6, Charleston, WV 25305; State Industrial Directories Corp., 2 Penn Plaza, New York, NY 10001

Wisconsin

STATE CAPITOL, MADISON, WI 53702
(608) 266-2211

INFORMATION OFFICES

Commerce/Economic Development
 Department of Business Development
 123 W. Washington Avenue
 Madison, WI 53702
Taxation
 Department of Revenue
 201 E. Washington Avenue
 Madison, WI 53703
State Chamber of Commerce
 Wisconsin Association of Manufacturers and Commerce
 111 E. Wisconsin Avenue
 Milwaukee, WI 53202
Small Business Administration
 212 E. Washington Avenue†
 Madison, WI 53703

 500 E. Barstow Street
 Eau Claire, WI 54701

 517 E. Wisconsin Avenue
 Milwaukee, WI 53202

PUBLICATIONS

Wisconsin Statistical Abstract, Department of Administration, Information Systems Unit, 101 S. Webster, Madison, WI 53702
Wisconsin Blue Book (population statistics, biennial), Legislative Reference Bureau, 201 N. State Capitol Street, Madison, WI 53702
Wisconsin Statistical Abstract (income statistics, biennial), Information Systems Unit, Wisconsin Department of Administration, 101 S. Webster, Madison, WI 53702
Wisconsin Work Force (employment statistics, monthly), Bureau of Research and Statistics Administration, Madison, WI 53702
New Industries and Plant Expansions (annual summary), *Available Industrial Buildings* (annual), *Available Industrial Sites* (annual), Wisconsin Department of Business Development, 123 W. Washington Avenue, Madison, WI 53702

INDUSTRIAL AND BUSINESS DIRECTORIES

Classified Directory of Wisconsin Manufacturers, Wisconsin Association of Manufacturers and Commerce, 111 E. Wisconsin Avenue, Milwaukee, WI 53202; State Industrial Directories Corp., 2 Penn Plaza, New York, NY 10001
Wisconsin Manufacturers Directory, Manufacturers' News, Inc., 3 E. Huron Street, Chicago, IL 60611
Wisconsin Local Development Organizations (annual), Wisconsin Department of Business Development, 123 W. Washington Avenue, Madison, WI 53702

Wyoming

STATE CAPITOL, CHEYENNE, WY 82002
(307) 777-7011

INFORMATION OFFICES

Commerce/Economic Development
 Department of Economic Planning and Development
 Barrett Building
 Cheyenne, WY 82002
Taxation
 Department of Revenue and Taxation
 2200 Carey Avenue
 Cheyenne, WY 82002
Small Business Administration
 100 E. B Street†
 Casper, WY 82601

PUBLICATIONS

Wyoming Data Book, University of Wyoming, Division of Business and Economic Research, Laramie, WY 82070
Report of Employment and Wages E.S.— 202 (income statistics, quarterly), Employment Security Commission, State Capitol Building, P.O. Box 2760, Casper, WY 82602
Employment and Total Payrolls by Industry Selected from Employer Quarterly Reports (employment statistics, quarterly), Employment Security Commission, P.O. Box 2760, Casper, WY 82601
Wyoming Labor Force Trends (monthly), Employment Security Commission, P.O. Box 2760, Casper, WY 82601
Biennial Report of the State Board of Equalization of the State of Wyoming (sales statistics, annual), Wyoming Board of Equalization, Department of Revenue, Supreme Court Building, Cheyenne, WY 82002

INDUSTRIAL AND BUSINESS DIRECTORIES

Wyoming Directory of Manufacturing and Mining, Manufacturers' News, Inc., 3 E. Huron Street, Chicago, IL 60611; Department of Economic Planning and Development, 720 W. 18th Street, Cheyenne, WY 82001; State Industrial Directories Corp. 2 Penn Plaza, New York, NY 10001

Puerto Rico

CAPITOL, SAN JUAN, PR 00901
(809) 723–6040

INFORMATION OFFICES

Commerce/Economic Development
Department of Commerce
Box S 4275
San Juan, PR 00905

Economic Development Administration
Box 2350
San Juan, PR 00936
Taxation
Income Tax Bureau
Department of Treasury
San Juan, PR 00905

Industrial Development Company
GPO Box 2350
San Juan, Puerto Rico 00936

Office of Industrial Tax Exemption
Fomento Building, 8th Floor
Hato Rey, Puerto Rico 00918

Government Development Bank
Box 42001
Minillas Station
Santurce, Puerto Rico 00940
Chamber of Commerce
Camara De Comercie de Puerto Rico
P.O. Box 3789
San Juan, PR 00904
Small Business Administration
Chardon and Bolivia Streets
Hato Rey, PR 00919

PUBLICATIONS

Statistical Yearbook, Bureau of Statistics, Planning Board, Santurce, PR 00940

INDUSTRIAL AND BUSINESS DIRECTORIES

Puerto Rico Official Industrial and Trade Directory, Witcom Group, Inc., P.O. Box 2310, San Juan, PR 00902
The Businessman's Guide to Puerto Rico, Puerto Rico Almanacs, Inc., P.O. Box 9582, Santurce, Puerto Rico 00908

INTERNATIONAL INFORMATION SOURCES

U.S. GOVERNMENT AGENCIES

Business people seeking information about foreign commercial opportunities or sources of business contacts have available a number of government and private services that are described in this and subsequent sections. The extensive nature of these services is not always fully appreciated by members of the business community. Some of the most helpful services are provided by the Industry and Trade Administration (ITA) of the Department of Commerce, described below. This agency is particularly helpful in establishing initial contacts and in evaluating foreign markets.

Business people traveling abroad will find the following services of help in initiating contacts:

1. U.S. Export Development Offices, U.S. Department of Commerce.
2. Commercial offices at U.S. embassies or consulates.

Foreign credit information sources are provided at the end of this section.

DEPARTMENT OF COMMERCE

Address: Constitution and 14th Street NW, Washington, DC 20230. Information phone: 202-377-4901.

The central information source within the Department of Commerce is the **Industry and Trade Administration** (ITA), which promotes the growth of U.S. industry and commerce, both foreign and domestic. The ITA consists of the following:

International Economic Policy and Research (IEPR) assists the department in research, analysis, and formulation of international economic programs.

The **Export Development** area (ED) helps U.S. business to sell its goods in international markets by providing commercial, economic, and marketing information. ED conducts export development activities including the management of trade fairs and export development facilities overseas (locations listed below). In addition, ED organizes trade missions for groups of business people interested in specific markets. Businesses interested in attracting foreign capital or in seeking foreign investment opportunities can also get help from ED.

World Traders Data Reports: ED provides very helpful reports on foreign firms in its *World Traders Data Reports* (WTDRS). Each report contains detailed commercial information on individual firms, including financial and credit references. The complete name and address of the foreign firm must be submitted when ordering WTDRS. To order, write Trade Facilitation and Services Division, Room 1033 WTDR, Washington, DC 20230.

Foreign Traders Index: Information on more than 140,000 foreign importing organizations in 130 countries is stored in ITA's *Foreign Traders Index* (FTI), a computerized file. New information on listed firms and information on newly identified firms are constantly added to the index. The information in the file is collected and supplied to Commerce by the U.S. Foreign Service—Department of State.

Most of the lists or services described here are products of the *Foreign Traders Index*. Some, however, are prepared from special source material.

Export Mailing List Service: U.S. firms wishing to make export contacts may obtain lists of foreign organizations selected by electronic data processing techniques from the *Foreign Traders Index*. Selection of firms in one or more countries or geographic areas may be made according to the products or product groups handled by the foreign organizations.

The information is available either on pressure-sensitive mailing labels or in standard printout format.

Data Tape Service: U.S. firms with computer facilities may purchase magnetic tapes containing information on all firms in selected countries or in all countries covered in the *Foreign Traders Index*. This service makes it possible for users to retrieve various segments of data from the *Foreign Traders Index* through their own computer facilities.

The Agent/Distributor Service: ITA's *Agent/Distributor Service* (A/DS) helps U.S. firms find agents or distributors for their products in almost every country of the world. U.S. commercial officers overseas will identify up to six foreign firms that have expressed interest in a specific U.S. proposal. The charge for this service is $25.

Application forms (ITA-424P) may be obtained from any Commerce Department district office. Trade specialists at district offices will help a U.S. firm prepare an application. They will offer guidance and determine whether there are factors to discourage a business relationship.

Trade List Service: The names and addresses of foreign distributors, agents, purchasers, and other firms, classified by products they handle and services they offer, are made available to U.S. firms through printed *Trade Lists* (TL). Some of the lists are produced from information in the *Foreign Traders Index*. Others are prepared from data compiled in connection with ITA's export promotion programs and from other sources.

Trade Opportunities Program: Up-to-the-minute direct sales leads and representation opportunities from overseas are now available to interested U.S. companies through a computerized mail service, the *Trade Opportunities Program* (TOP). A U.S. businessman, as a subscriber to TOP, specifies the products and the countries for which he wants trade opportunities, and that information is fed into the TOP computer.

Foreign Market Reports: Reports on commodities, industries, and economic conditions prepared by U.S. foreign service officers, and in-depth foreign market surveys prepared by private research organizations on a contract basis for ITA or by ITA's market research officers and U.S. foreign service officers are available for a nominal fee. Monthly indices list the reports and surveys in three sections—a numerical listing of documents, a country section, and the Standard Industrial Classification (SIC), and/or a general subject matter section.

Business Counseling Service: Counseling services are provided by the U.S. Departments of Commerce and State in Washington, DC, and by the Commerce district offices located in major commercial and industrial centers throughout the United States and Puerto Rico.

The Business Counseling Section of ITA's Office of Export Development in Washington offers guidance, in-depth counseling, and scheduling of appointments with appropriate Commerce officials as well as with officials in other agencies. This service is designed to give the businessperson a maximum amount of information in a minimum of time.

An important part of this program is an Export Information Reference Room where businesspeople can review a wide range of major foreign projects under consideration by international financial institutions—World Bank Group, Inter-American Development Bank, Asian Development Bank, and the United Nations Development Programme.

For further information on all of the above services, contact the nearest Department of Commerce District Office.

Trade Administration of ITA administers controls on exports that may be limited for national security, foreign policy, or short-supply reasons. This office also administers the antiforeign boycott program, U.S. foreign-trade zones program, and duty-free importation for scientific or educational reasons. The

bureau indicates quotas for duty-free import of watches and watch parts from the Virgin Islands, Guam, and American Samoa.

The Office of Business Liaison is a focal point for handling inquiries for business information as well as suggestions and complaints. Call 202–377–3176.

The Office of East-West Trade Development (OEWTD) coordinates programs and provides information with regard to commercial relations with the socialist nations. The (OEWTD) also manages export administration and issues export licenses, where required, for shipment to the Soviet bloc and China.

Information on specific countries may be obtained by calling the country marketing manager of ITA listed by region under Regional Marketing Managers, page 515. Assistance or information about marketing in these countries may be obtained by dialing these key people directly.

DISTRICT OFFICES OF THE U.S. DEPARTMENT OF COMMERCE

Alabama
Suite 200–201
908 So. 20th Street
Birmingham, AL 35205
Telephone: 205–254–1331

Alaska
701 C Street
P.O. Box 32
Anchorage, AK 99513
Telephone: 907–271–5041

Arizona
Suite 2950, Valley Bank Center
201 N. Central Avenue
Phoenix, AZ 85073
Telephone: 602–261–3285

Arkansas
320 W. Capitol Avenue
Suite 635
Little Rock, AR 77201
Telephone: 501–378–5794

P.O. Box 2525
ASU State University
Jonesboro, AR 72467*
Telephone: 501–792–4760

California
11777 San Vicente Boulevard
Los Angeles, CA 90049
Telephone: 213–824–7591

110 W. C Street
San Diego, CA 92101*
Telephone: 714–293–5395

Federal Building
Box 36013
450 Golden Gate Avenue
San Francisco, CA 94102
Telephone: 415–556–5860

Colorado
Room 165, New Customhouse
19th and Stout Streets
Denver, CO 80202
Telephone: 303–837–3246

Connecticut
Room 610-B, Federal Office Building
450 Main Street
Hartford, CT 06103
Telephone: 203–244–3530

Florida
Room 821
City National Bank Building
25 W. Flagler Street
Miami, FL 33130
Telephone: 305–350–5267

128 N. Osceola Avenue
Clearwater, FL 33515°
Telephone: 813–461–0011

815 S. Main Street
Suite 100
Jacksonville, FL 32207°
Telephone: 904–791–2796

Collins Building, Room G-20
Tallahassee, FL 32304°
Telephone: 904–488–6469

Georgia
Suite 600
1365 Peachtree Street NE
Atlanta, GA 30309
Telephone: 404–881–7000

222 U.S. Courthouse
P.O. Box 9746
125–29 Bull Street
Savannah, GA 31412
Telephone: 912–232–4321, ext. 204

Hawaii
4106 Federal Building
P.O. Box 50026
300 Ala Moana Boulevard
Honolulu, HI 96850
Telephone: 808–546–8694

Illinois
1406 Mid Continental Plaza Building
55 E. Monroe Street
Chicago, IL 60603
Telephone: 312–353–4450
Commerce Business Daily
Room 1304
433 W. Van Buren Street
Chicago, IL 60607°
Telephone: 312–353–2950

Indiana
357 U.S. Courthouse and Federal Office
    Building
46 E. Ohio Street
Indianapolis, IN 46204
Telephone: 317–269–6214

Iowa
817 Federal Building
210 Walnut Street
Des Moines, IA 50309
Telephone: 515–284–4222

Kentucky
U.S. Post Office and Court House Building
Room 636
Louisville, KY 40202
Telephone: 502–582–5066

Louisiana
432 International Trade Mart
No. 2 Canal Street
New Orleans, LA 70130
Telephone: 504–589–6546

Maine
Memorial Circle
40 Casco Bank Building
Augusta, ME 04333
Telephone: 207–623–2239

Maryland
415 U.S. Customhouse
Gay and Lombard Streets
Baltimore, MD 21202
Telephone: 301–962–3560

Massachusetts
441 Stuart Street, 10th floor
Boston, MA 02116
Telephone: 617–223–2312

Michigan
445 Federal Building
231 W. Lafayette
Detroit, MI 48226
Telephone: 313–226–3650

350 Ottawa Street NW
Grand Rapids, MI 49503°
Telephone: 616–456–2411/33

Minnesota
218 Federal Building
110 S. Fourth Street
Minneapolis, MN 55401
Telephone: 612–725–2133

Mississippi
Suite 550
200 E. Pascagoula
Jackson, MS 39201
Telephone: 601–969–4388

Missouri
120 S. Central Avenue
St. Louis, MO 63105
Telephone: 314–425–3302–4

Room 1840
601 E. 12th Street
Kansas City, MO 64106
Telephone: 816–374–3142

Nebraska
Capitol Plaza, Suite 703A
1815 Capitol Avenue
Omaha, NB 68102
Telephone: 402–221–3665

° Denotes trade specialist.

Nevada
777 W. 2nd Street, Room 120
Reno, NV 89503
Telephone: 702–784–5203

New Jersey
Gateway Building, 4th floor
Market Street and Penn Plaza
Newark, NJ 07102
Telephone: 201–645–6214

New Mexico
505 Marquette Avenue NW
Suite 1015
Albuquerque, NM 87102
Telephone: 505–766–2386

New York
1312 Federal Building
111 W. Huron Street
Buffalo, NY 14202
Telephone: 716–846–4191

Federal Office Building, Room 3718
26 Federal Plaza
Foley Square
New York, NY 10007
Telephone: 212–264–0634

North Carolina
203 Federal Building
West Market Street
P.O. Box 1950
Greensboro, NC 27402
Telephone: 919–378–5345

Ohio
10504 Federal Office Building
550 Main Street
Cincinnati, OH 45202
Telephone: 513–684–2944

666 Euclid Avenue, Room 600
Cleveland, OH 44114
Telephone: 216–522–4750

Oklahoma
4024 Lincoln Boulevard
Oklahoma City, OK 73105*
Telephone: 405–231–5302

Oregon
1220 S.W. 3d Avenue, Room 618
Portland, OR 97204
Telephone: 503–221–3001

Pennsylvania
9448 Federal Building
600 Arch Street
Philadelphia, PA 19106
Telephone: 215–597–2850

2002 Federal Building
1000 Liberty Avenue
Pittsburgh, PA 15222
Telephone: 412–644–2850

Puerto Rico
Federal Building
Room 659
San Juan, PR 00918
Telephone: 809–753–4555, ext. 555

Rhode Island
7 Jackson Walkway
Providence, RI 02903*
Telephone: 401–277–2505, ext. 22

South Carolina
Strom Thurmond Federal Building
1835 Assembly Street
Columbia, SC 29201
Telephone: 803–765–5345

505 Federal Building
334 Meeting Street
Charleston, SC 29403*
Telephone: 803–677–4361

Tennessee
147 Jefferson Avenue
Room 710
Memphis, TN 38103
Telephone: 901–521–3213

Andrew Jackson Office Building
Room 1020
Nashville, TN 37219
Telephone: 615–251–5161

Texas
1100 Commerce Street
Room 7A5
Dallas, TX 75242
Telephone: 214–767–0542

2625 Federal Building, Courthouse
515 Rusk Street
Houston, TX 77002
Telephone: 713–226–4231

Utah
1201 Federal Building
125 S. State Street
Salt Lake City, UT 84138
Telephone: 801–524–5116

Virginia
8010 Federal Building
400 N. 8th Street
Richmond, VA 23240
Telephone: 804–782–2246

8550 Arlington Boulevard
Fairfax, VA 22031*
Telephone: 703–560–6460

Washington
Lake Union Building, Room 706
1700 Westlake Avenue North
Seattle, WA 98109
Telephone: 206–442–5615

West Virginia
3000 New Federal Building
500 Quarrier Street
Charleston, WV 25301
Telephone: 304–343–6181, ext. 375

Wisconsin
Federal Building/U.S. Courthouse
517 E. Wisconsin Avenue
Milwaukee, WI 53202
Telephone: 414–291–3473

Wyoming
6022 O'Mahoney Federal Center
2120 Capitol Avenue
Cheyenne, WY 82001
Telephone: 307–778–2220, ext. 2151

PUBLICATIONS, DEPARTMENT OF COMMERCE

The following publications on international commerce are available from the Government Printing Office, Washington, DC 20402.

Foreign Trade Report FT 410: U.S. Exports Commodity by Country is one of the best sources for locating export markets. These monthly publications provide a statistical record of the shipments of all merchandise from the United States to foreign countries.

Market Share Reports. These annual reports provide a five-year record of U.S. participation in foreign markets for manufactured products. Both country and product series are available.

International Economic Indicators and Competitive Trends is a quarterly report providing basic international data.

Overseas Business Reports (OBR). These reports provide a great deal of basic background data for businessmen who are evaluating export markets. Each OBR discusses separate topics for a single country. About 80 reports per year are issued.

Global Market Surveys are in-depth reports covering 15 to 20 of the best foreign markets for a single industry or a group of related industries.

Foreign Economic Trends is an in-depth series of country-by-country reports prepared annually or semiannually by the U.S. Foreign Service of the Department of State that covers individually almost every country in the world. It gives the latest data on GNP, foreign trade, and wages and prices.

Special Reports. ITA publishes special reports detailing economic data, marketing, and trade opportunities.

Index to Business International Publications is an index to materials appearing in *Overseas Business Reports, Global Market Surveys, Foreign Economic Trends,* and *Special Reports.*

Country Market Surveys are in-depth reports covering the most promising U.S. export opportunities.

A Guide to Financing Exports. A summary of sources of credit and credit information for exports. Reviews services offered by Export-Import Bank.

International Marketing News Memo. This includes information bulletins received directly from the U.S. Foreign Service—reports prepared by U.S. businessmen or Department of Commerce officers. Reports cover a wide variety of industries, products, and countries.

Business America (formerly *Commerce Today*). This biweekly is the Commerce Department's principal periodical for domestic and international business news.

Commerce Business Daily is a daily record containing synopses of U.S. government procurement limitations, subcontracting leads, contract awards, sales of surplus property, and foreign business opportunities.

Commerce News. Published weekly, this publication lists books, pamphlets, and reports by the Department of Commerce.

The Overseas Export Promotion Calendar lists U.S. trade-promotion events held abroad. These include exhibitions, missions, and seminars featuring U.S. products and services. The calendar is indexed by product, gives the location and date of each event, and also identifies U.S. Export Development Offices (i.e., International Marketing Centers) promoting sales of U.S. goods and services. Subscription information may be obtained by calling ITA's Office of Export Promotion at 202–377–5783.

MARKETING DIRECTORY, DEPARTMENT OF COMMERCE

Current information relating to political, commercial, and economic developments in foreign countries and trade agreements is provided by a large staff of country specialists in the Department of Commerce.

If you are in the United States, a convenient way of obtaining information or contacting personnel is to call the Regional Marketing Managers (see below). You can also obtain information by writing to the U.S. Export Development Offices listed under that title, p. 517.

If you are traveling abroad, contact the local U.S. Commercial Attaché or the U.S. Export Development Offices overseas. In-country phone numbers are given on page 517.

REGIONAL MARKETING MANAGERS

Dial 202–377 plus the given extension.

United Kingdom/Canada 3337
  United Kingdom   Malta
  Canada   Ireland

France/Benelux 3337
  France   Luxembourg
  Belgium   The Netherlands

Germany/Nordic 3187
  Germany   Denmark
  Austria   Norway
  Finland   Iceland
  Sweden

Southern Europe 3944
  Italy
  Turkey
  Greece

Cyprus
Spain
Portugal
Yugoslavia
Switzerland
Andean/Caribbean 4673
Bahamas
Barbados
Belize
Bermuda
Bolivia
Chile
Colombia
Dominican Republic
Ecuador
French Guiana
French West Indies
Guyana
Haiti
Jamaica
Leeward Islands
Netherlands Antilles
Peru
Surinam
Trinidad/Tobago
Venezuela
Windward Islands
Mexico/Central America 2313
Costa Rica
El Salvador
Guatemala
Honduras
Mexico
Nicaragua
Panama
Brazil/River Plate 5427
Argentina
Brazil
Paraguay
Uruguay
Arab states 5767
Bahrain
Iraq
Jordan
Kuwait
Lebanon
Oman
Qatar
Saudi Arabia
People's Democratic
   Republic, Yemen
Syria
United Arab Emirates
Yemen Arab Republic
Arab countries of North Africa 4652
Algeria
Libya
Morocco
Tunisia
Egypt
Non-Arab countries of the Middle East 4652
Iran
Israel
Asia/India/Pakistan 2522
Singapore
Malaysia
Indonesia
Philippines
Thailand
India
Pakistan
Bangladesh
Afghanistan

Sri Lanka
Burma
Nepal
Bhutan
Maldives
Cambodia
Viet Nam
Laos
Brunei
East Asia/Taiwan/Australia/New Zealand .. 3646
Australia
New Zealand
Taiwan
Papua New Guinea
Fiji
Pacific Islands
Japan/Korea/Hong Kong 2896
Africa 4927
Angola
Benin
Botswana
Burundi
Cameroon
Cape Verde Islands
Central African Empire
Chad
Comoros
Congo (Brazzaville)
Djibouti
Equatorial Guinea
Ethiopia
Gabon
Gambia
Ghana
Guinea
Guinea-Bissau
Ivory Coast
Kenya
Lesotho
Liberia
Madagascar
Malawi
Mali
Mauritania
Mauritius
Mozambique
Niger
Nigeria
Rhodesia
Rwanda
Sao Tome and Principe
Senegal
Seychelles
Sierra Leone
Somalia
South Africa
Sudan
Swaziland
Tanzania
Togo
Uganda
Upper Volta
Zaire
Zambia
East-West Trade 2543
USSR Affairs Division 4505
Eastern European Affairs Division 3150
People's Republic of China Division 3583

U.S. EXPORT DEVELOPMENT OFFICES°

Milan
U.S. Export Development Office
c/o American Consulate General
APO New York 09689
Phone 469–6451

Sydney
U.S. Export Development Office
c/o American Consulate General
APO San Francisco 96209
Phone 929–0977

Singapore
U.S. Export Development Office
c/o American Embassy
30 Hill Street
FPO San Francisco 96699
Phone 373–1000

Tokyo
U.S. Export Development Office
c/o American Embassy
APO San Francisco 96503
Phone 987–244

Bonn
U.S. Export Development Office
c/o American Embassy, Bonn
APO New York 09080
Phone 330–045

London
U.S. Export Development Office
c/o American Embassy
FPO New York 09510
Phone 499–9000

Paris
U.S. Export Development Office
c/o American Embassy
APO New York 09777
Phone 624–3313

San Paulo
U.S. Export Development Office
c/o American Consulate General
APO Miami 34030
Phone 455–778

COMMERCIAL OFFICES OVERSEAS, DEPARTMENT OF COMMERCE°

Athens
Regional Trade Development Office
91 Vasilissi Sophia Boulevard (at the Embassy)
Athens, Greece
Phone 712–951

Moscow
U.S. Commercial Office
15 Chaykovskovo
Moscow, USSR
Phone 252–0011

° The phone numbers listed in this section are "in-country" numbers and are the most current available. Since phone numbers do change, it is best to check with U.S. Embassy to confirm them.

Nagoya
American Commercial Information Office
Aichiken Sangyo Boeki Kaikan,
Nishikan, 4–7
Marunouchi 2-chome, Naka-ku
Nagoya, Japan
Phone 231–7791

Osaka
U.S. American Merchandise Display
Sankei Kaikan Building
4–9, Umeda 2-chome
Osaka, Japan
Phone 341–2754

Vienna
U.S. East-West Trade Development Support Office
Vienna I, Friedrich Schmidt Platz 2
Austria
Phone 31–55–11

Warsaw
U.S. Trade Development Center
Ulica Wiejska, 20
Warsaw, Poland
Phone 21–45–15

U.S. DEPARTMENT OF STATE

Address: New State Building, 2201 C Street, NW, Washington, DC 20520.
Information: 202–632–9884.

PUBLICATIONS

Background Notes of the Countries of the World gives profiles of foreign countries.

Key Officers of Foreign Service Posts lists the addresses and phone numbers of all American embassies and consulates and their key personnel.

Department of State Bulletin is a weekly publication devoted to the latest developments in international politics and trade agreements.

UNITED STATES INTERNATIONAL TRADE COMMISSION

Address: 701 E Street NW, Washington, DC 20436. Information phone: 202–523–0161.

Formerly the U.S. Tariff Commission, the name was changed to the U.S. International Trade Commission in 1974.

The commission is given broad powers of investigation relating to the customs laws of the United States and foreign countries, the volume of importation in comparison with domestic production and consumption, the conditions, causes, and effects relating to competition of foreign industries with those of the United States and all other factors affecting competition between articles of the United States and imported articles.°

° Source: *Government Organization Manual.*

Businesspersons who believe they have been injured by unfair trade methods from abroad may file a complaint with this commission.

Summaries of trade and tariff information may be obtained directly from the commission.

The following agencies are important in arranging trade financing and credit insurance:

EXPORT-IMPORT BANK

Address: 811 Vermont Avenue NW, Washington, DC 20471. Phone: 202–566–8990.

FOREIGN CREDIT INSURANCE ASSOCIATION (FCIA)

Address: One World Trade Center, New York, NY 10048. Phone: 212–432–6200. Ombudsman: 212–432–6212.

The Export-Import Bank, established in 1934, is an independent agency of the U.S. government with the basic mission of encouraging U.S. exports. The policies of the bank recognize that credit terms are as important to foreign buyers as price and quality, and that U.S. exporters should be provided with financing that is competitive with that offered by foreign competitors. The bank cooperates with and supplements private capital sources. Loans to exporters are generally for specific purposes and most offer reasonable assurance of repayment.

A number of programs are offered by the Eximbank, including direct credit to foreign buyers, credit guarantees of commercial banks, loans to exporters, export credit insurance, and discount loans.

Credit insurance protection for exporters is provided by FCIA, an association of commercial insurance companies formed by the Eximbank and the insurance industry in 1961. Policies issued by FCIA insure repayment if the foreign buyer should default. The exporter may use FCIA insurance as collateral for obtaining a commercial loan.

The Eximbank will make a preliminary commitment concerning the amount it will guarantee or lend, a feature of particular value to U.S. importers submitting proposals in response to a foreign bid. The bank is also helpful in providing credit information on foreign buyers.

PUBLICATION

Eximbank: How It Works (free on writing to the Export-Import Bank).

OVERSEAS PRIVATE INVESTMENT CORPORATION (OPIC)

Address: 1129 20th Street NW, Washington, DC. Information phone: 202–632–1804.

OPIC, established in 1971, is an independent agency of the U.S. government with the mission of reducing or eliminating private investment risks in the developing countries. OPIC insures U.S. investors against political risks of expropriation, inconvertability of local currency holdings, and damage from war, revolution, or insurrection. The agency offers lenders protection by guaranteeing payment of principal, interest, and loans.

The corporation offers investment information and counseling to businesses and participates in the cost of locating and developing projects.

INTERNATIONAL ORGANIZATIONS

UNITED NATIONS (UN)

Address: New York, NY 10017. Information phone: 212–754–1234.

The UN and its affiliated organizations publish a large number of reports and statistical tables covering all member nations. Publications may be obtained by writing: Sales Section, United Nations Publications, New York, NY 10017. A periodic check list of UN publications is available on request.

PUBLICATIONS

Journal of Development Planning.

Guidelines for Contracting for Industrial Projects in Developing Countries.

World Economic Survey.

Annual Bulletin of Exports of Chemical Products.

Annual Bulletin of Coal Statistics for Europe.

Statistics of World Trade in Steel.

Annual Bulletin of Gas Statistics for Europe.

Annual Bulletin of Electric Energy Statistics for Europe.

Economic Bulletin for Europe.

Economic Bulletin for Asia and the Pacific.

Quarterly Bulletin of Statistics for Asia and the Pacific.

Statistical Yearbook for Asia and the Pacific.

Demographic Yearbook.

Yearbook of International Trade Statistics Vol. I: Trade by Country; Vol. II: Trade by Commodity.

Monthly Bulletin of Statistics provides monthly statistics on 70 subjects from more than 200 countries and territories together with special tables illustrating important economic developments. Quarterly data for significant world and regional aggregates are also prepared regularly for the bulletin.

Statistical Yearbook is a comprehensive compilation of international statistics relating to: population and manpower; agricultural, mineral, and manufacturing production; construction; energy; trade; transport; communications; consumption; balance of payments; wages and prices; national accounts; finance; development assistance; health; housing; education; science and technology; and culture.

Population and Vital Statistics Reports (quarterly).

Yearbook of National Accounts Statistics.

Yearbook of International Trade Statistics.

Yearbook of Construction Statistics.

Commodity Trade Statistics (quarterly).

World Trade Annual.

The Growth of World Industry: Vol. I General Industrial Statistics; Vol. II Commodities Production Data.

INTERNATIONAL MONETARY FUND (IMF)

Address: 19th and H Streets NW, Washington, DC 20431. Phone: 202–477–7000.

The IMF was organized in 1945 with the purpose of promoting international monetary cooperation and consultation. The fund also seeks to facilitate the expansion of international trade and currency exchange stability. The fund issues Special Drawing Rights (SDR), a form of reserve currency used by central banks for settling balance of payment obligations.

PUBLICATIONS

The IMF issues a broad range of publications (some in conjunction with the World Bank Group) of interest to the business community.

Foreign Trade Statistics. Series A. This monthly bulletin provides a breakdown of overall trade by main commodity categories and available indices of foreign trade unit values and volumes. *Series B. Trade by Commodities. Analytical Abstracts* (quarterly). *Series C. Trade by Commodities. Market Summaries* (yearly).

Provisional Oil Statistics (quarterly).

The Annual Report of the Executive Directors reviews the funds' activities, policies, organization, and administration and surveys the world economy, with special emphasis on international liquidity, payments problems, exchange rates, and world trade.

Annual Report on Exchange Restrictions reviews developments in exchange controls and restrictions and other measures that may have direct implications for the balance of payments of member countries.

International Financial Statistics (monthly) reports for most countries of the world current data needed for analyzing problems of international payments and inflation and deflation, i.e., data on exchange rates, international liquidity, money and banking, international trade, prices, production, government finance, interest rates, and other items. Information is presented in country tables for each country and in tables with area and world aggregates. Charts on each country page show recent changes in important series.

Balance of Payments Yearbook presents statistics in a standard form, expressed in a common unit of account, for countries that report information to the fund on their balance of payments transactions. In the tables that are designated as "standard presentations," these transactions are classified in terms of objective criteria; in the tables designated as "analytic presentations," they are regrouped to facilitate further analysis and certain cumulative balances are drawn.

Direction of Trade is published jointly by the International Monetary Fund and the International Bank for Reconstruction and Development. The monthly issues provide the latest available information on each country's direction of trade, with comparative data for the corresponding period of the preceding year.

The *IMF Survey* is a topical report of the fund's activities (including all press releases, texts of communiques and major statements, SDR valuations, and exchange rates) presented in the broader context of developments in national economics and international finance.

ORGANIZATION FOR ECONOMIC COOPERATION AND DEVELOPMENT (OECD)

Address: 2 Rue Andre Pascal, Paris, France.

1750 Pennsylvania Avenue NW, Washington, DC 20026. Phone: 202–724–1857.

The OECD, established in 1961, is an outgrowth of the Organization for European Economic Cooperation, set up under the Marshall Plan in 1948. It consists of 24 developed countries: Canada, United States, Japan, Australia, New Zealand, Austria, Belgium, Denmark, England, Finland, France, West Germany, Greece, Iceland, Italy, Luxembourg, Netherlands, Norway, Portugal, Spain, Sweden, Turkey, Switzerland, and Yugoslavia. Together, the OECD countries account for 20 percent of world population, 60 percent of world industrial production, and 73 percent of world trade.

PUBLICATIONS

OECD Observer is intended for people who are interested in and concerned with economic and social planning in the broadest sense and who want to have relevant information in the most succinct form possible. It presents in readable fashion the entire range of OECD's work—in economic affairs, trade, manpower, social affairs, science and education, the environment, financial affairs, and development assistance. (Published bimonthly.)

The *OECD Economic Outlook* is a twice yearly, detailed survey of economic trends and prospects for the immediate future.

OECD Financial Statistics supplies complete, up-to-date, authoritative information on financial markets in 16 European countries, the United States, Canada, and Japan. (Published yearly with bimonthly supplements.)

OECD Economic Surveys is an annual analysis of the economic policy of each OECD country as seen by the others.

Main Economic Indicators, a monthly publication, is an essential source of statistics for the student of the international business cycle.

GENERAL AGREEMENT ON TRADE AND TARIFFS (GATT)

Address: Centre William Rappard, 154 Rue de Lausanne, Geneva, Switzerland.

GATT is a multilateral trade treaty (entered into force in 1948) among 83 countries providing for the reduction of tariffs and other trade barriers, standardization of trade procedures, and the resolution of trade disputes. GATT publishes *Compilations of Basic Information on Export Markets; Guide to Sources of Foreign Trade Information; Analytical Bibliography: A Compendium of Sources: International Trade Statistics;* and *World Directory of Industry and Trade Associations.*

COMMERCIAL ORGANIZATIONS
DUN & BRADSTREET

Address: 99 Church Street, New York, NY. Phone: 212–285–7000.

Dun & Bradstreet provides a number of valuable services and publications in the area of international business, i.e., international credit reports on companies, international marketing guides and services, and directories of foreign firms. Dun & Bradstreet publishes the comprehensive annual, *Exporters Encyclopedia,* with monthly supplements. It details the rules and regulations in over 220 world markets and is arranged alphabetically by country and market area. *Principal International Businesses* is a useful marketing publication providing addresses, lines of business, sales figures, and other information on nearly 50,000 foreign firms.

INTERNATIONAL REPORTS

Address: 200 Park Avenue South, New York, NY 10003.

International Reports publishes reports on sources of worldwide export credit insurance, foreign investment guarantees, and export financing under the title of *Insurance in International Finance.*

It also publishes the monthly *International Commercial Finance Service,* containing extensive information and data on financing and interest rates, surveys of credit ratings, and foreign payment records of individual countries.

BUSINESS INTERNATIONAL

Address: One Dag Hammarskjold Plaza, New York, NY 10017. Phone: 212–750–6300.

Business International publishes a series of weekly reports: *Business International* (a global view of business); *Business Europe; Business Latin America; Business Asia; Eastern Europe Report; Business China* (People's Republic); *Business International Money Report; Investing, Licensing, Trading Report;* and *Financing Foreign Operations.* It publishes a multivolume series, *Doing Business with Eastern Europe.*

COMMERCE CLEARING HOUSE

Address: 4025 West Peterson Avenue, Chicago, IL 60646. Phone 312–583–8500.

Commerce Clearing House publishes a number of widely used looseleaf series updated on a weekly or monthly basis. In the international field these include: *Euromarket News; Doing Business in Europe; Balance of Payment Reports; Common Market Reports;* and *Income Taxes World Wide.* It also publishes a number of detailed tax and legal guides for specific countries, i.e., Canada, Mexico, Australia, England, and Germany.

OTHER PUBLICATIONS

Europa Year Book is an annual two-volume work covering a wide range of commercial, economic, and political statistics and information about every country in the world. Volume I deals with international organizations and the countries of Europe, while Volume II covers Africa, the Americas, Asia, and Australia. It is published by Europe Publications, Ltd., 18 Bedford Square, London, England.

Jane's Major Companies of Europe is an annual providing extensive information about all major European companies. It is available from Jane's Yearbooks, 8 Shepherdess, London N1 7LW, England.

SOURCES OF INTERNATIONAL CREDIT INFORMATION

Export Information Division, Domestic and International Business Administration, U.S. Department of Commerce, Washington, DC.

Dun & Bradstreet (address given above).

FCIB-NACM Corp., 475 Park Avenue South, New York, NY 10015.

Major Commercial Banks

INTERNATIONAL BUSINESS INFORMATION DIRECTORY

This Directory lists helpful addresses in the United States for those doing business with countries where business practices may present certain problems.

JAPAN

Exporters and importers generally find it essential to use the services of the Japanese trading companies, which offer a wide range of services including negotiation of overseas deals, transportation, storage, finance, and marketing. The ten largest trading companies are listed below. The small exporter will often do better using smaller trading companies that specialize in one or two types of products. Exporters seeking an appropriate trading company should contact the local office of the Japan Trade Center:

Bank of America Towers
555 S. Flower Street
Los Angeles, CA 90071

1737 Post Street
San Francisco, CA 94115

232 N. Michigan Avenue
Chicago, IL 60601

1221 Avenue of the Americas
New York, NY 10020

One World Trade Center
2100 Stemmons Freeway
Dallas, TX 75207

Melrose Boulevard
1127 Walker Street
Houston, TX 77002

P.O. Box 3356
Marina Station
Mayaguez, PR 00708

MAJOR TRADING COMPANIES (U.S. OFFICES)

Mitsubishi
277 Park Avenue
New York, NY 10017

601 California Street
San Francisco, CA 94108

Mitsui & Co. (USA), Inc.
200 Park Avenue
New York, NY 10166

611 W. Sixth Street
Los Angeles, CA 90017

Marubeni Corporation
200 Park Avenue
New York, NY 10166

One Wilshire Building
624 S. Grand Avenue
Los Angeles, CA 90017

C. Itoh & Co. (America), Inc.
270 Park Avenue
New York, NY 10017

555 S. Flower Street
Los Angeles, CA 90017

Sumitomo Shoji America, Inc.
345 Park Avenue
New York, NY 10022

606 S. Olive Street
Los Angeles, CA 90014

Nissho-Iwai American Corp.
1211 Avenue of the Americas
New York, NY 10036

One Wilshire Building
624 S. Grand Avenue
Los Angeles, CA 90017

Toyomenka (America), Inc.
One World Trade Center
New York, NY 10048

445 South Figueroa Street
Los Angeles, CA 90017

Kanematsu-Gosho (USA), Inc.
One World Trade Center
New York, NY 10048

350 California Street
San Francisco, CA 94104

Itoman USA Inc.
1211 Avenue of the Americas
New York, NY 10036

Nichimen Co., Inc.
1185 Avenue of the Americas
New York, NY 10036

Occidental Center
1150 S. Olive Street
Los Angeles, CA 90015

HELP FOR TRADING PROBLEMS IN JAPAN*

Help is available for firms, groups, and trade associations which have trouble gaining

---

* Source: *The Information Report*, Washington Researchers, 918 16th Street NW, Washington, DC 20006.

access to the Japanese market. The Joint U.S. Japan Trade Facilitation Committee staff will intervene with Japanese authorities on behalf of the U.S. companies or groups when Japanese regulations present trade problems.

For more information and aid, contact:

Trade Facilitation Committee
Industry and Trade Administration
Department of Commerce
14th & Constitution Ave. NW, Room 3053
Washington, DC 20230
202–377–5722

THE PEOPLE'S REPUBLIC OF CHINA

For information or advice on contacting the Chinese on commercial matters, call or write to:

U.S. Department of Commerce
Industry and Trade Administration
Office of East-West Country Affairs
PRC Affairs Division—Room 4044
Washington, DC 20230
Telephone: 202–377–3583/4681

Commercial Office
Embassy of the People's Republic of China
2300 Connecticut Avenue, N.W.
Washington, DC 20008

THE NATIONAL COUNCIL FOR U.S.-CHINA TRADE COUNCIL

Address: 1050 17th Street NW, Suite 350, Washington, DC 20036. Phone: 202–331–0290/0294.

The Council, a nonprofit, private organization maintaining close liaison with the U.S. government, serves as a forum for the discussion of trade policy and issues. It also serves as a focal point for business contact and the dissemination of information on marketing in the PRC. The council maintains a business counseling service; it also publishes the *China Business Review* bimonthly. The council facilitates the reciprocal arrangements of trade missions and trade exhibitions in the United States and China.

USSR AND EASTERN EUROPE

USSR

USSR Affairs Division, Office of East-West Country Affairs (202–377–4655). This division collects, analyzes, and disseminates current information on economic, commercial, and other developments in the USSR and estimates their impact on the U.S. business community. The division develops policy guidance in our commercial relationship with the Soviet Union and provides staff support to and representation on the Joint Commercial Commission.

It also maintains close contact with the U.S. Commercial Office in Moscow and with USSR commercial officials in the United States in order to initiate and pursue official representations on behalf of the American business community.

Office of East-West Trade Development. This office's Trade Promotion Division (202–377–2801) plans, organizes, and conducts the export promotion program of the Office of East-West Trade in the USSR, including participation in Soviet international trade fairs, staging seminar/exhibits in the Commercial Office, and participating in catalog shows. The Trade Development Assistance Division (202–377–2835) arranges contacts between businesspeople and appropriate Soviet officials, provides specialized guidance on contract negotiations and other commercial techniques, advises on obtaining necessary U.S. government clearances, and disseminates information about trade opportunities.

Office of East-West Policy and Planning (202–377–2456). This office identifies trade policy issues, conducts broad studies, reviews present and proposed legislation, and collects and disseminates detailed East-West trade statistics.

The Department of Commerce, Office of East-West Trade, USSR Affairs Division, and Trade Development Assistance Division, Washington, DC 20230. These two divisions together can provide businesspeople with foreign trade and economic data, five-year and annual plan targets, and advice on which organizations and personalities to contact in the USSR. The bureau should be a firm's first stop or call when it decides to do business with the USSR.

The U.S. Commercial Office (USCO), Moscow. The USCO should be a firm's first stop when visiting the USSR.

It may also be to the company's advantage to touch base with the following USSR commercial organizations in the United States to try to obtain some indication of Soviet interest and to identify contacts in the Soviet Union:

The Trade Representation of the USSR in the U.S.A., 2001 Connecticut Avenue NW, Washington, DC 20008, telephone 202–232–5988.

The Amtorg Trading Corporation, 750 Third Avenue, New York, NY, telephone 212–682–7404.

The staffs of both Amtorg and the Trade Representation include representatives of individual foreign trade organizations (FTOs).

The KAMA Purchasing Commission (KPC), General Motors Building, 767 Fifth Avenue, 6th floor, New York, NY 10022, telephone 212–593–2600. KPC was established in 1973 and

---

Source: Excerpted from Department of Commerce Overseas Reports, "Trading with the USSR."

serves as a direct channel to FTOs involved in procuring equipment and implementing contracts for five major projects currently underway in the USSR: the Kama River truck plant, the Cheboksary industrial tractor factory, the fertilizer complex at Tol'yatti, the International Trade Center in Moscow, and exploratory work in the Yakutsk natural gas fields. The KPC's staff has the authority to make purchasing decisions and to negotiate contracts; it is, therefore, an important contact point for preliminary discussions and after-sale follow-up for firms wishing to participate in the above projects.

The USSR Consulate General, 2790 Green Street, San Francisco, CA 94123, telephone 415–922–6642, may have information conveniently available for companies on the West Coast.

INSURANCE COVERAGE

Insurance coverage for U.S.–USSR trade is available from a number of U.S. insurance companies on a case-by-case basis in the areas of export insurance, transportation insurance, and insurance on fixed locations. No political or commercial credit risk coverage is currently available for the USSR from the Foreign Credit Insurance Association (FCIA) or the Export-Import Bank because of the 1974 Trade Act provisions. Many of the private U.S. companies, however, have established working and contractual relationships with the USSR State Insurance Company (Ingosstrakh) and with the wholly owned Soviet insurance companies, Black Sea and Baltic Company, Ltd., in London, Schwarzmeer und Ostee A.G. in Hamburg, and Garant A.G. in Vienna.

Private American insurers which write policies on some or all of the areas of standard property, casualty transportation, marine and war risk insurance, and more specialized insurance for Soviet-American cooperative projects in the USSR or a third country are:*

AFIA Reinsurance Insurance
North American Control Office
110 William Street
New York, NY 10038
Telephone: 212–732–9070

Members of the American Institute of
Marine Underwriters
14 Wall Street
New York, NY 10038
Telephone 212–233–0550

American International Underwriters
Corporation
70 Pine Street

* This listing is not to be considered an endorsement by the Department of Commerce, the U.S. government or the *Business Almanac.*

New York, NY 10005
Telephone: 212–770–7000

Chubb and Son, Inc.
International Department
100 William Street
New York, NY 10038
Telephone: 212–285–2850

Insurance Company of North America
International Insurance Section
2 INA Plaza
1600 Arch Street
Philadelphia, PA 19101
Telephone: 215–440–4100

EASTERN EUROPE

Commercial transactions with Bulgaria, Czechoslovakia, East Germany, Hungary, Poland, and Romania are similar to those with the USSR. Contracts are negotiated with the appropriate Foreign Trade Organization. For detailed information about trade shows, missions, export licenses, and FTOs, contact the Office of East-West Trade, Department of Commerce in Washington, or the Commerce Department Offices at the district level. Another key source of information is the U.S. East-West Trade Development Office in Vienna.

BULGARIA

Bulgarian Embassy
2100 16th Street NW
Washington, DC 20009

Bulgarian Commercial Counselor
50 E. 42nd Street
New York, NY 10017

CZECHOSLOVAKIA

Czechoslovakian Embassy
3900 Linnean Avenue NW
Washington, DC 20008

Office of the Czechoslovakian Commercial
Counselor
292 Madison Avenue
New York, NY 10016

EAST GERMANY
(German Democratic Republic)

Embassy of the German Democratic Republic
1717 Massachusetts Avenue NW
Washington, DC 20036

Permanent Mission of German Democratic
Republic to the United Nations

58 Park Avenue
New York, NY 10016

U.S. banks with offices in Berlin
Citibank, New York NY

HUNGARY

Embassy of Hungary to the United States
2437 15th Street NW
Washington, DC 20009

Office of the Commercial Counselor of the
    Embassy of Hungary
2401 Calvert Street
Washington, DC 20008

Trade Representation of the Hungarian
    People's Republic
150 E. 58th Street
New York, NY 10022

POLAND

Economic Counselor's Office
Embassy of the Polish People's Republic
2540 16th Street NW
Washington, DC 20008

Polish Consulate General
233 Madison Avenue
New York, NY 10016

Polish Commercial Counselor's Office
1 Daghammarskjold Plaza
New York, NY 10017

Office of Polish Commercial Consul
333 E. Ontario Street
Chicago, IL 60611

Polish Chamber of Foreign Trade
44 Montgomery Street
San Francisco, CA 94104

U.S. banks with offices in Warsaw
First National Bank, Chicago

ROMANIA

Romanian Embassy
1607 23rd Street NW
Washington, DC 20008

Romanian Office of the Economic Counselor
573–577 Madison Avenue
New York, NY 10016

Romanian Foreign Trade Promotion Office
100 W. Monroe Street
Chicago, IL 60603

Romanian Foreign Trade Promotion Office
22 Battery Street
San Francisco, CA 94111

U.S. banks with offices in Bucharest
Manufacturer's Hanover Trust, New York, NY

NEAR EAST AND NORTH AFRICA

The Commerce Action Group for the Near
East (CAGNE) within the International Trade
Administration serves as the focal point for the
U.S. Department of Commerce response to the
dramatically changed economic situation and
significant business opportunities in the Near
East and North Africa. The group assembles,
analyzes, and disseminates to the U.S. business
community information on economic conditions
and new opportunities in the area, provides
counseling for and makes representations on
behalf of U.S. exporters, and plans and organizes promotional programs to assist U.S. firms
to take advantage of the market boom. CAGNE
also coordinates Department of Commerce participation in joint commission activities.

To take advantage of these programs call
202–377–5767 (Arab Near East); 202–377–
5737 (North Africa); 202–377–3752 (Iran,
Israel, Egypt). For information concerning major projects, call 202–377–4441. The mailing
address is Commerce Action Group for the
Near East, International Trade Administration,
Room 3203, Washington, DC 20230.

ALGERIA

Embassy of Algeria
2118 Kalorama Road NW
Washington, DC 20008
Telephone: 202–234–7246

SONATRACH, Inc.
    (Algerian State Enterprise for Oil, Gas,
    Petrochemicals, Plastics, Fertilizers)
816 Connecticut Avenue NW
Washington, DC 20006
Telephone: 202–638–7180

BAHRAIN

Embassy of Bahrain
2600 Virginia Avenue NW
Washington, DC 20037
Telephone: 202–965–4930

ARAB REPUBLIC OF EGYPT

Embassy of the Arab Republic of Egypt
2310 Decatur Place NW
Washington, DC 20008
Telephone: 202–232–5400

Commercial and Economic Office
2715 Connecticut Avenue NW
Washington, DC 20008
Telephone: 202–234–1414

Source: *A Business Guide to the Near East & North
Africa*, Industry and Trade Association, U.S. Department of Commerce.

Consulate of the Arab Republic of Egypt
1110 Second Avenue
2nd Floor
New York, NY 10022
Telephone: 212–759–7120

Consulate of the Arab Republic of Egypt
3001 Pacific Avenue
San Francisco, CA 94115
Telephone: 415–346–9700

IRAQ

Iraqi Interests Section
Indian Embassy
1801 P Street NW
Washington, DC 20008
Telephone: 202–483–7500

ISRAEL

Embassy of Israel
1621 22nd Street NW
Washington, DC 20008
Telephone: 202–483–4100

Israel Consulates General
    Atlanta, Boston, Chicago, Houston, Los
    Angeles, New York City, Philadelphia, and
    San Francisco

Investment Authority and Branches:
350 Fifth Avenue
New York, NY 10001
Telephone: 212–560–0610

174 N. Michigan Avenue
Chicago, IL 60601
Telephone: 312–332–2160

Israel Trade Center
350 Fifth Avenue
New York, NY 10001
Telephone: 212–560–0680

6380 Wilshire Boulevard
Los Angeles, CA 90048
Telephone: 213–658–7924

805 Peachtree Street, NE
Atlanta, GA 30308
Telephone: 404–875–6947

JORDAN (HASHEMITE KINGDOM OF)

Embassy of Jordan
2319 Wyoming Avenue, NW
Washington, DC 20008
Telephone: 202–265–1606

Consulate General
866 U.N. Plaza
New York, NY 10017
Telephone: 212–752–0135

STATE OF KUWAIT

Embassy of Kuwait
2940 Tilden Street NW
Washington, DC 20008
Telephone: 202–966–0702

LEBANON

Embassy of Lebanon
2560 28th Street NW
Washington, DC 20008
Telephone: 202–332–0300

Consulate General
9 E. 76th Street
New York, NY 10021
Telephone 212–744–7905

Consulate General
1300 Lafayette East, Suite 407
Detroit, Michigan 48207
Telephone: 313–963–0233

LIBYA

Embassy of the Socialist People's Libyan Arab
    Jamakiriya
1118 22nd Street NW
Washington, DC 20037
Telephone: 202–452–1290

MOROCCO

Embassy of Morocco
1601 21st Street NW
Washington, DC 20009
Telephone: 202–462–7979/82

Consulate General
    (includes Moroccan National Tourist
    Office)
597 Fifth Avenue
New York, NY 10017
Telephone: 212–421–5771

OMAN

Embassy of the Sultanate of Oman
2342 Massachusetts Avenue NW
Washington, DC 20008
Telephone: 202–387–1980

Combined Consulate and Permanent Mission
    to the United Nations
605 Third Avenue
Room 3304
New York, NY 10016
Telephone: 202–682–0447

QATAR

Embassy of Qatar
600 New Hampshire Avenue NW
Washington, DC 20037
Telephone: 202–338–0111

SAUDI ARABIA

Saudi Arabian Embassy
1520 18th Street NW
Washington, DC 20036
Telephone: 202–483–2100

Consulate General
866 United Nations Plaza
New York, NY 10017
Telephone: 212–752–2740

SYRIAN ARAB REPUBLIC

Embassy of the Syrian Arab Republic
2215 Wyoming Avenue NW
Washington, DC 20008
Telephone: 202–232–6313

TUNISIA

Embassy of Tunisia
2408 Massachusetts Avenue NW
Washington, DC 20008
Telephone: 202–234–6644

Tunisian Investment Promotion Agency
Tunisian National Tourist Office
630 Fifth Avenue, Suite 863
New York, NY 10020
Telephone: 212–582–3760

UNITED ARAB EMIRATES

Embassy of the United Arab Emirates
Suite 740
600 New Hampshire Avenue, N.W.
Washington, DC 20037
Telephone: 202–338–6500

YEMEN ARAB REPUBLIC

Embassy of the Yemen Arab Republic
600 New Hampshire Avenue, NW
Suite 860
Washington, DC 20037
Telephone: 202–965–4760

Consulate of the Yemen Arab Republic
211 East 43rd Street
Room 2402
New York, NY 10017
Telephone: 212–986–0990

FAST—MATCH

A quick, easy way to match your international business requirements to the appropriate Government programs or services designed to satisfy those needs

IF YOU ARE SEEKING INFORMATION REGARDING ➡

USE ⬇

	Potential Markets	Market Research *	Direct Sales Leads	Agents/Distributors	Licenses	Credit Analysis	Financial Assistance	Risk Insurance	Tax Incentives
Foreign Trade Statistics (FT-410)	•								
Global Market Surveys	•	•							
Foreign Market Reports	•	•							
Market Share Reports	•	•							
Foreign Economic Trends	•	•							
Business America	•	•	•	•	•				
Commercial Exhibitions	**	**	•	•	•				
Overseas Business Reports (OBR)		•							
Overseas Private Investment Corp.		•					•	•	
Commerce Business Daily			•						
New Product Information Service			•	•	•				
Trade Opportunity Program (TOP)			•	•	•				
Industry Trade Lists			•	•	•				
Special Trade Lists			•	•	•				
Export Mailing List Service (EMLS)			•	•	•				
Agent/Distributor Service (ADS)				•					
World Traders Data Reports (WTDR)						•			
Export—Import Bank							•	•	
Foreign Credit Insurance Assoc. (FCIA)								•	
Domestic Int'l. Sales Corp. (DISC)							•		•

* Foreign Trade Outlook Market Profiles; Industry Trends; Distribution and Sales Channels; Transportation Facilities; Local Business Practices and Customs; Investment Criteria; Import Procedures and Trade Regulations; and Industrial Property Rights.

** Research material developed regarding a planned exhibition and released to support promotional activities.

Cost of services may be obtained from Commerce District Offices.

Source: Industry and Trade Administration, U.S. Department of Commerce.

Selected Business and Trade Organizations

Academy of Motion Picture Arts and Sciences
8949 Wilshire Boulevard
Beverly Hills, CA 90211

Administrative Management Society
Willow Grove, PA 19090

Advertising Research Foundation
3 E. 54th Street
New York, NY 10022

Aerospace Industries Association of America
1725 DeSales Street NW
Washington, DC 20036

Air Conditioning Contractors of America
1228 17th Street NW
Washington, DC 20036

Air Freight Forwarders Association of
America
1730 Rhode Island Avenue NW
Washington, DC 20036

Air Transport Association of America
1709 New York Avenue NW
Washington, DC 20006

Allied Trades of the Baking Industry
5240 W. Irving Park Road
Chicago, IL 60641

Aluminum Association
818 Connecticut Avenue NW
Washington, DC 20006

American Accounting Association
5717 Bessie Drive
Sarasota, FL 33581

American Advertising Federation
1225 Connecticut Avenue NW
Washington, DC 20036

American Apparel Manufacturers Association
1611 N. Kent Street
Arlington, VA 22209

American Arbitration Association
140 W. 51st Street
New York. NY 10020

American Association of Advertising Agencies
200 Park Avenue
New York, NY 10017

American Association of Attorney–Certified
Public Accountants
400 S. Beverly Drive, Suite 400
Beverly Hills, CA 90212

American Association of Equipment Lessors
5635 W. Douglas Avenue
Milwaukee, WI 53218

American Association of Meat Processors
224 E. High Street
Elizabethtown, PA 17022

American Automobile Association
8111 Gatehouse Road
Falls Church, VA 22042

American Automotive Leasing Association
5635 W. Douglas Avenue
Milwaukee, WI 53218

American Bankers Association
1120 Connecticut Avenue NW
Washington, DC 20036

American Booksellers Association
122 E. 42nd Street
New York. NY 10017

American Building Contractors Association
2476 Overland Avenue
Los Angeles, CA 90064

American Bureau of Metal Statistics
420 Lexington Avenue
New York, NY 10017

American Bureau of Shipping
65 Broadway
New York, NY 10006

American Business Communication
Association
317b David Kinley Hall
University of Illinois
Urbana, IL 61801

American Business Women's Association
9100 Ward Parkway
Kansas City, MO 64114

American Chemical Society
1155 16th Street NW
Washington, DC 20036

American Council of Life Insurance
1850 K Street NW
Washington, DC 20006

American Dairy Association
6300 N. River Road
Rosemont, IL 60018

Chamber of Commerce of the United States
1615 H Street NW
Washington, DC 20062

Clothing Manufacturers Association of the
U.S.A.
135 W. 50th Street
New York, NY 10020

Computer and Business Equipment
Manufacturer's Association
1828 L Street NW
Washington, DC 20036

Conference of American Small Business
Organizations, Inc.
407 S. Dearborn Street
Chicago, IL 60605

Construction Specifications Institute
1150 17th Street NW
Washington, DC 20036

Copper Development Association
405 Lexington Avenue
New York, NY 10017

Cotton Foundation, The
1918 North Parkway
Memphis, TN 38112

Council of Better Business Bureaus, Inc.
1150 17th Street NW
Washington, DC 20036

Council of the Americas
684 Park Avenue
New York, NY 10021

Dairy and Food Industries Supply
Association
5530 Wisconsin Avenue NW
Washington, DC 20015

Data Processing Management Association
505 Busse Highway
Park Ridge, IL 60068

Direct Mail/Marketing Association
6 E. 43rd Street
New York, NY 10017

Distilled Spirits Council of the United States
1300 Pennsylvania Building
Washington, DC 20004

Drug, Chemical and Allied Trades
Association
42–40 Bell Boulevard
Bayside, NY 11361

Edison Electric Institute
1140 Connecticut Avenue, NW
Washington, DC 20036

Electronic Industries Association
2001 Eye Street NW
Washington, DC 20006

Engineering Foundation
345 E. 47 Street
New York, NY 10017

Farm and Industrial Equipment Institute
410 N. Michigan Avenue
Chicago, IL 60611

Farm Equipment Manufacturers Association
230 S. Bemiston Avenue
St. Louis, MO 63105

FCIB-NACM (formerly Foreign Credit Interchange Bureau)
475 Park Avenue, So.
New York, NY 10016

Fertilizer Institute, The
1015 18th Street NW
Washington, DC 20036

Financial Analysts Federation
219 E. 42nd Street
New York, NY 10017

Financial Executives Institute
633 Third Avenue
New York, NY 10017

Food Distribution Research Society
Box 1843
Hyattsville, MD 20788

Food Marketing Institute
1750 K Street, NW
Washington, DC 20006

Foreign Credit Insurance Association
1 World Trade Center
New York, NY 10048

General Agreement on Tariffs and Trade
Centre William Rappard
154 Rue de Lausanne
Geneva 21, Switzerland

Health Insurance Association of America
1750 K Street NW
Washington, DC 20006

Independent Bankers Association of America
P.O. Box 267
Sauk Centre, MN 56378

Independent Insurance Agents of America
85 John Street
New York, NY 10038

Industrial Management Society
570 Northwest Highway
Des Plaines, IL 60016

Information Industry Association
316 Pennsylvania Avenue SE
Washington, DC 20003

Institute of Chartered Financial Analysts
P.O. Box 3668
University of Virginia
Charlottesville, VA 22903

Institute of Electrical and Electronics
Engineers
345 E. 47th Street
New York, NY 10017

Institute of Financial Education, The
111 E. Wacker Drive
Chicago, IL 60601

Institute of Gas Technology
3424 State Street
Chicago, IL 60616

Institute of Internal Auditors
249 Maitland Avenue
Altamonte Springs, FL 32701

Institute of Management Consultants
19 W. 44th Street
New York, NY 10036

Institute of Management Sciences, The
146 Westminster Street
Providence, RI 02903

Institute of Real Estate Management
430 N. Michigan Avenue
Chicago; IL 60611

Insurance Accounting and Statistical
   Association
Mutual Plaza
Durham, NC 27701

Insurance Services Office
2 World Trade Center
New York, NY 10048

International Advertising Association Inc.
475 5th Avenue
New York, NY 10017

International Air Transport Association
International Aviation Square
Montreal, PQ, Canada H3A2R4

International Airfreight Airforwarders and
   Agents Association
1300 Connecticut Avenue NW
Washington, DC 20036

International Association of Drilling
   Contractors
P.O. Box 4287
Houston, TX 77210

International Association of Exchange
   Dealers
16 Boulevard Montmartre
F–75009, Paris, France

International Bankers Association
P.O. Box 7780
Washington, DC 20005

International Coffee Organization
22 Berners Street
London WIP 4DD, England

International Confederation of Associations
   of Experts and Consultants.
Rue Ten Bosch, 85
B–1050, Brussels, Belgium

International Consumer Credit Association
243 N. Lindbergh Boulevard
St. Louis, MO 63114

International Copper Research Association
708 Third Avenue
New York, NY 10017

International Council for Small Business
University of Wisconsin Extension
929 N. Sixth Street
Milwaukee, WI 53203

International Council of Shopping Centers
665 Fifth Avenue
New York, NY 10022

International Executive Service Corps
622 Third Avenue
New York, NY 10017

International Executives Associations, Inc.
122 E. 42nd Street
New York, NY 10017

International Federation of Freight Forwarder
   Associations
P.O. Box 177
Ch-8026 Zurich, Switzerland

International Food Service Executives
   Association
3620 Rupp Drive
Fort Wayne, IN 46815

International Foundation of Employee
   Benefit Plans
18700 Blue Mound Road
Brookfield, WI 53005

International Franchise Association
7315 Wisconsin Avenue
Washington, DC 20014

International Television Association
26 South Street
New Providence, NJ 07974

International Iron and Steel Institute
Avenue Hamoir 12/14
B-1180, Brussels, Belgium

International Lead Zinc Research
   Organization, Inc.
292 Madison Avenue
New York, NY 10017

International Magnesium Association
c/o Bell Publicom
1406 Third National Building
Dayton, OH 45402

International Management Council
291 Broadway
New York, NY 10007

International Personnel Management
   Association
1850 K Street NW
Washington, DC 20006

Investment Company Institute
Suffridge Building
1775 K Street NW
Washington, DC 20006

Iron and Steel Society
410 Commonwealth Drive
Warrendale, PA 15086

Machinery and Allied Products Institute
1200 18th Street NW
Washington, DC 20036

Manufactured Housing Institute
1745 Jefferson Davis Highway
Arlington, VA 22202

Manufacturing Chemists Association
1825 Connecticut Avenue NW
Washington, DC 20009

Master Brewers Association of the Americas
4513 Vernon Boulevard
Madison, WI 53705

Master Furriers Guild of America
101 W. 30th Street
New York, NY 10001

Milk Industry Foundation
910 17th Street NW
Washington, DC 20006

Mortgage Bankers Association of America
1125 15th Street NW
Washington, DC 20005

Motor and Equipment Manufacturers
  Association
222 Cedar Lane
Teaneck, NJ 07666

Motor Vehicle Manufacturers Association
  of the United States
300 New Center Building
Detroit, MI 48202

National Academy of Television Arts and
  Sciences
110 W. 57th Street
New York, NY 10019

National Aeronautic Association of the USA
821 15th Street NW
Washington, DC 20005

National Agri-Marketing Association
8340 Mission Road
Prairie Village, KS 66206

National Air Transportation Associations
1010 Wisconsin Avenue NW
Washington, DC 20007

National Alcoholic Beverage Control
  Association
5454 Wisconsin Avenue NW
Chevy Chase, MD 20015

National Apartment Association
1825 K Street NW
Washington, DC 20006

National Association of Accountants
919 Third Avenue
New York, NY 10022

National Association of Alcoholic Beverage
  Importers
1025 Vermont Avenue NW
Washington, DC 20005

National Association of Bank Women
111 E. Wacker Drive
Chicago, IL 60601

National Association of Broadcasters
1771 N Street NW
Washington, DC 20036

National Association of Business Economists
28349 Chagrin Boulevard
Cleveland, OH 44122

National Association of Credit Management
475 Park Avenue So.
New York, NY 10016

National Association of Export Management
  Companies
65 Liberty Street
New York, NY 10005

National Association of Food Equipment
  Manufacturers
c/o Smith, Bucklin & Associates, Inc.
111 E. Wacker Drive
Chicago, IL 60601

National Association of Furniture
  Manufacturers
8401 Connecticut Avenue
Washington, DC 20015

National Association of Home Builders of the
  U.S.
15th and M Streets
Washington, DC 20005

National Association of Independent Food
  Retailers
125 W. 8 Mile Road
Detroit, MI 48203

National Association of Investment Clubs
1515 E. 11 Mile Road
Royal Oak, MI 48067

National Association of Life Underwriters
1922 F Street NW
Washington, DC 20006

National Association of Manufacturers
1776 F Street NW
Washington, DC 20006

National Association of Mutual Savings Banks
200 Park Avenue
New York, NY 10017

National Association of Pharmaceutical
  Manufacturers
747 Third Avenue
New York, NY 10017

National Association of Photographic
  Manufacturers
600 Mamaroneck Avenue
Harrison, NY 10528

National Association of Purchasing
  Management
11 Park Place
New York, NY 10007

National Association of Real Estate Brokers
1025 Vermont Avenue NW
Washington, DC 20005

National Association of Realtors
430 N. Michigan Avenue
Chicago, IL 60611

National Association of Retail Druggists
1750 K Street NW
Washington, DC 20006

National Association of Retail Grocers of the
  United States
P.O. Box 17208
Washington, DC 20041

National Association of Securities Dealers,
  Inc.
1735 K Street NW
Washington, DC 20006

National Association of Small Business
  Investment Companies
618 Washington Building
Washington, DC 20005

National Association of Women's and
  Children's Apparel Salesmen
1819 Peachtree Street NE
Atlanta, GA 30309

National Automobile Dealers Association
8400 Westpark Drive
McLean, VA 22102

National Business Aircraft Association
1 Farragut Square S.
Washington, DC 20006

National Business Forms Association
433 E. Monroe Avenue
Alexandria, VA 22301

National Business League
4324 Georgia Avenue NW
Washington, DC 20011

National Cable Television Association
918 16th Street NW
Washington, DC 20006

National Cattlemen's Association
1001 Lincoln Street
Denver, CO 80203

National Coal Association
1130 17th Street NW
Washington, DC 20036

National Coffee Association of U.S.A.
120 Wall Street
New York, NY 10005

National Consumer Finance Association
1000 16th Street NW
Washington, DC 20036

National Contract Management Association
2001 Jefferson Davis Highway
Arlington, VA 22202

National Council of Salesmen's Organizations
96 Fulton Street
New York, NY 10038

National Customs Brokers and Forwarders
  Association of America
1 World Trade Center
New York, NY 10048

National Electrical Manufacturers
  Association
2101 L Street NW
Washington, DC 20037

National Export Traffic League, Inc.
507 5th Avenue
New York, NY 10017

National Federation of Independent Business
150 W. 20th Avenue
San Mateo, CA 94403

National Food Brokers Association
1916 M Street NW
Washington, DC 20036

National Food Processors Association
1133 20th Street NW
Washington, DC 20036

National Foreign Trade Council, Inc.
10 Rockefeller Plaza
New York, NY 10020

National Foundation for Consumer Credit
1819 H Street NW
Washington, DC 20006

National Glass Dealers Association
1000 Connecticut Avenue NW
Washington, DC 20036

National Home Furnishings Association
405 Merchandise Mart Plaza
Chicago, IL 60654

National Independent Automobile Dealers
Association
Koger Executive Center
3700 National Drive
Raleigh, NC 27612

National Industrial Recreation Association
20 N. Wacker Drive
Chicago, IL 60606

National Licensed Beverage Association
309 N. Washington Street
Alexandria, VA 22314

National Liquor Stores Association
1025 Vermont Avenue NW
Washington, DC 20005

National Management Association
2210 Arbor Boulevard
Dayton, OH 45439

National Mass Retailing Institute
570 7th Avenue
New York, NY 10018

National Office Products Association
301 N. Fairfax Street
Alexandria, VA 22314

National Press Club
National Press Building
529 14th Street NW
Washington, DC 20045

National Restaurant Association
1 IBM Plaza
Chicago, IL 60611

National Retail Hardware Association
770 N. High School Road
Indianapolis, IN 46224

National Retail Merchants Association
100 W. 31st Street
New York, NY 10001

National Secretaries Association
2440 Pershing Road
Kansas City, MO 64108

National Small Business Association
1604 K Street NW
Washington, DC 20006

National Sporting Goods Association
717 N. Michigan Avenue
Chicago, IL 60611

National Tool, Die and Precision Machining
Association
9300 Livingston Road
Washington, DC 20022

National Trade Show Exhibitors Association
4300–L Lincoln Avenue
Rolling Meadows, IL 60008

National Waterways Conference
1130 17th Street NW
Washington, DC 20036

Organization of the Petroleum Exporting
Countries
Obere-Donaustrasse 93
A–1010, Vienna, Austria

Over-the-Counter Information Bureau
120 Broadway
New York, NY 10005

Overseas Automotive Club
475 Park Avenue, So.
New York, NY 10016

Overseas Press Club of America, Inc.
55 E. 43rd Street
New York, NY 10017

Packaging Institute
342 Madison Avenue
New York, NY 10017

Pharmaceutical Manufacturers Association
1155 15th Street NW
Washington, DC 20005

Planning Executives Institute
5500 College Corner Pike
Oxford, OH 45056

Prestressed Concrete Institute
20 N. Wacker Drive
Chicago, IL 60606

Printing Industries of America
1730 N. Lynn Street
Arlington, VA 22209

Professional Insurance Agents
400 N. Washington Street
Alexandria, VA 22314

Public Relations Society of America
845 Third Avenue
New York, NY 10022

Retail Advertising Conference
130 E. Randolph Street
Chicago, IL 60601

Robert Morris Associates
(National Association of Bank Loan and
Credit Officers)
Philadelphia National Bank Building
Philadelphia, PA 19107

Rubber Manufacturers Association
1901 Pennsylvania Avenue NW
Washington, DC 20006

Sales and Marketing Executives International
380 Lexington Avenue
New York, NY 10017

Sales Association of the Chemical Industry, Inc.
50 E. 41st Street
New York, NY 10017

Savings and Loan Foundation
1111 E Street NW
Washington, DC 20004

Securities Industry Association
20 Broad Street
New York, NY 10005

Service Corps of Retired Executives
1441 L Street NW
Washington, DC 20416

Silver Institute
1001 Connecticut Avenue NW
Washington, DC 20036

Society for Advancement of Management
135 W. 50th Street
New York, NY 10020

Society of Actuaries
208 S. LaSalle Street
Chicago, IL 60604

Society of Real Estate Appraisers
645 N. Michigan Avenue
Chicago, IL 60611

Specialty Equipment Market
  Association
11001 E. Valley Mall
El Monte, CA 91731

Sugar Association, Inc.
1511 K Street NW
Washington, DC 20005

Synthetic Organic Chemical Manufacturers
  Association
1075 Central Park Avenue
Scarsdale, NY 10583

Tanners' Council of America
411 Fifth Avenue
New York, NY 10016

Technical Association of the Pulp and Paper
  Industry
1 Dunwoody Park
Atlanta, GA 30338

Television Information Office
745 Fifth Avenue
New York, NY 10022

Tennessee Valley Public Power Association
831 Chestnut Street
Chattanooga, TN 37402

Textile Information Users Council
P.O. Box 7793
Greensboro, NC 27407

Tool and Die Institute
777 Busse Highway
Park Ridge, IL 60068

Toy Manufacturers of America
200 Fifth Avenue
New York, NY 10010

Transportation Association of America
1100 17th Street NW
Washington, DC 20036

Truck Body and Equipment Association
5530 Wisconsin Avenue
Washington, DC 20015

Underwriters Laboratories
207 E. Ohio Street
Chicago, IL 60611

United Fresh Fruit and Vegetable Association
N. Washington at Madison
Alexandria, VA 22314

United Press International
220 E. 42nd Street
New York, NY 10017

U.S. Council of the International
  Chamber of Commerce
1212 Avenue of the Americas
New York, NY 10036

United States League of Savings Associations
111 E. Wacker Drive
Chicago, IL 60601

U.S. Customs Information

U.S. CUSTOMS SERVICE

Headquarters: 1301 Constitution Avenue NW, Washington, DC 20229. Telephone information: 202–566–5286.

The major responsibility of the U.S. Customs Service is to administer the Tariff Act of 1930, as amended. Primary duties include the assessment and collection of all duties, taxes, and fees on imported merchandise, the enforcement of customs and related laws, and the administration of certain navigation laws and treaties. As a major enforcement organization, it engages in combating smuggling and frauds on the revenue and enforces the regulations of numerous other federal agencies at ports of entry and along the land and sea borders of the United States.

Under the President's Reorganization Plan No. 1 of 1965, the customs offices in the United States, Puerto Rico, and the Virgin Islands were reorganized into regions, districts, and port levels, headed respectively by regional commissioners of customs, district directors of customs, and port directors of customs. Regions receive primary direction from the Commissioner of Customs in Washington; while the districts and ports arranged under the nine regions derive their primary supervision from the regional commissioners.

Whenever it is suggested that you write to the district director of customs for information or a decision, the district director or port director referred to is the one at the port of entry through which your goods will be entered.

CUSTOMS REGIONS AND DISTRICTS

Region I—Boston, MA 02203
Information number: 617–223–7503
Districts:
Portland, ME 04111
St. Albans, VT 05478

Source: *Exporting to the United States*, U.S. Department of the Treasury.

Boston, MA 02109
Providence, RI 02903
Buffalo, NY 14202
Ogdensburg, NY 13669
Bridgeport, CT 06609
Region II—New York, NY 10048
Information number: 212–466–5550
Districts:
New York District, which is coextensive with the New York Region, has three administrative areas: Kennedy Airport Area, Newark Area, and New York Seaport Area.
Region III—Baltimore, MD 21202
Information number: 301–962–3288
Districts:
Philadelphia, PA 19106
Baltimore, MD 21202
Norfolk, VA 23510
Washington, DC 20018
Region IV—Miami, FL 33131
Information number: 305–350–5952
Districts:
Wilmington, NC 28401
San Juan, PR 00903
Charleston, SC 29402
Savannah, GA 31401
Tampa, FL 33601
Miami, FL 33132
St. Thomas, VI 00801
Region V—New Orleans, LA 70112
Information number: 504–589–2917
Districts:
Mobile, AL 36601
New Orleans, LA 70130
Region VI—Houston, TX 77002
Information number: 713–226–4891
Districts:
Port Arthur, TX 76640
Galveston, TX 77550
Houston, TX 77052
Laredo, TX 78040
El Paso, TX 79985
Region VII—Los Angeles, CA 90053
Information number: 213–688–5900
Districts:
Nogales, AZ 85621
San Diego, CA 92101
Los Angeles, CA 90731
San Pedro, CA 90731
Region VIII—San Francisco, CA 94105
Information number: 415–556–3500
Districts:
San Francisco, CA 94126
Honolulu, HI 96806

Portland, OR 97209
Seattle, WA 98104
Anchorage, AK 99501
Great Falls, MT 59401
Region IX—Chicago, IL 60603
Information number: 312–353–4733
Districts:
Chicago, IL 60607
Pembina, ND 58271
Minneapolis, MN 55401
Duluth, MN 55802
Milwaukee, WI 53202
Cleveland, OH 44114
St. Louis, MO 63105
Detroit, MI 48226

U.S. CUSTOMS OFFICES ABROAD

England
American Embassy
Room G94
24/32 Grosvenor Square
London, W.1
Canada
U.S. Consulate
Tour du Sud
Complex des Jardins
Montreal 45B 1G1, P.Q.

France
American Embassy Annex
58 Bis, Rue La Boetie
75008, Paris
Germany
American Embassy
Room 2069
Mehlemer Aue
53 Bonn-Bad Godesberg
Hong Kong
American Consulate General
26 Garden Road
Hong Kong
British Crown Colony
Italy
Consular Building
American Embassy
Room 302
Via Veneto 119
00187 Rome
Japan
American Embassy, Room 202
Akasaka, 1–Chome Minato-ku
Tokyo, 107
Mexico
American Embassy
Paseo de la Reforma 305
Colonia Cuahtemoc
Mexico, D.F.
Taiwan
2 Chun Hsaio West Road
Second Section
Taipei

Foreign Diplomatic Offices in the United States

The chancery is the name designating the building that houses the major components of the embassy in which the ambassador works.

A foreign consulate or embassy in the United States is where commercial, economic, and cultural information about a country can be obtained. It is also the place where an American can generally obtain a visa if one is needed for a particular country.

The State Department desk officer working at the U.S. State Department provides input for policy decisions relating to a specific country. Persons interested in doing business with a foreign country should contact the State Department desk officer (listed below) for that particular country. It is this officer who can direct him to additional sources of information at, for example, the Department of Commerce or the Agency for International Aid.

All chancery addresses in this section are, of course, in Washington, DC; all telephone numbers given in this section are in the 202 area code, unless otherwise indicated.

Afghanistan
Chancery: 2341 Wyoming Avenue, NW 20008; 234–3770.
State Department Desk Officer: 632–9552.
Albania
State Department Desk Officer: 632–1457.
Algeria
Chancery: 2118 Kalorama Road, NW 20008; 234–7246.
State Department Desk Officer: 632–0304.
Andorra
State Department Desk Officer: 632–2633.
Angola, Republic of
State Department Desk Officer: 632–0725.
Argentina
Chancery: 1600 New Hampshire Avenue, NW 20009; 387–0705.
State Department Desk Officer: 632–9166.
Australia
Chancery: 1601 Massachusetts Avenue, NW 20036; 797–3000.
State Department Desk Officer: 632–9690.

Austria
Chancery: 2343 Massachusetts Avenue, NW 20008; 483–4474.
State Department Desk Officer: 632–2005.
Bahamas, The Commonwealth of the
Chancery: Suite 865, 600 New Hampshire Avenue, NW 20037; 338–3940.
State Department Desk Officer: 632–6386.
Bahrain, State of
Chancery: 2600 Virginia Avenue, NW 20037; 342–0741.
State Department Desk Officer: 632–1794.
Bangladesh, People's Republic of
Chancery: 3421 Massachusetts Avenue, NW 20007; 337–6644.
State Department Desk Officer: 632–0466.
Barbados
Chancery: 2144 Wyoming Avenue, NW 20008; 387–7373.
State Department Desk Officer: 632–8451.
Belgium
Chancery: 3330 Garfield Street, NW 20008; 333–6900.
State Department Desk Officer: 632–0498.
Benin, Peoples Republic of
Chancery: 2737 Cathedral Avenue, NW 20008; 232–6656.
State Department Desk Officer: 632–0842.
Bhutan
State Department Desk Officer: 632–0653.
Bolivia
Chancery: 3014 Massachusetts Avenue, NW 20008; 483–4410.
State Department Desk Officer: 632–3076.
Botswana, Republic of
Chancery: Suite 404, 4301 Connecticut Avenue, NW 20008; 244–4990.
State Department Desk Officer: 632–0916.
Brazil
Chancery: 3006 Massachusetts Avenue, NW 20008; 797–0100.
State Department Desk Officer: 632–1245.
Brunei
State Department Desk Officer: 632–3276.
Bulgaria, People's Republic of
Chancery: 2100 16th Street, NW 20009; 387–7970.
State Department Desk Officer: 632—1457.
Burma, Socialist Republic of the Union of
Chancery: 2300 S Street, NW 20008; 332–9044.
State Department Desk Officer: 632–3276.

Source: "Foreign Consular Offices in the United States," "Diplomatic List," and U.S. Department of State information.

Burundi, Republic of
Chancery: 2717 Connecticut Avenue, NW 20008; 387–4477.
State Department Desk Officer: 632–3138.

Cambodia (see Khmer Republic)

Cameroon, United Republic of
Chancery: 2349 Massachusetts Avenue, NW 20008; 265–8790.
State Department Desk Officer: 632–0996.

Canada
Chancery: 1746 Massachusetts Avenue, NW 20036; 785–1400.
State Department Desk Officer: 632–2170.

Cape Verde, Republic of
Chancery: 1120 Connecticut Avenue, NW 20036; 659–3148.
State Department Desk Officer: 632–8436.

Central African Empire
Chancery: 1618 22d Street NW 20008; 265–5637.
State Department Desk Officer: 632–3138.

Ceylon (see Sri Lanka)

Chad, Republic of
Chancery: 2600 Virginia Avenue, NW 20037; 331–7697.
State Department Desk Officer: 632–3066.

Chile
Chancery: 1732 Massachusetts Avenue, NW 20036; 785–1746.
State Department Desk Officer: 632–2575.

China, People's Republic of
Embassy: 2300 Connecticut Avenue, NW 20008; 797–9000 (as of March 1, 1979).
State Department Desk Officer: 632–1004.

Colombia
Chancery: 2118 Leroy Place, NW 20008; 387–8338.
State Department Desk Officer: 632–3023.

Comores, The
Chancery: The Comores interests in the United States are represented by Tanzania, 2010 Massachusetts Avenue, NW 20036; 872–1005.
State Department Desk Officer: 632–0668.

Congo (Brazzaville)
Chancery: (temp.): 14 E. 65 Street, New York, NY 10021; 212–744–7840.
State Department Desk Officer: 632–0725.

Congo (Kinshasa) (see Zaire)

Costa Rica
Chancery: 2112 S Street, NW 20008; 234–2945.
State Department Desk Officer: 632–3385.

Cuba
Chancery: Cuba's interests in the United States are represented by Czechoslovakia.
State Department Desk Officer: 632–1476.

Cyprus
Chancery: 2211 R Street, NW 20008; 462–5772.
State Department Desk Officer: 632–1429.

Czechoslovakia
Chancery: 3900 Linnean Avenue, NW 20008; 363–6315.
State Department Desk Officer: 632–1457.

Dahomey (see Benin)

Denmark
Chancery: 3200 Whitehaven Street, NW 20008; 234–4300.
State Department Desk Officer: 632–1774.

Dominican Republic
Chancery: 1715 22d Street, NW 20008; 332–6280.
State Department Desk Officer: 632–3447.

Ecuador
Chancery: 2535 15th Street, NW 20009; 234–7200.
State Department Desk Officer: 632–5864.

Egypt, Arab Republic of
Chancery: 2310 Decatur Place, NW 20008; 232–5400.
State Department Desk Officer: 632–2365.

El Salvador
Chancery: 2308 California Street, NW 20008; 265–3480.
State Department Desk Officer: 632–8148.

Equatorial Guinea
Chancery: Equatorial Guinea's interests in the United States are represented by Cameroon, 2349 Massachusetts Avenue, NW 20008; 265–8790.
State Department Desk Officer: 632–0996.

Estonia, Legation of
Consulate General's Office: 9 Rockefeller Plaza, New York, NY 10020; (212) 247–1450.
State Department Desk Officer: 632–1739.

Ethiopia
Chancery: 2134 Kalorama Road 20008; 234–2281.
State Department Desk Officer: 632–3355.

Fiji
Chancery: Suite 520, 1629 K Street, NW 20006; 296–3928.
State Department Desk Officer: 632–3546.

Finland
Chancery: 3216 New Mexico Avenue, NW 20016; 363–2430.
State Department Desk Officer: 363–0624.

France
Chancery: 2535 Belmont Road, NW 20008; 234–0990.
State Department Desk Officer: 632–1412.

Gabon, Republic of
Chancery: 2034 20th Street, NW 20009; 797–1000.
State Department Desk Officer: 632–0996.

Gambia, The Republic of
Chancery: 1785 Massachusetts Avenue, NW 20036; 265–3252.
State Department Desk Officer: 632–2865.

German Democratic Republic (East)
Chancery: 1717 Massachusetts Avenue, NW 20036; 232–3134.
State Department Desk Officer: 632–2721.

Germany, Federal Republic of (West)
Chancery: 4645 Reservoir Road, NW 20007; 298–4000.
State Department Desk Officer: 632–2155.

Ghana
Chancery: 2460 16th Street, NW 20009; 462–0761.
State Department Desk Officer: 632–8436.

Great Britain
Chancery: 3100 Massachusetts Avenue, NW 20008; 462–1340.
State Department Desk Officer: 632–2622.

Greece
Chancery: 2221 Massachusetts Avenue, NW 20008; 667–3168.
State Department Desk Officer: 632–1563.

Grenada
Chancery: 1424 16th Street, NW 20005; 265–2561.
State Department Desk Officer: 632–8451.

Guatemala
Chancery: 2220 R Street, NW 20008; 332–2865.
State Department Desk Officer: 632–0467.

Guinea
Chancery: 2112 Leroy Place, NW 20008; 483–9420.
State Department Desk Officer: 632–0842.

Guinea-Bissau
Chancery: c/o Permanent Mission of Guinea-Bissau to the United Nations, Suite 604, 211 E. 43rd Street, New York, NY 10017; (212) 661–3977.
State Department Desk Officer: 632–8436.

Guyana
Chancery: 2490 Tracy Place, NW 20008; 265–6900.
State Department Desk Officer: 632–3449.

Haiti
Chancery: 4400 17th Street, NW 20011; 723–7000.
State Department Desk Officer: 632–3447.

Honduras
Chancery: Suite 408, 4301 Connecticut Avenue NW 20008; 966–7700.
State Department Desk Officer: 632–3385.

Hungary
Chancery: 3910 Shoemaker Street, NW 20008; 362–6730.
State Department Desk Officer: 632–1739.

Iceland
Chancery: 2022 Connecticut Avenue, NW 20008; 265–6653.
State Department Desk Officer: 632–1774.

India
Chancery: 2107 Massachusetts Avenue, NW 20008; 265–5050.
State Department Desk Officer: 632–1289.

Indonesia
Chancery: 2020 Massachusetts Avenue, NW 20036; 293–1745.
State Department Desk Officer: 632–3276.

Iran
Chancery: 3005 Massachusetts Avenue, NW 20008; 797–6500.
State Department Desk Officer: 632–0313.

Iraq
An Iraqi Interests Section is located in the Embassy of India at 1801 P Street, NW 20036; 483–7500.
State Department Desk Officer: 632–0695.

Ireland
Chancery: 2234 Massachusetts Avenue, NW 20008; 462–3939.
State Department Desk Officer: 632–1194.

Israel
Chancery: 1621 22d Street, NW 20008; 483–4100.
State Department Desk Officer: 632–3672.

Italy
Chancery: 1601 Fuller Street, NW 20009; 328–5500.
State Department Desk Officer: 632–2453.

Ivory Coast
Chancery: 2424 Massachusetts Avenue, NW 20008; 483–2400.
State Department Desk Officer: 632–0842.

Jamaica
Chancery: 1666 Connecticut Avenue, NW 20009; 387–1010.
State Department Desk Officer: 632–6386.

Japan
Chancery: 2520 Massachusetts Avenue, NW 20008; 234–2266.
State Department Desk Officer: 632–3152.

Jordan
Chancery: 2319 Wyoming Avenue, NW 20008; 265–1606.
State Department Desk Officer: 632–0791.

Kenya
Chancery: 2249 R Street, NW 20009; 387–6101.
State Department Desk Officer: 632–0857.

Khmer Republic (Cambodia)
State Department Desk Officer: 632–3132.

Korea, North and South
State Department Desk Officer: 632–7717.

Korea, Republic of
Chancery: 2320 Massachusetts Avenue, NW 20008; 483–7383.
State Department Desk Officer: 632–7717.

Kuwait
Chancery: 2940 Tilden Street, NW 20008; 966–0702.
State Department Desk Officer: 632–1334.

Laos
Chancery: 2222 S Street, NW 20008; 332–6416.
State Department Desk Officer: 632–3132.

Latvia
Chancery: 4325 17th Street, NW 20011; 726–8213.
State Department Desk Officer: 632–1739.
Lebanon
Chancery: 2560 28th Street, NW 20008; 462–8600.
State Department Desk Officer: 632–1018.
Lesotho
Chancery: Suite 300, Caravel Building, 1601 Connecticut Avenue, NW 20009; 462–4190.
State Department Desk Officer: 632–0916.
Liberia
Chancery: 5201 16th Street, NW 20011; 723–0437.
State Department Desk Officer: 632–8354.
Libya
Chancery: 1118 22d Street, NW 20037; 452–1290.
State Department Desk Officer: 632–9373.
Liechtenstein
State Department Desk Officer: 632–2005.
Lithuania
Chancery: 2622 16th Street, NW 20009; 234–5860.
State Department Desk Officer: 632–1739.
Luxembourg
Chancery: 2200 Massachusetts Avenue, NW 20008; 265–4171.
State Department Desk Officer: 632–0498.
Madagascar, Democratic Republic of
Chancery: 2374 Massachusetts Avenue, NW 20008; 265–5525.
State Department Desk Officer: 632–3040.
Malawi
Chancery: 1400 20th Street, NW 20036; 296–5530.
State Department Desk Officer: 632–8851.
Malaysia
Chancery: 2401 Massachusetts Avenue, NW 20008; 234–7600.
State Department Desk Officer: 632–3276.
Maldive, Republic of
State Department Desk Officer: 632–2351.
Mali
Chancery: 2130 R Street, NW 20008; 332–2249.
State Department Desk Officer: 632–2865.
Malta
Chancery: 2017 Connecticut Avenue, NW 20008; 462–3611.
State Department Desk Officer: 632–1726.
Mauritania
Chancery: 2129 Leroy Place, NW 20008; 232–5700.
State Department Desk Officer: 632–2865.
Mauritius
Chancery: Suite 134, 4301 Connecticut Avenue, NW 20008; 244–1491.
State Department Desk Officer: 632–3040.

Mexico
Chancery: 2829 16th Street, NW 20009; 234–6000.
State Department Desk Officer: 632–9364.
Morocco
Chancery: 1601 21st Street, NW 20009; 462–7979.
State Department Desk Officer: 632–0279.
Nepal
Chancery: 2131 Leroy Place, NW 20008; 667–4550.
State Department Desk Officer: 632–0653.
Netherlands
Chancery: 4200 Linnean Avenue, NW 20008; 244–5300.
State Department Desk Officer: 632–0498.
New Zealand
Chancery: 37 Observatory Circle, NW 20008; 328–4800.
State Department Desk Officer: 632–6386.
Nicaragua
Chancery: 1627 New Haupshire Avenue, NW 20009; 387–4371.
State Department Desk Officer: 632–2205.
Niger
Chancery: 2204 R Street, NW 20008; 483–4224.
State Department Desk Officer: 632–3066.
Nigeria
Chancery: 2201 M Street, NW 20037; 223–9300.
State Department Desk Officer: 632–3406 and 632–3468.
Northern Rhodesia (see Zambia)
Norway
Chancery: 2720 34th Street, NW 20008; 333–6000.
State Department Desk Officer: 632–1774.
Oman
Chancery: 2342 Massachusetts Avenue, NW 20008; 387–1980.
State Department Desk Officer: 632–1334.
Pakistan
Chancery: 2315 Massachusetts Avenue, NW 20008; 332–8330.
State Department Desk Officer: 632–9823.
Panama
Chancery: 2862 McGill Terrace, NW 20008; 483–4986.
State Department Desk Officer: 632–4980.
Papua New Guinea
Chancery: 1800 K Street, NW 20008; 659–0856.
State Department Desk Officer: 632–3546.
Paraguay
Chancery: 2400 Massachusetts Avenue, NW 20008; 483–6960.
State Department Desk Officer: 632–1551.
Peru
Chancery: 1700 Massachusetts Avenue, NW 20036; 833–9860.
State Department Desk Officer: 632–3360.

Philippines
Chancery: 1617 Massachusetts Avenue, NW 20036; 483–1414.
State Department Desk Officer: 632–1669.
Poland
Chancery: 2640 16th Street, NW 20009; 234–3800.
State Department Desk Officer: 632–3191.
Portugal
Chancery: 2125 Kalorama Road, NW 20008; 265–1643.
State Department Desk Officer: 632–0719.
Qatar
Chancery: Suite 1180, 600 New Hampshire Avenue, NW 20037; 338–0111.
State Department Desk Officer: 632–1794.
Rumania
Chancery: 1607 23d Street, NW 20008; 232–4747.
State Department Desk Officer: 632–3298.
Embassy at Washington, DC, has charge of the interests of Romanian nationals in the United States.
Rwanda
Chancery: 1714 New Hampshire Avenue, NW 20009; 232–2882.
State Department Desk Officer: 632–3138.
Samoa (see Western Samoa)
San Marino
State Department Desk Officer: 632–2453.
Sao Tome e Principe
State Department Desk Officer: 632–0996.
Saudi Arabia
Chancery: 1520 18th Street, NW 20036; 483–2100.
State Department Desk Officer: 632–0865.
Senegal
Chancery: 2112 Wyoming Avenue, NW 20008; 234–0540.
State Department Desk Officer: 632–2865.
Sierra Leone
Chancery: 1701 19th Street, NW 20009; 265–7700.
State Department Desk Officer: 632–8354.
Singapore
Chancery: 1824 R Street, NW 20009; 667–7555.
State Department Desk Officer: 632–3276.
Somalia
Chancery: Suite 710, 600 New Hampshire Avenue, NW 20037; 234–3261.
State Department Desk Officer: 632–0849.
South Africa, Republic of
Chancery: 3051 Massachusetts Avenue, NW 20008; 232–4400.
State Department Desk Officer: 632–3274.
Southern Rhodesia
State Department Desk Officer: 632–8252.
Spain
Chancery: 2700 15th Street, NW 20009; 265–0190.
State Department Desk Officer: 632–2633.

Spanish Guinea (see Equatorial Guinea)
Sri Lanka (Ceylon)
Chancery: 2148 Wyoming Avenue, NW 20008; 483–4025.
State Department Desk Officer: 632–2351.
Sudan
Chancery: Suite 400, 600 New Hampshire Avenue, NW 20037; 338–8565.
State Department Desk Officer: 632–0668.
Suriname, Republic of
Chancery: 2600 Virginia Avenue, NW 20037; 338–6980.
State Department Desk Officer: 632–3449.
Swaziland
Chancery: 4301 Connecticut Avenue, NW 20008; 362–6683.
State Department Desk Officer: 632–0916.
Sweden
Chancery: Suite 1200, 600 New Hampshire Avenue, NW 20037; 298–3500.
State Department Desk Officer: 632–0624.
Switzerland
Chancery: 2900 Cathedral Avenue, NW 20008; 462–1811.
State Department Desk Officer: 632–2005.
Syria
Chancery: 2215 Wyoming Avenue, NW 20008; 232–6313.
State Department Desk Officer: 632–4714.
Taiwan
The Coordination Council for North American Affairs (CCNA), 4301 Connecticut Avenue, NW 20010; 686–6400.
State Department Desk Officer: 657–2130.
Tanzania
Chancery: 2139 R Street, NW 20008; 232–0501.
State Department Desk Officer: 632–3040.
Thailand
Chancery: 2300 Kalorama Road, NW 20008; 667–1446.
State Department Desk Officer: 632–3276.
Togo
Chancery: 2208 Massachusetts Avenue, NW 20008; 234–4212.
State Department Desk Officer: 632–0842.
Tonga
State Department Desk Officer: 632–3546.
Trinidad and Tobago
Chancery: 1708 Massachusetts Avenue, NW 20036; 467–6490.
State Department Desk Officer: 632–3449.
Tunisia
Chancery: 2408 Massachusetts Avenue, NW 20008; 234–6644.
State Department Desk Officer: 632–3614.
Turkey
Chancery: 1606 23d Street, NW 20008; 667–6400.
State Department Desk Officer: 632–1562.

Uganda
Chancery: 5909 16th Street, NW 20011; 726–7100.
State Department Desk Officer: 632–0857.
Union of Soviet Socialist Republics
Chancery: 1125 16th Street, NW 20036; 628–7551.
State Department Desk Officer: 632–8671.
United Arab Emirates
Chancery: Suite 740, 600 New Hampshire Avenue, NW 20037; 338–6500.
State Department Desk Officer: 632–1794.
Upper Volta
Chancery: 5500 16th Street, NW 20011; 726–0992.
State Department Desk Officer: 632–3066.
Uruguay
Chancery: 1918 F Street, NW 20006; 331–1313.
State Department Desk Officer: 632–1551.
Vatican City
Apostolic Delegation (to U.S. Catholic Church): 3339 Massachusetts Avenue, NW 20008.
State Department Desk Officer: 632–8210.
Venezuela
Chancery: 2445 Massachusetts Avenue, NW 20008; 797–3800.
State Department Desk Officer: 632–3338.
Vietnam
State Department Desk Officer: 632–3132.
Western Samoa
Chancery: (temp.): Care of Permanent Mission of Samoa to the United Nations: 820 Second Avenue, Room 303, New York, NY 10017; 212–682–1482.
State Department Desk Officer: 632–3546.
Yemen Arab Republic
Chancery: Suite 860, 600 New Hampshire Avenue, NW 20037; 965–4760.
State Department Desk Officer: 632–3121.
Yemen, People's Democratic Republic of
State Department Desk Officer: 632–3121.

Yugoslavia
Chancery: 2410 California Street, NW 20008; 462–6566.
State Department Desk Officer: 632–3655.
Zaire, Republic of
Chancery: 1800 New Hampshire Avenue, NW 20009; 234–7690.
State Department Desk Officer: 632–2216.
Zambia, Republic of
Chancery: 2419 Massachusetts Avenue, NW 20008; 265–9717.
State Department Desk Officer: 632–8851.

INTERNATIONAL ORGANIZATIONS: STATE DEPARTMENT DESK OFFICE TELEPHONE NUMBERS

East African Community	632–2491
East-West Center	632–0896
Economic and Social Commission for Asia and the Pacific	632–1654
Economic Commission for Africa	632–1654
Economic Commission for Europe (ECE)	632–0315
Economic Commission of Latin America	632–1654
European Atomic Energy Commission (EURATOM)	632–0315
European Coal and Steel Community (ECSC)	632–1708
European Communities	632–1708
European Economic Community	632–1708
European Free Trade Association	632–0457
European Launcher Development Organization (ELDO)	632–0315
European Programs	632–9246
European Space Research Organization (ESRO)	632–0315
Organization for Economic Cooperation and Development	632–0326

Index

A

A&P, 34
Accounting Principles Board (APB)
  opinions, 77–78
  statements, 77
Accounting Research Bulletins (ARB), 77
Advertising
  expenditures by industry, 324–25
  50 top agencies, 326
  market areas of dominant influence ranked by TV, 327–30
  top 100 national advertisers, 322–23
Afghanistan, 1
Agriculture, Department of, 180–81
Air fares, 12, 22, 25, 40
Air Force, Department of, 176
Aircraft industry, financial statements in ratio format, 116–19
Alabama, state information guide, 482
Algeria
  business information, 524
  oil prices, 9
Aluminum industry, 14, 31
  labor contract, 29
Aluminum Company of America (ALCOA), 33
American Accounting Association (AAA), 76
American Broadcasting Company, 41
American Institute of Certified Public Accountants (AICPA), 76
American Motors Company, 11, 21, 34, 37, 44
American Natural Resources, 37
American Telephone and Telegraph Company, 39, 41
Antitrust Division (Department of Justice), 55–56
Antitrust legislation, 42
Arab Republic of Egypt, business information, 524–25
Arizona, state information guide, 483–84
Arkansas, state information guide, 484
Army, Department of, 175–76
Auto-leasing, 40
Automated Data and Telecommunications Services (ADTS), 177–78
Automobile industry
  competition, 8
  environmental regulations, 35
  federal aid, 35
  FTC investigation of defects, 8, 39
  imports, 25
  plant closings, 26, 28, 30, 32
  production, 1, 7, 12, 18, 19, 23, 27, 30, 42
  sales; see Car sales
Automobile parts suppliers, 33

B

Bache Halsey, 14, 17, 19, 29
Bahrain, business information, 524
Balance of payments, U.S., 15, 44
Balance sheet, 80–83
  ratios, 86–87
Bank cards, 12
Bank interest rates, 10
Banks
  financing exports, 435
  investments, 298–99
  lending terms, 284–85
  loans, 11, 13, 298–99
  reserves, 298–99
  300 largest commercial by states, 314–17
  25 largest commercial outside U.S., 312–13
  25 largest U.S. commercial, 310–11
Bankers Trust, 37
Bethlehem Steel, 9, 34, 36
Big Eight Accounting Firms, 76

Boeing, 16, 24
Bond market, 6, 8, 9, 10, 19, 20, 25, 28–29, 35, 38
Bonds
  corporate; see Corporate bonds
  government; see Government bonds
  investment returns on, 226–29
Bonneville Power Administration, 185
British pound, 30
Broadcast Bureau, 59
Brokerage firms, 36
Budget, federal
  deficit, 17, 31
  spending cuts, 37
Budgets for profit planning, 162–67
Building contracts, 17, 36, 39
Bulgaria, business information, 523
Bureau of Biologics, 66
Bureau of Drugs, 66
Bureau of Foods, 67
Bureau of Indian Affairs, 185
Bureau of Land Management, 185
Bureau of Medical Devices, 67
Bureau of Mines, 184
Bureau of Prisons, 185–86
Bureau of Radiological Health, 67
Bureau of Reclamation, 185
Business information directory
  corporate information, 471
  Department of Commerce sources, 478–81
  economic indicators, 472–73
  federal government developments, 471–72
  general sources, 470
  index publications, 472
  international; see International trade information sources
  state guides, 482–510
  useful contacts, 474–77
Business International, 520
Business inventories, 4, 9, 19–20, 31, 36, 40, 42
Business loans, 1
Business sales and inventories, 426–27
Business Services Directory, 191–93
Business spending, 3
Business and Trade Organizations, 528–36

C

Cable television, 37, 59
California, state information guide, 484–85
California Federal Savings, 33
Campbell Soup Company, 30
Canada
  commercial paper rates, 18
  interest rates, 18
Capital markets, 29
Capital spending, 14, 43
Car dealers, 34
Car sales, 2, 4, 5, 7, 9, 11, 12, 14, 16, 18, 20, 21, 24, 25, 28, 30, 37, 43, 44
Center for Disease Control, 183
Chain stores, 19, 24, 36
Changes over the life of the agreement, 355
Chase Manhattan Bank, 15, 17, 20, 21, 30, 40–41
Chemical Bank, 18, 39
Chemical industry, financial statements in ratio format, 100–103
Chicago White Sox, 40
China, business information, 522
Chrysler Corporation, 9
  layoffs, 21
  loans, 8, 19, 23, 31, 33, 36, 42
  losses, 24, 38
  marketing program, 5

Chrysler Corporation—*Cont.*
  recalls, 20
  sales, 7, 16, 18, 26, 37
  union bargaining, 1, 2
Citibank, 16, 19, 25, 32
Cities Service, 38
Clay industry, income statements in ratio format, 108–11
Clayton Act, 66
Clayton Brokerage, 41
"Clones", 16
Coal industry, financial statements in ratio format, 104–7
Colorado, state information guide, 485–86
Columbia Broadcasting Company, 41
Commerce, Department of, 181–82, 511–17
Commerce Action Group for the Near East (CAGNE), 524
Commerce Clearing House, 520
Commercial banks; *see* Banks
Commercial paper
  Moody's ratings, 291–92
  rates, U.S. and Canada, 450
  Standard and Poor ratings, 288
Commodities
  Dow Jones Index, 276
  monthly average spot price charts, 268–74
  trading, 20
Commodities Futures Trading Commission, 266
Commodity Exchanges, 267
Common Carrier Bureau, 60
Common stocks
  cash dividends and yields, 234
  50 leading stocks in market value, 242
  investment returns, 226–29
  price ratio scales, 275
  prices and yields, 198–99
  shares sold on registered exchanges, 235
Commonwealth Edison, 29
Computer equipment companies, 2
Congressional Budget Act of 1974, 416
Connecticut, state information guide, 486
Conoco, 38
Constant Dollar Dow, 205
Construction, 23, 33, 38–39, 42
  new construction, 425
  private housing, 424–25
Consumer credit, 2, 8, 13, 19, 24, 35, 39
Consumer Credit Protection Act, 64–65
Consumer installment credit, 2, 306–7
Consumer Price Index, 5, 228–29, 366, 367
  U.S. city average, 369–82
Consumer prices, 6, 16, 21, 37, 41, 44, 380–81
Consumer Product Safety Commission (CPSC), 56
Copper, 5, 9
Corn
  crop estimates, 39
  prices, 3
Corporate bonds
  foreign yields, 455
  investment returns, 226–29
  Moody's ratings, 290
  Standard and Poor's ratings, 287–88
Corporate profit, 15, 20, 26, 40, 400–401
Corporate-takeover, 10
Corporations
  new security issues, 301
  100 largest in U.S., 144–49
  100 largest outside U.S., 150–53
Cost Accounting Standards Board (CASB), 76
Credit
  consumer, 2, 8, 13, 19, 24, 35, 39
  demand, 1
  Federal Reserve policies, 2, 4, 8, 14, 16, 18, 20, 31, 34, 43, 44
  restrictions, 27
Credit cards, 12, 13, 15, 16, 20
Credit controls, 12, 16, 18, 20, 27, 34
Credit markets, U.S., funds raised, 302–4
Crocker National Bank of San Francisco, 20, 36

Crown-Zellerbach, 17
Customs information
  regions and districts, 537–38
  U.S. Customs Service, 537
  U.S. offices abroad, 538
Czechoslovakia, business information, 523

D

Dart Industries, 30
Debt ceiling, 12
Defense, Department of, 175
  surplus property sales, 190–91
Defense Logistics Agency, 176–77
Defense spending, 6
Delaware, state information guide, 486–87
Delta airlines, 38
Department store sales, 13
Direct costing, 168
Dodge, F. W., Company, 17, 36
Dollars, 1, 8, 10, 11, 13, 14, 16, 19, 24, 25, 28, 30, 31, 36
  price ratio scale, 275
Dow Jones Commodity Index, 276
Dow Jones Industrial averages, 2, 11, 14, 21, 28, 37, 39, 44
Dow Jones Industrial Transportation and Utility Averages, 202–4
Drug Enforcement Administration (DEA), 186
Drug industry, financial statements in ratio format, 100–103
Dun and Bradstreet, 520
Durable goods orders, 5, 26, 37, 41

E

Earnings, 348–51
  by industry, 350–51
Economic growth, 4, 10, 11, 15, 43
  downturn, 32, 33
Economic indicators, 1, 6, 34, 38, 42
  composite indexes and components, 383
  current data, 384–91
  developed countries, 456–62
  how to follow, 472–73
  selected business statistics, 392–93
Economic Regulatory Administration, 56
Effective wage-rate adjustments, 355
Egypt, business information, 524–25
Electrical and electronic equipment industry, financial statements in ratio format, 112–15
Employee Retirement Income Security Act of 1974 (ERISA), 69, 133
Employment, 7
  by industry, division and major manufacturing group, 344–45
  labor force status, 340–41
  nonagricultural, 346–47
  by sex, age and race, 418–19
Energy, Department of, 182–83
Energy conservation, 7
Energy legislation, 27, 33–34
Energy Research Development Administration, 182–83
Engelhard Minerals, 17
Environmental Protection Agency (EPA), 57–58, 187–88
Equal Opportunity Employment Commission (EEOC), 58–59
Equibank, 5
Europa Year Book, 520
Export-Import Bank (Eximbank), 435, 518
Export management companies, 435
Exports
  financing, 435
  to Soviet Union, 41
Express mail delivery, 20
Exxon, 3, 16, 21, 22, 31

F

Fabricated metal industry, financial statements in ratio format, 112–15
Factoring houses, 435

Factory operations, 15, 20, 32
Factory orders, 1, 7, 17, 29, 34
Fair Credit Reporting Act, 65
Farm prices, 1, 23, 29
Fast Match Chart, 527
Fastest growing small companies, 156–61
Federal Aviation Administration, 187
Federal budget, 414–15
   Congressional Budget Act of 1974, 416
   receipts, outlays and debts, 430–33
Federal Bureau of Investigation (FBI), 186
Federal Communications Commission (FCC), 59–61
Federal Energy Regulatory Commission, 57
Federal Highway Administration, 187
Federal Home Loan Bank Board, 16, 18, 22, 27
Federal Maritime Commission (FMC), 61–62
Federal National Mortgage Association, 39
Federal Preparedness Agency, 191
Federal Prison Industries, Inc., 185–86
Federal Railroad Administration, 187
Federal Reserve Board, 1
   bank reserves regulation, 13
   credit policies, 2, 4, 8, 14, 16, 18, 20, 31, 34, 43, 44
   discount rate, 24, 27, 28, 32
   member banks, 7
   money supply expansion, 10
   moratorium on foreign purchase of U.S. banks, 35
   regulatory powers expanded, 17
Federal Supply Service, 179–80
Federal Trade Commission (FTC), 62–66
Financial Accounting Standards Board (FASB), 25, 76
   statements, 78–79
   No. 33, 91
Financial companies, 25 largest diversified, 318–19
Financial Executives Institute (FEI), 76
Financial statements, 80–94
   analysis of, 85–94
   balance sheet, 80–83
      ratios, 86–87
   independent accountant report, 89–91
   income statements, 83–84
      ratios, 87–88
   inflation accounting, 91–93
   ratios by industry, 95–123
   segment information, 90, 91
   statements of accumulated retained earnings, 84
      ratios, 88–89
   statement of source and application of funds, 84–85
      ratios, 89
   ten-year financial summary, 93–94
Financial statement ratios by industry, 95–123
Financial terms, dictionary of, 246–65
Financing, 124
   plant expansion, 172–73
Finished goods prices, 3
Firestone, 28
First National Bank of Boston, 31
First National Bank of Chicago, 29
First National Bank in Dallas, 22
First Pennsylvania Corporation, 29
First-year wage settlement, 355
Fish and Wildlife Service, 185
Flood Insurance Administration, 184
Florida, state information guide, 487
Food industry, financial statements in ratio format, 96–99
Food and Drug Administration (FDA), 66–68, 183
Food prices, 40
Ford Motor Company, 1, 33, 36
   car prices, 1, 23
   layoffs, 22
   losses, 11, 25, 38
   plant closings, 3, 5, 7, 14
   recall, 31
   sales, 4, 9, 16, 18, 21, 26, 37
Foreign Credit Insurance Association (FCIA), 435
Foreign diplomatic offices in the United States, 539–44
Foreign investment in U.S., 41

Foreign securities listed on New York Stock Exchange, 232
Foreign trade of the United States, 440
Forest product industry, 17
Fuel conservation, 7
Fuel oil
   home heating, 3
   prices, 16
Fur Products Labeling Act, 65

G

Garnac Grain, 41
Gasoline
   prices, 15, 35, 38, 44
   rationing, 38
   sales, 41
   supply, 27
General Agreement on Trade and Tariffs (GATT), 520
General Dynamics, 16
General Electric Company, 40
General Motors Acceptance Corporation, 21
General Motors Corporation
   dividend cut, 24
   earnings, 21
   electric-powered cars, 35
   layoffs, 22
   new plant construction, 7
   plant closing, 8
   prices, 34
   safety investigation, 31
   sales, 4, 9, 18, 25, 37
   stock prices, 44
General Services Administration, 177–80
   surplus property sales, 190
Geological survey, 184
Georgia, state information guide, 487–88
Germany, East (German Democratic Republic), business information, 523–24
Getty Oil, 37, 38
GK Technologies, 35
Glass industry, financial statements in ratio format, 108–11
Gold
   discovery, 41
   prices, 1, 3, 4, 5, 6, 8, 9, 10, 11, 13, 14, 15, 19, 27, 28, 30, 31, 34, 36, 39, 42, 43
   ratio scale, 275
Gould, Inc., 34
Government bonds
   investment returns on, 226–29
   long-term yields, 226–29, 452–54
Grain
   price supports, 38
   prices, 2
   shipments to Russia, 2, 4, 32–33
Grand Metropolitan, 24
Gross domestic product, 462
Gross national product, 44, 394–99
   changes in measures, 398
   by country, 463–69
   implicit price deflation, 397
   selected components, 399
Gross private domestic investment, 402–3
Guided missile industry, financial statements in ratio format, 116–19
Gulf Oil Company, 38

H

Hawaii, state information guide, 488
Health, Education and Welfare, Department of, 183–84
Health Services Administration, 183
Home heating oil, 3
Home sales, 24, 31, 35, 39, 42
Honda, 3
Hostages in Iran, 9
Hotel Conquistador, Inc., 3
Household Finance, 20

Housing, 2
  new construction, 424–25
  prices, 2
  starts, 10, 15, 20, 36, 39, 40, 44
  vacancy rates, 424
Housing and Urban Development, Department of, 184
Hungary, business information, 524
Hunt brothers, 16, 17, 19, 22, 23, 28, 32, 40

I

Idaho, state information guide, 488–89
Illinois, state information guide, 489
Income statement, 83–84
  ratios, 87
India, 32
Indiana, state information guide, 489–90
Indiana Standard, 3, 9
Indonesia, oil prices, 26
Industrial corporations
  100 fastest growing small companies, 156–61
  100 largest in U.S., 144–49
  100 largest outside U.S., 150–53
Industrial production, 4, 20, 32, 34, 43
  developed countries, 458–59
  major market groups and selected manufacturers,
    422–23
Inflation, 10, 13, 23, 25, 26, 27, 30, 37
  anti-inflation legislation, 14
Inflation accounting, 91–93
Interest rates, 2, 12, 29, 30, 35, 38, 39–40, 42, 43
  bank, 10
  bond yields, 278–79
  capital markets, 280–81
  prime, 10, 11, 14, 15, 17, 18, 19, 21, 22, 26, 28,
    33, 37, 40, 283
  short term, 15, 21, 23, 34, 41, 451
  time and savings deposits, 282–83
Interior, Department of, 184–85
Internal Revenue Service, 9
International Monetary Fund, 519
International Reports, 520
International trade information sources
  business information directory, 521–26
  Business International, 520
  Commerce Clearing House, 520
  credit information, 521
  Department of Commerce, 511–17
  Dun and Bradstreet, 520
  Europa Year Book, 520
  Export-Import Bank, 518
  Fast Match, 527
  General Agreement on Trade and Tariffs, 520
  International Monetary Fund, 519
  International Reports, 520
  Jane's Major Companies of Europe, 520
  Organization for Economic Cooperation and De-
    velopment, 519–20
  Overseas Private Investment Corporation, 518
  United Nations, 518–19
  United States Department of State, 517
  United States Export Development Offices, 517
  United States International Trade Commission, 517–
    18
International trade, totals, 460–61
International transactions, U.S., 436–39
Interstate Commerce Commission (ICC), 68
Investment Advisers Act of 1940, 73
Investment Company Act of 1940, 72
Investment terms, dictionary of, 246–65
Iowa, state information guide, 489–90
Iran
  freezing of assets, 8
  petrochemical project, 24
  U.S. hostages, 9
Iraq
  business information, 525
  oil prices, 6, 33
Iron industry, financial statements in ratio format,
  108–11
Israel, business information, 525

J–K

Jane's Major Companies of Europe, 520
Japan
  auto imports to U.S., 6, 25
  business information, 521–22
Jordan, business information, 525
Justice, Department of, 185–86
K-mart, 13, 19
Kaiser Aluminum, 24
Kansas, state information guide, 490–91
Kentucky, state information guide, 491
Kodak, 9
Kraft, 30
Kuwait
  business information, 525
  Getty Oil deal, 37
  oil prices, 6, 23

L

Labor costs, 447
Labor management data, 355
Labor Management Reporting and Disclosure Act,
  69–70
Labor-Management Services Administration (LMSA),
  69–70
Lebanon, business information, 525
Legislation enacted, 51–54
Libya
  business information, 525
  oil prices, 26
Life insurance companies, 308–9
  25 largest, 320–21
Liggett, 24
Limited partnership, 126–27, 137
Liquid assets, 294–95
Lockheed, 25
Louisiana, state information guide, 491–92
Lower-of-cost-or-market accounting, 9

M

McGraw Hill, 36
Machine tool industry, 27
Magazines, circulation, 331–32
Mail rates, 34
Maine, state information guide, 492
Manufacturers Hanover, 29
Manufacturing
  shipments, inventories and orders, 428–29
  unit labor costs and productivity, 477
Margin requirements, 233
Maritime Administration, 182
Market areas of dominant influence ranked by TV
  households, 327–30
Maryland, state information guide, 493
Massachusetts, state information guide, 493
Merrill Lynch, 40
Merrill Lynch Ready Assets Trust, 15
Mexico
  natural gas prices, 17
  oil reserves, 4
MGM, 29
Michigan, state information guide, 493–94
Midland Bank, Ltd, 36
Military procurement programs, 175
Minnesota, state information guide, 494–95
Mining Enforcement and Safety Administration, 184–
  85
Mining industry, financial statements in ratio format,
  120–23
Mississippi, state information guide, 495
Missouri, state information guide, 495
Mitsubishi, 415
Mitsui & Company, 24
Mobil Oil, 9, 38
Mobile homes, 14
Monetary aggregates, newly defined, 141–43
Money, income velocity of, 296
Money market, 25
  bond equivalent yield on short term instruments,
    449
  interest rates, 15, 20

Money-market funds, 14–15, 16, 21
Money stock, 294–95
Money supply, 3, 4, 5, 7, 33
  new definitions, 8, 141
Money supply data, 141–43
Montana, state information guide, 496
Montgomery Ward, 13, 19, 24
Moody's ratings
  commercial paper, 291–92
  corporate bonds, 290
  municipal bonds, 289
  preferred stock, 291
  short-term loan ratings, 289–90
Morgan Guaranty Trust, 22, 37
Morocco, business information, 525
Mortgages, 2, 8, 13, 18, 19, 24, 25, 26, 33, 37, 43
  debt outstanding, 304–6
Motor vehicle equipment industry, financial statements
  in ratio format, 116–19
Mountain States Telephone, 41
Muncipal bonds
  Moody's ratings, 289
  Standard and Poor's ratings, 286–87
Mutual funds, 236–41

N

Nasdaq, 9
National Aeronautics and Space Administration
  (NASA), 188
National Association of Accountants (NAA), 76
National Association of Purchasing Management, 38,
  42
National Broadcasting Company, 41
National Bureau of Economic Research, 29
National Bureau of Standards, 182
National Center for Toxicological Research, 67
National Central Bank, 5
National income, 411–13
National Institute of Health, 183
National Oceanic and Atmospheric Administration, 182
National Park Service, 184
National Organization of State Boards of Accounting
  (NOSBA), 76
Natural gas, prices, 17
Navy, Department of, 176
Nebraska, state information guide, 496–97
Nevada, state information guide, 497
New England Telephone, 41
New Hampshire, state information guide, 497
New Jersey, state information guide, 498
New Mexico, state information guide, 498–99
New York, state information guide, 499
New York Futures Exchange, 35, 36
Nigeria, 18, 27
Nippon Steel, 9
Nissan, 3, 9, 19
Nonfarm, nonfinancial corporate business, 293
Nonferrous metal industry, financial statements in ratio
  format, 108–11
Nonfinancial corporations, 293, 297
Norfolk and Western Railway, 29
North Carolina, state information guide, 499–500
North Dakota, state information guide, 500
North Sea oil, 4

O

Occidental Petroleum, 43
Occupational Safety and Health Administration
  (OSHA), 70–71
OECD; see Organization for Economic Cooperation
  and Development
Office of Federal Contract Compliance (FCC), 71
Office of Human Development, 183
Ohio, state information guide, 500–51
Oil
  demand, 28, 33
  home heating, 3
  import fee, 25, 26, 30
  imports, 27, 40
  North Sea producers, 4

Oil—Cont.
  output, 13
  prices, 1, 2, 7, 16, 18, 32, 34, 37–38, 44
  profits, 21, 36, 37
  reduced consumption, 33
  reserves, 6
  spot prices, 1, 2
  stockpiling, 39
  windfall profits tax, 5, 8, 10, 11, 17, 18
Oklahoma, state information guide, 501–2
Oman, business information, 525
OPEC; see Organization of Petroleum Exporting Companies, 2
Oregon, state information guide, 502
Organization for Economic Cooperation and Development (OECD), 29, 30, 33, 519–20
Organization of Petroleum Exporting Companies, 1, 2,
  6, 10, 13–14, 17, 18, 25, 26, 27, 31, 34, 35,
  39, 43
Overseas Private Investment Corporation (OPIC), 518

P

Pacific Northwest Bell, 41
Pacific Telephone, 41
Pan American World Airways, Inc., 38
Paper industry, financial statements in ratio format,
  104–7
Patents on living organisms, 32
Penn Central Corporation, 35
Penney, J. C., Company, 7, 24, 26, 40
Pennsylvania, state information guide, 502–3
Pension and welfare plans, 25, 69
  multiemployer legislation, 44
Personal consumption expenditures, 410
Personal income, 15, 20, 26, 44, 406–10, 446
  disposition of, 408–9
  per capita and per square mile, 354
Petroleum industry
  financial statements in ratio format, 104–7
Petroleum stockpiling, 39
Peugeot, 8
Placid Oil Company, 22
Plant and equipment expenditures, 404–5
Plastics industry, financial statements in ratio format,
  104–7
Platinum, 3
Poland, business information, 524
Population, 338–39
  world data, 463–69
Postal service, 4, 189
  express mail delivery, 20
  rate increases, 21, 34
Preferred stocks
  cash dividend and yields, 234
  Moody's ratings, 291
  Standard and Poor's ratings, 288
Price guidelines, 7
Pricing, 168–71
Prime rate, 10, 11, 12, 14, 15, 17, 18, 19, 20, 21, 22,
  23, 24, 25, 26, 28, 29–30, 33, 35, 37, 40, 283
Printing and publishing industry, financial statements
  in ratio format, 100–103
Procter and Gamble, 29
Producer prices, 35
Producer price index, 35, 366–67
Productivity, 12, 22, 28, 38, 41, 447
  private business sector, 352–53
Profit planning, 162–67
Public Building Service, 178–79
Public Heath Services, 183
Public Utility Holding Company Act of 1935, 72
Puerto Rico
  corporate tax shelters, 9
  information guide, 510

Q–R

Qatar
  business information, 525
  oil prices, 6

Real estate, 129–31
Recession, 3, 6, 12, 20, 21, 22, 27, 29, 36, 42, 46–49
Retail industry, statements in ratio format, 120–23
Retail inventories, 15
Retail sales, 1, 3, 8, 13, 15, 19, 31, 35–36, 39, 42
   100 top markets, 333–35
   trends and projections, 336
Retained earnings statement ratio, 88–89
Revenue sharing, 33
Reynolds, R. J., Company, 5
Reynolds Metals, 24
Rhode Island, state information guide, 503
Robinson-Patman Act, 66
Romania, business information, 524
Rubber industry, financial statements in ratio format,
   104–7

                             S

Saint Lawrence Seaway Development Corporation, 187
Saudi Arabia
   business information, 526
   oil prices, 6, 23, 25, 26, 43, 44
   oil production, 13
   petrochemical plant, 35
Savings certificates, 10
Savings and Loan Associations, 16, 17, 18, 22, 24, 34,
   37, 43
Sea Land Service, 5
Sears Roebuck Company, 7, 13, 19, 24, 38
Securities Act of 1933, 71
Securities Exchange Act, 71
Securities and Exchange Commission (SEC), 71–74
   brokers commissions, 15
   commodity operations regulated, 23
   criticism by Congress, 43
   disclosure requirements, 3, 4
   reports
      8k, 244
      10k, 243–44
      10q, 244
      12k, 244
Segment reporting, 90–91
Shell Oil, 3, 35
Short-term loans, Moody's ratings, 289–90
Silver, 2, 3, 5
   Hunt brothers, 16, 17
   ratio scales, 275
Small Business Administration, 175
Small-saver certificates, 22
Social and Economics Statistics Administration, 182
Social and Rehabilitation Services, 183
Social Security Administration, 183
Social Security system, 32
Sohio, 23
South Carolina, state information guide, 503–4
South Dakota, state information guide, 504
South Korea, imports, 34
Southeastern Power Administration, 185
Southern Railway, 29
Southwestern Power Administration, 185
Soviet Union
   grain sales, 2, 4, 33
   U.S. exports, 41
Standard Brands, 24
Standard Industrial Classification (SIC), 194, 366
Standard Oil of Ohio, 38
Standard and Poor's ratings
   commercial paper, 288
   corporate bonds, 287–88
   municipal bonds, 287–88
   preferred stock, 288
State Department, U.S., 517
State information guides, 482–510; see also specific
   states
State and local governments, new security issues, 300
Statement of source and application of funds, 84
   ratios from, 89
Statement of accumulated retained earnings, 84
   ratios from, 89
Steel imports, 23

Steel industry
   demand, 14
   financial statements in ratio format, 108–11
   foreign competition, 23, 34
   orders, 36
   prices, 27
   production, 21, 29, 30–31, 36
Stock market, 2, 11, 14, 16–17, 21, 28, 36–37, 39,
   40, 42, 44
   averages, 200–201
   by industry, 207–25
   notable dates, 195–97
Stocks: see Common stocks and Preferred stocks
Stone products industry, financial statements in ratio
   format, 108–11
Strategic and Critical Materials Stock Piling Act, 191
Sugar, 43
Sun Oil Company, 38
Sweden, 25
Synthetic fuels, 12–13, 33, 35
Syrian Arab Republic, business information, 526

                             T

Taiwan, imports, 34
Tax cuts, 31, 33, 34, 37, 41
Tax-free versus taxable investments, 245
Tax shelters, 125–40
   agriculture, 132–33
   capital gains, 128–29
   cash flow, 128
   equipment leasing, 131–32
   glossary of terms, 135–40
   Keogh plans, 133
   municipal bonds, 133
   oil and gas, 131
   partnership, 126–27
   pension and profit-sharing plans, 133
   real estate, 129–31
Telecommunication companies, FCC regulation, 6
Telephone cost cutting, 174
Television, advertising, 328–31
10K Reports, 243–44
Tennessee, state information guide, 504–5
Tennessee Valley Authority, 188–89
Texaco, 38, 43
Texas, state information guide, 505–6
Texitile mill products, financial statements in ratio for-
   mat, 96–99
Textile Fiber Products Identification Act, 65
Thrift institutions, 308–9
Tobacco industry, financial statements in ratio format,
   96–99
Toyota, 3, 9, 19, 36
Trade deficit, 6, 8, 12, 22, 28, 33, 41
Trade-Mark Act of 1946, 63
Trade organizations, 528-36
Transportation, Department of, 187
Transportation industry, financial statements in ratio
   format, 116–19
Treasury, Department of, 186–87
Treasury bills, 12, 13, 16, 21, 41
   investment returns on, 226–29
   rates, 448
Treasury notes, 11, 30
Trucking industry deregulation, 13, 26, 33
Truth in Lending Act, 63, 65
Tunisia, business information, 526

                             U

UAW, 2
Unemployment, 3, 7, 18, 19, 23, 30, 34, 36, 37
   benefits, 44
   developed countries, 457
   selected rates, 342–43
Union addresses and membership, 361–65
Union Carbide, 30
United Arab Emirates, 6
   business information, 526
United Nations, 518–19
United States Coast Guard, 187

United States International Trade Commission, 517–18
United States Marshals Service, 186
United States Postal Service, 189
Uranium, 28
Union of Soviet Socialist Republics, business information, 522–23
Urban Mass Transportation Administration, 187
U.S. Army Materiel Development and Readiness Command (DARCOM), 175
U.S. Export Development Offices, 517
U.S. Steel
  contract with Nippon Steel, 9
  earnings, 6, 38
  plant closings, 25, 28
Utah, state information guide, 506
Utilities, 25 largest, 154–55

V

Venezuela, oil prices, 13, 16, 22
Venture capital, 124
Vermont, state information guide, 507
Veterans administration, 189–90
Vickers Favorite 50, 230–32
Virginia, state information guide, 507
Volkswagen of America, 16, 21, 26

W–Y

Wage and benefit settlement in major collective bargaining units, 358
Wage and Price Council, 15
Wage and price guidelines, 2, 14, 15, 17, 42
  mandatory controls, 11
  tax incentives, 21
Wages and salaries, 12, 28
  effective wage rate adjustments, 355, 359
Wall Street Journal, 33
Washington, state information guide, 507–8
West Germany, interest rates, 23
West Virginia, state information guide, 508–9
Wheat, prices, 13
Wholesale industry
  financial statements in ratio format, 120–23
  trends and projections, 337
Windfall profits tax, 5, 8, 10, 11, 17, 18
Wisconsin, state information guide, 509
Wool Products Labeling Act, 65
Woolworth, F. W., Company, 38
Work stoppage, 355–57
Wyoming, state information guide, 509–10
Xerox, 35
Yemen Arab Republic, business information, 526